Nineteenth-Century Literature Criticism

Guide to Gale Literary Criticism Series

For criticism on	Consult these Gale series
Authors now living or who died after December 31, 1959	*CONTEMPORARY LITERARY CRITICISM (CLC)*
Authors who died between 1900 and 1959	*TWENTIETH-CENTURY LITERARY CRITICISM (TCLC)*
Authors who died between 1800 and 1899	*NINETEENTH-CENTURY LITERATURE CRITICISM (NCLC)*
Authors who died between 1400 and 1799	*LITERATURE CRITICISM FROM 1400 TO 1800 (LC)* *SHAKESPEAREAN CRITICISM (SC)*
Authors who died before 1400	*CLASSICAL AND MEDIEVAL LITERATURE CRITICISM (CMLC)*
Black writers of the past two hundred years	*BLACK LITERATURE CRITICISM (BLC)*
Authors of books for children and young adults	*CHILDREN'S LITERATURE REVIEW (CLR)*
Dramatists	*DRAMA CRITICISM (DC)*
Hispanic writers of the late nineteenth and twentieth centuries	*HISPANIC LITERATURE CRITICISM (HLC)*
Native North American writers and orators of the eighteenth, nineteenth, and twentieth centuries	*NATIVE NORTH AMERICAN LITERATURE (NNAL)*
Poets	*POETRY CRITICISM (PC)*
Short story writers	*SHORT STORY CRITICISM (SSC)*
Major authors from the Renaissance to the present	*WORLD LITERATURE CRITICISM, 1500 TO THE PRESENT (WLC)*

ISSN 0732-1864

Volume 49

Nineteenth-Century Literature Criticism

*Criticism of the Works of
Novelists, Poets, Playwrights,
Short Story Writers, Philosophers, and Other
Creative Writers Who Died between 1800
and 1899, from the First Published Critical
Appraisals to Current Evaluations*

Marie Lazzari
Editor

Catherine C. Dominic
Associate Editor

 Gale Research Inc.

An International Thomson Publishing Company

I(T)P
Changing the Way the World Learns

 RK • LONDON • BONN • BOSTON • DETROIT • MADRID
URNE • MEXICO CITY • PARIS • SINGAPORE • TOKYO
O • WASHINGTON • ALBANY NY • BELMONT CA • CINCINNATI OH

STAFF

Marie Lazzari, *Editor*

Dana Ramel Barnes, Catherine C. Dominic, Jelena O. Krstović, *Associate Editors*

Matthew C. Altman, *Assistant Editors*

Marlene H. Lasky, *Permissions Manager*
Margaret A. Chamberlain, *Permissions Specialist*
Susan Brohman, Diane Cooper, Maria L. Franklin,
Arlene Johnson, Michele Lonoconus, Maureen Puhl, Shalice Shah,
Kimberly F. Smilay, Barbara A. Wallace, *Permissions Associates*
Edna Hedblad, Margaret McAvoy-Amato,
Tyra A. Phillips, Lori Schoenenberger, *Permissions Assistants*

Victoria B. Cariappa, *Research Manager*
Barbara McNeil, *Research Specialist*
Frank Vincent Castronova, Eva M. Felts, Mary Beth McElmeel, Donna Melnychenko,
Tamara C. Nott, Tracie A. Richardson, Norma Sawaya, *Research Associates*
Alicia Noel Biggers, Maria E. Bryson, Julia C. Daniel, Shirley Gates,
Michele P. Pica, Amy Terese Steel, Amy Beth Wieczorek, *Research Assistants*

Mary Beth Trimper, *Production Director*
Deborah L. Milliken, *Production Assistant*

Barbara J. Yarrow, *Graphic Services Supervisor*
Erin Martin, *Desktop Publisher*
Willie F. Mathis, *Camera Operator*
Pamela A. Hayes, *Photography Coordinator*

∞™ This book is printed on acid-free paper that meets the minimum requirements of American National Standard for Information Sciences—Permanence Paper for Printed Library Materials, ANSI Z39.48-1984.

Library of Congress Catalog Card Number 84-643008
ISBN 0-8103-8940-1
ISSN 0732-1864
Printed in the United States of America

I(T)P™   Gale Research Inc., an International Thomson Publishing Company.
ITP logo is a trademark under license.

10 9 8 7 6 5 4 3 2 1

Contents

Preface vii

Acknowledgments xi

Preface

Since its inception in 1981, *Nineteenth-Century Literature Criticism* has been a valuable resource for students and librarians seeking critical commentary on writers of this transitional period in world history. Designated an "Outstanding Reference Source" by the American Library Association with the publication of its first volume, *NCLC* has since been purchased by over 6,000 school, public, and university libraries. The series has covered more than 300 authors representing 26 nationalities and over 15,000 titles. No other reference source has surveyed the critical reaction to nineteenth-century authors and literature as thoroughly as *NCLC*.

Scope of the Series

NCLC is designed to introduce students and advanced readers to the authors of the nineteenth century, and to the most significant interpretations of these authors' works. The great poets, novelists, short story writers, playwrights, and philosophers of this period are frequently studied in high school and college literature courses. By organizing and reprinting commentary written on these authors, *NCLC* helps students develop valuable insight into literary history, promotes a better understanding of the texts, and sparks ideas for papers and assignments. Each entry in *NCLC* presents a comprehensive survey of an author's career or an individual work of literature and provides the user with a multiplicity of interpretations and assessments. Such variety allows students to pursue their own interests; furthermore, it fosters an awareness that literature is dynamic and responsive to many different opinions.

Every fourth volume of *NCLC* is devoted to literary topics that cannot be covered under the author approach used in the rest of the series. Such topics include literary movements, prominent themes in nineteenth-century literature, literary reaction to political and historical events, significant eras in literary history, prominent literary anniversaries, and the literatures of cultures that are often overlooked by English-speaking readers.

NCLC continues the survey of criticism of world literature begun by Gale's *Contemporary Literary Criticism (CLC)* and *Twentieth-Century Literary Criticism (TCLC)*, both of which excerpt and reprint commentary on authors of the twentieth century. For additional information about *TCLC, CLC*, and Gale's other criticism series, users should consult the Guide to Gale Literary Criticism Series preceding the title page in this volume.

Coverage

Each volume of *NCLC* is carefully compiled to present:

- criticism of authors, or literary topics, representing a variety of genres and nationalities
- both major and lesser-known writers and literary works of the period
- 7-10 authors or 4-6 topics per volume
- individual entries that survey critical response to an author's work or a topic in literary history, including early criticism to reflect initial reactions, later criticism to represent any rise or decline in reputation, and current retrospective analyses.

Organization

An author entry consists of the following elements: author heading, biographical and critical introduction, list of principal works, excerpts of criticism (each preceded by an annotation and followed by a bibliographic citation), and a bibliography of further reading.

- The **Author Heading** consists of the name under which the author most commonly wrote, followed by birth and death dates. If an author wrote consistently under a pseudonym, the pseudonym will be listed in the author heading and the real name given in parentheses on the first line of the biographical and critical introduction. Also located at the beginning of the introduction to the author entry are any name variations under which an author wrote, including transliterated forms for an author whose language uses a nonroman alphabet.

- The **Biographical and Critical Introduction** outlines the author's life and career, as well as the critical issues surrounding his or her work. References are provided to past volumes of *NCLC* in which further information about the author may be found.

- Most *NCLC* entries include a **Portrait** of the author. Many entries also contain reproductions of materials pertinent to an author's career, including manuscript pages, title pages, dust jackets, letters, and drawings, as well as photographs of important people, places, and events in an author's life.

- The list of **Principal Works** is chronological by date of first publication and identifies the genre of each work. In the case of foreign authors with both foreign-language publications and English translations, the English-language version is given in brackets. Unless otherwise indicated, dramas are dated by first performance, not first publication.

- **Criticism** in each author entry is arranged chronologically to provide a perspective on changes in critical evaluation over the years. All titles of works by the author featured in the entry are printed in boldface type to enable the user to easily locate discussion of particular works. Also for purposes of easier identification, the critic's name and the publication date of the essay are given at the beginning of each piece of criticism. Unsigned criticism is preceded by the title of the journal in which it appeared. Publication information (such as publisher names and book prices) and parenthetical numerical references (such as footnotes or page and line references to specific editions of works) have been deleted at the editors' discretion to provide smoother reading of the text.

- Critical excerpts are prefaced by **Annotations** providing the reader with information about both the critic and the criticism that follows. Included are the critic's reputation, individual approach to literary criticism, and particular expertise in an author's works. Also noted are the relative importance of a work of criticism, the scope of the excerpt, and the growth of critical controversy or changes in critical trends regarding an author. In some cases, these annotations cross-reference excerpts by critics who discuss each other's commentary.

- A complete **Bibliographic Citation** designed to facilitate location of the original essay or book follows each piece of criticism.

- An annotated list of **Further Reading** appearing at the end of each entry suggests secondary sources on the author. In some cases it includes essays for which the editors could not obtain reprint rights.

Cumulative Indexes

- Each volume of *NCLC* contains a cumulative **Author Index** listing all authors who have appeared in Gale's Literary Criticism Series, along with cross-references to such biographical series as *Contemporary Authors* and *Dictionary of Literary Biography*. Useful for locating authors within the various series, this index is particularly valuable for those authors who are identified with a certain period but who, because of their death dates, are placed in another, or for those authors whose careers span two periods. For example, Fyodor Dostoevsky is found in *NCLC*, yet Leo Tolstoy, another major nineteenth-century Russian novelist, is found in *TCLC* because he died after 1899.

- Each *NCLC* volume includes a cumulative **Nationality Index** which lists all authors who have appeared in *NCLC*, arranged alphabetically under their respective nationalities, as well as Topics volume entries devoted to particular national literatures.

- Each new volume in Gale's Literary Criticism Series includes a cumulative **Topic Index**, which lists all literary topics treated in *NCLC, TCLC, LC 1400-1800*, and the *CLC* Yearbook.

- Each new volume of *NCLC*, with the exception of the Topics volumes, contains a **Title Index** listing the titles of all literary works discussed in the volume. In response to numerous suggestions from librarians, Gale has also produced a **Special Paperbound Edition** of the *NCLC* title index. This annual cumulation lists all titles discussed in the series since its inception and is issued with the first volume of *NCLC* published each year. Additional copies of the index are available on request. Librarians and patrons have welcomed this separate index: it saves shelf space, is easy to use, and is recyclable upon receipt of the following year's cumulation. Titles discussed in the Topics volume entries are not included in the *NCLC* cumulative index.

Citing *Nineteenth-Century Literature Criticism*

When writing papers, students who quote directly from any volume in Gale's Literary Criticism Series may use the following general forms to footnote reprinted criticism. The first example pertains to material drawn from periodicals, the second to material reprinted from books:

[1]T.S. Eliot, "John Donne," *The Nation and Athenaeum*, 33 (9 June 1923), 321-32; excerpted and reprinted in *Literature Criticism from 1400-1800*, Vol. 10, ed. James E. Person, Jr. (Detroit: Gale Research, 1989), pp. 28-9.

[2]Clara G. Stillman, *Samuel Butler: A Mid-Victorian Modern* (Viking Press, 1932); excerpted and reprinted in *Twentieth-Century Literary Criticism*, Vol. 33, ed. Paula Kepos (Detroit: Gale Research, 1989), pp. 43-5.

Suggestions Are Welcome

In response to suggestions, several features have been added to *NCLC* since the series began, including annotations to excerpted criticism, a cumulative index to authors in all Gale literary criticism series, entries devoted to criticism on a single work by a major author, more illustrations, and a title index listing all literary works discussed in the series.

Readers who wish to suggest authors or topics to appear in future volumes, or who have other suggestions, are cordially invited to write the editors.

Acknowledgments

The editors wish to thank the copyright holders of the excerpted criticism included in this volume and the permissions managers of many book and magazine publishing companies for assisting us in securing reprint rights. We are also grateful to the staffs of the Detroit Public Library, the Library of Congress, the University of Detroit Mercy Library, Wayne State University Purdy/Kresge Library Complex, and the University of Michigan Libraries for making their resources available to us. Following is a list of the copyright holders who have granted us permission to reprint material in this volume of *NCLC*. Every effort has been made to trace copyright, but if omissions have been made, please let us know.

COPYRIGHTED EXCERPTS IN *NCLC*, VOLUME 49, WERE REPRINTED FROM THE FOLLOWING PERIODICALS:

American Imago, v. 31, Winter, 1974. Copyright 1974 by The Association for Applied Psychoanalysis, Inc. Reprinted by permission of the publisher.—*Arizona Quarterly*, v. 31 Spring, 1975 for "Eros and Thanatos in 'Bartleby'" by Ted Billy; v. 31, Spring, 1975 for "Bartleby and the Presentation of Self in Everyday Life" by Milton Kornfeld. Copyright © 1975 by *Arizona Quarterly*. Both reprinted by permission of the publisher and the author.—*Birmingham News*, March 2, 1980, for "Irrational Behavior? No, Historical Experience," by Russell Kirk. Reprinted by permission of the publisher and the Literary Estate of Russell Kirk.—*Bulletin of the Polish Institute*, 1948. Reprinted by permission of the publisher.—*The Centennial Review*, v. XIII, 1969 for "The Inner Conflicts of Maggie Tulliver: A Horneyan Analysis" by Bernard J. Paris. © 1969 by *The Centennial Review*. Reprinted by permission of the publisher and the author.—*Comparative Literature Studies*, v. 22, Spring, 1985; v. 24, 1987. Copyright © 1985, 1987 by The Pennsylvania State University. Both reprinted by permission of The Pennsylvania State University Press.—*Critical Inquiry*, v. 8, Winter, 1981. Copyright © 1981 by The University of Chicago. Reprinted by permission of the publisher.—*Early American Literature*, v. XIV, Spring, 1979 for "Strategies of Candor in 'The Federalist'" by Albert Furtwangler. Copyrighted, 1979, by the University of Massachusetts. Reprinted by permission of the publisher and the author.—*ELH*, v. 45, Fall, 1978. Copyright © 1978 by The Johns Hopkins University Press. All rights reserved. Reprinted by permission of the publisher.—*The Georgia Review*, v. XVIII, Summer, 1965. Copyright, 1964, renewed 1992 by the University of Georgia. Reprinted by permission of the publisher.—*German Life & Letters*, v. 18, 1964-65. Reprinted by permission of the publisher —*Indian Journal of American Studies*, v. 4, June-December, 1974. Copyright © 1974 by American Studies Research Centre. Reprinted by permission of the publisher.— *Nineteenth-Century Fiction*, v. 27, 1972-73; v. 30, September, 1975; v. 31, September, 1976. © 1973, 1975, 1976 by The Regents of the University of California. All reprinted by permission of the publisher.—*Oxford German Studies*, v. 16, 1985 for "Problems of Realism in Immermann's 'Die Epigonen'" by Michael Minden. Reprinted by permission of the author.—*Philological Quarterly*, v. 56, 1977 for "Authority in 'The Mill on the Floss'" by Janet Freeman. Copyright 1977 by The University of Iowa. Reprinted by permission of the publisher and the author.—*PMLA*, v. LXXX, September, 1965; v. 87, January, 1972. Copyright © 1965, renewed 1993; copyright © 1972 by the Modern Language Association of America. Reprinted by permission of the Modern Language Association of America.—*The Southern Literary Journal*, v. XXII, Fall, 1989. Copyright 1989 by the Department of English, University of North Carolina at Chapel Hill. Reprinted by permission of the publisher.—*The Southern Review*, Louisiana State University, v. X, Winter, 1974 for "'Bartleby', Melville's Circumscribed Scrivener" by Marvin Fisher. Copyright 1974 by Louisiana State University. Reprinted by permission of the author.—*Studies in English Literature, 1500-1900*, v. XIV, Autumn, 1974 for "Maggie Tulliver's Long Suicide" by Elizabeth Ermarth. © 1974 William Marsh Rice University. Reprinted by permission of the publisher and the author.—*Studies in Short Fiction*, v. 24, Fall, 1987. Copyright 1987 by Newberry College. Reprinted by permission of the publisher.—*Texas Studies in Literature and Language*, v. 1, Summer, 1959 for "Thomas Holley Chivers and the Kentucky Tragedy" by Richard Beale Davis. Copyright © 1959, renewed 1987 by the University of Texas Press. Reprinted by permission of the publisher.

COPYRIGHTED EXCERPTS IN *NCLC*, VOLUME 49, WERE REPRINTED FROM THE FOLLOWING BOOKS:

Baron, Hans. From *In Search of Florentine Civic Humanism: Essays on the Transaction from Medieval to Modern Thought, Vol. II.* Princeton University Press, 1988. Copyright © 1988 by Princeton University Press. All rights reserved. Reprinted by permission of the publisher.—Bellringer, Alan W. From *Modern Novelists: George Eliot.* St. Martin's Press, 1993. © Alan W. Bellringer 1993. All rights reserved. Reprinted with permission of St. Martin's Press, Inc. In the British Commonwealth by the author and Macmillan Press Ltd.—Blackwood, John. From a Letter in *The George Eliot Letters: 1859-1861, Vol. III.* Edited by George S. Haight. Yale University Press, 1954. Copyright, 1954, by Yale University Press. All rights reserved.—Carroll, David. From *George Eliot and the Conflict of Interpretations: A Reading of the Novels.* Cambridge University Press, 1992. © Cambridge University Press 1992. Reprinted with the permission of the publisher.—Chesterton, G. K. From *William Cobbett.* Dodd, Mead, 1926. Renewed 1953 by Oliver Chesterton.—Dyck, Ian. From *William Cobbett and Rural Popular Culture.* Cambridge University Press, 1992. © Cambridge University Press 1992. Reprinted by permission of the publisher.—Eliot, George. From a letter in the *George Eliot Letters, 1859-1861, Vol. III.* Edited by George S. Haight. Yale University Press, 1954. Copyright, 1954, by Yale University Press. All rights reserved.—Gilbert, Felix. From *History: Politics or Culture? Reflections on Ranke and Burckhardt.* Princeton University Press, 1990. Copyright © 1990 by Princeton University Press. All rights reserved. Reprinted by permission of the publisher.—Green, Daniel. From *Great Cobbett: The Noblest Agitator.* Hodder and Stoughton, 1982. ©Daniel Green 1982. All rights reserved. Reprinted by permission of the publisher.—Hardy, Barbara. From *Particularities: Readings in George Eliot.* Ohio University Press, 1982. © Barbara Hardy 1982. All rights reserved. Reprinted by permission of the publisher.—Heller, Erich. From *The Disinherited Mind: Essays in Modern German Literature and Thought.* Bowes & Bowes, 1975. Copyright © 1975 by Erich Heller. Reprinted by permission of the publisher.—Holst, Gunther. From "Karl Immermann and the Romantic Fairy Tale: Between Two Literary Poles," in *Vistas and Vectors: Essays Honoring the Memory of Helmut Rehder.* Edited by Lee B. Jennings and George Schulz-Behrend. University of Texas at Austin, 1979. Copyright © The University of Texas at Austin Department of Germanic Languages. All rights reserved. Reprinted by permission of the publisher.—Kaplan, Harold. From *Democratic Humanism and American Literature.* University of Chicago Press, 1972. © 1972 by The University of Chicago. All rights reserved. Reprinted by permission of the publisher.—Kaplan, Morton and Robert Kloss. From *The Unspoken Motive: A Guide to Psychoanalytic Literary Criticism.* Free Press, 1973. Copyright © 1973 by The Free Press. Reprinted with the permission of The Free Press, a Division of Simon & Schuster Inc.—Keene, Donald. From *Dawn to the West, Japanese Literature of the Modern Era: Fiction, Vol. 1.* Holt, Rinehart and Winston, 1984. Copyright © 1984 by Donald Keene. All rights reserved. Reprinted by permission of Henry Holt and Company, Inc. In the British Commonwealth by permission of Georges Borchardt, Inc. for the author.—Kerrigan, William, and Gordon Braden. From *The Idea of the Renaissance.* Johns Hopkins University Press, 1989. © 1989 The Johns Hopkins University Press. All rights reserved. Reprinted by permission of the publisher.—Kirk, Russell. From *The Conservative Mind: From Burke to Eliot.* Revised edition. Regnery Books, 1986. Copyright © 1953, 1960, 1972, 1978, and 1986 by Russell Kirk. All rights reserved. Reprinted by permission of the publisher.—Knoepflmacher, U.C. From *Laughter & Despair: Readings in Ten Novels of the Victorian Era.* University of California Press, 1971. Copyright © 1971 by The Regents of the University of California. Reprinted by permission of the publisher.—Lombard, Charles. From an introduction to *The Path of Sorrow.* By Thomas Holley Chivers. Scholars' Facsimiles & Reprints, 1979. © 1979 Scholars' Facsimiles & Reprints, Inc. All rights reserved. Reprinted by permission of the publisher.—Lowith, Karl. From *Meaning and History.* University of Chicago Press, 1949. Copyright 1949, renewed 1976 by The University of Chicago. All rights reserved. Reprinted by permission of the publisher.—Malone, Dumas. From "Jefferson, Hamilton, and the Constitution," in *The Theory and Practice in American Politics.* University of Chicago Press, 1964, © 1964, renewed 1992 by William Marsh Rice University. All rights reserved. Reprinted by permission of The University of Chicago Press.—McDonald, Forrest. From "The Rhetoric of Alexander Hamilton," in *Rhetoric and American Statesmanship.* Edited by Glen E. Thurow and Jeffrey D. Wallin. Carolina Academic Press and The Claremont Institute for the Study of Statesmanship and Political Philosophy, 1984. © Glen E. Thurow and Jeffrey D. Wallin. All rights reserved. Reprinted by permission of the publisher.—Mollinger, Robert N. From *Psychoanalysis and Literature: An*

Jacob Burckhardt

1818-1897

(Full name Jacob Christoph Burckhardt) Swiss historian and art critic.

INTRODUCTION

Burckhardt is remembered as the preeminent cultural historian of his era and the creator of the period concept of the Renaissance. His most important work, which gained a general as well as a scholarly readership, is *Die Kultur der Renaissance in Italien* (1860; *The Civilization of the Renaissance in Italy*). A notable stylist, Burckhardt was also an art critic, and his work is characterized by vivid description and an appreciation for detail.

Biographical Information

Burckhardt was born in Basel in 1818, the son of a pastor. His parents hailed from families that had long been prominent in the history of Basel, and this fact is often invoked to explain his later anti-democratic outlook. After abandoning theological studies at the University of Basel, Burckhardt traveled to Berlin, where he attended lectures by the noted historian Leopold von Ranke and the art historian Franz Kugler. Training as a historian himself, he focused his attention on northern European medieval art. Burckhardt returned to Basel in 1843, taking a position as a newspaper correspondent and lecturing at the University. In the following years, he made several extended journeys to Italy and became fascinated with the art and architecture of the Italian Renaissance. His first major publication was *Die Zeit Constantins des Grossen* (1852; *The Age of Constantine the Great*). Burckhardt then turned his attention to the Renaissance, first writing *Der Cicerone: Eine Einleitung zum Genuss Kunstwerke Italiens* (1855; *The Cicerone: A Guide to the Enjoyment of the Artworks of Italy*) and then his acknowledged masterwork, *The Civilization of the Renaissance in Italy.* In 1855 he was appointed professor of art history at Zurich, and in 1858 he became professor of history at the University of Basel. He subsequently focused all his energies on lecturing. Although he spent some time preparing his lectures for publication, he did not complete this project by the time of his death.

Major Works

The term Renaissance—referring to the revival of classical learning in the fourteenth, fifteenth, and sixteenth centuries in Italy— was already in use by the time Burckhardt wrote his *Civilization of the Renaissance in Italy.* However, Burckhardt was the first historian to attempt a broad description of Italian society, to capture the spirit of the age, to understand the lives and personalities of

Renaissance men. His understanding of the Italian Renaissance, with its emphasis on unbridled individualism, has been attacked from many directions, but the modern conception of the period—both scholarly and popular—is essentially that formulated by Burckhardt. *The Civilization of the Renaissance in Italy,* and to a lesser extent the earlier *Age of Constantine the Great* and the posthumous *Griechische Kulturgeschichte* (1898-1902; *The Cultural History of Greece*), also laid the foundations for contemporary cultural history and social history. Rejecting prevailing chronological history, Burckhardt declined to reconstruct past events, providing instead an image of a society in a given age by examining conditions, customs, world views, and motivations. To this end, he relied heavily on original sources, which he prized more for their "flavor" than their historical accuracy. His training and continuing research as an art historian also allowed him to draw on the art and architecture of the cultures he sought to portray. He chose as his subjects mainly periods of transition, times of upheaval when an old order had given way to a new age. Unlike most of his contemporaries, Burckhardt did not believe in progress, and this fact most likely contributed to his lack of interest in historical development. He also stood out for his refusal to develop a philosophy of history or a system by which to explain everything that had ever happened. He claimed he had no head for philosophy and no use for systems, insisting instead on an immediacy of perception enabled by immersion in the source material and visible culture of the societies he studied. His informal, flexible style, his eye for vivid detail and telling anecdote, and his mastery in assembling his materials allowed his readers to share in that perception. Burckhardt described his historical method most extensively in *Weltgeschichtliche Betrachtungen* (1905; *Reflections on World History*, a work also published as *Force and Freedom*), a posthumous publication prepared from his lecture notes.

Critical Reception

Although the works Burckhardt published during his lifetime generally received favorable notice, he was out of step with most of the historians of his own age. It was not until the twentieth century that his work, particularly the *Civilization of the Renaissance in Italy,* received widespread attention. This popularity resulted in the posthumous publication of lecture notes, letters, and other documents, most prominently the *Reflections on World History.* Not only his scholarship but his pessimism appealed to disillusioned audiences throughout western society. One unforeseen result was an almost equally widespread misreading of Burckhardt's conception of the Italian Renaissance. The popular version of his findings came under sharp attack. Among other things, he was accused of having ignored continuities between the Renaissance and the Middle Ages, of having misrepresented Renaissance attitudes to religion, and of having misunderstood the economic conditions that enabled the flowering of Renaissance culture. However, by the mid-twentieth century, in part through the work of such eminent Renaissance scholars as Wallace K. Ferguson and Hans Baron, a more balanced assessment in large part vindicated Burckhardt's scholarship. His historical method has fared less well. Philosophers Benedetto Croce and Reinhold Niebuhr have attacked his position, while a generation of scholars has identified a range of philosophical biases in what Burckhardt professed to be an approach free of philosophy.

PRINCIPAL WORKS

Die Zeit Constantins des Grossen [*The Age of Constantine the Great*] (history) 1852

Der Cicerone: Eine Einleitung zum Genuss der Kunstwerke Italiens [*The Cicerone: A Guide to the Enjoyment of the Artworks of Italy*] (guidebook) 1855

Die Kultur der Renaissance in Italien [*The Civilization of the Renaissance in Italy*] (history) 1860

Die Geschichte der Renaissance (history) 1867

Griechische Kulturgeschichte [*The Cultural History of Greece*] (history) 1898-1902

Weltgeschichtliche Betrachtungen [*Force and Freedom: Reflections on World History*] (essays) 1905

CRITICISM

Reinhold Niebuhr (essay date 1943)

SOURCE: "Jacob Burckhardt: *Force and Freedom: Reflections on History,*" in *A Reinhold Niebuhr Reader: Selected Essays, Articles, and Book Reviews,* edited by Charles C. Brown, Trinity Press International, 1992, pp. 138-40.

[*Niebuhr, considered one of the most important and influential Protestant theologians in twentieth-century America, is the author of* The Children of Light and the Children of Darkness *(1944) and* Christian Realism and Political Problems *(1953). In the following excerpt from a review originally published in the* Nation *in 1943, Niebuhr summarizes Burckhardt's philosophy as an historian and its significance to the modern world.*]

As a philosopher of history Burckhardt accepted neither the idea of progress which the French Enlightenment had popularized nor yet the cyclical interpretation of history which German romanticism had borrowed from classicism and which is best known to us in the thought of that late romantic, Oswald Spengler. On the whole he belonged in the tradition of Ranke, who sought to give history meaning not primarily as a continuum but in terms of the unique value of each moment and epoch. Burckhardt saw little more in the idea of progress than the vulgar illusion "that our time is the consummation of all time" and "that the whole past may be regarded as fulfilled in us."

In seeking to interpret the unique significance of various epochs he analyzed them from the standpoint of the particular balance achieved in each era among three factors—religion, culture, and the state. In making this analysis he refused to accept either the thesis that all cultural realities are but rationalizations of economic and political circumstances or the idealistic interpretation which makes cultural forces primary and all political and economic facts derivative. He had a lively sense of the constant interaction between civilization as the body of a culture and culture as the soul of a civilization, and his insights into these complexities represent a permanent antidote to simple deterministic theories, whether idealistic or materialistic.

Flourishing in the latter half of the nineteenth century and able to point up his historical reflections by contemporary observations which cover post-Napoleonic Europe until the Franco-German war, Burckhardt may be defined as a humanistic anti-democrat. He feared democracy because he thought it would contribute to the development of the totalitarian state. Some of his fears were prompted by the tragic history of France from the generous impulses of the Revolution to the sorry realities of the Napoleonic dictatorship. But it is not merely this bit of history that prompted his fears for the future but profound reflection on the necessity of a delicate balance between traditional cultural factors and emerging forces which he thought the rise of democracy had disturbed.

Though he had little understanding for the positive and creative elements in the bourgeois democratic movement and interpreted its passion for justice quite perversely, he must be credited with the most precise kind of prescience in regard to the twentieth century. No one predicted the modern totalitarian state more accurately. He was certain that its secularized power would be more vexatious than the sacred power of ancient states. He foresaw that peculiar relation between the industrial workshop and the battle-field, between industrial and military power, which characterizes modern militarism. He believed that modern tyrants would use methods which even the most terrible despots of the past would not have had the heart to use. "My mental picture of the *terribles simplificateurs* who will overrun Europe is not a pleasant one," he wrote a friend. Burckhardt even predicted fairly accurately to what degree a liberal culture in totalitarian countries would capitulate to tyranny through failure to understand the foe.

The accuracy of historical predictions does not necessarily validate the philosophical convictions upon which they are based. Burckhardt's thought, indeed, contains some apprehensions about democracy which history has refuted as definitely as it has justified his fears of the totalitarian state. Nevertheless, Burckhardt's view into the future was something more than successful guessing. He was one of the most profound historical minds of the last century, and he provides a quite unique illumination of our present difficulties.

Wallace K. Ferguson (essay date 1948)

SOURCE: "Burckhardt and the Formation of the Modern Concept," in *The Renaissance in Historical Thought: Five Centuries of Interpretation,* Houghton Mifflin Company, 1948, pp. 179-94.

[*In the following excerpt, Ferguson, a noted Renaissance historian, describes the structure and argument of Burckhardt's* The Civilization of the Renaissance in Italy, *and evaluates the continuing validity of Burckhardt's portrait of the age.*]

The Civilization of the Renaissance in Italy, Burckhardt's masterpiece, was planned as an investigation of the inner spirit of Italy during the Renaissance. . . . Its subtitle, "An Essay," was not merely the product of his accustomed ironical modesty. He did not intend it to be a comprehensive history nor a reference book. . . . Even in the use of illustrative material he practiced perpetual restraint. He congratulated himself that he had not made it "three times as thick," as he might easily have done. But he wanted nothing to confuse the essential thesis or mar the artistic form of the work. As a result, the architectural design stands out clearly and leaves the impression of a perfectly integrated synthesis.

To outline the argument of a book so well known may seem an unjustifiable waste of space, yet in no other way could one do justice to the organic construction which is one of its most effective features. Moreover, it is not impossible that there may be scholars whose familiarity with Burckhardt's interpretation of the Renaissance is based on something less than a complete reading of his work. The book is divided into six parts, each viewing the civilization of Italy from the beginning of the fourteenth to the beginning of the sixteenth century from a different angle. The first part establishes the general political background. Here Burckhardt approached most nearly to the narrative tradition, though even here narrative is strictly subordinated to topical discussion of a prevailing condition. The peculiar character of Italian politics he ascribed in general to the conflict between the emperors and the popes. But causation was not his major interest. The principal thesis of this part is indicated in the title: "The State as a Work of Art," a phrase reminiscent of Hegel's characterization of Greek civilization. There is just enough narrative to illustrate his conclusion that in the Italian states "the modern European state-spirit appeared for the first time, free to follow its own inclinations," and that with them "a new factor enters history, the state as a calculated, conscious creation, the state as a work of art." Interwoven with this major theme is the secondary one of the character of the Renaissance man as illustrated and conditioned by his political activity. The illegitimacy of despotic government and the party strife in the republics bred a new type of individual, wholly dependent on his own resources and therefore developing them to the fullest extent, seeking only egocentric ends, and uninhibited by sentimental or traditional standards. "The conscious calculation of all means, of which no prince outside of Italy had at that time any idea, combined with an almost absolute power within the limits of the state, produced here men and modes of life that were altogether peculiar."

From this Burckhardt proceeded naturally to the second part, devoted to the most significant thesis of the book: "The Development of the Individual," which he thought resulted in large part from the unique political condition of the Italian states.

> In the character of these states, whether republics or despotisms, lies not the only but the chief reason for the early evolution of the Italian into the modern man. That he became the first-born among the sons of modern Europe hangs on this point.

> In the Middle Ages both sides of human consciousness—that which turned outward toward the world and that which turned inward toward man himself—lay dreaming or half awake beneath a common veil. The veil was woven of faith, illusion, and childish prepossession, through which the world and history were seen clad in strange hues. Man was conscious of himself only as a member of a race, people, party, family, or corporation—only through some general category. In Italy this veil first melted into air; there developed an *objective* consideration and treatment of the state and of all things of this world; at the same time the *subjective* asserted itself with full power; man became a spiritual *individual* and recognized himself as such. In the same way the Greek had once distinguished himself from the barbarian. . . .

There are echoes of Hegel in this and a remarkable similarity to Voigt's analysis [in *Die Wiederbelebung des classischen Altertums*] of the corporate spirit of the Middle Ages and to his perception of Petrarch's consciousness of individual personality as the distinguishing trait of the "ancestor of the modern world." Yet Burckhardt had not read Voigt until his own work was almost through the press, and he need not have actually read Hegel. That individualism was the dominant trait of modern civilization and that it had first appeared during the Renaissance were ideas which had been in the air for some time. And the Romanticists had emphasized the unselfconscious, corporate qualities of medieval society *ad nauseam*. But no one had developed the concept of Renaissance individualism so fully in relation to every aspect of the culture of the age. Burckhardt made it the central point about which his whole synthesis was constructed. Perhaps for this reason, it remained a very protean concept. At times Burckhardt applied it to the individual's conscious dependence on his own resources for power and success in a hazardous society that had lost its traditional sanctions. Or again, it might denote the self-centered interests of "the private man, indifferent to politics and busied partly with serious pursuits, partly with the interests of a dilettante." In many instances it evidently meant a new moral autonomy or emancipation from inherited standards and authorities. Cosmopolitanism was still another of its occasional traits. In this section, where he developed the idea most specifically, Burckhardt stressed above all the stimulating consciousness of personality, and the resulting urge to give full expression to every talent and every facet of character. Leon Battista Alberti, the many-sided man and artist, is here the prototype. From this awareness of personality in oneself and in others resulted the modern idea of fame and its counterpart, the spiteful wit and satire of the humanists. Egotism was an ever-present ingredient in the compound, but more significant is the constant suggestion of a liberation, a new consciousness of spiritual freedom.

In the third part, and not till then, Burckhardt took up the "Revival of Antiquity," "the 'rebirth' of which has been one-sidedly chosen to sum up the whole period." And he began with the notable assertion that, though the influence of the ancients colored the civilization of the Renaissance in a thousand ways, it was not essential to its evolution. "The essence of the phenomena might have been the same without the classical revival."

> We must insist upon it [he added] as one of the chief propositions of this book, that it was not the revival of antiquity alone, but its union with the genius (Volksgeist) of the Italian people, which achieved the conquest of the Western World.

Here Burckhardt was running counter to a powerful tradition, though Hegel, Hagen, and, *mutatis mutandis,* Jules Michelet had already suggested that the classical revival was only one part of the Renaissance. Burckhardt went further than they, however, in demonstrating its relation to the major tendencies of the age as a result rather than cause.

For this [the Italian enthusiasm for antiquity] a development of civic life was required, which took place only in Italy, and there not till then [the fourteenth century]. It was needful that noble and burgher should first learn to dwell together on equal terms, and that a social world should arise which felt the want of culture and had the leisure and means to obtain it. But culture, when it first tried to free itself from the fantasies of the Middle Ages, could not find its way to knowledge of the physical and intellectual world by mere empiricism. It needed a guide, and found one in the ancient civilization with its wealth of objective, evident truth in every intellectual sphere.

For the rest, Burckhardt's account of the revival of antiquity is noteworthy chiefly for his description of the humanists as a new class in society and one marked by the modern traits of individualism and secularity. Their frequent character defects he ascribed to the hazards of their social position as well as to the influence of pagan antiquity.

Having thus established the bases of Renaissance civilization in the political situation, the emergence of the individual, and the revival of antiquity, Burckhardt devoted the remainder of the book to an analysis of the ways in which these factors operated in the cultural, social, and moral life of the age. Under the title, "The Discovery of the World and of Man," he expanded the concept and filled in the content of Michelet's famous phrase with a quantity of variegated illustrative material. To geographical exploration of the world, he added the discovery of natural beauty and progress in all the physical sciences. The greater part of this section, however, is devoted to the discovery of man, and the delineation of personality in the literature of the age. Here the development of the individual and consciousness of individuality is once more the keynote, conditioned in its expression by the influence of ancient literature. "But the power of perception lay in the age and in the nation."

In the fifth section, "Society and Festivals," Burckhardt proceeded to place the individual in his social setting. Here the prime factor is again the mingling of noble and burgher in an urban society founded on wealth and culture rather than on birth. As a result of this "the individual was forced to make the most of his personal qualities, and society to find its worth and charm in itself. The demeanor of individuals, and all the higher forms of social intercourse, became a free, consciously created work of art." Burckhardt's illustration of this theme is a veritable model for social *Kulturgeschichte* [cultural history].

Finally, in the last part, "Morality and Religion," Burckhardt turned, hesitatingly and with qualifications which his successors too frequently ignored, to judgment of the men of his favorite age. The tone of this part is set by Machiavelli's dictum: "We Italians are irreligious and corrupt above others." And Burckhardt concluded that "Italy at the beginning of the sixteenth century found itself in the midst of a grave moral crisis." With no moral supports left except the sense of personal honor, the upper classes gave free reign to imagination and passion, with results that were frequently deplorable. Burckhardt's conception of Renaissance morality was in the tradition of Heinse and Stendhal, with qualifications, but he did not idealize egotism and uninhibited passion. He may have felt unconsciously the fascination of forces of character which he himself lacked, but his Swiss Protestant morality was too firmly grounded to permit the suspension of moral judgment. He was far indeed from Nietzsche's positive approbation of the amoral superman. Burckhardt's apologia for the Renaissance man was based on purely historical grounds:

> The fundamental vice of this [the Italian] character was at the same time a condition of its greatness, namely excessive individualism. . . . But this individual development did not come upon him through any fault of his own, but rather through an historical necessity. It did not come upon him alone, but also, and chiefly by means of Italian culture, upon the other nations of Europe, and has constituted since then the higher atmosphere which they breathe. In itself it is neither good nor bad, but necessary; within it has grown up a modern standard of good and evil, which is essentially different from that which was familiar to the Middle Ages. But the Italian of the Renaissance had to bear the first mighty surging of a new age. . . .

This was as far as he could go in excusing the immorality of the Renaissance men, or their indifference to religion, for, like Pierre Bayle and Voltaire, he was convinced that they had but little religion, though he did note frequent signs of true piety. The irreligious tone of Renaissance society he thought was partly the fault of the Church, partly of reverence for pagan antiquity, but mostly it was the natural result of that same individualism that made the Renaissance Italian in all things the forerunner of the modern world.

> These modern men . . . were born with the same religious instincts as other medieval Europeans. But their more powerful individualism made them in religion as in other things altogether subjective, and the intense charm which the inner and outer universe exercised upon them rendered them markedly worldly. In the rest of Europe, religion remained till a much later period something given from without.

Thus, to the end, individualism and modernity remained for Burckhardt the twin keys to the interpretation of the Renaissance.

After generations of revisionism it is easy to discern the faults in Burckhardt's synthesis. It was too static, too sharply delimited in time and space, the contrast with the Middle Ages and the other European countries too strong. It was limited moreover, as Burckhardt himself was at times aware, to the upper classes of Italy. It omitted the economic life of Italy almost entirely and underestimated the effect of economic factors. It overstressed the individualism, and with it the immorality and irreligion of Renaissance society, as well as its creative energy. Finally, the whole synthesis was built upon an insecure foundation, upon the doubtful assumption that there was a specific spirit common to Italian society for a period of two hundred years, that it was born of the mystical cohabitation of the antique spirit with the Italian *Volksgeist* [spirit of the nation], and that it was essentially modern, the prototype of the modern world. Yet for all its faults of exaggeration, it contained much brilliantly penetrating analysis, and a great deal of evident truth. And it was no more one-sided than many of the later revisions.

Arnaldo Momigliano (essay date 1955)

SOURCE: "Introduction to the *Griechische Kulturgeschichte* by Jacob Burckhardt," in *Essays in Ancient and Modern Historiography,* Wesleyan University Press, 1977, pp. 295-305.

[*Originally published as the introduction to an Italian edition of* The Cultural History of Greece, *the following essay places Burckhardt's book in its contemporary intellectual context.*]

An inspired teacher with a natural aptitude for collecting together his researches and reflections and presenting them clearly and calmly, Burckhardt was able, as were few other historians, to express his ideas in courses of lectures. This is particularly true of the **Griechische Kulturgeschichte** [*The Cultural History of Greece*], a course of lectures given repeatedly between 1872 and 1885, which he had already started to think about shortly after 1860. Although he prepared it and even partly drafted it for future publication, he never considered it ready for the press, and in the end, in about 1880, he decided finally to abandon his attempt to turn it into a book. Whatever the reasons for this decision, the reader must remember that he has before him an unfinished work, indeed a course of lectures never approved by the author for publication.

Inevitably most courses of lectures aim at more than one end. In the case of the **Griechische Kulturgeschichte** it is easy to distinguish two tendencies. Burckhardt intended to offer his listeners a course in Greek history and antiquities that would be more satisfactory in method than those he had himself attended as a young man. At the same time he was communicating certain reflections on the nature of Greek civilization—reflections clearly connected with the course of lectures on the "Study of History" which he gave three times (in 1868-9, 1870-71, and 1872-3) and which were later published posthumously with the title **Weltgeschichtliche Betrachtungen** [**Reflections on World History**].

As we know from the letter quoted in the introduction by the editor J. Oeri, Burckhardt decided in 1868 to arrange his course on Greek culture in systematic, not chronological, order. He was not alone in these years in preferring the descriptive approach in historiography to the evolutionary scheme. In 1871 Mommsen published the first volume of his *Römisches Staatsrecht,* possibly the greatest descriptive work of modern historiography. Mommsen never really returned to evolutionary historiography: even the fifth volume of the *History of Rome,* which came out subsequently in 1885, is structurally descriptive and systematic.

Chronological order and systematic order have alternated in historical works since the fifth century B.C. At least from Varro onwards the two methods of arrangement have corresponded to two kinds of historiography, the one concerned with describing institutions and customs, the other with narrating events: the *Antiquitates* in systematic order went side by side with the *Annales* and *Historiae* in chronological order. But in the eighteenth century antiquarian research fell into disrepute with the majority of philosophically trained historians, and in the nineteenth century this disrepute was combined with a feeling of doubt as to whether such research could rightfully exist alongside narrative history. In the century of evolution it was easy to observe that even institutions and customs undergo evolution and should be studied in chronological order. Without wishing to simplify a complex situation, it is perhaps legitimate to assert that about 1870 antiquarianism was at best admitted as an inferior form of historiography.

It is to some degree surprising that just at that time Mommsen and Burckhardt should have had recourse to the systematic form typical of the study of antiquities. Both believed it necessary for their interpretations, and from different points of view they hoped for greater advantages from it than from the chronological form. Naturally neither intended to relapse into the antiquarian genre as such. While the traditional *Antiquitates* described all aspects of ancient life without attempting to look into their meaning, Burckhardt aimed at describing the Greek spirit as it emerged from an analysis of the institutions and forms of life in Greece. Furthermore, though systematic, he did not aim to review every aspect of Greek life: as is well known, he always claimed the right to a subjective choice of interesting details.

In the introduction to the course Burckhardt himself explains the advantages he attributes to his own method. Historiography in chronological order blurs the essential with the particular, the permanent with the changing, the typical with the accidental; furthermore it must inevitably involve endless discussion of the authenticity and chronological sequence of documents. In a *Kulturgeschichte* in systematic order a document stands on its own, as evidence of a state of mind, quite apart from the objective truth of the facts attested in it and its exact chronological position. The return to the systematic form therefore has the virtue not only of making possible an understanding of the spirit of the Greek world, but also of dispelling the doubts introduced by historical criticism concerning the value of the ancient sources. . . .

While Burckhardt was establishing a correlation between the systematic form and the presence of the Greek spirit, Mommsen was justifying the same form by adducing the organic nature of the state. . . .

In short, in both of them a descriptive and systematic historiography reaffirmed its right to exist—a type of historiography which was in danger, since it offended the evolutionary principle so widely accepted in the nineteenth century. The new antiquarianism of the nineteenth century, like that of the seventeenth and eighteenth centuries, was an answer to Pyrrhonism; but unlike the earlier antiquarianism it claimed to be able to penetrate beyond phenomena into the spirit of a people and the structure of a political organization. It was a study of antiquity revised in accordance with romantic notions of national character and the organic State, which in its turn paved the way for the sociological investigation of the ancient world introduced by Max Weber.

But the notion of the Greek spirit (like that of a political organization) is not in fact so simple and definite as to justify the abandoning of chronological order with no further discussion. And the solution of taking the evidence on its own, out of time, is at best only a partial reply to sceptical criticism. It is still necessary to decide if the historian is lying or mistaken about himself or things which happen during his lifetime. The method of *Kulturgeschichte* favoured by Burckhardt might make it possible to avoid the problem of whether Herodotus was well-informed about Gyges, but it does not free one from the task of deciding whether his picture of contemporary society corresponds to the facts or whether it is the product of his imagination. There is clearly a difference between a description of customs based on Herodotus or Tacitus and one based on unreliable writers such as Ctesias or the *Scriptores Historiae Augustae*. However, Burckhardt did not want completely to eliminate chronological order, and, like some earlier antiquarians and archaeologists, . . . he arrived at a rather cloudy compromise between systematic order and chronological order. For example, in the last volume he discussed the evolution of Greek man; but the types and characteristics were at least partly the same as those he had described in the preceding volumes without reference to their chronological context.

In abandoning chronological order Burckhardt laid himself open to the accusation . . . of lacking critical sense in the examination of evidence. The accusation was all the more easily made in that, unlike Mommsen, Burckhardt did not keep abreast of the progress made in classical studies after his youth (let us say, roughly speaking, after 1850) and for this reason often appeared out of date in the matter of details. But more serious still was his uncritical acceptance of the notion of the Greek spirit, even though this had been traditional in German historiography from Winckelmann onwards and was therefore far less irritating to Burckhardt's critics, who took no account of the fact that one of his reasons for adopting an a-temporal form was that it corresponded to an a-temporal Greek spirit. There is clearly no way of deciding *a priori* if those who understood one another by talking or writing one of the many varieties of the language we call Greek had mental habits and characteristics in common which could be designated a Greek 'spirit' or 'character'. Only a piece of research extending over the centuries and the various regions of the Greek world could establish whether Homer and Tzetzes, the Arcadian peasant of the fourth century B.C. and the Alexandrian intellectual of the sixth century A.D., reveal common mental character- istics, or whether on the other hand what is called the Greek spirit was the sum of intellectual qualities restrict- ed to a Greek-speaking group found in a particular chro- nological, geographical and social situation. Burckhardt and his predecessors were wrong not because they admit- ted the existence of the Greek spirit, but because they presupposed it. Far from justifying a non-chronological exposition, the question of the Greek spirit demands re- search in strictly chronological order. Even some more recent works inspired by Burckhardt or written in this same non-chronological order . . . arbitrarily extend ob- servations and reflections which are or could be true only of a limited section of the Greek-speaking peoples: their margin of error is directly proportional to the extension of the generalization. The question of the existence of the Greek spirit is open, because it has not yet been critically approached.

In so far as he offered a systematic description of the Greek spirit, Burckhardt satisfied a deeply felt need of the whole of nineteenth-century German culture. It is certain that he was strongly influenced by Boeckh; he not only attended Boeckh's lectures on Greek antiquities in 1839- 40, but also probably knew of his plan (which was never realized) for a *Culturgeschichte* of the Greeks with the title *Hellen.*

The section on the Greeks in Hegel's *History of Philos- ophy* was also a *Griechische Kulturgeschichte* in embryo. But the fact that Burckhardt was the first to present an extensive analysis of the Greek spirit shows that although the idea had been in the air for a century it was difficult to realize: it required a breadth of reading and a construc- tive ability that are rarely found. In this sense the **Kul- turgeschichte** of Burckhardt is a monument to the Ro- mantic spirit he had absorbed before 1848; a monument if not actually anachronistic, at least certainly created when the main German historians of the Greek world could no longer fail to see its defects.

. . . . .

There is, however, another aspect in which Burckhardt shows himself to be far more original, though here too it is possible to sense traces of Boeckh's teaching. The publication in 1905 of the **Weltgeschichtliche Betrach- tungen** revealed the thorough revision of values under- taken by Burckhardt in the years preceding and following the foundation of the German empire. The letters of this period (particularly those to F. von Preen), the text of certain lectures and the recollections of his pupils con- firm that Burckhardt not only cut himself off from Bis- marck's Germany, but showed a greater appreciation of Catholicism and modified his own ideas on the Middle Ages and Counter-Reformation. Religion appeared to him, at least in some cases, as a bulwark of the individual against the State: one such case was naturally the resis- tance of the Catholics in the *Kulturkampf.*

The **Weltgeschichtliche Betrachtungen** attempted to un- ravel the thread of an historical process in which democ- racy kills liberalism, the national State strangles the small regional and civic units, and the desire for power grows in inverse proportion to education in truth and beauty. But his pessimism in the face of the immediate future was tempered by his radical pessimism about all human histo- ry, since Burckhardt recognized that the historical forces regulating the present had also operated in the past, from which everything beautiful, good and true in the world had come. Though the State and religion could devitalize culture, culture would not exist without religion and the State. Precisely because he had no illusions about the cost of culture, Burckhardt was ready to recognize the condi- tions upon which culture depended. The analysis does not end in relativism. Two decisive chapters discuss historic "greatness" and the question of what constitutes a favour- able outcome (*Glück*) in history. The first, while it makes concessions to the relativity of points of view, reaffirms the possibility of an objective judgement on the greatness of individuals. The second calls for the replacement of the approximative and optimistic notion of the providen- tial by that of the evil which cannot be eliminated from history: the only consolation is knowledge.

Burckhardt saw that Greek civilization had experienced the same conflicts that were to be found in modern civ- ilization—those between material power and spiritual culture, between masses and individuals, between reli- gious subjection (and inspiration) and humanistic inde- pendence. He developed a sharp eye for the failings of the Greek world; but an awareness of the fragility of every culture also sharpened his perception of the greatness and variety of Greek culture. A tenderness, a warmth, a new intimacy in the contemplation of the Greek miracle were combined with a merciless analysis of those forces with which and against which Greek culture developed. Real- ism and pessimism colour Burckhardt's exposition: it is possible to recognize the roots of both of these in Bo- eckh's teaching at Berlin. Burckhardt established a new solidarity between Greek culture and modern culture on the basis of their common difficulties and common con- flicts. He explicitly repudiated the interpretation diffused by [Friedrich] Schiller and later by [Ernst] Curtius of the Greek world as a serene and beautiful world, undisturbed by anxieties about what lay beyond. Less explicitly, Burck- hardt also opposed the interpretation of [Geert] Grote and the other radicals for whom Greek democracy and sophis- tics were the height of Greek civilization.

In both these points . . . Burckhardt naturally agreed with Nietzsche. In those years of friendship between 1869 and 1872, Burckhardt and his young colleague must have said more to one another than has been documented. But the letters that Nietzsche, who was less reticent than Burck- hardt, wrote to Rohde are sufficient proof that fellow- feeling never actually amounted to collaboration. Nietzsche and Burckhardt, though encouraging and possibly inspir- ing one another, proceeded independently. There are few traces of Nietzsche in Burckhardt's work. Even the chap- ter on tragedy bears his mark only slightly. Dionysiac elation, let alone rebellion against morality, attracted Burckhardt little, being as he was cautious by nature and by now over fifty years old.

Burckhardt turned to the Greeks because they too derived a basically pessimistic conclusion about life from their own conflicts. His most telling pages concern Greek pessimism, and of these the ones dealing with the propensity to suicide, which are also particularly fully documented, are especially striking: the most carefully drawn figure, almost a self-portrait, is that of the pagan ascetic Diogenes the Cynic, *der heitere Pessimist*. Burckhardt was fully aware of the debt which Greek art and poetry owed to religion, but at the same time he believed that Greek religion was more a matter of imagination than moral energy. It was not in the myths, but in the pessimism of their ethics and their praxis that Burckhardt saw and loved the essential seriousness of the Greeks; and here his Calvinist heritage came to the fore. It is pointless to speculate on what would have been his reaction to the new trend which was started in the studies on Greek religion by E. Rohde and the Scandinavian school, if he had ever known about it. Burckhardt knew only the interpretation of Greek religion as the religion of an artistic people and accepted it as an indication that the moral strength of the Greek people was to be sought elsewhere.

Burckhardt appreciated Greek myth as an immediate apprehension and purification of reality, as a fruit of beauty; but believed that there was a tension between myth and the precepts of morality and reason. Among the Greeks pessimism was the complement of the mythical imagination; it sustained their moral life and made possible the coexistence of imagination and rational effort. Greek pessimism was therefore liberating and creative; it expressed itself in terms of knowledge and beauty and was thus inseparable from the Greek vocation for dispassionate contemplation. Prepared for death, the Greeks were also prepared for life. Unafflicted by a priestly religion, they could easily transform religious experience into a source of aesthetic pleasure. They had in fact to struggle not against the Church, but against the State. The basic conflict of the Greek world was between State and culture, not between religion and culture.

Burckhardt's antipathy to democracy explodes in the famous chapter in which the paradoxical thesis is expounded that the Greek culture of the fifth century was the product not of a golden age but of the resistance of the spirit to an age of iron. On the other hand admiration for Greek aristocracies led him to the definition of the agonistic, individualistic phase of Greek culture which, even if exaggerated by later scholars, is one of Burckhardt's genuine discoveries. In the world of archaic Greece the historian of the Renaissance found himself at home once more. He is not really praising the aristocratic state, but an aristocracy which lives according to its own rules of honour and its own artistic tastes. There is therefore no contradiction if subsequently he extends his sympathy to the apolitical individual of the Hellenistic period. Other extremely powerful passages examine the position of sculptors, painters and architects in a society which equated art with manual labour, but for this very reason left it undisturbed, while it tended to exert control over poetry, philosophy and science.

Burckhardt at the University of Basel, 1878.

Chiefly concerned with religion, State and culture, Burckhardt's exposition leaves out of account, for instance, law, finances, the art of war, education, family life, friendship and love. . . .

But the fact remains that much of the *Griechische Kulturgeschichte* was written not to analyse the conflicts of Greek civilization, but to provide a systematic treatment of Greek art, politics, religion and poetry. To express the conflicts between religion, State and culture, a representation of Greek civilization in movement would have been necessary, yet the antiquarian treatment is static. The result is uneven. The two tendencies hamper one another, and certain of the author's prejudices and shortcomings become more evident because of the work's lack of proportions. For example, the one-sidedness of the judgement of Greek democracy would be less offensive if Burckhardt had not taken upon himself the task of describing Greek democracy.

Anyone wanting to develop Burckhardt's ideas must have a clear knowledge of the difficulties inherent in his thought. His *Kulturgeschichte* belongs to two historical periods. As an analysis of the Greek spirit it is rooted in German

Romanticism and inherits the laziness with regard to chronology, as well as a certain indifference to source criticism, of some representatives of German Romantic thought. . . . As an examination of the complex and contradictory roots of Greek culture it is an anti-Romantic and revolutionary book, comparable with Nietzsche's *Die Geburt der Tragödie,* but, although sharing many of its prejudices, far more realistic and sincerely humane. Burckhardt's novelty lies in the intense, pessimistic concern with the position of a free culture *vis-à-vis* politics and religion. His ***Griechische Kulturgeschichte*** should therefore bear fruit in historians of a liberal turn of mind who read it together with Grote's *History of Greece* and are able to benefit from the pessimism combined with awareness of the good things of life which is the distinctive characteristic of Burckhardt.

Karl Löwith (essay date 1957)

SOURCE: "Burckhardt," in *Meaning in History,* The University of Chicago Press, 1957, pp. 20-32.

[*In the excerpt below, Löwith discusses Burckhardt's understanding of political continuity, with special reference to* Reflections on World History.]

The proper purpose of Burckhardt's lifelong study and teaching of history was neither to construct "world history" philosophically nor to promote technical scholarship but to develop the historical sense. His course on history was intended as an introduction to the study of "the Historical," in order to stimulate the genuine appropriation of those periods of our history which may appeal individually. For to him history was not an objective science concerning neutral facts but "the record of facts which one age finds remarkable in another." As a record it depends on remembering, and each generation, by a new effort of appropriation and interpretation, has to remember time and again its own past unless it wants to forget it and to lose the historical sense and substance of its own existence. Such interpretation implies selection, emphasis, and evaluation. They are not regrettable or avoidable subjectifications of neutral facts but creative in regard to historical understanding as well as to historical facts; for it is only by selective interpretation and evaluation that we can determine which are, after all, the historically relevant, remarkable, significant, and important facts. "There may be a fact of first importance in Thucydides which will only be recognized a hundred years from now." Far from being neutral and therefore incapable of judgment, Burckhardt was the most consciously selective and critical historian of the nineteenth century. But he never pretended to be a philosopher.

From the beginning, Burckhardt declares that his ***Reflections on [World] History*** cannot and will not compete with a philosophy of history. His task is more modest. He will merely "link up a number of observations and inquiries to a series of half-random thoughts." He rejects any attempt to form a "system" and any claim to historical "ideas." The philosophy of history is to him a contradiction in terms, inasmuch as history co-ordinates observations, while philosophy subordinates them to a principle. He dismisses likewise a theology of history. "The amelioration offered by religion is beyond our scope." The religious solution of the meaning of history belongs, he says, to a "special faculty" of man—to faith, which Burckhardt did not pretend to have.

He refers to Hegel and Augustine as the two who made the most outstanding attempts to explain history systematically by a principle: by God or the absolute Spirit, each working out his purpose in history. Against Hegel's theodicy, Burckhardt insists that the reasonableness of history is beyond our ken, for we are not privy to the purpose of eternal wisdom. Against Augustine's religious interpretation he says: "To us it does not matter." Both transcend our possible, purely human wisdom. Philosophy and theology of history have to deal with first beginnings and ultimate ends, and the profane historian cannot deal with either of them. The one point accessible to him is the permanent center of history: "man, as he is and was and ever shall be," striving, acting, suffering. The inevitable result of Burckhardt's refusal to deal with ultimate ends is his complementary resignation concerning ultimate meaning. He asks himself: "How far does this result in skepticism?" and he answers that true skepticism certainly has its place in a world where beginning and end are unknown and where the middle is in constant motion.

And yet there is some kind of permanence in the very flux of history, namely, its continuity. This is the only principle discernible in Burckhardt's ***Reflections on History,*** the one thin thread that holds together his observations after he has dismissed the systematic interpretations by philosophy and theology. The whole significance of history depends for Burckhardt on continuity as the common standard of all particular historical evaluations. If a radical crisis really disrupted history's continuity, it would be the end of a historical epoch, but not a "historical" crisis.

Continuity as understood by him is more than mere going on, and it is less than progressive development. It is less than progressive because it does not imply the complacent assumption that the whole process of history has the purpose of leading up to our contemporary mediocrity as its goal and fulfilment. According to Burckhardt, man's mind and soul were complete long ago. And continuity is more than mere going on, because it implies a conscious effort in remembering and renewing our heritage, instead of merely accepting the cake of custom. Conscious historical continuity constitutes tradition and frees us in relation to it. The only people who renounce this privilege of historical consciousness are primitive and civilized barbarians. Spiritual continuity, as constituted by historical consciousness, is "a prime concern of man's existence," because it is the only proof of the "significance of the duration of our existence." Hence we must urgently desire that the awareness of this continuity should remain alive in our minds. Whether such continuity exists outside our historical consciousness, in a divine mind concerned with human history, we can neither tell nor imagine.

Thus continuity points out not merely the significance of formal duration but also the need of preservation. The value of continuity consists in the conscious continuation of history as a tradition, and the historical tradition has to be continued and preserved against a revolutionary will to permanent revisions. Burckhardt's basic experience was that, since the French Revolution, Europe had been living in the state of a rapidly disintegrating tradition; and the fear of a threatening break with all that is precious and costly in European tradition was the background of his understanding of his historical mission. The personal motive of his study of history and of his almost desperate clinging to continuity was a passionate reaction against the revolutionary trend of his age. He realized that the restoration from 1815 to 1848 was but an "interlude" in a yet unfinished "era of revolutions," which began with the French Revolution and which proceeds in our days to the Bolshevist, the Fascist, and the National Socialist revolutions. By defending the mission of the historical consciousness, he tried at least to retard the imminent dissolution; and he defended his historical creed against the radical movement, in which some of his most intimate friends had taken an active part. He thought that a radically egalitarian democracy would not lead to individual liberty and responsibility but to a pretentious mediocrity and a new type of despotism. He feared that economic socialism would promote an overdeveloped state machine, which any bold demagogue might easily seize and exploit, combining social democracy with military dictatorship. This process seemed to him prefigured in the paradigmatic course of the French Revolution, for Napoleon's Caesarism was the logical consequence of the social revolution inaugurated by Rousseau and executed by the Jacobins. "The two claws of the pincers" between which so-called "culture" will then be caught are the emancipated working classes from below and the military hierarchy from above; for it is the emancipation of the modern masses from the ancient social hierarchy and religious authority which created on the Continent a nationalism and a corresponding militarism of a hitherto unknown thoroughness as the only remaining guaranty of social order.

Disgusted by contemporary history, Burckhardt escaped to Italy to write his *Cicerone* and to collect material for ***The Age of Constantine [the Great]***, which gave him a historical standard for an understanding and evaluation of contemporary events; for what happened in the third and fourth centuries, when the ancient world disintegrated, may occur once more: a radical change in the thoughts and hearts of men, from progressive optimism to ascetic pessimism. Feeling that minor amendments would not do when the whole social body is in anarchy, he resolved to retire into a sort of Stoic-Epicurean privacy. "Yes, I will escape them all: the radicals, the communists and industrialists, the sophisticated and presumptuous . . . the philosophers and sophists, the state-fanatics and idealists . . . . You do not realize what tyranny will be imposed upon the spiritual life on the pretext that higher education be a secret ally of capital which has to be destroyed." Thirty years after his first premonitions, Burckhardt became even more keen and specific in his prognostica-

tions. It is possible, he thought, that a few half-endurable decades may still be granted to us until Europe, after a series of terrific wars and upheavals, will settle down into a kind of *imperium Romanum,* centralized by a military-economic despotism to which liberal democrats and proletarians alike will have to submit; "for this fine century [the twentieth] is designed for anything rather than true democracy." The vulgarization and standardization of life seemed to him inevitable. Instead of a liberal democracy, he foresaw the totalitarian state governed by *terribles simplificateurs,* who will overrun old Europe and rule with absolute brutality, scornful of law and quite unconcerned with the people's freedom and sovereignty. He writes in 1871 to a German friend:

> I have a premonition, which sounds like utter folly and yet which positively will not leave me: the military state must become one great factory. Those hordes of men in the great industrial centers will not be left indefinitely to their greed and want. What must logically come is a fixed and supervised stint of misery, glorified by promotions and uniforms, daily begun and ended to the sound of drums. . . . Long voluntary subjection under individual *Führers* and usurpers is in prospect. People no longer believe in principles but will, periodically, probably believe in saviors. . . . For this reason authority will again raise its head in the pleasant twentieth century, and a terrible head.

But this new authority, by which nineteenth-century liberalism will find unexpected end, is no longer an authority of tradition but the result of a revolutionary reaction against nineteenth-century makeshift provisions. Seen in this historical context, Burckhardt's emphasis on continuity is certainly understandable and yet remains astounding because it is the only desideratum . . . which he exempts from his devastating criticism of desiderata as standards of historical judgments. Historical continuity and consciousness have an almost sacramental character for him; they are his "last religion." Only in regard to those events which have established a continuum of Western tradition does Burckhardt retain an element of teleological, if not providential, interpretation.

Our own historical continuity, he declares, was created primarily by the Hellenization of the East after Alexander, the political and cultural unification under Rome, and the preservation of the whole complex of ancient Western culture by the Christian church. Here we can discern a historical purpose on the grand scale which is, "to us at any rate," apparent, namely, the creation of a common world culture, which also made possible the spread of a world religion. Both were capable of being transmitted to the Teutonic barbarians of the *Völkerwanderung* as the future bond of a new Europe. He adds, however, that the Roman Empire was inaugurated by the most frightful methods and completed in rivers of blood. And the question as to whether the forces that succumbed were perhaps nobler and better cannot be silenced by reference to the fact that there is nothing more successful than success.

However creative great upheavals and destructions may turn out to be, evil remains evil, Burckhardt maintains, and we cannot fathom the economy of the world's history. If there is anything to be learned from the study of history, it is a sober insight into our real situation: struggle and suffering, short glories and long miseries, wars and intermittent periods of peace. All are equally significant, and none reveals an ultimate meaning in a final purpose. "Ripeness is all." The existence of the many is at all times and everywhere such that "it just compensates the trouble." The most grandiose decisions and efforts may result also in an ordinary destiny. The only sound conclusion to be drawn from this spectacle is not a consolation with a higher world plan but a more moderate "taxation" of our earthly existence. The historical greatness of a nation does not make up for the annihilation of one single individual, nor are nations as such entitled to permanent existence. The balance between fortune and misfortune in history is kept not by a providential design but by the frailty of gain as well as of loss, and we are at a loss when we try to assess the historical losses and gains.

At the beginning of his lecture on "Fortune and Misfortune in History" Burckhardt illustrates our average judgments as follows: It was fortunate that the Greeks conquered Persia; and Rome, Carthage; unfortunate that Athens was defeated by Sparta and that Caesar was murdered before he had had time to consolidate the Roman Empire. It was fortunate that Europe held Islam at bay, unfortunate that the German emperors were defeated in their struggle with the Papacy, and so on. But in the last analysis, Burckhardt says, all such judgments annul one another, and the nearer we come to the present, the more opinions diverge. If Burckhardt were alive today and were asked about his judgment of contemporary events, as a European he would probably say that the defeat of Nazi Germany was fortunate and desirable, the rise of Russia appalling and undesirable, though the first depends on the second. As a historian, however, he would refuse to predict whether the alliance and victory of the Allies is ultimately a "fortune" or a "misfortune" in this incalculable world-historical process.

It is obvious that, on the basis of such an outlook, neither a philosophy nor a theology of history can be constructed. The thin thread of mere continuity, without beginning, progress, and end, does not support such a system. And yet Burckhardt's is the soundest modern reflection on history. It is "modern," inasmuch as Burckhardt understands the classical as well as the Christian position, without committing himself to either of them. Over against the modern striving for social security, he praises the ancient greatness of passion and sacrifice for the sake of the city-state; over against the modern striving for a higher standard of living, he has a deep appreciation for the Christian conquest of all things earthly. At the same time he knows perfectly well that "the spirit of antiquity is not any longer our spirit" and that "from Christianity 1800 years are separating us." The Christian faith and hope in a moral purpose and meaning are toned down in Burckhardt's reflections to blind desiderata, "the deadly enemies of true historical insight." How different is this modern wisdom of Burckhardt's from all those philosophies of history—from Hegel to Augustine—which definitely knew, or professed to know, the true desirability of historical events and successions! They knew it, not as scientific historians, not even as philosophers, but as theologians who believed in history as a story of fulfilment.

Karl J. Weintraub (essay date 1966)

SOURCE: "Burckhardt, 1818-1897," in *Visions of Culture: Voltaire, Guizot, Burckhardt, Lamprecht, Huizinga, Ortega y Gasset,* University of Chicago Press, 1966, pp. 115-60.

[*In the excerpt below, Weintraub discusses Burckhardt's approach to art and art history.*]

Burckhardt's reluctance to theorize must not be confused with dislike for generalization or structuring principles, nor should he be compared with the hesitant factual historian who makes a meager virtue of accurate detail at the cost of any larger vision. Burckhardt had a pronounced love for details, but he criticized the busy piling-up of more and more unwanted facts. . . . As art historian he sought to rise above the "old cheese of the history of artists". . . by giving the "pure history of styles and forms." His formal analysis of Italian Renaissance architecture, *Die Geschichte der Renaissance in Italien,* was pioneering work for a methodologically independent art history. Burckhardt the cultural historian selected large topics which permitted him to characterize whole epochs or societies, or in other words, styles of life. He preferred to present the "small and single detail as symbol of a whole and large view, the biographical detail as symbol of a broader general aspect." Even with a more confined topic . . . he interlaced the more general concern with the specific. He sought as a historian the same harmony of detail and whole for which the Renaissance architect strove in his buildings. But for this immense task he had no principle of organization or a thought-out methodology. When a friend tried to persuade the young Burckhardt that historical labors need a philosophical position (preferably Hegel's), he was told: "By inclination I cling to the material, to the visible nature and to history. . . . Let me proceed with my humble point of view, let me sense and feel history instead of knowing her by first principles." And the old man simply repeated the point: "We are 'unscientific' . . . and have no method"—then adding, in his inimitable manner, "at least not that of the others."

The search for structure and order in Burckhardt's treatment of culture leads in two directions. Werner Kaegi, the greatest Burckhardt scholar, has pointed to one of these by drawing attention to an intellectual parallel between Burckhardt and Alexander von Humboldt. The young Swiss very probably met the great naturalist at the home of his most influential teacher, the art historian Franz Kugler, who was a personal friend of Humboldt. At the time when Burckhardt stayed in Kugler's home at Berlin, the old Humboldt had just begun to publish his *Kosmos.* There are statements of purpose and method in this comprehensive view of the physical world which anticipate

Burckhardt's historical program to an amazing degree. Humboldt strove to integrate the endless variety of natural phenomena into a total vision. He sought this not by subordination of concrete details to abstract natural laws, but by a descriptive mode . . . which co-ordinated related phenomena in comprehensible tableaux . . . Far from remaining static, this approach also sought to reveal the metamorphosis of types and the shifting interdependence of phenomena. The integrated conception of the cosmos did not result primarily from clear classification. Humboldt placed more emphasis on learning "to see" and "to visualize" an ordered universe. This involved a constant weighing, juxtaposing, and co-ordinating of phenomena until they formed a unifying vision in which the vital detail was preserved. The aim was *Weltanschauung* [vision of the world], a composite of meaningful . . . views, a combination of empirical insights integrated by the mind of the viewer. Thus Burckhardt found in the naturalist a companion who demonstrated a versatile art of viewing, of *Anschauung,* in one vast field of human knowledge. And, in addition, the cultural historian noted Humboldt's brilliant chapters on the changing conception of nature and the world through the ages. In his work on the Renaissance and the Greeks, the Swiss historian made similar attempts to trace the experience of nature which both peoples expressed. . . .

Extensive reading of Burckhardt's writings suggests the central importance of these words: harmony, organic, whole, true measure, and ideal form. His letters attest to the importance which the word "harmony" had for him in a variety of meanings. His desire for harmonious viewing grew in proportion to his anxious awareness of an age which surrendered harmony to fragmentation, specialization, uniformity, boundless subjectivism, dulling luxury, an all-devouring acquisitiveness, and the hustle of metropolitan life. He thirsted for a "refreshing bath" in the contemplation of beauty and harmony when overwhelmed by the "lack of the sweet pensive afternoon hours," or when he saw the "inner vacation" sacrificed to a constant preparedness to telegraph instantaneously for greater profit. And when Burckhardt spoke of such values as harmony and beauty and form, such words as "great" and "eternal" and "divine" also appeared.

What did this word "harmony" mean for Burckhardt and what significance did it have for his historical labor? The notion was not limited to the arts, but its fullest meaning emerges there. Harmony, or the organic, can exist only where the manifold diversity is valued, where preoccupation with the whole does not preclude respect for the part, where the total vision is an organic whole composed of many constitutive elements instead of a radical simplification. Art which sacrifices detail to the effect of the whole is boring and lacks greatness. "Just as there once was an abbé Trublet who infuriated Voltaire with a treatise 'On the true causes of boredom in the Henriade,' thus I am studying here [Rome] the true cause of boredom of many, though not all, paintings by the Caracci! But now I know the turning point, especially for Lodovico Caracci: it came when he merely gave the essence of his knowledge and when he no longer fought battles in his soul for

the individual figures and their action; when he finally noticed it himself, while working on the colossal Annunciation above the apse of Saint Peter's, he became melancholic and died. . . ." Burckhardt similarly criticized baroque artists who slurred over the details in their quest for an impressive effect. But no better, for him, is the artist who, reveling in detail, suffocates the living whole. The rococo as a play of merely decorative forms was never his favorite style, even if he valued individual expressions such as Poeppelmann's Zwinger at Dresden. Where the viewer must "think away" details to get at the whole, the artist has sinned against objective forms. Thus Burckhardt saw in Flemish painting an artistic product unbalanced by too loving a concern for the partial view. In contrast, great art presents an organic balance where no part can be "thought away" without upsetting the equilibrium. In a Doric temple, such as that of Paestum which Burckhardt knew from his early travels, the supported weights and the supporting structures melt into an organic whole; the slightly tapered columns, enlivened by subtle cannellation, presented for him an ideal form which transformed the mass into a structured totality with the semblance of organic life. No part could be exchanged without destroying the whole. In "the only other strictly organic style," the northern Gothic, the artists accomplished a perfect harmony of external and internal structures and a perfect integration of decorative detail with structural necessities. Similarly the great works of Renaissance architecture display a harmonious blend of structural forms and the love for pictorial . . . decoration characteristic of that tradition. In Raphael's painting, "the most comforting subject" for mortal men, "the forms are entirely beautiful, noble, and at the same time animated without harm to the whole. No detail obtrudes or crowds forward; the artist precisely understands the delicate life of his symbolic subjects, and knows how easily the separately interesting drowns the whole."

But Burckhardt learned more from his encounter with art than merely how to harmonize the detail with the whole. He wrote cultural history with a sure sense, harmonizing his objective and his expression. Harmony in a work of art involved for Burckhardt more than the mere balance of part and whole, of color and composition, of movement and perspective. This harmony depended upon more than the mere balancing of formal aspects. He deemed it necessary, for instance, that the chosen artistic medium be appropriate to the subject matter, that the formal execution of a work be adequate to its purpose, and that both subject matter and form be fused into one. In the great medieval cathedrals the structural forms were perfectly adapted to the functional objective of a ritual in which all eyes were focused on the sacramental acts performed at the altar. Function (or purpose) and form were balanced, as they should be. On the other hand, Burckhardt considered it inappropriate of Bernini to express the momentary floating ecstasy of Saint Theresa's heavenly vision in marble sculpture. He thought that the baroque love for clouds, baldachins, and tricky drapery, all executed in marble, attested to an imbalance of artistic conception and artistic means. Technical skill should be so fused with the artistic intention that neither the one nor the other jars the harmonious blending. Mere formal excellence was never sufficient for a great work of art.

A work of art is not only the fulfilment of aesthetic demands. It should also be an expression of the sublime, a bridge to the realm of values. A good artist unobtrusively communicates his "moral" commitment. This historian similarly strives for more than a merely pleasing aesthetic production; he seeks to contribute to the higher wisdom of man. Burckhardt especially valued the harmony of aesthetic and moral values . . . , but the word "moral" must be understood correctly. Few things could irritate the young Burckhardt more than "art pietists" who claimed that art must serve the higher values of religion and Christian morality. Such artistic moralism presumed the *subordination* of the aesthetic to the moral concerns. A true harmony of all values results instead from the *co-ordination* of all objectives. Burckhardt always had special praise for the artists who fully integrated the good and the beautiful, and harsh words for those who seemed insensitive to anything but their aesthetic tasks. Raphael's "greatness consists in the highest view of the spiritual nobility of human nature." Of Dutch landscape painters "by far the greatest is Jacob Ruisdael, . . . the painter of the divine in nature." One of Burckhardt's favorites, Claude Lorrain, "a pure-attuned soul, hears in nature the voice which above all was meant to comfort man, and he repeats her words." Great classical art unobtrusively joined the idealized human figure, even the nobility of classical dress, with the moral values of the culture. The famed Laocoön group led Burckhardt to remark: "As soon as one begins to account to oneself for the Why? of all single motives, of the mixture of physical and spiritual suffering, chasms of artistic wisdom open up. But the highest achievement is the struggle against pain, first noted by Winckelmann . . . . The moderation in misery has not merely an aesthetic but a moral reason." On the other hand, Burckhardt blamed Caravaggio, in spite of his great technical skill, for painting the apostles as a pack of ragamuffins. . . . In front of Bernini's Saint Theresa "one forgets all mere questions of style over the revolting degradation of the supernatural." And in Rembrandt, who, like Michelangelo, served Burckhardt as a crucial test of art, he mercilessly criticized the use of vulgar human types, of vulgar themes, and the total misuse of art for expressing the base and ugly. "He never denied that Rembrandt was a great painter, but the ability to paint was not the highest of goods for him, not even in painting." Real beauty must be linked to ideal forms and the nobility of the subject, even where this was the demonic and the gruesome.

Great art must represent a composite of values; no single value or concern may dominate; none is sufficient in isolation. The great artist balances "values of equal weight," what Burckhardt called *Aequivalente,* or equi-valents. The meaning of this notion is explained in Burckhardt's description of a painting by Rubens: the representation of the famous scene in which Saint Ambrose refuses to admit the impenitent Emperor Theodosius into his church at Milan.

> Here both groups are weighed out one against the other optically and morally: at the left the energetic imperator with his three adjutants, of whom the one or the other could easily settle the affair by the use of force, but this group has the light behind itself and has been placed in the shadow and two steps lower, one of which Theodosius is in process of ascending; on the steps to the right, stands the saint with his calm and mostly elderly companions, materially helpless, but in the full light, in a bright bishop's coat, and with majestic gesture and a most venerable expression.

Burckhardt was aware that the artist's ability to fuse all his equi-valents into a harmonic, organic whole depended on the artist's "moral" attitude. The harmony of creations— whether in art, in a work of history, or even a whole culture—has its origin in the internal harmony of the creators. The crucial virtue for Burckhardt was tact, *sophrosyne,* a virtue as much aesthetic as "moral." It involves the inner sense of measure, balance, and proportion, man's instinctive knowledge of limitation and ability, a sense of the possible, an inner restraint which preserves an inner harmony. It is the "sense of the fitting." Without this virtue the artist oversteps the bounds or laws of his subject matter, of his ability, of his medium, and of his tradition. This problem of the boundless—ultimately the problem of the subjective—was of such immense importance to Burckhardt because he was so strongly committed to the ideal of a harmonious existence. Artistically the issue was exemplified for him in the contrast between Raphael and Michelangelo. Raphael was the "predominantly healthy soul, the normal personality," the artist with "tact" and "conscience," "rich in all simplicity," the "most comforting subject," for whose art Burckhardt had a sense of "religious reverence." By contrast, Michelangelo was the "man of fate," for the arts as well as for modern man in general. "He led the three fine arts to the highest summit and then he himself took them down again." Why? This "titanic, demonic genius" sacrificed his own sense of harmony, and the laws of his artistic forms, to his desperate struggle "for ever greater creative freedom." In his later years, Michelangelo could not consider himself bound to any rules, to any tradition. Beyond such released subjectivity lay the realm of arbitrariness (a word which poorly expresses Burckhardt's use of *Willkür*) which would undermine art and modern life.

The fusion of all equi-valents into a harmonious whole culminated for Burckhardt in the problem of style. His conception of style is a difficult subject. For excellent reasons he used it sparingly. Yet it is a crucial term which could serve to pull his many ideas together. In its most important sense style is that unity of factors which constitutes a specific harmony. In that sense, man can give style to his life by integrating the diverse components of his existence into a related whole which preserves his many-sidedness. "Thus even the beggars have honor and style." The ideal which Burckhardt held up to modern man, who was in process of losing a clear sense of style and harmony, was not by accident that of the Renaissance man, who had no philosophy but a style of life, and the example of classical man, who had once aimed at the harmoniously formed human being. . . . If one looks further into this problem, it appears that styles of life, like styles of art, involve the acceptance of a tradition. The "normal personality" (as Burckhardt occasionally expressed it), therefore, will find the means for personal expression within the traditional forms of proven quality. The "titan," who breaks loose from all inheritance and seeks to create a unique existence out of nothing but his own inner resources, rarely is great enough to give a harmonious style to either his life or his art. Burckhardt illustrated this point again clearly in his thinking about art. The "basic trait of all classic artistic activity" was "the repetition of the acknowledged excellence." The Greeks did not demand from their artists originality in the modern sense, that is, they did not expect from them constant innovation in the forms of expression or in the themes expressed; when a subject had once found its highest expression, this remained the norm for centuries. In addition, the classical artist, like the medieval one, possessed an established stock of mythological and religious forms. Such artists did not need to invent their subject, but could truly re-experience its tested significance and thus endow it once more with that measure of personal life which it acquires from a sensitive personal experience. . . . For Burckhardt, it was again Michelangelo who exemplified the fatal break with tradition and who, stepping into the realm of *Willkür,* or subjective arbitrariness, sought all content and form within his own turbulent soul. "No time-honored myth guards and limits his fantasy." Raphael and Rubens, on the other hand, worked within a tradition and invested their great artistic talent in the re-interpretation, reformulation, and renewed expression of the society's rich stock of themes and myths. Both artists raised painting to new heights—but they stayed within the bounds of proven aesthetic canons. In back of all these arguments stands Burckhardt's deep conviction that man, divorced from tradition, is too weak and too poor a creature to create greatness out of himself. Instead, Burckhardt saw man's real chance for a decent life in the attempt to build upon the accumulated wealth of generations, to add to this by constant effort guided by proven norms, and thus slowly to transform the inheritance. So the argument has run full circle: without his past, man is a barbarian. And life is bearable only when related to a cultural continuum.

In the *Erinnerungen aus Rubens,* the last book published during his life, Burckhardt once more surveyed a great favorite at work. Perhaps the old historian also read his own way of composing a book into Rubens' art. Throughout, the reader is tempted to draw parallels between Burckhardt's image of Rubens and Burckhardt's own life: the early death of the mother, the search for harmony in life, the sense of proportion, the serene joy in landscapes, the quiet helpfulness toward others, and so forth. But the main parallel for us is the relevance of the painter's "method" to that of the cultural historian. After Rubens, on his Italian journey, had learned to see with Titian's eyes, he gradually found his own manner for "glorifying man in all his capacities." His cultural milieu still was a coherent unity. Rubens found the subjects of his art in the immense stock of biblical, legendary, mythological, allegorical, and historical figures in which the imaginative spirit of western man had summed up its rich experience. Rubens' "enormous inven-

tive powers were used essentially to experience these given matters anew and then to render them afresh." All individual parts of his subject were for him, to a high degree, components and expressive means of a highly vivid whole. From an early moment Rubens felt called upon to act as the "guardian of a higher harmony of presentation." "In painting he combined the most extensive symmetric handling of the different but 'similarly valuable,' the equivalents, with the most vivid, even the most vehement action, achieving thus that kind of successful effect which enchants the external view and the inner senses simultaneously. . . . These equi-valents do not appear separately but interpenetrate." Masses and colors, lines and forms and facial expressions are balanced, "and above all, he counterpoises optical values and ideal ones. The moving is balanced by the resting . . . and accents of the most differing types and dignity are brought together in one painting." "Only through the combination of such ability and such a will"—held together by a self-imposed discipline—"with the moving, actually the very vigorously moving and rich narrative, the amazing works are created which can only be explained by an inner process peculiar to Rubens." In a total vision the artist simultaneously balances all the equivalents, perceiving (as in a flash of the moment) all components in their proper relation. He became the master of moving scenes through this ability to solve the most momentous tasks of organization by an internal vision before he even began to draw. Rubens and Homer were thus the greatest narrators of mankind.

Burckhardt was correct in saying he had no "method," if method meant to organize historical data by means of the systematic use of logical tools. He was right to add "at least not the method of others," if the less conceptualized ordering of manifold impressions by the visual artist constitutes a method. Burckhardt had learned to see, to view contemplatively, and to form his views into larger visions. He had developed a sureness of judgment without relying on clearly reasoned principles of judgment. The consistent and subtle judgments on the whole realm of Italian art in a "fat, little book of a thousand pages," the *Cicerone,* is an astounding testimony of his highly developed "art of viewing." He applied this technique of viewing, the "gathering of the world as an external image," to the less immediate world of the past.

Hayden White (essay date 1973)

SOURCE: "Burckhardt: Historical Realism as Satire," in *Metahistory: The Historical Imagination in Nineteenth-Century Europe,* Johns Hopkins University Press, 1973, pp. 230-64.

[*Below, White analyzes Burckhardt's work within the framework of a structuralist theory of historiography. He emphasizes the influence of Arthur Schopenhauer on Burckhardt's thought.*]

The German philosopher and historian of ideas Karl Löwith argued that it was only with Burckhardt that the "idea of history" was finally liberated from myth, and

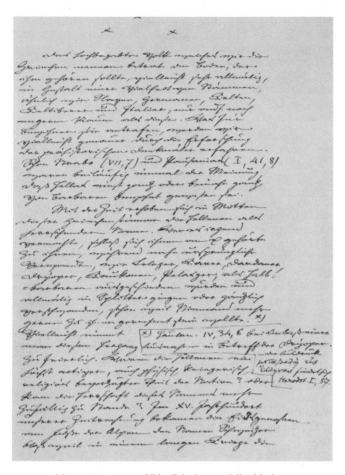

Manuscript page of Die Griechen und ihr Mythus.

from that nefarious "philosophy of history" spawned by the confusion of myth with historical knowledge which had dominated historical thought from the early Middle Ages to the middle of the nineteenth century. . . . Löwith did not see that the urbanity, the wit, the "realism," the desire to see "things as they are," and the Reactionary implications of knowledge as pure "seeing" which Burckhardt promoted were themselves elements of a specific kind of mythic consciousness. Burckhardt liberated historical thinking not from myth but only from the myths of history which had captured the imaginations of his age. . . . But in the process of liberating thought from these myths, he consigned it to the care of another, the *mythos* of Satire, in which historical knowledge is definitively separated from any relevance to the social and cultural problems of its own time and place. In Satire, history becomes a "work of art," but the concept of art which is presupposed in this formula is a purely "contemplative" one—Sisyphean rather than Promethean, passive rather than active, resigned rather than heroically turned to the illumination of current human life.

In general, there are two views on Burckhardt as historian. One sees him as a sensitive commentator on the degeneration of culture as a result of the nationalization,

industrialization, and massification of society. The other sees him as a fine intelligence possessed of an inadequate vision of history as *developmental process* and *causal analysis* resulting from a not very deeply buried Schopenhauerian conception of human nature, the world, and knowledge. The first view is inclined to overlook Burckhardt's shortcomings as a theorist in the interest of praising his "perception," and it makes of his doctrine of "seeing" (*Anschauen*) a historical method of timeless value. The second view homes in on Burckhardt's inadequacies as a philosopher and social theorist, criticizes the one-sidedness of his historical, as well as his ethical, ideas, and tends to relegate him to the status of a representative of his times, rather than to take seriously his ideas about the nature of the historical process.

The truth does not lie "between" these two views but beneath both of them. For the former, laudatory conception of Burckhardt's achievement obscures the ethical and ideological implications of the epistemological position that yields to Burckhardt both the originality of his conception of history and the authenticity of his way of writing it. And the second, derogatory conception of his achievement obscures the aesthetic justification of the ethical principles that it correctly exposes as evidence of Burckhardt's essential nihilism, egotism, and reactionary ideological position.

Burckhardt's historical vision began in that condition of Irony in which Tocqueville's ended. . . . Burckhardt surveyed a world in which virtue was usually betrayed, talent perverted, and power turned to service of the baser cause. He found very little virtue in his own time, and nothing to which he could give unqualified allegiance. His only devotion was to "the culture of *old* Europe." But he contemplated this culture of old Europe as a ruin. It was to him like one of those crumbling Roman monuments which stand in the midst of a Poussin landscape, all covered over with vines and grasses, resisting its reconfiscation by the "nature" against which it had been erected. He had no hope of restoring this ruin. He was satisfied simply to remember it.

But Burckhardt's attitude toward the past was not uncritical. Unlike Herder (whom he cited often, and approvingly), he was no uncritical advocate of everything old. Unlike Ranke, he entertained no illusions about things always working out for the best in the long run and in such a way as to translate private vice into public benefit. Unlike Tocqueville, he did not suppress his privately held worst fears, in the hope that reason and judicious language could contribute to the salvaging of something valuable from present conflicts. And—needless to say—unlike Michelet, he felt no *enthusiasm* for anything, for either the struggle or the prize. Burckhardt was ironic about everything, even himself. He did not really believe in his own seriousness. . . .

Burckhardt's major historical works are *The Age of Constantine the Great* (1852) and *The Civilization of the Renaissance in Italy* (1860), both of which were published during his own lifetime, and *The Cultural History of Greece* and **Reflections on World History,** published posthumously from lecture notes. The **Constantine,** a study of cultural decline, consciously evoked a comparison of the fall of the Roman Empire with the coming end of European civilization. The **Renaissance** was a *tour de force* in which Burckhardt all but single-handedly created the picture of that age of cultural flowering known to modern scholarship. But both books, the one of decline, the other of rebirth, dealt with a single problem: the fate of culture in times of crisis, its subjugation to, and liberation from, the great compulsive forces (*Potenzen*) of world history, conceived by Burckhardt to be religion and the state. The **Constantine** showed culture freed from the grip of the absolute state of the ancient world but tied by the constricting bonds of religion in the Middle Ages. The **Renaissance** dealt with the breakdown of the religious spirit and the flowering of the individualistic culture of the Renaissance prior to the foundation of the modern power state in the eighteenth century.

In his books Burckhardt's heroes, the representatives of culture, are always those dynamic personalities who are governed by their own inner vision of the world and who rise above the mundane conception of virtue. They either (like himself) withdraw from the world and cultivate their own autonomous personalities in secret or they rise above the ordinary human condition by supreme acts of will and submit the world to the domination of their own creative egos. Burckhardt found the former type represented in the Pythagoreans of ancient Greece and the anchorites of the Middle Ages; the latter type was represented by the artists and princes of the Renaissance. In short, Burckhardt's general theme was the interplay of great personalities and the compulsive forces of society, a theme which received full theoretical treatment in his **Reflections on World History**.

Burckhardt always denied that he had a "philosophy of history," and he spoke with open contempt of Hegel, who had presumed to deliver a *Weltplan* that explained everything and placed everything within a prearranged intellectual frame. Yet in his letters Burckhardt praised Taine, whose general purpose was much the same as Hegel's and whose "philosophy of history" was much less subtle and elastic. For Burckhardt the essential difference between Hegel and Taine lay in the fact that the former's philosophy of history was susceptible to, indeed invited, Radical conclusions, whereas that of the latter discouraged them. Actually, as Burckhardt well knew from the example of Ranke, to deny the possibility of a philosophy of history is in effect to affirm another philosophy of a particularly Conservative sort. For to deny the possibility of a philosophy of history is to deny either reason's capacity to find a pattern in events or the right of the will to impose a pattern on them. Like his master Ranke, Burckhardt wanted to remove history from the political squabbles of the time or at least to show that the study of history precluded every chance of deriving political doctrines from it—which would be a boon to the Conservative cause. So Burckhardt called his "philosophy of history" a "theory" of history, and presented it as nothing more than an "arbitrary" arrangement of the materials for

purposes of presentation and analysis. He could not attempt to give the "real nature" of the events, because his pessimism denied him the luxury of assuming that events had any "nature" at all. This pessimism found its intellectual justification in Burckhardt's mind in the philosophy of Schopenhauer. What Feuerbach was to Marx and the political Left, Schopenhauer was to Burckhardt and the political Right. . . .

Schopenhauer had no social theory or philosophy of history. Yet his whole system was a sustained attempt to show why social concerns and historical interests are unnecessary. Thus he had a negative theory of both. He provided an alternative to historicism in any form. Georg Lukács sees Schopenhauer as the ideologue of the German bourgeoisie after 1848, when the liberal, humanistic naturalism of Feuerbach was definitively abandoned and a reactionary, pessimistic, and egoistic world-view was required by the times and the situation in which the German middle class found itself. Schopenhauer was no simple ideologue, however, as was Spencer in England and Prévost-Paradol in France. According to Lukács, Schopenhauer was an *indirect apologist* for the style of life of a class which, in the face of its own affirmed ideals, had to find some reason for justifying its failure to act, and for denying, in the face of its prior talk of progress and enlightenment, the possibility of further reform. . . .

In one sense, of course, Schopenhauer was the ruthless critic of bourgeois values—that is, of interest in practical activity, the passion for security, and the merely formal adherence to Christian morality. He denied all the shibboleths of laissez-faire capitalist theory and of Ranke's pious historicism, the notion that a hidden hand directs society to the realization of a general good, that competition under law is really productive of cooperation, and the like. Instead, he professed to reveal life as it *really* is: a terrible, senseless striving after immortality, an awful isolation of man from man, a horrible subjection to desire, without end, purpose, or any real chance of success. But in the end, Schopenhauer's general world view leaves whatever happens to be the case at any particular time completely untouched, undermining any impulse *to act* out of any motives whatsoever, either selfish or unselfish. . . .

All human effort is grounded in a cycle of will-acts which is utterly without purpose or meaning, unsatisfactory, yet compelling until death releases the individual to the common natural ground out of which all individuated wills crystallize. Schopenhauer discovered that the sense of *Streben,* of aspiration, which had been triumphantly held up to man by Feuerbach as constituting his humanity and the justification of his pride, was both the fundamental fact and the fundamental burden of human existence. Human reason and knowledge were not construed by him as instruments for mediating the process of human growth through cooperative action or acts of love. Reason only informs you of your determinate quality; it locates the will in time and space, the sphere of complete determinateness, and thereby destroys in the individual any feeling that he can act as will at all. Reason allows man to survey his condition in the abstract, but it does not permit hope that any attempt to relieve suffering and pain will be successful.

On the strength of this argument, Schopenhauer had to consider the possibility of self-destruction as a way out of a life that was nothing but frustrated desire. He ruled this alternative out, however, insofar as, for him, it was less a solution to the problem of human existence than evidence that one was taking life too seriously. The suicide loves life but cannot bear the conditions under which life must be lived. He does not surrender the will to live; he surrenders only life. "The suicide denies only the individual, not the species. . . ."

Schopenhauer's aim was to "deny the species." And he saw man's power of imagistic representation as the means by which this could be accomplished. Man's true freedom lies in his image-making capacities. The will finds its freedom in its capacity to fashion a world out of perceptions as it chooses. It experiences its determinate nature only when it seeks to act on the basis of these fantasies. It follows, then, that the highest aim of the individual will is to experience its freedom, and that, if the only way it can do so is through the exercise of its fictive capability, the best life is that which uses phenomena only as material for fictive recreation.

Historical thought is bound to occupy a secondary position in such a schema, because it assumes that there is such a thing as real time, that human events have an objective reality apart from the consciousness which perceives them, and that the imagination is restricted to the use of causal categories when it seeks to make sense out of these events. As lived, historical existence is a changeless game of desire, the effort to satiate desire, the success or failure to do so, and the consequent impulsion to new desire when it is successful, to pain when it is not. It is a chaos of conflicting actions, all of which are masked behind motives, statements, and forms that can be shown, on analysis, to be nothing but blind, egoistic will.

The outer limits of the cycle are set by pain and boredom. This implies that great social events, such as wars, revolutions, and the like, have their real causes in some dissatisfaction felt by individual wills, and that the slogans under which they offer themselves for consideration are mere façades. But in its quintessential nature genius is not involvement in the historical process but the capacity to remain a pure spectator. The aim of genius is to complete in the mind's eye the form being striven for in the phenomenon. With respect to history, this means doing what one wants to with historical materials, accepting or rejecting them as one likes, in order to make of them a pleasing image for contemplation. . . .

History breeds a certain species consciousness by encouraging the search for variations on the human idea which every failure to attain a goal suggests to consciousness. Insofar as it tells us about these variations, however, history is the story of unrelieved disaster. It gives a sense of species consciousness only insofar as we are capable of completing *in our imaginations* the forms of which the

individual events are evidences of misfires. Thus, we attain to genuine humanity by our transcendence, not only of history, but of time itself. . . .

Schopenhauer's world view was perfectly suited to the needs of those parts of society which wanted to ignore social questions altogether. For anyone who found the tensions between the classes on the one hand and between the imperatives of tradition and innovation on the other too painful to contemplate, Schopenhauer's philosophy allowed them to believe that it was futile to contemplate them at all. At the same time, it allowed those still burdened by the necessity of having to study mankind as a way of defining their own humanity—as a way of avoiding solipsism—to study only those parts of history which gave them pleasure; or, better still, to study only those aspects of a given age which reinforced their pleasure in their own conception of themselves. Burckhardt wrote his one-sided and distorted picture of fifteenth-century Italy under the sway of these preconceptions; Nietzsche's study of Greek Tragedy was a product of it; Wagner's "total art form" was composed under its aegis; and Thomas Mann's *Buddenbrooks* was justified by it.

What was typical of all of these thinkers was a manifest disgust with the society in which they lived, but a refusal to countenance the notion that any public or private action could possibly change the society for the better. All of them showed an impulse to flee reality into artistic experience conceived not as something that unifies man with man in shared apprehensions of a minimal humanity but as something that isolates him within his own communings and prohibits any communication with society. Nietzsche and Mann later repudiated their early Schopenhauerian conception of art, correctly seeing that it was escapist and inconsistent with the notion of art as a human activity. Wagner remained true to the Schopenhauerian vision to the end, investigating its capacities for self-delusionment with consummate artistry and skill. And so did Jacob Burckhardt, perhaps the most talented historian of the second half of the nineteenth century.

Like Schopenhauer, Burckhardt was not much appreciated in his own time. Most historians felt that he was too irresponsible, too subjective, to merit their attention. It was only near the end of the century, when it became apparent that the Rankean approach left too many questions unanswered, and historically engaged thinkers began to realize that they would have to choose between the attitudes of Marx and those of Schopenhauer, that Burckhardt's star began to rise. It tells us something about both Burckhardt and late nineteenth-century scholarship that this Schopenhauerian pessimist who saw history as an egoistic artistic exercise came into his own at this time.

It was an age characterized by a sense of breakdown and decline but an age unwilling to admit it, an age which took refuge in a conception of art as an opiate, which Burckhardt finally won to his view of history. By that time Nietzsche had already discovered the worm in the core of Schopenhauerian philosophy and had exposed it for all to see as merely a fear of living. He had tried to warn Burckhardt of the dangers contained in it and had suggested that, although Burckhardt's history pointed the way to a new conception of society which might oppose the leveling tendencies of both Marx and Ranke, it was not enough. Burckhardt refused to respond to Nietzsche's criticism. This has often been put down to a commendable unwillingness to become embroiled in fruitless philosophical disputes, but there was nothing commendable about it. Burckhardt refused to become embroiled in intellectual disputes because he disliked disputes of any kind. Schopenhauer had shown him that exertion was futile and that a man lived well who did only that which pleased him, in thought as well as in action.

In his lectures on modern history, delivered at the University of Basel from 1865 to 1885, Burckhardt considered the sixteenth century to be a period of inauguration. It was followed, he said, by a set of "metastases," which is to say, sudden irrational displacements of powers and symptoms from one organ or part of the body social to another. . . . This concept of "metastasis" was a central Metaphor in Burckhardt's thinking about history. He did not purport to be able to account for these transfers, or shifts; they were mysterious. Their causes could not be specified, but their effects were manifest. This is why, even though one can offer no definitive explanation of why history develops as it does, one can at least break up the chronological record into discrete segments or provinces of occurrence. For example, just as in the fourteenth century, something new and mysterious made its appearance in the Italian city-states, so, too, in "the last decades before the French Revolution, events and personalities are of a specifically new kind" This means that the period between the Renaissance and the French Revolution had, in principle, the same kind of perceivable, though ultimately undefinable, coherence as the Renaissance itself. "In relation to the great beginnings of the modern world epoch after 1450 it is a continuation; in relation to the age of revolution it is only the termination of an earlier age and a preparation for the coming one." It, too, is an "entracte, or, rather, an interlude."

But the Age of Revolution was for Burckhardt, as it had been for Tocqueville, a "new and terrible thing." The Revolution, he wrote, "unfettered, first, all ideals and aspirations, then all passions and selfishness. It inherited and practiced a despotism which will serve as a model for all despotism for all eternity." There was none of Tocqueville's attempt to assay "what has been gained, and what lost" as a result of the birth of this new and terrible thing. For Burckhardt it was all loss. Looking back upon the period in which Tocqueville wrote, he said:

> To be sure, in the three decades in which we were born and grew up it was possible to believe that the revolution was something completed, which therefore might be described objectively.

> At that time there appeared those books, well written and even classic, which tried to present a general view of the years 1789-1815, as of a completed age—not impartial, to be sure, but trying to be fair and quietly

convincing. Now, however, we know that the very same tempest which has shaken humanity since 1789 bears us onward, too. We can asseverate our impartiality in good faith and yet unconsciously be caught up in extreme partiality.

For "the decisive new thing that has come into the world through the French Revolution is the permission and the will to change things, with public welfare as the goal." And the result has been to elevate politics to the highest position, but without any principle to guide it, except anarchy on the one side and tyranny on the other—"constantly endangered by the desire for revision, or as a despotic reaction with a breaking down of political forms."

The driving force behind this "demonry" was the "illusion" of "the goodness of human nature." "Idealistic minds" had let their "desires and fantasies batten upon a radiant vision of the future in which the spiritual world will be reconciled with nature, thought and life would be one," and so on. But all of this is the product of "illusion," Burckhardt said. A realist knows better, and a historian at least knows that "wishing" makes nothing so. Burckhardt's aim was to dissolve these illusions and to return human consciousness to the recognition of its own limitations, its finitude, and its incapacity ever to find happiness in this world. "Our task," he said, "in lieu of all wishing, is to free ourselves as much as possible from foolish joys and fears and to apply ourselves above all to the understanding of historical development." He recognized the difficulty of this task, for objectivity is the most difficult of all perspectives in history, "the most unscientific of all the sciences" . . . the more so since, "as soon as we become aware of our position" in our own times, "we find ourselves on a more or less defective ship which is drifting along on one wave among millions." And, he reminded his auditors, "one could also say that we ourselves are, in part, this wave. . . ." The best we can hope for, then, is certainly not prophecy, but the location of our *place* within a segment of history which began with the Revolution; the form that our understanding of history must take is nothing more than the identification of "which wave of the great storm-tossed sea we are drifting on."

Wave and metastasis—these two images sum up Burckhardt's conception of the historical process. The former image suggests the notion of constant change, the latter the lack of continuity between the impulses. His conception is not cyclical; there are no *necessary* rejuvenations after a fall. But the *falls* are necessary, or at least *inevitable* at some time. What have to be explained in history are the moments of cultural brilliance and achievement; *they* are the problem.

The will to power (the basis of political achievement) and the desire for redemption (the basis of religious commitment) need no explanation; they are the *fundamental* bases of human nature. And they ebb and flow constantly, both as to quantity and quality in a given civilization. By contrast, culture, Burckhardt asserted, is both discontinuous in its moments and incremental. That is to say, it produces qualitatively equal moments of brilliance and clarity of vision, but an infinite number of these, and with an effect which constantly enlarges the human spirit. Culture can flourish, however, only when the "compulsive" powers, the state and religion, are so weakened that they cannot frustrate its innermost impulses, and only when the material conditions are right for its flowering. . . .

This is what appears to have happened, in Burckhardt's estimation, during the Renaissance in Italy. No formal explanation of this period of cultural flowering is offered except the general notion of culture as an eternal moment in human nature which flowers when the compulsive powers are weak. That is to say, only a negative condition is postulated: because the church and the state were weak in Italy at the same time, and as a result of a millennial contest which had exhausted both, culture found room to grow, expand, and blossom. But the flowering itself is a mystery, or so it appears. For the springs of culture have their origins in the innermost vibrations of the human soul, and this is especially true of the arts:

> They arise from mysterious vibrations communicated to the soul. What is released by those vibrations has ceased to be individual and temporal and has become symbolically significant and immortal.

Alongside the practical life represented by the state and the illusory life represented by religion, culture raises a "second, ideal creation, the only perdurable thing on earth, exempt from the limitations of individual temporality, an earthly immortality, a language for all the nations." The outward form of this "ideal creation" is material and hence is subject to the ravages of time, but only a fragment is needed to suggest "the freedom, inspiration, and spiritual unity" of the images that originally inspired them. In fact, Burckhardt said, the fragment is "particularly poignant," for art is still art, "even in the excerpt, the outline, the mere allusion." And we can, "with the assistance of analogy," perceive the "whole from fragments."

The language in which Burckhardt dealt was the language of Irony, both in the form in which it was presented and in the content that it directed attention to as that which is to be most highly valued. And Burckhardt's manner of representing the Renaissance was that of the connoisseur beholding a heap of fragments assembled from an archeological dig, the context of which he divines "by analogy" from the part. But the form of the context can only be pointed to, not specified. It is like those "things in themselves" which Kant maintained we must postulate in order to account for our science, but about which we cannot *say* anything. The voice with which Burckhardt *addressed* his audience was that of the Ironist, the possessor of a higher, sadder wisdom than the audience itself possessed. He *viewed* his object of study, the historical field, Ironically, as a field whose meaning is elusive, unspecifiable, perceivable only to the refined intelligence, too subtle, to be taken by storm and too sublime to be ignored. He *apprehended* the world of historical objects as a literal "satura," stew or medley, fragments of objects detached from their original contexts or whose contexts

are unknowable, capable of being put together in a number of different ways, of figuring a host of different possible, and equally valid, meanings. "After all," he said in ***Force and Freedom*** [that is, ***Reflections on World History***], "our historical pictures are, for the most part, pure constructions." We can put the fragments together in a number of ways, though we ought not to put them together in such a way as either to foster illusions or to divert attention from the here and now. The *story* he told was Ironic, with its aphoristic style, anecdote, witticism, and throwaway (the revolutions of 1848 were caused by "ennui," Napoleon was defeated by his own "impatience," and so on). The *plot structure* of this story was Ironic; that is to say, "the point of it all" was that there is no "point" toward which things in general tend, no epiphanies of law, no ultimate reconciliations, no transcendence. In his epistemology he was a skeptic; in his psychology he was a pessimist. He took a dour delight in his own resistance to the forces that prevailed in his own time and to the direction in which he saw them tending. He had no respect for "mere narration," as he called it . . . because he not only refused to prophesy how "things will come out in the end," but did not even see any ultimately significant provisional terminations in the ambiguous meantime between unknowable beginning and unforeseeable end.

Yet, if anything was constant in Burckhardt's thought, it was the enemies he opposed. These enemies were for him, as for all Ironists, "illusions," and they came in two principal forms: metaphorical reduction, which gives birth to allegory; and excessive symbolization, which gives birth to metaphysics. In fact, his formal theory of history, with its conception of the threefold interaction of culture, religion, and the state, was really a reflection of his theory of culture, which consisted, in his view, of a threefold action of allegorical, symbolical, and historical sensibilities. This theory of culture, which was the very quintessence of Burckhardt's brand of realism, was not set forth in any of his formally theoretical works, and was probably not even admitted by him to be a theory. But it was present, and was presented quite clearly, in the section on Italian painting in his ***Cicerone***, a guidebook to the "enjoyment" of the artworks of Italy, published in 1855.

Erich Heller (essay date 1975)

SOURCE: "Burckhardt and Nietzsche," in *The Disinherited Mind: Essays in Modern German Literature and Thought,* Harcourt Brace Jovanovich, 1975, pp. 67-88.

[*In the excerpt below, Heller describes Burckhardt's approach to original source material, positing an affinity between that employed by the historian and by the poet Goethe.*]

When in 1495 Raphael was apprenticed to Pietro Perugino at Perugia, this city was one of the many Renaissance centres of political strife, moral outrage and ruthless violence. Matarazzo, the chronicler of the Perugia of that time, relates in some detail the story of the two rival families, the Oddi and the Baglioni, interlocked in a deadly struggle for the possession of the city. The Baglioni had been victorious and remained for some time the overlords of the Republic. The Oddi and their soldiers lived as exiles in the valley between Perugia and Assisi, being attacked by, and counter-attacking, the Baglioni in a perpetual war which devastated the rich Umbrian land, turned the peasants into beggars or robbers, and the vineyards into jungles where wolves fed on the dead of the battles. One day, however, the soldiers of the Oddi succeeded in taking Perugia by storm. Coming up from the valley, they overwhelmed the defenders at the city gates and reached the piazza. But there, in front of the cathedral, they were defeated by Astorre Baglione. The contemporary reporter describes the daring feat of courage and martial skill that Astorre performed; at the last moment and against superior numbers, he threw himself into the battle, sitting upright on his horse, with a falcon on his helmet and with his golden armour glittering in the sun. He looked and acted, Matarazzo says, like the God of War himself.

Jacob Burckhardt, in his *The Culture of the Renaissance in Italy,* draws freely on such sources, and, in this particular case, reflects whether it is not the hero of this episode whom we can see in Raphael's early paintings of St. George and St. Michael; adding that in the figure of the celestial rider in the Heliodorus fresco Astorre Baglione has found his final glorification.

Again, using Matarazzo as his source, Burckhardt tells the story of Atalanta, the beautiful mother of Grifone Baglione, who was for some time ruling prince of Perugia. He had fought his way to power against rival members of his own family. His mother Atalanta was on the side of his enemies. On her son's victory she cursed him and fled from the city. But Grifone's rule was shortlived. He was soon overpowered by his rivals and mortally wounded. When Atalanta heard he was dying, she returned with her daughter-in-law. At the approach of the two ladies, the tumultuous crowd on the piazza parted, both sides fearing the wrath of the bereaved mother. She, however, went straight to her son, and, far from contemplating further violence, implored him to forgive those who had dealt the deadly blow. After he had thus renounced the spirit of revenge, he died with the blessings of his mother. Then the two women left the city again, and the crowd, partisans of both camps, knelt down and wept as they crossed the piazza in their bloodstained garments. It was for this Atalanta that Raphael later painted his *Deposizione*. Thus, Burckhardt writes, "her own suffering was laid at the feet of the most sublime and sacred agony of a mother." After all this the cathedral of Perugia, which had stood in the midst of these many scenes of felony and murder, was washed with wine and consecrated anew.

Anecdotes of this kind occur frequently in Jacob Burckhardt's book on the Renaissance, which was first published in Basle in 1860, when its author had reached the age of forty-two. Are they, the historian of to-day may ask, worthy of a self-respecting scholar? Have they not the romantic flavour of a fanciful dramatization rather

Medal struck by Hans Frei in 1898 to honor the memory of Burckhardt.

than the authentic ring of precise recording? What is the value of a source like Matarazzo's chronicles? Was he not a partisan himself, bent upon building up a heroic reputation for the Baglioni, and, at the same time, a storyteller determined to entertain and edify his public rather than to instruct it?

We may, in the context of such queries, note that, when he began his university education in Basle as a student of theology, Jacob Burckhardt soon developed a very sceptical attitude towards his subject. He was the son of a Protestant minister of the Church, and it was his father's— and originally his own—wish that he should become a clergyman himself. Soon, however, he decided to give up theology because the rationalist Bible criticism of his teacher de Wette had undermined his faith in orthodox beliefs. "De Wette's system," he wrote in a letter to a friend, "grows before my eyes to colossal dimensions; one *must* follow him, nothing else is possible; but, alas, every day there disappears under his hands a fragment of the traditional teaching of the Church. To-day I have finally discovered that he regards the birth of Christ as a myth—and I with him. It was with a shudder that I thought of a number of reasons why it all but had to be like this. . . ." Did this critical passion leave him during his subsequent training as a historian? And, after all, this history of the Renaissance was published by a pupil of Ranke's—Ranke whom he always respected, though without much affection, and in whose seminar he had learned how to handle sources and be critical of them. Are we not, therefore, entitled to expect something more sophisticated than heroic tales from this Professor of History, holding a chair in the University of Basle?

Before raising such questions we may first ask ourselves: what is the picture produced in our minds by these unverified, and probably unverifiable, anecdotes? It is composed of intense evil and sublime beauty, of hatred and charity, of degradation and purification, of the unscrupulousness that inflicts pain, and the reverence felt for suffering, of sin, contrition and atonement. Indeed, the source from which it springs is not chosen for the sake of factual exactitude. Its authority is of a different nature. It has for Burckhardt the authenticity of the mind, imagination and spirit of the Renaissance, and if it yields a negligible *quantity* of reliable facts, it nevertheless reveals something more important to him: the *quality* of the life of the period, or as he would have called it, the Geist of the epoch. To reproduce this is the concern of what he calls History of Culture as distinct from Political History. If he is to recapture the quality of life lived by a certain age, the historian must bring to his study not only industry, intelligence and honesty, but also something of the sensibility and intuition of the artist. History of Culture has a critical method of its own, still more difficult to acquire than the ordinary techniques of critical investigation. In fact, it is not a technique at all, but rather creative sympathy. If we do not possess this we are perpetually misled by the egocentricity of our intellectual concepts; for we are prone to overrate the power as well as the range of application of our abstract thinking. Notions, for instance, like "freedom" and "slavery"; "tolerance" and "intolerance"; "tyranny," "aristocracy," "democracy"; "belief" and "superstition," which we believe we are using objectively, applying them to certain observed phenomena, are, in fact, value-judgments charged with all the sentiments and resentments of our contemporary perception of human affairs. The very sound in our ears of the word "slavery" may render our imagination impotent in its dealings with the particular quality of Greek civilization, and the emotional charge contained in the term "freedom of thought" or, indeed, "objectivity" itself, may practically blot out all our understanding of the quality of the knowledge and wisdom of a medieval sage. Yet there is a possible scale of human achievement on which a wretched feudal drudge may appear to approach the degree marking absolute freedom, and the constitutionally free citizen of a free republic the state of absolute slavery.

To come back to Burckhardt's Renaissance scenes: who can, as long as he remains within his restricted moral senses, assess the spiritual power present in a society and ready to be spent on the transformation of a ruthless prince into the Raphael picture of a warrior of Heaven, and of a cunning and power-seeking woman into a *mater doloro-sa?* And when it comes to our contemporary debates, we might become considerably more economical and subtle in drawing historical parallels and comparisons, if we were inspired by only one spark of what Burckhardt meant by historical understanding. We might not have to risk in every attempt at, for instance, appreciating the spiritual life and character of the Middle Ages, the release of cataracts of moralizing recriminations about religious wars, crusades, inquisitions and other pestilences.

Indeed, Burckhardt, like his teacher Ranke, is convinced of the fundamental importance of original sources and warns his pupils against text-books, digests and interpretations, not because he upholds the superstition of perfect objectivity emerging like the vision of a god from the assiduity of the source collector, but because he believes that the activity of the imagination can be stimulated as well as purified by an ever-renewed contact with the documents which reproduce the impact made by an event in human history upon particular minds. Such a mind—and here the method of the historian of a culture differs from that of the political or economic historian—may be a naïve chronicler like Matarazzo or, indeed, an inspired painter like Raphael. Did they report or paint what *really* happened? Of course not, if 'real' is to denote the pure abstract of an event, which is, in fact, no event whatsoever. For something that happens becomes an event only when it is mentally and emotionally perceived and registered. Matarazzo, therefore, in all his naïvety, and Raphael, with all the transforming power of his art, are both sources for the historian of a culture, who is, as Burckhardt once put it in his unphilosophical manner, as much concerned with "represented history" as with what "literally happened," forgetting that nothing happens literally—unless we are determined to make our own perception the criterion of the perception of truth itself, and to say that what *really* happens is precisely what we would have noticed had we been on the spot. Thus it is with some justification that Burckhardt maintains, in a neat over-statement, that for the history of culture the facts to be assessed are *identical* with the sources. Claiming for his method *primum gradum certitudinis* [the first degree of certitude], he upholds in defiance of the fact-worshippers that even records of things that have not happened at all may be important by virtue of the typical mode of their distortions and misinterpretations. Of Aeneas Silvius he says in his **Renaissance:** "One may distrust the testimony of that man completely, and yet one would have to admit that there are not many other men in whose minds the picture of the age and its intellectual culture is reflected with such perception and liveliness."

The idea, however, of arriving at any positive certainty by accumulating more and more sources until that point of completeness is reached at which we may, in Bury's words, "grasp the complete development of humanity," is, of course, dismissed by Burckhardt as a chimaera. The very attempt, he holds, would interfere with any comprehensiveness of vision. Pedantry to him is one of the most cunning enemies of truth, luring the search into the dusty lumber rooms of the past where only mice may hope to find something to eat. Mind and imagination must needs choke in them, and Buckle, for instance, he says, owes his paralysis of the brain to his exclusive obsession with the Scottish sermons of the seventeenth and eighteenth centuries. The very spiritual poverty of what Burckhardt calls his "pretty century" drives many of its academic studies into some narrow recess of the past where the ideal of precision and completeness may hide from the adept the absence of true comprehension. It is in those holes of the mind that the indiscriminate and diffused suspicion is bred which tends to dismiss as vague generalizations *all* historical assessments based on a broader vision. For the modern mind, in some of its most vocal representatives, has yielded to the inferior magic of facts, numbers, statistics, and to that sort of empiricism which, in its passion for concreteness, paradoxically reduces experience to a purely abstract notion of measurable data, having cast aside the "immeasurable wealth" of authentic experiences of the spirit and imagination. The specialization in trifles which results from such abstractions seeks its justification not only in the arithmetical deception that a thousand futilities add up to a large piece of significance, but also in the strange belief that the great issues have all been fully explored and the outstanding sources exhausted. For Burckhardt, however, it merely brings to light that waning sense of significance which he finds and deplores in his age, the crumbling of all central convictions and the spontaneous disinclination of mediocrity to expose itself to the impact of what is great. It may be, he says, "that there is still hidden in Thucydides a fact of capital importance which somebody will note in a hundred years time." For the present, Burckhardt maintains, "a single source, happily chosen, can, as it were, do duty for a whole multitude of possible other sources, since he who is really determined to learn, that is, to become rich in spirit, can, by a simple function of his mind, discern and feel the general in the particular."

This is an echo from Goethe's world. For Goethe knew the difference in quality between a writer who, starting with preconceived ideas, assembles his particulars to fit the needs of his generalities, and a poet who "discerns and feels" the universal in the particular phenomenon. Like Stifter, with whom he has so much in common, Burckhardt felt himself to be one of "Goethe's family." As a young man he hoped he would become a poet—and he actually did publish a number of poems—and throughout his life history remained for him a poetic activity. "As a historian," he once wrote, "I am lost where I cannot begin with *Anschauung*." It is a Goethean word and hardly translatable. Its connotations are visual, and it means the mental process by which we spontaneously grasp, through observation aided by intuition, a thing in its wholeness. Goethe uses it as the opposite of analysis, the mental approach which he feared would establish itself as the dominant habit of an age fascinated by Newtonian physics, only to destroy all culture of the intellect. Sometimes Burckhardt even felt it to be a nuisance that the historian, in presenting his historical narrative, was bound by the chronological order compelling him to tell one thing after the other, when the true order "could only be represented as a picture."

Russell Kirk (review date 1980)

SOURCE: "Irrational Behavior? No, Historical Experience," in *The Birmingham News*, March 2, 1980, p. E8.

[*An American historian, political theorist, novelist, journalist, and lecturer, Kirk was one of America's most eminent conservative intellectuals. His works have provided a major impetus to the conservative revival that has developed since the 1950s. In the following excerpt from a review of* Reflections on History, *Kirk offers high praise for Burckhardt as a wise and prescient historian.*]

[*Reflections on History*] is a handsomely produced edition of lectures delivered a century ago by the great Swiss historian [which] contains an informative preface by Prof. Gottfried Dietze. As Dietze reminds us, Burckhardt did not desire to have his lectures published. Had his wish been respected, we should have lost a wise book.

The kernel of these reflections is Burckhardt's discussion of "the three powers": The state, religion, and culture. Since Burckhardt lectured, the power of the state has increased monstrously, the power of religion has decayed, the power of culture has fallen into a confused condition. So Burckhardt expected.

We find ourselves in a time when crisis succeeds crisis. Here Burckhardt, somewhat unexpectedly, lets cheerfulness break in. As he puts the matter in his lecture on "The Crisis of History":

> Crises clear the ground, firstly of a host of institutions from which life has long since departed, and which, given their historical privilege, could not have been swept away in any other fashion. Further, of true pseudo- organisms which ought never to have existed, but which had nevertheless, in the course of time, gained a firm hold upon the fabric of life, and were, indeed, mainly to blame for the preference for mediocrity and the hatred of excellence. Crises also abolish the cumulative dread of "disturbance" and clear the way for strong personalities.

In 1980, any reflective man or woman, confronting crises political and intellectual, needs the philosophic habit of mind and the long-range views which a thorough knowledge of history may confer. To read Burckhardt is to be led toward such attainments.

Hans Baron (essay date 1988)

SOURCE: "The Limits of the Notion of 'Renaissance Individualism': Burckhardt after a Century," in *In Search of Florentine Civic Humanism: Essays on the Transition from Medieval to Modern Thought, Vol. II,* Princeton University Press, 1988, pp. 155-81.

[*In the excerpt below, Baron evaluates Burckhardt's concept of the Renaissance, assessing criticisms of it and outlining two areas of weakness in* The Civilization of the Renaissance in Italy.]

September 1960 marked the hundredth year since the appearance of Jacob Burckhardt's *Kultur der Renaissance in Italien*. No other work has had a comparable influence on the formation of the historical concept of the Renaissance, and during the last four decades before its centenary it became a classic read in all western countries. Since the republication of Burckhardt's original text by Walter Goetz in 1922, one German reprint has followed another. After the Second World War, the early Italian and English translations began to share in this ever-growing popularity (America has seen about half a dozen editions recently), while the first Spanish translation came out in South America in 1942.

How is the Renaissance scholar to evaluate this late triumph of a book whose slow acceptance by his contemporaries brought bitter disappointment to its author? About 1900, when a "revolt of medievalists" against the nineteenth-century conception of the Renaissance was in full swing, the usual reaction of scholars to Burckhardt's work was fear that an apparently irrepressible product of a period of historiography long passed might perpetuate an antiquated bias against the Middle Ages through a false image of the unscrupulous, ruthless and lusty "superman" of the Renaissance. Today, at a longer distance in time, little of that suspicion has survived. Many, of course, disagree with some aspects of Burckhardt's views, but few still think they are confronted with a work disfigured by strong prejudices against the medieval past. The reason is both a keener awareness of the role in modern historiography of the phenomena described in the *Civilization of the Renaissance* and a better knowledge of the mind and motives of its author.

To begin with the second point, in several respects our judgment of Burckhardt as the first historian of the Renaissance can be quite different today from what it was around 1900. There is no doubt that we see more clearly the injustice of too closely identifying the positions of Burckhardt and Jules Michelet, the two authors who first entitled books "The Renaissance"—even though it is true that Burckhardt borrowed the famous formula "the discovery of the world and of man" from Michelet. For whereas the letter, as heir to eighteenth-century attitudes, saw the Middle Ages as a time of "proscription" of nature and science, of "abdications successives de l'indépendance humaine" [successive renunciations of human independence], one finds no trace of such a disparagement in Burckhardt. That his work could at all be considered to reflect an antimedieval prejudice is explainable only by the circumstance that the terse and pointed comments of the *Kultur der Renaissance* cannot be read together with the originally planned companion volumes on the culture of the Middle Ages, which were never published (except for the previously written *Age of Constantine the Great*).

As an academic teacher in Zurich and Basel, Burckhardt often lectured on medieval history, and the carefully prepared manuscripts of these lectures, preserved in the Burckhardt archives in Basel, have been consulted in recent decades for the reconstruction of his historical ideas, particularly by Werner Kaegi for his fundamental biography of Burckhardt. In his courses in Zurich at the very time when he was working out the guiding principles of his *Kultur,* we find Burckhardt apologizing to his listeners for the adoption—"for want of something better"—of the fashionable term "Renaissance," even though the word sounded "as if during the Middle Ages all cultural life had been sound asleep." He talked about the "undying sympathy" that moves anyone who has grasped the spiritual harmony of medieval art, and even after the appearance of his book he never retracted in his lectures his positive approach to the Middle Ages. Although from the 1850s on, classic art became his greatest love, and although he now discovered the emergence of a new world of culture in the background of the art of the fifteenth and sixteenth centuries, he did not lose his responsiveness to medieval values. Rather, he set an example of empathic flexibility, thereby becoming one of the founding fathers of historicism.

There has been a corresponding change in appraising the precise nature of Burckhardt's influence on Renaissance historiography. When at about the turn of the century scholars began to criticize and repudiate the late nineteenth-century notion of the uninhibited, secular, and even pagan "man of the Renaissance," little distinction was made between John Addington Symonds' glorification of the fifteenth and sixteenth centuries, the effects of Nietzsche's teaching of the superman, and Burckhardt's own preceding ideas. Since World War II, however, a number of investigations, especially in Germany, have sharply brought out the difference in spirit that separated Burckhardt's attitude from Nietzsche's, a difference clearly noticed by Burckhardt himself. Wallace K. Ferguson's history of the interpretations of the Renaissance [in *The Renaissance in Historical Thought*] has also shown in detail that the presumed Burckhardtian elements which were attacked and pruned after 1900 were to a large extent not actually Burckhardt's own but modifications of his conception by late nineteenth century writers.

This sharper definition of Burckhardt's perspective has in turn influenced the long-standing controversy over his treatment of religion in Italy during the centuries of the Renaissance. To be sure, the religious attitudes of the fourteenth, fifteenth, and sixteenth centuries have remained a moot problem of Renaissance historiography, but the anti-Burckhardtian asperity of the time about 1900 has disappeared from most of these discussions. We have become more aware of Burckhardt's tendency to give due place to Christian devotion, and even to the impact of traditional medieval religion, alongside the agnosticism, skepticism, and disbelief which are stressed in his book. If these latter received more emphasis than most historians today assign to them, it is not so much, we now realize, because of any bias on Burckhardt's part as of his need to spell out, in his section on religion, the consequences, good and bad, of "Renaissance individualism." The challenge to traditional religion, which Burckhardt believed to be evident in the lives of many highly developed individuals, had to be put into proper focus by abundant illustration; but the reasoning he drew from it was hardly strained. If the astrological superstition which he considered a sign of growing religious disbelief in Renaissance Italy has turned out to be more typical of the late Middle Ages in general than he realized, it is easy enough to play down the effects of individualism in this one case without touching the core of his argument; and if today we know even more than Burckhardt did about the remarkable part played by the urge for a more spiritual religiosity in the cultured Italian society of the Renaissance, most of the recent corrections of Burckhardt fit quite well the picture offered in his book, which is highlighted by a sympathetic reference to the emergence of "theistic" tendencies among the Florentine Neoplatonists, "one of the most precious fruits of the discovery of the world and of man." Here again one has to conclude that the imperfections of Burckhardt's concept of the Renaissance are not so difficult for us to overcome.

Finally, criticism of Burckhardt has subsided markedly because of a growing realization that the idea of an Italian Renaissance was not contrived by him suddenly—and, therefore, perhaps rather willfully—but had been taking shape for generations before its mature formulation in his book. Many studies have established not only that the term "Renaissance" was already in wide use, especially among French scholars, when Burckhardt adopted it, but also that the view that Humanism represented the beginning of a stage of culture no longer medieval had, in essence, been championed by the Renaissance humanists themselves. . . .

An evolutional scheme of modern history that included basically what, since Burckhardt, we have come to call the Renaissance in Italy had, therefore, been in preparation for several centuries. What was new and important in Burckhardt's work was the degree of maturity and the profounder meaning he gave to an already established tradition. Having followed Romanticism in his youth, he was, unlike his predecessors, no longer ready to identify the spirit of Renaissance Italy with the infancy of the thought of the Enlightenment. Nor was he willing to agree with the neoclassicists, past and present, in according the most important role to the revival of ancient letters, not even to the degree to which this opinion was still usually accepted after Voltaire. Burckhardt's book, in fact, abounds with rebuttals of the classicists' beliefs. The "rebirth" of Antiquity, he objects, "has been arbitrarily chosen as the name to sum up the whole period"; yet the deliverance of the state and the individual in Italy from medieval ties "would have sufficed, apart from Antiquity, to shake and mature the national mind; and most of the intellectual tendencies . . . would be conceivable without it. . . . We must insist, as one of the chief propositions of this book, that it was not the revival of Antiquity alone, but its union with the genius of the Italian people, that achieved the conquest of the Western World." As for the exceptional influence of the Italian Trecento, Quattrocento, and Cinquecento in the history of European culture, Burckhardt saw eye to eye with his humanist predecessors and maintained their attribution to Italy of a unique and highly advanced position at the beginning of the modern age.

Some of Burckhardt's other guiding ideas were equally far from being personal idiosyncracies. They were borrowed from nineteenth-century literary movements in which he found support for his revolt against the romantic view of history to which he had adhered in his youth. The notion that at the end of the Middle Ages there occurred a "discovery of the world and of man" was shared by many who, after abandoning their romantic attitudes, wondered about the nature and origin of the world that had succeeded the age of feudalism and religious asceticism. While the succinct and elegant formula "la découverte du monde et . . . de l'homme" [the discovery of the world and . . . of man] came from France, a similar leitmotif was used in Germany. There Hegel and historians like Karl Hagen, who was influenced by Hegel, had begun to define the tendencies initiating the modern world in terms of a new self-respect, a vindication of family life and material goods, the dignity of labor, and a new interest in "man's inner life" and in "external nature."

Other parts of Burckhardt's key tenet of "the development of the individual" were derived from Goethe. To his German translation (published in 1803) of Benvenuto Cellini's sixteenth-century autobiography, Goethe had appended a sketch of Cellini and his world that turned the old, time-honored accusations against the wickedness and depravity of the sixteenth-century Italian into a searching psychological analysis. While studying Cellini, Goethe had conceived the notion of an age that brought forth men of rare passion, marked by gross sensuality and feverish, brutal vindictiveness, but also by higher yearnings: a sincere respect for religious and ethical values, for the genius of great men, and for noble enterprises. In Goethe's depiction, Cellini's impulsive nature yields to a thousand temptations but does not succumb in the end to lowly pleasures. The force of this psychology—as well as of some comparable portrayals of the sixteenth-century Italian by two other recent poets, Alfieri in Italy and Stendhal in France—is felt throughout Burckhardt's analysis of the development of the individual.

The fact that Burckhardt wove these various strands of thought into his ***Kultur der Renaissance in Italien*** does not detract from the originality of his vision. It is high praise to say of any historian's work that it has succeeded in making some of the most fruitful philosophical and psychological insights of his own period effective aids in the discovery and interpretation of a past age. In Burckhardt's case, this age comprised the Italian Trecento—especially from the generation of Petrarch onward—the Quattrocento, and the early Cinquecento; in other words, roughly the stretch of history to which the historiography of the humanists and of the Enlightenment had drawn attention long before Burckhardt.

Thus, Burckhardt's decisive step was to focus some of the basic historical queries of the early nineteenth century upon a long-favored portion of Italian history. In order to realize the originality of his conclusions, one needs to recall that Hegel, in attributing the beginning of the modern age to the German Reformation, and Michelet, in placing the dividing line between the Middle Ages and the modern world in the sixteenth century and chiefly outside Italy, had both expressly disparaged the civilization of Quattrocento Italy. The psychological observations and *aperçus* of poets and writers like Goethe, Alfieri, and Stendhal, on the other hand, had tended to concentrate upon sixteenth-century Italians and their characteristic state of mind, and none of them had paid attention to the consequences of the appearance of the new individualism for the historical concept of the transition from the Middle Ages to the modern age. Although Burckhardt adopted some of the queries of previous historians and of contemporary thinkers, it was only when three Italian centuries were systematically reviewed by him through the prism of early nineteenth-century ideas that the concept of those centuries changed from the long-familiar one of "a renaissance of the arts and letters in Italy" to the period concept of "the Italian Renaissance." . . .

Does the consensus about the solidity and scope of Burckhardt's attainment mean that his view of the place of the Italian Renaissance in European history has now, after a hundred years, finally won out?

Burckhardt's thesis, we must understand, is not identical with the notion that some basic elements of modern civilization and, in particular, of the modern mind, appeared in a rudimentary form in Italy during the fourteenth, fifteenth, and sixteenth centuries and afterwards spread through the northern countries. This was how humanistic scholars had always viewed the progress of their cause, at least from the Italian Quattrocento onward, and how eighteenth-century writers had conceived the course of history from the Medicean age to the French and English Enlightenment, with its "sound philosophy." But to the nineteenth-century generation that had abandoned Romanticism, the cardinal point seemed to be in what form, where, and when, after the decay of feudalism and a hierarchical order of life, there first appeared a type of society in which the social function of the individual, his sense of values, and his perceptive powers differed from those of men in the medieval centuries. Burckhardt was searching not so much for the roots of a gradual evolution toward the modern world as for the first appearance of a clearly modern pattern of culture and thought within the framework of a modern state and for the emergence of the psychological and intellectual characteristics of modern man. "The Renaissance will be presented," he explained during the preparation of his work, "in so far as it has become the mother and home of modern man"— that is, through the molding influence of the period on subsequent centuries; his book would point out, for Renaissance Italy, "a number of phenomena of the modern mind." No other leitmotif occurs as often in his text as the contention that the Italians of the Renaissance were the "firstborn among the sons of modern Europe," that "the Italian Renaissance must be called the leader of modern ages," and that "the first truly modern man," "a wholly recognizable prototype of modern man," appeared in the period of Petrarch and the Quattrocento. Only two other points are made as frequently, and these are always closely interrelated with the first. One is that the classical revival in literature and art was not the *cause* of the new

culture, although it was only in the revived classical form that the new intellectual tendencies could find a means of expression capable of influencing and changing the course of Western culture as a whole. The other points is that a new cultural growth took place in Italy because, as the book states on its first page, there, in contrast to all other European countries, "the feudal system" did not survive long but was transformed at an early date into the society of the modern world. Already by the end of the struggle between the popes and the Hohenstaufen emperors, feudalism "had been shaken off almost entirely." This made it possible, only a few generations later, for a new type of state to emerge in which the individual was delivered from his former bonds, and this, in turn, transformed secular values and generated critical thought to a degree unknown outside Italy until the sixteenth century or even later.

Couched in these precise terms, the Burckhardtian concept of the Renaissance is far from being on its way to unanimous adoption by present-day scholars. At least two other notions of the historical development of Europe at the time of the Renaissance, both intrinsically antagonistic to that of Burckhardt, have also made headway since the late nineteenth century. First, the classicistic view of history returned in a new guise, in spite of Burckhardt's caveat against treating the revival of classical studies as *causa prima*. As the role of classical models in medieval literature, philosophy, and art became better known, the history of European culture began to be viewed by some, especially literary scholars, as a continual oscillation between periods of greater or lesser influence of classical elements. In this view, Italian Humanism from the fourteenth to the sixteenth centuries occupies a position between a medieval phase and a modern phase of humanistic classicism, both under French leadership; and thus Renaissance Italy loses much of the newness which the Burckhardtian perspective gives to it. In France, and wherever interest in the medieval humanism of the twelfth century or in the humanistic aspects of Thomism during the thirteenth has been strong, the work of Buckhardt has not held much attraction for the general reader, nor has it had much effect on scholars.

At the opposite end of the spectrum are those who, instead of attributing more influence to the ancient heritage than Burckhardt would allow, wonder whether our standard for what was "modern" after 1300 has not, on the contrary, remained too close to the classicistic point of view; whether we are not wrong to exclude from our concept of the Renaissance the realistic, individualistic, and urban movements outside the classical tradition. Should we not include such European-wide currents of the fourteenth and fifteenth centuries as philosophical "nominalism" and Occamistic science, the naturalism inherent in the political philosophy which sprang from the clash between papal and secular powers, the mystical movements of the late Middle Ages, and the realism of Flemish art? Within this larger framework, can we attribute to the course of events in Italy more significance than that of a merely local or national variation of a European development?

This is not the place to attempt to weigh the relative merits of the three approaches, each representing a partial truth. The point here is that we have every reason to expect that they will be in vigorous contention for decades to come, and perhaps forever. What I wish to explore is to what extent those who believe that the Italian Renaissance can be considered a "prototype" of the modern age will still be able to rely on Burckhardt's book as a sufficient foundation. In order to answer this question, we must try to find any symptomatic lacunae in his definition of Italian culture during the fourteenth, fifteenth, and sixteenth centuries.

From the vantage point of present-day scholarship, Burckhardt's picture of the Renaissance and Humanism is, of course, incomplete because of his ignorance of countless facts, writings, and queries brought forward in recent years. But this is bound to be true of any historical work more than a hundred years old. A deeper problem raised by his book is whether, despite its many great qualities, it was sufficiently inclusive with respect to the historical questions that could be posed—and were posed—in its own time. The fact, already stressed, that Burckhardt's presentation shows an unusually broad response to the philosophical and literary issues of his generation and those immediately preceding would make any serious omission all the more remarkable and in need of explanation.

There have not been many investigations of how complete Burckhardt's reconstruction was relative to the scholarship of his own age. Nevertheless, one gap in his work is strikingly obvious. One would think that nothing would have appealed to Burckhardt as much as the idea, already formulated in the eighteenth century, that the vitality of the Italian communes was stimulated by their successful defense of political independence and republican freedom during the eleventh, twelfth, and thirteenth centuries, and that it was owing to this political stimulus that the arts and letters later matured so rapidly. Even before 1800, philosophers and historians in Europe had sought to identify the factors in Italian society that might have been responsible for the distinctive flowering of culture on the peninsula; and by the early nineteenth century, two main complementary theories had gradually emerged to account for it.

One ascribed it to the invigorating power of competition within and between free city-states; this was an English eighteenth-century idea traceable to Hume (who applied it to Antiquity but was too prejudiced against Italian politics and literature to apply it to the Italian city-republics of the late Middle Ages). It was proposed most maturely in Adam Ferguson's *Essay on the History of Civil Society* of 1767, where it is argued that when in free societies many different types of men react to a common challenge, every conceivable form of human energy is released, and engagement and "exertion" become the major stimuli for culture. Ancient "Greece, divided into many little states, and agitated beyond any spot on the globe by domestic contentions and foreign wars, set the example in every species of literature. The fire was communicated to Rome; not when the [Roman] state ceased to be warlike

and discontinued political agitations, but when she mixed the love of refinement and of pleasure with her national pursuits, and indulged an inclination to study in the midst of ferments occasioned by the wars and pretensions of opposite factions. It was revived in modern Europe among the turbulent states of modern Italy. . . ."

The second approach was stimulated by Rosseau's praise of popular sovereignty and direct democracy in small local states. Under the influence of his early life in Geneva, the participation of a full-fledged citizen in the government of his city *patria* had seemed to him an even more effective spur to civic vigor than "turbulence." At the time of Geneva's subjection to Napoleon, Rousseau's countryman Simonde de' Sismondi drew upon Rousseau's ideas for a comparative study of the effects of the ancient Greek and medieval Italian city-states on the behavior and outlook of their citizens. . . .

In the works of Adam Ferguson and Sismondi we find the seeds of an interpretation that intimately connects psychological and intellectual change with a citizen's political life. Some historians of the subsequent romantic period carried this approach still further. In 1844, the *Storia delle belle lettere in Italia* by Paolo Emiliani Guidici (like Ferguson's and Sismondi's works, a book that should have been known to Burckhardt) made a special plea for "a political interpretation of literature." . . .

Against this background one realizes that some approaches which had been taken long before 1860 were overlooked or quietly excluded when Burckhardt undertook to describe "the development of the individual" in Renaissance Italy. In the chapter so title, after insisting on the disappearance of medieval cast distinctions, he analyzes the growth of many new fields of knowledge, the changes in the evaluation of life, and especially the appearance of uniquely "rounded" personalities. All these—to him, outstanding—characteristics of the period he traces back not to the molding influence of a society in which citizens were exposed to competitive conditions and allowed to be rulers as well as ruled, but rather to the impact of the life of those who through avoidance of public duties gained leisure for cultural pursuits. The type of "private man, indifferent to politics and occupied partly . . . with the interests of a dilettante," is said to have developed primarily in those states in which despots had taken the burden of government and administration upon themselves and thus relieved their subjects of participation in the common pursuits. But similar conditions existed also in republics, where men in power often had "to make the utmost" of a short period of triumph and afterwards, defeated or exiled, found themselves "involuntarily at leisure." Like the subjects of despots, such citizens, recognizing "the dangers and thanklessness of public life," learned to prize "a developed private life" as the necessary basis for cultural pursuits.

Why did Burckhardt limit his interest to this one aspect? Why did he not make use of the rudimentary sociology of city-state life already prepared by historians of the Enlightenment and Romanticism? Certainly not because he misjudged the continued importance of the republics of Florence and Venice during the Renaissance. His book includes some of the most impressive and sympathetic pages ever written on achievements in the Florentine republic: the spread of political *raisonnement* and a keen sense of calculation among an entire people, and the priority in time of the patronage of Florentine citizens over that of the princes. He described the difference between Florentine historiography—written "by citizens for citizens, as the ancients did"—and the work of official, paid historiographers in most principalities, from whose propensity for the "servile citation" of ancient parallels to the actions of the prince "the great Florentine historians and statesmen are completely free . . . , because the nature of their political life necessarily fostered in them a mode of thought with some analogy to that of Antiquity"; and he cited the last, heroic defense of the city in 1529-1530, without which Florentine history "would have been the poorer by one of its greatest and most ennobling memories."

The reason why Burckhardt did not develop any such observations for his general conception of the period must be sought, rather, in the peculiar bent of his personal relationship to culture. During the mid-1840s, when he was not yet thirty years old, he had turned with abhorrence from the rising democratic trend, which seemed to him to represent a fatal peril to civilization, heralding an upsurge of the masses, brutal wars, and despotism. He felt that he himself in such an iron, barbaric age should lead a life of privacy and withdrawal, by which he might best help to preserve the old, aristocratic traditions of European culture. It is not a question here of how good a judge of his time and prophet of the future Burckhardt was, or how valid his appraisal of Europe's aristocratic past. What matters to us is the impact these passionate convictions had on his views and historical methodology. Although his political outlook was far from the "liberalism" of German *Neuhumanisten* [new humanists] like Wilhelm von Humboldt, whom he admired, in effect he adopted Humboldt's belief that true individual culture could develop only in separation from the state. It is true that Burckhardt feared the further rise of the nineteenth-century state, shocked as he was by the revolutions of the 1840s, while Humboldt had been afraid of the absolutist monarchy of the eighteenth century; but for both, the ultimate goal was the harmonious growth and training of all the potentialities of the proud, autarchic individual. . . .

These blind spots also affected Burckhardt's appreciation of Humanism. If it is true that the political thought and historical outlook of the Renaissance can be appraised only in the context of the feud between city-state republics and Renaissance despotism, our understanding of humanistic pursuits will suffer if they are viewed, in isolation from the vital struggles of the age, as contributions of self-sufficient dilettantes or scholars. . . .

We have . . . come to recognize that in the long period from the fourteenth to the sixteenth centuries, Humanism was a far more profoundly variable historical trend than Burckhardt knew, differing in structure and creativity, in ideas and values, and in political and social background. In fact, despite temporary setbacks, scholarship after Burckhardt has on the whole moved steadily in the direction of a conception of the Renaissance which recognizes—for Humanism as well as for art—two fundamentally different periods: the "Trecento" and the "Quattrocento," the first still basically medieval, the second the true beginning of the Renaissance. This important distinction had to be worked out in detail almost without the help of Burckhardt, who instead of differentiating the successive phases of the Renaissance, presented a comparatively static picture in which the rise of "individualism," "the discovery of the world and of man," and related themes are presented as features common to three centuries.

Does this criticism mean that our perspective of the Renaissance has so changed that we can no longer call ourselves "Burckhardtians"? Before drawing this conclusion, we should remember that as a young art historian, prior to writing his **Kultur der Renaissance,** Burckhardt had strongly emphasized the profundity of the changes at the beginning of the Quattrocento. In his **Cicerone,** a "Guide to the Art Treasures of Italy" written five years before the **Kultur,** he had dated the onset of "the true Renaissance" (*eigentliche Renaissance*) in architecture "about 1420," and had magnificently described the rise of "the new spirit" of Renaissance painting "during the first decades of the fifteenth century." Thus, Burckhardt was actually the provider of two heterogeneous period concepts, one of which brings out the crucial role of the first decades of the Quattrocento in the breakthrough of "the new spirit" that guided and animated the mature Renaissance in art.

We do not know whether he himself was aware of the antithetical character of his approaches to art on the one hand and to culture in general on the other when, five years later, he drew his picture of Renaissance culture. But even if he was aware of the inherent antagonism between the period divisions set forth in his two books, he could not reconcile them in his **Kultur der Renaissance** by pointing out the chronological parallel between the emergence in art of the "true Renaissance" and the emergence of "true" Humanism. For it is only thanks to post-Burckhardtian insights into the history of Humanism—the emergence among Italian humanists not only of phiological studies and rhetoric but also of a "new spirit" in their outlook on life, history, and politics—that students have become aware of the parallelism of the two revolutions in art and in Humanism. . . .

A belief in the great cultural creativity of city-state societies is in obvious harmony with some of the general historical assumptions of the century that has passed since his time. Increasing familiarity with the preceding civilizations of the ancient East has only helped to strengthen the conviction that Greek and Roman culture was different from that of the Orient because it was founded on the political liberty existing in city-states; that much of what was to remain the political, ethical, and cultural heritage of the Western world was first developed in the bracing atmosphere of small commonwealths. The more fully, therefore, we recognize the significance that city-state society had for the Italian Renaissance, the more the relationship of Renaissance culture to modern life is seen to be part of a wider manifestation: the unique affiliation of Western history with traditions inherited from poleis of some sort. With the growing attention paid to this historical phenomenon, the essence of the Burckhardtian conception—the "prototypical" character of the Renaissance in Italy—may carry even greater conviction in years to come. . . .

William Kerrigan and Gordon Braden (essay date 1989)

SOURCE: "Burckhardt's Renaissance," in *The Idea of the Renaissance,* The Johns Hopkins University Press, 1989, pp. 3-35.

[*In the following excerpt, Kerrigan and Braden analyze Burkhardt's understanding of Renaissance individualism and posit that, in Burckhardt's view, the concept of honor provides the only counterbalance to the destructiveness of unbridled individualism.*]

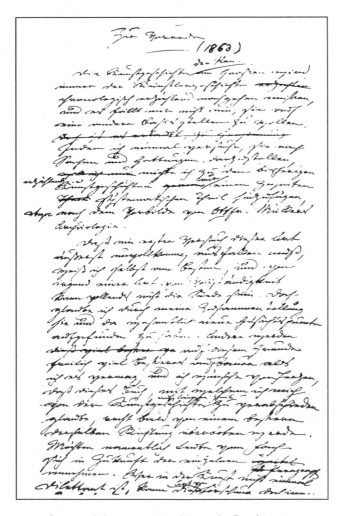

Portion of the manuscript of Kunst der Renaissance.

In the offing [in the stories about the spiteful wit Pietro Aretino] is one of Burckhardt's most troubled points about the individualism that he is sometimes taken merely to celebrate. Emperors aspire to uniqueness. A private selfhood that adopts in metaphorical form the authority and autonomy of political imperialism will adopt its aggression as well, a chronic irritability in the vicinity of others like itself. Part of what Burckhardt is establishing with his central contrast between the Renaissance and the Middle Ages is that representatives of the former will have a radical difficulty recognizing and working any secure common ground among them. Within the full picture of the period as Burckhardt understands it, that difficulty proves lethal.

The public part of the picture is the story that prompts the first modern political narrative, the story of how Italy lost control of its own destiny to become a battleground for foreign powers. Francesco Guicciardini's *History of Italy* begins with a celebration of the comparative peace achieved among the more important Italian states in the later fifteenth century, though it is not so much a settlement as an edgy balance of power:

> This alliance easily curbed the cupidity of the Venetian Senate, but it did not unite the allies in sincere and faithful friendship, insofar as, full of emulation and jealousy among themselves, they did not cease to assiduously observe what the others were doing, each of them reciprocally aborting all the plans whereby any of the others might become more powerful or renowned.

With the death of Lorenzo de' Medici—replaced by his erratic son Piero—and of Innocent VIII—replaced by the Borgia pope Alexander VI—the "pestiferous thirst for domination" which continues to animate the principals slips once more out of communal control to bring on what becomes known as the *calamità d'Italia* Italy's disaster. Lodovico Sforza thinks he is only strengthening his own hand against a perceived détente between Florence and Naples when he invites Charles VIII of France to make good on his claim to the Neapolitan throne. Before events play themselves out, Sforza is dead in a French prison and all of Italy, except a weakened Venice, is under the domination of Emperor Charles V. Guicciardini's political thought generally is much occupied with the ambition of *il particulare,* the political individual, whose drive is both an indispensable resource and a civic menace:

> Citizens who seek honor and glory in their city are praise worthy and useful. . . . Would to God our republic were full of such ambition! But citizens whose only goal is power are dangerous. For men who make power their idol cannot be restrained by any considerations of honor or justice, and they will step on anything and everything to attain that goal.

The *History* tells how the tragic potential of that drive came to dominate the Italian scene.

In the long view, Burckhardt sees the *calamità* as a greater disaster than even Guicciardini realized: the effectively suicidal end to the Italian Renaissance. Despite its organization into topics, "The State as a Work of Art" takes on conventional narrative form as it moves toward this conclusion, which for Burckhardt is a bitter lesson about the inability of Renaissance Italians to make common cause:

> When . . . in the political intercourse of the fifteenth century the common fatherland is sometimes emphatically named it is done in most cases to annoy some other Italian state. The first decades of the sixteenth century, the years when the Renaissance attained its fullest bloom, were not favorable to a revival of patriotism; the enjoyment of intellectual and artistic pleasures, the comforts and elegancies of life, and the supreme interests of self-development, destroyed or hampered the love of country. But those deeply serious and sorrowful appeals to national sentiment were not heard again till later, when the time for unity had gone by, when the country was inundated with Frenchmen and Spaniards, and when a German army had conquered Rome.

Individualism cannot defend its own nest.

This is the story that Burckhardt has to tell, the diachronic dimension recoverable from what is for the most part offered as a synchronic *Bildung* [image]. It was the diachronic dimension of Hegel's philosophy that most directly irritated Burckhardt, and there are good reasons for remarking on the general absence from the **Civilization** of any serious interest in the processes of historical change: "He regarded various aspects of the Renaissance, from politics to poetry, as objective historical entities whose temporal and spatial boundaries were clearly delimited. He was interested neither in where those entities came from nor in the directions in which they were tending." Yet we would argue that in at least one important regard Burckhardt's book is in the grip of an inclusive narrative, effaced to some degree it is so painful a story. Burckhardt's Renaissance destroys itself in following out the very logic of its own genius. The political fable has roots in received historiographic wisdom, but Burckhardt replicates it with striking originality on other levels, to make it a central part of his idea about the age.

The lengthy third section on "The Revival of Antiquity" ends, unexpectedly, with a section on the "Fall of the Humanists in the Sixteenth Century":

> After a brilliant succession of poet-scholars had . . . filled Italy and the world with the worship of antiquity, had determined the forms of education and culture, had often taken the lead in political affairs, and had, to no small extent, reproduced ancient literature—at length in the sixteenth century . . . the whole class fell into deep and general disgrace.

This is not a standard topic in the study of humanism. It is not there in the work of Burckhardt's contemporary Georg Voigt, and no particular consensus has evolved that any such phenomenon took place, aside from a general stagging of Italian culture under Spanish domination.

The early sixteenth century is if anything now remembered as the time when the alliance with printing celebrated and exploited by Erasmus enabled the movement to jump the Alps and achieve a new level of security and influence. Part of what concerns Burckhardt is the inevitably depersonalizing character of this success: "The spread of printed editions of the classics, and of large and well-arranged handbooks and dictionaries, went far to free the people from the necessity of personal intercourse with the humanists." A modern commentator might see no more here than the inevitable obsolescence of a certain style of heroic entrepreneurship. Burckhardt, however, detects something more virulent at work in a few extended attacks on the moral character of humanists as a group. The term *umanista* indeed makes its debut in Italian literature in the satire of Ariosto that Burckhardt cites:

> Senza quel vizio son pochi umanisti
> che fe' a Dio forza, non che persüase,
> di far Gomorra e i suoi vicini tristi . . .
>   Ride il volgo, se sente un ch'abbia vena
> di poesia, e poi dice:—È gran periglio
> a dormir seco e volgierli la schiena.

> Few humanists are without that vice which did not so much persuade, as forced, God to render Gomorrah and her neighbor wretched! . . . The vulgar laugh when they hear of someone who possesses a vein of poetry, and then they say, "It is a great peril to turn your back if you sleep next to him."

It is still possible to be unimpressed, especially since the most extensive text Burckhardt has to adduce is labeled by its own author a rhetorical *progymnasma,* or exercise. Burckhardt, however, is alert to a mirroring here of Italy's national fate: the generalized accusations of the sixteenth century merely repeat the *ad hominem* internal polemics of the fifteenth century as a brief against the whole profession. "The first to make these charges were certainly the humanists themselves. Of all men who ever formed a class, they had the least sense of their common interests, and least respected what there was of this sense." Like the *signori,* they are collectively betrayed by their incurable competitiveness.

The point opens onto something less vulnerable than some of the claims that lead up to it. The core of the chapter is Burckhardt's intuitive but compelling delineation of the psychic cost of the typical humanist career:

> For an ambitious youth, the fame and the brilliant position of the humanists were a perilous temptation; it seemed to him that he too "through inborn nobility could no longer regard the low and common things of life." He was thus led to plunge into a life of excitement and vicissitude, in which exhausting studies, tutorships, secretaryships, professorships, offices in princely households, mortal enmities and perils, luxury and beggary, boundless admiration and boundless contempt, followed confusedly one upon the other, and in which the most solid worth and learning were often pushed aside by superficial impudence. But the worst of all was that the position of the humanist was almost

incompatible with a fixed home, since it either made frequent changes of dwelling necessary for a livelihood, or so affected the mind of the individual that he could never be happy for long in one place.

Burckhardt had earlier quoted as if with approval the humanists' own boast about their homeless independence. Here that condition reappears not as a strength but as a curse. Burckhardt is probing a pathology that is built into the very structure of the individualism which he elsewhere praises:

> Such men can hardly be conceived to exist without an inordinate pride. They needed it, if only to keep their heads above water, and were confirmed in it by the admiration which alternated with hatred in the treatment they received from the world. They are the most striking examples and victims of an unbridled subjectivity.

The original detachment from group identity that made Renaissance individualism possible comes in the end to a willful and deathly solitude. Burckhardt's revision of Hegel's dialectic issues not in the higher realm of *unendende Subjectivität,* [unbounded subjectivity] but in an *entfesselte Subjectivität* [rootless subjectivity] that is actually a kind of suicide.

This intelligent ambivalence exerts pressure on the rest of Burckhardt's book and indeed much of his historical thought. The theorist of "*der Staat als Kunstwerk*" is also an impressive prophet of the state's demonic extremity in our own century, from which he recoils in horror: "Power is of its nature evil, whoever wields it. It is not a stability but a lust, and *ipso facto* insatiable, therefore unhappy in itself and doomed to make others unhappy." From his lecture notes we sense a deep pessimism about the modern world that the Renaissance initiates, as well as a strong attraction to the medieval dispensation that he became famous for scorning. Even within the **Civilization** Burckhardt does not imagine Renaissance man merely outgrowing the bonds that obligate him to others like himself. That those bonds become more difficult to recognize and respect was the age's great danger, the problem that most desperately needed to be solved.

The book's last section, "Morality and Religion," takes up directly the means by which combative individualism might be made social and accountable; it proves the most troubled section, awkwardly apologetic at the outset:

> The ultimate truth with respect to the character, the conscience, and the guilt of a people remains for ever a secret. . . . We must leave those who find a pleasure in passing sweeping censures on whole nations to do so as they like. The peoples of Europe can maltreat, but happily not judge, one another.

This is defensive prologue to Burckhardt's concession that the cliché of Italian wickedness in the Renaissance is neither inaccurate nor irrelevant: "It cannot be denied that Italy at the beginning of the sixteenth century found itself in the midst of a grave moral crisis, out of which the best men saw hardly any escape." By the end of the chapter, the formulation has become even more acute: "The fundamental vice of this character was at the same time a condition of its greatness—namely, developed individualism. . . . In face of all objective facts, of laws and restraints of whatever kind, he retains the feeling of his own sovereignty". The health and indeed survival of any individualistic civilization depends upon some external responsibility gaining purchase on that unfriendly surface. But so posed, the need seems almost a contradiction in terms.

Burckhardt himself highlights "the sentiment of honor" as "that moral force which was then the strongest bulwark against evil," and indeed one of the most important legacies of the Renaissance to later times: "This is that enigmatic mixture of conscience and egoism which often survives in modern after he has lost, whether by his own fault or not, faith, love, and hope. . . . It has become, in a far wider sense than is commonly believed, a decisive test of conduct in the minds of the cultivated Europeans of our own day." Not itself a moral code, honor is a means by which personal pride can be enlisted on the side of morality, protecting that morality against anomie, even to the point of thriving on it. The term indeed has a special aura in Renaissance culture, and it prompts some extravagant language. Burckhardt specifically quotes Rabelais on the Abbey of Théléme:

> In their rules there was only one clause:
>
> DO WHAT YOU WILL
>
> because people who are free, well-born, well-bred, and easy in honest company have a natural spur and instinct which drives them to virtuous deeds and deflects them from vice; and this they called honor.

Such honor implants the dictates of conscience so deeply into the individual psyche that no external constraints are necessary. Morality coincides precisely with impulse and desire, so that "Fais ce que voudras" is an injunction that does not threaten the social and civic fabric but is its great source of strength.

The briefness of Burckhardt's discussion of the matter, though, entails a recognition that the ideal is an intrinsically treacherous one. "This sense of honor," he concedes, "is compatible with much selfishness and great vices, and may be the victim of astonishing illusions." The mysterious chemistry that allows egoism to be shaped by conscience also allows conscience to be shaped by egoism. Burckhardt moves on to the most conspicuous specific, the cult of revenge:

> This personal need of vengeance felt by the cultivated and highly placed Italian, resting on the solid basis of an analogous popular custom, naturally displays itself under a thousand different aspects, and receives the unqualified approval of public opinion. . . . Only there must be art in the vengeance, and the satisfaction must

be compounded of the material injury and moral humiliation of the offender. A mere brutal, clumsy triumph of force was held by public opinion no satisfaction. The whole man with his sense of fame and of scorn, not only his fist, must be victorious.

Burckhardt gives several vivid examples of the vendetta *als Kunstwerk:* "After dinner he told him whose liver it was." The code is to prove one of Italy's most notorious exports, with private vengeance becoming a major concern for the governments of England, France, and Spain, and a dominant theme on their tragic stages. Burckhardt partly obscures the urgency of his point by ascribing this and other aberrations (such as gambling) to an unusually strong imagination (the Italian imagination kept the picture of the wrong alive with frightful vividness"). But the usually invoked motive for vengeance is honor, within whose cultus justice is effectively equated with self-respect. Renaissance literature gives some of its most memorable attention to the Herostratic potential of this noble word:

> —O thou Othello, that was once so good,
> Fall'n in the practice of a damned slave,
> What shall be said to thee?
> —   Why, any thing:
> An honorable murderer, if you will;
> For nought I did in hate, but all in honor.
>   (Othello 5.2.291-95)

Such demeanor had an authority and allure that troubled the very possibility of Renaissance civilization:

> When a murder was committed the sympathies of the people, before the circumstances of the case were known, ranged themselves instinctively on the side of the murderer. A proud, manly bearing before and at the execution excited such admiration that the narrator often forgets to tell us for what offence the criminal was put to death. But when we add to this inward contempt of law and to the countless grudges and enmities which called for satisfaction the impunity which crime enjoyed during times of political disturbance we can only wonder that the State and society were not utterly dissolved.

Burckhardt's Italy is a Thélème gone mad, in which "Fais ce que voudras" is, as we would normally expect, a call to anarchy.

Attempts were made in the Renaissance to define honor with enough care to avoid such consequences, primarily by internalizing it and (as Burckhardt does) distinguishing it from fame. But the ethical need it tries to fill finds a more decisive answer outside Burckhardt's territory. Burckhardt himself wonders why Italy did not produce a Reformation, and gives the "plausible answer": "The Italian mind . . . never went farther than the denial of hierarchy, while the origin and vigor of the German Reformation was due to its positive religious doctrines, most of all to the doctrines of justification by faith and of the inefficacy of good works." That is to beg the question of causality, but the contrast is revealing. For it is in Protes-

tant religious experience that conscience and egoism are reconciled by a mystery deeper than that of honor. Luther's account of Christian freedom is boldly paradoxical: "A Christian is a perfectly free lord of all, subject to none. A Christian is a perfectly dutiful servant of all, subject to all." These contrary propositions are interwoven in justification by faith, which begins with the acceptance of the harshest of moral judgments on oneself: "The moment you begin to have faith you learn that all things in you are altogether blameworthy, sinful, and damnable." Yet the certainty of never being able to merit salvation by any action or achievement is met by the promise of salvation *sola fide,* an inward emotional state which is everything: "a splendid privilege and hard to attain, a truly omnipotent power, a spiritual dominion in which there is nothing so good and nothing so evil but that it shall work together for good to me, if only I believe." Humiliation and submission, if sufficiently extreme, recover a primal sense of strength and confidence: "Who then can comprehend the lofty dignity of the Christian? By virtue of his royal power he rules over all things, death, life, and sin, and through his priestly glory is omnipotent with God because he does the things which God asks and desires." Selfishness here is both harshly straitened and grandiosely satisfied. Protestant theologians will develop the traditional Christian attack on individual pride with new force and sophistication; but as they do so, they also intensify the role of the individual conscience, and translate the institutional church into subjective terms that give individualism a new and potent dimension. The Italian project, we might say, was incomplete in subjectivizing only the state. The Reformation, subjectivizing the church as well, in this regard completes the Renaissance.

To put it that way is to gesture toward the *telos* for a general European Renaissance within which Burckhardt's Italy is only the opening chapter.

Felix Gilbert (essay date 1990)

SOURCE: "Burckhardt's Concept of Cultural History," in *History: Politics or Culture,* Princeton University Press, 1990, pp. 46-80.

[*In the following excerpt, Gilbert describes Burckhardt's intended projects in his early career and one of his early works,* The Age of Constantine the Great.]

When his years of study came to an end, Jacob Burckhardt decided to work in a particular field of history: in cultural history. What did that decision mean? What did he understand by this term? Did his conception of cultural history undergo significant changes in the course of his life? These are the questions with which this chapter is concerned.

In the early 1840s, cultural history was a small but recognized special field. Karl Dietrich Hüllmann was one of the few professors who offered lectures on cultural history, and he has left a description of what he considered cultural history to be: "So far," he stated, "history has always been treated in a very one-sided way; it has been exclusively concerned with those who have been influential and have written about their experiences. Scant attention has been paid to the lower classes [*Niedere Volk*] or to the age in general. This is the aim of cultural history, which, without regard to social status or to language, encompasses the whole of humanity. It illustrates the outstanding stages of development through which the prominent nations of the whole world have passed till they have reached the situation in which they are now."

This statement assigns to cultural history two related but distinctive functions. First of all cultural history has the task of recording the daily life of society and of all its groups. Indeed, in the six volumes in which Hüllmann described life in the towns of the Middle Ages, he dealt with the most varied aspects of urban life: guild regulations and festivities, drinking habits and gambling, the relation of dress to social standing, family life and prostitution—all aspects of what we would now call social history. It is no accident that Hüllmann's work in cultural history was centered on urban life. Towns were a favorite subject of cultural historians, and the connection between cultural history and towns had come to exist as the very words *culture* and *cultural* gained currency. These words had appeared in the German language only at the end of the eighteenth century and were then meant to signify the effort and the result of imposing reason and system on human activities. In this process of "cultivation" the development of towns was considered to have been of decisive importance; they were the focus of intense economic activity and they also stimulated intellectual life. At the end of the eighteenth century and the beginning of the nineteenth, the history of towns had a particular, almost personal interest to German academics. Towns had given rise to the middle classes and academics usually came from those classes, which were then struggling for a greater role in government and civic affairs.

According to Hüllmann's statement cultural history had a further purpose: to distinguish epochs of history from each other and to describe the stages of development through which the leading nations of the world had passed. One reason this function was ascribed to cultural history was the great popularity that the notion of *Zeitgeist* had acquired in the eighteenth century; those living in this enlightened age felt different from, and superior to, other periods of history. Voltaire had spread widely this view of the qualitative difference of historical periods with his distinction of "four brilliant ages" that stand out from the course of history: the times of Alexander and Pericles, of Caesar and Augustus, of the Medici, and of the "siècle de Louis XIV." Clearly, this kind of cultural history shifted emphasis to the preeminent classes of society, to literature and art, and to education and scholarly activities.

In the early years of his scholarly career, when Burckhardt referred to cultural history, his notions were similar to those of Hüllmann and other cultural historians of that time. Burckhardt's dissertation on Konrad von Hochstaden, published in 1843, contains detailed descriptions of social life. When in 1848—after six somewhat restless years in Berlin, Basel, and Italy—Burckhardt decided to accept a position in Basel as teacher of history at the university and at the Pädagogium, he came with a plan to edit a library of cultural history. It was to consist of a number of small, relatively cheap volumes aimed at the general public. Burckhardt's plan gives the titles of the prospective volumes: *The Age of Pericles, The Times of the Later Roman Emperors, The Century of Charlemagne, The Period of the Hohenstaufen, German Life in the Fifteenth Century, The Age of Raphael*. The criterion Burckhardt used for giving each volume a special theme was the cultural distinctiveness and coherence of an epoch. An example of what Burckhardt expected these volumes to contain is revealed in a course of lectures he gave in Basel in the winter of 1849-50, which fell under the rubric of "The Heyday of the Middle Ages" and treated the European Middle Ages from the eleventh to the fourteenth century as a coherent and unified period, distinctly separated from the preceding and the following centuries. At the outset of this course of lectures Burckhardt made it clear that he did not intend to discuss political developments, chronology, and geography. Rather he would lecture on medieval life in its relation to the spiritual trends that were at work throughout the entire period and created a common attitude in the various European nations. Evidently Burckhardt intended to combine a description of the varieties of life with an analysis of the all-pervasive, unique character of the period. In the course of these lectures Burckhardt discussed the organization and the impact of the Church, the rise of the towns, and the origin of the mendicant orders, and he offered an appraisal of what he called the greatest artistic achievement of the Middle Ages, the Gothic cathedral. But his lectures were primarily concerned with the dominant social class of that time: the knights. Burckhardt regarded them as crucially important because their ideals permeated the period, inspiring a sense of honor that the ancient world had not known, and creating the conditions for the emergence of knightly epic and poetry.

We do not know whether this picture of the culture of the High Middle Ages was meant to be a model of what the single volumes of Burckhardt's projected library were to contain, or whether, in these lectures, he made use of material he had collected for a particular volume in this series that was now no longer needed for this purpose. Soon after Burckhardt settled in Basel, he abandoned his plan for a library of cultural history.

Burckhardt turned to another subject: in 1852 **The Age of Constantine the Great** appeared, the first of Burckhardt's three cultural histories. **The Age of Constantine** was followed by **The Civilization of the Renaissance in Italy** in 1860, and by the **Greek Cultural History** in 1898. **The Age of Constantine** has particular importance for the development of Burckhardt's concept of cultural history. When he began writing it, he intended it to conform to the prevailing notions of this genre. As he worked his way into the topic he found himself increasingly restricted by these notions. He began, then, to examine them critically and to chart his own course.

Not until twenty-eight years after its first appearance, in the preface to the second edition of the *Constantine,* did Burckhardt call this work a cultural history; such a characterization is not to be found in the text of the book. At the time of its first publication in 1853, Burckhardt made remarks which suggest that he had intended to write a cultural history but that he had encountered difficulties. His aim had been to "bring together the significant characteristic aspects of the world of that time in a vivid picture," that is, to achieve what was regarded as the particular task of cultural history. However, he continued, he had not been able to carry out this plan because wide areas of the life of that time, particularly its economic and financial aspects, had not yet been sufficiently explored. However, a letter written at about the same time indicates that this was hardly the main reason for what Burckhardt then called the "unevenness of the book." The difficulty he had encountered was to fit into the existing framework of cultural history an evaluation of the contribution that a particular period had made to the development of world history.

In writing *The Age of Constantine* Burckhardt became aware that it was not possible to treat a period of the past as a separate or independent unit. The historian is interested in the past because of its bearing upon the present, and the contribution of a past period to the course of world history must form an integral element of every evaluation of the past. Awareness of the interrelationship between past and present became a crucial element in Burckhardt's concept of cultural history. *Constantine* is the first expression of what became a fundamental characteristic of his approach to the past.

For a young scholar who had worked on German medieval history and on art history, the choice of the Age of Constantine as a subject of extended historical research is astonishing and deserves some attention. It seems likely, almost certain, that Burckhardt received the first impulse for the *Constantine* in the summer semester of 1841, when he studied in Bonn. There he was a member of the group around Gottfried Kinkel, and he became Kinkel's particular friend. One of Kinkel's most popular lecture courses at the university was "The History of Paganism." This course represented the outline of a book in which Kinkel intended to write about the first three centuries after the birth of Christ, analyzing the political and intellectual developments in the course of which the victory of Christianity became a "historical necessity." After Burckhardt had left Bonn, Kinkel's plans for this book were often mentioned in the correspondence between the two men. Burckhardt seems to have concentrated fully on *The Age of Constantine* only after it had become clear to him that Kinkel would never write a book on this topic.

The dominating issue of *The Age of Constantine*—the victory of Christianity over paganism—had interest and significance because it seemed a mirror image of the recent German past, when a new attitude toward life and ethics based on philosophy and neoclassicism was undermining the validity of traditional church doctrines. The times when the old gods were sinking had a seductive attraction in a time when they were rising again. Moreover, Burckhardt was personally involved in the debate about the relevance of the doctrines and teachings of the Protestant church. A descendant of a long line of Protestant ministers, Burckhardt was expected to follow in their footsteps and had indeed begun to study theology. He had lost his faith, however, and changed to the study of history. But among those with whom he had studied—in Switzerland, in Berlin, and Bonn—were several theologians, and the role of Christianity in the modern world remained vital in discussions with his friends.

When Burckhardt was a student in Bonn this issue did not remain on a theoretical level. It created a serious conflict in which Kinkel was the chief figure. Kinkel too had started out as a theologian. He was a lecturer in the theological faculty of Bonn University, gave religious instruction in a school in Bonn, and preached in a Cologne parish. But Kinkel became attached to a married woman, who although seeking a divorce was still legally married, thus arousing strong disapproval in Protestant circles. Kinkel was forced to give up preaching and teaching school and, with some difficulties, he moved from the theological to the philosophical faculty of Bonn University. Not surprisingly, Kinkel turned away from Christianity and adopted a pantheistic outlook. Burckhardt watched closely as this drama unfolded. It must have been a concrete demonstration of the pressure that society, institutions, and political power could exert on an individual's personal life and religious beliefs. It gave some reality to what had happened in the times of Constantine.

Events of the recent past seemed to throw further light on the period of Constantine. Burckhardt's book is called *The Age of Constantine the Great,* a title that underlines its thesis of the overwhelming impact which a powerful personality can have on the course of history. In Burckhardt's book the victory of Christianity and the transformation of the Roman Empire from paganism to Christianity are presented as the work of one great individual, Constantine. Behind Burckhardt's belief in Constantine's ability to shape the course of history stood the figure who dominated Burckhardt's own time: Napoleon. In reporting about Constantine's campaign against Maxentius, Burckhardt compared it to "the Italian campaign of the youthful Napoleon with which it has more than one battlefield in common," and a reference to Napoleon occurs again when Burckhardt sums up his picture of Constantine as "a genius in stature who knew no moral scruple in politics and regarded the religious question exclusively from the point of view of political expediency."

Two of Burckhardt's teachers at the University of Berlin had frequently lectured on periods of transition in which two civilizations clashed. Johann Gustav Droysen had coined the term "Hellenism" to characterize the new civilization that arose from the establishment of Greek rule in Asia Minor and Egypt. And for Ranke the invasion of the German tribes into the Latin world of the Roman Empire signified the beginning of a new historical period, that of European history. In scrutinizing the process by which the victory of Christianity was attained in the Roman world, Burckhardt investigated a historical moment to which Ranke assigned crucial importance for the development of European history.

When Burckhardt wrote about the importance of Constantine he stated: "It is a remarkable concatenation of deeds and destiny to which ambitious men who are highly gifted are drawn as by some mysterious power." The Great Man acts by the principle of "necessity." While he "believes that he himself is ruling his age and determining its character," in reality "an epoch is expressed in his person"—that is why he is able to determine and change the course of history.

This view of the historical significance of a great personality hardly permits the presentation of a past era in accordance with the prevailing notions of cultural history. The world of action and the world of daily life seem far apart. Descriptions of a static character, which cultural history demanded, could not explain why this was a period of transition in which a decisive change in world history took place.

Nevertheless, Burckhardt's concern with fulfilling the demands of conventional cultural history is very noticeable in the **Constantine**. Burckhardt describes in detail the differences in the habits and behavior of the Gauls, the Britons, and the Germans, thereby directing attention to the problems involved in maintaining control over an empire of such varied composition. Cultural differences emerge sharply in Burckhardt's characterization of the great metropolitan centers: Alexandria, "which no other city of the world could equal in splendor in material as well as spiritual activities but also in corruption," and Rome, with both a refined Christian and pagan high society and masses craving for spectacles. Some of the most interesting passages of the book deal with life in the caves and huts to which the first eremites retired; the reader is made aware of the existence of strains and attitudes that came to full development in medieval Christianity. Because of these descriptions of situations in the various parts of the empire, the book has a remarkable liveliness.

By describing individual situations with concreteness and precision Burckhardt showed his intent to fit his work into the accepted pattern of cultural history, but it lacks, as Burckhardt himself remarked, "a consistent principle of presentation." There was a marked difference between the detailed account of a static situation and the explanation of the dynamic development that made the age of Constantine a crucial factor in the formation of modern Europe.

FURTHER READING

Biography

Kaegi, Werner. *Jacob Burckhardt: Eine Biographie.* 8 vols. Basel: Schwabe, 1947-85.
  Standard biography, in German.

Criticism

Gay, Peter. "Burckhardt: The Poet of Truth." In his *Style in History,* pp. 139-82. New York: Basic Books, 1974.
  Analyzes Burkhardt's literary style, with particular regard to *The Civilization of the Renaissance in Italy.*

Jensen, De Lamar. "Burckhardt's Renaissance: A Centenary Appraisal." *Western Humanities Review* XV, No. 4 (Autumn 1961): 309-24.
  Detailed discussion of the reception of *The Civilization of the Renaissance in Italy.*

Neff, Emery. *The Poetry of History: The Contribution of Literature and Literary Scholarship to the Writings of History Since Voltaire.* New York: Columbia University Press, 1947, 258 p.
  Contains a discussion of the place of poetry in Burckhardt's work.

Nichols, James Hastings. "Jacob Burckhardt." In *Force and Freedom: Refection on History,* by Jacob Burckhardt, pp. 3-76. Boston: Beacon Press, 1964.
  Provides a general introduction to Burckhardt's historical method.

Trevor-Roper, H. R. "The Faustian Historian: Jacob Burckhardt." In his *Men and Events: Historical Essays,* pp. 273-78. New York: Harper & Brothers, 1957.
  Discusses Burckhardt's political stance and traces his prescience with regard to nineteenth- and twentieth-century political developments, noting as well his insights as an historian and humanist.

Thomas Holley Chivers

1809-1858

American poet and essayist.

INTRODUCTION

Chivers was a Southern poet considered by his contemporaries and by many modern readers to be a literary curiosity due to his eccentric nature and his obsession with sorrow, loss, and death. Although some scholars find significant literary value in his poetry, Chivers is typically remembered for his association with Edgar Allan Poe, who Chivers claimed plagiarized his work.

Biographical Information

The son of a wealthy Georgia plantation owner, Chivers was born on October 18, 1809. He was educated as a physician at Transylvania University in Kentucky and received his medical degree in 1830, although he never practiced medicine. In 1827 Chivers married his 16-year-old cousin, Frances Elizabeth Chivers. The couple separated due to alleged abuse. Chivers's wife subsequently refused to let her husband see his daughter, who was born in 1828 after the separation. This loss provides the overall theme of *The Path of Sorrow; or The Lament of Youth: A Poem* (1832). In 1834, Chivers married Harriet Hunt. Their oldest daughter, Florence Allegra, died in 1842, and her sister and two brothers died in 1848. Later, two daughters and a son were born, all of whom survived their father. Throughout most of his literary career, Chivers corresponded with Poe. Chivers's affection for his friend is revealed in one letter in which Chivers offers to support Poe for the rest of his life. Their relationship continued until Poe's death in 1849. Chivers died on December 18, 1858.

Major Works

Chivers's first volume of poetry, *The Path of Sorrow,* reflects the poet's own experiences with loss and death. In 1834 Chivers completed *Conrad and Eudora; or, The Death of Alonzo,* a dramatic version of an actual 1825 murder case that came to be known as the "Kentucky Tragedy." Chivers's account of the case, when compared to modern renditions, has been called "the most bloodthirsty" by William Goldhurst. Another drama, *Leoni, the Orphan of Venice,* is similar in theme to *Conrad and Eudora* and was published in 1851, although an early version of the manuscript was completed in 1834. *The Lost Pleiad; and Other Poems* (1845), focusing on such somber themes as death and sorrow, features Chivers's exploration of the possibilities for new rhyme patterns in the sonnet form. *Eonchs of Ruby* (1851) includes a variety of poems which demonstrate Chivers's affinity to-

ward folklore and music and which challenge the boundaries of traditional patterns of poetry through metrical experimentation. In discussing the similarity of the work of Chivers and Poe, Charles Lombard comments that the "aims and techniques" of the poetry in this volume are common to both poets. Chivers's last volume of poetry, *Virginalia; or Songs of My Summer Nights,* (1853) continues to explore such topics as folklore, nature, and religion. The volume also displays Chivers's ability to stimulate the senses through unique connotative word combinations. Chivers also wrote several unpublished dramas and *Chivers' Life of Poe,* a biography which was published posthumously in 1952.

Critical Reception

Lombard characterized the critical reception to Chivers's work when he remarked that the volume *Virginalia,* typically judged Chivers's best work, received some praise in addition to "the usual caustic remarks that greeted any new volume he dared to publish. . . ." In response to Chivers's claims that Poe borrowed from his poetry, critics such as Joel Benton admit that Chivers's works, "which suggest the mechanism and flavor of Poe" in meter, rhythm, and use of refrain, for example, antedate the period of Poe's literary activity. However, these scholars also argue that Poe improved upon the use of such devises to the extent that Chivers actually contributed little to Poe's work. Poe himself stated, in a review of *The Lost Pleiad* written with Henry Watson, that many of the poems in the volume possess "merit of a very lofty—if not of the very loftiest order." These comments reflect the opinion of several modern scholars, including Lombard, S. Foster Damon, and Wilbur Scott, who have discussed Chivers as an accomplished poet in his own right. Like Poe, contemporary critics recognize Chivers's work as noteworthy in that he achieves effects with metrical variation and imitative sound that few other poets have successfully accomplished.

PRINCIPAL WORKS

The Path of Sorrow; or, The Lament of Youth: A Poem (poetry) 1832

Conrad and Eudora; or, The Death of Alonzo (drama) 1834

Nacoochee; or, The Beautiful Star, with Other Poems (poetry) 1837

The Lost Pleiad; and Other Poems (poetry) 1845

Search after Truth; or, A New Revelation of the Psycho-Physiological Nature of Man (essay) 1848

Eonchs of Ruby (poetry) 1851

Leoni, the Orphan of Venice (drama) 1851

Atlanta; or, The True Blessed Island of Poesy. A Paul Epic—In Three Lustra (drama) 1853

Memoralia; or Phials of Amber Full of the Tears of Love (poetry) 1853

Virginalia; or Songs of My Summer Nights (poetry) 1853

Birth-day Song of Liberty: A Pæon of Glory for the Heroes of Freedom (essay) 1856

The Sons of Usna: A Tragi-Apotheosis (drama) 1858

Chivers' Life of Poe (biography) 1952

*Privately published by Chivers.

CRITICISM

Edgar A. Poe and Henry C. Watson (essay date 1845)

SOURCE: A review of *The Lost Pleiad; and other Poems,* in *The Broadway Journal,* Vol. 2, No. 4, August 2, 1845, pp. 55-6.

[*Considered one of America's outstanding men of letters, Poe was a distinguished poet, novelist, essayist, journalist, short story writer, editor, and critic. In the following essay, Poe and Watson assess Chivers's* The Lost Pleiad; and Other Poems, *stating that many of the poems in the volume possess "merit of a very lofty—if not the very loftiest order."*]

This volume is evidently the honest and fervent utterance of an exquisitely sensitive heart which has suffered much and long. The poems are numerous, but the thesis is one—*death*—the death of beloved friends. The poet seems to have dwelt among the shadows of tombs, until his very soul has become a shadow. Here, indeed, is no mere Byronic affectation of melancholy. No man who has ever mourned the loss of a dear friend, can read these poems without instantly admitting the palpable truth which glows upon every page.

The tone of the composition is, in these latter days, a marvel, and as a marvel we commend it to our readers. It belongs to the first era of a nation's literature—to the era of impulse—in contra-distinction to the era of criticism— to the Chaucerian rather than to the Cowperian days. As for the *trans*-civilization epoch, Doctor Chivers' poems have really nothing of affinity with it—and this we look upon as the greatest miracle of all. Is it not, indeed, a miracle that *today* a poet shall compose sixty or seventy poems, in which there shall be discoverable *no* taint— absolutely none—of either Byron, or Shelley, or Wordsworth, or Coleridge, or Tennyson? In a word, the volume before us is the work of that *rara avis,* an educated, passionate, yet unaffectedly simple-minded and single-minded man, writing from his own vigorous impulses— from the necessity of giving utterance to poetic passion— and thus writing *not* to mankind, but solely to himself. The whole volume has, in fact, the air of a rapt soliloquy.

We have leisure this week only to give, without comment, a few extracts at random—but we shall take an opportunity of recurring to the subject.

> I hear thy spirit calling unto me
> From out the Deep,
> Like Arcbytas from out Venetia's Sea,
> While I here weep;
> Saying, Come, strew my body with the sand,
> And bury me upon the land, the land!
>
> Oh, never, never more! no, never more!
> Lost in the Deep!
> Will thy sweet beauty visit this dark shore,
> While I here weep;
> For thou art gone forever more from me,
> Sweet Mariner! lost—murdered by the Sea!
>
> Ever—forever more, bright, glorious One!
> Drowned in the Deep!
> In Spring-time—Summer—Winter—all alone—
> Must I here weep!
> Thou Spirit of my soul! thou light of life!
> While thou art absent, SHELLEY! from thy wife!
>
> Celestial pleasure once to contemplate
> Thy power, great Deep!
> Possessed my soul; but ever more shall hate,
> While I here weep,

Crowd out thy memory from my soul, Oh,
    Sea!
For killing him who was so dear to me!

He was the incarnation of pure Truth,
    Oh, mighty Deep!
And thou didst murder him in prime of
    youth,
    For whom I weep;
And, murdering him, didst *more* than
    murder me,
Who was my Heaven on earth, Oh,
    treacherous Sea!

My spirit wearied not to succor his,
    Oh, mighty Deep!
The oftener done, the greater was the bliss;
    But now I weep;
And where his beauty lay, unceasing pain
Now dwells—my heart can know no joy
    again!

God of my fathers! God of that bright One
    Lost in the Deep!
Shall we not meet again beyond the sun—
    No more to weep?
Yes, I shall meet him there—the lost—the
    bright—
The glorious SHELLEY! spring of my
delight!

Ah, like Orion on some Autumn night
    Above the Deep;
I see his soul look down from Heaven—
    how bright!
    While here I weep!
And there, like Hesperus, the stars of even
Beacon my soul away to him in Heaven!

—

    When thou wert in this world with me,
Bright ANGEL of the HEAVENLY LANDS!
Thou wert not fed by mortal hands,
But by the NYMPHS, who gave to thou
The bread of immortality—
Such as thy spirit now doth eat
    In that high world of endless love,
While walking with thy snowy feet
Along the sapphire-paven street,
    Before the jasper-walls above,
And list'ning to the music sweet
Of Angels in that heavenly HYMN
Sung by the lips of CHERUBIM
In Paradise, before the fall,
In glory bright, outshining all
In that great City of pure gold,
The Angels talked about of old, ·

Because of thine untimely fate,
Am I thus left disconsolate!
Because thou wilt return to be

No more in this dark world with me,
Must these salt tears of sorrow flow
    Out of my heart forever more!
Forever more as they do now!
    Out of my heart forever more!

Thou wert my snow-white JESSAMINE—
My little ANGEL-EGLANTINE!
My saintly LILY! who didst grow
Upon my mother's arms of snow—
Of whom thou wert the image true—
Whose tears fell on thy leaves for dew—
All but those deep blue eyes of thine—
They were the miniatures of mine,
Thou Blossom of that heavenly TREE,
Whose boughs are barren now for thee!
The sweetest bud she ever bore!
    Who art transplanted to the skies
To blossom there forever more
    Amid the FLOWERS OF PARADISE

—

Thus shalt thou leave this world of sin,
    And soar into the sky,
Where angels wait to let thee in
    To immortality.
And those who had nowhere to rest
    Their wearied limbs at night,
Shall lay their heads upon God's breast,
    And sleep in sweet delight.

There, Death's dark shades no more shall be
    The mystic veil between
The World which we desire to see,
    And that which we have seen.
There, father, brother, husband, wife—
    There, mother, sister, friend—
Shall be united, as in life,
    In joys that never end.

No pangs shall there disturbs the thrills
    Which animate thy breast;
But Angels, on the Heavenly Hills,
    Shall sing thee into rest.
No slanderous tongue shall there inflame
    Thy heart with words of gall;
For all shall be in Heaven the same,
    And God shall be in all.

—

As graceful as the Babylonian willow
    Bending, at noontide, over some clear
        stream
In Palestine, in beauty did she seem
Upon the eygnet-down of her soft pillow;
And now her breast heaved like some gentle
        billow
    Swayed by the presence of the full round
        moon—
    Voluptuous as the summer South at noon—

Her cheeks as rosy as the radiant dawn,
    When heaven is cloudless! When she
        breathed, the air
Around was perfume! Timid as the fawn,
    And meeker than the dove, her soft words
        were
Like gentle music heard at night, when all
    Around is still—until the soul of care
Was soothed, as noontide by some waterfall.

The poems of Dr. Chivers abound in what must undoubtedly be considered as gross demerit, if we admit the prevalent canons of criticism. But it may safely be maintained that these prevalent canons have, in great part, no surer foundation than arrant conventionality. Be these things as they may, we have no hesitation in saying that we consider many of the pieces in the volume before us as possessing merit of a very lofty—if not of the very loftiest order.

Joel Benton (essay date 1897)

SOURCE: "Was Poe a Plagiarist?" in *Forum,* Vol. XXIII, March-August, 1897.

[*In the following essay, Benton examines Chivers's accusations of plagiarism against Edgar Allan Poe.*]

Very few people to-day, even in literary circles, know anything about Thomas Holley Chivers, M.D. And even these know very little. He was a poet of at least one book before Bryant made that brief anthology of sixty or more American poets in 1840;—mostly names that have vanished long since into the everlasting inane;—but he was not there represented. His first volume of verse appeared in 1837, though fugitive lyrics from his pen were doubtless afloat on the periodical seas long before that year. Poems over his signature were contributed as late as 1853 to *Graham's Magazine* and to the *Waverley Magazine* of Boston.

It is, however, simply repeating an indubitable fact, to say that a large part of the poetry of Chivers is mainly trash,—of no account whatever, and not above the reams of stanzas which from time immemorial have decorated as "original" the country newspaper's poet's corner. But now and then he struck a note quite above this dead and wide-pervading commonplace; and, whenever he did, the verses brought forth were apt to suggest the mechanism and flavor of Poe. He not only said at various times—especially in a series of letters which he wrote to Mr. Rufus W. Griswold, Poe's biographer, and which are now in the possession of his son—that Poe had borrowed largely from him, but he put the transaction in much bolder terms. The charge of flagrant plagiarism of himself by Poe, in respect even of "The Raven" and "Annabel Lee," was not withheld, but was violently advanced by Chivers. Nor was he alone in making this charge. Some of his friends took it up and repeated it with a vehemence and an ability worthy of a most sacred cause. There is circumstance enough about this, to say nothing of its singularity, to elevate Chivers into something of a topic,—one worth considering at least for a moment.

What is known about this author is, that he published seven or eight volumes of poems between, and inclusive of, 1837 and 1858,—a period of twenty-one years. Many of them antedate Poe's period of literary activity, and not a few have the Poe afflatus and melody so strongly inherent in them that even the non-critical reader could not mistake their related quality. In Chivers's **"Lily Adair,"** which crowns his high-water mark of poetic achievement, the Poe manner stands out conspicuously. This refrain from it, for instance, varied in some details at the end of each stanza, illustrates what I mean:—

In her chariot of fire translated,
    Like Elijah, she passed through the air,
To the city of God golden-gated—
The home of my Lily Adair—
Of my star-crowned Lily Adair—
Of my God-loved Lily Adair—
Of my beautiful, dutiful Lily Adair.

Chivers, in this poem, and in others which resemble Poe's work, made Biblical allusion a dominant trait to an extent that Poe did not, and really attained, though not always with perfect sanity, to much of Poe's witchery and charm.

It is not my intention in this article to repeat the history and evidence which I presented and published elsewhere a year and a half ago concerning Chivers's claims against Poe. It will be sufficient for the purpose now in hand if I report, as briefly as may be, what Chivers and his friends, and those who antagonized the Chivers assumption, had to say about it forty-four years ago.

. . . [A] large part of the poetry of Chivers is mainly trash,—of no account whatever, and not above the reams of stanzas which from time immemorial have decorated as "original" the country newspaper's poet's corner.

— *Joel Benton*

In a quite able and stalwart way Chivers himself opened the contest, under the *nom de plume* of "Fiat Justitia," in the *Waverley Magazine* of July 30, 1853. In a long article, entitled **"Origin of Poe's 'Raven,'"** he claims that the laudators of Poe—particularly N.P. Willis, who said of "The Raven" that it "electrified the world of imaginative readers, and has become the type of a school of poetry of its own"—"betray not only a deplorable ignorance of the current literature of the day, but the most abject poverty of mind in the knowledge of the true nature of poetry." He then quotes from his own book, *The Lost Pleiad,* the following lines from the poem **"To Allegra in Heaven,"** which was published in 1842,—a few years before "The Raven" appeared. He asserts that these lines "show the intelligent reader the true and only source from which Poe obtained his style" in that poem:—

Holy angels now are bending to receive thy soul
  ascending
    Up to Heaven to joys unending, and to bliss
    which is divine;
While thy pale cold form is fading under
  Death's dark wings now shading
    Thee with gloom which is pervading this
    poor broken heart of mine!
And as God doth lift the spirit up to Heaven
  there to inherit
    Those rewards which it doth merit, such as
    none have reaped before;
Thy dear father will to-morrow lay thy body
  with deep sorrow,
    In the grave which is so narrow, there to
    rest forevermore.

In this article Chivers also says that Poe is not entitled to priority in the use of the refrain "Nevermore." It was Chivers, he says (still writing under his *nom de plume*), who originated this in a poem entitled **"Lament on the Death of my Mother,"** published in 1837 in the Middletown, Connecticut, *Sentinel and Witness.* The following extract from it is the proof he offers:—

Not in the mighty realms of human thought,
  Nor in the kingdom of the earth around;
Nor where the pleasures of the world are sought,
  Nor where the sorrows of the earth are
  found—
Nor on the borders of the great deep sea,
Wilt thou return again from heaven to me—
    No, nevermore!

The reader, I imagine, will be likely to think that Poe gave this refrain a more potent and appalling quality.

It is urged that Poe knew of Chivers's **The Lost Pleiad, and Other Poems,** as he "spoke of it in the highest terms in the *Broadway Journal* in 1845 [Vol. 2, No. 4]." The writer admits that "Poe was a great artist, a consummate genius; no man that ever lived having possessed a higher sense of the poetic art than he did." But he urges that this fact must not obliterate the other; viz., that he took the liberty, arrogated by genius, to borrow.

After saying that Chivers (he speaks of himself all along as another person) was the first poet to make the trochaic rhythm express an elegiac theme, and the first to use the euphonic alliteration adopted by Poe, he cites the following extract from a poem of his published before Poe's masterpiece in verse appeared:—

As an egg, when broken, never can be mended,
  but must ever
    Be the same crushed egg forever, so shall
    this dark heart of mine,
Which, though broken, is still breaking, and
  shall nevermore cease aching,
    For the sleep which has no waking—for the
    sleep which now is thine!

To step up to "The Raven" from so grotesquely low a level, one might easily consider—even were the charge of plagiarism proved—a complete absolution of blame.

And, if this is admitted to be the fountain whence Poe got his form, an irreverent critic might say he reproduced it with unsurpassable effect and dissociated from it the atmosphere of Humpty-Dumpty.

In the *Waverley Magazine* of August 13 of the same year, "Fiat Justitia" (Chivers) is taken in hand by "H. S. C." and "J. J. P.," on behalf of Poe. The difference in altitude and genius of the two writers is emphasized by them. Poe's personal character is palliated; but the question of priority in the use of the Poe alliterative rhythm is not argued. The only reply touching this is by the first of the two writers, who shows that "Nevermore," as a refrain, is nobody's trademark, since it has been used even earlier than Chivers's employment of it. As an instance buttressing this statement, he offers the following stanzas from a very old scrap-book in which the poem of which they are a part is credited to the Cheshire, England, *Herald*:—

Now the holy pansies bloom
Round about thy lonely tomb;
All thy little woes are o'er;
We shall meet thee here no more—
      Nevermore!

But the robin loves to sing
Near thee in the early spring;
Thee his song will cheer no more
By our trellised cottage door
      Nevermore!

The same writer asks if his antagonist cannot, by his form of logic, prove that Poe stole his poem of "The Bells" from the nursery rhyme of "Ding Dong Bell." A week later than this, "Fiat Justitia" reappears in the *Waverley Magazine,* together with an ally signing himself "Felix Forresti" (possibly Chivers again), who, seeing him attacked by two knights of the pen, "takes up the cudgels" for Chivers. In fact, to be more truthful, all these writers—speaking metaphorically—take up pitchforks and machetes. Their Billingsgate style savors of the Arizona *Howler,* and seems impossible to Boston. In this week's onslaught, however, no point of note occurs, except that the latter writer exhumes from a poem by Chivers, upon Poe, which was published in the Georgia *Citizen* about 1850, the following lines:—

Like the great prophet in the desert lone,
He stood here waiting for the golden morning;
From Death's dark vale I hear his distant moan
Coming to scourge the world he was adorning—
Scorning, in glory now, their impotence of
  scorning.
And now in apotheosis divine,
He stands enthroned upon the immortal
  mountains
Of God's eternity, for evermore to shine—
Star-crowned, all purified with oil-anointings—

Drinking with Ulalume from out th' eternal
  fountains.

And the writer adds: "Until both . . . champions [of Poe]
can write just such lines as these, they had better 'shut up
shop.'"

But neither side "shut up shop" just then. In the issue of
September 10, "Fiat Justitia" and "J. J. P." reappear. The
former occupies nearly three columns with extracts from
Chivers's poems to show the Poe manner, and to prove
that it was in these poems Poe found it. The following
sample is from *The Lost Pleiad*:—

And though my grief is more than vain,
  Yet shall I never cease to grieve;
Because no more, while I shall live,
  Will I behold thy face again!
No more while I have life or breath,
  No more till I shall turn to dust!
But I shall see thee after death,
  And in the heavens above I trust.

The following extract is from Chivers's *Memoralia*:—

I shall never more see pleasure,
Pleasure nevermore, but pain—
Pleasure, losing that dear treasure
Whom I loved here without measure,
Whose sweet eyes were Heaven's own azure,
Speaking, mild, like sunny rain;
I shall nevermore see pleasure
For his coming back again!

Of *The Lost Pleiad* volume, "Fiat Justitia" says that a
Cincinnati reviewer declared, some years ago, that "there
is nothing in the wide scope of literature, where passion,
pathos, and pure art are combined, more touchingly tender than this whole unsurpassed and (in our opinion)
unsurpassable poem."

Another sample of Chivers's pre-Poe likeness the writer finds
in a poem titled **"Ellen Æyre,"** which was printed in a
Philadelphia paper in 1836. He gives this stanza from it:—

Like the Lamb's wife, seen in vision,
  Coming down from heaven above,
Making earth like Fields Elysian,
  Golden city of God's love—
Pure as jasper—clear as crystal—
  Decked with twelve gates richly rare—
Statued with twelve angels vestal—
  Was the form of Ellen Æyre—
  Gentle girl so debonair—
Whitest, brightest of all cities, saintly angel,
  Ellen Æyre.

Very many other Poe-resembling extracts are given; but
these must suffice from the verse. To show that Poe borrowed from Chivers in a prose criticism, our writer copies
the following passage from an article by Chivers in the
Atlanta *Luminary*:—

There is poetry in the music of the birds—in the
diamond radiance of the evening star—in the sun-
illumined whiteness of the fleecy clouds—in the open
frankness of the radiant fields—in the soft, retiring
mystery of the vales—in the cloud-sustaining grandeur
of the many-folded hills—in the revolutions of the
spheres—in the roll of rivers, and the run of rills.

Now look on this, from Poe's "The Poetic Principle":—

He recognizes the ambrosia, which nourishes his soul,
in the bright orbs that shine in heaven . . . in the
waving of the grain-fields—in the blue distance of
mountains—in the grouping of clouds . . . in the
twinkling of the half-hidden brooks—in the gleaming
of silver rivers—in the repose of sequestered lakes—
in the star-mirroring depths of lonely wells . . . in the
song of birds—in the sighing of the night-wind . . . in
the fresh breath of the woods, etc.

Triumphantly the writer says, "Now . . . you will no longer wonder where Poe obtained his very delightful knowledge of the art of poetry." Not only the Chivers prose
extract, but also the verse passages quoted by him were
written, he affirms, "long anterior" to the parallel passages in Poe.

In the *Waverley* of September 24 following, "J. J. P."
quotes Poe as saying of "The Raven," "I pretend to no
originality in either the rhythm or metre." He also quotes
Poe as saying of the passage by Chivers containing the
egg simile: "That the lines very narrowly missed *sublimity* we will grant; that they came within a step of it we
admit; but, unhappily, the step is that *one* step which,
time out of mind, has intervened between the *sublime* and
the *ridiculous*."

The whole controversy was continued with warmth in the
Waverley Magazine of October 1, 1853, by "Fiat Justitia," who began it. I am told, too, that it was reopened in
a later volume. As the *Magazine* office files were long
ago destroyed by fire, I cannot say how the renewed
controversy fared; though it probably closed with nothing
fresher than new epithets coined by the combatants. Nor
is anything that is particularly new added by this article.
It was mainly a threshing of the old straw, which, all the
way through, was supplemented by a rhythm analysis that
would take too much space to follow. From the Chivers
poem **"To Allegra in Heaven"** he adduces this thereto-
fore unquoted line,

Like some snow-white cloud just under Heaven
  some breeze

                    has torn asunder—

which he thinks suggested Poe's two lines:—

And the silken sad uncertain rustling of each
  purple curtain—
            . . . . .

Much I marvelled this ungainly fowl to hear
  discourse so plainly.

Chivers, it seems, wrote for a variety of periodicals, among which were *Graham's Magazine* and *Peterson's*; and in the year this controversy was raging he contributed poems to the *Waverley Magazine* itself. In "Fiat Justitia's" contention, it is said that Poe was obliged to reply in the *Broadway Journal,* in defence of the plagiaristic charge, to some writer using somewhere the *nom de plume* of "Outis." There was, in connection with the Chivers assumption and advocacy, a surprisingly earnest and hot assault. Only one more of these militant articles (possibly by Chivers again) shall I notice here. He, signing himself "Philo Veritas" in the *Waverley Magazine* of October 8, 1853, communicates a **"Railroad Song"** taken from *Graham's,* which was written by Chivers, and which he terms "a truly *original* poem." He does so in part for the purpose of "exposing one of the most pitiful plagiarisms" known— the "wishy-washy thing" entitled "Railroad Lyric," that had appeared in *Putnam's Monthly* of the previous May. Here are some lines from the one hundred and thirteen composing Chivers's poem:—

> All aboard! Yes! Tingle, tingle,
> Goes the bell as we all mingle—
> No one sitting solely single—
> As the steam begins to fizzle—
> With a kind of sighing sizzle—
> Ending in a piercing whistle—
>
> . . . . .
>
> And the cars begin to rattle,
> And the springs go tittle-tattle—
> Driving off the grazing cattle,
> As if Death were Hell pursuing
> To his uttermost undoing,
> Down the iron road to ruin—
> With a clitter, clatter, clatter,
> Like the Devil beating batter
> Up in Hell in iron platter,
> As if something was the matter;
> Then it changes to a clanking,
> And a clinking and a clanking,
> And a clanking and a clanking—
>
> . . . . .
>
> As if Hell for our damnation,
> Had come down with desolation
>
> . . . . .
>
> While the engine overteeming
> With excruciating screaming,
> Spits his vengeance out in steaming.
>
> . . . . .
>
> Still repeating clitter, clatter
> Clitter, clatter, clitter, clatter
> As if something was the matter—
> While the woodlands all are ringing,

> And the birds forget their singing,
> And away to Heaven go winging.
>
> . . . . .
>
> Then returns again to clatter
> Clitter, clatter, clitter, clatter
> Like the Devil beating batter
> Up in Hell in iron platter—
> Which subsides into a clankey,
> And a clinkey and a clankey
> And a clankey and a clinkey
> And a clinkey, clankey, clankey—
> Then to witchey, witchey, witchey,
> Chewey-witchey, chewey-witchey—
> Chewey-witchey, witchey, witchey,
> Then returns again to fizzle,
> With a kind of sighing sizzle—
> Ending in a piercing whistle—
> And the song that I now offer
> For Apollo's golden coffer—
> With the friendship that I proffer—
> Is for riding on a Rail.

There was one poem of Chivers's, entitled **"The Little Boy Blue,"** copied in the *Waverley Magazine,* which is singularly saturated with the nomenclature and manner that Poe affected. Here are a few illustrative stanzas out of the thirty-seven to which it extended:—

> The little boy blue
>   Was the boy that was born
> In the forests of Dew
>   On the Mountains of Morn.
>
> . . . . .
>
> There the pomegranate bells—
>   They were made to denote
> How much music now dwells
>   In the nightingale's throat.
>
> . . . . .
>
> On the green banks of On,
>   By the city of No,
> There he taught the wild swan
>   Her white bugle to blow.
>
> . . . . .
>
> Where the cherubim rode
>   On four lions of gold,
> There this cherub abode
>   Making new what was old.
>
> . . . . .
>
> When the angels came down
>   To the shepherds at night,
> Near to Bethlehem Town
>   Clad in garments of light,

There the little Boy Blue
    Blew aloud on his horn,
Songs as soft as the dew
    From the Mountains of Morn.

. . . . .

But another bright place
    I would stop to declare,
For the Angel of the Face
    Of Jehovah was there.

. . . . .

Now this happy soul dwells
    Where the waters are sweet,
Near the Seven-fold Wells
    Made by Jesus's feet.

Not only are the Poe phrases here, but here, too, is the tossing, tumultuous imagination of William Blake. I know of no writer who, so much as Chivers did, fell into Blake's phantasmagorial extravagance.

The upshot of this cursory consideration of the voluminous controversy—beginning before Poe died, and virulently continued for some years after his death—shows that Poe knew Chivers's work and paid attention to him in more than one reference. The literary representatives of the minor poet appear, also, to bring forward some striking examples of verse which he wrote, which was outwardly like Poe's, and which considerably antedated "The Bells," "The Raven," and "Annabel Lee," on which Poe's poetic fame rests.

What conclusion must be drawn from these facts? Each reader will be certain to make his own. No critic will doubt that to Poe belonged the wonderful magic and mastery of this species of song. If to him who says a thing best the thing belongs, no one will hesitate to decide that Poe is entitled to the bays which crown him. It is a fact, that, with all the contemporary airing of the subject, it is Poe's celebrity and not Chivers's that remains. The finer instinct and touch are what the world takes account of. Chivers, except at rare intervals, did not approach near enough to the true altitude. He put no boundary between what was grotesque and what was inspired. He was too short-breathed to stay poised on the heights, and was but accidentally poetic. But we may accord him a single leaf of laurel, if no more, for what he came so near achieving in the musical lyric of **"Lily Adair."** Truly enough Shakespeare says:—

The lunatic, the lover and the poet,
Are of imagination all compact . . .

Their mental and spiritual territories interblend. The same frenzy is the endowment of each—as charcoal is in essence the diamond. As you differentiate and develop it you make your titular distinction and place. But it is not a small thing to have been mingled in some slight association with genius, and to have some credit you with it.

In an Oriental poem the clay pipe speaks of its contentment, since it cannot be a rose, of having, by a fortunate association, attained to some of the rose's fragrance.

Wilbur S. Scott (essay date 1944)

SOURCE: "The Astonishing Chivers: Poet for Plagiarists," in *The Princeton University Library Chronicle,* Vol. V, No. 4, June, 1944, pp. 150-53.

[*In the following essay, Scott provides a brief overview of Chivers's work and discusses the relationship between Chivers and Edgar Allan Poe.*]

If you know Chivers, give me your hand
             —Swinburne

Among the more interesting possessions of its Treasure Room, Princeton is fortunate to own some rare first editions of one of the most striking, albeit obscure figures of American literature. These are four books of poems, *Nacoochee* (1837), *The Lost Pleiad* (1845), *Eonchs of Ruby* (1851), and *Memoralia* (1853) by Thomas Holley Chivers.

Chivers was born in Georgia in 1809, the year which also marked the birth of Poe, with whose career that of Chivers is curiously woven. Before he was twenty, Chivers married and shortly found himself the victim of his first tragedy. The happiness of this marriage was terminated when Mrs. Chivers, apparently influenced by some sort of scandal now unknown to us, left her young husband and refused to allow him even to see their child. As an escape, the young man matriculated at Transylvania University, Kentucky, and there found some relief in writing poetry. Unfortunately some of his worst and most melodramatic lines are concerned with this affair.

The birth in 1839 of Allegra, his first child by a second wife, introduces another tragedy of Chivers' life, and reveals an interesting aspect of his personality—his mysticism. Eight years before, he had had a vision of two angels; now, in 1839, he recognized that Allegra was none other than the first angel. The second child materialized in the form of a son a year later. In 1842 Chivers was heartbroken at the death of Allegra, and the death, too, was accompanied by another preternatural experience, during which he seemed to hear the song the child had sung earlier as an angel.

Such experiences encouraged Chivers to support the spiritualism that blossomed in the 1840's. Many of these he published in *Univercoleum,* the publication of Andrew Jackson Davis, a famous clairvoyant of the time. But after the death of his friend, Poe, he no longer sympathized with the movement, because he could accept neither such childish ghostly manifestations as spirit rappings, nor the published verses which mediums asserted were dictated to them by the dead Poe.

Meanwhile, of course, he was writing poetry. Aside from his contributions to magazines, he published eleven volumes which today are exceedingly rare. Two are poetic dramas (and bad ones); one is an "Epic—in three Lustra"; another is a philosophical prose work; and the remaining seven are collections of poems.

Taken generally, the poems exhibit two tendencies, both remarkable for their time. First, Chivers frequently employed words more for their connotative than their denotative effect. The poem **"Georgia Waters,"** is a good example of this characteristic:

> On thy waters, thy sweet valley-waters,
> Oh! Georgia! how happy were we!
> When thy daughters, thy sweet smiling
>   daughters,
> First gathered sweet-william for me,
> Then thy wildwood, thy dark, shady wildwood
> Had many bright visions for me!
> For my childhood, my bright rosy childhood
> Was cradled, dear Georgia! in thee—
> Bright land of my childhood, in thee!

This, of course, places Chivers in the Poe and Coleridge tradition.

A second tendency, writing poetry which approaches imitative sound, establishes him as a precursor of Vachel Lindsay. It is really quite startling to come across his **"Railroad Song,"** for example:

> Clitta, clatta, clatta, clatter,
> Like the devil beating batter
> Down below in iron platter—
> Which subsides into a clanky,
> And a clinky, and a clanky,
> And a clinky, clanky, clanky,
> And a clanky, clinky, clanky;
> And the song that I now offer
> For Apollo's Golden Coffer—
> With the friendship that I proffer—
> Is for Riding on a Rail.

His first volume, **Path of Sorrow** (1832), is interesting in several ways. Technically, it is extremely varied and shows its author as a bold experimenter in metrics. But his interest in linguistic experiments is also obvious. For example, he uses such words as "congretion," "oblectation," "pedigal," and "sanguinize."

Nacoochee (1837), the second volume, is also the title of the initial poem, a symbolical and incomplete love story with an American Indian setting. Most of the remaining poems are lyrics, some being reprints from earlier publication, some original.

The third volume, **The Lost Pleiad** (1845), shows a better control of the technique of verse. In theme it is his gloomiest book, containing elegies on deceased members of his families and on dead celebrities. The style of many of these poems is simpler, with more normal word order and better handling of metre and rhyme.

Eonchs of Ruby (1851) has so much bad verse in it and so much good that it represents a true cross section of Chivers' talent. In this volume he returns to his love of experiment, metrical and linguistic. The title itself is of his own creation; his explanation reveals both his ingenuity and his learning:

> The word *Eonch* is the same as *Concha Marina—Shell of the Sea. Eonch* is used instead of *Concha,* merely for its euphony. It is the same as the *Kaur Gaur* of the Hebrews. Ruby signifies, in the language of Correspondence, *Divine Love.* The word *Eonch* is used, as a title, by metonymy, for *Songs.* The meaning of the title is, therefore, apparent—namely, *Songs of Divine Love.* The clouds, I hope, are now dispelled; and the mystery, I presume, evaporates. I hope the day will continue clear.

Virginalia (1853) contains some verse which reminds one of Poe in its successful use of the emotional value of sound which denotatively means little. This volume was followed the same year by **Memoralia,** which contains several new poems and many of those printed in the poorly selling **Eonchs of Ruby.**

But it was not Chivers' poetry which perpetuated his name so much as it was his friendship with Poe, and certain unusual consequences of that relationship. Their first contact occurred in 1835 when a notice, probably written by Poe, appeared in *The Southern Literary Messenger.* A correspondence ensued, but it was not until 1845 that the two poets met and became more than epistolary acquaintances. Their friendship, based on mutual respect, mutual interest in literature, and, on Chivers' part, concern for and tolerance of the eccentricities of Poe's character, lasted until Poe's death in 1849.

Out of this relationship arose an interesting critical controversy. When **Eonchs of Ruby** appeared, many critics accused the author of having plagiarized from the works of Poe. Chivers, in answering the attack, over-stated his case and in support of his position used one of his most unfortunate pieces of verse. This opened him to most unfair ridicule and as a result, for many years he was thought of merely as a literary curiosity who exploited the talent of his friend.

In fact, however, Chivers' position is quite defensible. In the most famous item of the controversy—the charge that he plagiarized from Poe's "The Raven"—the credit is all on Chivers' side. In the idea, in the unusual refrain, in the metre, and to some extent in the atmosphere, Chivers actually had precedence. And in other matters Chivers and Poe borrowed from each other, casually and openly. This unacknowledged borrowing was, for that matter, a common practice among writers of the day, and ordinarily considered no violation of auctorial ethics. It was the more natural for two persons of similar poetic temperament, however distant their accomplishments.

At any rate, owing to this charge of plagiarism, Chivers remained from 1858, the year of his death, until very recently, an obscure figure. This he did not deserve; as a personality, few contemporaries can make such a strong appeal, and as a poet, although he is surely not of the first rank, he occasionally reached heights which make his place in American letters secure.

Charles Henry Watts, II (essay date 1956)

SOURCE: "Technique," in *Thomas Holley Chivers: His Literary Career and His Poetry,* University of Georgia Press, 1956, pp. 211-48.

[*In the essay that follows, Watts provides examination of Chivers's poetic technique.*]

THEORY OF POETRY

Perhaps the measure of [Thomas Holley] Chivers' success with the themes most typical of his poetry may be in part determined by an examination of his theory of poetry, and his understanding of the duties and desires of the poet. Not an analytical critic or a particularly acute surveyor of the contemporary literary scene, he wrote few objective reviews, most of his expression on literary theory occurring in the Prefaces to *Nacoochee, Memoralia,* and *Atlanta.* Very often such discussion becomes a defense of his own poetry.

Chivers did not greatly modify his poetic beliefs as expressed early in *The Path of Sorrow;* his later theories are, in large part, developments of his determination in 1832 to write from the world of his imagination, and his certainty that the true poet was divinely inspired. As he wrote and experimented further, he came to change the terms of these theories; but they remain, in principle.

One of his earliest decisions was no doubt brought about by his own distress and grief over his first marriage. He will sing, he says, only of grief; there is reason to believe that his early tragedy focused his desire to write poetry. He had been happy, and indeed in early youth had composed a number of incidental verses, but after a period of mourning, grief "tuned up [his] heart strings to music again." Chivers' belief that sorrow could draw the poetry from him was never changed; *The Lost Pleiad* (1845) is a volume which testifies to the seemingly endless variety he could achieve upon the single theme of death and sorrow, and while such melancholia was quite in keeping with Romantic tendencies, it is obvious that he felt more than a theoretical motivation.

But even the most depressed of poets needs must find relief from such woe, and Chivers' most important interpretation of his calling arose from the necessity to find another outlet, another world in which he could create all that this one, he believed, had failed to supply him with. The mystical world of the terrestrial Eden and the emotional evocations of Heaven which are such an important part of his poetry provided the necessary outlet. His understanding of that world came from within himself; so there was no need to square it with the reality he saw

about him. He speaks often enough of the horrors of this world, of loss, death, and loneliness, but never does he evoke Hell; his glance moved only upward (if inward), a move which he once developed a metaphor to describe:

> As the penitent Pilgrim, on his way to Mount Zion, reclines, at the noontide hour of the day, from the burning heat of the tropical sun, in the cool refreshing shadow of the Rock of Rimmon, so does my wearied soul hide itself away into an ecstasy underneath the odoriferous dovewings of the Divine Queen of Heaven.

It is not difficult to understand the motivation for such a hiding away; the world would not receive his poetry in the manner he believed it deserved; his happiness with his second wife hardly compensated for the death of four of his children; and as a Southern Transcendentalist, he found himself out of place in both North and South.

The result of his inward-turning is such a poem as **"The Poet of Love,"** in which he attempts to explain his source of inspiration and to exhibit its effects at the same time:

> The Poet of Love receives divine ovation;
>> Not only from Angels' hands while here on
> earth,
> But all the Ages echo back with salutation
>> The trumpet of the Skies in praises of his
> worth;
>>> And all the islands of the Sea
>>> Of the vast immensity
>>> Echo the music of the Morns
>>> Blown through the Corybantine Horns
>>> Down the dark vistas of the reboantic
> Norns,
>>> By the great Angel of Eternity,
>>> Thundering, *Come to me! come to me!*
>
> From the inflorescence of his own high soul
>> The incense of his Eden-song doth rise,
> Whose golden river of pure redolence doth roll
>> Down the dark vistas of all time in
> melodies—
>>> Echoing the Islands of the Sea
>>> Of the vast immensity,
>>> And the loud music of the Morns
>>> Blown through the Conchimarian Horns
>>> Down the dark vistas of the reboantic
> Norns,
>>> By the great Angel of Eternity,
>>> Thundering, *Come to me! come to me!*
>
> With the white lightnings of his still small voice,
>> Deep as the thunders of the azure Silence—
> He makes dumb the oracular Cymbals with their
> noise,
>> Till BEAUTY flourish Amaranthine on the
> Islands
>>> Of the loud tumultuous Sea
>>> Of the vast immensity,
>>> Echoing the music of the Morns

Blown through the Chrysomelian Horns
Down the dark vistas of the reboantic Norns
By the great Angel of Eternty,
Thundering, COME TO ME! COME TO ME!

The excesses of the poem are perhaps annoying; yet it is successful, I believe, in the effect Chivers desired to create, for not only does it explain an important theme, but also it attempts to recreate the emotional state of the poet as he experienced that theme.

Furthermore, it exhibits almost all of the theories Chivers developed in prose regarding his theory of poetry. Chivers drew a distinction between the poem as such and experience as such which modern critics have found valid, and he would answer the critic who objected to the excesses of such a poem as this by saying, "There is nothing in the world that is not equivalent in brightness to the poetical manifestations of it. People too often mistake the *relations* of things for the *things* themselves." That is, the experience he creates here was, to him, the experiencer, just as frantic and bright as the poem in which he tries to explain it. Many of Chivers' poems are of the same sort; seldom have we found him as interested in the "brightness" of "things," although their brightness is insisted upon, as in the actual experience of his appreciation of that brightness. A nice distinction, perhaps, but a necessary one, and one which helps to explain Chivers' statement that all true poetry is dramatic, for at first glance his poetry appears to be singularly undramatic. What he means is that the true poet describes not the scene before him, but his experience in reacting to it. Because of his participation in the scene it becomes dramatic, animated, although the drama is usually implicit.

"The Poet of Love," by its very title, suggests further explanations. God, he believed, was Love. The true poet partakes of that Love and attempts to express it. In what may it be found? In the poet himself. What inspires it? His answer helps explain his poetry:

> . . . Poetry is the soul of his nature, whereby, from communing with the beauties of this earth, he is capable of giving birth to other beings brighter than himself; and of lifting up his spirit to the presence of those things which he shall enjoy in another state; and which he manifests to *this* [world] through the instrumentality of certain words and sentences melodiously concatenated; and such as correspond with the definite and wise configurations of the mouth in the communication of thought through language.

I very much doubt that any poet writing in the South in 1837, except perhaps Poe, had developed his own aesthetic so completely; Chivers' beliefs may not be suitable for the twentieth century, or, for that matter, popular in the early nineteenth, but they were definite and defined. We have grown away from any theory of poetry which depends upon inspiration of such a seemingly nebulous character; Chivers was close to it, and he depended upon it to write poetry. He said, in the Preface to **Birth-Day Song of Liberty,**

Inspired by that self-rewarding enthusiasm which always fills the heart with rapture—being the first-born Cherub of the soul's rapport with the infinite splendor of God—I composed the following Paean of Glory. . . .

Sometimes his sense of this identification may have been self-induced. That is not as important as the fact that it *was* induced. Poetry was not a matter of incidental composition to Chivers; it was tied very closely to his deep belief in an after life which would compensate for the toils and turmoil of this one. So when he soars upward in his description of Heaven, he is tasting joys which, to him, were just as much reality as the earthly vistas about him.

But those earthly vistas were, as he notes, important to evoke the needed inspiration. And since the following development of his theory comes close to that expressed by Poe in *The Philosophy of Composition* (1846), it is necessary to point out that Chivers had established, to his own satisfaction, the basis of his later expression in the Preface to **Nacoochee** (1837): by communing with "beauties" he will be empowered to produce further beauty which will in turn produce a "lifting up [of] his spirit." I do not suggest that Poe derived his belief that poetry's province was that of beauty which produced "pleasurable elevation, of the soul" from Chivers, but that such similarity as exists here is further evidence of a more inclusive similarity of judgment and taste. Poe's language apparently impressed him, however, for Chivers depended more and more upon the word *beauty* to express his desires after Poe's statement was published.

Poe believed poetry should concern itself with beauty, not with passion or with truth; Chivers disagreed, insisting that passion was an integral part of any poem and that Poe's poetry suffered from its absence. And Chivers' interpretation of beauty differed in an important point from Poe's; it was *divine* beauty that Chivers sought, in connection with his belief that poetry was a vehicle by which the soul might rise to God. Chivers attempted to set up an interesting distinction between earthly beauty and the divine, a distinction which probably resulted from his personal failure to find heavenly beauty in the physical world:

> No Nation, with the exception of the Hebrews, ever enjoyed so serene a vision of the Divine Glory as did the Greeks. Their religion was Beauty. It was out of the manifold analysis of Nature that they created their world-renowned Synthesis of Beauty, called *The Venus de Medicis* [sic]. For, as there was nothing in Nature perfect enough to represent the Divine Beauty, they had to resort to Art, which is the Synthesis of the highest sensation united to the loftiest thought. Thus, by glorifying sensation, which is finite, into thought, which is infinite, thereby creating an Image, they gave birth to the Apollo. . . .

> Now, the more palpably this thought is made manifest in the IMAGE, through Art, the more lucid will be the *Revelation of the Divine Idea.*

Having established the fact that he was reaching toward a purpose which was as much ethical as aesthetic, Chivers goes on to define the difference between Art and Thought, which taken together produce Divine Beauty. Every poem contains two beauties, the outward, that of form, the vehicle, and the inward, that of passion, of Nature; when they are correctly combined a "pure" poem results, one which will "enchant the souls of men." Passion, to Chivers, represented both thought and action, both the consciousness that contact with God could be established and the act of identification itself. A transcendental belief, surely, the transcendental nature of which is even clearer when Chivers speaks of the poet as having "the perfectly couched eyes of an illuminated Seer," to whom "all things appear beautiful that are *really* so."

As seer, or prophet, it is the poet's job to become the mediator "of the revelation of the influx of the Divine Life of God into the soul" of man; he is the voice of God and the echo of Nature.

In statements such as these, Chivers tried to define why he wrote as he did; occasionally he went on to speak of how the true poem might achieve the desired ends. He agreed with Poe that no true poem was anything but a lyric. Although he did not set as definite a limit on the length of a poem as Poe did, he based his objections to epic poetry on much the same belief as that which Poe had, that the soul wearies after a time and cannot absorb the beauties before it. A poem must be complete in itself, and the only way a long poem might be written was through the method Chivers used in *Atlanta,* by creating a narrative or symbolic framework against which separate images may be placed. These images, Chivers believed, must constantly be varied; the "true mystery" of angelic pleasure is the continual reception of varying delights.

One device which is helpful in producing this necessary variation is the refrain, which is not simply an ornament to a poem, but part of that poem's "essence": he describes its importance in typically Chiversian terms.

> It is a Poem precisely what Ovid says of the outward golden tire of the many-spoked wheels of the Chariot of Apollo, that makes a continual, ever-recurring Auroral chime at every revolution of the wheels, proportionate to their velocity, which is never lost, or dies away into an echo, but forever returns upon itself, like the menstrual changes of the Moon, but only to be made the same sweet Moon—the same sweet Auroral chime.

Again a reference to **"The Poet of Love"** will indicate Chivers' meaning; the refrain returns the poem and the reader's attention to the central theme once more, or, as in a poem like **"Rosalie Lee,"** it provides a melodious and slightly varying structure about which the theme is developed. Chivers experimented with the refrain, varying its place in the stanza (beginning, middle, or end), shifting its content slightly each time (as Poe did in "The Raven"), or using it to establish the desired rhythm.

Rhythm was particularly important, and although Chivers' statement of its importance was undoubtedly derived from Poe, he was experimenting with it before Poe defined a poem as "the rhythmical creation of beauty." Interested in music, and familiar with the Negro songs of the South, which he praises highly, Chivers would naturally utilize strong rhythm to produce the essentially hypnotic effect of some of his evocations of Heaven.

And although he never fully stated his implicit belief that the poet's province entitled him to coin whatever words were necessary to express his emotions, it is clear that when he says that no poem can be wholly successful unless the poet has "the highest knowledge of the true Art of musical language," he means just that. Much of the unique effect some of his poems have is derived from his interest in sound as such, which often demanded that he invent onomatopoetic words.

Chivers insisted that the Age does not make the poet, but that the poet establishes the essential character of the Age. Insofar as he adhered to the standards and theories which have been elaborated here, Chivers spoke the truth about himself. Although certain elements of his belief can be traced to New England Transcendentalism, and the wording of others to Poe, the poetry which resulted from the application of his theories is virtually unique in any anthology of nineteenth century American verse. Concerned with establishing his identification with what Emerson called the over-soul and with what he called Heavenly Beauty or Divine Beauty, he was very much of the nineteenth century, however, in the essentially theological base he chose to give his poetry. Furthermore, that poetry of his which does not concern itself with Divine Beauty, as a considerable amount does not, is typical of the magazine expression of his Age. No better proof than his intermittent application of his poetic beliefs, as well as the nature of those beliefs themselves, could be offered in testimony to the fact that Chivers was both a product of the nineteenth century and his own master.

FORM AND STRUCTURE

The development of Chivers' technical ability throughout his publishing career is a gradual one, moving from the use of standard *abab* quatrains, which were so simple and so popular, to a manipulation of stanza form and meter to achieve unique poetic effects. Chivers was a conscious artist, deeply concerned over the appropriate form his expression might take.

His very first volume, ***The Path of Sorrow,*** indicates that the young medical student had been paying as much attention to form and structure as to the woes he wished to express. Although depending largely on single and double quatrains for the majority of his poems, he experimented, at this beginning point in his career, with such diverse forms as Spenserians and blank verse, even pausing to invent a nine line stanza, *ababcdcdd,* which he hoped might round out the formal double quatrain to something more organic. Throughout his career he experimented with the basic eight line stanza, varying the pattern to such extremes as *aaaabbbb* and *abaabbaa,* and while many of these efforts are not successful, the fact of his experimenting, occurring as it does so early and continuing so long, helps to present another perspective on his nature. He was not simply a theorizer, but an artisan, attempting to mold his forms to particular ends. His second and third volumes indicate an early and sustained interest in the use of the refrain, an interest quite in accordance with his poetic theory, and the third, *Nacoochee,* contains **"Malavolti,"** a poem which, as Professor Damon points out, may well have been inspired by Coleridge, whose "Christabel" utilizes varying forms to suit the several moods; in **"Malavolti"** Chivers includes stanzas of *abab* rhymes, *aaaabbbb* rhymes, couplets, and an *abbacca* form.

The Lost Pleiad (1845) marks Chivers' first use of the sonnet, and his attempts to evolve a new pattern of rhyme for this form are as numerous as they are unsuccessful. All told, Chivers tried eighteen different variations, the majority involving changes in the Shakespearian sonnet, although he also tried to manipulate the octave and sestet of the Petrarchan form. However, he lacked the precise control necessary to achieve variation within the strict form of the sonnet, and most of his efforts indicate he understood the sonnet to be simply a fourteen line lyric. **"The Grave,"** for example, rhymes, in iambic pentameter, *ababacacacacac,* and although it is an effective lyric, it hardly illustrates the subtleties of a sonnet.

His last three books, **Eonchs of Ruby, Virginalia,** and **Atlanta,** are more interesting in terms of diction and sound than of form, although his early interest in the refrain here becomes almost an obsession. Usually he used his refrain to carry certain repeating hypnotic or melodic effects through the poem; so its use must have sprung directly out of his interest in sound and rhythm rather than from any artificial influence or example.

Chivers' forms are seldom completely orthodox. If he utilizes a simple double quatrain, he is likely to make it unique by alternating trimeter, tetrameter, and pentameter lines. His stanzas vary from tercets to an eleven line stanza. Blank verse appealed to him in his early work, although he used it only twice after 1837. It will be worth while to examine the effect of some of his less orthodox attempts.

Chivers' new stanza, *ababcdcdd,* a variation from the Spenserian, is usually marred by the obviousness of the experimentation. **"The Prophet's Dream,"** for example, concludes many of its stanzas with the final line beginning with an all-too-obvious *And,* the result of which is not all that Chivers was hoping for. He speaks of the coming of Christ:

> His hand shall help creation's alien race;
> His wings shall hover o'er the contrite child!
> The mighty men of earth shall see his face,
> But no man shall presume to say, He smil'd.
> He shall be sanctified by heaven's dew,
> And he shall be a stone—a steadfast rock!

> And he that doth his path, in love, pursue,
> Shall shine again, exempt from hell's foul shock;
> And He shall be a pillar on Jehovah's rock.

Perhaps Chivers realized that he had not fully integrated the final line with the rest of the stanza, for in **"Apollo,"** many years later, he used the same scheme but changed the repeating final rhyme into a varying refrain.

> Like some deep, impetuous river from the
>   fountains everlasting,
>   Down the serpentine soft valley of the vistas
> of all Time,
> Over cataracts of adamant uplifted into
> mountains,
>   Soared his soul to God in thunder on the
> wings of thought sublime.
> With the rising golden glory of the sun in
> ministrations,
>   Making oceans metropolitan of splendor for
> the dawn—
> Piling pyramid on pyramid of music for the
> nations—
>   Sings the Angel who sits shining everlasting
> in the sun,
>   For the stars, which are the echoes of the
> shining of the sun.

The repeating final phrase of the seventh line does help to control the long varying lines. Chivers' efforts to thus end-stop the double quatrain are effective only when he so arranged his content that the added line does not appear tacked on.

The blank verse which Chivers used in the three long autobiographical poems of **The Path of Sorrow** is of a particularly unique kind. Chivers knew Byron, but that poet's adept manipulation of the line apparently did not have as much effect upon him as his own wish to achieve a coherence through some sort of a carry-over from line to line. Realizing perhaps that steady, regularly accented pentameter lines might not achieve the flow he desired, Chivers tried to create something more organic by dividing his lines after the fourth or fifth beat in the line, and placing the resulting extra syllables at the beginning of the next line. The effect does not always succeed, partly because he often utilized this method artificially and without reference to the content of the line:

>   My
> Soul is drunk with thy omnipotence. There
> Seems to be, within my very life, a
> Longing after immortality, in love.
> There is an ideal something in my soul,
> Which swells my bosom lord nigh bursting!
>   What
> Is it?—from the very morning when I
> Woke a child of sorrow, I have espoused
> The cause of nature; and I love the world——
> Not that I feel adhesiveness for man——
> For sinful man! but, there is a glory
> In its contemplation, which pervades my

Very being. There is a fixedness,
Undaring purpose in my heart, which time,
With all her multitude of ills, shall not
Eradicate. The basis of my heart——
The center of my being—shall remain
As firm and steadfast as the wreckless rock
Of Heaven! it shall endure, though hell, with all
Her panoplied and plumed array, consign
Me to their grief.

Chivers' method creates a caesural pause before the fourth or fifth beat of the line. It seems probable that by this pattern he hoped to achieve something like Milton's blank verse paragraphs. The subtleties of Milton's technique escaped him, and his enjambment does not always create the organic effect he desired; while his attempt shows his lack of experience as a poet, it also shows his interest in technique itself. But in his poems written in this enjambed blank verse, he is trying to duplicate the emotional effects of an experience (not the experience itself), and the surge of each line into the next is occasionally successful in its context, even though the tendency toward regularity of enjambment is in itself static.

Not all of Chivers' blank verse attempts such carry-over. **"The Soaring Swan,"** whose subject is a symbol of Chivers' own desires, keeps its accents:

Thou art soaring around the throne of light,
Bathed in the tingling radiance of the sun
Whose bright effulgence, gilding thine abyss
Of burnished glory, scales the heights of heaven!
For on the velvet vesture of the hills,
Throned in the fulgence of the hills,
In desert embrace—bosomed by the groves—
And where the liquid flowings of the waves
Woo the enamoured banks—thy home shall be.

But blank verse could not serve him long, for his spirit would rise as does his swan, and the broken lines of **"The Death of Adaline"** or the long paragraphs of **"The Lament of Youth"** soon give way to more complex patterns, forms in which Chivers might establish a rhythm and break it where he wished.

One of Chivers' answers to this problem, the necessity of finding a strict form which might be endlessly varied, led him to utilize more and more the refrain, before, within, or at the end of each stanza, with the hope of thereby achieving a varying continuity, change plus exact cadence. In the Preface to *Virginalia,* he compared the refrain to the recurring chime at each revolution of the wheels of "the Chariot of Apollo"; but, he notes, the wheels' sound (i.e., the refrain's effect) is "proportionate," in terms of the metaphor, to the "velocity" of the chariot's wheels, or, to the desired motion of the poem. Since this desired variation is close to Poe's theory as stated in *The Philosophy of Composition,* it is interesting that Chivers experimented with such refrains as early as 1834.

Chivers developed his use of the refrain gradually, from the simple one line final refrain in his 1834 volume to a

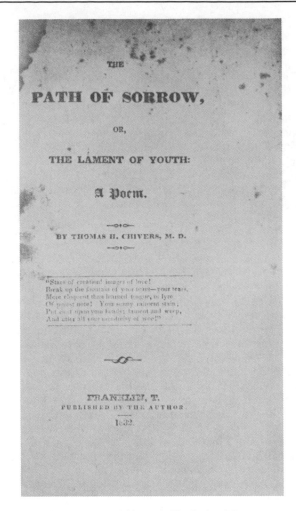

The title page of Chivers's The Path of Sorrow.

complex seven line refrain containing elements of both theme and mood in 1856; generally, the advance in complexity was steady. *The Path of Sorrow* (1832) makes no use of the refrain at all, while *Virginalia* (1853) contains only a few poems which avoid it. Such a steady progress toward the organic type of refrain which he desired shows constant attention to the problem, and makes it doubtful that any particular outside influence determined his interest.

The orthodox use of refrain as a continuing set-piece appears throughout Chivers poetry; often it is there simply to provide atmosphere for the body of the poem. **"To a China Tree,"** describing the idyllic surroundings of his early childhood, ends each stanza with "And shot with my cross-bow—my mulberry cross-bow—/ The robins that perched on the boughs near the gate." Not an effective refrain, surely, but the type is familiar. He achieved a variation on the same type in one of the **"Songs"** of *Nacoochee:*

Blessed of heaven! thy home shall be
In the bright green isle of my love for thee,

When thy form shall rest on my spirit bright
Like the silver moon on the starry night;
When thy voice shall float on my soul awake,
Like the gentle swan on the azure lake—
Blessed of heaven! thy home shall be
In the bright green isle of my love for thee.

Gradually Chivers' attempt to create an organic refrain evolved from simple parlor verse like the above. **"Choral Song of the Temperance Legions"** is an experiment that failed. Here he repeated, in each stanza, the first, seventh and eighth, and fourteenth lines of an odd fourteen line stanza, which attempts, as do a number of his poems, to present a shouted chant. The refrain lines presumably welded each bulky stanza to the next.

"The Angel's Whisper" is one of the more complex of his poems which attempt to integrate the refrain within the stanza. Following an *ababbab* scheme, Chivers used the fourth, fifth, and seventh lines as a constant refrain, and made the sixth line a repetition of the third. The result is a poem which depends for its effect almost entirely upon the varying content of the third line, which, by its repetition as the sixth line, a line contained within the refrain, determines the meaning of the refrain, allowing it to develop and change with each stanza.

Much of the same ballad-like quality is found in a series of poems which make use of the repeated rhyme in the refrain without attempting to insert it within the body of the stanza. **"Lily Adair"** and **"Rosalie Lee"** are familiar to Chivers readers, and their background extends as far back as 1836, to a poem entitled **"Ellen Aeyre,"** where the basic stanza form and refrain may be found. Again the simple double quatrain, *ababcdcd,* is the basis, but a *ddd* refrain is added to utilize the final pair of rhymes, the final *d* of the refrain doubling the length of the line.

Like the Lamb's wife, seen in vision,
    Coming down from heaven above,
Making earth like Fields Elysian,
    Golden city of God's love—
Pure as jasper—clear as crystal—
    Decked with twelve gates richly rare—
Statued with twelve angels vestal—
    Was the form of Ellen Aeyre—
    Of my saint-like Ellen Aeyre—
    Gentle girl so debonair—
Whitest, brightest of all cities, saintly
        angel, Ellen Aeyre.

When Chivers came to write **"Lily Adair"** he had only to shorten the third line of the refrain:

Where the Oreads played in the Highlands,
    And the Water-Nymphs bathed in the
    streams,
In the tall Jasper Reeds of the Islands—
    She wandered in life's early dreams.
For the Wood-Nymphs then brought from the
    Wildwood
    The turtle doves Venus kept there,

Which the Dryades tamed, in his childhood,
    For Cupid, to Lily Adair—
    To my Dove-like Lily Adair—
    To my lamb-like Lily Adair—
    To my beautiful, dutiful Lily Adair.

The same format for the refrain is found again in **"Rosalie Lee,"** with the same varied prepositions and descriptive phrases in the final three lines. Each refrain of these poems contains different descriptions of the heroine, each changing the reader's understanding of her a slight amount. The lulling, melodic effect of such refrains was part of what Chivers was seeking; it helped to weave an aura of vague ethereal beauty about his subject, which was the only way he could effectively describe female beauty.

Eonchs of Ruby and *Virginalia* in particular show how much Chivers depended upon this strict *ababcdcd* structure to provide a pattern from which he might deviate. **"The Place Where I Was Born,"** for example, presents this form, but subtracts the last three lines and makes them the basis of a *dcddd* refrain. **"The Moon of Mobile"** follows the double quatrain with a refrain of *efefff;* again Chivers seeks the hypnotic effect. **"Avalon,"** a poem typical of Chivers and one of his best, utilizes the repeating refrain for atmospheric effects:

Thy soul did soar up to the Gates of God,
    Oh, Lark-like Child!
And poured Heaven's Bowers of Bliss, by
    Angels trod,
        Poured Wood-notes wild!
In emulation of that Bird, which stood,
In solemn silence, listening to thy flood
Of golden Melody deluge the wood
        Where thou art lying
        Beside the beautiful undying
In the Valley of the Pausing of the Moon,
    Oh! Avalon! my son! my son!

Such an atmospheric refrain was necessary, Chivers believed, not as an ornament, or as embroidery, but to complete the theme; statement was never as effective as suggestion.

The refrain might be made a part of the whole in other ways, too. Any repetition of thematic lines would draw the various stanzas together and create a unified effect. Perhaps I take liberties with strict meaning when I call the following repeating and organic lines a refrain, yet I think that Chivers would have cited this poem as one which achieved the continuity plus variation which he desired, and so I have included it here. **"The Dying Beauty"** repeats the introductory statement in the first line eight times, and it is followed on each occasion by an extended simile; the whole poem, by virtue of these varying images within the static structure, creates a veiled and romantic picture of the death of a woman:

She died in beauty, like the morn that rose
In golden glory on the brow of night,
And passed off gently like the evening's close,

When day's last steps upon the heavens are
   bright.
She died in beauty, like the trampled flower
That yields its fragrance to the passer's feet,
For all her life was as an April shower,
That kept the tear-drops of her parting sweet.
And like the rainbows of the sunny skies,
The dew-drop fillet of the brow of even—
That blends its colours as the evening dies—
Her beauty melted in the light of heaven.

She died in softness, like the last sad tone
That lingers gently on the midnight ear,
When beauty wanders from her bower alone,
And no one answers, but the voice is near.
She died in beauty, like the lonesome dove
That seeks her fledglings in the desert air,
And hastes away from out the flowery grove
To seek the little ones that nestled there.
And like the humming-bird that seeks the bower,
But wings her swiftly from the place away,
And bears the dew-drop from the fading
   flower—
Her spirit wandered to the isle of day.

Several of the similes are effective; others are not, but whatever general success the poem has stems from the rigidity tempered by variation which the repeated line provides. Conscious, perhaps, that he had achieved something of his aim, Chivers used this formula in two other poems. **"To My Mother in Heaven,"** published in the following year, begins each stanza with "I see thee not!" and then enumerates, by stanza, the facets of his sense of loss. **"Uranothen,"** published in *Virginalia,* is a revision of **"The Heavenly Vision,"** which depends upon a repeating final line in each stanza, "She came from Heaven to tell me she was blest," to coordinate an essentially loose poem. In its revised form Chivers made the repetition less obvious, relegating it to the end position in the final line:

   The hyaline wavelets of her voice of love
      Rose on the boundless ether-sea's calm
   breast;
   Amid the interstarry realms above,
      To God in Heaven, telling me she was
   blest.

There are endless examples of Chivers' structural devices, but most of them stem from the two categories developed here. He was constantly interested in involved stanza forms; **"Threnody,"** written at the death of his son Tommy, indicates that he could be absorbed in the intricacies of form even in the midst of grief. In an attempt to slow down the movement of the opening of each stanza, he repeats the end-rhyme of the first stanza line as the first word in stanza lines two and three. The result is trickier than it is successful.

   How I miss him in the summer,
      Summer of the Golden Grain—
   Summer. . . .

What Chivers could achieve by use of the basic *abab* quatrain in his attempt to create certain hypnotic, semirhythmic effects was paralleled by his use of this form to produce a species of declamatory poetry which cannot easily be duplicated in the nineteenth century until Whitman turned it into a philosophy and an ideal. Like Whitman, he begins his stylistic ventures by adhering to orthodox forms; like him, too, he threw them away when certain inspirations were before him. Unlike the Camden seer, he did not utilize his declamations to present any but the most orthodox sentiments.

The development of Chivers' style was of course gradual, and we have just seen to what ends he put his experiments in the use of the refrain. There are suggestions of his declamatory style in his first tragedy, **Conrad and Eudora,** in 1834, although they are overwhelmed almost always by metaphysical imagery or Shakespearian rhetoric. Perhaps the earliest inspiration for his use of the style was from Byron, for a poem like **"Anastasius"** follows his formula for the narrative verse tragedy while it shows signs of declamation, unsuccessful as they are, which are absent from the other poetry of Chivers' first three volumes. Whenever an artificially imposed dramatic situation is present in his early poetry, as it rarely is, most of the poems being lyrical, Chivers attempts a rhetoric totally unlike the intimate style of his love songs or personal elegies. There is, however, a parallel between his development of the evocative, hypnotic effect which is exemplified in his later use of the refrain and the declamatory poetry under study here. In both styles he is likely to give way to exclamation and shouting which often obscure form, although the strictness superimposed by the varying refrain demands and gets attention where the blank verse or paeon-filled declamatory verse flows on from line to line without more than superficial notice of structure.

A series of what may be called patriotic poems best illustrates the development of this experiment. Chivers' quickly-incited fervor over any contest between liberty and tyranny was in some ways bound up with his desire to evoke or create the beauty of a Terrestrial Eden, for the Eden Isle is not far distant from the New Jerusalem which he saw embodied in nineteenth-century America. And when Chivers chooses Heaven or its earthly counterpart as subject, he seldom tries to limit his effects. The emotion within him can best be expressed by exultation.

Yet it may not be said that Chivers lost sight of the less ethereal details of his world; we find the clearest beginning of his declamatory style in the **"Choral Song of the Temperance Legions."** The poem is a series of trimeter quatrains arranged in the form of a chant, wherein the Legions shout their strength and purity to be answered by various Echoes—of the Sun, Moon, Constellations, or Angels. Its failure and its experimental nature are testified to by the fact he could revise it to **"The Cry of Hungary"** by changing little more than its title and omitting the identification of the Echoes; their lines become a widely varying refrain. The evocation, this time of freedom, is equally vague. Such vagueness would not necessarily harm a declamatory poem, but as yet Chivers had not found the meter to create the necessary carry-over from line to line which would unify the poem despite its looseness.

It was in 1854 that Chivers found and elaborated the form necessary to make his declamation effective. **"To Allegra Florence in Heaven"** had been written in lines which, although tetrameter in appearance, were actually broken octameters. In **"Where Liberty Was Born"** Chivers developed this meter in his favorite *abab* quatrain and kept the second and fourth lines catalectic. Like his earlier experiments in declamatory verse, the poem is marred by its extremes of imagery and diction, but the longer line goes far toward the effect of oration which Chivers was seeking.

"The Roll of Fame" is his most successful attempt in this direction, and its long, pulsing lines almost discard the stanza form and meter to achieve a rolling cadence now reminiscent of Whitman's carefully unmetered lines:

> In the Autumn of the world, when the honey of
> the Summer still lay on the flowers of the
> years,
> > I stood on the evergreen banks of the
> > beautiful River of Time,
> And there I heard the loud thunders, rolled off
> from the prows of the crystalline Spheres,
> > Break calmly against the white shore of my
> > panting soul in utterance sublime.
>
> . . . . .
>
> Then the tranced Silence, wakened from her
> peaceful slumber
> > In the Oasian Ocean of Saharah, hearing her
> > mournful voice
> Breaking against the Hills of Nubia, listening
> without number,—
> > Fled to the Pacific Islands in those Seas
> > whose billows make no noise.
>
> But still it was far sweeter the Muezzin's
> mournful crying
> > Uttered at daybreak from the Dome of the
> > beautiful Omar,
> Looking from the top of Zion up to the
> Mountain that is undying—
> > Like the first great golden Iliad bursting
> > from the soul of Homer.
>
> . . . . .
>
> Then, like the unfolding of some antediluvian
> iron Scroll,
> > With repercussive clang, like storm-winds
> > when they rend the bosom of the Deep,
> The Vail of Isis was rent in Twain, revealing
> unto my more than raptured soul
> > The dark Aenigma of the grave, written in
> > Dreams in the House of Sleep.

> . . . . .
>
> Then I heard iron words, spoken as if by
> clanking chains
> > Rattling in bottomless vaults rusted by tears
> > wept by the utterless Tomb—
> Followed by rumbling thunders-after which there
> fell down hailing rains,
> > As if hail fell instead of rain—freezing my
> > lips to dumbness doubly dumb!

The control afforded by meter is here discarded in favor of a series of chanted lines which, although the rhyme is kept, flow on without pause. The whole poem, thirty-four stanzas long, lacks any really vital organization, but moves from stanza to stanza within a very general framework of an emotional vision, in which Chivers sees the Heavenly kingdom spread before him. The effect of these short stanzas with their rolling lines, unhampered by any strict progression, is of a series of impressionistic and sometimes symbolic images flashed before the reader. Like the majority of Whitman's long catalogues of images, they demand that the reader supply most of the pictorial detail, and depend for their effect upon the continuing cadence lines, lines which sometimes include as many as fourteen accents.

This is the furthest approach Chivers made toward the effects Whitman was to make notorious and then famous less than a year later. Published only four years before Chivers' death, a poem like **"The Roll of Fame"** indicates the extent of his interest in form as controlled only by cadence and sound. The 1850's saw the fullest development of Chivers' powers as a poet, and the poems of these years help to show the distance he has travelled since 1832. Never content with existing forms or methods, Chivers sought to expand the power and scope of poetry, and his attempt ought to entitle him to a position at least part way removed from the limited horizons of the mid-nineteenth century "public Renaissance" and nearer the broader and deeper limits of the true American Renaissance of *Leaves of Grass*.

SOUND AND RHYTHM

A considerable part of the effect of Chivers' most characteristic poems stems from their often unique diction. His habits of language indicate that descriptive or suggestive words that appealed to him found a repository either in his memory or in some sort of a card file. Images and phrases become familiar to the reader of Chivers, and sometimes their change and development may be followed throughout his volumes.

The Path of Sorrow (1832) marks the beginning of his experiments with various types of diction. The product of a young, inexperienced poet, that it should contain coinage of his own is surprising at first glance, but when we recall that he tried many varieties of meter and stanza form in the same volume, *obsecration, unburlesqued, gnomen,* or *domil* further the belief that *The Path of Sorrow* was a thoroughly unusual first book. Attempting to find a vehicle for the untutored poetry he had within him, Chivers misuses and coins words whenever it serves his purpose to do so. The prophet, Chivers says, moves

>   far
> Beyond sycophants of terrene strife,—
> While scintillations from his mighty star,
> Shall pilot him to that eternal life,
> Where oblectations shine, devoid of grief.

Such diction is self-conscious and not entirely typical of the style he later developed. It does show, however, something more than early self-consciousness. Its essentially pedantic nature indicates that he was trying to mold what he thought of as esoteric diction to fit his own needs. An *orrery of tears,* an *ultramontaine sphere,* the *domil sun* are neither provocative nor suggestive unless they appear natural in their respective stanzas, and the poems of *The Path of Sorrow* are notable for their combination of standard poetic diction with such unique phrases as these. Delighted with unusual diction, Chivers had not yet found that it was possible to create poetry dependent almost entirely upon sound. The volume contains few color adjectives, and the greater part of the adjective usage is quite conventional in nature.

The urge to experiment in diction is not so much present in *Conrad and Eudora,* for the short lyrics in the book are, as has been suggested before, standard love songs whose content offered little or no incentive. The title drama indicates he knew his Shakespeare, although he cannot succeed in coordinating seventeenth-century soliloquy with nineteenth-century diction. And while a *run-mad heart* seems his own, Eudora says, echoing the Bible with some incoherence, "He, once the 'apple of mine eye,' cast off! / If it offend thee, pluck it out!" The violent rhetoric of the play is not good oration, but occasionally he succeeds:

> This fountain, which is stirred to bitter wrath,
> Which that insatiate wretch so rudely stung,
> And wounded with the arrows of his lust!—
> Shall turn an August to his life, and thirst
> For every drop that palpitates his heart!

Chivers revised and improved the play later as *Leoni; or, the Orphan of Venice.* Here the rhetoric is improved, and lines which were loose and vague in *Conrad and Eudora* appear in a more effective, concise style. The Shakespearian diction is still present, but Chivers has managed to develop his own images:

> . . . never shall my soul find rest,
> Until the purple mirror of his blood
> Reflect the deep damnation of his deeds. . . .

The fault of nineteenth-century colloquialism is still present, however, and exclamations of "By Jove!" appear violently out of place.

But the rhetoric which occupied Chivers in his plays does not often appear in his lyric poetry, except in the patriotic chants discussed earlier. He was busy developing what may be called his later style, which takes many of the unusual words of his earlier poetry and places them in a context which fits their nature. Compounds are very frequent, and *smile-beams, sapphire-paven,* or *zephyr-dimpled lake* become typical of the atmosphere he is trying to create. *Nacoochee* (1837) shows that it did not take Chivers long to realize the inadequacy of his earlier diction, or, rather, that that diction would not fulfill the purposes which were now uppermost in his mind. To paraphrase his own language, he would speak in *shell-tones,* moving in *pearl-tinct azure* (the sky) over the *crystalline deep sea* to the *island-clouds* of Heaven. The title poem of the volume and **"The Soaring Swan"** contain the clearest examples of this later preoccupation; the other poems follow the essentially orthodox style of the lyrics in **Conrad and Eudora.** Some time in the years just preceding **Nacoochee,** he saw the collected poetry of Coleridge as it appeared in the Galignani edition republished in Philadelphia. The sight of "Kubla Khan" and "The Ancient Mariner" must have excited Chivers as much as Keats or Shelley did, for here was confirmation that he was right in believing that the boundaries of poetic diction might be extended. But surely he saw too the hypnotic effect Coleridge's romantic images created in "Kubla Khan"; and "Alph, the sacred river" as well as "Mount Abora" may well have drawn his attention to the fact that a wholly unreal image could be created by the judicious use of exotic diction. It did not matter whether or not Mount Abora could be traced on a map; taken in its context it suggested just the remote romanticism that Chivers came to delight in.

Although Chivers learned more than exotic place names from Coleridge, his imagination was capable of producing such exoticisms as *Chalcedony, Boscobella, Oossanalla,* and *Meru,* and their use follows the date at which it is presumed he first saw Coleridge. **"The Soaring Swan"** (1837) suggests that he was either immediately inspired by Coleridge or had been experimenting on his own:

>   For there shall flow
> From out the circlings of thy floating form,
> Bathed in the flickering dalliance of the gems
> Of thy sun-cinctured dimples, like the pearl
> Of ocean set in beryl by the deep—
> A shell-toned music. . . .

Such a picture is not realistic, nor is it detailed in the sense of being exact; it might better be called provocative, in that it attempts to set the reader's imagination to work with the poet's, suggesting colors and hues which may be filled in as the reader chooses.

Eonchs of Ruby and **Virginalia** mark Chivers' primary effort in the use of imagery that depends wholly upon suggestive diction, and the second volume indicates his increasing interest in the effect and theory of pure sound. Stanzas of **"Rosalie Lee"** have already been quoted to indicate Chivers' delight in certain passages from Keats, notable for this same suggestiveness. **Eonchs of Ruby** contains diction which still startles:

In the mild month of October,
           As we did go
Through the fields of Cooly Rauber,
           No one can know,
But the great Archangel Auber,
           What songs did flow. . . .

That Chivers is interested in the suggestive connotation of a phrase like *Cooly Rauber* rather than its denotation is indicated by the fact that the cooly rauber is a vegetable, a cross between a cabbage and a turnip. The same poem describes the "thousand oceans spooming" (l. 82). Or he could describe a natural scene in these terms:

The cloud-sustaining, many-folded Hills—
       The soft, retiring mystery of the Vallies—
The open frankness of the verdant Fields—
       The winding labyrinths of the emerald
Alleys—
       The bending Heavens, with all the Stars in
cyclic sallies—

Lily Adair resides

Where the Oreads played in the Highlands,
       And the Water-Nymphs bathed in the
streams,
In the tall Jasper Reeds of the Islands—

Examples like these can be culled from a large number of the poems in these volumes, and they indicate a general trend. Chivers was less concerned with the denotation of his words than with the possible connotations dictated by the context of the poem; frequently he goes beyond the dictionary, to a land where the moon becomes a *melologue* (a word coined by Thomas Moore) and makes the *icy azure / Argently clear*. That is, Chivers could coin or distort language until it supplied him with the suggestiveness, the fantasy, he often desired. His imagination was not pictorial, nor was it, actually, dependent upon color so much as upon the connotations of the colors of precious stones; gem-mad, if you will, in the stanza from **"Rosalie Lee"** which he based on a scene from "The Eve of St. Agnes," he is interested in apples seen as "Ruby-rimmed Beryline buckets," and cucumbers as "emerald," "like Chrysopraz." His descriptions of Heaven depend largely upon the twenty-first chapter of the Revelation of St. John, where the City of God is described in terms of precious stones.

Exotic place names, figures from Greek mythology, Biblical names, precious stones—all contribute toward the diction of Chivers' later style. Most frequently he utilizes the more unusual words as end-rhymes, realizing the emphasis thus obtained. There was an interesting connection in Chivers' mind between color and sound. He added a note to the phrase "Soft as the liquid tones of Heaven," saying that he was "Alluding to the harmony between a soft sound and a blue color." Twentieth-century psychologists, and even home decorators would agree, perhaps, and it seems probable, that Chivers' growing interest in color and its suggestive powers led him to experiment

with the nature of pure sound in poetry. The mind that can record color in terms of sound clearly was sensitive to mutations in sound itself. Interest in suggestions of sound through alliteration and assonance led Chivers to write poems in which sound dominates, the thematic sense of the poem being of little importance. Coleridge certainly helped to lead him to such experimentation, and some of his lines are worthy of the English poet. Earlier he had written that the vultures "cleave their curve in the charnal air," a line which immediately suggests Gerard Manley Hopkins, and that his love's eyes were "Like the Lioness', lazy, their hazel hue." He once tried to put this interest into concrete terms: the Angelus is described as

              A wave-like, azure sound,
Upon the pavement of new-fallen snow,
       Pure as an Angel's garment on the
       ground—
Trembling the atmosphere with its soft flow—
Comes swiftly, with its Heaven-dilating swell,
From the Noon-ringing of yon far-off Bell.

An *azure* sound suggests the nature of Chivers' ear, but here he depends, successfully, at least partially upon the picture suggested. **"The Poet of Love,"** on the other hand, dispenses with such pictorial detail and relies upon the sweep of his language:

With the white lightnings of his still small voice,
       Deep as the thunders of the azure Silence—
He makes dumb the oracular Cymbals with their
       noise,
       Till BEAUTY flourish Amaranthine on the
Islands
       Of all the loud tumultuous Sea
       Of the vast immensity,
       Echoing the music of the Morns,
       Blown through the Chrysomelian Horns
       Down the dark vistas of the reboantic Norns
       By the great Angel of Eternity,
       Thundering, *Come to me! come to me!*

"Apollo" achieves much the same effect:

Like the lightning piled on lightning, ever rising,
       never reaching,
       In one monument of glory towards the
golden gates of God—
Voicing out themselves in thunder upon thunder
       in their preaching,
       Piled this Cyeclop [*sic*] up his Epic where
the Angels never trod.
Like the fountains everlasting that forever more
       are flowing
       From the throne within the centre of the
City built on high,
With their genial irrigation life forever more
       bestowing—
       Flows his lucid, liquid river through the
gardens of the sky,
       For the stars forever blooming in the
gardens of the sky.

The images of such poetry are not to be taken out of context, nor are they to be asked to produce their effects unless surrounded by others of the same nature. In these poems Chivers depends upon the multiplicity of his imagery, which in its suggestiveness often goes beyond intellectual comprehension, to produce an effect that is wholly of the senses. The reader is asked to forego his stable position and transport himself to Chivers' world, a world where "Chrysomelian Horns" and the "gardens of the sky" are wholly in place. The subject matter of poetry of this sort matters less than the emotional hypnosis the vast images and the exotic diction produce. It is not quite Xanadu, but it is not far from it.

Coleridge's world is most clearly evoked in a strange poem of Chivers' entitled **"The Little Boy Blue,"** a title as deceptive as any ever offered. The poem tells the story of the poet's wanderings across the earth, led on always by the song of the little boy blue. It becomes clear only after some little time that this figure symbolizes Chivers' poetic inspiration, and the places they visit are suggestive of the wild heights of Chivers' imagination. It matters not at all what the exact sense of the stanza may be; the thirty-seven quatrains that make up the poem establish a cadence which, while it is completely different from the whirling lines of the poems quoted above, carries the reader through the exotic lands of Chivers' inner world.

> The little boy blue
>   Was the boy that was born
> In the forest of Dru,
>   On the mountains of Morn.
>
> Where the tongue of the sea
>   Piles the dirges on Lorn
> There he warbled for me
>   Mellow lays on his horn.
>
> Where the dregs of his moan
>   Shingle-sanded the shore,
> There he built all alone
>   Lays that live evermore.
>
>   . . . . .
>
> By the cool crystal rills,
>   That meandered Lahawn,
> All along the green hills,
>   There he wandered at dawn—
> From the forests of Dru,
>   On the Mountains of Morn,
> Blowing songs ever new
>   Through the throat of his horn.
>
> From the island of Arran,
>   To the Vale of Lahore,
> Where the fields are all barren—
>   There he walked evermore.
>
> On the green banks of On,
>   By the City of No,
> There he taught the wild swan
>   Her white bugle to blow.

> First, he sang of the land,
>   Then he sang of the sea,
> Then he wrote on the sand
>   What I write now for thee.

And it does not seem imperative that the reader recognize symbolic meaning in such stanzas; their primary effect, obviously, is to establish the atmosphere of another world.

Although **"The Little Boy Blue"** depends for many of its effects upon strange end-rhymes, the true nature of Chivers' interest in sound itself becomes clearer from an examination of his **"Chinese Serenade."** The poem is divided into six irregular stanzas, the first three introduced by lines which attempt to approximate the sound of a Chinese stringed instrument:

> Tien-Tsze
> Tu Du
> Skies Blue—
> All clear—
> Fourth year,
> Third Moon,
> High Noon
> At night. . . .

Strange music indeed for the stable pages of a reputable literary magazine! The subtly cadenced music of the Chinese appealed to Chivers, and his attempt to reproduce it is successful as far as it goes. The main body of the first three stanzas does not continue the music, however, as it tells the story of the love and the "King of Son-Tay." The final stanzas of the poem are an attempt to convey the sound of a gong:

> Bo-au-awng, ba-ang, bing!
>   Bee-ee-eeing, ba-ang, bong!
> So-au-awng, sa-ang, sing!
>   See-ee-eeing, sa-ang, song!
>   Bing, bang, bong!

Here he has gone beyond poetry to a type of phonetic reproduction which is less effective than the tonal music of the first lines. Chivers' ear was not always acute, but melody and certain rhythms attracted him, and his attempts to create poetry which might approximate what he heard are a fascinating undercurrent in American literature. The songs of birds attracted him, and he tried several times to spell them out. In one of his letters to the *Georgia Citizen,* he speaks of his "recently written ***Theory of a true Poetical Language,***" and it may be presumed that this essay, were it extant, would lead up to a full understanding of his hopes to create a diction depending more upon connotation that denotation, and of his onomatopoetic attempts.

The presence of a strong rhythm in much of Chivers' experimental poetry is best accounted for by remembering his boyhood among his father's slaves. He writes that "there is absolutely more *real* and *soul thrilling* music made audible, (but still unwritten,) by the impassioned utterance of the *negroes* in the South . . . than can be found . . . in these whole Northern regions. . . ." Earlier he had noted that he had a large collection of such songs, and had praised them for their "simplicity" and natural perfection of rhythm. Cultural historians and jazz enthusiasts of the twentieth century have agreed, and Chivers' own day of course saw the beginning of the famed Christy minstrels. Whether the **"Corn Shucking Song"** Chivers published in 1855 in his own work and the result of many hours listening to work songs, or whether it is a literal transcription is difficult to tell. An earlier Negro melody, "De Ole Gray Hoss," contains the lines, "Oh! whar did you kum fum/Kum fum, kum fum—," the substance and rhythm of which can be found in many of that race's songs today, and the rhythm of the following seems legitimately derived from Negro melody:

> Shuck de Cawn, Niggers! oh! shuck de Cawn,
> Darkies!
>   De Mawnin' Staws a-risin' to bring de
> brake o' day;
> Shout aloud, Darkies! oh! shout aloud, Niggers!
>   De Oberseer's watin' to cawl us awl away.
> Wawk yore tawk, Jawbone! oh! wawk yore tawk
> wakin'!
>   For old Massa's dreamin' about de brake o'
> day;
> Bress yore soles, Darkies! de Oberseer's akin!
>   To gib us awl de cowhide, before we go
> away!
> *Git away de Cawn, Boys! git away de Cawn!*
>   *Oh! git away de Cawn, Boys! git away de*
> *Cawn!*
> *Linkydum-a-hydum, a linkydum-a-ho!*
>   *Holler, Boys! holler! de Cawn is gettin'*
> *low.*

Chivers evidently delighted in such exaggerated colloquialisms, for "De Ole Gray Hoss," mentioned above, is a comic lyric, and "The Death of the Devil," a low comedy farce built around one man's efforts to hoodwink another, makes use of exactly such stage-darky diction as we have above, unfortunately lacking the rhythms that make the **"Corn-Shucking Song"** successful.

Rhythm and onomatopoetic diction came together again in Chivers' attempt to reproduce the effect of a railroad train leaving the station. This is tour de force work, but nonetheless interesting as it exhibits his deep interest in an experiment with hypnotic effects. The images that are scattered throughout the poem resemble some of those he used to produce the sweeping effects of **"The Poet of Love"** or **"Apollo"** in that they are entirely suggestive, and totally unrelated to the realistic scene portrayed.

> All aboard! Yes—Tingle, tingle,
> Goes the bell as we all mingle—
> No one sitting solely single—
> As the steam begins to fizzle
> With a kind of sighing sizzle—
> Ending in a piercing whistle—
> As the fireman builds his fire,
> And the steam gets higher, higher—

> Thus fulfilling his desire—
> Which forever he keeps feeding
> With the pine-knots he is needing,
> As he on his way goes speeding—
> Till the Iron Horse goes rushing,
> With his fiery face all flushing—
> Every thing before him crushing—
> While the smoke goes upward curling,
> Spark-bespangled in unfurling
> And the iron wheels go whirling,
> Like two mighty millstones grinding,
> When no miller is them minding—
> All the eye with grit-dust blinding—
> And the cars begin to rattle,
> And the springs go tittle-tattle—
> Driving off the grazing cattle—
> As if Death were Hell pursuing
> To his uttermost undoing,
> Down the iron road to ruin—
> With a clitta, clatta, clatter,
> Like the Devil beating batter
> Up in Hell, in iron platter. . . .

These poems emphasize the continual necessity Chivers felt to expand the limits of poetic theory and practice as he knew it. They are not uniformly successful, but they are strong indication of his distinction from the common. He had imagination, an ear which could catch tonal differences and melodic rhythms, and often the talent to turn what he heard and felt into effective poetry. His diction varies from the dream world of **"The Little Boy Blue"** to such realism as we have just seen, a scope indicative of his interest in deriving meaning from the manipulation of sound itself.

POETIC DEVICES

Chivers' creative process was a religious one; his moments of inspiration are akin to the mystic's consciousness of his at-oneness with God. Chivers made the relation between the artistic and the religious experience concrete and factual by proclaiming that his poetry was an evocation of divinity, of the divine presence. Unlike most mystics, he felt no sense of awe upon establishing this identification. Supremely confident of his own abilities, he comments on the fact of the nature of poetry rather than on the technique used to create the poetry.

Expressing himself in exultant terms in his prefaces and prose statements, Chivers seldom speaks of his conscious effort to achieve something new in form and technique. Indeed, the majority of these statements have proved to be his efforts to explain the true quality of his subject matter, rather than explications of his method.

In line with this silence about his technical experiments is the absence of any general statement on imagery, beyond his assertion that "the more palpably [Divine Beauty] is made manifest in the IMAGE, through Art, the more lucid will be the *Revelation of the Divine Idea*." In introducing this comment, Chivers insisted that the image is derived "by glorying sensation, which is finite, into thought, which is infinite. . . ." Such a statement could come only from a poet who reacted to experience, to stimuli of any sort, by his senses alone. A ratiocinative poet, for example, would place his emphasis upon the Art, which Chivers does include in his theorem, rather than upon the sensation. When Chivers said Poe failed in certain poetic areas because he lacked passion, what he meant was that the Art, the craftsmanship of the poet, had become too obvious, that the fire of inspiration had been extinguished before the calculation of means to achieve the desired effect. Such an objection sums up the failure of certain of Poe's poems quite exactly; it also clarifies Chivers' own theory and practice. For while he objected that Poe stressed the necessary Art to the exclusion of the necessary Passion, Chivers himself delighted in the Passion to a point where some of his poems lose form and shape before its onslaught.

But it is not to be imagined that Chivers held entirely to the notion that Passion, or exalted emotion, was a poem's only necessary ingredient. His experiments in diction and form have already testified to his interest in technical matters, and his use of imagery furthers the belief that while he could speak of poetry only in terms of its ultimate purpose and divine nature, he was deeply if silently concerned with the problems of the working artist. Just as we have seen that his efforts to extend the boundaries of poetic form and language resulted from certain basic beliefs which he held, so will we see that his use of imagery derives from his insistence that an image is basically sensation "glorified" or raised into thought.

The explication of such a statement is relatively simple once Chivers' prose is understood: sensation, the reaction of the poet as he stands in the face of the given experience, when placed in the context of the poem's theme becomes more than simply emotional response; it becomes the true interpretation of the experience, for the poet sees with the eyes of the seer. His reaction, then, expressed in terms of imagery, gives the facts or details of the experience the inspired quality which makes them the "Revelation of the Divine Idea."

With such a belief behind it, Chivers' poetry takes on new meaning, particularly when his subject matter is concerned with divinity or the divine, that which is in some way at a remove from this earth. His more conventional pieces, those devoted to standard romantic themes of earthly love, parting, or sorrow, for example, seldom make use of imagery. But the poems which transcend the earthly toward the divine contain images which are distinctly unusual in the work of an American poet of the 1840's and 1850's.

While this theory lies behind virtually all of Chivers' more unusual imagery, his use of the simile seems to derive directly from an outside influence rather than from his poetic theory. In many of the poems following the middle years of the 1830's, presumably after he had seen Shelley's collected works for the first time, Chivers depends wholly upon the parallel construction made possible by repetition of the simile. Shelley's influence seems clear, for his work abounds in such usage; this has already been noted in reference to Chivers' **"To Allegra Florence in Heaven."**

Yet in another way Chivers' use of the simile derives from the emotional and sometimes erratic quality of his mind. Where a poet like Edward Taylor, rational in at least certain elements of his Puritan thinking, seldom leaves an image until he has exhausted all its involutions and possibilities, Chivers, moved by emotion and not by intellectual or rationalistic stimuli, seldom investigates an image beyond its surface connections with the subject at hand. One aspect of a comparison catches his attention, and he builds a simile about it; another, perhaps illustrating a second comparison, may be added to the first—and so on. Rather than utilizing a single fully developed metaphor or image, Chivers' poetry is characterized by a loose, inclusive structure, typical in many ways of Shelley. Borne upward by emotion, his mind and imagination play over a series of comparisons, delighting in each for a moment before going on to the next. The effect of such composition is sometimes erratic, while at other times the spread of his series of pictures gives just the quality of totality which he desired. **"The Dying Beauty,"** a poem written soon after he had first studied Shelley, is typical:

> She died in meekness, like the noiseless lamb
> When slain upon the altar by the knife,
> And lay reclining on her couch so calm,
> That all who saw her said she still had life.
> She died in softness, like the Dorian flute,
> When heard melodious on the hills at night,
> When every voice but that loved one is mute,
> And all the holy heavens above are bright.
> And like the turtle that has lost her love,
> She hastened quickly from the world to rest;
> And passed off gently to the realms above,
> To reign forever in her FATHER's breast.

The majority of Chivers' similes utilize the word *like,* and frequently it is given a primary position in the line. Others use a moderately extended simile bounded formally by *as* and *so;* apparently the strict format of such a construction helped Chivers to achieve a tighter structure. **"Caelicola,"** an elegy on Poe, begins,

> Like that sweet bird of night,
> Startling the ebon silence from repose,
> Until the stars appear to burn more bright
> From its excessive gush of song which flows
> Like some impetuous river to the sea—
> So thou did'st flood the world with melody.
>
> For as the evening star
> Pants with its "silver lightnings" for the high
> And holy Heavens—the azure calm afar—
> Climbing with labor now the bending sky
> To lead Night's Navy through the upper sea—
> So thou did'st pant for immortality.

Such usage is not always effective, for the structure of the stanza dominates its content instead of containing it.

Chivers' mind, with a wide enough grasp to delight in virtually unrelated similes, occasionally achieved a yoking of disparate elements reminiscent of John Donne. When lust attacks virtue, Chivers says in **Conrad and Eudora,** "Then fix a pivot in thy heart for doubt to turn on!" Violent and forceful images of this sort do not occur often in his work, but their presence, as in the following example, is another instance of that facility of imagination which characterizes Chivers' poetry:

> Thou wert as mild as an incarnate Moon,
> Making his soul the satellite of mine—
> Round which thou didst revolve in joy,
>   as soon
> As my fond soul could shed its light on thine.

The Path of Sorrow (1832) and **Conrad and Eudora** (1834) do not develop in this imaginative usage very far. Generally, the poems in the first volume utilize direct statement of emotion or reaction rather than the indirection of the simile or metaphor. **"Songs of the Heart"** of **Conrad and Eudora** contains fewer of such personal revelations, but the format normally involves an artificial situation or theme, and such notable imagery as is found there seems orthodox romanticism. Occasionally Chivers developed an atmospheric effect through the use of an imaginative image: his sister's dying eyes mirrored sights to him which were "the whisperings of bliss, / Uttered by silence. . . ." The significance of silence seems to be the beginning of his almost mystic insight into sensory reaction:

> my chamber has become an alcove
> For the watchers of the sky! and in my
> Bed, at midnight of my sleep, I people
> Worlds, and dream unnumbered things; till
>   silence
> Wakes from lethargy, and shocks my burning
> Brain. . . .

In these two random examples, Chivers has had comparative success with a device which he was to use more and more frequently. By personalizing or animating the abstract, he attaches a physical dimension to his otherwise prosaic statement.

This same device is elaborated in **Nacoochee** (1837), and we find "An angel fondling with the locks of even . . ." or with "the locks of love!" His Heaven is made physical, if not visual, and thus susceptible to sensory reaction. He came to use this device most frequently when he attempted to envision vast or distant or indistinct forces. The earth, in her last convulsion at Judgment Day, is seen as an animated being:

> the far-stretching solitudes were torn
> By the tempestuous whirlwinds, as they came
> From out the nostril of the dying sea!
> And when the pantings of his collapsed sides
> Gave out the last Lunarian sigh to heaven,
> That sent prolific torpor through his limbs;
> And when the voiceless confines of his waves
> Lay back within the pulseless arms of his

> Peninsulas, with one far-spreading seethe
> Of songless palsy—down his bosom sank!

He attempts the same visual effect in **"The Death of Time"**:

> A mournful anthem comes from out the moon!
> For she has found her grave-clothes in the
>   clouds!
> And frightened at the widowhood of earth,
> She wanders blindfolded from her wonted path,
> And, wailing for her ocean-lord, she puts
> On sackcloth for the dying sun, and sets
> Behind Eternity to rise no more!

Such an image is both pictorial and suggestive; the reader cannot visualize its full extent, but because of the animation of forces and bodies not normally capable of feeling or emotion, Chivers has made an otherwise unimaginable circumstance vivid.

Imagery of this sort depends for its effect upon and helps explain extensions beyond the normal boundaries of experience. When Chivers says "Before [God] laid the world's foundation stone / High on the nothing of primeval night," he intends that the reader understand by visualizing the action. God fixing the cornerstone of the world led to more unusual work. By the same token that Chivers is able to accept and utilize the metaphor of an artisan constructing the world is he able to provide an almost surrealistic effect when he imagines his own death:

> The great golden hand on the Adamant Dial
> Of the Clock of Eternity pauses in Heaven!
> From Death's bony hand I now empty the
>   Phial—
> And the Morning is just like the Even!

It is a sensory reaction that Chivers demands of the reader. By an extension of the physical reality of this world to a plane which is usually dealt with only in abstract terms, he presents an image which can be visualized by the imagination. I say "by the imagination," because Chivers seldom uses intimate detail of the physical world in his imagery. The scene set by "Death, from out Hell's bars, / Looked lean for want of life!" is one which can be seen, but seen only by the inward, imaginative eye. The following description of a dead woman's hair moving slightly in the wind sets a scene clearly enough, but it is one which draws the imagination into the reader's reaction; where much romantic imagery provides a familiar or quickly visualized setting, the following scene exists in a separate world, a world which, I believe, existed within Chivers' own consciousness:

> the whispers of the odorous Breeze,
> Lifting her raven locks with spirit-hands,
> And weaving, with their glossy curls, the woof
> Wherein to hide the fragrance he had stolen—

Or, more exactly, when he speaks of his own emotions Chivers turns to an imaginative world which is not far distant from that which provided such imagery as we have been examining. Here the metaphor is standard in its limits, until the final lines:

> The last dark wave that lashed affection's shore,
>> Is pausing now upon my weary soul!
> Thy syren mistress of its tides shall be
>> A lamp hung out beyond eternity!

Chivers' imagination and mind were extensive enough to grasp such an image, and through the use of them in his poetry he hoped to achieve the revelation of the nature of his reaction to certain situations. When the situation was one which included Heaven, then his inward reactions became the true image of that Heaven, or when it was of lesser import, as the one above, he could suggest the extreme nature of his reaction by images which immediately force the reader to abandon his grasp upon the physical world and to enter into Chivers' consciousness, which, partially at least, becomes just as visible and real as the world the reader has left.

The images we have examined so far have all dealt in visual and sometimes imaginative terms; they are the sensory reactions Chivers has spoken of which both explain the poet's response and demand intuitive comprehension by the reader. But Chivers depended less upon his visual sense for his most striking images, than upon a combination of his auditory and olfactory senses. At times such imagery approached sense confusion, but almost always such multiplicity of sensory response is intentional. It might better be called ambiguity than confusion of sensory response. When Emily Dickinson described a humming bird as "A resonance of emerald," she was uniting the reaction of her eye with that of her ear; such unification is of course intentional and it suggests the totality or the multiplicity of her understanding of the bird. Chivers also makes use (perhaps to a greater degree even than Emily Dickinson) of this totality of the senses.

When Chivers speaks of the "Incense-smoke of pain" arising from the crucified Christ, he combines odor with emotion, as it were, in almost symbolic terms, demanding that the reader experience as well as understand the scene. A more complicated image attempts to describe the murmur of a sea shell when held close to the ear: "Here, in its labyrinthine curve, it leaves / The footprints of its song in many dyes; / And here, incessantly, it ever weaves / The rainbow-tissue of its melodies." Song, personified, is equated with color in such an image, and the effect is one of purposeful ambiguity or sense confusion.

It would seem that Chivers' ear supplied him with virtually all the ambiguities of sense imagery which he uses. This fact perhaps explains as well as depends upon his understanding of Heaven as a state of music. The inward world out of which almost all his more vivid imagery comes was one in which abstractions could have their own particular sound (and sometimes odor), and where vast forces are understood best in terms of their sound. Only once did Chivers attempt to describe his reaction definitively: entitled **"The Voice of Thought,"** the fol-

lowing poem presents an explanation of what occurred during his moments of inspiration.

> Faint as the far-down tone
>> Beneath the sounding sea,
> Muffled, by its own moan,
>> To silent melody;
> So faint we cannot tell
>> But that the sound we hear
> Is some sweet rose's smell
>> That falls upon our ear;
> (As if the Butterfly,
>> Shaking the Lily-bell,
> While drinking joyfully,
>> Should toll its own death-knell!)
> Sweeter than Hope's sweet lute
>> Singing of joys to be
> When Pain's harsh voice is mute,
>> Is the Soul's sweet song to me.

The poem's title helps us understand Chivers' method of sensory perception; thought, an abstraction, is given a voice, and that voice is best understood by Chivers when likened to the odor of a rose. The voice, he says ambiguously, is silent, yet that silence stirs a certain sensory reaction within him.

By such reaction as this, Chivers could achieve a variety of effects. The vastness of space and Heaven, which he so often spoke of in his poetry, gathers sound unto itself, much in the manner of the belief of Pythagoras in the music of spheres:

>> the rolling spheres
> Diffuse their circular orbit-tones on high—
> Spreading till they embrace th' Eternal Years
> With their dilating, wave-like melody—
> Winnowing the calm, clear, interstellar air—

Or he can turn the device about and give physical qualities to sound itself:

> Tempestuous whirlwinds of deep melody
>> Dash from his orb-prow on his spheric
> road—
> Rolling in mountain-billows on Heaven's sea
>> Against the white shore of the feet of God.

The image becomes vast and all-inclusive as the singer's melody becomes a vessel moving through an ocean; the poem from which the image comes is an attempt to recreate an astronomer's sense of exultation as he discovers a new planet, and in its context the image serves to increase and broaden the reader's response to the poem.

But such sensory effects as Chivers desires were not always of such huge size. By taking the physical quality of one physical situation and giving it to another, he produced a visual image which is at once real and imaginative:

> Silver twilight softly snowing
>> On the earth and on the sea,

All the darkness overflowing—
Rode the moon. . . .

This entire image depends for its effect upon the use of the word *snowing* in connection with *twilight;* indeed, many of Chivers' most interesting images stem from his ability to snatch a word from a familiar context and put it in another, where it both describes the image and suggests the one from which it was taken.

But sound imagery, which is the particular fascination of so many of his poems, can be carried further, sometimes too far. A harpist is described:

While from his fingers' ends the dews of sound
Dript, changing into Jewels as they fall,
Bright as stalactites of crystal. . . .

The imagery which has been described here is not unusual in Chivers' poetry; it is not chosen with any purpose other than to present his most typical and yet most unorthodox images. There are, of course, numbers of poems which are wholly standard in imagery: here the wind is personified.

Thou wringest, with thy invisible hand, the foam
Out of the emerald drapery of the sea,
Beneath whose foldings lies the Sea-Nymph's
home—
Lifted, to make it visible, by thee. . . .

But even as standard a romantic image as this indicates Chivers' primary interest and effect; it is an imaginative, visual, yet suggestive world out of which he would write. His attempt to recreate the totality of his sense response to particular situations through ambiguity is only a symptom of the completeness with which his emotions responded to certain stimuli.

The manner in which Chivers often strings a series of similes together to illustrate his reaction to an experience indicates further his attempt to make the Divine Idea, to use his words, clear to the reader. By comparing his subject with a variety of partially similar subjects or experiences, he hopes to illustrate the basic quality of that subject. These similes, as well as certain of his almost metaphysical conceits, frequently deal in terms of the poet's senses, for, as has been noted, Chivers would change sensation into thought or understanding, and one of the surest ways of achieving such a change is to force the reader to respond with his own senses in a variety of ways until the subject of the poem becomes an actual experience for him just as it was for the poet.

S. Foster Damon   (essay date 1957)

SOURCE: An introduction to *The Complete Works of Thomas Holley Chivers, Volume I,* edited by Emma Lester Chase and Lois Ferry Parks, Brown University Press, 1957, pp. xiii-xv.

[*Known as an expert on the work of William Blake, Damon was also highly regarded as the biographer of Chivers and American poet and critic Amy Lowell. In the following essay, Damon comments on Chivers's personality, reputation, and literary style.*]

Of all the figures in American literature, Thomas Holley Chivers, M.D., was certainly one of the most extraordinary. You may not like him, but you cannot ignore him. His poetry ranged from markedly original fantasies, in which the music transcends the sense, to verses so bathetic as to be immortally ridiculous. But Chivers was also a playwright, cosmic philosopher, essayist, controversialist, fascinating newspaper columnist, and at one time was even appointed a college professor. Yet he was also a lonely person, a nomad in our sprawling states, who until the end of his life did not find that uncritical admiration which alone made him feel secure.

Edgar Allan Poe comments on the work of Chivers:

Dr. Thomas Holley Chivers, of New York, is at the same time one of the best and one of the worst poets in America. His productions affect one as a wild dream—strange, incongruous, full of images of more than arabesque monstrosity, and snatches of sweet unsustained song. Even his worst nonsense (and some of it is horrible) has an indefinite charm of sentiment and melody. We can never be sure that there is *any* meaning in his words—neither is there any meaning in many of our finest musical airs—but the effect is very similar in both. His figures of speech are metaphor run mad, and his grammar is often none at all. Yet there are as fine individual passages to be found in the poems of Dr. Chivers, as in those of any poet whatsoever.

His MS. resembles that of P. P. Cooke very nearly, and in poetical character the two gentlemen are closely akin. Mr. Cooke is, by much, the more *correct;* while Dr. Chivers is sometimes the more poetic. Mr. C. always sustains himself; Dr. C. never.

Edgar A. Poe in Graham's Magazine, *Vol. XIX, No. 6, December, 1841.*

He was obsessed and driven by three separate demons: his family, his genius, and his pose.

The Chiverses were a proud, turbulent family. The father, Colonel Robert Chivers, made a fortune in cotton, which left his sons wealthy slave-owners. In the near-frontier conditions which then prevailed in Georgia, everything they did ran to excess. Their pride swelled into arrogance; their quarrels crowded the law-courts; their romances constantly broke out into scandals.

The poet was a Chivers to the full. As the eldest son he inherited the old homestead; he also had a town house in Washington, Georgia. He owned many slaves, whom he hired out when convenient, and for whom he bought bacon by the thousand pounds. He was also one of our first literary men to appreciate the original rhythms of their music, and to record one of their songs.

A rich man, he lived lavishly, as was the custom of the southern aristocracy. But like many another rich man, he was cautious to an extreme about lending money to others; and his letters prove that he seldom knew the moment when to be generous. He never sent Poe the expected $50 when Poe needed it desperately, and he even made the strapped actor Dickinson pay the postage on a letter which did not contain the half-promised remittance. (It was Longfellow who finally got Dickinson out of his difficulties.) Chivers evidently would not buy his way into the American Parnassus; probably he also wanted to keep his friendships clear of pecuniary involvements. But it must also be remembered that once he offered to support Poe for the rest of his life.

His early first marriage broke up almost immediately, and before the divorce proceedings were quite concluded, he married again—legally, according to Georgian law. His second marriage ceremony, to a girl from Springfield, Massachusetts, was performed in New York; it sounds like an elopement. Thereafter, he preferred to live in the north; and when he finally did return home to live, he had to remove suddenly to Decatur, the strong local tradition insisting that he was helped out of town because of the way he treated his wife.

His literary genius was also one of excess. He pushed his medium—the music of words and resonance of ideas—to such extremes that his poems were never valued as they should have been. Simms once wrote him an earnest letter of honest advice, pointing out his supposed faults. Chivers preserved the letter, but fortunately paid no heed to its suggestions. Had he done so, he would have shorn his work of all of its especial excellences.

His pose, however, was a genuine danger. Not content to write unappreciated poems, Chivers also wanted to enact the role of Poet in the eyes of the world. Therefore he tried to make himself into what the world supposed a poet should be—remote, crushed with secret sorrows, mysterious, profound. Like Young, he made literary capital of his personal tragedies, until his obsession with the grave became a bore. "You ask me why I hate the world," one of his letters begins; and we know we are in for an essay in his most solemn but fashionable manner. It is well done, but we don't like the type any more.

He never resolved this conflict between poetry and pose; he never knew that there might be a conflict. Lacking any trace of humor—and what other man could possibly take seriously the burlesque "Presentation of the Wooden Spoon" at Yale?—he also lacked self-criticism. And nobody ever told him the difference between his best and his worst work. Nobody could.

But the ego of Chivers was too demonic ever to be crushed by Fate or anything else. To the end he kept on writing, publishing, fighting for a reputation, and corresponding. He might be infuriated by neglect, but he never once doubted his own genius.

Yet he was lonely. Much of his correspondence consists of attempts to establish cultural friendships, which he learned to hold only towards the end of his life. He was in touch with almost everybody, and almost everybody was alternately attracted and repelled by his magnetic personality. His letters therefore illuminate many a corner in our literary history. The elaborate annotations to these letters contain biographies and other data hitherto unavailable. Sometimes they are more interesting than the letters themselves.

More than that, they illuminate Chivers himself, with his insuperable arrogance, his real and exaggerated melancholy, his rages, his brassy mendacities, his metaphysical ecstasies, his curious scholarship, his startling metaphors and gorgeous platitudes. Irritating though he often is, one cannot help admiring him. And what a relief he is!—what a phenomenon!—in the dead level of the respectably genteel verse of his times!

Richard Beale Davis (essay date 1959)

SOURCE: "Thomas Holley Chivers and the Kentucky Tragedy," in *Texas Studies in Literature and Language*, Vol. 1, No. 2, Summer, 1959, pp. 281-88.

[*An educator and scholar, Davis is best known for his writings on Southern life and literature. In the following essay, Davis compares Chivers's* Conrad and Eudora *and* Leoni, *contending that they are different versions of the same work and that they reveal Chivers's "abilities as a self-critic."*]

The Kentucky Tragedy stands as one of the three great historical events, matters, or themes which American writers have drawn upon in creating fiction, poetry, and drama. Only Pocahontas and Merry Mount rival it. This dark tale of violence and sentiment fitted the temper of the violent and emotional age in which it was born. "No more thrilling, no more romantic tragedy did ever the brain of poet conceive than was the tragedy of Sharpe and Beauchampe," Poe once remarked in reviewing a novel on the subject by William Gilmore Simms [*Graham's Magazine*, XX (May, 1842)]. It has continued to have its appeal down to the present time, to an age less sentimental but hardly less violent, an age which sees in this theme the eternal problem of order versus violence. Poe himself was among those who attempted a romantic and melodramatic play (*Politian*) on the subject, and in our time Robert Penn Warren has set in this same event his novel *World Enough and Time,* one of his most sensitive presentations of man's search for justice and for an explanation of his relation to the universe.

In certain respects the first published belletristic work based on the theme is the most interesting, both for itself and as indication of the tastes and creative capacities of its author. This work is a play, by Thomas Holley Chivers, or rather three plays based on the same materials, the first of which was written only seven or eight years after the event it depicts. This Georgia poet, now properly given a significant place among Southern antebellum writers, is perhaps better known for his slender volumes of lyric verse than for his plays. But his three versions of the Kentucky Tragedy are fairly representative of his peculiar rhetoric, imagery, and versification, and indicate a number of things about his peculiar genius.

In 1834 Chivers published in book form his first play on the subject, **Conrad and Eudora,** a volume as difficult to come by now as are his other books. About 1838 or 1839, he composed a quite different play on the same theme, calling it **Leoni, the Orphan of Venice**. The manuscript, now in the Harvard Library, really represents two stages of this second play, for there are markings through and obliterations which are more than mere cuttings. These alterations may have been made about 1845, as suggested below, and clearly before 1851. For in 1851 he published in the *Georgia Citizen* a third version, improved and condensed, with the title of the second play, **Leoni**. At least one of these three, that in manuscript, was read by Poe, though too late to influence his own work on the subject. The three taken together well indicate Chivers' ability to criticize and improve upon his own work. All three are literary exercises characteristic of our American romantic period, employing a native theme in partly native, partly exotic settings.

The historical significance of these plays lies somewhat in the fact that the first of them is an early, if not the earliest literary and dramatic presentation of the notorious series of events which occurred at Frankfort, Kentucky, in 1825-1826. At dawn of November 7, 1825, Colonel Solomon P. Sharp, an able lawyer and widely known politician who had just been elected to the Kentucky legislature, was called to the door of his home in the state capital and stabbed fatally by Jereboam O. Beauchamp, a young lawyer who had been a friend and perhaps protégé of his victim. Sharp had earlier been a member of the legislature, from 1813 to 1817 a member of Congress, and just before 1825 attorney-general, a position he resigned in order to enter the race for representative of Franklin County on the Relief or New Court Party ticket. James Madison called him "the ablest man of his age who had represented the west."

Beauchamp, destined to be executed at twenty-four, had married Anne Cooke, a Southern Kentucky belle, who accepted him on the condition that he kill her seducer, Colonel Sharp. After the assassination Beauchamp, who earlier had been heard to threaten the older man, was arrested on suspicion. Motivated at least in part by personal and political antagonisms, the grand jury indicated Beauchamp. He was tried and convicted. His wife, who had been released for lack of evidence, insisted on spending the last days with her husband in the dungeon of the Frankfort jail. After pleas by the two Beauchamps' political friends failed, the married pair entered into a suicide pact and swallowed laudanum. The drug failed in the desired effect, and they stabbed themselves with a small case knife on the morning of the day set for the execution, July 7, 1826. Mrs. Beauchamp died immediately, and her husband, though weakened by his wound and partially drugged, was hanged on the public gallows.

The trial had been flamboyant, and the Kentucky newspapers sensationalized the case. The strong sentimental appeal of the story—seduction! love! revenge! suicide! hanging!—caused it to be copied in journals all over the country. News ballads, long and lugubrious, were soon spreading the facts, or alleged facts, through rural America. Moreover, Beauchamp had in the weeks between conviction and execution composed a *Confession,* a curiously introspective *apologia* reviewing the events, printed immediately after his death and widely circulated. This *Confession* has become one of the major "old yellow books" of American literature. Cheap reprints of the "document" in dime-novel format continued to be in demand through the 1850's. It has been used by almost every writer—poet, playwright, or novelist—who developed the theme, from Chivers in 1833-1834 to Warren in 1950. A volume of Anne Cooke's letters and the dismal ballads mentioned above are among other contemporary or nearly contemporary materials employed by certain later writers.

Sentimentalizers of the story in the nineteenth century ignored the claims of the Sharp supporters that Anne Cooke was a sophisticated, scheming woman of unprepossessing appearance and of worse than doubtful reputation, a hellion whose personality disgusted the jury; they ignored the claim that Beauchamp may have been merely an infatuated, hysterical swain certainly half a generation younger than his deviously plotting wife. Anne became Innocence Betrayed; Jereboam was the Heroic Avenger. Upon this tale of the Dark and Bloody Ground the American writer built many imaginatively and dramatically interesting edifices.

There may have been one unpublished play on the subject before Chivers'; if so, it has disappeared. As this letter dated 1834 prefacing the 1851 printing of **Leoni** states, Chivers read the *Confession,* or most of it, while he was a medical student at Transylvania University in Lexington, Kentucky (1828-1830). Also he seems to have been the preparatory-school pupil of the same Thomas Lacey who acted as one of Beauchamp's counsels. Chivers generally sticks close to the *Confession* in his plots, but his more realistic portrayal of Anne Cooke's vengeful nature may have come to him orally from Lacey. At all events, as a student in Lexington he must have had many opportunities to talk to people who saw or knew something of the events mentioned in the *Confession.* One does not need to take seriously his 1834 dating of his prefatory letter to **Leoni,** for in 1851 he certainly used the names from his 1838-1851 play versions, not the names from the 1834 **Conrad and Eudora**. Clearly he had not in 1834 written "the following play," i.e., **Leoni,** as it appears in the *Georgia Citizen* of 1851. The letter does indicate that he himself considered **Conrad and Eudora** and the two versions of **Leoni** as essentially one work.

As suggested above, by 1834 Chivers had written the first of his three plays. The setting is Frankfort, Kentucky, but the principal characters with one exception are given fictitious and exotic names. **Conrad and Eudora** was published in Philadelphia at about the time of Chivers' twenty-fifth birthday, in a volume bearing the play's title but also containing forty-nine lyrics. Presumably the author paid for it himself, as he did for most of his other books. Though the poetry of the play is predominantly blank verse, there are in the dialogues rhyming couplets, and in the speeches alternating rhyme. Also there are songs in other meters. The language is stilted, rhetorical, too-often suggestive of Chivers' lyrics at their worst; it rarely if ever comes up to their best. Though the play apparently was written in the fashion of the closet dramas of the day, it should not act badly. The five acts develop naturally the seduction, the oath of vengeance and of eternal love, the assassination, the death penalty, and the suicide-execution. The action moves much more swiftly than in the other plays on the subject, including Poe's, perhaps because Chivers had dramatized the crime so literally, almost without change.

Though the settings remain in Kentucky, the "Cottage in the Country" (II,i,iii;III,iii;IV,ii) is in the romantic-dramatic tradition, and most of the scenes could occur anywhere. The innkeeper's speech may be incongruous set against such high-flown language, but it is colloquial and therefore to us rather effective:

> Innkeeper.   Killed him! was he murdered!
> merciful heavens! I never heard the like in all
> my life.

The French-Italian-Spanish names of the principal characters are natural to the poetic tradition in which Chivers was working, and they have individually been traced to such classics as Byron, Sheridan, and Shakespeare. The diatribes against seduction and the praise of female virtue, the pathos of orphan and orphan's illegitimate child are characteristic of the same tradition. Actually Chivers is not nearly so baldly didactic as some of his successors in Kentucky Tragedy dramatization, writers like Charlotte Barnes in *Octavia Bragaldi.*

Motivation remains weak and often obscure. The lyric quality, including the songs, is more marked in *Conrad and Eudora* than in Chivers' later versions of the tragedy. The characters have usually been called stereotypes, and certainly Alonzo (Sharp) is the dastardly and cowardly villain, Conrad (Beauchamp) the sentimental hero, and Eudora (Anne Cooke) the wronged, weeping, noble-hearted heroine of sentimental melodrama. But there is some individualization, even of the two male principals, for they frequently suggest peculiar traits of character indicated in the *Confession.* And the pure and clinging-vine Eudora of the early scenes who after her seduction becomes, perhaps somewhat inconsistently, the bloodthirsty and indomitable wronged woman in search of revenge strongly suggests in her later qualities what appears to have been the actual Anne Cooke.

Chivers at his best is never too far from the ridiculous. At times in *Conrad and Eudora* he is absurd—in some of the stilted dialogue, the word inventions, the lapses in grammar, the repetitions of lines he deemed especially good, and the grandiloquent metaphor of some of his

soliloquies. Quasi-Shakespearean diction is everywhere, particularly reminiscent of *King Lear, Macbeth,* and *Romeo and Juliet.* Byronic phrase and figure are also frequent, not too happily rendered. Yet one should keep in mind that Chivers seems to have been the first to appreciate the literary potentialities of the Beauchamp-Sharp affair, and that he dramatized its details more effectively than did his successors. The year after *Conrad and Eudora* was published, Poe tried his hand with the same material in his never-completed *Politian,* greatly superior in poetry to Chivers' work, but hardly as good theater. Charlotte Barnes' *Octavia Bragaldi* in 1837 was an overly complicated yet fairly actable melodrama on the same subject, and between 1858 and 1865 there were other plays. The novels of Charles Fenno Hoffman in 1840, of Simms in 1842 and 1856, and of Warren in 1950 are the best-known works of fiction on the theme. There is a formidable list of poems, ballads, and stories concerned with the same ill-starred lovers and their oppressor-victim.

But Chivers was by no means through with this plot when he published *Conrad and Eudora* in 1834. Perhaps because of the death of his beloved mother soon after its publication, he did not touch the play for some time; but we know that he was again at work on it by 1837-1838. In March 1838 he wrote to the Philadelphia actor-manager Conner (husband of Charlotte Barnes), asking for professional criticism of the new play *Leoni.* The manuscript version we now have seems to have been written between early 1838 and April 5, 1839. Apparently Conner did not see the text, for in a later letter of May 28, 1851, Chivers again recommended the play to him and sent him a copy of the first act from the *Georgia Citizen.*

The title-page of the Harvard manuscript of *Leoni* bears the date 1838 changed to 1839, good indications of the time of composition of this form of the play. The markings through or blottings out of the whole or parts of speeches would indicate that we have here a working copy, perhaps representing two stages of the play's development, as suggested above.

For, despite the fact that Chivers seemed always to have thought of *Conrad and Eudora* and *Leoni* as one play, a new play, and a new play in two or three versions, the latter certainly is in its surviving copies. Chivers had seen much of the theater in Northern cities since his earlier excursion into playwriting, and he had matured somewhat as a poet. He seems to have been aware of many of the "imperfections" of *Conrad and Eudora.* He cut, transposed, rephrased, reversified. The scene was shifted from Kentucky to Venice; the principal characters all have new names, though the new suggest the old. The seduction itself is omitted; the action begins *in medias res,* with Leoni's desertion by her seducer, Count Alvar. To bring the length to nineteenth-century five-act normal, Chivers added a new sub-plot, closely integrated with the main thread of action. The old minor characters—Eudora's mother, for example—are eliminated to make room for the sub-plot group. The new plot element necessitates a slight alteration in the catastrophe. Good lyrical lines of certain songs and soliloquies are ruthlessly deleted, some

Edgar Allan Poe, friend of Chivers.

of them better in image and rhythm than what the author substituted. But the result was a much better play: *Leoni, the Orphan of Venice,* a full-length blank verse tragedy, with a title derived from two plays by Otway.

Later, in 1851, perhaps despairing of publication or production, Chivers had *Leoni* printed in five issues of the *Georgia Citizen* of May and June, the newspaper in which so much of his prose and poetry first appeared. As we have seen, this 1851 version is prefaced by a letter dated 1834 which suggests that this is the play Chivers wrote before that earlier date. Actually it is not even one form of the 1838-1839 play of the Harvard manuscript, but a further condensed and somewhat revised version of that manuscript. The two *Leoni*'s must be considered together, for they share the same characters, scenes, and action.

In *Leoni* the title character is at last worthy of her original. None of the inconsistency of Eudora is here. Leoni pursues her vengeance relentlessly from beginning to end. She calls upon a former suitor to do the deed, making the bargain of marriage (though love does develop—or was already smoldering). All the major characters are less stereotyped. The villainous Count Alvar is genuinely in love with his wife Theresa. Don Carlos, center of the sub-plot, is vengeful, affectionate, proud, but self-recriminating. Don Pedro is unscrupulous but his love for Elvira, sister of Don Carlos, dominates his actions. Alvino (Beauchamp) is the simplest and weakest, but even he has his complexities.

Here the blank verse is less rhetorical, less madly metaphoric. It occasionally verges on the absurd, but the author through the three stages of *Leoni* (uncut manuscript, cut manuscript, and *Georgia Citizen*) is consciously reducing length and exaggerated imagery. The language becomes gradually simpler.

In a letter of November 1, 1845, Chivers wrote that "In 1834 I wrote a Play in Five Acts, which received the commendations of the greatest men in the world, yet it has never been published up to this hour . . . [It] is now in the possession of M*r* Poe, one of the greatest men that ever lived." Though the inaccuracy of the statement as to publication is obvious, the information that Poe had in his possession about 1845 a version of *Leoni* (and there is no reason to doubt Chivers' statement) is most interesting. It may be that the obliterations and other excisions on the Harvard manuscript are his or were suggested by him, or it may be that the condensed 1851 *Georgia Citizen* printed version is the result of his critical comment. The conjecture is pleasant to entertain, at all events. And certainly Poe and Chivers in 1845 were for some time in almost daily communication.

Though the *Georgia Citizen* printed version of *Leoni* is superior to the manuscript version primarily because of the condensation and elimination of large sections of the latter, the former is most clearly understood after reading the latter. In other words, the revisions were hasty. For example, marked through in the manuscript is a statement that the time of the action is compressed into two days and nights, and the following day until evening. This tight or unified time-scheme, though probably not precisely that intended in the *Georgia Citizen* play, does help to explain the positive statements of the characters in both versions that an assassination has to take place "tonight," or that something is to happen tomorrow, or did happen yesterday or today, events which in truth took place weeks or months apart. Again, Elvira's part, and her motives, in enticing Don Pedro to his death are not entirely clear in either version, but the longer speeches of the manuscript explain several things about the Don Carlos-Elvira-Don Pedro relationship which in the printed *Leoni* remain puzzling (e.g., III, ii, of the manuscript).

Though the action proceeds through the two *Leoni*'s in the same order, the texts differ in phrase and even in whole speeches quite considerably. Strikingly different speeches, for example, by different characters, introduce I, i. In the Harvard manuscript, Count Alvar begins with

> Now shall the mild Ænigma, told in tears,
> Be solved.

In the same place in the *Georgia Citizen,* Leoni is first speaking, clearly in the revenge-tragedy tradition, and employs a line Chivers uses elsewhere in the other versions:

> Revenge in woman hath no limitations.

Cutting, of course, produced many or most of the changes between the two later versions. In Act II, scenes i and ii of the manuscript are telescoped into scene i of the *Georgia Citizen*. In a few instances speeches are transferred from one character to another. There are sections, too, of rephrased dialogue.

In conclusion, it may be pertinent to point out that the most successful creations in verse and prose from the Kentucky Tragedy have all been done by Southerners—Chivers of Georgia, Simms of South Carolina, Poe of Virginia, and Warren of Kentucky. The last of these, Warren, has employed the material to present his frequently recurring motif of the struggle of order against violence. Simms and Chivers likewise were concerned with this problem, though in terms of an earlier culture. They seemed more concerned with *honor* and violence, but honor too may be a form of order, a sense of order. Chivers in the matter of his three plays presents Southern as well as sentimental concepts of honor and the means of its redemption and preservation. In his style he affords the reader generous specimens of his unusual poetic genius—his strange imagery—and of his abilities as self-critic.

John Olin Eidson (essay date 1964)

SOURCE: "The Letters of Thomas Holley Chivers," in *The Georgia Review,* Vol. XVIII, No. 2, Summer, 1964, pp. 143-49.

[*In the essay that follows, Eidson assesses Chivers's correspondence and what personal details it reveals.*]

In many ways the personal letters of Thomas Holley Chivers tell us more about him than a biography. And what they reveal is a strange and curious phenomenon. In his arrogant pride, his tremendous egotism, his complete lack of humor, all mixed in with a broad knowledge and detailed scholarship on the strangest of subjects, Chivers is a literary curiosity which one would go far to match. Practically every letter is revealing. Few are routine, because to Chivers nothing was. He could blow up the simplest detail into the grand and dramatic. In his quarrels—over the price of potatoes, the delivery of a book, the pronunciation of a word—, his posing, his sermonizing—"My dear Poe! you must not practice lip service with me. . . . Never touch another drop of liquor. . . . Nothing in a corrupt age will sell but *corruption*"—, he often shows himself at his worst, but he is never dull. He is often unbelievable, but he is also unforgettable.

Chivers' correspondents form a heterogeneous group: poets, actors, editors and publishers, literary critics ("biped Asses," "two-legged serpents," "my sap-headed enemies"), lawyers, theologians, business men. Emerson says that great men in their writing introduce us to their subjects, little men to themselves. The letters of Chivers place him in the second category. They tell us much more about him than anything else. He corresponded with Poe, Simms, Kennedy, Jenny Lind, Edwin Forrest, George K. Dickinson, Alexander H. Stephens, but when the subject strays to them, he shortly brings it back. When Poe tells of his plans for the *Penn Magazine,* Chivers ignores them and

replies with detailed accounts of his own troubles, and to Dickinson's tales of woe about problems in the theater, Chivers replies with descriptions of his own plays and his vain efforts to get them on the stage.

He wrote numbers of letters for the sole purpose of promoting his own work and trying to get it published. Dozens of letters were written to publishers and friends of publishers in his desperate attempt to get his biography of Poe published. In the many letters which he wrote charging that Poe plagiarized him, he praised his own work so highly and had such an exaggerated opinion of his own genius that he greatly weakened his case.

To Chivers, his correspondence was a forum—an arena for debate. It was deadly serious. He tolerated no levity. His letter was often the presentation of his side of a debate, and he demanded a reply. To one of Chivers' long arguments about the interpretation of a passage in Proverbs, the Biblical scholar George Bush replied, "I cannot now possibly go into [it], as it would take a great deal of time & after all would be left just as uncertain as ever. . . . Your kindness will excuse me." He knew what Chivers expected and was trying to beg off, but Chivers' "kindness" did not excuse. Likewise, Poe's remonstrance "What is the use of disputing an obvious point?" did not let him out. "I have given you thunder in this letter," Chivers wrote, "and I now wish you to answer it." Chivers often closed his letters with statements that he expected an immediate reply. He once wrote to Poe that he was coming to New York and that if Poe did not answer his letter before that time, "you may expect to be passed in the street without ever being recognized by me. Remember! I give you warning."

Chivers yearned for an audience, and the letter gave him an opportunity. While he lived on his plantation near Washington, Georgia, letters were for months at a time practically his only contact with the outside world. Most of his literary acquaintances he knew entirely through correspondence. The Reverend John Gierlow, whom Chivers named as his literary executor and with whom he corresponded constantly. he never saw in person, though Gierlow lived in Macon, less than a hundred miles away.

When Chivers begins a letter with "You ask me why I hate the world" or "My belief in the fall of man is Pelagian," a long, solemn, and philosophical disquisition is underway. It is erudite, filled with classical and Biblical allusions, and carefully worked out to the last detail. Each point is elaborately supported, and on each one, first to last, he stood ready to defend it to the last gasp. Often a letter would begin with a defense of a minor point with which someone had disagreed—or a violent attack on the pest, fool, or ass who had had the temerity. One correspondent protested, "Calling an opponent a 'dunderhead' . . . is no argument. . . . Be calm, and give proof of your positions." But calmness was not in Chivers' make-up.

Often a reviewer whose review of a Chivers book was ninety percent favorable would get a vitriolic letter about the remainder. Publishers would refuse to give him the names of reviewers and proof-readers, and he would go to lengths to find them out. A single typographical error could become a major matter. The "mutilations" of one Boston proof-reader made Chivers "weep for this Copper Age of Typography": "the proof-reader ought to be taken to Frog-Pond and baptized into a New Era." Either a disagreement in an argument or an error in a poem, he took "with the same feelings that you would resent an insult offered to one of your children."

In view of Chivers' careful scholarship and his demand for correctness in others, it is surprising to find in his letters numerous examples of bad grammar, poor punctuation, and misspellings. Proper names he made little attempt to get right: Emmerson, Tenneyson, Lowel. The Georgia country in which he lived—Wilkes—was misspelled Wilks, and his plantation was sometimes Oaky Grove and sometimes Oakey Grove.

These were matters beneath his attention. He was following "mighty dreams" which carried him far above such considerations—and even "above the use" of money. But at the same time that he is adjuring his correspondents to connect none of his actions "with any worldly matter," he exhibits a queer mixture of the spiritual and the mundane. While staving off requests for money—from Poe, Mrs. Clemm, or Dickinson—with high-flown protestations of its worldliness, he haggles endlessly over the price of bacon or lard, or the postage on a letter.

He often quoted to his friends the Platonic distinction between Venus Urania (intellectual beauty) and Venus Pandemos (sexual attachment) with the strongest condemnation of the latter. Dickinson, who had a girl friend whom Chivers learned about, objected to a "horrible" letter "with your Venus this & Venus to'ther." But Chivers' letters give ample evidence that he himself valued both Venuses very highly. His most eloquent flights often drop sharply to the materialistic. He "dreams mighty dreams" in his wife's presence "sometimes." He assures Poe that he holds him in the highest esteem, that Poe's motives and conceptions are the loftiest, and that he would like to unite with him "provided it would be to my interest to do so." This trait, along with his utter lack of a sense of humor, might help to explain his mixing the unpoetic with the poetic in so many of his poems.

Chivers never for a moment doubted his own genius. There was not to be the least questioning of that. He understood and could create the Divinely Beautiful. In all seriousness, he offered to Poe for the *Broadway Journal* an article which would give a "death blow to materialism" for all time; and to George Rex Graham for *Graham's Magazine* he offered poems which would do "what never has been done before, namely, make a perfect unition, or marriage of Art with Passion" and articles which would "unfold—(what never has been done—) the true nature of the Poetic Art." Neither editor thought the proffered material worthy of publishing. To Simms he wrote that he had found the one clear insight into Art. It was a "most wonderful thing" that no one else had "the most distant dreams of what constitutes the Art of Poetry." But he had.

And in quite a different field, he condescendingly assured Alexander H. Stephens, then a member of the Georgia legislature, "I could be of more intrinsick advantage to you than any other living being." Chivers never lacked self-confidence.

His letters give numerous examples of his dramatizing himself. He wrote the actor E. S. Connor, "Dramatic Literature is my chief delight," and his love of the dramatic situation—centered around himself—shows again and again in the letters. A letter from "a Friend" requesting a specimen of his early writing brought a thirteen-page effusion in which, page after page, he leads his friend along "the long avenue of Cypress Months which stand, Nunlike, weeping along the dark Vistas of the mournful years which lead me back into the beautiful Edens of the Past."

This could become monotonous, and it did. It sometimes became ridiculous, and showed clearer than ever Chivers' utter lack of self-criticism. Just as he could not be reasoned with, he could not be mildly advised. When Poe thought Chivers had forgotten something and asked him what he could have been thinking about, Chivers immediately came back with "What can *you* be thinking about to ask me what *I* could have been thinking about. . . ." There was no getting through.

Chivers was the martyr, as he felt a poet should be, and he made the most of his personal tragedies, his vain efforts to win recognition, and all the injustices done him— both real and imagined. He became obsessed with the idea of defeat, frustration, and death. Death came to mean release, perfect bliss, as it did in his poems. He often uses it in that connotation in his letters. Alexander H. Stephens must have received a shock when Chivers ended a long and friendly letter to him with "I now conclude, wishing you immediate death."

Often called a Southern Transcendentalist, Chivers deserved the title. Differing strongly with Poe, he thought highly of Emerson and *The Dial,* and lectured on the subject, getting him to the point of writing in one letter, "You mistake me in supposing I dislike the transcendentalists—it is only the pretenders and sophists among them." Chivers called some of his letters "meanderings of metaphysic thought." Many of his ideas and phrases are Swedenborgian. He read avidly Swedenborg's mystical discussions of the connection between God and Man, wrote long letters to the spiritualist Samuel Byron Brittan, and offered to join with Brittan in publishing a spiritualist journal. In a letter to Poe he defined transcendentalism:

> It is taking the swan of thought, which has floated on the crystalline water of the *familiar* in this world, and giving it wings, whereby it may ascend into the regions of the unfamiliar, and there, in that divine attitude, become the recipient of that lore which is the harmony of the Angels. All our knowledge comes from the relations which subsist between us and the external world. And what is Revelation, but Transcendentalism?

He thought of language as the manifestation of these relations to the external world, but he was determined in his use of language to "soar up from the palpable and the material, to the impalpable, spiritual, and immaterial." This led him to some of the most amazing examples of "fine writing" to be found anywhere in American literary correspondence. He praised Edwin Forrest for his "able out-breathings of the genius of the immortal Bard of Avon," and wrote Jenny Lind that she had "with the genius of an Angel, exalted the souls of [her] Audience by reechoing the words of Memory wedded to the songs of Apollo which were better than the Muses themselves." Chivers spoke of his "Adamic life" in Boston, "afar off in this Land of Banishment" as not at all "like those Idylic Days which I spent in the morning side of my life, when I played on the borders of the clear crystal streams which meandered the Meadowy Seas of the Lost Edens of my youth." To let a correspondent know that he was writing many poems, he wrote, "The embers of enthusiasm are still glowing with a quenchless heat in the center of my heart." And one of the best examples is the letter that he wrote to John Sullivan Dwight to let Dwight know that he liked the first issues of *Dwight's Journal of Music* and thought the magazine had a good future:

> Methinks that I can now see the Angels with their ploughs of Pearl breaking up the fallow lands of the Oriental Fields of Heaven into Auroral furrows. From the Pisgah-top of the Present I look abroad upon the far-reaching Fields of the Future, and behold that Promised land of the Beautiful, through whose verdant Vallies the rivers of milk and honey flow.

Some of the most flowery passages in the letters, Chivers used again almost word for word in poems or prefaces. The paragraph quoted above appeared again in the Preface to *Atlanta*.

Chivers was as wild and unrestrained in his superlatives as in his similes and metaphors. Nothing was ordinary and everyday. Poe and a number of others were the noblest of all his friends, and there was no man living "whose good opinion he valued more" than Simms's. Numbers of his plays and poems were the greatest ever written. The *New York Herald,* which did not agree with this evaluation, had "done more evil than all the papers on earth put together." There was "a more elaborate perfection in the Poems of Tennyson than in any Poet that ever lived." But, in another breath, "America has produced the best Lyrical Poetry of any land under the sun."

Simms called Chivers a "wild Mazeppa" of literature, and Chivers' letters bear this out. To E. C. Stedman he was "a sort of Poe-run-mad." The letters to and from Poe, covering an eight-year period, with Chivers writing about three letters to Poe's one, are the most valuable part of the Chivers correspondence. They do not, however, deal with the matter of plagiarism. These charges and counter-charges came after Poe's death, with Chivers writing to Augustine Duganne, "Poe stole all his 'Raven' from me," and to Simms, "I am the Southern man who taught Mr. Poe all these things." Then followed the bitterest of letters in which Chivers made extravagant claims and charges that greatly hurt his own reputation.

Many of the Poe-Chivers letters are taken up with Poe's desperate appeals for money and Chivers' staving them off. Poe appealed again and again but apparently never received over five dollars. By the time Chivers got around to his magnanimous offer "If you will come to the South to live, I will take care of you as long as you live," Poe had already stopped taking Chivers' offers seriously, and did not even reply. It is unfortunate that Chivers' stinginess drew a barrier between the two, who had so much in common. Poe was undoubtedly sincere when he wrote Chivers that with no other man had he ever felt so strongly "that intimate *sympathy* (of intellect as well as soul) which is the sole basis of friendship." "There is nothing," wrote Poe, "which gives me more sincere pleasure than the receipt of your letters."

The "Lost Poet" of Georgia is now well on the way to being found. A good biography and a sound critical study have been done, and now a four-volume edition of *The Complete Works of Thomas Holley Chivers* is in preparation and will make all of his writings easily available.

Chivers' personal letters will not do much to enhance his fame. They make it harder to separate the poet of real stature from the strange and forbidding personality. They form a queer collection, fitting no pattern that one can imagine. But one might say of them what Chivers' biographer says of Chivers: You may not like them, but you cannot ignore them. They throw interesting and important light upon one of literature's strangest phenomena.

Edward Dahlberg (essay date 1964)

SOURCE: "Chivers and Poe," in *Alms for Oblivion,* University of Minnesota Press, 1964, pp. 73-6.

[*An essayist, poet, philosopher, and literary critic, Dahlberg's eccentric writing style caused him to be recognized as a phenomenon of sorts in American letters during his lifetime. In the following essay, Dahlberg comments on Chivers's biography of Poe and on the relationship between the two poets.*]

The Small Life of Poe by Dr. Thomas Holley Chivers was perhaps finished in 1857, a year before Chivers' death, and has been mummified in the Huntington Library until recently. As an ode in prose to Poe, it is false, orphic sublimity, but the homage is tender and just and comes from a quick, interior nature alien to gross matter. Despite the biographies of Poe, and his current revivification, the author of "The Raven" still stands as a great, ruined obelisk in American literature. His genius is a monumental waste; his marvelous tales, gothic cabala, are transhuman and inscrutable.

Chivers has left us some swollen dithyrambs on Poe's person. "The Messiah of melody," as Chivers describes his hero, had a pensive, Grecian bend when he walked, and a long, slender neck which made him appear taller when seated. Poe had feminine hands and considerable knowledge in the "aesthetics of dress." He carried a cane, and I imagine he would have worn the vests of Bacchus or Heinrich Heine, or been as modish as Baudelaire, if he had possessed the money. Chivers' remark that money would have ruined Poe shows abundant wisdom, for though many writers have been harmed by penury, more have suffered damage from lucre.

Poe gave readings to ladies' societies dedicated to gabbling. He had a chaste voice, but he lacked the humbug actor's inflections needed for success in such groups. He was very vain, as all good writers are (the meek ones are furtive, belonging to another tribe). He had told Chivers that every article in the last number of the *Broadway Journal* was remarkable and had been written by himself, with the exception of one poem which Chivers claimed was also by Poe. Poe had a testy temperament, an occupational trait of the writer, but he also had a good digestion, which Chivers asserts is not a scholarly sign.

Emily Dickinson had no one to turn to except that drab ecclesiastic of letters, Thomas Wentworth Higginson, who was astonished at the reception the posthumous publication of her verse received. Poe, no less unfortunate than Miss Dickinson, had as his literary executor the Reverend Rufus Griswold. Griswold wrote a memoir about Poe which in pure weight of spite took care of the same amount of genius Griswold lacked. This stygian piece of literary Calvinism endured, and for a hundred years what has concerned the attention of exsanguine critics was Poe's drunkenness. There was also small pardon in the ashy hearts of the critics for the poet's marriage to Virginia Clemm, his cousin, when she was thirteen.

Along with Rufus Griswold and the other predatory prudes on lower Broadway who could not abide Poe's rancor or his astonishing abilities was Margaret Fuller. A rude, bellicose crone of the arts, Miss Fuller got up a delegation which demanded that Mrs. Osgood relinquish Poe's friendship!

There were other recondite scandals in Poe's life. He had had a fugitive liaison with one of the lady poets of the time. Eros is cold and altogether reposeful in the "Tales," though Poe was a toady to any Ophelia. He could pen a frightening invective against almost any man who malpracticed verse, but he was the serpent and dove with the lady poetasters. Poe found in many of these dear sibyls, whose sighs were more beatific than their poems, the most valorous defenders of his character and afflatus. There were Sarah Helen Whitman, Mrs. Osgood, and Emilie Weltby who had pulsed to Poe's genius and manners and august face. Maria Clemm, the mother of his bride, loved her two occult children, and Mrs. R. S. Nichols, another defender, wrote the monody, "let him rest by lost 'Lenore.'"

"Israfel" was a greater original than Byron, Shelley, or Keats. Poe's verse is very inferior to Keats's "Hyperion" or to the "Endymion," but the form of Poe's prose poems is aboriginal. He was an abstruse psalmist, a saturnine Saul who had stature of soul. "Ligeia," "Eleonora," "Berenice," "The Fall of the House of Usher," are Arabic music of the soul fit for an Antony or the seraglio in Mahomet's Paradise, but of what profit to human wisdom or to the spirit in its transient, purblind earthly pilgrimage? Chivers said of Poe that he "always wrote as though all Poetry consisted more in the Poetry of the language than in the passions of the heart to be expressed through that language."

Without Poe's "Tales," *Les Fleurs du Mal* could not have been born in Baudelaire's mind. Each morning before starting to write, Baudelaire prayed to the Virgin Mary, to his mother, and to Edgar Poe. That poems should be cold, passionless objectivism is the creed of the imagists, who, in part, are the heirs of Poe. The "Tales" are flowers in hell, and they have the odor of Persephone. It is with the most obdurate reluctance that I suggest that they are the fallen angelic parent of today's cankered mystery story. Poe's belief that a poem ought to be governed by the ratiocinative intellect rather than by the controlled tumult of feeling has been taken up by today's Brahmins of aesthetics. Poe so hated the forerunners of these Brahmins, the mandarins of Beacon Hill of the nineteenth century, that he always said he was born in Baltimore, though his birthplace was actually in Boston.

There were some arguments between Poe and Chivers. Poe admired some of Lowell's verse; Chivers thought Poe had overpraised Lowell. Poe regarded Tennyson as a great bard; Chivers' regarded him as "a phlegmatic fat baby." Sharing Chivers' feeling, James Joyce called the poet "Alfred Lawn Tennyson."

Dr. Chivers was a marvelous friend, for he was a poet himself. (Cézanne once said that it takes one writer to catch another.) Chivers did not have to wait a century to be an enthusiast of a contemporary genius. He wrote: "I allude . . . to those who dispraised him in his lifetime, on account of envy of his genius, as well as to those still more despicable souls who pretend to defend him on the still basic principle of wishing the world to believe that they are . . . the faithful Apostles of his greatness." Any writer reading this prayer cannot help but say in his own conceited heart, "I wish that Dr. Thomas Holley Chivers had known me!"

Charles Lombard (essay date 1979)

SOURCE: An introduction to *The Path of Sorrow* by Thomas Holley Chivers, Scholars' Facsimiles & Reprints, 1979, pp. v-xxxi.

[*In the following essay, Lombard provides a detailed study of several of Chivers's major works.*]

THE PATH OF SORROW

When only nineteen Thomas Holley Chivers in 1827 married his sixteen-year-old cousin, Frances Elizabeth

Chivers. Within a year she left him because of alleged cruelty. He was never allowed to see his daughter, born in 1828 after the separation. The chief culprit in the destruction of his marriage was, according to Chivers, Franky Albert, a relative who was a malicious gossip. Since litigation failed to win him a divorce, Chivers finally took advantage of a Georgia law on desertion of one's marital partner. Having established Frances' absence for over five years, he was free to find another wife. In 1837 Chivers married Harriet Hunt of Springfield, Massachusetts, and enjoyed twenty years of happiness with her.

The Path of Sorrow, or, the Lament of Youth: A Poem, was published at Chivers' expense by the *Weekly Review* of Franklin, Tennessee, late in 1832. Just a few volumes were printed and only several known original copies exist today. The poems were highly personal in nature and Chivers may have wished to confide his lyrical outpourings and anguish over a broken home only to trusted friends and relatives. Members of the immediate family might have destroyed copies to avoid further gossip and scandal and close friends probably did not let strangers read it out of respect for Chivers' feelings. There is also reason to believe that once he had released his pentup emotions by publishing the poems, he felt indisposed to give them wide circulation. Chivers made no effort to retain the manuscripts and any critical comments on *The Path of Sorrow,* contrary to his usual custom of carefully recording and preserving all manuscripts in orderly fashion together with pertinent magazine articles. Only later, by chance, did he come across the original manuscripts of his published volume of poetry. In all probability he wished to forget the period of despondency and self-imposed exile spent away from Georgia and in the wilderness beyond St. Louis and Cincinnati.

The preface is dedicated to John Rhay, Esq., and dated November 15, 1832. He mentions to Rhay that many of the poems were written in 1828-29 during his period as a student at Transylvania University. Rhay was apparently a fellow student and familiar with Chivers' interest in poetry. Some of the verses in the volume may have been known already to Rhay from their college days.

The first poem, **"The Dream,"** is important in content, if of limited literary value. Chivers broaches a subject which was to become of increasing interest to him, the nature of sleep, the subconscious, and visions. From metaphysical speculations Chivers goes on to deal with his rupture with Frances. The poet recalls the happy days that first marked his marriage, the bliss of two teenagers fully aware of the sincerity and intensity of their love. Chivers' personal involvement with the events recorded in **"The Dream"** can be sensed in his recounting of the courtship, wedding, and the joyful days as man and wife, abruptly disrupted by an obnoxious busy-body who permanently destroys their idyl. Angrily Chivers tells the story from the standpoint of a heartbroken young husband.

Not satisfied by the mention of one detail in his domestic misfortune, the intervention of an unpleasant relative, Chivers proceeds to reproach his faithless wife for refus-ing to allow him to see his own child, born after their separation. Recalling her heartless attitude, Chivers suddenly excoriates a cruel wife and looks elsewhere for love and companionship. Another woman enters the narrative at this point and momentarily promises to make him forget his misfortune, but happiness, he discovers, does not succeed sorrow so quickly. Legal obstacles prevent a swift marriage with his second love.

Patterned closely after Byron's poem of the same name, **"The Dream"** is an example of the Byronic fad in American Romanticism. Chivers empathized with Byron, who also lost his wife and child through malignant gossip. In defending Chivers against plagiarism, it should be noted that he was not the only imitator of Byron at that time in America. A distinction should also be made between Chivers' use of the general outline of Byron's poem and those elements that for all their faults are strikingly Chiversian.

One aspect of **"The Dream"** has yet to be clarified. In a poem where most of the autobiographic details correspond closely to known events in Chivers' life there is still one allusion that gives rise to speculation. Who was the young lady, mentioned at the end of the poem, he was prevented by law from marrying? The incidents in Chivers' life from 1829-32 are not too closely documented. An impulsive person of Chivers' disposition could easily have sought solace elsewhere. Mention of another woman in a poem so patently autobiographic would be one way to get the news indirectly to his wife, in whose defense something should be said. Her side of the story has never been heard, although court records do indicate she filed a suit for alimony on the grounds of extreme cruelty.

Earlier in life Chivers experienced even greater tragedy in the loss of a favorite sister, referred to as "Adaline" in his poems. Relating his father's reaction to her demise in **"On the Death of Adaline,"** Chivers tells how an angel takes charge of Adaline's soul. Momentary doubts about the existence of a benevolent God disappear when in a vision Adaline is heard conversing with an angel as the poet is elevated to the World of Spirits.

The appearance of the angel in the vision may not seem at first glance of any significance until Chivers' subsequent conversion to Swedenborgianism is recalled. The mention of angels then takes on a new dimension. Swedenborg stressed the existence of angels who attended humans and were present at all phases of man's life and at death. Both Adaline's conversation with the angel and Chivers' vision of "sublunary things" have a distinctly Swedenborgian flavor. The Swedish mystic often recorded how his soul left the body to wander about in the World of Spirits and speak with angels. If Chivers at this stage was not fully converted to the theology and revelations of Swedenborg, he was at the very least favorably disposed to accept such views at a later date by reason of his early belief in supernatural experience and visions.

"On the Death of Adaline" also contains a reference to one of Chivers' more mundane interests, the folk music of his native region. When the poet summons the heavens and hills to celebrate the ascension of his sister's innocent soul into heaven, he calls for a melody to be played on instruments brought over to the southern colonies from England. The psaltry and dulcimer were among the early folk instruments used in the American colonies when English immigrants played and sang the songs of their native land.

"What is Life?" brings to mind the lugubrious lines of Young's *Night Thoughts,* a work that furnished many themes of lamentation and melancholy which were destined to become commonplace among Romantic writers in America and France. One stanza, despite the clichès, supplies the motif of *The Path of Sorrow:*

> Our life is that asperity which rends
> The heart, in sorrow's path—a piercing thorn!
> 'Tis that pernicity of doubt, which ends
> In immortality at that great morn—
> The resurrection far beyond the skies;
> And blessings of the soul which never dies!

Pernicity, one of a list of terms coined by Chivers and used in *The Path of Sorrow,* lends to the stanza a tone that sets it apart from the usual sentimental verse of the period. If there is sadness in the world, muses Chivers, there are as well mysteries, concealed by the outward appearance of things, whose presence the poet senses, nonetheless, and whose meaning he seeks to fathom.

From the death of loved ones Chivers returns to the main theme of *The Path of Sorrow,* the loss through separation and incompatibility of his first wife and child. The trauma of that agonizing moment is recalled in **"The Minstrel's Valedictory."** Relatives and associates apparently advised him reconciliation was out of the question and separation the only solution. Chivers discloses unknowingly an argument for his estranged wife's side of the story. Artlessly and fatuously he announces in all seriousness the nature of his relationship to his mother. If anything he presents a picture of himself as a rather spoiled adolescent.

Putting aside bitter memories, Chivers bids farewell to his native soil and family in a homespun fashion that has its own quaint dignity. He yearns to break forth in song but finds himself too overburdened with grief and unequal to the task. The verses are unquestionably original, bearing, as they do, the imprint of his florid rhetoric and far-fetched imagery:

> Farewell! ye groves and hillocks, dales and
>   brooks,
> And evergreens which stood before my view—
> Which caught, in morn of life, my youthful
>   looks—
> I bid you all farewell! a long adieu!

Watts has indicated Chivers' borrowings from *Childe Harold,* although the Byronic tenor and pose of **"The Minstrel's Valedictory"** would seem at best superficial. In the lines cited above Chivers is addressing himself to

the crucial and personal decision he has to make in leaving family and homestead to forget his grief in the wilderness. The folkloric aspect of Chivers' work manifests itself here in the direct and unsophisticated farewell to familiar scenes. In speaking of the resumption of his "minstrelsy" and his "song" Chivers sounds more like a Georgian balladeer composing for the popular market and not a conventional poet addressing himself to a cultivated society. What some may judge a defect is more likely one of the few vigorous and redeeming features of *The Path of Sorrow*.

Throughout most of the poems Chivers manages to inject a personal note, even though the framework of a particular poem and the lines themselves may be ostensibly modeled on Byron, Young, or some other poet. A case in point is **"The Prophet's Dream,"** purportedly an Old Testament writer's vision of Christ's coming. Actually it is an excuse for Chivers to define his role as poet:

> Eternal Spirit! lend thy spark, to raise my
> Thought above the mountain of my heart! breath
> On the flambeau of my youthful soul—
> Ask in love! Do thou inspire my song! . . .

It was difficult for Chivers to be the sedate and genteel writer. He was too much the independent maverick who would coin unusual words if he found the old ones unsuitable. Two Chiversian terms, *terrene* and *oblectations,* are used in the following passage:

> He shall protect him with his outstretched hands;
> And lead him, as a faithful steward, far
> Beyond the sycophants of terrene strife,—
> While scintillations from his mighty star,
> Shall pilot him to the eternal life,
> Where oblectations shine, devoid of grief.

The unevenness of Chivers' style notwithstanding, he was at an early date bringing rhythm and melody to many lines. A reading of the dry and stilted poetasters of the times is convincing proof of his originality. Even in a stanza replete with platitudes there is conveyed to the reader a sense of Chivers' strength and conviction.

Not always involved with themes drawn from personal experiences and suffering, Chivers treated historical subjects. **"The Siege of Vienna"** retells the rescue of the city from the Turkish army by Sobieski's legions. In nineteenth century America there was considerable empathy with the nationalist movement in Poland. Americans sympathized with the subjugated Poles and recalled the contributions of Kosciusko and Pulaski. Polish writers and leaders who emigrated to America helped to keep the public here aware of Poland's plight. Since Byron too dealt with Sobieski's heroism, Chivers in predictable fashion profited by the Englishman's work.

"The Lament of Youth" is a fairly long poem, consisting of two cantos and covering about twenty-five pages of *The Path of Sorrow;* its length emphasizes the extent to which personal problems motivated Chivers in composing the major part of the work. His estranged wife, Frances, called Angeline in **"The Lament of Youth,"** is addressed with rather mixed feelings as Chivers alternately relives their happy days together and reproaches her for infidelity. Eventually the poet overcame the sad memories of his first marriage, but the depth of passion displayed in *The Path of Sorrow* indicates a state of mind that was transmitted to later poems.

After the painful soul-searching in **"The Lament of Youth"** Chivers appears exhausted in **"The Retrospect"** and prematurely aged:

> I am now, not what I have been in youth!
> The light which first awoke me, glimmers now,
> To shine no more!—the starlight which I made
> My banquet, and the sunbeam which my soul
> Did seek as nutriment has faded! . . .

One poem in *The Path of Sorrow* prefigures perhaps more than any other the future course of Chivers' poetry. **"Let My Name Survive"** gives the impression that the poet was groping for the symbolism and cadence achieved in subsequent poems. There is present the Chiversian touch, that wistful and charming manner that characterized the best of his later poetry.:

> In the wilderness there is a tree—
> In the bower there springs up a vine—
> Any my soul in its mystical visions can see,
> When my heart shall embrace them as mine.

"An Elegy," dedicated to Thomas Lacey, one of the poet's teachers at Transylvania University, reveals some of the sensuous imagery Chivers would later employ rather effectively;

> Nature summons my body to death!
> My soul bursts the bonds of regret;
> And inspires this undying breath,
> With the bliss I can never forget.
> Let the wings of heaven bear the sound,
> Let the whirlwinds of glory be driven—
> Let the hearse of mortality's sound,
> Conduct such a rapture to heaven!

The volume concludes with **"To My Mother,"** where Chivers gives vent to his nostalgia and longing for the relatively uncomplicated and peaceful years of childhood. Like many Romantics, Chivers was given to regression when adulthood confronted him with oppressing problems. The internal evidence in the poem would seem to point to a rather long period of absence from home during the poet's voluntary exile, inasmuch as he complains of the length of separation.

Watts and Damon find *The Path of Sorrow* important as a starting point in a study of Chivers' development. He had not yet formulated the concept of a poetry whose esthetic merit was primarily in its sound value. Some tendency in that direction can be seen in the willingness to coin *domil, oblectation, pernicity,* and other terms in passages that were otherwise specimens of conformity to commonplace Romantic standards. Chivers was also tinkering with versification and meter and invented a new stanza with an *ababcdcdd* rhyme scheme. If unsuccessful in his attempts, he did try out spenserians and heroic quatrains. Finding blank verse rather dull, he used a ten-syllable line and allowed the accent to fall where it normally would. Often this resulted in monotonous lines, but on occasion Chivers achieved novel effects.

The Path of Sorrow is of importance as a documentation of his initial attempt at writing poetry. The emotions expressed by Chivers were in the main heartfelt and genuine. In spite of its flaws the volume expresses Chivers' fondness for Georgia and its folk songs and is a simple declaration of his faith in Christ. Signs of the value placed on his poetic calling are discernible in the sacerdotal role he assumes. Also present in *The Path of Sorrow* are definite indications of Chivers' fascination with visions and dreams concerning death and the afterlife. Not to be disregarded as the youthful blunders of an untutored poet, *The Path of Sorrow,* by reason of its autobiographic data and evidence of Chivers' evolving interests, is a necessary point of departure in any serious study of the poet.

EONCHS OF RUBY

In 1851 Thomas Holley Chivers paid Spalding and Shepard of New York to publish *Eonchs of Ruby, A Gift of Love.* A definition of the work's odd title was later provided by the poet in the *Georgia Citizen* (June 28, 1851): "The Word *Eonch* is the same as *Concha Marina—Shell of the Sea. Eonch* is used instead of *Concha,* merely for its euphony. It is the same as the Kaur Gaur of the Hebrews. Ruby signifies, in the language of correspondence, *Divine Love.* The word Eonch is used, as a title, by metonymy, for *Songs.* The meaning of the title is, therefore, apparent, namely, *Songs of Divine Love.* The clouds, I hope, are now dispelled; and the mystery, I presume, evaporates. I hope the day will continue clear."

The subtitle indicates Chivers' desire to capitalize on the contemporary fetish for gift books, but he was also keeping pace with another trend by using an obscure title that required an occultist explanation. Mediums and spiritualists, very much in vogue, used to utter strange sounds, purportedly the speech of the spirit world. Swedenborgians were studying the description of angelic language, which, according to *Heaven and Hell,* consisted only of vowel sounds. Chivers' endebtedness to Swedenborg is disclosed in his definition of "Ruby" as "Divine Love" in the "language of Correspondence." To the Swedish mystic precious stones were emblems of supernatural truths.

About half of the forty poems in *Eonchs of Ruby* had previously appeared in magazines; and since Chivers' name was fairly well known by 1851, the work at first drew the attention of readers and critics. Some had favorable comments, but there were enough caustic remarks to irk the hypersensitive Chivers. Those poems with a Poesque flavor were later to set off an argument over the extent to which the Georgian had plagiarized Poe.

Since the first poem, **"The Vigil in Aiden,"** is a homage to Poe, any borrowing in this instance could be condoned, for Chivers was paying tribute to his colleague. The opening lines have a cadence and melody that recall Poe's best lyrics:

> In the Rosy Bowers of Aiden,
> With her ruby-lips love-laden,
> Dwelt the mild, the modest Maiden
> Whom POLITIAN called LENORE.
> As the Churches, with their whiteness
> Clothe the earth, with her uprightness
> Clothed she now his soul with brightness,
>   Breathing out her heart's love-lore;

Politian, none other than Poe in a thinly veiled disguise, mourns the impending loss of Lenore. The mood and rhythm of "The Raven" are invoked by Chivers to picture the sorrowful Politan inquiring of his beloved whether their two souls will meet again. Chivers' imitation of Poe here is quite acceptable.

If the structure of **"The Vigil in Aiden"** is Poesque, the theology is definitely Chiversian. Poe was indifferent to religion, unlike Chivers, who eagerly depicts his ubiquitous band of angels waiting to whisk some fortunate soul off to heaven; in this instance Lenore is the lucky one.

The second poem in the volume, **"The Mighty Dead,"** is also a lengthy elegy. Among the famous figures Chivers eulogized here is William Henry Harrison (1773-1841), for whom he has a few Swedenborgian words of wisdom about the happy destiny of the spiritual body: the association of Swedenborg with American liberty is implied by Chivers, who assigns to Harrison a hieratic role in leading Americans to a New Jerusalem, the Swedish mystic's term for a revitalized spiritual order.

Among the other persons praised in **"The Mighty Dead,"** some remain well known today; others are given little or no attention. Consider the current fame of Washington, Milton, and Shakespeare, for example, as compared to that now of Felicia Hemans, Edward Young, and Marco Botzaris. The last three, familiar only to readers of the nineteenth century, demonstrate by their oblivion the mercurial nature of popular taste and acclaim.

The third poem, also an elegy of considerable length, concerns four of Chivers' children who died in the span of a year. His oldest son, Eugene Percy, is commemorated in **"Avalon."** Here Chivers' love of nature in springtime blends with an unaffected expression of grief and with a desperate plea to God to assuage his sorrow: earnest and profound emotions furnish Chivers with what he considers to be some of the best and most human themes expressed in poetry. Among European Romantics meditation on the death of loved ones was a common subject, but they were more inclined to be deists and not as orthodox in their attitude towards Christianity as Chivers. In fact adherence to a more traditional, Christian view distinguished many American Romantics from their confrères in Europe. In America, Romanticism was closely linked to the Protestant ethic and the Second Great Awakening; as a writer of the first half of the nineteenth century, Chivers in his poetry reflects those trends.

The hymnal quality of **"Avalon"** and the directness achieved by its refrains make the lines ring true. Awkwardness in some of the rhymes does not detract greatly from the overall effect of the poem. In moments like these Chivers, despite his stylistic shortcomings, produced poetry that in its simplicity, religious spirit, and provincialism fulfilled some of the requirements of the so-called true American lyric that many contemporary exponents of a native literature were demanding.

A plausible explanation for the seemingly ridiculous aspects of another poem **"The Lusiad,"** lies in Chivers' affinity to folk music. In the *Georgia Citizen* of March 24, 1854, he referred to G.P. Morris's "Southern Refrain" and its use of the repetend "Long time ago" as being of "nigger origin." While Watts feels that Chivers borrowed from Morris, it is more likely that the individualistic Georgian spontaneously inserted a refrain from a familiar old folk tune. If one views **"The Lusiad"** as a ballad, there is little reason to question Chivers' use of outlandish metaphors and similes. What is objectionable in more conventional lyrics is often admissible in the ballad. **"The Lusiad"** has also been considered a parody of Poe's "The Haunted Palace." While the meter is trochaic in both poems, there is little other similarity.

It is doubtful that any other poet of the time wrote and felt in quite the same fashion Chivers did. He was not an ignorant man, but, being largely self-taught and having traveled little, he had a rustic response to the wonders of the big city. A concert in New York by Mme Caradori Allen prompted the enthusiastic strains of **"To Cecilia":**

> Like mellow moonlight in the month of June,
>   Waning serenely on some far-off sea,
> Died the soft pathos of that spiritual tune—
>   Soft as the liquid hues of Heaven to me.

Chivers provides an *explication de texte* for "liquid hues," by stating that it alludes "to harmony between a soft sound and a blue color," in a manner reminiscent of Baudelaire's comment on one of his own poems.

From Shelley, Chivers acquired the shell image; but the American poet's use in **"The Shell"** gives it a broader meaning and makes it a symbol of the mysteries of the universe. The shell in the Swedenborgian system of correspondences, as interpreted by Chivers, is an emblem of the arcana that the poet alone is capable of fathoming. To Chivers, the shell also symbolizes the world of sensory impressions yet to be fully described by the poet; that realm is one in which music, the spoken word, and a painting can be united in their mutual expression of the beauty of the universe.

"Leaving the rapt World mute with supernatural wonder," Chivers in **"The Dying Swan"** tries to stimulate the reader's imagination to the point of furnishing sensations and impressions of sound and color to complete further the word portrait of the universe's reaction to the Day of Judgment. A cascade-like effect is derived from reading its lines. From time to time in the *Eonchs of Ruby* Chivers succeeds in realizing new perspectives and in freeing poetry from rigid and traditional patterns, as he does in "Isadore," another step away from the grotesque verse of his contemporaries. For obvious reasons the poem figures prominently in the Poe-Chivers controversy.

Following right after the musicality and charm of "Isadore," the choppy verse of "The Gospel of Love" is a sharp reminder of the ease with which Chivers could lapse into mediocrity. One element makes "The Gospel of Love" worthy of mention. It is one of the few poems in which Chivers shows definite signs of social consciousness when he deplores inadequate care for the insane. A surprising modernness of perception on the problems of mental health is coupled with a very progressive outlook, for the time, on penal reform. Chivers states his unqualified disapproval of capital punishment, for God alone bestows life on man and has the right to take it away.

The central idea of "The Gospel of Love" is the proper care of children, who should be reared by loving and tender parents. Chivers may well have been thinking of some of his own children, taken from him by untimely deaths, and of how he would have attended to their needs with paternal solicitude had they lived. However, though social insights are all very fine, they have no place in a poem if they are not expressed in an esthetically appealing style.

Chivers returns to better form in "Evening" when depicting the effect of the sun's rays shining on rapidly flowing water and a school of fish swimming in the current:

> Down in the acromatic streams,
> Meeting the luminiferous beams
> With which the air forever teems,
> The golden mail of minnows gleams.

Equally effective is the panorama of the heavens in the initial stanza of "The Chaplet of Cypress." an elegy written for one of his sisters, Florence. Chivers was unusually adept at creating the sensation of literally soaring through space:

> Up through the hyaline ether-sea,
> Star-diademed, in chariot of pure pain,
> Through th' empyreal star-fires radiantly,
> Triumphant over Death in Heaven to reign . . .

Poetry that would otherwise be of no consequence has a redeeming feature when Chivers adds a distinctive note that reflects his personal concerns, whether he mourns the loss of loved ones or expresses his regionalism. The love of homeland finds expression in poems, mediocre from a strictly literary standpoint but valuable as evidence of Chiver's folklorism. "Song from the Inner Life" terminates in a stanza that has the rough and honest outlines of a Negro spiritual or a hymn sung by the congregation of a Baptist church. This poem resounds with Chivers' provincial and rustic impulse to portray the feelings and emotions associated with his youth and early manhood in Georgia, a reminder of the essentially frontier society in which he was reared.

On another theme, one which represents a different kind of religious experience, the "Song of LeVerrier on Discovering a New Planet" is an effort to relive the astronomer's emotions when confirming the existence of Neptune through mathematical analysis. Once again Chivers displays his ability to grasp the tremendous significance of infinity and literally to whirl his readers with him through space. By alliteration and metaphor he achieves a measure of sublimity. The general impact of the poem is unified and forceful, and shows that Chivers' forte lies in shorter poems.

Undoubtedly Swedenborg's views on the intermingling of sensory impressions, all derived from one source or central sense, helped to shape Chivers' thinking. The poet attempts in the "Voice of Thought" to convey his impression of immaterial concepts through specific physical sensations. In this instance thought has a voice and is compared to the fragrance of a rose. The notion of speech expressed through silence recalls some of Swedenborg's remarks on silence as one characteristic of angelic language. From this poem the reader can derive a picture of Chivers' own internal state when composing poetry; as described by him, his spirit is like a combined sound chamber and flower bed filled with an aromatic music.

Chivers had something in common with Poe in the use of the refrain and in the conjuring-up of sensory images. However the mere coincidence that both poets used the same title for some of their poems need not produce speculation about possible plagiarism. Except in title, for example, there is little similarity between Poe's "Eulalie" and Chivers' poem of the same name. The Georgian's mark is deeply imprinted on his own version, in which his flamboyant imagery is redeemed by a certain gracefulness. Memories of Poe are also invoked by titles such as "Lily Adair." If Chivers lacked Poe's technique and level of performance, he was frequently more original in his philosophy and use of subject matter; he was incapable of consciously indulging in the slavish imitation of any poet.

Deeply religious by nature, the Baptist converted to Swedenborg combined the austerity of his childhood beliefs with the intriguing mysticism of the New Church. The concept of the spiritual body continuing life in the celestial sphere fascinated Chivers. He yearned to communicate with angels in heaven, and he counted the steps in perfection necessary to achieve the closest possible union with God. In voicing his longing for the other world Chivers sought objects in the physical world that served as harbingers of things to come. This search resulted in a fusion of sensory images in keeping with Swedenborg's concept of the fundamental union of sensations. What was a useful poetic technique had a theological basis. Chivers was more consistent in one respect than poets merely interested in the esthetic advantages afforded by Swedenborg. A convinced disciple of the Scandanavian seer, the Georgian regarded his efforts in the lyric as an exposition of theological truths. In many poets such an assumption would be judged unwarranted; in Chivers the statement of his beliefs, whether in poetry or in prose, is clear and unequivocal. He was too unsophisticated to indulge in ambiguous subtleties. From Swedenborg's revelations he undoubtedly acquired the impulse to picture man soaring through space and the heavens.

With a similar naiveté and brashness Chivers made no pretense of concealing his unaffected regionalism and provincial background. His very outlandishness stemmed from a frankly nationalistic as well as a Georgian orientation. The reiterative and simple strains of Baptist hymns were to him fitting models for elegies or religious lyrics. As for his nationalism, Chivers may have voiced his sentiments with less polish than continental writers, but pride in one's country to the point of chauvinism was fashionable in the nineteenth century.

The variation in the quality of Chivers' verse is understandable in terms of his own unpredictable and chameleonic temperament. He could write atrocious lines one moment and then compose a moving passage on the death of his children; such personal notes are endearing for their lack of affectation. Although seldom given to crusading in the cause of social reform, he could voice a concern about injustices which showed his profound awareness of the ills of society.

Some poems in the *Eonchs of Ruby,* while they do provide justifiable grounds for speculation on the extent of Chivers' borrowing from Poe, usually point only to aims and techniques common to both poets. A more profitable subject of inquiry would be the manner in which Chivers and Poe represented a unique trend in American poetry, one apart from the main current. Baudelaire, and later the French Symbolists, found much to admire in Poe. Chivers in *Eonchs of Ruby* also probed, albeit briefly, into the sound value of words alone with little regard for their literal meaning, a technique to be developed in detail by Mallarmé and his school. As conventional as Chivers often was in his choice of thematic material, he still achieved, for a regional poet, unexpected and startling effects of rhyme, meter, and imagery. For this reason the *Eonchs of Ruby* is of interest to the literary historian.

MEMORALIA

In January of 1853 Chivers decided to publish a revised edition of the *Eonchs of Ruby*. It was printed by Lippincott in Philadelphia under the title *Memoralia; or, Phials of Amber Full of the Tears of Love, A Gift for the Beautiful*. Actually only one poem, **"The Vigil in Aiden,"** was omitted. The *Memoralia* was merely a reissue of the *Eonchs* to which a long preface and six new poems had been added. The preface contained further reflections on Chivers' Swedenborgian esthetics and was the volume's most valuable addition. Of the six poems **"Bochsa"** was generally judged the best; here Chivers pictured an indi-

vidual who could elevate himself to the World of Spirits and enjoyed the pristine insights of Edenic man.

The sales of the *Eonchs of Ruby* had been decreasing, so Chivers felt a reissue under a different title would attract buyers, who would consider the *Memoralia* an entirely new volume of poetry. What Chivers did was a fairly common practice at the time, but unhappily the second edition did little to increase the Georgian's profits from his writing.

VIRGINALIA

Virginalia, or Songs of My Summer Nights was printed at Philadelphia in 1853 by Lippincott. Chivers did not use one lengthy poem as the principal selection to which a collection of shorter lyrics was appended. Instead, almost all the poems are under two hundred lines in length. About one-half of them had previously appeared in magazines. A few commentators perceived some merit in Chivers' latest work, but the Georgian was, nonetheless, the recipient of the usual caustic remarks that greeted any new volume he dared to publish.

As was his custom, Chivers expounded in the preface the philosophical and esthetic notions central to *Virginalia*. Swedenborg's use of the polished diamond to symbolize heavenly truths is adapted to fit Chivers' theory of the preternatural function of poetry as an expression of divine truth.

Diamonds to Swedenborg were the emblems of celestial love; the successive degrees of color and the varieties of refraction in a diamond corresponded to the different phases of good and truth in heaven. The diamond also signified spiritual light for, as Swedenborg explained, the influx of light into a diamond had a correspondential relationship to the supreme degree of spiritual life a soul could receive. The "crystalline revelation of the Divine Idea" is Chivers' reference to the mystical sense attributed to crystal by Böhme and Swedenborg. For the Swedish mystic this transparent substance connoted the shining light of divine truth as well as those believers who dwell in the knowledge which that light provides. To Chivers any revelation of God's will to the poet furnished special insights into supernatural secrets hidden from ordinary mortals and, to verify this point, he discourses on the function of the repetend in mystical terms.

The refrain already appears in the first poem **"Chactas; or, the Lament of the Harmonious Voice,"** which bears the explanatory caption "Founded on Chateaubriand's Atala." In the poem Chivers centers largely on building the suspense to the moment when Chactas is rescued by a strange Indian maid; the French writer inspired much of his work:

> The night arrived. The pale Moon seemed to
> glide,
> Weeping through Heaven, like Sorrow by my
> side—
> When, lo'! before me, swaying down the grass,

A Maiden, beautiful as Heaven, did pass,
With noiseless steps, upon the silver sands,—
Then, turning round, untied my fettered hands.

Another poem in the collection, **"Ganymede,"** marks a continuation of the religious preoccupation typical of Chivers. The subject, he claimed, was based on an actual experience. Impelled by a mysterious impulse, he had climbed to the heights of a hill and at the summit he had a vision of George Washington and the future greatness of America. The crowning point of his revery is the realization of the supernatural character of his vision;

For Beauty, with her love divine,
Intoxicates the soul like wine.
Thus, glory-crowned, in robes of light,
He soared up from the World's dark night.
And sitting on the highest Sills,
With Angels, on the Eternal Hills,
Hears Heaven's immortal music roll
Down God's great Ages through his soul.
Te Deum Laudamus!

Less inspired moments are handsomely redeemed by **"Apollo,"** recognized by Bayard Taylor as one of the best poems in *Virginalia;* Taylor was expecially impressed by the imagery in the third and sixth lines of the following stanza:

Like some deep, impetuous river from the
     fountains everlasting,
Down the serpentine soft valley of the vistas of
     all Time,
Over cataracts of adamant uplifted into
     mountains,
Soared his soul to God in thunder on the wings
     of thought Sublime,

With the rising golden glory of the sun in
     ministrations
Making oceans metropolitan of splendor for the
     dawn—
Piling pyramid on pyramid of music for the
     nations—
Sings the angel who sits shining everlasting in
     the sun,
For the stars, which are the echoes of the
     shining of the sun.

Unlike other poems with only a few good passages, **"Apollo"** conveys an even, sustained impression. The rough edges have been smoothed and the result is an excellent short poem of three stanzas with polished meter and rhythm. Noticeably absent is the far-fetched imagery in which Chivers was often inclined to indulge.

"Lily Adair," while longer in length, has much the same quality as **"Apollo";** in addition, the terminal rhyme scheme, *dddd,* is utilized adroitly to enhance the musicality of the stanza. Chivers also displays finesse in merely hinting at the general outlines of maidenly comeliness.

Thus she stood on the arabesque borders
     Of the beautiful blossoms that blew
On the banks of the crystalline waters,
     Every morn, in the diaphane dew.
The flowers, they were radiant with glory,
     And shed such perfume on the air,
That my soul now to want them, feels sorry,
     And bleeds for my Lily Adair—
For my much-loved Lily Adair—
     For my long-lost Lily Adair—
     For my beautiful, dutiful Lily Adair.

Like **"Lily Adair,"** **"Valete Omnia"** also enjoys an uninterrupted harmony thanks to the absence of any infelicitous metaphors. Another notable feature is the refrain, which is reminiscent of previous ballad-like verse written by Chivers in which he successfully combines his musical and folkloric insights; the imagery is also quite striking:

The great golden hand on the Adamant Dial
Of the Clock of Eternity pauses in Heaven!
From Death's bony hand I now empty the
     Phial—
And the Morning is just like the Even!

"The Fall of Usher," which has been criticized for its obvious Poe-isms, was written as a tribute to Chivers' late colleague. Borrowings from Poe were, therefore, both understandable and justifiable. To Chivers' credit, he did not join the current trend to demean the dead writer but paid him just tribute:

"Thou art gone to the grave!" thou art silently
     sleeping
     A sleep which no sorrow shall ever molest;
And, in longing for which, my poor heart now is
     keeping
     This silent lament in its grave in my breast!
     Like Shelley for Keats, in its grave in my
breast!

Unlike the better poems in this collection, **"Rosalie Lee"** marks Chivers' lapse into the old habit of wildly choosing metaphors and of displaying almost complete disregard for common sense. What botanist has discovered cucumbers growing on a tree, or, for that matter, how many poets compare that succulent vegetable to a goblet?

Many mellow Cydonian Suckets,
Sweet apples, anthosmial, divine,
From the Ruby-rimmed Beryline buckets,
     Star-gemmed, lily-shaped, hyaline—
Like that sweet golden goblet found growing
     On the wild emerald Cucumber-tree—

Although referring once more to "Cydonian Suckets," the title **"Pas d'Extase"** suggests that this poem was gaily dashed off after seeing a company of ballerinas perform. Various Chiversian elements are combined in what begins like a sybaritic ditty and ends in the ecstatic ascent of the poet's soul to heaven. Chivers employs mythological imagery with the zest and vigor of a Georgian farmer who derived lusty enjoyment from his Classical studies. References to revelry and the imbibing of alcoholic spirits remind us of earlier poems. Allusions to the death bed recall the elegies to deceased loved ones. Paradoxically he was a teetotaler and gave temperance lectures:

> Like those sweet Cydonian Suckets
> Herbe brings in crystal Buckets
> To the Gods in Heaven above,
> When they drink, forever quaffing
> Fiery draughts of living wine—
> Sometimes shouting, sometimes laughing
> With the heavenly bliss divine. . . .

By its energy and vitality **"Pas d'Extase"** provides a striking study of Chivers. Several motifs are once more combined; what seemed a bacchanalian revelry in a provincial Georgian setting is slowly transformed into a mystical anticipation of celestial joys in the afterlife. The immediacy of angelic presences quickens the poet's sensation of climbing a ladder that leads to heaven.

Chivers' ability to picture humble flora and fauna in unusual, original terms is again demonstrated in **"Bessie Bell."** Few poets would speak of the action of a butterfly's wings as "psychical," but Chivers does so because he has a spiritualist's view of nature. **"Bessie Bell"** has one of the several references to Israfel that caused Poe's constituents to suspect plagiarism; the meter has been traced to the four-stressed trochaic of Tennyson's "Locksley Hall." While Chivers might have imitated the British poet in using this particular meter, the imagery and subject matter are undeniably his own:

> Like the psychical vibration
> Of the BUTTERFLY's soft wings,
> Dallying with the rich CARNATION—
> Played her fingers with the strings.
> Israfelian in its dearness—
> All her heart's deep love to tell—
> Bell-like, silver in its clearness,
> Fell the voice of BESSIE BELL.

The death of Henry Clay prompted Chivers to compose **"Morcia Funebre,"** in which he achieved unique results in evoking the pealing of bells. The very words by their strength and resonance reproduce the alternate strokes of a clapper hitting the sides of a bell. Chivers borrowed from Poe's "The Bells," but, unlike that poem, **"Morcia Funebre"** is more thunderous and resounding in its effects:

> Toll, toll, toll!
> Let your great Thor-hammer strike upon the bell,
> Crushing from out his iron heart the dole—
> To sable all the world with his funeral knell!
> For the passing into glory of his soul—
> For the Requiem of the soaring into glory of his
>   soul!
> Then toll, toll, toll!

At times Chivers put aside his ingrained provincialism to view the world on a wider scale. When surveying the situation in Europe, he could not resist the impulse to proclaim America the leader of freedom and the model to be emulated by enslaved peoples, even though ironically he was a slaveholder. There is a pre-Whitmanic strain in Chivers' vision of the United States' role and his sense of manifest destiny. While only a faint suggestion of Whitman's mighty lines is found in Chivers' **"The Rising of the Nations,"** his poem foreshadows some of the pageantry of *Leaves of Grass:*

> Now louder than the loud tumultuous Ocean
> Stormed into passion by the ever-roaring
>   Winds—
> Come the loud shouts from all those multitudes
>   in motion,
> Chorusing the lightnings of these million mighty
>   minds—
> Answering the Bugle-blasts from out the
>   Mountains,
> Blown from the lips of ever-living Liberty—
> Louder than thunders of ten thousand fountains
> Leaping down cataracts of Adamant exultingly
> Impatient to become the Children of the Sea!

In *Virginalia* Chivers' poetic principles are put into practice with fair success. Romanticism, to be sure, is present in subjects carried over from previous works; Chateaubriandesque Indians, patriotic fervor, outbursts of melancholy, and glorification of feminine beauty all remind readers of

The first page of a letter from Chivers to Edgar Allan Poe.

Chivers' conventional side. To these elements might also be added a continuing interest in folklore, ballads, and nature; this last serves as a link between Chivers' conformity to the prevailing Romantic vogue and a solitary search for a deep theological meaning in the universe. This religious search was tightly bound to a quest for a new poetics, a quest that comes closer to realization in *Virginalia* than in previous works. Evidence in the poems of *Virginalia* indicates Swedenborg was still the primary source of inspiration for Chivers that made him seek invigorating imagery in the world about him to express the arcana which, the Swedish mystic maintained, were hidden in nature.

Chivers sets out boldly to accomplish what he considers his mission, the development of poetry as an instrument of sonification, in a physical as well as in an intellectual sense. At times this results in poems that, when read aloud, produce a series of irregularly recurring impulses painful to hear. Quite often, however, Chivers generates a sustained vibrational energy from felicitous word combinations that convey to the reader not just concepts alone but impressions and sensations that bring into play all the reader's faculties; mind, imagination, and intuition are simultaneously stimulated. For these reasons *Virginalia* is usually judged Chivers' best work.

THE SONS OF USNA

In the preface to *The Sons of Usna,* dated November 7, 1854, Mount Vernon, New York, Chivers gratefully acknowledges his debt to Theophilus O'Flanagan's *Daidra, or the Lamentable Fate of The Sons of Usnach.* Chivers had become acquainted with O'Flanagan's work thanks to a footnote to Thomas Moore's *Irish Melodies.* Through it he was referred to the *Transactions of the Gaelic Society of Dublin.* Probably in about 1845 Chivers took an interest in the Deidre legend and, judging from the date given in the preface, he had the manuscript of *The Sons of Usna* ready for publication in 1854. By that time Chivers expected little support from editors and was reconciled to paying the printing costs in 1858 to C. Sherman and Son in Philadelphia.

O'Flanagan's observation on the antiquity and purity of Gaelic and his remark that the Irish tongue was "the language of Japhet, spoken before the Deluge, and probably the Language of Paradise" would have instantly impressed Chivers as a reflection of his own views on the pristine nature of ancient languages and poetry. In his effusive panegyric of Gaelic O'Flanagan sounded almost Chiversian:

> The beauties and excellence of our language must soon be seen and admired; a language copious, elegant, and harmonious, ancient above all the languages of the world, yielding to none, not even to the Greek, in the beauty and elegance of its cadences, and peculiar aptness for music and poetry; a language, in fine, highly cultivated and admired . . . at a time when the Gauls alone, of all the nations in Europe, were free from barbarism and ignorance, and stood unrivaled in the cultivation of letters. . . .

Towards the end of his life Chivers apparently discovered in the rhythm and musicality of Gaelic a primitive poetry of the highest order. The desire to produce a dramatic version in English of the story of Deidre and the sons of Usna is explainable both by Chivers' personal esthetic principles and his continuing interest in the theatre.

In consulting various sources Chivers must have read Thomas Moore's *The History of Ireland* (1835), where Deidre and the sons of Usnach are mentioned as the leading figures in one of the most famous Celtic epics. Here he would have found a detailed description of the function of the druids which may have inspired him to expand the role of Caffa in his play. In the *Irish Melodies,* besides calling attention to "the very ancient Irish story" of Deidre as related by O'Flanagan, Moore also composed a poem on the Usnach theme entitled "Avenging and Bright."

A summary of *The Sons of Usna* is sufficient to illustrate the hodgepodge of divergent ideas and notions in Chivers' play, destined to remain a closet drama. Shakespearean allusions are very much in evidence, since *Macbeth* especially was one of Chivers's favorite sources for dream symbols and portents of disaster. Conor, at the end of the *The Sons of Usna,* indulges in several lengthy monologues and is haunted by a series of ghosts that make the apparition of Banquo rather tame by Comparison.

Lavercam, when not occupied with her celestial assignment of watching over Daidra and Caffa, plays a rather roguish nurse similar to her counterpart in *Romeo and Juliet.* For an angel she is devilishly clever in arousing Naisa's passions by a glowing description of Daidra: "Whose irresistible Art outcharms all / Studied ingenuity of artfulness."

Caffa, the high priest, is an odd product of an unintentional ecumenism on Chivers' part. He speaks the language of the druid, performs incantations, conjures up spirits, and restores the dead to life, all the while propounding a theology that is basically Christian. He waxes Baptist at one point when intoning a hymn: "This is the burden of our song—/ How long? Oh, Lord! how long?"

On the subject of sacred hymns Caffa gives a Chiversian description of the divine music heard in the everyday world: "The Eden-crystalline songs that Nature sings—/ Filled every human heart with joy."

Another favorite theme of Chivers is represented by Lavercam, a Swedenborgian-type angel who was once a mortal. Her function, no doubt, is to remind readers of the presence of angels among men to ward off evil influences. Lavercam, whose methods tend at times to be a bit devious, is well chosen to work in this primitive court where King Conor resorts to violence and treachery on the slightest pretext.

Caffa is also a wily rascal who discourses glibly about Christian truths and, like Lavercam, deceives time and again an incredibly gullible Conor, a typical Chiversian character who probably survives until the end of the play because Caffa has his hands full with Lucifer; the latter insists on appearing at most inopportune moments to distract the druid from more serious matters. The archdevil has spotted Caffa as one of God's elect and his fiendish suspicions are confirmed when an angel appears to hand the priest a scroll containing the key to celestial wisdom. Resorting on one occasion to a description of the millenium, when eventually even evil spirits will be restored to divine favor, Lucifer does his best to talk Caffa into giving him the scroll. Blandishments diabolical have no effect whatsoever on the tricky Caffa, who takes delight in teasing Lucifer and testing the devil on various points of theology and biblical history. Determined to seize the scroll, Lucifer makes one last effort in the final act, just before Conor dies, only to be thwarted by a thunderbolt from heaven that sends the ineffectual devil scurrying back to hell.

There are various subplots that slow down the action considerably and give the impression that Chivers' play is little better than a haphazard combination of several totally unrelated scripts. Still there are a few scenes and passages that retain some of the spirit of the original Celtic tale. In one such scene Conor, by a tricky method of interrogation, tries to get one of his followers to participate in the assassination of the Usnas. He puts the same question to Conol Carnach, Cuchullan, and Fergus:

> What would you do, should Usna's Sons be
>   slain
> Under my guarantee?

The first two refuse to cooperate with Conor but Fergus gives an ambiguous reply, typical of the old Gaelic epics:

> Why by my soul.
> Although I swear not to attempt thy life,
> They all should die together as one man.

Daidra's description of her dream lover also captures a bit of the flavor of the original tale of the Usnas:

> The husband I would have, must be a man
> Whose hair is like that Raven's wing; his cheeks
> As red as blood; his skin as white as snow.

The translation from the Gaelic by O'Flanagan relates how Daidra describes to Lavercam the ideal husband, "his hair of the colour of the raven, his cheek of the colour of the calf's blood, and his skin of the colour of the snow." These are the three colors she has just seen. Here, as elsewhere, Chivers adheres rather closely to the original story.

The same fidelity to the O'Flanagan translation is also found in Conor's description of Daidra's birth and the sparing of her life through his intervention:

> . . . You know she owes her life to me.
> When Feidlim's, son of Delas, wife lay in
> With her, Caffa, the Druid, prophesied

> That she would bring destruction on the land—
> Alarm—that Morning Star of heavenly love
> Whose rising brings monition to the world.

An excerpt from O'Flanagan's reference to Daidra's birth is of interest for purposes of comparison:

> On a certain day that Conor, King of Ulster, went to partake of an entertainment at the mansion . . . Feilims' [*sic*] wife lay in of a fair daughter, during the entertainment; and Caffa the Druid, who was then of the company, foreboded and prophesied for the daughter . . . numerous mischiefs. . . . Upon hearing this, the nobles proposed putting her to death forthwith. Let it not be done so, said Conor, but I will take her with me, and send her to be reared, that she may become my only own wife. The Druid, Caffa, named her Deidri. . . .

A footnote by O'Flanagan explains that the Gaelic equivalent of "Deidri" is "Alarm"; the information, which Chivers expands with Shakespearean gusto in the reference to the "Morning Star," serves as a warning to the world. While not an exceptional poetic *tour de force,* the passage shows no mean facility on Chivers' part in adapting the prose of O'Flanagan to blank verse. With similar ease Chivers handles the scene, taken directly from the Gaelic accounts, in which Conor has to approach three different noblemen before he gets an ambiguous pledge from the third one, Fergus, to lead the sons of Usna into a trap.

From this point Chivers' play follows the general outline of the old Irish versions. Daidra, who has seen omens of disaster, is unable to keep Naisa from accepting Fergus' offer of safe conduct back to Conor's kingdom. Her husband rejects a second warning from Daidra when he goes to the Red Branch, a castle where he quarters his brothers and their men. They are soon attacked there by Conor's soldiers, but the latter cannot prevail against the onslaught of the Usnas until Caffa's magic conjures up a huge wave engulfing and disarming Naisa and his brothers. Breaking a promise to Caffa to spare the Usnas, Conor has them slain by Manani with a mighty sword offered by Naisa to insure an instant and merciful death for the three Usnas. According to Gaelic tradition Daidra either dies or commits suicide not long afterwards. Chiversian logic, however, would require a happy ending; therefore Caffa must restore the Usnas to life, reunite Naisa and Daidra, and make sure Conor receives his just deserts.

Chivers took some liberties in the use of names. In Macpherson's account Darthula is Naisa's wife and Slissama the mother of the Usnas; Chivers changes their roles respectively to that of the daughter of the king of Scotland and the spirit of Caffa's wife embodied in Lavercam. There are also variations in spelling; names like Caffa, Lavercam, Daidra, and Manani represent Chivers' orthography, which differs from Gaelic equivalents such as Cathbad, Leabharcham, Deidre, and Maini. The Georgian probably felt justified in altering the names in order to make them more poetic. O'Flanagan's narrative is fragmentary and uneven, and Dr. Jeoffrey Keating's *The*

General History of Ireland, which Chivers also undoubtedly used, gives only the bare outline of the Usna tragedy. Chivers became convinced substantial changes were in order if the tale was to be successfully adapted to the stage. In some respects he could defend his alterations on the basis of vague hints in the original versions concerning the sympathies and inclinations of certain characters. Since Caffa and Lavercam indicate they tend to favor the Usnas and Daidra, Chivers places them squarely in the camp opposed to Conor. Other changes are more drastic. Eogan Mor, the slayer of the brothers in the Keating version of the legend, becomes the king of Scotland's henchman in *The Sons of Usna.* Fergus' role does not differ greatly from the one he plays in the O'Flanagan translation, although his support of the Usnas after Conor's betrayal seems half-hearted.

Certain elements Chivers added to the plot make it burdensome. The last minute decision of the king of Scotland and the queen of Connaught to join forces with the resurrected Usnas against Conor resembles an episode from the *Arabian Nights.* The combination of Baptist moralizing and Swedenborgian metaphysics that Chivers adds to the dramatic ingredients produces a confusing mixture which at times borders on the ludicrous.

One exception may be seen in the scenes that involve Caffa and Lucifer. Here the inspiration most likely comes from Byron's *Cain* rather than Marlowe's *Dr. Faustus* or Philip J. Bailey's *Festus.* None of Marlowe's rhetoric is even faintly suggested in *The Sons of Usna* when Lucifer appears. Bailey, chief of what W.E. Aytoun called the "spasmodic" school of poets, wrote a long contemporary interpretation of *Faust* in which both Festus and Lucifer emerge as rather wishy-washy characters. Some of Bailey's Victorian moralizing may have rubbed off on Chivers, but in general *Festus* would appear only a remote source of inspiration.

Chivers' Lucifer and Caffa engage in a theological dispute in which the druid finally gets the upper hand. The devil is unable to disarm Caffa with beguiling chatter about heaven. Instead he is a ready foil for Caffa similar to a straight man in a standard comedy routine. In Byron's *Cain* such banter is absent, but, unlike the lackadaisical pair in *Festus,* Adam's son and Lucifer are equally aggressive individuals. Cain takes nothing for granted and often derides the devil.

The witty exchanges between Caffa and Lucifer that brighten *The Sons of Usna* recall Byron's irony rather than Bailey's maudlin sermonizing or Marlowe's lofty oratory. Another source also must not be ruled out, the popular belief in the devil among poor Southern whites and blacks. Chivers had capitalized on this theme in **"The Death of the Devil,"** published in the *Georgia Citizen* in 1852. There were also popular ditties in which a sharp operator frequently outfoxed old Satan himself.

Of great concern to Chivers are Swedenborgian themes he feels obliged to interpose at one point or another. The bantering between Caffa and Lucifer takes on a sober tone when the subject of angels and their presence among men is brought up in relation to the need for spiritual regeneration. Naisa, in the midst of embracing Daidra, makes passing reference to a cardinal point in Swedenborg's teachings, the influx of God's life into man's soul.

Some understanding of the author's objective in *The Sons of Usna* may be acquired from a manuscript in the Duke University Library Collection, "Introduction to a Drama," dated August 12, 1856, Villa Allegra, Georgia. Chivers reasons that the "Protoplay" composed by God with Adam and Eve the featured players, had tragic and comic elements. And while Christ's crucifixion was tragedy in its most sublime sense, like the story of Eden the drama of the cross gave "pleasing sensations." This to Chivers seemed perfectly logical, for if a tragedy was to arouse terror or pity, it had to be tempered by a message of reconciliation or "enthusiastic hope." Shakespeare's tragedies had this principle of "enthusiastic hope" through the "New Dispensation," namely, the gospel of Christ.

If there is ever a museum founded in which will be displayed the "awful examples" of bad, nonsensical poetry, Chivers will be king, though we might easily cite lines by Shelley, Poe, Browning, Mrs. Browning, and Swinburne that make for nonsense, though often resounding.

James Huneker, in **The Pathos of Distance: A Book of a Thousand and One Moments,** *1913*.

In seeking to provide a theological basis for his dramatic theory Chivers was at heart a Romantic when it came to enunciating what he deemed the fundamental esthetics of dramaturgy. "Gothic Dramatic is not logic of grammar, but of Passion." The underlying motivation of human conduct was to be found in the emotions of man; this principle furnished the true test of dramatic excellence, borne out by Shakespeare's works. Thus Chivers rejects implicitly the Aristotelian concept that a tragedy arises from a major flaw in the character of the central figure in a play. True tragedy, he goes on to explain, is "the result of a combination of virtues and perfections" and has "a higher source than mere murder." Returning to the prototypes of comedy and tragedy in the Bible, Chivers again cites respectively, as an example of each genre, the "Protoplay of Eden" and the crucifixion. Since "a tragedy proper does not consist in abstract suffering," it follows that tragedy and comedy, in the absolute sense, must both have "vis poetica" or "passion." The best of Shakespeare, Chivers emphasized, was inferior to the drama of Eden and the Cross. The one in Eden took place when the world was "young and full of beauty" and the Crucifixion occurred in a world already "old and full of ugliness."

In attempting to unite his theological and esthetic views, Shakespeare found sublime inspiration in the Eden of his own soul, which often resulted in what Chivers considered a true play, that is, one that would be like heavenly music to the audience. From Chivers' remarks it is clear that the ideal tragedy would end not in death but instead with the promise of eternal life. When referring to events in Eden as a comedy, Chivers must have had in mind a comic situation so lifelike that it had in it the makings of tragedy.

The Georgian was realistic, however, about the practical difficulties of staging a play. He recognized in another manuscript, probably intended as a preface to *Charles Stuart,* two kinds of plays, the poetic, customarily assigned to the closet, and the usual prose drama that was a commercial hit. Undaunted, nonetheless, Chivers refused to concede that a play written in verse was necessarily marked for failure. If *Romeo and Juliet* could succeed, Chivers saw no reason why the poetry of his play *Charles Stuart* would fail to charm an audience with its "fortuitousness."

If the foregoing principles represent Chivers' concept of the theatre, what is their relation to *The Sons of Usna?* While not set in Edenic times, the author chose a relatively primitive period of Irish history, when passions were more spontaneous and "fortuitous." The death and subsequent restoration to life of the Usnas seem intended to recall Christ's crucifixion and resurrection and Caffa's being raised to Heaven by a band of angels obviously reminds readers of Jesus' ascension. By the same token Caffa's frequent debates with Lucifer, from which the priest emerges victorious, may have been Chivers' way of underscoring the comic aspects of man's constant bouts with the devil despite the seriousness of the ever-present threat of eternal damnation. As for "enthusiastic hope" and the existence of a celestial message, these are provided by Lavercam, whose very presence as an angel symbolizes the promise of salvation. The play does not end in "mere murder," since Caffa summons the Usnas back to life and Conor dies of a guilty conscience. Chivers' expectations that *The Sons of Usna* might prove successful on the stage may have come from his belief that its source, a primitive epic, possessed the germs of pure poetry unspoiled by a modern society that had lost its appreciation of fresh and untained beauty. Unhappily the play did not live up to Chivers' rather lofty ambitions. Today *The Sons of Usna* is of importance largely as a document of literary history. As in most of the Georgian's works there are delightful and charming passages, and he was successful at times in capturing some of the original flavor of the Irish tale. Still the Swedenborgian speculations of Caffa and Lavercam slow down the play's action and deprive it of a certain degree of verisimilitude. Many scenes serve only as padding; one frightful example is the incident, borrowed from *Count Julian,* in which Naisa kisses the sleeping Darthula by mistake, much to Daidra's distress. Eogan Mor's lust for Darthula and other needless trivia also show that Chivers had much to learn about dramatic technique.

In the final analysis *The Sons of Usna* is Chivers' best poetic drama, but it still lacks the power and realism of *Conrad and Eudora,* as deficient as the bloodcurdling melodrama is in many respects. The historical significance of *The Sons of Usna* is that it is the first modern literary work based on the Deidre legend.

William Goldhurst (essay date 1989)

SOURCE: "The New Revenge Tragedy: Comparative Treatments of the Beauchamp Case," in *The Southern Literary Journal,* Vol. XXII, No. 1, Fall, 1989, pp. 117-27.

[*In the essay that follows, Goldhurst compares various dramatizations of the Beauchamp-Sharp murder case, arguing that Chivers's 1834 version is "the most bloodthirsty" of all the treatments.*]

Poe's strategy of setting an American literary situation in a remote and exotic environment has a special and complex application in the verse drama *Politian,* written in 1835. Set in Rome during the Renaissance, the play is a retelling of the Beauchamp-Sharp murder case, which took place in Frankfort, Kentucky, in 1825 and is known to historians as the Kentucky Tragedy. The story has attracted the notice of numerous authors from Poe's day to our own, including Thomas Holley Chivers, William Gilmore Simms, Charles Fenno Hoffman and Robert Penn Warren.

The lurid aspects of the sordid affair needed little blowing up to please sensation seekers of the period. Sex and violence are the foundation, while seduction, pregnancy, desertion, slander and revenge all play vivid roles in the elaboration. There is no single climax; but a bloody murder and then a trial ending in a guilty verdict, a suicide pact, and a public hanging are high points of intensity near the conclusion.

Two components of this story line are perhaps more compelling than the others: the idea that the seducer must die, and the character of Ann Cooke, who offered herself to Beauchamp on the condition that he kill for her. Of course young Beauchamp made her quarrel his own, and swore that he was acting on moral principle, as if Sharp had wronged not only a provincial maiden, but all decent men and women. Most likely Beauchamp eventually came to believe his own internal propaganda; but it was Ann Cooke who breathed life into his anger and kindled his blood lust.

According to Beauchamp's *Confession,* Cooke told him her heart would cease to ache only when Colonel Sharp was killed and not by a stranger to her tragedy, but by *her* agent acting under her direction. She was willing to kiss the hand of the person who avenged her, Ann was; and furthermore would remain forever in his debt. Later Beauchamp taught her how to shoot his pistol and she contemplated killing Sharp herself. But this plan was soon scrapped and the agent idea reinstated. When Beauchamp inquired if he should kill Sharp's brother, too, Cooke said no—not because she cared to spare the innocent, but knowing how the brother worshipped the colonel, she thought he would suffer more if left alive.

Eventually the plan was put into effect, Sharp was tricked into opening his front door and stabbed in his own vestibule, and a triumphant Beauchamp returned to an ecstatic Ann Cooke, who fell to her knees, kissed Beauchamp's hand, and begged to hear all the details of "the glorious deed."

At the end, Cooke visited Beauchamp in prison, bringing laudanum. The dose did not "take," and upon recovering they agreed to use a knife, which Cooke had smuggled into the cell. "I can refuse her nothing she prays of me to do," writes Beauchamp as his execution hour approaches. He raises the dagger and plunges it into his side, but Cooke deflects the blow, grabs the blade and directs the thrust into her own abdomen. Cooke dies of her wound; Beauchamp goes bleeding to the gallows.

The Letters of Ann Cooke provides an interesting glimpse (if they can be believed) into Cooke's feelings as she went from innocent maid to mistress to avenger. On the fatal night of her seduction, Sharp invited her to a ball, where she was "carried away" with the lights, the music, the dancing, and the wine her escort forced upon her. Acting under the influence of all these powerful and unaccustomed stimuli, Cooke says her "reason was subdued by the power of a resistless passion," etc. Before the year was out, she heard that Sharp intended to marry someone else. When she learned from Sharp himself that this was true, she sank to the floor in a faint and spent the next several weeks in her bed with a raging fever. Some months later, her baby died and Ann Cooke began to lapse into "a settled melancholy."

Eventually she emerged from her depression sufficiently to entertain Beauchamp's proposals. Yet she told him she felt she could never again experience happiness in this life, so deep was the trauma Sharp had inflicted. She believed Beauchamp thought her "degraded and unworthy" because she had been another man's fool.

Still, she was beginning to enjoy life again until she learned of Sharp's latest treachery: he was circulating a story that her baby was fathered by a negro and had even had a forged birth certificate drawn up as proof of her indiscretion. According to the *Letters,* it was at this point that Cooke invoked the Erinyes. "We took a solemn oath," she says, "that nothing but the heart's blood of the slanderer and betrayer should atone for the deep and horrible injury he had inflicted." As Beauchamp evolved from visitor to suitor to fiancé he and Cooke shared her gradually mounting anger over the injustices done her by Sharp. In calmer moments, she reminded Beauchamp that the world regarded her as "guilty and polluted." He responded by insisting that she was the innocent victim of a scoundrel's treachery.

They marry. The plan to avenge her wrongs is set in motion. Sharp is killed. Beauchamp is tried and convict-ed. Cooke commits suicide in his presence and he is soon afterward hanged as a felon.

Ann Cooke represents the dark side of the naive American *Frauendienst*—the habit of dehumanizing women of the time by investing them with an unrealistic purity, spirituality, and vulnerability. Individual women who swallowed the mythology whole and then exaggerated its effects could easily assume a becoming narcissism, with attendant feelings of self-pity over life's injustices and a brutal attitude toward the men who had wronged them.

The real Ann Cooke is difficult to identify. Certainly she did not resemble the portrait circulated by Sharp's defenders, where she is pictured as a "waning flirt of 35" who had lost her front teeth and had no chin, etc. Most likely she was average in appearance, if not beautiful, and Sharp did seduce her and then left her to marry another woman. Perhaps a healthy attitude at that point might have been a sense of shared irresponsibility. But the very definition of seduction, with its implication that the man took advantage, pressured the woman to succumb, etc., involves the idea of misconduct on the part of the male acting out a power charade against the passive female. From this assumption to: the seducer must pay! is only a short logical step.

To be sure, the early American seduction novels placed some of the blame upon the female victim, implying or stating explicitly that she was guilty of romantic fantasizing or frivolity. Still, the notion of exploitation of the female persisted, with many of Poe's contemporaries sharing the view that seducers deserved to die for offending against morality and violating the integrity of the social structure.

George Lippard certainly endorsed this view. His *The Monks of Monk Hall* concludes with the murder (or as Lippard would have us believe, the execution) of the seducer Gus Lorrimer by Byrnewood Arlington, brother of Lorrimer's victim, Mary Arlington. Byrnewood gloats over the corpse of the seducer with typical Lippard verbosity: "Ha, ha! Here is blood warm, warm, aye, warm and gushing—that gushing of the Wronger's blood!" And so on.

Earlier, Mary's seduction is accomplished with all the imagined sentiments of the stereotyped sexual villain. "Force—violence" muses the handsome Lorrimer, who says he has deeper means than force. "My victim is the instrument of her own ruin—without one rude grasp from my hand, without one threatening word, she swims willingly to my arms!"

Not only did Lippard celebrate the murder of Lorrimer in his novel, but his inflamed rhetoric resulted in a wave of public opinion (according to Leslie Fiedler's Introduction to *Monks*) that led to passage of an anti-seduction law in New York state in 1849. Death to the seducer became an ingrained formula in the urban consciousness at least, often invoked to explain the sudden or mysterious death of popular controversial figures. An irate husband or brother beat him to death: so people whispered about Poe following his collapse in Baltimore. Years later the same rumor would be circulated about Louis Gottschalk, who in fact suffered peritonitis from months of overwork.

"The seduction of a poor and innocent girl is a deed altogether as criminal as deliberate murder. It is worse than the murder of the body, for it is the assassination of the soul. If the murderer deserves death by the gallows, then the assassin of chastity and maidenhood is worthy of death by the hands of any man, and in any place," says the *Monks* author.

Lippard's revenge melodrama has much in common with the Kentucky Tragedy; the author might have had Sharp and Beauchamp and Cooke in mind when fashioning Lorrimer, Byrnewood and Mary. One conspicuous difference, however, is in his portrayal of the ruined maid. Mary Arlington, while suffering from severe depression after her "fall," assumes that her pollution and worthlessness are irredeemable; but unlike Cooke she tries to prevent any moves toward retaliation. "The wrong has been done," says Mary to her brother, "but do not, I beseech you, visit his (that is, Lorrimer's) head with a curse—." In Lippard's scheme of things, most women are pure, long-suffering, uncomplicated, and forgiving. The concept of a vindictive woman he found not unthinkable, but offensive.

Other authors of Poe's time discovered similar difficulties in attempting to portray Ann Cooke in drama or fiction. After all, weren't women, according to the popular stereotype, flawless, as well as spiritual, sentimental, loving, caring, uplifting, weak, helpless, ill, refined and self-sacrificing? How, then, with this idealized image in the popular mind, depict a vengeful, vindictive, obsessed, insane, bloodthirsty female without surrendering reader sympathy in the portrayal? It would seem that Poe and his contemporaries in this extremely revealing instance had three alternatives: 1) paint her black, make her the villain; 2) change her character, as Lippard did, omitting whatever ugly motives and emotions readers might find objectionable; or 3) complicate her character: make her vindictive, but with mitigating traits—confusion, distraction or insanity. Most authors, as we shall see, chose this third alternative.

In his verse drama ***Conrad and Eudora; or The Death of Alonzo,*** (1834), Thomas Holley Chivers believes along with Lippard that the crime of seduction is grievous and deserves to be punished by death. Early in the play Conrad (Beauchamp) is talking to a friend who says Alonzo (Sharp) is guilty of murder, treason, rape because he seduced Eudora and thereby "ruined the sweetest thing on earth." Conrad has a moral scale upon which he measures the degree of a seducer's guilt: "If she loved him well, and he deceived her / The crime falls heavier on his heart / Than on them both, did both love equally." Later another friend tells Conrad that "a woman's virtue robbed, like loss of sight, / Can never be restored." When Conrad says he will try to cheer Eudora up, the friend says "You can not mend a broken egg." Still later, the Innkeeper hears

that Conrad might be the man who murdered Alonzo and suggests that the fault might be Eudora's: he flatly asserts that no man should be killed over a woman. But when he is told that Alonzo promised to marry Eudora and then ruined her, he says: "Then damn him—let him die." All Chivers's characters are in accord on the severity of Alonzo's crime.

The character of Ann Cooke as portrayed by Chivers is predominantly vengeful and vindictive, as she appears in Beauchamp's *Confession*. In fact she seems more bloodthirsty in ***Conrad and Eudora*** than she was in real life. After Conrad confronts Alonzo for the first time, issuing a death threat but relenting and letting Alonzo go, Eudora says:

> Had I been with thee, he had died so sweet
> Where he within this proud arm's reach—this
>   stroke
> Should be effected and bring his lowness low
> I'd tramp me in his blood, and smile with joy.

Of course, earlier Eudora tells her mother, "I would not harm the simplest thing on earth!" But she follows this statement with a lengthy speech about how deeply she has been wounded by Sharp, for whom she feels "endless hate"; and she closes with a promise to pursue him to the ends of the earth to make him pay with his life. Her mother replies: "Oh! my child! my child! thou art run mad!" Eudora denies that she is mad, but reminds her mother that "Revenge in woman hath no limitations!"

But a moment later Eudora breaks down and asks her mother to teach her how not to hate. Eudora's mother says: "Thou art distracted—oh! that I were dead!" By such means as these the playwright can have it both ways. The heroine is possibly estranged from her true nature (passive and loving) by reason of insanity. At the same time she is sane but driven by extreme emotions to act out her homicidal plan, which makes for good melodrama.

The key to this solution was provided by Cooke herself (or by the anonymous author of *The Letters*) when Ann says that Beauchamp spoke to her about the cruel treatment she had received from Sharp. "That was a chord that was never struck without producing agony and madness." The single sentence inspired more than one author of the time who was struggling with the problem of making Cooke palatable.

Greyslaer: A Romance of the Mohawk, by Charles Fenno Hoffman, originally published in 1840, is so long and diffuse that one can truthfully say the Kentucky Tragedy is buried in the narrative. Hoffman's novel is devoted more to the theme of America's emerging independence from Great Britain, with an emphasis upon Indian ways and outlaw life along the New York frontier, than it is to the affair of a wronged woman. Nonetheless some of the familiar ingredients are immediately apparent. The seduction of the heroine, Alida de Roos, leaves her scarred, psychologically speaking, for years. After her "fall," her eyes have a "bright and glassy stare," as if to indicate that she lives in a state of shock. She confesses to the hero, Greyslaer, that she is practicing with a pistol in order to avenge herself on someone; at which point Greyslaer says he loves her and would willingly become the agent of her revenge. In this version of the story, as in *Monks of Monk Hall,* the seduction of Cooke-Alida is accomplished by means of a faked marriage ceremony; and the villain undergoes character-splitting, emerging as the German immigrant Voltmeyer and the rejected suitor Bradshawe. When Alida and Greyslaer fall in love, the sentiment has a softening influence: she yields up all thoughts of retribution, and his hunger for revenge grows fainter as he enlarges his circle of acquaintances and meets more sophisticated men and women.

However, when Bradshawe hears that Alida and Greyslaer are contemplating marriage, he circulates the story that Alida has borne a child to an Indian. The slander "unhinges" Greyslaer and he begins to think of nothing but revenge. Eventually he confronts Bradshawe, but they are interrupted by Voltmeyer, whom Greyslaer kills. Arrested for this crime, Greyslaer receives a visit in prison from Alida. She expresses regret that she ever planted the idea of revenge in his mind. He says it was all an "hallucination" of her earlier years. She begs him to give up all thought of harming Bradshawe. (Later Bradshawe is shot and killed in battle.)

Hoffman's intention in *Greyslaer* was clearly to humanize the main characters of the Kentucky Tragedy. Alida's passion for blood is lukewarm most of the time; she is basically the sweet and loving woman of the sentimental tradition. Greyslaer's obsession with vengeance is short-lived and the result of temporary insanity. The author has an obvious affection for both characters; and at the end he has them fall in love, get married and live happily ever after. Like Chivers, Hoffman wants his heroine both ways—sweet and vicious. But instead of accommodating this concept by making Alida insane when she concentrates on murder, he transfers the madness to the hero and has his heroine achieve true feminity through the love of a good man. Still, for all the thought that went into Hoffman's portrayal, Alida remains a flat character, undeveloped and relatively uninteresting. In this work, at least, the author is better at portraying action than character.

The most interesting, fleshed-out depiction of Ann Cooke appears in William Gilmore Simms's novel, *Beauchamp or The Kentucky Tragedy,* published the same year as *Greyslaer.* Beauchamp is introduced as a young attorney who under extreme circumstances is capable of wild behavior. Cooke is sensitive, melancholy and capable of subtle feeling: at first she resists falling in love with Beauchamp because she fears she will use him to fulfill her "dark purpose." As other authors of the period attempted by various means to present a two-sided or ambiguous Ann Cooke—by having her basically loving, with her revenge obsession emerging out of temporary insanity, so Simms makes his heroine a combination of paradoxical traits—strength and weakness. After telling Beauchamp her story and making murder a condition of inti-

macy, she faints. She was "wonderfully strong," says Simms, but she was "yet a woman"—a diagnosis that explains her "sinking to the sward unconscious."

Later, her vengeful impulse becomes softened, as with Hoffman's heroine, under the influence of love; but Simms gives his heroine additional motives that help to round her out. She wants Beauchamp to *avoid* Sharp because she fears the consequences of their actions. In all the treatments of these characters from that period, including the real life models, none express this sort of very likely apprehension about the community's reaction to the murder of a high state official. The usual presentation shows Cooke and Beauchamp relishing the idea of homocide with only faint thoughts, or none at all, about consequences. The way Simm's Cooke is drawn, she qualifies as the most intelligent and the most human of all the portrayals. She is also long-suffering and tolerant, far beyond what one would expect from a knowledge of the original. Simms's Cooke releases Beauchamp from his blood oath and begs him to remain with her in the country, obscure and happy, rather than highly visible in town, where he is bound to confront Sharp.

Toward the conclusion, by a complex twist of the plot, Sharp winds up a houseguest in the Beauchamp home, his crime against Ann concealed from her husband. Sharp renews his attempts at seduction of Ann; he promises to make her husband's fortune, then threatens to tell Beauchamp the truth if Cooke does not yield. Carried away by physical desire, ironically Sharp does not stop to consider what will happen to *him* if he reveals his part in Ann's ruin. Simms is the only author of the period to display the feelings involved in the Kentucky Tragedy in an ironic light.

Simms also portrays Sharp more realistically than the others. In Beauchamp's *Confession,* in the *Letters,* and in fictional or dramatic portrayals, Sharp is an abject coward. In Simm's novel, he is gutsy, sneaky and opportunistic.

The actual homicide is committed by a "maddened" Beauchamp; Cooke has begged him to leave her and avoid risking his life for her. After Beauchamp departs on his mission of murder, Cooke delivers a soliloquy showing her confusion. What good will come of this crime? she asks. But then, thinking of the way Sharp intruded into her home, even at this late stage of their history, she wonders if she will ever be free of his evil presence. Cooke concludes the speech with the idea that it might be best to kill Sharp, after all; and Simms concludes the passage by saying: "the world will not willingly account this madness. It matters not greatly by what name you call a passion which has broken bounds and disdains the right angles of convention." Unmistakably one senses that the highly civilized Simms wishes he could alter the story a la Charles Fenno Hoffman, and spare his heroine the guilt of complicity and the gruesome fate of the real Ann Cooke. Not that Simms creates profound characters in *Beauchamp,* but his Sharp and Cooke are deeper and more lifelike than other depictions of the period.

Poe's Ann Cooke, called Lelage in the verse drama *Politian,* bears little resemblance to her real-life counterpart in the Kentucky Tragedy. Instead of the depressed, melancholy, vindictive and obsessed heroine of the *Letters* and the *Confession,* Lalage is much simpler, less visible, and more pathetic than Cooke or any of her fictional incarnations.

We first hear of her from one of the servants in the home of the Duke di Broglio, Lalage's custodian:

> I saw her yester eve thro' the lattice-work
> Of her chamber-window sobbing upon her knees
> And ever and anon amid her sobs
> She murmured forth Castiglioni's name
> Rupert, she loves him still!

Later, as if to emphasize her sense of what today we call low self-esteem, her servant-girl abuses her, leaving Lalage to bemoan her altered physical appearance and imminent death as a "ruined maid." Today's readers might identify all of these character traits as obvious neuroses, but the nineteenth-century audience found the pathetic heroine appealing. Or was Poe playing psychologist here, consciously endowing Lalage with sick attitudes because he believed Ann Cooke to be unappetizing? We know Poe was not satisfied with *Politian,* that he left if unfinished, and years later in a review of Simm's *Beauchamp* he observed: "Historical truth has somewhat hampered the artist." Poe might have experienced the same difficulty himself, attempting to create a sympathetic heroine from a model he could not admire.

As for Lalage's vengeful feelings and craving for the blood of her seducer—elements that form the foundation of the living story—Poe has a scene where a friendly monk enters Lalage's apartment and asks her to think of her soul and pray. Lalage says she can only think of her present misery. When the holy man offers her a crucifix, she draws a dagger and holds it high by the blade. "Behold the cross wherewith a vow like mine / Is written in Heaven!" she cries, adding that the deed, the vow, and the symbol of the deed should tally. Thus Poe preserves the essential character element of vengeful feeling, but reduces it to an oblique reference and a metaphorical gesture. Still later, in Scene VII, after Politian has declared his love for Lalage and she has revealed to him the cause of her anguish, he begs her to come away with him to America. Lalage replies: "A deed is to be done—Castiglioni lives!" To which Politian says "And he shall die!" Then he exits in a rage.

The speech that follows is extremely revealing of Poe's attitude toward his heroine. Although Lalage displays none of the fury of Ann Cooke, she has stipulated that Politian avenge the wrong she has suffered by killing Castiglioni. The fact that the promise is exacted offstage is itself significant, for it spares the audience a view of the vicious original while adhering to the basic story line. Furthermore, as soon as Politian exits on his homicidal mission, Lalage immediately regrets their compact. She calls out,

> Thou art gone—thou art not gone, Politian!
> I feel thou art not gone—yet dare not look,
> Lest I behold thee not; thou couldst not go
> With those words upon thy lips. . . .

Next, after showing Lalage as a tender and regretful, nonviolent version of Cooke, Poe has her conclude the speech with something of Cooke's resolution:

> Gone—gone [referring to Politian]
> Where am I? 'tis well—'tis very well!
> So that the blade be keen—the blow be sure—
> 'Tis well, 'tis very well—alas! alas!

The final exclamations reverse the image of the heroine yet again, so that the audience might conclude that Lalage is a) in a distracted, deeply confused state of mind or b) at the mercy of forces she can not control, even though she is an active participant in and inspirer of the events that now overwhelm her.

At the conclusion, when it is clear that Politian is planning to murder Castiglioni while his marriage ceremony is in progress, Lalage cries, "Farewell, Castiglioni, and farewell my hope in heaven."

All these details of presentation—from Lelage's introduction into the drama singing sweet and mournful tunes, to her suffering abuse from her servant, to her eliciting the fateful pledge from Politian offstage, to her swearing an oath the content of which is left unspecified, to her terrible confusion when Politian goes off to avenge her, to her obvious repentance at the conclusion—accumulate to create a much softened, pathetic, vulnerable and humanized Ann Cooke. Poe's attitude toward women as ethereal, as evidenced in such early poems as "Al Aaraaf" and "To Helen," might explain his reluctance to deal with the ugly aspects of the Kentucky Tragedy, while his concern over audience reaction to his work might also have played a part in the Lalage characterization.

Of all the treatments of Cooke considered here, Lippard's is the most innocent and at the same time the most insipid. Chivers's is the most bloodthirsty, but this is mitigated (in **Conrad and Eudora**) by the possibility that she is mad. Hoffman's portrayal is the most sentimental and nonthreatening; Simm's is the most intelligent, rounded, and interesting, while Poe's is unquestionably the most pathetic.

FURTHER READING

Bell, Landon, C. *Poe and Chivers.* Columbus: Trowbridge, 1931, 101 p.

> Faults S. Foster Damon for his praise of Chivers in *Thomas Holley Chivers: Friend of Poe* (1930).

Benton, Joel. "The Poe-Chivers Controversy," and "Thomas Holley Chivers." In *In the Poe Circle,* pp. 31-53, 61-8. New York: M. F. Mansfield & A. Wessels, 1899.

Summarizes the Poe-Chivers plagiarism controversy and provides an account of the relationship between the two poets.

Lombard, Charles. Introduction to *Search after Truth, The Lost Pleiad, and Atlanta,* by Thomas Holley Chivers. Delmar, N.Y.: Scholars' Facsimiles & Reprints, 1976, pp. v-xiii.

Offers a brief summary and analysis of the three works.

————. Introduction to *Conrad and Eudora (1834) and Birth-Day Song of Liberty (1856)* by Thomas Holley Chivers. Delmar, N.Y.: Scholars' Facsimiles & Reprints, 1978, pp. v-xii.

Discusses the details of the Beauchamp-Sharpe murder case upon which *Conrad and Eudora* is based and provides a brief summary and analysis of the two works.

————. *Thomas Holley Chivers.* Twayne's United States Authors Series, edited by Lewis Leary. Boston: Twayne Publishers, 1979, 148 p.

Provides extensive biographical information, analyses of Chivers's major works, and discussion of the Chivers-Poe controversy.

————. Introduction to *The Unpublished Plays of Thomas Holley Chivers.* Delmar, N.Y.: Scholars' Facsimiles & Reprints, 1980, pp. v-xxvii.

Provides a detailed discussion of Chivers's unpublished plays, including *Count Julian, Osceola, Charles Stuart,* and *Leoni.*

William Cobbett

1763-1835

English journalist and essayist.

INTRODUCTION

Cobbett was a leading advocate of parliamentary reform in the quarter century before the Reform Bill of 1832. A lifelong advocate of social justice for England's rural poor and a defender of freedom of the press, he sought to break the power of the ruling oligarchy of politics and business to restore what he perceived as an earlier, better England. Superficially radical and profoundly conservative, Cobbett despised political parties and industrialism, championing an ideal of the common people. He crafted a distinctly vigorous, biting prose style, which characterizes both his voluminous journalism and the two works considered his most distinguished, *Rural Rides* (1830) and *Advice to Young Men* (1831).

Biographical Information

Cobbett was born into an innkeeper's family in Farnham, Surrey. He had little formal education and left home at age 20, working as a clerk and then becoming a soldier. Assigned to work as a copyist for a garrison commandant, Cobbett was compelled to improve his writing and grammatical skills. He read and reread Robert Lowth's eight-volume *Short Introduction to English Grammar* (1762) until he had memorized it. While in the military, he witnessed and documented numerous cases of abuse and corruption in his unit; discharged with the rank of sergeant-major in 1791, Cobbett filed complaints against the government for the misdeeds he had seen. When a hearing was eventually scheduled on his charges, Cobbett left the country, convinced that he had no chance of winning his case. He lived in France for a year, then fled to America as the prospect loomed of war between France and Britain. In America, Cobbett established himself as a journalist, living in Philadelphia and publishing a daily journal, *Porcupine's Gazette,* under the pseudonym Peter Porcupine. Returning to England in 1800, he opened a bookshop and founded the most acclaimed of the fourteen or more periodicals he started during his lifetime, *Cobbett's Weekly Political Register,* which he published until his death. Initially Cobbett devoted the *Political Register* and his other pamphleteering to support of the government against "Jacobinism" at home and French imperialism abroad. Gradually, though, he came to believe that the real enemy of the English common people, with whom Cobbett identified, was not France but Prime Minister William Pitt's financial system of paper money, stock jobbing, taxation, placement, and sinecurists. He formed the conviction that there were no true political

parties in England, only coalitions of selfish men bent on plunder and power. Opposing this system, Cobbett adapted to the revolutionary world of 1800 many of the notions of a Tory squire of 1700, becoming a leader of industrial, working-class radicalism. His writings called for reform of English laws to make life more amenable for working-class families, especially farmers, whose livlihood was threatened by the growth of industrialization. In early 1817, largely in an effort to stifle Cobbett, Parliament passed the Power of Imprisonment Bill, which made it easier to successfully prosecute seditious writing and allowed the suspension of habeas corpus. Cobbett retreated to America, where he leased a farm on Long Island for two years. During this time he continued publishing the *Register* and wrote his *Grammar of the English Language* (1818) and *A Year's Residence in the United States of America* (1818). Cobbett returned to England in late 1819; two years later he took the first of his "rural rides," travelling by horseback throughout southern England to observe and report on the condition of the poor and to speak on parliamentary reform. He harangued for reform for the rest of his life, eventually seeing a degree of progress when Parliament passed the moderate Reform Bill of 1832, which made for fairer parliamentary representation among the laboring centers of England and extended the franchise to the propertied middle class. Cobbett was himself elected to Parliament within a year of the Reform Bill's passage, but was not an effective representative: he refused to master the rules of the House of Commons, was rude to his opponents during debates, and had difficulty adjusting to Parliament's nocturnal schedule. During his last years, and in declining health, he divided his time between London and his farm in Surrey, where he died of influenza at age seventy-two.

Major Works

Cobbett's effectiveness lay less in his theories about paper money, electoral reform, or whatever, than in his creation of a mythical, but not insubstantial, lost Eden of old rural England. Cobbett glorified agricultural labor in its hardihood, innocence, and usefulness—and by its associations with patriotism, morality, and the beauties of nature. Cobbett exaggerated the material comforts of laborers in Old England, but he did not exaggerate the beauty of the man-made (yet natural) landscape where they worked and the decency of a life regulated by the cycle of the seasons rather than the steam engine. Cobbett's readers may have been mostly in the industrial towns, but many of them had only recently abandoned an agricultural way of life. Cobbett kept alive in the consciousness of urban workers a folk memory of rural beauty and seemliness, and an allied sense of lost rights in the land. On this theme, his *Rural Rides* (1830) has proved his most enduring work. It is a collection of journals written during his tours on horseback between 1822 and 1826, observing rural conditions and discussing the political perceptions of the agricultural community. Another enduring work is his *Advice to Young Men* (1829-1830). While not primarily political, in this work Cobbett counters the denunciations of his character by government officials and churchmen, providing a self-portrait demonstrating all the benefits of industry, sobriety, independence, and thrift. Cobbett also involved himself in the struggle for Roman Catholic emancipation; to that end he wrote his best-selling *A History of the Protestant "Reformation" in England and Ireland* (1824-1826). His theme is that the Reformation was not an act of purification but one of bloody devastation, a fraud "engendered in lust and brought forth in hypocrisy and perfidy," which had engendered more and more monstrous "reformations" in the shape of Oliver Cromwell's Commonwealth and the "Glorious Revolution," which had brought into being the national debt and all present woe. Here as in his other books, an ideal pre-Reformation England is contrasted to a miserable present reality.

Critical Reception

Much of what Cobbett wrote was ephemeral, addressing small but important events of his own era. Despised by business and political leaders during his lifetime, he was recognized by even those critics who opposed his ideas as the writer of vigorous, effective, clear prose, what William Hazlitt called "plain, broad, downright English,"

without artifice. With the triumph of large-scale industrialism and the decline of agricultural small-holding, much of what Cobbett wrote has been deemed dated and at best quaint, despite the passage of successive labor reforms in England for which he was undeniably a major if indirect source. Much criticism today focuses on *Rural Rides*, a work which is seen as a pleasant and appealing portrait of both the author and of a homely, rural England which is, for the most part, no more.

PRINCIPAL WORKS

Observation on the Emigration of Dr. Joseph Priestley and on the Several Addresses Delivered to Him on His Arrival at New York (essay) 1794

Le tuteur anglais, ou grammaire régulière de la langue anglaise (grammar) 1795

The Life and Adventures of Peter Porcupine (autobiography) 1796

Porcupine's Gazette and United States Daily Advertiser (journal) 1797-1800

The Rush-Light (journal) 1800

Porcupine's Works. 12 vols. (pamphlets) 1801

Cobbett's Weekly Political Register. 89 vols. (journal) 1802-35

A Grammar of the English Language (grammar) 1818

A Journal of a Year's Residence in the United States. 3 vols. (journal) 1818-19

The American Gardener (nonfiction) 1821

Cobbett's Sermons (sermons) 1821-22

Cottage Economy: Containing Information Relating to the Brewing of Beer, Making of Bread, Keeping of Cows . . . (treatise) 1822

A History of the Prostestant "Reformation" in England and Ireland. 2 vols. (history) 1824-27

Cobbett's Poor Man's Friend (journal) 1826-27

The Woodlands; or, A Treatise on the Preparation of the Ground for Planting (treatise) 1828

The English Gardener (nonfiction) 1829

Rural Rides in the Counties of Surrey, Kent, Sussex, Hampshire, Wiltshire, Gloucestershire, Herefordshire, Worcestershire, Somersetshire, Oxfordshire, Berkshire, Essex, Suffolk, Norfolk, and Hertfordshire (essay) 1830

Advice to Young Men and (Incidentally) to Young Women (essay) 1831

Cobbett's Twopenny Trash (journal) 1830-32

Life of Andrew Jackson (biography) 1834

Selections from Cobbett's Political Works. 6 vols. (essays and treatises) 1835-37

CRITICISM

Francis Jeffrey (review date 1807)

SOURCE: A review of *Cobbett's Political Register,* in *The Edinburgh Review,* Vol. X, No. 20, July, 1807, pp. 386-421.

[*Jeffrey was a founder and editor of the* Edinburgh Review, *one of the most influential nineteenth-century British magazines. A liberal Whig, he often allowed his political beliefs to color his critical opinions. In the following excerpt, Jeffrey writes of Cobbett as a political opportunist who overstates the issue of corruption in British politics.*]

We are induced to take some notice of [*Cobbett's Political Register*] because we are persuaded that it has more influence with that most important and most independent class of society, which stands just above the lowest, than was ever possessed before by any similar publication. Its circulation and its popularity are, we think, upon the whole, very creditable to the country. It is written with great freedom, and often with great force of argument. It flatters few national prejudices—except our love of detraction and abuse; and has often had the merit of maintaining bold truths, both against the party in power, and the prevailing sentiments of the nation. It consists, in general, of solid argument and copious detail; with little relief of general declamation, and no attraction of playfulness. It is a good sign of a people, we think, when a work of this description is generally read and studied among them. It can only be acceptable to men of some vigour of intellect, and some independence of principle; and it was, upon the whole, with feelings of pride and satisfaction, that we learned the extent of its circulation among the middling classes of the community, and the great superiority of its influence over that of the timid and venal prints, which subsist by flattering the prejudices of a party, or of the nation at large.

The author's original anti-Jacobinism was, like all other anti-Jacobinism after 1800, extravagant, scurrilous, and revolting. But this died away; and, for the three or four last years, till very lately, his influence, we believe, has been rather salutary, and we have been well pleased that such a journal should be in existence. Disgusted as we have often been with his arrogance; irritated by his coarse and clamorous abuse; and wearied with the needless vehemence and disproportioned fury with which he frequently descanted on trifles, we could still admire his intrepidity, and respect his force of understanding; and were glad to have a journal in which salutary truths could be strongly spoken, and which might serve as a vehicle for independent sentiments, and a record of necessary, but unpopular accusations. With this general impression, we could easily make allowance for the excesses into which the author was habitually betrayed, either by the defects of his education, or by his known political partialities; and after setting aside his raving about the funds and the committee at Lloyd's—his trash about the learned languages—and his ignorant scurrility about Mr Malthus—we had still some toleration in store for his zeal for the Bourbons, his horror at revolutions, and his jealousy of the democratical part of our constitution.

Within the last six months, however, he has undergone a most extraordinary and portentous transformation. Instead of the champion of establishment, of loyalty, and eternal war with all revolutionary agency, he has become the patron of reform and reformers; talks hopefully of revolutions; scoffingly of Parliament; and cavalierly of the Sovereign; and declaims upon the state of the representation, and on the iniquities of placemen and pensioners, in the very phrases which have been for some time laid aside by those whom he used to call levellers and Jacobins.

The inconsistencies and apostasies of a common journalist, certainly are neither so rare nor of such importance as to deserve any notice from us. But Mr Cobbett is not quite a common journalist; and his case is somewhat peculiar. He has more influence, we believe, than all the other journalists put together; and that influence is still maintained, in a good degree, by the force of his personal character. He holds a high tone of patriotism and independence; he puts his name to all his publications; and manfully invites all who dissent from his opinions, to meet him in the fair field of public disputation. Another peculiarity in Mr Cobbett's case is, that he still stoutly asserts his consistency; and maintains, that with a very moderate allowance for the exaggerations of a disputant, and for actual changes in the position of our affairs, the doctrines which he now promulgates are the same which he has held and expressed from the beginning. He has neither professed to be converted like Mr Redhead Yorke, nor attempted to sneak silently to the other side like the herd of venal pamphleteers. Though our quarrel with him, therefore, be entirely on the score of the tendency of his later productions, the question of their consistency or inconsistency with his former professions is by no means indifferent to the issue. There are many who believe in him, partly at least, on account of the sturdy honesty to which he lays claim, and the tone of confidence with which he predicts what is to come, and pretends to have predicted whatever has actually occurred; and there are few, perhaps, of those who have received any impression from his writings, whose faith in his reasonings would not be diminished by a conviction of the inconsistency or versatility of his successive opinions, or a suspicion of the share that passion or party may have had in their formation. It is not, therefore, from any paltry or vindictive motive, but for the purpose of reducing his *authority* to its just standard, that we think it necessary, before entering upon the examination of his late doctrines, to make a few remarks on his title to the praise of consistency, and to exhibit some instances of what has certainly appeared to us as the most glaring and outrageous contradiction.

The first thing that would strike any one who had only known Mr Cobbett as the author of the *Porcupine,* and the earlier volumes of the *Political Register,* on looking into any of his later numbers, would be the terms of high and unmeasured praise with which he speaks of the political principles and proceedings of Sir Francis Burdett. We were perfectly certain, that these same principles had formerly been the object of his most furious reprobation, and had an obscure recollection that the worthy Baronet himself had occasionally been subjected to the discipline of his pen. . . .

Now, what is it that we infer from this strange alternation of praise and blame in the pages of Mr Cobbett? Why, that nobody should care much for either; that they are bestowed from passion or party prejudice, and not from any sound principles of judgement; and that it must be the most foolish of all things to take our impressions of the merit of any individual, from a man whose own opinions have not only varied, but been absolutely reversed, within these four years. The consideration of this versatility in Mr Cobbett's likings and dislikings, has, we will confess, been a considerable encouragement to us in the task of reviewing his lucubrations. When we first felt it to be our duty to point out the pernicious parts of his tenets, we were a little appalled by the prospect of the weekly abuse with which we lay our account with being rewarded; but when we discovered in the course of our reading, how kindly he repays the victims of his occasional reprobation, we grew quite easy upon that subject;—satisfied that, if he should abuse us for a month or two to come, he will make us ample amends in the long-run, and end by being the most devoted of our admirers. . . .

The points upon which Mr Cobbett has descanted with the greatest zeal and animation for the last four months, are, 1st, The necessity of a reform in the representation: 2d, The benefit of frequent elections; and, 3d, The necessity of removing all placemen, as well as pensioners, from the houses of Parliament. . . .

Mr Cobbett's great modern theme, however, is his detestation of placemen and pensioners; and the leading argument—if we must call it argument—of his late Numbers, is directed to show, that there can be no salvation for England till every individual of this hateful description be excluded from the Houses of Parliament. This, so far as we can gather, is the sum and substance, the beginning and end of the reform by which alone we can be saved from destruction. We are wearied now of turning over the close-printed pages of his former Numbers for doctrines exactly opposed to this. We are very much mistaken, however, if they are not to be found there; and are perfectly positive that no hints of this new creed are to be met with in any writing of his published so long as two years ago. This, of itself, is quite decisive as to the state of his former opinions. Placemen and pensioners have sat in Parliament for upwards of a hundred years; and yet Mr Cobbett had been ten years a patriotic journalist in this country, before he found it necessary to say one word against this dreadful abuse. He will scarcely pretend that there are more placemen now in Parliament than there were three years ago; and if their existence there be now so mortal to the constitution that nothing short of their total expulsion can give us a chance for its preservation, it surely must have been his duty to have proposed such a measure before Sir Francis Burdett put it into his famous address to the Electors of Middlesex. The merits of the doctrine itself we shall consider immediately. We are now speaking only of Mr Cobbett's consistency in insisting on it as obviously indispensable to our salvation. We have just fallen by accident upon the following passage, in an abusive letter to Mr Wilberforce in December 1802, in which the propriety and legality of placemen sitting in Parliament seems to be pretty clearly taken for granted. Discoursing of Parliamentary disinterestedness, he says—

Though present experience teaches us that some men certainly wish for office, to gratify their own covetousness and vanity; there are others, and, I trust, *a far greater number,* who, in their pursuit of power, are actuated by the noble motive of advancing the power and happiness of their Sovereign and their country. That considerations of a private nature,—the desire of posthumous, and even of present fame, may mix themselves along with this great leading public motive, I allow:—But, Sir, I defy you to show me, in the conduct of a *placeman* of this description, any presumption that he has made the choice of his *electors* subservient to his own interest or aggrandisement, which will not apply with equal, or with greater, force to yourself, &c.

There is only one other subject, we think, upon which Mr Cobbett used formerly to enlarge with such frequency and zeal as to make it one of the fair characteristics of his peculiar opinions; we mean his ardent love and veneration for the person and family of the Sovereign, and for royalty indeed in general. In his earlier volumes, there is much fulsome cant and disgusting raving of this sort; but since he has embraced the creed of Sir Francis Burdett, this fine spirit of devoted loyalty seems to be pretty well evaporated. In his number for 24th March 1807, he defends the toast of 'our Sovereign the people,' given at one of the worthy Baronet's dinners, and says, he has no other objection to it than that 'it is not of plain unequivocal meaning.' He treats with considerable derision a loyal correspondent, who had said, he trusted every true Englishman would shed the last drop of his blood in support of his King;—tells him the King has about 200,000 gentlemen in red and blue jackets whose business it is to support him, and that he is able to take care of himself;—and that such views of devotion may be reasonable and manly when we see the King giving up any point whatever, however loudly called for, or from whatever quarter. After this he proceeds to justify the party at the said dinner for omitting to drink the King's health;—contends that this is merely a voluntary expression of admiration of his conduct,—and that, for his own part, since the introduction of so many Hanoverian soldiers, the exemption of the King's property from the income-tax, and one or two other suspicious things of the same description, he has not felt quite so much of that admiration, and does not choose voluntarily to come forward with expressions of that sentiment, &c. Is it too much to say, that the zealous advocate of the Bourbons, and of all their connexions, might have been expected to speak of the sons of his own Sovereign in terms of less contempt and acrimony? His observations on the Dukes of York and Clarence, though we had no great objection to their substance, are certainly too much in the style of the professed enemies of royalty.

We have dwelt on this subject too long; but we conceive that the charge of inconsistency is made out completely: and though we do not by any means marvel, as Mr Cobbett is moved to do on a similar occasion, 'how a man can hold up his head, or even exist, under the proof of such glaring tergiversation,' we do think ourselves entitled to say, that the proof which we have now detailed should disable his judgement, and detract from his authority, upon all the subjects to which that proof is applicable. Whatever influence or reputation he may have acquired by his earlier writings, should operate against the doctrines which he is now employed in promulgating; and all the effect which his arguments have produced on his admirers, should turn to the prejudice of the maxims to which he now requires their assent. A man who had never been zealous for his party or his opinions, may desert them without much reproach; but it must always be an awkward evolution for one who had been distinguished for confidence and clamour, and who has no sooner made the transition, than he renews the violence and abuse which he had formerly exerted on the opposite side. By the uncharitable, such a man will always be regarded as a professional bully, without principle or sincerity,—whose services may be bought by any one who will pay their price to his avarice or other passions;—and the most liberal must consider him as a person without any steadiness or depth of judgement;—accustomed to be led away by hasty views and occasional impressions;—entitled to no weight or authority in questions of delicacy or importance; and likely to be found in arms against his old associates on every material change in his own condition, or that of the country.

The only important question, however, as we have more than once intimated already, is not whether Mr Cobbett's recent doctrines are reconcileable to those which he formerly maintained, but whether they are reconcileable to truth and to the interests of the country. It is only with his recent doctrines,—the current series of his opinions—that we have any interest or concern;—his earlier volumes are beyond our reach;—they have done their work of mischief or utility, and passed away;—and the effect which they have produced, can no longer be either enforced or counteracted. He has been busied, however, for some months past, in a task which is not yet finished, and is still in the act of enforcing certain positions, the general adoption or rejection of which, may produce, as it appears to us, very important effects on the interests and happiness of the whole community. It is not too late, therefore, to inquire, whether those effects are likely to be pernicious or salutary,—to detect what is deleterious in the nostrum that is just handing out among the multitude,—and to exhibit an antidote to the poison, of which the doses are at this moment making up.

We have not the slightest hesitation in saying, that the doctrines maintained by Mr Cobbett, for the last four months, and especially since he has espoused the cause of Sir Francis Burdett, are in the highest degree pernicious and reprehensible; and that it is solely for the purpose of exposing and discrediting them, that we have been induced to enter upon our present irksome task. The sum and substance of our objections to the recent numbers of the *Political Register,* is, that they are all obviously intended to beget a distrust and contempt of every individual connected with public life, except only Sir Francis Burdett and his adherents,—to spread abroad a general discontent and disrespect for the constitution, usages, principles and proceedings of Parliament,—to communicate a very exaggerated and unfair impression of the evils, abuses and inconveniences, which arise from the present system of government,—and to hold out the absolute impossibility of correcting or amending these, without some great internal change of the nature of a political revolution. Under the present system, Mr Cobbett maintains, that our only rational feelings, are contempt and detestation of our rulers, and despair of any relief or improvement, except by its total subversion; and with this impression, it will easily be understood, that he looks forward to a revolution, not only without sadness, or dismay, but with a kind of vindictive eagerness and delight. He foretells it with much confidence and complacency; and does his utmost, we may say, to accomplish his own prediction. The natural conclusion from all this is, that a state of things, so miserable and so desperate, is not worth contending for; and that foreign conquest would not be so very great an evil as our rulers would fain persuade us to imagine. We do not say, that Mr Cobbett directly draws this last conclusion; but it seems to follow inevitably from his premises; and he does make use of expressions, which satisfy us that he has had it in contemplation, without being much appalled or startled at its aspect. . . .

We have but a word or two to say on the subject of venal boroughs, and we shall take our leave of Mr Cobbett, and relieve our readers from this unreasonable demand on their attention. We [say] that a man who takes a bribe is despicable, and that the man who offers it is in some measure dishonoured. We leave the individuals, therefore, who are concerned in this traffic, to the indignation of Mr Cobbett, without any qualification. But we are by no means certain that its consequences are so extremely injurious to the constitution as he appears to imagine. A venal borough is a borough which Government has not bought; and which may therefore be bought by Mr Cobbett, or any other independent man. When a seat in Parliament is advertized for sale, a pretty fair competition, we think, is opened to politicians of all descriptions. The independent and well-affected part of the nation is far richer than the government, or the peerage; and if all seats in parliament could be honestly and openly sold for ready money, we have no sort of doubt that a very great majority would be purchased by persons unconnected with the Treasury, or the House of Lords. Wealth is one of the *democratical* elements in this trading and opulent country; and an arrangement which gave it more immediate political efficacy, probably would not be at all unfavourable to that part of our constitution.

The great objection, on the other hand, is, that no honourable man will purchase a seat, and that those who do pay money for one, may be presumed to intend to make money by it, and to sell themselves the first good opportunity. The first observation sounds plausible; and yet every body knows it not to be true. There certainly are many men whose private honour is unimpeachable, who sit for venal boroughs. How this is managed we do not exactly know. Whether the end is thought to sanctify the means, or whether the frequency of the transaction has legalized it in the ideas of the world, like the orchard thefts of schoolboys, and the plunder of Border chieftains of old;—or whether the seat is bought *for* the young patriot, as the living is bought for the young priest, while they themselves are kept pure from the stain of bribery or simony—we really do not pretend to understand. With regard to the other conclusion, that when the seat is bought, the sitter must mean to be sold,—it is as certainly at variance with fact, and has a smaller share of probability. The most moderate contest will generally cost more than the dearest borough in the market; and as, in trying times, contests will be very frequent, it must be the most economical and prudent way for a patriotic party to provide for as many as they can by purchase, before they try the more costly and honourable road of open competition. On the whole, however, we have no great affection for rotten boroughs; but chiefly, because we think that the practice of purchasing them tends to abate the love of liberty, and the pride of independence among the people; and that it is to their feelings, and not to the composition of the Legislature, that we must always look for the fountain and vital spring of our freedom.

Upon the whole, we hope we have said something to justify our love of our actual constitution—our aversion to Mr Cobbett's scheme of reform—and our indignation at his attempts to weaken the respect and attachment of the people to forms and establishments, without which, we are persuaded, there would be no security for their freedom. To some among the higher classes of our readers, an apology may appear to be requisite for the time and attention we have bestowed on a writer of this description. The higher orders of society, however, we are afraid, are but little aware, either of the great influence which such a writer possesses, or of the extent to which many of his sentiments prevail among the middling classes of the community. In his contempt for the Legislature, and his despair of public virtue or energy, Mr Cobbett, we believe, has rather followed than fashioned the impressions of those for whom his publications are intended. *There is* a very general spirit of discontent, distrust, and contempt for public characters, among the more intelligent and resolute portion of the inferior ranks of society. We can see, as well as Mr Cobbett, the seeds of a revolution in the present aspect and temper of the nation; and though we look forward to it, we trust, with other feelings and other dispositions, we are not the less sensible of the hazard in which we are placed. We anticipate little from such an event, but general degradation and misery; we have stepped beyond the limits of our duty, to express our horror at the suggestion; and have contributed our feeble aid to rouse or to undeceive those who may have been misled by different anticipations. At the same time, we cannot be blind to the tendency of public opinion; and are afraid that, in the event of any great emergency or disaster, no reasonings, and no motives of prudence, will be sufficient to uphold the established forms of the constitution, unless some effort be made on the part of public men to wipe off the imputations which are now thrown upon their characters,—to show that, in a great crisis, they can forget party, and prejudice, and self-interest,—and that they have either talents to form plans adequate to the emergency, and resolution to carry them into execution,—or magnanimity to retire from a situa-tion, to the duties of which they are unequal, and to give place to those, upon whose firmness, and prudence, and talents, the nation can rely with assurance. We do not think that this would be done, by making Sir Francis Burdett first Lord of the Treasury, and Mr Horne Tooke secretary for the Home Department. But much must be done,—and more desisted from,—before they and their advocates are disarmed of their most effectual means of delusion.

Leigh Hunt   (essay date 1820)

SOURCE: "Mr. Cobbett, and What is Wanted in Parliament," in *Leigh Hunt's Political and Occasional Essays,* edited by Lawrence Huston Houtchens and Carolyn Washburn Houtchens, Columbia University Press, 1962, pp. 228-35.

[*An English poet and essayist, Hunt as literary critic encouraged and influenced several Romantic poets, especially John Keats and Percy Bysshe Shelley. Hunt was a cofounder of the weekly liberal newspaper the* Examiner. *In the following excerpt from an essay originally published in the* Examiner *in 1820, Hunt proclaims the salutary effect of Cobbett's pending election to Parliament.*]

There are things in Mr. Cobbett which are not to our "fastidious" taste; but we should like much to see him in Parliament. His interests, small as well as great, are those of the age; and he has sense enough to perceive it. Then he has a considerable knowledge of statistics; he speaks as he writes, a good clear idiomatic style; he is quick at detecting such absurdities as ministerial men commit; he is healthy, active, and zealous; he has had experience of several conditions of life; and lastly, he has risen, not merely from the people, but from their very poorest ranks, and is therefore a striking specimen of that intellectual power, and that ascendancy of opinion and acquirement, which has come up in these latter times to confront and pull down the otherwise victorious assumptions of brute authority.

There has been a great talk of grenades, and of the confusion which their explosion would have made among the Members of Government. But of all implements to be pitched among a set of Ministers, and to confuse and scatter their faculties, commend us to the Cobbett. Neither grenade from Cato-street, nor shell from Copenhagen, no, nor even Infernal Machine from Paris, could carry such inevitable worry and horror among the Treasury benches, as the appearance of this blowing-up figure. How genteelly would the slender mightiness of my Lord Castlereagh recoil! What would be the petty perturbutions of Mr. Vansittart! What the queer consciousness of Mr. Croker! What the affected indifference of the counter orb of Mr. Canning! Think also of the sidelong glances of Mr. Tierney; of the solemn expectations of the country gentlemen; of the careless pride and perplexity of the young politicians; of the proud but scrambling resort of the young members in general to their university common-places; and last but not least, of the disjointed and whiffling confidence of that old babe of grace, Mr. Wilberforce.

But here some creature of parliamentary habit may exclaim, "Cobbett! What can *he* do? He, who has no parliamentary influence, no connexions, no money, no tactics? He may speak occasionally; but who will listen?"

The People.

The country is in great want of such a Member of Parliament as Cobbett; of one who has none of the usual drawbacks arising from place, or pension, or titled connexions, or the indolent possession of wealth, or the interchange of endearments in St. James's-street, or a hundred other "delicacies," which do and must "awe a man from the career of his humour." When he shall think of any plan that may benefit his country, he will have no need to consider what Tomkins will say to it. He need not waive inquiring into this or that matter, out of deference to Blenkinsop. There will not be infinite things to be concealed and dallied with between him and the consciences of office. If ever he should be in the humour to coalesce with the corrupt, he is not a man to be coalesced with. Power and privilege will do every thing they can, rather than let in among them the plebeian faculty,—the mere untitled, and unprivileged, and unpolite, and uninheriting possession of intellect. It has been said that all classes of mental, as well as pecuniary property, find their representatives in the House of Commons. It is a saying as false as an allied monarch. Its object is to smooth down the popular intellect, and to pretend that its rights are not only recognized, but taken care of; whereas the popular intellect, taking such a man as Cobbett for its representative has never yet made its way into that House. Neither the popular, nor, if we are to believe the strange warning of a Noble and accomplished Member of the other House, the unpopular intellect, has yet found its representative in Parliament; for as there has never yet been a Member to lay the same zealous and sympathetic stress on the claims and knowledge of the poorer orders, while there are hundreds to take infinite care of all the rest, so there was not a man in Parliament the other day, who in this denounced age of infidelity, ventured a syllable in behalf of an honest want of religious faith. We once heard an eminent Counsel say before the Lord Chancellor, and without any one's thinking of contradicting him, though he had opponents enough,—that Deism, or the belief in a God separated from any other faith, was notoriously the religion of almost all the literati of Europe. Has the literary religion of Europe then a representative in the House of Commons? Yes; many in secret; but what is a secret representative? What would secret representatives of Protestantism have done for the growth of religious liberty, if they had contented themselves with keeping their testimonies to their own book-cases, and continued to vote with Popery? So much for the "unpopular" intellect. The popular, we fear, has not even this kind of coy image, afraid of beholding too much sincerity in its looking-glass. Doubtless, besides Whigs and Tories, there are members who are neither Whig nor Tory; at least, who go all lengths with neither, and who sometimes say and do very useful and very popular things. We admire those sayings and those deeds accordingly; especially when we consider all the habits and other temptations which might have prevented them. These are men also extremely useful and respectable, even as a class by themselves. Neither do we mean to assert here, that a proper quantum of Toryism may not have its representative, with advantage to existing institutions. It has plenty at all events;—a great deal too many. But what the country wants in Parliament, is men who can come forward and state plainly, without any reserve whatsoever, the very same arguments and feelings which occupy the enlightened part of the poorer orders; men, who have been of that class themselves; who have acquired knowledge enough of their own to see beyond the superficial assumption of others, and to denounce them; who will not be content with saving the reputation of their better wits by hinting a joke at Lord Castlereagh, but will get up and say plainly, that he is a very shallow person, and prove him so in good round terms and logic,—who will discuss an income tax without mere reference to the purses present;—who will handle a corn bill, not with tenderness to the value of the sheaves, but to the wants of the people's pockets and stomachs;— who will take a leading part in questions of finance, and not suffer them to be lorded over by placemen and ex-placemen; who will regard the heavy assumptions of Grenvilles, and the genteeler fopperies of Castlereaghs, and the Tory-propping opposition of mere Whigs, and the shambling independence of Saints, as a heap of impertinence which it becomes the age to leave behind it:—in short, who will not merely declaim once and away on the subject of Reform, but talk of it, and urge it without ceasing; who will tell us all plainly what he means by it, and what we have a right to possess; and who will expose all the contented and contenting sophistry, the nonsense, solemn or smiling, the round-about stuff, bad grammar, and mincing parliamentary cant of those, whose corruptions are "as notorious as the sun at noon-day."

If Mr. Brougham, a Whig by connexion, a lawyer by education, and a patrician by birth, is nevertheless a most liberal representative of law and jurisprudence, especially in those noble toils of his for the schools;—if Sir Francis Burdett, considering his wealth, rank, and propensity to enjoyment, deserves the praise and gratitude of his country for being so good a representative of the independent English gentlemen; and if Mr. Hobhouse would make a good, indignant representative of the more intelligent and independent part of the younger men of the same class, disgusted at seeing the affairs of the world lorded over by their inferiors; still there wants somebody to speak the sense and feelings of the largest and most important class of the community, who are the pith of the body politic, and without a perfect understanding of whose rights and feelings, it may still turn to a mass of corruption.

Now, we know of no man, whose experience, whose interest, and whose acquirements, point him out as a fitter person to be such a representative than Mr. Cobbett; and therefore we cordially wish to see him in his place. We are the more anxious to see him there, because, whatever the House may in the first instance affect to think him, we are persuaded that no man will supply a more desirable share of the Parliamentary Reports; and our anxiety is increased by a supposition which seems prevalent, that the general returns to Parliament will be favourable to Ministers. And why will they be so? Because corruption, after provoking violence, is enabled to take advantage of its misdeeds by the hypocritical fears of the *expedient* and *accommodating*. These alleged conspirators in Cato-street would no doubt have done something for the corruptions which provoked them, out of the mere blindness and stupidity of those who cannot see the provocation; but the timidity, which leads people to blink the real question, and to answer to the menacing and impudent call of the corrupt upon all "loyal and honest men" for their denouncement of assassination, will do infinitely more. Fear and insincerity are always thus hindering the progress of knowledge and justice: and therefore, for our parts, nothing upon earth shall induce us to truckle to either.

William Hazlitt (essay date 1821)

SOURCE: "Character of Cobbett," in *The College Book of Essays,* edited by John Abbott Clark, Henry Holt and Company, 1939, pp. 517-28.

[*One of the most important commentators of the Romantic age, Hazlitt was an English critic and journalist. He is best known for his descriptive criticism in which he stressed that no motives beyond judgment and analysis are necessary on the part of the critic. In the following essay, originally written in 1821, Hazlitt examines Cobbett's character as reflected in his writings, offering numerous illustrations.*]

People have about as substantial an idea of Cobbett as they have of Cribb. His blows are as hard, and he himself is as impenetrable. One has no notion of him as making use of a fine pen, but a great mutton-fist; his style stuns his readers, and he "fillips the ear of the public with a three-man beetle." He is too much for any single newspaper antagonist; "lays waste" a city orator or Member of Parliament, and bears hard upon the government itself. He is a kind of *fourth estate* in the politics of the country. He is not only unquestionably the most powerful political writer of the present day, but one of the best writers in the language. He speaks and thinks plain, broad, downright English. He might be said to have the clearness of Swift, the naturalness of Defoe, and the picturesque satirical description of Mandeville; if all such comparisons were not impertinent. A really great and original writer is like nobody but himself. In one sense, Sterne was not a wit, nor Shakespear a poet. It is easy to describe second-rate talents, because they fall into a class, and enlist under a standard: but first-rate powers defy calculation or comparison, and can be defined only by themselves. They are *sui generis,* and make the class to which they belong. I have tried half a dozen times to describe Burke's style without ever succeeding;—its severe extravagance; its literal boldness; its matter-of-fact hyperboles; its running away with a subject, and from it at the same time—but there is no making it out, for there is no example of the same thing any where else. We have no common measure to refer to; and his qualities contradict even themselves.

Cobbett is not so difficult. He has been compared to Paine; and so far it is true there are no two writers who come more into juxtaposition from the nature of their subjects, from the internal resources on which they draw, and from the popular effect of their writings, and their adaptation (though that is a bad word in the present case) to the capacity of every reader. But still if we turn to a volume of Paine's (his *Common Sense* or *Rights of Man*), we are struck (not to say somewhat refreshed) by the difference. Paine is a much more sententious writer than Cobbett. You cannot open a page in any of his best and earlier works without meeting with some maxim, some antithetical and memorable saying, which is a sort of starting-place for the argument, and the goal to which it returns. There is not a single *bon-mot,* a single sentence in Cobbett that has ever been quoted again. If any thing is ever quoted from him, it is an epithet of abuse or a nickname. He is an excellent hand at invention in that way, and has "damnable iteration in him." What could be better than his pestering Erskine year after year with his second title of Baron Clackmannan? He is rather too fond of *The Sons and Daughters of Corruption.* Paine affected to reduce things to first principles, to announce self-evident truths. Cobbett troubles himself about little but the details and local circumstances. The first appeared to have made up his mind beforehand to certain opinions, and to try to find the most compendious and pointed expressions for them: his successor appears to have no clue, no fixed or leading principles, nor ever to have thought on a question till he sits down to write about it; but then there seems no end of his matters of fact and raw materials, which are brought out in all their strength and sharpness from not having been squared or frittered down or vamped up to suit a theory—he goes on with his descriptions and illustrations as if he would never come to a stop; they have all the force of novelty with all the familiarity of old acquaintance; his knowledge grows out of the subject, and his style is that of a man who has an absolute intuition of what he is talking about, and never thinks of any thing else. He deals in premises and speaks to evidence—the coming to a conclusion and summing up (which was Paine's *forte*) lies in a smaller compass. The one could not compose an elementary treatise on politics to become a manual for the popular reader; nor could the other in all probability have kept up a weekly journal for the same number of years with the same spirit, interest, and untired perseverance. Paine's writings are a sort of introduction to political arithmetic on a new plan: Cobbett keeps a day-book and makes an entry at full of all the occurrences and troublesome questions that start up throughout the year. Cobbett, with vast industry, vast information, and the utmost power of making what he says intelligible, never seems to get at the beginning or come to the end of any question: Paine, in a few short sentences, seems by his peremptory manner "to clear it from all controversy, past, present, and to come." Paine takes a bird's-eye view of things. Cobbett sticks close to them, inspects the component parts, and keeps fast hold of the smallest advantages they afford him. Or, if I might here be indulged in a pastoral allusion, Paine tries to enclose his ideas in a fold for security and repose: Cobbett lets *his* pour out upon the plain like a flock of sheep to feed and batten. Cobbett is a pleasanter writer for those to read who do not agree with him; for he is less dogmatical, goes more into the common grounds of fact and argument to which all appeal, is more desultory and various, and appears less to be driving at a previous conclusion than urged on by the force of present conviction. He is therefore tolerated by all parties, though he has made himself by turns obnoxious to all; and even those he abuses read him. The Reformers read him when he was a Tory, and the Tories read him now that he is a Reformer. He must, I think, however, be *caviare* to the Whigs.

If he is less metaphysical and poetical than his celebrated prototype, he is more picturesque and dramatic. His episodes, which are numerous as they are pertinent, are striking, interesting, full of life and *naïveté*, minute, double measure running over, but never tedious—*nunquam sufflaminandus erat*. He is one of those writers who can never tire us, not even of himself; and the reason is, he is always "full of matter." He never runs to lees, never gives us the vapid leavings of himself, is never "weary, stale, and unprofitable," but always setting out afresh on his journey, clearing away some old nuisance, and turning up new mould. His egotism is delightful, for there is no affectation in it. He does not talk of himself for lack of something to write about, but because some circumstance that has happened to himself is the best possible illustration of the subject, and he is not the man to shrink from giving the best possible illustration of the subject from a squeamish delicacy. He likes both himself and his subject too well. He does not put himself before it, and say—"admire me first"—but places us in the same situation with himself, and makes us see all that he does. There is no blindman's-buff, no conscious hints, no awkward ventriloquism, no testimonies of applause, no abstract, senseless self-complacency, no smuggled admiration of his own person by proxy: it is all plain and above-board. He writes himself plain William Cobbett, strips himself quite as naked as any body would wish—in a word, his egotism is full of individuality, and has room for very little vanity in it. We feel delighted, rub our hands, and draw our chair to the fire, when we come to a passage of this sort: we know it will be something new and good, manly and simple, not the same insipid story of self over again. We sit down at table with the writer, but it is to a course of rich viands, flesh, fish, and wild-fowl, and not to a nominal entertainment, like that given by the Barmecide in the Arabian Nights, who put off his visitors with calling for a number of exquisite things that never appeared, and with the honour of his company. Mr. Cobbett is not a *make-believe* writer. His worst enemy cannot say that of him. Still less is he a vulgar one. He must be a puny, common-place critic indeed, who thinks him so. How fine were the graphical descriptions he sent us from America: what a transatlantic flavour, what a native *gusto*, what a fine *sauce-piquante* of contempt they were seasoned with! If he had sat down to look at himself in the glass, instead of looking about him like Adam in Paradise, he would not have got up these articles in so capital a style. What

a noble account of his first breakfast after his arrival in America! It might serve for a month. There is no scene on the stage more amusing. How well he paints the gold and scarlet plumage of the American birds, only to lament more pathetically the want of the wild wood-notes of his native land! The groves of the Ohio that had just fallen beneath the axe's stroke "live in his description," and the turnips that he transplanted from Botley "look green" in prose! How well at another time he describes the poor sheep that had got the tick, and had tumbled down in the agonies of death! It is a portrait in the manner of Bewick, with the strength, the simplicity, and feeling of that great naturalist. What havoc he makes, when he pleases, of the curls of Dr. Parr's wig and of the Whig consistency of Mr.———! His *Grammar* too is as entertaining as a story-book. He is too hard upon the style of others, and not enough (sometimes) on his own.

As a political partisan, no one can stand against him. With his brandished club, like Giant Despair in the Pilgrim's Progress, he knocks out their brains; and not only no individual, but no corrupt system could hold out against his powerful and repeated attacks, but with the same weapon, swung round like a flail, that he levels his antagonists, he lays his friends low, and puts his own party *hors de combat*. This is a bad propensity, and a worse principle in political tactics, though a common one. If his blows were straight forward and steadily directed to the same object, no unpopular Minister could live before him; instead of which he lays about right and left, impartially and remorselessly, makes a clear stage, has all the ring to himself, and then runs out of it, just when he should stand his ground. He throws his head into his adversary's stomach, and takes away from him all inclination for the fight, hits fair or foul, strikes at every thing, and as you come up to his aid or stand ready to pursue his advantage, trips up your heels or lays you sprawling, and pummels you when down as much to his heart's content as ever the Yanguesian carriers belaboured Rosinante with their packstaves. *"He has the back-trick simply the best of any man in Illyria."* He pays off both scores of old friendship and new-acquired enmity in a breath, in one perpetual volley, one raking fire of "arrowy sleet" shot from his pen. However his own reputation or the cause may suffer in consequence, he cares not one pin about that, so that he disables all who oppose, or who pretend to help him. In fact, he cannot bear success of any kind, not even of his own views or party; and if any principle were likely to become popular, would turn round against it to shew his power in shouldering it on one side. In short, wherever power is, there is he against it: he naturally butts at all obstacles, as unicorns are attracted to oak-trees, and feels his own strength only by resistance to the opinions and wishes of the rest of the world. To sail with the stream, to agree with the company, is not his humour. If he could bring about a Reform in Parliament, the odds are that he would instantly fall foul of and try to mar his own handy-work; and he quarrels with his own creatures as soon as he has written them into a little vogue—and a prison. I do not think this is vanity or fickleness so much as a pugnacious disposition, that must have an antagonist power to contend with, and only finds itself at ease in systematic opposition. If it were not for this, the high towers and rotten places of the world would fall before the battering-ram of his hard-headed reasoning: but if he once found them tottering, he would apply his strength to prop them up, and disappoint the expectations of his followers. He cannot agree to any thing established, nor to set up any thing else in its stead. While it is established, he presses hard against it, because it presses upon him, at least in imagination. Let it crumble under his grasp, and the motive to resistance is gone. He then requires some other grievance to set his face against. His principle is repulsion, his nature contradiction: he is made up of mere antipathies, an Ishmaelite indeed without a fellow. He is always playing at *hunt-the-slipper* in politics. He turns round upon whoever is next him. The way to wean him from any opinion, and make him conceive an intolerable hatred against it, would be to place somebody near him who was perpetually dinning it in his ears. When he is in England, he does nothing but abuse the Boroughmongers, and laugh at the whole system: when he is in America, he grows impatient of freedom and a republic. If he had staid there a little longer, he would have become a loyal and a loving subject of his Majesty King George IV. He lampooned the French Revolution when it was hailed as the dawn of liberty by millions: by the time it was brought into almost universal ill-odour by some means or other (partly no doubt by himself) he had turned, with one or two or three others, staunch Buonapartist. He is always of the militant, not of the triumphant party: so far he bears a gallant shew of magnanimity; but his gallantry is hardly of the right stamp. It wants principle: for though he is not servile or mercenary, he is the victim of self-will. He must pull down and pull in pieces: it is not his disposition to do otherwise. It is a pity; for with his great talents he might do great things, if he would go right forward to any useful object, make thorough-stitch work of any question, or join hand and heart with any principle. He changes his opinions as he does his friends, and much on the same account. He has no comfort in fixed principles: as soon as any thing is settled in his own mind, he quarrels with it. He has no satisfaction but in the chase after truth, runs a question down, worries and kills it, then quits it like vermin, and starts some new game, to lead him a new dance, and give him a fresh breathing through bog and brake, with the rabble yelping at his heels, and the leaders perpetually at fault. This he calls sport-royal. He thinks it as good as cudgel-playing or single-stick, or any thing else that has life in it. He likes the cut and thrust, the falls, bruises, and dry blows of an argument: as to any good or useful results that may come of the amicable settling of it, any one is welcome to them for him. The amusement is over, when the matter is once fairly decided.

There is another point of view in which this may be put. I might say that Mr. Cobbett is a very honest man with a total want of principle, and I might explain this paradox thus. I mean that he is, I think, in downright earnest in what he says, in the part he takes at the time; but in taking that part, he is led entirely by headstrong obstinacy, caprice, novelty, pique or personal motive of some sort, and not by a stedfast regard for truth, or habitual anxiety for what is right uppermost in his mind. He is not

a feed, timeserving, shuffling advocate (no man could write as he does who did not believe himself sincere)—but his understanding is the dupe and slave of his momentary, violent, and irritable humours. He does not adopt an opinion "deliberately or for money;" yet his conscience is at the mercy of the first provocation he receives, of the first whim he takes in his head; he sees things through the medium of heat and passion, not with reference to any general principles, and his whole system of thinking is deranged by the first object that strikes his fancy or sours his temper.—One cause of this phenomenon is perhaps his want of a regular education. He is a self-taught man, and has the faults as well as excellences of that class of persons in their most striking and glaring excess. It must be acknowledged that the Editor of the *Political Register* (the *Two-Penny Trash,* as it was called, till a bill passed the House to raise the price to sixpence) is not "the gentleman and scholar:" though he has qualities that, with a little better management, would be worth (to the public) both those titles. For want of knowing what has been discovered before him, he has not certain general landmarks to refer to, or a general standard of thought to apply to individual cases. He relies on his own acuteness and the immediate evidence, without being acquainted with the comparative anatomy or philosophical structure of opinion. He does not view things on a large scale or at the horizon (dim and airy enough perhaps)—but as they affect himself, close, palpable, tangible. Whatever he finds out, is his own, and he only knows what he finds out. He is in the constant hurry and fever of gestation: his brain teems incessantly with some fresh project. Every new light is the birth of a new system, the dawn of a new world to him. He is continually outstripping and overreaching himself. The last opinion is the only true one. He is wiser today than he was yesterday. Why should he not be wiser to-morrow than he was to-day?—Men of a learned education are not so sharp-witted as clever men without it: but they know the balance of the human intellect better; if they are more stupid, they are more steady; and are less liable to be led astray by their own sagacity and the overweening petulance of hard-earned and late-acquired wisdom. They do not fall in love with every meretricious extravagance at first sight, or mistake an old battered hypothesis for a vestal, because they are new to the ways of this old world. They do not seize upon it as a prize, but are safe from gross imposition by being as wise and no wiser than those who went before them.

Paine said on some occasion—"What I have written, I have written"—as rendering any farther declaration of his principles unnecessary. Not so Mr. Cobbett. What he has written is no rule to him what he is to write. He learns something every day, and every week he takes the field to maintain the opinions of the last six days against friend or foe. I doubt whether this outrageous inconsistency, this headstrong fickleness, this understood want of all rule and method, does not enable him to go on with the spirit, vigour, and variety that he does. He is not pledged to repeat himself. Every new *Register* is a kind of new Prospectus. He blesses himself from all ties and shackles on his understanding; he has no mortgages on his brain; his notions are free and unincumbered. If he was put in tram-

Cobbett as an M.P. in the House of Commons,
as sketched by Daniel Maclise.

mels, he might become a vile hack like so many more. But he gives himself "ample scope and verge enough." He takes both sides of a question, and maintains one as sturdily as the other. If nobody else can argue against him, he is a very good match for himself. He writes better in favour of Reform than any body else; he used to write better against it. Wherever he is, there is the tug of war, the weight of the argument, the strength of abuse. He is not like a man in danger of being *bed-rid* in his faculties—He tosses and tumbles about his unwieldy bulk, and when he is tired of lying on one side, relieves himself by turning on the other. His shifting his point of view from time to time not merely adds variety and greater compass to his topics (so that the ***Political Register*** is an armoury and magazine for all the materials and weapons of political warfare), but it gives a greater zest and liveliness to his manner of treating them. Mr. Cobbett takes nothing for granted as what he has proved before; he does not write a book of reference. We see his ideas in their first concoction, fermenting and overflowing with the ebullitions of a lively conception. We look on at the actual process, and are put in immediate possession of the grounds and materials on which he forms his sanguine,

unsettled conclusions. He does not give us samples of reasoning, but the whole solid mass, refuse and all.

—He pours out all as plain
As downright Shippen or as old Montaigne.

This is one cause of the clearness and force of his writings. An argument does not stop to stagnate and muddle in his brain, but passes at once to his paper. His ideas are served up, like pancakes, hot and hot. Fresh theories give him fresh courage. He is like a young and lusty bridegroom that divorces a favourite speculation every morning, and marries a new one every night. He is not wedded to his notions, not he. He has not one Mrs. Cobbett among all his opinions. He makes the most of the last thought that has come in his way, seizes fast hold of it, rumples it about in all directions with rough strong hands, has his wicked will of it, takes a surfeit, and throws it away.— Our author's changing his opinions for new ones is not so wonderful: what is more remarkable is his facility in forgetting his old ones. He does not pretend to consistency (like Mr. Coleridge); he frankly disavows all connexion with himself. He feels no personal responsibility in this way, and cuts a friend or principle with the same decided indifference that Antipholis of Ephesus cuts Aegeon of Syracuse. It is a hollow thing. The only time he ever grew romantic was in bringing over the relics of Mr. Thomas Paine with him from America to go a progress with them through the disaffected districts. Scarce had he landed in Liverpool when he left the bones of a great man to shift for themselves; and no sooner did he arrive in London than he made a speech to disclaim all participation in the political and theological sentiments of his late idol, and to place the whole stock of his admiration and enthusiasm towards him to the account of his financial speculations, and of his having predicted the fate of paper-money. If he had erected a little gold statue to him, it might have proved the sincerity of this assertion: but to make a martyr and a patron-saint of a man, and to dig up "his canonised bones" in order to expose them as objects of devotion to the rabble's gaze, asks something that has more life and spirit in it, more mind and vivifying soul, than has to do with any calculation of pounds, shillings, and pence! The fact is, he *ratted* from his own project. He found the thing not so ripe as he had expected. His heart failed him: his enthusiasm fled, and he made his retractation. His admiration is short-lived: his contempt only is rooted, and his resentment lasting.—The above was only one instance of his building too much on practical *data*. He has an ill habit of prophesying, and goes on, though still deceived. The art of prophesying does not suit Mr. Cobbett's style. He has a knack of fixing names and times and places. According to him, the Reformed Parliament was to meet in March, 1818—it did not, and we heard no more of the matter. When his predictions fail, he takes no farther notice of them, but applies himself to new ones—like the country-people who turn to see what weather there is in the almanac for the next week, though it has been out in its reckoning every day of the last.

Mr. Cobbett is great in attack, not in defence: he cannot fight an up-hill battle. He will not bear the least punishing. If any one turns upon him (which few people like to do) he immediately turns tail. Like an overgrown school-boy, he is so used to have it all his own way, that he cannot submit to any thing like competition or a struggle for the mastery; he must lay on all the blows, and take none. He is bullying and cowardly; a Big Ben in politics, who will fall upon others and crush them by his weight, but is not prepared for resistance, and is soon staggered by a few smart blows. Whenever he has been set upon he has slunk out of the controversy. *The Edinburgh Review* made (what is called) a dead set at him some years ago, to which he only retorted by an eulogy on the superior neatness of an English kitchen-garden to a Scotch one. I remember going one day into a bookseller's shop in Fleet-street to ask for the *Review;* and on my expressing my opinion to a young Scotchman, who stood behind the counter, that Mr. Cobbett might hit as hard in his reply, the North Briton said with some alarm—"But you don't think, Sir, Mr. Cobbett will be able to injure the Scottish nation?" I said I could not speak to that point, but I thought he was very well able to defend himself. He however did not, but has borne a grudge to the *Edinburgh Review* ever since, which he hates worse than the *Quarterly*. I cannot say I do.

William Cobbett (review date 1829)

SOURCE: "On His Writings," in *The Opinions of William Cobbett* by William Cobbett, edited by G. D. H. Cole and Margaret Cole, The Cobbett Publishing Co. Ltd., 1944, pp. 42-3.

[*In the following excerpt from an essay originally published in 1829, Cobbett expresses contempt for critics while stating the intent of his own writing.*]

As to merit, as an author or writer, I have always despised what is generally called criticism. I know well that those who carry on the trade of critics are a base and hireling crew; more corrupt, perhaps, than any other set of beings in the world. The only critics that I look to are the public; and my mode of estimating a writing, is by the *effect* which it produces. If there be two writings, having the accomplishment of the same object in view, that writing which soonest and most completely accomplishes its objects, is the *best* of the two. I listen to nothing about *style* as it is called; or any thing else. As the man, who soonest and best weaves a yard of cloth, is the best weaver; so the man, who soonest and best accomplishes an object with his pen, is the best writer. Taking this as my standard, I know very well, that I am a very good one: but it does, nevertheless, give me singular pleasure to hear you say that you have been taught by me. Perhaps there is no pleasure so great as that which we derive from a conviction that we have produced great effect upon the minds of great multitudes of persons; and especially when we are able to reflect that, as in the present case, the effect has been produced by calm and dispassionate reasoning upon serious and important subjects. Who, besides myself, has, in our day, attempted to gain popularity by dint of fact and of argument, unmixed with any thing to

amuse the human mind? If, at any time, I have indulged in a sort of jest I have been almost ashamed of the momentary triumph thereby acquired. I have rested my reputation upon the success of truth supported by dry argument. I knew well that the seeds must lie long in the ground; that the vegetation of the plants must be slow; but I knew also that the growth of them would be sure and that their nature would be durable. *"Cast your bread upon the waters,"* has always been at my tongue's end, when, many years ago, I perceived a disinclination in the People to hear, and when almost any other man would have thrown down the pen in despair. I knew, however, that I was gradually making converts, though I very seldom saw any outward proof of the fact. I waited also for the misery which I knew would be the final consequence, and which I also knew would open the ears of the nation. When that misery came, I redoubled my efforts; and the effect has been that universal conviction of the utility of my efforts, and with regard to which conviction you speak only the voice of the nation at large.

James Fitzjames Stephen (review date 1866)

SOURCE: A review of *Selections from Cobbett's Political Works,* in *The Saturday Review,* London, Vol. 22, No. 558, July 7, 1866, pp. 17-20.

[*James Fitzjames Stephen was an English jurist and literary critic, best known for his* Liberty, Equality, Fraternity *(1873), a detailed, conservative counterblast to John Stuart Mill's* On Liberty *(1859). In the following excerpt, he attempts "to give some estimate of the man [Cobbett] himself, and some account of his more characteristic opinions."*]

If we had to take a representative man from each of the three kingdoms, Cobbett, O'Connell, and Walter Scott would be by no means bad men to choose. Cobbett was a model John Bull. He had all the characteristics of the race in an exaggerated from, and the chief interest which now attaches to his opinions arises from the degree in which they illustrate the strength and the weakness of a thorough-bred Englishman of much more than average power, but not of more than average enlightenment. Cobbett's great qualities were immense vigour, resource, energy, and courage, joined to a force of understanding, a degree of logical power, and above all a force of expression, which have rarely been equalled. His weakness lay in his incredible self-confidence, his monstrous prejudices, his extreme coarseness and occasional ferocity, and the thoroughly invincible ignorance with which, when he had got any ideas into his head, he clung to them and defended them against all comers. As life went on, his style to some extent degenerated, and became, as the style of all journalists tends to become, turgid and cumbrous; but his best performances are models of vigour and pungency. These qualities, together with his energetic, rather domineering, character, are displayed in great abundance in the most unlikely places. Nothing, for instance, can be racier or more amusing than many parts of his French and English Grammars. No other man, in all probability, would ever have thought of making such books the vehicle of the keenest political satire. Cobbett contrived to do so by choosing his examples of bad grammar from despatches, King's Speeches, and other public papers. For instance, the Prince Regent in 1814 said:—

> "Although this war originated in the most unprovoked aggression on the part of the Government of the United States . . . I never have ceased to entertain a sincere desire to bring it to a conclusion on just and honourable terms."

> Does the Prince [asks Cobbett] mean that he would be justified in wanting to make peace on unjust and dishonourable terms because the enemy had been the aggressor? He might, indeed, wish to make it on terms dishonourable and even disgraceful to the enemy; but could he possibly wish to make it on unjust terms? Does he mean that an aggression, however wicked and unprovoked, would give him a right to do injustice? Yet if he do not mean this, what does he mean?

He concludes the letter in which this occurs by saying to his son, to whom the letters are addressed, that when he comes to hear the people who write King's Speeches making speeches in Parliament themselves, "Your wonder will be, not that they wrote a King's Speech so badly, but that they contrived to put upon paper sentences sufficiently grammatical to enable us to guess at the meaning." The French Grammar is as remarkable in some ways as the English one. It contains, for instance, directions for learning the French genders, which are most characteristic both of the energy and of the clumsiness of the man who invented them. Take, he says, a little book, each page of which is divided into two columns. Write out all the masculine words in one set of columns, and all the feminine words in the other, and read them over and over again at odd times until you know them all by heart. The hatred of rules and the readiness for labour which this plan shows—for it was the plan which Cobbett himself followed—are not less remarkable than the fact that, having adopted it when he was a sergeant in a marching regiment, he recommended it to others between thirty and forty years afterwards. It never appears to have occurred to him that, as five French nouns out of six are masculine, a list of the feminine nouns only would have saved five-sixths of the trouble.

Illustrations of the peculiarities of his style might be multiplied to any extent. His name, so to speak, is signed upon every page of all his writings. It will be better worth while to attempt to give a short account of the general cast of his political opinions. He was in no sense a party writer. From first to last he expressed his own views in his own way upon all sorts of subjects; and whatever the subject in hand may be, there is one uniform cast of thought about all his opinions as distinctive as the style in which it finds expression. They changed a good deal as he grew older, more passionate, and more accustomed to feel and to exert the singular powers which he possessed; but the progress of the change can be traced from month to month and year to year, and it is obvious enough that,

under the varieties of opinion which he held at different times, he was always the same man. The leading idea on political subjects in Cobbett's mind was that all legislation ought to have for its object the production of a certain rough kind of prosperity and plenty, diffused throughout the whole population. There never was such an energetic believer in the theory of a good old time when every man was fed on beef, or at least bacon, and beer, and clothed in good woollens made from the fleeces of English sheep, and in shoes made out of English hides, when there were hardly any imports and very few taxes, and when there were no paupers. He appears to have believed that for several centuries this actually was the state of things in England, and that it had passed away only in very modern times by reason of the system of taxation and paper money and funding, which he never ceased to denounce as the source of every kind of national evil. As he read the history of England, "the thing called the Reformation" was the source of all our evils. Up to that time things had on the whole gone on well, and in particular the Church had provided for the poor so largely and so plentifully that there had been none of the grinding poverty which was witnessed in later times. The Reformation he viewed as having been, in a political point of view, nothing but a vast aristocratic job and robbery of the poor. Before that event a large proportion of the revenues of the Church went to the poor. After it the whole went into the hands of private persons or of a married priesthood, who, as far as the poor were concerned, were little better. Still Queen Elizabeth's Poor-law was some compensation, and, notwithstanding the gross injustice which had been inflicted on them, the common people got on pretty well till the aristocracy invented the never-sufficiently-to-be-cursed funding system, whereby they were enabled to live out of the taxes in a constantly increasing ratio. What with constant borrowing, and what with paper money and indirect taxation, which raised the price of all food, drink, clothing, and lodging to an incredible pitch, the poor became poorer, and the rich richer, till at last, towards the time when the *Political Register* was at the height of its influence, the labourers were ground down to an extreme degree of misery, the old landlords were reduced to poverty, and Jews and fund-holders (so he loved to put it) lived in brutal luxury out of the taxes. The burden of large parts of the *Political Register* and other works, especially of the delightful book—for such it is, notwithstanding many obvious blemishes—called *Rural Rides,* is that the taxes were squandered in supporting luxury. The population in the country, it is constantly repeated, was decaying, and was being collected into the great towns—or, as Cobbett always calls them, the Wens—there to be devoured by the "Wen devils":—

> The land is now used [he says in one of his rides] to raise food and drink for the monopolizers and the tax-eaters and their purveyors and lackeys and harlots; and they get together in Wens. Of all the mean, all the cowardly reptiles that ever crawled on the face of the earth, the English landowners are the most mean and the most cowardly; for while they see the population drawn away from their parishes to the Wens, while they are taxed to keep the people in the Wens, and while they see their own parsons pocket the tithes and

the glebe rents, and suffer the parsonage-houses to fall down; while they see all this, they, without uttering a word in the way of complaint, suffer themselves to be taxed to build new churches for the monopolizers and tax-eaters in those Wens! Never was there in this world a set of reptiles so base as this.

Nothing in Cobbett is more remarkable than the fact that, though he was regarded for many years as the incarnation of radicalism and revolution, he was no Radical at all in spirit and sentiment; at least he was not what is usually understood by that name. The whole of the Young England theory of things is nothing more than an effeminate parody of one side of his views. He was, as we have already said, the most English of Englishmen, as full of every English prejudice as an egg is full of meat. He always speaks with reverential tenderness of every old institution or building. The old churches and old cathedrals fill him with admiration. He had a great tenderness for the old religion, though he had no love for the despotic or priestcraft side of Popery, which he sometimes attacked in his characteristic style, and he despised Unitarians and Methodists and Jews about equally. His account of Unitarians is eminently characteristic, and contains a good deal of his grotesque humour. Baron Maseres

> went on at a great rate laughing about the Trinity, and I remember he repeated the Unitarian distich which makes a joke of the idea of there being a devil, and which they all repeat to you, and at the same time laugh and look as cunning and priggish as jackdaws, just as if they were wiser than all the rest of the world. I do most heartily despise this priggish set for their conceit and impudence; but seeing that they want reason for the Incarnation, seeing that they will have effects here ascribed to none but usual causes, let me put a question or two to them.

Then follow seven questions, the last of which is, "What causes flounders, real little flat fish, brown on one side, white on the other, mouth sideways, with tails, fins, and all, leaping alive in the inside of a rotten sheep's, and of every rotten sheep's liver?" Jews, Methodists, and Quakers come off quite as ill. The Quakers are "base vermin" and "unbaptized blackguards." The Methodists are a "bawling, canting crew" of "roving fanatics." The Jews are "Christ-killing rascals"; and "Christ-killer" is his favourite pseudonym for a Jew, if one is to be introduced into an imaginary conversation or semi-dramatic scene in one of his letters. The Scotch and Irish are served in the same way. He had no opinion of the Irish. One of the most stinging and crushing letters he ever wrote is devoted to the demolition of a speech of O'Connell's in his usual vein (*Register,* January 1832). Churchill and Johnson were not harder on the Scotch. "The Scotch beggars would make us believe that we sprang from beggars. The impudent scribes would make us believe that England was formerly nothing at all till they came to enlighten it and fatten upon it." He carried his John Bull pride indeed to a positively ludicrous pitch, for in a letter to Lord Fitzwilliam, in 1817, he reproaches him bitterly for being a party to the renunciation by George III. of the title of King of France. "Had I been in Parliament I would have made

every stand inch by inch in order to expose, at any rate, the abandonment of a plume won by the valour of my forefathers. . . . The abandonment of the title of King of France was an act of baseness without a parallel." We are acquainted with no English writer who illustrates in a more pointed manner the vein of poetry and romance which runs through every part of the English character, though in a form so strange, so subtle, and at times so grotesque, that it is continually overlooked or mistaken by superficial observers. It requires a far closer knowledge of the John Bull nature than most people possess to understand how the same man should burst into fiery indignation about the baseness of abandoning the perfectly senseless title of King of France, and should observe, "Talk of 'liberty,' indeed, 'civil and religious liberty,' the Inquisition with a bellyfull is far preferable to a state of things like this," and declare elsewhere that the religion for him was a religion which filled people's bellies.

It is most remarkable that Cobbett, who passed his life in the most passionate advocacy of Radical Reform, and who denounced rotten boroughs and all the works of boroughmongers, fund-holders, stock-jobbers, and other "wen devils," every day and all day long for some forty years, was opposed to all characteristically liberal measures. He denounced schemes of popular education. For instance, in December 1813, he published a letter to Alderman Wood **"On teaching the Children of the Poor to Read,"** the gist of which is that there is nothing wholesome for them to read, and that they had much better not learn. They cannot understand the Bible, and the newspapers are all corrupted by the Government. In another letter he says that, in his experience of the army, he always found that the scholars in a regiment were "generally dirty and drunkards," "the conceit makes them saucy"; and their characters are so bad that men who can neither read nor write are frequently made non-commissioned officers because of the superiority of their moral character, notwithstanding the inconvenience of their ignorance. In much the same spirit of bigoted love to all that was old-fashioned, he admired the old laws against forestalling and regrating, and considered shops a mischievous innovation upon the good old fashion of fairs and markets. His view of facts was as much perverted by this state of mind as his theories. He continually maintained that it was a gross and ludicrous error to believe that the population was rapidly increasing. A man who could believe in the correctness of the census returns would be capable of believing that the moon was made of green cheese.

These were a few of the most important and characteristic of the political views of this remarkable man. They are interesting at present chiefly because they show the cast of thought which gave the most popular of all English political writers his great hold over the minds of a larger section of his countrymen than any other writer of the same class ever had for an equal time, and because they thus afford decisive proof of the strength of Conservative tendencies in this country even at a time in which party feeling ran higher than it probably ever did at any other period in our history. No one ever attacked either individuals or classes in this country with such unsparing violence as Cobbett, and yet his attachment to what he regarded as the genuine constitution of the country was undoubtedly sincere, and was exceedingly strong. He goes so far as to speak with kindness, and even with a certain sort of regret, of the feudal system. When the matter is considered attentively, it is obvious enough that the doctrines which we are so much accustomed to see recognised, professed, and extolled in all directions—the doctrine of universal competition, free-trade, religious equality, and the like—however true they may be, are popular only by accident. They are not the natural and appropriate creed of the great masses of the population. Liberalism is in many respects an aristocratic creed, inasmuch as the essence of it is to produce a condition of things in which the energies of every individual will have the fullest possible scope, and produce the most permanent results. The vigorous man will, under this system, get a maximum of advantage from his superior strength, and will transmit to his descendants the advantages which he has acquired. The apparent tendency of unrestricted free-trade and unlimited competition is to throw wealth, and everything that depends upon and is derived from it, into comparatively few hands. What the average man likes is an artificial system which provides as large a number of persons as possible with a reasonable level of comfort. When people talk of good old times, the state of things present to their imagination, rightly or wrongly, is a state in which there was less trouble and anxiety, and fewer vicissitudes in life, than in the time of which they are speaking. The ideal age of most men is an age in which the common run of people got along pretty comfortably without much trouble. It does no doubt so happen that, in our own times, the extraordinary inventions which have changed the face of society, and have poured over us a flood of wealth unexampled in former times, have produced a state of feeling to which we are so accustomed that we do not see that it is exceptional. There never was an age in which the go-ahead spirit was so powerful, but even in these days there are considerable exceptions to this state of feeling. Trades' unions are a good illustration. They show that the great bulk of the class of mechanics have hardly any sympathy with free-trade, and comparatively little ambition. Let us, say they in effect, have fair wages and short hours, and let both time and wages be regulated by the work of the average man, not by the powers of those who rise above the average. The following passage is at once an excellent specimen of Cobbett's best style and a short summary of his most characteristic doctrine:—

> The state of the people relative to the nobility and gentry used to be such as to be productive of great advantages to both. The labourers were happy. Each had his little home. He had things about him worth possessing and worth preserving. His clock, which had come to him from his father, in many cases, and from his grandfather, was preserved with as much care and veneration as you would preserve your title-deeds, or any building upon your estates. Men lived in the same cottage from the day of their marriage till the day of their death. They worked for the same masters for many years. They were so well off that there was no desire for change. Whole families were in the service of the same nobleman or gentleman, without any legal engagement, and without any other dependence than that occasioned by respect and good-will. In numerous instances, son succeeded father, generation after generation, as the workman or servant of son after father. The liberality and kindness of the employer were repaid by the respect and fidelity of the servant. All this is now swept away. That inexorable system of taxation, that fraudulent and ruinous system of funding, which have enabled the borough holders in England to smother liberty and reinstate despotism in Europe, have, at last, almost wholly destroyed this most beautiful and happy state of society, and, in the place of mutual confidence and mutual good-will, have introduced mutual distrust and mutual hatred. The American war, as I said before, gave the nation a great blow. That blow, however, might have been overcome; but the blow given by the late wars never can be overcome, except by that regeneration which a Parliamentary reform would produce.

What degree of truth was there in these views? The question is one which could be adequately discussed only in a large work spreading over a great variety of subjects, but one remark about it may be made with confidence. Cobbett altogether overstated his case, and pertinaciously shut his eyes to the real progress which the nation was most undoubtedly making in the midst of much suffering and a great deal of jobbery and corruption. The vast load of indirect taxation was no doubt cruel and mischievous. The abuses of Government were very great, but, notwithstanding all that, the wealth of the country did increase enormously, and so, whatever Cobbett thought about it, did the population, all through the great war and down to our times. He put his finger on the real evil when he complained of the way in which property is distributed, and when he pointed out the excessive hardship upon the poor of the system of indirect taxation; but he was mistaken when he underrated the powers of production in the country, and was utterly wrong when he denied its increase in population. He was also wrong, as it appears to us, in the notion that it is possible by any artificial means to arrest the natural progress of society, and to make the general diffusion of rough plenty the principal ideal of such a nation and such an age as our own.

We have given only a slight outline of one part of Cobbett's views. His occasional writings on all manner of practical subjects are eminently characteristic, and for the most part well worth reading. Whoever wishes to get a vivid picture of the man, his thoughts, his views on all subjects, and his personal adventures, intermixed with most picturesque and beautiful descriptions of every part of the country, and of most classes of its inhabitants, may find all this, and much more, in the *Rural Rides*—a delightful book, with all its occasional coarseness and ferocity. We have omitted all notice of Cobbett's wars with private persons, many of which were exceedingly violent. They make up a great part of his writings, but their interest has now entirely passed away. To those who are accustomed to the gentler manners of our own time they are wearisome, and sometimes disgusting. We have also left unnoticed many of his special opinions, and many of the recommendations which he made from time to time. They are characteristic enough, and in some cases very absurd; but they were made under violent excitement, and may as well be forgotten.

Hugh E. Egerton (essay date 1885)

SOURCE: "A Scarce Book," in *The National Review,* London, Vol. V, No. 27, May, 1885, pp. 413-28.

[*In the following excerpt, Egerton discusses* Rural Rides, *citing several lengthy quotations to illustrate Cobbett's handling of various concerns and emphases.*]

Were the well-meaning persons to have their way who long for the establishment of an English Academy, one wonders what would be the attitude of such an august body towards a writer like Cobbett. And yet his claim to rank as a classic admits, I suppose, of little question. The position he holds among the immortals he has taken, as it were, by storm; and what no favour of literary clique helped to gain, no passing whim of favour can take away. It is indeed possible that as the English language comes more and more to savour of the dissecting-room and the studio, and the form of its literature to sink beneath the weight of its matter, criticism may attach a yet greater importance to the style as opposed to the substance of an author, and the surrounding desert render yet more gracious such wells as still exist of "English pure and undefiled." But of the merits of Cobbett's style there can be no question. In his moods of most frantic violence, dancing a war-dance around Lord Castlereagh's dead body, or covering with the foulest abuse the honoured name of Burke, the manner of his writing never lacks in skill. We may not approve the music it gives forth, but we cannot but allow that the pipe is never out of tune. Nor is the secret of the merits of his style far to seek. Of none other does the saying of Buffon hold more profoundly true that *"le style c'est l'homme."* His very weaknesses as a man lent strength to his writing. Because he was obstinate, narrow-minded, and could see only the one side of a question, therefore his sight had nothing to distract it from seeing what he did see with perfect distinctness, and from describing that with perfect accuracy. It is surely no mere coincidence that in our times a similar intellectual soil has produced for us a similar intellectual harvest, and that the greatest of living English orators recalls in his obstinacy and in his self-sufficiency, no less than by the spell of his eloquence, the memory of Cobbett.

To good writing, profound knowledge is often a hindrance rather than a help. The author's sentences become loaded with parentheses, because his mind is being crossed by contrary currents of thought. The panting expression toils in vain after the conception; the most notable instance of which tendency is to be found in the style of Thucydides, the rush of whose meaning, very often, scarcely contains itself within the banks of grammar. So, too, we have been lately told that the strange vocabulary of "immensities," "eternities," &c. which Carlyle was continually employing, was in great measure due to the awkwardness with which he approached subjects too deep for words.

No such difficulty attended the steps of Cobbett. The native hue of his argument, in all conscience resolute enough, is never sicklied o'er by any pale cast of thought. "His Minerva is born in panoply." "The twilight of dubiety never falls upon him." *"Res duplex."* But could Cobbett have understood the saying he would have answered, "Yes, to the double-faced." Of all writers who have lived, he is the most frankly and completely materialist. "In the groves of *his* academy at the end of every *visto* we see nothing but"—the stomach. "Whose God is their belly." Only it is but fair to say that, himself the most frugal of men, it is for the belly of others that he is concerned. "I have observed, and I beseech you to attend to it," he wrote to the English people,

> that the words *liberty, freedom, rights,* and the rest of the catalogue, which hypocritical knaves send rolling off the tongue, are worth nothing at all. It is things that we want. Those men who make a fuss about sorts of Government, and who tell us about the good things which arise from the Republican Government of America, deceive themselves or deceive others. It is not because the government is Republican, but because it is cheap; and it is cheap not because it is Republican, but because the people choose those who make the laws and vote the taxes. If the President of America were called King of America instead of being called President, it would be of no consequence to the people, if the King cost no more than the President now costs. Nothing is worth looking at; nothing is worth talking about but the cost, because it is this that comes and takes the dinner from the labourer and that takes the coat off his back.

It is not surprising that a writer of this stamp should be neglected at the present day. Alike in his merits and in his faults Cobbett appeals but little to a modern taste. The gulf which divides Gillray from Tenniel, is not wider than that which separates Cobbett from the modern controversialist. We may have become, as he complained, "a hollow and trivial nation," "frivolous, effeminate, and senseless," but at least we have the qualities of our defects, and are not, like him, *brutal.* Some of us are, perhaps, still capable of removing our neighbour's land-mark, but we are careful to do so with "agricultural implements." Moreover, Cobbett was, to the very depths of his innermost being, a Philistine of the Philistines, and we are nothing if not "cultured." In his youth, when in America, and fighting single-handed the battles of the English people and Constitution, he heard himself described one day by the English Consul as "a wild fellow." It is as "a wild fellow" that he takes his place in the republic of letters, and, therefore, it is no wonder that the guides and cicerones of that republic should prefer to give him a wide berth.

After all, however, the main reason of the neglect which has overtaken Cobbett lies in what, when he was alive, undoubtedly constituted his strength, namely, his exclusive attention to politics. Now, freshness being desirable in all things, there is, perhaps, nothing so unsavoury as stale politics. And the political beliefs of Cobbett belong, and have for many years belonged, to the limbo of the past; gone, if not "to the tomb of all the Capulets," perhaps to a warmer place! That the English people were once free, prosperous, and contented: that it was "this vile paper-money and funding system; this system of Dutch descent, begotten by Bishop Burnett, and born in Hell," which had changed that state of things: that to support this system (the tendency of which was to divert their estates into the hands of Jews and money-jobbers), the aristocracy had to be bribed by places and pensions; that its maintenance involved so grievous a burden of taxation upon all the necessaries of life, as to reduce the labouring classes to very starvation. That the remedy lay in such an "equitable adjustment" as should give, to the public creditor and the public pensioner, only what remained after that the condition of the people had been rendered tolerable; that such an equitable adjustment could only be obtained in a Reformed Parliament, and that, therefore, and for no other reason, Reform was desirable. In these propositions may be roughly summarised the main articles of Cobbett's political creed. But the mere statement of them proves better than the most eloquent argument how wholly they belong to the past. There may be much that still requires remedy in the condition of the labouring classes, but no honest man can say that it is the result of excessive taxation falling upon the necessaries of life. And the "facts and fallacies" of the "Financial Reform Almanack" are at most the mere ground-swell of what was once an angry sea. *Quisque suos manes patimur;* but a society which has survived the cannonading of Cobbett may await, perhaps, with confidence the Greek fire of Messrs. Chamberlain and Henry George.

It follows from what has been said that the task of commenting on any book written by Cobbett, without continually trespassing upon the field of politics, is one of no little difficulty; yet in the case of his **Rural Rides** it may be attempted. The fate of this book very strongly bears out my statement as to the neglect of Cobbett's writing by the general public. The shelves of Mudie know it not, and it has become so scarce, that a book published at the price of a few shillings can now with difficulty be obtained for thirty. It was, I believe, the intention of a lately-deceased publisher to issue a new edition of the work. Whether such an undertaking would be rewarded with much success is, I think, very questionable. Let no one expect in Cobbett the account of a mere tour of pleasure. The stern utilitarian who, somewhere, tells us that he had never in his life gone for a walk save with an object at the end of it, was not likely to ride, as he did, many hundreds of miles through England merely to enjoy the views and afterwards to describe them. "My object was not to see inns and turn-pike roads, but to see *the country*; to see the farmers at home and to see the labourers in the fields, and to do this you must travel on foot or on horseback. With a gig you cannot get about among bye-ways and across fields, through bridle-ways and hunting-gates." Again: "I wish to see many people, and to talk to them; and there are a great many people who wish to see and talk to me. What better reason can be given for a man's going about the country and dining at fairs and markets." "Thus, Sir," in another place he writes, "I have led you about the country. All sorts of things have I talked of, to be sure,

but there are very few of these things which have not their interest one way or another. At the end of a hundred miles or two of travelling, stopping here and there, talking freely with everybody; hearing what gentlemen, farmers, tradesmen, journeymen, labourers, women, girls, boys, and all have to say; reasoning with some, laughing with others, and observing all that passes; and especially if your manner be such as to remove every kind of reserve from every class; at the end of a tramp like this you get impressed upon your mind a true picture not only of the taste of the country, but of the state of the people's minds throughout the country."

Nevertheless, freely granting that his main object is political, there is much in the book which the most frivolous readers cannot fail to find very entertaining. To begin with, it abounds in those autobiographical references, which, to lovers of Cobbett, form one great charm of his writings. His moral ideals were, as has been already hinted, very far from the highest; but, unlike nearly all professional moralists, his practice corresponded with his precepts. In widening the area of the affections there is, without doubt, grave danger lest we diminish their depth. Most people will prefer Cobbett to Rousseau; the lover of his kindred to the lover of his kind; the indifferent citizen of the world to the fervid philanthropist, who left his children to the tender mercies of the public hospital. The following passage throws a flood of very pleasant light upon the burly demagogue in his family relations.

> Before we [*i.e.* his son Richard and he] got this supply of bread and cheese, we, though in ordinary times a couple of singularly jovial companions, and seldom going a hundred yards (except going very fast) without one or the other speaking, began to grow *dull,* or, rather, *glum.* The way seemed long, and when I had to speak in answer to Richard, the speaking was as brief as might be. Unfortunately just at this critical period, one of the loops that held the straps of Richard's little portmanteau broke, and it became necessary for me to fasten the portmanteau on before me, upon my saddle. This, which was not the work of more than five minutes, would, had I had *a breakfast,* have been nothing at all, indeed, matter for laughter. But *now* it was something. It was his *"fault"* for capering and jerking about *"so."* I jumped off, saying, "Here, I'll carry it *myself."* And then I began to take off the remaining strap, pulling with great violence and in great haste. Just at this time, my eye met his, in which I saw *great surprise;* and feeling the just rebuke, feeling heartily ashamed of myself, I instantly changed my tone and manner, cast the blame upon the saddles, and talked of the effectual means which we would take to prevent the like in future.

Although Cobbett is divided, *toto cælo,* from the landscape wordpainters of our own day, no one had a keener eye for the beautiful or a more vivid pen in its description. Witness the following examples:—

> Woodland countries are interesting on many accounts, not so much on account of their masses of green leaves, as on account of the variety of sights and sounds and incidents that they afford. Even in winter the coppices

Elliott's elegy to Cobbett:

Oh, bear him where the rain can fall,
 And where the winds can blow,
And let the sun weep o'er his pall,
 As to the grave ye go.

And in some little lone churchyard,
 Beside the growing corn,
Lay gentle nature's stern prose bard—
 Her mightiest peasant-born!

Yes, let the wild flower wed his grave,
 That bees may murmur near,
When o'er his last home bend the brave,
 And say, "A MAN lies here."

For Briton's honour, Cobbett's name,
 Though rashly oft he spoke;
And none can scorn, and few will blame,
 The low-laid heart of oak.

See, o'er his prostrate branches, see
 Ev'n factious hate consents
To reverence in the fallen tree
 His British lineaments!

Though gnarl'd the storm-toss'd boughs that braved
 The thunder's gather'd scowl,
Not always through his darkness raved
 The storm-winds of the soul.

Oh, no! in hours of golden calm
 Morn met his forehead bold;
And breezy evening sung her psalm
 Beneath his dew-dropp'd gold.

The wren its crest of fibred fire
 With his rich bronze compared,
While many a youngling's songful sire
 His acorn'd twiglets shared.

The lark, above, sweet tribute paid,
 Where clouds with light were riven;
And true-love sought his blue-bell'd shade,
 "To bless the hour of Heav'n."

Ev'n when his stormy voice was loud,
 And guilt quaked at the sound,
Beneath the frown that shook the proud,
 The poor a shelter found.

Dead Oak, thou liv'st! Thy smitten hands,
 The thunder of thy brow,
Speak, with strange tongues in many lands,
 And tyrants hear thee NOW!

Ebenezer Elliott, "William Cobbett," in The Life of
William Cobbett, Dedicated to His Sons, *E. L. Carey
and A. Hart, 1835.*

are beautiful to the eye, while they comfort the mind with the idea of shelter and warmth. In spring they change their hue from day to day during two whole months, which is about the time from the first appearance of the delicate leaves of the birch to the full expansion of those of the ash; and even before the leaves come at all to intercept the view, what in the vegetable creation is so delightful to behold as the beds of a coppice bespangled with primroses and blue-bells? The opening of the birch leaves is the signal for the pheasant to begin to crow, for the blackbird to whistle and the thrush to sing; and just when the oak buds begin to look reddish, and not a day before, the whole tribes of finches burst forth in song from every bough, while the lark, imitating them all, carries the joyous sound to the sky.

. . . . .

The custom is, in this part of Hertfordshire (and I am told it continues into Bedfordshire) to leave a *border* round the ploughed part of the fields to bear grass, and to make hay from, so that the grass being now made into hay, every corn-field has a closely-mowed grass-walk about ten feet wide all round it, between the corn and the hedge. This is most beautiful! The hedges are full now of the shepherd's rose, honey-suckle, and all sorts of wild flowers, so that you are upon a grass-walk with this most beautiful of all flower-gardens and shrubberies on your one hand, and with the corn on the other. And thus you go from field to field (on foot or on horseback), the sort of corn, the sort of underwood and timber, the shape and size of the fields, the height of the hedgerows, the height of the trees, all continually varying. Talk of *pleasure-grounds,* indeed! What that man ever invented under the name of pleasure-grounds can equal these fields in Hertfordshire?

Upon the songs and habits of birds, we may add the following:—

There is one deficiency, and that, with me, a great one, throughout this county of corn and grass and oxen and sheep, that I have come over during the last three weeks, namely, the want of *singing birds.* We are now just in that season when they sing most. Here, in all this county, I have seen and heard only about four skylarks, and not one other singing bird of any description; and of the small birds that do not sing I have seen only one *yellow-hammer,* and it was perched on the rail of a pond between Boston and Sibrey. Oh! the thousands of linnets all singing together on one tree in the sand-hills of Surrey! Oh! the carolling in the coppices and dingles of Hampshire and Sussex and Kent! At this moment (five o'clock in the morning) the groves at Barn Elm are echoing with the warbling of thousands upon thousands of birds. The *thrush* begins a little before it is light; next the *blackbird;* next the larks begin to rise; all the rest begin the moment the sun gives the signal; and from the hedges, the bushes, from the middle and the topmost twigs of the trees, comes the singing of endless variety; from the long dead grass comes the sound of the sweet and soft voice of the *white-throat* or *nettle-tom,* while the loud and merry song of the lark (the songster himself out of sight) seems to descend from the skies. Milton, in his description of Paradise, has not omitted the "song of earliest birds."

. . . . .

Here I heard the first singing of the birds this year; and I here observed an instance of that *petticoat government* which apparently pervades the whole of animated nature. A lark very near to me in a ploughed field rose from the ground, and was saluting the sun with his delightful song. He was got about as high as the dome of St. Paul's (having me for a motionless and admiring auditor) when the hen started up from nearly the same spot whence the cock had risen, flew up and passed close by him. I could not hear what she said, but supposed that she must have given him a pretty smart reprimand, for down she came upon the ground, and he, ceasing to sing, took a twirl in the air and came down after her. Others have, I dare say, seen this a thousand times over; but I never observed it before.

It is pleasant to know that the practice referred to in the following paragraph still holds amongst English labourers:—

You see here (*i.e.* Buckinghamshire), as in Kent, Sussex, Surrey, and Hampshire, and, indeed, in almost every part of England, that most interesting of all objects, that which is such an honour to England, and that which distinguishes it from all the rest of the world, namely, those *neatly kept and productive little gardens round the labourers' houses,* which are seldom un-ornamented with more or less of flowers. We have only to look at these to know what sort of people English labourers are. These gardens are the answer to the Malthuses and the Scarletts. Shut your mouths, you Scotch economists; cease bawling, Mr. Brougham and you *Edinburgh Review*ers, till *you* can show us something, not *like,* but approaching towards a likeness of *this!*

Apropos of Scotchmen, here is his opinion of that canny race:—

Scotchmen toil hard enough in Scotland, but when they go from home it is not to *work,* if you please. They are found in gardens, and especially in gentlemen's gardens. Tying up flowers, picking dead leaves off exotics, peeping into melon-frames, publishing the banns of marriage between the "male" and "female" blossoms, tap-tap-tapping against a wall with a hammer that weighs half-an-ounce. They have backs as straight, and shoulders as square, as heroes of Waterloo; and who can blame them? The digging, the mowing, the carrying of loads; all the break-back and sweat-extracting work, they leave to be performed by those who have less *prudence* than they have. The great purpose of human art, the great end of human study, is to obtain *ease,* to throw the burden of labour from our own shoulders, and to fix it on those of others.

He has already been compared in some respects to Mr. Bright, but, to judge from the following, such a compar-

ison would have seemed to him far from flattering. He is speaking of the Quakers.

Here is a sect of non-labourers. One would think that their religion bound them under a curse not to work. Some part of the people of all other sects work, sweat at work; do something that is useful to other people; but here is a sect of buyers and sellers. They make nothing, they cause nothing to come; they breed as well as other sects, but they make none of the raiment or houses, and cause none of the food to come. In order to justify some measure for paring the nails of this greedy sect, it is enough to say of them, which we may with perfect truth, that, if all the other sects were to act like them, *the community must perish.* This is quite enough to say of this sect, of the monstrous privileges of whom we shall, I hope, one of these days see an end. If I had the dealing of them, I would soon teach them to use the *spade,* and the *plough,* and the *musket* too when necessary.

Very seasonable just now appears his general appreciation of middle-men. "Does not everyone see, in a minute, how the exchanging of fairs and markets for shops creates *idlers and traffickers,* creates those locusts called middle-men, who create nothing, who add to the value of nothing, who improve nothing, but who live in idleness and who live well, too, out of the labour of the producer and the consumer. The fair and the market, those wise institutions of our forefathers, and with regard to the management of which they were so scrupulously careful; the fair and the market bring the producer and the consumer in contact with each other. Whatever is gained, is at any rate gained by one or the other of these. The fair and the market bring them together, and enable them to act for their mutual interest and convenience. The shop and the trafficker keep them apart; the shop hides from both producer and consumer the real state of matters. The fair and market lay everything open. Going to either, you see the state of things at once, and the transactions are fair and just; not disfigured, too, by falsehood, and by those attempts at deception which disgrace trafficking in general."

Here, as so often, Cobbett makes the great mistake of wishing to put back the clock of history; nevertheless, the evil to which he alludes is a very real one, and to remedy it would be to supply the answer to what is undoubtedly one of the most pressing social questions of the day.

In reading Cobbett, one must always bear in mind the character of the times in which he lived. It is this which explains, and in a great measure justifies, his attitude towards the Church Establishment. A not wholly base indignation may have moved him, when he saw that estate of the Church, which Mr. Disraeli termed "the estate of the poor," diverted from its rightful purpose, and serving to maintain absentee parsons in the assembly rooms of Bath and Cheltenham. "This parish," he writes, probably with exaggeration, but with a certain substratum of truth, "of Weston is remarkable for having a rector *who has constantly resided for twenty years!* I do not believe that there is an instance to match this in the whole kingdom." "It is very true that the labouring people have in a great measure ceased to go to church. There were scarcely any of that class in this (Goudhurst) great country church to-day. I do not believe there were ten."

What would have been Cobbett's opinion (assuming always, as I see no reason to doubt, that he honestly held the views he professed) upon the question of the Established Church, could he have lived to witness that great revival by which its dry bones have become animated with new being and new life, it were idle to inquire. Probably his prejudices had become too deeply rooted to be extirpated. On many questions, however, his views, starting from very different premises, curiously anticipate those of the later High Church party.

"Let it be observed," he writes,

> that when these churches were built, people had not yet thought of cramming them with pews, as a stable is filled with stalls. Those who built these churches had no idea that worshipping God meant going to *sit* to hear a man talk out what he called preaching. By *worship,* they meant very different things; and, above all things, when they had made a fine and noble building, they did not dream of disfiguring the inside of it by filling its floors with large and deep boxes made of deal boards. In short, the floor was the place for worshippers to stand or to kneel, and there was *no distinction;* no *high* place, and no *low* place; all were upon a level *before God* at any rate. Some were not stuck into pews lined with green or red cloth, while others were crammed into corners, to stand erect or sit on the floor. These odious distinctions are of Protestant origin and growth. The lazy lolling in pews we owe to what is called *the Reformation.*

Again,

> St. Botolph, to whom this church (Boston) is dedicated, while he (if Saints see and hear what is passing on earth) must lament that the piety-inspiring mass has been in this noble edifice supplanted by the monstrous humming of an oaken hutch, has not the mortification of seeing his church treated in a manner as if the new possessors sighed for the hour of its destruction. It is taken great care of; and though it has suffered from *Protestant repairs;* though the images are gone and the stained glass, and though the glazing is now in squares instead of lozenges; though the nave is stuffed with *pens* called pews; and though other changes have taken place, detracting from the beauty of the edifice, great care is taken of it, as it now is, and the inside is not disfigured and disgraced by a *gallery,* that great characteristic mark of Protestant taste, which, as nearly as may be, makes a church like a playhouse.

In this connection we may note the following:—

> Hearing the bells of the Cathedral, I took Richard to show him that ancient and most magnificent pile, and particularly to show him the tomb of that famous Bishop of Winchester, William of Wykham, who was the chancellor and minister of that great and glorious King, Edward III.; who sprang from poor parents in the little village of Wykham, three miles from Botley; and who, amongst other great and most munificent deeds, founded the famous college, or school, of Winchester, and also one of the colleges at Oxford. I told Richard about this, as we went from the inn down to the Cathedral; and when I *showed him the tomb* where the bishop lies on his back, in his Catholic robes, with his mitre on his head, his shepherd's crook by his side, with little children at his feet, their hands put together in a praying attitude, he looked with a degree of inquisitive earnestness that pleased me very much. I took him, as far as I could, about the cathedral. The "service" was now begun. There is a *dean,* and God knows how many *prebends,* belonging to this immensely rich bishopric and chapter; and there were at this 'service' *two or three men and five or six boys* in white surplices, with a congregation of *fifteen women* and *four men.* Gracious God! If William of Wykham could at that moment have been raised from his tomb! If St. Swithin, whose name the Cathedral bears, or Alfred the Great, to whom St. Swithin was tutor: if either of these could have come or had been told that *that* was what was now carried on, by men who talked of the "damnable errors" of those who founded that very Church! . . .

> For my part I could not look up at the spire and at the whole of the Church of Salisbury without *feeling* that I lived in degenerate times. Such a thing never could be made *now.* We feel *that,* as we look at the building. It really does appear that if our forefathers had not made these buildings, we should have forgotten before now what the Christian religion was!

Of course it would be easy to make too much of all this. Where Cobbett is, there, we may be sure, politics are not far off. And his enthusiasm for William of Wykham is mainly due to the fact that in the times of that worthy there were as yet no poor rates. It would be an idle, as well as somewhat ludicrous endeavour, to wrap his brawny form in a ritualist cassock, or represent the man who brought Tom Paine's body home to England as a Tractarian born out of due time: nevertheless, the form in which his natural tastes and instincts embodied his attacks upon the Church of his day is, I think, not a little curious.

Upon the subject of sport, Cobbett is always good reading. He was, his son tells us, while at Botley for years a strict preserver of game, though no "shot," keeping sometimes from thirty to forty dogs, greyhounds, pointers, setters, and spaniels. He had a cart's bed, full of live hares, brought from Yorkshire, to turn down on his own farms.

At Uphusband, in Hampshire, he is reminded how he once saw at Netherhaven, Mr. Hick Beech's, an "acre of hares." "Mr. Beech received us very politely. He took us into a wheat stubble close by his paddock; his son took a gallop round, cracking his whip at the same time; the hares (which were very thickly in sight before) started all over the field, ran into a *flock* like sheep, and we all agreed that the flock did cover an acre of ground." . . .

The attitude of Cobbett towards the "landed interest" was one altogether peculiar to himself. His natural prejudices were in favour of the old country squire, as opposed to the "lord of the loom" and the loanmonger. He speaks with respect and enthusiasm of "a resident native gentry, attached to the soil, known to every farmer and labourer from their childhood, frequently mixing with them in those pursuits where all artificial distinctions are lost, practising hospitality without ceremony, from habit and not on calculation." But on the other hand the interests of the aristocracy seemed closely identified with those of the "system," and with "the system" Cobbett had declared war to the death. And so it happened that he became the most bitter enemy of his natural friends, constituted under a commission signed and sealed by his own arrogance to be a "scourge and minister." But, just as in his quarrel with the Church we found him curiously anticipating the notes of the Oxford movement, so, in his opinions upon social questions he is often the precursor of the "Young England" party.

> Hume and other historians rail against the *feudal* system, and we "enlightened" and "free" creatures, as we are, look back with contempt, or at least with surprise and pity, to the "vassalage" of our forefathers. But if the matter were well inquired into, not slurred over, but well and truly examined, we should find that the people of these villages were as free in the days of William Rufus, as are the people of the present day; and that vassalage, only under other names, exists now as completely as it existed then. Well, but out of this, if true, arises another question, namely, whether the million would derive any benefit from being transferred from these great lords, who possess them by hundreds, to Jews and jobbers who would possess them by half-dozens or by couples? . . . Talk of vassals! talk of villains! talk of serfs! Are there any of them, or did feudal times ever see any of them, so debased, so absolutely slaves, as the poor creatures who, in the "enlightened" North, are compelled to work fourteen hours in a day, in a heat of eighty-four degrees, and who are liable to punishment for looking out at a window of the factory!

Different as was in many ways the England of Cobbett from the England of to-day, there are yet some observations in *Rural Rides* that would apply very well to the state of things around us. "Agricultural distress," he writes in 1821, "is the great topic of general conversation." And the burden of the following lament is still heard in the land.

> Those [*i.e.* the farm-houses] that are now erected are mere painted shells, with a mistress within, who is stuck up in a place she calls a *parlour*, with, if she have children, the "young ladies and gentlemen" about her: some showy chairs and a sofa (a *sofa* by all means); half a dozen prints in gilt frames hanging up; some swinging book-shelves with novels and tracts upon them; a dinner brought in by a girl that is perhaps better educated than she; two or three nick-nacks to eat, instead of a piece of bacon and a pudding; the house too neat for a dirty-shoed carter to be allowed to come into; and everything proclaiming to every sensible beholder that there is here a constant anxiety

to make a *show* not warranted by the reality. The children (which is the worst part of it) are all too clever to work. They are all to be *gentle-folks*. Go to plough? Good God! What! young gentlemen go to plough! They become clerks, or some skimming-dish thing or other. They flee from the dirty *work*, as cunning horses do from the bridle.

The following passage upon the working of the old Poor Law, is worthy to be placed beside the memorable account, in *Past and Present*, of what Carlyle saw outside the workhouse at St. Ives. It detracts nothing from the merit of Cobbett's description that he altogether misread the moral of the picture, and fiercely opposed that change in the law which was to render such a state of things for the future impossible.

> Here we found a parcel of labourers at parish work. Amongst them was an old playmate of mine. The account they gave of their situation was very dismal. The harvest was over early; the hop-picking is now over; and now they are *employed by the parish*, that is to say, not absolutely digging holes one day and filling them up the next, but, at the expense of half-ruined farmers, and tradesmen, and landlords, to break stones into very small pieces, to make nice smooth roads, lest the jolting in going along them should create bile in the stomach of the over-fed tax-eaters. I call upon mankind to witness this scene, and to say whether ever the like of this was heard of before. It is a state of things wherein all is out of order; where self-preservation, that great law of nature, seems to be set at defiance; for here are farmers unable to pay men for working for them, and yet compelled to pay them for working in doing that which is really of no use to any human being. There lie the hop-poles unstripped. You see a hundred things in the neighbouring fields that want doing. The fences are not nearly what they ought to be. The very meadows to our right and left in crossing this little valley would occupy these men advantageously until the setting in of the frost; and here are they not, as I said before, actually digging holes one day and filling them up the next, but to all intents and purposes as uselessly employed.

Even in his maladies Cobbett could not be like other people, nor would it be wise to try as a remedy for the *whooping cough*, the riding wet to the skin two or three hours amongst the clouds on the South Downs, because in his case it appears to have been efficacious. The dogged obstinacy which was his characteristic finds an amusing illustration in the story of his ride from Hambledon to Thursley. If he had taken the regular road he would have passed over Hindhead, *which he was determined to avoid*. He accomplishes his object as far as a village called Headley, by going across a forest. But from Headley his troubles begin. He rashly sets out in the dark with a guide who manages to lose his way. The end of it being that they arrive at Thursley, but only *after having crossed Hindhead*. Whereupon Cobbett, *more suo*, refuses the guide the three shillings that he had agreed to give him for showing him the way. "Either you did not know the way well," he says, "or you did: if the former, it was dishonest in you to undertake to guide me; if the latter, you have wilfully led me miles out of my way." "The guide grumbled, but off he went!"

This experience suggests to him the old moral "how differently one is affected by the same sight under different circumstances. At the 'Holly Bush' at Headley, there was a room full of fellows in white smock-frocks, drinking and smoking and talking, and I, who was then dry and warm, *moralized* within myself on their *folly* in spending their time in such a way. But when I got down from Hindhead to the public-house at Road Lane, with my skin soaking and my teeth chattering, I thought just such another group, whom I saw through the window, sitting round a good fire, with pipes in their mouths, the *wisest assembly* I had ever set my eyes on. A real *collective wisdom!"* In the manufacture of nick-names or of "catch" sentences Cobbett was proverbially happy. Little did Gambetta think, when he coined the famous expression "Se sommettre ou se démettre," that he was merely putting into French Cobbett's advice to Sir Francis Burdett, which occurs in the **Rural Rides,** that he must "turn to or turn out."

COBBETT'S

TWO-PENNY TRASH;

OR,

POLITICS FOR THE POOR.

VOLUME I.

FROM JULY 1830, TO JUNE, 1831, INCLUSIVE.

LONDON:
PRINTED BY THE AUTHOR, AND SOLD AT No. 11, BOLT-COURT, FLEET-STREET, AND MAY BE HAD OF ALL BOOKSELLERS.

1831.

Title page of Cobbett's Two-Penny Trash, *a periodical concerned with the grievances of laborers.*

In the foregoing pages an attempt has been made to give, by means of copious extracts, some idea of a book now scarce, written by an author now, I believe, neglected; but who, in the memory of men still living, was a great power in the land. Fifty years have well nigh passed since Cobbett's death, and the country people whom he loved well, if not wisely, are at last entering upon that promised land of political citizenship which is, they are told, to be flowing for them with the milk and honey of others' storing. And men are awaiting, some with insolent exultation and others with fear and trembling, and others yet again with hope not unmixed with apprehension, the event. At such a time an additional interest lends itself to the one eminent author whom the farm-labourers of England can claim as their own. The grandson of a day-labourer, the son of a small farmer, in his youth himself a plough-boy, growing up, a common soldier among comrades recruited from the lowest classes, Cobbett, with all his individual peculiarities, yet everywhere smacks of the deep clays and sands of his native Surrey. To him may we apply with truth the expression of Balzac "Il pue le peuple." What light then, however fitful and dubious, do Cobbett's writings throw upon the probable action of our new masters? In the first place, if we are to accept him as security, the *Pall Mall Gazette* is clearly right, and Manchester Liberalism will soon, at the hands of an enfranchised Democracy, receive its quietus. Talk of war and empire being the dreams of an idle aristocracy! Why, Cobbett considered that the first act of a Reformed Parliament, after settling the question of the Debt, should be to build such a fleet as should curb once and for ever the insolence of cousin Jonathan! Upon the grave question how far the Democracy will be able to keep clear of the dangerous rocks of Socialism, the answer from Cobbett is less certain. Upon the one hand he has all a Democracy's hatred and contempt for political economy, for that "feelosophy" which he does not care to comprehend. He believes that the condition of the people may in many ways be bettered by Acts of Parliament, and very often he comes very near to Socialism; but on the other hand his roots grow deep in the past; he has the Englishman's contempt for Utopian system-mongers (witness the way in which he speaks of "Owen that 'humane' half-mad fellow"), and the English tolerance of what is logically anomalous, so long as in fact it works well; he may assume the rags and ribbons of Jacobin Paris, but the smock-frock of his fathers is his natural wear. With all his violence there is in him not a little of that English "good humour" which Clarendon has noted in a sentence which Bolingbroke could never read without tears. Thus musing, one seems to discern, hardly and indistinctly, through the dense fog of bygone controversies, the figure of another Cobbett, whom neglect has not piqued, nor persecution maddened; a figure not wholly inauspicious for the success of our new departure. These, however, are high themes, upon which I have neither the desire nor the capacity to enter. Enough to have been allowed to suspend in the temple of Toryism a wreath, however short-lived, to the memory of one with whom, a Radical of Radicals, we have this much in common, that he did not love the Whigs, and that he loved England.

George Saintsbury (essay date 1891)

SOURCE: "William Cobbett," in *The Collected Essays and Papers of George Saintsbury, 1875-1920, Vol. I,* J. M. Dent & Sons, Ltd., 1923, pp. 269-301.

[*Saintsbury was a late-nineteenth and early-twentieth-century English literary historian and critic. Hugely prolific, he composed histories of English and European literature as well as numerous critical works on individual authors, styles, and periods. In the following essay, originally published in* Macmillan's Magazine *in 1891, Saintsbury discusses Cobbett's career and significance.*]

To acquaint oneself properly with the works of Cobbett is no child's play. It requires some money, a great deal of time, still more patience, and a certain freedom from superfineness. For, as few of his books have recently been reprinted, and as they were all very popular when they appeared, it is frequently necessary to put up with copies exhibiting the marks of that popularity in a form with which Coleridge and Lamb professed to be delighted, but to which I own that I am churl enough to prefer the clean, fresh leaves of even the most modern reprint.

And the total is huge; for Cobbett's industry and facility of work were both appalling, and while his good work is constantly disfigured by rubbish, there is hardly a single parcel of his rubbish in which there is not good work. Of the seventy-four articles which compose his bibliography, some of the most portentous, such as the *State Trials* (afterwards known as Howell's) and the *Parliamentary Debates* (afterwards known as Hansard's), may be disregarded as simple compilation; and it is scarcely necessary for any one to read the thirty years of **The Register** through, seeing that almost everything in it that is most characteristic reappeared in other forms. But this leaves a formidable residue. The **Works of Peter Porcupine,** in which most of Cobbett's writings earlier than the nineteenth century and a few later are collected, fill twelve volumes of fair size. The only other collection, the **Political Works,** made up by his sons after his death from **The Register** and other sources, is in six volumes, none of which contains less than five hundred, while one contains more than eight hundred large pages, so closely printed that each represents two if not three of the usual library octavo. The **Rural Rides** fill two stout volumes in the last edition: besides which there are before me literally dozens of mostly rather grubby volumes of every size from Tull's *Husbandry,* in a portly octavo, to the *Legacy to Labourers,* about as big as a lady's card-case. If a man be virtuous enough, or rash enough, to stray further into anti-Cobbett pamphlets (of which I once bought an extremely grimy bundle for a sovereign) he may go on in that path almost for ever. And I see no rest for the sole of his foot till he has read through the whole of "the bloody old *Times*" or "that foolish drab Anna Brodie's rubbish," as Cobbett used with indifferent geniality to call that newspaper,—the last elegant description being solely due to the fact that he had become aware that a poor lady of the name was a shareholder.

Let it be added that this vast mass is devoted almost impartially to as vast a number of subjects, that it displays throughout the queerest and (till you are well acquainted with it) the most incredible mixture of sense and nonsense, folly and wit, ignorance and knowledge, good temper and bad blood, sheer egotism and sincere desire to benefit the country. Cobbett will write upon politics and upon economics, upon history ecclesiastical and civil, upon grammar, cookery, gardening, wood-craft, standing armies, population, ice-houses, and almost every other conceivable subject, with the same undoubting confidence that he is and must be right. In what plain men still call inconsistency there never was his equal. He was approaching middle life when he was still writing cheerful pamphlets and tracts with such titles as **The Bloody Buoy, The Cannibal's Progress,** and so on, destined to hold up the French Revolution to the horror of mankind; he had not passed middle life when he discovered that the said Revolution was only a natural and necessary consequence of the same system of taxation which was grinding down England. He denied stoutly that he was anything but a friend to monarchical government, and asseverated a thousand times over that he had not the slightest wish to deprive landlords or any one else of their property. Yet for the last twenty years of his life he was constantly holding up the happy state of those republicans, the profligacy, injustice, and tyranny of whose government he had earlier denounced. He frequently came near, if he did not openly avow, the "hold-the-harvest" doctrine; and he deliberately proposed that the national creditor should be defrauded of his interest, and therefore practically of his capital.

A very shrewd man naturally, and by no means an ill-informed one in some ways, there was no assertion too wildly contradictory of facts, no assumption too flagrantly opposed to common sense, for him to make when he had an argument to further or a craze to support. "My opinion is," says he very gravely, "that Lincolnshire alone contains more of those fine buildings [churches] than the whole continent of Europe." The churches of Lincolnshire are certainly fine; but imagine all the churches of even the western continent of Europe, from the abbey of Batalha to Cologne Cathedral, and from Santa Rosalia to the Folgoët, crammed and crouching under the shadow of Boston Stump! He "dared say that Ely probably contained from fifty to a hundred thousand people" at a time when it is rather improbable that London contained the larger number of the two. Only mention Jews, Scotchmen, the National Debt, the standing army, pensions, poetry, tea, potatoes, larch trees, and a great many other things, and Cobbett becomes a mere, though a very amusing, maniac. Let him come across in one of his peregrinations, or remember in the course of a book or article, some magistrate who gave a decision unfavourable to him twenty years before, some lawyer who took a side against him, some journalist who opposed his pamphlets, and a torrent of half humorous but wholly vindictive Billingsgate follows; while if the luckless one has lost his estate, or in any way come to misfortune meanwhile, Cobbett will jeer and whoop and triumph over him like an Indian squaw over a hostile brave at the stake. Mixed with all this you shall find such plain shrewd common sense, such an incomparable power of clear exposition of any subject that the writer himself understands, such homely but genuine humour, such untiring energy, and such a hearty desire for the comfort of everybody who is not a Jew or a jobber or a tax-eater, as few public writers have ever displayed. And (which is the most important thing for us) you shall also find sense and nonsense alike, rancorous and mischievous diatribes as well as sober discourses, politics as well as trade-puffery (for Cobbett puffed his own wares unblushingly), all set forth in such a style as not more than two other Englishmen, whose names are Defoe and Bunyan, can equal.

Like theirs it is a style wholly natural and unstudied. It is often said, and he himself confesses, that as a young man he gave his days and nights to the reading of Swift. But except in the absence of adornment, and the uncompromising plainness of speech, there is really very little resemblance between them, and what there is is chiefly due to Cobbett's following of the *Drapier's Letters,* where Swift, admirable as he is, is clearly using a falsetto. For one thing, the main characteristic of Swift—the perpetual unforced unflagging irony which is the blood and the life of his style—is utterly absent from Cobbett. On the other hand, if Cobbett imitated little, he was imitated much. Although his accounts of the circulation of his works are doubtless exaggerated as he exaggerated everything connected with himself, it was certainly very large; and though they were no doubt less read by the literary than by the non-literary class, they have left traces everywhere. As a whole Cobbett is not imitable; the very reasons which gave him the style forbade another to borrow it. But certain tricks of his reappear in places both likely and unlikely; and since I have been thoroughly acquainted with him I think I can see the ancestry of some of the mannerisms of two writers whose filiation had hitherto puzzled me—Peacock and Borrow. In the latter case there is no doubt whatever; indeed the kinship between Borrow and Cobbett is very strong in many ways. Even in the former I do not think there is much doubt, though Peacock's thorough scholarship and Cobbett's boisterous unscholarliness make it one of thought rather than of form, and of a small part of thought only.

Therefore Cobbett is very well worthy studying, the study being part of that never-ending and delightful game of tracing literary genealogies, of filling in the literary maps, which is at once the business and the pastime of the critic. His political importance has seldom been questioned, and I think that on the whole it has been even underrated. His personality is extremely interesting and nearly always amusing, though the amusement may sometimes go a little close to disgust,—for no man ever illustrated both the faults and the merits of *l'Anglais,* if not of *l'homme sensuel moyen,* as did Cobbett. And last of all, though to me not least, there are few more simply delightful writers to read without bothering yourself at all about literary filiations or ancestries, about political revolutions or conversations, about Cobbett the man, or England the nation. It is indeed true (and this is the curse of all political writing, though less of his than of most) that the lapse of time has

made it impossible to leave all trouble about politics aside, unless you happen to be thoroughly well acquainted with politics. Even the ***Rural Rides,*** even the ***English Gardener,*** nay, even the very ***Grammar*** itself, cannot be read currently if you do not know who and what "the Thing" and "the Wen" and "the Fool-Liar" and "Anna Brodie" and "my dignitary Dr Black" were; if you are not acquainted with all the circumstances which made the very words "tea" or "taxes," "paper-money" or "potatoes," throw Cobbett into a kind of epilepsy; if you are not in the secret of his perpetual divagations on locust-trees and swede turnips, on "Cobbett's corn" and ridge cultivation. But my experience is that, when you once do know these things, you bother yourself very little about them afterwards so far as the mere reading of Cobbett goes. The hottest Tory gospeller could not think of getting angry with Cobbett, or indeed getting into controversy with him at all; and I should doubt whether even our modern Socialists, though some of his ideas are very like theirs, would greet him very warmly as an ally. He *disreasons* too much (to use a word which is very much wanted in English and has the strictest titles to admission), and his disreasoning, powerful as it was at the time, has lost too much of its hold on present thought and present circumstance.

He has left an agreeable and often quoted account of his own early life in an autobiographic fragment written to confound his enemies in America. He was born on 9th March, 1762, at Farnham; and the chief of his interests during his life centred round the counties of Hampshire and Surrey, with Berkshire and Wiltshire thrown in as benefiting by neighbourhood. His father was a small farmer, not quite uneducated, but not much in means or rank above a labourer, and all the family were brought up to work hard. After some unimportant vicissitudes, William ran away to London and, attempting quill-driving in an attorney's office for a time, soon got tired of it and enlisted in a marching regiment which was sent to Nova Scotia. This was in the spring of 1784. As he was steady, intelligent, and not uneducated, he very soon rose from the ranks, and was sergeant-major for some years. During his service with the colours he made acquaintance with his future wife (a gunner's daughter of the literal and amiable kind), and with Lord Edward Fitzgerald. The regiment came home in 1792, and Cobbett got his discharge, married his beloved, and went to France. Unfortunately he had other reasons besides love and a desire to learn French for quitting British shores. He had discovered, or imagined, that some of his officers were guilty of malversation of regimental money, he abused his position as sergeant-major to take secret copies of regimental documents, and when he had got his discharge he lodged his accusation. A court-martial was granted. When it met, however, there was no accuser, for Cobbett had gone to France. Long afterwards, when the facts were cast up against him, he attempted a defence. The matter is one of considerable intricacies and of no great moment. Against Cobbett it may be said to be one of the facts which prove (what indeed hardly needs proving), that he was not a man of any chivalrous delicacy of feeling, and did not see that in no circumstances can it be justifiable to bring accusations of disgraceful conduct against others and then run away. In his favour it may be said that, though not a very young man, he was not in the least a man of the world, and was no doubt sincerely surprised and horrified to find that his complaint was not to be judged off-hand and Cadi-fashion, but with all sorts of cumbrous and expensive forms.

However this may be, he went off with his wife and his savings to France; and enjoyed himself there for some months, tackling diligently to French the while, until the Revolution (it was, let it be remembered, in 1792) made the country too hot for him. He determined to go to Philadelphia, where, and elsewhere in the United States, he passed the next seven years. They were seven years of a very lively character; for it was the nature of Cobbett to find quarrels, and he found plenty of them here. Some accounts of his exploits in offence and defence may be found in the biographies, fuller ones in the books of the chronicles of Peter Porcupine, his *nom da guerre* in pamphleteering and journalism. Cobbett was at this time, despite his transactions with the Judge Advocate General, his flight and his selection of France and America for sojourn, a red-hot Tory and a true Briton, and he engaged in a violent controversy, or series of controversies, with the pro-Gallic and anti-English party in the States. The works of Peter, besides the above-quoted *Bloody Buoy* and *Cannibal's Progress,* contain in their five thousand pages or thereabouts, other cheerfully named documents, such as: *A Bone to Gnaw for the Democrats, A Kick for a Bite, The Diplomatic Blunderbuss, The American Rushlight,* and so on. This last had mainly to do with a non-political quarrel into which Cobbett got with a person of some professional fame, the "American Sydenham," otherwise Dr Benjamin Rush. Rush got Cobbett cast in heavy damages for libel; and though these were paid by subscription, the affair seems to have disgusted our pamphleteer and he sailed for England on 1st June, 1800.

There can be little doubt, though Cobbett's own bragging and the bickering of his biographers have rather darkened than illuminated the matter, that he came home with pretty definite and very fair prospects of Government patronage. More than one of his Anti-Jacobin pamphlets had been reprinted for English consumption. He had already arranged for the London edition of "Porcupine's" *Works* which appeared subsequently; and he had attracted attention not merely from literary understrappers of Government but from men like Windham. Very soon after his return Windham asked him to dinner, to meet not merely Canning, Ellis, Frere, Malone and others, but Pitt himself. The publication of the host's diary long afterwards clearly established the fact, which had been rather idly contested or doubted by some commentators.

How or why Cobbett fell away from Pitt's party is not exactly known, and is easier to understand than definitely to explain; even when he left it is not certain. He was offered, he says, a Government paper or even two; but he refused and published his own *Porcupine,* which lasted for some time till it lapsed (with intermediate stages) into the famous *Weekly Register*. In both, and in their inter-

mediates for some three or four years at least, the general policy of the Government, and especially the war with France, was stoutly supported. But Cobbett was a freelance born and bred, and he never during the whole of his life succeeded in working under any other command than his own, or with any one on equal terms. He got into trouble before very long owing to some letters, signed *Juverna,* on the Irish executive; and though his contributor (one Johnson, afterwards a judge) gave himself up, and Cobbett escaped the fines which had been imposed on him, his susceptible vanity had no doubt been touched. It was also beyond doubt a disgust to his self-educated mind to find himself regarded as an inferior by the regularly trained wits and scholars of the Government press; and I should be afraid that he was annoyed at Pitt's taking no notice of him. But, to do Cobbett justice, there were other and nobler reasons for his revolt. His ideal of politics and economics (of which more presently), though an impossible one, was sincere and not ungenerous; and he could not but perceive that a dozen years of war had made its contrast with the actual state of the British farmer and labourer more glaring than ever.

The influence which he soon wielded through the *Register,* and the profit which he derived from it, at once puffed him up and legitimately encouraged the development of his views. He bought, or rather (a sad thing for such a denouncer of "paper"), obtained, subject to heavy mortgages, a considerable estate of several farms at and near Botley, in Hampshire. Here for some five years (1804 to 1809), he lived the life of a very substantial yeoman, almost a squire, entertaining freely, farming, coursing, encouraging boxing and single-stick, fishing with dragnets, and editing the *Register* partly in person and partly by deputy. Of these deputies, the chief were his partner, and afterwards foe, the printer Wright, and Howell of the *State Trials*. This latter, being unluckily a gentleman and a university man, comes in for one of Cobbett's characteristic flings as "one of your college gentlemen," who "have and always will have the insolence to think themselves our betters; and our superior talents, industry and weight only excite their envy." Prosperity is rarely good for an Englishman of Cobbett's stamp, and he seems at this time to have decidedly lost his head. He had long been a pronounced Radical, thundering or guffawing in the *Register* at pensions, sinecures, the debt, paper-money, the game-laws (though he himself preserved), and so forth; and the authorities naturally enough only waited for an opportunity of explaining to him that immortal maxim which directs the expectations of those who play at any kind of bowls.

In July, 1809, he let them in by an article of the most violent character on the suppression of a mutiny among the Ely Militia. This had been put down, and the ringleaders flogged by some cavalry of the German Legion; and Cobbett took advantage of it to beat John Bull's drum furiously. It has been the custom to turn up the whites of the eyes at Lord Ellenborough who tried the case, and Sir Vicary Gibbs who prosecuted; but I do not think any sane man who remembers what the importance of discipline in the army was in 1809, can find fault with the jury who, and not Ellenborough or Gibbs, had to settle the matter, and who found Cobbett guilty. The sentence no doubt was severe,—as such sentences in such cases were then wont to be—two years in Newgate, a fine of a thousand pounds, and security in the same amount for seven years to come. Here, no doubt, Ellenborough's responsibility comes in, and he may be thought to have looked before and after as well as at the present. But the *Register* was not stopped, and Cobbett was allowed to continue therein without hindrance a polemic which was not likely to grow milder. For he never forgot or forgave an injury to his interests, or an insult to his vanity; and he was besides becoming, quite honestly and disinterestedly, more and more of a fanatic on divers points both of economics and of politics proper.

I cannot myself attach much importance to the undoubted fact that after the trial, which happened in June, 1810, but before judgment, Cobbett, aghast for a moment at the apparent ruin impending, made (as he certainly did make) some overtures of surrender and discontinuance of the *Register*. Such a course in a man with a large family and no means of supporting it but his pen, would have been, if not heroic, not disgraceful. But the negotiation somehow fell through. Unluckily for Cobbett, he on two subsequent occasions practically denied that he had ever made any offer at all; and the truth only came out when he and Wright quarrelled, nearly a dozen years later. This, the affair of the court-martial, and another to be mentioned shortly, are the only blots on his conduct as a man that I know, and in such an Ishmael as he was they are not very fatal.

He devoted the greater part of his time, during the easy, though rather costly, imprisonment of those days, to his *Paper against Gold,* in which, with next to no knowledge of the matter, he attacked probably the thorniest of all subjects, that of the currency; and the *Register* went on. He came out of Newgate in July, 1812, naturally in no very amiable temper. A mixture of private and public griefs almost immediately brought him into collision with the authorities of the Church. He had long been at loggerheads with those of the State; and it was now that he became more than ever the advocate (and the most popular advocate it had) of Parliamentary Reform. He was, however, pretty quiet for three or four years, but at the end of that time, in September, 1816, he acted on a suggestion of Lord Cochrane's, cheapened the *Register* from one shilling to two-pence, and opened the new series with one of his best pamphlet-addresses, **"To the Journeymen and Labourers of England, Wales, Scotland and Ireland."** For a time he was very much in the mouths of men; but Ministers were not idle, and the suspension of the Habeas Corpus and the famous *Six Acts* prepared for him a state of things still hotter than he had experienced before. Cobbett did not give it time to heat itself specially for him. He turned his eyes once more to America, and, very much to the general surprise, suddenly left Liverpool on 22nd March, 1817, arriving in May at New York, whence he proceeded to Long Island, and established himself on a farm there. Unluckily there were other reasons for his flight besides political ones. His affairs had

become much muddled during his imprisonment, and had not mended since; while though his assets were considerable they were of a kind not easy to realise. There seems no doubt that Cobbett was generally thought to have run away from a gaol in more senses than one, and that the thought did him no good.

But he was an impossible person to put down; even his own mistakes, which were pretty considerable, could not do it. His flight, as it was called, gave handles to his enemies, and not least to certain former friends, including such very different persons as Orator Hunt and Sir Francis Burdett; it caused a certain belatedness, and, for a time, a certain intermittency, in his contributions to the *Register;* it confirmed him in his financial crazes, and it may possibly have supported him in a sort of private repudiation of his own debts, which he executed even before becoming legally a bankrupt. Finally it led him to the most foolish act of his life, the lugging of Tom Paine's bones back to a country which, though not prosperous, could at any rate provide itself with better manure than that. In this famous absurdity the purely silly side of Cobbett's character comes out. For some time after he returned he was at low water both in finances and in popularity; while such political sanity as he ever possessed may be said to have wholly vanished. Yet, oddly enough, or not oddly, the transplanting and the re-transplanting seem to have had a refreshing effect on his literary production. He never indeed again produced anything so vigorous as the best of his earlier political works, but in non-political and mixed styles he even improved; and though he is more extravagant than ever in substance occasionally, there is a certain mellowness of form which is very remarkable. He was not far short of sixty when he returned in 1819; but the space of his life, subsequent to his flight, yielded the *Year's Residence in America,* the *English Grammar,* the *Twelve Sermons,* the *Cottage Economy,* the *English* (altered from a previous *American*) *Gardener,* the *History of the Reformation,* the *Woodlands, Cobbett's Corn,* the *Advice to Young Men,* and a dozen other works original or compiled, besides the *Rural Rides* and his other contributions to the *Register*.

He could not have lived at Botley any longer if he would, for the place was mortgaged up to the eyes. But to live in a town was abhorrent to him; and he had in America rather increased than satisfied his old fancy for rural occupations. So he set up house at Kensington, where he used a large garden (soon supplemented by more land at Barnes, and in his very last years by a place near Ash, in his native district) as a kind of seed farm, selling the produce at the same shop with his *Registers*. He also utilised his now frequent rural rides—partly to provide himself with political subjects and to deliver political addresses, partly as commercial travelling for the diffusion of locust-trees, swede turnip seed, and "Cobbett's corn"—a peculiar kind of maize, the virtues of which he vaunted loudly.

Also he began to think seriously of sitting in Parliament. At the general election after George the Third's death he contested Coventry, but without even coming near success. Soon afterwards he had an opportunity of increasing his general popularity—which, owing to his flight, his repudiation, and the foolery about Paine's bones, had sunk very low—by vigorously taking Queen Caroline's side. But he was not more fortunate in his next Parliamentary attempt at Preston, in 1826. Preston, even before the Reform Bill, was, though the Stanley influence was strong, a comparatively open borough, and had a large electorate; but it would not have Cobbett, nor was he ever successful till after the Bill passed. Before its passing the very Whig Government which had charge of it was obliged to pull him up. If he had been treated with undeserved severity before he was extremely fortunate now, though his rage against his unsuccessful Whig prosecutors was, naturally enough, much fiercer than it had been against his old Tory enemies. I do not think that any fair-minded person who reads the papers in the *Register,* and the cheaper and therefore more mischievous *Twopenny Trash,* devoted to the subject of "Swing," can fail to see that under a thin cloak of denunciation and dissuasion their real purport is "Don't put him under the pump," varied and set off by suggestions how extremely easy it would be to put him under the pump, how well he deserves it, and how improbable detection or punishment is. And nobody, further, who reads the accounts of the famous Bristol riots can fail to see how much Cobbett (who had been in Bristol just before in full cry against "Tax-Eaters" and "Tithe-Eaters") had to do with them. It was probably lucky for him that he was tried before instead of after the Bristol matter, and even as it was he was not acquitted; the jury disagreed. After the Bill, his election somewhere was a certainty, and he sat for Oldham till his death. Except for a little tomfoolery at first, and at intervals afterwards, he was inoffensive enough in the House. Nor did he survive his inclusion in that Collective Wisdom at which he had so often laughed many years, but died on 19th June, 1835, at the age of seventy-three. If medical opinion is right the Collective Wisdom had the last laugh; for its late hours and confinement seem to have had more to do with his death than any disease.

I have said that it is of great importance to get if possible a preliminary idea of Cobbett's general views on politics. This not only adds to the understanding of his work, but prevents perpetual surprise and possible fretting at his individual flings and crazes. To do him justice there was from first to last very little change in his own political ideal; though there was the greatest possible change in his views of systems, governments, and individuals in their relations to that ideal and to his own private interests or vanities. In this latter respect Cobbett was very human indeed. The son of a farmer-labourer, and himself passionately interested in agricultural pursuits, he may be said never, from the day he first took to politics to the day of his death, to have really and directly considered the welfare of any other class than the classes occupied with tilling or holding land. In one place he frantically applauds a real or supposed project of King Ferdinand of Spain for taxing every commercial person who sold, or bought to sell again, goods not of his own production or manufacture. If he to a certain extent tolerated manufactures, other than those carried on at home for immediate

use, it was grudgingly, and indeed inconsistently with his general scheme. He frequently protests against the substitution of the shop for the fair or market; and so jealous is he of things passing otherwise than by actual delivery in exchange for actual coin or payment in kind, that he grumbles at one market (I think Devizes) because the corn is sold by sample and not pitched in bulk on the market-floor.

It is evident that if he possibly could have it, he would have a society purely agricultural, men making what things the earth does not directly produce as much as possible for themselves in their own houses during the intervals of field-labour. He quarrels with none of the three orders,— labourer, farmer, and landowner—as such; he does not want "the land for the people," or the landlord's rent for the farmer. Nor does he want any of the lower class to live in even mitigated idleness. Eight hours' days have no place in Cobbett's scheme; still less relief of children from labour for the sake of education. Everybody in the labouring class, women and children included, is to work and work pretty hard; while the landlord may have as much sport as ever he likes provided he allows a certain share to his tenant at times. But the labourer and his family are to have "full bellies" (it would be harsh but not entirely unjust to say that the full belly is the beginning and end of Cobbett's theory), plenty of good beer, warm clothes, staunch and comfortably furnished houses. And that they may have these things they must have good wages; though Cobbett does not at all object to the truck or even the "Tommy" system. He seems to have, like a half socialist as he is, no affection for saving, and he once, with rather disastrous consequences, took to paying his own farm-labourers entirely in kind. In the same way the farmer is to have full stack-yards, a snug farm-house, with orchards and gardens thoroughly plenished. But he must not drink wine or tea, and his daughters must work and not play the piano.

Squires there may be of all sorts, from the substantial yeoman to the lord (Cobbett has no objection to lords), and they may, I think, meet in some way or other to counsel the king (for Cobbett has no objection to kings). There is to be a militia for the defence of the country, and there might be an Established Church provided that the tithes were largely, if not wholly, devoted to the relief of the poor and the exercise of hospitality. Everybody, provided he works, is to marry the prettiest girl he can find (Cobbett had a most generous weakness for pretty girls) as early as possible, and have any number of children. But though there is to be plenty of game, there are to be no game-laws. There is to be no standing army, though there may be a navy. There is to be no, or the very smallest, civil service. It stands to reason that there is to be no public debt; and the taxes are to be as low and as uniform as possible. Commerce, even on the direct scale, if that scale be large, is to be discouraged, and any kind of middleman absolutely exterminated. There is not to be any poetry (Cobbett does sometimes quote Pope, but always with a gibe), no general literature (for though Cobbett's own works are excellent, and indeed indispensable, that is chiefly because of the corruptions of the times), no fine arts—though Cobbett has a certain weakness for church architecture, mainly for a reason presently to be explained. Above all there is to be no such thing as what is called abroad a *rentier*. No one is to "live on his means," unless these means come directly from the owning or the tilling of land. The harmless fund-holder with his three or four hundred a year, the dockyard official, the half-pay officer, are as abhorrent to Cobbett as the pensioner for nothing and the sinecurist. This is the state of things which he loves, and it is because the actual state of things is so different, and for no other reason, that he is a Radical Reformer.

I need not say that no such connected picture as I have endeavoured to draw will be found in any part of Cobbett's works. The strokes which compose it are taken from a thousand different places and filled in to a certain extent by guess-work. But I am sure it is faithful to what he would have drawn himself if he had been given to imaginative construction. It will be seen at once that it is a sort of parallel in drab homespun, a more practical double (if the adjective may be used of two impracticable things), of Mr William Morris's agreeable dreams. The artistic tobacco-pouches and the museums, the young men hanging about off Biffin's to give any one a free row on the river, and so forth, were not in Cobbett's way. But the canvas, and even the main composition of the picture, is the same. Of course the ideal State never existed anywhere, and never could continue to exist long if it were set up in full working order to-morrow. Labourer *A* would produce too many children, work too few hours, and stick too close to the ale-pot; farmer *B* would be ruined by a bad year or a murrain; squire *C* would outrun the non-existent constable and find a Jew to help him, even if Cobbett made an exception to his hatred of placemen for the sake of a Crown tooth-drawer. One of the tradesmen who were permitted on sufferance to supply the brass kettles and the grandfathers' clocks which Cobbett loves would produce better goods and take better care of the proceeds than another, with the result of a better business and hoarded wealth. In short, men would be men, and the world the world, in spite of Cobbett and Mr Morris alike.

I doubt whether Cobbett, who knew something of history, ever succeeded in deceiving himself, great as were his powers that way, into believing that this State ever had existed. He would have no doubt gone into a paroxysm of rage, and have called me as bad names as it was in his heart to apply to any Hampshire man, if I had suggested that such an approach to it as existed in his beloved fifteenth century was due to the Black Death, the French wars, and those of the Roses. But the fair vision ever fled before him day and night, and made him more and more furious with the actual state of England,—which was no doubt bad enough. The labourers with their eight or ten shillings a week and their Banyan diet, the farmers getting half-price for their ewes and their barley, the squires ousted by Jews and jobbers, filled his soul with a certainly not ignoble rage, only tempered by a sort of exultation to think in the last case that the fools had brought their ruin on their own heads by truckling to "the Thing." "The Thing" was the whole actual social and political state of England; and on everything and everybody that had brought "the Thing" about he poured impartial vitriol. The war which had run up the debt and increased the tax-eaters at the same time; the borough-mongers who had countenanced the war, the Jews and jobbers that negotiated and dealt in the loans; the parsons that ate the tithes; the lawyers that did Government work,—Cobbett thundered against them all.

But his wrath also descended upon far different, and one would have thought sufficiently guiltless, things and persons. The potato, the "soul-destroying root" so easy to grow (Cobbett did not live to see the potato famine, or I fear he would have been rather hideous in his joy), so innutritious, so exclusive of sound beef and bread, has worse language than even a stock-jobber or a sinecurist. Tea, the expeller of beer, the pamperer of foreign commerce, the waster of the time of farmers' wives, is nearly as bad as the potato. I could not within any possible or probable space accorded me follow out a tithe or a hundredth part of the strange ramifications and divagations of Cobbett's grand economic craze. The most comical branch perhaps is his patronage of the Roman Catholic Church, and the most comical twig of that branch his firm belief that the abundance and size of English churches testify to an infinitely larger population in England of old than at the present day. His rage at the impudent Scotchman who put the population at two millions when he is sure it was twenty, and the earnestness with which he proves that a certain Wiltshire vale, having so many churches capable of containing so many people must have once had so many score thousand inhabitants, are about equally amusing. That in the days which he praises so much, and in which these churches were built, the notion of building a church to "seat so many," or with regard to the population at all, would have been regarded as unintelligible if not blasphemous; that in the first place the church was an offering to God, not a provision for getting worship done; and that in the second, the worship of old, with its processions, its numerous altars in the same churches, and so on, made a disproportionate amount of room absolutely necessary,—these were things you could no more have taught Cobbett than you could have taught him to like *Marmion* or read the *Witch of Atlas*.

It is however time, and more than time, to follow him rapidly through the curious labyrinth of work in which, constantly though often very unconsciously keeping in sight this ideal, he wandered from Pittite Toryism to the extreme of half socialist and wholly radical Reform. His sons, very naturally but rather unwisely, have in the great selection of the ***Political Works*** drawn very sparingly on Peter Porcupine. But no estimate of Cobbett that neglects the results of this, his first, phase will ever be satisfactory. It is by no means the most amusing division of Cobbett's works; but it is not the least characteristic, and it is full of interest for the study both of English and of American politics. The very best account that I know of the original American Constitution, and of the party strife that followed the peace with England, is contained in the Summary that opens the ***Works***. Then for some years we find Cobbett engaged in fighting the Jacobin party, the fight constantly turning into skirmishes on his private account, conducted with singular vigour if at a length disproportionate to the present interest of the subject. Here is the autobiography before noticed, and in all the volumes, especially the earlier ones, the following of Swift, often by no means unhappy, is very noticeable. It is a little unlucky that a great part of the whole consists of selections from *Porcupine's Gazette,* that is to say, of actual newspaper matter of the time,—"slag-heaps," to use Carlyle's excellent phrase, from which the metal of present application has been smelted out and used up long ago.

This inconvenience also and of necessity applies to the still larger collection, duplicating, as has been said, a little from Porcupine, but principally selected from the *Register,* which was published after Cobbett's death. But this is of far greater general importance, for it contains the pith and marrow of all his writings on the subject to which he gave most of his heart. Here, in the first volume, besides the selection from Porcupine, are the masterly *Letters to Addington on the Peace of Amiens,* in which that most foolish of the foolish things called armistices is treated as it deserved, and with a combination of vigour and statesmanship which Cobbett never showed after he lost the benefit of Windham's patronage and (probably) inspiration. Here too is a defence of bull-baiting after Windham's own heart. The volume ends with the *Letters to William Pitt,* in which Cobbett declared and defended his defection from Pitt's system generally. The whole method and conduct of the writings of this time are so different from the rambling denunciations of Cobbett's later days, and from the acute but rather desultory and extremely personal Porcupinades, that one is almost driven to accept the theory of "inspiration." The literary model too has shifted from Swift to Burke—Burke upon whom Cobbett was later to pour torrents of his foolishest abuse; and both in this first and in the second volume the reformer, wandering about in search of subjects not merely political but general—Crim. Con., Poor-laws, and so forth—appears. But in the second volume we have to notice a paper, still in the old style and full of good sense, on Boxing.

In the third Cobbett is in full Radical cry. Here is the article which sent him to Newgate; and long before it a series of virulent attacks on the Duke of York in the matter of Mrs Clarke, together with onslaughts on those Anti-Jacobins to whom Cobbett had once been proud to belong. It also includes a very curious *Plan for an Army,* which marks a sort of middle stage in Cobbett's views on that subject. The latter part of it, and the whole of the next (the fourth) consists mainly of long series on the Regency (the last and permanent Regency), on the Regent's disputes with his wife, and on the American War. All this part displays Cobbett's growing ill-temper, and also the growing wildness of his schemes—one of which is a sliding-scale adjusting all salaries, from the civil list to the soldier's pay, according to the price of corn. But there is still no loss of vigour, if some of sanity; and the opening paper of the fifth volume, the famous Address to the Labourers aforesaid, is, as I have said, perhaps the

climax of Cobbett's political writing in point of force and form—which thing I say utterly disagreeing with almost all its substance. This same fifth volume contains another remarkable instance of Cobbett's extraordinary knack of writing, as well as of his rapidly decreasing judgment, in the *Letter to Jack Harrow, an English labourer, on the new Cheat of Savings Banks*.

At least half of the volume dates after Cobbett's flight, while some is posterior to his return. The characteristics which distinguish his later years, his wild crotchets and his fantastic running-a-muck at all public men of all parties, and not least at his own former friends, appear both in it and in the sixth and last, which carries the selection down to his death. Yet even in such things as the *Letter to Old George Rose* and that from *The Labourers of the ten little Hard Parishes* [this was Cobbett's name for the district between Winchester and Whitchurch, much of which had recently been acquired by the predecessors of Lord Northbrook] *to Alexander Baring, Loan-monger,* we can see, at a considerable distance of time, the strength and the weakness of this odd person in conspicuous mixture. He is as rude, as coarse, as personal as may be; he is grossly unjust to individuals and wildly flighty in principle and argument; it is almost impossible to imagine a more dangerous counsellor in such, or indeed in any times. Except that he is harder-headed and absolutely unchivalrous, his politics are very much those of Colonel Newcome. And yet the vigour of the style is still so great, the flame and heat of the man's conviction are so genuine, his desire according to the best he knows to benefit his clients, and his unselfishness in taking up those clients, are so unquestionable that it is impossible not to feel both sympathy and admiration. If I had been dictator about 1830 I think I should have hanged Cobbett; but I should have sent for him first and asked leave to shake hands with him before he went to the gallows.

These collections are invaluable to the political and historical student; and I hardly know any better models, not for the exclusive, but for the eclectic attention of the political writer, especially if his education be academic and his tastes rather anti-popular. But there is better pasture for the general student in the immense variety of the works, which, though they cannot be called wholly non-political—Cobbett would have introduced politics into arithmetic and astronomy, as he actually does into grammar—are non-political in main substance and purport. They belong almost entirely, as has been said, to the last seventeen or eighteen years of Cobbett's life; and putting the *Year's Residence* aside, the *English Grammar* is the earliest. It is couched in a series of letters to his son James, who had been brought up to the age of fourteen on the principle (by no means a bad one) of letting him pick up the Three R's as he pleased, and leaving him for the rest "To ride and hunt and shoot, to dig the beds in the garden, to trim the flowers, and to prune the trees." It is like all Cobbett's books, on whatsoever subject, a wonderful mixture of imperfect information, shrewd sense, and fantastic crotchet. On one page Cobbett calmly instructs his son that "prosody" means "pronunciation"; on another, he confuses "etymology" with "accidence." This may give the malicious college-bred man cause to be envious of his superior genius; but there is no doubt that the book contains about as clear an account of the practical and working nature and use of sound English speech and writing as can anywhere be found.

The grammar was published in 1818, and Cobbett's next book of note was *Religious Tracts,* afterwards called *Twelve Sermons*. He says that many persons had the good sense to preach them; and indeed, a few of his usual outbursts excepted, they are as sound specimens of moral exhortation as anybody need wish to hear or deliver. They are completed characteristically enough by a wild onslaught on the Jews, separately paged as if Cobbett was a little ashamed of it. Then came the *Cottage Economy,* instructing and exhorting the English labourer in the arts of brewing, baking, stock-keeping of all sorts, straw-bonnet making, and ice-house building. This is perhaps the most agreeable of all Cobbett's minor books, next to the *Rural Rides*. The descriptions are as vivid as *Robinson Crusoe,* and are further lit up by flashes of the genuine man. Thus, after a most peaceable and practical discourse on the making of rushlights, he writes: "You may do any sort of work by this light; and if reading be your taste you may read the foul libels, the lies, and abuse which are circulated gratis about *me* by the Society for Promoting Christian Knowledge." Here too is a charming piece of frankness: "Any beer is better than water; but it should have *some* strength and *some* weeks of age at any rate."

A rearrangement of the *Horse-hoeing Industry* of Jethro Tull, barrister, and the *French Grammar,* hardly count among his purely and originally literary work; but the *History of the Reformation* is one of its most characteristic if not of its most admirable parts. Cobbett's feud with the clergy was now at its height; he had long before been at daggers drawn with his own parson at Botley. The gradual hardening of his economic crazes made him more and more hate "Tithe-Eaters," and his wrath with them was made hotter by the fact that they were as a body opponents of Reform. So with a mixture of astounding ignorance and of self-confidence equally amazing, he set to work to put the crudest Roman view of the Reformation and of earlier times into his own forcible English. The book is very amusing; but it is so grossly ignorant, and the virulence of its tirades against Henry VIII and the rest so palpable, that even in that heated time it would not do. It may be gathered from some remarks of Cobbett's own that he felt it a practical failure; though he never gave up his views, and constantly in his latest articles and speeches invited everybody to search it for the foundation of all truth about the Church of England.

The more important of his next batch of publications, the *Woodlands, The English Gardener, Cobbett's Corn,* restore a cooler atmosphere; though even here there are the usual spurts. Very amusing is the suppressed wrath of the potato article in the *English Gardener,* with its magnanimous admission that "there appears to be nothing unwholesome about it; and it does very well to qualify the effects of the meat or to assist in the swallowing of quan-

tities of butter." Pleasing too is the remark, "If this turnip really did come from Scotland, there is something good that is Scotch." *Cobbett's Corn,* already noticed, is one of the most curious of all his books, and an instance of his singular vigour in taking up fancies. Although he sold the seed, it does not appear that he could in any case have made much profit out of it; and he gave it away so freely that it would, had it succeeded, soon have been obtainable from any seedsman in the kingdom. Yet he wrote a stout volume about it, and seems to have taken wonderful interest in its propagation, chiefly because he hoped it would drive out his enemy the potato. The English climate was naturally too much for it; but the most amusing thing, to me at least, about the whole matter is the remembrance that the "yellow meal" which it, like other maize, produced, became, a short time after Cobbett's own death, the utter loathing and abomination of English and Irish paupers and labourers, a sort of sign and symbol of capitalist tyranny. Soon afterwards came the last of Cobbett's really remarkable and excellent works, the *Advice to Young Men and Incidentally to Young Women,* one of the kindliest and most sensible books of its kind ever written. The other books of Cobbett's later years are of little account in any way; and in the three little *Legacies (to Labourers, to Peel,* and *to Parsons*) there is a double portion of now cut-and-dried crotchet in matter, and hardly any of the old power in form.

Yet to the last, or at any rate till his disastrous election, Cobbett was Cobbett. The *Rural Rides,* though his own collection of them stopped at 1830, went on to 1832. This, the only one of his books, so far as I know, that has been repeatedly and recently reprinted, shows him at his best and his worst; but almost always at his best in form. Indeed, the reader for mere pleasure need hardly read anything else, and will find therein to the full the delightful descriptions of rural England, the quaint, confident, racy, wrong-headed opinions, the command over the English language, and the ardent affection for the English soil and its children, that distinguish Cobbett at his very best.

I have unavoidably spent so much time on this account of Cobbett's own works—an account which without copious extract must be, I fear, still inadequate—that the anti-Cobbett polemic must go with hardly any notice at all. Towards the crises of the Reform Bill it became very active, and at times remarkable. Among two collections which I possess, one of bound tracts dating from this period, the other of loose pamphlets ranging over the greater part of Cobbett's life, the keenest by far is a certain publication called *Cobbett's Penny Trash,* which figures in both, though one or two others have no small point. The enemy naturally made the utmost of the statement of the condemned labourer Goodman, who lay in Horsham Gaol under sentence of death for arson, that he had been stirred up by Cobbett's addresses to commit the crime; but still better game was made controversially of his flagrant and life-long inconsistencies, of his enormous egotism, of his tergiversation in the matter of the offer to discontinue the *Register,* and of his repudiation of his debt to Sir Francis Burdett. And the main sting of the

Penny Trash, which must have been written by a very clever fellow indeed, is the imitation of Cobbett's own later style, its italics, its repetitions, its quaint mannerisms of fling and vaunt. The example of this had of course been set much earlier by the Smiths in *Rejected Addresses,* but it was even better done here.

Cobbett was indeed vulnerable enough. He, if any one, is the justification of the theory of Time, Country, and *Milieu,* and perhaps the fact that it only adjusts itself to such persons as he is the chief condemnation of that theory. Even with him it fails to account for the personal genius which after all is the only thing that makes him tolerable, and which, when he is once tolerated, makes him almost admirable. Only an English *Terræ Filius,* destitute of the education which the traditional *Terræ Filius* had, writing too in the stress of the great Revolutionary struggle and at hand-grips with the inevitable abuses which that struggle at once left unbettered, after the usual gradual fashion of English betterment, and aggravated by the pressure of economic changes—could have ventured to write with so little knowledge or range of logical power, and yet have written with such individual force and adaptation of style to the temper of his audience. At a later period and in different circumstances Cobbett could hardly have been so acrimonious, so wildly fantastic, so grossly and almost impudently ignorant, or if he had been he would have been simply laughed at or unread. At an earlier period, or in another country, he would have been bought off or cut off. Even at this very time the mere circumstantial fact of the connection of most educated and well-informed writers with the Government or at least with the regular Opposition, gave such a Free-lance as this an unequalled opportunity of making himself heard. His very inconsistency, his very ferocity, his very ignorance, gave him the key of the hearts of the multitude, who just then were the persons of most importance. And to these persons that characteristic of his which is either most laughable or most disgusting to the educated—his most unparalleled, his almost inconceivable egotism—was no drawback. When Cobbett with many italics in an advertisement to all his later books told them, "When I am asked what books a young man or young woman ought to read I always answer: 'Let him or her read *all the books that I have written,*'" proceeding to show in detail that this was no humorous gasconade but a serious recommendation, one "which it is my *duty* to give," the classes laughed consumedly. But the masses felt that Cobbett was at any rate a much cleverer and more learned person than themselves, had no objection on the score of taste, and were naturally conciliated by his partisanship on their own side. And, clever as he was, he was not too clever for them. He always hit them between wind and water. He knew that they cared nothing about consistency, nothing about chivalry, nothing about logic. He could make just enough and not too much parade of facts and figures to impress them. And above all he had that invaluable gift of belief in himself and in his own fallacies which no demagogue can do without. I do not know a more fatal delusion than the notion, entertained by many persons, that a mere charlatan, a conscious charlatan, can be effective as a statesman, especially on the popular side. Such a one may be

an excellent understrapper; but he will never be a real leader.

In this respect, however, Cobbett is only a lesson, a memory, and an example, which are all rather dead things. In respect of his own native literary genius he is still a thing alive and delectable. I have endeavoured, so far as has been possible in treating a large subject in little room, to point out his characteristics in this respect also. But, as happens with all writers of his kidney, he is not easily to be characterised. Like certain wines he has the *goût du terroir;* and that gust is rarely or never definable in words. It is however I think critically safe to say that the intensity and peculiarity of Cobbett's literary savour is in the ratio of his limitation. He was content to ignore so vast a number of things, he so bravely pushed his ignorance into contempt of them and almost into denial of their real existence, that the other things are real for him and in his writings to a degree almost unexampled. I am not the first by many to suggest that we are too diffuse in our modern imagination, that we are cumbered about too many things. No one could bring this accusation against Cobbett; for immense as his variety is in particulars, these particulars group themselves under comparatively few general heads. I do not think I have been unjust in suggesting that this ideal was little more than the belly-full, that Messer Gaster was not only his first but his one and sufficient master of arts. He was not irreligious, he was not immoral; but his religion and his morality were of the simplest and most matter-of-fact kind. Philosophy, æsthetics, literature, the more abstract sciences, even refinements of sensual comfort and luxury he cared nothing for. Indeed he had a strong dislike to most of them. He must always have been fighting about something; but I think his polemics might have been harmlessly parochial at another time. It is marvellous how this resolute confinement of view sharpens the eyesight within the confines. He has somewhere a really beautiful and almost poetical passage of enthusiasm over a great herd of oxen as "so much splendid meat." He can see the swells of the downs, the flashing of the winterbournes as they spring from the turf where they have lain hid, the fantastic outline of the oak woods, the reddening sweep of the great autumn fields of corn, as few have seen them, and can express them all with rare force and beauty in words. But he sees all these things conjointly and primarily from the point of view of the mutton that the downs will breed and the rivers water, the faggots that the labourer will bring home at evening, the bread he will bake and the beer he will brew—strictly according to the precepts of **Cottage Economy**.

This may be to some minds a strange and almost incredible combination. It is not so to mine, and I am sure that by dint of it and by dint of holding himself to it he achieved his actual success of literary production. To believe in nothing very much, or in a vast number of things dispersedly, may be the secret of criticism; but to believe in something definite, were it only the belly-full, and to believe in it furiously and exclusively is, with almost all men, the secret of original art.

Leslie Stephen (essay date 1893)

SOURCE: "William Cobbett," in *The New Review*, Vol. 9, No. 54, November 1893, pp. 482-93.

[*Stephen is considered one of the most important English literary critics of the late Victorian and early Edwardian era. In his criticism, which was often moralistic, he argued that all literature is nothing more than an imaginative rendering, in concrete terms, of a writer's philosophy or beliefs. It is the role of criticism, he contended, to translate into intellectual terms what the writer has told the reader through character, symbol, and plot. In the following excerpt, Stephen provides an overview of Cobbett's beliefs regarding numerous social issues.*]

Cobbett somehow or other fought through his troubles; brought up his family; heartily enjoyed life till the end; and was even regarded with a certain tolerance by his opponents. They did not take him quite seriously, and thought that his rough abuse was after all the cover of a certain bluff, genial good humour which merely used bad language as it is used by the vulgar—not in its real force, but as a conventional ornament of speech. Even Tories looked with a not unkindly curiosity at the stalwart British farmer, snuff-waistcoated and blue-coated, with his twinkling eyes and broad humorous grin, who took his seat for Oldham in the first Reformed Parliament. Cobbett, entering that assembly at the age of seventy, naturally failed to make a mark and when he died on June 18th, 1835, left no very perceptible gap. He had become a representative of a past order of things.

It is the more remarkable, when we remember the follies and failures of this last period [1815 to 1835], that Cobbett's powers as a writer were never greater. It was during these years that he published in the *Register* those *Rural Rides* which are among the favourite books of all lovers of English scenery. The *Advice to Young Men* is another really charming book, which, though the advice may be summed up in the words, "Be Cobbett if you can"—be, that is, models of all domestic and manly virtues—contains some of the most charming bits of autobiography ever written; and it was at this time, too, that he published one of the most remarkable and popular of his books, the *History of the Protestant Reformation*. With the help of these and of the facts already noticed, let me try to sum up Cobbett's real position. It is easy to show that Cobbett was in one sense the most inconsistent of mankind. Lord Dalling wrote a very interesting essay upon him as the type of the "contentious" man; and Hazlitt describes him in the same sense as a simple lover of contradiction. He was a journalist, bound to keep himself before the public eye by assaulting someone, even, it might be, his own old friends or his former self. He began as an Anti-Jacobin, and ended as a Radical; he passionately advocated and then passionately denounced the war; and he vehemently declared that the war had always had the same principles; he reviled Americans, and then found out that Americans were the only people worth admiring. He stuck meanwhile to some old prejudices which conflict strangely with his new doctrines. He hated the Jews; he hated the Scotch, the Irish, and the French; he hated Unitarians with a special hatred; he hated all Dissenters as hypocrites and humbugs; and some of these hatreds fitted in awkwardly with the Liberal programme. He boasted in his early *Registers* that he had always defended the slave trade, and he abused the anti-slavery agitators to the end of his life; he defended bull-baiting and prize-fighting to the last; he denounced schools for the people, when Whitbread first proposed a scheme of national education in 1807; argued with his odd mixture of sense and perversity how much might be learnt without books; and talked with profound scorn of "Heddekashun," when in later days Brougham declared that the "schoolmaster was abroad." He reviled savings banks, because he thought that they would give the poor an interest in the Funds; and he attacks and supports the Poor Laws in the same breath, alternately considering them as grossly demoralising and as the natural right of the poor man. These are queer doctrines for a reformer. And yet there is no difficulty in seeing that Cobbett was in his way thoroughly consistent. To explain such a man we must consider his innate prejudices, not the logic by which he has learnt to defend his views. He has simply certain sympathies and antipathies which never weaken or alter; he runs like a bull at a red rag at whatever for the moment repels him; and the strength of his indignation disqualifies him from framing any general theory or bringing his various utterances into apparent harmony.

Cobbett, I need hardly repeat, is simply the voice of the English peasant. He is the translation into sturdy vernacular of the dumb unreasoning sentiments of the class which was then most cruelly suffering from causes only half intelligible, though their effects were painfully manifest. He is the cry of blind anger, indignation, and remonstrance rising from the social stratum which, being the weakest, was being most crushed and degraded in the gigantic struggle of the revolutionary wars. The peasant of Cobbett's youth had been fairly prosperous; he had, if Cobbett be a fair specimen, none of the accumulated bitterness against his social superiors which was to be shown by his fellows in France. When the squire of the Windham type rode out hunting, farmer and ploughboy joined heartily in the sport. The splendid prelate, Bishop of Winchester, with his gardens and palace, was a natural ornament of the soil, like the giant oaks of the forest. Cobbett felt a certain patriotic pride in the whole system. He loved, he says, "the name and fame of England . . . above all, her deeds in arms, her military glory." He resented the abandonment of the absurd old claim to the Kingdom of France because the farmer would no longer be asked to explain it to his boys and have to tell them the old stories of Crécy and Agincourt. Like Shakespeare's Henry V., he believed in the good yeomen whose limbs were made in England; and only desired them to show their old mettle. Cobbett, if any one, was a believer in the "good old times," the belief in which used to vex the soul of Macaulay. When he returned from America, still thrilling with the emotions of battle against Jacobin levellers and the wretches who had not the virtue of being born in England, he became aware of the industrial revolution which was taking place in his native country; the substitution of factories for the domestic system of manufacture, and the dismissal of the labourer, who in the old days had been one of the farmer's family, to live in a wretched hovel and depend upon the parish rates. He began by calling this change the ruin of the old families and the rise of the new men, stockjobbers, and the pensioners who had bought Waverley Abbey and Moor Park, and had even designs against the Episcopal palaces. But the love of the old Norman families was a bit of surface sentimentalism; it was the ill fortunes of the peasant that really touched his heart. He was shocked to see the miserable scarecrows swilling their tea instead of drinking home-brewed beer, living on dry bread instead of partaking the farmer's coarse plenty, while the farmer himself was aping the gentry, drinking wine at his ordinaries, and letting his wife and daughters wear silk and play on the piano. Enclosures had taken away the poor man's cow and left him to eke out his wretched means by whining for parish charities. That was the scene—exaggerated or not—which really stirred Cobbett's wrath.

The old families and the old institutions! They, he soon saw, had become mere appendages of the "Thing"—the hideous, corrupt, boroughmongering, pension-distributing gang of plunderers who were waxing fat as the peasant grew lean. The Radicals, after the peace, were attacking the governing classes, and, above all, were aiming at the Church. That Prince-Bishop of Winchester, for example, who used to drive about, in the memory of men not yet old, in a chariot with four horses and outriders, in wig and full canonicals, with two chaplains sitting on stools with their backs to the horses; who had won his preferment by favour of the virtuous Prince Regent—was he not a fine mark for a popular writer? Utilitarians and Liberals asked whether he might not be carved for the public benefit; and readers of Newman's *Apologia* will remember how their proposals of confiscation shocked the Churchmen of the day. The remedy desired by Newman and his friends was to restore the more spiritual view of the Church, or to find another Church freer from the degrading bonds of the State. Cobbett's view, though partly analogous, was different. He cared absolutely nothing for theology; religion, as a clergyman once remarked to him, was for him merely a matter of politics; but the Bishop and his like strengthened him in a theory which he had long maintained. He did not complain that the Church was worldly, but that it was a robbery of the poor. He looked back to the good old times of his imagination and found a historical theory, given by Blackstone, for example, though not, I believe, to be received as accurate, which stated that a certain proportion of the tithes was originally devoted to the support of the poor. This bloated Bishop, then, was really fattening upon an income which ought to have gone to the support of the agricultural labourer. This doctrine became the kernel of his popular book upon the Protestant Reformation. The agitation for Catholic Emancipation, as well as the attacks upon the pluralism and other abuses of the Church of England, had brought such questions to the foreground. What right had this Protestant Church to the incomes which it was so vigorously defending against the united assaults of Catholics and Radicals? The answer, according to Cobbett,

was plain. The Church was the creation of the Tudor Parliaments, and the revenues came from the systematic plundering of the Reformation. The poor man's share of the tithes had been already partly appropriated by monasteries, and the revenues of the monasteries had been grabbed by the favourites of those brutal tyrants, Henry VIII. and Elizabeth. A married clergy meanwhile was bringing up its families on the incomes which should have been devoted in part to the same end. Briefly, this fat, lazy band of pluralists, sinecurists, and bloated bishops, was fattening on funds belonging of right to the agricultural labourer.

That was Cobbett's doctrine, of which I need not discuss the value. Anyhow, he put it with immense energy, and, though his research was shallow enough, he showed no little shrewdness and sense of the true ends of history. He took, of course, the narrow view of a great revolution. A journalist who makes the Pitt and Canning of his own time responsible for all the evils of the day naturally attributes all the evils of the past to a Henry VIII. and a Thomas Cromwell. He was unable to gauge the general significance of vast historical processes, of which even the Reformation was only one symptom. And yet, of the many writers who have said the same thing since, I think that few have said better than Cobbett how important it is to make history more than a mere biography of kings and generals. It is, he says, of little more use to read about battles and intrigues than to read a romance. The important thing is to ascertain the state of the people in the past. To do that, compare the price of labour with the price of food. You hear enough of the glorious wars of Edward III.—not too much, he adds, for he could never forget that King of France business; but historians don't condescend to tell you that in those days a common labourer earned three-pence-halfpenny a day, while a fat sheep was sold for one shilling and two-pence, and a fat goose for twopence-halfpenny; that old women got a penny a day for haymaking, and that a gallon of red wine was sold for fourpence. Cobbett's facts may often be disputable. He had only glanced at a few Acts of Parliament or taken them at second-hand. He argued persistently and with some ingenuity, that the population of England had been as great in the Middle Ages as in his own time; and when some of his conclusions were dispersed by the census he thought it a sufficient answer to call the returning officers monstrous liars. But he insisted upon facts which have rightly received more attention of late. He dimly saw what Thorold Rogers' work has made familiar—the prosperous state of the labourer in the fourteenth and fifteenth centuries; and I may add that Rogers coincides curiously in some of his views with other positions maintained by Cobbett. Rogers could himself be only a pioneer in a most important field of inquiry, and Cobbett certainly deserves the credit of having very distinctly pointed to the great importance of such researches.

Cobbett's whole position rests on the same sentiment. He is one continuous protest against the degradation of the agricultural labourer. His history, his politics, his economic theories, so far as they are not mere journalism for the moment, have no other aim. It is the centre of all his thoughts. Nor could anyone speak with stronger common-sense. No one pointed out more clearly how the system of paying wages partly out of the rates injured the pauper; how the labourer came to reckon the parish chest among his ways and means; hid his earnings to cheat the parish; and lost all his old horror of dependence. Charity, he says, is a premium on hypocrisy. His own labourers were what some people called "saucy"; he liked them "saucy"; they were what Englishmen should be; they gave him labour and took his money, and there was no obligation either way. He never employed a pauper but he gave good wages, and paid them all the year round. He acted, he says, not from charity, but for his own interest. One of his men was worth two or three half-famished paupers. The first thing to be done, he says, is to encourage the labourer to be honest and truthful. To be honest and truthful "he must have his bellyful and be free from fear; and his bellyful must come from his wages and not from benevolence." A labourer's cottage, he said, on a Sunday, with husband or wife carrying a baby and two or three elder children playing in the garden, is the "most interesting object that eyes ever beheld" to which this John Bull adds that it can only be seen in England. He once met such a party by a cottage in Sussex, and asked the father how many children he expected to have. "I don't care how many," was the reply; "God never sends mouths without sending food." "Did you never hear of Parson Malthus?" asked Cobbett, and proceeded to explain that gentleman's theories, to the amazement of the couple, who had five children though the wife was only twenty-two. That is the genuine Cobbett. Nobody could tell more plainly the demoralising effects of the Poor Law; but when it came to remedying the abuses his old vein of sentimentalism came to the surface. Malthus, in particular, evoked his bitterest hatred. The phrase, "surplus population"—a favourite with the Malthusians—always rouses him to fury. There was not, and could not be, and never had been, a surplus population, let census gatherers say what they pleased. All that really happened was a drain from the country to the monstrous wen, which was already, as he observes in 1822, prolonging its hideous arms six or seven miles along the road to Cambridge. The economists were humbugs. One number of his "twopenny trash" was worth all that Adam Smith ever wrote. And, therefore, when a real reform of the Poor Laws was proposed, Cobbett was its bitterest enemy; abused Scottish "feelosophers," as he called them, and Mill and MacCulloch and the stockjobbing Ricardo, and the paper which he pleasantly calls "the bloody old *Times,*" for it was one of the favourite tenets of this peculiar Radical that the Press was on the whole (wholly, indeed, with the exception of the *Register*) a mischievous institution and one of the numerous instruments of corruption at the disposal of the "Thing."

Cobbett's alliance with the Radicals was thus always superficial. To them the freedom of industry, the encouragement of manufactures, and of the growth of capital were the great ends, and if they attacked the aristocracy, they objected to the ancient system, not to the new aristocracy of wealth. They shared the prejudices of the commercial and the middle classes. Cobbett's sentiment was

entirely different. In his early period, he adopted a phrase attributed (though wrongly, it seems) to Windham, "Perish Commerce." Not, of course, that he objected to commerce in itself; but he held that all the real wealth of the country came from the land; and he defended the war on the ground that we could lose little by a destruction of trade, which was after all of doubtful benefit. In speaking of the capitalist he uses language which might commend itself to some of our Socialist friends. What, he asks, is capital? It is "money taken from the labouring classes, which being given to army tailors and such like, enables them to keep fox-hounds and trace their descent from the Normans." To Cobbett, in short, the existing order was bad, but for the ideal order which was to replace it he looked backwards. The stockjobber, not the old noble, was the real enemy. The Socialist Owen said much the same. Cobbett's pet political project was the destruction of the debt, and therefore, as he thought, of excessive taxation and of the whole machinery by which the stockjobber lived upon the poor man. The old days of Crécy and Agincourt, the times when the labourer could buy a fat goose for his day's work, was the true period of English glory and happiness. He looked back through that mirage of boyish happiness which makes so many of us fancy that the world grows worse as we grow older. He repeats in his later years the wish which I have before quoted, the desire to restore to the "labouring classes that happiness which in my youth I saw them enjoy and enjoyed with them." That Cobbett felt that wish so sincerely is his true title to our good will; his expression of it in many detached passages and the light which it infuses into his account of country scenery, gives a fascination to some of his writings, the *Rural Rides* in particular, which is not quenched even though it is set in the midst of reckless declamation and bewildered ravings and brutal abuse of men and things which he only half understood. To the last, he is still at bottom the hearty, jovial countryman, coarse-mouthed, and too often a mere blatant demagogue, and yet with a certain genial breath of emphatic, full-blooded enjoyment of the good things of the world, the homely affections of commonplace mankind, which we cannot help recognising.

Two people have left descriptions of Cobbett which may complete his picture. Miss Mitford was at Botley about 1806-7; she saw the jolly British yeoman, an English version of Dandie Dinmont, in a big farmhouse, where he could accommodate a dozen guests, clergymen, politicians, and men of letters. She never saw heartier hospitality. He gathered his neighbours for country games—wrestling, cudgel playing, and running; his gardens were full of flowers and fruit; and everything was jovial and pleasant, till some explosion of prejudice produced a little social tempest, without which Cobbett could hardly be complete. A greater writer visited England in Cobbett's later days. "Old Cobbett," says Heine, "English bulldog, I don't love you; every vulgar nature is revolting to me, but I pity you in my deepest soul, when I see you unable to break your chain and reach the thieves (the 'Thing,' that is) who carry off their booty before your eyes and mock at your impotent howls." Put the two pictures together, and we have the two sides of Cobbett. Would you, I wonder, rather be the man of exquisite genius, nailed down in later years to his bed of misery and suffering the penalty of overwrought nerves, or this huge British bulldog, who had no nerves at all, and, if genius, a genius of the commonplace kind, who blustered and bullied his way through the world, enjoyed himself to the end, and stood so firmly on his feet that all the abuse of the "Thing" and its slaves appeared to him to be nothing but an involuntary testimony to his superlative merits?

John Freeman (essay date 1921)

SOURCE: "William Cobbett," in *English Portraits and Essays,* Hodder and Stoughton, 1924, pp. 61-86.

[*In the following excerpt from an essay originally published in the* London Mercury *in 1921, Freeman surveys Cobbett's career and his reputation among his contemporaries.*]

Born in 1762 at Farnham (Surrey) in a house upon which amused and affectionate eyes may, I think, still fall; guiltless of any enforced education other than lessons at a dame's school and, on winter evenings, from his father at home; walking to London when he was about thirteen and spending his last coppers on *A Tale of a Tub* by that earlier pamphleteer whose more powerful and sombre genius was to vivify his own; enlisting in a lawyer's office and then in that scarcely more unconscionable school, His Majesty's Army; serving in that Army until 1791, and all the while plucking (or was it not, in a common soldier, poaching?) grammar, French, and other strange fruits from the wrinkled Tree of Knowledge whose branches did not then, as now, caress and darken the whole earth; rising to sergeant-major and obtaining his discharge after service in England and New Brunswick, in order that he might begin his career of political bruiser by charging his late officers with theft; developing a quick discretion for the lack of which martyrs have become martyrs, and evading by flight to France the revenges which he was sensible of provoking; settling at Philadelphia, and there pursuing that querulous and quixotic course for which his temperament found unfailing justification in circumstance; returning to England in 1800, famous and courted; quickly proving himself unpliable to a Tory Government and devoting his powers with greater joy to attack; attacking, then, and attacked, in prison and in peril of prison, broken and renewed, savage and untamable yet with brief revulsions and obscure returns which he is not always able to illustrate; riding through England between 1821 and 1832, sometimes like a farmer and sometimes like a conqueror; entering Parliament in 1832 and emitting prompt contempt upon his fellow-members; incessantly writing and speaking and farming and planting, incessantly boasting and performing; having outlived many enemies and more friends and welcomed hatred as others enjoy servility, at length [Cobbett] died, in 1835, in the full consciousness of a happy life of which the only constant stars had been his faith in himself, his affection for his family, and his passionate belief in the inheritance of every Englishman in the virtue, abundance, and beauty of his native country.

Cobbett's introduction to his *Advice to Young Men* contains a characteristic vaunt of his activity as a writer. It was an incredible activity. For over thirty years he wrote all but single-handed and published all but uninterruptedly *Cobbett's Political Register,* a weekly review which provoked sometimes the crowd and sometimes the Government, and made its author a constant energy amid the lethargy and corruption of English politics. He has told how it was his practice to dictate the *Register* to his young children, and how proud he was to send what he had dictated without revision to the printer. An earlier journal had been published in America with the title or in the name of *Peter Porcupine;* it ended with an action by an unhappy leech for libel and a verdict which almost broke Cobbett; it was revived in London, and gave equal offence. But it was the *Political Register* that brought Cobbett's chief opportunity of suffering for righteousness' sake. The militia at Ely mutinied because of a stoppage for their knapsacks, and four squadrons of the German Legion were called in to suppress the rising. Five of the men were sentenced to receive five hundred lashes each, and did, in fact, receive as many as their backs could endure. Cobbett, remembering his own eight years in the Army, was maddened.

> Five hundred lashes each! Aye, that is right! Flog them; flog them; flog them! They deserve it, and a great deal more. They deserve a flogging at every meal-time. 'Lash them daily, lash them duly!' What, shall the rascals dare to mutiny, and that too when the German Legion is so near at hand! Lash them, lash them, lash them! They deserve it. Oh yes; they merit a double-tailed cat. Base dogs! What, mutiny for the sake of the price of a knapsack. Lash them! Flog them! Base rascals! Mutiny for the price of a goat's skin; and, then, upon the appearance of the German soldiers, they take a flogging as quietly as so many trunks of trees! I do not know what sort of a place Ely is; but I really would like to know how the inhabitants looked one another in the face while this scene was exhibiting in their town.

For this he was prosecuted, convicted, and sentenced to imprisonment and a ruinous fine. Snatched from his farm at Botley, the development of which was another of his extravagances, he spent two years in prison, sustaining himself and his family by the faithful pen and avowing the deadliest vindictiveness towards his enemies. "I have three sons; and if any one of them ever forgets this . . . may he become both rotten and mad. May he, after having been a gabbling, slavering half-idiot all the prime of his life, become in his last days loathsome to the sight and stinking to the nostril!" Each of the sons became a lawyer. Years after he wrote of the effect upon them of the news of his sentence, and added:

> How I despise the wretches who talk of my vindictiveness; of my exultation at the confusion of those who inflicted those sufferings! How I despise the base creatures, the crawling slaves, the callous and cowardly hypocrites, who affect to be 'shocked' (tender souls!) at my expressions of joy, and at the death of Gibbs, Ellenborough, Perceval, Liverpool, Canning, and the rest of the tribe that I have already seen out,

and at the fatal workings of that system, for endeavouring to check which I was thus punished! How I despise these wretches, and how I, above all things, enjoy their ruin, and anticipate their utter beggary! What! I am to forgive, am I, injuries like this; and that, too, without any atonement? Oh no! I have not so read the Holy Scriptures.

And when, twenty years after the flogging, his rural rides took him into the eastern counties, he rode on to Ely in order to see the spot where the German Legion flogged the English militia, and make an opportunity of retelling the story as publicly as he could. He found one of the victims still alive.

About the time of this visit to Ely, Cobbett founded the *Twopenny Trash,* gladly adopting a poor taunt as title; and in it he boasted of the influence of his own writings, which had brought petitions for Parliamentary reform:

> The answers to these petitions were laws to enable Ministers to take, at their pleasure, any man that they might suspect of treasonable intentions; to put him into any jail and any dungeon that they might choose; to keep him there for any time that they might choose . . . on their own mere will, and at their sole pleasure, without regular commitment, without confronting him with his accuser, without letting him know who was his accuser, and without stating even to himself what was his offence.

How modern and familiar an echo does this recital raise; yet it is actually so long ago as 1817 that he is writing of, and not the period of our late war and uneasy peace.

Once again Cobbett found it necessary to fly, and *A Year's Residence in America* (1818) was the happiest result, a book in which his free humour had easier play and his denunciations were singularly free from bitterness; as, for example, in his reference to "little Jerry Bentham. . . . This everlasting babbler has aimed a sort of stiletto stroke at me; for what God knows, except it be to act a consistent part, by endeavouring to murder the man whom he has so frequently robbed, and whose facts and thoughts, though disguised and disgraced by the robber's quaint phraseology, constitute the better part of his book—Jerry, who was made a reformer by Pitt's refusal to give him a contract to build a penitentiary." Age as well as distance may have lent a little lightness to his attack. In the *English Grammar,* published some years after his brief exile was ended, he chooses passages of prose for castigation not from obscure contemporary writers, but from Johnson and the King's Speech; as to the latter picturing the joint labours of the Ministry in concocting this "pretty stuff. . . . If you should hear them there (in 'the Thieves' Houses') stammering and repeating and putting forth their nonsense, your wonder will be, not that they wrote a King's Speech so badly, but that they contrived to put upon paper sentences sufficiently grammatical to enable us to guess at the meaning." His own first speech in Parliament sounded the same note of pleasant arrogance: "It appears to me that since I have been sitting here I have heard a great

deal of vain and unprofitable conversation." Such phrases did not lose by falling from humorous lips. At seventy he was six feet in height and one of the stoutest men in the House; his hair was milk-white, his complexion still ruddy; but it was his small, sparkling, laughing eyes that chiefly struck an observer. One of his speeches was as delightful (save for the unpitiable victim) as anything that he wrote; it was an attack on Lord Plunkett, who had sworn opposition to the Act of Union and devoted his children to eternal hostility against the invaders of his country's freedom:

> Where is the man who held this language? Is he in England, or is he in Ireland? Is he in the ranks of the Ministerialists opposite, or in the ranks of the repealers around me? He is in Ireland. But what is he there? Is he Lord Chancellor? Yes! This old Hannibal is actually Lord Chancellor of Ireland. . . .

And he reinforced the onslaught, in which these clublike phrases played only a part, though not the meanest part, by giving the names, the places, and the emoluments of all the Lord Chancellor's sons, the numerous "young Hannibals" who were indeed guiltless only of their country's blood.

Cobbett spoke as he wrote, and his writing was but a lightly sophisticated speech. Whether writing or speaking, invective was his chief weapon. Attacking Malthus and all other theorists, absentee parsons, upstart landowners, soldiers turned statesmen and statesmen turned thieves; denouncing potatoes, tea-drinking, poets and historians, education and educators, aristocrats and democrats; deploring rural depopulation and urban herding—in all these vigorous exercises he delighted in coarse abuse, and indeed it was wanted in his time to sustain the ancient method of defence. Nicknames gave him a boyish satisfaction—"Dread-death and dread-devil Johnson," and "Stern-path-of-duty-man" Lord Liverpool, and "M. de Snip," an Army clothing contractor and Member of Parliament. He was, in fact, driven to exaggerating the anger or the contempt he felt by his sharp sense of the advantages conferred on his opponents by rank, wealth, and culture.

Yet it would be wrong to think of him as merely a literary or political bully. He loved contention, and none the less remained a true peasant in his domestic affections, satisfactions, and fidelities. I cannot conceive of a political England in which he would have rested content and inactive; but he was a born writer, and had his temper been less often exasperated by privilege and injustice he would have written another and still more attractive *Rural Rides,* a yet happier *Year's Residence in America.* A clear hint of the writer that was half lost to letters may be found in one of many passages describing the education of his children:

> The first thing of all was health, which was secured by the deeply interesting and never-ending sports of the field and pleasures of the garden. Luckily these things were treated of in books and pictures of endless variety;

so that on wet days, in long evenings, these came into play. A large, strong table in the middle of the room, their mother sitting at her work, used to be surrounded with them, the baby, if big enough, sat up in a high chair. Here were inkstands, pens, pencil, indiarubber, and paper, all in abundance, and every one scrabbled about as he or she pleased. There were prints of animals of all sorts; books treating of them; others treating of gardening, of flowers, of husbandry, of hunting, coursing, shooting, fishing, planting, and, in short, of everything, with regard to which we had something to do. One would be trying to imitate a bit of my writing, another drawing the pictures of some of our dogs or horses, a third poking over Bewick's *Quadrupeds* and picking out what he said about them; but one book of never-failing resource was the French *Maison Rustique,* or Farm House, which, it is said, was the book that first tempted Duquesnois (I think that was the name), the famous physician, in the reign of Louis XIV., to learn to read. . . . I never have been without a copy of this book for forty years, except during the time that I was fleeing from the dungeons of Castlereagh and Sidmouth, in 1817; and when I got to Long Island the first book I bought was another *Maison Rustique.*

Best of all had he written an autobiography untinctured by libels and lamentations, for in the writing of such a book, which he seems always on the verge of attempting, he would have had the advantage of a vivid memory and the minutest familiarity with the aspects and conditions of rural life as it touches the farmer and his labourers. Quieter days bringing reflection, and a more frequent reverie over the things which had taken the deepest root in his immature mind, he would have left us a book better than his best passages, flushed with the unaccountable brightness of a child's universe. But, alas! the literature of autobiography remained neglected in England, to be fulfilled in another tongue. For Cobbett's most expressive prose we must turn to a chapter which rings with the eloquence of an orator:

> Go to the site of some once opulent convent. Look at the cloister, now become in the hands of some rack-renter the receptacle for dung, fodder, and faggot-wood. See the hall where for ages the widow, the orphan, the aged, and the stranger found a table ready spread. See a bit of its wall now helping to make a cattle-shed, the rest having been hauled away to build a warehouse. Recognise in the side of a barn a part of the once magnificent chapel; and if, chained to the spot by your melancholy musings, you be admonished of the approach of night by the voice of the screech-owl from those arches, which once at the same hour resounded with the vespers of the monk, and which have for seven hundred years been assailed by storms and tempests in vain; if thus admonished of the necessity of seeking food, shelter, and a bed, lift up your eyes, and look at the whitewashed and dry-rotten shed on the hill called the 'Gentleman's House'; and apprised of the 'board wages' and 'spring guns,' which are the signs of his hospitality, turn your head, jog away from the scene of former comfort and grandeur; and with old English welcoming in your mind, reach the nearest inn, and then in a room half-warmed and half-lighted, with a reception precisely proportioned to the presumed length of your purse, sit down and listen to an account

of the hypocritical pretences, the base motives, the tyrannical and bloody means, under which, from which, and by which the ruin you have been witnessing was effected, and the hospitality you have lost was for ever banished from the land.

That Ruskin expanded prose of this noble cadence into his own wilder and looser laments need not diminish our sense of its virtue.

Hazlitt reports James Northcote as saying that Cobbett was a giant who tore up a subject by the roots, and used a homely, familiar way of writing, not from necessity or vulgarity, but to show his contempt for aristocratic pride and arrogance. Both Hazlitt and Carlyle contrasted him with Scott, Carlyle seeing in Cobbett the pattern John Bull of his century, strong as the rhinoceros, with singular humanities and genialities shining through his thick skin; one of the healthiest of men, a great improviser, whose writing is wonderful in quality and quantity. "Poor old Cobbett!" wrote Heine. "England's watch-dog! I have no love for thee, for every brutish nature revolts me; but I pity thee from my inmost soul as I see how thou strainest in vain to break loose and get at those thieves." All Cobbett is open to us now, and it is not pity that should be given to the man who wrote to his friends on leaving England:

> I will never become a subject or a citizen in any other State, and will always be a foreigner in every country but England. Any foible that may belong to your character I shall always willingly allow to belong to my own . . . and my beloved countrymen, be you well assured, that the last beatings of my heart will be love for the people, for the happiness and the renown of England; and hatred of their corrupt, hypocritical, dastardly, and merciless foes.

Like Blake, though wielding weapons all unlike Blake's, he would not cease from mental fight until he too had built a new Jerusalem in England's green and pleasant land.

Leonard Woolf (review date 1923)

SOURCE: "An Englishman," in *Essays on Literature, History, Politics, Etc.,* Harcourt Brace Jovanovich, 1927, pp. 26-30.

[Woolf is best known as one of the leaders of the Bloomsbury Group of artists and thinkers, and as the husband of novelist Virginia Woolf, with whom he founded the Hogarth Press. A Fabian socialist during the World War I era, he became a regular contributor to the socialist New Statesman *and later served as literary editor of the* Nation *and the* Athenaeum, *in which much of his literary criticism is found. In the following essay, originally published in 1923 in the* Nation *and the* Athenaeum, *he focuses on* Rural Rides *in discussing Cobbett's contributions to England's cultural and literary history.*]

Cobbett's *Rural Rides* and selections from his writings have been recently published for use in schools. I hope that this means that there is a revival in the appreciation of Cobbett. Nations, like individuals, are more often proud of their bad than of their good qualities, and, on this account, one may not feel altogether comfortable as to the spirit in which Cobbett will be taught and learnt in schools. He had all the vices as well as all the virtues of the typical John Bull, and in some schools and by some schoolmasters I can imagine the vices being taken for virtues and the virtues themselves being overlooked. Nevertheless, the good things in him are so many and so good that it seems absurd to feel anything but pleasure at boys and girls being brought up on the *Rural Rides* instead of Smiles or Mrs. Hemans.

First among Cobbett's virtues I place his English style. I cannot imagine any English prose more suitable to be given as a pattern and model to the ordinary man and woman. If England ever becomes a civilized country, 90 per cent of the population will write like William Cobbett. His English is plain, absolutely unaffected, vigorous and supple, beautiful. He knows instinctively not only exactly what he wants to say, but also the words which will most naturally and harmoniously express his meaning. I get something of the same kind of pleasure in watching the way in which his words clothe his thoughts as I do in watching the satiny coat of a race-horse ripple over the muscles as he walks. In each case the "fit" is so perfect and so natural. Cobbett's style is extraordinarily English. There are, of course, far greater English prose-writers than he is, but no one, I believe, has ever written sentences which are more perfectly in keeping with the peculiar genius of the English language. (It is because this faculty is natural and unconscious in him that I say that in an English Utopia we ordinary persons would all write like Cobbett.) When you read a paragraph of Cobbett, all you can say is: "Well, that simply *is* English"; you cannot say the same of Sir Thomas Browne or of Milton or of many far less Latinized prose-writers.

Cobbett seems to me to get into his sentences something of the atmosphere of the English country and the English climate as well as of the English language and the English character. This is true of all his writings, even of his tedious, bullying, blustering political abuse, but it is what gives a peculiar quality and charm to his descriptions of English country and so to his *Rural Rides*. What could be simpler or apparently more easy to write than the following passages, yet how many people could ride out on a January morning from Kensington and return with this in their note-books?—

> However, man was not the maker of the land; and, as to human happiness, I am of opinion that as much, and even more, falls to the lot of the leather-legged chaps that live in and rove about amongst those clays and woods as to the more regularly disciplined labourers of the rich and prime parts of England. As "God has made the back to the burthen", so the clay and coppice people make the dress to the stubs and bushes. Under the sole of the shoe is *iron;* from the sole six inches upwards is a highlow; then comes a pair of leather breeches; then comes a stout doublet; over this comes a smock-frock; and the wearer sets brush and stubs and thorns and mire at defiance. I have always observed that woodland and forest labourers are best off in the main. The coppices give them pleasant and profitable work in winter. If they have not so great a corn-harvest, they have a three weeks' harvest in April or May; that is to say, in the season of barking, which in Hampshire is called *stripping,* and in Sussex *flaying,* which employs women and children as well as men. . . .

> Even in winter the coppices are beautiful to the eye, while they comfort the mind with the idea of shelter and warmth. In spring they change their hue from day to day during two whole months, which is about the time from the first appearance of the delicate leaves of the birch to the full expansion of those of the ash; and even before the leaves come at all to intercept the view, what in the vegetable creation is so delightful to behold as the bed of a coppice bespangled with primroses and bluebells? The opening of the birch leaves is the signal for the pheasant to begin to crow, for the blackbird to whistle, and the thrush to sing; and just when the oak-buds begin to look reddish, and not a day before, the whole tribe of finches burst forth in songs from every bough, while the lark, imitating them all, carries the joyous sounds to the sky.

Cobbett is as English in his thoughts as he is in his style. But at this point it is impossible to speak of the virtues without also mentioning the vices. He belongs to the same breed as Dr. Johnson. His opinions were nearly always prejudices, often grotesque prejudices, and yet, even when most grotesque, always springing, in a peculiarly English way, from a subsoil of native "common-sense". When Cobbett writes that the trade of shoemaker "numbers more men of sense and of public spirit than any other in the kingdom", I feel a little glow of smiling pleasure, just as I do when Dr. Johnson remarks that all foreigners are fools. Each of these beliefs is a prejudice which I personally do not happen to share, yet I cannot but recognize that each has its roots just touching that deep subsoil of British common-sense. It is impossible not to feel affection for a man who holds Cobbett's view of shoemakers or Dr. Johnson's view of foreigners. And when one happens to share Cobbett's prejudices, as, for instance, his hatred of sham Gothic arches or fir-trees or paper money or war, then the blunt, honest vigour with which he expresses them is very refreshing. Even when he is wrong—and nine times out of ten he is hopelessly, incredibly wrong—you always see, as in the case of Dr. Johnson's wrong-headednesses, what is at the root of them, and feel a certain sympathy with it. But—and now I come to the faults and vices of Cobbett. But, after all, it is fortunately unnecessary to say more than a word about his vices, for they are very fully, clearly, and ably dissected by Hazlitt in his essay. The worst of Cobbett is that he always has someone and something which he wants to abuse and beat and bully. He must always have a prejudice *against* something or someone. And he cannot leave this butt for his contempt or abuse alone. He drags it in again and again to spoil his sentence or his paragraph and to weary his reader. But all that is in Hazlitt.

G. D. H. Cole (essay date 1924)

SOURCE: "Advice to Young Men," in *The Life of William Cobbett,* Harcourt Brace Jovanovich, 1924, pp. 306-18.

[Cole wrote extensively on Cobbett's life and work and was the author of a Cobbett biography long considered definitive. In the following excerpt, he comments on Advice to Young Men.]

[*Advice to Young Men*] was not intended mainly for a working-class public. The advice was addressed "to young men and (incidentally) to young women in the middle and higher ranks of life." It took the form, a favourite form with Cobbett, of letters to "a Youth, a Bachelor, a Lover, a Husband, a Father, a Citizen or a Subject." Its purpose was not primarily political, though it contains many political allusions. It is, in fact, a series of straight talks on the various concerns of life, simply and directly written, and plentifully illustrated with incidents from Cobbett's own life. It is egotistic, of course: all he wrote was that. But the egotism is pleasant, because the matter and manner do not bring Cobbett's good opinion of himself into sharp and constant contrast with his low opinion of all those with whom he had a difference of opinion. It is a good-humoured book, recalling the manner of his **Sermons,** but improving on them because there is less in it of desire to score off either political opponents or tract purveyors of the conventional type.

Cobbett was, in the fullest sense of the word, a self-made man. He had raised himself to his position of power—and power, he said, was always above all the object of his desire—entirely by his own efforts. He had taught himself to form opinions, to write, to speak, to play a part in public life, to be feared even where he was not respected. He had begun as a ploughboy: he had become the most powerful political writer in England. He was intensely proud of his achievement, and also intensely conscious that it was all his own. It seemed to him the result, not of any inborn gift or genius, but merely of will-power and steady application. Robust health was indeed the foundation of his success; but he attributed his health also to himself—to his sobriety, frugality, habits of early rising, love of exercise and the open air—qualities, these too, of the will. All that he had done, he maintained that others could do. *Advice to Young Men* was an appeal to youth to follow in the steps by which he had made William Cobbett what he was.

All this, and much more, he now set down. "It is the duty, and ought to be the pleasure, of age and experience to warn and instruct youth, and to come to the aid of inexperience. When sailors have discovered rocks or breakers, and have had the good luck to escape with life from amidst them, they, unless they be pirates or barbarians as well as sailors, point out the spots for the placing of buoys and of lights, in order that others may be not exposed to the danger which they have so narrowly escaped. What man of common humanity, having, by good luck, missed being engulfed in a quagmire or quicksand, will withhold from his neighbours a knowledge of the peril without which the dangerous spots are not to be approached." . . .

[Since *Advice to Young Men*] is the work in which, above all, Cobbett sets down his personal philosophy of life, apart from his political convictions, we must pause to consider what is the gist of the advice which he has to give. Men must work, both because it is their duty to themselves, their children, and their fellow-men, and because useful work is the key to happiness. "Happiness ought to be your great object, and it is to be found only in *independence.*" Genius, or natural talent, will accomplish little by itself: countless men have failed, though they had it, for lack of other qualities. "There must be something more than genius: there must be industry: there must be perseverance: there must be, before the eyes of the nation, proofs of extraordinary exertion. . . . These are the things, and *not genius,* which have caused my labours to be so incessant and so successful." Frugality and simplicity of manners, too, are vital. "A great misfortune of the present day is, that every one is, in his own estimate, *raised above his real state of life.*" Gluttony and drunkenness are beastly and destructive vices: tea-drinking an insidious and time-wasting pest. So Cobbett's prejudices mingle always with his sound counsel.

Advice to Young Men is really a sort of novel, with Cobbett for the blameless, but by no means colourless, hero. It celebrates what he has done, tells the story of his life with as definite a purpose as *The Pilgrim's Progress,* records not merely his successful search for power, but above all his successful search for happiness. It is the book of a man happy in achievement, happy in his work, happy in his family life; celebrating all his happiness as the triumph of the virtues he possesses, passing by, or rather totally unconscious of his besetting vices, because they have not managed to make him unhappy, or to interfere at all with the steady contentment of his inner life. He can catalogue in cold blood the qualities that a man should seek in a wife. "The things which you ought to desire in a wife are, 1. chastity; 2. sobriety; 3. industry; 4. frugality; 5. cleanliness; 6. knowledge of domestic affairs; 7. good temper; 8. beauty." But he could also conceive and expound these qualities as a portrait of his own wife, and make of them a real and living picture of married life and fellowship. Isolated sentences from the *Advice* have often a priggish sound: there never was a less priggish book; for it abounds everywhere in a sense of happiness and cheerful enjoyment of the good things of life. It takes a great man—a great personality—to moralise without sounding a prig. Cobbett could do it: his egotism, assertive rather than limiting, lustily abusive rather than censorious, helped him. A man who is really happy cannot be a prig.

Faults in any number one can find. Cobbett had none of the liberal virtues. He was not broad-minded or tolerant, or considerate or forgiving, or humble or charitable, or slow to anger or plenteous in mercy. His morality was of a fighting, self-assertive sort. He proclaimed duties as well as rights, but he made the duties means to the exercise of the rights, and not virtues for their own sake. He claimed for all men the rights which he claimed for himself; but he would have agreed with Walt Whitman.

> What others give as duties I give as living
>   impulses.
> Shall I give the heart's action as a duty?

His whole emphasis is on "selfhood," not because he preaches selfishness, but because he wants each man, and each woman, to find happiness in the successful exercise of his own will, the successful development of his own powers, the expression to the last drop of all the goodness he can squeeze out of himself. He would have men drive themselves hard. Recreation he approves; but let it be not of a lazy sort, like card-playing or play-going, but of good vigorous sort, like country dancing or the sports of the field. Education is good and useful; but it is best when a man teaches himself, not when he is taught by others. Hence his dislike of schools and projects of public education. The schoolmaster will pump knowledge into the child: learning at home can give, if it is done as Cobbett did it with his own children, the best impetus to the child to teach itself. And if we must send our children to school, let the school at least be small. Numbers corrupt: the big school is like "jails, barracks, factories," which corrupt not "by their walls, but by their condensed numbers." He cannot bear education in the mass: it must be something individual, something done for and by each child and each adult.

"Be just, be industrious, be sober, and be happy." Thus Cobbett sums up his advice, and he conceived that in his own life he had carried out these precepts. Just to individuals he had certainly not been; just to the common people and his conception of their rights he had been consistently from the time of his political awakening. Industrious he had been in an incredible degree, and sober always in the things of the body. But above all he had been happy, and had the art, in his best work, of communicating that sense of happiness in activity which was really the foundation of all his achievements.

G. K. Chesterton (essay date 1926)

SOURCE: "The Revival of Cobbett" and "Last Days and Death," in *William Cobbett,* Dodd, Mead & Company, 1926, pp. 3-25, 219-54.

[*Regarded as one of England's premier men of letters during the first half of the twentieth century, Chesterton is best known today as a colorful bon vivant, a witty essayist, and as the creator of the Father Brown mysteries. Chesterton shared Cobbett's belief that the Reformation brought on many of modern Europe's social problems. In the excerpt below, Chesterton discursively examines the paradoxes of Cobbett's beliefs and the significance of his work as a reformer, comparing Cobbett's thought with that of Edmund Burke and Thomas Carlyle.*]

It is but a year or two ago that I had the great and (it is to be feared) the undeserved honour of reading a paper on

Satirical depiction of Cobbett writing to Henry Hunt from his Long Island farm.

the subject [of Cobbett] to the Royal Society of Literature on my admission to that body, which certainly consists almost entirely of men who know much more about literature than I do. It was a graceful formality on such an occasion for the least learned person in the room to lecture to all the rest. Yet on that occasion the chairman, who was much more of a literary expert than I am, remarked on my having chosen an obscure and largely forgotten writer, just as if I had been lecturing on one of the last and least of the Greek sophists, or one of the numberless and nameless lyrists among the Cavaliers. Between then and now the change from neglect to revival has taken place. It is true that it is not until the first beginnings of the revival that we ever even hear of the neglect. Until that moment even the neglect is neglected. When I delivered the highly amateur address in question, the memory was already stirring, in others besides myself. But it is not out of egotism that I give this example; but because it happens to illustrate the first fact to be realized about the present position of Cobbett.

In one sense, of course, Cobbett has never been neglected. He has only been admired in the way in which he would have specially hated to be admired. He who was full of his subject has been valued only for his style. He who was so stuffed with matter has been admired for his manner; though not perhaps for his manners. He shouted to the uproarious many, and his voice in a faint whisper has reached the refined few; who delicately applauded a turn of diction or a flight of syntax. But if such applause be rather disconcerting to the demagogue, the real revival of his demagogy would be even more disconcerting to the academic admirer. Now I mean by the revival of Cobbett the revival of the things that Cobbett wished to revive. They were things which until a little while ago nobody imagined there was the slightest chance of reviving; such as liberty, England, the family, the honour of the yeoman, and so on. Many of the learned who, on the occasion above mentioned, were very indulgent to my own eccentric enthusiasm, would even now be a little puzzled if that enthusiasm became something more than an eccentricity. Cobbett had been for them a man who praised an extravagant and impossible England in exact and excellent English. It must seem strange indeed that one who can never hope to write such English can yet hope to see such an England. The critics must feel like cultivated gentlemen who, after long relishing Jeremy Taylor's diction, should abruptly receive an unwelcome invitation to give an exhibition of Holy Dying. They must feel like scholars who should have lingered lovingly all their lives over the lapidary Babylonian jests and vast verbal incantations of the wonderful essay on Urn-Burial; and then have lived to see it sold by the hundred as the popular pamphlet of a bustling modern movement in favour of cremation.

Nevertheless, this classic preservation of Cobbett in an urn, in the form of ashes, has not been quite consistent with itself. Even now it would seem that the ashes were still a little too hot to touch. And I only mentioned my own little effort in academic lecturing because it concerned something that may be repeated here, as relevant to the first essentials of the subject. Many professors have in a merely literary sense recognized Cobbett as a model; but few have modelled themselves upon their model. They were always ready to hope that their pupils would write such good English. But they would have been mildly surprised if any pupil had written such plain English. Yet, as I pointed out on that occasion, the strongest quality of Cobbett as a stylist is in the use he made of a certain kind of language: the sort of use commonly called abuse. It is especially his bad language that is always good. It is precisely the passages that have always been recognized as good style that would now be regarded as bad form. And it is precisely these violent passages that especially bring out not only the best capacities of Cobbett but also the best capacities of English. I was and am therefore ready to repeat what I said in my little lecture, and to repeat it quite seriously, though it was the subject at the time of merely amused comment. I pointed out that in the formation of the noble and beautiful English language, out of so many local elements, nothing had emerged more truly beautiful than the sort of English that has been localized under the name of Billingsgate. I pointed out that English excels in certain angular consonants and abrupt terminations that make it extraordinarily effective for the expression of the fighting spirit and a fierce contempt. How fortunate is the condition of the Englishman who can kick people; and how relatively melancholy that of the Frenchman who can only give them a blow of the foot! If we say that two people fight like cat and dog, the very words seem to have in them a shindy of snaps and screams and scratches. If we say *"comme le chat et le chien,"* we are depressed with the suggestion of comparative peace. French has of course its own depths of resounding power: but not this sort of battering-ram of bathos. Now nobody denies that Cobbett and his enemies did fight like cat and dog, but it is precisely his fighting passages that contain some of the finest examples of a style as English as the word dog or the word cat. So far as this goes the point has nothing to do with political or

moral sympathy with Cobbett's cause. The beauty of his incessant abuse is a matter of art for art's sake. The pleasure which an educated taste would receive in hearing Cobbett call a duchess an old cat or a bishop a dirty dog is almost onomatopœic, in its love of a melody all but detached from meaning. In saying this, it might be supposed, I was indeed meeting the purely artistic and academic critic half way, and might well have been welcomed, so to speak, with an embrace of reconciliation. This is indeed the reason why most lovers of English letters have at least kept alive a purely literary tradition of Cobbett. But, as it happened, I added some words which I will also take the liberty of mentioning, because they exactly illustrate the stages of this re-emergence of the great writer's fame from the field of literature to the field of life.

> There is a serious danger that this charm in English literature may be lost. The comparative absence of abuse in social and senatorial life may take away one of the beauties of our beautiful and historic speech. Words like "scamp" and "scoundrel," which have the unique strength of English in them, are likely to grow unfamiliar through lack of use, though certainly not through lack of opportunity for use. It is indeed strange that when public life presents so wide and promising a field for the use of these terms, they should be suffered to drop into desuetude. It seems singular that when the careers of our public men, the character of our commercial triumphs, and the general culture and ethic of the modern world seem so specially to invite and, as it were, to cry aloud for the use of such language, the secret of such language should be in danger of being lost.

Now, when I drew the attention of those authoritative guardians of English literature, responsible for the preservation of the purity of the English language, to this deplorable state of things—to the words that are like weapons rusting on the wall, to the most choice terms of abuse becoming obsolete in face of rich and even bewildering opportunities in the way of public persons to apply them to—when I appealed against this neglect of our noble tongue, I am sorry to say that my appeal was received with heartless laughter and was genially criticized in the newspapers as a joke. It was regarded not only as a piece of mild buffoonery but as a sort of eighteenth-century masquerade; as if I only wished to bring back cudgels and cutlasses along with wigs and three-cornered hats. It was assumed that nobody could possibly seriously hope, or even seriously expect, to hear again the old Billingsgate of the hustings and the election fight. And yet, since those criticisms were written, only a very little time ago, that sort of very Early English has suddenly been heard, if not in journalism, at least in politics. By a strange paradox, even the House of Commons has heard the sound of common speech, not wholly unconnected with common sense.

The cudgel has come back like a boomerang: and the common Englishman, so long content with taking half a loaf, may yet in the same tradition of compromise confine himself to heaving half a brick. The reason why Parliamentary language is unparliamentary and Westminster has been joined to Billingsgate, the reason why the English poor in many places are no longer grumbling or even growling but rather howling, the reason why there is a new note in our old polite politics, is a reason that vitally concerns the subject of this little study. There are a great many ways of stating that reason; but the way most relevant here is this. All this is happening because the critics have been all wrong about Cobbett. I mean they were specially wrong about what he represented. It is happening because Cobbett was *not* what they have always represented him as being; not even what they have always praised him as being. It is happening because Cobbett stood for a reality of quite another sort; and realities can return whether we understand them or not. Cobbett was *not* merely a wrong-headed fellow with a knack of saying the right word about the wrong thing. Cobbett was *not* merely an angry and antiquated old farmer who thought the country must be going to the dogs because the whole world was not given up to the cows. Cobbett was not merely a man with a lot of nonsensical notions that could be exploded by political economy; a man looking to turn England into an Eden that should grow nothing but Cobbett's Corn. What he saw was not an Eden that cannot exist but rather an Inferno that can exist, and even that does exist. What he saw was the perishing of the whole English power of self-support, the growth of cities that drain and dry up the countryside, the growth of dense dependent populations incapable of finding their own food, the toppling triumph of machines over men, the sprawling omnipotence of financiers over patriots, the herding of humanity in nomadic masses whose very homes are homeless, the terrible necessity of peace and the terrible probability of war, all the loading up of our little island like a sinking ship; the wealth that may mean famine and the culture that may mean despair; the bread of Midas and the sword of Damocles. In a word, he saw what we see, but he saw it when it was not there. And some cannot see it—even when it is there.

It is the paradox of his life that he loved the past, and he alone really lived in the future. That is, he alone lived in the real future. The future was a fog, as it always is; and in some ways his largely instinctive intelligence was foggy enough about it. But he and he alone had some notion of the sort of London fog that it was going to be. He was in France during the French Revolution; amid all that world of carnage and classical quotations, of Greek names and very Latin riots. He must have looked, as he stood there with his big heavy figure and black beaver hat, as solemn and solid a specimen as ever was seen of the Englishman abroad—the sort of Englishman who is very much abroad. He went to America just after the American Revolution; and played the part of the old Tory farmer, waving the beaver hat and calling on those astonished republicans for three cheers for King George. Everywhere, amid all that dance of humanitarian hopes, he seemed like a survival and a relic of times gone by. And he alone was in any living touch with the times that were to come. . . .

Nobody else had felt the future; nobody else had smelt the fog; nobody else had any notion of what was really coming upon the world.

I mean that if you had gone to Jefferson at the moment when he was writing the Declaration of Independence, and shown him the exact picture of an Oil Trust, and its present position in America, he would have said, "It is not to be believed." If you had gone to Cobbett, and shown him the same thing, he would have said, like the bearded old gentleman in the rhyme, "It is just as I feared." If you had confronted Carnot with Caillaux, the old revolutionist would have wondered what inconceivable curse could have fallen on great France of the soldiers. If you had confronted Cobbett with some of our similar specimens, he would have said it was what might be expected when you gave over great England to the stock-jobbers. For men like Jefferson and Carnot were thinking of an ancient agricultural society merely changing from inequality to equality. They were thinking of Greek and Roman villages in which democracy had driven out oligarchy. They were thinking of a mediæval manor that had become a mediæval commune. The merchant and man of affairs was a small and harmless by-product of their system; they had no notion that it would grow large enough to swallow all the rest. The point about Cobbett is that he alone really knew that *there* and not in kings or republics, Jacobins or Anti-Jacobins, lay the peril and oppression of the times to come.

It is the riddle of the man that if he was wrong then, he is right now. As a dead man fighting with dead men, he can still very easily be covered with derision; but if we imagine him still alive and talking to living men, his remarks are rather uncomfortably like life. The very words that we should once have read as the most faded and antiquated history can now be read as the most startling and topical journalism. Let it be granted that the denunciation was not always correct about Dr. Priestley or Dr. Rush; that the abuse was not really applicable to Mr. Hunt or Mr. Wright; let us console ourselves with the fact that the abuse is quite applicable to us. We at least have done all that Cobbett's enemies were accused of doing. We have fulfilled all those wild prophecies; we have justified all those most unjustifiable aspersions; we have come into the world as if to embody and fulfil in a belated fashion that highly improbable prediction. Cobbett's enemies may or may not have ruined agriculture; but anyhow we have. Cobbett's contemporaries may or may not have decreased the national wealth; but it is decreased. Paper money may not have driven out gold in his lifetime, but we have been more privileged than he. In a mere quarrel between the eighteenth century and the nineteenth century he may easily appear wrong; but in a quarrel between the nineteenth century and the twentieth century he is right. He did not always draw precise diagrams of things as they were. He only had frantic and fantastic nightmares of things as they are. The fame of Cobbett faded and indeed completely vanished during our time of prosperity; or what is counted our time of prosperity. For in fact it was only the prosperity of the prosperous. But during all that time his version of the doubts about what Carlyle called the profit-and-loss philosophy practically disappeared from the modern mind. I have mentioned Carlyle; but as expressed by Carlyle the same doubts were not the same thing. Carlyle would have turned capitalism into a sort of feudalism, with the feudal loyalty on the one side and the feudal liberality on the other. He meant by the profit-and-loss philosophy a small and mean philosophy that could not face a small loss even for the sake of a great profit. But he never denied that there could be a great profit; he never contradicted the whole trend of the age as Cobbett did. On the contrary, Carlyle called the capitalist by a romantic name, where Cobbett would have called him by a shockingly realistic name. Carlyle called the capitalist a captain of industry; a very sad scrap of Victorian sentimentalism. That romantic evasion misses the whole point; the point which Cobbett kept steadily in sight all his life. Militarism would be much less respectable and respected if the captain of a line regiment had pocketed the rent of every acre that he fought for in Flanders. Capitalism would be much more respectable and respected if all the master-builders climbed to the tops of towers and fell off; if there were as many capitalists knocked on the head by bricks as there were captains killed at the front by bullets. But as I pointed out in a connection already mentioned, Carlyle was really rather an optimist than a pessimist. Certainly Carlyle was an optimist where Cobbett was a pessimist. Cobbett dug much deeper: he not only called a spade a spade, but he used it like a resurrectionist—not merely like a reformer weeding out small evils. We might say that the mere reformer calls a spade a spud. Carlyle gave hints and suggestions rather darkly that the whole business might end badly; but he never really dared to wish that it had never begun. He told the rich sternly how they should dispose of their wealth; he did not, like Cobbett, tell them coarsely how they had collected it. The consequence was that Carlyle has been exhibited as a Puritan, a pessimist, a prophet of woe. Cobbett has not been exhibited at all. Carlyle has been set over against Mill and Macaulay as a sort of official opposition; but Cobbett's opposition was not sufficiently official. Carlyle has been allowed to grumble like a choleric old major much respected in the club. Cobbett has been entirely removed, like the *enfant terrible,* kicking and screaming, lest he should say something dreadful in the drawing-room. Hence the big secret with which he was bursting has actually been too big to be uttered; his condemnation was so large and sweeping that it had to be hidden in a hole. The Victorians were quite cultivated enough and broad-minded enough to realize that there must be some reminder amid their rejoicings of human fallibility and frailty; lest Mr. George Augustus Sala should seem a creature all too bright and good for human nature's daily food. They had something of the imperial imagination and philosophic outlook of the ancient Egyptians, who set a skeleton at the banquet to remind them of mortality and a more melancholy mood that might mingle harmlessly with the mood of joy. Carlyle was the skeleton of the feast. But Cobbett was not the skeleton of the feast; he was the skeleton in the cupboard.

In short, Carlyle did criticize the profit-and-loss school, but not the profitableness of the whole world in which it was made. Certainly he did not question the assumption that it was at least profitable in the sense of being practicable. But since then deeper forces have moved and darker riddles begun to be murmured amongst us; and it

is not the superficial abnormalities and accidents but the whole main movement and purpose of the nineteenth century that is brought in question. We have come back to doing what Carlyle never really did, what Cobbett always wanted to do, to make a real reckoning of ultimate loss and profit on the profit-and-loss philosophy. Even in the economic sphere the answer has been looking more and more doubtful. We talk of it as the age of profiteers; but it is a question how long even profiteers will make profits. We talk of it as capitalism; and so it is, in the rather sinister sense of living on capital.

. . . . .

Cobbett had no power of illusion at all; that is why he was not what people call a practical man. That was especially why he could never manage to be a Whig; however much he might be called a Tory or a Radical. He could never have understood the sincerity there was in the self-deception of a man like Burke, who could look back on the oligarchical intrigues of 1688 and onwards in a glow of Constitutional enthusiasm. Perhaps to say that he was never a Whig is but another way of saying that he was not an aristocrat. History was not a hobby; politics were not a game, even a game played for money. He had that indefinable attitude which marks the man who has always had to earn his own living. He wanted history and politics to be useful; in that sense he was quite utilitarian. In the strict sense of the word, he was not a gentleman—he was a yeoman. He was a farmer who worked for a harvest; not a landscape-painter or even a landscape-gardener. All his wild life long he was working for a harvest; even when men thought he was sowing the wild oats of fanaticism; even when they thought he was sowing the dragon's teeth of revolution. He was trying to get results; and did not mind how hard he worked to get them. He worked to get a reform of Parliament; he worked to get a more popular control of Parliament; not because he particularly wanted to see the working of a new constitution in the abstract, but because he thought the old constitution was delaying the harvest. He worked for a right to take a hand in the work. He worked for a place among the new rulers of a new realm. He worked for a seat at Westminster because he really believed, more or less, that it would be a sort of throne from which he would see all England rejoicing in the new liberty; since the hirelings and hacks of the wicked squires were gone and there had been summoned in the ancient language of English liberty, a Free Parliament. The height from which he would look over that landscape of liberty would be higher than the Accursed Hill. He would see a New Sarum almost as ideal as the New Jerusalem, if not descending out of heaven from God, at least lifted towards heaven by the giant limbs of liberated man; by the proud toil and spontaneous prudence of the free. The new Parliament was meant to make a new people. And almost the first thing it did was to pass the New Poor Law. Almost the first thing it did was to hand over little Oliver Twist to be starved and beaten by Bumble and Claypole: and sell English children into slavery for being poor.

There is an irony that is like an agony and is beyond speech or measure. It were vain to wonder, in the normal way, what manner of words would have come to those all too tempestuous lips; what lucid violence of logic as of light through rending rocks would have tried to do justice to that towering contradiction, in the days when the giant was young. Much he did say, of course, in his own way. But there was something in that final contradiction that could not so be contradicted finally or fully: and when Cobbett came with the clearer eyes of later life to look at the Reform Parliament, to look steadily at its Reformers and its Parliamentarians, to absorb the whole scene of how such laws are made and how such men make them; to sit in his seat in silence for a little, and take in all that enormous thing calmly and completely—then he made the only comment at all commensurate with it, or equal in eloquence to the occasion: he died.

Chesterton on Cobbett:

I saw great Cobbett riding,
The horseman of the shires;
And his face was red with judgment
And a light of Luddite fires:
And south to Sussex and the sea the lights leapt
    up for liberty,
The trumpet of the yeomanry, the hammer of the
    squires;
For bars of iron rust away, rust away, rust away,
Rend before the hammer and the horseman
    riding in,
Crying that all men at the last, and at the worst
    and at the last,
Have found the place where England ends and
    England can begin.

His horse-hoofs go before you,
Far beyond your bursting tyres;
And time is bridged behind him
And our sons are with our sires.

A trailing meteor on the Downs he rides above
    the rotting towns,
The Horseman of Apocalypse, the Rider of the
    Shires.
For London Bridge is broken down, broken
    down, broken down;
Blow the horn of Huntingdon from Scotland to
    the sea—
. . . Only a flash of thunder-light, a flying dream
    of thunder-light,
Had shown under the shattered sky a people that
    were free.

    G. K. Chesterton, *in* The Collected Poems of G. K.
    Chesterton, *Dodd, Mead & Company, 1980.*

The great world with its wheels of progress that went rolling over him did not understand his death any more than his life. A hundred years afterwards he is perhaps better known than he was ten years afterwards, or even ten minutes afterwards. Two hundred years afterwards,

perhaps, he will be known better still. Johnson is more human and familiar to every casual reader to-day than he was to Churchill or Horace Walpole; but Johnson had a bodyguard of faithful friends who really understood him, his quaint weaknesses and his mighty worth. Cobbett hardly had a friend outside his family; and it is doubtful whether there had ever been one human being who really understood what he meant. His political allies were not friends; and they were not generally for very long allies. And the reason was that not one of them could enlarge his mind to understand the mind of Cobbett; or that immense desire for the deliverance and perpetuation of the whole huge humanity of England. The makers of the French Pantheon, wisely combining republican and royal and imperial trophies, have inscribed their common monument, "To All the Glories of France." If any man as wise had stood by the little gravestone in the churchyard of Farnham, he might have traced the words, "To All the Glories of England." All the other leaders were falling apart into foolish party systems and false antitheses; into Tories who were mere squires, and Radicals who were mere merchants. Windham had been his friend; but who could expect Windham to understand what he felt about the wild justice of the Luddite fires? Orator Hunt had been his ally; but who could expect Hunt to know what Cobbett was talking about when he praised the spires of the Gothic churches or the saints of the Dark Ages? This uneducated man was too well educated for all his contemporaries. He stood in a world which believed that it was broadening; and the whole mind of that world was narrower than his own. It believed itself to be growing modern and many-sided; and he alone saw that it was growing monomaniac and mean. And that larger vision died with him: and vanished for a hundred years.

Cobbett was only too ready to give people, the language of the comic landlady, a piece of his mind. But the accidental phrase is after all an accurate phrase. It was only a piece of his mind that was ever given to anybody; a rather ragged piece often torn off in a rather random fashion: but not the whole truth that he really meant, for that he had great difficulty in giving to anybody, perhaps even to himself. Talkative as he was, it may be that he never said enough; and lucid as he was, it may be that he never quite got to the point. But the point was a whole point of view. And whether it was his fault or the other people's fault, that point of view was never really taken by anybody else: nobody stood exactly where he stood or saw the world exactly as he saw it; or others would have realized that, amid all his contradictory phrases and combative passions, he did in a real sense of his own see life steadily and see it whole. As we look back on his life, even with the views that were not consistent with each other seem to be consistent with him. A friend would not deny that he contradicted himself; but a friend would be able to guess when and where he would probably contradict himself. Only in this sense it is true to say that he never had a friend. He had affections, and he had alliances; but not one true intellectual friendship.

There was this true distinction in the mind of the self-taught farmer: that his mind is a place where extremes meet. When it can be said of a man that the Tories thought him a Radical, and the Radicals thought him a Tory, the first thing that will occur to us is that he is a moderate. It can truly be said of Cobbett; and the very last thing that would occur to anybody would be to call him a moderate. He was not only the reverse of a moderate, he was something that would be utterly bewildering to any moderate. He was an extremist all round. He was more Tory than most Tories, and more Radical than most Radicals. In other words, it was because he was original; but it was also because he was universal. He did not altogether understand his own universality; and he expressed it mostly in the form of inconsistency. He was fanatical, but he was not narrow. With all his fanaticism, he was really looking at things from too many points of view at once to be understood by those who wore the blinkers of a party or even a theory. He seemed to be at all extremes, because he had in some sense encircled and surrounded his whole generation. Ignorant and violent as he seemed on the surface, his spirit was like one that had lived before and after. He was there before they were all born, in the crowded mediæval churches. He was there after they were all dead, in the crowded congresses of the Trades Unions. It was not knowledge, but it was understanding, in the sense of sympathy. When we find this sort of universality we find, I think, a thing on the heroic scale. It would surely be no bad definition of greatness in a man, to say that we can strike out in any direction and still find the circumference of his mind.

There was never a Cobbettite except Cobbett. That gives him an absolute quality not without a sort of authority. He was a full man and a ready man, but he was not an exact man. He was not a scientific man or in the orderly and conscious sense even a philosophical man. But he was, by this rather determining test, a great man. He was large enough to be lonely. He had more inside him than he could easily find satisfied outside him. He meant more by what he said even than the other men who said it. He was one of the rare men to whom the truisms are truths. This union of different things in his thoughts was not sufficiently thought out; but it was a union. It was not a compromise; it was a man. That is what is meant by saying that it was also a great man. There was something in him that the world had not taught him; even if it was too vast and vague for him to teach it to the world. Things were part of that thing that could not be parts of any other thing. That is why he had no real intellectual friendships among the intellectuals of his day, when all allowance is made for his real faults of vanity and violence and readiness to quarrel. It is easy to argue about how he came to quarrel with his best friends. It is more penetrating to ask how he could ever come to agree with them. Even to the best of them his whole outlook, which seemed to him so simple, would have been bewildering. How was Orator Hunt to understand that the great empty churches with their gaping mouths cried aloud that they also belonged to the future, because they belonged to the past? How was the Right Honourable William Windham to understand that riotous artisans in the Black Country were also appealing to the past, as well as threatening the future? How was Mr. Carlile the atheist bookseller to know that

a ruined abbey and a raging mob were one thing; and that thing liberty? How was Lord Brougham to understand that a field of clover and a grotesque gridiron were one thing; and that thing England?

That is the paradox of Cobbett; that in a sense he quarrelled with everybody because he reconciled everything. From him, at least, so many men were divided, because in him so many things were unified. He appeared inconsistent enough in the thousand things that he reviled; but he would have appeared far more inconsistent in the things that he accepted. The breadth of his sympathy would have been stranger than all his antipathies, and his peace was more provocative than war. Therefore it is that our last impression of him is of a loneliness not wholly due to his hatreds, but partly also to his loves. For the desires of his intellect and imagination never met anything but thwarting and wounding in this world; and though the ordinary part of him was often happy enough, the superior part was never satisfied. He never came quite near enough to a religion that might have satisfied him. But with philosophies he would never have been satisfied, especially the mean and meagre philosophies of his day. The cause he felt within him was too mighty and multiform to have been fed with anything less than the Faith. Therefore it was that when he lay dying in his farmhouse on the hills, those he had loved best in his simple fashion were near to his heart; but of all the millions of the outer world there was none near to his mind, and all that he meant escaped and went its way, like a great wind that roars over the rolling downs.

This book began with an indefensible piece of personal recollection, and I fear it will have to end with another. Perhaps I might plead the influence of the man I have been studying and trying to understand; who has been called egotistical, though I should be content to call him autobiographical. As Mr. Cole pointed out in his admirable biography, Cobbett treated his ego as an emblematic figure of England, as Whitman did his of America. My own memories can have no such symbolic excuse; but I passed much of my childhood along that main thoroughfare where Cobbett had his seed-farm at Kensington; and one of the last things my own father told me was a tale of a strange object hanging above the road, before alterations and destructions removed it; one glimpse of a symbolic shape more ugly and ungainly than a gallows in the sunlight: the Gridiron.

All that he hated has triumphed on that spot. The ordinary shop that he thought a nuisance has swelled into the big emporium he would have thought a nightmare; the suburb has sunk deep into the new London; but the road still runs westward down which he went riding so often, heading for the open country, and leaving the Wen as far as possible behind. The Wen has pursued him, shooting out further and further in telescopic perspective, past Hammersmith and Chiswick and Richmond; and still I seem to see the back of that vanishing rider ever ahead, and lessening amid changing scenery; hills turning about him like a transformation scene, away almost to the stormy wall of Wales. It was as if he were riding further and further westward, following towards the sunset the road of the fallen kings; where a low red light glows for ever upon things forgotten and the last ruins of the Round Table. And yet I am not sure of such a view of history; it seems to me that with us also things change and even change places; and the war does not always go one way. When I used to go out as a boy into the green twilight, having written nonsense all night (fortunately unpublished), and drink coffee at a stall in the street, brooding upon all these things, it seemed then as if the tide were running high enough in the one direction; but I have since had a notion that high tides can turn. The enormous buildings, seen in outline like uncouth drawings, seem to stand up more insecurely against an altered sky; with some change in it too subtle yet to be called the twilight. I discovered, at least, that even in all that labyrinth of the new London by night there is an unvisited hour of almost utter stillness, before the creaking carts begin to come in from the market-gardens, to remind us that there is still somewhere a countryside. And in that stillness I have sometimes fancied I heard, tiny and infinitely far away, something like a faint voice hallooing and the sound of horse-hoofs that return.

Edmund Blunden (essay date 1930)

SOURCE: "Rural Rides," in *Votive Tablets: Studies Chiefly Appreciative of English Authors and Books,* Cobden-Sanderson, 1931, pp. 268-80.

[*Blunden was associated with the Georgians, an early twentieth-century group of English poets who reacted against the prevalent contemporary mood of disillusionment and the rise of artistic modernism by seeking to return to the pastoral, nineteenth-century poetic traditions associated with William Wordsworth. As a literary critic and essayist, he often wrote of the lesser-known figures of the Romantic era as well as of the pleasures of English country life. In the following essay, originally published in the* Times Literary Supplement *in 1930, Blunden examines* Rural Rides.]

No title could sound simpler than that which was applied many years ago to William Cobbett—"the Last of the Saxons"—unless it were the title of Cobbett's book, *Rural Rides;* and yet the man and his book alike are complexities from which a modern mind without abundant leisure might turn in despair. I say "his book" because the *Rural Rides* is the confluence of many Cobbettian streams, and his fantastic mass of printed declarations, decimations, didactics appears in it to reach a certain degree of maturity and compactness; and then again, except for the mighty hunter of old editions, Cobbett is accessible as a writer mainly in reprints of *Rural Rides*. There is still another reason: the political arena of the Regency is at best a hot, dusty, uproarious scene, and in it the figure of Cobbett is perhaps unusually hot, dusty and uproarious; but the title of *Rural Rides* steals upon the ear

> Sweet as the shepherd's pipe upon the
> mountains,

and promises an almost aquatint easiness of spirit in the lanes and bridle-paths of this country before we yielded to speed.

Such a notion would doubtless have amused and infuriated Cobbett at the time when he was proceeding with his *Rides*. He had other things than aquatints to attend to. He was the bringer of light and fire to the cold, dark regions of Hodge and Dobbin. He was the crusader of the Locust-tree—

> those who will be born *sixty* years hence, will think that Locust-trees have *always been* the most numerous trees in England; and some curious writer of a century or two hence, will tell his readers that, *wonderful* as it may seem, "the Locust was hardly known in England until about the year 1823, when the nation was introduced to a knowledge of it by WILLIAM COBBETT." What he will say of me besides, I do not know; but I know that he will say this of me.

Besides his occupation of awakening the countryside to the marvels of the locust-tree (or acacia), and Cobbett's Corn (or maize, "if the instructions in my Book be followed"), and "the converting of English Grass, and Grain Plants cut green, into Straw, for the purpose of making Plat for Hats and Bonnets" (see Mr. Cobbett's *Cottage Economy*)—besides these and similar creative iterations, the horseman was not likely to forget his mission of clearing the land of men who represented the wrong institutions. This set of ogres was ever increasing. Of all the caricaturists Cobbett was the most spontaneous. He travelled the country, so to speak, with an unparalleled gallery of grinning effigies, and dashed along his row of rifles knocking out their teeth too fast for his clients to get their shots in.

But even Cobbett had his times when political war was suddenly interrupted: when other interests led him, almost unwittingly, away from the ruling passion of flaying "all the Rag-Rooks, big and little, and all the Jews, and all the Jobbers, and all the loanmongers, and all the lords of the loom and the anvil." In his *Political Register* we see him suddenly withdraw from some formidable dispute, in which "to repeal the malt tax" (for example) "would be a blessed revolution," in an unexpected direction. The politician even becomes the literary leader:

> *Shakespeare Hoax.* I have at various times and in sundry parts of my voluminous writings, expressed my contempt of those who, by enthusiastic men, or knavish traders in plays and pamphlets, have been induced to look upon the plays of this old author as *something almost divine*. The words *"immortal bard,"* applied to this man, have always appeared to me such a monstrous perversion of terms, such an insult to my understanding, that I have many times expressed my contempt of the persons making use of the appellation as thus applied.

With what delight Cobbett goes on to point out that "learned Doctors" accepted the impostures of a sixteen-year-old boy as the genuine production of Shakespeare!

And, after shedding his ink on their abhorred names, how naïvely he makes one of his many requests to readers of the Register: "It is curious that I never saw a copy of these famous *Shakespearian remains*. I wish some one would lend me the book for a day or two."

Soon after the appearance of W. H. Ireland himself with the desired book at 183, Fleet Street, Cobbett began advertising (December 12, 1829) the work on which, we say, his chances of being heard nowadays mainly depend.

> *Rural Rides*. I have now collected these, and published them, in one volume of considerable size, price 10*s*. Many persons have wished to possess them in this form; and, therefore, I have thus published them. I say *published;* but, perhaps, the volume will not be ready for sale until next week.

And meanwhile Cobbett went off on a new Ride—a Northern Tour.

His book appeared with date 1830. In spite of its considerable size, it did not include a large number of Rides which had been described in the **Register** between 1821 and 1826, nor any of those subsequent to 1826. It remained for Mr. and Mrs. G. D. H. Cole, in a remarkable centennial edition, to do for Cobbett's masterpiece what neither he nor his numerous editors did (though James Paul Cobbett, in 1853, made some show of enlarging the view of his father's travels in prose). With splendid loyalty they collected from the **Register** in their exact form all the Rides that were printed there from 1821 to 1834, these including Cobbett's **Tour in Scotland** (which he printed as a book in 1833) and his **Tour in Ireland** (which took the form of letters to his labourer Charles Marshall); and in addition they supplied many concise and valuable annotations, a biographical directory of the famous and, not less, the obscure persons whom Cobbett names "for bale or balm," and a preliminary essay. Theirs is the only edition of the **Rural Rides** which, from its publication, will be consulted with certainty; and, if I may mention my one lack in it, I could wish that the portrait of Cobbett had been included besides the embellishments drawn by Mr. John Nash and the map Cobbett's Country—from Gloucester to Rye—by Mr. A. E. Taylor.

In the introduction the reader is given a good opportunity to prepare himself for the **Rural Rides** without courting bewilderment among the stack of volumes containing Cobbett's journalism, or even that smaller stack intended as a poor man's practical university—or "the literature which, compendiously called 'Anti-Cobbett,' takes up a pretty large space in the catalogue of the British Museum Library." The begetting and nourishment of his principal hobgoblin may be comprehended for immediate needs from these pages; the outline appears of that

> system which Cobbett called *"the Thing"*—a *Thing* which seemed so vividly personal to him that one is tempted to believe he must have seen it in his dreams as something like Peer Gynt's Great Boyg, a vast immovable object which bore the face now of Pitt, now of Malthus, now of Baring, and now of Castlereagh.

It is a suggestion kindled with imaginative insight. A thousand writers have likened Cobbett to the typical John Bull; but what is the almost delirious gulf of horrid shapes and shrieks and sights unholy in which this "plain man" plunges himself? His talent for the sarcastic nickname has been noticed again and again; but is it not something apart from the mere dexterity of a popular opinion-maker? It is shrill, forlorn, more private than public, much like the contemporary ululation of the painter Haydon in his pamphlets and his journals. Even when the abusive element disappears, Cobbett can still seem talking to himself in his solitary Apollyoniad.

> Having heard that *Dundas* would be out with the hounds, I rode to the place of meeting, in order to look him in the face, and to give him an opportunity to notice, on his peculiar dunghill, what I had said of him at Newbury. He came, I rode up to him and about him; but, *he said not a word*. The company entered the wood, and I rode back towards my quarters. They found a fox, and quickly lost him. Then they came out of the wood and came back along the road, and met me, and passed me, they as well as I going at a foot pace. I had plenty of time to survey them all well, and to mark their looks. I watched *Dundas*'s eyes, but the devil a bit could I get them to turn my way.

All this sounds more akin to some ghostly ballad than to the material business of the **Political Register**.

Towards the close of the introduction, the editors contribute much to their readers' understanding of Cobbett by answering a question likely to be asked more lethargically now than formerly: "Was William Cobbett a failure?" As time runs on, the miseries of the past are hidden away, and men and women who have been greatly instrumental in reforming them utterly tend to vanish from the new consciousness as well. "Whole buried towns support the dancer's heel"; and the names to conjure with that once were conspicuous are now mentioned with some difficulty. To indicate the connection between Cobbett and the world about us would be hard work; even the small farmer does not speak of "Cobbett's Corn." But, once beyond the general barrier, one hears Cobbett's editors clearly maintaining the position of success which Cobbett held for so many years; which Cobbett held in spite of his peculiar, inherent weaknesses. How capably Hazlitt in 1825 delineated the genius of Cobbett for achieving no actual aim!

> If he could bring about a Reform in Parliament, the odds are that he would instantly fall foul of and try to mar his own handy-work; and he quarrels with his own creatures as soon as he has written them into a little vogue—and a prison. I do not think this is vanity or fickleness so much as a pugnacious disposition, that must have an antagonist power to contend with, and only finds itself at ease in systematic opposition. If it were not for this, the high towers and rotten places of the world would fall before the battering-ram of his hard-headed reasoning: but if he once found them

tottering, he would apply his strength to prop them up, and disappoint the expectations of his followers.

The new essay in my hands gives a short catalogue of those matters in the state of England which Cobbett most obviously intended to destroy or purify, and which were going on little altered, or altered for the worse, when he ended his campaign.

But his success transcended these confusions. Cobbett was a presence and an impulse where without him there certainly was a want of light and fire.

> In the strictest possible sense of the word [as his editors write] Cobbett, through the dark years, *upheld* the working-class. At a time when those who professed most sympathy with the labourer vied with his open enemies in telling him that he was a poor creature whose whole duty was to restrain his natural impulses and to be obedient and grateful to all set in authority over him, Cobbett, almost alone, told him that he was a man, and that by holding up his head and bearing himself manfully he might gain a man's inheritance. No oppression enraged him so much as the insidious propaganda which hinted that the labourer was not capable of knowing his own mind or thinking for himself.

Even here one recalls the Cobbettian inconsistency; one thinks of Cobbett advertising for ploughboys who "*must never, on any account, go into a public-house.* None will be hired that do not come in smock-frocks." However, so long as the labourer had Cobbett to talk to him of "Pitt's false money, Peel's flimsy dresses, Wilberforce's potatoe diet, Castlereagh's and Mackintosh's oratory, Walter Scott's poems, Walter's and Stoddart's paragraphs" and the rest, he could certainly feel that the world was not constructed to impose upon him perpetual imprisonment of spirit and the routine of inferiority.

I turn from Cobbett's career and value in public affairs to his works considered as literature, and the question whether he succeeded or failed with his pen. To that there is the immediate answer that "at its height, the unstamped *Register* had a sale of sixty thousand copies," and that nearly everything that Cobbett put forth had a large audience. Reformers of his own day—I have quoted one of them on Cobbett—admired his power of downright English; and it remains as it was, individual and insistent. But Cobbett, profusely as he wrote, had no very clear notion of literary purpose, and was nearly always intent on some victory of the minute. He sometimes took a subject for a book rather than a periodical or pamphlet treatment, but even so he went to work without conceptions of a far future, or of style regarded in an extensive way. His *Woodlands* is a book of which he instantly decides the limits:

> Some writers give you the mere *botany* of the tree; others its qualities as *timber;* others tell you what *ground* it delights in; others treat of the act of *planting;* others of *pruning* and *cultivation;* but no book that I ever yet saw told me *everything* that I ought to know, from the *gathering of the seed,* to the rearing up and the cutting down of the tree.

And yet, a little farther on, he denies that he is bringing out the book merely "to promote public and private utility." He confesses another motive—"the indulgence of my own delight in talking about trees." In the text he sometimes catches himself talking about them:

> It is also well known, that the Ash is a beautiful tree. Gilpin calls it the Venus of the woods. It has, however, one great disadvantage: that is, that it puts on its leaves later in the spring, and loses them earlier in the fall, than any other English tree. But perhaps Gilpin was thinking of a *naked* Venus, and then, indeed, the Ash claims the pre-eminence in our woods. Laying aside this nonsense, however, of poets and painters, we have no tree of such various and extensive use as the Ash.

It would be foolish to pretend that Cobbett does not often write in a masterly strain when he is severely practical: but his feelings are not of that reach and fineness which could respond fully to the promising theme of *The Woodlands*.

Of the *Rural Rides,* again, the origin was a definite, a transitory one. Agricultural distress followed the war; a committee in 1821 proposed remedies, Cobbett cursed their remedies; and he "made up his mind to see things for himself, and to enforce, by actual observation of rural conditions, the statements he had made in answer to the arguments of the landlords before the Agricultural Committee." Such a statistical necessity might seem from the outset to threaten a type of *Rural Rides* which would be over and done when the bad times and the committee were over and done. But, happily, there was ever in Cobbett that gift for being called away from his wrathful business by some topic of which the life is longer; once away from "The Wen," he surrendered himself quite frequently to the appeals of country life and scenery; and in that manner "the *Rides* themselves are very much more than the propagandist's tour which their origin suggests." They will never be a favourite book—though they will continue to be read—in the sense that *Selborne* is, and many lesser works with the grace of unity. The interventions are too many, the sentences too flinty, the descriptions too little mellowed with impression, for Cobbett's entire book to be affectionately perused. "There is nothing in English," his editors say, "which gives better than this book the sensation of starting out on a fresh summer day in glorious country, healthy and full of vigour, to do work which really needs to be done—." A careful and a wise estimate.

On the other hand, the *Rural Rides* affords a capital opportunity to enjoy the choleric outbursts and the sarcasms of Cobbett without being overwhelmed by too long tirades against extinct monsters. At Oxford, gazing at the buildings:

> I could not help reflecting on the drones that they contain and the wasps they send forth! . . . As I looked up at what they call *University Hall,* I could not help reflecting that what I had written, even since I left Kensington on the 29th of October [it was then the

18th of November] would produce more effect, and do more good in the world, than all that had, for a hundred years, been written by all the members of this University, who devour, perhaps, not less than *a million pounds* a year, arising from property, completely at the disposal of the "Great Council of the Nation."

At Brighton, Cobbett had no difficulty in detecting a swarm of *"expectants"*: "you may always know them by their lank jaws, the stiffeners round their necks, their hidden or *no* shirts, their stays, their false shoulders, hips and haunches, their half-whiskers, and by their skins, colour of veal kidney-suet, warmed a little, and then powdered with dirty dust." It must have gone hard with Brighton and its "Kremlin" or "Norfolk-turnip" had not Cobbett encountered in the evening some reformers, "who, though plain tradesmen and mechanics, know, I am quite satisfied, more about the questions that agitate the country, than any equal number of Lords." At Chilworth, "where the nightingales are to be heard earlier and later in the year than in any other part of England," he found that gunpowder and banknotes were being made. The gunpowder, he reflected, might be sometimes "innocently and meritoriously employed," but the banknotes!

> To think that the springs which God has commanded to flow from the sides of these happy hills, for the comfort and the delight of man; to think that these springs should be perverted into means of spreading misery over a whole nation; and that, too, under the base and hypocritical pretence of promoting its *credit* and maintaining its *honour* and its *faith!*

It was some comfort to remember "that a part of these springs have, at times, assisted in turning rags into *Registers*"; but none the less, Cobbett rode on to Albury in a very melancholy mood.

At New Romney he was quietly jogging along, surveying sea, and cattle, and corn, when "a *great round building*" and then twenty or thirty others came into sight. He exclaimed, "in a voice that made his horse bound, 'THE MARTELLO TOWERS, by———!'" The faces of Pitt, Dundas, Perceval seemed staring at him, instead of cannons, from these "ridiculous things. . . . I dare say they cost MILLIONS." In this rage he toured the Kentish coast, and really one is rather relieved when he leaves the county. But he could never avoid rotten boroughs and the grimaces of the Thing. Old Sarum magnetised him.

> I resolved to ride over this ACCURSED HILL. As I was going up a field towards it, I met a man going home from work. I asked how he *got on*. He said, very badly. I asked him what was the cause of it. He said the *hard times*. "What times," said I; "was there ever a finer summer, a finer harvest, and is there not an *old* wheat-rick in every farm-yard?" "Ah!" said he "*they* make it bad for poor people, for all that." *"They?"* said I, "who is *they?*" He was silent. "Oh, no no! my friend," said I, "it is not *they;* it is that ACCURSED HILL that has robbed you of the supper that you ought to find smoking on the table when you get home." I gave him the price of a pot of beer, and on I went, leaving the poor dejected assemblage of skin and bone to wonder at my words.

Perhaps Cheltenham inspired the most complete displays of Cobbett's indignation; it was, he averred, another Wen:

> A place to which East India plunderers, West India floggers, English tax-gorgers, together with gluttons, drunkards, and debauchees of all descriptions, *female* as well as male, resort, at the suggestion of silently laughing quacks, in the hope of getting rid of the bodily consequences of their manifold sins and iniquities.

His disapproval was tempered a little by the thought that "the place really appears to be sinking fast." In a year or two—Cobbett's prophecies were numerous—it would all be deserted—"Liverpool-Cottage, Canning-Cottage, Peel-Cottage."

But the loud condemnations, the invincibly exploding economic arguments, the broad satirical sketches, the laments for vanished ages of wealth and prosperity and populous market-places, are not the most insistent passages of **Rural Rides**. Cobbett's England is not, after all, a squalid ruin through the gloomy, disease-ridden air of which creeps a broken race, and out of which the "reptile" landlords are saving themselves with whatever they can extort from those wretched bondmen. It is, with all its faults, its spring-guns and its tithe-tables, a bright and various landscape, which on a closer view is a pattern of active and fertile farms and sweet-scented gardens, of rich plantations, of cathedrals, of squarely built towns, and villages that seem to grow as their sheltering elm-trees do. The shadows that fall upon this country, which Cobbett explains with the strenuous disgust of the partisan and the additional projections of his own mind, do not ultimately impair its fine influence and countenance. Bedevilled by the sufferings, real and speculative, which his hated "people at Westminster" have sown throughout these coloured counties, our farmer-politician is for ever returning to sources of—one might also use the expression even for this champion of the cudgel—sweetness and light.

It is so in other books of Cobbett's; after all the scourging, the morning breaks anew, the hills are tipped with gold. There is a moment in the **Rural Rides** which especially forms a symbol or reflection of this inbred, Waltonish, natural piety; he writes from Horncastle:

> There is one deficiency, and that, with me, a great one throughout this country of corn and grass and oxen and sheep, that I have come over during the last three weeks; namely, the want of *singing birds*. . . . Oh! the thousands of linnets all singing together on one tree, in the sand-hills of Surrey! Oh! the carolling in the coppices and the dingles of Hampshire and Sussex and Kent! At this moment (5 o'clock in the morning) the groves at Barn-Elm are echoing with the warblings of thousands upon thousands of birds. The *thrush* begins a little before it is light; next the *blackbird;* next the *larks* begin to rise; all the rest begin the moment the sun gives the signal; and from the hedges,

the bushes, from the middle and the top-most twigs of the trees, comes the singing of endless variety; from the long dead grass comes the sound of the sweet and soft voice of the *white-throat,* or *nettle-tom,* while the loud and merry song of the *lark* (the songster himself out of sight) seems to descend from the skies.

None of Cobbett's little georgics are premeditated; they occur to him, as though a rustling wind or a sudden twinkling of light on a mill-pond told him what to write next. He is not among the subtlest artists of the English seasons and atmosphere even in these interludes; but he has an eye and a style for the form of the land, and the inhabitants and their homes as part of the picture. He cannot choose but see—and communicate; he falls into the spirit that creates greater books than his *Rural Rides,* which is only a book at all by chance.

> The farmyard is surrounded by lofty and beautiful trees. In the rick-yard I counted twenty-two ricks of one sort and another. The hills shelter the house and the yard and the trees, most completely, from every wind but the south. The arable land goes down before the house, and spreads along the edge of the down, going, with a gentle slope, down to the meadows. So that, going along the turnpike road, which runs between the lower fields of the arable land, you see the large and beautiful flocks of sheep upon the sides of the down, while the horn-cattle are up to their eyes in grass in the meadows. Just when I was coming along here, the sun was about half an hour high; it shined through the trees most brilliantly; and to crown the whole, I met, just as I was entering the village, a very pretty girl, who was, apparently, going a gleaning in the fields. I asked her the name of the place, and when she told me it was Bishopstrow, she pointed to the situation of the church, which, she said, was on the other side of the river.

That was all; one may omit the sentence which Cobbett adds in order to work in a blow at a landlord. What had his early encounter in the happy fields of Bishopstrow to do with readers of the *Political Register,* or the battle between the son of freedom and guilty tyrants for the better state of the agricultural labourer and the annihilation of paper money? Nothing: Cobbett has deserted them, hearing horns of elf-land faintly blowing. Had he suspected that this was going on, he might have done something to stop it. But so little did he suspect the possibility of his being romanticised in the midst of his warfare that he even became musical in the cadence of the sentences; and this distinctly contravened his argument in the *English Grammar* that writing is not singing and needs no rules of melody. There was another principle in the *Grammar* to the effect that one should only write what one understands; but Cobbett, touring his country with an object burning before him, is often made to deviate and pause and talk to himself, and us, by something that he does not understand as he understands mangel-wurzel.

Crane Brinton   (essay date 1933)

SOURCE: "The Revolution of 1832: Cobbett," in *English Political Thought in the Nineteenth Century,* Ernest Benn Limited, 1933, pp. 61-74.

[*In the following excerpt, Brinton provides an overview of Cobbett's political thought, especially in regard to its effect on the Reform Bill of 1832.*]

To write about Cobbett as a political thinker implies, in a sense, a false start. For, properly speaking, Cobbett never thought at all. Let us hasten to add that this remark is not a snobbishly intellectualist condemnation of Cobbett, but an attempt to give to the word thought a decently precise meaning. To think implies an effort on the part of the thinker to construct a coherent scheme out of the material of his experience, yet independent of his desires. The possibility of complete detachment on the part of the thinker may well be an illusion, but it is an indispensable illusion. Without it, thought is as immediate, as private, and as unreal as the rest of our sense-experience. Now Cobbett never made any attempt to get outside himself. His responses to experience are as self-centred as a child's. He was naturally enough never really troubled by the reproaches of moral inconsistency to which his career gave rise, and which were on the whole unjust; but, had he been able even to suspect the meaning of the phrase, he would have been equally untroubled by the reproach of logical inconsistency. Put him over against Bentham, Brougham, and Owen, and the contrast is remarkable. Each of these former drew certain assumptions from his temperament and experience; but they erected on these assumptions systems which have a certain amount of what the world has agreed to call logical consistency. Cobbett, too, harboured innumerable generalizations; and he could draw logical inferences in specific cases. But he has nothing like a system. His judgments of value have a peculiar directness and privacy. He actually *felt* about ideas the way most men—and none more strongly than Cobbett—feel about food and drink. He disliked paper money exactly as he disliked tea. There is no separating the operations of his consciousness. To say that he was prejudiced is quite inadequate. He was not even capable of framing a notion as to the difference between a prejudiced judgment and an unprejudiced one. He was always "morally certain"—that dreadful, and in this world perhaps the sole, form of certitude.

This childish directness which could never distinguish between an appetite and a principle has given Cobbett's work the charm it holds for such men as Mr. Chesterton. Cobbett affords a standing invitation to paradox. Any critic can find him as full of surprises as a human being can be. He had no interest in the imaginative literature of his time; yet in one of the most obvious senses of the word, he was more romantic than Keats or Shelley. For romanticism was in part an attempt to recapture the childhood of the race. Cobbett was—though Wordsworth would have been horrified at the thought—the "mighty prophet, seer blest" of the famous ode. Now this kind of romanticism seeks the richness of sense-life not staled by unduly analytical reflection. It would revive, if we may use the word without Christian overtones of condemnation, the sentient animal in man. Animals are notoriously conservative. They like to be comfortable and undisturbed. Cobbett was a true conservative. What he valued was the good, simple, hearty life of the Englishman of fable—

good food, good drink, good labour of the soil that pricks the appetites, the comfortable family life of the den. It is the intellect that finds satisfaction in novelty. Bodily necessity may be the mother of protest, but not of invention. The scheming intellect, then, is the real radical. Now Cobbett lived in a very radical and very uncomfortable age. All the old ways were disappearing. Englishmen were drinking tea and other slops; even their beer was brewed for them, and was acquiring a synthetic, manufactured flavour. Cobbett hated machinery as an animal must hate a treadmill. Moreover, the good life of the human animal, at least, must be a tribal life. Part of its satisfactions must lie in loyalty to a fixed and recognizable group. But the industrial revolution was successful only because it broke up the fixed loyalties of old England. The model for the factory was not, and could not be, the mediaeval parish. Therefore the conservative Cobbett—and this is a paradox Mr. Chesterton makes the most of—became the leading English Radical. But he was a Radical only in the shallow and obvious sense of the word which involves resistance to the existing order. He was a peer of Bentham's only in that he wanted very much less of that of which the utilitarians wanted a great deal more. That both Cobbett and the utilitarians hoped a reform of Parliament would give them what they wanted afforded an accidental common rallying-point.

Cobbett notoriously began his career as a Tory of Tories. Few writers were more vituperative towards the French Revolution, that compound of "Atheism, Robbery, Unitarianism, Swindling, Jacobinism, Massacres, Civic Feasts, and Insurrections." Later he could write of that movement: "In judging the French Revolution, we are not to inquire what fooleries or violences were committed during its progress; but, we are to ask, what has it produced in the end?" In the end, he continues, it has destroyed Bourbon tyranny and given the land to the peasant. The Revolution is justified in its results. Yet few men, not excepting Burke, deserve less to be called turncoats. Cobbett's conversion does not even, as does the conversion in the other direction of the Lake poets, present a subtle problem in psychology. He is an articulate Tory first in America, where the enemies of the England he could not help loving were democrats, Jacobins. On his return to England, he naturally continued to support the Tory party. But as early as 1804 he began to distrust Pitt for his financial measures and his obvious leanings towards the commercial classes. Cobbett was a Tory because he supposed the Tories, like himself, wanted to retain the old England of the soil, the England of manly rural simplicity, the England of hearty squires and heartier yeomen. Melville's impeachment opened his eyes to the existence of financial corruption which he simply had been too faithful to see. The Tory party was sold to the "fund-lords" as completely as the Whigs. Seats in Parliament were actually advertised *for sale* in the London dailies.

How could one who loathed the cash nexus defend such a state of affairs? Cobbett clung hopefully a while longer to his benefactor Windham. But by 1807 he has given up hope in the Tories. The **Political Register** has turned to the people of England, still uncorrupted at heart. Their governors have betrayed them. Reform is the only way out. We may take Cobbett at his own word, when, in reply to the *Elements of Reform,* a pamphlet in which his enemies reprinted some of the bitterest tirades of Porcupine against reformers, he asserted that he had mistaken his men, but not his goal. "The doctrine of *consistency,* as now in vogue, is the most absurd that ever was broached. It teaches, that, if you once think well of any person or thing, you must always think well of that person or thing." You change your mind, not Yourself.

Cobbett had those gifts of the artist which are indispensable to the journalist and agitator, and which were so sadly lacking in the utilitarians. He could be interesting because he could use hard, tangible phrases that got to work at once on the senses of his readers. He could move men because he felt as they did. He could create in thousands and thousands of men that almost magical cohesion which it is out of the power of the thinker to create. The **Political Register,** become proudly **Twopenny Trash,** was the first really popular English journal. After all, the men of England were animals like himself. They, too, found the industrial revolution uncomfortable. It is one of the ironies of history that he pushed them on towards the political capping of the new movement, towards that Reform of 1832, which is the English Revolution of 1789. The survival of mediaeval land tenure in France, and the complete failure of its aristocracy to adjust itself to the new commerce, gave the French Revolution an emotional hold over ordinary Frenchmen which enabled its leaders to overcome the inertia of the many, and achieve the rare miracle of a violent social and political change. In England, conditions for such a miracle were lacking. Thanks to Cobbett, however, Englishmen became excited over the Reform Bill. He made reform seem the common thing, the *res publica* which it was not.

Any study of Cobbett's political ideas must be an analysis of his likes and dislikes. It must try to illustrate concretely the daily life of his old England, which was simply an extension to others of his own daily life. The basis of that life was domestic. Cobbett valued highly all that Owen so disliked in the family. "Give me, for a beautiful sight, a neat and smart woman, heating her oven and setting in her bread! And, if the bustle do make the sign of labour glisten on her brow, where is the man that would not kiss that off, rather than lick the plaster from the cheek of a duchess." He loved young children, and writes reverently of their "almost boneless limbs" and touching helplessness. This he characteristically erects into a moral absolute. "I never knew a man that was good for *much* who had a dislike for little children; and I never knew a woman of that taste who was good for anything at all."

Women he worshipped after a satisfying image of his own. "It is, I should imagine, pretty difficult to keep love alive towards a woman who *never sees the dew,* never beholds the *rising sun,* and who constantly comes directly from a reeking bed to the breakfast table, and there chews about, without appetite, the choicest morsels of human food." Women must be pure. "It is not enough that a young woman abstain from everything approaching to-wards indecorum in her behaviour towards men; it is, with me, not enough that she cast down her eyes, or turn aside her head with a smile, when she hears an indelicate allusion: she ought to appear *not to understand* it, and to receive from it no more impression than if she were a post." She must love her children, and suckle them herself. Cobbett devoted a sermon to "The Unnatural Mother," which shows him at his most domestic. "The motives [for employing a wet-nurse] are two in number, the one, that her *beauty* may not suffer from the performance of her most sacred duty; the *other,* too gross, too beastly, to be named, except within the walls of a brothel. Let it be observed, however, that, as to the first motive, it is pretty sure to *fail,* if beauty be valued on account of its power over *the husband.* For, the flame of love being past, the fire is kept alive by nothing so effectually as by the fruit of it; and, what becomes of this, if the child be banished to a hireling breast?"

For Cobbett's was a highly decent, almost Victorian, nature. There are no pathological depths in him. He never behaves the way pessimistic Christian ethics assume it is natural for the human animal to behave. His appetites are all healthy. Gluttony he abhors as "the indulgence beyond the absolute demands of nature." He asserts proudly that he never "spent more than *thirty-five minutes a day at table,* including all the meals of the day." He never played cards, nor wasted time in public houses. He estimates that the fifteen pounds a year the average man throws away in public houses would amount, in the course of a trades-man's life, to a decent fortune for a child. Men spend too much time outside the family circle. He himself had never been an absentee husband. Much of his work was written while the babies were crying—that never disturbed him. He thought the text beginning "Go to the ant, thou slug-gard" one of the most beautiful ever penned.

Domestic happiness and natural sobriety formed the foundations of his good life. Work, for its own sake, was an essential. "To wish to live on the labour of others is, besides the folly of it, to contemplate a *fraud* at the least, and, under certain circumstances, to meditate oppression and robbery." And this must be independent work, work like that of the farmer who reaps where he has sown. It must rest on the institution of private property. These independent workers are united in a society by common tastes, by common forbearances, and by a common love of country. Cobbett never worried over the intellectual opposition between the individual and the group. "A man is so identified with his country, that he cannot, do what he will, wholly alienate himself from it: it can know no triumph, nor any disgrace, which does not, in part, belong to him: parents, brethren, relations, friends, neighbours, make, all taken together, a good half of one's self."

Cobbett, as we have said, never thought of criticizing, or rounding out this moral world of his into a system. He loved the look of the English countryside. He also wanted Englishmen to produce their own food. When, therefore, he ardently defends live and wasteful hedges in contrast to dead and efficient fences, he simply sinks the weaker

desire in the stronger. He ought to have felt some sympathy—if sympathies only went by ought to's—for Samuel Johnson, whom he nevertheless calls "old dread-death and dread-devil Johnson, that teacher of moping and melancholy." He disliked the false modesty of "genteelisms" and attacked expressions like "small-clothes"; yet in the very same passage he denies that any modest woman could allow a man to attend her at childbirth. He would have none of Jenner's vaccination—naturally enough he distrusted physicians—but he defends inoculation with smallpox itself. Perhaps the most striking example of his inability to allow facts to influence his judgment is his determined insistence that, census figures to the contrary notwithstanding, the population of England had not greatly increased between 1801 and 1821. Since England took a century, he says, to grow from five millions to eight, it could not possibly have grown from eight millions to eleven in twenty years. This is not *a priori* reasoning; it is pure romance.

When Cobbett ventures, as he has to venture, into political generalizations, this picturesque immediacy of judgment betrays him. These generalizations carry with them concrete consequences. They influence, according to a law of their own, the very world of likes and dislikes which for Cobbett never changed. The social contract theory and the patriarchal theory do not affect political practice in the same way. Cobbett, as a matter of fact, held them both in a fraternal and unnatural embrace. His political theories are, to use the cant word, rationalizations. But rationalizations do a work of their own in this world, a work Cobbett simply could not understand. Property he thought with Locke was crystallized labour. To live without labour he thought immoral, "unless you have ample fortune whereon to live clear of debt." That rigid adherence to his definition of property would destroy most property in his England apparently did not enter his mind. He did not like property in stocks and bonds, because he did not like the new rich. He thought men of property should care for the poor. He wanted the poor to be self-respecting, and to own a little property of their own. It is all very confusing, and very well meant.

Cobbett accepts an extraordinary amount of the fashionable political theory of the Enlightenment. "These truths are written on the heart of man: that all men are, by nature, *equal;* that civil society can never have arisen from any motive other than that of the *benefit of the whole;* that, whenever civil society makes the greater part of the people *worse off* than they were under the Law of Nature, the civil compact is, in conscience, dissolved, and all the rights of nature return; that, in civil society, the *rights and the duties go hand in hand,* and that, when the former are taken away, the latter cease to exist . . . rights going before duties, as value received goes before payment." Freedom he defined as Macaulay might have defined it: "Freedom is not an empty sound; it is not an abstract idea; it is not a thing that nobody can feel. It means, and it means *nothing else, the full and quiet enjoyment of your own property.* "

Now these free and equal men, banded together under the social contract, each with his own property, will govern themselves by a representative Parliament. "The great right, therefore, of *every man,* the right of rights, is the right of having a share in the making of the laws, to which the good of the whole makes it his duty to submit." This right is no mere abstract principle. It is a practical matter, for a man who pays taxes should help decide how much he pays and for what purpose the money is spent. Once the whole people share in determining taxation, a lessening of governmental expenditure is inevitable. Cobbett actually uses the Broughamese phrase to describe the ultimate end of government—"cheapness." His government will not even interfere to provide compulsory education. "The general taste of parents and their naturally high opinion of their children's capacities, are quite sufficient to furnish the schools, without the aid of another Act of Parliament and *another cursed tax.*" Finally, he is an exponent of Free Trade.

This is certainly a pretty complete outline of a *laissez-faire* political philosophy, most of it, let it be noted, in Cobbett's own words. Nothing could be more contrary to what Cobbett really wanted. He had, it is true, that English devotion to the yeomanry ideal, that notion of the individual independent in the castle of his home, which gives a more than abstract force to his distrust of the State. He had an unquestioning devotion to the historical paraphernalia of English rights. But above all he hated the England of fund-lords and manufacturers, and he loved the England of the common people. To protect the common people, to restore them to what he imagined had been their old status, he is willing to use any possible method. "I wish to see the poor men of England what the poor men of England were when I was born," he said in a famous phrase. He is an interventionist in spirit. The tragedy of his life lies in his conviction that the Reformed Parliament would intervene as he desired. He lived to see that Parliament, of which he was a member, pass the new Poor Law.

This desire to intervene in the free play of economic life to protect the poor comes out in all his work. He admired the Church of the Middle Ages because it was the "guardian of the common people," and he is as bitter as Disraeli on the spoliation by which the English Reformation robbed a common thing for the good of a few. Absolute ownership of the land is un-English. "Men lawfully possess only the USE of land and of things attached to the land; and they must take care that in USING them, they do not do injury to any other part of the community, or to the whole of the community taken together." Cobbett brings forward a long list of things a man may *not* do with his own—such as producing unnecessary noises, smoke, other nuisances, allowing stallions to roam on commons, and so on; he concludes that landlords may not drive tenants and cottagers off their land, that on the contrary they must provide for them. "That there ought to *be no legal provision for the poor and destitute;* that all such provision is *essentially bad;* that such provision, *even for the aged and infirm,* ought not to be made; and that even the *giving of alms to the wretched is an evil:* these assertions of MALTHUS and BROUGHAM . . . demand a serious, and, at the same time, an indignant and scornful, refutation."

Cobbett was even willing to achieve his desires by so revolutionary a step as expropriation. He suggests that, if conditions get worse, it may be necessary to make every tenant of house or land worth less than ten pounds a year an owner in fee-simple, indemnifying the present owners with money saved by Governmental economies. His natural conservatism comes out in his respect for a real landed aristocracy, for an aristocracy built on the true patriarchal principle. He contrasts the old "resident *native* gentry, attached to the soil, known to every farmer and labourer from their childhood, frequently mixing with them in those pursuits where all artificial distinctions are lost," and the modern non-resident gentleman, who merely recuperates on his acres from city dissipations.

Nor are Cobbett's economic notions orthodox. Something—he is never quite sure what—must call a halt to the immoral expansion of wealth. He looks back fondly on the mediaeval prohibition of interest, and regrets that men have abandoned the teaching of the Fathers in this as in so many other respects. Paper money and the whole machinery of credit he loathed. It made possible the sponging existence of the speculator. It upset everyone with the false hope of unearned riches. Accidental success in the hurly-burly turned "those whom nature and good laws [note the phrase 'nature and good laws'] made to black shoes, sweep chimnies or the streets," into men "rolling in carriages, or sitting in saloons surrounded by gaudy footmen with napkins twisted round their thumbs." Paper money brought inevitable inflation, and inflation benefited the adventurer, the man whose assets were as mobile as his principles, and injured the sober, steady man whose assets were fixed. It injured the workman, for wages never rise as rapidly as prices. Yet deflation would bring an unearned gain to all those who had lent money to the nation at the high price level. Cobbett's remedy was characteristically simple and unburdened with theoretical scruples: reduce the interest rate on the national debt. He thought no other solution possible, and offered to allow himself to be broiled alive if the return to a gold basis as provided for in Peel's Bill proved possible. Cobbett never understood the incredible powers of the new industry. In the end, England actually produced enough new goods to balance the increase in the quantity of money brought on by the expenses of the Government in the Napoleonic wars. The new wealth undoubtedly created the world of speculation Cobbett disliked; it undoubtedly corrupted, and then destroyed, his beloved rural England; but it certainly was no fiction.

Cobbett's great failure, after all, was a failure of the understanding. So many of his outraged feelings are the feelings of all honest men that we are inclined to overmuch sympathy with him. We, too, dislike the England of his wrath, "the capacious jails and penitentiaries; the stock exchange; the hot and ancle and knee-swelling, and lung-destroying cotton-factories; the whiskered standing army and its splendid barracks; the parson-captains, parson-lieutenants, parson-ensigns and parson-justices; the poor rates and pauper houses; and by no means forgetting, that blessing which is peculiarly and doubly and 'gloriously' protestant, the NATIONAL DEBT." But our sympathies, and the

Contemporary caricature of Cobbett after he personally disinterred Tom Paine's bones and transported them from the United States to England.

attraction which so able a master of the concrete in words must have for us, ought not to conceal from us Cobbett's weakness as a prophet. With his diagnosis of the political and social evils of his time we may easily agree. In the name of economic freedom, men were exploiting other men. Somehow, the assurance of regularity had gone out of life. For that part of their nature that demands something fixed and eternal, men could find no satisfaction. Cobbett, though he never used the phrase, was as aware as St. Simon or Comte that what his century lacked was a unified scheme of social reconstruction, a universal faith.

But any such faith is a constructive effort of the whole of man's faculties. Men build abiding faiths out of the world of sense-experience in which they live. But what gives to faith an apparent independence of the chaos of experience is the intellectual effort which has gone into the absorption of this experience. In spite of what is still current opinion to the contrary, effective human belief has always an element of reason. For human reason alone can make the adjustment between novelties forced on human experience—the machine, for instance—and habit. Now Cobbett, as we have tried to show, never made this effort of adjustment. In purely personal terms, he merely growled at being disturbed in his habits. In a wider sense applying to the system of ideas he had after all to work with, he sought to maintain the old frame of society, the old specific adjustments to a given situation, and to destroy, or neglect, he was never quite sure which, the

new situation. He says definitely that he never sought to *change* or *destroy* the institutions of England, but to do away with innovations upon them, the encroachments of aristocracy, and especially of the usurers' aristocracy, new treason laws, combination laws, Bourbon-police laws, taxation, standing armies, *agents provocateurs,* and so on. Most deeply rooted in Cobbett was that kind of moral solipsism which is the source of much of what goes by the name of Conservatism. He could never even admit the existence of moral values outside himself. Therefore the question of adjusting his scheme of values to altered conditions never troubled him. For as Cobbett lacked the intellectual detachment which would have allowed him to criticize his own habits, so he lacked the imaginative capacity which would have enabled him to salvage those habits, in part at least, in a new faith.

He was, however, too uncomfortable to keep quiet. The very intensity with which he felt a conservative's unhappiness in a changing world prevented his making the compromises with novelty by which most conservatives cheat themselves. He was no Eldon. Something had to be done. We have already explained the pathetic fervour with which he took up the Radical cause. His blundering enthusiasm led him to do the thing most contrary to his ultimate hopes. Were he alive to-day, he would surely be even more unhappy than he was in the England of the Regency. Yet most of what he fought for politically has been achieved. The men of England were no Cobbetts. They were either far more flexible, or far more cowardly, than he. The England of universal suffrage has not proved to be the England of *Cottage Economy.* Just why Cobbett was so wrong cannot be answered in a formula. Yet it seems most likely that he carried the natural conservatism of the average man to heroism. We may worship heroes, but we do not imitate them. Not even the Englishman will really die for his beer. Indeed, the only kind of heroism that comes near being practical is heroism in defence of the abstract. Cobbett was too attached to common things to be a successful defender of them. We return to his fundamental failure—his failure to use his intellect to correct, build up, and render systematic, and thus shareable with other men, his prejudices.

A. R. Orage (essay date 1934?)

SOURCE: "Purified Talk," in *Selected Essays and Critical Writings,* edited by Herbert Read and Denis Saurat, Stanley Nott, 1935, pp. 23-4.

[*Orage was an English editor, reviewer, and essayist who edited the influential periodical* New Age *from 1907 to 1922. In 1932 he founded the* New English Weekly, *which he edited until his death two years later. In the following essay, he praises the simplicity and naturalness of Cobbett's prose.*]

Cobbett does not deserve what Green says of him, that he was 'the greatest tribune the English poor ever possessed'. Cobbett had not sufficient appreciation of the real enemy of the English poor, and it is safe to say of his projects of reform, as of so many others, that if they could all have been carried, the English poor would have remained the English poor. A much more lasting effect and testimony to his tribuneship is to be found in his style, which is as near an approach to good spoken English as any writer is ever likely to make. Not to English as spoken by the educated classes; still less to English as spoken by the uneducated. It has neither class distinction nor distinction of dialect; but it is what we call plain English. Mark how closely his sentences follow speech in both vocabulary and construction:

> The farmers here, as everywhere else, complain most bitterly; but they hang on, like sailors to the masts or hull of a wreck.

> It [the land system] is staggering about like a sheep with water in the head, turning its pate up on one side, seeming to listen, but it has no hearing; seeming to look, but it has no sight; one day it capers and dances; the next it mopes and seems ready to die.

> Old dread-death and dread-devil Johnson, that teacher of moping and melancholy! If the writings of this time-serving, mean, dastardly old pensioner had got a firm hold of the minds of the people at large, the people would have been bereft of their very souls.

The qualities of such writing are hard to define for the very reason that they are so well concealed. There is no appearance of art; and I should fancy that Cobbett never saw the end of the sentence in writing, as we do not in speech, before beginning it. It is writ straight on as we talk straight on. But anybody who thinks it easy to imitate on that account will discover his mistake upon trial. Cobbett's style was Cobbett. On the other hand, it would be to fall into no less a mistake to suppose that the acquirement of his style was never any effort to Cobbett himself. We are told that while in the army he read and got by heart an English grammar, which he used to repeat while doing sentry. We know also that he wrote one of the best English grammars even now in existence. His simplicity, though natural, had to be maintained and developed. For it is just the natural and the simple that needs the greatest art.

V. S. Pritchett (essay date 1941)

SOURCE: "Current Literature," in *The New Statesman and Nation,* Vol. XXI, No. 517, January 18, 1941, pp. 62, 64.

[*Pritchett, a modern British writer, is respected for his mastery of the short story and for what critics describe as his judicious, reliable, and insightful literary criticism. In the following excerpt, he focuses on the paradoxical nature of Cobbett's character as reflected in his writings.*]

In the panorama of English history from the time of the French revolution to the Reform, the huge steam-rolling person of Wm. Cobbett stands out among his contemporaries like a figure drawn out of scale. There are more sensational, more momentous and more intricate characters in the picture than his, yet as a man he dwarfs them. He is one of Morland's farmers who appears in a Whig drawing-room, twinkling with pleasure at the memory of a good sight of swedes, and hectoring the company with the temper (if not the blasphemy) of an ex-company sergeant-major. Where the rest are historical personages whose minds and actions have made the fate of Europe, Cobbett stands out by the blunt originality of being, simply, a man. Even more, he is a reminder, as we consider the close parallel of his period and his case with our own, of that enormous variant, that untutored political force which gets left out of political theory—human nature.

How close the parallel between Napoleonic times and the present is, must be left to political palmists. Was 1789 our 1917? Was the Treaty of Amiens our Munich, or is it yet to come? With Pitt we fought for the Old Order against the New Order to defeat a foreign imperialist and, in doing so, killed both the Old Order and the immediate possibility of a new one. It came, but after what repression! If the public was united, the intellectuals were not—Hazlitt might be called a fifth columnist—and, as with us to-day, most men actively concerned in politics held equivocal positions. In times of transition people rush to cover their nakedness with what "lesser evils" they can get together, but these, like shirts that are too short, expose regions which are irresistible to the unbenevolent eye of the party enemy. All this is of our time and if a study of the revolutionary and Napoleonic periods does not answer our questions it supplies us with a commentary. Some dates from Wm. Cobbett's life show how near his course may be to ours. He was twenty-six when the Bastille fell, thirty-nine at the Peace of Amiens which he patriotically opposed, fifty-two at Waterloo (by which time he had repented) and—to jump into our future—sixty-nine when the Reform Bill became law.

Taking the long view of Cobbett's life, English writers have thought of him as a survival, a kind of sport in politics, a short-tempered, thick-skinned, likeable John Bull, with honest instincts but muddled ideas. He is the reactionary-revolutionary, a cross between two centuries, a present for Mr. Chesterton. He believes not in the New Dawn, but in the good old times. He is seen as a symbol of the English nature undergoing the martyrdom of being turned from countryman into townsman and shouting to go back and go forward at the same moment. What he hates is the New Order. He hates it as a Radical, not as a Tory; he hates it as an Anarchist hates the Communist and Fascist, the Socialist and the Capitalist, for being the same dogs with different collars.

This is not an untrue reading of Cobbett's career. The proper, attendant irony is that even in his widest radicalism Cobbett did not understand the new industrial working class and, in the end, won Reform not for the poor whom he helped (and lectured), but for the new genteel, the clerk, the shopkeeper, the nineteenth century's David Copperfields whose passion for going up in the world and keeping a servant enraged him. But to think of Cobbett as a survival is nevertheless only half true. Cobbett brings something quite new into English life. He is a new kind of Englishman, as new in his time and as isolated as Defoe was in an earlier century of change. Cobbett was the product of a revolution which had nothing to do with the pros and cons of Jacobinism. He had been touched by the true English revolution, the one which pre-dated the French and took place in America. It is picturesque to see Cobbett as the last John Bull of the eighteenth century; he was really the new John Bull made in the United States. . . .

Cobbett attacked emigration on patriotic and economic grounds: he returned from the United States the complete, emancipated emigrant. He had experienced for many years, liberty, equality and fraternity—well, perhaps not fraternity. He had made money. He had left England, an insubordinate sergeant-major, the self-taught know-all and ruler of the regiment who had been diddled by the War Office; he returned free of the English caste system, established as a journalist and business man. Cobbett advocated frugality, the bleak habits of a set peasant life; yet his financial history, his speculative instinct, the huge "indemnity" he asked for—it was £10,000—when at the end of his days he was asked to stand for Oldham, have a transatlantic air. And in America there was relative abundance, there was opportunity, there was space. The famous description of Nova Scotia in *Advice to Young Men,* when he is confessing to his second love affair, indicates his feeling for the country, but is a picture of his ideal country life. Dying in England, in America it had room to live in. From hard abstract thinking the English reformers and early socialists had laid it down that a man's labour was property; Cobbett in America, untrained in abstract thought, had seen this to be true with his eyes. The emigrant's labour, to the active and industrious, became his property with no squire nor tithe-eating priest to rob him. Independence Cobbett put first among the things that make a good life, and when he wrote of manners he said he wished "every English youth could see those of the United States; always civil, never servile." (If he was never servile, Cobbett was often pretty uncivil.) There is even something very American in another sentence in *Cottage Economy* in the section on How to Keep Geese— his handbooks on gardening and smallholding are not only very readable but really useful—in which, like some dry-voiced Yankee, he says "The reader will be apt to exclaim, as my friends very often do, 'Cobbett's geese are all swans.' Well, better that way than not to be pleased with what one has." It was a typical piece of American showmanship to arrive in England with the bones of Tom Paine—of whom he was not a follower—to propose to take them on a triumphal tour of England—and to drop the whole business suddenly when he saw it was going to be a flop.

Though part of Cobbett seems either to be an essential kind of old Englishman set free or a new kind altogether, Cobbett remained without successors in England. In these times, so like his, is there a contemporary sergeant-major, suddenly promoted over the heads of thirty others, the self-appointed indispensable, quietly teaching himself to write English, writing at the same time a book on how to

teach oneself, preparing a case against the War Office, working to expose official corruption? Transition brings out the reactionary-adventurer-revolutionary, the strong-willed egotist: is there now, hotly and wrong-headedly placed in the wrong political party, a Cobbett of the machines, the man who will take his motor bicycle over northern England and note, here, a good piece of boiler making, there, the lost art of making the private wireless set and the craftsmanship of private enterprise, as Cobbett wrote about bee-keeping, swedes and barley? Who will curse the new monopolies, the new taxes, mass-production and emigration once more—a sure post-war movement—and yet mix up this Old Guard stuff with a fierce new radicalism, so that he will be an embarrassment to all political parties and quarrelling with his own on bitter personal grounds. H. G. Wells has foreseen such a type among the *petit bourgeois.* There have been attempts at Cobbettry. Where they have failed is in the element of character. The method can be followed but not the man. The *petit bourgeois* conception of freedom has been imaginative, a fantasy, a dream; it does not spring from the *habit* of liberty, kept loose in the shoulders. It is clever, but it is not practical nor very moral.

What we read of Cobbett to-day—*The Rural Rides, Cottage Economy,* the *Grammar of the English Language,* the *Advice to Young Men,* and, I would like to add because of the war, the excellent *English Garden,* after reading which you seem to feel Cobbett's own hand guiding yours as you hole in your plants—we read, of course, for his character. It is his original achievement not only to have drawn himself well, but to have made the common character of the egotist, of all kinds the least sympathetic to draw, absorbingly attractive. Unlike Montaigne, he is not intensely self-curious; Cobbett takes it for granted that the curiosity is yours, that you will profit by anything he writes about himself. He is always right. His books are the most famous in the world, he has worked harder than any man on earth, he has enormous talents but they did not come from Heaven; on the contrary, will, industry, self-discipline have made them; there is almost a Cobbett method; squeamish authors cannot write while their children yell, but he has written really great works in snatches between nursing and generally looking after a house full of screaming babies; he is an early riser, his good health itself is a virtue due to his sober habits; he takes less time for eating than any other man he knows and for two years had a mutton chop every day for lunch and never got tired of it. Incidentally, he always shaves in cold water.

It is an appalling character; one is not surprised that his sons were mediocrities brought up by such a monster of vehement perfections. And yet his is an altogether charming portrait because it is entirely unselfconscious and without priggishness. He is definite but never censorious. It is the easy portrait, a continual autobiography running through all his books, of a natural man whose greatest experience in his life was the discovery, made by himself, of how to write so that he could pour out the pleasure of having a pugnacious, independent, extravert nature. Robinson Crusoe, the only too practical Crusoe, was a bore with his planks and his nails and his bad conscience; Cobbett's conscience is as good as his health; he conveys to one all the pleasure of the things he has found out for himself. A man like Crusoe is consistent; Cobbett is full of contradictions. An inveterate traveller, he curses the restlessness of the age with the solemnity of a gaffer who has never budged from his own doorstep. Uprooted and risen above his own station, he angrily assures us that the evil of the age lies in the number of people who think themselves risen above their origins. The sublime unconsciousness of it all reduces us to admiration.

W. Baring Pemberton (essay date 1949)

SOURCE: A chapter in *William Cobbett,* Penguin Books, 1949, pp. 180-85.

[*Below, Pemberton summarizes Cobbett's accomplishment as a rough-hewn thinker and his significance to the future of English culture.*]

With the death of William Cobbett it was as if a blustering gale from off the saltings had ceased abruptly. It had been a gale which, according to the politics of a man, intoxicated him like wine or doubled him up as with a blow in the pit of the stomach. In either case it had been a gale to which all had become accustomed and when it blew no more it was as if a familiar sound had ended. With his ***Weekly Political Registers,*** his rural ridings, his lectures and speeches and prodigious literary output Cobbett had engrossed the attention of the country; he had become an institution, a national habit. The question 'What does Cobbett say about it?' was heard from Treasury Bench to cottage settle. And on every subject he had something, right or wrong, to say; and he said it in loud, blunt and unequivocal language. In power and in popularity he had become a writer such as England had never known before and is unlikely to know again.

And yet, this position, akin (as Hazlitt said) to a Fourth Estate of the Realm, was achieved by a man who was neither a profound nor a logical thinker. For all his early rising Cobbett never had the time (nor indeed the inclination) to reflect deeply. Cause and effect were with him hopelessly confused. Perversity and egotism distorted his vision. Every event, every question, was considered in relation to his own instinctive feelings. His confidence in his own judgment was so enormous that he saw no need for any laborious process of thought. Impressions came to him with the swiftness of an exposure upon a photographic plate. Whatever failed to impinge itself upon his senses he ignored; what did not pass before his immediate vision had no real existence. Any point of view other than his own was to him incomprehensible. Unable to think in the abstract, he personified with childlike naïvety his ideas and grievances. It was so much easier for him to tilt at coercion, birth-control and papermoney by calling them Castlereagh, Malthus and Pitt.

While a passionate conviction that he alone was right gave strength to his arm, it tended to obscure the direction of his aim. Like some fanatical knight-errant Cobbett laid wildly about him. Down went his enemies, but down too went his friends if they shifted their ground by so much as an inch. In his blinding sincerity he would make no allowances, admit no compromise, accept no excuses, recognize no neutrality. Men were either good or bad; Cobbettites or anti-Cobbettites. Like George III with whom he had much in common, he took opposition as a personal affront, if not a sign of criminal lunacy. To acquire and retain the friendship of Cobbett was a task beyond the competence of any man of spirit. And when he dropped off, a friend forfeited all claims upon Cobbett's charity and was consigned to the same bottomless hell whither Pitt and Castlereagh had preceded him.

Cobbett has been acclaimed 'the greatest of Radicals'; and so he would have considered himself. But from the distance of more than a century we see that he was at heart nothing of the kind. So raging an individualist could conform to no party. He was a political Ishmaelite; 'The Contentious Man' as Bulwer called him. He took orders or advice from no one. He stood for his own programme. He had his own conception of what England should be and it was not that of Robert Owen or Jeremy Bentham. Reform meant to him, not as it did to orthodox Radicals a change to something new and progressive, but a return to old ways and hallowed customs. Though it has accepted him as a pioneer, the Socialist movement owes nothing to Cobbett. A socialist England with its emphasis upon the community rather than the individual he would have attacked with all the rancour of a die-hard Tory. The only function of the State in his eyes was to ensure its people lived full, contented and therefore independent lives. To that end he saw no need for popular education, a vast Whitehall honeycomb, an expanding bureaucracy. These things had not existed in the Middle Ages when he believed the peasant went well-fed and well-clothed. But in the Middle Ages, Kings, Lords and Commons had flourished, and a resident body of country gentlemen had administered local justice. These things he would not change, except to ensure that the Commons did really represent the Commonalty. Nor, unlike many of his contemporary Radicals, was he a leveller. 'An aristocracy of *title and privilege* when kept within due and constitutional bounds, brings none of the oppression upon the people which is always brought upon them by a *damned aristocracy of money.*' It was perhaps as well that Cobbett died before what he called the Lords of the Spinning Jennies and the Seigneurs of the Twist came flooding into the House of Lords.

Cobbett belonged to no party but he did emphatically belong to an age—to the age of Gillray and Rowlandson, when controversy was fierce and unflattering; when hard words were used and no quarter was asked or given. If he disliked a man or a thing he said so in matchless invective. And it is in his angry moods that Cobbett is at his best and is most lovable. Then he spared neither the feelings of his victims nor the stomachs of his readers. Yet coarse though his language could be, it was never vulgar; for nothing can be vulgar which comes white-hot from the heart. To-day invective and plain speaking are out of fashion, and for that, if for no other reason, there could be no twentieth-century Cobbett.

But to say that Cobbett could not exist to-day is not to imply that he has no interest for us—no message to convey. On the contrary, it is the twentieth century emerging from the complacency of the nineteenth century which has rediscovered Cobbett. To-day no historian would think it necessary (as was done in 1871) to remind his readers that Cobbett had existed. As agricultural depression deepened, and the industrial prospect darkened, Cobbett has emerged from the obscurity to which Victorian prosperity consigned him. In a world of strikes and lock-outs, of cartels and combines, of slumps and booms and uncertain markets, he stands for the serenity and security of a solid rural economy. If he championed an England which had gone beyond recall, in that championship he had expressed a philosophy which was at once simple and eternal. To the poor be charitable; to the lowly be merciful; to all be just. To a generation which has seen the violent dissolution of traditional values and the unparalleled inhumanity of man to man, the voice of Cobbett comes down the decades like the encouraging words of a physician in the ears of the fevered patient:

> What is the object of government? To cause men to live *happily*. They cannot be happy without a sufficiency of food and raiment. Good government means a state of things in which the main body are well fed and clothed. It is the chief business of a government to take care that one part of the people do not cause the other part to lead miserable lives.

Cobbett died a splendid failure, his life's purposes unachieved. He had failed to resuscitate an independent peasantry; he had failed to prevent the continued degradation of the labouring poor; the forces of The Thing only slightly expurgated by Reform swept over him in triumphant unconcern. But no man can be regarded as an unqualified failure who continues to be held in affectionate remembrance. And this will be the achievement of William Cobbett as long as there lives one Englishman who loves his countryside and who dares to doubt whether material progress is a sure guarantee of increasing happiness.

James Sambrook (essay date 1973)

SOURCE: "*Rural Rides* and *Advice to Young Men:* 1830," in *William Cobbett,* Routledge & Kegan Paul, 1973, pp. 143-64.

[*In the following chapter from his critical biography of Cobbett, Sambrook examines* Rural Rides *and* Advice to Young Men, *quoting at length from each to illustrate the characteristics of Cobbett's thought.*]

Towards the end of 1829 Cobbett announced the forthcoming publication of a collection of the 'Rural Rides' which had first appeared in the *Political Register,* but the book did not appear until October 1830. Though the con-

fused pagination and unaccountable omission of parts of certain 'Rides' indicate some carelessness on the part of the compiler, the principle of selection for **Rural Rides** appears to have been to include only the tours made on horseback between September 1822 and October 1826 in the area south and east of a line from Norwich to Hereford—Cobbett's 'home-ground'. By omitting tours undertaken partly by coach in 1821-2 and the northern tours of 1828-9, he achieved a kind of unity of time, place and locomotion. The 'Rides' are reprinted exactly as they appeared in the **Political Register,** so that Cobbett's narrative retains all the freshness and immediacy of its original form as a daybook written in snatches. He rode on horseback, rather than by coach, to see the country and to meet country people of his own choosing. For a man of sixty, Cobbett displayed (and boasted of) great hardiness, for he was often in the saddle fasting from daybreak to sunset in all weathers—on one occasion riding for two hours wet to the skin in order to rid himself of the 'hooping cough'. He was usually accompanied by one of his sons or a friend, and, whenever he could, he stayed with a farmer or landowner friend.

The main object was to see the condition of the country folk and talk politics to them. So he delivered his formal 'Rustic Harangues' on tithes, taxes, corn laws, placemen, paper-money and the need for Reform, to meetings of farmers and freeholders in market towns, but he also spoke with the labourers in the fields as he passed. Thus as he rode towards that most 'rotten' of boroughs, the accursed hill of Old Sarum:

> I met a man going home from work. I asked how he *got on*. He said, very badly. I asked him what was the cause of it. He said the *hard times*. 'What *times,*' said I; 'was there ever a finer summer, a finer harvest, and is there not an *old* wheat-rick in every farm-yard?' 'Ah!' said he, '*they* make it bad for poor people, for all that.' '*They?*' said I, 'who is *they?*' He was silent. 'Oh, no no! my friend,' said I, 'it is not *they;* it is that Accursed Hill that has robbed you of the supper that you ought to find smoking on the table when you get home.' I gave him the price of a pot of beer, and on I went, leaving the poor dejected assemblage of skin and bone to wonder at my words.

Near the very hop-gardens at Farnham where Cobbett himself had worked as a boy he found an old playmate of his in a gang of labourers at parish-work, that is, 'at the expense of half-ruined farmers and tradesmen and landlords, to break stones into very small pieces to make nice smooth roads lest the jolting in going along them, should create bile in the stomachs of the overfed tax-eaters'. Better roads brought readier access to town markets and benefited all engaged in agriculture (not excluding labourers)—as Cobbett knew when he helped to project and build the new turnpike through Botley—but in his present state of mind the spectacle of labourers mending roads was 'a state of things, where all is out of order':

> here are farmers *unable* to pay men for working for them, and yet compelled to pay them for working in

doing that which is really of no use to any human being. There lie the hop-poles unstripped. You see a hundred things in the neighbouring fields that want doing. The fences are not nearly what they ought to be. The very meadows, to our right and our left in crossing this little valley, would occupy these men advantageously until the setting in of the frost.

So Cobbett spoke to them of the true causes of their misery: 'However, in speaking of their low wages, I told them, that the farmers and hop-planters were as much objects of compassion as themselves, which they acknowledge.' Farmers could not afford to pay a living wage to their labourers, because they were so heavily taxed to support the 'dead-weight' of pensioners, sinecurists, fund-holders and a thundering standing army in time of peace. Loanmongers and stock-jobbers became rich and with their financial power propped up a corrupt government which ruled in their interest and retained perpetual power by its control of rotten boroughs. The once independent landed gentry had enough political power to check all this, but, in order to share the places and pensions, they had cravenly thrown in their lot with the moneyed men. However, they would find soon that the moneyed men had eaten them all up; the gentry would follow the farmers and the labourers in a total ruin of what had once been the 'landed interest'. So, riding with a sense of relief out of Tunbridge Wells, Cobbett reflected that this 'toad-stool' town is a product of the gambling system brought in by the moneyed men. The means for this gamble 'are *now* coming out of the farmer's capital and out of the landlord's estate; the labourers are stripped; they can give no more: the saddle is now fixing itself upon the right back'.

So the farmworkers starved amid plenty. They were pauperized, while their share of food and raiment was taken off to support the Debt, the 'dead-weight' and the standing army. At Cricklade, Cobbett came to a farm near the new canal:

> I saw in *one single farm-yard* here more food than enough for four times the inhabitants of the parish . . . but, while the poor creatures that raise the wheat and the barley and cheese and the mutton and the beef are living upon potatoes, an accursed *Canal* comes kindly through the parish to convey away the wheat and all the *good food* to the tax-eaters and their attendants in the Wen. . . . We have very nearly come to the system of Hindoostan, where the farmer is allowed by the Aumil, or tax-contractor, only *so much* of the produce of his farm to eat in the year! The thing is not done in so undisguised a manner here; here are *assessor, collector, exciseman, supervisor, informer, constable, justice, sheriff, jailor, judge, jury, jack-sketch, barrack-man.* Here is a great deal of *ceremony* about it.

The canal, like the road at Farnham, is an unlikely agent of villainy, but it is something new, and that is enough. Cobbett's fancy takes fire, generating a grotesque string of professional oppressors who constitute a kind of Asiatic despotism. The bizarre comparison and the list of assorted professions both have in them a hint of Swift.

According to Cobbett, this ceremonious process has beggared the countryside in order to enrich the towns, so urban growth is itself a sign of rural decay. Continually he denounces the Great Wen itself and its satellites: Sunning Hill near Windsor 'is a spot all made into *"grounds"* and gardens by *tax-eaters*. The inhabitants of it have beggared twenty agricultural villages and hamlets.' He denounces garrison towns, such as 'odious, hellish' Portsmouth, and even towns which have had industrial growth, such as Frome with its 'swaggering inns', but some of his bitterest invectives are reserved for Cheltenham:

> which is what they call a *'watering place'*; that is to say, a place, to which East India plunderers, West India floggers, English tax-gorgers, together with gluttons, drunkards, and debauchees of all descriptions, *female* as well as male, resort, at the suggestion of silently laughing quacks, in the hope of getting rid of the bodily consequences of their manifold sins and iniquities. When I enter a place like this, I always feel disposed to squeeze up my nose with my fingers. It is nonsense, to be sure; but I conceit that every two-legged creature, that I see coming near me, is about to cover me with the poisonous proceeds of its impurities. To places like this come all that is knavish and all that is foolish and all that is base; gamesters, pick-pockets, and harlots; young wife-hunters in search of rich and ugly and old women, and young husband-hunters in search of rich and wrinkled or half-rotten men, the former resolutely bent, be the means what they may, to give the latter heirs to their lands and tenements.

Cobbett is attacking in the conventional way a common eighteenth-century satirical target; he is almost Smollett's Matthew Bramble to the life. But, more than this, the physical and moral infirmities of the watering place's visitors symbolize the diseased condition of the whole corrupt and corrupting carcase of the 'Thing', while indicating that the death of the 'Thing' cannot be long delayed.

At Cheltenham, Cobbett recalled a speech made twenty years earlier in the House of Commons *'in favour of the non-residence of the Clergy'* which 'expressly said, that they and their families ought to appear at watering places, and that this was amongst the means of *making them respected by their flocks'*. In every parish that he visited he looked at the parsonage and, as often as not, damned some fat absentee parson who has deserted his moral and legal duty to live with his flock, but who continued to sack the produce of tithe and glebe. Coming to one of the six parishes of which the highly-connected Reverend John Dampier was rector, he exclaimed:

> It is a part of our system to have certain *families,* who have no particular merit; but who are to be maintained, without why or wherefore, at the public expense. . . . If you look through the old lists of pensioners, sinecurists, parsons, and the like, you will find the same names everlastingly recurring. They seem to be a sort of creatures that have an *inheritance in the public carcass,* like the maggots that some people have in their skins. The family of Dampier seems to be one of those.

The 'famous cock-parson, the "Honourable and Reverend" George Herbert' was another. Herbert was Lord Carnarvon's brother and rector of Burghclere where Cobbett frequently stayed with his farmer friend, William Budd. Herbert 'had grafted the *parson* upon the *soldier* and the *justice* upon the parson; for, he died, a little while ago, *a half-pay officer in the army, rector of two parishes, and chairman of the quarter sessions.*' In fact, he had six ecclesiastical livings, worth three-thousand pounds a year in all.

Cobbett, as the writer of sermons, has much to say of the preaching. On a typical Sunday (31 August 1823), riding through Kent from Goudhurst to Tenterden, he hears four or five sermons. Three of them are from Methodists. One is 'shaking the brimstone bag most furiously' at a congregation of Sunday-school boys and girls; he is a sleek fellow who probably eats as much meat as any ten of his charges. Another ought to be put in the stocks. A third, worst of all, is preaching the doctrine of election: 'He distinctly told us, that a man *perfectly moral*, might be *damned*; and that "the *vilest of the vile*, and the *basest of the base*" (I quote his very words) "would be saved if they became *regenerate*".' This outrages all Cobbett's religious instincts. The Anglican parson at Goudhurst was inviting his congregation to give money to the Society for Promoting Christian Knowledge; Cobbett, while he was not computing the size of the church and reckoning to what extent population had declined since the Reformation, was wondering why 'all the deacons, priests, curates perpetual, vicars, rectors, prebends, doctors, deans, archdeacons and fathers in God, right reverend and most reverend' were not capable of promoting Christian knowledge themselves. At Tenterden Church, looking at the pews, he commented on the odious social distinctions brought into Christian worship as a result of the Reformation.

Cobbett's rides took him to many medieval parish churches and all the cathedrals in his area. His comments are always those of a politician, not an antiquarian, but amid his invectives a sense of wonder is faintly discernible. In Salisbury Cathedral he marvels at the impudence of men who represent as ignorant and benighted their medieval forefathers who 'conceived the grand design, and who executed the scientific and costly work', who 'carried so far towards the skies that beautiful and matchless spire'. 'These fellows, in big white wigs, of the size of half a bushel, have the audacity, even within the walls of the Cathedrals themselves, to rail against those who founded them.' Among the few surviving ruins of Malmesbury Abbey

> there is now a *door-way*, which is the most beautiful thing I ever saw, and which was nevertheless, built in Saxon times, in 'the *dark* ages', and was built by men, who were not begotten by Pitt nor by Jubilee-George. What *fools*, as well as ungrateful creatures, we have been and are! There is a broken arch, standing off from the sound part of the building, at which one cannot look up without feeling shame at the thought of ever having abused the men who made it. No one need *tell* any man of sense; he *feels* our inferiority to our fathers, upon merely beholding the remains of their efforts to

ornament their country and elevate the minds of the people.

Everywhere, of course, he finds huge and magnificent parish churches in poor villages with only a handful of inhabitants, and asks whence came the means and the hands to build these churches if there has not been considerable rural depopulation since the Middle Ages.

Cobbett's imaginary medieval world fulfilled completely his ideal of a society of well-fed, well-clothed husbandmen living on the land and enjoying the best from it, but—compared with the miserable present—the England of his own youth, we are not surprised to learn, was close to the ideal. He writes a great deal in familiar and traditional vein about the engrossing of farms and rural depopulation. At Burghclere, for instance:

> one single farmer holds by lease, under Lord Carnarvon, as one farm, the lands that men, now living, can remember to have formed *fourteen farms*, bringing up, in a respectable way, *fourteen families*. In some instances these small farm-houses and homesteads are completely gone; in others the buildings remain, but in a tumble-down state; in others the house is gone, leaving the barn for use as a barn or as a cattle-shed; in others, the out-buildings are gone, and the house, with rotten thatch, broken windows, rotten door-sills, and all threatening to fall, remains as the dwelling of a half-starved and ragged family of labourers, the grand-children, perhaps, of the decent family of small farmers that formerly lived happily in this very house. This, with few exceptions, is the case all over England; and, if we duly consider the nature and tendency of the hellish system of taxing, of funding and of paper-money *it must be so.*

Where much engrossing had occurred the farmers, needless to say, had acquired luxurious habits and sought to ape the manners of the gentry. Cobbett came to a farm-sale near Reigate where there was a parlour, a carpet, a mahogany table, decanters and a bell-pull, and where the farmer had evidently found it cheaper and more gentleman-like to pay his labourers starvation wages and let them look after themselves, than to board and feed them in the old-fashioned way. This farmer's father, 'I dare say' (an habitual phrase with Cobbett), used 'to sit at the head of the oak-table [in the kitchen] along with his men, say grace to them, and cut up the meat and the pudding'; so Cobbett, reflecting 'on the thousands of scores of bacon and thousands of bushels of bread' that had been eaten from the table, vowed to buy it 'for all the good it has done in the world'. This was a very proper resolution for the man who boasted that 'I have bought and have roasted more whole sirloins of beef than any man in England.' The oak table where master and men used to sit down together was a favourite symbol in the myth of happy old rural England; among contemporary poets it appeared for instance in Bloomfield's *The Farmer's Boy* and Clare's *The Parish*.

The richer the land, the more likelihood there was of engrossing and enclosure and of the impoverishing of the labourer; conversely on poorer lands where there were still unenclosed wastes the labourer fared better. Cobbett came to a hamlet in the rich corn-land of the Isle of Thanet:

> The labourers' houses, all along through this island, beggarly in extreme. The people dirty, poor-looking; ragged, but particularly *dirty*. The men and boys with dirty faces, and dirty smock-frocks, and dirty shirts; and, good God! what a difference between the wife of a labouring man here, and the wife of a labouring man in the forests and woodlands of Hampshire and Sussex! Invariably have I observed, that the richer the soil, and the more destitute of woods; that is to say, the more purely a corn country, the more miserable the labourers. The cause is this, the great, the big bull frog grasps all. In this beautiful island every inch of land is appropriated by the rich. No hedges, no ditches, no commons, no grassy lanes: a country divided into great farms; a few trees surround the great farm-house. All the rest is bare of trees; and the wretched labourer has not a stick of wood, and has no place for a pig or cow to graze, or even to lie down upon. The rabbit countries are the countries for labouring men. There the ground is not so valuable. There it is not so easily appropriated by the few.

Writers who before Cobbett's birth had commented on the greater independence and insubordination of woodland and heath men, as compared with men living in open lowland, were observing the same difference.

According to Cobbett engrossing was operating higher in the social scale. Between Warminster and Devizes, 'All the way along, the *mansion-houses* are nearly all gone. There is now and then a *great place,* belonging to a *borough-monger,* or some one connected with borough-mongers; but all the *little gentlemen* are gone.' Time and again he notes where old estates have fallen into the clutches of Jews and jobbers. In Herefordshire and Worcestershire he observes that the great family of financiers and boroughmongers, the Barings, are 'adding field to field and tract to tract . . . depositing their eggs about, like cunning old guinea-hens, in sly places, besides the great open, showy nests that they have'. One of their larger estates in Hampshire had been bought from the Russells, but the Russells had received it as part of the loot disbursed by the old wife-killer, Henry VIII, so that there is a kind of justice in the long working-out of the 'System'. Looking at the great estates of new moneyed men or placemen, Cobbett has a physical sense of the weight of corruption and of the 'Thing'. Thus, passing through Kent,

> I asked a man whose fine woods those were that I pointed to, and I fairly gave *a start,* when he said, the Marquis Camden's. Milton talks of the *Leviathan* in a way to make one draw in one's shoulders with fear; and I appeal to any one, who has been at sea when a whale has come near the ship, whether he has not, at the first sight of the monster, made a sort of involuntary movement, as if to *get out of the way.* Such was the movement that I now made. . . . It is Bayham Abbey that this great and awful sinecure placeman owns in this part of the county. Another great estate he owns near *Sevenoaks.* But here alone he spreads his length and breadth over more, they say, than *ten or twelve thousand acres of land.*

Landowners new and old have betrayed their trust in allying themselves with the wealthy against the poor:

> the foul, the stinking, the carrion baseness, of the fellows that call themselves *'country gentlemen',* is, that the wretches, while railing against the poor and the poor-rates; while affecting to believe, that the poor are wicked and lazy . . . they never even whisper a word against pensioners, placemen, soldiers, parsons, fundholders, tax-gatherers, or tax-eaters.

They support a system of taxation which benefits the 'dead-weight', they bring in Corn Laws to keep prices high and they conduct a little one-sided rural war of their own in enforcing the Game Laws. Riding through Kent, Cobbett's attention is caught by a notice-board 'standing in a garden near a neat little box of a house. The words were these. "Paradise Place. *Spring guns and steel traps are set here.*"' One case in particular under the Game Laws horrified him, and he refers to it several times in *Rural Rides.* At the Lent Assizes at Winchester in 1822, James Turner was accused of helping to kill a gamekeeper employed by the famous sportsman Thomas Assheton Smith, and Charles Smith was accused of shooting, but not killing, one of Lord Palmerston's gamekeepers. Both were sentenced to death and they were hanged on the same gallows. At the same Assizes sixteen other prisoners were condemned to death but the two poachers were the only ones hanged. Cobbett had presented a petition to Parliament referring to these cases, urging that the severity of the Game Laws made it inevitable that poachers should attempt to defend themselves against gamekeepers, and that the remedy lay in amending the laws.

Against these monstrosities Cobbett can set the activities of good landlords who have kept up the labourers' wages, who know their tenants and mix with them on the hunting field—rather than indulge in the selfish, solitary sport of shooting. Plenty of these appear in *Rural Rides,* and even where Cobbett has no direct evidence of a landowner's virtues he can readily infer them from the appearance of the labourers. Thus, of the Duke of Buckingham's turnip-hoers at Avington in Hampshire:

> These girls were all tall, straight, fair, round-faced, excellent complexion, and uncommonly gay. They were well dressed, too, and I observed the same of all the men that I saw down at Avington. This could not be the case if the Duke were a cruel or hard master.

There is plenty of denunciation in *Rural Rides* but no despair. Nature may be perverted where, for the present, labourers starve amid plenty, stock-jobbers build their 'suburban boxes on spewy gravel', or the waters of a lovely stream drive a mill that manufactures banknotes, but the heart of the land is sound, and in many places man and nature are what they should be. At Bishopstrow in Wiltshire, land, houses and girls are neat and pretty, as they all should be:

> The arable land goes down before the house, and spreads along the edge of the down, going, with a

gentle slope, down to the meadows. So that, going along the turnpike road, which runs between the lower fields of the arable land, you see the large and beautiful flocks of sheep upon the sides of the down, while the horn-cattle are up to their eyes in grass in the meadows. Just when I was coming along here, the sun was about half an hour high; it shined through the trees most brilliantly; and, to crown the whole, I met, just as I was entering the village, a very pretty girl, who was apparently, going a gleaning in the fields.

In West Sussex:

> I called to me a young man, who, along with other turnip-hoers, was sitting under the shelter of a hedge at breakfast. He came running to me with his victuals in his hand; and, I was glad to see, that his food consisted of a good lump of household *bread* and not a very small piece of *bacon*. . . . In parting with him, I said, 'You do get some *bacon* then?' 'Oh, yes! Sir,' said he, and with an emphasis and a swag of the head which seemed to say, 'We *must* and *will* have *that*.' I saw, and with great delight, a pig at almost every labourer's house. The houses are good and warm; and the gardens some of the very best that I have seen in England.

In the same area Cobbett saw a woman bleaching her home-spun and home-woven linen, and elsewhere he found cottagers making gloves, and, of course, the famous straw-plait, using the methods publicized in *Cottage Economy*. In all the little corners of England where domestic industry survived, where women and girls could be put to their 'natural employment,' labourers' families would always rise above pauperism; in these places the 'Lords of the Loom' were being successfully defied, and their system which drew wealth into great masses.

Everywhere Cobbett rides as a farmer, with an eye to the lie of the land, the soil, the drainage, the condition of the crops and livestock. Good husbandry is his first concern, and whenever he comes to a new scene he first describes the nature of the soil and says what it will best grow. Thus, between Selborne and Thursley, 'I am here got into some of the very best barely-land in the kingdom; a fine, buttery, stoneless loam, upon a bottom of sand or sand-stone. Finer barley and turnip-land it is impossible to see.' In the Vale of Pewsey he is not indulging in anthropomorphic fancy when he says that the trees, 'generally *elms,* with some *ashes* . . . delight in the soil that they find here'. He feels the wholeness of nature, and of man in nature, because he is constantly alive to the physical character of the land and the manner in which it shapes, and is shaped by, the working lives of husbandmen. For instance, every one of his journeys took him at some point or other into the downland; so we find him frequently discussing the merits of a well-draining chalk bottom. Near Winchester:

> The country where the soil is stiff loam upon chalk, is never bad for corn. Not rich, but never poor. There is at no time any thing deserving to be called dirt in the roads. The buildings last a long time, from the absence

of fogs and also the absence of humidity in the ground. The absence of dirt makes the people habitually cleanly; and all along through this country the people appear in general to be very neat. It is a country for sheep, which are always sound and good upon this iron soil.

Near Andover the surface of the land:

> presents, in the size and form of the fields, in the woods, the hedge-rows, the sainfoin, the young wheat, the turnips, the tares, the fallows, the sheep-folds and the flocks . . . that which I, at any rate, could look at with pleasure for ever . . . there are no ditches, no water-furrows, no dirt, and *never any drought* to cause inconvenience. The *chalk* is at bottom and it takes care of all.

This is down to earth in every way, but Cobbett also senses the strangeness and wonder of the land itself. Looking at the three hills called 'The Devil's Jumps' near Farnham, he asks:

> How could waters rolling about have formed such hills? How could such hills have bubbled up from beneath? But, in short, it is all wonderful alike: the stripes of loam running down through the chalk-hills; the circular parcels of loam in the midst of chalk-hills; the lines of flint running parallel with each other horizontally along the chalk-hills; the flints placed in circles as true as a hair in the chalk-hills; the layers of stone at the bottom of the hills of loam; the chalk first soft, then some miles farther on, becoming chalk-stone; then, after another distance, becoming burr-stone, as they call it; and at last, becoming hard, white stone, fit for any buildings.

Then, Cobbett finds the formulations of his own mind as unexpected, wonderful and natural as the flint formations in the chalk hills. Sitting in a comfortable Wiltshire inn he is amazed to discover himself suddenly thinking about Grimshaw, the mayor of Preston, who had rigged the election against Cobbett in several ways, one of which was in the construction of restricted approaches (called 'ditches') to the polling-booths:

> I am now sitting at one of the southern windows of this inn, looking across the garden towards the rookery. It is nearly sunsetting; the rooks are skimming and curving over the tops of the trees; while, under the branches, I see a flock of several hundred sheep, coming nibbling their way in from the Down, and going to their fold.

> Now, what ill-natured devil could bring Old Nic Grimshaw into my head in company with these innocent sheep? Why, the truth is this: nothing is *so swift as thought:* it runs over a life-time in a moment; and, while I was writing the last sentence of the foregoing paragraph, *thought* took me up at the time when I used to wear a smock-frock and to carry a wooden bottle like that shepherd's boy; and, in an instant, it hurried me along through my no very short life of adventure, of toil, of peril, of pleasure, of ardent friendship and not less ardent enmity; and after filling me with wonder, that a heart and mind so wrapped up

in every thing belonging to the gardens, the fields and the woods, should have been condemned to waste themselves away amidst the stench, the noise and the strife of cities, it brought me *to the present moment,* and sent my mind back to what I have yet to perform about Nicholas Grimshaw and his *ditches.*

Cobbett has several audiences. He is reviewing the state of the countryside, reporting back to readers of the *Political Register* and proposing his usual remedies for social, economic and political ills; he is addressing his farmer and freeholder audiences with 'Rustic Harangues', and cottagers and labourers by the wayside; he is conversing with his companion, usually one of his sons, about what they see as they ride; but, significantly he is often, as here, simply talking to himself.

There is no kind of formal unity in *Rural Rides,* but all is connected within Cobbett's consciousness, and this is nowhere clearer than in those places where the landscape is a landscape of memory. Thus he shows his son, James, one of the haunts of his youth at Farnham:

> There is a little hop-garden in which I used to work when from eight to ten years' old; from which I have scores of times run to follow the hounds, leaving the hoe to do the best that it could to destroy the weeds; but the most interesting thing was, a *sand-hill,* which goes from a part of the heath down to the rivulet. As a due mixture of pleasure with toil, I, with two brothers, used occasionally to *desport* ourselves, as the lawyers call it, at this sandhill. Our diversion was this: we used to go to the top of the hill, which was steeper than the roof of a house; one used to draw his arms out of the sleeves of his smock-frock, and lay himself down with his arms by his sides; and then the others, one at head and the other at feet, sent him rolling down the hill like a barrel or a log of wood. By the time he got to the bottom, his hair, eyes, ears, nose and mouth, were all full of this loose sand; then the others took their turn, and at every roll, there was a monstrous spell of laughter. . . . This was the spot where I was receiving my *education;* and this was the sort of education; and I am perfectly satisfied that if I had not received such an education, or something very much like it; that, if I had been brought up a milksop, with a nursery-maid everlastingly at my heels; I should have been at this day as great a fool, as inefficient a mortal, as any of those frivolous idiots that are turned out from Winchester and Westminster School, or from any of those dens of dunces called Colleges and Universities.

Of course this passage has the raucousness that tends to appear whenever Cobbett admits himself 'perfectly satisfied that . . . ', but as his memory sets to work the sand-hill becomes a concrete symbol of his own sturdy self-reliance, of permanent characteristics which unite the child and the man, and which, it is implied, have been transmitted to the man's child, who also is to be spared school and university.

Three years later, with his youngest son, Richard, Cobbett is back at Farnham, again showing that his life is all of a piece and that the child is father of the man:

> I showed him the spot where the strawberry garden was, and where I, when sent to gather *hautboys,* used to eat every *remarkably fine one,* instead of letting it go to be eaten by Sir Robert Rich. I showed him a tree, close by the ruins of the Abbey, from a limb of which I once fell into the river, in an attempt to take the nest of a *crow,* which had artfully placed it upon a branch so far from the trunk as not to be able to bear the weight of a boy eight years old. I showed him an old elm tree, which was hollow even then, into which I, when a very little boy, once saw *a cat go,* that was *as big as a middle-sized spaniel dog,* for relating which I got a great scolding, for standing to which I, at last, got a beating; but, stand to which I still did.

He is still standing to it.

Rural Rides is Cobbett himself—cantankerous, naïve, unfair, preposterously conceited, but innocently and splendidly responsive to the life of man in nature. The only work that contains as much of his personality is his *Advice to Young Men* (published in fourteen sixpenny parts between July 1829 and September 1830). This work is addressed to men (and women) 'in the Middle and Higher Ranks of Life' and is not primarily political in intention; nevertheless it is something of a Radical's *apologia pro vita sua.* For years, government supporters and churchmen had denounced the Reformers as examples of every vice, but here Cobbett replied with a self-portrait of all the benefits of industry, sobriety, independence and thrift. He quoted, approvingly, Rousseau's observation that 'men are happy, first, in proportion to their virtue, and next, in proportion to their *independence',* and illustrated it from his own life.

Cobbett's first piece of advice is that men must work, not only because this is their duty to their dependants and fellow men, but because useful work is the clue to happiness. He was in no doubt that his public success and private happiness were triumphs of will, effort and character-training, and he saw that others could achieve similar happiness if they would develop their own powers as fully and strenuously as he had. Entirely by his own exertions, Cobbett has raised himself from common ploughboy to one of the most powerful political writers in the land. He was fortunate in enjoying good health, of course, but even this was self-made, for it was attributable to self-imposed habits of early-rising, sobriety and frugality, and love of exercise and fresh air. His physical regimen and love of hard work even gave him a moral advantage over other political writers, for, as he had never been debased by luxury, he had never become a drone or slave. How different from Dr Johnson, says Cobbett—a man of great genius, and, for a time, of great industry, who accepted a pension merely in order to indulge in the pleasures of the table, even though he had, in his *Dictionary,* correctly defined 'Pensioner' as 'A slave of state', but 'When this celebrated author wrote his Dictionary, he had not been debased by luxurious enjoyments.' As a dastardly state-pensioner, Johnson wrote *Taxation no Tyranny* which 'defended, and greatly assisted to produce, that unjust and bloody war' which severed the United States from England. William Gifford's was an even worse case, but:

Endless are the instances of men of bright parts and high spirit having been, by degrees, rendered powerless and despicable, by their imaginary wants. . . . Dryden, Parnell, Gay, Thomson, in short, what poet have we had, or have we, Pope only excepted, who was not, or is not, a pensioner, or a sinecure placeman, or the wretched dependent of some sort of the Aristocracy?

Cobbett scatters his literary judgments, or prejudices, freely through the *Advice.* Addison, Blair, Johnson and 'the punning and smutty Shakespeare' come under his lash as usual, but he seems to distrust most literature, since most poets, playwrights and romancers teach bad morality. Thus *Cymbeline* and the once-popular *Douglas* by John Home (a 'base parasite', like Shakespeare) perpetrate the pernicious falsehood 'that there is in *high birth,* something of *superior nature,* instinctive courage, honour, and talent'. This is how Cobbett describes *Tom Jones:*

Here are two young men put before us, both sons of the same mother; the one a *bastard* (and by a parson too), the other a *legitimate child;* the former wild, disobedient, and squandering; the latter steady, sober, obedient, and frugal; the former every thing that is frank and generous in his nature, the latter a greedy hypocrite; the former rewarded with the most beautiful and virtuous of women and a double estate, the latter punished by being made an outcast. How is it possible for young people to read such a book, and to look upon orderliness, sobriety, obedience, and frugality, as *virtues?* And this is the tenor of almost every romance, and of almost every play, in our language. In the 'School for Scandal,' for instance, we see, two brothers; the one a prudent and frugal man, and, to all appearance, a moral man, the other a hair-brained squanderer, laughing at the morality of his brother; the former turns out to be a base hypocrite and seducer, and is brought to shame and disgrace; while the latter is found to be full of generous sentiment, and Heaven itself seems to interfere to give him fortune and fame. In short, the direct tendency of the far greater part of these books, is, to cause young people to despise all those virtues, without the practice of which they must be a curse to their parents, a burden to the community, and must, except by mere accident, lead wretched lives.

More than he cared to admit, Cobbett shared the views of the contemporary Evangelicals he despised so much.

The *Advice,* like the *Grammar* and everything else that Cobbett wrote, is full of political asides, but its last paragraphs make an excursion, unusual for him, into general political theory, when he takes, and greatly simplifies, the notions of Locke and Rousseau concerning the 'social contract', and adapts them to the aims of the Parliamentary reformers, just as in the *Poor Man's Friend* (1826-7) he had adapted them to a defence of the existing Poor Law. So, in the *Advice,* he again tells how civil society arose when, in order to secure mutual protection, men divided the land over which, according to the Law of Nature, they had all formerly ranged freely, and established a law of property based upon labour. In time inequalities of property arose:

but these truths are written on the heart of man: that all men are, by nature, *equal;* that civil society can never have arisen from any motive other than that of the *benefit of the whole;* that, whenever civil society makes the greater part of the people *worse off* than they were under the Law of Nature, the civil compact is, in conscience, dissolved, and all the rights of nature return.

These rights include

the right of enjoying life and property; the right of exerting our physical and mental powers in an innocent manner; but, the great right of all, and without which there is, in fact, *no right,* is, the right of *taking a part in the making of* the laws by *which we are governed.*

The purpose of government is to secure the well-being of the common people, that is, to restore the labourer's life to what it was when Cobbett was a boy. Denunciation and retrospective idyll play in counterpoint, as they do in so much of his political writing, but, refreshingly, in the *Advice* the idyllic tones are dominant:

Those who have, as I so many hundreds of times have, seen the labourers in the woodland parts of Hampshire and Sussex, coming, at night-fall, towards their cottage-wickets, laden with fuel for a day or two; whoever has seen three or four little creatures looking out for the father's approach, running in to announce the glad tidings, and then scampering out to meet him, clinging round his knees, or hanging on his skirts; whoever has witnessed scenes like this, to witness which has formed one of the greatest delights of my life, will hesitate long before he prefer a life of ease to a life of labour. . . . This used to be the way of life amongst the labouring people; and from this way of life arose the most able and most moral people that the world ever saw, until grinding taxation took from them the means of obtaining a sufficiency of food and of raiment; plunged the whole, good and bad, into one indiscriminate mass, under the degrading and hateful name of paupers.

The sentimentalized, retrospective Arcadia is a world of domestic virtues, but it is not an utterly lost world, for these virtues survive, he implies, in Cobbett himself, who, in this as in much else, sees himself as a living image of Old England.

The dominant theme of the *Advice* is Cobbett's domestic happiness. All his public success he attributes to the fact that he is happily married, and in unaffectedly idyllic terms he writes of a courtship and married life marked throughout by mutual consideration, loyalty, trust and respect. Cobbett writes with his usual unashamed egotism, but upon subjects more likely than usual to engage his readers' sympathies. Thus, of an episode of his early married life in Philadelphia:

that famous Grammar for teaching French people English, which has been for thirty years, and still is, the great work of this kind, throughout all America, and in every nation in Europe, was written by me, in hours not employed in business, and, in great part, during my share in the night-watchings over a sick, and then only child, who, after lingering many months, died in my arms.

Or, at Botley, writing those powerful *Political Registers,* 'many a score papers have I written amidst the noise of children, and in my whole life never bade them be still. . . . That which you are *pleased with,* however noisy, does not disturb you.' Cobbett's tender domestic relations are the obverse of his violent public controversies, and his hatred of his enemies is all the more extreme when they seem to threaten his family. As he will never forget the tears of his young children when he was torn from his family and thrown into prison on that unhappy day in 1810, so he rejoices in the deaths of many of the men then ranged against him—Gibbs, Ellenborough, Perceval, Liverpool and Canning. He hated Malthus because that audacious and merciless person has declared war on the poor labourer's family.

Malthus is hateful on another score, for Cobbett detests the 'filthiness' of birth-control. Running through the entire *Advice,* indeed, is a prudery which, though some might call it 'Victorian', is in fact very characteristic of Cobbett's age—Mrs Grundy was invented in the eighteenth century and Bowdler was born before Cobbett. So Cobbett condemns the indelicacy of women who employ man-midwives, or use 'hireling breasts' to feed their children. The woman who hires a wet-nurse does so from the worst of motives, that is, 'to *hasten back,* unbridled and undisfigured, to those enjoyments, to have an eagerness for which, a really delicate woman will shudder at the thought of being suspected'. His sense of delicacy is offended even by the thought of a widow remarrying, for she 'has *a second time* undergone that surrender, to which nothing but the most ardent affection, could ever reconcile a chaste and delicate woman'.

If Cobbett was as strict as the most prudish Evangelical in sexual matters, his notions of child-rearing were very free. Hannah More had written that it was a 'fundamental error to consider children as innocent beings', rather they were creatures of 'a corrupt nature and evil dispositions.' John Wesley agreed:

> Break their wills betimes. Begin this work before they can run alone, before they can speak plain, perhaps before they can speak at all. . . . Let a child from a year old be taught to fear the rod and to cry softly; from that age make him do as he is bid, if you whip him ten times running to effect it. . . . Break his will now, and his soul shall live, and he will probably bless you to all eternity.

Cobbett, by contrast, boasted that he had never struck any of his children, and had always enjoyed their respect, love and obedience. In the passages of the *Advice* dealing with education he is the avowed disciple of Rousseau, whose *Émile* he had read in those early years as a language tutor in Philadelphia:

> I have always admired the sentiment of Rousseau upon this subject. 'The boy dies, perhaps, at the age of ten

or twelve. Of what *use,* then, all the restraints, all the privations, all the pain, that you have inflicted upon him? He falls, and leaves your mind to brood over the possibility of your having abridged a life so dear to you. I do not recollect the very words; but the passage made a deep impression upon my mind, just at the time, too, when I was about to become a father; and I was resolved never to bring upon myself remorse from a such a cause. . . . I was resolved that, as long as I could cause them to do it, my children should lead happy lives.

Cobbett shared Rousseau's notions concerning the spontaneous development of the child, and carried them into effect in the education of his own children. Rousseau had said that the child's natural teachers are his parents, and his best environment the countryside; Cobbett's children secured both advantages when the family settled at Botley, and some of the most delightful passages of the *Advice* are Cobbett's fresh, easy accounts of the way he reared his children there:

> The mind as well as the body, requires time to come to its strength; the way to have it possess, at last, its natural strength, is not to attempt to load it too soon; and to favour it in its progress by giving to the body good and plentiful food, sweet air, and abundant exercise, accompanied with as little discontent or uneasiness as possible.

So the Cobbett children were first introduced to useful, innocent, practical pursuits:

> Each his flower-bed, little garden, plantation of trees; rabbits, dogs, asses, horses, pheasants and hares; hoes, spades, whips, guns; always some object of lively interest, and as much *earnestness* and *bustle* about the various objects as if our living had solely depended upon them.

Young children cannot understand ideas or mere words, but *things* will educate them; the child must come to book-learning only when he is ready and eager for it. Then:

> A large, strong table, in the middle of the room, their mother sitting at her work, used to be surrounded with [the children], the baby, if big enough, set up in a high chair. Here were ink-stands, pens, pencils, India rubber, and paper, all in abundance, and every one scrabbled about as he or she pleased. There were prints of animals of all sorts: others treating of gardening, of flowers, of husbandry, of hunting, coursing, shooting, fishing, planting, and, in short, of every thing, with regard to which *we had something to do.* One would be trying to imitate a bit of my writing, another *drawing* the pictures of some of our dogs or horses, a third poking over *Bewick's Quadrupeds,* and picking out what he said about them; but our book of never-failing resource was the French *Maison Rustique,* or *Farm-House.* . . . I never have been without a copy of this book for forty years, except during the time that I was fleeing from the dungeons of Castlereagh and Sidmouth in 1817; and, when I got to Long Island, the *first book I bought* was another *Maison Rustique.*

What need had we of *schools?* What need of *teachers?* What need of *scolding* and *force,* to induce children to read, write, and love books?

The reference to Castlereagh and Sidmouth reminds Cobbett's reader of the threatening presences which lay, and in new embodiments still lie, beyond the charmed family circle of health and virtue.

Formal 'education' might be as much of a threat to domestic virtue and happiness as those 'dungeons' were. It was wrong to gather any human beings into large, systemized masses, and doubly wrong so to gather children. Large schools are like gaols, barracks and factories, which corrupt not 'by their walls, but by their condensed numbers'. Worse, any scheme of national public education would place in the hands of the government of the day a new tool for indoctrination and intimidation. It already seemed that the principal aim of Sunday schools (which had spread widely since the foundation of the Sunday School Society in 1785) was to extend work-discipline into the seventh day, and thus make poor children more orderly, tractable, submissive and dutiful in the factories, workshops or fields on the other six days of the week. All men could not be Cobbetts, but given decent living conditions and freedom from the 'comforting' interference of his so-called betters, any man could establish a happy, virtuous home in which he could create the physical conditions, and set the parental example, by which his children could healthfully and happily educate themselves.

The *Advice to Young Men* is Cobbett's happiest book:

> Born and bred up in the sweet air myself, I was resolved that they should be bred up in it too. Enjoying rural scenes and sports, as I had done, when a boy, as much as any one that ever was born, I was resolved, that they should have the same enjoyments tendered to them. When I was a very little boy, I was, in the barley-sowing season, going along by the side of a field, near Waverley Abbey; the primroses and bluebells bespangling the banks on both sides of me; a thousand linnets singing in a spreading oak over my head; while the jingling of the traces and the whistling of the ploughboys saluted my ear from over the hedge; and, as it were to snatch me from the enchantment, the hounds, at that instant, having started a hare in the hanger on the other side of the field, came up scampering over it in full cry, taking me after them many a mile. I was not more than eight years old; but this particular scene has presented itself to my mind many times every year from that day to this. I always enjoy it over again; and I was resolved to give, if possible, the same enjoyments to my children.

It is characteristic of Cobbett that he should still enjoy this childhood experience, unclouded by the sense of mortality and mutability with which many a man would have recalled an event in his own life sixty years earlier. Thanks to the power of memory, Cobbett's sensuous joy in life at sixty-six is as fresh and whole-hearted as a child's. He recreates a childhood experience in its time, place and circumstance, giving us a sense of the wholesomeness of work and play in the countryside; and the leaping delight that runs through his recollection is more than sufficient warrant for the rightness of his views on child-rearing. There is a no less beautiful, though more self-consciously idyllic, passage in the *Advice* where he describes his flirtation with a New Brunswick girl, and where, again, the emotions of his youth rush back into his heart and pen at the moment of writing. As in some of the freshest parts of *Rural Rides,* the landscape that Cobbett sees best and loves best of all is the landscape of memory.

George Spater   (essay date 1982)

SOURCE: "The Writer," in *William Cobbett: The Poor Man's Friend, Vol. 2,* Cambridge University Press, 1982, pp. 427-56.

[*Spater's* William Cobbett: The Poor Man's Friend *(1982) is considered the definitive biography of Cobbett. In the following excerpt, he offers a broad, thematic survey of Cobbett's writings.*]

Nearly all of Cobbett's writing that was published in book form was for the purpose of instruction, and nearly all the instruction related to four subjects: language, gardening or farming, personal behavior, and government affairs, with a goodly amount of overlap among categories. The language books of this period include a grammar for use by those who wished to learn French, a French—English dictionary, and a spelling book. "For once in my life," wrote Cobbett announcing publication of the grammar, "I have written a book without a word of politics in it . . . while all will agree, that the book cannot be the worse for such exclusion." As Cobbett predicted, the lacuna was no deterrent to the aspiring linguist. The book was printed and reprinted in a large but unknown number of editions— there were at least fifteen by the middle of the century— and Cobbett claimed that "More young men have, I dare say, learned French from it, than from all the other books that have been published in English for the last fifty years."

Cobbett produced five gardening or farming books after the move to Kensington. The contrast between the traditional English kitchen garden ("nicely laid out and the paths bordered with flowers") and the barren farmyards Cobbett saw on Long Island during his 1817-19 stay stimulated him to write *The American Gardener* (1821), which, published in at least a dozen editions, became the vade mecum for several generations of American housewives. In 1828 Cobbett published *The English Gardener*. Superficially, this was a revision and expansion of the earlier work, but the revision and expansion were so extensive as to constitute an entirely new book. The American instructions on how to eat an artichoke, for instance, were deleted, presumably being unnecessary for the more sophisticated English; the bare two pages accorded the cucumber in the American edition became more than a dozen for the English reader; the potato was dismissed in the earlier volume with no more than "Every body knows how to cultivate this plant," while the later book contained eight pages of discussion, starting with the criticism of the potato as a substitute for bread, but with the begrudging admission that "as a mere vegetable, or sauce, as the country people call it, it does well to qualify the effects of fat meat, or to assist in the swallowing of quantities of butter." Cobbett never ate it himself, "finding so many other things far preferable." One is apt to forget, among such endearing marks of eccentricity, Cobbett's real genius for exposition. *The English Gardener,* like all his books of instruction, is a model of good writing: strong, lucid, plain, well ordered. Viewed solely from that point of view, it is a masterpiece. Generations of readers who bought the book without regard to the beauty of the writing have testified to the practical value of its contents. And finally, the book served a further purpose. Cobbett's advertisement describing *The English Gardener* invited the gentlemen of the time, who rarely took spade in hand, to free themselves from the tyranny of their gardeners: "The book, if read with attention, will soon qualify any gentleman for knowing, at least, when his garden is well managed." And so it proved. A few years after it was published, an unidentified correspondent wrote to the horticulturalist John Loudon: "I have reason to believe that Mr. Cobbett's book has been extensively influential among the higher orders of society; and that . . . it has been a means of raising disputes between gardeners and their employers." Whether this stimulated or deterred sales is impossible to say. The book went through a number of editions in the nineteenth century and was reprinted as recently as 1980.

The Woodlands was also published in 1828. "Many years ago," Cobbett explained in the preface, "I wished to know whether I could raise Birch trees from the seed. I looked into two French books and into two English ones without being able to learn a word about the matter. I then looked into the great book of knowledge, the *Encyclopedia Britannica*: there I found in the general dictionary, 'Birch Tree, see Betula: Botany Index'. I hastened to Betula, with great eagerness; and there I found, 'Betula, see Birch Tree'." Cobbett's book, in contrast, told everything "from the gathering of the seed, to the rearing up and the cutting down of the trees"—not only of the birch, but of fifty or so others as well. The locust occupied the center of the stage in *The Woodlands* and in many *Political Register* articles. It was not unknown to English horticulturalists. There were specimens here and there, and the merits of the locust were described in several old books on tree culture. "Notwithstanding this, we never heard of a man in England that ever planted this tree, until I took the matter in hand, except as a thing of mere ornament." Unfortunately for Cobbett's nursery business, the interest he aroused in the locust was in the seedlings he offered, rather than in the young trees which he had gone to the expense of planting a few years earlier. John Loudon, after visiting Kensington in 1828, reported that "while all sorts of trees, with the exception of a few varieties of the apples, are growing old in the nurseries, from being but little asked for, Mr. Cobbett cannot raise a sufficiency of seedlings to supply the demand." He sold over a million locust seedlings. Those that went to Sir Thomas Beevor of Hargham Hall, near Norwich, were still producing valuable timber in the 1970s, more than a hundred and fifty years after they had been planted. In general, how-

ever, the wood of the locust had only a brief popularity. Its marine use disappeared with the wooden ship. Another short span of interest occurred during the period when the spokes of motorcar wheels were made of wood. And although as gate and fencing posts the locust is still "unrivaled for strength and durability by any native timber except that of the yew," it is only rarely used for that purpose in England. Cobbett's book *The Woodlands* was not a commercial success and has never been reprinted. Yet an authoritative twentieth-century publication confirms that it "continues to be worth reading."

The other farming text published in 1828 met a similar commercial fate. It was *A Treatise on Cobbett's Corn,* dealing with the cultivation of Indian corn, or maize, which, in the author's egocentric hands, was transmuted into "Cobbett's Corn." The primary purpose of taking the eighty-acre farm at Barn Elm was to determine whether this product could be successfully grown in England. Cobbett succeeded in producing a crop of nearly a hundred bushels an acre, which, with his usual excess of optimism, he figured was worth three times the cash yield of an acre of wheat. Cobbett predicted that "you will see this corn in the field of every farmer, and in the garden of every cottager in England." The results of his experiments were heralded in letters from Cobbett to the editors of London newspapers who were sent ears of corn in the husk and loaves of bread made of two parts maize, one part rye. A continuous flow of "Cobbett's Corn" articles appeared in the *Political Register*. The claims for the product became more and more exaggerated. "In a few years it will put an end to the importation of corn [wheat and other grain] and flour forever." It would assist in making perfect the changes to be brought about by parliamentary reform: "It will prevent the labourers from ever being slaves again; it will inevitably re-produce small farms; it will make the labourers more independent of their employers; it will bring back, it will hasten back, the country towards its former happy state." Barn Elm farm was thrown open to the public so the curious might see for themselves. They came, so Cobbett claimed, by the thousands. Specimens of Cobbett's corn were sent off to agricultural shows, and letters went out to editors of country papers. Cobbett extolled the virtues of beer made from the stalks of the corn. "My men are now drinking this beer, and I taste no other beer myself." Several thousand ears of corn were offered free to laborers in the southern counties of England. In 1831 the *Political Register* publicized the success of a large number of Cobbett fans in growing small patches of maize; one had been able to produce a crop as far north as Paisley in Scotland. But none of this had any long-run impact on the English farming community as a whole, either in the planting of maize or the purchase of Cobbett's book. There was a second edition of the work, and that was all. Yet its relaxed style and amusing digressions make it an entertaining book, even for one whose farming experience has been limited to the care of a single potted geranium. A perceptive contemporary review began:

> It is a property of genius, not only to be in love with
> its chosen pursuit, but at the same time to make others

in love with it. Mr. Cobbett writes about his own beloved corn, as he calls it, with an enthusiastic freshness that communicates itself to the most listless reader: it is hardly possible to keep the plough out of the ground as you read his description of the plant and the history of its cultivation.

Despite this appeal, the plough was rather generally kept out of the ground insofar as the cultivation of Cobbett's corn was concerned. More than twenty years elapsed after the book was published before small, but increasing, quantities of maize began to be imported into England. But not until the twentieth century, long after Cobbett's efforts had been forgotten, did the sceptical farmers of England accept the product as a valuable crop for animal feed and begin to reap some of the benefits Cobbett had proclaimed a hundred years earlier. The first edition of **Cobbett's Corn** (but not the second) had its title page and table of contents printed on paper made of maize husks. This, the wrapper covering the early parts of **Advice to Young Men,** and one issue of the **Political Register** are the only known uses of the results of Cobbett's paper experiments.

The most famous of Cobbett's works related to farming was **Cottage Economy** (1822), which dealt to a large extent with life inside the farmhouse itself. It was written for the purpose of showing a farm laborer's family how to get the most out of their small income. They should brew their own beer and drink it instead of tea, which was more expensive, had no strength in it, caused sleeplessness, and weakened the nerves. "Put it to the test with a lean hog: give him the fifteen bushels of malt, and he will repay you in ten score of bacon or thereabouts. But give him the 730 tea messes, or rather, begin to give them to him, and give him nothing else, and he is dead with hunger and bequeaths you his skeleton, at the end of about seven days." The laborer's family should eat bread, baked at home, in preference to the beastly potatoes—bread was more nourishing and was cheaper. They should keep poultry and bees and pigs and a cow (the produce of a cow was equal to half a man's wages), and this could be done on a quarter of an acre. Cobbett's detailed explanation of how to do all these things was accompanied by comments on the education of children and an aesthetic appreciation of the hardworking wife: "Give me for a beautiful sight, a neat and smart woman, heating her oven and setting in her bread!" **Cottage Economy** was an immediate success. The *Edinburgh Review* found it "an excellent little book—written not only with admirable clearness and good sense, but in a very earnest and entertaining manner—and abounding with kind and good feelings as well as most valuable information." It urged "all persons in easy circumstances, who live in the country" to distribute "these little books." Cobbett himself modestly claimed that "every parson ought, upon pain of loss of ears, to present [a copy] to every girl he marries, rich or poor." In the first ten years, 100,000 copies were sold; in all, more than twenty editions were printed, including three in the twentieth century. It is in print today.

Cobbett's contributions to the agricultural field were not limited to his own writing, since in 1822 he resurrected and reprinted a "lost" classic: Jethro Tull's *Horse-Hoeing Husbandry,* originally published in 1731. Tull advocated planting in rows spaced sufficiently far apart to allow easy tillage during the growing period, as contrasted with the ancient practice of sowing seeds broadcast. This method, which had been in large part forgotten, was popularized by Cobbett first in America and then in England. "I have obtained the premium of five guineas from the Wharfedale Agricultural Society for the best crop of Swede Turnips, grown from your seed, and after your plan," read one of the many letters Cobbett received.

Three of Cobbett's books are mainly devoted to instruction on matters of personal behavior: **Cobbett's Sermons** (1822), **The Emigrant's Guide** (1829), and **Advice to Young Men and (Incidentally) to Young Women** (1830). The sermons were first issued in parts beginning in March 1821 and were published in book form in the following year. They had all the outward manifestations of what an intelligent vicar might deliver from the pulpit on a Sunday morning. They discussed such subjects as "Hypocrisy," "Drunkenness," and "Gaming." They were replete with biblical quotations. Yet there is the strong suspicion that they had another purpose: that, for example, the sermon on "Hypocrisy" was directed at Wilberforce; that the sermon on "The Sin of Forbidding Marriage" was for the benefit of Malthus and his followers; and that the sermon entitled "God's Vengeance against Murderers," dealing with the cruelty of a husband toward his wife, was intended for George IV, whose wife had died the month before the sermon appeared. By 1825 they had attained a circulation of 240,000, so that Cobbett was able to declare that more of his sermons had been purchased than those of all the clergy of England combined. He presumably also enjoyed his impish utilization of the legal provision which exempted "religious" tracts from the stamp tax.

The Emigrant's Guide is a charming little book which, regrettably, has been out of print for more than a hundred years. A modern-day reader cannot fail to be entertained by the twenty-odd letters from former Sussex residents in America to their relations in England; by bits of practical information on life aboard ship, including an explanation of how women in the steerage can dress and undress without offense to their sensibilities; and by Cobbett's description of the puritanical ways of the Americans and how newcomers will be expected to behave.

The Emigrant's Guide was closely followed in time, and in style, by **Advice to Young Men and (Incidentally) to Young Women,** which ranks high, perhaps highest, among all of Cobbett's works for amusement and edification. "Happiness ought to be your great object," Cobbett says almost at the outset, and this is what the book was about. It was a healthy and worldly book, possibly intended as an answer to the solemn and otherworldly advice commonly preached to the lower classes. The advice which Cobbett offered was in the form of six letters addressed, successively, to a youth, a young man, a lover, a husband, a father, and a citizen. Much of the material was autobiographical—but, one suspects, slightly romanticized at almost every point, so that the author appears somewhat more heroic, more understanding, more lovable, and more sympathetic than in real life. *Advice* is the source of Cobbett's account of learning grammar in an army barracks and his selection of Nancy Reid as the girl he wanted to marry, as well as most of the description of life at Botley when the children were small. These and other anecdotes were used to illustrate the standards of conduct most likely to produce the greatest happiness. Many of the social customs of 1830 are now archaic, and some of Cobbett's notions were eccentric even then, but the main thrust of the advice is as appropriate today as when it was written. Cobbett's stories frequently have a wider application than the narrow terms in which they were stated. To cite an example: "It was said of a famous French commander, that, in attacking an enemy, he did not say to his men 'go on', but, 'come on'; and whoever have well observed the movements of servants, must know what a prodigious difference there is in the effect of the words *go* and *come*." The nineteenth century produced a number of books on how to lead a good and happy life, but *Advice to Young Men* is the only one that has survived. Seven new editions have been published in the twentieth century.

The final category of Cobbett's works is those chiefly concerned with the system of government and, in particular, the impact of government on the working man. This single subject was year after year the main burden of the *Political Register,* and it is natural that the theme should predominate in *Rural Rides,* which appeared serially in the current issues of the *Political Register* from 1822 to 1826. Published in book form in 1830, it is the work for which Cobbett is best known today, and it is one of his most enjoyable for the general reader, taking its place, in that respect, with *The Life and Adventures of Peter Porcupine, A Year's Residence in the United States, The Emigrant's Guide,* and *Advice to Young Men and (Incidentally) to Young Women.*

Rural Rides begins in September 1822: "This morning I set off in rather a drizzling rain, from Kensington, on horse-back, accompanied by my son James . . . my object was, not to see the inns and turnpike-roads, but to see the country; to see the farmers at work, and to see the labourers in the fields." This purpose was amply fulfilled. On each leg of each journey Cobbett described the soil, the crops, the condition of the farmers and of their laborers. He said in *Advice to Young Men* that "To come at the true history of a country you must read its laws; you must read books treating of its usages and customs in former times; you must particularly inform yourself of the prices of labour and of food." In *Rural Rides* Cobbett left, for those who want to come at the true history of England, an unequalled picture of the early nineteenth century, written by a man well qualified to observe and to comment. Yet it is not a dull collection of statistics. We read about the shepherd who knew he had thirteen score and five sheep, but was unable to say how many hundred; about the belief that "a great nut year [is] a great bastard year"; about the sign standing in a garden near a neat little box of a house, reading "PARADISE PLACE. *Spring guns and*

steel traps are set here." Small episodes yield the full savor of the country and its people. Many of the incidents involve Cobbett himself. In October 1825 he and his youngest son, Richard, rode their horses north from Winchester:

> After, however, crossing the village, and beginning again to ascend the downs, we came to a labourer's (once a farm house), where I asked the man, whether he had any bread and cheese, and was not a little pleased to hear him say "Yes". Then I asked him to give us a bit, protesting that we had not yet broken our fast. He answered in the affirmative, at once, though I did not talk of payment. His wife brought out the cut loaf, and a piece of Wiltshire cheese, and I took them in hand, gave Richard a good hunch, and took another for myself. I verily believe, that all the pleasure of eating enjoyed by all the feeders in London in a whole year, does not equal that which we enjoyed in gnawing this bread and cheese, as we rode over this cold down, whip and bridle-reins in one hand, and the hunch in the other. Richard, who was purse bearer, gave the woman, by my direction, about enough to buy two quartern loaves; for she told me, that they had to buy their bread at the mill, not being able to bake themselves for want of fuel.

Fortunately for us, Cobbett did not stick precisely to his objective of seeing the country, the farmers, and the laborers. Inevitably, there is something that sets him off on a digression relating to one of his favorite topics: himself, his grievances, his theories, and his crotchets. A small boy wearing a smock frock causes him to recall his own childhood; a plantation of scotch firs and oaks reminds him of the superiority of locust trees; an eighty-year-old laborer cutting grass evokes Cobbett's self-satisfied comment that the mower does not know how to hold the scythe properly. Cobbett's long memory for his grievances produced remarks on the 1810 trial for libel, the suspension of habeas corpus in 1817, the Coventry election of 1820—even on the villainy of Judge McKean that had occurred a quarter century before.

Many of the apparent digressions were not that at all; almost all of them relate to subjects which had an impact on the farmers and their workers; subjects such as the enclosures, the game laws, the tithes, the salt tax—a cruel burden to those whose only meat was bacon cured with salt. When Matthew Arnold said that "Cobbett's politics were at bottom always governed by one master-thought—the thought of the evil condition of the English labourer," he was too restrictive. Not simply Cobbett's *politics,* but his idiosyncratic views of social, economic, and religious issues were so governed. He hated the methodists because they taught the poor to be satisfied with their lot in this life, issuing "nonsensical little books . . . to make you believe that it is necessary for you to be starved to death in order to ensure you a place in heaven after you are dead." He hated the middlemen who did not increase the quantity or quality of goods produced, but added to the cost of articles purchased by the working man. Much better than the village stores were the markets and fairs of olden times which brought the producer and consumer face to face without a burdensome intermediary. His dislike of the quakers and Jews stemmed from this objection to nonproducers. The quakers were forestallers, buying from the farmers and holding to sell at the most advantageous prices; they were "jews in grain," and "worse than the Jews." Both quakers and Jews were jobbers and money-lenders. In his campaign against unlawfully charged turn-pike tolls, Cobbett discovered that many of the turnpikes around London were farmed by Jews. The word "Jews" as used by Cobbett often referred to those engaged in occupations similar to those of Jews: he spoke of jobbers and money-lenders as "Jews or Jewish Christians," or "Jews and Jew-like Christians." The quakers were "broad-brimmed Jews" or "buttonless Jews." Paper money was a "Scotch, Jew, Quaker trap." Cobbett resented Ricardo's fortune derived from "watching a turn in the market," since the half million gained by Ricardo had to come out of the pockets of those doing productive work. He had no dislike of quakers so long as they were engaged in some productive activity. The quakers of Pennsylvania, mostly farmers, were "the best people in the world." His dislike of Jews was more complicated: It was partly because of occupation, partly because they were "foreigners," and partly because of their blasphemy against Christianity. He specifically disclaimed any intention that the Jews be persecuted, but they were not to be encouraged either, as to do so would "join in the blasphemy."

Cobbett thought that the potato was less nourishing and more expensive than bread, making elaborate computations to show that this was so. However, his principal objection to the potato was based on an issue of human dignity. The English farm worker for generations had been accustomed to eat bread as the chief item of his diet, supplemented, when available, by cheese or bacon. The potato in most English farming communities was boiled up to feed pigs. It was an affront to the laborer to be asked to eat pig food, "and bad pig meat too." The Irish custom of raking potatoes out of the coals and eating them with the fingers without utensils was especially degrading. Cobbett's inveterate habit of gross exaggeration, plus his sense of humor, produced statements like this:

> A potato is the worst of all things for man. There needs nothing more to inflict scrofula on a whole nation. It distends the stomach, it swells the heels, and enfeebles the mind. I have no doubt, that a whole people would become ideots in time by feeding *solely* upon potatoes. Like other vegetables, this root, in moderate quantity, is well enough in the way of sauce; but, as the main article of the meal, as the joint to dine on, it is monstrous, or, rather beastly, to think of it.

Another of Cobbett's crotchets that repeatedly appeared in *Rural Rides,* and was only partially explained there, was his view that the population of England was declining, rather than increasing. Everywhere he travelled, he observed large churches and decaying villages. The church at Old Romney, for example, could hold 1,500 persons, and there were only twenty-two or twenty-three houses remaining in the parish. The first census in Britain was taken in 1801. Cobbett was able to point out what he thought were discrepancies between this data and that produced at subsequent ten-year intervals. He had other reasons to disbelieve the objectivity of government reporting, and thought that the claimed increases were part of a propaganda campaign to prove that prosperity existed at a time when the poor of England were suffering great privation. He also suspected that the figures were for the purpose of supporting the claimed need, by Malthus and others, for population control among those receiving parish aid. The "main drift of these writings is to impute all these [the miseries of the country] to the people themselves and not to their rulers; and, at the same time, to find an apology for the rich in suffering the poor to be reduced to starvation." No one suggested controlling the breeding of the clergy, the sinecurists, and the "dead-weight," all nonproductive classes supported by public money. "It is the *working* population, those who raise the food and the clothing, that he [Malthus] and Scarlett want to put a stop to the breeding of!"

Cobbett's dislike of London, the "wen," was partly because of the noise, smoke, and crime of the city, but to a greater extent because it represented a parasite whose swelling was at the expense of the impoverished country people. The wen was the residence of the nonproductive class made up of tax-eaters, sinecurists, deadweights, middlemen, "jobbers and Jews"—all depending for their income on the rest of the population and eating the food that had been taken away from the communities where it had been grown: "go to the *villages,*" Cobbett wrote in an open letter to Canning, "and see the misery of the labourers; see their misery, compared to the happy state in which they lived before the swellings out of this corrupt and all devouring wen."

Rural Rides concentrated on one principal aspect of the problem of the laborer: it revealed his poverty, and the reasons for it as seen by Cobbett. Heavy taxes and paper money were at the root, abetted by such ancillary evils as the enclosures, the game laws, the Speenhamland system. The other principal aspect of the laborer's problem with which Cobbett was concerned was the inadequacy of payments under the poor law to those in distress, and the imminent danger that such payments might be further reduced or even eliminated. The complaints of those paying poor rates were made respectable by Malthus's assertion that the poor laws only tended to defeat their own purpose by creating more poverty. Legislation consistent with this view was introduced in parliament by William Sturges Bourne and James Scarlett. The premise underlying Malthus's proposals was his belief that the poor had no right to relief. In Malthus's own words, a laborer out of work "has no claim of right on society for the smallest portion of food," and "the laws of nature, which are the laws of God, had doomed him and his family to suffer for disobeying their repeated admonitions"—that is, had doomed them to starve. It was to this premise that Cobbett directed his attack in two other works: *A History of the Protestant "Reformation"* and the *Poor Man's Friend.* The *History* was originally published in parts from 1824 to 1826, and the *Poor Man's Friend* was published in

1826, while Cobbett was still engaged in the journeys described in *Rural Rides.* Stated briefly, Cobbett argued that the laws of nature ("the principles of society") demand that each person be provided with the necessities of life; that before the Reformation this provision was made by the church, which was required to set aside a third of its revenue for the benefit of the poor and sick; that after the Reformation (the church property having been appropriated by the king and his rich friends), provision for the impoverished was made by the poor law statute enacted during the reign of Queen Elizabeth I; and that, in the event that the poor were not thereby provided with the necessaries of life, they had the right to be maintained "out of the lands, or other property, of the rich." It was left to Cobbett's speeches, the *Political Register,* and a later book, *Cobbett's Legacy to Labourers* (1835), to declare openly what was so obviously implied:

> Well, then, what is the conclusion to which we come at last? Why, that the labourers have a right to subsistence out of the land, in all cases of inability to labour; that all those who are able to labour have a right to subsistence out of the land, in exchange for their labour; and that, if the holders of the land will not give them subsistence, in exchange for their labour, they have a right to the land itself. Thus we come to the conclusion, that, if these new, inhuman and diabolical doctrines were acted upon, instead of giving that "security to property," which is their pretence, there would be an end of all respect for, and of all right to, property of every description!

A History of the Protestant "Reformation", using materials derived from a recent book written by the English historian John Lingard, was almost wholly devoted to a demonstration that the so-called Reformation was engendered in the "beastly lust" of Henry VIII and forced on an unwilling people by acts of unprecedented ferocity and greed sanctioned by that monarch and his protestant successors, and that it was not a reformation at all, but a "devastation." ". . . it is my chief business," Cobbett declared, "to show that this devastation impoverished and degraded the main body of the people." Cobbett's enthusiasm for the task led him into a much wider range of controversial subjects relating to the history of the English church (and the sex life of the "virgin queen") than would have been necessary if he had confined himself to proving his ultimate conclusion. The story that he unfolded made the catholic position—"the religion of our forefathers"—far more appealing than most protestants liked to admit. Because of this, the book proved to be the most explosive of all Cobbett's works. It was execrated by church of England clergymen. It was extolled by the Roman catholics. "I have published a book that has exceeded all others in circulation, the Bible only excepted," declared Cobbett. By 1828 the total sale of the sixteen separate numbers, published in book form beginning in 1826, had attained 700,000. This did not include those printed in Ireland, America, France, Spain, Switzerland, Italy, Portugal, Romania, Germany, Holland, Australia, and Venezuela. In America the sale was said to exceed 100,000. In Paris there were "three different booksellers selling three different translations." A stream of irate replies flowed from the printing presses, and Cobbett was forced to defend himself from the charge that he had become a convert to Rome. It is a mere quibble to contend, as some have done, that Cobbett's polemic was erroneous in detail and gave an exaggerated account of the Reformation. If Cobbett too warmly urged that everything in the old religion had been good and that the change was made solely for sordid reasons, this was only a fair counterbalance to three centuries of erroneous and exaggerated propaganda to the opposite effect. John Ruskin put it nicely: "the sum of my forty-four years of thinking on the matter, from an entirely outside standpoint—as nearly as possible that of a Turk—has led me to agree with Cobbett in all his main ideas, and there is no question whatever, that Protestant writers are, as a rule, ignorant and false in what they say of Catholics—while Catholic writers are as a rule both well-informed and fair."

As might be expected, Cobbett revelled in the controversy he had provoked: He enjoyed anything that might be upsetting to the contemporary clergy of the church of England, who often lived in unChristian splendor, rendered little service, and supported the oppressive measures of the establishment; he disliked the arrogance of the rich whig families who had been among the principal beneficiaries of the Reformation; he had always contended that the poor men of England had been better off in ancient times than they were in the nineteenth century; and he had, for years, been a strong advocate of catholic emancipation. Perhaps, too, the implication that the English might do well to return to catholicism was a humorous reply to Wilberforce's irrational belief that the Irish could be converted to protestantism.

It is amazing, after surveying the mountainous output of writing, to find the quality as good as it is. There are dull passages, plenty of them; there are repetitions, too many of them. But on average the quality was high. Southey's comment that "there never was a better or more forcible writer" is demonstrated by the extent and character of Cobbett's readership. No journalist ever attained such eminence. He was read by all his contemporaries: by the prime ministers of England, by the presidents of the United States, by Napoleon and Talleyrand. As Cobbett himself said, "there is no piece of earth which has any thing worthy of a government, where the *Register* is not read, and that too, by persons composing the government. He was read, during the French wars, on ships at sea and in army mess halls. He was read by Carlyle and Macaulay; by Byron, Shelley, Lamb, Coleridge, Wordsworth, Southey, Hazlitt, Peacock, Tom Moore, Leigh Hunt, Matthew Arnold; by Philip Freneau, Emerson, and James Fenimore Cooper; by the German poet Heine; by Ricardo, Malthus, Bentham, James Mill, John Stuart Mill, and Karl Marx. He is mentioned in novels by George Borrow, George Eliot, and Benjamin Disraeli. He was caricatured by Gillray, Cruikshank, and Doyle. He was the subject of a parody—along with Coleridge, Byron, Sir Walter Scott, and other literary luminaries of the day—in *Rejected Addresses* (1812) by James and Horace Smith, a work that was reprinted some twenty or thirty times, and he was the subject of an ode in the Smiths' *Horace in London* (1813); he was included with a similarly distinguished group in another volume of parodies called *Rejected Articles* (1826) by P. G. Patmore. The appeal of Cobbett's writing to his contemporaries was described by one of them, Sir Henry Lytton Bulwer:

> Whatever a man's talents, whatever a man's opinions, he sought the **Register** on the day of its appearance with eagerness, and read it with amusement, partly, perhaps, if De la Rochefoucauld is right, because, whatever his party, he was sure to see his friends abused. But partly also because he was certain to find, amidst a great many lies and abundance of impudence, some felicitous nickname, some excellent piece of practical-looking argument, some capital expressions, and very often some marvellously-fine writing, all the finer for being carelessly fine, and exhibiting whatever figure or sentiment it set forth in the simplest as well as the most striking dress.

Lies? That there were occasional lies cannot be doubted. Misstatements of fact are inevitable even in a modern newspaper with its superior information-gathering services. And in Cobbett's case his radical opinions and hyperbole were readily translated into lies by his opponents.

Cobbett's hope that the "whole world" would want to read his writing was largely realized. But despite the large numbers sold of many of his books, Cobbett was unable to release himself, except for occasional sunny intervals, from the financial straits that had become a way of life. He seems to have regularly underpriced his publications to get the maximum number of readers, and, to get the unit cost down to where he could justify the low price, frequently ordered more copies than he was able to sell expeditiously, leaving him with a large inventory of unrealizable assets. Two of the bestsellers, **Cottage Economy** and the **Sermons,** were issued in parts at threepence a number, and in bound volumes at only sixpence more than the price of the separate issues. When **Cottage Economy** was enlarged to include instructions on the production of the straw plait, Cobbett stated: "The book is nearly double the bulk that it was at first: but I have never altered the price of it, because I would do nothing to put it beyond the reach of poor people, for whose benefit it was written." The **Poor Man's Friend** was sold at twopence a part; the five parts when bound were offered at a shilling. "This is not the way to get money," wrote Cobbett, "but my object was to put this little book within the reach of almost every body." On occasion his books were pirated and he received nothing for them. When this happened to **The American Gardener,** Cobbett's response was to castigate the pirate (a Baltimore printer) for omitting the dedication to Mrs. Tredwell, Cobbett's neighbor on Long Island. Although we lack precise figures for his publishing business, it is plain that the profits were not enough to support his family and carry on his extraneous ventures. In 1827 we find Cobbett sending John Dean, in charge of the shop in Fleet Street, a message of the sort he once sent to John Wright: "The sum of money that I wrote to you about I *must have,* on the 19th instant. Whether it be yours or mine, it signifies not: that sum I must have, and on that day, which is this day week." As

early as 1828 Cobbett was once again compelled to borrow money. And there is a letter from John Cobbett to his father in 1832 urging him to reduce the printing order for the French—English dictionary. He was fearful of "having all this immense stock on our hands . . . when it . . . is not without difficulty that I can meet all the bills now out."

Money, however, was never a major consideration with Cobbett. His passion was for something more honorable or, at least, more difficult to attain. He craved a heroic role in serving the world, and in particular, that part of the world which few cared to serve: the poor and the friendless. The fact that few cared to assume this burden and that it was the heaviest and most difficult of all burdens that could be assumed only made the cause more attractive to him. The reward he sought for this service was not worldly goods, as we have seen; nor was it mere inner satisfaction or recognition in heaven. He openly and unashamedly declared that what he wanted was "fame." "I care not for their money or their estates," he once said of the aristocracy, "but I care for my fame, and that I will not fail to secure."

Although this avowal was made when Cobbett was about sixty years old, the strong aggressive component in his nature, which accounted for his constant striving for superiority, had been manifest since childhood. Later, when entered upon his career, he quickly proved his superiority as a soldier, rising from private to sergeant major in three years and establishing himself, in the process, as a dominant force in the regiment, even among the officers. He just as rapidly proved his superiority as a writer, first in America and then in England. But he was not content to be a superior soldier, or a superior writer; he insisted on his superiority as a husband, as a father, as an employer, as a farmer, as an economist, as a teacher, as a . . . whatever role he was playing at the moment. The introduction of a better fireplace or domestic straw plait, or a demonstration of how the laws should be enforced against wrongdoers, were means of proving his superiority in the same way as were the introduction of a better tree or a better apple or a better method of cultivating turnips, or a sounder system of currency.

This enormous aggressive force had been met, almost at the outset of Cobbett's career, by the first of a series of frustrations that continued for the next twenty-five years. His effort to expose the corruption that existed in the army forced him to flee from England in 1792. His attacks on Rush's false cure for yellow fever stripped him of his earnings and drove him back to England in 1800. His condemnation of flogging put him in prison from 1810 to 1812. His efforts to relieve the distresses of the poor people of England through reform of a corrupt government led to another exile from 1817 to 1819. Not only were good deeds met with punishment, but the punishment was accompanied by vilification from the press and from the establishment to which the press pandered. The vilification did not stop with known facts; outright falsehoods were circulated. While he was in America, the *Courier,* a ministerial paper, claimed that Cobbett had been fined $700 for writing against the American govern-ment. This was a complete fabrication; there had never even been a charge lodged against him. Charles Dundas, member of parliament for Berkshire and cousin of Lord Melville, declared that Cobbett had been an associate of Arthur Thistlewood, who had been hanged for high trea-son in 1820, whereas Cobbett had never seen or corre-sponded with Thistlewood. The *New Times* and *Courier* falsely claimed that Cobbett, in buying a house, had paid the "required premium of £500 by a check on the Cath-olic Association"—for which, as Cobbett pointed out, "there is not even the shadow of a pretence." In 1822 *The Times* claimed that Cobbett was in the pay of the English treasury! In 1823 the whig papers implied that Cobbett was in the pay of the Bourbon government of France. The allegation that Cobbett had been a British-paid spy in America prior to 1800 and had subsequently been dis-missed from that service was a constantly renewed false-hood. The great *Times*, the newspaper that declared on Cobbett's death that he was "in some respects a more extraordinary Englishman than any other of his time," had hardly a civil word to say of him while he was living. The general view taken by that paper and the balance of the "respectable" press, as well as by most of the gentle-men in and out of parliament, was that Cobbett was some kind of renegade, an outlaw, a traitor, a blackguard, a mountebank, whose sole motivation was in the large profits he allegedly derived from his activities.

Cobbett's literary efforts were met by a conspiracy of silence among the leading contemporary newspapers and journals. Neither his *History of the Protestant "Reforma-tion,"* which had an unparalleled sale throughout the western world, nor any of the many other successful books published by him, was ever noticed by a paper or journal, with the single exception of the enthusiastic review of *Cottage Economy* by the *Edinburgh Review*. And his frus-trations took one further form: At the same time as he was being denied merit for the views espoused in his writings, these views, often only slightly disguised, fre-quently reappeared in the rival press, on the floor of par-liament, and in the mouths of speakers at public meet-ings. The snobbery of the period was reluctant to admit much merit in the ideas of a humbly born, uneducated, renegade newspaper editor. William Carpenter, radical reformer and publisher of *Political Letters and Pamphlets,* spoke of the surprising extent to which Cobbett's "views and arguments are made use of by men who never think of avowing to whom they are indebted for their borrowed plumes." William Smart, no admirer of Cobbett, wrote: "it is impossible not to see that his main ideas were taken, without acknowledgement as he complained, by politi-cians and statesmen, as well as by farmers and landown-ers." The high tory newspaper, the *Standard,* claimed that speeches of Grey, Brougham, Durham, Graham, and Macaulay, as well as opinions expressed in *The Times* "and other more respectable journals," were derived from Cobbett's writings.

It comes as no surprise, therefore, that when Cobbett later asserted: "I wrote for fame," he immediately added "and was urged forward by ill-treatment and by the desire to triumph over my enemies." The 1810 libel prosecution, in particular, was never far from his thoughts. Mentioned again and again in his writings, often when its relevance is difficult to detect, it became Cobbett's hair shirt. He could not clear his mind of the unfairness of being sent to jail like a common criminal for having condemned the flogging of young boys in the militia who had complained of not being paid what the law required. This incident had taken him away from his family and from the farm that he loved nearly as much as his family, and had precipi-tated the financial distress from which he had never re-covered. No effort was made by the government to right the wrong, even after protests against flogging had be-come an accepted part of the scene and were no longer prosecuted. Attempts made by Cobbett in 1828 and again in 1832 to have the £1,000 fine remitted, which might have constituted a token admission that a wrong had been done, were peremptorily rejected. After being turned down in 1828, Cobbett wrote: "I had not forgotten, nor have I yet forgotten, nor shall I ever forget or forgive, the treat-ment which I have received from persons in power in England. But, they are *not England;* they are not *my country;* my country is unhappy, in misery, sinking in character, and it is my duty to endeavour to restore her to her former state . . . but above all things, it is my duty . . . to better the lot of the labouring classes." The injustice from which Cobbett personally suffered he equated with the injustices suffered by the entire class from which he had sprung. They did the work and received a niggardly share of the benefits. Cobbett, harried and persecuted for his efforts to serve the public, saw liberal rewards heaped on those who, in his eyes at least, had added nothing to the well-being of the country.

Cobbett's response to these repeated rebuffs took two predictable courses: praise of himself and abuse of others. Everything Cobbett did, from the most simple to the most elaborate, was heralded by him as of unique importance. "So help me God, I would rather see a full-sized ripe apple from one of these graffs than I would see myself made a knight of the Garter." Indian corn was "the great-est blessing that God gave to man." It was not mere chance that it had been Cobbett, of all the inhabitants of England, who was responsible for this boon: "The truth is, that I know how to make things move. Another man might have written about the thing to all eternity; and his writing might be better than mine; but very few men could, like me, have made the thing move." And so it went. "I have done a great many wonderful things . . . my name will live many score years after me." "When I am asked what books a young man or young woman ought to read, I always answer: Let him or her read all the books that I have written." "Ten thousand times my ears have been saluted, from the lips of men that I have never seen be-fore . . . 'Here's the cleverest man in England'."

To the cries of "egotism" that met this type of effusion Cobbett responded, "mock-modesty . . . is, in fact, only another term for hypocrisy." "A great deal of what passes for 'modesty' ought to pass for cowardice or servility." Cobbett was only saying out loud what "more civilized" men keep to themselves, as we see in the conduct of the small child who is not old enough to have been inhibited by social convention. Cobbett made no secret that he thought himself superior to the public figures of his day. When George Canning became minister for foreign affairs and leader of the House of Commons on Castlereagh's death in 1822, he was taken "regularly to school" by Cobbett in a series of six articles. It was not presumptuous of Cobbett to instruct Canning, because "as to all the chief matters appertaining to your office, I have greater ability than you." And Cobbett proceeded to demonstrate this assertion: Cobbett had more accurately predicted the course of events in the past; Cobbett was Canning's literary superior; Cobbett could write and speak French better than Canning "and, perhaps, better even than any of your interpreters"; Cobbett knew the principles and practice of public law (he had translated Martens's *Law of Nations*) as well as Canning and could write on them more forcibly than Canning; and so on—an extraordinary exercise. Shocking? But who is such a hypocrite as to assert that he has never had similar thoughts in the privacy of his bedroom?

As time passed and frustrations increased, Cobbett's ambition mounted. The fame that Cobbett had in mind was not merely public recognition that he was industrious, virtuous, and able. It was that, but much more besides. He wanted to be called by the nation to a place of power from which he could relieve the poor and administer justice. He was grossly offended by a statement of Castlereagh in 1817 that the petitions for reform that were pouring into parliament were due to "the instigations of men, who, without any pretensions, were aspiring to high office." Cobbett testily replied that while Castlereagh might think he had no pretensions, "there are hundreds of thousands of persons, and sensible persons too, in this kingdom, who think I have." In 1825 Cobbett predicted that the people would soon be saying "how unfortunate for us that Mr. Cobbett had not been the minister of England twenty years ago." Two years later, when it was rumored that Lord Goderich would be succeeded as prime minister by Dudley Ryder (the rumor was wrong; Wellington won the post), Cobbett offered himself in an open letter to the king: "there is not one man in Your Majesty's dominions, who will not unhesitatingly declare, that I am a thousand times as fit to be your minister as he is, and that I am, at this moment, more fit for that office than any other man in the kingdom." Although the offer as worded must be regarded as a bit of Cobbettian humor, he certainly thought himself fully capable of filling the office.

It would hardly be urged that all the abuse that flowed from Cobbett's pen was attributable to the conduct of his adversaries. Much of it was a part of his natural aggression and came effortlessly, almost unconsciously. A man so constituted needed enemies. When accused of having unfairly assaulted others, he declared: "that which is true, though it may be seriously censorious, can never be called abusive." Seriously censorious, indeed, were some of the terms Cobbett applied from time to time to whoever might be his target at the moment. Canning was an "impudent mountebank," a "jack-pudding," a "loathsome dish." Burdett was a "base paltroon." Castlereagh was a "shal-

low pated ass." Liverpool was a "pick-nose wiseacre." Brougham was "all jaw and no judgment." Wilberforce was "the prince of hypocrites." Bentham was "Old Jerry the Rump Cock." These are only the briefest sample of the hundreds of epithets which Cobbett, presumably, thought not abusive. Nor was he a believer in *de mortuis nil nisi bonum:* it "is a foolish maxim that says we are not to speak evil of the dead: it is the maxim of knaves imposed on fools. We are to say nothing but the truth of the dead, and the same rule we ought to observe towards the living." When the recently dead Duke of York, a notorious lecher and coward, was portrayed as a saint and hero by the London newspapers, Cobbett courageously set forth the true facts. "If these praises of the Duke of York be suffered to pass without comment, who shall say that a young man will be wrong if he endeavour, or, permit himself to imitate the life and actions of the Duke of York?" This worshipper of the truth also believed that calling attention to the faults of his friends was as essential as pointing out the virtues of his enemies. "I like the Americans very much; and that, if there were no other, would be a reason for my not hiding their faults." Thus, among his friends, he publicly criticized William Windham for his opposition to a bill allowing distillers to use sugar in place of grain; Lord Cochrane for his stock dealings; Lord Folkestone for his refusal to submit a petition of Cobbett's to the House of Commons (and much more besides); Daniel O'Connell for his mishandling of the Catholic Emancipation Bill in 1825. He occasionally found good things to say about those he did not agree with: Sir Francis Burdett was "an English gentleman . . . wholly beyond the reach of everything that leads to dirty compromises, and of talent . . . equal to this or to any other undertaking." Peel "appears to me to have a solider head than any minister that I have ever yet seen in power." Canning was "a correct, a clear and elegant writer; an acute reasoner; has, in speaking, a perfect command of words, and may be said to be truly eloquent." Wellington was better fitted for prime minister than "any one of the nine who have gone before him." George III, despite his many faults, was no hypocrite.

The secret of this apparent evenhandedness among friends and foes was that Cobbett was attached to causes, not to men. He commended acts that were consistent with the position he espoused, and attacked those he thought were inconsistent with it. He did not hesitate to attack this week a man he had applauded the week before, and vice versa. In this respect he was the opposite of Wilberforce, who sided first with Pitt, then with Perceval, then with Liverpool and his henchmen Sidmouth and Castlereagh—and thus was guilty of supporting one piece of oppressive legislation after another by smugly reposing his confidence in whoever was the prime minister. Cobbett, in contrast, was rarely motivated by personal relationships. He had fixed notions of what was right and wrong, and these rather than friendship governed his conduct. His son James (making notes in preparation for a biography of his father, which he barely started) wrote:

> He had but little individual attachment. Liked people's company; & they liked his (when he was agreeable).

But he formed very little of *friendship*. And wd. break off with any one, however old an acquaintance, on any affront, or being crossed in his will.

In **Rural Rides** . . . he speaks of his "ardent friendship and not less ardent enmity." But he was not steady or constant in either; excepting that, as to the enmity, *public* causes were continually arising to keep the enmity renewed, or to revive it . . . He was engrossed with the effect he sought to produce on society at large. So that, after all, there was with him but little banding together with others for a common end, as with many men inspired by the "patriotic" sentiment. He might be sd. to *use* others, rather than to act with them.

James, born in 1803, could have had little recollection of his father before the harrowing Newgate experience of 1810-12, when Cobbett was nearly fifty years old; hence, James's comments cannot be applied unqualifiedly to the earlier years of Cobbett's life, when he seems to have had a fair number of real friends. Cobbett would have claimed that he had a great many friends in his later years; but most of those he included in that category were more properly "devoted admirers": They were delighted to entertain the great man as a guest in their homes or to do the various favors he from time to time asked of them. There rarely was any two-way flow of respect and affection that is characteristic of typical friendships. Cobbett was oblivious of this: "as to my family and friends, I leave them to say whether there is the company of any person on earth, in which they delight more than they do in mine. I do not believe, that I have experienced the breaking off of friendship with ten persons in the whole course of my life. . . . Why the devil then, am I to suppose myself unamiable?" Cobbett had answered his own question several months earlier when he wrote: "It is, in short, the caring nothing for any body, that has enabled me to obtain something like justice for myself."

That the later Cobbett seldom made an effort to ingratiate himself is reflected in his relations with Francis Douce, former keeper of manuscripts in the British Museum and Cobbett's neighbor in Kensington. To Douce, just around the corner in Kensington Square, Cobbett sent a letter via one of his daughters, complaining that slugs and snails from Douce's garden were invading Cobbett's garden and feeding on his vegetables. Was he joking, or was he serious?—Douce was unable to decide, but his reply covered both eventualities. He pointed out to Cobbett that his own cabbages had been ravaged by "the legions of vermin in question from your premises," while his nerves were being impaired by the howling of Cobbett's dogs, "an infliction worse than the pains of purgatory." To cite another instance, Cobbett told, with obvious amusement, an account of a Scotch pedlar on Long Island,

who, on finding my doors wide open on a summer's day, walked into the hall, and then into the parlour where I was sitting, and, turning round at the end of the table, placed, without saying a word, his pack upon it, pulling his arms out of the straps of the pack, which I, with reciprocal taciturnity, took hold of and tossed

out of the window, which, being a free country, was standing wide open, as it were, on purpose to admit of the ejectment. It was not till after this that the Scotchman spoke, which he did in a manner that would certainly have procured him the honour of following the pack, if he had not, upon due notice given, taken the more circuitous route by the door.

No further examples are necessary to show why Cobbett stood alone in the world in his battle for what he thought right. When he was gently chided for being bitter, unforgiving, and uncompromising, he asserted that the large numbers of persons who composed his following, and particularly the new generation of young men who had begun to make their appearance on the political scene in the late 1820s, "are bound to me, because I am *bitter;* because I am *unforgiving;* because I am *uncompromising* with what they deem would be hostile to them as well as myself."

Daniel Green   (essay date 1983)

SOURCE: "The Climactic Years," in *Great Cobbett: The Noblest Agitator,* 1983. Reprint by Oxford University Press, Inc., 1985, pp. 423-54.

[*In the following excerpt, Green discusses Cobbett's skill as a writer and the characteristics of his thought, touching on a wide range of Cobbett's writings.*]

Because Cobbett's most enduring achievement was to turn author at a comparatively late stage in his career, it is, in the end, not his politics nor his journalism nor even his character that we have to examine, but his books. There is more of the real William Cobbett in them than there was in the ageing, failing and increasingly erratic man who finally achieved what contemporaries considered to be his greatest political success at a time when his fortunes and his happiness had most completely failed. His journalism, to a certain extent, reflected both his successes and his failures, but neither, it would seem, influenced his books. They, since he was essentially an Arcadian, reflect the ideal rather than the actual; and they show few or no signs of deterioration.

Between 1818, when he first turned author proper, and 1833, when the **Northern Tour** was published, he produced over twenty works that can properly be described as books rather than pamphlets. Of these, no fewer than six have survived as minor classics. Those critics who have thought to see a falling-off in his writing towards the end have to be reminded that **Advice to Young Men** was written in 1829 and the **Northern Tour** in 1832. G. D. H. Cole argued that this last failed to equal the earlier **Rides,** being too shrilly polemical. It was, indeed, polemical and contained even more puffs for himself, in the shape of Congratulatory Addresses, than usual. On the other hand, he had converted what had been thought of as a venture into hostile territory into a triumphal progression, and he was entitled to proclaim that fact to his enemies. His descriptions of the Scottish scene, whether

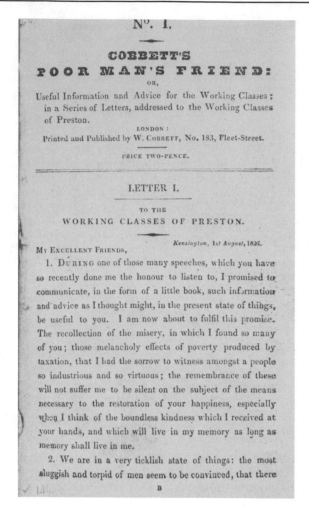

Title page of Cobbett's Poor Man's Friend, *a work called by its author "the most learned book that I ever wrote."*

making and selling of books. These would include his *Spelling-Book,* the *Geographical Dictionary of England and Wales* and *A New French and English Dictionary.* What it did include is best left to Cobbett to describe:

> When I am asked what books a young man or young woman ought to read, I always answer, Let him or her read *all that I have written.* This does, it will doubtless be said, *smell of the shop.* No matter. It is what I recommended; and experience has taught me that it is my duty to give that recommendation. I am speaking here of books other than THE REGISTER; and even these, that I call my LIBRARY, consist of *twenty-six* distinct books; two of them being TRANSLATIONS; *six* of them being written BY MY SONS; *one* (TULL'S HUSBANDRY) revised and edited, and one published by me and written by the Rev. Mr. O'CALLAGHAN, a most virtuous Catholic Priest. I divide these books into classes, as follows. 1. Books for TEACHING LANGUAGES; 2. On DOMESTIC MANAGEMENT AND DUTIES; 3. RURAL AFFAIRS; 4. On THE MANAGEMENT OF NATIONAL AFFAIRS; 5. HISTORY; 6. TRAVELS; 7. LAWS; 8. MISCELLANEOUS POLITICS. Here is a great variety of subjects; and all of them very *dry*; nevertheless the manner of treating them is, in general, such as to induce the reader to *go through the book,* when he once has begun it. . . .

In the list that followed, the puffs he attached to each title are not without interest. Of his *English Grammar:* "This is a book of *principles* clearly laid down; and when once these are got into the mind they never quit it." Of his *French Grammar:* "More young men have, I dare say, learned French from it, than from all the other books that have been published in English for the last fifty years." Of *Cobbett's Sermons:* "More of these Sermons have been *sold* than of the Sermons of all the Church-parsons put together since mine were published." Of *Rural Rides:* "If the members of the Government had *read* these Rides, only just *read* them, last year, when they were collected and printed in a volume, they *could not have helped* fore-seeing all the violences that have now taken place, and especially *in these very counties;* and foreseeing them, they must have been devils in reality, if they had not done something to prevent them." Of *Cobbett's Poor Man's Friend:* "This is my *favourite* work. I bestowed more labour upon it than upon any large volume that I ever wrote."

This somewhat unusual advertisement ended in the following way: "This is the Library that I have *created.* It really makes a tolerable *shelf of books;* a man who understands the contents of which may be deemed a man of great information. In about every one of these works I have pleaded the cause of the *working people,* and I shall now see that cause triumph, in spite of all that can be done to prevent it." This political note was followed by a prudently commercial one. "N.B. A whole *set* of these books at the above prices amounts to 7£.0s.2d.; but if a whole set be taken together, the price is 6£. And here is a stock of knowledge sufficient for any young man in the world."

Cobbett not only enjoyed the advantage of being able, as a publisher, to recommend himself as an author. He could

in the Lothians or on the banks of the Clyde, were as fresh and as vivid as any of his other pieces of descriptive writing. Nor had he become any less perceptive: his accounts of both life and his two *Letters to the Chopsticks* are, in some respects, better than any other of his many socio-political analyses of rural life amongst the poor. The best of him in these last years was contained in his books rather than in his politics.

As his titles accumulated, advertisements for what was called *The Cobbett-Library* began to appear in the *Register* and various others of Cobbett's publications. What Cobbett himself thought of his 'Library' and how he divided it into its various subjects provides, perhaps, the only *catalogue raisonné* that is needed. The advertisement that follows was included in Cobbett's *Two-Penny Trash* of 1 July 1831. It does not, therefore, include later works, such as *Cobbett's Tour in Scotland,* his *Life of Andrew Jackson,* his *Manchester Lectures* or his *Lectures on the French and Belgian Revolutions*. It also omits the obvious pot-boilers he published at the end of his career in a desperate attempt to raise money by the also, as a newspaper proprietor, advertise both publisher and author for nothing. But what modern publisher would have the honesty to admit that all the books he offered dealt with "dry" subjects? And for how many of his authors could he honestly claim the ability to make "dry" subjects readable?

Indeed Cobbett's books, or at the least large parts of them, are still readable, which is somewhat remarkable considering the subjects he chose and the fact that it was always his purpose to be didactic, moralistic or politically partisan. It is not thus that a modern bestseller is produced. And yet Cobbett's books were, and to a limited extent still are, bestsellers. Contemporary readers can still, if they persevere, find in each one of them at least some moments of sudden and unexpected delight. There will, of course, be *longueurs* arising from what Hazlitt described as Cobbett's "damnable habit of iteration". There will be political arguments lost or won so long ago that they are now interesting only to historians. There will be scurrilous attacks on people long dead and references to scandals long forgotten that will have to be explained to become amusing.

Yet one cannot go far in any of his books without coming across a fine piece of descriptive writing or a passage in which something complicated has been so lucidly and simply laid out that his interpretation of it seems both convincing and elegant. Every now and again, and generally when it is least expected, his sense of humour, which was both sly and savage, will surface. His polemics always owe something to his appreciation of all that is ridiculous in a situation or an individual and it is often when he is at his most solemn that something truly comical emerges. His overstocked and underdisciplined mind leads him off into digressions that generally seem more interesting than anything he digressed from. When the reader has resigned himself to the tedium of one of his prolonged political or economic diatribes he will suddenly be jolted into attention by a completely unexpected word or phrase which only on second thought seems apposite and difficult to better. If his language seems plainer than that of his contemporaries, his constructions are often daringly complicated, yet he generally emerges from them with both his meaning and his syntax intact. He is not a writer to be read rapidly or skippingly or the best of him, which is his ability to surprise his reader, will be lost.

A writer's skills can only be properly judged by the effect he has on his reader. Cobbett, by that criterion, was amongst the most skilful, for his works still produce the effects he intended. In another writer this would probably be attributed to his style, but we tend to take Cobbett's style somewhat for granted. This may be because his works have provided so much material for politicians, historians, and even biographers to work on that attention has always been focussed on what he had to say rather than on the manner in which he said it.

Hazlitt, that shrewd literary critic, refrained from analysing Cobbett's style, explaining that "He might be said to have the clearness of Swift, the naturalness of Defoe, the picturesque satirical description of Mandeville, if all such comparisons were not impertinent. A really great and original writer is like nobody but himself". He added, however, that Cobbett "speaks and thinks plain, broad, downright English", and that, perhaps, brought him halfway to the truth. Cobbett was, in fact, too complex a man to *think* "plain English", but he did *write* it. That in an age when most educated men had been brought up to believe that in order to write English well one must study and imitate the Romans, made him an original.

Such greatness as Cobbett had as a writer arose, however, out of his love of the English language which was, in its turn, the product of his early circumstances. As a self-educated man he had, in so far as that was possible, escaped the influences of a classical education. He had, instead, read a great deal of English literature and, if he had done so indiscriminately, his natural taste exposed him to the influences of the better rather than the lesser writers. Although in later years he turned ostentatiously Philistine and decried all novelists, most poets and all dramatists, his writings are full of quotations from and references to Shakespeare and Milton, Dryden and Pope, Fielding and Goldsmith, Wycherley and Congreve.

Even more important, he had turned himself into a more than competent grammarian and had become enough of an etymologist to be able to correct and rebuke his opponents whenever they used a word in a way which revealed that they were ignorant of its origins and true meaning. A man elects to educate himself in that manner only if he delights in words and language, and this Cobbett very obviously did. As for the way in which he made use of that language, it possibly owed something to the years he spent in the orderly room writing out regimental orders. That could have taught him the value of clarity and precision though it did not appear to have taught him anything about being concise.

But the easy, conversational style he eventually evolved was probably never consciously adopted but was rather an inevitable product of his politics. Once he had turned politician, whether as a Tory or a Radical, he saw himself as a demagogue, in the original meaning of that word, which the dictionary gives as "a leader of the people as against the other parties in the state". As Peter Porcupine, he set out to persuade ordinary Americans to abandon their almost traditional attachment to the French alliance. As a Radical, he attempted to persuade ordinary Englishmen to reject the political and economic system imposed on them by the Whigs as much as the Tories. In each case he opposed the Establishment and appealed to the commons.

Whoever appeals to the people must do so, if he is to succeed, in the demotic, or at least in something that resembles it, and if the appeal is a written one, it must come as close as the written language will allow to the spoken word. These were the effects Cobbett's conversational style allowed him to achieve. His more artless readers, at least, did not feel that they were reading, but were rather listening to someone who talked to, reasoned with and argued at them in a style they found congenial and in language they could comprehend. But if they were artless enough to believe that they were being addressed by some acquaintance from across a table, the man who created that illusion was far from artless. Indeed, more writing arts have to be deployed to sustain the conversational style than are used by those who, recognising the fundamental differences between the spoken and written languages, accept the limitations involved, even though these mean distancing themselves from their readers.

Cobbett accepted no such limitations, possibly because he had acquired sufficient skills to do otherwise. He could give to his writing some of the pace and rhythms of speech and was able to create the impression that his words came hot from his mouth instead of being prepared and meditated on before ever they were written. Some of this *trompe-l'oeil* effect was achieved through the constructions he used. He varied the length of his sentences so as to make them resemble the hesitations and overflowings of speech. Some were little more than ejaculations that concluded in an exclamation mark. Others seemed interminable and contained the explanations, recapitulations, parentheses and asides of the spoken language, which can never, by its nature, be as well-organised as the written one. The enthusiasm, passion and humour with which he wrote gave some of the spontaneity of speech to his work and, although he used words more exactly and more correctly than they are used in conversation, he seldom used ones that are not commonly used, or misused, when people speak to one another.

His punctuation, which he used in accordance with the old rules of grammar, that is to say immoderately, was an essential part of his style. Commas separated every clause, and this allowed him to construct sentences in which the clauses could accumulate without the thread being lost. He marched semi-colons, colons and exclamation marks across the page in much the same way as he had once marched soldiers across a barrack square and, perhaps another military touch, he numbered his paragraphs, which made for orderly reading but was typographically ugly.

He made lavish use of another typographical device which, because it is now seldom used, can be irritating. He scattered italics across every page in much the same way, and for much the same reason, as a composer places his markings over every few bars of his score. This was, once again, part of his conversational style. The italicised words marked the places where, if he had actually been talking, he would have raised his voice or have given a knowing wink or have banged his first on the table. Occasionally, when he wanted that bang to be particularly significant, he would substitute upper case for italics, whether it was in the middle of the sentence or not.

He had a remarkably quick eye for the ridiculous. Although it won him more readers than any other of his accomplishments, he was, in his later days, humorous almost in despite of himself. He was enormously proud of his powers of reasoning—which were always suspect—

but far less proud, by then, of his undoubted ability to inspire laughter. 'Who, besides myself,' he wrote in the *Register,* 'has, in our day, attempted to gain popularity by dint of fact and of argument, unmixed with anything to amuse the human mind? If, at any time, I have indulged in a sort of jest I have been almost ashamed of the momentary triumph thereby acquired.'

The Cobbett who wrote that passage had clearly lost the delight in humour that had once made Peter Porcupine so proud that he had 'endeavoured to make America laugh'. For the older man, humour had become a more serious business, a cudgel to be taken out and used on wrongdoers rather than the necessary seasoning to all that he thought and all that he wrote. But he could still make the nation laugh. Even his victims grinned as they squirmed under his attacks. Cobbett never developed, however, into the truly comical writer Porcupine might have become if he had been able to keep away from politics. Nor, on the other hand, did he grow into the great satirist he wanted to be. Irony, sarcasm and vituperation can all, in the hands of a man as witty as Cobbett, earn our laughter, but neither severally nor singly do they amount to satire.

True satire starts from that form of self-knowledge that inspires a high and wholesome degree of self-disgust. Cobbett's self-knowledge was woefully limited. What he did know about himself inspired complacency rather than disgust. Swift, the only man Cobbett ever took as his literary model and guide, was a true satirist because what he hated in the Yahoos was what he hated in himself, whilst all that was noble and benign in the Houyhnhnms was all that was most notably lacking in every forked radish calling himself a man, including, of course, Jonathan Swift.

The distinction is, perhaps, best brought out in one of Swift's best-known sayings: 'Principally I hate and detest that animal called man; although I heartily love John, Peter, Thomas and so forth.' Yet Swift, for all his savage satires on society, was deeply loved by all who knew him and by many who did not. Cobbett, on the other hand, frequently expressed his love for mankind or, at least, for sections of it such as his starving and ill-treated chopsticks or the virtuous, freedom-loving and well-fed Americans. This was, however, an abstract and politically based sort of love that inspired no love in return. Cobbett was often admired and sometimes adulated, but he was seldom liked, for he lacked the gift of friendship. After his death his son James, preparing notes for a biography that was never completed, wrote that his father had been 'steady and constant' only in his hatreds. 'He had but little individual attachment. Liked people's company; & they liked his (when he was agreeable). But he formed very little of *friendship*. And wd. break off with any one, however old an acquaintance, on any affront, or being crossed in his will.'

Cobbett, in spite of all his writings and protestations to the contrary, lacked affection. A man without affection finds it difficult to understand others, and without an understanding of men there can be no true satire. His attacks on the follies, vices and crimes of his enemies were often witty and sometimes funny, for few men have ever handled abuse and ridicule more effectively. But, although he thought of himself as one, he was never a satirist. Yet he could have become a memorable one if only he could have seen in himself the folly he so easily saw in others and if he had had more liking for 'John, Peter and Thomas'.

If his character prevented him from being a satirist, circumstance did something to prevent him from being an even better writer than he was. The need to fill the columns of each week's *Register* forced him to write too much, too often and too quickly, and the state of his finances led him to do the same as an author. He was probably the most prolific of all English writers, and much of his work was dictated to a secretary to be sent, unpolished and unrevised, straight to the printer.

Whilst authors can sometimes, if they need to, make a success of journalism, it is more difficult for journalists to succeed as authors. If Cobbett succeeded in crossing the gulf that separates the one from the other, his books, nevertheless, reveal the price he had to pay for having been first, and primarily, a journalist. Some of his books, *Rural Rides* especially, were no more than collections of *Register* articles that had not even been worked over to prepare them for publication in book form. They lacked, therefore, the discipline and the organisation one expects from a book. It is relevant that Cobbett, both as journalist and author, always acted as his own publisher, editor, and, to a large extent, distributor. This meant that he had only himself and his readers to please and be disciplined by and, since he was an undisciplined thinker and a wordy, repetitive writer who had to follow every hare that he started, this shows in his work.

An outside publisher and editors might well have disciplined him into making his books move steadily and logically forwards, and it was his inability to do this that his contemporaries criticised. Hazlitt wrote that 'Cobbett, with vast industry, vast information, and the utmost power of making what he says intelligible, never seems to get at the beginning or come to the end of any question'. Today, when we read him for entertainment rather than to be informed, we enjoy his digressions and meanderings more than we do the subjects he originally set out to deal with. Who, except Cobbett, would insert into a chapter dealing with potato-growing, a large section criticising the works of Shakespeare and Milton and ridiculing all those Bardolators who had made such public fools of themselves over William Ireland's forgeries? Or who, in the same treatise on farming, would have included in a chapter on pig management such a passionate defence of that animal's sagacity, or have ended by asserting that no sow was properly housed unless her winter quarters were so warm that her owner would be prepared to share them with her?

It is delightful that Cobbett should have strayed into such arguments which few other potato-growers or pig-farmers could have thought of. Nevertheless it was, in a writer, a form of self-indulgence, and self-indulgent writing, most publishers would agree, must always be discouraged. It wastes paper and print, slows the pace of the work, and intervenes between the author and what ought to be his purpose. They would, in Cobbett's case, be no more than partially right, for not all of his digressions were as delightful as these. The merest mention of, say, William Pitt, or paper money, or Old Sarum would set him off at a tangent into digressions that were all the more tedious because they had developed into reflex reactions.

It is not fanciful to believe that Cobbett's particular experiences as a journalist had trained him in this self-indulgence. His absolute control over the *Register* allowed him to say anything and everything that he wanted to say at no matter what length. If he was interested in the subject he would not remain content with a 10,000 word article in a single Number of that paper, but he would chase it through subsequent Numbers until he had ended up with a book-length serial in which everything had been said two or three times over. *Register* readers accepted this because it was, in an indirect way, a guarantee of Cobbett's integrity. Other journalists might have to write to length and to order, but Cobbett was proprietor, editor and journalist all in one, and the very length of his articles proved that there was no one who could bribe, bully or cajole him into his opinions. Journalistic independence, however admirable though it was, bred bad habits in the author.

Yet it is where one would have expected Cobbett's work as a journalist to have influenced his work as an author most that it influenced it not at all. Since he had never used 'journalese' as a journalist he had no need to struggle against it as an author. He never elevated or lowered his style as he alternated between authorship and journalism, but always, as Hazlitt put it, 'wrote himself plain William Cobbett'. His avoidance of 'journalese' was a more considerable feat than the laymen will credit. Most journalists, sooner or later, adopt its convenient shorthand, whether they use it in the high mandarin style of a *Times* leader writer, or the cheerfully vulgar one of the gossip columnist. Cobbett was not above using clichés to save having to use language, but they were generally ones of his own inventing, such as 'the Wen', the 'Sons of Corruption', 'the tax-eaters' or 'the half-pay gentry'. He was remarkably ingenious with nicknames, generally choosing to impale his victims on some laudatory phrase from their pasts. The conceit became irritating, however, when used for the hundredth time, however amusing it had been when Pitt was first referred to as 'the Pilot', Wellington as 'the great Captain' and Goderich as 'Prosperity Robinson'.

Although Cobbett was almost inordinately proud of the books he wrote, he possibly never thought of himself as primarily an author. Indeed, there was a time, when he was farming out much of the *Register* and all of his *Parliamentary History* to Wright, and his *State Trials* to Howell, when he thought it more important to be a publisher. Then, forgetting his early days in Philadelphia when he had raged against Carey and Bradford, he affected, as publishers sometimes do, to despise mere authors. In

December 1808 he had written to Wright about Howell saying: 'I know that he is what the French call *un homme à grandes pretensions,* as, indeed, all your authors are . . . Their conceit is so intolerable that I would sooner have dealings with an old lecherous woman that would be tearing open my cod-piece fifty times a day.'

Taking Cobbett all in all, however, as journalist and author, what must impress any professional writer is his complete professionalism. He achieved that most difficult of all feats, writing to please himself and getting well paid for it. He never flattered, or pampered, or even considered his readers, and yet he never wrote anything except **Important Considerations,** that did not earn him money. To that extent he agreed with Doctor Johnson's dictum that 'no man but a blockhead ever wrote, except for money'.

He never wasted a single thought or a single sentence that could be used again in a different context. A speech or a letter would be resurrected as an article, that article would be republished as a pamphlet, and the pamphlet would be used to furnish a book. He was quite extraordinarily versatile, attempted every form apart from fiction, and wrote, with apparent authority, on almost everything. If he could have known little about the subject before he had started, he could create the impression of knowing everything about it before he had finished. And he could do this without allowing either his initial ignorance nor his subsequent researches to show.

As a consequence, he wrote as an expert on economics, foreign affairs, military matters, household matters, travel, farming, gardening and forestry in addition to writing endlessly about politics. He produced sermons, fables, grammars, biographies, histories and dictionaries. He could achieve almost any effect, being alternately moralistic, dogmatic, scientific, picaresque, sentimental, ribald, polemical and scurrilous. He could make his passions seem justified, his prejudices reasonable and his hatreds ordained by the Deity.

Yet for all his versatility, he never gave the impression of being superficial. His arguments were so well conducted that those who agreed with them were strengthened in their convictions and those who did not were inspired to counter-argument. He was not, in either case, a man to be ignored or lightly dismissed. Since he frequently indulged in argument for argument's sake, he could leave his readers wondering whether white was, indeed, as light as they had thought, and black quite as dark.

It is thought derogatory to refer to any writer as a hack but it is easier to understand the word if one turns to the world of the horse, where a hack can be described as a most useful, all-purpose sort of animal which goes well at all paces and in all gears. It is perhaps in that sense that Cobbett can be described as the greatest hack in the history of English literature.

But he was also, of course, something more. He was a master of English prose. As a political writer he stands level with Paine and a little below Burke. No writer on country subjects has ever shown a better understanding of the life and the nature of the English countryside. He was an outstanding polemicist who has made it seem as if all his successors have been firing off squibs where he fired off siege guns. He was, within his limited range, an excellent humorist. He was, in the truest sense of the word, an original, for he owed nothing to other writers, most of whom he despised, and he has had, more's the pity, no successors. He was a man of the eighteenth century whose arguments still echo in our minds at the end of the twentieth century for he is, in many ways, closer to us than he was to the Victorians. He still offers the best of company to any reader who has the sense to listen to him, the spirit to argue with him, enough humour to be able to laugh both with him and at him, and, above all, a sufficient liking for the language and for singularity to enjoy him.

Roger Sale (essay date 1986)

SOURCE: "William Cobbett," in *Closer to Home: Writers and Places in England, 1780-1830,* Cambridge, Mass.: Harvard University Press, 1986, pp. 67-86.

[*In the following essay, Sale discourses on Cobbett's significance and the nature of his philosophical outlook, referring recurrently to* Rural Rides.]

Cobbett wrote a shelf of books, including the **Political Register,** which once a week for many years offered itself as the political and economic conscience of England. He was born in 1763 and had a long career that to some looks like failure and to others like success. For instance, it is frequently said that Cobbett was the single person most responsible for the passage of the Reform Bill of 1832; he has admirers who feel he was wrong to settle for so little an achievement. Presumably because he is not "literary," he is missing from most anthologies of English literature, even one that devotes seventy-five pages to Carlyle. For students of literature he remains not someone to know so much as to know about.

Cobbett's most famous book is **Rural Rides** (1830), and we can restrict our attention to this volume because it represents his important contribution to the literature of place. But we will have to alter our bearings to show this. Cobbett had a home place that shaped him as much as any home place shaped anyone in this period, with the possible exception of Clare, and I will note more than once that Cobbett's outlook is nostalgic, his youth having given him all his essential standards of comparison. But he is a rural rider, a traveler whose places are ones he will be in today but not tonight or tomorrow, and this affects both the way he writes and the way we look at him. Though his sojourns are necessarily brief, Cobbett exudes confidence that from them he can learn the state and fate of England. He gives us a chance to concern ourselves more with what was happening to the English countryside than we have thus far.

Cobbett's instinctive ambition was to speak for England, or at least for its conscience, its right knowledge. In the old culture the two voices that in theory could speak for England were those of the monarch and the church, but the basis of the claim was an understanding of symbolic, or magical, relations between monarch or clergy and the subjects, the sheep of the pasture. The execution of Charles I "ruined the great work of time," and after the Glorious Revolution a generation later the only ones who believed in magical relations between king and subjects were the loyal followers of the Stuart cause in the Highlands of Scotland. Elsewhere it was understood that the monarchy was an arrangement born of a series of accommodations among power groups; how else could it be understood if, at the time of the Hanoverian succession in 1714, there were fifty-seven people who had a better claim to the crown than did George I? What had been magic had become settlement, a matter of borrowing money and collecting taxes; the king not only could not speak for England but could not speak English. So too with the church and clergy. The great energies that built the cathedrals and the huge parish churches between 1100 and 1500 seemed able to unite and express a people, especially in comparison with events after the Reformation. After Henry VIII broke with Rome and the monasteries were closed, the crown gave their lands to its favored subjects, and gradually Anglicanism became a sect rather than a national church, and a persecuting sect at that; a great pastoral power was secularized into pious manners and a tithe-collecting arm of the propertied class. At the very least, then, if a voice *could* speak for England, it was not going to be one of the traditionally powerful voices, and, on the face of it, no unifying power larger than the human voice was there to serve as successor or replacement.

Traditionally, pastoral was the mode that expressed magical or symbolic relations, and by the eighteenth century it is not surprising to find an inability to understand how the hungry sheep could ever have looked up and *been* fed. Indeed, in his denunciation of the church Milton still imagines that traditional language is viable, whereas a century later Johnson can imagine it is a relevant criticism of "Lycidas" that Milton and Edward King were never shepherds. Wordsworth calls "Michael" a pastoral poem because by the beginning of the nineteenth century "pastoral" had become a synonym for "rural"; the magical and symbolic relations are gone, and place has become particular and local.

If Cobbett had been told he sought to be a pastoral figure in the earlier sense of the term, he might well have concluded he was being addressed by "one of those frivolous idiots that was turned out from Westminster and Winchester School, or from any of those dens of dunces called Colleges and Universities," or perhaps someone from London, the GREAT WEN, "Jews, loan-jobbers, stock-jobbers, placemen, pensioners, sinecure people, and people of the *dead weight*." The voice, clearly, is coarse, but in his time and place a certain coarseness may have been integral to his effort to harmonize the human and the natural and to denounce all that threatened that harmony.

Rural Rides is a journal of a number of journeys Cobbett took between 1822 and 1826 through the southern counties of England. He may have little bits of business to do here and there, but for the most part he rides because he wants to see and to report on what he sees, and he wants to take what he sees as evidence of what the state of England is, not just where he is but everywhere. He does not, of course, assume that the same thing is happening everywhere—no need to take journeys at all if that were so—but he always wants to interpret material facts as evidence and to read much into his interpretation. His crudeness is not the result of being afraid he will not be heard and has no hint of underlying defensiveness or uncertainty. It is part and parcel of his confidence. Thus it is unsurprising that he is given to superlatives; "Thus ended the most interesting day, as far as I know, I ever passed in all my life"; "Here I am, then, just going to bed after having spent as pleasant a day as I ever spent in my life"; "I never saw anything to please me like this valley of the Avon"; "It is impossible for the eyes of man to be fixed on a finer country than that between the village of Coxford and the town of Warminster"; in Warminster itself are "the finest veal and lamb that I had ever seen in my life," and a little farther on "there are the most beautiful trees that I ever saw in my life." As one might well imagine, when Cobbett turns that language on himself, he can be mightily pleased; "I got many blows in the sides, and if I had been either a short or a weak man, I would have been pressed underfoot and inevitably killed"; "During the whole of this ride I was very rarely abed after daylight; I drank neither wine nor spirits. I ate no vegetables, and only a very moderate quantity of meat." Though he never seems to see himself as a writer, he feeds on his own words.

In these excerpts Cobbett fills up too much of the space in his pictures, the natural surroundings and the human community serving as background for self-portraits in landscapes with low horizon lines, Cobbett and his horse dominating the scene. One might, seeing this, think how much more companionable is Defoe in his *Tour of England and Wales,* written about a century before ***Rural Rides*** and filled with much soberly presented lore and observation that seldom seeks to make more of what it offers than a local citizen would. But Defoe's modesty cannot guarantee that he can find enough for himself or for us to be truly interested in, because he is unable to connect, to point up relevance, to make his journey seem other than one place following another. There is, by comparison, hardly a page of ***Rural Rides*** that does not have its passionate outburst, its insistence that what happens to the land, and the people on the land, matters tremendously.

Many things feed this passion, one of which is Cobbett's skewed sense of history, without which he never could have proceeded so confidently or achieved so much. On their journeys, both Defoe and Cobbett come to Winchester, and both offer homage to William of Wickham, founder of Winchester Cathedral. I need not quote Defoe; his account characteristically is full of lore that Defoe need never have been in Winchester or seen its cathedral to report, place for him being a generator of lore. Here is Cobbett:

> I took Richard to show him that ancient and most magnificent pile, and particularly to show him the tomb of that famous Bishop of Winchester, WILLIAM OF WYKHAM; who was Chancellor and the Minister of the great and glorious king, Edward III; who sprang from poor parents in the little village of WYKHAM, three miles from Botley; and who, amongst other great and munificent deeds, founded the famous College, or School, of Winchester, and also one of the Colleges at Oxford. I told Richard about this as we went from the inn down to the cathedral; and when I *showed him the tomb,* where the bishop lies on his back, in his Catholic robes, with his mitre on his head, his shepherd's crook by his side, with little children at his feet, the hands put together in a praying attitude, he looked with a degree of inquisitive earnestness that pleased me very much.

Cobbett is more personal than Defoe as he offers his recital of facts, but, more important, he senses a break with the past, believes in old magical relations that are gone now, and wants his son to understand history in terms of the contrast of past to present.

Up to this point in his story, Cobbett sees nothing to ignite him, but soon he gets what he needs:

> The *"service"* was now begun. There is a *dean,* and God knows how many *prebends* belonging to this *immensely rich* bishopric and chapter: and there were, at this *"service,"* two or three men and *five or six boys* in white surplices, with a congregation of *fifteen women* and *four men!* Gracious God! If WILLIAM of WYKHAM could, at that moment, have raised from his tomb!. . . . and had been told, that *that* was *now* what was carried on by men, who talked of the *"damnable* errors" of those who founded that very church!

So, when Richard says no one could make such a cathedral now, Cobbett replies: "That building was made when there were no poor wretches in England, called *paupers;* when there were no *poor-rates;* when every laboring man was clothed in good woollen cloth; and when all had plenty of meat and bread and beer." Cobbett is right in saying that no one was called "pauper" and no one paid "poor-rates" in fourteenth-century England; no one did in the years of his youth either. But of course Winchester Cathedral was built at the time of the Black Plague, when good woolen cloth, meat, bread, and beer were neither in plentiful supply nor enough to prevent the deaths of a third of the population.

Decidedly Cobbett is a shortsighted historian; if he can remember (rightly or wrongly) something as having been true in his early years, he can insist it was always thus, and (always) when he sees a church that can seat a thousand people or a cathedral that can seat five thousand, he imagines that once these places were filled to capacity and infers that the total population of England has fallen since the Middle Ages. If this were all, his confidence

would be only another name for pig-headed delusion, and Cobbett would only be offering ample evidence that in the early nineteenth century no voice could possibly claim, at least successfully, all that he claimed. But I think someone who had been more cautious about knowing the past would have been more cautious about knowing the present as well, and in Cobbett's case his active historical sense was food for his larger sense that the life of a society, of people, place, event, past and present, was intelligible, and this is what gave his rural rides, his descriptions of places where he would be today but not tonight or tomorrow, such impressive resonance. He looks at what Crabbe and Austen look at quite often, but where they claim that only small communities are knowable, he claims the ability to generalize from minutely observed evidence to the national scene.

Thus in the Isle of Thanet, in Kent, one of the richest wheat areas in England, Cobbett sees:

> The people dirty, poor-looking; ragged, but particularly *dirty.* The men and boys with dirty faces, and dirty-smock-frocks, and dirty shirts; and good God! what a difference between the wife of a labouring man here and the wife of a labouring man in the forests and woodlands of Hampshire and Sussex!

If this seems paradoxical, Cobbett can explain:

> Invariably I have observed that the richer the soil, the more destitute of woods; that is to say, the more purely a corn country, the more miserable the labourers.

That is acutely observed, and observation leads to generalization:

> The cause is this, the great big bull frog grasps all. In this beautiful island every inch of land is appropriated by the rich. No hedges, no ditches, no commons, no grassy lanes; a country divided into great farms; a few trees surround the great farmhouses. All the rest is bare of trees; and the wretched labourer has not a stick of wood, and has no place for a pig or a cow to graze, or even to lie down upon.

What his observation tells him is indeed the case, and the contrast between the rich corn country of Kent and the forests and woodlands of Hampshire and Sussex is enough to tell him why the laborers are dirtier and poorer in one area than the other.

Cobbett is right enough in one sense, but in fact there never had been hedges, ditches, common land, or grassy lanes in Kent, since the farms had been enclosed there when the land was first cleared, in the Middle Ages. He did not know this, and was inclined to think the great big bullfrog had been created in his lifetime. But this only means that here Cobbett had his history askew. The essential point about rich land yielding poor laborers remains intact, and, as a general rule, it can be said that when Cobbett is acute in his observations he will have at least something important to offer in his generalizations.

He keeps his eyes on the object on this ride and therefore does not fall into two arguments he was fond of using, either of which would have betrayed his historical ignorance. He might have claimed that in olden times the laborers were more prosperous, and he might have claimed that it is London's rapacious demand for the countryside's produce that impoverishes these rural workers. Avoiding these, he rightly says that in areas farther west the land was poorer and therefore the cottagers lived better, because the landowners had not insisted upon a ruthless cultivation of the soil.

With Austen one is inclined to feel, for all her placing of some crucial scenes in Derbyshire and Northamptonshire where she had never been, that she seeks to write of what she knows on long acquaintance, and so too with Crabbe. Cobbett is in his rural rides a tourist—his book is travel literature, in effect—but, lacking Austen's or Crabbe's discretion, he draws more inferences from what he sees than they ever would. Thus, a few miles from the Isle of Thanet but still in Kent, he goes to Dover and scores wonderful direct hits:

> Here is a hill containing probably a couple of square miles or more, hollowed like a honeycomb. Here are line upon line, trench upon trench, cavern upon cavern, bomb-proof upon bomb-proof; in short the very sight of the thing convinces you that either madness the most humiliating, or profligacy the most scandalous must have been at work here for years. The questions that every man of sense asks is: What reason had you to suppose that the *French would come to this hill,* to attack it, while the rest of the country was so much more easy to assail? . . . This is, perhaps, the only set of fortifications in the world ever framed for mere *hiding.*

The castle itself had been there since William I conquered the island by conquering its coastline, but in the two decades of the wars against France, 1793-1815, the land surrounding Dover Castle had indeed been fortified, as Cobbett says, "Just as if they would not go (if they came at all) and land in Romney Marsh, or on Pevensey Level, or anywhere else, rather than come to this hill."

The point of the observation is already clear, but we can note that in the observing Cobbett rises to a level of generalization that is not usual for Austen or Crabbe, and he follows it up by questioning Pitt and the others responsible for this folly: "The money must have been squandered purposely, and for the worst ends." He is one of the first to discover the secret of military expenditure in modern nations:

> What they wanted, was to prevent the landing, not of Frenchmen, but of French principles; that is to say, to prevent the example of the French from being alluring to the people of England.

There, it seems to me, is the pastoral voice, the conscience, speaking. Cobbett assumes, rightly or wrongly, that the English had nothing to fear from French principles, but on seeing the fortifications at Dover he could insist that the country was thereby threatened with the loss of a harmony that existed before the money was "squandered purposely, and for the worst ends." Though I am unable to add to or subtract from this as an accurate historical account, I can say that the evidence offered by Wordsworth in *The Prelude,* by Coleridge in the *Biographia Literaria,* by Charlotte Brontë in *Shirley,* and by Elizabeth Gaskell in *Sylvia's Lovers* is ample and eloquent on the fierceness, the repressiveness, and the stupidity of the English in their fear of the French in the years during and after the French Revolution. It is out of the experience of these years, especially but far from exclusively as seen by Cobbett, that English radicalism was born. E. P. Thompson says: "It is as if the English nation entered a crucible in the 1790s and emerged after the wars in a different form."

Cobbett himself is not necessarily at his sharpest on the coast of Kent, where the fortification of Dover Castle practically hands him a vision of foreign policy seen from a single hill. He is not so much at home in Kent, whose countryside had been developed in its contemporary form many centuries earlier and did not show as many signs of the great growth of London as did Surrey and Hampshire. In his riding about these counties, Cobbett does not claim the special pride of knowledge he has of his home places, but his observation there is especially sharp and can show us most fully the possibilities and the limits of his ability to generalize from careful observation. Here he is at the sale of a farm in Surrey, only a few miles from where Emma Woodhouse faced the yellow curtains in Vicarage-lane in Highbury:

> Oak clothes-chests, oak bedsteads, oak chests of drawers, and oak tables to eat on, long, strong, and well supplied with joint stools. Some of the things were many hundreds of years old. But all appeared to be in a state of decay and nearly of *disuse.* There appeared to have been hardly any *family* in that house, where formerly there were, in all probability, from ten to fifteen men, boys, and maids: and, which was worst of all, there was a *parlour!* Aye, and a *carpet* and *bell-pull* too!

The crudeness here is muted, the nostalgia working to some point, so we know that Cobbett has found a true Cobbett place:

> One end of the front of this once plain and substantial house had been moulded into a *parlour;* and there was the mahogany table, and the fine chairs, and the fine glass, and all as barefaced upstart as any stock-jobber in the kingdom can boast of.

When one catches the scorn that lies behind that "mahogany table," in contrast with all the oak furniture being put up for sale, one sees also why SIR WALTER RALEIGH "was one of the greatest villains on earth," for introducing potatoes to England. England has no need of potatoes, or mahogany, and Lord knows how long the list might be extended; Cobbett could not distinguish Bishop Wilberforce from Dickens' do-gooding Mrs. Jellyby, because

Wilberforce was raising a hue and cry about slaves when he should have been worrying about native English laborers.

But this *is* Cobbett at his best, and it is important not to become distracted:

> And there were the decanters, the glasses, the "dinner-set" of crockery, and all just in true stock-jobber style. And I dare say it has been *Squire* Charington and the *Miss* Charingtons; and not plain Master Charington, and his son Hodge, and his daughter Betty Charington, all of whom this cursed system has, in all likelihood, transmuted into a species of mock gentlefolks, while it has ground the labourers down into real slaves. Why do not farmers now *feed* and *lodge* their work-people, as they did formerly? Because they cannot keep them *upon so little* as they give them in wages. This is the real cause of the change.

Think of Penshurst, and of Ben Jonson's celebration of magical relations between classes offered as a triumphant harmony, as if of people with nature—some of that lies behind Cobbett's scorn of what is for him a new establishment of class relations, snooty and aloof on the part of the owners. Once you create the parlor and the oak furniture goes into disuse, it follows that the laborers will no longer be fed and housed properly because the new class distinctions are based on cost effectiveness: "and yet so much does he gain by pinching them in wages that he lets all these things remain as of no use, rather than feed labourers in the house. Judge, then, of the *change* . . . and be astonished, if you can, at the *pauperism* and the *crimes* that now disgrace this once happy and moral England." He has probably gone too far, slid off into easier generalizing than in the previous passage, but remember, there are no longer agreed-upon ways and means of generalizing, and Cobbett has little to rely on to help him except instinct; so of course he can easily and frequently overstep himself, as when he is recalling, a latter-day John of Gaunt, "this once happy and moral England."

Cobbett excels at observation and at passionate bursts of generalization from observation, and that is why *Rural Rides* is better than most of the hundreds of issues of the *Political Register* and his various advice books. When he is out riding, there is always the possibility of a visual challenge that can turn the crude thinker into the pastoral knower. Faced with a book by Malthus or a speech by Canning, Cobbett knows so well what he thinks beforehand that he can never be more than momentarily impressive rhetorically; he just falls back on his preconceived opinion, facing no challenge. Even out in the countryside he had little of Defoe's ability to be simply interested in things. How did Dunwich fall, how was Lyme's harbor built, how far from London does London's marketing grasp extend—Defoe can ask these questions and be satisfied with the received answers. Faced with the same questions, Cobbett would tend to bluster, to make a point and not to worry if that point made little sense.

Thus when Cobbett sees churches too large for the existing population of a parish, he presumes that the population in these parishes was once large enough to fill the churches, a presumption so preposterous it makes one wonder what England would have been like had it been built from the beginning on Cobbett's principles. Cobbett then says England's population must therefore be declining—in fact, it doubled in Cobbett's lifetime—and that anyone who doubts this must be able to "literally believe, that *the moon is made of green cheese.*" There are other instances. Selborne Hanger, one of the highest hills Cobbett has seen, must consequently be "among the highest hills in England," being in fact a quarter to a third the height of most of the bigger mountains in the Pennines and the Lake District. Or, if an area produces more food than it can eat, it is obvious that Quakers ("a sect of non-labourers") must be at work, since they are "as to the products of the earth, what the Jews are to gold and silver."

These are the consequences of Cobbett's pulling the trigger too quickly, as he also was wont to do even when his clearest observation led to some of his richest generalizing. We have looked at his insights about rich land and poor workers, about the fortifications against French ideas, about the Charington parlor and mahogany table. He might have asked himself how all these were related, but to do that would have required a sense of history that Cobbett did not have; for him it was enough to treat landscape as text and to follow with sermon. In fact, and these were not facts totally unavailable to Cobbett, London had been a Great Wen well before he was born; the capitalist system he saw invading the countryside had been expanding, and creating and defining the landed gentry, for two centuries and more, so that what Cobbett saw was neither new nor so impressively expanding as to be news just then.

There had been a huge inflation in farm prices and a corresponding rise in farm rents during the years of the Napoleonic wars. After Waterloo prices fell but rents did not; many landowners were therefore squeezed and became inclined to squeeze their workers, especially if they had undertaken the considerable expense of enclosing their land in false expectation of prices' remaining high. As a result the 1820s, the decade of *Rural Rides,* was one of the worst ever for rural workers, and the situation was not helped by the great shifting in land ownership throughout the period, which meant that many new owners like Henry Crawford had never known a relation between land, owner, and worker that was not capitalist.

Cobbett could see some of this at least, but he saw it either as a single great blob called London, or as little bits that could not be synthesized into a single view no matter how hard he tried, or as a matter of England's needing nothing so much as a return to the time of Cobbett's youth. The blob was the WEN, London, run by the THING, and the THING controlled England by means of rotten boroughs, paper money, taxes, poor laws, national debt, standing armies, and the granting of power to the likes of Dissenters and Jews. In the place of analysis Cobbett made lists, especially of villains, but the flaw of drawing up lists and of hurling words into block capitals was that they suited Cobbett's temperament all too well and thereby rendered his shrewd perceptiveness quiescent.

"Here I am, in Kent and Christendom," wrote Thomas Wyatt to his own John Poins three centuries earlier. It is a way of speaking Cobbett loved, for it places the voice at the center of the universe. But much had changed in three centuries. Wyatt speaks from a generalized place and feels no need to comment on the particular place; "Kent" is a part of Christendom as good as any other, and as long as it stands apart from the court it is an address from which letters are written. Knowing a place, in our sense of the term, was seldom relevant. A familiar place provided material, lore, and suggested the best available metaphor, but places never demanded perceptive scrutiny of particulars. "Kent" for Cobbett, though, *is* its own place, not a generalized one, and to the extent that he wanted or needed to separate Kent from the rest of Christendom, to say how its farms and people were different from those in Sussex and Hampshire, to that extent the generalizations he could make about one place were restricted to that place, as surely as Gilbert White's observations and generalizations about the behavior of sand martins and swallows applied only to them and not to nightingales, to say nothing of squirrels. To that extent Cobbett was always on dangerous ground when he tried to look at a place and intone about the fate of England. In its moving stages, his generalizing is often wonderfully good. It is in moving from the particulars and his early generalizations to his attempts to state larger conclusions that he most often gets into trouble, falling back on his prejudice or his shortsighted sense of history.

The task he had given himself, however, was difficult, more difficult than he knew, certainly. What helps Cobbett is his love of details, and this keeps him from trying to generalize without regard to anything local or particular. As for what might happen when such a thing was attempted, take these lines of Wordsworth's:

> Milton! thou shouldst be living at this hour:
> England hath need of thee; she is a fen
> Of stagnant waters: altar, sword, and pen,
> Fireside, the heroic wealth of hall and bower,
> Have forfeited their ancient English dower
> Of inward happiness.

It would be interesting to juxtapose "On the late massacre at Piedmont" to see Milton mixing the general with the particular. But here it is enough to say that it does not help us, or Wordsworth, to call this poem "London, 1802" because it remains all stance, attitude, vague gesture. By some unknown process halls, bowers, and firesides lose "inward happiness" and thereby become fens, and Milton, of all people, is called upon to observe or reverse this miracle of catastrophe. It is a poem that needs space and time coordinates, and something like Cobbett's shrewd eyes, to keep it from being mumbo-jumbo, feeling and bluster. We will have ample occasion later to see what wonderful generalizing Wordsworth could do when starting from haunting particulars, but even great writers are at risk when they fail to see how things change, history

happens, and the possibilities for successful utterance thereby are altered.

Jane Austen offers splendid confirmation. Because we often understand her as the heir of Dr. Johnson, our instinct may tell us to think of her as a novelist given to more generalizing than later writers. But her most famous generalization belongs to the feeble understanding of Mrs. Bennet, and ironically, despite her husband's ridicule, Mrs. Bennet's statement about single men in possession of a good fortune is perhaps the only generalization that all six novels uphold. Except for that one, if we think of the subjects in which Austen shares an interest with Cobbett, such as money, class, property, or London, it is surprising to note that she, like him, is always confident but, unlike him, avoids generalizations and makes it difficult for others to generalize about her. She shares Cobbett's feelings about London, presumably, but her only characters who actually live there, the Gardiners and John and Isabella Knightley, are just about everyone's, including Austen's, favorite minor characters in her fiction. Her clergymen are a mixed lot: Henry Tilney, Edward Ferrars, William Collins, Edmund Bertram, Philip Elton, and Charles Hayter. Her improving landowners are Mr. Rushworth, Henry Crawford—and George Knightley. Her titled aristocrats are dreadful—Lady Catherine de Bourgh, Sir Thomas Bertram, Sir Walter Elliot—but her greatest hero is aristocrat in all but title. Her new-rich are Augusta Hawkins—and Frederick Wentworth. In the four major novels the social range from top to bottom is large, but no class or profession, and no attitude about money, learning, travel, or society outside the family is built up as a structure of emphasis or preference we can call Austen's own. Of course there are generalizations in her fiction, but I think scrutiny would show that they are mostly dramatic, offered as hypotheses rather than received truths. It may well be that those who have found her narrow because she ignores the rural poor or the Napoleonic wars are in fact responding to her variousness, which demands from her readers an absorption in this time and that place that makes generalization difficult.

The shift we have been following, from the generalized to the particular place, turns out to have little-seen consequences, one of the most important being the shift in the nature of generalizing, in the structure of successful generalization. To look at almost any twenty or thirty lines of a Shakespeare play is to see speeches that move back and forth from the detailed to the generalized as if the act were as simple as breathing:

> Give me a cup of sack, rogue—Is there no virtue
>   extant?
>
> My lord, here are letters for you—
> O gentlemen, the time of life is short. . . .
>
> The queen, my lord, is dead.
> —Tomorrow, and tomorrow, and tomorrow. . . .

The movement from detail to generalization is easy enough, but the presence or absence of sack does not mean there is, or is not, any virtue extant. We cannot say of these generalizations that they succeed or fail. Nor is the situation much different if we start with the generalizations, as with "The quality of mercy is not strained" or "To be or not to be." Modern readers have learned to distinguish detail, or particular, from generalization, and we have to work to learn that in earlier centuries that distinction was much less clearly defined or felt. In our period, the transition between then and now, it may be said that for the first time it became possible for a generalization to fail.

"A mind lively and at ease," Austen writes, "can do with seeing nothing, and can see nothing that will not answer." Cobbett, hearing this, would have ground his teeth. *His* mind could never do with seeing nothing and could never imagine it was nothing that he was seeing, because his perception must answer to his mind's need to be lively and to know the meaning of what he is seeing. In these circumstances he must generalize, and it is possible for the generalizations to fail.

Cobbett is in Whiteflood, on the Hampshire downs— "These hills are amongst the most barren of the Downs of England; yet a part of these was broken up during the rage for improvements." The result was a disaster—"A man must be mad, or nearly mad, to sow wheat on such a spot." If not strictly true, it is fair enough, and Cobbett, had he been asked, could have given the farmer warning. But here is Cobbett's conclusion:

> And this was *augmenting the capital of the nation.* These new enclosure-bills were boasted of by George Rose and by Pitt as proofs of national prosperity! When men in power are ignorant to this extent, who is to expect anything but consequences such as now we behold.

From a madman to a mad nation. It does not work, but it is important to ask why.

"Improvements, Ma'am!" is Cobbett's shorthand term of contempt for enclosures, and it is hardly surprising that agriculturalists, enclosure commissioners, and surveyors all had a bad smell for him, since they were a new sort of person and were not satisfied with the England of his youth. The very idea that the capital of the nation could be increased sounded fishy to him, like paper money. In an 1813 *Political Register* he objected to a general enclosure law because he was sure it was not possible to increase the food supply without increasing the population. So he is pleased to note the failure of the mad Hampshire farmer's ploughed downland because it "proved" that enclosure, which in this case would have allowed sheep or cattle to be removed from the land, could not augment the capital of the nation. It can be presumed that in the particular case Cobbett could have been right, but in the general case he was quite wrong. The wealth of the nation increased greatly during the period of the greatest enclosures, and because of them in part: not so much in Hampshire as elsewhere, not so much or so quickly as many enclosers hoped, and not so much by the single act of

enclosing as by the accompanying changes in husbandry, crop rotation, ditching, and drainage. Cobbett is a farmer, he sees the broken-out land and the poor yield, and, not content to say the farmer is a fool, he generalizes, and suddenly enclosures in Norfolk, Leicestershire, and Yorkshire, all successful and all unknown to Cobbett, are the work of fools. Surely they must be—since here is Cobbett, in Hampshire and Christendom, is he not?

I do not intend to scorn so much as to indicate the precariousness of the enterprise, and I need to end with what I take to be a brilliant sequence showing how, in the period when generalizing itself was becoming more perilous, Cobbett could relate observation to generalization splendidly. Cobbett's ride down the valley of the Avon to Salisbury, on August 30, 1826, in which he is retracing a route he had taken almost twenty years earlier, yielded one of his finest sustained pieces of writing. The following may need a larger context to show all its strengths, but it clearly shows the shrewd eye of the superb early classifier and generalizer:

> I found the place *altered* a good deal; out of repair: the gates rather rotten; and (a very bad sign!) the roof of the dog-kennel falling in! There is a church, at this village of Netheravon, large enough to hold *a thousand or two* of people, and the whole parish contains only 350 men, women, and children. This Netheravon was formerly a great lordship, and in the parish there were three considerable mansion-houses, besides the one near the church. These mansions are all down now; and it is curious enough to see the former *walled gardens* become orchards, together with other changes, all tending to prove the gradual decay in all except what appertains merely to *the land* as a thing of production for the distant market.

Until this last phrase, it is unclear what direction Cobbett intends to take, but the observation is clear and shrewd, so the yield should be rich; Cobbett can "see" decay in the fallen-in roof of the kennel and paradoxically also in the productiveness of the orchards.

"But indeed, the people and the means of enjoyment *must go away.*" Most writers, including Cobbett himself when less alert, would have written "employment" rather than "enjoyment," and thereby lose the sense that what the walled gardens as well as the kennel are concerned with is not productivity but quality of life:

> They are drawn away by the taxes and the paper-money. How are *twenty thousand new houses* to be, all at once, building in the WEN, without people and food and raiment going from this valley towards the WEN? It must be so; and this unnatural, this dilapidating, this ruining and debasing work must go on, until that which produces it be destroyed.

This may not be entirely clear. Earlier in his account of this day, Cobbett insists that "though paper-money could CREATE nothing of value, it was able to TRANSFER everything of value." Further, he had noted that the women of this valley once had full employment carding and spinning wool, and their work had ceased with the widespread use of the spinning jenny and the factories to house it.

Here Cobbett sees what he often is blind to elsewhere, that a decline in rural population did not mean a decline in national population but a transfer of people; and the kennel, the disappearance of the three mansion houses, and the appearance of orchards where walled gardens had been are all observations leading to the generalization about rural neglect, loss of enjoyment, and transfer of wealth and people to the WEN where twenty thousand new houses were being built. About London itself Cobbett may have been shortsighted, because his WEN was the city being built by John Soane and John Nash, but he is dead right about the relation of Netheravon to London. If, as Cobbett suspects, the disappearance of the mansion houses and walled gardens was the result of enclosures, then his point about the effects of a new kind of people coming to the countryside is secure. Crabbe speaks often about the difference between the sloppy old farmer who had a good relation with the people on his land and the classy efficient new farmer who is all capitalism and productivity. And what Crabbe notes in his fine wry way, indicating a value but not raising his voice, is food and drink to Cobbett. Even Crabbe would not have seen the dog kennel as revealingly as Cobbett does.

All this is to say that Cobbett at his best can sound a note that Jane Austen cannot. She is seldom foolish, especially in the folly of generalizing, because she is so carefully absorbed in her people of this time and that place. But such absorption did not affect her assumption that money and land were simply different forms of wealth; and if there ever was a relation of land, landowner, and worker that was not capitalist, she neither knew nor cared. It can be said for Cobbett that he has just enough history, along with a different and richer sense of the countryside than Austen's, to yield him a much more resonant sense of the value of land, and of people working with it and on it, than she could possibly have. Her confidence lies in her absorption, in the sense of intimacy of places; Cobbett's lies in his wonderfully interpreting observations, and what they lead him to, wrong and wrong-headed though his points of rest often are. Thus her fiction had no successors, in part because her generalizations broke down as they were supposed to do and yielded only the local truths they could. Raymond Williams is right to suggest that Cobbett's attempts to generalize about land, class, and money are precursors of the fiction of George Eliot and Hardy; what Cobbett reached to conclude about the new and the old relations to land, and the classes of people engendered by the new relations, is appropriated by the novelists as rich material for their fictions.

Cobbett is crude, Cobbett is a little-Britain bigot, Cobbett is a biased historian and, quite often, a desperate generalizer. Yet Cobbett is the first major voice of modern English radicalism, and radicalism has played an important and distinguished role in English thought and letters. The problem is not so much that of deciding which aspect is the most in need of being stressed as that of trying to write about him from a point of view different from that of most of the people who have so carefully preserved his memory. It is a great shame that he is so little known except as part of that radical tradition. An admiring but unradical American would like to make Cobbett's writing known and his presence felt among many to whom he is merely a name that begins with C and isn't Cowper, Clare, or Crabbe, and to admit to feeling ambivalent about him in ways his radical heirs need not feel.

"I have never gone out to 'take a walk' in the whole course of my life," Cobbett writes, striking a characteristic pose, "nor to take a ride; there had to be something to make me take one or the other." I tend to feel combative about such swaggering, knowing that he is one person and I another. I could, I answer, simultaneously take a walk and have something to make me take one: something, indeed, like *Rural Rides*. I could walk a rural ride, avoid Hindhead, stop at the Holly Bush in Headley, note the scrabbly common land nearby that both Cobbett and Defoe found shocking.

The two signs I love most in England and miss in America are those that announce a pub and those that proclaim a Public Footpath. In accepting their announcements and proclamations, especially in places in the southern counties well known to Cobbett, I have come to hear a voice, blustery and outraged:

> Public footpath! Gracious God, could there be a clearer sign that the WEN keeps moving, out from its center, by *taking a walk*, no less. And why? Because some nabob, or stock-jobber, some pensioner or admiral, has taken over a perfectly good farm. In the wake of all his Improvements, Ma'am, he has the gall to announce just where our feet and the hooves of our horses can be put, as if any decent traveler might want to trample his corn. The tide moving out from the WEN may think it is being "nicely treated," thank you, by this sign of PUBLIC FOOTPATH, but when the nabob restricts the common right to one pulling track, the beast will soon want to remove the track as well.

And then:

> In any decently regulated country, one finds public houses, and travelers know their gratitude for them. But here is THE WHITE HORSE, a sign painted by a man showing in every stroke of the brush that he had never seen the same, at least could not tell it from THE WHITE HART! Pretty signs indeed! To delight the Tourists that now crowd into the turnpikes. So people are *hired* to entice those who lately left a decent countryside and who now desire to visit it *on holiday*, to leave the WEN and to mar the land with these "signs" of public accommodation and national ignorance. And who, visiting these coaching inns, knows that wherever the cottager has ceased to make his own beer, in that place "Improvements, Ma'am,!" have invaded. So we have ever-so-pretty signs saying THE GREEN MAN by those who do not know the man, and others nearby announce the ruin of the country with their sign of PUBLIC FOOTPATH.

Walking from Selborne to Thursley, along the route of a Rural Ride, I cleverly give Hindhead a miss, as Cobbett has instructed. But I love the Holly Bush in Headley, which he hated, and what, I wonder, would be his response to my spending the night at the Pride of the Valley, a Best Western Hotel, right outside the Thursley that Cobbett always liked? How to placate his ghost, since the Pride of the Valley caters to outgrowths from the WEN and I pay for my lodging with a credit card? Gracious God!

The walk ends in Farnham, at what was the Jolly Farmer, on Bridge Street, where the man himself was born. It is now called The William Cobbett, and is filled with small rooms housing video games, and television sets which blink the Pages from Seefax. During a Happy Hour I was served a hamburger covered with an excellent Stilton sauce. Except for the portrait of Cobbett on the sign, one finds little trace of the master, and, given the noise, it is hard to hear, though easy to listen for, the sound of Cobbett rolling over in his grave.

Propped up by Satan, Tom Paine returns from death to haunt Cobbett.

David A. Wilson (essay date 1988)

SOURCE: "Epilogue," in *Paine and Cobbett: The Trans-atlantic Connection,* McGill-Queen's University Press, 1988, pp. 184-92.

[*Below, Wilson summarizes the findings of his full-length comparison of Paine and Cobbett's political thought.*]

Tom Paine and William Cobbett, founding fathers of British popular Radicalism, developed their ideology in an Anglo-American context during the Atlantic Revolution. They responded to the American Empire of Liberty in separate and distinct ways, although they eventually came to share many ideas about political liberty in the United States and its relevance to Britain. For Paine, the American experience was central. He became aware of Real Whig and republican ideas early in life, participated in the radical transformation of those ideas in America, and transmitted democratic republican ideology back to Britain. The United States, in Paine's view, supplied a model of the benefits of government based on the rights of man, where hereditary rule had been rejected and the "productive classes" had come into their own.

In Cobbett's case, the pattern was different. An idealistic Paineite and admirer of American liberty in his youth, Cobbett became disillusioned with democratic republicanism shortly after moving to the United States in 1792. By the time he returned home in 1800, Cobbett had become a John Bull High Tory who idealized England and who believed that American ideology and imperialist ambitions seriously threatened his country. Yet in much the same way that the United States had failed to live up to Cobbett's Utopian expectations, his image of English liberty and justice began to crack under the pressure of reality. With much difficulty, and using Paine's financial writings as a lever, Cobbett lurched uneasily towards a populist brand of socially conservative political Radicalism. Although he remained deeply suspicious of Ameri-

can imperialism, he increasingly believed that many aspects of the American political system could inspire the reform movement in Britain.

As he developed this view, Cobbett's comments about the United States became increasingly "Paineite" in tone and content. Nevertheless, there were still real differences between the two men. While Paine hoped that the symbolic power of the United States would impel British Radicals towards democratic republicanism, Cobbett used the American example to further the cause of parliamentary reform and lead Britain out of the modern world towards the ancient constitution, traditional liberties, and national glory. And in contrast to Paine's democratic internationalism, Cobbett remained a patriotic Englishman, continually worrying that American imperial power could contradict the ends that he wanted the example of American liberty to serve in Britain.

Despite these differences, Paine and Cobbett had much in common. In a sense, their complementarity stemmed from the complementarity of the traditions on which they drew. Paine transformed eighteenth-century Real Whig thought into a new form of democratic republicanism; Cobbett developed eighteenth-century Country Party ideology into a new form of Tory-Radicalism. Although the original traditions started from opposite ends of the political spectrum, they converged at a number of key points. Real Whig and Country Party writers alike denounced corruption, patronage, and the insidious influence of high finance in eighteenth-century politics. Because Real Whigs and the Country Party Opposition attacked the same targets, and because the new order appeared to threaten the "natural magistracy" as much as the "people," there was an odd compatibility between eighteenth-century Radicals and Tories; the essentially conservative outlook of the Country Party contained radical tendencies within itself.

If we cast the net forward to the late eighteenth and early nineteenth centuries, we find that even as Paine and Cobbett transformed their respective traditions they inherited the common ground which those traditions had occupied. While Paine approached politics from the democratic "left" and Cobbett embraced an agrarian conservatism, both men eventually became united in their struggle against the oligarchical political establishment in Britain. Like their Real Whig and Country Party predecessors, both men attacked placemen, sinecures, the debt, taxation, and the whole web of manipulative politics which enveloped the country. It is significant, moreover, that the bridge between the Radical Paine and the Tory Cobbett was effected through Paine's critique of the English financial system, since that critique itself had its roots in common Real Whig and Country Party attitudes to the financial revolution. Having identified the problems facing his country, Cobbett pushed the radical elements within Country Party thought to their democratic extreme, sounding in the process remarkably—and in some respects, deceptively—like Paine.

By transforming earlier traditions, both Paine and Cobbett attempted to realize different visions of an alternative society. Paine wanted to establish a democracy of small-scale property owners and producers, in which free competition underpinned by a social welfare scheme would benefit men of talent but prevent excessive inequality. This was not, Paine insisted, a Utopian dream. In the United States, he argued, the "productive classes" had already shaken off the oppressive weight of monarchy, aristocracy, and established religion; the point now was to establish in Britain the conditions of liberty which existed in America. In contrast, Cobbett wanted to recreate Old England. Beneath his toughest, most pragmatic political writings, behind his changing, contradictory, and incoherent political outlook, lay a strikingly consistent purpose: to re-establish a paternalistic, hierarchical, agrarian society in which well-fed, well-clad, honest industrious labourers respected and were respected by a virtuous, patriotic, and God-fearing landed gentry. Everything—including his image of America—was subordinated to that aim.

Yet there was an inescapable paradox in their position. Products of the Age of Revolution, the process of revolutionary change which brought Paine and Cobbett to prominence also made their visions increasingly anachronistic and unattainable. The Industrial Revolution, with its class conflict, unprecedented economic growth, and massive capital accumulation, left them gasping on the pre-industrial shore. Paine belonged to eighteenth-century Philadelphia, not nineteenth-century Manchester. He assumed an identity of interests among the "productive classes" against the aristocracy, and did not think in terms of "middle class" and "working class." On both sides of the Atlantic, he attempted to unite labourers, artisans, manufacturers, merchants, and professional men behind the rights of man. But on both sides of the Atlantic, industrial change was increasingly dividing society along class lines.

In the United States, the labour conspiracy trials of 1806 and 1809 against combinations of journeymen-shoemak-ers signalled the emergence of a distinct working-class consciousness which implicitly challenged Paineite notions of republican harmony. As Richard Twomey has shown, American Jacobins displayed a uniform and deep hostility to such trade unions, which they saw as a threat to the common good. In England, many Paineites of the 1790s wound up as successful businessmen in the early nineteenth century. At a meeting in 1822 to celebrate the twenty-eighth anniversary of Thomas Hardy's acquittal on charges of high treason, Francis Place noted that many of the central figures in the London Corresponding Society had risen from shopmen to journeymen to become "all in business all flourishing men, some of them were rich." But many more artisan supporters of Paine, reeling from the impact of technological innovation, unskilled labour, and increased concentration of ownership, were driven down into the working class rather than up into the middle class. Under the pressure of class conflict, Paine's Anglo-American social ideal could not be sustained.

More obviously, the Industrial Revolution also made Cobbett's return to the past utterly impossible to achieve. Applying pre-industrial solutions to industrial problems, and only dimly aware of the factory system, Cobbett focused all his attention on the unholy trinity of the national debt, paper money, and taxation. Class conflict, in his view, was a kind of false consciousness which diverted attention away from the real struggle against the "Pitt system." Cobbett believed that employers and labourers had the same interests, and insisted that "when journeymen find their wages reduced, they should take time *to reflect on the real cause,* before they fly upon their employers, who are, in many cases, in as great, or greater, distress than themselves." For Cobbett, class conflict was essentially a symptom of the financial system; once that system was overthrown, employers could afford to pay decent wages, and all classes would share in the general prosperity. The irony, as Marx pointed out, was that Cobbett, through trying to establish an alliance of all the "productive classes" against the "system" of fund-holders and borough-mongers, actually lent support to the very middle class that was undermining Cobbett's own ideal of traditional English liberties.

The process of industrialism not only subverted Paine's and Cobbett's social visions, but also worked against their strategies for change. Both men eventually pinned their faith on the conjunction of "objective" and "subjective" forces; the advent of inevitable financial collapse together with the pressure of massive popular democratic sentiment would, they believed, produce revolution or radical reform. Yet this approach had serious difficulties at each major point. Paine's and Cobbett's financial predictions suffered from internal problems of logic and external industrial developments. The arguments of Paine's *Decline and Fall* were overly mechanistic, transforming insights about the inflationary consequences of war into an iron law of impending bankruptcy. Similarly, Cobbett viewed paper money simply as an unmitigated evil once it exceeded the quantity of gold and silver it promised to pay; he refused to recognize any connection between the financial revolution and Britain's economic growth. But beyond this, the enormous increase in wealth produced during the Industrial Revolution pulled the government through the financial crisis of 1796 and 1797, and enabled the "system" to stay alive long after Paine's predicted date of expiry. Under these circumstances, the "objective" conditions for political change could not be met.

In the absence of financial collapse, the weakness of the "subjective" component in their strategies became apparent. For both men, public opinion guided by truth and reason would overawe an increasingly crisis-stricken government. Cobbett put so much faith in *"Petition and Remonstrance"* that he explicitly rejected "all sorts of *combinations, associations, and correspondencies of societies"* which attempted to give the reform movement organizational and institutional expression. And although Paine supported democratic clubs and regarded petitions as a humiliating waste of time, he could also argue in the *Rights of Man* that "Reason, like time, will make its own way." Yet even in the context of national bankruptcy, the force of argument backed by the sheer weight of numbers would not have been sufficient to make the government back down; in what became a common Radical weakness, the strength of the state was underestimated. In his darker moments, Cobbett conceded as much, adding gloomily that without reform "the people would become the most beggarly and slavish of mankind, and nothing would be left of England but the mere name." Massive popular sentiment, truth, and reason would not in themselves dislodge powerful vested interests backed up with significant powers of coercion.

Furthermore, even had these difficulties been overcome and either republican democracy or fundamental parliamentary reform been established, it is far from certain that such political changes would have produced the social order Paine and Cobbett envisaged. With their absolute faith in democratic reform as a panacea for Britain's problems, Paine and Cobbett did not pay enough attention to the relationship between political power and socio-economic developments. In their view, political democracy could control social and economic change; it did not occur to them that social and economic changes might strongly influence the nature of political democracy, that representative government could coexist with glaring inequalities of property or that political emancipation was partial emancipation.

We cannot know how Paine would have reacted to the United States over two hundred years after *Common Sense;* it can be said, however, that the modern capitalist industrial order contradicted the kind of small-scale property-owning, harmonious, roughly egalitarian society which Paine had associated with republican democracy. And just as the financial system did not destroy the British government, democracy in Britain did not destroy the financial system; Cobbett's Utopia remained unfulfilled.

All this helps to explain the failure of their visions; it does not imply that their views are "irrelevant" or that their arguments should be consigned to the pre-industrial scrap heap. Yet the question of "relevance" is a complex

and contradictory one. Paine and Cobbett were men whose ideas were grounded in eighteenth-century Anglo-American Radicalism; once their ideas were torn out of this context and transposed onto the nineteenth- and twentieth-century world, ambiguities were bound to appear and tensions were bound to be magnified. The ambiguities and tensions are apparent in the shifting images of Paine and Cobbett in America and Britain. For a century and a half, they had almost no image at all in the United States; they became famous in the land that neglected them, and neglected in the land that made them famous. It is true that a minority of "freethinking" deists, reinforced by Radical British immigrants, honoured Paine's memory in the nineteenth century, but it was not until the mid-twentieth century that Paine was rehabilitated into the American mainstream.

This was the Paine of the *American Crisis* papers, the Paine whose "tyranny, like hell, is not easily conquered" became the motto of General Patton's army. But it was also the Paine of the American Progressives, the Paine called into life by Howard Fast's novel: a down-and-out corset maker who came to the New World from the gutters of England, who was dirty, insecure, abrasive, and self-pitying, but who knew in his heart how working people thought and felt, and who stood up for the common man against the rich, the powerful, and the corrupt. After World War II, both the American left and the right claimed Paine as one of their own. Many modern American radicals admired his democracy, his faith in the common people, and his humanitarianism. On the other hand, right wing Republicans such as presidents Ford and Reagan approvingly quoted Paine as an apostle of *laissez-faire* individualism and as a spokesperson for America's mission to free the world by making it more American.

Cobbett, in contrast, could not be pressed into such service; indeed, he has been almost completely ignored in the United States. Cobbett's opinions were too closely linked with another country and another political system to be "serviceable" to most Americans; moreover, those intellectuals who compared America's position in the Cold War with Britain's position in the 1790s were attracted to the more sophisticated thought of Burke rather than the polemics of Cobbett.

In Britain, Paine and Cobbett left a deeper and different mark. At much the same time that modern American Republicans were moving towards aspects of Paine's thought, Conservative councillors in his native Thetford were outraged by a Labour Party proposal to erect a statue of Paine and one resigned in protest. In Britain, it was the politically blasphemous Paine who was remembered; this was the Paine who attacked and ridiculed the monarchy and the aristocracy, the Paine who poured scorn on revealed religion, the Paine whose social program appeared as a precursor of the welfare state. A powerful presence through the Chartist movement, Paine's political and religious writings became an important strand of the labour movement, where they became entwined with Owenism and the emerging socialism of men like Bronterre O'Brien and William Thompson. It all depended on what elements of Paine's thought were selected and how they were transformed to meet changing conditions; at any rate, the Paine whom the Labour councillors revered at Thetford was very different from the Paine whose faith in the free market and whose hostility to government and taxation appealed so much to contemporary American conservatives.

As for Cobbett, the tensions within his thought are reflected in current images. He has attracted more attention and approval from the left than from the right, but his writings flow into both radical and Tory traditions; one can focus on his critique of corruption, his sympathy with ordinary people and his attack on the political and financial élite, or one can embrace his anti-Jacobin writings and his consistent social conservatism. On the one hand, Raymond Williams has written a penetrating essay on the contemporary relevance of Cobbett's thought to the British left. On the other, Cobbett has been treated with sympathy and admiration by Daniel Green, a conservative former agricultural correspondent with the *Daily Telegraph.* And in another development, Cobbett's agrarian writings have been picked up by the "back-to-the-land" movement, which itself contains both radical and conservative tendencies. Clearly, Paine's and Cobbett's work has been used to realize new visions which often contradict one another and which are far removed from each man's original intentions.

This continuing process of renewal and reinterpretation not only testifies to the persistence of Paine's and Cobbett's influence, but also has its own strengths and weaknesses. To the extent that their thought has been ransacked to find support for *a priori* political positions, their work has been seriously distorted. But we can also draw on the insights and limitations of their ideas, methods, and goals within their specific historical context to shed light on present dilemmas, such as the problems facing those who believe that our present conditions are unjust and irrational and who seek to realize their own radical alternative visions. To do this, however, it is essential to recognize the wide gulf that separates us from them.

Paine thought that he was on the threshold of a new era, and in a very real sense he was. But it was not the kind of future he had anticipated. When he wrote of progress, commercial growth, social welfare, and democracy, Paine was trying to refashion pre-industrial society along American lines; he was not heralding an Industrial Revolution which eventually shattered his social vision. Nor could Cobbett turn the clock back, despite a stridency which became more pronounced as his agrarian ideal became less likely. Both men developed their ideas in an eighteenth-century world of Anglo-American Radical discourse which preceded the emergence of modern industrial class-based society. Paine and Cobbett were not the first men of a new world; they were the last men of a dying one.

Ian Dyck (essay date 1992)

SOURCE: "Cottage Economy," in *William Cobbett and Rural Popular Culture,* Cambridge University Press, 1992, pp. 107-24.

[In the following chapter, Dyck discusses the background, intent, and critical reception of Cottage Economy.*]*

In 1823 *The Edinburgh Review* imposed a sudden if temporary ceasefire in its fifteen-year battle with Cobbett's politics and economics by declaring his new work *Cottage Economy* to be 'an excellent little book . . . abounding with kind and good feelings, as well as with most valuable information'. The *Review* (Henry Brougham was the author of the praise) recognized that Cobbett's work was addressed to 'them', or 'the labouring classes', but it encouraged the rich to enlist the text in Whig educational service as a 'really useful' publication. Tories, for their part, did not publicize their opinions on *Cottage Economy,* but much of Cobbett's enthusiasm for an independent cottage economy was echoed in Robert Southey's essays on the 'peasantry' for *The Quarterly Review.* Thus we might ask: was Cobbett absolving employers and the state of responsibility for rural poverty, or was *Cottage Economy* misinterpreted by the élite? Wholly the latter, [as I] will argue, for in its political suppositions, and above all in its revisionist model of agrarian capitalism, Cobbett's strictures on cottage technology parted company with Whig improvement theory and with Tory prescriptions on the means of creating independent cottagers out of proletarian economic conditions.

Programmes of self-help, such as that espoused in *Cottage Economy,* were not the preserve of Whigs and Tories. A central theme of popular rural song throughout the first half of the nineteenth century was the struggle between economic determinism and the people's own agency in the attainment of domestic happiness. When traditional ballads treating of the chivalry of the nobility fell out of favour after 1815, the labourers turned not only to overt protest verse but to a genre of cottage songs whose heroes and heroines were humble country men and women who lived by the sweat of their brows, and who strove to maintain hospitality and happiness in the face of material hardship. At first glance the cottage songs appear to conform to the values promoted by the dominant culture's intrusions into the rural song market, but where the latter decree that the poor are too often idle and dissolute, the cottage songs suggest that these vices afflict the rich more than the poor. The songs acknowledge that honesty is an important virtue, but they proceed to remark that grinding poverty and unjust laws frequently oblige the poor to supplement their household economy by poaching and other extra-legal endeavours. Happiness, the songs observe, cannot be found in the face of poverty and exhaustion, but they encourage the poor to maintain their spirits, to seek out political solutions to their problems and to do whatever they must to make cottage life bearable and efficient. Thus, contrary to the élitist caricature of the farm workers as violent and misanthropic boors, the cottage songs reveal a class of people who strove to solve their social and cultural problems according to their own values and moral priorities. Indeed, the songs underwrite Cobbett's dictum that 'though we are oppressed, there is always something that we can do ourselves'.

During his twenty-two years as a practising farmer Cobbett delighted in growing two blades of grass where only one grew before; he experimented with tree culture, Tullian drill husbandry, Indian corn, cottage manufacturing and the importation of merino sheep. Not all of these projects were successful (the sheep, for example, developed an incurable foot-rot on the wetter English pastures), but it is simply wrong to suggest that his agricultural projects were ill-conceived or demonstrative of his inability 'to innovate'. He was indeed 'bereft of allies' in his husbandry, but only because of his opposition to the capital-intensive and market-oriented agriculture conducted at Holkham, Woburn and Petworth. As he explained to Thomas Coke, he was an improver with a difference:

> [Improvement] is a mark of good taste, and it is a pursuit attended with more pleasure, perhaps, than any other. But, if the thing cannot be accomplished without producing the fall, the degradation and misery of *millions,* it is not improvement . . . The gay farmhouses with pianos within were not *improvements*. The pulling down of 200,000 small houses and making the inhabitants paupers was not an *improvement*. The gutting of the cottages of their clocks and brass-kettles and brewing-tackle was no *improvement*.

In Cobbett's 'radical' husbandry, as he called it, improvement was a technological innovation which added to the food, dress and happiness of those who worked the land. While the agricultural societies of the farmers and landlords ('nests of conspirators against the labourer', in Cobbett's view) awarded premiums to employers who cultivated the most land with the fewest hands, Cobbett's experiments were manpower intensive, even to the point where he once worked 100 men upon 4 acres at Kensington. The great object of Cobbett's agricultural experiments was to elevate labourers into self-sufficient smallholders, and in the process to undermine the high capitalism of large farmers and shopkeepers. Not in so many words did he encourage labourers to cease waged employment, but nor did he disguise the fact that the introduction of more non-wage forms of survival would reverse proletarianization and reduce the pool of reserve labour upon which large-scale capitalist agriculture depended.

Cobbett deplored the word 'peasantry' on account of its implication of a 'degraded caste of persons', but he was strongly supportive of many of the occupational characteristics that rural historians have assigned to an objective or idealized peasantry. Indeed, Cobbett's assumption in **Cottage Economy** that many village workers extracted part of their subsistence from self-employments, cottage gardens and other diverse ingenuities goes some way towards reinforcing the suggestions by Mick Reed and Dennis Mills that peasants or household producers were more common in nineteenth-century rural England than we have been in the habit of thinking. Cobbett certainly remarked upon a trend in his day towards a threefold tiering of rural society—namely landlords, tenant farmers and hired labourers—but he also observed that many agricultural workers in the rural South derived a portion of their livelihood by productive modes that were distinct from market-oriented capital on one hand, and from proletarian labour on the other.

For Cobbett, the most important means of self-sufficiency was access to the soil, whether in the form of common land, cottage gardens or small farms. Even at Botley, where he cobbled together farms to a total of some 600 acres (mostly during his anti-Jacobin years, but still an embarrassment to a future critic of engrossment), he stood opposed to enclosure schemes which would have contributed more acres to his personal holdings. These stands against enclosure were hardly acts of great charity, but he also pursued more direct initiatives in support of landholding among the rural poor. During the scarcity of 1816, according to the vestry minutes of Bishop's Waltham, he used his influence as one of the larger landholders in the parish to call a special vestry meeting to obtain leave from the Lord of the Manor and the copyhold tenants

> to enclose small parcels of Waste-Land in order to assist them in the support of their families. *Second,* to consult on the propriety of making application to the Lord of the Manor and the tenants to grant Copies for the said enclosures, and also for all enclosures already made in the manor by Encroachers, if the said Encroachers be poor men or women belonging to this Parish.

The proposal, according to the minutes, 'was rejected, their [*sic*] being only Mr. Cobbett to vote for the Propositions'. Among those who voted against the initiatives were two leasers of pauper labour and three large farmers: the first claimed that the parcels of land would make the labourers more 'saucy', the second argued that it would cause them to breed more rapidly and the third suggested that it would lead them to demand higher wages. Not only was the plan lost but within two years the vestry voted to throw open the existing encroachments which Cobbett had sought to have certified in deed.

Although not resident at Botley after his bankruptcy of 1820, Cobbett maintained a close interest in the welfare of the labourers and cottagers in his former parishes. In 1826 he opposed a petition by local farmers and landlords to enclose the 1,300 acres of Waltham Chase, on which lived a thousand cottagers who drew a large portion of their living from the cows, pigs and forest horses that they grazed on the common. The petitioners' claim that the land was 'unproductive in its present state' was sufficient word for the House of Commons, which drafted and passed a bill allowing the enclosure to proceed. Much to Cobbett's gratification, however, the Lords, to whom he had submitted evidence on both the productive use of the Chase and the hardship that its enclosure would cause, inspected the bill in committee and refused to proceed with it. 'Judge you of [the farmers'] mortification', said Cobbett to the cottagers:

> You have seen an egg-sucking cur, when an egg-shell fitted with hot coals has been crammed into his mouth; and you have seen him twist his jaws about, and stare like mad. Like these curs were the graspers, when the House of Lords refused to give them the power of

robbing the poor of Waltham Chase of the last blade of grass.

It was Cobbett's experience that commons and small farms bred a spirit of independence and self-confidence among the rural poor. His favourite agricultural scientist, Jethro Tull, had complained bitterly during the early eighteenth century of 'saucy' labourers who defied their masters and insisted that they be addressed 'in a very humble persuasive manner'. This was all to the good in Cobbett's view. While admitting that there might be some 'inconvenience' in brashness, he much preferred 'the saucy daring fellow' over the 'poor, crawling, feeble wretch, who is not saucy, only, perhaps, because he feels that he has not the power to maintain himself'.

Cobbett also knew that labourers and cottagers were efficient and productive cultivators in their own right. Turning to Coke of Norfolk as an apologist for large farms and capital-intensive agriculture, he asserted that ten farms of 100 acres would yield more than one farm of 1,000 acres, for much agricultural produce, especially poultry, milk and honey, was more the result of time and care than of capital. The large farm, he claimed, only *appeared* more productive, with its large wagons rumbling to market along impressive new turnpikes. Large farmers knew as much, hence their bitter and irrational denunciations of cottagers as a 'new class of producer' who had the arrogance (in the words of one employer) to 'show us how to farm'. As one steward learned, 'it is by no means uncommon for a farmer who holds three or four hundred acres of land to complain, when his landlord interferes to take from him three or four acres for a cottager, that his farm is essentially injured by it'. In Wiltshire in 1806, recalled the rector of Broad Somerford, some parcels of land that farmers proved unable to reclaim were allotted to labourers, and soon 'cultivated in such perfection that . . . it is a disgrace to the farmer's cultivation'.

Cobbett knew many instances of cottagers succeeding at labour-intensive husbandry. Known to him since his youth were the Surrey 'Bourners' who put their spades to the tiny green patches between the heath-covered hills to the south of Farnham. 'The land being generally too poor to attract the rich,' Cobbett observed, 'this common has escaped enclosure bills; and every little green dip is now become a cottager's garden or field . . . till they have formed a grand community of cottages, each with its own plot of ground and its pigsty. Similar to the 'Bourners' were the cottagers of the New Forest who managed a prosperous and efficient agriculture which included a pig, sometimes a cow and pony, customary access to peat, wood and turf, as well as rights of grazing and mast. The pig was the certain thing: on one visit Cobbett counted some 140 within 60 yards of his horse. New Forest pigs, according to the topographers Brayley and Britton, produced the best bacon in the country, and reached weights of between 300 and 800 pounds apiece. Yet this dynamic economy of the foresters invited charges that they were so many thieves, prostitutes, smugglers and poachers. The agricultural improver Charles Vancouver pleaded on 'moral' grounds for the removal of the encroachers on the

Forest's edge, while William Gilpin represented the entire population as 'an indolent race; poor and wretched in the extreme'. All their manifold advantages in way of fuel and livestock, he claimed, 'procure them not half the enjoyments of common day-labourers'. Cobbett, on the other hand, found them 'happy and well' with neat cottages, abundant fuel, a pig or two and sometimes a cow.

The pattern to emerge from Cobbett's detailed studies of forests and commons was that the poorer the soil the better off the labourers. At Swing-torn Micheldever in Hampshire he found newly enclosed commons, large farms and hungry labourers, whereas south of Winchester on the Mildmay estates, amid poorer soil, smaller farms and abundant woods and commons, the labourers had gardens, pigs and 'none of that haggard look which is so painful to my eyes in the north of Hampshire'. At Hurstbourne Tarrant the soil was rich and the agriculture advanced, but the labourers among the poorest in the county. To the south and east on the difficult soil of the Sussex woodlands, the labourers and cottagers were better off than their fellows in the corn-growing regions, for 'all is not appropriated where there are coppices and woods, where the cultivation is not so easy and the produce so very large'. In the forests near Tunbridge Wells, for example, he found that the labouring people looked 'pretty well' and had pigs in their sties; while in more arable areas, such as the Isle of Thanet, they 'suffer from the want of fuel, and they have nothing but their *bare pay*'. Scenes of poverty amid plenty were observed by Cobbett in the valley of the Avon, East Anglia and most often in north Hampshire and Wiltshire, where he found the labourers at the 'inferno potato level' with 'worse gardens than anywhere else'.

Of all country workers it was the 'clay and coppice' people of the southern weald that Cobbett most admired, and it was among them that he researched and compiled the recipes and instructions of *Cottage Economy*. These workers were unlettered and superstitious, but from the awkward wealden soils they extracted a hearty living 'by hook or by crook'. They had pigs, cows in some cases, winter employment in the coppices and a ready supply of wood for fuel, pig-sties, cow-sheds and hop-poles. These people were not confronted by enclosure schemes or by engrossing farmers; they secured their subsistence independently of the rich, who despised them for it. These 'leather-legged chaps', as Cobbett called them, were neither capitalist nor proletarian; they produced for their own consumption, exchanged produce with their friends and neighbours and had only occasional recourse to the commercial market. It was Cobbett's observation that they were able to maintain their independent economy, not so much because of any uniquely 'entrepreneurial' disposition, but because their property was 'deemed worth *nothing*' by the large landholders.

Much in contrast with the clay and coppice people were the labourers of arable districts who were often obliged to pay £4 or £5 a year, or a quarter of the man's earnings, for wood, peat or coal. Some Wiltshire labourers, Cobbett observed, scrambled for fuel merely to boil water for tea.

These 'local disadvantages', as Frederick Eden glibly called them, were not sympathetically treated by the labourers' critics: a Surrey farmer, for example, *seemed* to have the right idea when he urged his workers to diversify their diet by boiling rather than broiling their meat, but after a fair trial his workers complained that they could not afford the additional fuel involved. Cobbett understood the problem: at Botley he included a constant supply of fuel in his workers' wages; he also ensured that his cottages were fitted with large ovens. But these were extraordinary practices; the first cottage of Joseph and Hannah Ashby, for example, had no range for cooking, 'only an open fire with a shallow oven of seventeenth-century pattern under it'. Such an obvious disadvantage, however, did not prevent a visitor to Tysoe from publicly condemning the 'improvidence and cooking of the cottage women', which charge would have gone unchallenged had not Joseph, like Cobbett, possessed the exceptional ability to launch a written defence of the skills and efficiency of his class.

Ill-informed criticism of the labourers' 'improvidence' was commonplace in nineteenth-century cottage manuals. But while Cobbett's treatise was a rare exception, it did not pretend to approve of all of the labourers' domestic habits. Not intending that the book be read by employers or Whig educators, he dealt frankly with domestic inefficiencies, calling upon rural workers to make the best use of their raw materials. There 'are very few gardens of the labourers in the country', he observed, 'unless where they have been totally stripped by the bull-frog system of enclosure, which do not contain twenty or thirty rods each'. He instructed his readers in how to turn these few rods to full advantage, and at the same time to cease all unnecessary indulgences which imbalanced the cottage budget. His most controversial advice pertained to bread—the *'staff of life'* which he insisted upon for every farm worker. A man earning 10s. a week, with four children, an industrious wife and a quarter acre garden, he calculated, should not have his children crying for bread, even with flour at 6d. a bushel. The woman's duty was to bake the bread; that of the man was not to complain that a coarser loaf was not good enough—'it was good enough for his forefathers who were too proud to be paupers'. These heady words were more pleasing to the readers of *The Edinburgh Review* than to the southern rural workers, who associated the coarse and heavy flour of Cobbett's recommendation with extraordinary scarcity, the olden times and the fare of the Midlands and North. But unlike other commentators who criticized the labourers' insistence upon the wheaten loaf, Cobbett ensured that he also offered advice on the means of securing the other two-thirds of the three Bs: bacon and beer.

In a small way *Cottage Economy* indulged the southern farm worker by refusing to recommend the more flexible diet of the labourer of the North and Scotland. It was Cobbett's boast that a Sussex labourer would not adopt a northern diet unless the rich 'broke every limb in his body', destroyed the coppices and woods and force-fed him *'oat-cakes, pea-bunnochs, and burgoo'*. Thus no sooner was he across the Tweed in 1832 than he began composing broadsides for the southern chopsticks about the scarcity of villages, churches, alehouses, flower-gardens, and pigs and geese, while ridiculing the bothies where the Scottish labourers kept residence and prepared their meals from their allowances of potatoes, oats, barley and milk. 'If this be the effect of [Scottish] light,' he declared, 'give me the darkness o' tha' Sooth', and on he went to urge the southern labourers to go to any length to preserve their gardens, Poor Laws and what remained of their bread, bacon and beer. This was indulgence of a sort, but it was also the commission of the southern labourers' own songs, which refused to relinquish a claim to the three Bs, even if it meant foregoing the more varied fare of their Scottish brothers and sisters.

The Edinburgh Review was able to embrace **Cottage Economy** on account that its editors did not detect Cobbett's unofficial sub-text which invited the labourers to steal fuel and fodder, to poach as required and to evade the exciseman whenever possible. Such practices were condoned by Cobbett on account of his belief that the labourers already performed adequate services for their rulers and employers, who in turn bore much of the responsibility for the erosion of organic relationships within the cottage. The state taxed leather, salt, candles, soap, malt and hops, while employers often refused to break bulk or to retail small portions of food to their workers. The result was a dependence upon shopkeepers which crippled the cottage budget by appending to food costs the profits of farmer, miller, mealman and retailer, which in many cases amounted to the difference between indebtedness and solvency within the cottage. A cycle was thereby set in motion that saw the labourers mortgage their harvest earnings by July, fall into debt by early winter, and have their credit vanish by the start of the new year. Among Cobbett's official remedies were his campaigns against excise duties, his lectures to farmers on the virtues of the farm-gate sale and his support for the cottage cow-keeping programmes of Lords Brownlow, Carrington, Stanhope and Winchelsea, but he did not hold his breath for these reforms, advising the labourers in the meantime to do what they had to do—legal or otherwise—to avoid the shopkeeper and the purchase of taxable commodities.

After the quarter-acre garden or its pilfered equivalent the cornerstone of Cobbett's writing on cottage economics was the pig. It was the national animal, according to Cobbett and the labourers—unmatched in taste and culinary versatility. Cobbett was even moved to suggest that a flitch in the larder was more important and meaningful than a complete set of the **Political Register;** it prompted peace, goodwill and happiness in a way that nothing else could. As Walter Rose later observed, the flitch 'formed the purtiest picture in the house', and 'to understand why, you must know not only the labourers' habit of mind but the poverty from which his stock had sprung'. Cobbett well understood this state of mind, but first he got down to advising the labourers on the means of fattening hogs upon a wide variety of fodders amenable to spade husbandry, including potatoes, pease, beans, cabbages, turnips and Indian corn, together with the familiar roadside acquisitions that inclined some Dorset farmers to declare that 'no labourer can be honest and feed a pig'. It was in pig-keeping that labourers and cottagers most ably demonstrated the 'hook or crook' ingenuity that Cobbett wished to see extended to all aspects of the rural domestic experience, for despite a decline in the number of cottage pigs in some regions, Cobbett found many sties still occupied, especially in Gloucestershire, Worcestershire, Kent, the Isle of Wight and the fens of Lincolnshire and Cambridgeshire. Exact figures are hard to come by, but there seems to have been a pig in about 40 per cent of cottage gardens.

Like Flora Thompson, Cobbett revelled in the lore of the pig. He spoke in metaphysical tone about the sagacity and discriminating palate of the hog, and happily conformed with the countryman's penchant for scratching a pig's back with a walking stick while entertaining passers-by with tall stories about the hog's wisdom. One of his yarns, though 'true beyond all doubt', pertained to a gamekeeper who had taught a pig to point to partridges and other fallen game in the manner of a pointer dog. Accordingly, Cobbett insisted upon first-class accommodation for his swine: 'When I make up my hogs' lodging place for winter, I look well at it, and consider, whether, upon a pinch, I could, for once and away, make shift to lodge in it myself. If I *shiver at the thought,* the place is not good enough for my hogs.' During his stay in America in 1817-18, he went as far as to accommodate a large sow inside his Long Island farmhouse, much to the irritation of his son John who was kept awake at night by the incessant grunts of the boarder. If in some ways Cobbett lived an absurd and obsessive life, this was not one of them: the pig is a tidy and intelligent animal maligned only by urban prejudice. Its well-being was the most important concern of a pig-keeping household; when the bacon chest ran low, Cobbett observed, the pig-keeper's discourse evolved from 'd—d hog' to 'pretty piggy'; and as slaughter-day approached, the atmosphere in the cottage became one of nervous anticipation. Along with the labourers, Cobbett remembered the procedures of the butchering with proverbs and rituals, knowing that the job had to be done methodically and with a mystical reverence, not in the haphazard and secular manner of Hardy's Jude. For a small minority of countrymen, such as Joseph Ashby, the mentality associated with pig-keeping was intellectually debilitating; Cobbett preferred to see it as an example of the importance of tradition, neighbourliness and good living in the village community.

Cobbett's greatest contribution to pig-keeping was his introduction to England of 'Cobbett's Corn': a dwarf variety of Continental maize which he proved would ripen in England and provide an excellent source of both animal fodder and of human food. As small a crop as 10 rods, he claimed, could fatten a pig to 1,000 pounds; or if the labourer preferred, five pigs to 200 pounds. The crop had much to commend it in Cobbett's agrarian economics: it required no capital and no barn, it could be worked by women and children, with the entire family spending the winter months shelling ears at the fireside. Cobbett further predicted that cottagers with 20 rods of his corn would aspire to 10 acres, and subsequently to a

small farm. In this way the corn would produce *'real emancipation:* it is the *poor man's plant:* it is the *plant of liberty;* the *plant of independence',* and of insurance: 'It will *prevent the labourers from ever being slaves again;* it will inevitably re-produce *small farms;* it will make labourers more independent of their employers; it will bring back, it will *hasten* back, the country towards its former happy state.' Cobbett's expectations were not met, but in the face of derision from *The Times* and the *Farmer's Journal,* the crop met with substantial, if temporary, success. From his experimental farm in Surrey (the cost of the experiments ran into the 'thousands' according to his daughter Susan), 'Cobbett's Corn' spread in patchwork from Scotland to the Channel Islands, enabling a number of labourers to keep a pig for the first time. Early in 1831, on account of the excellent public response to the corn, Cobbett arranged to distribute free packages of seed to the Swing counties, each of which was to receive 200 ears for its labourers, with the exception of Kent, which was to receive 500 in unsubtle commemoration of the starting point of the rising. It was Cobbett's intention to distribute the corn in person, 'but I do not want to be hanged; and, I know, that no place is safe for me; which is not at a *good* distance from the ricks and barns, and furnishes me with an alibi'. When the torches were laid to rest, Cobbett hurried to the Swing-torn parishes of Sussex and north Hampshire, where he organized the planting of the corn in the face of derision from large farmers, the London press and an estranged Henry Hunt. All that mattered to Cobbett was the response of the labourers, who seem to have appreciated the gesture. One elderly labourer refused to accept payment from Cobbett for two exemplary ears: 'I planted 24 corns, and I have these bunches of fine ears, I have put some short ones by for seed and Mr. Cobbett, God bless him, he is welcome to the whole of them if he wishes it.' The local scribe who passed on the message might have coloured its contents to curry favour with Cobbett; nevertheless the corn was not the hoax that many alleged, even some of Cobbett's political adversaries admitted as much. Still, not even Cobbett himself boasted complete success, for the new crop failed to bring an end to the human consumption of potatoes.

It is understandable that late twentieth-century Britons—the world's foremost consumers of potatoes—should find novelty and amusement in Cobbett's diatribes against 'the root of extreme unction', but dietary dignity is relative. If today's North Americans feel no cultural imposition in gnawing 'Cobbett's Corn' directly off the cob, the same cannot be said for many aghast British observers, who sometimes marvel at the culinary simplicity and apparent indignity of the spectacle. Cobbett ate his sweet corn directly off the cob, yet he deplored the sight of labourers unearthing potatoes, tossing them unwashed into a pot, and carrying them cold to the fields in their satchels. It was not so much the taste or the foreign origins of the potato that most unnerved him (nor its status as an innovative crop: his own sweet corn was an even newer arrival), but rather the 'slovenly and beastly habits' which he associated with its production and consumption. The vigour of Cobbett's opposition to the 'villainous root' had much to do with with his recollection of a potato-free Farnham:

> I can remember when the first acre of potatoes was planted in a field, in the neighbourhood of the place where I was born; and I very well remember, that even the poorest of the people would not eat them. They called them hog-potatoes; but now, they are become a considerable portion of the diet of those who raise the bread for others to eat.

Although carrying his opposition to the ridiculous heights of threatening to inflict penalties upon anyone who transported potatoes onto his own farms, he had important scientific and economic objections to the root. First, it contributed little to the organic relationships in the cottage garden, yielding no straw for pig-bedding and returning few nutrients to the soil. Second, he joined the labourers in objecting to potatoes, not as a dietary supplement, but as the 'sole food of man'. Finally, he strongly rejected the uncharitable idea (often expressed in Cobbett's own day, and later by J. H. Clapham) that potatoes were adequate compensation for the labourers' losses in other vegetable fare. The labourers of 1830 were 'almost wholly supplied with potatoes', according to one observer: 'breakfast and dinner brought to them in the fields, and nothing but potatoes'. In 1826, not a particularly hungry year, Alexander Somerville was obliged to do with his crop of potatoes 'what I intended a pig to do—eat them'. Most emphatically of all, Cobbett opposed the potato because it allowed rural employers to add to the exploitation of their workers. Farmers represented the potato plot as 'a blessing to all the lower classes of the community', for it meant that their labourers might survive on 7s. or 8s. a week. In the words of one agricultural reporter, the new crop kept the labourers 'more under subjection' by discouraging them from 'leaving their master during the summer; as in that case the crop would be forfeited'.

Potato-eating, according to Cobbett, was not an isolated practice but 'a component part of the tea-drinking system' which cumulatively robbed the labourers of time, money and good health. In advising English workers to refrain from tea, he joined the company of John Wesley, Arthur Young, Frederick Eden, William Howitt and Sir John Sinclair—Tories in the main. These men looked back to an older, more virile and 'manly' England; they parted company with Cobbett on political matters but believed in fair play and hard work, which according to most genuine countrymen, required an ample supply of beer. For William Marshall, the speed at which harvest work was performed stood in inverse relationship with the amount of beer consumed. The same observation was made all over the Kingdom, including by a Shropshire farmer who after complaining of the *excessive quantity* of beverage' allowed to the farm workers of his county, proceeded to observe (without relating cause and effect) that 'there are few parts of England, where the harvest is got in with such spirit and expedition'. Cobbett was in no doubt that beer was a necessity of life for those who lived by their labour. As an employer he discovered that one labourer

'well lined with meat and beer is worth two or three creatures swelled out with warm water, under the name of tea'. In terms of the labourers' overall diet, he rated beer next in importance to bread and meat, and as far more important than cheese or butter.

Opposition to beer came from the advocates (mainly Whigs and Peelites) of an urban-based English culture. The younger Peel, whom Cobbett later confronted in Parliament for a repeal of the malt duty, defended tea as a moral refreshment and as 'our national beverage'. Cobbett and his men could only laugh at these suggestions; they saw the advertisers of tea in the same light as they saw temperance reformers: as 'despicable drivelling quacks'. This is not to say that Cobbett approved of immoderate consumption or drunkenness. He carefully calculated his workers' allowances at two quarts per day in winter, three in spring and five in summer; this much the labourers must have, he argued, otherwise they would turn to the alehouse with ruinous frequency.

Cobbett was far from alone in condemning the decline in cottage brewing precipitated by the leap in the malt tax from 10s. 6d. per quarter in 1791 to 38s. 8d. in 1804. Farmer John Ellman of Glynde in Sussex informed the 1821 Select Committee on Agriculture that when he began farming in the 1770s, every family in his parish brewed their own beer—'there are few of them now that do, unless I give them the malt'. Ellman was no Radical, and partly for this reason Cobbett extracted abundant mileage from the testimony, referring to it not fewer than twenty times. Many other commentators supplied similar evidence. At Chailey in Sussex during the 1790s it was observed that 'since the advance in the price of malt, both the brewing and consumption of beer have been much discontinued; and tea and spirits have been very greatly substituted'. In nearby Offham there was said to be tea but no beer in the cottages. In Berkshire, according to David Davies, home-brewing fell off markedly during the early 1790s on account of a doubling of the taxes on malt and hops. During the 1780s, remembered an Isle of Thanet farmer, every labourer 'had a barrel of beer in his cellar', but such was not the case by the 1830s. Home-brewing, said Frederick Eden in 1797, 'even amongst small farmers is at an end. The Poor drink tea at all their meals.' The labourers were 'worse workmen' as a result, added a Gloucestershire farmer, 'for they have not now strength sufficient to perform their work properly, from the want of a nutritive and invigorating beverage, which the removal of the Tax upon Malt would supply'.

Some of Cobbett's archest political foes, including the Hampshire MP Willis Fleming and Thomas Coke of Holkham, lamented the passing of cottage brewing. Many farmers, to be sure, were less interested in cheap beer than in markets for their barley, but some were genuinely distressed at the sight of their workers attempting to quench their thirst at the water-pump. In some cases these farmers continued to brew, despite the high costs. A large Kentish farmer claimed that his brewing expenses amounted to £2,000 between 1831 and 1834; another announced that he tolerated a high malt bill because 'a man cannot work without beer'. Still, such sensitivity was the exception. The Essex farmer and political reformer Montagu Burgoyne, for example, was party to a local decision to pay weekly wages of 8s. with beer, or 9s. without. 'I am laughed at by all gentlemen farmers for preferring the former', he remarked, 'I know that it is attended with inconvenience; but it is no small comfort to the poor man; and trouble, in such a case, is a duty.'

Thus, while the commercial production of beer continued to rise after 1790, the decline of home-brewing meant a decrease in the rates of *per capita* consumption, which is to say that English rural workers doubtless consumed more beer in the 1720s than in the 1820s, despite a modest reduction in the malt duty in 1822. Moreover, the beer consumed in Regency times was largely purchased from the public house, where until 1830 it was taxed at the rate of 200 per cent. The bottle-crook that Cobbett had carried to the field in his youth became a rare sight. 'While this tax lasts', he argued,

> working men have *no home;* no fireside, no family; they are driven to prowl about for drink like cattle in a dry summer. In short, this tax must be repealed, or we must prepare ourselves for everlasting strife, and everlasting confusion. Tax the wine, tax the spirits, tax the sugar, tax the tea, tax anything but the malt.

The malt duty was worse than plague, famine or civil war, he claimed, it was 'the main instrument in the ruin of England'. Given cheap malt, the labourers would brew again; their beer would cost them a penny a quart and they could dispense with the tea-kettle 'that boileth without ceasing, like the bowels of Mount-Edna'. In the meantime he urged his own workers to make their own malt behind the back of the exciseman, 'and good jovial lives they led'.

Along with the Poor Law Bill, the malt duty was Cobbett's first priority as a member of Parliament, and he died fighting for its repeal against the Whigs and Tories who cared little about the labourers and their mascot John Barleycorn. Home-brewing would ultimately return to the cottage, but not until later in the century, in the communities of Richard Jefferies and Flora Thompson, by which time tea was commonplace and the standing of beer reduced in rural culture. Even a countryman of the calibre of W. H. Hudson would assume that neatness and civic pride in Wiltshire villages implied temperance among the inhabitants. He was surprised to learn that the villagers brewed their own beer and drank of it daily. Doubtless the village was sober not despite its home-brewing but because of it, just as Cobbett would have anticipated.

The great explanation for Cobbett's long-standing opposition to Regency tax schedules lies not in the **Political Register** but in **Cottage Economy**. The approximately 40 percent of the labourers' earnings that went to the taxman were the ways in which the 'system' contributed to the corruption of the labourers' economy. Salt quarried in Hampshire cost 2s. 6d. in the state of New York, but 19s. at the quarry itself. Legislators seemed unaware that salt

was required in the making of butter, cheese and, above all, bacon. The labourer Thomas Smart, in giving evidence to the 1824 parliamentary committee on agricultural wages, complained that the salt tax prevented him from keeping a pig, for the three pecks needed to salt a good-sized hog were elevated by the tax from 6d. to 10s. 6d. The pig might also have to go if the farmer refused to sell the odd bushel of wheat to the labourer, for that was the source of bran that best concluded the fattening process. The demise of home-brewing also had implications for pig-keeping inasmuch as used malt was often applied to the same purpose. Without a pig, in turn, there was neither bacon in the cottage nor natural fertilizer for the garden; nor was there lard for cooking or (to return to the decline of home-brewing) yeast for the baking of bread. Cottagers had either to buy these supplies at the inflated prices of the shopkeeper, publican and baker, or they went without their traditional fare.

The last great compromise of the organic potential of the cottage lay in the removal of manufacturing from the countryside. Cobbett is often criticized for his prosaic appeals for a return to 'the *dark ages*' when women spun wool and knitted stockings, but it is seldom observed that he tackled the problem directly by reviving the straw-plait industry which had entered a depression during the 1820s on account of the importation of straw hats from Tuscany. His plan was to grow in England the same grasses that were used in the Italian and American manufacture, which in a limited way he succeeded in doing. Among those to prosper at his industry were two Botley girls who earned more at plaiting than did their father at agricultural labour. A crippled Kentish worker who was unable to perform field labour mastered the craft of plaiting from the book by 'Mr. Caubitt'. Even as far north as the Orkneys there was introduced the 'Cobbett-Bonnet' industry, which, according to one observer, added £20,000 a year to the regional economy. For his efforts Cobbett was awarded the silver medal of the Society of Arts (he thought that he deserved the gold), which he accepted in a frank speech condemning 'that despicable cant, which was constantly dinned into the ears of the labouring classes; who, if they complained of their situation, were immediately told, that they ought to be contented with the state of paupers'. Mixed with the applause of Society members, according to *The Times* correspondent, was 'some slight disapprobation'. A certain amount of disapprobation was inevitable for Cobbett was attracted to the industry because it engendered no urban masses, 'calico-lords' or Combination Acts. He also liked the fact that it required little capital, and that it was 'a great deal better employment than singing hymns, listening to the bawling of the Methodist parson, or in reading those lying blackguard things called religious tracts'.

Cottage Economy sought to rebuild the cottage as a viable economic organism at the same time as Cobbett campaigned against legislation prejudicial to the labourers' independence and happiness. At one level it is a practical text on cookery, but when set beside Cobbett's other ventures on behalf of the village economy, it becomes a highly political text in a way that *The Edinburgh Review* did not perceive. Even on points where Cobbett and the ruling class seemed to be in essential agreement, such as on the merits of the straw-plait industry, or on the virtues of home-brewed ale, they were at political and economic odds; for while most legislators and employers were not exactly opposed to improvements in the labourers' happiness and material circumstances, they were not prepared to run any risk of esteeming labour ahead of capital. Cobbett, on the other hand, perceived the cottage, and indeed the entire industry of agriculture, as a family unit of peasant production which would have all but destroyed capitalist agriculture. *Cottage Economy* worked in close collaboration with the labourers' own cultural priorities, while giving them hard advice on how to brew affordable beer (even with the malt tax in place), to build ice-houses and to keep bees. Although stopping short of the more collectivist agrarianism of the Owenites or Spenceans, Cobbett was adamant that his readers not be content as waged labourers or even as cottagers; he wanted a nation of peasants or 'household producers' who exchanged goods and services in kind, cultivated their own lands with family hands and avoided the capitalist market except to sell by barter some excess produce at traditional fairs:

> I hold a return to *small farms* to be absolutely necessary to a restoration of any thing like an English community; and I am quite sure, that the ruin of the present race of farmers, generally, is a necessary preliminary to this . . . Men, not only without *capital,* but who have never so much as heard the coxcomical word, must be put to cultivate farms. Farms will be divided again.

And so sang the labourers, who called for ten farms to be made of one. But small farms did not return, and the primacy of capital was not reduced. Even the later allotment movement was viewed by many employers with grave suspicion: as a Suffolk labourer recalled, 'the landowners and gentry were as much against our desire for allotments as if we had claimed universal suffrage'.

FURTHER READING

Biography

Bowen, Marjorie. *Peter Porcupine: A Study of William Cobbett, 1762-1835.* London: Longmans, Green and Co., 1935, 312 p.

Broad-stroked life of Cobbett which attempts "to reduce to their simplest elements the problems that vexed Cobbett and his contemporaries. . . ."

Briggs, Asa. *William Cobbett.* London: Oxford University Press, 1967, 63 p.

Succinct, well-informed, illustrated biography.

Clarke, John. *The Price of Progress: Cobbett's England, 1780-1835.* London: Granada Publishing, 1977, 200 p.

Supplies background on the state of agricultural England during the years 1780 to 1835, and places Cobbett amid that milieu.

Johnson, D. C. "William Cobbett: 1762-1835." In her *Pioneers of Reform: Cobbett, Owen, Place, Shaftesbury, Cobden, Bright,* pp. 23-54. 1929. Reprint. New York: Burt Franklin, 1968.

Emphasizes Cobbett's agitation for cultural change, finding that though he did not accomplish what he wished, "He made known some of the under side of the 'progress' which few cared to observe; he played an effective part in developing early democratic activity," among other accomplishments.

Moore, John. "Politics and Swedes." In his *Country Men,* pp. 108-56. 1935. Reprint. Freeport, N.Y.: Books for Libraries Press, 1969.

Lively biographical essay which presents Cobbett as a blustering, changeable, opinionated rustic in whom a high degree of intelligence and common sense coexisted with stupidity and rude intolerance.

Sales, Roger. "The Unacceptable Face of Rural Society." In his *English Literature in History, 1780-1830: Pastoral and Politics,* pp. 70-87. New York: St. Martin's Press, 1983.

On the true state of rural England during the time of Cobbett's *Rural Rides,* with illustrations from history of the poverty under which the "chopsticks" labored. Sales finds *Rural Rides* a convincing argument against returning to the values of a romanticized "Merrie England" of the popular imagination.

Thomas, Edward. "William Cobbett." In his *A Literary Pilgrim in England,* pp. 117-25. London: Methuen & Co., 1917.

Focuses upon Cobbett's favorable perceptions of the English countryside in which he and his ancestors lived and worked.

Bibliography

Gaines, Pierce W. *William Cobbett and the United States, 1792-1835: A Bibliography with Notes and Extracts.* Worcester, Mass.: American Antiquarian Society, 1971, 249 p.

Exhaustive bibliography of Cobbett's works "written in the United States and published here or abroad, or written elsewhere and published here, or written and published elsewhere but related in a major way to the United States."

Pearl, M. L. *William Cobbett: A Bibliographical Account of His Life and Times.* London: Oxford University Press, 1953, 266 p.

Thorough, detailed bibliography of writings by and about Cobbett.

Criticism

Aarts, F. G. A. M. "William Cobbett: Radical, Reactionary and Poor Man's Grammarian." *Neophilologus* LXX, No. 4 (October 1986): 603-14.

Clear, succinct biographical and critical essay on Cobbett's life and career, focusing upon his *Le tuteur anglais, ou grammaire régulière de la langue anglaise,*

A Grammar of the English Language, and his *Spelling Book, with Appropriate Lessons in Reading and with a Stepping-Stone to English Grammar.*

Chandler, Alice. "Historical Background: Cobbett." In her *A Dream of Order: The Medieval Ideal in Nineteenth-Century English Literature,* pp. 52-82. London: Routledge & Kegan Paul, 1971.

On Cobbett as an "archexemplar" in propounding an early nineteenth-century "medieval revival." Chandler claims that Cobbett's "regret for a pastoral, more prosperous, smock-frocked England captures the spirit of the age."

Chesterton, G. K. Preface to *Cottage Economy,* by William Cobbett, pp. vii-x. London: Peter Davies, 1926.

Praises Cobbett as a champion of the poor and a revivifier of medieval English values in regard to the cottager and the land. He describes *Cottage Economy* as a valuable, practical work.

————. "Cobbett's View of History" and "Cobbett and the Neglected Truth." In his *The Collected Works of G. K. Chesterton, Vol. XXXIII: "The Illustrated London News," 1923-1925,* edited by Lawrence J. Clipper, pp. 582-87, 587-90. San Francisco: Ignatius Press, 1990.

Two-part commentary upon G. D. H. Cole's biography, emphasizing Cobbett's "medievalism" and characteristics as a political thinker.

Duff, Gerald. "William Cobbett and the Prose of Revelation." *Texas Studies in Literature and Language* 11, No. 4 (Winter 1970): 1349-65.

Examines Cobbett's prose style, finding that as a satirist, "Cobbett attacks in English society what he sees to be false, hypocritical, and selfish," but that in order to communicate with his readers, "he takes the idiom of the common people, clears it of its disorder and awkwardness, and puts it on the page in a manner comprehensible to the ordinary laborer."

Jensen, Jay. "William Cobbett: John Bull as Jouralist." *The Emory University Quarterly* XXI, No. 3 (Fall 1965): 173-82.

Thematic general essay on Cobbett's journalism, concluding that "his genius for expressing in concrete terms the interests and sentiments of the working classes made him the most popular and influential English journalist of his time."

Joad, C. E. M. "Books in General." *The New Statesman and Nation* XXIX, No. 734 (17 March 1945): 175.

Reviews *The Opinions of William Cobbett,* edited by G. D. H. and Margaret Cole. Joad discusses Cobbett's beliefs, comparing them with those of Bernard Shaw and John Stuart Mill. He concludes that it is the "conjunction of country roots and urban flowering, of Tory tastes and Radical opinions, that endears Cobbett to the heart of the present reviewer; it also, I think makes him unique."

Lemrow, Lynne. "William Cobbett's Journalism for the Lower Orders." *Victorian Periodicals Review* XV, No. 1 (Spring 1982): 11-20.

Explores Cobbett's skill in implementing "a style of writing uniquely suited to the needs of his audience, a newly literate laboring class made up of the journeymen and laborers of England, Scotland, Wales, and Ireland."

Osborne, John W. *William Cobbett: His Thought and His Times.* New Brunswick, N.J.: Rutgers University Press, 1966, 272 p.

Seeks "to analyze Cobbett's ideas and their relation to the England of his time."

————. "William Cobbett and Ireland." *Studies: An Irish Quarterly Review* LXX, Nos. 278-79 (Summer-Autumn 1981): 187-95.

Offers a detailed examination of what Cobbett said about Ireland in his journalism and during his term in the House of Commons.

Pritchett, V. S. "Cobbett or His Horse." *The New Statesman* LVII, No. 1457 (14 February 1959): 225-26.

Reviews a contemporary edition of *Rural Rides* and discusses Cobbett as a "surly, burly homely taker-on of all comers."

Rickword, Edgell. "William Cobbett's *Twopenny Trash.*" In *Rebels and Their Causes: Essays in Honour of A. L. Morton,* edited by Maurice Cornforth, pp. 141-49. London: Lawrence and Wishart, 1978.

On Cobbett's significance as an advocate of reform, focusing upon his twopenny monthly tract, priced for accessibility by the common folk, which became "a documentary record of the tragic dénouement of the economic-political system, whose instability Cobbett had been fore-telling for years."

Taylor, A. J. P. "Books in General." *The New Statesman and Nation* XLVI, No. 1173 (29 August 1953): 236-67.

Amused assessment of Cobbett as a critic of "the Thing"—the cultural and political establishment—who was something of a dilettante in his role as social critic and agriculturalist.

Wiener, Martin J. "The Changing Image of William Cobbett." *The Journal of British Studies* XIII, No. 2 (May 1974): 135-54.

Surveys trends in critical perception of Cobbett's significance in the years since his death. Weiner demonstrates that "Cobbett's changing reputation has come full circle: from posthumous dismissal to rehabilitation, in several distinct ways, to a renewed note of dismissal."

Williams, Raymond. "Contrasts: Edmund Burke and William Cobbett." In his *Culture and Society, 1750-1950,* pp. 3-20. New York: Columbia University Press, 1958.

Compares and contrasts the political views of Burke and Cobbett, finding each valuable in his own way as interpreters of the state of England.

The Mill on the Floss

George Eliot

The following entry presents criticism of Eliot's novel *The Mill on the Floss* (1860). For a discussion of Eliot's complete career, see *NCLC,* Volume 4; for criticism devoted to her novels *Middlemarch, Daniel Deronda,* and *Silas Marner,* see *NCLC,* Volumes 13, 23, and 41, respectively.

INTRODUCTION

The Mill on the Floss is George Eliot's second novel and her most autobiographical work of fiction. It tells the story of Maggie Tulliver, detailing her relationship with her brother Tom and her inability to conform to the rigidly traditional society in which she lives. Commentary on *The Mill on the Floss* has focused on its conclusion—which many critics consider abrupt—and on its complex characterizations and sociological insights.

Biographical Information

In its portrayal of the childhood, adolescence, and young womanhood of Maggie Tulliver, *The Mill on the Floss* is closely identified with Eliot herself—intellectually gifted, impulsive and passionate by nature, and living in a familial and social setting that did not value these qualities in her. In particular, her focus on her protagonist's relationship with a beloved but tyrannical and disapproving older brother closely mirrors Eliot's own relationship with her brother: Maggie and Tom Tulliver are given the same birthdates as Eliot and her brother, who for twenty years spurned Eliot while she lived with the married philosopher and essayist George Henry Lewes. It was not until Lewes died and Eliot married that the rift with her brother was mended. Maggie's need for Tom's love and acceptance has often been compared to Eliot's desire for her brother's acceptance; Barbara Hardy asserts: "As she dwells on the relationship between a brother and sister we can discern an understandable and undisfiguring nostalgia; a need to explain and justify in concretely imagined terms; and the falsifying pressures of a wish-fulfilling reconciliation."

Plot and Major Characters

Written in seven books, *The Mill on the Floss* chronicles Maggie and Tom Tulliver's lives from childhood to young adulthood. Books I and II concentrate on Maggie's childhood, establishing her impulsive temperament and her dependence on Tom. Eliot recounts several episodes be-

tween brother and sister, and, as John Hagan has noted, "in nearly every one . . . there emerges a sequence of actions which dramatizes Maggie's hunger for Tom's love, the frustration of that hunger, her rebellion, and the pleasure she receives from reconciliation." This section has been described as one of the most sympathetic and psychologically acute literary portrayals of girlhood in English literature. In the following books, the Tulliver family becomes impoverished and Maggie grows increasingly estranged from her father and brother. She becomes involved with the son of the man who bankrupted her father, and is also attracted to another man who is engaged to marry her cousin. On learning of these relationships, Tom turns Maggie out of his house and refuses to speak to her. Maggie's subsequent life is spent in service as a governess and in struggle with temptation and self-renunciation. As George Levine has noted, she ultimately submits herself "to the higher responsibility despite the loss of the possibility of self-fulfillment." Just as she offers up a prayer to the "Unseen Pity," the river begins to rise, and she sees Tom being swept away by the flood. Maggie rushes to Tom's rescue, and they drown in each other's arms, fulfilling the novel's epitaph, "In death they were not divided."

Major Themes

Critics assert that Maggie's need for love and acceptance is her underlying motivation throughout *The Mill on the Floss,* and the conflicts that arise in the novel often stem from her frustrated attempts at gaining this acceptance. Alan Bellringer has commented, "The two main themes of the novel, growing up and falling in love, lend themselves to amusement, but it is stunted growth and frustrated love that are emphasized." Commentators have often focused on the constant rejection of Maggie's talents and mannerisms by her family and society. Even the cultural norms of her community deny her intellectual and spiritual growth, according to Elizabeth Ermarth, "They are norms according to which she is an inferior, dependent creature who will never go far in anything, and which consequently are a denial of her full humanity."

Critical Reception

Commentators have varied in their analyses of *The Mill on the Floss.* Many critics concur with U. C. Knoepflmacher's assessment of the novel's conclusion as "at best pathetic, for it asks us to believe that the muddy waters of the Floss have briefly restored an Eden that never existed," but others defend the ending as appropriate and inevitable, consistent with the details of the plot and the novel's themes. The autobiographical nature of *The Mill on the Floss* has been deemed aesthetically damaging by some critics because, they charge, it led Eliot to place disproportionate emphasis on the first two books. However, Bernard J. Paris contends "that the novel's weaknesses are closely related to its strengths, for if George Eliot had not been so intimately identified with Maggie she could hardly have given us a portrait of such subtlety and interest." Critics consistently praise Eliot's touching portrayal of Maggie Tulliver's childhood; the novelist Henry James stated in an early review of the novel, "English novels abound in pictures of childhood; but I know of none more truthful and touching than the early pages of this work."

CRITICISM

George Eliot (letter date 1860)

SOURCE: A letter to John Blackwood on July 9, 1860, in *The George Eliot Letters, Vol. III: 1859-1861,* edited by Gordon S. Haight, Yale University Press, 1954, pp. 317-18.

[*In the following letter to her publisher, Eliot responds to Edward Bulwer-Lytton's criticism of* The Mill on the Floss.]

My dear Sir

I return Sir Edward's critical letter, which I have read with much interest. On two points I recognize the justice of his criticism. First, that Maggie is made to appear too passive in the scene of quarrel in the Red Deeps. If my

book were still in MS., I should—now that the defect is suggested to me—alter, or rather expand that scene. Secondly, that the tragedy is not adequately prepared. This is a defect which I felt even while writing the third volume, and have felt ever since the MS. left me. The *"epische Breite"* into which I was beguiled by love of my subject in the two first volumes, caused a want of proportionate fullness in the treatment of the third, which I shall always regret.

The other chief point of criticism—Maggie's position towards Stephen—is too vital a part of my whole conception and purpose for me to be converted to the condemnation of it. If I am wrong there—if I did not really know what my heroine would feel and do under the circumstances in which I deliberately placed her, I ought not to have written this book at all, but quite a different book, if any. If the ethics of art do not admit the truthful presentation of a character essentially noble but liable to great error—error that is anguish to its own nobleness—*then,* it seems to me, the ethics of art are too narrow, and must be widened to correspond with a widening psychology.

But it is good for me to know how my tendencies as a writer clash with the conclusions of a highly accomplished mind, that I may be warned into examining well whether my discordancy with those conclusions may not arise rather from an idiosyncrasy of mine, than from a conviction which is argumentatively justifiable.

I hope you will thank Sir Edward on my behalf for the trouble he has taken to put his criticism into a form specific enough to be useful. I feel his taking such trouble to be at once a tribute and a kindness. If printed criticisms were usually written with only half the same warrant of knowledge, and with an equal sincerity of intention, I should read them without fear of fruitless annoyance. I remain, my dear Sir,

Always yours truly

Marian Evans Lewes.

John Blackwood (letter date 1860)

SOURCE: A letter to George Eliot on March 20, 1860, in *The George Eliot Letters, Vol. III: 1859-1861,* edited by Gordon S. Haight, Yale University Press, 1954, pp. 276-77.

[*In the following letter written to Eliot, her publisher praises the manuscript of* The Mill on the Floss.]

My Dear Madam

Your second last chapter arrived safely today and will go out in proof to you along with this. I must write you a line of congratulation without waiting for the last chapter, which I hope to see on Thursday morning. *The Mill on the Floss* is safe for immortality.

Of course in spite of Lewes' strict injunctions I fastened upon these two last chapters the moment I secured them. Nothing short of a point of honour would have restrained me.

Bob Jakin's attempt to convey his sympathy to Maggie is beyond price. Never surely were pathos and exquisite humour more beautifully combined. Bob is the prince of packmen and a gentleman. In his reply to Dr. Kenn he will have the ardent sympathy of every one who has groaned under the inforced idleness of a dull sermon, and who has not?

I do not envy the man who can read the scene where Lucy appears and falls on Maggie's neck without being affected to tears. It is overpowering and touching and beautiful and is moreover exactly what was wanted to relieve the reader's feelings as well as Maggie's. The skill too with which it is indicated that dear Lucy's is a sorrow which may not be without hope like poor Maggie's is very fine.

I early foresaw that good Dr. Kenn would play a part and he comes in most happily. The illustration that his effort to put Maggie's character in the right light was as hopeless as a struggle to change the shape of bonnets made me burst out laughing. Aunt Glegg is great. Several times in reading these last chapters I have found myself start from my seat and walk to the Major's adjoining room exclaiming "By God she is a *wonderful* woman." The exclamation was irreverent, quite superfluous, and has a rude sound but I felt impelled to speak and the emphasis conveyed volumes of heartfelt admiration, so I hope to be excused.

I await with trembling impatience the Catastrophe.

ever yours truly

John Blackwood.

Henry James (essay date 1866)

SOURCE: "The Novels of George Eliot," in *George Eliot and Her Readers: A Selection of Contemporary Reviews,* edited by John Holmstrom and Laurence Lerner, Barnes & Noble, 1966, pp. 42-4.

[*James was an American novelist, short story writer, critic, and essayist of the late nineteenth and early twentieth centuries. Regarded as one of the greatest novelists of the English language, he is also admired as a lucid and insightful critic. In this article, first published in the* Atlantic Monthly *in 1866, James offers an early and largely favorable review of* The Mill on the Floss.]

. . . Of the four English studies, **The Mill on the Floss** seems to me to have most dramatic continuity, in distinction from that descriptive, discursive method of narration which I have attempted to indicate. After Hetty Sorrel, I think Maggie Tulliver the most successful of the author's young women, and after Tito Melema, Tom Tulliver the

best of her young men. English novels abound in pictures of childhood; but I know of none more truthful and touching than the early pages of this work. Poor erratic Maggie is worth a hundred of her positive brother, and yet on the very threshold of life she is compelled to accept him as her master. He falls naturally into the man's privilege of always being in the right. The following scene is more than a reminiscence; it is a real retrospect. Tom and Maggie are sitting upon the bough of an elder-tree, eating jam-puffs. At last only one remains, and Tom undertakes to divide it.

> The knife descended on the puff, and it was in two; but the result was not satisfactory to Tom, for he still eyed the halves doubtfully. At last he said, "Shut your eyes, Maggie."
>
> "What for?"
>
> "You never mind what for,—shut 'em when I tell you."
>
> Maggie obeyed.
>
> "Now, which'll you have, Maggie, right hand or left?"
>
> "I'll have that one with the jam run out," said Maggie, keeping her eyes shut to please Tom.
>
> "Why, you don't like that, you silly. You may have it if it comes to you fair, but I sha'n't give it to you without. Right or left,—you choose now. Ha-a-a!" said Tom, in a tone of exasperation, as Maggie peeped. "You keep your eyes shut now, else you sha'n't have any."
>
> Maggie's power of sacrifice did not extend so far; indeed, I fear she cared less that Tom should enjoy the utmost possible amount of puff, than that he should be pleased with her for giving him the best bit. So she shut her eyes quite close until Tom told her to "say which," and then she said, "Left hand."
>
> "You've got it," said Tom, in rather a bitter tone.
>
> "What! the bit with the jam run out?"
>
> "No; here, take it," said Tom, firmly, handing decidedly the best piece to Maggie.
>
> "O, please, Tom, have it; I don't mind,—I like the other; please take this."
>
> "No, I shan't," said Tom, almost crossly, beginning on his own inferior piece.
>
> Maggie, thinking it was of no use to contend further, began too, and ate up her half puff with considerable relish as well as rapidity. But Tom had finished first, and had to look on while Maggie ate her last morsel or two, feeling in himself a capacity for more. *Maggie didn't know Tom was looking at her: she was see-sawing on the elder-bough, lost to everything but a vague sense of jam and idleness.*

"O, you greedy thing!" said Tom, when she had swallowed the last morsel.

The portions of the story which bear upon the Dodson family are in their way not unworthy of Balzac; only that, while our author has treated its peculiarities humourously, Balzac would have treated them seriously, almost solemnly. We are reminded of him by the attempt to classify the Dodsons socially in a scientific manner, and to accumulate small examples of their idiosyncrasies. I do not mean to say that the resemblance is very deep.

The chief defect—indeed, the only serious one—in *The Mill on the Floss* is its conclusion. Such a conclusion is in itself assuredly not illegitimate, and there is nothing in the fact of the flood, to my knowledge, essentially unnatural: what I object to is its relation to the preceding part of the story. The story is told as if it were destined to have, if not a strictly happy termination, at least one within ordinary probabilities. As it stands, the *dénouement* shocks the reader most painfully. Nothing has prepared him for it; the story does not move towards it; it casts no shadow before it. Did such a *dénouement* lie within the author's intentions from the first, or was it a tardy expedient for the solution of Maggie's difficulties? This question the reader asks himself, but of course he asks it in vain.

For my part, although, as long as humanity is subject to floods and earthquakes, I have no objection to see them made use of in novels, I would in this particular case have infinitely preferred that Maggie should have been left to her own devices. I understand the author's scruples, and to a certain degree I respect them. A lonely spinsterhood seemed but a dismal consummation of her generous life; and yet, as the author conceives, it was unlikely that she would return to Stephen Guest. I respect Maggie profoundly; but nevertheless I ask, Was this after all so unlikely? I will not try to answer the question. I have shown enough courage in asking it. But one thing is certain: a *dénouement* by which Maggie should have called Stephen back would have been extremely interesting, and would have had far more in its favour than can be put to confusion by a mere exclamation of horror. . . .

Jerome Thale (essay date 1959)

SOURCE: "The Social View: *The Mill on the Floss,*" in *The Novels of George Eliot,* Columbia University Press, 1959, pp. 36-57.

[*In the following excerpt, Thale analyzes* The Mill on the Floss *as a sociological study.*]

The Mill on the Floss has been most often remembered as the idyl of Tom and Maggie Tulliver's early years; we recall the account of Maggie's enthusiasm and warmth, the powerful figure of Mr. Tulliver, and the remarkable gallery of aunts and uncles. We are inclined to think of *The Mill on the Floss* as among the very best of Victorian novels, with the characteristic defect of the type, imperfect structure, and its characteristic strength, an

abundance of what the Victorian critics called life. The characters and the setting in *The Mill on the Floss* are first of all simply there, in remarkable fullness and immediacy. But for us vividness, fullness, sense of life are discredited as sole criteria for excellence in fiction: we look for more than presentation and feel that there ought to be some pattern or structure which evaluates and gives significance to that which is presented. Thus *David Copperfield*—to take another novel of childhood—seems to us to have serious defects. Although many of the things in it—Mr. Micawber, David's desolation at the wine warehouse—are unforgettable, it does not bring all these things together as functioning parts of one novel. Its strength seems to us to lie almost wholly in presentation, and we ask more than that of fiction.

The role of the river in *The Mill on the Floss*:

. . . The notion of predestined calamity, though never brought prominently forward, is vaguely hinted at from the commencement and never lost sight of throughout the narrative. A unity and completeness of effect is thus attained, as rare as it is excellent. The story opens with a description of the water-mill on the borders of the river Floss, and the key note is at once struck, which first comes trembling on the ear, then increases in its ominous sound, till it shatters two lives in its reverberating shock. We are first introduced to the mill-owner through 'a great curtain of sound,' caused by the 'rush of the water and the booming of the mill:' it is the water which has a special attraction for Tom and Maggie; the law-suit consequent on a fancied infringement of Mr. Tulliver's share of water-power ends in his ruin; again, the water is the medium for the elopement of Maggie with her cousin's suitor: and it is the water, in its flooded rage, close to the old mill, which brings swift justice and everlasting rest to brother and sister. In all this, the hand of the artist is apparent. . . .

A review of The Mill on the Floss, *in* The Atlas, *April 14, 1860. Reprinted in* George Eliot and her Readers, *edited by John Holmstrom and Laurence Lerner, Barnes & Noble, 1966.*

Of course, a reading of *The Mill on the Floss* as presentation, as life rather than art, would still give us a great deal, for so much is vivid and memorable. But to take the novel chiefly as a kind of emotion recollected in tranquility is to underestimate in several ways the toughness and complexity of the work.

The Mill on the Floss does have structural defects. They are not the ordinary ones of the ill-made novel, unevenness, incoherence, disorganization, sentimentality, or dullness. But there is a certain disproportionate fullness in the account of the early years. As George Eliot said, "My delight in the pictures of childhood led me into what the Germans call an 'epic breadth.'" But this does not mean that the novel is formless or episodic. "I could not," said George Eliot, "develop as fully as I wished the concluding 'Book' in which the tragedy occurs, and which I had looked forward to with much attention and premeditation from the beginning." The "concluding 'Book'" means the last of the seven books of the novel, and "attention and premeditation" indicate the author's concern for over-all form. Granted that the end is not developed as fully as it might be, we can still assert that, if seen rightly, the structure of the novel is strong and clear. The emphasis falls, as George Eliot meant it to fall, not on the ordinary events of most novels—falling in love, marriage—not on the things Maggie does, but on Maggie's response to her world and its effects upon her. Although the first section is full, everything in it is meaningful and essential in terms of what happens later in the novel.

Indeed it would be impossible to understand Maggie's renunciation and the necessity of her death at the end without such things as the aunts and the lawsuits about the Mill. They are not only the necessary background but the means by which Maggie's history—which contains only a few outward events and which is so much a record of her inner life—is given largeness of meaning. And it has meaning in many dimensions, for in *The Mill on the Floss* George Eliot, who was always profoundly interested in ideas, studies character in relation to theology, economics, and general culture. Thus *The Mill on the Floss* is a good deal more than a combination of liberal tragedy and pastoral. Like *Middlemarch,* which is subtitled *A Study of Provincial Life,* it is a presentation of the interaction of character, manners, and morals in a particular society.

Certain novelists use society in the same way that others use manners. Just as *Pride and Prejudice* uses the matter of courtship rituals, balls, and visits as a means of defining character and as the material of the characters' problems, so novels like *The Mill on the Floss* use the workings of society to define and objectify their characters. Since there is no term for what we have been describing, we have to speak of George Eliot's concern with society, or her sociological interest. It is perhaps true that both the novel and the science of sociology owe their success in the nineteenth century to the final breakdown of the old hierarchic order and to the great social dislocations which accompanied it. Certainly the sociological habit of mind is peculiarly suited to the novel, to its "circumstantial view of life." The novel's very inclusiveness in social fact demands some sort of organizing insights, and the categories of the sociologists are in a sense the only ones available. George Eliot was one of the first of a long series of novelists who drew upon the insights of sociology. She is also one of the first to treat the relation of the individual and society (a problem, as Ian Watt points out, basic to fiction since *Robinson Crusoe*) with any great sociological thoroughness.

Even before she began to write fiction, George Eliot had indicated this habit of mind. In a review entitled "The Natural History of German Life: Riehl," she complains "How little the real characteristics of the working-classes are known to those who are outside them . . . is sufficiently disclosed by our Art." She proposes what we should recognize today as essentially a sociological study, to be undertaken by a "man of sufficient moral and intellectual breadth, whose observations would not be vitiated by a foregone conclusion, or by a professional point of view." It would devote itself "to studying the natural history of our social classes, especially of the small shopkeepers, artisans, and peasantry,—the degree in which they are influenced by local conditions, their maxims and habits, the points of view from which they regard their religious teachers, and the degree in which they are influenced by religious doctrines, the interaction of the various classes on each other, and what are the tendencies in their position towards disintegration or towards development." She was not of course describing what the novel should do, but her references to social portraiture in Dickens, Kingsley, and Scott make clear that she has the novel in mind, and her discussion of English social life contains a number of details which suggest the novels that were to come.

As a sociologist George Eliot was of course very little like the sociologist as we know him, or like her great contemporaries Herbert Spencer and Auguste Comte, whose work she knew well. On the immediate surface of her novels there is little suggestion of the abstractism of these social theorists, and if their science enters into her work it is not in the form of theory but of their way of looking at things, their habit of ordering social fact, of seeking the unity of diverse phenomena, of a unitary vision of culture. If George Eliot was interested in theory, she was first of all a novelist and she approached her materials empirically without attempt to find an abstract formulation. She does not give us the theoretical formulations of the sociologists but, much more than a social critic like Thackeray, she operates out of some sense of the anatomy and physiology of society.

There may be a causal connection between George Eliot's interest in contemporary social thinkers and her own work, but she is interesting to us for a reason other than an application of the ideas of other thinkers. Disclaiming the title of discoverer of the unconscious, Freud protested that the poets had discovered it and that he had merely formulated it. The novel, at least the English novel, because of its empiricism and lack of controlling theoretical bias, has often presented and sometimes analyzed social phenomena before they were clearly formulated by theorists, just as Sophocles and Shakespeare presented the materials that Freud later systematized. *The Mill on the Floss* suggests many of the sociological insights formulated by such thinkers as Marx, Weber, Sombart, and Tawney.

To say that George Eliot makes use of the sociologist's way of looking at things when she presents character does not, in our time, seem to be saying a great deal, for this approach has become commonplace. There is much social fact in earlier novels, in *Roderick Random* or *Tom Jones,* but it seems to be there incidentally, as part of the realistic picture, and is presented neither in great detail nor in significant relation to the main characters. Unlike the earlier novelists George Eliot presents a good deal of detail as causally connected to the formation of the characters. And that is not always an easy thing to do. Often enough these things can be a deterrent to effective characterization, a way of making characters the sum of their parts.

A mass of detail is likely to produce a social history, not a full consideration of character. Proust and Joyce do it splendidly, but not many others. Perhaps George Eliot gained some advantage here from coming to the insights when they were fresh.

The Mill on the Floss is, as I have said, a presentation of the interaction of character, manners, and morals in a particular society. How it is all these things, and all of them at once, can be seen in its rich surface texture, its abundance of detail that is at once thematically relevant and part of the concreteness that satisfies our curiosity and convinces us that this world must be real. George Eliot had the fine discrimination which could make the world both spectacle and vehicle. The Dodsons (Tom and Maggie's maternal aunts), for example, are as significant as they are live. Touch them on their domestic side and you see closets, linen, wills, sugar tongs. These minutiae are in fact the outward signs of a code which embraces and penetrates every aspect of life for the Dodsons, and which arises from ethical and metaphysical attitudes.

> Mrs Glegg had doubtless the glossiest and crispest brown curls in her drawers, as well as curls in various degrees of fuzzy laxness; but to look out on the weekday world from under a crisp and glossy front, would be to introduce a most dreamlike and unpleasant confusion between the sacred and the secular. Occasionally, indeed, Mrs Glegg wore one of her third-best fronts on a week-day visit, but not at a sister's house.

> When one of the family was in trouble or sickness, all the rest went to visit the unfortunate member, usually at the same time, and did not shrink from uttering the most disagreeable truths that correct family feeling dictated.

And there are rules to govern what one serves to company, what one accepts at strange houses, what quality of linen one provides.

These pieties of the Dodson life are more than an object of satire for George Eliot. It is part of the richness of her art that she is able to see the pieties from so many aspects. Aunt Pullet's correctness makes visits to her miserable for Tom and Maggie—they have to scrape their feet carefully on the second scraper, not the ornamental one, before they can enter her house. But the same kind of correctness makes Aunt Glegg defend Maggie after she has lost her character. In Mrs. Tulliver, the "weakest vessel," the code is pathetic and absurd. When the family has been sold up she is unable to sleep nights thinking of her linen scattered all over England. Because she lacks her sisters' rigidity and clear-sightedness, one part of the code, the domestic, comes into conflict with another, the acceptance of fact. In the other sisters the strength of the code enables them to order their lives successfully. For them domestic rites and duties operate within larger sets of moral stringencies.

The Dodson code also has certain somber implications, not so immediately evident, but suggested through images of keys, locks, darkened closets, mould, and mildew. When Mrs. Pullet gives an advance glimpse at her new bonnet (she does not intend to wear it for some years, but "'There's no knowing what may happen'"), she unlocks a wardrobe, looks under several layers of linen for the key to the best room, and "unlocked a door which opened on something still more solemn than the passage: a darkened room, in which the outer light, entering feebly, showed what looked like the corpses of furniture in white shrouds. . . . Aunt Pullet half-opened the shutter and then unlocked the wardrobe, with a melancholy deliberateness which was quite in keeping with the funereal solemnity of the scene." We are reminded of the Clennam house in *Little Dorrit;* and like Dickens, George Eliot suggests a connection between this kind of code and a sense of mortality.

The world of these two novels is like the world Gabriel Marcel knew as a child, "hedged with moral restrictions and ravaged by despair. . . . A world subject to the strangest condominium of morality and of death." In *The Mill on the Floss* the note of mortality is muted by the humor and by the idyllic strain, but it comes through, ironically, in the images of death surrounding the code. "Other women, if they liked, might have their best thread-lace in every wash; but when Mrs Glegg died, it would be found that she had better lace laid by . . . than ever Mrs Wooll of St Ogg's had bought in her life, although Mrs Wooll wore her lace before it was paid for." The Dodson code, so exacting, and so demanding of continual self-denial, seems directed toward one thing—mortality. And it has its last triumph at death. "'Pullet keeps all my physic-bottles. . . . He says it's nothing but right folks should see 'em when I'm gone. They fill two o' the long store-room shelves a'ready—but . . . it's well if they ever fill three. I may go before I've made up the dozen o' these last sizes.'" The same motif appears in the discussions of one of the citadels of correct dealings with one's family, strictly equal distribution of inheritance, regardless of attachments or merit. Appealing to Tom's sense of family, Mrs. Glegg says, "'As if I wasn't my nephey's own aunt, . . . and laid by guineas, all full weight, for him—as he'll know who to respect when I'm laid in my coffin.'" And again, "'There was never any failures, nor lawing, nor wastefulness in our family—nor dying without wills—' 'No, nor sudden deaths,' said aunt Pullet; 'allays the doctor called in.'"

Placed against the Dodsons are the Tullivers, Chiefly Mr. Tulliver. The huge mill-like man, with his strong passions and animal stubbornness, is the equal of the whole Dodson clan. If the images to characterize the Dodsons are linen, locks, mould, wills—images drawn from domesticity and mortality—those to characterize Mr. Tulliver are the mill, the river, the outdoors, horses—images suggesting strength and elemental energy. We think of the Dodsons closed up in their houses fingering their keys and documents, but Mr. Tulliver we picture swaggering about, superintending, looking like a man of substance.

In economic terms Glegg and Pullet are the old middle class who have more than they show, cautious families who have accumulated wealth slowly. Mr. Tulliver is the man who appears more than he is. But economic categories will not do for Mr. Tulliver; he is totally unfit for economic life. And this is at the root of the inadequacy of the Tulliver way. Mr. Tulliver has too little control over himself, is too much the victim of his passions, to succeed either in the way of Mr. Glegg or in the more spectacular way of Mr. Deane, who has risen rapidly through a connection with capital. Mr. Tulliver is even too restless and sanguine to be a laborer or an artisan. I do not think George Eliot is suggesting that he represents a way of life that is being destroyed by industrialism. In fact the immediate cause of his trouble is simply his insistence on going to law to defend what he thinks are his rights. Mr. Tulliver's tragedy is that, in spite of so much generosity and commitment to life, he has so little control over himself that he cannot cope with life. Economics is only the most disastrous way in which his flaw manifests itself.

Theology, like economics, can be seen as a manifestation of character, as, conversely, economics and theology shape character, and George Eliot exploits these complex relationships. To be sure, the Dodsons and the Tullivers cannot be said to have any articulated theology. Mr. Tulliver's only religious act is the curse upon Lawyer Wakem and the promise of revenge which he makes Tom write in the Bible. The Dodsons do have a set of rites, which carry the value of religion for them and which are as strictly observed. And here manners, theology, and character are fused. The Dodsons save their money, lock their doors, and frown on pleasure, because they see the world and the self as things to be conquered and controlled. For them life is a conflict with the forces of evil within and without: man's calling is struggle and discipline. Mr. Tulliver, before his law trouble at least, is more nearly at one with the world: he sees it as a harmonious and agreeable arrangement, in which he pursues his own will and asserts himself, and in which obstacles are temporary and accidental.

These two worlds, Dodson and Tulliver, are presented so fully and occupy so much of a book about Tom and Maggie because it is in terms of their milieu, especially their families, that George Eliot establishes Tom's and Maggie's characters. She may be concerned with heredity, but she uses it poetically or symbolically, rather than scientifically, as the French naturalists were to do. Tom and Maggie are on the one hand merely focuses, part-for-the-whole metonymies, of the conflict between different kinds of character in society. On the other hand, the society objectifies and magnifies those problems which Tom and Maggie must work out within themselves; it is only a projection, though a causally related one, of the individual's conflicts, enabling us to see the elements of the conflict largely and simply. Between Tom and Maggie and their world, between symbol and the thing symbolized, there is a certain equivocality. It is part of George Eliot's art that the novel is at once the story of Maggie and of two different ways of life. The emphasis and most immediate interest is of course that given by plot; the story is to be read first as about Tom and Maggie, and second as about the two ways of life, with Tom and Maggie

as extensions and combinations, means of exhibiting the two ways and bringing them to test.

Tulliver and Dodson do not mix, do not even understand each other. They are radically separate and antagonistic. Yet each could use something of the other, Mr. Tulliver some of the Dodson prudence and restraint, and the Dodsons something of Mr. Tulliver's warmth. The fact that the two ways are antagonistic and yet complementary is dramatized in the account of Tom and Maggie's growing up, and is the very center of their problem.

Maggie is essentially a Tulliver. Though she lacks her father's stubbornness, she has his warmth: she needs to give and receive love and is miserable under reproach. Along with this warmth she has her father's heedlessness of consequences; she wants reality to conform to her love, not her love to reality. At the beginning of the novel she is heartbroken because she has forgotten to feed Tom's rabbits, and at the end, against her firm decision, she lets herself drift down the river with Stephen Guest Tom is a Dodson. He has their inflexibility, their clear vision of their own interest (though he is seriously blinded by his Tulliver stubbornness), and their devotion to principle; and he is scornful of anyone who lacks either principle or the will to live up to it. There is one of those large and obvious ironies, so common in fiction, in the wrongness of the combinations: without the Tulliver stubbornness Tom would do well enough as a Dodson; without the Dodson moral code Maggie would do well enough as a Tulliver.

The novel, to put it most simply, is about Tom and Maggie's growing up, their deciding who they will be, which of the two ways they will follow. It is part of their tragedy that the people, the ways of life, that their limited experience presents, are imperfect. The Dodsons and Tullivers, in spite of a certain adequacy with the world, are yet deficient as human beings. Mr. Tulliver is like a child in his defiance of reality. He is incomprehending of the claims of other people or of law, that symbol of fact and reality. He sees any obstacles and difficulties—law, creditors, bankruptcy—as acts of personal hostility and as fundamental disruptions of reality. "'It's the fault o' the law—it's none o' mine. . . . It's the fault o' raskills.'" This blindness to reality, to responsibility, starts the chain of misery: the conviction that Wakem is plotting against him, the need to be avenged, the curse, and the burden laid upon Tom that destroys both Tom and Maggie's chances for happiness.

Beside Mr. Tulliver the Dodsons look very grown-up. Moral responsibility and clear-sightedness are at the very center of their lives. When Mr. Tulliver has the chance to become mill manager under his adversary Wakem, the uncles and aunts think the proposition ought not to be rejected "when there was nothing in the way but a feeling in Mr. Tulliver's mind, which . . . was regarded as entirely unreasonable and childish—indeed, as a transferring towards Wakem of that indignation and hatred which Mr. Tulliver ought properly to have directed against himself." The Dodsons, unlike Mr. Tulliver, who always approves of himself, would never hesitate to reproach themselves for a mistake. It is for fear of giving occasion for self-reproach that they tread so cautiously. While their awareness of responsibility for their actions is a sign of maturity, the Dodsons are in other ways as immature as Mr. Tulliver. However heedless of consequences, Mr. Tulliver at least does act. The Dodsons avoid action; they guard against, fence out the challenge and the danger of choice by a network of rituals, imperatives, and rules. For choice involves the possibility of being wrong, committing one's self, or risking. The Dodsons see contingency and chance in the world, but they overestimate the danger and challenge of them, they are terrified by them and sacrifice the freedom of acting for the security of not taking risk. This view of the world shows up in economics, which is a kind of metaphor for the whole attitude; the Dodsons are willing to accept low-interest-bearing notes that are safe. Within the code there is no danger of risk, everything is taken care of through the crushing of passion and of the self. This is why they feel superior when Tulliver goes bankrupt. Yet the hedging out of choice, of everything that does not contribute to living up to the code, is as immature as Mr. Tulliver's irresponsibility, and more dangerous, since it seems to succeed and yet cuts off so much of life.

Our knowledge of their double heritage and its weaknesses makes clear to us the problems that Tom and Maggie face in growing up. I do not think George Eliot means to suggest that one part Tulliver plus one part Dodson, mixed well, will result in wholeness or maturity. In fact the two ways will not readily mix, for each seems entire and all of a piece. It is Tom and Maggie's misfortune that the ways they have before them are so imperfect, but the choice before them seems to them an either/or, and a choice not simply of one aspect but the whole way of life. Tom and Maggie, however, are not trapped by their environment; though the environment imposes a certain necessity, it does not destroy freedom. Even though they have to make a choice between Dodson and Tulliver, they should be able to see that the way they choose must be tempered, limited, and guarded by the knowledge of the other way. Maggie ought to temper the Tulliver warmth and generosity with some of the Dodson prudence and restraint. Tom ought to see in Maggie and his father not just irresponsibility but also the love whose absence makes the Dodson world so barren.

Both Tom and Maggie fail. Tom fails, to put it in terms of heredity, because in him the worst qualities of two breeds have come together with almost none of the redeeming qualities of either. Tom has all the rigorous and unloving strength of the Dodsons; and to this he adds what must be disastrous, the passion and obstinacy of his father. Tom had shown signs of coming to terms with hard adult reality very early, as when he stopped Maggie from arguing with Aunt Glegg because he recognized that it was futile. He has always believed in the outer world rather than the inner, in facts rather than sentiment. The turning point for Tom, the point at which he must decide whether and how he will grow up, comes at the family bankruptcy, when he is only sixteen. His hardness helps

him start paying his father's debts. But, as he grows older, he does not mature by tempering his attitudes. Burdened so precociously he stiffens, attempts to take an even clearer view of the world and a stronger grasp on himself. He does make good, but he never really grows up: his reaction to Philip Wakem remains adolescent, and, more important, his attitude toward himself and toward Maggie does not develop beyond that of the self-righteous schoolboy. Tom's ferocious and one-sided coming to terms with reality is a growing up only in a superficial sense.

Though it does in the end amount to a failure to grow up, Maggie's difficulty is not to be described so simply. It is tempting to see her as the victim of society, a soul striving for largeness yet caught in a narrow provincial world and deprived of the fulfillment that her nature demands. Such a reading is true enough, but it is not complete. To see the novel as simple conflict between Maggie and her world is to mistake the matter of the problem for the problem itself. Though Maggie's world does not offer her much, her real problem is internal and lies in the way that she deals with that world. On a matter-of-fact level, her problems-chiefly whether to accept Stephen-are not so great that they cannot be solved by common sense. Maggie's attitudes compel her to make more of the problems than she need.

On the most obvious level, the problems are those of love and duty; more relevantly they are the assertion or renunciation of the will. Maggie is a Tulliver, and love is a necessity of her nature. The withdrawal of Tom's love—it is his method of punishing people—is the most terrible thing that happens to her, and her misery as a child when Tom is angry with her for letting the rabbits die is prophetic of their future. For Maggie, love is associated with other spontaneous and free acts, imagination, poetry, and she sees it as opposed to the unpoetic and prudential life, the life of control rather than spontaneity.

Maggie's internal problem is objectified for her in the two families. She has to decide whether she will be Dodson or Tulliver, which she will allow to be dominant in her nature. Thus the vehicle for the choice is the families, but the choice itself is about herself. In her childhood she is thoroughly Tulliver. But after the loss of the Mill she becomes a follower of à Kempis, and the lesson she learns from him is the renunciation of the will. She discovers that she has been too much bound up in her own feelings, too little regardful of duty. There is a certain irony in her learning from à Kempis the same wisdom which is so unlovely in the Dodsons. Thus far, however, she is in the right way, and may develop some restraint upon the Tulliver warmth.

But Maggie reacts too violently. For both her and Tom the first trial, the bankruptcy of their father, brings an excessive reaction that will lead to disaster. Maggie thinks that giving up one's own will means rejecting everything that is easy and pleasant. When Philip offers her a book, saying it will give her pleasure, she refuses it because "'It would make me in love with this world again . . . it would make me long for a full life.'" Philip argues that poetry, art, and knowledge are sacred and pure. And Maggie replies, "'But not for me. . . . I should want too much,'" and she calls Philip a tempter.

What is at fault is not Maggie's principle of selflessness (though in her it is at bottom egotistic, a false transcendence, driving out self with self), but that in applying it she accepts the false description of moral reality that is the basis of the Dodson way: the cleavage between duty and pleasure, the conviction that whatever is enjoyable must be wrong, that man's desires are essentially evil. In this view of life as a struggle against a hostile and evil world, we can come through unscathed only by command of the self and rejection of the lures offered by the world and the appetites. The Calvinism of the Dodsons is essentially "this worldly": they check the indulgence of the will in order to get on in the world better. In them this spirit is mean and bourgeois, for the restraint is imposed for no large object—not at all for the love or fear of God, not even for power or ambition—but out of fear and for a very limited economic security. They see that the indulgence of the will, the doing of what one wants, stands in the way of getting ahead, of making one's self secure in a precarious world. Maggie has a large and high, if undefined, object, but like the Dodsons she sees desire as evil, a thing to be conquered and controlled for higher reasons, and the more it is controlled the better. This is the basis of Maggie's "'longings after perfect goodness.'"

It is these longings after perfect goodness that make Maggie reject Stephen's love. She convinces herself that loving him is opposed to duty, that their love is forbidden by his tacit engagement to Lucy and by Maggie's loyalty to her cousin. Stephen points out realistically that much more harm is done to everyone if Maggie rejects him and he marries Lucy, whom he no longer loves. But for Maggie, love is selfishness; "'Faithfulness and constancy mean something else besides doing what is easiest and pleasantest to ourselves.'" To such a state have Maggie's zeal and warmth, her generosity, brought her at last—to the Calvinist vision of life as a struggle against the self. As George Eliot describes it, Maggie has rejected "the delicious dreaminess of gliding on the river" and chosen to "struggle against this current, soft and yet strong as the summer stream."

This imagery, and it is repeated, suggests the sexual aspect of Maggie's problem. Philip warns Maggie, "You will be thrown into the world some day, and then every rational satisfaction of your nature that you deny now, will assault you like a savage appetite." Savage appetites are not discussed in Victorian fiction, but George Eliot tells us, "her whole frame was set to joy and tenderness. . . . She might expand unrestrainedly in the warmth of the present." Yet when Stephen kisses her arm, she reacts violently, feeling that the kiss is "punishment . . . for the sin of allowing a moment's happiness that was treachery to Lucy, to Philip—to her own better soul."

Maggie has gone the full circle and, like the Dodsons, rejected love and poetry. In each case the renunciation is

an escape from commitment, from the burden of adulthood. For Maggie this makes for an intolerable contradiction, for she is a Tulliver, and her nature demands commitment, love.

The Mill on the Floss opens with Maggie as a child of nine eagerly waiting for her brother Tom to come home from school. It takes them through their formative years, and it ends with their drowning together. The ending, though plausible, is somewhat too convenient; symbolically it is apt in that it represents their failure to grow up, the disaster of their not maturing. If the novel is the story of Tom and Maggie it is also a great deal more. The concern with society, economics, manners, theology, adds interest and richness, and even after a century makes George Eliot's vision of the world seem modern. Like the older novelists she makes us live in a world that is immensely real, but at the same time she makes us understand and judge that world, not just as a society to be analyzed, but as the place where tragedies like Tom's and Maggie's take place.

Stephen praises the character of Maggie:

The Mill on the Floss, indeed, considered simply as a story, obviously suffers from the disproportionate development of the earlier part; but I do not think that any reader could wish for a change which would sacrifice the revelation of character to the requirements of the plot. Taken by itself, the first part of *The Mill* represents to my mind the culmination of George Eliot's power. Maggie is one example of the feminine type which occurs with important modifications in most of the other stories. But George Eliot throws herself so frankly into Maggie's position, gives her "double" such reality by the wayward foibles associated with her nobler impulses, and dwells so lovingly upon all her joys and sorrows, that the character glows with a more tender and poetic charm than any of her other heroines. I suppose that Dinah Morris would be placed higher in the scale of morality; but if the test of a heroine's merits be the reader's disposition to fall in love with her (and that, I confess, is my own), I hold that Maggie is worth a wilderness of Dinahs.

Leslie Stephen; in George Eliot; 1902. Reprint by Macmillan and Co., Limited, 1909.

George Levine (essay date 1965)

SOURCE: "Intelligence as Deception: *The Mill on the Floss,*" in *PMLA,* Vol. LXXX, September, 1965, pp. 402-09.

[*In the essay below, Levine explores unity of intellect and emotion as the theme of* The Mill on the Floss.]

With only small exceptions, *The Mill on the Floss* can be seen as adequately representative of even the most mature of George Eliot's art—morally energetic yet unsentimentally perceptive about the meaning of experience. Like all of her works, it is thoroughly coherent and gains its coherence from a unified vision. But the vision, here as elsewhere, is, I would argue, incomplete. There were elements in experience, that is, which she was never fully able to assimilate and which, as was true of most of the major Victorian writers, she was genuinely unable to see. She pushed the boundaries of Victorian experience as far as any of her contemporaries and moved to the brink from which one can observe the modern sensibility, but inevitably she pulled back.

The point at which she stopped is the point at which *The Mill on the Floss*—which remains one of the very great novels of the period—goes wrong. The difficulty, I would suggest, is not merely George Eliot's excessive moral energy nor even, exclusively, her too close identification, criticised by F. R. Leavis [in his *The Great Tradition*, 1954], with her heroine. Rather, it seems to me to result from a complex mode of self-deceit—from a combination of high intelligence with powerful moral revulsion from what that intelligence tended to reveal.

I

It is important, at the outset, to remember that George Eliot's intelligence was at home with several highly elaborated intellectual systems which, she believed, could largely—if not entirely—account for the experience being narrated. Of course, her works cannot be reduced simply to any one set of rationally coherent ideas; but it is certainly true that her empirical and rationalist biases (modified though they were by her total commitment to "truth of feeling") demanded an explanation of experience consistent with reason, and that the explanation she accepted influenced certain crucial elements in her novels. Determinism is the central and dominant explanation of the facts of the experience; the moral direction of those facts is controlled largely by many ideas which might be traced to Comte and Feuerbach. All of these ideas are woven inextricably into the very texture of *The Mill on the Floss,* but I shall argue that there came a recognizable point at which, especially in her use of Feuerbach, George Eliot employs them in such a way as to help her escape the implications of her own most deeply felt insights.

To begin with, then, it is necessary to clarify what the informing ideas of *The Mill on the Floss* meant to George Eliot. For her, determinism . . . entailed a total commitment to the notion that every action has its causes, and only by a meticulous examination of those causes can any action be seen as comprehensible. She also argued, however, that determinism does not entail belief in inefficacy of the will. Since, that is, a man's character is always an element in his choice, he must be seen as responsible. Finally, whatever the intellectual formulation might be, to excuse a man on the basis of an abstract theory of determinism is altogether irrelevant to his evil; as Adam Bede remarks, "I see plain enough we shall never do it without a resolution, and that's enough for me."

All the major themes of *The Mill on the Floss,* as well as its structure, are related to determinism. It is a commonplace that the novel develops as Tom and Maggie grow: it sets them within the framework of a family and society which extensively determine what they become, shows the inevitable development of their characters according to the pressures of heredity and irrevocable events, and traces their destinies chronologically from love, to division, to unity in death. The simple narrative progression is incremental and stresses the ineluctable dependence of every act and thought on acts and thoughts which preceded them.

Both in its personal drama and in its vividly imagined description of a period of social transition the novel seems illustrative also of many of Comte's and Feuerbach's notions of social and moral growth. In a letter to John Blackwood comparing *Adam Bede* to *The Mill on the Floss,* which was then in progress, George Eliot noted that the characters in the latter "are on a lower level generally." Quite deliberately, she was creating a society which has not as yet moved beyond the egoism of man's animal beginnings to the sympathy and benevolence which Feuerbach and Comte believed would grow out of egoism. Among other things, the frequency with which all the characters are compared to insects and animals makes plain that George Eliot does not see them as ready for any but the slightest advance toward the full intellectual and moral development from egoism to intelligent sympathy towards which she aspired.

Aside from working out George Eliot's characteristic theme [in J. W. Cross's *George Eliot's Life*] of "the adjustment of our individual needs to the dire necessities of our lot," Maggie's story is also a dramatization of Feuerbach's religion of suffering—the "suffering, whether of martyr or victim, which belongs to every historical advance of mankind." Through suffering the "obscure vitality" of the "emmet-like Dodsons and Tullivers" will be transcended, will be "swept into the same oblivion with the generations of ants and beavers," and man will move slowly towards his full humanity. The immersion in water, which in the final chapter is the form which the suffering takes, is, in Feuerbach's view [in his *Essence of Christianity*], an annihilation of consciousness: it is the first step towards regeneration, but the regeneration itself must be active, not passive, the assertion of "the power of mind, of consciousness, of man." Maggie's world lacks the moral guidance Comte insisted was necessary for that regeneration or for the achievement of a satisfactory society: it had "no standard but hereditary custom".

Ideas such as these form the intellectual framework of *The Mill on the Floss.* The ideas and the experience, however, are two aspects of the same thing. Here at least one feels no tension between the two halves of the almost schizophrenic (intellectual vs. emotional) George Eliot that critics have taken to creating. For all but a brief section of the book the experience itself seems a necessary and convincing source of the ideas; although the world the novel describes is entirely deterministic and largely positivistic, the "system" does not distort the experience. But since the details of the novel are so widely known, I shall concentrate on the relation between the ideas and the experience—rather than on the experience itself—in order to suggest how George Eliot's extraordinarily tough-minded and complicated analysis of personal and social experience could have concluded [as stated by Miriam Allott, "George Eliot in the 1860's," *Victorian Studies,* V, 1961] in a "comfortingly conventional" way, "its tone barely distinguishable from hundreds of pious and exemplary tales where salvation comes through sacrifice and love triumphs over death."

II

George Eliot's "love of the childhood scenes" is not likely to have carried her to such lengthy description as we have in the early books had she not felt those scenes were important, both intrinsically and for the development of the novel as a whole. They are in fact a demonstration of the idea which she found confirmed in Comte, of whom she said that "no one has more clearly seen the truth, that the past rules the present, lives in it, and that we are but the growth and outcome of the past." The focus on family in the first book relates directly to the Comtean notion (shared by Feuerbach) that the family is the primary means by which man can transcend his egoism and animality. These early scenes establish that the characters are, in Feuerbach's terms, in a "natural" state, beneath the level of full humanity. It is no accident, for example, that the novel's first speech by an important character—Mr. Tulliver—should begin, "What I want," nor that George Eliot should pointedly repeat the clause. "The oppressive narrowness" of the Dodsons and Tullivers creates a tension for both readers and characters. On the one hand, it is what must be transcended by Maggie if she is to rise above "the mental level of the generation before" her. On the other, she is tied to that generation "by the strongest fibres of" her heart. In "the onward tendency of human things" the Dodsons and Tullivers must go, but they cannot be ignored and they must, indeed, be loved.

The notions explicit in this view suggest how the story points towards both personal and social growth; and these notions are worked out in almost every detail of the novel. The town of St. Ogg's, to use only one example, has grown in a slow, incremental, entirely unplanned way. It has roots deep in the past, and every part of it is "familiar with forgotten years." Under the slow pressure of time the processes of cause and effect have built it, almost as a natural growth. And George Eliot certainly means to imply a parallel between social and natural law which is central to the beliefs we have been examining:

> It is one of those old, old towns which impress one as a continuation and outgrowth of nature, as much as the nests of the bower-birds or the winding galleries of the white ants: a town which carries the traces of its long growth and history like a millennial tree, and has sprung up and developed in the same spot between the river and the low hill from the time when the Roman legions turned their backs on it from the camp on the hillside, and the long-haired sea-kings came up the river and looked with fierce eager eyes at the fatness of the land.

Even the architecture suggests the natural connections with the primitive sea-kings; equally, the citizens of St. Ogg's are what they are because of the past: inconsistent, old-fashioned, egocentric, crude, but sympathetic because they inherit—even without being aware of it—the best (along with the worst) of what men have thought and felt. But because they lack the clarity of vision Feuerbach desiderated they are determined: they "inherited a long past without thinking of it".

The Dodsons and Tullivers, of course, are the dramatic embodiments of the town's essential nature, and they confirm the notion that for George Eliot determinism is both dangerous and morally essential. She saw with Feuerbach that society included not merely rigid conventions but also the slowly, painfully earned developments in man's intelligence and sensibility. Maggie, then, must learn what other characters suffer by not learning—that everything must be judged on its unique merits, that no laws, habits, or traditions can apply indiscriminately in all situations. On the other hand, much of what she does learn in this way turns out to be a "relearning" of the values already implicit in social conventions. The trouble with the Dodsons and Tullivers is that they fail to establish an adequate relation to their own traditions and are therefore unable to understand their own motives derived from myriad causes out of the past. Neither they nor Maggie quite attain the "objectivity" Feuerbach requires, the ability, that is, to see "the real relation of things." They cannot achieve that "right understanding" of "the unchangeable Order of the world" which Comte says [in his *A General View of Positivism*] "is the principal object of our actions."

The predominant theme of the novel then, as George Eliot makes explicit, is the quest for unity—social, familial, and personal—that fusion of imagination and will which leads to sympathetic action. A convenient summary of Feuerbach's views [Bernard Paris, "George Eliot's Religion of Humanity," *ELH,* XXIX, 1962] will suggest the direction George Eliot wants Maggie's history to take:

> The individual who has a strongly sympathetic nature combined with profound experience and the ability to imagine the inner states of others has a moral life that is independent of traditions; he has a more highly developed conscience and a truer sense of good and evil than tradition, in its present state of development, could supply. The sympathetic tendencies can lead a person to rebel against the harsh usages of tradition, even when such rebellion involves great personal risk.

But this combination of qualities, which can lead justifiably to a rebellion against convention, was more George Eliot's than Maggie's. It would not be stretching things to consider the possibility that these views of Feuerbach helped George Eliot justify to herself her decision to live with G. H. Lewes. But Maggie needs yet to unify her desires with her intentions, to discipline her passions in keeping with an objective view of possibility—"knowledge of the irreversible laws within and without her, which, governing the habits, becomes morality, and developing the feelings of submission and dependence, becomes religion".

Socially, the quest is for unity between public opinion and individual sensibility. Comte places heavy emphasis on the value of public opinion in a way relevant to *The Mill on the Floss*. "The principal feature of the state to which we are tending," he says, "will be the increased influence which Public Opinion is destined to exercise. It is in this beneficial influence that we shall find the surest guarantee for morality. . . . Except the noblest of joys, that which springs from social sympathy when called into constant exercise, there is no reward for doing right so satisfactory as the approval of our fellow-beings." Maggie's relation to public opinion seems different, but that is partially because the society in which she lives is at such a primitive stage of development. George Eliot is certainly suggesting in the final chapters both the power of public opinion and the need to develop it more consistently to a higher level of social sympathy. The society of St. Ogg's, however, is disintegrating, as Dr. Kenn says, under the pressure of modern life, "seems tending toward the relaxation of ties—towards the substitution of wayward choice for adherence to obligation, which has its roots in the past".

All aspects of the theme of unity are worked out in three of Maggie's moments of choice: her interview with Philip Wakem in the Red Deeps, her rowing party with Stephen Guest, and her refusal to stay with Stephen after they arrive at Mudport. The two earlier decisions show that Maggie has not achieved that personal unity which is essential to moral well-being. Philip is obviously right when, attacking her new-found asceticism, he warns her that if she persists in mere negations she will find that when she is "thrown upon the world . . . every rational satisfaction of your nature that you deny now, will assault you like a savage appetite". Unfortunately, of course, even this sensible argument serves to weaken Maggie because it is not disinterested, but designed to keep her from leaving Philip altogether. The truth in this case is a lie, and deceit in the complicated deterministic universe of George Eliot is a form of moral disease whose dangers are far-reaching. It may be, as Maggie recognizes, that "it is other people's wrong feelings that make concealment necessary; but concealment is bad, however it may be caused".

Nor has Maggie achieved unity by the time she meets Stephen Guest. Whatever one's objections to Stephen as a character, it is obvious that here as elsewhere George Eliot has been extremely careful to work out the reason for the action. What Maggie does with Stephen is determined by a past in which egotism and personal wilfulness keep her from moral integrity. There is no need here to list all the causes, but it is interesting to note how down to the finest details it is possible to observe kinship with the thought of Feuerbach and Comte. One of the things, for instance, which attracts Maggie to Stephen is his singing, and Maggie is deeply susceptible to music. Feuerbach argues strongly for the power of music: "What would man be without feeling?" he asks. "It is the musical power in man. But what would man be without music? Just as man has a musical faculty and feels an inward necessity to breathe out his feelings in song; so, by a like necessity,

he, in religious sighs and tears, streams forth the nature of feeling as an objective, divine nature." Music, George Eliot remarks, "could hardly be without some intoxicating effect on her, after years of privation." It should be noted also that Maggie's desperate need to be admired and loved, one of the causes of her fall, corresponds closely to Comte's sense of what makes people behave as they do.

Because Maggie succumbs at her second moment of choice with Stephen, she is faced with a dilemma which is, in some ways, the purest in all of George Eliot's novels. Maggie's decision now cannot be in passive accordance with the push of circumstance; it depends on her understanding of the particular situation and cannot be governed by conventions. Simply by following out the implications of her complex attitudes towards tradition and modernity, self-control and self-assertion, George Eliot here arrives at a point where tradition cannot supply an adequate answer but where her heroine's character is inadequate to the task of Feuerbach's sympathetic rebellion. Maggie cannot even decide on the basis of the likely consequences of her actions because the damage has already been done and misery will be the consequence of either choice.

Thus, in making this third choice, Maggie achieves the highest level of consciousness of which a St. Ogg's citizen is capable. She reveals an awareness of the "real relation of things" by accepting both the irrevocability of her act and the fact that it "must blot her life" and bring sorrow into lives that were "knit up with hers by trust and love." She is aware that she has broken all "the ties that had given meaning to duty, and had made herself an outlawed soul," having lost the relation to community which, in Comte's sense, provides moral guidance; she was left with "no guide but the wayward choice of her own soul". Recognizing this loss and its dangers, Maggie attempts to turn to the past and inherited traditions. "If the past is not to bind us," she says to Stephen, "where can duty lie: We have not law but the inclination of the moment". Through the past she attempts to overcome the persistent fragmentation of self which has hitherto left her vulnerable to the past's uncomprehended forces.

She struggles against committing herself to a "momentary triumph of my feeling," to an evil which will form a habit of surrender to impulse and fragmentation. One of George Eliot's primary insights, dramatized in the curious passivity of her characters at their moments of choice, is that "character" as it has been formed over a lifetime finally determines how one will behave in a crisis. Untrained will is unequal to the pressures of the moment; the training of the will into a habit of goodness is essential because "moral behavior is only to be found in the spontaneous exercise of moral emotion. Moral action is not the result of a decision to act morally; it is the result of moral feeling, forcing itself into practice" [Michael Wolff, "Marian Evans to George Eliot: The Moral and Intellectual Foundation of her Career," 1958]. At her present stage of development, Maggie must still labor at her choice, but she does move towards the unity of self which makes moral action a habit by recognizing that mind, memories, obligations are all part of what a man is, fully as important as natural feelings; and she tries to bring her feelings into conformity with her conscious intentions. The renunciation of Stephen moves one step beyond her immature asceticism, not based on a sense of the real relation of things, which Philip had criticized in the Red Deeps.

III

In keeping with her deterministic insistence on the pressure of ordinary events, her Comtean awareness of the moral pressures of public opinion, and the deep psychological perceptions she shared with Feuerbach about the nature of human suffering and morality, George Eliot could not allow Maggie's resolution yet to be final. Resolutions must be tested moment by moment and day by day and they must establish themselves in relation not only to the complete self but to the community. Thus, all the influences so carefully prepared through the apparently leisurely movement of the early stages of the novel come into play in the last book.

The tensions between the Dodsons and the Tullivers—between the two modes of egoism represented by the forces of convention uncomprehended and rigidified and the forces of blind spontaneity of feeling—now become in a more complex way the tensions between Maggie and the town. All of Maggie's past—not understood—contributed to her fatal lapse with Stephen; so all of Maggie's past—now largely if incompletely understood—contributes to her decision to return to St. Ogg's. Equally, all the seemingly innocuous circumstances which precede Maggie's lapse help determine the rigidly conventional—that is, unimaginative and therefore unsympathetic—response of the townspeople to Maggie. In language which suggests the quite conscious influence of both Comte and Feuerbach, George Eliot describes the "ladies of St. Ogg's" as "not beguiled by any wide speculative conceptions; but they had their favourite abstraction called society which seemed to make their consciences perfectly easy in doing what satisfied their egoism". George Eliot's revulsion from abstractions is widely known, and in its temperamental character it is much more skin to Feuerbach than to Comte, who, though he insisted always on the positive and scientific, was himself the victim of abstractions. But this passage certainly evokes Comte, who, according to John Stuart Mill [in *Auguste Comte and Positivism*], described the "Metaphysical Stage" of human development as the stage which "accounts for phenomena by ascribing them, not to volitions either sublunary or celestial, but to realized abstractions. In this stage it is no longer a god that causes and directs each of the various agencies of nature: it is a power, or a force, or an occult quality, considered as real existence, inherent in but distinct from concrete bodies in which they reside, and which they in a manner animate."

The traditions animating the kind of Dodsonian behavior which condemns Maggie are given new life and meaning by the eldest of the Dodsons, Mrs. Glegg, who is capable of dealing with new kinds of experience because she is the strongest willed and most intelligent of the clan. Her willingness to oppose public opinion and convention is certainly intended as at least in part a dramatization of the way in which family unity—recognized by both Comte and Feuerbach as the source of morality—is the first step toward community, the first means of transcending the "I" for the "Thou," for breaking away from the narrow egoism which governs the action of ordinary men. It is the source of Maggie's higher sensibility, and as it is revivified in Mrs. Glegg it helps us to understand George Eliot's commitment to the sustaining power of tradition.

Despite Mrs. Glegg's help, however, the pressures on Maggie become strong enough to make her feel again the temptation to return to Stephen. She must once again work out the relation between self-will and self-denial, and George Eliot's comment on the problem reveals the impasse at which both author and heroine have arrived: "The great problem of the shifting relation between passion and duty is clear to no man who is capable of apprehending it: the question whether the moment has come in which a man has fallen below the possibility of a renunciation that will carry any efficacy, and must accept the sway of passion against which he had struggled as a trespass, is one for which we have no master-key that will fit all cases". As the book has demonstrated, only in a society where egoism and self-will are not driven as in Maggie's case into excessive self-denial or, as in Tom's case, into respectability and moral brutality, does the problem of the shifting relation have a chance to be resolved. But such a positivist utopia, in which the individual and society are allied in one will, was, as George Eliot knew, a mere dream of the future, and one could only move towards it through the slow increment of wasted lives, of suffering such as Maggie's and Dorothea Brooke's, from which new moral insight can be assimilated into man's consciousness. Maggie is at an impasse which everything in the book has suggested is unresolvable. And Dr. Kenn's comment that any action she might take would be "clogged with evil" is undeniably true.

IV

The continuity of George Eliot's views is suggested by the similarity between Maggie's conflict as she battles temptation in the dark night preceding the flood and that of Dorothea on the night she resolves to accept Casaubon's unexplained demands. Both characters submit themselves to the higher responsibility despite the loss of the possibility of self-fulfillment. But neither character is made to face the full implications of such renunciation. Certainly, Dorothea does not achieve a fate with Ladislaw equal to her own large possibilities. Moreover, George Eliot means us to understand that her marriage to him will evoke considerable public disapprobation. But she is certainly not at such a primitive stage of development as Maggie, and Casaubon's death does save her from total and pointless frustration. This death follows almost immediately after her resolution, just as Maggie's death follows her own final renunciation.

In her first spontaneously moral action, she rushes to Tom's rescue and is swept to death in his arms, as though one were meant to see in that death her reconciliation to all those forces to which she could by temperament and action never be reconciled. Maggie's final action, however, can be seen as the last stage in the progress of her growth according to Feuerbach's principle and therefore altogether consistent with what has gone before. Beginning in mere egoism and rebellion, she moves on to the incomplete sympathy—as a result of family pressures—of her asceticism; the suffering which she endures intensifies that sympathy and produces in her a surer vision of reality so as to make her capable of a deliberate act of renunciation with Stephen; her rescue of Tom, however, is to be seen as a spontaneous moral action which suggests the real beginning of Feuerbach's genuinely noble man. But Maggie's newly earned "nobility" is once again exercised in the direction of her family, and will, moreover, never be tested in that infinitely more complicated social world which posed her moral dilemma. The escape, then, is thematically consistent, but it can be seen also as external and fortuitous, an intrusion of that "Favourable Chance" which George Eliot anathematized in *Silas Marner*.

One can only speculate on the reasons for such a lapse, characteristic not only of George Eliot's work but of much of the best work of the time. Perhaps Matthew Arnold's explanation of why he removed "Empedocles on Etna" from his 1853 *Poems* will throw light on the problem. Arnold, it will be remembered, asked with Schiller for an art "dedicated to Joy," since "there is no higher and more serious problem, than how to make men happy." George Eliot, for her part, during the decade following *The Mill on the Floss,* wrote that "the art which leaves the soul in despair is laming to the soul, and is denounced by the healthy sentiment of an active community." She is likely to have agreed with Arnold that there were certain situations, "from the representation of which, though accurate, no poetical enjoyment can be derived. They are those in which the suffering finds no vent in action; in which a continuous state of mental distress is prolonged, unrelieved by incident, hope, or resistance; in which there is everything to be endured, nothing to be done" ["Preface" to the 1853 edition of Arnold's poems, reprinted in *Mixed Essays, Irish Essays, and Others,* 1883]. This is Maggie's condition before the flood.

For Arnold, the solution was to abandon art for criticism; George Eliot, also too intelligent and too responsible to let need consciously dictate to art, allowed herself to flaw her art, I would suggest, by deceiving herself with her own intelligence. She could, consistently with her own view of experience, avoid the condition Arnold described by leaning on Comte and Feuerbach; and in this way she could give Maggie the heroic, tragic, but largely affirmative action with which she dies. This action is consistent not only with the details of the plot as she carefully worked them out, but with the very themes which give the novel so much of its richness.

Moreover, within the system of Feuerbachian thought, the death by water makes good symbolic sense. Water, for Feuerbach, is one of the two major sacraments, the other and more important one being the bread and wine of the Lord's Supper. But although, as has been shown [by U. C. Knoepflmacher, "George Eliot, Feuerbach, and the Question of Criticism," *Victorian Studies,* VII, 1964], much symbolic use of this sacrament occurs in *Adam Bede* there is apparently no such use in *The Mill on the Floss*. The crucial dinner scene in the first book marks not harmony but the beginning of the division between the Tullivers and Dodsons. The reason seems to be that *The Mill on the Floss* concerns itself with people on "a lower level generally"—not "lower" in class but in the development of their moral perceptions—with a society not prepared for the higher sacrament. Indeed, it is likely that George Eliot sees Maggie's death by water as a preparation for the condition in which the society would be prepared.

Water, for Feuerbach, is the sacrament which symbolically asserts man's dependence on nature; the flood served to remind man of this. Curiously, in water "the scales fall from [man's] eyes: he sees and thinks more clearly," and at the same time "human mental activity is nullified." Both these effects of water operate in *The Mill on the Floss*. With Stephen Maggie falls into oblivion as she floats downstream; by contrast, with Tom the scales fall from her eyes as she reflects: "what quarrel, what harshness, what unbelief in each other can subsist in the presence of a great calamity, when all the artificial vesture of our life is gone, and we are all one with each other in primitive mortal needs". Here, appropriately, Maggie not only "sees and thinks more clearly," but she is forced to these reflections by the power of Nature over the merely "artificial." And, of course, in the death which follows, consciousness is nullified, but only after, by symbolically crying "Maggie," Tom avers the love which dominated in the natural state of childhood. The death is a purification of both Maggie and Tom: "To purify oneself," as Feuerbach says, "to bathe, is the first, though the lowest of virtues."

This, it seems to me, is George Eliot's attitude toward the final catastrophe; Tom and Maggie must achieve "the first, though the lowest of virtues" because even now neither they nor St. Ogg's is ready for the higher, active, creative virtues of man's full consciousness and power.

One more quotation from Feuerbach should suggest other ways in which the conclusion of *The Mill on the Floss* was firmly a part of the intellectual structure of the book: "It needs only that the ordinary course of things be interrupted in order to vindicate to common things an uncommon significance, *to life, as such, a religious import.* Therefore let bread be sacred for us, let wine be sacred, and also let water be sacred! Amen." For George Eliot, the inability to see the extraordinariness of the ordinary is an aspect of that egoism and lack of imagination which characterizes the society of St. Ogg's. She insists on the religious import, surely in Feuerbach's sense, of the ordinary, and thus follows Feuerbach by introducing into the novel the extraordinary—the flood—which is in fact only an extreme development of the ordinary and which in its extreme quality takes on the nature of a ritual. It is curious how so many of George Eliot's novels, however much the great bulk of events they include are assertively ordinary, turn on events which seem to come directly out of melodrama—Arthur Donnithorne's last-minute rescue of Hetty, the final meeting of Bladassarre and Tito, Grandcourt's drowning and Mordecai's mystical Zionist visions, the revelation of Transome's relation to the lawyer Jermyn.

It is perhaps too simple to suggest that this sort of refusal to face the total implication of her own ideas and of her very temperament was the result of George Eliot's conscious effort to protect "her readers from any 'laming' effects." Obviously George Eliot did seek moral order in the bleakest and most amoral elements of the world. But she was too intelligent to be satisfied with emotional need unsustained by intellectual conviction. Feuerbach, at least in *The Mill on the Floss,* seems to have supplied her with an intellectually satisfying and emotionally acceptable answer. Because we take George Eliot's perceptions to the point of the modern vision, where the only affirmation is personal, inward, and isolated, we tend to believe that in honesty she needed to do the same thing. But she turns away with characteristic Victorian strength and integrity in search of meaning, justice, and the organic community. We could do much worse.

Bernard J. Paris (essay date 1969)

SOURCE: "The Inner Conflicts of Maggie Tulliver: A Horneyan Analysis," in *The Centennial Review,* Vol. XIII, No. 2, 1969, pp. 166-99.

[*In the following essay, Paris examines the psychology of the character of Maggie Tulliver using Karen Horney's theories of neurosis.*]

I

In *The Great Tradition* [1950] F. R. Leavis argues that Maggie Tulliver's "emotional and spiritual stresses, her exaltations and renunciations, exhibit . . . all the marks of immaturity," but that George Eliot, because her own needs or hungers lead her to over-identify with Maggie, has little awareness of the inadequacy of her heroine's solutions:

> There is nothing against George Eliot's presenting this immaturity with tender sympathy; but we ask, and ought to ask, of a great novelist something more. 'Sympathy and understanding' is the common formula of praise, but understanding, in any strict sense, is just what she doesn't show. To understand immaturity would be to 'place' it, with however subtle an implication, by relating it to mature experience.

In two previous discussions of *The Mill on the Floss* ["Toward a Revaluation of George Eliot's *The Mill on the Floss*," *Nineteenth Century Fiction,* XI, 1956, and *Experiments in Life: George Eliot's Quest for Values,* 1965] I have quarrelled with Dr. Leavis's response, arguing, in both, that Maggie's is a story of moral education and that by the end she has resolved her inner conflicts and

achieved an adequate philosophy. I still have reservations about Dr. Leavis's critical position, but I now agree with many of his judgments. Maggie's "hunger for ideal exaltations" *is* immature; her "lack of self-knowledge" *is* "shared by George Eliot"; and the ending *is* "a kind of daydream indulgence".

My change of mind does not mean that I repudiate my previous interpretations of *The Mill on the Floss*. I believe them to be valid readings of the novel in its own terms. They give Maggie's story the significance that the novel means it to have, and they account for Maggie's behavior in terms of the novel's own analysis of motives. What my change of mind means is that now I, like Dr. Leavis, see Maggie from the perspective of a value system other than that of the novel, and that my interpretation of Maggie's psychology differs from George Eliot's.

George Eliot's characterization of Maggie is brilliant; and, given brilliant characterization, we must say that, in one sense, the author has understood the character perfectly. George Eliot's intuitive grasp and mimetic presentation of Maggie's psychology are flawless; her attitudes, values and analyses are considerably less trustworthy. There is often a disparity between the novel's representation of Maggie and the novel's interpretation of Maggie. In the past I have been so busy showing Maggie's function in the novel's overall thematic structure that I have failed to see how much of Maggie escapes such analysis, how little she can be understood as a character in this way. In order to understand the character that George Eliot has actually presented (rather than the one she *thinks* she has presented) it is necessary to employ not thematic, but psychological analysis.

A psychological study of *The Mill on the Floss* will heighten our awareness of values to which other approaches give little emphasis. As [Robert] Scholes and [Robert] Kellogg point out in *The Nature of Narrative* [1966], there is behind realistic fiction a strong "psychological impulse" that "tends toward the presentation of highly individualized figures who resist abstraction and generalization, and whose motivation is not susceptible to rigid ethical interpretation." In some realistic novels, and *The Mill on the Floss* is one, the central characters have very important thematic (or "illustrative") functions; but, even so, they exist primarily as mimetic portraits whose intricacies continually escape the moral and symbolic meanings assigned to them. It is only when we see such a novel from the perspective afforded by psychological analysis that we can properly appreciate the depth and subtlety of its characterizations.

In this essay I shall analyze Maggie Tulliver in the light of Karen Horney's theories of neurosis [in her *Neurosis and Human Growth: The Struggle Toward Self-Realization,* (1950)]. My use of Horney does not mean that I assume the universal applicability of her theories or that I am chiefly interested in Maggie Tulliver as a type of neurotic. My object is the illumination of the literary text, and I use Horney's analysis of the structure of neurosis because it helps me, first, to understand the character of

Maggie Tulliver; next, to see "what the weaknesses of *The Mill on the Floss* really are", and, finally, to appreciate the novel's excellence, the nature of its achievement. Since some literary critics may be unfamiliar with the work of Karen Horney, I shall begin by presenting an outline of her system.

II

In an atmosphere of warmth, security and esteem, says Horney, a child "will develop . . . the unique alive forces of his real self: the clarity and depth of his own feelings, thoughts, wishes, interests . . . : the special capacities or gifts he may have; the faculty to express himself, and to relate himself to others with his spontaneous feelings. All this will in time enable him to find his set of values and his aims in life." Under unfavorable conditions, when the people around him are prevented by their own neurotic needs from relating to him with love and respect, the child develops a "feeling of being isolated and helpless in a world conceived as potentially hostile". This feeling of "basic anxiety" makes the child fearful of spontaneity; and, forsaking his real self, he develops neurotic strategies for coping with his environment.

These strategies are of three kinds: the individual can adopt the self-effacing or compliant solution and move toward people; he can develop the aggressive or expansive solution and move against people; or he can become withdrawn or resigned and move away from people. Each of these solutions produces its own set of character traits and beliefs.

The person in whom self-effacing trends are dominant becomes weak, humble and dependent; he values goodness and love above all else. He tries to overcome his basic anxiety by gaining approval and by controlling others through his need of them. He believes in turning the other cheek, and he tends to see the world as displaying a providential order in which virtue is rewarded. He needs to feel himself a part of something larger and more powerful than himself. This need often manifests itself as religious devotion.

The predominantly aggressive person tries to be strong, efficient and exploitative. What appeals to him most is not love, but mastery. He is ruthless and cynical. He believes that might makes right and that the world is a jungle in which each man is out for himself. His object is to defeat others before they defeat him. There are three expansive types, the narcissistic, the perfectionistic and the arrogant-vindictive:

> . . . they all aim at mastering life. This is their way of conquering fears and anxieties. . . . They try to achieve such mastery in different ways: by self-admiration and the exercise of charm; by compelling fate through the height of their standards; by being invincible and conquering life in the spirit of a vindictive triumph.

The basically withdrawn person worships freedom and strives to be independent of both outer and inner demands.

He cultivates detachment and self-sufficiency and handles a threatening world by removing himself from its power, by shutting others out of his inner life. He tries to subdue his inner cravings and to be content with little. Whereas the compliant person tends toward a Christian and the aggressive person toward a Nietzschean philosophy, the withdrawn person's beliefs are stoic in nature.

In the course of neurotic development, the individual will come to make all three of the defensive moves compulsively; and, since they involve incompatible character structures and value systems, he will be torn by inner conflicts. In order to gain some sense of wholeness, he will emphasize one move more than the others and will become predominantly self-effacing, expansive, or resigned. The other trends will continue to exist quite powerfully, but they will be condemned and suppressed. The "basic conflict" will not have been resolved, but will simply have gone underground. When the submerged trends are for some reason brought closer to the surface, the individual will experience severe inner turmoil, and he may be paralyzed, unable to move in any direction at all.

His defensive strategies for coping with other people are designed to reduce the individual's anxiety by giving him a feeling of safety, but in reality they are destructive to him, and this for several reasons. His compulsive behavior makes his human relations more rather than less disturbed. His self-protective moves create a basic inner conflict (primarily between aggressive and compliant trends) which threatens to tear him apart. His choice of safety over spontaneous growth leads to greater and greater self-alienation, for his artificial strategies create a system of neurotic feelings which has little to do with the feelings of his real self. Finally, his self-alienation intensifies his original feelings of weakness, and his self-betrayal intensifies his feeling of worthlessness; for every time he chooses against the interests of his real self he incurs self-hatred.

While interpersonal difficulties are creating the movements toward, against and away from people, and the basic conflict, the concomitant intra-psychic problems are producing their own self-defeating defensive strategies. The destructive attitudes of others, his alienation from his real self and his self-hatred make the individual feel terribly weak and worthless. To compensate for this he creates, with the aid of his imagination, an "idealized image" of himself: "In this process he endows himself with unlimited powers and with exalted faculties; he becomes a hero, a genius, a supreme lover, a saint, a god". Thus begins his "search for glory," as "the energies driving toward self-realization are shifted to the aim of actualizing the idealized self". The search for glory often takes the form of a quest of the absolute: "All the drives for glory have in common the reaching out for greater knowledge, wisdom, virtue, or powers than are given to human beings. . . . Nothing short of absolute fearlessness, mastery, or saintliness has any appeal . . . ".

The creation of the idealized image produces not only the search for glory but a whole structure of neurotic strate-

Robert Evans, George Eliot's father. Evans was the basis for the character of Mr. Tulliver in The Mill on the Floss.

gies which Horney calls "the pride system." The idealized image leads the individual to make both exaggerated *claims for* himself and excessive *demands upon* himself. He takes an intense pride ("neurotic pride") in the attributes of his idealized self, and on the basis of these attributes he makes "neurotic claims" upon others. He feels outraged unless he is treated in a way appropriate to his status as a very special being. His neurotic claims make him extremely vulnerable, of course, for their frustration threatens to confront him with his "despised self," with the sense of worthlessness from which he is fleeing. Either he is all, or he is nothing. Indeed, it is because he feels himself to be nothing that he must claim to be all: he who can be a man does not need to be God.

The individual's pride in his idealized self also leads him to impose stringent demands and taboos upon himself ("the tyranny of the should"). The function of the shoulds is "to make oneself over into one's idealized self: *the premise on which they operate is that nothing should be, or is, impossible for oneself.*" Since the idealized image is for the most part a glorification of the self-effacing, expansive, and resigned solutions, the individual's shoulds are determined largely by the character traits and values as-

sociated with his predominant trend. The shoulds are a defense against self-loathing, but, like other neurotic defenses, they tend to aggravate the condition they are employed to cure. Not only do they increase self-alienation, but they also intensify self-hate for they are impossible to live up to. The penalty for failure is the most severe feeling of worthlessness and self-contempt. This, indeed, is why the shoulds have such a tyrannical power.

Here we have another vicious circle: self-contempt gives rise to the pride system, the pride system cannot work and only intensifies self-contempt, greater self-contempt can be compensated for only by greater self-glorification, and so on. The individual suffers greatly, but his suffering is in no way educative. It may lead him to change, but the change will only be from one neurotic solution to another. The nature of neurotic development is such that, if no positive forces intervene, the condition is far more likely to get worse than it is to get better.

It is time to look at Maggie Tulliver.

III

It is not difficult to identify the destructive forces at work in Maggie's environment. George Eliot speaks of the "painful collisions" that are bound to occur when there is a marked "contrast between the outward and the inward". The collisions in Maggie's case are, at least initially, between her given nature and the rigid ideas held by her society and her family of what she ought to be. Not only are Maggie's aesthetic and intellectual faculties starved in the oppressively narrow medium of St. Ogg's, they are regarded as inappropriate for a girl and hence contribute to Maggie's uncertainty about her worth. She is not only a girl, and hence an inferior being; she is an inferior girl. In talents, manners and appearance, she is the opposite of what the Dodson's value in a female (Lucy embodies their ideal), and Mrs. Tulliver is engaged in a constant battle to transform her into an acceptable child. When Maggie resists or fights back, her mother retaliates with further rejection.

It is primarily through her mother that the negative attitudes of her culture towards her kind of person are transmitted to Maggie. Mrs. Tulliver gets her sense of worth and of orientation in the world through her conformity to the ways and values of the Dodson clan. Maggie's deviations from the Dodson ideal fill her with anxiety, and she is deeply ashamed of her daughter. Mrs. Tulliver's displeasure manifests itself in an "habitual deprecation" of Maggie, and her daughter's self-esteem wilts under her ceaseless criticism.

Her mother's attitudes are echoed, of course, by the whole Dodson side of the family. After she cuts her hair and after she makes Tom spill his wine at Garum Firs, everyone scolds her, and Maggie seems "to be listening to a chorus of reproach and derision". She is so hurt by the rejection she experiences after the latter incident that she runs away to the gypsies, seeking "a refuge from all the blighting obloquy that had pursued her in civilized life".

Maggie's vulnerability to criticism is not simply a sign of her sensitive nature; it is also a manifestation of her profound insecurity. Since she has never been able to develop a healthy self-esteem, she is "as dependent on kind or cold words as a daisy on the sunshine or the cloud". Her sense of worth soars or plunges in accordance with the treatment she receives. Maggie is so easily elated and deflated because at bottom she thinks very little of herself.

There are a number of ways in which Maggie tries to compensate for her feelings of inferiority. Even though he says that "a woman's no business wi' being so clever," Mr. Tulliver takes great pride in his daughter's intelligence, and Maggie, quite naturally, seizes upon intellectual preeminence as the readiest means to self-esteem. Maggie's sense of worth is dependent upon the recognition by others of her cleverness, and she welcomes opportunities to demonstrate her superiority. After her father's failure, she turns to masculine learning in her search for an explanation of life:

> Not that the yearning for effectual wisdom was quite unmixed: a certain mirage would now and then rise on the desert of the future, in which she seemed to see herself honoured for her surprising attainments. And so the poor child, with her soul's hunger and her illusions of self-flattery, began to nibble at this thick-rinded fruit of the tree of knowledge . . . feeling a gleam of triumph now and then that her understanding was quite equal to these peculiarly masculine studies.

Her quickness being the only thing for which Maggie has received praise, it is no wonder that she fastens on to it as the means to vindication and mastery.

Her need for compensations being strong, and her triumphs in life being few, it is no wonder, also, that Maggie creates a fantasy world in which she receives the love, admiration and glory for which she hungers. The fantasy that most vividly reveals the co-existence in Maggie of self-rejection and a search for glory is the one in which she dreams of being a queen: "She was fond of fancying a world where the people never got any larger than children of their own age, and she made the queen of it just like Lucy, with a little crown on her head, and a little sceptre in her hand. . . . only the queen was Maggie herself in Lucy's form". As she grows up, Maggie gives up her childish fantasies, but the desire for preeminence which they express, the need to be somebody very special, remains with her to the end.

Maggie employs all three of Horney's defensive strategies in her relations with other people. Her withdrawal into a world of books and daydreams is an attempt to escape her dependence upon the real, unsatisfactory people around her. Her desire to be a queen and her displays of cleverness reveal expansive drives; she seeks a sense of safety and worth through mastery and recognition. Her aggressive trends are most clearly seen in her relations with her mother and her aunts, towards whom she is quite rebellious. She deeply resents these stifling, rejecting

women, and her anger manifests itself in frequent outbursts of hostility and vindictiveness, as well as in behavior of a more subtly thwarting kind.

Maggie is full of rage, and of powerful cravings to get revenge—to thwart, hurt and humiliate her tormentors. When she is in the grip of her fury she is capable of openly vindictive acts against even Tom and Lucy, whom she usually tries to please. Her sadistic trends are most vividly manifested in her use of "a Fetish which she punished for all her misfortunes":

> This was the trunk of a large wooden doll, which once stared with the roundest of eyes above the reddest of cheeks; but was now entirely defaced by a long career of vicarious suffering. Three nails driven into the head commemorated as many crises in Maggie's nine years of earthly struggle; that luxury of vengeance having been suggested to her by the picture of Jael destroying Sisera in the old Bible. The last nail had been driven in with a fiercer stroke than usual, for the Fetish on that occasion represented aunt Glegg. But immediately afterwards Maggie had reflected that if she drove many nails in, she would not be so well able to fancy that the head was hurt when she knocked it against the wall, nor to comfort it, and make believe to poultice it, when her fury was abated; for even aunt Glegg would be pitiable when she had been hurt very much, and thoroughly humiliated, so as to beg her niece's pardon.

Maggie's triumphs of vengeance, like her triumphs of recognition, are most completely realized in her fantasy life.

Although Maggie has strong tendencies in all three directions, her predominant solution is to move not away from or against, but toward people. She tries to gain affection, approval, and care by being good and loving. Whenever there is a conflict between her desires for glory or revenge and her need of being loved, her need for love always subdues her. When Tom behaves vindictively toward her, Maggie's first reaction is often anger and a desire to make him sorry, but it is always she who ends up pleading for forgiveness:

> . . . her need of love had triumphed over her pride, and she was going down with her swollen eyes and dishevelled hair to beg for pity. . . . It is a wonderful subduer, this need for love—this hunger of the heart—as peremptory as that other hunger by which Nature forces us to submit to the yoke, and change the face of the world . . . she rushed to him and clung round his neck, sobbing, "O Tom, please forgive me—I can't bear it—I will always be good—always remember things—do love me—please, dear Tom!"

The meaning of life for Maggie lies in being loved by her father and by Tom: " . . . if life had no love in it, what else was there for Maggie?" Her father's affection means a great deal to Maggie, but the most important person in her life is Tom—"What was the use of anything, if Tom didn't love her?"—and her life goal is to secure his favor.

Her mother's approval seems inaccessible, and, besides, Mrs. Tulliver's weakness makes her support of little value. The love of her father and brother is of such value mainly because they are arrogant-vindictive types and, as such, powerful figures who can fight her battles for her:

> "O how brave you are, Tom! I think you're like Samson. If there came a lion roaring at me, I think you'd fight him—wouldn't you, Tom? . . ."
>
> "But the lion *isn't* coming. What's the use of talking?"
>
> "But I like to fancy how it would be," said Maggie, following him. "Just think what you would do, Tom."

Maggie strongly identifies with her father and brother, partly because she wants them to identify with her in return, and partly because through them she can vicariously experience her aggressive drives:

> We might naively expect [explains Horney] that this type would rather abhor aggressive, arrogant or vindictive traits in others. But actually his attitude is divided. He does abhor them but also secretly or openly adores them . . . he admires in an aggressive type the expansive drives which for the sake of his integration he must so deeply suppress in himself. This disavowing of his own pride and aggressiveness, but admiring them in others, plays a great part in his morbid dependency. . . .

Maggie's relation with Tom, so much at the center both of her life and of the novel, is one to which Horney's analysis of morbid dependency is perfectly applicable. Tom thinks Maggie a silly thing, but Maggie glorifies his boyish accomplishments: "Maggie thought this sort of knowledge was very wonderful—much more difficult than remembering what was in the books; and she was rather in awe of Tom's superiority, for he was the only person who called her knowledge 'stuff,' and did not feel surprised at her cleverness". Though with part of her being Maggie wants recognition for her cleverness, another part of her needs to see Tom as far stronger and wiser than she. Tom's scorn of her, even though it is undermining, is part of his appeal for Maggie. The self-effacing person is drawn to the arrogant-vindictive person not only because he needs to be protected by and to live vicariously through someone who can master life aggressively, but also because he can only love someone who can "knock his own pride out from under him. . . . Insulting behavior frequently precipitates a dependent relationship". The self-effacing person "craves to surrender himself body and soul, but can do so only if his pride is bent or broken". Her father, Philip and Stephen are all important to Maggie; but they feed rather than break her pride; and they cannot, therefore, master her as does Tom.

In childhood, then, Maggie's predominant solution is to attach herself to Tom; and it is because she compulsively needs his approval and protection that her feelings toward him of love, awe, admiration and fear are all so exaggerated. Maggie's character structure and value system are the opposite of Tom's; but, because of her suppressed aggressive trends and her morbid dependency, she cannot help having "a certain awe as well as admiration of Tom's firmer and more effective character". "Maggie had an awe of him, against which she struggled as something unfair to her consciousness of wider thoughts and deeper motives; but it was of no use to struggle". George Eliot grasps perfectly the compulsiveness of Maggie's feelings toward her brother.

The chief source of Tom's power over Maggie is her fear; she "dreaded Tom's anger of all things":

> Her brother was the human being of whom she had been most afraid, from her childhood upwards: afraid with that fear which springs in us when we love one who is inexorable, unbending, unmodifiable—with a mind that we can never mould ourselves upon, and yet that we cannot endure to alienate from us. That deep-rooted fear was shaking Maggie now. . . .

When Tom is cruel or unloving, Maggie is torn by feelings of fright and rage. Because she needs to love Tom so that he will love her, she suppresses awareness of her vindictive drives and acts them out only in indirect or disguised ways: she forgets to feed Tom's rabbits, she accidentally knocks over his house of cards, she poisons his moment of triumph by drifting away with Stephen Guest. While behaving destructively, Maggie never "means" any harm. (Except toward her mother, Maggie rarely expresses anger directly and on her own behalf. When she denounces the Dodson aunts for criticizing her father and Tom for his cruelty to Philip, she is able to give vent to her pent-up rage only because she is defending another. Maggie's handling of resentments follows the typical compliant pattern: her taboos against feeling and expressing anger are lifted only when she is fighting someone else's battle, when she is angry in a good cause.)

If Maggie had developed in a healthy way, she could have endured an alienation from Tom; indeed, she would have chosen it rather than have Tom thwart her growth. But, as it is, she can do nothing that will disrupt her relation with her brother; and Tom, knowing this, is able to impose his will upon her. Maggie fears Tom's rejection so because it leaves her feeling alone and helpless in a hostile world: submission to Tom is the chief means by which she fends off her basic anxiety. Her dread of Tom is a dread of her own anxiety, and the intensity of her fear is a direct revelation of the weakness of her real self. With her self-esteem resting upon Tom's love and approval, she compulsively sacrifices her own legitimate claims in order to appease him.

IV

Now that we have some idea of Maggie's character, we need to examine her history. "Her history," as George Eliot says, "is a thing hardly to be predicted even from the completest knowledge of characteristics. For the tragedy of our lives is not created entirely from within". Much of Maggie's fate *is,* of course, created from within. Her solutions, being neurotic, can never work. Her compliance, even when it brings approval from without, weakens her real self and hence heightens her anxiety and self-rejection. The idealization of her self-effacing qualities (which we shall soon examine) increases rather than allays her self-hate, for she can never become the saint that she needs to be. But the tragedy of her life does not follow inevitably from her neurosis. If circumstances had permitted her to devote herself to a partner whose neurosis complemented her own, her inner conflicts and her suffering would have been much less severe. As it is, Maggie has the misfortune of finding not only her real self, but also her neurotic solutions frustrated by particularly unfavorable environmental conditions.

The first big change in Maggie's life comes with her father's failure and subsequent illness. At first Maggie derives an intense satisfaction from the new opportunity for devotedness. But the privation of all aesthetic and intellectual satisfactions and the fact that now she gets "no answer to her little caresses, either from her father or from Tom—the two idols of her life" eventually makes her more unhappy than she has ever been. She turns to masculine learning for the secret that will enable her to understand "and, in understanding, endure"; and she dreams, as we have seen, of being "honoured for her surprising attainments". She entertains "wild romances of a flight from home in search of something less sordid and dreary: she would go to some great man—Walter Scott, perhaps—and tell him how wretched and how clever she was, and he would surely do something for her". She rebels against her lot: " . . . fits even of anger towards her father and mother . . . —towards Tom, who checked her . . . —would flow out over her affections and conscience like a lava stream, and frighten her with a sense that it was not difficult for her to become a demon".

George Eliot attributes Maggie's neurotic sufferings, as she had earlier attributed Mr. Tulliver's compulsive vindictiveness, to inadequate culture. Maggie came "out of her school-life with a soul untrained for inevitable struggles—with no other part of her inherited share in the hard-won treasures of thought, which generations of painful toil have laid up for the race of men, than shreds and patches of feeble literature and false history". She is put in touch with the moral tradition of the race through Bob Jakin's gift of a copy of *The Imitation of Christ.* The impact of Thomas à Kempis upon Maggie is, indeed, great; but this is not, as George Eliot would have it, because he provides a moral wisdom that is new to Maggie. *The Imitation of Christ* is a classic statement of the self-effacing solution, and it comes to Maggie "as an unquestioned message" because it articulates attitudes that exist in her already. Given her compliant trends, the activation of her inner conflicts, and the fact that submission to Tom and her father has proven to be an inadequate solution, it is not surprising that Maggie is profoundly receptive to à Kempis's assurances that the total subduing of self-love will bring "great peace and tranquility". The search for

calm that is so central to Maggie's history is in reality a search for freedom from her inner conflicts, and in this quest the philosophy of Thomas à Kempis henceforth occupies a central position.

À Kempis proposes a solution that is far more rigorous and far less vulnerable than any which Maggie has been able to devise by herself. His strategy is to suppress all expansive drives, to resign himself to suffering in this life, and to give up the fight for self-realization. Earthly joys and frustrations are unimportant, for one's true dwelling is in heaven. Instead of depending on other people, one submits oneself to God, who completely loves and rewards his self-effacing subjects. In God, moreover, one finds the perfect being—all powerful, all-wise, all-loving—with whom to merge oneself. God takes the place of Tom for Maggie. Through her submission and feeling of helplessness Maggie gains a sense of being taken care of. Her solution is to remain a child, to refuse to take over the direction of her own existence: "'I think'" she tells Philip, "'we are only like children, that some one who is wiser is taking care of. Is it not right to resign ourselves entirely, whatever may be denied us? I have found great peace in that for the last two or three years—even joy in subduing my own will'."

Maggie does, indeed, find joy in self-renunciation. Thomas à Kempis offers his followers not only "inward peace" but also "an everlasting crown". Before she reads à Kempis, Maggie feels that it is part of the hardness of her life "that there was laid upon her the burthen of larger wants than others seemed to feel—that she had to endure this wide hopeless yearning for that something, whatever it was, that was greatest and best on this earth". George Eliot seems to regard Maggie's spiritual cravings as part of her essential nobility of nature, but they are much more satisfactorily explained as manifestations of her search for glory. "'I used to think,'" Maggie later tells Philip, "'I could never bear life if it kept on being the same every day, and I must always be doing things of no consequence, and never know anything greater'." The "strange thrill of awe" that passes through Maggie when she reads *The Imitation* comes, in part at least, from the book's revelation that the path to glory is through self-effacing goodness. Her yearning for the greatest and best is no longer hopeless. By renunciation Maggie at once escapes frustration ("'I was never satisfied with a *little* of anything'") and fulfills her ambition for preeminence.

Under the influence of à Kempis, Maggie's idealized image becomes fully articulated and her shoulds are firmly established. She forms plans of "self-humiliation and entire devotedness" and is "in ecstasy" because she thinks she has found the key to happiness. She denies herself even the most innocent pleasures and spends nights lying "on the hard floor for a penance" when she fails to live up to her perfectionistic standards. Her behavior changes so much that her mother feels "a sort of puzzled wonder that Maggie should be 'growing up so good;' it was amazing that this once 'contrary' child was becoming so submissive, so backward to assert her own will".

V

The serenity which Maggie achieves through total self-effacement is lost when the return of Philip Wakem stirs up her desires for love and a fuller life. She is so vulnerable to Philip's temptations because she has only repressed, not really resolved, her inner conflicts. In response to Philip's attentions there rises again "her innate delight in admiration and love", but she feels that she must renounce friendship with him because of her family's enmity toward lawyer Wakem. When Philip argues that it is not "right to sacrifice everything to other people's unreasonable feelings," Maggie replies:

> "I don't know. . . . Often, when I have been angry and discontented, it has seemed to me that I was not bound to give up anything; and I have gone on thinking till it has seemed to me that I could think away all my duty. But no good has ever come of that—it was an evil state of mind. I'm quite sure that whatever I might do, I should wish in the end that I had gone without anything for myself, rather than have made my father's life harder to him."

Maggie sees rebellion and callousness, the whole system of aggressive attitudes, as the only alternative to self-effacement. She cannot conceive of a healthy self-assertion, a self-assertion that respects the rights of others but insists upon one's own rights as well. The alternative to seeing Philip secretly is giving him up. It occurs neither to Maggie nor to the author that Maggie might assert her right to a relationship with Philip. Philip's position is a sounder one than Maggie's, and it is treated with some sympathy, but the narrator tells us that we "can hardly help blaming him severely" for tempting Maggie into a secret relation. Though Maggie's decision is presented as an extremely difficult one, with much to be said on both sides, the novel clearly leaves the impression that by continuing to see Philip, Maggie makes the wrong choice. She does, of course: she should have fought for her self-realization. As her dilemma is structured by the author, and by her own psychology, Maggie has a choice only of neurotic solutions. She can callously rebel against her family, she can sacrifice her own legitimate claims to other people's unreasonable feelings, or she can at once take what she wants and avoid conflict by engaging in a morally destructive act of deception. There is no escape from pain, for even a healthy solution would involve great friction between Maggie and her family, but a person in Maggie's position need not behave self-destructively. Maggie, of course, behaves as she must.

There are a number of reasons why Maggie cannot fight for her growth and autonomy, the chief of which is that she is afraid to jeopardize the precarious peace she has achieved by suppressing both her self-realizing and her expansive drives. She feels that her impoverished existence is "like death", but she is fearful of anything that might rouse her to life. Because she is afraid of being rejected, and, even more, of being bad, Maggie is terrified of hurting others. Self-assertion would mean violating her taboos against egoism and giving up her image of herself as a saint and martyr. It would mean giving up her suffering. Maggie displays the masochistic tendencies typical of the self-effacing person for whom suffering is both a way of life and a claim to virtue and superiority. Finally, as Maggie's spontaneous feelings have been replaced by a system of neurotic motivations, her legitimate desires have been transformed into insatiable cravings for the absolute. When Philip argues against her "narrow asceticism" and proclaims that "poetry and art and knowledge are sacred and pure," Maggie replies: "'But not for me—not for me. . . . Because I should want too much. I must wait—this life will not last long'."

After much inner conflict, Maggie drifts into a secret relation with Philip, the allurements of knowledge, beauty and love overcoming her "dread" of doing "something that, if discovered, must cause anger and pain". It is his offer of worshipful devotion that, more than anything else, makes Philip irresistible to Maggie. On her way to tell Philip that they must part, Maggie looks forward eagerly "to the affectionate admiring looks that would meet her", and her face, under Philip's influence, is "like that of a divinity well pleased to be worshipped". Philip loves her as, in her fantasies, she had always imagined herself being loved by Tom.

When Maggie found that she could not have love, she turned, as we have seen, to renunciation and goodness for her sense of safety and worth. With the reappearance of Philip, she is once again drawn by the appeal of love. Because of the feud between Tulliver and Wakem, her need for goodness and her need for love (both aspects of her self-effacing solution) are in conflict with each other. She cannot be loyal to her father without giving up Philip, and she cannot see Philip without feeling very sinful.

The weakness and dependency which make Philip so appealing to Maggie are also responsible for the absence in Maggie's feelings of the intensity that characterizes her relations to Tom and Stephen. The self-effacing person, says Horney,

> externalizes his own expansive drives and admires them in others. It is their pride and arrogance that touch him to the core. Not knowing that he can solve his conflict in himself only, he tries to solve it by love. To love a proud person, to merge with him, to live vicariously through him would allow him to participate in the mastery of life without having to own it to himself. . . .

> On the other hand a person with self-effacing trends does not appeal to him as a sexual partner. He may like him as a friend because he finds in him more sympathy, understanding, or devotion than in others. But when starting a more intimate relationship with him, he may feel even repelled. . . . He sees in him, as in a mirror, his own weakness. . . . He is . . . afraid of the clinging-vine attitude of such a partner because the mere idea that he himself must be the stronger one terrifies him.

Maggie's beauty and intelligence make her a worthy prize in Philip's eyes, the object of a grand passion; but Maggie does not reciprocate Philip's feeling and is never quite easy about regarding him as a lover. When Tom forbids them to see each other, Maggie is enraged at his cruelty and is full of a "just indignation"; but she is also "conscious of a certain dim background of relief in the forced separation from Philip". Maggie feels relief partly because she has been rescued from evil and partly because she has been punished, but mostly, I suspect, because she has been delivered by a harshness not her own from an oppressive relationship.

VI

Maggie is drawn to Stephen Guest by many of the same hungers that made her consent to a clandestine relation with Philip. With her separation from Philip, the death of her father, and the harshness of Tom, Maggie has been deprived of all warmth and companionship. Her life as a teacher in a third-rate boarding school has been lonely, barren and oppressive. With no one to appreciate her sacrifices, and with a future that seems "likely to be worse than her past," Maggie, "after her years of contented renunciation," has "slipped back into desire and longing." Stephen offers her the things for which she is most starved—admiration, devotion, opportunities for culture and enjoyment—and in "poor Maggie's highly-strung, hungry nature" there is, initially at least, little power of resistance.

But we have not yet explained the overwhelming force of Maggie's attraction to Stephen. Philip, too, offers adoration and escape from a dreary existence; but we cannot imagine Maggie, at this point in her life, being seduced by *him* into a violation of all of her feelings of duty. Maggie's deepest craving, as we have seen, is to have Tom, or someone like Tom, love "her—oh, so much,—more, even than she loved him, so that he would always want to have her with him and be afraid of vexing her". Philip loves her "devotedly, as she had always longed to be loved", but he can never satisfy, as Stephen can, her need to submit and her desires for protection and conquest. When she trips and Stephen holds her up "with a firm grasp," Maggie finds it "very charming to be taken care of in that kind graceful manner by some one taller and stronger than one's self". She is always looking *down* into Philip's pale, pleading, feminine face. Stephen's easy arrogance, so annoying to the critics, at once offends Maggie and fascinates her. On the disastrous boating expedition, Maggie submits herself with exquisite pleasure to the "stronger presence that seemed to bear her along without any act of her own will, like the added self which comes with the sudden exalting influence of a strong tonic". "Maggie obeyed: there was an unspeakable charm in being told what to do, and having everything decided for her".

Stephen is an aggressive person of the narcissistic type who is drawn to Maggie partly because "to see such a creature subdued by love for one would be a lot worth having". One of the reasons why Stephen's love is so precious to Maggie is that through it she can satisfy her own expansive drives. Her "passionate sensibility," George Eliot tells us, "prevented her vanity from taking the form of mere feminine coquetry and device, and gave it the poetry of ambition". Maggie has always been helpless, odd, deprived. All this can be changed by the love of St. Ogg's richest and handsomest young man, the scion of the town's most powerful and respected family. By becoming the beloved of Stephen Guest, Maggie can achieve the position of preeminence, of "acknowledged supremacy", for which she has always longed. She cannot resist Stephen's professions of devotion: " . . . that to satisfy her lightest wish was dearer to him than all other bliss . . . he would belong to her for ever, and all that was his was hers—had no value for him except as it was hers. Such things, uttered in low broken tones . . . were like nectar held close to thirsty lips . . . "

Even though there is little direct evidence in the text, it is tempting to believe that Maggie's drifting away with Stephen is partly motivated by an unconscious desire for revenge on Tom. Nothing Maggie could do would hurt Tom more; and the disgrace comes just as Tom has, with great effort, redeemed the family's losses and reestablished its traditions by returning to the mill. There is ample evidence, however, that her conquest of Stephen satisfies Maggie's deep, though suppressed, desire for a vindictive triumph over Lucy, in whose shadow she has always been. In her childhood fantasies she imagined Lucy as a queen and dreamt of taking her place. Several years before she meets Stephen, Maggie returns *Corinne* to Philip unfinished, telling him that she is "determined to read no more books where the blond-haired women carry away all the happiness":

> "If you could give me some story, now, where the dark woman triumphs, it would restore the balance. I want to avenge Rebecca and Flora McIvor, and Minna and all the rest of the dark unhappy ones. . . . "

> "Well, perhaps you will avenge the dark women in your own person and carry away all the love from your cousin Lucy. She is sure to have some handsome young man of St. Ogg's at her feet now: and you have only to shine upon him—your fair little cousin will be quite quenched in your beams."

> "Philip, that is not pretty of you, to apply my nonsense to anything real," said Maggie, looking hurt. "As if I, with my old gowns and want of all accomplishment, could be a rival of dear little Lucy, who knows and does all sorts of charming things, and is ten times prettier than I am—even if I were odious and base enough to wish to be her rival. . . . "

> "Maggie," said Philip, with surprise, "it is not like you to take playfulness literally."

Maggie's defensive reaction is a clear sign that Philip has brought to light a fantasy that attracts Maggie strongly, but against which she has powerful taboos. This interpretation is confirmed by an episode after her flirtation with

Stephen has begun in which Maggie is afraid that Philip remembers the conversation just quoted:

> Had his mind flown back to something that *she* now remembered?—something about a lover of Lucy's? It was a thought that made her shudder: it gave new definiteness to her present position. . . . Philip must not have that odious thought in his mind: she would banish it from her own.

Maggie suffers "horrible tumult within" because, strong as are the drives which compel her into a relation with Stephen, the drives which forbid such a relation are even stronger. For one thing, Maggie's own sufferings, combined with her highly developed powers of sympathy, make her shrink from inflicting pain upon others. This, of course, is the novel's explanation of Maggie's behavior, and it has its truth; but it does not, I think, account for the intensity of Maggie's inner conflict or for her persistent refusal, after she has already compromised all the affected relationships, to consider marriage with Stephen. Maggie tells Stephen at Garum Firs that she would "rather die than fall into" the "temptation" of marrying him because, whatever her cravings might be for triumph and fulfillment, her self-esteem depends upon her being good and doing her duty. What George Eliot interprets as "the gathered spiritual force of painful years coming" to Maggie's "aid in this extremity" I would explain as the persistence of Maggie's powerful self-effacing trends and a resurgence of the philosophy of renunciation articulated by Thomas à Kempis.

Given her feelings before she succumbs to Stephen's temptation, it is inevitable that Maggie should be appalled when she awakens to the discovery that she has acted out her secret (and, in some cases, unconscious) wishes. Her first awareness of what she has done comes in the dream in which she is in a boat with Stephen and she sees Tom row past without looking at her: " . . . she rose to stretch out her arms and call to him, and their own boat turned over with the movement, and they began to sink, till with one spasm of dread she seemed to awake, and find she was a child again in the parlor at evening twilight, and Tom was not really angry". Earlier we are told that "to have no cloud between herself and Tom was still a perpetual yearning in her, that had its root deeper than all change". Despite his charm, eminence and conceit, Stephen cannot replace Tom for Maggie. As a suffering lover he can appeal to her sympathies, but he lacks Tom's power to chasten her pride and to master her will and conscience. By marrying Stephen Maggie will cut herself off forever from Tom's approval; by returning to accept judgment and punishment at his hands, she maintains the possibility of an eventual rapprochement.

In addition to cutting herself off from others whose approval she needs, Maggie has violated the strictest taboos of the self-effacing solution and has thereby roused up her profoundest feelings of anxiety and of self-contempt. I have no wish to deny the moral nobility of some of Maggie's feelings: she has a vividly imaginative sympathy with those whom she has injured, and she profoundly

regrets having brought them so much pain. But her subsequent behavior, which is compulsive in nature, has much more to do with reestablishing her relation to herself, with repairing her defenses, than with minimizing or repairing the damage she has done to others.

Maggie once again gives up all thought of earthly happiness and turns to renunciation as a refuge from her own nature and from the conflicts and imperfections of the human condition. This time the author unreservedly approves of her renunciation, for Maggie has learned that resignation is not joy but sorrow borne willingly. Maggie has not given up her search for glory and accepted the pain of being human: rather, she has learned the high price of perfect goodness and is compelled to pay it.

I cannot agree with those who argue that George Eliot at the end is aware of Maggie's limitations. Though there are differences in the perspectives of Maggie and of the novel as a whole through most of the story, at the end these points of view seem to coalesce: Maggie's self-abnegation is presented as the "clue of life." In terms of the novel's thematic structure, Maggie's fall is in many ways a fortunate one, for it brings her firmly back to the philosophy of Thomas à Kempis, which she now properly understands. Her struggles of conscience mark her as a morally superior person, a being far above those who condemn her. One detects a kind of pride in Maggie and, even more, in the narrator at how "good" Maggie was to have returned, even though this is impractical and makes no sense to the world. Maggie is so noble that she does not even claim a right to be indignant at the terribly unjust treatment that she receives in St. Ogg's: "There was no home, no help for the erring: even those who pitied were constrained to hardness. But ought she to complain? Ought she to shrink from the long penance of life, which was all the possibility she had of lightening the load to some other sufferers, and so changing the passionate error into a new force of unselfish human love?" Maggie suffers horribly from mistreatment and from her own errors, which are presented as the result, in part, of her superior endowment. But her suffering, instead of embittering her, is transformed by her nobility of nature into a powerful force for goodness: "Surely there was something taught her by this experience of great need; and she must be learning a secret of human tenderness and long-suffering, that the less erring could hardly know?" I see no distinction here between Maggie's view of herself and the author's view of her.

Maggie is presented so sympathetically because the perspective of the novel as a whole is that of the self-effacing solution at which she arrives by the end. The clue of life is total renunciation. There is nothing in the novel to suggest that Maggie's solution is not a good one, but only one to which she has unfortunately been driven by her nature and by the unfavorable circumstances of her life. Maggie's suffering is pitied, but it is presented as ennobling rather than as destructive. Maggie's earlier renunciation was defective because she had hoped through goodness to achieve happiness. At the end Maggie resigns herself to a suffering from which there is no relief and devotes herself to a goodness for which there is no re-ward. The novel's conclusion, which is a fantasy of the compliant solution working to perfection, releases Mag-gie from her suffering and rewards her goodness. It has often been noted that the goodness of George Eliot's heroines is magically followed by plot occurrences in their favor.

Maggie's solution has its rewards, of course, even be-fore the happy ending. There is the reward of feeling perfectly good and completely misunderstood. George Eliot's emphasis upon true resignation as pain borne willingly without hope of gratification is but a refine-ment of Maggie's earlier religious ardor. The most glo-rious thing of all is to do without glory. All satisfactions are given up, but there remains the pride in being *really* perfectly good, a pride which is attended, of course, by intense satisfaction. There is no awareness in the novel that Maggie at the end is still engaged in a neurotic search for glory. Indeed, the novel itself invests her fi-nal sufferings and renunciations with an exalted glam-our. Maggie, with her crown of thorns, is another Christ: "'I have received Cross,'" she exclaims, "'I have re-ceived it from Thy hand; I will bear it, and bear it till death, as Thou has laid it upon me'."

The ending vindicates Maggie to the world. With the coming of the flood Maggie feels as though she has en-tered upon a new life; for she senses that this is her op-portunity to redeem herself in the eyes of others, to have her goodness recognized. Her torpor passes away, and she is filled with a glorious energy. She feels herself to be divinely protected, an agent of God, who has always seen in her the nobility to which men have been blind. Her moment of ecstatic triumph comes when Tom, "pale with a certain awe and humiliation", realizes how wrong he has been about her and gives Maggie the love and hom-age she has always wanted: "Maggie could make no an-swer but a long deep sob of that mysterious happiness that is one with pain". The novel's epigraph—"In their death they were not divided"—indicates that the author gives as much importance as does Maggie herself to the climactic reunion with Tom. Maggie's death preserves forever the glorious victory which she has wrested from defeat.

At the moment of her death Maggie has that which she has most wanted from life. Had she lived on there would have been renewed turmoil and failure to mar her victory. For Maggie has not resolved her inner conflicts; she has only repressed them by totally inhibiting both her self-realizing and her expansive drives. After their quarrel over Philip releases her anger toward Tom, Maggie moves for a while toward autonomy. She refuses the stifling protec-tion both of her brother and her aunts, and she goes off to teach, to earn her own way in the world. When, later, Tom complains that she won't be guided by his better judgment, Maggie replies: "'I am grateful to you. But, indeed, you can't quite judge for me—our natures are very different'." She tells Lucy: "'I must not stay here long. It would unfit me for the life I must begin again at last. I can't live in dependence—I can't live with my

brother . . . that would be intolerable to me'." But Maggie has not the strength to become her own person. At school she is starved for the warmth and approval that she needs so much, and this makes her particularly vulnerable to Stephen's attentions. After she compromises herself with Stephen, she becomes totally incapable of self-assertion and is entirely at the mercy of her "dread." She reverts to a childish dependence and returns to Tom for punishment and for protection from herself.

Maggie is terribly afraid of herself, and with good reason; for her compulsive acts have wrought great harm. When Tom rejects her, she clings desperately to St. Ogg's and to her family, symbols of restraint and of security, and refuses all opportunities to make a new life for herself elsewhere.

"All she craved," we are told, "was something to guaran-tee her from more falling: her own weakness haunted her like a vision of hideous possibilities, that made no peace conceivable except such as lay in the sense of a sure refuge". Maggie sees no prospect of happiness (she is afraid, of course, of wanting anything for herself); her only recourse is to live out the self-effacing solution for the rest of her days. But she knows that there are power-ful forces in her working against this solution, and she is oppressed by the fear that she will succumb to them. She has promised to bear the Cross till death: "'But how long it will be before death comes! . . . How shall I have patience and strength? Am I to struggle and fall and re-pent again'?—has life other trials as hard for me still?'" There is in Maggie a profound wish for death, for only in death is there the peace of a sure refuge. Not only is her wish for death granted, and not only does she die before she falls again, but her death comes, as we have seen, in her moment of highest glory. Even when the flood comes and Maggie feels that she has "suddenly passed away from that life which she had been dreading" her desire is to be reconciled to Tom and then to die. How else can one explain the fact that she is afraid, as she rows up the Ripple, that the floating masses in it "might dash against her boat as she passed, and cause her to perish *too soon*"? (my italics.)

My thesis, then, is that Maggie at the end has adopted an extreme form of the self-effacing solution. She wishes to die so that she might remain good. Death is, of course, the ultimate self-effacement. She senses, quite correctly, that if she lives she will be torn by endless conflicts. She will violate her inner dictates again and again, and every time she will be confronted by her profound dread and self-loathing. The novel succeeds brilliantly in its charac-terization of Maggie, but it fails to interpret her correctly and to see the destructiveness of her solution—though it dramatizes that destructiveness with great penetration. The ending is artistically weak because, though the action of the novel has everywhere else been realistic, it seems here to be controlled by the wishes and fantasies of the hero-ine. In her over-identification with Maggie, George Eliot loses sight of that disparity between inward and outward, wish and reality, which is usually a controlling principle in her fictional universe. The novel prepares us for catastrophe—or, at least, for the frustration of the heroine—but it gives us instead, as Leavis says, "the dreamed-of perfect accident that gives us the opportunity for the dreamed-of heroic act—the act that shall vindicate us against a harshly misjudging world, bring emotional fulfillment and . . . provide a gloriously tragic curtain".

VII

F. R. Leavis is right in saying that George Eliot does not "understand" Maggie Tulliver's immaturity; but he is wrong, I think, in feeling that we "ought to ask" this kind of understanding "of a great novelist." We must regret George Eliot's over-identification with Maggie because it results in aesthetic failings—such as the inconsistent handling of distance, the disparities between representation and interpretation, and the mixing of realism and fantasy; but this is not Dr. Leavis's point. He wants George Eliot to understand Maggie from without as well as from within, to have a set of mature values against which Maggie's immaturity can be seen. I respect the importance of this kind of understanding as much as does Dr. Leavis; but I do not think that we find much of it in fiction; and I feel that its absence is regrettable only when, as in *The Mill on the Floss,* it is damaging aesthetically. Even in such a case we should note that the novel's weaknesses are closely related to its strengths, for if George Eliot had not been so intimately identified with Maggie she could hardly have given us a portrait of such subtlety and interest.

My disagreement with Dr. Leavis does not mean that I am denying to fiction an illuminative value; it means, rather, that I look for a different kind of illumination than he seems to be demanding. What is enduringly valuable about realistic fiction as a source of knowledge is not its moral or intellectual insight, but its phenomenological grasp of experience. Such fiction lets us know how it is inside to be a certain kind of person with a certain kind of destiny. Through mimetic portraits of character, novels like *The Mill on the Floss* provide us with artistic formulations of experience which are permanent, irreplaceable, and of a quite different order than the discursive formulations of philosophy or of systematic psychology. And, if we view him as a fictional persona, as another character, rather than as a source of wisdom, the implied author, too, enlarges our knowledge of the human psyche. For through the novel's rhetoric we become aware of the meaning which the characters' experience has for a mind like that of the implied author, and we enter thus into his subjective world. The communication of healthy norms and a balanced view of life is simply *not* the kind of illumination that is proper to fiction—even if the novelist himself makes the mistake of thinking that it is.

George Eliot, of course, made this mistake, and she invites, therefore, the kind of criticism in which Dr. Leavis and other moral critics engage. I engaged in such criticism myself in *Experiments in Life,* where I not only expounded, but also tacitly assented to George Eliot's theory of fiction and valued her novels—in part, at least—for the soundness of their moral vision. In a letter to Dr. Joseph Frank Payne, George Eliot described her novels as "simply a set of experiments in life—an endeavor to see what our thought and emotion may be capable of—what stores of motive, actual or hinted as possible, give promise of a better after which we may strive—what gains from past discipline we must strive to keep hold of as something more sure than shifting theory." "The empirical epistemology," I explained,

> with its emphasis upon the concrete, the particular, the experienced as the source and test of truth, led George Eliot to distrust abstractions and systems . . . and to rely upon art in her search for moral truths. Feuerbach . . . claims validity for his method because "both in substance and in speech, it places philosophy in the *negation of philosophy, i.e.,* it declares *that* alone to be the true philosophy which is converted in *succum et sanguinem,* which is incarnate in Man." The novel, which deals pre-eminently with flesh and blood experience, and which is produced by "emotion blending with thought" . . . is, then, clearly a vehicle of true philosophy.

There is here the rejection of abstractions and of systems that is common to both Romanticism and Existentialism. Caught, like ourselves, in a time of social and intellectual fragmentation, George Eliot despaired of arriving at intellectual formulations which would be widely accepted. She hoped, however, to discover through her fiction truths of feeling in which men would perceive unquestioned values and by which they would recognize themselves as brothers. If a moral posture could be shown to derive from life as felt rather than from life as thought, it would have an impressive claim to validity and would flash conviction upon the world.

This is an inviting view of art, one that is very much in harmony with some major trends in twentieth century thought; but it is not compatible with our growing awareness of the psychological origins of our value systems. I do not deny that if the configuration of experience presented in fiction corresponds in some significant way to our own sense of the world, the moral affirmations of the work may come, as did the philosophy of Thomas à Kempis to Maggie Tulliver, as an unquestioned message. But experiences of the world differ greatly, and we in fact respond strongly to only a small percentage of the works that we read. We are, to a large degree, predisposed by our strategies of defense to certain attitudes, values and beliefs. When we encounter works of fiction in which our feelings about life are more fully and subtly articulated, we have a sense of being profoundly influenced and of our lives being made more meaningful. But the attitudes and values which are thus reenforced are, from an ethical standpoint, not necessarily good ones.

The novelist may feel, as did George Eliot, that the ability of a formula to get itself "clothed" for him "in some human figure and individual experience" attests to its validity; but he creates his picture of life out of his own prior sense of the world, and he is no more likely than his reader to be convinced by a picture to which he has not assented (perhaps unconsciously) at the outset. The author, in the act of writing, and the audience, in the act of reading, may have a sense of discovering moral truths; but it is more likely that what they are discovering is themselves, the potentialities for ramification and rationalization of their own position.

From the point of view of the psychological theories which inform this essay, the novel *could* be an instrument of moral discovery if the author were psychologically healthy, or if he were in the process of working out his problems. According to Abraham Maslow [in his *Toward a Psychology of Being*, 1962], it is possible to arrive at a universally valid humanistic ethic, but in order to do so we must ignore the choices, or values, of neurotic people and focus on the choices of healthy (self-actualizing) people:

> To average the choices of good and bad choosers, of healthy and sick people is useless. Only the choices and tastes and judgments of healthy human beings will tell us much about what is good for the human species in the long run. The choices of neurotic people can tell us mostly what is good for keeping a neurosis stabilized . . . I think that this is the main reef on which most hedonistic value theories and ethical theories have foundered.

The main problem in Maslow's position (and it is, I think, an insoluble one) is that there is no way of validating, for those who are not already convinced, the criteria of psychological health, the criteria by which the good choosers are chosen. I believe that Maslow's criteria are sound ones; and if, as he claims, we make continual discoveries of the good by observing the lives of healthy people, then fiction that was written from a healthy perspective or that depicted healthy characters could, indeed, fulfill the objectives that George Eliot defined for her own novels. George Eliot, however, for all her genius as an artist, did not possess the qualifications necessary for conducting such experiments in life.

I do not discover in *The Mill on the Floss,* therefore, either healthy solutions for problems such as Maggie's or a vision of "a better after which we may strive." I discover how it is to be a Maggie Tulliver and what values such a person must have. I discover what the experience of a Maggie Tulliver means, intellectually and emotionally, to a consciousness like that of the implied author. But this is a great deal; and there is, of course, more in the same kind. Even though I no longer go to George Eliot as a great sage, I still value her highly and go to her as a great artist who gives me a kind of knowledge that I find nowhere else of certain patterns of experience. George Eliot's experiments in life do present enduring truths, but they are not the truths for which she was searching.

Barbara Hardy (essay date 1970)

SOURCE: *"The Mill on the Floss,"* in *Particularities: Readings in George Eliot,* Ohio University Press, 1983, pp. 58-74.

[*In the following essay, first published in 1970 in her* Critical Essays on George Eliot, *Hardy explores the conclusion of* The Mill on the Floss *as an example of authorial fantasy.*]

I take it that **The Mill on the Floss** is the novel most visibly close to George Eliot's life. As in many novels loosely classed as autobiographical, this closeness to life has advantages and disadvantages, and shows itself in various ways. It creates the loving and seemingly accurate chronicle of actual events; the successfully externalized conscious and unconscious disguise and transformation; and the glib, inventive fantasy of dreaming and wishing. I am separating these processes for the purpose of announcing my analysis, but the novel blurs the edges and blends the kinds. It is a novel where the author is recalling the landscape and feelings of her childhood, in ways both gratifyingly indulgent and rationally analytic. As she dwells on the relationship between a brother and sister we can discern an understandable and undisfiguring nostalgia; a need to explain and justify in concretely imagined terms; and the falsifying pressures of a wish-fulfilling reconciliation. Where she modifies experience, in order to hide or reveal, we can find resemblance with difference: she brings out order and meaning, discovers and argues her case, by summoning variety and antithesis, by trying out her particular conclusions and experience in the generalizing process of ordered invention, which accumulates and patterns fresh particulars. The submission to pressures of wishing and dreaming shows itself in a failure to particularize, in a movement away from the scrupulous testing process into simplifications of symbol and plot. **The Mill on the Floss** is especially interesting as a novel because it sets up an expressive form which betrays itself, and because in so doing reveals the varying relationships between the work of art and the materials of life.

The uneven and complex relation between the work of art and its sources—which we can usually only guess at—is perhaps most clearly introduced by taking a look at some similar cases in the art of fiction. Like **The Mill on the Floss,** Charlotte Brontë's *Jane Eyre* and Dickens's *David Copperfield* also combine a strongly contrasted particularity with an uncontrolled submission to fantasy. Not surprisingly, all three novels sharply betray this submissiveness in the testing ground where the novelist solves his problems and reaches his conclusions—at the end of the story. At the end of novels of education the novelist stands back and defines the nature and meaning of the process, the development, the *Bildung.* His conclusion is a conclusion in both senses: an end and an arrival at meaning. Behind such problem-solving lies the more or less invisible pressure of the artist's personal problems, and it is characteristic of such mid-Victorian novels that they should arrive at conclusions which are affirmative, reconciliatory, and final. Charlotte Brontë, Dickens, and George Eliot do not exactly create simple fables for their time, but achieve affirmation and finality by crushing a complex experience into narrow simplifications of plot and symbolism. The endings of all three novels are religious or quasi-religious, and are marked by a strong emotional crescendo which betrays the uncontrolled urge to reach an end. They make an under-distanced appeal which can command the assent of tears or the dissent of stony recognition—or both. Charlotte Brontë kills off Rochester's mad wife, and brings him through the fire, multilated and penitent, to Jane's arms: there is the triumphant reconciliation after all that pain, and the triumphant discovery of meaning. Dickens kills off David's child-wife, Dora, and brings him through visionary experience in the high and lonely Alps to Agnes's arms: there is the triumphant reconciliation after all that pain, and the triumphant discovery of meaning. George Eliot kills off Tom and Maggie, bringing them through the waters of the flood into each other's arms: there is the triumphant feeling after all that pain, and the triumphant discovery of meaning. Each novel ends with a double Eureka feeling: the final embrace of the loved-one and the vision of meaning. The blinded Rochester now sees the pattern in his life and Jane's; David ceases to be metaphorically 'blind, blind, blind'; and Tom Tulliver at last sees (and Maggie sees that he sees) 'the depths in life, that had lain beyond his vision which he had fancied so keen and clear'. The imagery of blindness and good vision is there in each novel.

In *Jane Eyre* and *David Copperfield* the fantasy runs as a vivid unreal thread through the novel, and is particularly associated with Rochester and Agnes. In both novels there is an increase in authorial magic at the end, but the wish-fulfilment also shapes a kind of character who will make for that end, fantastically idealized and simplified. In *The Mill on the Floss* there is no such character—not even Maggie—and the drop, or rise, into the heights of the false Sublime and a false catharsis is therefore especially violent. All three novels show a controlled and controlling particularity *and* an abrupt movement into unparticularized consolations and conclusions. Whether we see the novel as an imitation of reality or as an expressive form creating virtual experience, it seems right to speak of partial failure. Each novel seems to fail for a good reason: the solutions and conclusions are so visibly needed by the artist, not by the tale. Each novel is an instance of technique acting, not as discovery, but as obscuring fantasy.

Perhaps all we can really say about autobiographical novels is that they are novels which reveal this connection between the life-need and the completed form. Novels which seem more objectified are often novels which we simply cannot check against biographical data. The weakness in Coleridge's distinction between the Shakespearian or Spinozan imagination which becomes all things and the Miltonic imagination which brings all things into itself, or in Keats's distinction between the chameleon poet and the Wordsworthian or egotistical Sublime, is their reliance on the distinction between an artist's life about which little is known and an artist's life about which a great deal is known. We happen to be in a position to say that Charlotte's sexual and social experiences may well explain her need for a sexual and religious solution like the one provided by the conclusion to *Jane Eyre,* to see that Dickens's marriage encouraged fantasy, and to see that

George Eliot's break with family and society shaped the form and content of her solution. The actual prayers of Jane, David, and Maggie all correspond closely with the needs of their authors, and the needs produce the facile sublimity of the answers. But we do not find that the novel is totally falsified, wholly shaped by the fantasy of wishing and dreaming: each novel challenges the notion of an evenly objectified and totally realized work of art.

Each novel happens not only to betray wish-fulfilment, but to discuss it. If there is the self-indulgence of fantasy here, it is not the gross indulgence of ignorant artists, but the fine indulgence of intelligent artists, alive to the nature and dangers of romantic fantasy. Dickens creates a comic inflation and deflation of the fantasy and romantic imagery of David's immature loves. Charlotte Brontë has an intense analysis of the nature and the origin of fantasy in Jane's deprivation and ennui before she meets Rochester. George Eliot discusses and dramatizes Maggie's needs for various opiates—in daydreams, literature, religion, and personal relationships. The existence of this discussion of fantasy could mean no more than the unsurprising combination of rational insight with irrational blindness, but it happens also to be accompanied by a very strenuous effort to shape experience, to distinguish between dreaming and waking, and to break with the simplifications and stereotypes of fantasy.

The Mill on the Floss explores the realities of character and event by exposing human beings to life without opiate, but in the end it succumbs itself, as a work of art, to the kind of unreality it has been criticizing. The process by which it succumbs is not a simple one. I do not see the novel in terms of a polarity of soft dream and hard, daylight experience. There is a toughness and openness, a kind of pragmatism which shows itself especially in a movement away from heavy plotting and shaping of character development; there is a successful and transforming use of the personal experience of religious crisis and conversion; there is a successfully particularized though more personally interested transformation of George Eliot's sexual crisis; and there is a final unsuccessful resort to solution by fantasy. I want to take these four aspects of the novel in reverse order, beginning at the end.

The case against the concluding Providential fantasy has perhaps been won too easily, whether by Henry James or Joan Bennett or Dr Leavis, who have all written finely but not lengthily on the subject. I assume that all readers of George Eliot will agree on the importance of a sense of unity and continuity in her life and her novels. The two major crises of her life, the one a crisis of belief and the other a crisis of ethical choice, and many less climactic occasions of depression and anxiety, were all marked by a frightening sense of dislocation and loss of identity. Behind the loving chronicle of childhood and the fantastic problem-solving in *The Mill on the Floss* lies the estrangement from her early past. The breach with her brother Isaac was not mended until 1880, when she married John Cross, and received the famous letter of forgiveness:

I have much pleasure in availing myself of the present opportunity to break the long silence which has existed between us.

To which she replied:

It was a great joy to me to have your kind words of sympathy, for our long silence has never broken the affection for you which began when we were little ones.

It is no act of wild speculation which finds personal pressures at work in the childhood scenes of *The Mill on the Floss,* in the nostalgic and analytic treatment of brother and sister, in some aspects of Tom's character, and in the subject of the break and the reconciliation. The emotional centrality of the relationship is significant, and so is the intensity of the final embrace—'In their death they were not divided'.

The conclusion still needs to be closely evaluated. We can only defend it, I think, on very restricted aesthetic grounds. We may say that the novel's ending is prepared from its beginning, in the doom-laden references to death by drowning, in the river-imagery, and in the threads of pagan and Christian lore that run through the reminiscences of past floods, the legend of St Ogg and the folk-superstition that 'when the mill changes hands, the river's angry'. George Eliot is all too plainly preparing for her dénouement. This is what Henry James had to say about the dénouement in his essay, 'The Novels of George Eliot', in *The Atlantic Monthly,* October 1866:

The dénouement shocks the reader most painfully. Nothing has prepared him for it; the story does not move towards it; it casts no shadow before it.

James is wrong about nothing preparing us, wrong too about no shadow being cast, but he is quite right to say that 'the story does not move towards it'. Almost everything moves except the story. Even the characters are ingeniously though artificially involved in the pre-echoes as Mrs Tulliver fretfully worries about her children being brought home drowned, or about Maggie tumbling in some day, and as Philip teases Maggie about selling her soul to the ghostly boatman on the Floss. The foreshadowings strike us as artificial because they are uninvolved with action. There is the sense of a restless preparation in rhetoric which does not move dynamically with events and characters. Mrs Tulliver's nagging worries attach themselves clearly enough to the Maggie who pushes Lucy into the mud, but scarcely to the flood and the heroic rescue. If Maggie were to fall in carelessly, or throw herself in recklessly, there would be a relation between prolepsis and action. Or if those legends about the river and the great set-piece descriptions of its transiently tamed powers were part of a presentation of man at work in and against Nature, there could have been such a relation. But such descriptions remain figures in the frame, not in the picture. The imagery that Henry James uses of Isabel Archer not only hints at danger, but is fully related to the action: Ralph does something very like putting wind in

her sails, and the audacity, responsibility, freedom, and danger involved in the figure are fully worked out in event and character. The animation that Thomas Hardy bestows on Nature is revealed throughout *The Return of the Native* or *Far from the Madding Crowd,* and Nature and Man are related at every turn of the action. But the river-imagery and the descriptions of Nature in *The Mill on the Floss* expose instead of disguising those gaps in the action. Most of the hints and images and descriptions could be cut without much loss of lucidity; Tulliver is a marvellous study in reduced pride and love and temper, but not the hero or victim of a story of man against nature. The novel has a unity in imagery, and this has a strong mnemonic force, but it does not prepare us for the part played by the river in reaching the conclusion and solving the problem. What we are prepared for is the struggle between the energetic human spirit and a limited and limiting society: such struggles are not settled by floods.

Woolf discusses Eliot's development of her heroine Maggie Tulliver:

The noble and beautiful girl who insisted upon being born into the Mill on the Floss is the most obvious example of the ruin which a heroine can strew about her. Humour controls her and keeps her lovable so long as she is small and can be satisfied by eloping with the gipsies or hammering nails into her doll; but she develops; and before George Eliot knows what has happened she has a full-grown woman on her hands demanding what neither gipsies nor dolls, nor St. Ogg's itself is capable of giving her. First Philip Wakem is produced, and later Stephen Guest. The weakness of the one and the coarseness of the other have often been pointed out; but both, in their weakness and coarseness, illustrate not so much George Eliot's inability to draw the portrait of a man, as the uncertainty, the infirmity, and the fumbling which shook her hand when she had to conceive a fit mate for a heroine.

Virginia Woolf, in The Common Reader, *Harcourt, Brace and Co., 1925.*

The flood is the Providence of the novel. It would not be quite true to say that religion is rushed in at the end without being earlier involved with action and character. The community of St Ogg's is most carefully analysed as a mixed pagan and Christian society, and a very large number of the characters are placed in religious tradition, belief, and feeling. Maggie's religious experience is central to the novel, but I do not think it prepares us for the miraculous aura, however delicately adjusted, which surrounds her in the last pages. It is interesting that a scholar who has made a special study of George Eliot's treatment of religion, Martin J. Svaglic, observes that 'Maggie and Dorothea, in their moments of greatest crisis, do not pray.' Gordon Haight rightly corrects him about Maggie (in a footnote to the reprinted article in *A Century of George Eliot Criticism*). Yet there is a sense, I think, in which we can see why Svaglic can say that Maggie, like Dorothea, does not pray. Her prayer is in no way formal, her God can merge into the God of our anguished cries to no God, her voice is not raised to be heard—only compare her prayer with Jane Eyre's. But he is wrong, for the vague appeal is instantly answered, pat, like the prayers in *Jane Eyre,* with comfort and solution. When she is faced with a crisis of decision (which is what Svaglic may have meant by her moment of greatest crisis), she does not make her decision by referring to any laws or values that are not human. Dorothea's critics knew very well that her decisions and values were revealingly humane, void of supernatural reference, and Maggie feels, thinks, and chooses in the same humanly reliant way. True, there is the conversion by the aid of Thomas à Kempis, but there is absolutely nothing in it that does not pertain to George Eliot's Feuerbachian creed. Here is the third Positive, Duty, which she allowed to Myers in the garden of Trinity, Cambridge, but no trace of the first two, God and Immortality. If we look carefully, we see that George Eliot makes the religious conversion insistently human: the value is that of selflessness; there is a conversion of ethic, not of belief. George Eliot's emphasis is on the human agents, on Thomas himself, but also on the conveying human agent, whose 'hand' made the marginal marks and helped Maggie read and emphasize. There may be some slight trace of her own Evangelicalism in Maggie's adolescent histrionics, and it is, of course, interesting that this is the part of the conversion that is criticized and rejected. But the chief emphasis is human, though by this stage George Eliot could take and indeed represent human duty and fellowship in a solvent of religious symbolism and association. What is emphasized in the conversion is the human element, but what is emphasized at the end in the final chapter, despite the tactful and tactical ambiguities of 'almost miraculous divinely-protected effort, and the dream of the Virgin in the boat, is the superhuman:

> Her soul went out to the Unseen Pity that would be with her to the end. Surely there was something being taught her by this experience of great need; and she must be learning a secret of human tenderness and long-suffering, that the less erring could hardly know? 'O God, if my life is to be long, let me live to bless and comfort—'

> At that moment Maggie felt a starling sensation of sudden cold about her knees and feet: it was water flowing under her.

What turns a great psychological novel into a Providence novel at the end is not simply this magical coincidence of prayer and answer in the 'water flowing under her': it is the appearance of exactly the wrong kind of problem-solving. Throughout the novel there have been two chief implications in the action and relationships—implications which at times rise into explicit formulation: one, the Novalis aphorism that 'character is destiny', which is qualified by George Eliot's words 'But not the whole of our destiny', emphasizing not only social determinism and large human influence, but the sheer chanciness of life; the other, that 'The highest "calling and election" is to *do without opium*', a belief central to George Eliot's rejection of Christianity, which remained with her all her life, which is fully and strongly borne out in all her novels,

and which seems to be the standard by which maturity is described and measured in *The Mill on the Floss*. Maggie's 'process' is more complex than any extracted pattern, but one of the strands in the extracted pattern must be her rejection of the opiates of daydream, literature, and religion. When she is able to make no dream-worlds any more, and when literary dream-worlds fail her, she finds a new and subtly effective drug in the religion of self-denial. Philip—and the novel's course—make it plain to her that she is now substituting another harder fantasy for the older fragile ones. She acts her renunciations, and Philip prophesies, while the novel's course reveals that she has fallen into the fantasy of choosing renunciations—little ones that will not hurt too much. The final experience is the lengthy painfulness of renunciation, and George Eliot takes great pains to show this, even in the last fore-shortened book of the novel, by making Maggie try to live with the renunciation, and by making her go through it a second time. She dramatizes most movingly the difference between giving up passion in passion and giving it up in deprivation. Laurence Lerner, in *The Truthtellers,* seems to me to be right off the track when he says that the second renunciation is theoretic, because the actual presences of the victims have gone. The second renunciation is, on the contrary, a proof of the untheoretic nature of her choice: she has lived with it. Imagination can people Maggie's world with her victims, just as it makes her 'hear' Stephen's voice as she reads his letter—a true and acute touch about the physiological pressures of imagination. George Eliot is showing implicitly what she made Philip tell Maggie explicitly—that renunciation hurts, that pain is unpleasant, that deprivation is destructive. My reason for making such an elaborate attack on the end of this novel is not a high regard for aesthetic unity and distress over an unprepared ending: it is an objection to the bad faith that contrasts so strongly with the authenticity of everything that comes before. George Eliot insists that renunciation does not make you feel noble and striking and secure, but empties life, depresses the spirit, and disrupts a sense of meaning. Little renunciations and sacrifices, such as doing plain sewing and being nice to your mother, are enjoyable because painless, and are no kind of rehearsal for the real thing. George Eliot makes this point as toughly as James was later to do in *The Portrait of a Lady,* but she then goes back on it, softens it, tacks on the least appropriate conclusion. She gives Maggie rewards and triumphs after all, not just by answering the despairing prayer, but by taking her to Tom and allowing her, before they drown together, to see that change of vision in his eyes. The novel has been about living without fantasy and opiate, and ends with a combination of several strong fantasies. There is the fantasy of death, the fantasy of reconciliation, and the fantasy of being finally righted and understood. Henry James's suggestion that Maggie might call back Stephen was nowhere within range of the novel's contingencies: Maggie could either have thrown herself into the river or carried on, and the point which the whole novel had been sharpening would then have been driven against the reader's breast.

I do not see this novel as sharply divided into 'realism' and fantasy. We can see the way the end undermines the strength of the analysis of moral choice, and we can see personal reasons behind the shift into such blatant fantasy. In the rest of the novel there are other visible personal pressures at work, which are far from being destructive and falsifying. If the final fantasy is a response to her personal break with the past and her brother, so the crisis of renunciation seems also to be propelled by a personal need. There is some relation, at each stage in the novel, between a great personal need and the artistic shaping. The renunciation of Stephen seems to me to be a typical and successful instance of personal problem-solving: in it George Eliot transfers the ethical issues involved in her own sexual choice to a different situation which will generalize, justify, and explain. George Eliot violently and predictably rejected the renunciation in *Jane Eyre*—a renunciation made in the interests of 'a diabolical law which chains a man soul and body to a putrefying carcase'. *The Mill on the Floss* reverses the situation in *Jane Eyre* in a way that can be seen as an argument with Charlotte Brontë. But I would scarcely wish to put it so theoretically. George Eliot went to live with Lewes in what was technically an adulterous union; her heroine refuses to marry a man who is unofficially engaged. George Eliot is not affecting moral delicacy (as some hostile readers thought) but inventing a situation which brings out her own defence, which eliminates all the personal particulars and invents new ones which generalize her argument. In her own case there is the breaking of a social, moral and religious 'law'; in Maggie's case nothing approaching law or contract. In her own case there are no human victims, but George Eliot's own freedom and isolation, and Lewes's already wrecked relationship with his unfaithful wife; in Maggie's case there are two human beings, Lucy and Philip, out of whose painful deprivation would be taken her joy. The novel's apologia says, in effect: had human ties been involved, I would not even have broken the faintest commitment; since there were none, I was prepared to break social laws and commandments. Here is another personal pressure shaping the novel, but it works lucidly, logically and imaginatively: the argument is sharpened as artistic argument must be, through particulars of feeling and relationship.

George Eliot's presentation of sexual-ethical choice is very far from being disinterested, but it in no way distorts the solidity and effective particularity of the novel. The same may be said for her presentation of religious conversion. Here we have something which seems also to have a source in personal experience, though George Eliot's change of faith is probably further 'behind' Maggie Tulliver's conversion than her sexual choice lies 'behind' Maggie's. At this point in the novel, we are midway between invention and experience, and it is, of course, true that crises of decision and vision which are to be found in most of the other novels can also be so described. Romola's decision to reject Savonarola's rigid doctrine for her human ethic is very close to George Eliot's arguments for Maggie's renunciation, but the situation in which Maggie is placed is plainly closer to personal experience. There is the continuity and stability of the ethic: her moral arguments are not purely pragmatic, and her reasons for living with Lewes

are perfectly compatible with her humanist ethic as reasons, not as rationalizations. But just as the inventions are closer to the personal crises elsewhere, so they are, I think, in the religious crisis. Once again there is involvement, but no loss of clarity. The artist seems to be using invention in order to see experience straight, or in order to validate fantasy. Maggie's conversion to an ethic of love and sacrifice draws on George Eliot's own conversion from Christianity. As in *Silas Marner,* the religion to which she gives fullest sympathy is a religion of personal love, so that it is not true to say that experience is reversed. Characteristic of her own experience is the sense of false conversion and the restoration to continuity: George Eliot dramatized her 'conversion' in much the way Maggie does, by refusing to go to church, by taking the risk of a break with her father. Afterwards came not only a loving need to compromise and conform, but a tolerance which refused to draw lines between right and wrong belief. The element of egoism in Maggie's altruism, of new fantasy in her apparent rejection of fantasy, makes the presentation psychologically alive and morally interesting.

But this interestingness depends on much more than the ability to criticize and generalize moral experience. It depends also on the imaginative representation of ethics and psychology, on the ability to make us feel that the artist is enlarging investigation, not restricting it. At the end of the novel we feel this restriction with particular force, not simply because it goes against the grain of the truths the novel is trying to utter, but because the presentation of character has been remarkably open and unformed by the usual *Bildungsroman* conventions. E. S. Dallas, in his review of the novel in *The Times* (19 May, 1860), spoke with fine penetration of George Eliot's 'effortlessness', observing that 'even when she has reached her climaxes she is entirely at her ease'. Maggie's character is presented in the medium of pity which has made it possible for Dr Leavis and other critics to see in it elements of indulgence and self-gratification, but it also comes very close to an existential openness, freedom, and pragmatism. Right up to the bad faith of the conclusion, we are presented with characters who are defined by the process of experiencing. Such closeness to experience is a rich theft from life by art, and all too rare in the great Victorian novelists. There is a tendency in modern criticism to argue or assume that closeness to life has the disadvantage of imperfect externalization, but it may also bring with it the advantage of unformed experience—of intransigence and a denial of form. The characteristic formal movement of novels of education is a progressive and evolutionary one, but even though *The Mill on the Floss* is a very Darwinian novel, its debt to Darwin is to be found in its hard and pessimistic look at struggle and survival, rather than in its optimistic treatment of personal evolutions. If we feel effortlessness in the climaxes, this is to some extent the result of a refusal to let climax determine and change character too markedly. To compare the process of Maggie Tulliver with the process of Janet Dempster or Adam Bede is to see George Eliot presenting character still sunk in the inchoate eddies of living.

Maggie is a character who believes herself to be converted and transformed, but who is incorrigibly herself. I speak relatively: of course, she does learn to live in a reserved and controlled way, but this lesson is scarcely a dramatic change, being a part of social education hard for sane and sensitive creatures to escape. But her change is minimal. George Eliot creates a pattern of apparent *Bildung,* but undermines and flattens its gains and crises. I do not know what Lady Ritchie had in mind when she said in her essay on Mrs Gaskell (*Blackstick Papers*) that George Eliot seldom becomes subject to her creations, but seems to watch them from afar, except in the case of Maggie, where for once she is apparently 'writing of herself'. Apart from the sources of personal experience I have been speaking of, there is this lack of patterning, which also seems to have come out of the closeness to life. Writing out of personal dreams and urges has many effects, moves art in contrary directions. Here perhaps it moves it in the direction of a static concept of moral character in marked opposition to the models of development and deterioration found in earlier and later novels, where the heroes and heroines seem smoothly and steadily to ascend and descend their moral staircases.

It is possible to describe Maggie's progress in the diagrammatic form of such an ascent: her childhood is marked by the habit of creative and drugging fantasy, by the need to be loved and admired, by recklessness and absentmindedness, by pride and masochism; she moves to more subtly effective fantasies, in art and religion, her need to be loved and admired is controlled and subdued, and modified by her need to argue her values, she softens her pride; but the final stages show the weakness of her masochistic and unreal religiosity, and recklessness and dreaminess are finally triumphed over in the renunciation of Stephen: Maggie emerges from illusion and self-love. My account of her process is the more distorting for being faithfully close to the climaxes of the novel. What happens, however, is that the climaxes are reached and then denied. Maggie ascends and descends. It is a process more like an eddy than a directing current. It is true that Maggie is 'converted' to self-abnegation and the life of duty, and true, too, that Thomas à Kempis brings into her life something which changes it and does not entirely disappear. But it is a much weaker influence than we may remember. Before Philip tells her that fanaticism brings its own perils and that renunciation may have a terrible backlash, she is already moving out of that violent act of histrionic repression. She is very easily persuaded by Philip to move into a world of emotional and intellectual gratification, but a world that is the adult equivalent of her old dream-worlds. George Eliot shows the backward movement very gently and unfussily. The climax of vision and decision is not utterly undone, but its effects are largely erased:

> (Could she really do him good? It would be very hard to say 'good-bye' this day, and not speak to him again. Here was a new interest to vary the days—it was so much easier to renounce the interest before it came.)

This mild and muted irony does not hold up its hands and exclaim in horror that on the preceding page Maggie had been saying 'it makes the mind very free when we give up wishing, and only think of bearing what is laid upon us, and doing what is given us to do'. George Eliot does not shirk showing the dividedness of Maggie's mind, and the shifting dialogue between the two voices, one sweet, one stern, which comes close on the passage just quoted, is Clough-like in its refusal to set a good angel against a bad. Maggie postpones conflict and drifts with the conversation, until she hits against 'an old impression' revived 'with overmastering force'. Philip offers to lend her *The Pirate,* and she feels the old wind blowing on her from Scott's rough sea, and puts the book aside: 'It would make me in love with this world again . . . it would make me long for a full life.' Philip tempts her then with sacredness and purity of 'Poetry and art and knowledge', relying ruefully on the lack of sexual temptation his friendship offers. Maggie replies with fair self-knowledge, and a better instinct about the sacredness and purity of the arts, 'But not for me. . . . Because I should want too much. I must wait—this life will not last long.' The debate is lengthily repeated once more in the third chapter of Book Five, and once more there comes an interval in which it is dropped. In the less intense and argumentative talk in the interval there is another aesthetic temptation as Philip sings 'Love in her eyes sits playing'. The argument and the song end very undramatically, with little comment from the author, as Philip offers his sophistry, 'If I meet you by chance, there is no concealment in that?' which Maggie snatches at. The long, reflective passages which follow do not exclaim at the shortlived nature of Maggie's renunciations, but are given up to Philip. And in the following chapter, which moves on nearly a year, Maggie is back again reading Scott, identifying with the dark-haired heroines, telling Philip that their renewed friendship has indeed made her restless and occupied with 'the world', and referring to the time when she was 'benumbed' as past time. What happens next is one of those unexpected eddying movements: Philip asks her to love him, she accepts and assents, and what has seemed a source of dream and love and richness for the mind is set out as a new renunciation: 'if there were sacrifices in this love, it was all the richer and more satisfying' and 'The tissue of vague dreams must now get narrower and narrower'.

The web is a complex one: just when Maggie seems to be most enticed by the old voice 'that made sweet music', George Eliot shows that the relation with Philip is made up of renunciation as well as indulgence. At each step of apparent progress, when Maggie says most confidently that she has made up her mind, she is shown, very quietly, as moving back on her word. This eddying process shows itself not only in each detail of apparent change, but throughout the whole broad pattern of growing up. The Maggie who pushed Lucy into the mud, who ran away, who used her doll as a scapegoat, who cut off her hair, who wanted to give Tom the bigger half of the jam-puff and immediately forgot his existence in devouring it, this Maggie is still present in the older Maggie, with adult appetites, adult control over trivial acts, and adult lack of control over grave ones. The strength of personal love which animates her sense of duty as she renounces Stephen owes something to the stern voice she listened to in Thomas à Kempis, and forgot, and heard again, but much to the generous lovingness that was there in the little girl. He *experience* changes: she finds that renunciation is hard and destructive, but her *character* is not transformed by this discovery. Character is not cut in marble, George Eliot tells us in **Middlemarch,** but although the motion of Maggie's character is dynamic, it is no case of progress, like Silas Marner's. It is not very easy to say what George Eliot is doing in creating this oscillation and eddy. It may be that she saw herself as writing a tidy *Bildungsroman,* as she was in her other novels, but that the very closeness to life, so falsifying at the end, paradoxically broke the pattern by its fidelity to the stubborn and unchanging nature of human character. It may have been Maggie's refusal to be a tragic and evolutionary heroine (like Morel's refusal to be a villain in *Sons and Lovers*) that brought about the final swing into dreaming and wishing.

On the sociology and psychology of *The Mill on the Floss:*

The Mill on the Floss enabled George Eliot to be "born a little sister" again and carried her readers back to the early morn of their lives, bathed in a new light. Like Dickens, she relived childhood for her generation, universalizing it into the childhood of humanity, but for her it was regarded as a stage in the life of man and in the evolution of human culture, traced through its later development in her succeeding novels. With Thackeray, she recognized the mixture of good and evil in us all, but her closer knowledge of man's physiological and nervous composition led her to a subtler insight into motivation. She brought, therefore, a new precision to the analysis of the irrational that Charlotte Brontë recognized as a phase of the human condition. Lewes applied physiology to common life; she gave life to physiology, revealing man in his totality as a subtle knot of instinct, emotion, reason, and conscience. George Eliot is the most "modern" of Victorian novelists in her psychosomatic representation of character and yet very much of her age in her elevation of ethics above aesthetics. **The Mill on the Floss** in its ennobling of domestic life and its preoccupation with "natural piety" . . . is rooted in the social and literary milieu of its times, but its poetry rises above them and its thought and psychology moved ahead of them.

Robert A. Colby, in Fiction With a Purpose: Major and Minor Nineteenth-Century Novels, *Indiana University Press, 1967.*

One last word. It is not a novel where one character shows this openness and freedom while others remain conventionally grouped around that live centre. The stubborn and unchanging nature of character is shown dynamically, not statically, and the whole psychological notation of the novel keeps us in touch with mobility and complexity. This stubbornness is seen outside Maggie, for instance, in Tom, and perhaps most movingly in Mr Tulliver. One of the finest examples, to my mind, comes in two adjacent scenes, which show Tulliver's recovery after his stroke. One marks a crisis of change, the other undercuts and makes an almost cancelling movement. 'Almost cancel-

ling'—it is necessary to say 'almost', because although the novel is constantly showing characters apparently changing and thinking themselves changed, it is also showing that what seemed so influential is not utterly to pass without trace. Maggie does hear the stern voice at the end. And though Mr Tulliver feels the Christian sacramental demands of his family Bible, and is led to an action which he tries to cancel in an act of pagan revenge, set out in that same Bible, the first submissive act does hold good, does affect events. It is rather that George Eliot shows people acting out of character, in obedience to strong external pressures, and then shows the recoil, in obedience to the principle of self. In Book Three, Chapter 8, Mr Tulliver is apparently transformed, rather like Maggie, on the day when he comes down from his sickbed to face the daylit emptiness of his house after the bankruptcy and sale. He picks up the family Bible and traces in it the cyclical history and ritual of birth, marriage, and death: his mother's death, his own marriage, his children's births. His wife wails in terms reduced to sacrament and proverb, speaking in the urgent voice of traditions larger than herself:

' . . . we promised one another for better and for worse. . . . ' 'But I never thought it 'ud be for so worse as this. . . . '

and

'Then we might stay here and get a living, and I might keep among my own sisters . . . and me been such a good wife to you, and never crossed you from week's end to week's end . . . and they all say so . . . they said it 'ud be nothing but right . . . only you're so turned against Wakem.' . . .

'Let her be,' said Mr Tulliver.

There is a strange unreality and foreignness in Tulliver's feelings in this chapter: he speaks in a voice of feeling unnaturally enlarged by awe and suffering and responsibility and illness. What George Eliot knows, and clearly shows that she knows, is that such high tide-marks of feeling, as she calls them elsewhere, when speaking of Maggie's deceptive acquiescence in Philip's love, may take us out of character, but do not transform us. It is the same intuition about moral change which lets her show Rosamond briefly and warmly responding to Dorothea, then living on to be Lydgate's basil plant. In the very next chapter Tulliver's return to health and routine, his habituation to what shocked him out of character, makes him speak and act from the feelings of an older and for him more native religion of vengeance, curse, and feud:

—That first moment of renunciation and submission was followed by days of violent struggle . . . he had promised her without knowing what she was going to say. . . .

Here again it is easy to set out a plain, unblurred antithesis, missing the nuances. George Eliot does not show a straight swing of the pendulum, any more than she does with Maggie's 'submission' to Philip. Tulliver's old vigour returns, not simply to show him the difficulty of that vow made out of character, but also to bring up feelings that argued on the side of that vow, feelings that were not relevant when it was made, but which crop up later to arrest the pendulum, feelings of practical advantage, feelings of love for his past and his home. Here too, George Eliot uses her authorial reserve, saying nothing to interrupt the swing from tugging nostalgia to the violent decision to curse Wakem. There are times when her refusal to comment on the relation between two contrary states of mind points to the subterranean workings of conflict and decision. Tulliver repeats that vow out of character, 'I'll be as good as my word to you,' but makes Tom write—in that same Bible whose ritual influence helped to take him out of character—the words of unforgiveness and hate: 'I wish evil may befall him.'

The novel whose chapters and divisions are so marked by quotations and images from Bunyan is no simple pilgrim's progress, but is indeed the least progressive of all George Eliot's studies in character and morality. This denial of progress in character, this flattening and erasing of the conventional diagram of moral evolution (conventional in moral thinking as well as in art) is a source of the truthfulness of a great but flawed novel, a novel whose merits and flaws show how art can tell difficult truths and consoling lies.

U. C. Knoepflmacher (essay date 1971)

SOURCE: "The Intrusion of Tragedy: *The Ordeal of Richard Feverel* and *The Mill on the Floss*," in *Laughter & Despair: Readings in Ten Novels of the Victorian Era,* University of California Press, 1971, pp. 109-35.

[*In this excerpt, Knoepflmacher compares Eliot's* The Mill on the Floss *to George Meredith's* The Ordeal of Richard Feverel, *noting that these novels do not effectively negotiate the split between romance and realism.*]

The Ordeal of Richard Feverel: A History of Father and Son (1859) and **The Mill on the Floss** (1860) are shaped by a vision of change and disorder which, though inherent also in the comedy of Trollope and Thackeray and in Emily Brontë's romance [*Wuthering Heights*], acquires far more despairing overtones in the form chosen by George Meredith and George Eliot. Both novels are relatively early works written by intellectuals who were newcomers to the field of Victorian fiction. Meredith, who started out in the romance tradition of the Brontës, had written the Arabian extravaganza *The Shaving of Shagpat* in 1855 and *Farina: A Legend of Cologne* in 1857. George Eliot, continuing the more "realistic" vein of Thackeray, conquered the Victorian reading public with her sketches of provincial life in **Scenes of Clerical Life** (1857-1858) and **Adam Bede** (1859). For their third work each novelist chose the form of the *Bildungsroman* or novel of education, a form popular with Victorian novelists ever since Thomas Carlyle had translated Goethe's *Wilhelm Meister* in his *Specimens of German Romance* (1827).

Goethe's *Bildungsroman* had served as a model for several major English novels written before *The Ordeal* and **The Mill**. Dickens' *David Copperfield* (1849-1850), Charlotte Brontë's *Jane Eyre* (1847), and Thackeray's *Pendennis* (1848-1850) had all depicted the growth of a child through adolescence to adulthood. The development of the protagonists of these earlier novels was inevitably crowned with success: though initially at odds with society, each protagonist profited from the tests and "ordeals" to which he was exposed and eventually managed to win a place in society, even if, as in the case of Thackeray's Pendennis, his position might remain precarious. Meredith and George Eliot, however, depart from this practice. They impose on the form of the *Bildungsroman* a tragic outcome that is more in the vein of Goethe's *Sorrows of Young Werther,* in which the romantic aspirations of the young protagonist are cut short by his untimely death.

Richard Feverel and Tom and Maggie Tulliver are not allowed the social integration possible for Jane Eyre or David Copperfield. In denying their creations even the compromises possible for Thackeray's Pendennis or Dobbin, Meredith and George Eliot anticipate the bleak conditions faced by the protagonists of later *Bildungsromane,* such as Hardy's Jude Fawley and Butler's Ernest Pontifex . . . or Lawrence's Paul Morel and Joyce's Stephen Dedalus. The orphaned Jane Eyre and the orphaned David Copperfield still follow in the path of those fatherless figures who, in eighteenth-century novels like *Tom Jones* or *Humphry Clinker,* could find their identity restored to them by a providential dispensation; Richard Feverel and Tom and Maggie, however, are wantonly destroyed by the mistakes of their parents. It is in the relentless portrayal of the breakdown of a family—that hallowed Victorian institution—that Meredith and George Eliot differ most significantly from their predecessors.

Usually written early in a novelist's career, the *Bildungsroman* allows the artist to objectify his private traumas and regrets. In creating Sir Austin Feverel and Richard, Maggie and Tom, their creators tried to mend deep personal wounds. It is undoubtedly relevant to Richard Feverel's fictional ordeal that Meredith should have lost his own mother as a small child and, more important, that he was faced with the bitterness of his wife's desertion and the task of raising an infant son while at work on his novel. Similarly, there is an unquestionable link between Marian Evans' despair over her brother's intransigence after her elopement with a married man and Maggie Tulliver's alienation from her brother, Tom ("George Eliot" was born in 1819, as is Maggie; her brother Isaac Evans in 1816, as is Tom).

Still, Meredith's *Ordeal* and George Eliot's **Mill** contain more than a private record of their creators' attempts to counter a deep personal disorientation. To an extent, any novel is shaped by the private experiences of its author. Thackeray's depiction of Georgy Osborne's precarious growth without a father can be attributed to his own fatherless childhood; Trollope's persistent characterization of weak men and domineering women, to his formidable mother. In *The Ordeal of Richard Feverel* and **The Mill** *on the Floss,* the disruption of the harmony of family life carries the same universal implications as in Emily Brontë's *Wuthering Heights*. By giving an even greater prominence to the clash between two generations than the novelists before them, Meredith and George Eliot brought to the fore the more acute severance between past and present felt by the mid-Victorians of the late 1850s.

. . . . .

It is no coincidence that Meredith's *Ordeal* should have been published, and George Eliot's *Mill* composed, in 1859, a year commonly accepted as a turning point in Victorian sensibility. The fathers of the mid-Victorians became to their children symbols for past solutions and past attempts at order which no longer seemed practicable in a present marked by the evolutionary theories of Spencer and Darwin, whose *Origin of Species* appeared in 1859. John Stuart Mill, whose *On Liberty* was published in 1859, had been molded by James Mill, who, like Sir Austin Feverel, relied on Reason and Locke. Matthew Arnold, who in 1859 ceased to be a despairing poet and wrote his first polemical essay, had been shaped by Thomas Arnold, the stern master of Rugby. James Mill was an atheist; Thomas Arnold, a Christian. Yet each man had a "system," and each son reacted against that system.

The differences between parents and children became to the Victorians a prime metaphor illustrating not only the artist's concern with his own threatened identity but also with the identity of all men in a world which more than ever seemed fortuitous and erratic. "This is a changing world," says Mrs. Deane in *The Mill on the Floss* to her sister Mrs. Tulliver, who soon proves to be utterly incapable of protecting her children from that changing world, "and we don't know today what may happen to-morrow. But it's right to be prepared for all things and if trouble's sent, to remember that it isn't sent without a cause." This belief in a just providence belongs to the earlier generation; it is not shared by George Eliot's narrator, who, for all his desire to vindicate the "cause" for the troubles to be visited on the Tullivers, complains that Tom and Maggie have risen too rapidly "above the mental level of the generation before them". Their suffering, the narrator suggests, is that of "martyr or victim" and "belongs to every historical advance of mankind."

Increasingly insecure about the future, the mid-Victorians found a bittersweet delight in recording the breakdown of a heroic past. In 1859 Tennyson published the first four parts of his *Idylls of the King,* in which he portrayed the dissolution of an ideal order headed by the paternalistic King Arthur. The cohesion which, in an earlier generation, writers like Sir Walter Scott still sought in a wishful, feudal past was no longer possible. *The Mill* portrays the loss of an ancestral fief held by the descendants of Ralph Tulliver; *The Ordeal* depicts the decay of the family who pretend to hark back to the Norman Fiervarelles (the chivalric elements in Meredith's novel are treated with devastating irony).

In varying degrees, history to the mid-Victorians seemed a record of struggles and failures. George Eliot's narrator uncovers the layers of historical strata on which the present of St. Ogg's is built to show that the intermittent floods have merely separated one age of strife from another. The present warehouses of Guest & Co. rest on the site where Roman legions were displaced by Vikings, where Danes and Normans slaughtered Saxon settlers, and where Puritans and Cavaliers butchered each other. Though less explicit, Meredith's narrator suggests ominously that the curse in the Feverel blood, "Mrs. Malediction," has manifested itself again and again throughout the family's checkered history—in war, as well as in times of peace.

To elude the determinism of the past seemed an irresistible temptation. It was in 1859 also that Edward FitzGerald presented his translation of the *Rub iyát of Omar Khayyám,* in which he refracted Victorian pessimism into an attitude of cynical escapism:

> Ah, my beloved, fill the Cup that clears
>   Today of past Regrets and Future Fears
> Tomorrow?—Why Tomorrow I may be
> Myself with Yesterday's seven thousand years.

FitzGerald's hedonistic speaker offers an escape route entertained by Richard Feverel [in *The Ordeal of Richard Feverel,* edited by Charles J. Hill, 1964] as well as by Maggie Tulliver. Both Richard and Maggie try to escape a world of painful responsibilities. Both are prevented by their moralistic creators. Richard must reject the seductiveness of Bella as well as the self-indulgent attitude of his false tutor, Adrian Harley, "an Epicurean of our modern notions"; Maggie Tulliver must deny the blandishments offered by her specious lover, Stephen Guest, for whom "the inclination of the moment" is the only true "law." They must face, rather than avoid, the insecurities of past and future.

These insecurities already existed in varying degrees of intensity in the three novels we have considered so far. Like Meredith and George Eliot, the earlier novelists availed themselves of the divisions separating parents and children; like them, they linked these divisions to the disruptions they saw in the world at large. The misunderstandings that alienate Eleanor Bold from her father in *Barchester Towers* were directly connected by Trollope to the disorder caused by the Londoners who disrupt Barchester's harmony. Thackeray likewise linked Osborne's ugly behavior toward his only son and Becky's rejection of little Rawdon to the misplaced values of the shifting Fair. And, in *Wuthering Heights,* as we saw, the rigidity of old Earnshaw—so like Sir Austin's own Puritanical severity—became emblematic of a world no longer bound by love.

Yet in *Barchester Towers* and in *Wuthering Heights* these conflicts ceased when the comic endings devised by each novelist allowed a return to sanity and order. Affinities that were threatened are restored; identities that seemed interrupted are continued. Far from remaining at odds with his daughter, Mr. Harding discovers that she has chosen to marry a man who is almost a double for himself; far from being disrupted by the excesses of Catherine and Heathcliff, the union of Hareton and the second Cathy blends the best of the Earnshaw and Linton lines and bypasses Heathcliff and his withered son. Even in *Vanity Fair,* where the Showman's pessimism survives, Thackeray manages to soften the abrasive quality of a world in which parents are inevitably pitted against their offspring: Dobbin's belated exaltation into fatherhood at least augurs a mildly better future for a Georgy and Janey who may grow up without the vanities that crippled two previous generations.

In the more tragic worlds devised by Meredith and George Eliot, such resolutions are impossible. The bond between parents and children becomes a destructive one. While Emily Brontë countered the tragic waste of Heathcliff and Catherine with a comic resolution, both of these novelists reverse the process by converting a childhood comedy into the tragedy of mature experience. Both works ostensibly begin in a comic vein. Meredith's aphoristic narrator matches witty epigrams with Sir Austin; George Eliot's ironic observer treats the insufficiencies of Mr. and Mrs. Tulliver with tongue-in-cheek. In *The Ordeal* the females who converge on Raynham Abbey to challenge Sir Austin's defiance of their sex—Miss Joy Blewins the blue-stocking, Mrs. Cashentire the banker's wife, the swift Camilla—are comic stereotypes similar to the Barchester ladies who engage in Trollope's version of the battle of the sexes. In *The Mill* the humorous clash between the proud Mr. Tulliver and his henlike Dodson wife is reminiscent of the confrontation between Mr. and Mrs. Bennet in the opening pages of Jane Austen's *Pride and Prejudice.* But the comic control exerted by each novelist vanishes. When reversals of fortune cut short the reader's expectations of a happy ending, Meredith and George Eliot obscure themselves. In the earlier novels, the tone established by Trollope's jovial narrator, by Thackeray's Showman, and by the cheerful Nelly Dean is maintained to the very end. Meredith, however, deliberately relies on Lady Blandish's despairing letter to inform the reader of the aftermath of Richard's duel and Lucy's pathetic derangement and death. George Eliot likewise dispenses with the stable voice of the narrator who had acted as the reader's guide and alternates between bursts of indignation and pauses of helpless silence as she documents Maggie's final trials and melodramatic drowning.

In both novels the gap between past and present proves to be impassable; the potentially paradisial Raynham Abbey and Dorlcote Mill are irrevocably lost. Moreover, the tragic conclusions augur no better future for those who remain behind. . . .

The ending of *The Mill on the Floss* . . . depicts a future that has been blocked. In the novel's "Conclusion" the wharves on the Floss are busy again "with echoes of eager voices, with hopeful lading and unlading." But the reader, like the small band visiting the tombs of Tom and Maggie, cannot participate in this hopefulness. The emphasis on the busy traffic on the river forces us to return in circular fashion to the book's opening paragraphs, in which

the narrator who surveys the laden "black ships" was led to recollect the tiny child who stood absorbed by the churning mill wheel, so unconscious of her future. Lost in his reverie, the narrator managed to escape the weight of time, only to discover that his transcendence was shortlived. Like the widowed Richard Feverel, desperately "striving to image" Lucy "on his brain", this time-burdened narrator sadly concludes even then that he was merely "dreaming" of an irrecoverable past.

The Ordeal of Richard Feverel and **The Mill on the Floss** represent their respective creators' attempts to master a temporal reality which had become even more intractable by the end of the 1850s than it had seemed to Thackeray in 1848. Both novelists try to prepare the reader for the tragic conclusions they deem irresistible; both narrators make sure to hint that mistakes in childhood can prefigure the catastrophes of adult life. Meredith's narrator warns the reader that Austin Wentworth could have prevented Richard's downfall: "very different for young Richard would it have been, had Austin taken his right place in the Baronet's favor". George Eliot's narrator counters Mr. Tulliver's plan for Tom's education by stressing the miller's hopeless ignorance of "the world": "Nature," the narrator informs us, "has the deep cunning which hides itself under the appearance of openness". Childhood pranks are revealed to be far from trivialities. Richard's vengeful burning of Farmer Blaize's hay-rick foreshadows his disastrous duel with Mountfalcon; Maggie's impulsive dunking of her cousin Lucy and her consequent flight foreshadow her later escape by water with Lucy's fiancé. Fire in *The Ordeal* and water in **The Mill** provide a symbolic patterning for novelists who, in the words of George Eliot's narrator, always prove themselves eager to connect "the smallest things with the greatest".

In their efforts to interpret the larger reality that thwarts the education of Richard, Tom, and Maggie, Meredith and George Eliot meet with difficulties not experienced by the comic novelists before them. As novelists of a more "philosophical" cast of mind, they are forced to explain, as well as to illustrate—they are burdened with the task of educating the reader in the ways of that "Nature" which is ignored in the educations devised by Sir Austin and Mr. Tulliver. George Eliot's description of her heroine's plight thus acts as an apt description of the novelist's own predicament: rejecting the "absorbing fancies" of the romances of Scott and Byron as well as refusing to make "dream worlds of her own," Maggie demands "some explanation of this hard, real life: the unhappy-looking father, seated at the dull breakfast-table; the childish, bewildered mother; the little sordid tasks that filled the hours".

By using the novel in a far more exploratory fashion, by seeking, like Maggie, "some key that would enable" them "to understand," George Eliot and Meredith no longer possess the artistic self-assurance and self-sufficiency of their predecessors. Trollope, Brontë, and Thackeray managed to generate an internal logic in the invented worlds of their novels. We do not ask what power it is that re-

Isaac Pearson Evans, George Eliot's brother. Many critics believe that the relationship between Maggie Tulliver and her brother, Tom, was based on that of Eliot and Evans.

myth of the cursed Feverel blood; the overtly realistic George Eliot, however, finds it far more difficult to accommodate reason and hope, explanation and yearning. . . .

When Maggie Tulliver makes her first appearance in chapter two of *The Mill on the Floss,* her mother asks her to go on with her "pretty patchwork, to make a counterpane" for her aunt Glegg. Maggie contemptuously rejects Mrs. Tulliver's invitation to act "like a little lady" and refuses. "'It's foolish work,' said Maggie with a toss of her mane,—'tearing things to pieces to sew 'em together again. And I don't want to do anything for my aunt Glegg—I don't like her.'" While Mrs. Tulliver is dumbfounded by her daughter's defiance, her husband "laughs audibly" at the little girl's sally.

The event, though seemingly inconsequential, contains all the ingredients for the later Tulliver tragedy. Maggie's asocial nature, her charm and intelligence, Mrs. Tulliver's impotence, and her husband's indulgence of the "little wench" he prefers to his Dodson son, are all incapsulated in this minuscule action. Maggie later defies conventional duties again when, after having lost her father and become alienated from Tom, she tries to escape the puerilities of St. Ogg's with Stephen Guest (to Maggie's surprise, it is the aunt she least likes, Mrs. Glegg, who stands by her after her disgrace). Moreover, although the child does not yet know this at the time, her words are rather prophetic. At this very moment, the father who laughs at her wit has already begun to "tear things apart." By trying to fight the "puzzling world" he finds so threatening, Mr. Tulliver will never be able to sew things "together again." The education he is about to bestow on Tom proves useless; the litigations he is about to enter cause his downfall.

The Tulliver children are unable to reverse the breakup begun by their father. Inheriting the miller's impulsiveness Maggie can only help to rend things apart. Although Tom unlearns his false "education," his efforts to mend the past prove fruitless. At the end of the novel, the river, that ominous embodiment of that "Nature" so often invoked by the narrator, swells. The waters of the flood both span the irreconcilably opposed worlds of St. Ogg's and Dorlcote Mill and unite the pragmatic Tom and the romantic Maggie. Their union is short-lived. The river which tears off the "huge fragments" that slay Tom and Maggie cannot sew things together again. In *The Ordeal of Richard Feverel* the sudden death of Lucy is designed to mock her husband's defiance of a potentially beneficent order. But in the *Mill on the Floss* Tom and Maggie's capricious drowning signifies their creator's secret despair over a temporal order in which unity can only be found through death.

In the novel's conclusion the narrator tells us: "Nature repairs her ravages—but not all. The uptorn trees are not rooted again; the parted hills are left scarred: if there is a new growth, the trees are not the same as the old, and the hills underneath their green vesture bear the marks of past rending. To the eyes that have dwelt on the past there is

stores order to Barchester or pause to question whether it was heredity or environment which led Catherine Earnshaw to prefer Edgar over Heathcliff. Yet, alerted by the novelists' own desperate search for "some explanation," we do wonder whether the fates of Richard Feverel and Maggie Tulliver could have been reversed and do want to know who is to blame for their destinies. Determinism and free will, chance and design, environment and heredity—terms so dear to the intellectual circles to which Meredith and George Eliot belonged—are far more relevant to their own brand of fiction than to the earlier novels.

Like the three novelists we have considered, Meredith and George Eliot are moralists eager to fight off despair by denying the logic of a totally anarchic universe. Resisting the nihilism of a Hardy, both are therefore led to extract a moral order from the "hard, real life" they find so intractable. Both try to suggest how a true understanding of the world might have prevented the tragedy to which their creations succumb. But although Meredith's "explanations" do not considerably vary from George Eliot's own, the two writers differ markedly in their method. The covertly romantic Meredith can ultimately avoid the need for explanations by falling back on the no thorough repair." Nature thus seems to confirm Maggie's initial statement: it is foolish, because impossible, to tear things to pieces to sew them together again. Still, this is exactly what George Eliot, like the novelists before her, sets out to do. By tearing a family to pieces she wants to direct the reader towards a "new growth," to leave us purged, through pity and fear, first, by Mr. Tulliver's death, and then, all the more by Maggie's immolation.

Like *The Ordeal,* George Eliot's novel is structured to make the reader anticipate the failures of the children in the failures of their parents. The book falls into two distinct movements: in the first Mr. Tulliver vainly tries to shore his present against the impending future; in the second, where that future becomes the present of his children, Tom and Maggie vainly try to recover the idyllic past of Dorlcote Mill amidst the hard reality of St. Ogg's. The novel is divided into seven books. Maggie's story is subordinated to her father's in the first book. By book five, which concludes the second volume and ends with the miller's death, her unsatisfied yearnings for fulfillment are given prominence. The last two books, in the third volume, are taken up entirely with her destiny.

Like Meredith, George Eliot pretends to be as critical of a father's faulty "system" as of his children's mistakes. Mr. Tulliver's distrust of "the world" he deems to be ruled by the devil resembles Sir Austin's own secret Manichaeism; Maggie's passionate excesses as a child are treated with the same irony devoted to the impulsive actions of Richard the rick-burner. In *The Ordeal* Sir Austin's selection of "a pale, languid, inexperienced woman" who is his distinct inferior proves to be as disastrous as Mr. Tulliver's own choice of a woman who "from the cradle upwards had been healthy, fair, plump, and dullwitted." The calculating baronet's choice is his one concession to sentiment; the hot-headed miller, on the other hand, deliberately picks the least pugnacious of the Dodsons because "she wasn't o'er cute," like her sisters, but "a bit weak, like; for I wasn't agoin' to be told the rights o' things by my own fireside." Mr. Tulliver's experiment in natural selection misfires when his "cute" daughter inherits the genes of the fiery Tullivers and Tom the stolid practicality of the Dodsons. "It's like as if the world was turned topsy-turvy," Mr. Tulliver complains.

The miller contributes to his children's unfitness to cope with a topsy-turvy world by thwarting his son's development and by indulging Maggie's fantasies. George Eliot makes it clear that the classical education Mr. Tulliver imposes on Tom would have been ideal only for Maggie. Just as Meredith demonstrates that Richard, though an emotionalist, is very much his phlegmatic father's son, so does George Eliot stress that, despite her greater intellect, the imaginative Maggie is very much her father's daughter. Both novelists equate imagination with passion. The same imagination that Richard drew upon as a child flares up when he vows revenge for imagined indignities: the adolescent who dreams of himself as the "chief of an Arab tribe," flying on his mare in the moonlight, soon finds his fancy rekindled by the masquerading Bella. Maggie, too, is a dreamer who takes refuge in fantasies. The child who wanted to be crowned as queen of the gypsies, who invented a world in which her cousin Lucy was queen, "though the queen was herself in Lucy's form", will try, unsuccessfully, to escape the prosaic reality of St. Ogg's by fleeing with Lucy's Prince Charming.

In her treatment of the adult Maggie, however, George Eliot loses the ironic detachment maintained in the earlier portions of her book. Meredith indicted both son and father through the unexpected catastrophe of Lucy's death. George Eliot, however, becomes increasingly uneasy as she moves closer to the expected tragedy so carefully built up from the beginning. Whereas her characterization of Mr. Tulliver's imprudence and downfall, her sympathy with the plight of an extraordinary child, and her insights into the differences that separate Maggie from Tom are almost unmatched in Victorian fiction in their veracity and psychological penetration, George Eliot falters when she converts the tiny malcontent of the first half into a noble victim of epic proportions to reconcile herself to the girl's destiny.

In Meredith's scheme Richard's sexual entanglement with Bella can be forgiven, even if Richard is incapable of forgiving himself. The ideal is in Richard's grasp; Lucy, the "Angel" whose ineffable beauty Lady Blandish describes in her letter, is idealized, but she is wholly credible as Richard's better nature. In George Eliot's scheme, however, Maggie's far more harmless elopement with Stephen Guest is forgiven only by Philip Wakem, who believes in Maggie's innocence and attributes her lapse to "that partial, divided action of our nature which makes half the tragedy of the human lot". Philip himself remains inactive. Whereas Austin Wentworth gives Richard a chance to embrace his better self, Philip can merely pity Maggie's self-division. Maggie, too, becomes hopelessly paralyzed. Unlike the impenitent Richard, she has returned to atone only to find that expiation proves impossible. The fulfillment possible for Richard is denied in the world of St. Ogg's. Richard refuses to reign at Raynham; the girl with the "queenly" coronet of black hair lacks even the subjects her father possessed. She is disenfranchised. The same Raynham Abbey which once curbed Richard's growth now offers him unbridled happiness; Maggie, however, can only yearn neurotically for her lost childhood at Dorlcote Mill. St. Ogg's refuses to shelter this sufferer "tossed by the waves." The wholesomeness available to Richard is represented by Austin and Lucy; in George Eliot's novel, however, neither the understanding Philip nor the benevolent Dr. Kenn can assist Maggie. In *The Ordeal,* the humorous point of view of Mrs. Berry remains intact even in the face of the final catastrophe; in *The Mill,* the comical tone of Bob Jakin jars with George Eliot's canonization of a martyr awaiting her last ordeal. The normally loquacious Bob finds "his tongue unmanageable in quite a new fashion" when he fathoms Maggie's despair. Awkwardly, he asks her to take his baby into her arms, "if you'd be so good. For we made free to name it after you, and it 'ud be better for your takin' a bit o' notice on it." As soon as Bob's tongue is "loosed from its unwonted bondage," however, he waxes "timid" again; for he has realized that his attempts at therapy have been of little use.

Richard Feverel chooses to destroy his better self to avoid condemnation; Maggie Tulliver finds herself condemned, regardless of her choice. The moral which the shrewd little girl drew from *The History of the Devil* applies to her later history in St. Ogg's: "Oh, I'll tell you what that means. It's a dreadful picture, isn't it? But I can't help looking at it. That old woman in the water's a witch—they've put her in to find out whether she's a witch or no, and if she swims she's a witch, and if she's drowned—and killed, you know—she's innocent, and not a witch, but only a poor silly old woman. But what good would it do her then, you know, when she was drowned?" The question is all the more poignant in light of the answer framed by the child herself: "Only, I suppose, she'd go to heaven, and God would make it up to her." As an adult, Maggie is denied even this consolation. Like Meredith, George Eliot no longer could believe in a providentially ordered world; but, unlike Meredith, she also found it impossible to romanticize "Nature." Thus she had to convert Maggie into a martyr, for only by doing so could she "make it up" to this choiceless victim in a godless world.

Both Meredith and George Eliot are guilty of inconsistencies in their efforts to vindicate and explain the ways of "Nature" denied by their characters. Meredith resolves these inconsistencies by relying on paradox: although Sir Austin is satirized for believing that the world is well designed, the novelist manages to suggest that a beneficent order does exist. The lyricism with which Meredith portrays landscape is Wordsworthian. Richard's encounter with Lucy on an island removed by water from the mists of Raynham and from the lucubrations of the Scientific Humanist implies—like the later scene in the rain—the presence "of something far more deeply interfused," "a motion and a spirit" akin to that force intuitively felt by Wordsworth in "Tintern Abbey." George Eliot, too, alternates between satire and lyricism, irony and symbol. Unlike Meredith, however, she finds herself unable to balance these extremes when she depicts Maggie's plight at St. Ogg's. Her Thackerayan satire of the society which spurns Maggie clashes with the last-minute exaltation of an idyllic, Wordsworthian childhood. Whereas Meredith's treatment of the rainstorm suggests the existence of a regenerative force, George Eliot's reliance on the flood as a deus ex machina remains a mechanical device to bring about a harmony that brother and sister never experienced while alive. Meredith's ending is tragic because it suggests that the Paradise lost by Richard was in his grasp; George Eliot's ending is at best pathetic, for it asks us to believe that the muddy waters of the Floss have briefly restored an Eden that never existed.

George Eliot is guilty of sentimentalizing Maggie's childhood by claiming that in death brother and sister are allowed to relive "the days when they had clasped their little hands in love, and roamed the daisied fields together." There were few instances when Maggie the child was allowed to hold her brother's hand. The little girl asked by Tom to choose between two halves of a muffin found then, as well as later, that any choice would make her unhappy. By forgetting that her heroine's ordeals began as a child, George Eliot conveniently glossed over the "realism" with which she had presented that childhood. The narrator was able to expose Mr. Tulliver's insufficiencies by showing that the miller's vision of the world as evil was merely the product of his evasions of reality. Yet, even though this narrator wants us to believe that Maggie possesses the same "soul untrained for inevitable struggles" that led to her father's ruin, he cannot bring himself to accept that explanation. Mr. Tulliver blamed "old Harry" for his misfortunes; the intelligent narrator who exposed the simplicity of such an explanation now resorts to a fiction of his own. He lashes out against "the world's wife," the abstraction that Dickens was to call "the voice of Society," and blames this imaginary figure for Maggie's suffering in order to exorcise the novelist's mounting revulsion over the "oppressive narrowness" to which Maggie is condemned.

The concluding portions of *The Mill* reveal George Eliot's acute split between realism and romance. Eager to dispel her own Thackerayan insistence on the world as it is, she desperately tried to infuse the world with the higher emotions of sympathy and love. In her desperation the novelist denied herself an opportunity to make the symbolic flood seem a more plausible agent of justice. Had the flood made its appearance at the time of Maggie's and Stephen's escape, had it then prompted the girl's remorse and led her to honor her past ties by returning to the Mill and to Tom, a logical connection between her willfulness and her bondage to the past might at least have been established. But the author wanted Maggie to become a noble sufferer, whose ordeals in St. Ogg's would provide a true "Imitation of Christ." The break in continuity, though allowing the narrator to pour his satire on the "world's wife," unfortunately also has the effect of making Maggie seem all the more a victim of accident and chance.

George Eliot was forced to resort to Maggie's martyrdom to counter a Manichaeism which seemed to deny her trust in goodness and love. Meredith, too, sacrificed a heroine to vindicate such a trust. But Maggie the helpless victim of chance is unlike the blameless Lucy who must die to remind others of their mistakes. Meredith's description of Austin Wentworth applies to George Eliot's heroine: "For a fault in early youth, redeemed by him nobly, according to his light, he was condemned to undergo the world's harsh judgment: not for the fault—for its atonement". Austin remained behind as an example of his creator's belief that the world can be remade; only by dying can Maggie escape the harsh judgment of St. Ogg's. Though meant to inspire its inhabitants, her death also signifies George Eliot's despair over the reality of that City of Destruction. Unlike Christiana in *The Pilgrim's Progress,* which Maggie read as a child, she is unable to ford the river.

Thus it is that George Eliot in *The Mill on the Floss* found that, her intentions notwithstanding, it was hard work to tear things to pieces to put them together again. Her Thackerayan emphasis on the world-as-is and her thwarted idealism ultimately found a compromise in her greatest novel, *Middlemarch*. . . . But it was Charles Dickens who, in his last complete work, was able to achieve what she could not do in *The Mill on the Floss*. By carrying the form of the romance beyond Meredith and even Emily Brontë, the Dickens of *Our Mutual Friend* methodically tears apart the world as he finds it and then proceeds to put it together again before the reader's startled eyes. George Eliot the realist was forced to sacrifice Maggie the dreamer, but Dickens the myth-maker destroys the logic of the actual world by defiantly superimposing on it the logic of the fairy tale. Out of the fragments of a sterile material existence he sews together a fantastic ideal order, and, through the force of his art, compels us to accept his patchwork in place of the reality he has displaced.

The Mill on the Floss as a family history:

The Mill on the Floss is unusual in George Eliot's fiction in the dominant role played by secondary characters. In tracing the destinies of Tom and Maggie from childhood on this novel also necessarily focuses on their family, with its uncles and aunts as well as more immediate parents. Most of the novel—up until the final book, where the children are more autonomous young adults—can be read as the story of that family, and particularly as the story of the destiny of Mr Tulliver, whose choleric, impulsive nature is brought into confrontation with that of the more respectable Dodsons.

Ian Adam, in George Eliot, *Humanities Press, 1969.*

John Hagan (essay date 1972)

SOURCE: "A Reinterpretation of *The Mill on the Floss*," in *PMLA*, Vol. 87, No. 1, January, 1972, pp. 53-63.

[*In the following essay, Hagan challenges the conclusions drawn by several earlier critics, maintaining that the relationship between Maggie Tulliver, her brother Tom, and by extension their father, is the main concern of* The Mill on the Floss.]

The salient fact about the most significant and representative of the recent interpretations of *The Mill on the Floss* is the extent to which they have become polarized, with William R. Steinhoff and Jerome Thale exemplifying one kind of reading and Bernard J. Paris, Reva Stump, and George Levine the other [respectively, in "Intent and Fulfillment in the Ending of *The Mill on the Floss*," in *The Image of the Work*, edited by B. H. Lehman et al., 1955; "Intelligence as Deception: *The Mill on the Floss*," *PMLA*, 80, September 1965; "Toward a Revaluation of George Eliot's *The Mill on the Floss*," *Nineteenth Centu-*

ry Fiction, 11, June 1956; *Movement and Vision in George Eliot's Novels,* 1959; and *The Novels of George Eliot,* 1959]. Each of these critics has made valuable contributions to our understanding of various aspects of this novel, and I trust that whatever I say here will not be taken as ignoring this fact. Yet the way in which, between them, they dichotomize the novel's vision does essentially simplify its complex wholeness. I will try to demonstrate this by analyzing both approaches in turn, and then by offering a reading of my own.

I

For the first two critics, the novel is a tragedy of repression and regression. Maggie Tulliver's life culminates in her downfall, and she herself is responsible for this because she is flawed by her acceptance of an unnatural philosophy of renunciation and by a morbid, infantile fixation upon her father and brother; both flaws fatally pull against her legitimate desire and need for a life of wider fulfillment. Steinhoff puts the case as follows:

Throughout the novel Maggie is revealed to be gradually losing buoyancy in her repeated failures to reconcile her individual demands with the pressures of family and society. At each failure she turns naturally back to a period of relative happiness and security, her childhood, in which her father and brother are permanent sources of comfort and authority. Gradually there is built up in her a mistrust of her own adventuring spirit, a fear of independent action, and, as a corollary, a tendency to equate self-martyrdom with goodness. . . .

The irony in her final decision [to rescue Tom from the flood], and the reason why the novel has to culminate in an event that is both "glorious" and "tragic," is that while renunciation seems to Maggie the only right course, it is at the same time a surrender to narrowness and conventionality. She is giving in to her weakness: a fatal timidity toward life. . . . [an] inability to choose adult experience at the expense of being uprooted from family life.

One of the most serious and obvious errors in this reading is the misunderstanding of George Eliot's attitude toward the philosophy of Thomas à Kempis, with which Maggie becomes acquainted in Book IV. The degree to which Maggie can live, or at least struggle to live, by that philosophy does become one of the major issues of the novel. But Steinhoff and Thale fail to perceive the moral perspective from which George Eliot treats this issue. For them, all of Maggie's attempts to live in accord with Kempis' teachings are utterly misguided. Indeed, these attempts are the essence of her tragedy, for by struggling to repress the most vital desires of her nature, according to Kempis' prescriptions, which Thale sees as essentially "the same wisdom which is so unlovely in the Dodsons," she denies herself all possibility of adult fulfillment and regressively surrenders to "narrowness and conventionality." In Steinhoff's and Thale's view the moral norm of the novel is announced not by Kempis, but by Philip in the Red Deeps when he warns Maggie that her efforts at renunciation are unnatural and dangerous. To accept Philip's view as the author's is, however, a mistake. The very chapter in which Maggie reads Kempis for the first time contains a passage of authorial commentary honoring the saint's words in the highest terms and it seems perfectly clear that the tone with which George Eliot treats Maggie's struggles to renounce her desires is deeply sympathetic throughout. Maggie's rejection of Stephen Guest, in particular, is surely represented as an act of the greatest moral heroism.

It is true, of course, that because of Maggie's passionate and imaginative nature, her vitality and youth, her intense need to love and be loved and her urgent yearnings for a wider, fuller, richer life than that afforded by the oppressive narrowness of her environment, we would certainly prefer that she did *not* have to renounce. We recognize the legitimacy of her desires, and wish that she lived in an ideal world where they could be satisfied without guilt. In such a world Philip's warnings against repression would be valid. But Maggie does not live in an ideal world. Given the fact that she profoundly loves her father and brother; that both adamantly oppose her having anything to do with Philip; that Stephen has led Lucy to believe that he will marry her; and that Philip remains faithful to his love for Maggie herself, renunciation first of Philip and then of Stephen is the only morally admirable course open to her. Had she gone on to love and marry Philip against her father's and Tom's wishes, she would have been betraying their "primary natural claim on her," a claim rooted in blood and a common past alike. And had she run away and married Stephen, she would have been betraying the sacred trust vested in her by Philip and Lucy. To have acted, under these particular circumstances, only in accord with her own desires for love and happiness would have been to "justify breaking the most sacred ties that can ever be formed on earth'." Philip is certainly right in predicting that the desires she represses will later assault her "'like a savage appetite'," for this is precisely what happens when she meets Stephen. But this does not mean that Maggie's repression is wrong per se; it is the very essence of her tragedy that at every turn the choices which are morally right should also have terrible consequences.

Steinhoff's and Thale's misunderstanding of George Eliot's attitude toward this issue does not, however, exist in isolation. Because they believe that Maggie's renunciation of Philip, in the spirit of Kempis, is wrong, and because they see that it is her love for her father and brother which causes her to renounce Philip out of respect for their disapproval, they conclude that this love itself is wrong. Though fully recognizing its intensity, they deny that it ought to have the morally binding force on her which it does. Maggie's struggles to live by Kempis' teachings, her filial and sisterly devotion, and her final attempt to rescue Tom from the flood at the risk of her own life are thus all indiscriminately grouped together as "a surrender to narrowness and conventionality," "weakness," and "a fatal timidity toward life." But this interpretation, like that of the significance of Kempis, surely ignores the attitude of the author herself. Though the point is almost impossible to demonstrate without referring the reader to

large parts of the text, I submit that whenever George Eliot represents or comments upon Maggie's attachment to Tulliver and Tom, she does so with the deepest respect and sympathy. Even single phrases like "simple primitive love," "primary natural claim," and "a perpetual yearning . . . that had its roots deeper than all change," which George Eliot uses at different times with reference to this attachment, have an honorific ring in themselves. Furthermore, one simply must not ignore the relevance to this question of either the extremely revealing authorial description in v, ii, of family relations as "the most sacred relations of our lives" or the two famous Wordsworthian and Proustian passages of authorial commentary at the end of I, v, and II, i, which develop the theme that "the loves and sanctities of our life" have their "deep immovable roots" in memories of childhood. George Eliot's insistence in the former passage that "our delight in the sunshine on the deep-bladed grass to-day might be no more than the faint perception of wearied souls, if it were not for the sunshine and the grass in the far off years which still live in us, and transform our perception into love" is prefaced by an explicit statement that the unbreakable bond between Maggie and Tom was forged of precisely such beneficent childhood experiences as these.

It seems clear, then, that the two features of Maggie's psychology that Steinhoff and Thale regard as flaws—her love for her father and brother, and her desire to live by the philosophy of Kempis—are among the very things which ought most to enlist the reader's respect and sympathy. In addition, these critics' assumption that Maggie's tragedy is the result of some kind of flaw in her character is itself open to objection on still other grounds. For George Eliot, after carefully making an explicit distinction between two kinds of tragedy—the Naturalistic tragedy of circumstance and the Aristotelian tragedy of flawed character—relates Maggie's father to the second, but Maggie herself to the first:

> . . . you have known Maggie a long while, and need to be told, not her characteristics but her history, which is a thing hardly to be predicted even from the completest knowledge of characteristics. For the tragedy of our lives is not created entirely from within. "Character," says Novalis, in one of his questionable aphorisms—"character is destiny." But not the whole of our destiny. Hamlet, Prince of Denmark, was speculative and irresolute, and we have a great tragedy in consequence. But if his father had lived to a good old age, and his uncle had died an early death, we can conceive Hamlet's having married Ophelia, and got through life with a reputation of sanity, notwithstanding many soliloquies, and some moody sarcasms towards the fair daughter of Polonius, to say nothing of the frankest incivility to his father-in-law.

This passage is of crucial importance in defining the perspective in which Maggie's story must finally be viewed. Her destiny is a tragic one; this tragedy is primarily determined not by her character but by the particular circumstances in which she finds herself; and, as the last sentence hints, the most decisive of these circumstances is comprised in the characters and actions of her close relations—her father and her brother. As I shall emphasize, it is the latter who reveal an increasing inability, after a certain point in the story, to reciprocate her love, and this development becomes the crux of the whole plot—the pivot on which Maggie's tragedy ultimately turns.

II

It may be argued, of course, that Maggie's character is flawed, but that she overcomes this flaw and that her destiny consists chiefly of this very process of spiritual development. This is the position taken, in fact, by the second group of critics whom I have mentioned—Paris, Stump, and Levine. Whereas Steinhoff and Thale maintain that Maggie's search for love and happiness outside her family and immediate society is good, and that her attempts at renunciation and her attachment to her father and brother which inhibit and thwart this search are a tragic mistake, these other critics maintain the opposite. Correctly seeing that George Eliot intends us to admire equally Maggie's struggles to live by Kempis' philosophy and her devotion to Tom and Tulliver, they conclude that, because this is so, Maggie's efforts to transcend her environment must be wrong, and that these efforts spring from a flaw in her character which can be identified as "egoism." As Paris has put it, "Maggie's desires for beauty and pleasure are essentially selfish or egoistic in their nature. Although gratification of those desires would enable Maggie to realize a higher and more desirable level of civilization than that which prevails in St. Ogg's, it is only by a renunciation of the desires of the self that Maggie can truly realize her 'higher faculties'." Accordingly, the process by which Maggie struggles toward this renunciation and finally achieves it by making the triumphant self-sacrifices of twice rejecting Stephen and then of attempting to rescue Tom from the flood becomes the main subject of the novel.

Perhaps the most obvious objection to this interpretation is that it ignores George Eliot's clear directive, just cited, that we view Maggie's story as a specific kind of tragedy. While not denying the presence of tragic elements in that story, it tends to place it on the whole in the category of the *Bildungsroman*. It is a reading which also suffers from lack of clarity. If the contention that Maggie is flawed because her desires for beauty and pleasure are "essentially selfish or egoistic" means simply that, under the special circumstances in which Maggie finds herself, her desires for personal happiness ought to take second place to the moral duties she feels toward others (Tom, Philip, and Lucy) and that insofar as they do not they constitute flaws in her character, then such a description of the situation is valid—though in this case to speak of her desires as "selfish" or "egoistic" is surely somewhat misleading. But if, as I suspect, what is meant is that Maggie is flawed because her desires per se are selfish and egoistic, then this reading is unacceptable. The great attention George Eliot devotes to her largely satirical representations of the oppressive narrowness of provincial society in the persons of Mrs. Tulliver, the Gleggs, the Pullets, Mr. Stelling, and others inevitably encourages us to view with deep sympathy Maggie's longings to escape that

environment. And certainly such sympathy is the dominant tone of the numerous passages in which these longings themselves are represented. If George Eliot wants us to feel that in renouncing Philip and Stephen Maggie is doing the right thing, she also wants us to feel that the yearnings which she renounces are no less right. Indeed, it is precisely because they are right that when circumstances make it morally necessary for her to give them up her story becomes genuinely tragic.

But there are still more fundamental objections to the Paris-Stump-Levine interpretation of the novel. Even granting that Maggie's desires for personal happiness are "egoistic" only in the sense that I have accepted, the problem remains as to whether her successive renunciations of those desires constitute a moral progression of the sort this interpretation indicates. All three critics maintain that by the time Maggie is able to reject Stephen and, later, to risk her life in order to save Tom from the flood, she has reached a point in her development where she is able to act in accord with Kempis' philosophy to a degree she would not have been able to act earlier. But their defense of this conclusion is very inadequate. Although, for example, Maggie performed the morally heroic act of renouncing Philip over two years before she even met Stephen, this is a crucial phase of her life—a phase occupying almost the whole of Book v—to which none of these critics gives more than casual attention. Even if one were to argue, as I think one must, that the moral significance of her renunciation of Philip is much less than that of the renunciation of Stephen, in that the former was enjoined by Tom, whereas the latter is self-motivated, there still exists the great difficulty of regarding her attempted rescue of Tom as the logical culmination of this series. Levine, for instance, sees the rescue as the fullest achievement of that selflessness toward which Maggie has been steadily growing, because it is wholly instinctive—"her first spontaneously moral action." But this interpretation is implausible, for given one of the premises on which the whole novel is based—that is, the peculiar depth, intensity, and constancy of Maggie's love for her brother, who, along with her father, is one of "the two idols of her life"—the probability is clearly established that if Tom's life had been threatened at any point earlier in the novel Maggie would have reacted in exactly the same way; she would have tried to rescue him whether she had read Kempis or not. The only reason she risks her life to save him at the end of the novel is simply that the opportunity to do so did not arise before the time of the flood.

Moreover, to return to Maggie's rejections of Philip and Stephen, if what is meant by moral development is that Maggie achieves complete acceptance of Kempis' philosophy, then it must be objected that there is no ground whatsoever for concluding that the latter rejection shows this any more than did the former. Maggie's final struggle, which occurs as a result of Stephen's importunate letter in VII, V, ends quite inconclusively. Indeed, in view of the fact that she achieved "contented renunciation" once before at the time she lived away from home for two years as a governess only to have this destroyed when she met Stephen, there is no certainty that because she has now renounced Stephen she will not falter again. Although she piously murmurs Kempis' words and burns Stephen's letter, vowing that tomorrow she will write him "the last word of parting," these words and actions are followed by a "cry of self-despair": "'How shall I have patience and strength? Am I to struggle and fall and repent again?— has life other trials as hard for me still?'" To these important questions the novel provides no answer. For, though Maggie falls to her knees and begins to pray for strength, her prayer is suddenly cut off by the flood in which she and Tom drown. Maggie is *trying* to live by her choice, and this attempt does have immense moral value, but there is no guarantee that she actually *can*.

But even accepting those aspects of the Paris-Stump-Levine interpretation of Maggie's development which I think can properly be admitted—namely, that Kempis' philosophy does define one of George Eliot's moral norms, that Maggie does significantly struggle to live by this philosophy, and that she does morally develop insofar as she can at least temporarily renounce first Philip and then Stephen—the most important question of all is still left open: What precisely is the importance of this subject in relation to the novel as a whole? That the degree to which Maggie can live, or struggle to live, by Kempis' philosophy is *one* of the major issues of the novel is perfectly clear. But Paris, Stump, and Levine insist that it is *the* major issue—the central subject of the whole book—a point on which Steinhoff and Thale, in spite of their misinterpretation of George Eliot's attitude toward Kempis, wholly agree. This is the very point on which I wish to challenge all of these critics at length by offering an interpretation of the novel's central subject which is quite different. In the last analysis, the matter is a delicate problem of emphasis, and one of the cruxes of this problem lies in what we make of the novel's much criticized ending, which deals with the flood and its aftermath. Since this subject, as I have just noted, has an entirely different kind of significance from Maggie's attempts to live by the philosophy of Kempis, it is strange that if the novel as a whole is primarily concerned with the latter it should place its final emphasis on the former; and it is doubly strange that the very last words of the book—the words of Maggie and Tom's epitaph, "In death they were not divided," which focus on the subject of the brother's and sister's relationship not only in death but, by implication, in life too—should also appear as the novel's epigraph and thereby give that subject even greater emphasis. What the ending and the epigraph provide, I submit, is a vital clue as to what the main concern of the novel really is— namely, the nature of Maggie's relation to Tom (and, by extension, to her father) and the tragic effects of this relation on her life. Everything else in the novel, including Maggie's own moral development in terms of Kempis' philosophy (important though the latter certainly is), is ultimately subordinate to that.

III

One of the reasons the critics I have been considering offer a questionable interpretation of the novel's tragic central subject is that they narrow the range of George Eliot's outlook and thus create a polarization which does not exist in the novel itself. Each reading ignores the explicit indication of her perspective which she provides near the beginning of Book IV, where, after explaining that she has been depicting the "oppressive narrowness" of Tom's and Maggie's environment in order that the reader may understand "how it has acted on young natures in many generations," she identifies the young natures with whom she is specifically concerned as those "that in the onward tendency of human things have risen above the mental level of the generation before them, to which they have been nevertheless tied by the strongest fibres of their hearts." Applied to Maggie, this passage makes clear that the yearnings for a wider life which spring from the fact that Maggie has "risen above the mental level of the generation before" her and the love which ties her to her brother, her father, and her past by "the strongest fibres" of her heart are to be regarded as *equally legitimate, equally* worthy of fulfillment. By not allowing that both kinds of need deserve satisfaction, that it would be best for Maggie if neither had to be sacrificed, one misses either the fact that her life is a tragedy, or the fact that the essential nature of that tragedy is one of having to choose between goals that are equally good but incompatible.

This incompatibility is not inherent in the goals themselves (the desire to marry Philip and the desire to remain loyal to Tom, for example, are not intrinsically irreconcilable), but is the result of circumstance. Nor is this circumstance chiefly "social," for to whatever degree the narrowness of thought and feeling which is characteristic of Maggie's social environment thwarts her desires, it comes to play upon her chiefly through the characters and actions of Tom and Tulliver. Maggie has intense desires for a full and rich life which Tom and Tulliver can neither comprehend nor sympathize with, but she is, at the same time, bound to them by a noble love which makes her renunciation of those desires morally necessary. From this situation spring directly or indirectly all the decisive frustrations of her life and hence the tragedy which is at the center of the novel. A detailed analysis of the structure of the plot will I believe, demonstrate this.

The first segment, which comprises Books I and II, centers on Maggie's late childhood and establishes the premises about her psychology and her relations to Tom, her father, and her society in general on which the rest of the novel depends. The major emphasis is placed on precisely those two aspects of her character and situation which, as I have just noted, are explicitly singled out at the beginning of Book IV: that is, her intellectual and spiritual superiority to her environment and the fact that she is "nevertheless tied" to this environment by "the strongest fibres" of her heart. On the one hand, extensive, primarily satirical portraits of her mother and her maternal aunts and uncles, who lack Maggie's sensitivity, and who habitually misunderstand, criticize, and reject her, make clear the degree to which her position in this society is an isolated and painful one. On the other hand, George Eliot shows that Maggie is dominated by a great need to love and be loved by Tom and Tulliver, which impels her to turn to them in times of trouble, and enables her to find in this uncomprehending and otherwise intolerable environment a spiritual home. The essential fact is that, during this period of her life, her father and brother reciprocate her love. This is why at the end of Book II, when Maggie's childhood is coming to an end, George Eliot can refer to it as having been an Eden, and why at the end of the novel the last thing Maggie remembers before she drowns is the time when she and Tom, like a kind of Adam and Eve, "had clasped their little hands in love, and roamed the daisied fields together." The point is not that Maggie's childhood is an unadulterated idyll (it obviously is not), but that this is the time when her need to be loved and accepted by her brother and father is most fully satisfied. It is true, of course, that even in this period Tom's need to love Maggie is much less than hers to love him. But it is also true that, in comparison to the later periods of her life, Maggie's childhood is the period of least frustration and greatest fulfillment. It becomes for her the touchstone of what her loving relations to her brother and father should be.

The relations to her brother, in particular, are defined most clearly by a series of parallel episodes which give Book I its structural backbone (the episode on the dead rabbits, of the jam-puff, of the haircutting, of the mud, and, climactically, of the gypsies, and in nearly every one of which there emerges a sequence of actions which dramatizes Maggie's hunger for Tom's love, the frustration of that hunger, her rebellion, and the pleasure she receives from reconciliation. At this period of her life such reconciliation and the consequent fulfillment of her need to be loved by her brother satisfy Maggie's deepest instincts. Her need to rebel is decidedly secondary, and is primarily a response to her brother's rejections. When Maggie's craving to love and be loved by her brother asserts itself, as sooner or later it always does, her desire to rebel is suppressed; and when that craving is satisfied, as sooner or later it always is, she is reconciled to her otherwise hostile environment.

In Book III, however, with the father's financial and mental collapse, begins the process which results in the cruel frustration of that craving and in the tragic search for alternative sources of fulfillment. This Book is thus the pivot on which the central action of the novel turns. Its title, "The Downfall," refers not only to the misfortunes which befall Tulliver, but to the fact that those misfortunes expel Maggie from the "Eden" of her childhood by progressively alienating from her the father's and brother's love on which she has come so deeply to depend.

Her initial inclination is to seek escape from her daily miseries by retreating into "wild romances of a flight from home . . . to some great man," like Walter Scott, who would understand and "surely do something for her." Such fancies led her in childhood to seek compensation for Tom's rejection by running away to the gypsies. But this kind of solution will no longer work, for by now Tulliv-

er's plight has inculcated Maggie with a strong sense of moral responsibility. The object of her first quest becomes, therefore, a way not of fleeing her world, but of enduring it, and the key ready to hand turns out, of course, to be Thomas à Kempis, in the spirit of whose philosophy of renunciation and resignation Maggie hopes to solve the problem of her frustrated desire for her father's and brother's love and for the happiness of her childhood by crushing that desire itself. This quest is the main subject of Book IV, Chapter iii.

That it fails—as the two different quests which follow it in Books V and VI will also fail—is clear. The crucial question is why it fails. In one sense, obviously, the fault is Maggie's: her longings for a happiness which will compensate for the emptiness of her life after her father's downfall are so great that the effort of renunciation becomes for her a source of that very happiness which she is supposedly renouncing. George Eliot's ironical attitude toward this piece of self-deception is quite explicit. Yet it is also true, as I have shown, that Maggie's longings arouse George Eliot's deepest sympathies. To deny their legitimacy would be to insist absurdly that she alter her very nature and completely subdue herself to the oppressive narrowness of the provincial world around her. Thus, it might seem to follow that the fault lies instead in Kempis' philosophy itself: Kempis' demand that legitimate yearnings such as Maggie's be suppressed is unnatural. Yet, again as I have shown, George Eliot's sympathy for this philosophy is as great as her sympathy for the passions it would deny. Under the circumstances, Maggie's attempt to live by it—to endure suffering rather than to seek escape in romantic daydreams—not only makes good sense, but is even morally noble. The issue, therefore, comes down to the existence of the circumstances themselves—circumstances which decree that what is morally noble should also be unnatural. To ask why Maggie's first quest fails is to ask what has brought these circumstances into being.

And the answer to that can only be the flaws in the characters of her father and brother. Maggie's frustration and her struggles to endure that frustration by means of renunciation are the direct consequences of Tom's and Tulliver's failure, at this stage in her life, to perceive, to understand, and to reciprocate her love. Were they to respond to her now as they did in her childhood, Maggie's happiness would be restored, and any futile attempts to deny her need for happiness would therefore no longer need to be made. But such a response has become impossible for them: their mutual hatred of Wakem, their acute sense of disgrace, and their grim determination to restore the family fortunes imprison them in a world of gloomy obsessions from which Maggie is wholly excluded. The conflict which thus results is the conflict which appears in all George Eliot's novels—that between two radically different kinds of characters; on the one hand, the large-souled, who, like "all of us" (as George Eliot puts it in *Middlemarch,* Ch. xxi), are "born in moral stupidity, taking the world as an udder to feed our supreme selves," but are sensitive and imaginative enough ultimately to transcend this limitation and see that others possess "an equivalent center of self," and, on the other hand, the narrow-souled, who are incapable of this kind of vision, and remain permanently trapped in the confines of the egoistic self.

The conflict between these two kinds of characters which begins to emerge as the novels' central tragic issue in Book IV becomes even more intense, however, in Book V, when Maggie begins her second quest for fulfillment, the result of which is her involvement with Philip Wakem. The futility of her attempt to live by Kempis' philosophy which was demonstrated in Book IV by her self-deception is demonstrated even more clearly now, three years later, by the flaring-up of her erotic passion for "the only person who had ever seemed to love her devotedly, as she had always longed to be loved." Her need to love and to be loved by her father and brother and to win their approval remains as compelling and legitimate as ever; she continues to be bound to them by "the strongest fibres" of her heart. But now, partly because Tom and Tulliver continue to frustrate her demand, and partly because Maggie is going through a natural process of maturation, which, in accord with "the onward tendency of human things," enables her to rise even farther "above . . . [their] mental level" than previously, this need is balanced by an equally strong, legitimate, and autonomous desire to find additional fulfillment from sources beyond them. Both kinds of fulfillment have become essential to her. Yet, because of the "moral stupidity" of Tom and her father, she will get neither. This is the basic tragic situation of the novel which now definitely takes shape.

The obvious solution to Maggie's hunger for a new life in Book V is for her and Philip to marry; she is nearly seventeen by this time, and he is twenty-one. Near the end of a year of secret meetings in the Red Deeps, she kisses him, admits that she loves him, confesses that she has found in him the greatest happiness since her childhood with Tom, and implicitly tells him that, though the thought is new to her, she would willingly marry him if there were no obstacle. But the crux of the situation is precisely that there *is* an obstacle, and that because of it her second quest proves as futile as the first. Superficially, of course, that obstacle is in Maggie herself—in her profound attachment to her father and brother, both of whom oppose not only marriage but even friendship between Maggie and Philip because of their long-standing hatred of Philip's father. If Maggie's attachment to them were not so deep, she could disregard the voice of her guilty conscience which urges her to renounce Philip, defy their ban, and find an escape from her frustration. But it does not follow from this that her attachment is wrong. George Eliot explicitly states that Philip's arguments for continuing to meet Maggie in the Red Deeps are "sophistry" and "subterfuge"; and she calls Maggie's "prompting against a concealment that would introduce doubleness into her own mind, and might cause new misery to those [Tom and Tulliver] who had the primary natural claim on her" a "true" prompting. Given Maggie's deep loyalty to her father and brother, and given George Eliot's complete sympathy with that loyalty, Maggie's scruples of conscience are wholly justified. The real obstacle to her ful-

fillment lies, as in her first quest, in the flawed characters of Tom and Tulliver, whose opposition to Philip springs from their narrow prejudice against Wakem and their complete failure to appreciate the depth of Maggie's need for a fuller life. The most active opposition comes, of course, from Tom, who cruelly forces upon Maggie an absolute choice between Philip and himself. Were it not for Tom's fanaticism, Maggie could be loyal to him and marry Philip at the same time; in themselves both goals are completely compatible and completely desirable. The necessity of choosing between them is an artificial one forced upon Maggie by Tom's insensitivity. The situation is very similar, indeed, to that in *Middlemarch,* when Mr. Casaubon cruelly contrives his will so as to force Dorothea to choose between inheriting his property and marrying Ladislaw. As George Eliot sums up at the end of Book VI, Chapter xii, Tom belongs to a class of minds to which

> prejudices come as the natural food of tendencies which can get no sustenance out of that complex, fragmentary, doubt-provoking knowledge which we call truth. . . . however it [a prejudice] may come, those minds will give it a habitation: it is something to assert strongly and bravely, something to fill up the void of spontaneous ideas, something to impose on others with the authority of conscious right: it is at once a staff and a baton. Every prejudice that will answer these prejudices is self-evident.

The nature of the tragic contrast between the two kinds of characters represented by Maggie and Tom and its decisive effect on Maggie's destiny could hardly be spelled out more distinctly.

By the middle of Book VI, however, the situation has been complicated by an additional factor: Maggie is reluctant to marry Philip not only because of Tom's continued opposition, but because of her growing attraction to Stephen Guest, whom she met at Lucy's home upon her return to St. Ogg's after her two years' absence as a governess, and whose admiration has become one of the chief causes of her renewed discontent. The two things with which Stephen is most frequently associated—music and the river—come to epitomize the irresistible force of the intoxication which she increasingly feels in his presence. To satisfy her newly aroused yearnings for love and life by surrendering herself to Stephen has now become, in fact, her third and final quest.

This quest fails, of course, no less than did the others. Maggie has to renounce Stephen, just as she renounced Philip, and, as a result, the frustration of her life reaches its tragic climax. The pattern of futile quests which has been taking shape since the last chapter of Book IV is thus logically completed and the novel's true central subject is fully defined. The relation of this failure to the two preceding ones, however, needs careful clarification. The first two quests failed, as we have seen, because of the flaws in the characters of Maggie's father and brother, who were unable to reciprocate her love and opposed her marriage to Philip. But the third quest fails for a different reason: Maggie gives up Stephen, not (as in Philip's case) because she is intimidated into doing so and wishes to avoid betraying Tom and her father, but because of her own free choice and her desire not to betray Philip and Lucy, to whom she and Stephen are tacitly engaged. In this decision Tom plays no role whatsoever. Nevertheless, he is decisively related to the failure of Maggie's third quest in other ways which keep the conflict between him and Maggie—and, by implication, the larger conflict between the kinds of characters which they respectively represent—the tragic focal point of the novel to the very end.

To begin with, though Maggie renounces Stephen of her own free will, both her involvement with him in the first place and the great intensity of that involvement are direct consequences of the earlier renunciation of Philip which Tom virtually forced upon her. Philip's warning at the time—namely, that "'You will be thrown into the world some day, and then every rational satisfaction of your nature that you deny now, will assault you like a savage appetite'"—is precisely what happens later when she meets Stephen. Had she been able to marry Philip with Tom's approval in Book V, this tragic development would presumably have been impossible. Tom has helped to create the very predicament for which Maggie herself must pay the tragic price.

Moreover, almost equally influential in Maggie's destiny is the continuation of Tom's ban on Philip not only to the beginning of Book VI, but even to the end. The obvious solution to her suffering after her renunciation of Stephen at the end of Book VI would be to return to Philip and marry him, just as this was the obvious solution at the beginning of this Book, when she came back to St. Ogg's. Philip's letter clearly implies that if Maggie were to return to him, he would accept her. But, even if she were able to overcome her remorse and the infatuation she still strongly feels for Stephen, the insuperable barrier of Tom's ban on Philip would still remain. Tom's "bitter repugnance to Philip" is the same after the trip down the river as it was before—the same at the end of her final quest as it was at the beginning. The "something" for which Maggie had earlier hoped "to soften him" has still not occurred.

But the most important way in which Tom is related to the failure of Maggie's final quest is through his reaction to her renunciation itself. This reaction is, indeed, the central subject of all but the last chapter and the brief "Conclusion" of Book VII, a fact which strikingly differentiates this Book from the three preceding ones (which are centrally concerned with Maggie's quests themselves), and thus makes clear the decisive thematic significance George Eliot wishes to attach to it. Maggie's renunciation of Stephen is climactic: uncompelled by anything but the voice of honor and conscience, and carried out in opposition to the strongest, most sensual passion for love and a rich life she has known, it represents the moment in the novel when her success in living by Kempis' philosophy is most complete. Only later, when temptation in the form of Stephen's letter assaults her again, does her hold on

this philosophy slacken. Yet the point of the first four chapters of Book VII is that if Maggie's self-discipline has reached its height, so too, in ironic counterpoint, has Tom's blindness and opposition. The heroism of her renunciation of Stephen, instead of at last winning her brother's understanding, respect, and love, as it should, is powerless against the alienation of his sympathy which has been caused by the river journey itself. Completely oblivious to the moral grandeur of that renunciation, he rejects her more brutally than ever before, and Maggie, of course, is crushed.

With the exception of the malicious town gossips, no one else in her world is so cruel to her. In fact, after the rejection scene in Chapter i, nearly every other episode in the first four chapters of Book VII is carefully designed by George Eliot to emphasize the key importance of that scene by contrasting Tom with characters and actions which put him in the worst possible light: Bob Jakin climaxes an earlier series of benevolent actions by chivalrously taking Maggie into his home as a lodger; Dr. Kenn gives her sympathetic counsel, and, failing in his efforts to find her employment elsewhere, takes her on as a governess to his own children; Philip declares not only that he forgives Maggie and still loves her, but that in loving her he has attained to a new and enlarged life of selflessness; Lucy too has forgiven her; and even Aunt Glegg, although motivated by family pride, comes staunchly to her defense on the ground that she should be punished only in proportion to the misdeeds actually proved against her, rather than those merely alleged. Especially important is the contrast between Tom and Dr. Kenn. Whereas the latter can appreciate Maggie's spiritual conflicts because he is a man of "broad, strong sense" who can "discern that the mysterious complexity of our life is not to be embraced by maxims, and that to lace ourselves up in formulas of that sort is to repress all the divine promptings and inspirations that spring from growing insight and sympathy," Tom is the "man of maxims" par excellence—a representative of all those "minds that are guided in their moral judgment solely by general rules, thinking that these will lead them to justice by a ready-made patent method, without the trouble of exerting patience, discrimination, impartiality—without any care to assure themselves whether they have the insight that comes from a hardly-earned estimate of temptation, or from a life vivid and intense enough to have created a wide fellow-feeling with all that is human". This passage, echoing the earlier one on Tom as a man of prejudice, emphatically defines again the crucial distinction between the two types of human character which underlies the tragic contrast and conflict between Tom and Maggie herself.

But, if it is true that Tom's climactic rejection of Maggie is the central subject of most of Book VII, this has the crucial effect of placing the drama of her fall and recovery in Book VI in a wholly new perspective. What now becomes clear is that the struggle leading up to her renunciation of Stephen and the renunciation itself have been fully and emphatically rendered by George Eliot not because they themselves are the novel's central subject, but because they provide the occasion for the rejection which is the culminating revelation of Tom's insensitivity, and because only in relation to their nobility can the horror of that rejection and insensitivity be fully measured. The ultimate importance of the entire affair with Stephen which constitutes Book VI is not that it brings to a climax Maggie's efforts to live by Kempis' philosophy (though this does happen), but rather that it brings to a climax Tom's failure to understand his sister's needs and reciprocate her love. By the end of Book VII, Chapter iv, then, the drama of Maggie's tragic frustration is complete in all essentials, and has emerged as the true center of the novel. Each of her three vitally necessary quests for love and a wider life, which were originally incited by the alienation of her father's and brother's love at the time of the family downfall, and were later broadened and intensified by the natural process of her maturation, has ended in failure. And the failure in each case is related in some vital way to the flawed characters of Tom or Tulliver or both, who are far inferior to Maggie in spiritual sensitivity, but to whom she is nevertheless bound by the noblest feelings of loyalty and devotion.

There still remains, of course, the important question of how this drama is related to another one, namely, that of the flood and its aftermath, which comprises the main action of Book VII, Chapter V, and the "Conclusion." As is well known, this part of the novel has given critics more trouble than any other; there is almost universal agreement that for one reason or another it is unsatisfactory. That the action is melodramatic and indeed almost comic in its foreshortening and fortuity; that it is sentimental in the abruptness with which Tom at last awakens to Maggie's nobility and in the description of their death embrace; and that it has the defect of imposing a somewhat mechanical finality, a formal "ending," upon a struggle in Maggie's soul which, as long as Tom's opposition exists, can only remain inconclusive—all are points that can be conceded at once. But the question of the thematic relevance of this action to the rest of the novel may still be profitably reconsidered. For if the flood sequence is seen as functioning primarily to clarify and reinforce the tragic central theme of the novel I have been defining, its logic becomes inescapable. When Maggie begins her prayer to the "Unseen Pity" in Book VII, Chapter V, that theme has been developed as far as strict dramatic necessity requires: as a result of the attitudes of her father and brother various frustrations have been built up in her which there is no way of enduring except by struggling again, as we see her doing, to renounce all her desires. The flood sequence, though it carries the action farther, adds nothing new to this theme. But it does serve as a rhetorical device for giving it maximum final emphasis. A series of ironies focuses all the major issues. That the "something" which Maggie had earlier hoped would "soften" Tom has finally occurred, so that he begins to awaken to her greatness of soul and to reciprocate her love, accentuates the momentous significance of his earlier blindness and spirit of opposition; that this awakening occurs only because Maggie is sacrificing herself to save *him* highlights the importance of his selfishness; that now it comes too late to alter Maggie's destiny confirms our sense of the deci-

sive difference for the better it could have made earlier; that she and Tom are killed by floating "machinery" symbolizes how destructive have been the effects on her of her father's and brother's prosaic materialism; and finally, that their epitaph reads "In death they were not divided" comments definitively on how much Maggie and Tom were divided in life. With this epitaph, indeed, as I suggested earlier, the thematic center of the novel is established conclusively: appearing as both the last words and again as the epigraph, it unmistakably implies that the whole of Maggie's story must be seen with reference to her tragic relationship with Tom—and, of course, by extension, her father. The key concept of the novel, it emphatically announces, is "division"—the division between the large-souled woman, whose profound love for her father and brother is one of the proofs of her spiritual greatness, and the narrow-souled father and brother themselves, whose inability to reciprocate that love or grasp the validity and urgency of her other needs destroys her life.

Elizabeth Ermarth (essay date 1974)

SOURCE: "Maggie Tulliver's Long Suicide," in *Studies in English Literature 1500-1900,* Vol. XIV, No. 4, Autumn, 1974, pp. 587-601.

[Here, Ermarth explores the influence of restrictive societal norms on the character of Maggie Tulliver.]

George Eliot makes it clear in **The Mill on the Floss** that the social norms of St. Oggs exert a heavy influence on Maggie's development. This fact has long been obvious but less obvious, perhaps, is that fact that the norms Maggie struggles with are sexist. They are norms according to which she is an inferior, dependent creature who will never go far in anything, and which consequently are a denial of her full humanity. Years of such denial teach Maggie to repress herself so effectively that she cannot mobilize the inner resources that might have saved her. By internalizing crippling norms, by learning to rely on approval, to fear ridicule and to avoid conflict, Maggie grows up fatally weak. In place of a habit of self-actualization she has learned a habit of self-denial which Philip rightly calls a "long suicide." Both she and Tom feel the crippling influence of these norms but we will focus here on Maggie and on how being female is an important key to her tragedy.

George Eliot said several times that the first part of this novel, which deals with Maggie's childhood development, had such importance for her that she devoted an amount of time to it that might seem disproportionate. Maggie's fate develops out of her social experience, particularly out of the local attitudes toward sex roles and out of the assumptions behind those attitudes. We can begin with the Dodsons' emphasis on rules and measuring and with their correlative faith in the clear difference between right and wrong.

The Dodsons' "faithfulness to admitted rules" results in two equally dangerous habits: an utter inability to question themselves and a correlative habit of questioning everybody else. The Dodson sisters have codified their need to feel "right" into a whole social and economic position. I am what I am, they day, because I am not that inferior thing. One is either a Dodson or not a Dodson, but the category of not-Dodson contains no valid or interesting possibilities. To be not-Dodson is simply to be wrong or at best unfortunate. Of course, the harmony established on the basis of such narrow exclusiveness is constantly threatened both from within by atrophy and from without by excluded forces. It is Mr. Tulliver's keen consciousness of being "right" that prompts him always to be "going to law" with his neighbors and finally to ruin himself and his family; it is Maggie's sense of being continually "wrong" and her need always to measure up to standards not her own, that encourages the disaster. However, during Maggie's childhood at least, the family and communal rules are strong by their very negations. Nearly everyone is bent on being "right": from little Lucy Deane with her perfect dress and demeanor to the Rev. Walter Stelling who teaches his pupils in the "right" way: indeed, the narrator tells us, "he knew no other".

This emphasis on rules and measuring connects naturally with a tendency to value the measurable, a tendency which is expressed in the materialism of St. Oggs, where most of the respectable citizens are in trade, and which finds its most grotesque elaboration in the Dodson sisters' household religion. Their peculiar view of human priorities puts a premium on physical manifestations and leaves little room for deviation. The important differences between people are usually physical, as with the Dodson kinship which is an affinity of blood not spirit. "There were some Dodsons less like the family than others—that was admitted; but in so far as they were 'kin' they were of necessity better than those who were 'no kin'." In a similar way the correct appearance and behavior for little girls is already established, too rigidly to allow for the internal, individual imperatives Maggie feels. Maggie's physical characteristics—her unruly hair, her unruly manners, her physical robustness as a young woman—all inappropriate for a Dodson girl, generally convince her relations that she is a "mistake of nature": a deformity just as surely as Philip Wakem with his hunchback.

The same logic of right and wrong that holds in social and economic matters also holds for the sexes. If one is either right or not right, of course the second alternative merely means to be wrong. In St. Oggs one is either male or not-male, and while there may be a way to be a proper female, in a deeper way to be not-male means merely to be wrong or inferior in some essential way. For a woman in this society to be "right" means accepting a place that is defined for inferior creatures, always adjunct to the more significant activities of men. As the hard-headed Wakem says bluntly, "We don't ask what a woman does— we ask whom she belongs to".

Most men in the novel have a deep, unselfconscious belief that they are innately superior to women, even to the women they most care about. Although Maggie is Mr. Tulliver's favorite child, he deplores her acuteness. In discussing the important question of a child's education he says of her simply, it's a pity she wasn't a boy, she is "too 'cute for a woman. . . . It's no mischief while she's a little 'un, but an over-'cute woman's no better nor a long-tailed sheep—she'll fetch none the bigger price for that." Both Mr. Tulliver and Stephen Guest look for a certain weakness when choosing their spouses. Mr. Tulliver confides to Mr. Riley, "I picked the mother because she wasn't o'er 'cute—being a good-looking woman, too an' come of a rare family for managing; but I picked her from her sisters o' purpose, 'cause she was a bit weak, like; for I wasn't agoin' to be told the rights o' things by my own fireside". Mr. Stephen Guest, the "odiforous result of the largest oil mill and the most extensive wharf in St. Oggs", is a "patronising" lover who finds charm in silliness. When Stephen directs Lucy to sing "the whole duty of woman—'And from obedience grows my pride and happiness'," his banter has a point. He chooses the wife "who was likely to make him happy," which means that he has a norm Lucy happens to fit, not that he derives his norm from knowing her qualities. "He meant to choose Lucy: she was a little darling, and exactly the sort of woman he had always most admired".

As a growing boy Tom struggles anxiously to be superior. For him equality is confusing and inferiority insupportable. He is baffled by Bob Jakin's different ways and standards and by the fact that he cannot assert mastery because Bob does not care for Tom's approval. Tom makes the most of his opportunities with Maggie, who does care. He feels the flattery of her emotional dependence on him and he gives his affection chiefly as a reward for submission. "He was very fond of his sister, and meant always to take care of her, make her his housekeeper, and punish her when she did wrong". When Tom takes an equal chance with Maggie for the unevenly divided jam-puff, he cannot accept either the fact that she wins the big half or the fact that she offered it to him anyway, so he turns the incident into another instance of Maggie's inferiority. She is made to feel that she is somehow mysteriously at fault: a "fact" she knows for certain because Tom withdraws his affection as punishment.

Tom's affections for his absent sister are strongest when his ego is most in jeopardy, under his tutelage at Mr. Stelling's. His difficulties with Euclid and Latin and the long lonely evenings crush his spirit and give him a "girl's susceptibility." "He couldn't help thinking with some affection even of Spouncer, whom he used to fight and quarrel with; he would have felt at home with Spouncer, and in a condition of superiority". When Philip Wakem arrives it is even worse for Tom since Philip is much more accomplished, and so Tom is delighted when Maggie arrives to visit. Now he can measure his ability in Latin against her non-existent one. How important condescension to "girls" is to Tom, and how readily he gets corroboration in this from adults, appears in this exchange with Stelling:

"Girls can't do Euclid: can they sir?"

"They can pick up a little of everything, I daresay," said Mr. Stelling. "They've a great deal of superficial cleverness; but they couldn't go far in anything. They're quick and shallow."

Tom, delighted with this verdict, telegraphed his triumph by wagging his head at Maggie behind Mr. Stelling's chair. As for Maggie, she had hardly ever been so mortified. She had been so proud to be called 'quick' all her little life, and now it appeared that this quickness was the brand of inferiority. It would have been better to be slow, like Tom.

"Ha, ha! Miss Maggie!" said Tom, when they were alone; "you see it's not such a fine thing to be quick. You'll never go far in anything, you know."

And Maggie was so oppressed by this dreadful destiny that she had no spirit for a retort.

At the end of a scene like this Tom's prophecy promises to be self-fulfilling. Mr. Stelling, so long as he can patronize her, actually enjoys her talk; and Tom actually learns through Maggie to take more interest in Latin. But neither Tom nor his teacher can admit to themselves that she has intellectual potential, and when Maggie demands recognition they resort to that old and effective cruelty, ridicule: Tom with conscious delight and Mr. Stelling, at his more advanced stage of masculine development, without thinking.

The women in the novel accept their place willingly. Lucy knows her lover thinks her silly and that he likes insipid women, but she does not think of challenging this view of her character. She is complacent in her "small egoisms" and "small benevolences", fond in her turn of patronizing dependent creatures like Mrs. Tulliver and even Maggie. The most Lucy's talents run to, given the limits of her options, is to manage and manipulate people by strategem into better dealings with one another: not a bad cause, perhaps, but in her case pitifully circumscribed. "I'm very wise," she tells her papa, "I've got all your business talents". She probably does, poor thing. Within her scope she manages but her scope is small and her influence peripheral to the real business of people's lives. She derives her strength from her security and hence does not dream of asserting herself.

Like Lucy, Mrs. Tulliver was a good child. She never cried, she was "healthy, fair, plump, and dull-witted; in short, the flower of her sex for beauty and amiability." She is like the early madonnas of Raphael, says the narrator (reminding us of the venerable age of this tradition of feminine virtue) with their "blond faces and somewhat stupid expression" who were probably equally as "ineffectual" as Mrs. Tulliver and Lucy. Mrs. Tulliver's view of the whole duty of women befits a Dodson sister: it is to make beautiful elderflower wine; it is to keep her clothes tidy so no one can speak ill of her, for she does not "wish anybody any harm" (implying with her usual logic that if she keeps her clothes neat she will somehow be wishing her neighbors well); it is to make pie fit to "show with the best" and to keep her linen "so in order, as if I was to die tomorrow I shouldn't be ashamed." As she concludes with

unwitting penetration, "a woman can do no more nor she can."

Maggie, too, learns the family pieties, though not so willingly. She is strong enough to be suffocated by her narrow life, but not strong enough to escape it. Responsive and flexible, she resents the narrow restrictiveness of her environment and she struggles valiantly against it. But because she is completely alone in this struggle her small force is too feeble to prevail. Her family's constant opposition to her aspirations gradually teaches her a habit of self-distrust which over-powers her better self and which perverts her energies. This habit is already well-developed on the morning she goes off to fish with Tom. "Maggie thought it probable that the small fish would come to her hook, and the large one to Tom's." Soon Tom sees she has one and he whispers excitedly,

> "Look, look Maggie," and running to prevent her from snatching her line away.

> Maggie was frightened lest she had been doing something wrong, as usual.

The family pieties, unflattering though they are and in conflict with her inner imperatives, are inseparable from her sense of identity. She feels she must be wrong, not according to any standard of her own but according to some external authority which she barely understands and yet which, as a child, she implicitly trusts more than she trusts herself.

She has already learned to defer to others in place of developing a sense of her own authority; hence what she learns to fear most is the withdrawal of approval. In the jam-puff episode this is Tom's device for enforcing her submission and he has learned it from his elders. Maggie's mother uses the same device to control her troublesome daughter. On the morning Tom is to be brought home from school, for example, Maggie is prevented from going along because the morning was too wet "for a little girl to go out in her best bonnet." When Maggie tries to assert herself against these unfair restrictions by ducking her curls in water, she gets the following response: "'Maggie, Maggie,' exclaimed Mrs. Tulliver, sitting stout and helpless with the brushes on her lap, 'what is to become of you if you're so naughty: I'll tell your aunt Glegg and your aunt Pullet when they come next week, and they'll never love you any more'." Of course, Maggie and Tom are none too fond of their aunts—their mother says this is "more natural in a boy than a gell"—but the important point is that Maggie is threatened with the withdrawal of approval or love as punishment for being the wrong kind of little girl. She is referred to a standard she does not accept or understand (the value of her aunts' love) and for which her own mother will betray her or "tell" on her.

Insulting behavior causes dependency, as Bernard Paris has shown in his "[The Conflicts of Maggie Tulliver: A] Horneyan analysis" [*Centennial Review*, 12, 1969] of

Maggie's neurosis. With her pride constantly knocked away from under her, Maggie responds by becoming self-effacing and dependent, buying her identity at the price of her autonomy. The narrator suggests in the first Book that "the dark-eyed, demonstrative, rebellious girl may after all turn out to be a passive being compared with this pink-and-white bit of masculinity with the indeterminate features". If Maggie wants to be accepted she must learn to submit to the control of others who will then reward her obedience with affection. Without this affection Maggie has no identity, and so it happens that "the strongest need in poor Maggie's nature" develops, the "need of being loved".

As a child Maggie has no adult reserve about her feelings so it is then that her need to be loved is most apparent. Tom has no sooner arrived from school than he is teasing her and she is having to beg, "*Please* be good to me". When he wants to punish her for not being sure his rabbits were fed, he says, "I'm sorry I brought you the fish-line. I don't love you". And Maggie begs: "'O, please forgive me, Tom; my heart will break,' said Maggie shaking with sobs, clinging to Tom's arm, and laying her wet cheek on his shoulder. . . . What was the use of anything, if Tom didn't love her?" Alone in her attic, just as "her need of love had triumphed over her pride" and she is going down "to beg for pity" she hears Tom's step on the stair. "Her heart began to beat violently with the sudden shock of hope. He only stood still at the top of the stairs and said, 'Maggie, you're to come down.' But she rushed to him and clung round his neck, sobbing, 'O Tom, please forgive me—I can't bear it—I will always be good—always remember things—do love me—please dear Tom!'" Her need for love, inculcated by her bitter experience, overthrows her pride so completely that it also overthrows her integrity. She cannot exercise independent judgment. She will promise to be something she cannot be (always good, always remember things): anything, so long as the essential support is not withdrawn. Her need for love is a morbid dependency, and Tom uses it to master her, threatening to hate her if she is not just what he requires.

Maggie's dependency is re-inforced continually by ridicule and disapproval. When she shows her precious picture book to Mr. Riley she has the sense, not that he thinks the *book* silly but that *she* was "silly and of no consequence." No matter what Maggie does on her own initiative she usually regrets it. For example, on the visit to aunt Pullet, while Lucy characteristically waits without eagerness until she's told to eat, Maggie "as usual" becomes fascinated by a print of Ulysses, drops her cake underfoot, and earns the general disapprobation once again. The next minute, when the musical snuff-box excites her feelings, she runs to hug Tom and spills his wine.

"Why don't you sit still, Maggie?" her mother said, peevishly.

"Little gells mustn't come to see me if they behave in that way," said aunt Pullet.

"Why, you're too rough, little miss," said uncle Pullet.

Poor Maggie sat down again, with the music all chased out of her soul, and the seven small demons all in again.

When she resolves on a "decided course of action" in regard to her troublesome hair and cuts it all off, she is again met with disapproval and ridicule. "She didn't want her hair to look pretty—that was out of the question—she only wanted people to think her a clever little girl, and not to find fault with her." But Tom's response brings an "unexpected pang" of regret. "'Don't laugh at me, Tom,' said Maggie, in a passionate tone, with an outburst of angry tears . . . ". The impulsiveness of her actions and the rapidity of her regret seem to be consequences of her persistent sense of inferiority, a sense which is further reinforced on this occasion. She is met in the dining room with "a chorus of reproach and derision" so that, when Tom unexpectedly adds his own, "her feeble power of defiance left her in an instant, her heart swelled, and, getting up from her chair, she ran to her father, hid her face on his shoulder, and burst out into loud sobbing". Nearly the only source of sweetness in her early life comes when she throws herself on this source of support, never from her own powers, which only bring her ridicule and shame. The love she gets is nearly always payment for humiliation. It is not surprising, then, that she learns to distrust her own powers and to develop a fatal sense of the sweetness of submission.

Maggie's rapid shift from defiance to despair suggest the fatal instability that is developing in her. Potentially she could develop a strong, flexible character, given her inclinations and her gifts; but actually she is preparing for disaster because she never has an opportunity to make her own choices or to develop her own judgment. Whatever she attempts, the withdrawal of approval is so great a threat—almost an ontological threat—that she cannot proceed in the face of contradiction. In her later struggles with St. Oggs Maggie does not struggle like Antigone to hold her own against social norms because, in a fundamental way, she has no force of her own. She has assimilated the social norms and if she fights against them she must fight against herself. *She* believes the lie, that she is inferior, or wrong, or not to be taken seriously. She has learned to collaborate in her own defeat.

The same self-defeating habits occur in the second stage of her life, when Maggie must face the family disaster and when she establishes important relationships outside her family (with Philip and Stephen). As a child Maggie gives up her will for the reward of acceptance and affection; after the downfall when her family seem like strangers and she is driven more into herself she develops a new rationale for the old habit, she gives up things on principle. It is perfectly in keeping with her childhood need to be loved that an adolescent Maggie resolves to meet the family misfortune by "plans of self-humiliation and entire devotedness" (notice the familiar connection between devotion and the necessity for self-humiliation). She succeeds so well that her mother is amazed "that this once 'contrary' child was become so submissive, so backward to assert her own will". But the motives are still what they were. As the narrator warned, her rebelliousness was weaker than her need to be loved and it has turned into a strange passivity. She *likes* to give up her will or, rather, to exert her will only against herself. She now can do to herself what others used to do to her, and it gives her the sense of being "right" for the first time in her life. Being "right" requires Maggie to turn against herself.

The morbidity of her so-called renunciation is obvious to Philip Wakem. She refuses even to read or hear music because "it would make me in love with this world again, as I used to be—it would make me long to see and know many things—it would make me long for a full life". Philip tells her she has "wrong ideas of self-conquest". "It is mere cowardice to seek safety in negations. No character becomes strong in that way. You will be thrown into the world some day, and then every rational satisfaction of your nature that you deny now will assult you like a savage appetite. . . . It is less wrong that you should see me than that you should be committing this long suicide". Philip's own self-interest in the matter does not invalidate the accuracy of his observations on her "wilful, senseless privation" and "self-torture". He perceives that the fatal weakness Maggie is cultivating is a form of suicide.

Of course self-privation suggests there is something of which to deprive herself. Unlike Lucy, who renounces personal desires so completely that she effectively has none, Maggie has desires that might be fulfilled. She is responsive to the appeal of books, of music, of conversation with Philip, and she feels her life growing again through these experiences. In particular she begins to feel need for a life outside love, as if she is beginning to understand that what she has called love is really a self-defeating, neurotic compulsion. "I begin to think there can never come much happiness to me from loving. I have always had so much pain mingled with it. I wish I could make myself a world outside it, as men do". A true prompting, this wish for a life outside affection. George Eliot wrote to her friend Mrs. Robert Lytton:

> We women are always in danger of living too exclusively in the affections; and though our affections are perhaps the best gifts we have, we ought also to have our share of the more independent life—some joy in things for their own sake. It is piteous to see the helplessness of some sweet women when their affections are disappointed—because all their teaching has been, that they can only delight in study of any kind for the sake of a personal love. They have never contemplated an independent delight in ideas as an experience which they could confess without being laughed at. Yet surely women need this sort of defense against passionate affliction even more than men.

The important themes of the novel are recapitulated here: the importance to a woman of a life outside love, the danger of ridicule in pursuing it, the unhealthiness of confinement to the affections. Maggie might have become a woman who, like Madame de Sablé [in "Woman in France: Madame de Sablé," *Essays of George Eliot,* ed. Thomas Pinney, 1963], was a woman "men could more than love—whom they could make their friend, confidante, and counsellor; the sharer, not of their joys and sorrows only, but of their ideas and aims." But to make a life outside love one needs experience of actual dealings with the actual world, experience from which Maggie has always been cruelly "protected." Even in her statement to Philip it is clear that she has in mind vague hopes but no real alternative.

While Maggie's inner promptings to a wider life do exist, they are not stronger than her habit of self-denial as, I think, her rejection of Philip shows. Maggie obeys Tom's insistence that she break with Philip ostensibly out of duty to her father, but there may be some argument about her motives. She feels an unaccountable relief when her relations with Philip are cut off, a relief which seems to me to have reference to the demands Philip has been making on her: that she be herself and trust her interests. But responsibility for herself is something she has learned to avoid, and so her relief seems a clear assertion of an old reluctance to assert herself and not, as has been thought, a sexual repulsion to Philip. George Eliot has spent most of her time showing that Maggie is not chiefly a sexual creature but a social creature, and so it is plausible, given the whole direction of the novel, that Maggie is simply glad the inner conflict and need for decision are over.

Much as she may wish for a life outside love, the undertow of her dependency is too strong a force with her, preventing her from dealing with the conflicts of adult life. Her clandestine association with Philip, which by definition is a separate reality from her home life, inevitably results in a conflict with her family once the protection of secrecy disappears. Yet she is emotionally unprepared to accept the fact that her two worlds are separate and unreconcilable. Tom says that since she can do nothing in the world she should "submit to those that can," still assuming that it is her nature to depend and be capable of nothing. Maggie cries, "you are a man, Tom, and have power, and can do something in the world"; but these poignant words are lost on Tom Tulliver and, with Maggie's acquiescence he makes her choice for her, literally requiring her to speak the words he gives her: "'Do as I require,' said Tom. 'I can't trust you, Maggie. There is no consistency in you. Put your hand on this Bible, and say, I renounce all private speech and intercourse with Philip Wakem from this time forth'." Maggie gives her word, although in this context it hardly can be called hers. Her private reflections after this scene reveal how fully she wishes to escape from conflicts she cannot resolve:

> She used to think in that time that she had made great conquests, and won a lasting stand on serene heights above worldly temptations and conflict. And here she was down again in the thick of a hot strife with her own and others' passions. Life was not so short, then,

and perfect rest was not so near as she had dreamed when she was two years younger. There was more struggle for her—perhaps more falling. If she had felt that she was entirely wrong, and that Tom had been entirely right, she could sooner have recovered more inward harmony. . . .

She would rather be "wrong" and submit to the "right" than to continue in a struggle she is unequipped for, or to support the painful consciousness that she is responsible for defending a valid position, but that, at the same time, she is without the resources necessary to the task.

Maggie seems to acknowledge that this promise she made for Tom was not really hers when she asks him to release her from it, two years later. But the scene in which Tom gives her her freedom has a bitterly ironic quality, since it actually confirms in other ways how little strength she has for bearing freedom. "When Maggie was not angry, she was as dependent on kind or cold words as a daisy on the sunshine or the cloud: the need of being loved would always subdue her, as, in old days, it subdued her in the worm-eaten attic". It subdues her again. Tom releases her, but with resentment and criticism. She sees the "terrible cutting truth" in Tom's remark that she has "no judgment and self-command" without seeing that this is true because she has always been commanded, that even now she is seeking to be commanded to do what she herself wants to do. Her one clear response, through the confusion of inner voices which condemn both herself and Tom, is despair at being shut out from acceptance by Tom.

The same weakness for substituting another's will for her own plays a crucial role in her relationship with Stephen, when she falls in love with him as well as when she leaves him. Initially she feels a sense of relief at being able to depend on Stephen, first when she slips in the boat and is supported by his firm grasp, and later when he takes her arm in the garden. "There is something strangely winning to most women in that offer of the firm arm: the help is not wanted physically at that moment, but the sense of help—the presence of strength that is outside them and yet theirs—meets a continual want of the imagination". Being used to treatment that is indifferent and pre-emptive, Maggie is more at the mercy of such flattery which, when it comes "will summon a little of the too-ready, traitorous tenderness into a woman's eyes, compelled as she is in her girlish time to learn her life-lessons in very trivial language". Maggie's love for Stephen is traitorous dependence because it fulfills her need to be supported from without, rather than from within, and it thus acts as one further encouragement to deny herself.

In the light of her development it seems clear that Maggie rejects Stephen out of the same weakness that made her accept him. She rejects him, not out of moral principle, but out of the same, deep-rooted, unhealthy instincts that made her give up Philip and music and books. Both Philip and Stephen ask in different ways that she assert her will against the wills of others and that is what she cannot do (of course, Stephen also asks for a personal submission to himself that Philip does not ask). Now, far from being a virtue in Maggie this unassertiveness is perverse. George Eliot makes it crystalline in her novels and letters and essays ["The Antigone and Its Moral," *Essays of George Eliot,* ed. Thomas Pinney, 1963] that one must not only learn to renounce (i.e., submit to actual conditions that cannot be changed) but also to act (i.e., shape the conditions that can be changed). One must even "dare to be wrong." So when Maggie returns to St. Oggs for the third time, when she clings to those who ostracize her, saying—"I have no heart to begin a strange life again. I should have no stay. I should feel like a lonely wanderer—cut off from the past"—George Eliot is not praising Maggie out of Maggie's own mouth for acting on principle or for respecting the past. While George Eliot valued those things, she also valued realism. Maggie is merely expressing her insistence on having what, by definition, she cannot have: acceptance of herself by her brother and by St. Oggs.

The confusion and ambivalence we feel so keenly in the final chapters reflects accurately Maggie's own confusion and ambivalence at the painful conflict in her life between aspiration and fact [as stated by R. T. Jones in *George Eliot,* 1970]: "It is no moral philosophy that determines her decision, but a far deeper moral sense, which turns out to be hardly distinguishable from a sense of what she *is*. It is a clear recognition that there is no escape from what she is, however bitterly she might wish there were." This interpretation makes clear the essential importance of the full portrait of Maggie's childhood. It is not the happiness of her childhood that finally brings her down but the intensity of it. She speaks to Stephen of Philip's claims, yet neither she nor Philip ever recognized the kind of formal relationship she implies; she speaks of the past that sanctifies one's life, but we know her past has hardly done that; and finally, when Stephen presses her, her reasons disappear and she responds just as she did to the prospect of leaving St. Oggs: her "heart" won't let her. "'O, I can't do it,' she said, in a voice almost of agony—'Stephen—don't ask me—don't urge me. I can't argue any longer—I don't know what is wise; but my heart will not let me do it'." The past is her "stay": from which it does not follow that for her this is the best, but merely that it is for her the case. She is still looking to the same source for resolution of conflict, for rest from the too-feeble effort that always seems to turn back on itself and achieve nothing. When she leaves Stephen her mind is

unswervingly bent on returning to her brother, as the natural refuge that had been given her. In her deep humiliation under the retrospect of her own weakness— in her anguish at the injury she had inflicted—she almost desired to endure the severity of Tom's reproof, to submit in patient silence to that harsh disapproving judgment against which she had so often rebelled. . . . She craved that outward help to her better purpose which would come from complete, submissive confession—from being in the presence of those whose looks and words would be a reflection of her own conscience.

Given other conditions these instincts might not be entirely wrong (although the masochistic note here is hard to miss), but she has chosen the wrong object in Tom, and she perseveres, like the goldfish still endeavoring to swim in a straight line beyond the glass, in spite of the actual condition.

When Tom rejects her, she looks for some other "sure refuge" or stay to "guarantee her from falling", and lacking any, she only continues to vacillate between her conflicting feelings. She denies Stephen and then is inclined to yield because she begins to "doubt in the justice of her own resolve"; then, having decided to accept him, "close upon that decisive act her mind recoiled; and the sense of contradiction with her past self in her moments of strength and clearness came upon her like a pang of conscious degradation. No—she must wait . . . for the light that would surely come again". The confusion in interpreting this part of the novel is owing partly to Maggie's confusion. Her course is as erratic as a boat loose on the flood. Philip does have a claim, and so does Tom and even Stephen; but their claims conflict and Maggie has not learned the strength to do what she must, which is to choose one particular course and let another go. Her only instinct is to wait passively for help.

"'O God, where am I? Which is the way home?' she cried out, in the dim loneliness." In the flood, at night, her boat leaves its mooring at Bob Jakin's and floats away: a "transition of death" which is only the last in a series of fatal transitions which began in her childhood and which in a few moments will finally carry her under. As she floats and then rows towards home she is finally able to see the "light" she waited for: "the dawning seemed to advance more swiftly, now she was in action". What seems to be a dawning is a fatal illusion, because it is death she is heading for. Maggie is looking for a "reconcilement with her brother: what quarrel, what harshness, what unbelief in each other can subsist in the presence of a great calamity . . . ?" The undertow of dependency carries her back, and only with it can she act decisively: "as if her life were a stored-up force that was being spent in this hour, unneeded for any future".

The final scene where Tom reverts to the "childish" nickname for his sister, the scene which ends in a recollection of "the days when they had clasped their little hands in love, and roamed the daisied fields together" seems not saccharine and sentimental but, in light of the present interpretation, harsh and grim. Such sentimentality as there is echoes Maggie's longing for an impossible reconciliation. (When did they ever roam the fields in love?) And the words suggest that, since she was shaped to be a child by the family pieties, it is fitting that her life ends in a reversion to childhood where her energies to be an adult, tragically, are "unneeded."

George Eliot, born the same year as Maggie, left her brother Isaac, who was born the same year as Tom; she left her home of thirty years for London and despite the hard and lonely beginning she never went back. Maggie went back and her fate is the strongest possible argument and justification for doing the opposite: for doing precisely what George Eliot did in leaving her home behind. George Eliot does not try to disguise the tremendous difficulties in making the endless, painful effort required of such a woman, nor does she disguise the importance to such a woman of some support in making the effort; but in counterpoint she offers a grim warning as to the consequences of avoiding that effort. For Maggie the price of "feminine" affection and "feminine" self-sacrifice is suicide. Just as a fully human life is constituted of mind, imagination, and feeling, not only biological conditions, so equally, human death comes not only with the deprivation of oxygen but with the deprivation of mental, imaginative, and emotional life. Maggie's literal drowning is merely physical corroboration of the more important disaster.

Nina Auerbach (essay date 1975)

SOURCE: "The Power of Hunger: Demonism and Maggie Tulliver," in *Nineteenth-Century Fiction*, Vol. 30, No. 2, September, 1975, pp. 150-71.

[*In the following essay, Auerbach analyzes* The Mill on the Floss *as a Gothic romance, noting that it is a novel of sensation rather than naturalism.*]

We do not expect to meet vampires and demons on the flat plains of George Eliot's St. Ogg's, or to find witches spying on the regular rotations of the mill on the Floss. George Eliot's insistence on a moral apprehension of the real seems to banish all such strange shapes from her landscape.

But the stolid world of **The Mill on the Floss** is more receptive to the uncanny than its surface appears to be. The novel is often condemned for a loss of moral balance arising from George Eliot's overidentification with her heroine, Maggie Tulliver. It is true that Maggie's pull on the novel causes George Eliot to relinquish her sharply defined moral perspective in favor of a sense of immediate immersion in "the depths in life"—a loss of perspective that is in many ways a gain, as the author herself seems to realize, for she begins the novel by abandoning herself to her material in a refusal to be our sage. The first voice we hear is the narrator's cry for submergence in a half-drowned landscape, a defiance of the perspective of the normal: "I am in love with moistness, and envy the white ducks that are dipping their heads far into the water here among the withes, unmindful of the awkward appearance they make in the drier world above."

In chapter 4, Maggie mimics the ducks' defiance of dryness and perspective by suddenly plunging her head into a basin of water, "in the vindictive determination that there should be no more chance of curls that day." The repetition of this gesture suggests an important area of experience in the novel, one that the narrator leans toward herself: plunging one's head underwater entails the exchange of a clear vision for a swimming vision, a submergence in experience at the cost of objectivity and judgment. Maggie Tulliver lives in such a swimming perspective, and *The Mill on the Floss* is her story.

Though many critics find loss of perspective to be the besetting artistic sin of *The Mill on the Floss,* the experience of perspectivelessness is in part what the novel is about. In one of its many nostalgic evocations, it defines childhood vision as "the strangely perspectiveless conception of life that gave the bitterness its intensity," admonishing us that if we could recapture this intense vision, "we should not pooh-pooh the griefs of our children." But it is part of Maggie's nature that, like Peter Pan, she never grows away from her capacity to plunge into the moment, to submerge herself exclusively in what is near. In her first intense awareness of Stephen Guest, she is "absorbed in the direct, immediate experience, without any energy left for taking account of it and reasoning about it." When she drifts down the river with him, her sensations are described as unique in their passionately immediate perspective, which gives to objects usually seen at a distance the fractured intensity of an impressionist painting: "Such things, uttered in low broken tones by the one voice that has first stirred the fibre of young passion, have only a feeble effect—on experienced minds *at a distance* from them. To poor Maggie *they were very near:* . . . and the vision for the time excluded all realities—all except the returning sun-gleams which broke out on the waters as the evening approached, and mingled with the visionary sunlight of promised happiness—all except the hand that pressed hers, and the voice that spoke to her, and the eyes that looked at her with grave, unspeakable love" (my italics). Here as so often in Maggie's life, reality is what the senses swallow undigested.

Maggie's—and George Eliot's—capacity to dissolve experience into its constituent vivid moments and sensations looks forward to Pater as much as her fostering of memory looks forward to Proust. In its emotional vividness, Maggie's renunciation seems as gratifying as her abandonment to passion, for in it she achieves not the "stupefaction" Philip envisions, but a state George Eliot defines more equivocally as "that mysterious wondrous happiness that is one with pain." What post-Freudian critics might be tempted to dismiss as Maggie's "masochism," a neurosis that should be beneath George Eliot's noble gaze, becomes for George Eliot herself part of the virtuosity in suffering that makes a heroine: "But if Maggie had been that [wealthy and contented] young lady, you would probably have known nothing about her: her life would have had so few vicissitudes that it could hardly have been written; for the happiest women, like the happiest nations, have no history." In such passages as this, George Eliot seems to be abandoning moral placement entirely and applying a Paterian criterion of intensity to Maggie's history: the well-lived life is the vividly felt life that feeds into art. Seen in this light, the flood that justifies Maggie's life and destroys it is her only adequate consummation, because only through an upheaval of this magnitude can she attain, not merely her brother's love, but the intensity she craves from existence and cannot find there.

The fervor with which Maggie sees and is seen is thrown into relief by the emotional deadness of the medium she lives in. It is true that as a moral commentator, George Eliot gave scrupulous due to the tenacity and respectability of Tom and the Dodsons, as she herself asserted in response to Eneas Sweetland Dallas's review of the novel: "I have certainly fulfilled my intention very badly if I have made the Dodson honesty appear 'mean and uninteresting,' or made the payment of one's debts appear a contemptible virtue in comparison with any sort of 'Bohemian' qualities. So far as my own feelings and intentions are concerned, no one class of persons or form of character is held up to reprobation or to exclusive admiration. Tom is painted with as much love and pity as Maggie, and I am so far from hating the Dodsons myself, that I am rather aghast to find them ticketed with such very ugly adjectives." But no matter how tolerant and broad-minded a moralist George Eliot may be, she is disingenuous here about herself as an artist. Tom's self-denying struggle to pay his father's debts and restore the mill to the family is simply subordinated to the high drama of Maggie's love affairs with Philip and Stephen. Though we are told about his honor and ability, we are rarely allowed to see Tom at his disciplined, determined best, but only as Maggie's vindictive prosecuting angel. As for the Dodsons, occasional pious commentary about their honest virtues does not obscure the narrator's glee at the overwhelming ridiculousness of Aunt Pullet and Aunt Glegg and their muttering husbands. Nor does it counterbalance such authorial outbursts as: "A vigorous superstition, that lashes its gods or lashes its own back, seems to be more congruous with the mystery of the human lot, than the mental condition of these emmet-like Dodsons and Tullivers". This sudden endorsement of sheer intensity seems to overwhelm the novel's carefully constructed, moral antitheses.

The narrator's outburst in favor of a "vigorous," even a violent, superstition is at one with her impulse to follow the ducks and Maggie in plunging her head under water in revolt against a drier world's perspective. This tendency in *The Mill on the Floss* to oppose provincial respectability with an ambiguous emotional explosiveness that culminates in pain allies the novel with a Victorian sub-genre of dubious respectability: the novel of sensation and, more particularly, the Gothic romance.

Of course, Gothic romance is in many ways alien to the George Eliot that most of us know. Her rootedness in the near mitigates against it, for Gothicism is a call of the wild, the remote in time and space. As Jane Austen's Catherine Morland puts it after Henry Tilney has led her into the sunlight of British common sense: "Among the Alps and the Pyrenees, perhaps, there were no mixed characters. There, such as were not as spotless as an angel, might have the dispositions of a fiend. But in England it was not so; among the English, she believed, in their hearts and habits, there was a general though unequal mixture of good and bad." To be Gothic is to be unadulterated and therefore un-English; and George Eliot's native tolerance seems to eschew the violent moral extremes of foreign landscapes.

Gothicism, too, is a summons from a remoter past than George Eliot wants to know; *Romola,* her one excursion into the Italian Renaissance, endows even the wild-eyed Savonarola with the secular bias and ideological complexity of an enlightened Victorian sage. Ann Radcliffe's Emily St. Aubert, on the other hand, must journey from the sunlight of home and the enlightenment of the Renaissance to a medieval Catholic setting before she can palpitate to the terrors of obscurity and night. Coleridge's ancient mariner sails from the Christian Middle Ages into a pagan and primitive seascape. Bram Stoker's Jonathan Harker and Joseph Conrad's Marlow also journey from secular contemporaneity into a haunted past, the realm of "a vigorous superstition, that lashes its gods . . . [and] lashes its own back": the world that George Eliot invokes but does not inhabit in *The Mill on the Floss.* Even Victor Frankenstein, whose researches suggest the Promethean aspirations of the "modern" scientist, travels into the past in the course of his narrative, going from the relatively stable community of an English ship to increasingly wild Alpine landscapes until he touches the primitive solitudes of Coleridge's "land of mist and snow"; moreover, his research is inspired in the first place by the medieval pseudoscience of alchemy. All Gothic journeys seem to take place in time machines.

St. Ogg's, too, "carries the traces of its long growth and history like a millennial tree," and "the Catholics," those traditional conduits of Gothic terror, are a vague threat in the novel due to the rumblings of Catholic Emancipation. But St. Ogg's is prosaically immune to its haunted past: "The mind of St Ogg's did not look extensively before or after. . . . the present time was like the level plain where men lose their belief in volcanoes and earthquakes, thinking to-morrow will be as yesterday, and the giant forces that used to shake the earth are for ever laid to sleep." The sensibly level vision of St. Ogg's is as perspectiveless as Maggie's intensely momentary one, denying the wide swings through time and space that constitute the rhythms of Gothic fiction.

George Eliot's sympathetic naturalism and her tendency to make the boundaries of the community the boundaries of reality are in some ways like the vision of St. Ogg's. Her humanistic bias is suspicious of solitary aberration, emphasizing always the "threads of connection" rather than the potentially grotesque disjunctions between people. In a famous passage from *Romola,* which is often taken as George Eliot's central statement of belief, Romola banishes the shadows of the self:

> What reasonable warrant could she have had for believing in . . . [Dino's mystical and solitary] vision and acting on it? None. True as the voice of foreboding had proved, Romola saw with unshaken conviction that to have renounced Tito in obedience to a warning like that, would have been meagre-hearted folly. Her trust had been delusive, but she would have chosen over again to have acted on it rather than be a creature led by phantoms and disjointed whispers in a world where there was the large music of reasonable speech, and the warm grasp of living hands.

Yet even within *Romola,* this declaration is ambivalent, for the solitary and irrational whisper of foreboding has proved true; and throughout the novels, George Eliot's characters turn with longing to the "disjointed whispers" of uncertain origin that come only in solitude. At the end of her career, the visionary Mordecai in *Daniel Deronda* is apotheosized as an inspired descendant of the Hebrew prophets. George Eliot's reason and trust did indeed shun solitary Gothic shadows, but her imagination did not: just before beginning *The Mill on the Floss,* she turned from the rather overinsistent naturalism of *Scenes of Clerical Life* and *Adam Bede* to write "The Lifted Veil," a short story in which Gothic fantasies run wild. Latimer, the story's misanthropic, clairvoyant hero, comes together rather uneasily with the story's *Frankenstein*-like Alpine setting at the beginning and its reanimated corpse at the end, and George Eliot was probably right to deny her authorship of the story until 1877; but it gives us a telling glimpse of the shadows that were moving through her mind when she envisioned the dark and dreaming figure of Maggie Tulliver, standing rapt on a bridge under "the deepening grey of the sky," "like a wild thing" refusing to take her place around the family fire.

The intonations of Gothicism that run through the language of *The Mill on the Floss* converge in the "loving, large-souled" figure of Maggie, who broods over its landscape. The turbulent hair that is her bane as a child is an emblem of destructive powers she is only half aware of and unable to control; its roots reach back to the serpent tresses of the Greek Medusa, peer through the "wanton ringlets" of Milton's Eve, and stretch down from mythology into Gothicism when the female narrator of a late Victorian vampire story—Eric, Count Stenbock's "The True Story of a Vampire" (1894)—describes her "long tangled hair [which] was always all over the place, and never would be combed straight." The traditionally demonic connotations of unruly hair are reinforced by Maggie's life. The intensity with which she flings herself at the moment contains a certain murderousness, even when she is nursing a doll "towards which she [has] an occasional fit of fondness in Tom's absence, neglecting its toilette, but lavishing so many warm kisses on it that the waxen cheeks [have] a wasted unhealthy appearance". From the beginning, Maggie's kisses tend to take life rather than bestow it.

In her worm-eaten attic, she keeps another doll as a fetish, whose head she mauls and pounds into unrecognizability during outbursts of sheer violence which do not take the shape of love. Pounding her fetish, Maggie embodies "the vigorous superstition, that lashes its gods or lashes its own back" for which the narrator will pine in the desert of Dodson modernity. She turns from these two "love-dismembered" dolls to Tom, on whose neck she hangs "in rather a strangling fashion" throughout the novel, though adulthood brings her greater awareness of the draining tendency in her love: "I think I am quite wicked with roses—I like to gather them and smell them till they have no scent left." Maggie's rapacity has something in common with that of Tennyson's Ulysses, who sails away from commonality proclaiming "I will drink life to the lees"; and something else in common with that of Sheridan Le Fanu's Carmilla, a demure vampire who literally does so.

Maggie's recurrent pattern of action is to enter worlds and explode them. Her destructive aura takes shape in the associations of demonism, witchery, and vampirism that surround her, which will be examined more closely below, and which, despite the narrator's insistence on the prosaic narrowness of Lincolnshire village life, are in part an outgrowth of the environment defined by the "emmet-like Dodsons and Tullivers."

"Emmet-like" is actually an unfair dismissal of the intricacies of Dodson and Tulliver perceptions. Part, at least, of the elaborate Dodson metaphysic can be summed up in a single penetrating sentence: "it was necessary to be baptised, else one could not be buried in the churchyard." Given their tendency to embalm life's great crises in layers of ritual, it does not seem unfair to the spirit of the Dodsons to translate this sentence as, "it was necessary to be born, else one could not die." Life for the Dodsons is a tedious rehearsal for the triumphant performance of death. Aunt Glegg secretes her best hairpieces and linen, Aunt Pullet her treasured medicine bottles, Mrs. Tulliver (before the bankruptcy) her best china, so that they will be intact and pristine when that great day arrives. The aunts admire pink-and-white little Lucy, primarily because she is able to simulate the deathlike immobility of an icon: "And there's Lucy Deane's such a good child—you may set her on a stool, and there she'll sit for an hour together, and never offer to get off." It is one of the novel's muted ironies that only Aunt Deane, the most shadowy because the least Dodsonian of the sisters, achieves death in the course of the narrative. The other aunts are forced to survive beyond the end, presumably still quoting their wills and rehearsing their funerals. In a moment of uncharacteristic self-transcendence, Aunt Glegg places her husband's death before her own in this wistful reverie about the consummation of her widowhood:

> It would be affecting to think of him, poor man, when he was gone; and even his foolish fuss about the flowers and garden-stuff, and his insistance on the subject of snails, would be touching when it was once fairly at an end. To survive Mr Glegg, and talk eulogistically of him as a man who might have his weaknesses, but who had done the right thing by her . . . all this made a flattering and conciliatory view of the future.

The bristlingly proper Aunt Glegg takes the romantic Liebestod a step beyond itself: death is not merely love's climax, but its birth. Like Poe's protagonists or the converts of vampire literature, she venerates death not as a gateway to the hereafter, but as a state complete in itself, and for her its trappings and machinery are objects of fascination and delight. We need think only of such embalmed Victorian icons as Little Nell in her tomb, Tennyson's Elaine in her coffin, Millais' lavishly drowned Ophelia, to recall the loving fascination with which high Victorian art embraces and embellishes its corpses.

This reverence for and simulation of death is a pall that winds through Maggie's childhood and survives in the strikingly unnurturing quality of her love, which eats rather than nourishes its objects. When Tom comes home from school for the first time, her suggestively sterile love token is a hutch of dead rabbits for him—a symbol that Lawrence may have borrowed for *Women in Love,* in which a paralyzed rabbit becomes a token of the deathly kinship between Gerald and Gudrun. The defaced dolls, shattered cardhouses, and spoiled hopes with which Maggie's life is littered suggest that in her own messy, over-heated Tulliver fashion, she inherits the Dodson penchant for death and its trappings, carrying it from respectability down toward Gothicism. The cake she crushes and the wine she spills at Aunt Pullet's have a touch of black mass in them, for example; and her love-dismembered dolls anticipate the children from whose blood all the female vampires in *Dracula* take life instead of giving it. The unwomanly, because unnurturing, woman of whom Maggie Tulliver is a small type will come into her own in vampire literature, to be hymned most erotically in the ecstatically infertile lesbianism of *Carmilla.*

Maggie's faint taste of demonism is also shot through with Tulliver blood, in an inheritance more complex than mere impulsiveness. In fact, despite her father's proud claims for his sister, Maggie's love is sufficiently non-generative to align her with the Dodson sisters rather than with the wearily prolific Aunt Gritty, whom we can never envision defacing a doll rather than nourishing it. Maggie is closer to her father in her capacity to destroy things with the most loving of intentions, and her demonic leanings reveal an affinity with him that is intellectual as well as temperamental:

> Mr Tulliver was, on the whole, a man of safe traditional opinions; but on one or two points he had trusted to his unassisted intellect, and had arrived at several questionable conclusions; among the rest, that rats, weevils, and lawyers were created by Old Harry. Unhappily he had no one to tell him that this was rampant Manichaeism, else he might have seen his error.

The Manichaean heresy, which defines evil as an active, autonomous, and potent force rather than as the mere absence of good, expresses perfectly a world Mr. Tulliver sees madly twisting in the grip of Old Harry and his progeny. In granting to evil its own independent and powerful existence, Manichaeism is the necessary premise of Gothic sensationalism, and, like the Dodson worship of death and the deathlike, it has a powerful effect on young Maggie's sense of who she is and where she will find her life.

For Maggie's philosophical isolation, the fact that she has access to no ideology other than that of her family, is stressed again and again. Nor is the narrator able to provide one, for Maggie or for us. Her assertion of Maggie's tragic ignorance of "the irreversible laws within and without her, which, governing the habits, becomes morality, and, developing the feelings of submission and dependence, becomes religion" seems, like so much Victorian affirmation, a sonorous hedge: these "laws" are a vague postulate, unrealized in the explosive course of a novel, the mystery of whose workings may after all be most appropriately productive of a primitive and pain-ridden superstition. Lacking an overall rational structure to define our experience while reading, we are thrown back with Maggie on an ethos of sensationalism, even of demonism. To unravel her world, Maggie turns naturally to books; but they cannot provide for her the key "that would link together the wonderful impressions of this mysterious life, and give her soul a sense of home in it." Instead of opening a window into spaciousness and coherence, Maggie's books become a mirror reflecting her own dark impulses. In fact, an examination of the world she sees in books provides us with a striking portrait of Maggie herself.

As a child, Maggie invokes her demonic self out of her books. On our first extended view of her, she is poring over a picture of a witch: "O, I'll tell you what that means. It's a dreadful picture, isn't it? But I can't help looking at it. That old woman in the water's a witch—they've put her in to find out whether she's a witch or no, and if she swims she's a witch, and if she's drowned—and killed, you know—she's innocent, and not a witch, but only a poor silly old woman. But what good would it do her then, you know, when she was drowned? Only, I suppose, she'd go to heaven, and God would make it up to her."

In a passage that recalls Latimer in its near clairvoyance, Maggie projects the ambiguity of her own nature and destiny. Her interpretation of the picture is a miniature reflection of the narrator's attitude toward her: a mélange of demonism, rationalism, and a wistful faith that, after all, God will apologize in the end and redeem her innocence. But Maggie's first intuition springs out in a searing declarative statement: the woman in the water's a witch. Is Maggie? Witchery is entangled in her pull toward the smoky, nocturnal underworld of the gypsies, in "the night of her massy hair" with its suggestion of a somewhat smothering sexuality, and, most interestingly, in her charged relationship both to animals and to the natural world.

Traditional accounts of witchcraft place the witch in an intense and equivocal relationship to the animal kingdom. Animal masks are worn at the witches' Sabbath, where Satan frequently presides in the costume of a bull; animals are worshipped and used as conduits for spells, the witch's nature seeming at times interchangeable with that of her familiar. But one of the commonest manifestations of witchery is the power to blight and cause disease in the animal kingdom. Here we can see the affinity between the legends of the witch and those of the vampire. The vampire too has a magical sympathetic kinship with animals, being able to assume the shape of dog and wolf as well as bat. But in some legends, animals shun him: he is a scourge of cattle and sheep, and dogs howl and even die in terror at his approach. Both witch and vampire simultaneously spring from animals and are fatal to them.

Maggie too both blights animals and becomes them. The hutch of starved rabbits is presented as the first symbol of her love for Tom, suggesting a silent murderousness of which the animals are conduit and fetish. Yet much of the animal imagery in the novel clusters around Maggie. Her affinities with animals range from simple descriptive similes—she shakes the water from her hair "like a Skye terrier escaped from his bath"—to intimations of metamorphosis that carry magical suggestions, such as this image of Philip's: "What was it, he wondered, that made Maggie's dark eyes remind him of the stories about princesses being turned into animals? . . . I think it was that her eyes were full of unsatisfied intelligence, and unsatisfied, beseeching affection". Philip's vocabulary and the narrator's reassuring explication soften the power of the picture, which is sinister. Witches in folklore are more likely to turn into animals than princesses are; and as well as expressing the rootedness of the witch in her familiar, the image evokes a string of pagan goddesses with the bodies of animals and the heads of women, of whom the lamia, the vampire's pagan ancestor, is one of the darkest.

Maggie's alliance with trees also connotes witchcraft, which is traditionally linked to tree worship: the dance around the fairy tree and invocation to it are perennial features of witches' Sabbath rituals in England. The tree appears first when little Maggie is possessed by "small demons": "a small Medusa with her snakes cropped," she pushes Lucy into the mud and retreats impenitently to the roots of a tree, to glower at Tom and Lucy "with her small Medusa face." In the sequence with Philip in the Red Deeps, the association recurs, amplified and beautified: "With her dark colouring and jet crown surmounting her tall figure, she seems to have a sort of kinship with the grand Scotch firs, at which she is looking up as if she loved them well." Philip, who seems possessed by the association of Maggie with metamorphosis, insists upon this kinship, finally painting Maggie as "a tall Hamadryad, dark and strong and noble, just issued from one of the fir-trees". Philip's artist's eye continually captures Maggie in the process of equivocal transformation, which his less true language muffles by such adjectives as "noble." To one familiar with English witchcraft legends and rituals, these images of Maggie carry their own undercurrents, which hardly need Lucy's more explicit reinforcement later on: "I can't think what witchery it is in you, Maggie, that makes you look best in shabby clothes." Another of Lucy's innocent remarks, about the secret liaison with Philip, carries more complex ironies: "Ah, now I see how it is you know Shakespeare and everything, and have learned so much since you left school; which always seemed to me witchcraft before—part of your general uncanniness." Lucy's initial intuition is correct, for Maggie learned about Shakespeare in the Red Deeps, which, as Philip senses, is the proper setting for and a powerful projection of her "general uncanniness."

But in the prophetic doppelgänger that arrests the young Maggie from the pages of Defoe, the witch is not lodged in an animal or a tree; she is bobbing in water, an element that follows Maggie and shapes her life. The origin of the English ducking ritual places the witch in a typically ambiguous relationship to water. In theory, a witch will not drown because the pure baptismal element must cast out the evil thing. But there is an obverse explanation of the witch's ability to float: perhaps her magical kinship with a more darkly defined water allies her with the element and prevents it from destroying her. The witch's dual relationship to nature is evident in the ducking ritual as it is in her power over animals: do they feed on or repel each other? Is the witch a growth from or an enemy of the natural world?

The vampire's relationship to water is as ambiguous as the witch's. In many versions of the legend, he is unable to cross running water on his own power. This abrupt paralysis is a suggestive dark gloss on the figure of the Virgin of the Flood, Maggie's holy analogue in *The Mill on the Floss,* whom local legends depict wailing by the river bank to be ferried across, unable to work her magical transformation until Beorl has allowed her to enter his boat. But Maggie's "almost miraculous" flight across the river to Tom shows her powers gushing out on the water, and so, in some stories, do the vampire's. Count Dracula feasts triumphantly on the ship's crew during an ocean voyage; he is able to control storms and tides; and Mina Harker's unholy "marriage" to him is revealed under hypnosis through a shared sense of "the lapping of water . . . gurgling by." The implicit question that runs through the legends of witches and vampires also runs through Maggie's voyages in *The Mill on the Floss:* is the pure baptismal element itself a conduit blending what is unholy with what is potentially divine?

Like the crises in the lives of Romola, Gwendolen Harleth, and Daniel Deronda, the great crises in Maggie's life come when she abandons herself to the movement of the tides. We first see her staring intently over the gloomy water; before we hear her speak, her mother prophesies darkly about her proclivity for "wanderin' up an' down by the water, like a wild thing"; her father's mad fear that irrigation will drain the mill of its water deprives her of her childhood home; the flight with Stephen that uproots so many lives takes place by water; and so, of course, do Maggie's much-criticized apotheosis and death in the final flood, which raise more questions than they resolve.

These questions are the same as those raised by the childish Maggie about the witch in Defoe who is her psychic mirror: is the woman in the water a witch or not? Does she float or sink? Is water her friend or foe, condemning her to spiritual exile forever or sweeping her to final vindication and "home"? "'O God, where am I? Which is the way home?' she crie[s] out, in the dim loneliness" of a flooded world, and the book's conclusion only echoes this cry. Everything has plunged its head under water with the ducks, as the narrator had yearned to do at the beginning. The difficult ending will always be unsatisfactory for those seeking a drier world's perspective, but it is at one with the ethos of Gothic romance as Robert Kiely defines it: "We have seen over and over again that

romantic novels have troubled and unsatisfactory endings. One may say that a resistance to conclusion is one of the distinguishing characteristics of [Gothic] romantic fiction" [*The Romantic Novel in England,* 1972]. Kiely gives a darker and more detailed account of these concluding visions in his discussion of *The Monk,* which can be translated illuminatingly into the world of *The Mill on the Floss:* "Lewis's final vision is of a chaos which neither man nor art has the capacity to control or avoid. Indeed, uncontrollable energy would seem to be the only energy there is in the world of *The Monk.* The artist, like the monk who seeks liberation from lifeless conventions, is apt to find himself unexpectedly on the side of the flood."

Certainly, Maggie seems to be on the side of the flood, since it seeps into the house as an efficacious, though indirect, answer to her despairing prayer. Does she "cause" it, as the vampire evokes storms and controls the tides? Are the waves on which she magically rides her final destructive ally against the commonality that expels and entices her? To some extent, at least, the flood is Maggie's last and strongest familiar, and it is not described through a soothing haze of death and rebirth imagery, but as a fury that crashes through houses, destroys livestock, and drowns crops. "Nature repairs her ravages—but not all" is the narrator's final quiet statement about a phenomenon that uproots and scars more life than it restores.

But it preserves Maggie until she has obtained Tom. Floating toward him, she is envisioned ambiguously with "her wet clothes [clinging] round her, and her streaming hair . . . dashed about by the wind." Like the witch's watery cousin, the Lorelei or mermaid, she lures Tom out of the house where he has found temporary protection—for the waters have stopped rising—into the dangerous tides. The loosely sacramental language of the ending tells us that preternatural forces have been evoked and revealed without disclosing their source. Tom is possessed by the "revelation to his spirit, of the depths in life, that had lain beyond his vision," leaving him "pale with a certain awe and humiliation. At last, "a mist gather[s] over the blue-grey eyes," he falls under Maggie's spell, rows the boat into the dangerous current, clings to her, and sinks, a devotee at last.

The mist that gathers over Tom's eyes at the end concludes the pattern of imagery that centers around what I have called the "swimming vision," a vision of eyes that project upon rather than reflect the world, associated in the novel with explosions of undirected energy reminiscent of sensationalism. Like the witch that leaps at Maggie from the pages of Defoe, the shining eyes the child sees in Bunyan reflect her own in the mask of the devil: "'Here he is,' she said, running back to Mr Riley, 'and Tom coloured him for me with his paints when he was at home last holidays—the body all black, you know, and the eyes red, like fire, because he's all fire inside, and it shines out at his eyes'."

Throughout the novel, Maggie's potent power shines out at her eyes as the devil's does. Shortly after the above speech, we learn that the powdery white of the mill makes "her dark eyes flash out with new fire." When "small demons" impel her to push Lucy into the mud, the Medusa-like power of her eyes is referred to twice and is demonstrated later in her bewitching effect on Philip and Stephen. Her eyes evoke Philip's vision of her as a woman metamorphosed into an animal, with its suggestions of witch, vampire, and lamia; and Stephen, after remarking prophetically "an alarming amount of devil there," falls under Maggie's spell and thirsts obsessively for her *look*. Burning or swimming, Maggie's eyes invoke or transmit more than they see, suggesting an infernal dimension to "the depths in life," that new realm which the intensity of her gaze reveals to Tom in the boat.

If Maggie uses books primarily to invoke mirror images of her own demonic tendencies, the reflections they show her may not always be malign. Bob Jakin's present of Thomas à Kempis's *Imitation of Christ* reveals to her a doctrine of renunciation and self-suppression which some critics, at least, interpret as Maggie's true path to whatever salvation the novel has to offer. At the very least, Thomas à Kempis presents Maggie with a new, celestial image of herself which prompts her to reject the books Philip offers to entice her out of isolation: Madame de Staël and Walter Scott, with their familiar, banished reflections of the "dark, unhappy ones."

But whatever Thomas à Kempis's doctrine may be in itself, it becomes in Maggie's hands another "fetish" that explodes communities and blights lives. The "law of consequences," that ethical variant of utilitarianism which operated so stringently against Arthur and Hetty in *Adam Bede,* judges actions according to their detonations on others, not the high-minded hopes that accompany them; and by its criteria at least, Maggie's applications of Kempis's strictures are disastrous. In her first liaison with Philip, renunciation erupts into hunger for love and talk and books, and clouds over Tom's triumphant restoration of the family honor—an effect which is dwelt on with greater immediacy than the checkered fulfillment of her meetings with Philip in the Red Deeps. When she falls in love with Stephen's strong arm, she renounces renunciation and momentarily abandons herself to the tides of her feeling for him; but when morning comes, the "law" she had found in Thomas à Kempis returns, somewhat transmuted in form, but even more disastrous in effect.

Maggie's second dedication to renunciation takes the form not of mystical quietism, but of a humanistic reverence for ties sanctioned by the past and kept alive by memory: "If the past is not to bind us, where can duty lie? We should have no law but the inclination of the moment." Through this new application of Kempis, Maggie attempts to free herself from the momentariness bordering on sensationalism that has possessed her throughout her life. The "memory" she invokes is actually a myth-making faculty that makes of the past a sanctuary against the present rather than its seeding ground; and the narrator has reminded us earlier that such memories sculpted into myths can be a saving anchor against the chaos of space:

"But heaven knows where that striving might lead us, if our affections had not a trick of twining round those old inferior things—if the loves and sanctities of our life had no deep immovable roots in memory."

But while adherence to memory can be a ballast, the retreat from Stephen which it results in can at that point produce only chaos. The ties to Philip and Lucy to which Maggie declares allegiance have already been snapped by her flight; Tom, the protective deity of her earliest memory, must repudiate her; memory casts her out into a present which denies her as well, containing only a shamed family, an irate community, and a devastated lover. The novel's heavy irony against "the world's wife" does not mean the wife is wrong in seeing that Maggie's wild swerve toward renunciation and her solitary return after the fact are the most destructive choices she can make. Marriage to Stephen would have hurt fewer people than a renunciation whose consequences fling Maggie and all the characters attached to her into a morass where, as the well-meaning Dr. Kenn perceives, each immediate step is "clogged with evil." In terms of its effect on other lives, even a potentially celestial book like Thomas à Kempis's can be a source of evil in Maggie's hands because, once it finds its way into her life, it does evil things.

Though in several forms the world inside books is a demonic mirror for Maggie, turning away from it to the world outside seems demonic as well. If one motif shows her avidly devouring books, another shows her obliterating them in dreams or flinging them aside. When we first meet her, she is "dreaming over her book" instead of reading it, and upon hearing Tom's name, she jumps "up from her stool, forgetting all about her heavy book, which [falls] with a bang within the fender". This sound reverberates through her first visit to Tom at school, when her abandon at seeing him again sends a fat dictionary crashing to the floor. Later on, caught in her family's dreary poverty, she dreams intermittently of using her learning to invade the world of men and so escape from home; but "somehow, when she sat at the window with her book, her eyes *would* fix themselves blankly on the out-door sunshine; then they would fill with tears, and sometimes, if her mother was not in the room, the studies would all end in sobbing." The swimming vision which is her motif in the novel leads her eyes from book to window, and thence to "fits even of anger and hatred" which "flow out over her affections and conscience like a lava stream, and frighten her with a sense that it [is] not difficult for her to become a demon." The path outward from book to nature makes of the window a demonic mirror as well, and at Lucy's house later on, her eyes move from book to window for the last time: "Lucy hurried out of the room, but Maggie did not take the opportunity of opening her book: she let it fall on her knees, while her eyes wandered to the window." Soon afterward, Maggie and Stephen will pass through this same window toward the river, in a voyage whose destructive effects we have already looked at. Both the world in books and the world beyond them are for Maggie reflections of "the depths in life" whose emissary she is forced to be in "the drier world above."

Chap 1   Outside Dorlcote Mill

A wide plain, where the broadening Floss hurries on between its green banks to the Northern Sea, & the loving tide, rushing to meet it, checks its passage with an impetuous embrace. On this mighty tide the black ships — laden with the fresh-scented fir-planks, with rounded sacks of oil-bearing seed, or with the dark ... of coal — are borne along to the town of St Ogg's, which shows its aged, fluted red roofs & the ... gables, of its wharves between the green ... & the river brink, tinging the water with a soft purple hue under the transient glance of the February sun. Far away on each hand stretch the rich pastures, & the patches of dark earth made ready for the seed of broad-leaved green crops, or touched already with the tint of the tender bladed, autumn sown corn. There is a remnant still of the last year's golden clusters of bee hive ricks rising at intervals beyond the hedge rows; & everywhere the hedge rows are studded with trees; the distant ships seem to be lifting, their masts & stretching their red brown sails close among the branches of the spreading ash. Just by the red ...

First page of the manuscript for The Mill on the Floss.

For whether they are devouring books or thirsting toward the world beyond the window, Maggie's eyes have the demonic power of transfixing and transforming what they illuminate into their own images. The power of transformation has always been central in witchcraft legends; the witch's ability to impress herself on others by fixing on them the evil eye or making of them a waxen effigy strikes at the heart of our fear that we will disappear into the image of ourselves that others see. In the two most famous nineteenth-century novels of terror, *Frankenstein* and *Dracula,* the demon's power of transformation takes on sweeping racial overtones: both the monster and Dracula threaten the human species with extinction by their hunger to propagate their own corpselike kind. If, as was said above, such female demons as Carmilla absorb some of their power from their perverse infertility, a demon with reproductive organs is more demonic still. In such a vision, evolutionary fears join with the fertility of death and the weariness of rebirth in a concluding cycle of life evolving forever into death, death into life again. The prolific destructiveness of Maggie Tulliver, the mode in which she spills into her environment by breaking and overturning things, has some of this aura. But the blight she is able to spread is crystalized in the figure of the thoroughly demonic Bertha in "The Lifted Veil," as she sits eyeing a corpse: "but I asked myself how that face of hers could ever have seemed to me the face of a woman born of woman, with memories of childhood, capable of pain, needing to be fondled? The features at that moment seemed so preternaturally sharp, the eyes were so hard and eager—she looked like a cruel immortal, finding her spiritual feast in the agonies of a dying race."

In the ensuing action of the story, the corpse Bertha eyes hungrily is actually restored to "life." Though in terms of the plot's rather awkward and incoherent machinery the reanimated corpse is Bertha's Nemesis, the conjunction between female demon with feasting eyes and the renewal of life in death is suggestive, if not causal. It reminds us that because of her fertility, the female monster in *Frankenstein* is more deadly than the male, and must be ripped savagely apart before she has been born. Apparently the nineteenth-century fear that evolution will lead to an Armageddon of demons subsuming life into death eternally is still with us, on the evidence of two contemporary American Gothic novels, Ira Levin's *Rosemary's Baby* and Thomas Tryon's *Harvest Home.* Both are pristine antifertility myths, in which the women's hunger to reproduce threatens all the norms we are supposed to cherish. Once she has been supernaturally infected the "natural" woman casts the most dangerous shadow of all, for she is able to breed within her the germ of a new death.

George Eliot seems aware of this deeper note in her passage from the unnatural Bertha Latimer to Maggie Tulliver, who is unmistakably a woman as the author defines the species above: she is flooded by memories of childhood, an awareness of pain, and the need to be fondled. The intensity with which her womanliness is realized may obscure the extent to which Maggie, like Bertha, is spir-

itually feasting on the world she lives in. The language of hunger and thirst is used to define her as frequently as the nearly ubiquitous water imagery is, and its implications crystallize in an attempt to explain Philip's pull toward Maggie: "The temptations of beauty are much dwelt upon, but I fancy they only bear the same relation to those of ugliness, as the temptation to excess at a feast, where the delights are varied for eye and ear as well as palate, bears to the temptations that assail the desperation of hunger. Does not the Hunger Tower stand as the type of the utmost trial to what is human in us?"

The allusion is to the Hunger Tower where Ugolino is imprisoned in Canto 33 of Dante's *Inferno.* The emotional complexity of *The Mill on the Floss* finds a precise illustration in Ugolino's life and his afterlife. In the *Inferno,* the scent of cannibalism hovers even over the love between parent and child, and its final implicit suggestion that the pain of the man who must eat is far more excruciating than that of the man who is eaten is an instructive gloss on the intimations of vampirism we have found in Maggie's avid love. Unlike that of the vampire, the horror of whose being lies in the fact that he is a body without a soul, Maggie's hunger is never denied its spirituality. Its essence is captured in a beautifully resonant line from Richard Wilbur's poem, "The Undead," an elegy for a creature who is abandoned "To pray on life forever and not possess it." The power of hunger is at one with the wish of a loving prayer. The final flood that sweeps over the novel and ravages its landscape is the last yearning efflorescence of a young woman who prays from her soul.

The suggestions of demonism we have found in Maggie Tulliver are by no means unique in George Eliot's female characters. We have already looked at the preternaturally evil Bertha in "The Lifted Veil," who in Latimer's first vision of her swims in the water imagery that always engulfs Maggie: "The pale-green dress, and the green leaves that seemed to form a border about her pale blond hair, made me think of a Water-Nixie,—for my mind was full of German lyrics, and this pale, fatal-eyed woman, with the green weeds, looked like a birth from some cold sedgy stream, the daughter of an aged river." Some of this "water-nixie" imagery also surrounds the more convincingly murderous Rosamond in *Middlemarch,* and it swarms over Gwendolen Harleth in *Daniel Deronda,* with her "lamia beauty," her green-and-white colors, her blond pallor, her sinister associations with drowning and the sea.

But George Eliot allows us to doubt whether the loveless Bertha, Rosamond, and Gwendolen are "woman born of woman." Bertha is "sarcastic," "without a grain of romance in her"; Rosamond is coldly ambitious, the riding accident that causes her to miscarry bringing with it faint memories of Hetty Sorrel's infanticide; and the involutions of Gwendolen's psychic frigidity and hatred of love are brilliantly traced. But in *The Mill on the Floss,* "if life had no love in it, what else was there for Maggie?" Although Maggie does say at one point, "I wish I could make myself a world outside [loving], as men do," George

Eliot's sharp delineation of her fitful, solipsistic reading reveals that her efforts in this direction are not great. The demonism of Maggie Tulliver is planted in her very womanliness—as George Eliot defines it—and adds another dimension to the author's attitude toward a character whom many critics have accused her of overfondling. Her overt moral statements about Maggie are not always clear, but her feelings seem to have been: in Maggie Tulliver, she reveals a woman whose primordially feminine hunger for love is at one with her instinct to kill and to die. And she expresses her intertwined sense of Maggie, not in the explicit idiom of the "masculine intellect" critics have praised her for, but in the conventionally "feminine," subterranean language of the George Eliot that many deplore: the language of Gothic romance.

The Mill on the Floss as spiritual autobiography:

In her homeward journey George Eliot was come now to the innermost places, to where she was face to face with herself, and it was that self's face she now drew. It is her own Odyssey whose Ithaca is always behind and not before. It is George Eliot at her best, full of her "manifold but disinterested and impartially observant sympathy." It seems her childish pain had entered into its life of memory at last and had been changed into compassion.

Anne Fremantle, in George Eliot, *Haskell House Publishers Ltd., 1972.*

Janet H. Freeman (essay date 1977)

SOURCE: "Authority in *The Mill on the Floss*," in *Philological Quarterly,* Vol. 56, 1977, pp. 374-88.

[*In this essay, Freeman contends that the omniscient narration of* The Mill on the Floss *renders the novel's ending appropriate.*]

> "By God she is a *wonderful* woman."—John Blackwood, upon reading the next-to-last chapter of *The Mill on the Floss*

Looking up from *The Mill on the Floss,* generations of readers have been drawn to comment on George Eliot herself—often without John Blackwood's admiring enthusiasm, but nearly always with the sense that the history of Maggie and Tom Tulliver is a highly personal narrative, as significant to the storyteller as it is to her audience. Significant, yet at the same time troubling: "What does it all come to except that human life is inexplicable, and that women who feel this find the feeling painful?" This nicely alliterative response [*"The Mill on the Floss," Saturday Review,* 9, 14, April 1860] appeared in print ten days after the novel was first published. It took some time for readers of *The Mill on the Floss* to focus their criticisms, to reach a consensus. Gordon S. Haight summed it up a hundred and one years later [in his introduction to *The Mill on the Floss,* 1961], when he observed that "dissatisfaction with the catastrophic ending is almost

universal." Today there is little reason to revise that estimate, though efforts to account for the belief that the novelist falters as she brings her story to a close continue to accumulate.

They are not easy to summarize. A long, carefully documented, and fully realized narrative stretching over some ten years ends in a sudden natural disaster which snuffs out the lives of her hero and heroine immediately after the "one supreme moment" in which their lifelong division was finally healed. This catastrophe, seemingly at odds with all that precedes it, has led critics to a number of suggestions: indulgence in wish fullfillment, lapse into self-deceit, failure of nerve, or some other more charitable explanation. Nearly every case carries the implication of weakness on George Eliot's part.

That the passage of time has not silenced readers of *The Mill on the Floss* as it has the woman who wrote it and herself looked back on it with as much regret as satisfaction, is less disheartening than perhaps it ought to be: the novel continues, alive, to reach out. One may be touched, however, at any number of points. In this essay, I propose to attend as much to the narrator who tells about Maggie and Tom as to the short lives they live out. I propose further to consider that narrator as a full participant in the fiction George Eliot created. Her history, as generously as the history of the Tulliver family and the history of George Eliot herself, rewards contemplation. A crucial element of the novel's aesthetic structure, it too has a beginning and an end, a past and a future. And the memory of how her narration began can make what it becomes in the end intelligible—in fact, moving. George Eliot, I would argue, has admirably realized not only the tale her narrator tells, but also—and just as vividly—the intense experience of telling it. Once the story within *The Mill on the Floss* is perceived *as told,* the ending of the novel, taken by so many to be an aesthetic lapse, is just, appropriate, and inevitable.

To participate in *The Mill on the Floss* is to exist in time, as much for the narrator as for the characters she describes. In the end, simple chronology subdues them all. But in the beginning, the narrator is all mastery; perfectly recapturing the past ("I remember those large dipping willows. I remember the stone bridge—", she enters it herself and leaning on the bridge looks across the water at the motionless little girl. The sound of the rushing water and the booming mill curtains her off from "the world beyond," she says, as if that solitude were a necessary condition to her inspiration. It enables her to invite us to enter too, to look and see (those are her verbs) for ourselves. It frees her to remember, to animate the water, the horses, and the ducks, to read the tardy waggoner's mind, and to bring that child back to life. Bringing Maggie Tulliver within reach, George Eliot's narrator has defied the death that is to come.

W. J. Harvey [in *The Art of George Eliot,* 1963] calls this power "audacious," and he deems it successful. Yet this inspired possession—and the narrator is as much possessed as possessing—does not endure. The world does not withdraw permanently, nor the child remain motionless. Nor does time stand still: from the moment the narrator realizes she is dreaming in her chair, the years it will take before Maggie and Tom die together begin inexorably to pass. Her confident ability to bring a lost world back to life and invite us to enter it with her, sharing her perfect sympathy and understanding and recognizing her authority to achieve this miracle, dies with them.

Look at the conclusion. Here, the passage of time, no longer extinguished by the narrator's strong and willing memory, is carefully noted, its effects acknowledged, especially its awful power to erase: "The desolation wrought by that flood, had left little visible trace on the face of the earth, five years later. The fifth autumn was rich in golden corn-stacks, rising in thick clusters among the distant hedgerows; the wharves and warehouses on the Floss were busy again, with echoes of eager voices, with hopeful lading and unlading". Surrendering her former visionary power to the bountiful yet indifferent seasons and the unflagging energy of British commerce, the narrator no longer boldly enters into what she sees, inviting our attention. Instead, we watch her in retreat. "To the eyes that have dwelt on the past, there is no thorough repair" refers not to her own desolation—at least not directly—but to marks on hills and trees. Whatever human sorrow remains is experienced in private, for now the narrator's observation keeps its distance; now, she notices only visible facts, public knowledge, the *face* of the earth. The two men who wordlessly visit Dorlcote churchyard (and they visit separately) go unnamed. And as if memory itself were failing her, she must look on their tomb for the names of the two bodies "found in close embrace" five years before. Her final act is to repeat the sentence she sees engraved there, so that in the end even her words are not her own. "In their death, they were not divided" appeared on the title page of *The Mill on the Floss,* before its narrator ever began to speak. It has silenced her at last.

This transformation in George Eliot's narrator, however, is not so abrupt as it seems. It works itself out gradually, as the passing years steadily undermine her initial authority. Time imposes the terms of that erosion; even to describe it, therefore, is a form of submission, demanding that the reader of *The Mill on the Floss* participate in the novel's reality, as much a creature of time as the narrator herself or the story she tells. We must look to the future, to the present, and to the past, the three sources of narrative authority in the novel. Each perspective is eventually closed off.

The sense of a significant future has no part in the watches kept by Philip, Stephen, and the "sweet face beside him" long after the flood has receded, just as the close embrace of brother and sister exists within their tomb, not beyond it. To know what is to come makes no difference to any of them. They share this deprivation with George Eliot's narrator, whose story, now futureless, is at an end. But there was a time when every character in *The Mill on the Floss* was obsessed with thoughts of what the future might hold, and only the narrator had the answer. That

Mrs. Tulliver's children might drown some day is by no means the only prediction made in the novel, though it is usually the only one noticed. Mr. Tulliver fears that Tom might take the mill away from him, he fears that Maggie's cleverness will "turn to trouble", Mrs. Tulliver fears that she might not be able to wash Tom's linen at his new school; Maggie hopefully intends to keep Tom's house when they grow up; Tom expects always to take care of her. The Dodson clan, though they fear for the future of Maggie and Tom, tainted by Tulliver blood, outwits the future's power over their own respectability by the strict commands of their respective Wills. Mr. Tulliver, after he loses the mill not to Tom but to Wakem, makes a fierce gesture against contingency when he forces his son to record in the family Bible that he will have his revenge, that the future will somehow provide his satisfaction.

Tedious to list but useful to recognize, these habitual expressions of the wish to know and control the future saturate the novel, all of them either ironically wrong or ironically right, all of them guesswork. And not only in the beginning. Philip Wakem is good at it, too—witness his timid witticism to Maggie, predicting that she may some day "carry away all the love" from her cousin Lucy, or the dozing dream that comes to him in his "vague dread" of the future, in which he "fancied Maggie was slipping down a glistening, green, slimy channel of a waterfall, and he was looking on helpless". And as the Great Temptation gathers together, Lucy—too innocent to fear for herself—plans to save Maggie from more drudgery as a governess by marrying her to Philip. "Wouldn't that be a pretty ending to all my poor, poor Maggie's troubles?" she asks, happily.

Maggie reacts with a shiver, a "sudden chill." She too is preoccupied with endings. From the time when, as a remorseful child—remorseful in this case over the death of Tom's rabbits—she wished that the subsequent history of the Prodigal Son had not been "left a blank", through her futile efforts to imagine a happy finish for Scott's *The Pirate* ("I could never make a happy ending out of that beginning"), and on to her "presentiment of a troublous future" in her own life, Maggie has struggled to see ahead, to finish the story for herself. She never abandons the effort. Even her last, penitential return to St. Ogg's is in part an act of defiance. "I will not go away because people say false things of me," she tells Dr. Kenn, "They shall learn to retract them". And her last words before the flood waters finally reach her betray the same preoccupation: "O God, if my life is to be long, let me live to bless and comfort—".

Death, however, is only a few hours away. How could she have guessed? The reader of *The Mill on the Floss* has long since been taught the rule Maggie Tulliver never learns to follow, that to make predictions is to make mistakes. Only George Eliot's narrator—at least in the beginning—is secure in her knowledge of what's to come. "Nature," she points out sententiously when young Tom comes home to the mill for the first time, "has the deep cunning which hides itself under the appearance of openness, so that simple people think they can see through her quite well, and all the while she is secretly preparing a refutation of their confident prophecies". Special pains are taken more than once to see that we remain uncertain—even Mr. Riley's motives when he suggests a teacher for Tom are not what "a too sagacious observer" might expect. We are in the dark, as we watch Maggie and Tom as children trot along and sit down together, "with no thought that life would ever change for them: they would only get bigger and not go to school, and it would always be like the holidays; they would always live together and be fond of each other". We only know that their predictions must be wrong.

"Life did change for Tom and Maggie," the narrator comments, but she won't say how. Alone in her knowledge of the future (earned, of course, by that initial step backwards in time), her authority seems complete. Only Maggie, who remains incorrigible, comes to challenge it; only Maggie takes the future into her own hands and, in the end, succeeds. But long before that happens there are signs of this growing energy, aside from Maggie's very interesting penchant for finishing romantic novels herself. While at the beginning of *The Mill on the Floss* we are repeatedly advised to take Maggie's childish sorrows seriously, as if to trivialize her experience were to miss it altogether, as time passes Maggie's feelings take on a potential significance no authorial apology can augment. She contains her own future in the smoldering fires of her developing nature. Trapped at home with her impoverished family,

> . . . she rebelled against her lot, she fainted under its loneliness, and fits even of anger and hatred toward her father and mother, who were so unlike what she would have them to be—toward Tom, who checked her, and met her thought or feeling always by some thwarting difference—would flow out over her affections and conscience like a lava stream, and frighten her with a sense that it was not difficult for her to become a demon.

This hidden passion becomes increasingly forbidding as Maggie becomes increasingly adult. To watch the child Maggie passionately chop her hair off is touching—but only faintly disquieting; indeed, the narrator uses the occasion to remind us that Maggie's trouble is not to be sneered at. Watching her enter the Red Deeps six years later, however, her hair grown into a "jet crown," one feels intimidated,

> . . . one has a sense of uneasiness in looking at her— a sense of opposing elements, of which a fierce collision is imminent: surely there is a hushed expression, such as one often sees in older faces under borderless caps, out of keeping with the resistant youth, which one expects to flash out in a sudden, passionate glance, that will dissipate all the quietude, like a damp fire leaping out again when all seemed safe.

Now, the narrator herself is disturbed by Maggie's latent force. The dangerous future—once safely distant, when it

was as yet untold—is slowly making itself known. And she herself, like the Dodsons and the Tullivers, has come to fear for it. Two more years of Maggie's life pass and we are told outright that though we have known Maggie "a long while" and are familiar with her characteristics, her history cannot be predicted even by the most privileged of observers: "Maggie's destiny . . . is at present hidden, and we must wait for it to reveal itself like the course of an unmapped river: we only know that the river is full and rapid, and that for all rivers there is the same final home".

And so we wait, reader and narrator alike witnessing Maggie's passionate attraction to and abandonment of Stephen Guest, until at last the unmapped river floods St. Ogg's and Maggie, alone, takes control of her future. She does so in order to renounce it, in a gesture unthinkable to any other character in the novel and independent of the foresight of its narrator. Only moments before, Maggie saw the remaining years of her life as a series of penitent, hurtful, and repeated self-denials. On the instant, however, her fear and despair leave her. She thinks of nothing "but that she had suddenly passed away from that life which she had been dreading", and she calls up her energy "as if her life were a stored-up force that was being spent in this hour, unneeded for any future". On her way home for the last time, Maggie's only wish is that she not die before she gets there, that she not "perish too soon". The extinction of the long years ahead is a price Maggie willingly pays, as she finds her way across the flood to Tom. On her own authority and to her own satisfaction, she at last finishes the story.

Once George Eliot's narrator accomplishes her visionary leap into the past, *The Mill on the Floss* is relentlessly chronological. Her omniscience very rarely disobeys the law that connects past, present, and future in an unbroken chain. Foreknowledge is a powerful instrument to that omniscience, so long as she alone knows what the next link will be. So also is her insight into the immediate present, an insight exhibiting both tact and wisdom—a far-reaching authoritative perspective on the present, that carefully schools us into understanding. For a time, at least, we learn to watch the unfolding present with sympathy, the virtue in which George Eliot's narrators consistently specialize. We pity the young Maggie for her "perspectiveless conception of life". We feel for young Tom, boxed in by Mr. Stelling's rigid belief that a single educational regimen must do for all minds and unable to see beyond his present misery. We are invited to share the narrator's "sense of oppressive narrowness" generated by "these emmet-like Dodsons and Tullivers", even as we learn to join their small preoccupations to her wide experience of life, literature, science, and history, and to become accustomed to that celebrated tone of sympathetic wisdom. "Mr. Tulliver had a destiny as well as Oedipus", we are told, in a characteristic reminder that the tiny doings of a "miller and maltster" can have wide application. Or again: "Mr. Tulliver, you perceive . . . was as proud and obstinate as if he had been a very lofty personage".

Mr. Tulliver himself perceives no such thing. Both the Dodsons and the Tullivers, in fact, lack any capacity to conceive their own experience in the light of lives and times other than their own, just as they lack the "highly modifying influence" George Eliot's narrator habitually provides for her reader. "In natural science," she tells us with familiar authority, ". . . there is nothing petty to the mind that has a large vision of relations . . . It is surely the same with human life". So the lesson goes. The baffled wish to preach it not to us but to Maggie, "as lonely in her trouble as if every other girl besides herself had been cherished and watched over by elder minds, not forgetful of their own early time", seems unmistakable, however, especially when the lonely child comes across *The Imitation of Christ* and finds on its pages the notations of a "quiet hand" and the words of a "supreme Teacher," the "direct communication of a human soul's belief and experience". It is an interesting moment in the novel, for here the narrator's capacity to instruct her reader seems no longer a sufficient motive; here her sympathy as well as our own seem no longer a sufficient motive; here her sympathy as well as our own seem no longer to the point. Maggie is being instructed, but by whom?

She lectures us nonetheless, in what appears to be an inappropriate diatribe against high society, "its claret and its velvet-carpets, its dinner-engagements six weeks deep, its opera and its faery ball-rooms", the object of a scorn quite out of keeping with the sympathetic good humor she has hitherto striven to maintain. Meanwhile, Maggie, "without the aid of established authorities and appointed guides", reads on. And our carefully nurtured understanding of her, though it too can never touch her directly, is now taken for granted: "From what you know of her, you will not be surprised [and of course we are not] that she threw some exaggeration and willfulness, some pride and impetuosity, even into her self-renunciation".

Maggie, that is to say, learns her lesson incompletely. As yet unlearned in the pain of genuine renunciation, she firmly turns her mirror to the wall. But George Eliot's narrator, not able to shed the light of her own wise counsel on Maggie herself in her hour of need, is also unable to maintain her sense that the reader continues to benefit by it. By the time the recalcitrant Maggie, her determination to resist the alms of her family having forced her to take the traditionally onerous post of a governess, begins to enjoy the luxuries of a stylish vacation with her cousin Lucy, our sympathy comes openly into doubt. Our "large vision" of the relation of the petty to the large, it seems, ceases to function when it comes to the behavior of St. Ogg's fashionable sons and daughters. For instance, Maggie is said to look flushed at the end of a busy day. "Had anything remarkable happened?" asks the narrator—and immediately offers the following disagreeable reply: "Nothing that you are not likely to consider in the highest degree unimportant". We also are said to consider it "incredible" that Lucy and Maggie talk together before going to bed and "inexplicable" that Lucy should welcome Maggie into her happy life with the adoring Stephen.

One resents this imputed hostility, after having been ceaselessly indoctrinated into the habit of sympathy. One does not asily give up the narrator's former willingness to teach. Yet that authority seeps away, as *The Mill on the Floss* moves out into the world, as the world (and the world's wife) comes into its own. For when Maggie returns to St. Ogg's for the last time, bringing her broken reputation with her and looking only for a refuge, the virtue of a widened understanding of events is once and for all put to the test, and in an arena over which George Eliot's narrator, enraged at the judgments of those smug matrons as if she herself had forgotten how to sympathize with "small minds," has no influence whatever. One incident after another is referred to this issue. Tom's cruel rejection of Maggie is the consequence of his being "imprisoned within the limits of his own nature," his fatal lack of "the wider vision." The ladies of the town, in their unwavering condemnation, are not "beguiled by any wide speculative conceptions" Philip painfully learns the blessings of an "enlarged life," the "birth of strong sympathy"; but since he is never seen out of doors this lesson is of little significance to the world. Lucy learns to forgive Maggie, to see her ("You are better than I am—") sympathetically; but she too remains secluded. Dr. Kenn, whose popularity with his female parishioners is very nearly extinguished because of his sympathy for Maggie, in the end advises her to leave town.

The test results, in short, are negative. And as they come in, one by one, George Eliot's narrator herself lays aside the effort. The swift pace of the last two books of *The Mill on the Floss* is often noticed. The cause, I think, is not merely George Eliot's wish to get to Rome for Holy Week. Both the scrupulous endeavor of her narrator to solicit her reader's sympathy and the task of exhibiting her own are plainly irrelevant to the march of events that leads up to and follows the prodigal's return. Maggie's fate at the hands of the ladies of St. Ogg's comes to pass, whether or no.

Thus knowledge of the future and widely sympathetic insight into the present gradually lose their authority in *The Mill on the Floss* as the story moves closer and closer to its catastrophe. The fate of the narrator's memory, her ability to recover the past, is similar; but this loss devastates far more seriously than those other failures, since memory is not only the source of her inspiration as a storyteller, it is also her salvation as an individual—indeed, it is the only mode of salvation offered in the novel. She spells out this blessing very early, in a fervently detailed revelation of her own experience as a perceiving mind with the gift of loving speech. It occurs in Book One:

> The woods I walk in on this mild May day, with the young yellow-brown foliage of the oaks between me and the blue sky, the white star-flowers and the blue-eyed speedwell and the ground ivy at my feet—what grove of tropic palms, what strange ferns or splendid broad-petalled blossoms, could ever thrill such deep and delicate fibres within me as this home-scene? These

familiar flowers, these well-remembered bird-notes, this sky, with its fitful brightness, these furrowed and grassy fields, each with a sort of personality given to it by the capricious hedgerows—such things as these are the mother tongue of our imagination, the language that is laden with all the subtle inextricable associations the fleeting hours of our childhood left behind them. Our delight in the sunshine on the deep-bladed grass to-day, might be no more than the faint perception of wearied souls, if it were not for the sunshine and the grass in the far-off years which still live in us, and transform our perception into love.

Without this commitment to the past, George Eliot's narrator could not speak at all; she could never have arrived at Dorlcote Mill in the first place. The subtle modulation from "my" to "our," an assumed solidarity between narrator and reader rare enough to pause over, allows us to share the reward of an awakened perception and the language in which to utter it truly. Furthermore, we share it with Maggie and Tom, as they grow out of their early ignorance and into a sense of the past. Learning to see themselves in time, not outside it, they acquire what Maggie later calls "the divine voice within us" that reminds us of "all the motives that sanctify our lives". No wonder the invocation of the voice of memory is potent enough to resolve for the moment all our differences. It is our common bond, our common salvation.

Listening to that voice, Maggie is about to leave Stephen and go back to St. Ogg's. Her return, the most important decision she has ever made, is an emblem of its saving guidance—but this time salvation does not inevitably follow. The pattern was established when the storyteller first left "the world beyond" and made her way to the mill, he memory leading her back to that chilly February afternoon; it was renewed when Tom returned home at Christmas the following year, seeing "the bright light in the parlour at home, as the gig passed noiselessly over the . . . bridge"—details which deliberately recall the opening of the novel; and it is repeated throughout the various homecomings to follow. Its symbolic authority is lost, however, when Maggie goes home only to be denied her brother's roof and forced to meet the world. Once again, Maggie's history threatens her historian.

It has taken Maggie many years of struggle to acquire the docility that leads her to renounce Stephen and face the music back home. Her painfully learned obedience to the principle that the past will guide her rightly is profoundly different from the willing commitment made by George Eliot's narrator to the same imperative; but surely her ultimate tenacity deserves the prize. The forgetful child who left her brother's rabbits to die, who ran away from home to wander with the gypsies, who was jolted into an awareness of the value of the past by the loss of all its amenities, who was persuaded into secret meetings in the Red Deeps by the revival of an early affection, and who floated downstream with the wrong man only so long as her memory remained quiescent, earns her virtue. Her difficult experience of life grants her the authority to question the "natural law" her lover relies on and to ar-

ticulate in her own words a loyalty we at one time were told was below the level of speech:

> "I have tried to think it again and again; but I see, if we judged that way, there would be a warrant for all the treachery and cruelty—we should justify breaking the most sacred ties that can ever be formed on earth. If the past is not to bind us, where can duty lie? We should have no law but the inclination of the moment."

Maggie has finally found her inspiration. Speaking for herself at last—no more does the narrator remind us that Maggie needs "established authorities"—she now possesses and obeys the guiding, saving memory that the entire narration of *The Mill on the Floss* has tried to honor. It guides her to the end; and in the end, as she sets out over the floodwaters, it means more to her than life.

Maggie's sacrifice of herself to the god of recollection easily outdistances whatever other pieties the novel offers. But Maggie's is not the only memory that must finally be satisfied. The long substantiation of Maggie and Tom's childhood serves us as well as them—we too can remember, if we will. We can inquire into the accuracy of Maggie's dream of her happy childhood; we can question her habitual tendency to become a child again; we can see how the past has in fact tyrannized over Maggie's future by providing her with needs she never outgrows, even as it tyrannizes over Tom by ingraining in him a rigidity only his sister's last act of rashness—not by any means her first—can soften:

> There had arisen in him a repulsion towards Maggie that derived its very intensity from their early childish love in the time when they had clasped tiny fingers together, and their later sense of nearness in a common duty and a common sorrow: the sight of her, as he had told her, was hateful to him.

Tom's cruelty is the result of the same loyalty Maggie becomes willing to die for. Which, one wonders, is the deadlier consequence? How can this novel celebrate the divine guidance only memory can give, when those who follow it end up dead and we who observe it end up unconvinced?

We come to these subversive questions by summoning up our own accumulated memory of Maggie and Tom's past—that is, we participate in the same process by which George Eliot's narrator began to tell their story, looking confidently back to her vivid memory of the large dipping willows, the stone bridge, and the mill. The loss of that early confidence, as the task of realizing Maggie and Tom's "joy-in-death or death-in-joy" looms larger and larger, means that she has come to them too. Maggie and Tom have had their reconciliations before, of course, each one exacting its own harsh penalty; but this time, since it costs them their lives, the price is clearly exorbitant. That they die happy adds to the tragedy—eliciting a horror felt as much by the narrator, who must finish what she began and honor that happiness, as it is by the reader, who looks on in helpless dismay.

The heightened immediacy and eloquence of "The Last Conflict" are indirect expressions of this increasing dread. Maggie's consciousness is given with a conspicuous absence of authorial intervention, as she struggles to find her direction across the floodwaters:

> "O God, where am I? Which is the way home?" she cried out, in the dim loneliness.

> What was happening to them at the Mill? The flood had once nearly destroyed it. They might be in danger—in distress; her mother and her brother, alone there, beyond reach of help!

This final homeward journey, in all its heroism, danger, and exhaustion, is utterly different from the dreamlike, inspiring return with which the novel began. The wheel has not come full circle—for the direction George Eliot's narrator took when she began is contradicted by the direction her heroine takes in the end. The intensity of Maggie's effort is rewarded by "one supreme moment" of memory, reaching back to "the days when they had clasped their little hands in love, and roamed the daisied fields together". George Eliot's narrator, however, had scrupulously remembered everything— the fetish, the floury spiders, the "pretty" patchwork, and the dead moles nailed to the stable wall. She renounces it all, in the simplifying eloquence of those little clasped hands. Maggie's version of the past, like her heroic effort to retrieve it, is all that remains.

Readers of *The Mill on the Floss* have never hesitated to point out the haste and tension of its closing pages. These excesses signify the lessening poise of a narrator who can feel her authority waver, but who even so continues to the end, when the inscription on Maggie and Tom's tomb speaks for itself. That early mastery, easy in its knowledge of the distant unnamed future, its sure and sympathetic grasp of the present moment, and its earnest conviction that remembering the past can both inspire and guide, has vanished in the act of telling over a history that gradually undermines the validity of all three. Whatever authority endures—once Maggie and Tom drown together—is possessed by the waters that close over them. "I am in love with moistness," George Eliot's narrator said as she watched the white ducks dip their heads in the murmuring Ripple; but time, like the river's gentle current, does not stop in response to that loving impulse. The stone bridge on which she leaned in order to look across the water at the silent little girl is eventually swept away.

And so George Eliot's narrator, who would speak to Maggie Tulliver if she could, is finally overwhelmed. Unable to alter the course of the unmapped river she saw as Maggie's destiny, she too must submit. In that submission, however, she enters the tragic world of *The Mill on the Floss* more truly than any expression of authorial sympathy, foreknowledge, or memory could possibly permit, having earned her union with those other victims in the inevitability of their common fate.

Mary Jacobus (essay date 1981)

SOURCE: "Men of Maxims and *The Mill on the Floss*," in *Reading Woman: Essays in Feminist Criticism,* Columbia University Press, 1986, pp. 62-79.

[*In the following excerpt, first published in* Critical Inquiry *in 1981, Jacobus applies a critical feminist perspective to the language of* The Mill on the Floss.]

Nancy Miller's "maxims that pass for the truth of human experience" [in her "Emphasis Added: Plots and Plausibilities in Women's Fiction," *PMLA*, January 1981] allude to Eliot's remark near the end of *The Mill on the Floss* that "the man of maxims is the popular representative of the minds that are guided in their moral judgment solely by general rules." Miller's concern is the accusation of implausibility leveled at the plots of women's novels: Eliot's concern is the "special case" of Maggie Tulliver—"to lace ourselves up in formulas" is to ignore "the special circumstances that mark the individual lot." An argument for the individual makes itself felt as an argument against generalities. For Eliot herself, as for Dr. Kenn (the repository of her knowledge at this point in the novel), "the mysterious complexity of our life is not to be embraced by maxims". Though the context is the making of moral, not critical, judgments, I think that Eliot, as so often at such moments, is concerned also with both the making and the reading of fiction; with the making of another kind of special case. Though Maggie may be an "exceptional" woman, the ugly duckling of St. Ogg's, her story contravenes the norm, and in that respect it could be said to be all women's story. We recall an earlier moment, that of Tom Tulliver's harsh judgment of his sister ("You have not resolution to resist a thing that you know to be wrong"), and Maggie's rebellious murmuring that her life is "a planless riddle to him" only because he's incapable of feeling the mental needs which impel her, in his eyes, to wrongdoing or absurdity. To Tom, the novel's chief upholder of general rules and patriarchal law (he makes his sister swear obedience to his prohibitions on the family Bible), the planless riddle of Maggie's life is only made sense of by a "Final Rescue" which involves her death: "In their death they were not divided." But the reunion of brother and sister in the floodwaters of the Ripple enacts both reconciliation and revenge, consummation and cataclysm; powerful authorial desires are at work. To simplify this irreducible swirl of contradictory desire in the deluge that "rescues" Maggie as well as her brother would be to salvage a maxim as "jejune" as *"Mors omnibus est communis"* (one of the tags Maggie finds when she dips into her brother's Latin grammar) stripped of its saving Latin. We might go further and say that to substitute a generality for the riddle of Maggie's life and death, or to translate Latin maxims into English commonplaces, would constitute a misreading of the novel as inept as Tom's misconstruction of his sister, or his Latin. Maggie's incomprehensible foreignness, her drift into error or impropriety on the river with Stephen Guest, is a "lapse" understood by the latitudinarian Dr. Kenn. For us, it also involves an understanding that planlessness, riddles, and impropriety—the enigmas, accidents, and incorrectness of language itself—are at odds with the closures of plot (here, the plot of incestuous reunion) and with interpretation itself, as well as with the finality of the maxims denounced by Eliot.

For all its healing of division, *The Mill on the Floss* uncovers the divide between the language or maxims of the dominant culture and the language itself which undoes them. In life, at any rate, they remain divided—indeed, death may be the price of unity—and feminist criticism might be said to install itself in the gap. A frequent move on the part of feminist criticism is to challenge the norms and aesthetic criteria of the dominant culture (as Miller does in defending Eliot), claiming, in effect, that "incorrectness" makes visible what is specific to women's writing. The culturally imposed or assumed "lapses" of women's writing are turned against the system that brings them into being—a system women writers necessarily inhabit. What surfaces in this gesture is the all-important question of women's access to knowledge and culture and to the power that goes with them. In writing by women, the question is often explicitly thematized in terms of education. Eliot's account of Tom's schooling in "School-Time," the opening chapter of Book 2, provides just such a thematic treatment—a lesson in antifeminist pedagogy which goes beyond its immediate implications for women's education to raise more far-reaching questions about the functioning of both sexual ideology and language. Take Maggie's puzzlement at one of the many maxims found in the Eton Grammar, a required text for the unfortunate Tom. As often, rules and examples prove hard to tell apart:

> The astronomer who hated women generally caused [Maggie] so much puzzling speculation that she one day asked Mr. Stelling if all astronomers hated women, or whether it was only this particular astronomer. But, forestalling his answer, she said,

> "I suppose it's all astronomers: because you know, they live up in high towers, and if the women came there, they might talk and hinder them from looking at the stars."

> Mr. Stelling liked her prattle immensely.

What we see here is a textbook example of the way in which individual misogyny becomes generalized—"maximized," as it were—in the form of a patriarchal putdown. Maggie may have trouble construing *"ad unam mulieres,"* or "all to a woman," but in essence she has got it right. Just to prove her point, Mr. Stelling (who himself prefers the talk of women to star gazing) likes her "prattle," a term used only of the talk of women and children. Reduced to his idea of her, Maggie can only mimic man's talk.

Inappropriate as he is in other respects for Tom's future career, Mr. Stelling thus proves an excellent schoolmaster to his latent misogyny. His classroom is also an important

scene of instruction for Maggie, who learns not only that all astronomers to a man hate women in general but that girls can't learn Latin; that they are quick and shallow, mere imitators ("this small apparatus of shallow quickness," Eliot playfully repeats); and that everybody hates clever women, even if they are amused by the prattle of clever little girls. It's hard not to read with one eye on her creator. Maggie, it emerges, rather fancies herself as a linguist, and Eliot too seems wishfully to imply that she has what one might call a "gift" for languages—a gift, perhaps, for ambiguity too. Women, we learn, don't just talk, they double-talk, like language itself; that's just the trouble for boys like Tom:

> "I know what Latin is very well," said Maggie, confidently. "Latin's a language. There are Latin words in the Dictionary. There's bonus, a gift."

> "Now, you're just wrong there, Miss Maggie!" said Tom, secretly astonished. "You think you're very wise! But 'bonus' means 'good,' as it happens—bonus, bona, bonum."

> "Well, that's no reason why it shouldn't mean 'gift,'" said Maggie stoutly. "It may mean several things. Almost every word does."

And if words may mean several things, general rules or maxims may prove less universal than they claim to be and lose their authority. Perhaps only "this particular astronomer" was a woman-hater or hated only one woman in particular. Special cases or particular contexts—"the special circumstances that mark the individual lot"—determine or render indeterminate not only judgment but meaning too. The rules of language itself make Tom's rote learning troublesome to him. How can he hope to construe his sister when her relation to language proves so treacherous—her difference so shifting a play of possibility, like the difference within language itself, destabilizing terms such as "wrong" and "good"?

Maggie, a little parody of her author's procedures in *The Mill on the Floss,* decides "to skip the rule in the syntax—the examples became so absorbing":

> These mysterious sentences snatched from an unknown context,—like strange horns of beasts and leaves of unknown plants, brought from some far-off region, gave boundless scope to her imagination, and were all the more fascinating because they were in a peculiar tongue of their own, which she could learn to interpret. It was really very interesting—the Latin Grammar that Tom had said no girls could learn: and she was proud because she found it interesting. The most fragmentary examples were her favourites. *Mors omnibus est communis* would have been jejune, only she liked to know the Latin; but the fortunate gentleman whom every one congratulated because he had a son "endowed with *such* a disposition" afforded her a great deal of pleasant conjecture, and she was quite lost in the "thick grove penetrable by no star," when Tom called out,

> "Now, then, Magsie, give us the Grammar!"

Whereas maxims lace her up in formulas, "these mysterious sentences" give boundless scope to Maggie's imagination; for her, as for her author (who makes them foretell her story), they are whole fictional worlds, alternative realities, transformations of the familiar into the exotic and strange. In their foreignness she finds herself, until roused by Tom's peremptory call, as she is later to be recalled by his voice from the Red Deeps. Here, however, it is Maggie who teaches Tom his most important lesson, that the "dead" languages had once been living: "that there had once been people upon the earth who were so fortunate as to know Latin without learning it through the medium of the Eton Grammar." The idea—or, rather, fantasy—of a language that is innate rather than acquired, native rather than incomprehensibly foreign, is a consoling one for the unbookish miller's son; but it holds out hope for Maggie too, and presumably also for her creator. Though Latin stands in for cultural imperialism and for the outlines of a peculiarly masculine and elitist classical education from which women have traditionally been excluded, Maggie can learn to interpret it. The "peculiar tongue" had once been spoken by women, after all—and they had not needed to learn it from Mr. Stelling or the institutions he perpetuates. Who knows, she might even become an astronomer herself, or, like Eliot, a writer who by her pen name had refused the institutionalization of sexual difference as cultural exclusion. Tom and Mr. Stelling tell Maggie that "Girls never learn such things"; "They've a great deal of superficial cleverness but they couldn't go far into anything." But going far into things— and going far—is the author's prerogative in *The Mill on the Floss*. Though Maggie's quest for knowledge ends in death, as Virginia Woolf [in "George Eliot," *Collected Essays of Virginia Woolf*] thought Eliot's own had ended, killing off this small apparatus of shallow quickness may have been the necessary sacrifice in order for Eliot herself to become an interpreter of the exotic possibilities contained in mysterious sentences. Maggie—unassimilable, incomprehensible, "fallen"—is her text, a "dead" language which thereby gives all the greater scope to authorial imaginings, making it possible for the writer to come into being.

We recognize in "School-Time" Eliot's investment—humorous, affectionate, and rather innocently self-lovingly—in Maggie's gifts and haphazard acquisition of knowledge. In particular, we recognize a defense of the "irregular" education which until recently had been the lot of most women, it educated at all. Earlier in the same chapter, in the context of Mr. Stelling's teaching methods (that is, his unquestioning reliance on Euclid and the Eton Grammar), Eliot refers whimsically to "Mr. Broderip's amiable beaver" which "busied himself as earnestly in constructing a dam, in a room up three pairs of stairs in London, as if he had been laying his foundation in a stream or lake in Upper Canada. It was 'Binny's' function to build." Binny the beaver, a pet from the pages of W. J. Broderip's *Leaves from the Note Book of a Naturalist* (1852), constructed his dam with sweeping brushes and warming pans, "hand-brushes, rush-baskets, books, boots, sticks, clothes, dried turf or anything portable." A domesticated *bricoleur,* Binny makes do with what he

can find. A few lines later, we hear of Mr. Stelling's "educated" condescension toward "the display of various or special knowledge made by irregularly educated people." Mr. Broderip's beaver, it turns out, does double duty as an illustration of Mr. Stelling's "regular" (not to say "rote") mode of instruction—he can do no otherwise, conditioned as he is—and as a defense of Eliot's own display of irregularly acquired "various or special knowledge." Like Maggie's, this is knowledge drawn directly from books, without the aid of a patriarchal pedagogue. Mr. Stelling and the institutions he subscribes to (Aristotle, deaneries, prebends, Great Britain, and Protestantism—the Establishment, in fact) are lined up against the author-as-eager-beaver. Eliot's mischievous impugning of authority and authorities—specifically, cultural authority—becomes increasingly explicit until, a page or so later, culture itelf comes under attack. Finding Tom's brain "peculiarly impervious to etymology and demonstration," Mr. Stelling concludes that it "was peculiarly in need of being ploughed and harrowed by these patent implements: it was his favourite metaphor, that the classics and geometry constituted that culture of the mind which prepared it for the reception of any subsequent crop." As Eliot rather wittily observes, the regimen proves "as uncomfortable for Tom Tulliver as if he had been plied with cheese in order to remedy a gastric weakness which prevented him from digesting it." Nor is Eliot only, or simply, being funny. The bonus or gift of language is at work here, translating dead metaphor into organic tract.

Like Maggie herself, the metaphor here is improper, disrespectful of authorities, and, as Tom later complains of his sister, not to be relied on. Developing the implications of changing her metaphor from agriculture to digestion, Eliot drastically undermines the realist illusion of her fictional world, revealing it to be no more than a blank page inscribed with a succession of arbitrary metaphoric substitutions:

> It is astonishing what a different result one gets by changing the metaphor! Once call the brain an intellectual stomach, and one's ingenious conception of the classics and geometry as ploughs and harrows seems to settle nothing. But then, it is open to some one else to follow great authorities and call the mind a sheet of white paper or a mirror, in which case one's knowledge of the digestive process becomes quite irrelevant. It was doubtless an ingenious idea to call the camel the ship of the desert, but it would hardly lead one far in training that useful beast. O Aristotle! if you had had the advantage of being "the freshest modern" instead of the greatest ancient, would you not have mingled your praise of metaphorical speech as a sign of high intelligence, with a lamentation that intelligence so rarely shows itself in speech without metaphor,—that we can so seldom declare what a thing is, except by saying it is something else?

In the *Poetics* Aristotle says: "It is a great thing to make use of . . . double words and rare words . . . but by far the greatest thing is the use of metaphor. That alone cannot be learned; it is the token of genius. *For the right use of metaphor means an eye for resemblances.*" Of course there's authorial self-congratulation lurking in this passage, as there is in Eliot's affectionate parade of Maggie's gifts. But an eye for resemblances (between Binny and Mr. Stelling, for instance, or brain and stomach) is also here a satiric eye. Culture as (in)digestion makes Euclid and the Eton Grammer hard to swallow; Aristotle loses his authority to the author herself. On one level, this is science calling culture into question, making empiricism the order of the day. But there's something unsettling to the mind, or, rather, stomach, in this dizzy progression from culture, digestive tract, and tabula rasa to ship of the desert (which sounds like a textbook example of metaphor). The blank page may take what imprint the author chooses to give it. But the price one pays for such freedom is the recognition that language, thus viewed, is endlessly duplicitous rather than single-minded (as Tom would have it be); that metaphor is a kind of impropriety or oxymoronic otherness; and that "we can so seldom declare what a thing is, except by saying it is something else."

Error, then, must creep in where there's a story to tell, especially a woman's story. Maggie's "wrong-doing and absurdity," as the fall of women often does, not only puts her on the side of error in Tom's scheme of things but gives her a history; "the happiest women," Eliot reminds us, "like the happiest nations, have no history." Impropriety and metaphor belong together on the same side as a fall from absolute truth or unitary schemes of knowledge (maxims). Knowledge in *The Mill on the Floss* is guarded by a traditional patriarchal prohibition which, by a curious slippage, makes the fruit itself as indigestible as the ban and its thick rind. The adolescent Maggie, "with her soul's hunger and her illusions of self-flattery," begins "to nibble at this thick-rinded fruit of the tree of knowledge, filling her vacant hours with Latin, geometry, and the forms of the syllogism." But the Latin, Euclid, and Logic, which Maggie imagines "would surely be a considerable step in masculine wisdom," leave her dissatisfied, like a thirsty traveler in a trackless desert. What does Eliot substitute for this mental diet? After Maggie's chance discovery of Thomas à Kempis, we're told that "the old books, Virgil, Euclid, and Aldrich—that wrinkled fruit of the tree of knowledge—had been all laid by" for a doctrine that announces: "And if he should attain to all knowledge, he is yet far off." Though the fruits of patriarchal knowledge no longer seem worth the eating, can we view Thomas à Kempis as anything more than an opiate for the hunger pains of oppression? Surely not. The morality of submission and renunciation is only a sublimated version of Tom's plainspoken patriarchal prohibition, as the satanic mocker, Philip Wakem, doesn't fail to point out. Yet in the last resort, Eliot makes her heroine live and die by this inherited morality of female suffering—as if, in the economy of the text, it was necessary for Maggie to die renouncing in order for her author to release the flood of desire that is language itself. Why?

The Mill on the Floss gestures toward a largely unacted error, the elopement with Stephen Guest which would have placed Maggie finally outside the laws of St. Ogg's.

Instead of this unrealized fall, we are offered a moment of attempted transcendence in the timeless death embrace which abolishes the history of division between brother and sister—"living through again in one supreme moment, the days when they had clasped their little hands in love." What is striking about the novel's ending is its banishing not simply of division but of sexual difference as the origin of that division. The fantasy is of a world where brother and sister might roam together, "indifferently," as it were, without either conflict or hierarchy. We know that their childhood was not like that at all, and we can scarcely avoid concluding that death is a high price to pay for such imaginary union. In another sense, too, the abolition of difference marks the death of desire for Maggie; "The Last Conflict" (the title of the book's closing chapter) is resolved by her final renunciation of Guest, resolved, moreover, with the help of "the little old book that she had long ago learned by heart." Through Thomas à Kempis, Eliot achieves a simultaneous management of both knowledge and desire, evoking an "invisible" or "supreme teacher" within the soul, whose voice promises "entrance into that satisfaction which [Maggie] had so long been craving in vain." Repressing the problematic issue of book learning, this "invisible teacher" is an aspect of the self which one might call the voice of conscience or, alternatively, sublimated maxims. In "the little old book," Maggie finds the authorized version of her own and Eliot's story, "written down by a hand that waited for the heart's prompting . . . the chronicle of a solitary, hidden anguish . . . a lasting record of human needs and human consolations, the voice of a brother who, ages ago, felt and suffered and renounced."

Where might we look for an alternative version or, for that matter, for another model of difference, one that did not merely substitute unity for division and did not pay the price of death or transcendence? Back to the schoolroom, where we find Tom painfully committing to memory the Eton Grammar's "Rules for the Genders of Nouns," the names of trees being feminine, while some birds, animals, and fish "*dicta epicoena . . .* are said to be epicene." In epicene language, as distinct from language imagined as either neutral or androgynous, gender is variable at will, a mere metaphor. The rules for the genders of nouns, like prescriptions about "masculine" or "feminine" species of knowledge, are seen to be entirely arbitrary. Thus the lament of David for Saul and Jonathan can be appropriated as the epitaph of brother and sister ("In their death they were not divided"), and "the voice of a brother who, ages ago, felt and suffered and renounced" can double as the voice of a sister-author, the passionately epicene George Eliot. One answer, then, to my earlier question (why does Eliot sacrifice her heroine to the morality of renunciation?) is that Eliot saw in Thomas à Kempis a language of desire, but desire managed as knowledge is also managed—sublimated, that is, not as renunciation but as writing. In such epicene writing, the woman writer finds herself, or finds herself in metaphor.

For [Luce] Irigaray, the price paid by the woman writer for attempting to inscribe the claims of women "within an order prescribed by the masculine" may ultimately be death; the problem as she sees it is this: "[How can we] disengage ourselves, *alive,* from their concepts?" The final, lyrical chapter of *This Sex Which Is Not One,* "When Our Lips Speak Together," is, or tries to be, the alternative she proposes. It begins boldly: "If we keep on speaking the same language together, we're going to reproduce the same history." This would be a history of disappropriation, the record of the woman writer's self loss as, attempting to swallow or incorporate an alien language, she is swallowed up by it in turn:

> Outside, you try to conform to an alien order. Exiled from yourself, you fuse with everything you meet. You imitate whatever comes close. You become whatever touches you. In your eagerness to find yourself again, you move indefinitely far from yourself. From me. Taking one model after another, passing from master to master, changing face, form, and language with each new power that dominates you. You/we are sundered; as you allow yourself to be abused, you become an impassive travesty.

This, perhaps, is what Miller means by "a posture of imposture," "the uncomfortable posture of all woman writers in our culture, within and without the text." Miming has become absorption into an alien order. One thinks of Maggie, a consumer who is in turn consumed by what she reads, an imitative "apparatus" who, like the alienated women imagined by Irigaray, can only speak their desire as "spoken machines, speaking machines." Speaking the same language, spoken in the language of the Same ("If we keep on speaking sameness, if we speak to each other as men have been doing for centuries, as we have been taught to speak, we'll miss each other, fail ourselves"), she can only be reproduced as the history of a fall or a failure. Eliot herself, of course, never so much as gestures toward Irigaray's jubilant utopian love language between two women—a language of desire whose object ("my indifferent one") is that internal (in)difference which, in another context, Barbara Johnson [*The Critical Difference*] calls "not a difference between . . . but a difference within. Far from constituting the text's unique identity, it is that which subverts the very idea of identity." What is destroyed, conceptually, is the "unequivocal domination of one mode of signifying over another." Irigaray's experiment in "When Our Lips Speak Together" is of this kind, an attempt to release the subtext of female desire, thereby undoing repression and depriving metalanguage of its claim to truth. "The exhausting labor of copying, miming" is no longer enough.

But for all Irigaray's experimentalism, the "difference" is not to be located at the level of the sentence, as Miller reminds us. Rather, what we find in "When Our Lips Speak Together" is writing designed to indicate the cultural determinants that bound the woman writer and, for Irigaray, deprive her of her most fundamental relationship: her relationship to herself. In fact, what seems most specifically "feminine" about Irigaray's practice is not its experimentalism as such but its dialogue of one/two, its fantasy of the two-in-one: "In *life* they are not divided," to rephrase David's lament. The lips that speak together (the lips of female lovers) are here imagined as initiating a dialogue not of conflict or reunion, like Maggie and Tom's, but of mutuality, lack of boundaries, continuity. If both Irigaray and Eliot kill off the woman engulfed by masculine logic and language, both end also—and need to end—by releasing a swirl of (im)possibility:

> These rivers flow into no single, definitive sea. These streams are without fixed banks, this body without fixed boundaries. This unceasing mobility. This life—which will perhaps be called our restlessness, whims, pretenses, or lies. All this remains very strange to anyone claiming to stand on solid ground.

Is that, finally, why Maggie must be drowned, sacrificed as a mimetic "apparatus" (much as the solidity of St. Ogg's is swept away) to the flood whose murmuring waters swell the "low murmur" of Maggie's lips as they repeat the words of Thomas à Kempis? When the praying Maggie feels the flow of water at her knees, the literal seems to have merged with a figural flow; as Eliot writes, "the whole thing had been so rapid—so dream-like—that the threads of ordinary association were broken." It is surely at this moment in the novel that we move most clearly into the unbounded realm of desire, if not of wish fulfillment. It is at this moment of inundation, in fact, that the thematics of female desire surface most clearly.

We will look in vain for a specifically feminine linguistic practice in *The Mill on the Floss;* "a possible operation of the feminine in language" is always elsewhere, not yet, not here, unless it simply reinscribes the exclusions, confines, and irregularities of Maggie's education. But what we may find in both Eliot and Irigaray is a critique which gestures beyond cultural boundaries, indicating the perimeters within which their writing is produced. For the astronomer who hates women in general, the feminist critic may wish to substitute an author who vindicates one woman in particular or, like Irigaray, inscribes the claims of all women. In part a critic of ideology, she will also want to uncover the ways in which maxims or *idées reçues* function in the service of institutionalizing and "maximizing" misogyny, or simply deny difference. But in the last resort, her practice and her theory come together in Eliot's lament about metaphor—"that we can so seldom declare what a thing is, except by saying it is something else." The necessary utopianism of feminist criticism may be the attempt to declare what is by saying something else—that "something else" which presses both Irigaray and Eliot to conclude their very different works with an imaginative reaching beyond analytic and realistic modes to the metaphors of unbounded female desire in which each finds herself as a woman writing.

David Carroll (essay date 1992)

SOURCE: *"The Mill on the Floss:* Growing Up in St. Ogg's," in *George Eliot and the Conflict of Interpretations: A Reading of the Novels,* Cambridge University Press, 1992, pp. 106-39.

[*In this essay, Carroll examines the world-views of the Dodsons and Tullivers and their effect on Tom and Maggie's "search for an interpretative key to life."*]

In both *Adam Bede* and *The Mill on the Floss,* George Eliot interrupts her narrative to deliver a lengthy apologia for the kind of novel she is writing. It is prompted in each case by what appears to be an anomaly. In *Adam Bede,* the vicar of Hayslope fails as Christian mentor and appears to a putative reader as 'little better than a pagan'. Chapter seventeen which follows is the famous aesthetic justification based on a contrast between the 'secret of proportion' of classical art and 'the secret of deep human sympathy' of Dutch realism. Only sympathy can understand and interpret the human anomalies who fail to measure up to the conventional types and contrasts of high art. The apologia in *The Mill on the Floss* is very different. This is again prompted by an apparent conflict between Christian and pagan values. Mr Tulliver, though a regular churchgoer, has just recorded his desire for vengeance against one of his enemies on the fly-leaf of the family Bible. The chapter which follows, 'A Variation of Protestantism Unknown to Bossuet', defines the strategies which this novel has adopted to interpret such heretical behaviour.

Once again a contrast is established between two forms of life, symbolised on this occasion by the ruins of the Rhine and the Rhône. The former represent a time of romance when moral categories were clear and antithetical, when the great cathedrals were built and the known world was intelligible through the world-shattering opposition of Christian and pagan values: 'did not great emperors leave their Western palaces to die before the infidel strongholds in the sacred East?' This is George Eliot's version of Ruskin's 'The Nature of Gothic', a brief re-creation of a dramatically coherent world in which art and religion reflect each other. That such coherence has been lost in the world of *The Mill on the Floss* is clear from the anomalous action of Mr Tulliver which confuses these clear categories. His provincial world is more fittingly symbolised by the ruins on the Rhône, the remnants of a 'narrow, ugly, grovelling existence, which even calamity does not elevate' and which can only be understood by careful investigation and interpretation, not through simple contrast and literary convention. But what is going on here, and 'by hundreds of obscure hearths' cannot be ignored. It too belongs to the 'historical advance of mankind' but it needs a different approach to understand it: 'we need not shrink from this comparison of small things with great; for does not science tell us that its highest striving is after the ascertainment of a unity which shall bind the smallest things with the greatest?' This is a different kind of hermeneutical language from that used in *Adam Bede*. Here the narrator is not evoking 'the secret of deep human sympathy', but recommending a scientific examination of the 'theory of life' of the Dodsons and Tullivers. His justification follows: 'In natural science, I have understood, there is nothing petty to the mind that has a large vision of relations, and to which every single object suggests a vast sum of conditions. It is surely the same with the observation of human life.' This explains why *The Mill on the Floss,* as it traces the natural history of these provincial families and their strange tribal customs, is the most anthropological of George Eliot's novels. It deploys also a wide range of analogies and metaphors from classical literature and the natural sciences, but it does so ironically, as if to establish its own fictional mode in the territory between, traditionally that of the folklorist and anthropologist.

The remainder of the chapter puts the method vividly into practice. The theory of life of the Dodsons and Tullivers is too specific and eccentric 'to be arrived at deductively, from the statement that they were part of the Protestant population of Great Britain.' The 'large vision' and the 'single object' must be held in a flexible, dialectical relationship. Where the theologians fail, the trained folklorist is more likely to succeed: 'If, in the maiden days of the Dodson sisters, their Bibles opened more easily at some parts than others, it was because of dried tulip-petals, which had been distributed quite impartially, without preference for the historical, devotional, or doctrinal.' Such practices belong to the 'eternal fitness of things,' in the same way as the mutton-bone Mrs Glegg carries in her pocket protects her against cramp. By representing such esoteric customs and elaborate rituals, George Eliot both distances the world of the novel and then, through the children, brings it close as she uncovers its assumptions and values. What is being uncovered is—in that crucial term—a world-view. In other words, the narrator as anthropologist is interpreting this way of life itself as an interpretative grid, a collage of pagan and Christian elements, which mediates between the families and their conditions. His careful fieldwork will eventually elicit the founding myth of the society to which they belong. At the end of this apologia, the narrator assumes that the reader will no longer be surprised by Mr Tulliver's action.

Such a narrative stance, which predominates in the childhood half of the novel, foregrounds the problems of interpretation in quite a different way from *Adam Bede,* where Hayslope at the turn of the century is presented through pastoral norms and types. In *The Mill on the Floss,* by contrast, the narrator allies himself with the cultivated reader in the difficult task of decoding this oppressively narrow and eccentric form of provincial life in the more recent past (1829-39). And there is a second feature of the novel which foregrounds interpretation in a decisive way. *The Mill on the Floss* is a critical adaptation of the *Bildungsroman* and, as such, shows Tom and Maggie struggling to adapt their inherited world-view to the conditions in which they are growing up—'in the onward tendency of human things that have risen above the mental level of the generation before them, to which they have been nevertheless tied by the strongest fibres of their hearts.' What epitomises this most clearly is their desire— expressed as a refrain in the novel—for a 'key' to 'the painful riddle of this world.' As their dilemmas crowd in upon the children, these two dimensions of the novel are seen to be inseparable: the family world-view they have inherited (which requires the skills of the anthropologist to interpret) is both the origin and the obstacle to their own search for an interpretative key to life. This chapter will examine first the lives of the Tullivers and Dodsons, George Eliot's most detailed piece of ethnography, and then the struggles of Tom and Maggie for a coherent view of the world.

. . . . .

The co-ordinates of the children's world are the respective codes of their parents' families, the Dodsons and Tullivers. Other Victorian writers are fond of binary oppositions in their definitions of culture: Hebraism and Hellenism (Arnold), mechanical and organic (Carlyle), Gothic and classical (Ruskin), or, as we have seen, Christian and pagan. George Eliot domesticates with sustained irony her fundamental binary opposition in these two provincial families, so that the values and assumptions of the Dodsons and Tullivers become the building blocks out of which Tom and Maggie have to construct their world-views. From a distance, provincial life may appear uniformly and oppressively narrow; on a closer look, crucial differences emerge. As these are investigated by the narrator, he uncovers two quite different logics, each of which seeks and fails to control the uncertainties of life.

For Mr Tulliver, the mill is the centre of his emotional and imaginative life. It links his present existence directly to that prelapsarian state when he was a child within the security of the family, bound by the kind of close personal relationships he still maintains with his sister Gritty. One of his earliest memories is of the completion of the malt-house and his childhood anticipation of a future replete with plum puddings. But this future never materialised, and the more confusing life becomes, the more his mind harks back to that time of simple, unquestioned verities before the devil, in the shape of the lawyers, began to interfere in the affairs of the world. The puzzling world in which he now finds himself can only be explained by his increasingly 'rampant Manichaeism' which tells him that 'rats, weevils, and lawyers were created by Old Harry,' and somehow these have gained access to his Eden. The lawyers are particularly dangerous because the prelapsarian identification of words and things, signifiers and signifieds, has been fractured: 'Not but what, if the world had been left as God made it, I could ha' seen my way, and held my own wi' the best of 'em; but things have got so twisted round and wrapped up i' unreasonable words, as aren't a bit like 'em, as I'm clean at fault, often an' often.' In this gap, the lawyers machinate. 'Everything winds about so— the more straightforward you are, the more you're puzzled.' And this is the fallen world for which Tom is to be prepared—according to Tulliver's muddled plans— by knowing 'a good lot o' words as don't mean much, so as you can't lay hold of 'em i' law.'

Mr Tulliver is vulnerable because the mill is not only the centre of his emotional life, it is also a piece of mortgaged property. And it is here, in the public domain, in that other reality made up of laws, money, debts, and interest rates, that he appears so deficient and his enemies so cunning. He is a man of ends not means; of metaphoric

identification ('water is water') not of metonymic accretion. The more he identifies himself with the absolutes of water, land, and mill, the more unintelligible the contemporaneous, changing, provincial world becomes. He has to keep creating in explanation new enemies: 'his entanglements in this puzzling world . . . required the hypothesis of a very active diabolical agency to explain them.' Anyone who challenges his predominance is quickly placed in the devilish half of his Manichean universe— lawyers, Dodsons, Pivart, Papists, even Tom and Maggie at different times. When he becomes sufficiently incensed by his enemies' effrontery, he has no choice but to make an aggressive foray to defend his possessions, for they are 'part of his life, part of himself.' As the novel opens, he has just made what is to be his last successful skirmish over his irrigation rights; from this point his attacks become increasingly rash and intemperate and the destructive rhythm of his life is accentuated. A violent counter-attack on his encircling enemies is followed, after the inevitable defeat, by a retreat to the security of the mill and its memories based on the inalienable values of the land, river, and water-power, in a world of pastoral equipoise. As these oscillations become increasingly violent during the first half of the novel, the mill becomes more and more necessary to Tulliver as a refuge, but also more and more vulnerable in the public domain where his Manicheism prevents him dealing with the simplest problems. He even revokes the Dodson loan in one of his rages. Finally, the public domain in the person of his enemy Wakem gets control of the mortgage to the mill and then the prising apart of the world and what it signifies is complete. The centre of his emotional life has been invaded and possessed by the evil principle.

Tulliver is by his very nature unable to accept this contradiction inherent in his theory of life. His paralysis is the sign of this impasse from which family memories briefly revive him, only to be superseded by the rages which conjure up further devilish enemies and return him to his living death. As he gradually recovers, he is forced by his wife to come to terms with financial reality; it was she who in the first place provided Wakem with the opportunity of causing Tulliver this 'most deadly mortification.' The Dodson and Tulliver principles, though complementary, are in their partiality in deadly opposition, as Mrs Tulliver discovers to her cost during the bankruptcy. Now, Tulliver is faced with an impossible choice, the kind of choice which the dialectical narrative of *The Mill on the Floss* repeatedly generates to challenge every fixed world-view. He can stay at the mill, the only place where his life has continuity and meaning, if he is prepared to work for Wakem's wages, thereby humbling his pride and sacrificing his independence. The alternative is to salvage his pride (as Tom wishes) by leaving the mill and handing it over to the evil principle. In either direction lies renunciation, and like Wordsworth's Michael, which this part of the novel movingly recalls, he chooses to stay at the mill sustained by the memories of his forefathers, but truncated—'a tree as is broke'—in the present. He is defeated, but the god of his Manichean world will not allow him to forgive his enemies, as he records in the Bible: 'I'll serve him honest, I with evil may befall him.'

This is an animus the commercial Dodsons do not understand, but Tulliver keeps it alive until the moment when all his debts are paid off, a remnant of his pride returns, and then he is empowered to attack once again. His physical assault on Wakem is the final violent oscillation in his life's rhythm as he tries to rout the devil, is frustrated by Maggie, and dies still hating his enemies.

At the very end, however, in the most moving phase of Mr Tulliver's confused life, there is a suggestion that he transcends briefly the rigid dichotomy of the Manichean world which has betrayed him. It is Maggie who prompts this awareness: she had protected the defenceless Wakem and now, as her father is dying, she asks him if he forgives his enemy. He can't love a rascal, he replies, but she prompts in him a final question. While '[h]is hands moved uneasily, as if he wanted them to remove some obstruction that weighed upon him', he asks, 'Does God forgive raskills? . . . but if He does, He won't be hard wi' me.' At the last, Tulliver struggles hesitantly out of the constraints of his world and dimly acknowledges the possibility of a god who might conceivably forgive the devil's party which, for the moment, comes to share the same puzzling human reality as himself. It is the briefest moment of puzzled transcendence, but it re-enacts that crucial paradigm in George Eliot's fiction in its fundamental form: the claims of the two Manichean interpretative schemes are perfectly balanced in a moment of equipoise. Can they turn into a dialectic out of which a new vision of life will come? Or, in Mr Tulliver's terms, is there a god able to forgive both himself and rascals in his divided world?

The contrasting world of the Dodsons is experienced by the children through their mother and her three sisters who live in the nearby town of St Ogg's. This contrast, as it shows itself within the family, is dramatised in the opening conversation of the novel between Mr and Mrs Tulliver. He is seeking to outflank his enemies by sending Tom, his agent, away to school for a superior education. To each of his muddled arguments his wife simply responds with a practical suggestion—to kill a couple of fowl, to wash Tom's clothes, to air the sheets for the best bed. The husband plans, the wife translates the plans into objects. Ends—the ultimate defeat of his enemies—are instantly reduced to means, to objects in a world which the Dodsons know how to control and in which Mr Tulliver has little interest. In contrast to the rashness, generosity, and emotional warmth of the Tullivers, the Dodson theory of life is cautious, ritualised, and impersonal. Any account of it rapidly turns into a list of objects, sacred and profane:

> A Dodson would not be taxed with the omission of anything that was becoming, or that belonged to the eternal fitness of things which was plainly indicated in the practice of the most substantial parishioners, and in the family traditions—such as, obedience to parents, faithfulness to kindred, industry, rigid honesty, thrift, the thorough scouring of wooden and copper utensils, the hoarding of coins likely to disappear from the currency, the production of first-rate commodities for the market, and the general preference for whatever was home-made.

It is an ethic expressed in negative and precautionary terms, in the avoidance of omission: 'it was necessary to be baptized, else one could not be buried in the churchyard, and to take the sacrament before death as a security against more dimly understood perils.' But their world is not full of enemies. More Augustinian than Manichean, evil for them consists in the absence of good.

The concern with objects is, of course, common to both families, but there are crucial differences. For Mr Tulliver the mill, the water, and the land are co-extensive with his emotional life. He has remained in the pre-industrialised, pre-commercial rural world, expressed most vividly in the novel as the pastoral of childhood, 'where objects became dear to us before we had known the labour of choice, and where the outer world seemed only an extension of our own personality: we accepted and loved it as we accepted our own sense of existence and our own limbs.' This is very different from the facticity of the Dodsons. Their spontaneous, inner life has all gone into their objects—the teaspoons, the teapots, their bonnets—and congealed there. Consequently, they are able to manipulate these objects adeptly, according to their family rituals and without emotional complications. Within the family they communicate with each other, expressing their firmly controlled feeling, in a sign system which almost precludes the use of words. Its main purpose is keeping errant members of the family up to the mark. 'So if Mrs Glegg's front to-day was more fuzzy and lax than usual, she had a design under it: she intended the most pointed and cutting allusion to Mrs Tulliver's bunches of blond curls, separated from each other by a due wave of smoothness on each side of the parting.' In contrast to Mr Tulliver's intemperate outbursts, Dodson emotion is expressed through subtle deviations from the norm which can only be properly analysed by the skilled anthropologist, as we see when sister Pullet seeks to express her grief: 'From the sorrow of a Hottentot to that of a woman in large buckram sleeves, with several bracelets on each arm, an architectural bonnet, and delicate ribbon-strings—what a long series of graduations!' Grief checked by ritual 'produces a composition of forces' which only a Dodson can decode.

All the sisters, with the exception of Mrs Tulliver, are firmly linked to the commercial world of St Ogg's through their successful husbands, so that they see even their marriages as important business deals. They have invested so many years of their lives, plus their hand-embroidered tablecloths, in return for the legacies they anticipate at their husbands' deaths. Mrs Glegg, for example, is quickly reconciled to her husband after one of their rows at the thought of the 'testamentary tenderness' she is sure will be forthcoming. This is the reverse side of the Dodson solidarity, loyalty, and sense of duty. Personal relations must take second place to the laws of exchange, legacies, and interest rates. Tenderness is testamentary. This is harshly demonstrated at the Tulliver bankruptcy when the Dodson sisters refuse to recover their sister's precious objects—her 'seraphim or household gods'—and, apart from a few things they need themselves, allow everything to be sold. Affection must not interfere with the judgment expressed through the ineluctable workings of the market: as Mrs Glegg says, 'The disgrace is, for one o' the family to ha' married a man as has brought her to beggary. The disgrace is, as they're to be sold up. We can't hinder the country from knowing that.' Unlike the good-natured Tulliver who lends money for sentimental reasons and creates the impression that he is 'a much more substantial man than he really was,' the Dodsons through their careful and relentless hoarding of money turn means once again into ends. The purpose of life becomes 'an ingenious process of nibbling out one's livelihood without leaving any perceptible deficit.' And it is the money market which determines the Dodson attitude to time: they are constantly anticipating the maturing of their investments and the regular payments of interest. Unlike Mr Tulliver, fearful of the future 'when the country would become utterly the prey of Papists and Radicals,' they look ahead confidently to a time when all preparations in the form of tablecloths, clothes, even burial sheets, have been made in advance—and their account with life closed. Then, they are forced willy-nilly to contemplate death.

Here, means become ends in the most striking way. Compared to the Tullivers, the Dodsons are practical people with great skills of survival in their changing provincial world. But death is their constant concern and topic of conversation. It is the final contingency they are all seeking to prepare for, control, and survive. At the beginning of the novel, Mrs Tulliver reassures her husband that if he were to die tomorrow the laying-out sheets are 'mangled beautiful' and ready for use. 'Funerals were always conducted with peculiar propriety in the Dodson family,' we are told. But these careful preparations for death seek to deny its reality through the assumption that the dead Dodson will be present to enjoy her triumph. When Mrs Glegg's will is read out, no one must be able to say 'that she had not divided her money with perfect fairness among her own kin.' Preparations are made for the final settlement, death is jumped over, and the deceased Dodsons will still be there commenting on their own wills, their laying-out sheets, and their superior lace. The practical preparations for death become ends in themselves. In a world of solid, valuable objects death has no place. All the proprieties will have been observed and death will have become so much a part of the public domain that it will not be experienced as a personal, private experience. If their possessions survive, they will too. Mr Tulliver's failure was his inability to recognise a public world independent of himself; the Dodson failure is the opposite— the inability to acknowledge the end of the self which has become so completely ritualised and objectified in the public domain.

George Eliot plays several variations on the self-confident Dodsons' ritualised attempts to defeat that final end which their means seek to pre-empt. Aunt Pullet's constant topic of conversation is illness and its remedies, and the pills and medicines with which she keeps death at bay. But, in a characteristic Dodson reversal, the remedies—or at least their containers—become themselves the justification of the life they are seeking to extend. Mr

Pullet, she announces, keeps all her old medicine bottles, and her only concern is that 'I may go before I've made up the dozen o' these last sizes.' The aim of life becomes the collection of medicine bottles, and the sorrow of death lies in the failure to collect enough. Similarly, the awesome viewing of aunt Pullet's new bonnet becomes the opposite of what is intended. The imagined triumph turns to ashes as she realises that a death in the family would prevent her wearing her masterpiece until it was out of fashion. The hidden keys, the darkened corridors and rooms, all become pointless as time triumphs again, and the shrouds turn the furniture into 'corpses', the solemnity becomes 'funereal', and the shrine a mausoleum. The alternative strategy of stockpiling clothes regardless of fashion is practised by aunt Glegg, but this also defeats itself. She becomes walking testimony to time's decay as she uncovers the next ancient stratum of clothes to wear: her gowns, covered in damp spots, give off 'a mouldy odour,' while at one especially awe-inspiring moment she appears at a family crisis in 'garments which appeared to have had a recent resurrection from a rather creasy form of burial.

The Dodsons don't only value material objects. Their clan is a network of human relationships within which they have clear obligations: 'The right thing must always be done towards kindred.' But these obligations have been externalised to such an extent that the only relations which have any validity are guaranteed blood relationships. The result is a clan system with virtually no emotional validation: 'And it is remarkable that while no individual Dodson was satisfied with any other individual Dodson, each was satisfied, not only with him or her self, but with the Dodsons collectively.' What is lacking, of course, is an infusion of the Tulliver spontaneity and warmth. Their only concern is public disgrace. Theirs is no Manichean world: if someone fails, they deserve it. And Mrs Tulliver herself movingly accepts this view, as 'her old self' in the shape of her precious objects 'which had made the world quite comprehensible to her for a quarter of a century' is sold off. Mr Tulliver's final baffled question was, why should evil triumph? His wife asks, what have I done wrong? In her 'helpless imbecility,' bewildered and cut off from the security of her own clan, Mrs Tulliver makes a feeble and pathetic attempt to break through the Dodson constraints. She turns away at the end of the novel from the externals of respectability, away even from Tom— that true Dodson—to the previously despised Maggie, to the life of personal affection discovered through her suffering. In the valley of his humiliation, Mr Tulliver similarly reversed his natural tendency in a desperate attempt to come to terms with the world which had destroyed him, becoming increasingly attached to Tom as the only person likely to re-establish the family fortunes. But it is too late for either husband or wife to rescue the wholeness of the worlds they have lost.

The answer to both their perplexed questions is that they have married each other. Dodsons and Tullivers embody vital but partial truths which, when they meet within the family, proceed to destroy each other. Mr Tulliver's imaginary battles with the evil principle astonish her, while his wife's appeals to Dodson traditions enrage him: 'Mrs

Tulliver had lived fourteen years with her husband, yet she retained in all the freshness of her early married life a facility of saying things which drove him in the opposite direction to the one she desired'. The plotting of the first half of the novel demonstrates this mutual destruction which culminates in the bankruptcy. Mrs Tulliver's fatal interference results in the loss of the mill and her husband's 'deadly mortification' in being forced to work for the devil's wages, a tragedy dismissed by the Dodsons as 'but a feeling in Mr Tulliver's mind.' But it works the other way also. He brings upon his wife her most 'deadly mortification' with the financial disgrace and the loss of her household gods. With remorseless logic, the two theories of life probe, interrogate, undermine, and finally destroy each other.

What, finally, are the controlling myths which underpin these contrasting, complementary, and fallible theories? Both seek worlds beyond the reach of time, either before the narrative began or after it has ended. Tulliver is sustained by the prelapsarian world of his childhood to which things will return once he has defeated the evil principle and its agents, whereas the Dodsons look beyond the final contingency of death, to a time when all their accounts will have been settled, their wills read, and all the proprieties observed. Then, they will be able to enter into full enjoyment of their possessions, safe from the anxieties of the moths that consume and the thieves that break in. Death itself has been elided in both scenarios but, unfortunately, the eternal verities embodied in the mill and the Dodson household gods prove not to be inalienable. At the climax of the novel, Tom and Maggie subsume both of these family myths—pre-and post-lapsarian—in their final reconciliation.

The general ambience in which the children grow up, then, is one in which life, 'a painful riddle', is lived in 'the maze of this puzzling world' without any obvious key. And the narrator, as ironic anthropologist, frequently expresses this through the bewildered natives' attempts to make sense of things. Mr Glegg, for example, in his retirement has two hermeneutic obsessions. First, he has noticed remarkable but unexplained coincidences between 'zoological phenomena' in his garden and 'the great events of that time', such as the burning of York Minster. A parody of the narrator, he too is seeking that 'unity which shall bind the smallest things with greatest'. And secondly, he is bewildered by the fact that Mrs Glegg—'a creature made . . . out of a man's rib'—should be in a state of permanent contradictoriness. This 'was a mystery in the scheme of things to which he had often in vain sought a clue in the early chapters of Genesis.' St Ogg's, it is clear, is an ethos very different from Hayslope and its confident theodicies, one in which the search for keys, clues, and origins is never ending and never satisfied. It is, in fact, a community in transition between the verities of Tulliver's rural traditionalism ('water is water') and the new commercial capitalism (bringing steam-power to the mill) which has produced the Dodsons. The result is a fragmentation of values into sects, schisms and, as we have seen, families: 'Public spirit was not held in high esteem at St Ogg's'.

The fragmented world of the present contains within it, however, evidences of the founding faith of the original community. This is 'a town which carries the traces of its long growth and history like a millenial tree', and the narrator turned antiquarian is able to decipher these traces of mainly architectural evidence. The old Norman hall incorporating the older half-timbered banqueting-hall is still in use, comments the narrator, but is itself pre-dated by a piece of wall in the parish church, 'said to be a remnant of the original chapel dedicated to St Ogg, the patron saint of this ancient town, of whose history I possess several manuscript versions.' Reading the evidence of the stones in this way, the narrator cautiously arrives at the founding myth in manuscript form and then relates its briefest version—commenting with ironic pedantry that, 'since, if it should not be wholly true, it is at least likely to contain the least falsehood'—the legend of Ogg ferrying the woman in rags and her child across the river. Revealing herself to be the Blessed Virgin, the woman sanctifies Ogg and blesses his boat; 'thou didst not question and wrangle with the heart's need, but wast smitten with pity, and didst straightway relieve the same'. It is a complex historical account in which the narrative moves back to an uncertain legend, forward to the time of narration, and then back again thirty years to the Dodsons and Gleggs, deciphering the layers of history like a palimpsest. But the interpretative pressure exerted brings to light the crucial foundational story. This, by definition, needs no interpretation ('didst not question . . . straightway relieve'). But it has been forgotten, for 'the days were gone when people could be greatly wrought upon by their faith, still less change it'. The churches of all denominations are either lax or schismatic. It is a diagnosis confirmed by Dr Kenn at the end of the novel in accounting to Maggie for the absence of a shared ethic in the community.

By planting this kernel of the legend of origins in the first book of the novel in this way, George Eliot is sketching a possible closure to *The Mill on the Floss*. Is it possible, the narrative implies, for the neglected type—like Dinah's opening sermon in *Adam Bede*—still to foreshadow and be fulfilled by its antitype in the present? In the puzzling world of St Ogg's, made up as it were from the fragments of this primal ethic—and of which the Dodsons and Tullivers are schismatic elements—is it possible to reconstitute, however briefly and circuitously, a world of transparent ethical meaning?

. . . . .

Tom and Maggie are hybrids born into a world which believes in the fixity of species. Their dilemma, representative in one sense, is acute because of the comprehensive opposition between their parents' theories of life; the sisters agree 'that the Tulliver blood did not mix well with the Dodson blood.' The problem the novel examines in its brilliant first phase is; how do they begin to create their own world-views from these opposing elements out of which they are constituted?

The children's growth into self-consciousness is measured nostalgically against the unified world of the pastoral of childhood, that 'Eden before the seasons were divided, and when the starry blossoms grew side by side with the ripening peach.' A world without time is also a world 'where objects became dear to us before we had known the labour of choice, and where the outer world seemed only an extension of our own personality.' This is an absolute reality when a view of the world is, by definition, impossible. The world is the self, and the self is the world: 'the pattern of the rug and the grate and the fire-irons were "first ideas" that it was no more possible to criticize than the solidity and extension of matter.' It is a world so identical with itself that it can only be described in philosophical terms which have no relevance to it. It is, in fact, a pre-linguistic world where the physical, natural objects of flowers, fields, and hedgerows form a fully semiotic system: 'such things as these are the mother tongue of our imagination, the language that is laden with all the subtle inextricable associations the fleeting hours of our childhood left behind them.' It is also a non-narratable world which can only be glimpsed during pauses in the narrative, or before the narrative begins, and after it ends, as in the prelude to the novel. Here, in a scene of equipoise—river and sea, town and country, seed and harvest, man and nature—Maggie is transfixed in a time-less moment, 'rapt' as she watches the mill-wheel turning in 'dreamy deafness' and cut off by 'a great curtain of sound . . . from the world beyond.' In its fine balance between stillness and motion, the episode recalls a Wordsworthian 'spot of time' when the child, suddenly stationary, experiences the earth rolling 'With visible motion her diurnal round'. It is a moment safe from narrative temporality, cut off in its circularity not only by the curtain of sound but also by a time-gap of thirty years which the narrator's memory suddenly bridges.

This is the reality which the Dodsons and Tullivers have divided between them and, as soon as the narrative proper begins, Maggie is summoned into the house where her parents are quarrelling. Even this moment by the mill-wheel, at the age of nine, proves to be already a recovery of an earlier state, a brief ekstasis from the problems of her world which arise initially from the fact that both children are perceived as anomalies, mistakes of nature, by the two families. The Dodsons decide early that Tom belongs to their species—'in liking salt and eating beans'—while Mr Tulliver constantly sees his mother and sister in Maggie. The first difficulty with this is that the Dodson-Tulliver classification contradicts classification by gender. Dodson values are supposed to be transmitted through the women, Tulliver values through the men. Mrs Tulliver, therefore, wants a Dodson daughter as neat, pretty, and docile as her niece Lucy; while Mr Tulliver wants a son with the skills necessary to run rings round the lawyers—someone like himself, he imagines, with a little more education. Both are disappointed. Even the fixity of species can no longer be relied on in this puzzling world, concludes Mr Tulliver: 'That's the worst on't wi' the crossing o' breeds, you can never justly calkilate what'll come on't'.

Nevertheless, the two families don't give up easily. Maggie is tortured in various Dodson ways when she refuses to conform—'Little gells as cut their own hair', announc-es aunt Glegg, 'should be whipped and fed on bread-and-water'—while Tom is sent off to school to his ordeal by Latin grammar, a teaching device compared by the narrator to 'that ingenious instrument the thumb-screw.' Both regimens achieve the opposite of what they intend. The more Maggie is forced into the Dodson mould, the more her Tulliver characteristics of spontaneity and rebellion assert themselves; 'the small demons who had taken possession of Maggie's soul' become so strong that her actions become unintelligible to her mother. Similarly with Tom. His confident Dodson sense of the factual and the physical is undermined by the conventional and highly abstract education provided by the Rev. Stelling. As a manuscript deletion expressed it at this point, Tom's brain could 'mov[e] with much vigour and ability among things themselves, but [was] helpless among the signs and definitions of things.' His nature is emasculated. The perversity of the children's treatment is dramatised when Maggie visits Tom at his school and to everyone's surprise—considering the universal and 'superficial cleverness' of young girls—moves with vigour and ability among the signs and definitions of things in her own imaginative way. She has learnt, like her father, that there is no singular relationship between words and things, that a word, as she explains to a sceptical Tom, 'may mean several things—almost every word does.' This is a linguistic discovery sadly confirmed by the narrator when he questions Aristotle's praise of metaphorical speech—that ubiquitous tendency of 'so seldom declar[ing] what a thing is, except by saying it is something else'.

With the family bankruptcy, any hope of the children reconciling the opposing sides of their natures in a satisfactory way is lost. Tom leaves school, puts aside dreams and ambitions linking him with his father, and hands himself over to the Dodson side of the family to be fitted into the world of commerce. The pragmatic language of the self-made Mr Deane drastically reduces life's possibilities: 'If you want to slip into a round hole, you must make ball of yourself—that's where it is.' And to find out 'what the world is made of', Tom has to 'learn the smell of things' in the warehouse. Now it is the Dodsons' turn to educate him according to their lights into the role of the Industrious Apprentice—this part of *The Mill on the Floss* is a critique of that influential Victorian genre—but again the children evade this simple dualism. Tom does submit himself to learning the ways of the mercantile world of St Ogg's, yet his underlying single motive is eventually to re-possess the mill, the charged symbol of his father's life, and wipe out the family disgrace. The Dodsons never understand how this can take precedence over the accumulation of capital. As Tom excludes more and more from his life in order to achieve this end, his career becomes a slow and undramatic suicide. From the opposing elements he has inherited, circumstances have required him to combine his strong Tulliver pride with his pragmatic Dodson sense of fact into a formidable combination, binding 'together his integrity, his pride, his family regrets, and his personal ambition.' The two complementary but restricted sides of his nature fit together, denying him the obvious satisfactions of either the Dodsons or the Tullivers.

Maggie's career provides a very different model of the *Bildungsroman*. Cut off abruptly by the bankruptcy from her previous memories and satisfactions, Maggie's 'conflict between the inward impulse and outward fact, which is the lot of every imaginative and passionate nature' is exacerbated. Instead of Tom's concentration of purpose, there is increasing instability and oscillation. This is *her* long suicide. In many ways, the rhythm of her life is similar to her father's—a destructive oscillation between moods of emotional aggrandisement and fulfilment in which reality conforms briefly to the demands of the self, followed by moods of despair and fury when these demands are thwarted by an unmalleable world. When the disenchantments occur, something like her father's uncontrollable fury takes over: fits of 'anger and hatred . . . would flow out over her affections and conscience like a lava stream, and frighten her with a sense that it was not difficult for her to become a demon.' But hers cannot be a simple repetition of her father's Manichean struggle. With her passionate Tulliver nature there is combined a strong sense of external obligations, characteristic of the Dodsons, which denies her any clear-cut victories over the evil principle. The result is that whereas Tom fits together, through abstinence and self-denial, elements from the two families into a limited but unified purpose, Maggie embodies the more positive qualities—Tulliver spontaneous affection and Dodson sense of loyalty—in a life of increasing oscillation. These two versions of the *Bildungsroman,* masculine and feminine, constitute **The Mill on the Floss** even as they deconstruct each other.

We can now see that the conflict between their parents' families, which bankrupts and destroys the family at the mill, is internalised in the children's careers. This is what creates the powerful sense of unity and development in the novel, both organic and dialectical. In the background of the children's struggles are the shadowy paradigms of Dodson and Tulliver which are now being re-enacted in more complex permutations. For Tom and Maggie, this is both an opportunity and a premonition; it is, says the narrator, the situation of each generation which seeks within the dialectic of the family 'to rise above the level of the preceding generation'. But in this case the terms have been too rigidly established. What happens, therefore, between brother and sister is a new and more extreme—because more intimately personal—polarisation than the original Dodson and Tulliver conflict. It is also more anguished because their relationship inevitably con-

Griff House, Arbury, childhood home of Mary Ann Evans.

tains all the components of their family inheritance; it recalls that holistic unity of childhood, lost before the novel begins, but present in their memories. Both the Dodsons' and Tullivers' 'theory of life had its core of soundness' despite their inner contradictions, but the children never establish such a core. Tom's self-willed denials create a united but truncated life, while Maggie's character is continually decentered by the oscillations of clashing elements. Because of these differences, they quarrel with increasing violence, and yet they know that they need each other, that growth into a fuller life from their abbreviated childhood cannot be achieved separately. It is this which controls the pattern of their later lives, as it did their childhood: again and again they drift apart in alienation and misunderstanding, only to be re-united with increasing desperation and relief. Each character represents a discrete phase of a complete dialectical movement: Maggie's response to life is the prolonged and unresolvable oscillation of antinomies, Tom's is a premature and drawn-out synthesis. Her world is subject to a dramatic catastrophism spinning out of control; his is controlled by an undramatic gradualism slowly running down.

The title of the novel underlines both the similarity and conflict in the children's careers. Both are seeking to recover the mill which has been lost. Tom is intent on re-possessing it as a piece of property, free of debt, to restore the family's pride; Maggie is seeking to recover the state of unified consciousness which the mill has symbolised since childhood. The plotting of the novel shows their aims becoming increasingly antagonistic as their quests intensify: Tom becomes more single-minded than any Dodson, while Maggie's inner conflicts are more turbulent than even her father's puzzlement. As this occurs, each comes to represent and force on the other what they have rejected from their combined inheritance.

To achieve his purpose, Tom submits himself completely and at great emotional cost to the commercial system which defeated his father. Maggie, in contrast, seeks to recover everything that he has rejected—the dreams and demands of the self reconciled to the world through a reciprocated love—all fused into the unified consciousness of childhood at the mill. After each attempt and failure to achieve this—her childhood flight to the gypsies establishes the pattern—she must return to the mill for security and recuperation. Only from there can she start again. After Mr Tulliver's death, these departures and returns take the form of quarrels and reconciliations with Tom. If the present can't provide the key to the unity she is seeking, then her brother, her complementary half, is the means to the pastoral holism of childhood. The first separation occurs when Tom goes away to school and ends with the bankruptcy: the 'two poor things clung closer to each other.' They drift apart again and are brought together by their father's death: " 'Tom, forgive me—let us always love each other,' "says Maggie, 'and they clung and wept together.' Each time they move further apart as they seek their own fulfilments—each time it requires a more serious crisis to bring them together, until only the final ca-

tastrophe of the flood can achieve this. The progression of both their careers is, in their contrasting ways, back to the mill and what it symbolises—their interdependence and alienation.

From his position of self-denial, Tom sceptically observes and judges Maggie's erratic career. Until the very last, she refuses to accept the truth of the novel's realism that there is always a discrepancy between the inner desire and the outward fact. This can be denied, regretted, ignored in various ways; the Dodsons sought to circumvent it by curtailing the inner life, Tulliver by outmanoeuvring the devil's party which was gaining control of the world. Maggie uses both methods in various forms, unwilling to accept the impossibility of complete fulfilment. This unacceptable truth, which she has to win through to (and transform) at the end of her suffering, is stated early in her career by Thomas à Kempis: 'for in everything somewhat will be wanting, and in every place there will be some that will cross thee.' But characteristically, Maggie deploys the *Imitation of Christ* to satisfy separately both sides of her nature, so turning the message of renunciation into a precarious means of satisfaction. The Dodson belief in external obligation, and the determinism which accompanies this, are spiritualised into the ability 'of taking her stand out of herself, and looking at her own life as an insignificant part of a divinely-guided whole.' In parallel fashion, the Tulliver conviction that the world is really co-extensive with the self converts this form of self-abnegation into a creation of her own mind: 'Here, then, was a secret of life that would enable her to renounce all other secrets—here was a sublime height to be reached without the help of outward things—here was insight, and strength, and conquest, to be won by means entirely within her own soul, where a supreme Teacher was waiting to be heard.' In this way, the conflicting claims of the self and the world are reconciled, not through genuine renunciation, but through satisfying both sides of her divided nature in a temporary truce. 'Yet', says the narrator, 'one has a sense of uneasiness in looking at her—a sense of opposing elements, of which a fierce collision is imminent.'

Unlike Tom, what Maggie has not grasped is that 'renunciation remains sorrow'. She was 'still panting for happiness, and was in ecstasy because she had found the key to it.' The *Imitation,* she eventually discovers, offers a 'clue' to a life to be lived rather than a 'key' to be applied, a pattern or type to be fulfilled rather than a formula to be copied. These are two forms of repetition and imitation which the climax of the novel holds in tension. But the crucial importance of Thomas à Kempis's work—the most extensive example of intertextuality in George Eliot's fiction—lies in Maggie's persistent misinterpretations, mistranslations, and evasions of its real meaning—a meaning redefined, in her own way, by the novelist. The text is presented as a voice which speaks quietly but persistently through the novel, its crucial truths marked in the margins by 'the quiet hand' which indicates their importance to Maggie. This is the kind of interpretative mediation George Eliot is so aware of: the *Imitation,* itself a (translated) collage of biblical texts, is subjected to the marginal selection by an unknown hand in a copy sympathetically handed on to Maggie by Bob Jakin. And it is through Thomas à Kempis that her definition of ekstasis begins, from wish-fulfilment to 'an emphatic belief', a genuine 'enthusiasm'—'something, clearly, that lies outside personal desires, that includes resignation for ourselves and active love for what is not ourselves.'

Maggie is now seventeen, and this particular state of equilibrium can only be maintained by suppressing the full demands of her nature. Philip, on his re-appearance, makes her realise this—'Stupefaction is not resignation'—as he gradually insinuates his own claims and appeal into her life. As a result, 'a doubleness' creeps between her family loyalty and her friendship with the son of the man her father has cursed. Philip's attraction is that he seems to reconcile in his character the elements previously opposed in her life, the attachment to her brother and the desire for emotional and artistic fulfilment. As well as his intellectual and artistic interests, he is gentle, sympathetic, and understanding. He would be an ideal replacement for Tom: 'You would have loved me well enough to bear with me, and forgive me everything. That was what I always longed that Tom should do.' But although Philip offers a seductive synthesis, she tells him she cannot reject Tom. 'Maggie felt a great relief in adjourning the decision. She was free now to enjoy the minutes of companionship.' It is in these moments of adjournment, through a kind of psychological legerdemain, that Maggie characteristically achieves a brief fulfilment by acknowledging and suspending the discrepancies in her life—until Tom forces upon her the necessity of choice.

These choices, under which Maggie 'writhes,' become increasingly unacceptable and anguished because she accepts both the truth and the incompleteness of Tom's position. Whereas Tom acknowledges no disparity between conduct and feeling, Maggie stresses the inability of the former to express the latter: 'sometimes when I have done wrong, it has been because I have feelings that you would be better for, if you had them.' But Tom's reply contains a 'demonstrable truth' which he has lived by in the other half of this double *Bildungsroman:* 'if your feelings are so much better than mine, let me see you show them in some other way than by conduct that's likely to disgrace us all—than by ridiculous flights first into one extreme and then into another.' The language of this bitter confrontation echoes that of George Eliot's essay on Sophocles' *Antigone* [in *Essays of George Eliot,* edited by Thomas Pinney, 1963] which defines that 'antagonism between valid claims' in which neither side can be exonerated as 'blameless martyr' or condemned as 'hypocritical tyrant'. Here, they have been domesticated into an extreme form of 'that family repulsion which spoils the most sacred relations of our lives' These are the unpalatable truths that the brother and sister force on each other, and on this occasion it takes the death of their father to bring them together again.

After three years of teaching and submission, Maggie returns to St Ogg's for the final phase of her struggle and temptation. Coming under the influence of Stephen Guest,

the 'negative peace' of her life is disturbed irrevocably as she glimpses again the 'brighter aërial world' of her hopes. Again, she is seeking to balance in a state of unresolved equipoise her loyalty to Tom and her affection for Philip, each compensating for the other's deficiencies and so creating for herself a world without the labour of choice. (The earlier Philip who had seemed to reconcile her previous conflict has now become one antinomy in this next stage of the dialectic.) Tom's demands enable her to keep at bay Philip's emotional claims, while Philip provides her with the affection Tom denies. While the two men neutralise each other in this way, other appetites which they do not include assail and get possession of Maggie. Stephen's impact is so powerful because he not only brings the new element of sexual attraction, but he also duplicates, subsumes, and reconciles in his character the conflicting qualities of Tom and Philip. He is strong, influential, and decisive in the world of men, business, and action—the world, for example, where the future of the mill will be determined—and, as the son of the firm, he has achieved his position without the grinding effort which has stunted Tom. At the same time, he represents like Philip the world of art and intellect—as well as being an amateur geologist—but without Philip's uncertainty and physical disability. Stephen's presence, of course, briefly neutralises rather than resolves the others' claims, so that he becomes simply the next stage in the destructive dialectic of Maggie's career.

In this final stage, the concealed desires of both Maggie and Stephen are so intense, and yet their public obligations so clear, that they have to consign their feelings to the twilight world below the level of conduct and action where they can allow their minds to deceive themselves that nothing is happening. It is another form of the 'adjournment' of decision and choice at which Maggie has become so expert. The growth of their intimacy is a wonderfully dramatised piece of self-deception, as they continually assert their obligations to others while at the same time drifting together, like sleep-walkers in a timeless world without memory or choice. Stephen, like Maggie, 'wilfully abstained from self-questioning, and would not admit to himself that he felt an influence which was to have any determining effect on his conduct.' It is here, in the gap between feeling and conduct, words and actions, that their infatuation is allowed to develop. And it can do so the more easily because Maggie's commitment to Philip is an unspoken one, while Stephen and Lucy are in 'that stage of courtship . . . when each is sure of the other's love, but no formal declaration has been made.' What George Eliot captures so compellingly is the involuntary nature of their deepening attraction, once the earlier decision not to make decisions has been made. They become monomaniacs in a dream of their own emotions, out of contract with the external world which, paradoxically therefore, when it does impinge controls them helplessly and effortlessly. Afterwards it is possible to plead, as Stephen does, that their actions were determined for them, that their love was not of their own choosing.

Of special appeal to Maggie is the fact that this man, who apparently reconciles the clashing polarities of her previous life, is not only attracted by her—he is submissive. When he offers her his arm it is as if, at last, the unmodifiable empirical world of fact is amenable to her desire: 'the help is not wanted physically at that moment, but the sense of help—the presence of strength that is outside them and yet theirs—meets a continual want of the imagination.' In other words, it is another of those moments of ekstasis which provide Maggie with the outside standing-ground from which all conflicts can be reconciled and lifted to a higher unity. The dialectic of her life is punctuated by such moments, as we have seen, all of which are repetitions, anti-types of the holistic experience of childhood, symbolised by the trance in the presence of the mill-wheel: 'the presence of strength that is outside them and yet theirs'. But far from returning her to an earlier simplicity, these moments compound her conflicting loyalties when she has to return to the world of time and choice.

Stephen, in contrast, is fascinated by the alternations in Maggie's moods as she switches from her opium dream to resistance when her sense of duty re-asserts itself, and back again. This unpredictability, so different from Lucy's docility, captivates and challenges: 'such eyes—defying and deprecating, contradictory and clinging, imperious and beseeching—full of delicious opposites. To see such a creature subdued by love for one would be a lot worth having.' There is a considerable distance from this provincial infatuation to Grandcourt's sinister and sadistic subduing of Gwendolen's 'iridescence', but in both cases George Eliot juxtaposes male power and female plenitude. The delicious opposites represent possibilities as well as a challenge to masculine values; in their oscillations they articulate a vital spark which the men—Tom, Philip, Stephen—seek to appropriate and subdue. In other words, Maggie's search for, and inability to find, a 'key' to this puzzling world is now recognised as an inability to categorise her. If character is world-view, then this is inevitable; unable to impose a coherent interpretation upon the world, she is herself uninterpretable. Everyone knows where they stand with Tom, 'a character at unity with itself,' whereas they find Maggie baffling. For Stephen she is a 'dark-eyed nymph' with 'an alarming amount of devil'; while for Lucy her wide learning 'always seemed to me witchcraft before—part of your general uncanniness.' These are more sophisticated versions of Maggie's hybrid nature as a child, which baffled the family, and they develop the premonitory hints of the inevitable end to which such an innocent witch will come.

She bewilders and fascinates the fashionable and snobbish provincial world of St Ogg's in the same way. She challenges, as we have seen, the categories upon which its view of the world is constructed, and succeeds in confusing all her friends. As Stephen, for example, struggles against his betrayal of Lucy, fluctuating between his love for Maggie and his attempt to suppress and conceal it, his conduct comes to appear to Philip hypocritical. But this is a falsification: 'The conduct that issues from a moral conflict has often so close a resemblance to vice, that the distinction escapes all outward judgments, founded on a mere comparison of actions.' This is the ambig-

uous terrain into which Maggie is leading her friends and St Ogg's in general. Stephen, we are assured, was not a hypocrite, 'capable of deliberate doubleness for a selfish end,' yet his response to Maggie can only be constructed in these terms. The final phase of the novel is constructed to demonstrate the unreliability of this mode of interpretation and judgment. The signs are increasingly misread. Tom, Philip, and Lucy misconstrue the relationship between Maggie and Stephen, and unwittingly bring them closer together. As the world of feelings and motives drifts away from the world of actions and consequences, we seem to be entering a realm of experience where inner and outer bear only a fortuitous relation to each other. But Maggie is not prepared to abandon the idea of meaningful action. As Stephen forces his love upon her, she begins to articulate the problems and paradoxes that have bedevilled her life. One side of her nature agrees that their love is 'natural—it has taken hold of me in spite of every effort I have made to resist it,' but she opposes to this her sense of faithfulness and duty. So that when Stephen pleads he was not officially engaged to Lucy anyway, Maggie replies that 'the real tie lies in the feelings and expectations we have raised in other minds.' Dodson and Tulliver values are being synthesised belatedly into a more coherent world-view: the former provides the crucial significance of temporal priorities, the latter charges this with feeling. What reconciles them is the renunciation which Tom has been demonstrating in his parallel career and which has just enabled him to recover the mill.

As the structure of their careers suggests, Tom's character has become focused most narrowly and rigidly just as Maggie's conflict between the two sides of her nature is most unstable. She has begun to formulate a theory of renunciation, a restatement of Thomas à Kempis, but to put it into practice she has to resist the hypnotic fascination of Stephen. Renunciation must begin now 'when something like that fulness of existence—love, wealth, ease, refinement, all that her nature craved—was brought within her reach.' It is, of course, too late as the boating episode proves. Stephen seems to offer a momentary reconciliation of the previously competing elements of her life. She knows it will cut across and compound her existing obligations, but, when he presents himself, she is prepared once again to adjourn her moral dilemmas. It is another moment of false ekstasis as she stands outside her own life and allows the embodiment and reconciler of her inner conflicts to take control. 'Maggie felt that she was being led down the garden among the roses . . . all by this stronger presence that seemed to bear her along without any act of her own will, like the added self which comes with the sudden exalting influence of a strong tonic—and she felt nothing else. Memory was excluded.' The puzzling world, now in the shape of Stephen, at last seems amenable and submissive, and suddenly circumstances have combined to make their final meeting possible, perhaps inevitable. In this fatal moment of adjournment, they persuade themselves that everything is being determined by forces outside their control. It is another misapplication of Thomas à Kempis ('Forsake thyself, resign thyself, and thou shalt enjoy much inward peace') through which Maggie still seeks the atemporal world of childhood. The drifting on the river is a fine expression of this adjournment in which, inevitably, decisions are being made by their apparent postponement.

. . . . .

The more the factitious ekstasis excludes, the more devastating and problematic is the backlash of conscience. Up to now Maggie has tried to keep separate the legitimate, though narrow, claims of her family from the more attractive ones which corresponded to her own desires. But just when—here, on the drifting boat—she realises she has betrayed the former and is prompted to renounce the latter, she becomes aware of Stephen's own suffering. Suddenly the categories dissolve and merge: 'This yielding to the idea of Stephen's suffering was more fatal than the other yielding, because it was less distinguishable from that sense of others' claims which was the moral basis of her resistance.' Once the temporal priority of moral claims has been ignored, then subsequent claims begin to establish their own validity. But equally, as events force upon Maggie the consequences of her actions, the two sides of her nature—desire and duty—are being revealed as only artificially separated. The implications of this discovery, however, here at the end of Maggie's day of wish-fulfilment on the river with Stephen, are again adjourned: 'then came food, and then quiet reclining on the cushions, with the sense that no new resolution *could* be taken that day. Everything must wait till to-morrow.'

Between falling asleep in the sunset and waking to reality in the dawn, Maggie experiences a complex dream. Throughout the novel, as her dilemmas have multiplied, she has repeatedly longed to 'wake back' into an earlier time before fatal choices had to be made. In the dream there is a double return into the past. First, the myth of St Ogg's is re-created with Tom, Lucy, and Philip acting out its foundational ethic from which she and Stephen are excluded as their boat turns over and they begin to sink, clutched in each other's arms. Such an isolated and alienated future for the lovers is one possible ending of the novel. The second part of the dream into which Maggie 'wakes' from this nightmare is a return, not to the mythic, but to the familial past: 'she was a child again in the parlour at evening twilight, and Tom was not really angry'. This is another possible, though increasingly unlikely, ending. When she awakes properly, however, it is to a realisation that neither of these dream solutions is permissible; while, on the one hand, the 'irrevocable wrong that must blot her life had been committed', alienating her from family and friends, on the other, 'her soul, though betrayed, beguiled, ensnared, could never deliberately consent to a choice of the lower'. She is in limbo. She has 'rent the ties that had given meaning to duty, and had made herself an outlawed soul', but thanks to the other side of her nature, 'the consequences of such a fall had come before the outward act was completed.' She is neither able to go forward into an alienated future with Stephen or back into the past to rejoin her betrayed family and friends. And yet as always with Maggie, the nature of her impossible dilemma also defines the possibilities of her character. Can the mythic and familial be synthesised?

Through this dilemma, she comes finally to a true understanding of the meaning of renunciation: 'she had thought it was quiet ecstasy; she saw it face to face now—that sad patient loving strength which holds the clue to life—and saw that the thorns were for ever pressing on its brow.' Now, in her genuine *imitatio Christi,* suffering is accepted not as the key to life but simply as a 'clue'—and it is a clue to the fact that there is no final interpretative key, that there is always a discrepancy between inner and outer, and that this form of suffering is the meaning of renunciation. The crucifixion image expresses the genuine ekstasis which transforms, without adjourning or abandoning, the conflict between desire and duty. This, like her father's final puzzled questioning of his Manichean world, is a move to a genuine synthesis which gives her the strength and confidence to rebut Stephen's renewed arguments the next morning. She rejects his antithesis between natural law and outward ties, and in doing so moves beyond the Dodson-Tulliver conflict, which has bedevilled her life, towards a genuine reconciliation. Outward ties, she now sees, are not merely ritualised (Dodson) bonds; she redefines them as an acknowledgement of 'the reliance others have in us'. In other words, they must be transformed by an infusion of Tulliver emotion and fellow-feeling. She now begins to formulate a creed in which claims and feeling define and reinforce each other: 'if I had been better, nobler, those claims would have been so strongly present with me—I should have felt them pressing on my heart so continually, just as they do now and in the moments when my conscience is awake—that the opposite feeling would never have grown in me, as it has done: it would have been quenched at once.' Maggie is only enabled to say this because she has both fallen, and resisted the fall, into temptation; the drifting with the tide, followed by the refusal to complete the outward act, are the correlatives of this.

The temporary fall from grace has provided Maggie with a true glimpse of the meaning of renunciation. Duty and desire can be grasped simultaneously and, as they come together, they change their natures: outward claims become inner faithfulness, while emotional desires become loving sympathy. This accounts for the poignancy of her rejection of Stephen. Just as she has gained a new sense of the outer claims which she will now seek to honour, so her wish-fulfilling desire for Stephen is transformed into a loving sympathy with its own valid claims. Painful renunciation lies either way; each course of action both fulfils and denies legitimate claims, each victory is simultaneously a defeat. Only her idealism tells her that she must try to attain once more—this time through the rejection of all subsequent claims—the simplicity and unity of her childhood relationship. What view of the world does this finally represent? It is a martyrdom in which the full possibilities of life—those 'delicious opposites'—have been given full expression until, in the limbo where all categories have dissolved and merged into each other, Maggie has grasped the genuine clue of renunciation, the crown of thorns, which underpins and holds together all the antinomies in conflict. George Eliot redefines martyr-dom, most publicly in the life of Savonarola, not as a witnessing to some accepted truth, but as the acting out of the 'antagonism of valid claims'. The martyr embodies this antagonism, out of which the conflict of interpreta-tion arises.

The question now is, how will the moral conundrum of Maggie's renunciation be interpreted? As we have seen, in reaching it she has revealed the inadequacy of all cri-teria except for that moral intuition of which her whole life is the culmination. She has grasped the clue that there is no key to life, only the renunciation upon which her actions are finally based. How will such an interpretation be interpreted? The final book of *The Mill on the Floss* is occupied with this question in the same way that the final phase of *Adam Bede* shows Hayslope trying to come to terms with Hetty's infanticide. This is Maggie's trial and it consists of a series of interpretations (followed by judgments) of Maggie's rejection of Stephen and her re-turn to St Ogg's, the action which has confounded every-one's expectations.

The first and crucial reaction is Tom's. Not only is it essential for Maggie to re-establish their relationship, but her return to the mill is a sign of her new submis-sion, 'to submit in patient silence to that harsh disap-proving judgment against which she had so often re-belled.' In a limited sense Tom has been all along the embodiment of the renunciation she has at last discov-ered, as he indicates when she pleads with him: 'You struggled with your feelings, you say. Yes! *I* have had feelings to struggle with; but I conquered them.' This reminds us again that the novel is a double *Bildungsro-man* and that Tom has been making hard choices which have just resulted in the recovery of the mill, the mill which Maggie now needs as an emotional symbol of her new life. He interprets her liaison with Stephen in the harshest light as another attempt to sabotage his hard-won success. By turning her away from the mill, Tom now sabotages, in turn, her planned life of belated re-nunciation, for she needs him as 'a mind that we can never mould ourselves upon, and yet that we cannot endure to alienate from us.' In this penultimate meeting, they represent a confrontation between two contradicto-ry forms of renunciation, the only possible theories of life to come out of their hybrid natures. Tom's career of grinding endeavour and self-denial began began in re-nunciation and has apparently succeeded in its ultimate aim; in reality, his residence at the mill is the conclusion of a long suicide which has withered all feeling and sympathy. He has recovered the family home in order to turn his sister away in her need. In contrast, Maggie has refused the hard choices of life and allowed the oscilla-tions of her character to end in repeated defeats; in re-ality, her failures have led to the final discovery of true renunciation which the symmetrical paradoxes of the novel define as success. The irony of Tom's rejection is that it springs from the same source as Maggie's need: his repulsion towards her 'derived its very intensity from their early childish love in the time when they had clasped tiny fingers together, and their later sense of nearness in

a common duty and a common sorrow.' By his lights he has remained true to that early love, so that the logic of his life of renunciation is now to reject her in her be-trayal of it. The logic of Maggie's oscillating life is leading her to the discovery of a very different kind of renunciation. Her rejection by Tom prevents her putting into practice her sacrifice of expiation. This is the stale-mate their lives have reached before the flood.

The next attempt to interpret Maggie's actions is made by public opinion or, more specifically, 'the world's wife' in the chapter entitled 'St Ogg's Passes Judgment'. It is strik-ing how many times and in different ways the boating episode is scrutinised and its ambiguities interpreted ac-cording to different keys. St Ogg's interprets by results—'how else?—not knowing the process by which results are arrived at'—and we are provided with two contrasting assessments of Maggie's behaviour, the first on the as-sumption that she would return to the town as Mrs Stephen Guest, the second in the knowledge that she 'had returned without a *trousseau,* without a husband.' The favourable, though hypocritical, extenuation of the first version is replaced by the harsh, equally hypocritical, re-interpreta-tion of the second. As examples of a utilitarian calculus, both are rejected by the novel out of hand. Having shown how the dialectic of Maggie's life deconstructs all crite-ria, George Eliot becomes incensed in her satire when anyone seeks to judge her heroine. One is reminded of that intemperate paragraph in the Finale of *Middlemarch* which the novelist felt obliged to revise.

Even by the calculus of results, Maggie is condemned either way: if she came back married she could be looked down on in her lapse, if unmarried then she must have failed in her scheming. As she comes to be the scapegoat upon which St Ogg's heaps its hypocrisies, we are re-minded of the story Maggie herself recounts at the begin-ning of the novel from Defoe's *The History of the Devil:* 'That old woman in the water's a witch—they've put her in to find out whether she's a witch or no, and if she swims she's a witch, and if she's drowned—and killed, you know—she's innocent, and not a witch, but only a poor silly old woman. But what good would it do her then, you know, when she was drowned?' The inadequa-cy of such a hermeneutic is analysed most explicitly by Dr Kenn, the author's voice at this point and the next interpreter of Maggie's choice. He considers her desire to come back to St Ogg's, 'to remain where all the ties of your life have been formed—is a true prompting' to which the Church, representing the community, should respond by receiving the penitent with open arms. But, because 'the ideas of discipline and Christian fraternity . . . can hardly be said to exist in the public mind,' he lacks the confidence to advise her either to stay or leave. And the way in which the parish turns against him in his continu-ing support of the scapegoat confirms his diagnosis; he is tarnished and bewildered—like generations of readers—by the ambiguities she embodies. In the absence of a coherent community, all he can conclude is that 'her conscience must not be tampered with: the principle on which she had acted was a safer guide than any balancing of consequences.'

The principle Dr Kenn recommends is, of course, a denial of principle, a moral intuition not a general idea. As the narrator makes clear at the end of the chapter, in rejecting 'the men of maxims' with their 'general rules' and 'ready-made patent method' in favour of the maligned casuists: 'their perverted spirit of minute discrimination was the shadow of a truth to which eyes and hearts are too often fatally sealed—the truth, that moral judgments must remain false and hollow, unless they are checked and enlightened by a perpetual reference to the special circumstances that mark the individual lot.' This is casuistry seen in terms of the hypothetical method—tentative, dialectical, never finalised. But not only does it reject general rules, it seems unwilling in Maggie's case to formulate a tentative hypothesis: 'the question whether the moment has come in which a man has fallen below the possibility of a renunciation that will carry any efficacy, and must accept the sway of a passion against which he had struggled as a trespass, is one for which we have no master-key that will fit all cases.' Indeed, if you are able to 'apprehend' the problem, says the narrator, you are unable *ipso facto* to propose a solution. This exegesis is, of course, what Maggie, the exegete of her own life, had already discovered.

Judging by results is crass, the balancing of consequences is dangerous, general rules are reductive, and even casuistry hesitates to formulate a specific hypothesis. In effect, the final isolated phase of Maggie's career consists of a series of responses and reports, a kind of forensic commentary made up of conflicting opinions on her conduct. They alternate between support and rejection. Mrs Glegg is prepared to stand by her kin according to the Dodson ethic, which echoes Kenn's words in schismatic form: 'it was not for her own friends . . . to cast her out from family shelter to the scorn of the outer world, until she had become unequivocally a family disgrace.' But she is unable to overcome the stronger opposition of Tom. Next, Maggie receives a letter from Philip who has witnessed her martyrdom and through it been transformed: his own search for personal ekstasis has been succeeded by an 'enlarged life which grows and grows by appropriating the life of others.' But opposition and rumours of further scandal about Maggie spread through St Ogg's, so that the Miss Guests are in no doubt she must be prevented from ever marrying their brother. The scales are tipped again when Lucy visits Maggie and expresses her belief in her, but then in the final chapter Stephen's letter of reproach arrives and the oscillations intensify with Maggie 'battling with the old shadowy enemies that were for ever slain and rising again.' The 'long penance of life' in which she might change 'that passionate error into a new force of unselfish human love' now seems increasingly unattainable.

All of these reactions, these voices, reflect publicly the inner conflict Maggie has been unable to resolve, frustrated by Tom's final rejection which is the expression of his own impasse. As she sits in the darkness alone, this plethora of interpretations is reduced to two, those of Stephen and of Thomas à Kempis, texts which become alternate voices speaking through her. 'The words that were marked by the quiet hand in the little old book . . . rushed even to her lips . . . "I have received the Cross, I have received it from Thy hand: I will bear it, and bear it till death, as Thou has laid it upon me".' But equally strongly come Stephen's pleadings in his letter to which she can only beg forgiveness. There is no resolution to Maggie's dark night of the soul, only the 'cry of self-despair', her cry of dereliction: 'Am I to struggle and fall and repent again?' But then out of her despair comes again a movement towards the renunciation and self-abnegation she had glimpsed before Tom's rejection: 'O God, if my life is to be long, let me live to bless and comfort—'. Here, effectively, Maggie's unresolvable conflict ends and with it the novel. 'At that moment' the water rises, Maggie sets off on her rescue attempt, and verisimilitude is suspended: 'The whole thing had been so rapid—so dream-like—that the threads of ordinary association were broken.' The typology of the imitation of Christ is being fulfilled. After Gethsemane and the trial, after the crucifixion and the cry of dereliction, the final episode of the novel represents a brief resurrection: 'In the first moments Maggie felt nothing, thought of nothing, but that she had suddenly passed away from that life which she had been dreading: it was the transition of death, without its agony—and she was alone in the darkness with God.' As with **Adam Bede,** the whole narrative has been driving towards this point of uninterpretability—in that case, Dinah and Hetty sink in the darkness and come together in prayer and confession, here Maggie enters the darkness to be released from her intolerable struggle. She is allowed to begin life again, to emerge out of the darkness—her first memory was holding hands with Tom by the side of the Floss, 'everything before that is dark to me'—and be reconciled with her brother, not by expiation, but through the self-sacrifice of redemption. This is the form her resurrection takes because her faith ('Let me live to bless and comfort') has remained inviolate.

Maggie's conflict, dramatised in the earlier boating episode, could not be resolved, interpreted, or judged according to any principle or maxim. As the narrative became clogged with commentary, the heroine's dilemma became more and more intractable. Now, suddenly, narrative is transformed into simple story: the flood rises, Maggie rescues Tom from the mill, and they are drowned in each other's arms. These events take place in a world without introspection or prevarication, a world where 'we are all one with each other in primitive mortal needs.' 'Maggie knew it was the flood' and there is 'great calm in her' as she acts 'without a moment's shudder of fear'. 'In the first moments Maggie felt nothing, thought of nothing, but that she had suddenly passed away from that life which she had been dreading.' When she becomes aware of her situation on the water she remembers her old home: 'Her whole soul was strained now on that thought.' As she sets out to rescue Tom, she is 'hardly conscious of any bodily sensations—except a sensation of strength, inspired by mighty emotion', and, despite the obvious dangers, 'there was no choice of course, no room for hesitation.' There is no gap here between conduct and motive, actions and feeling; everything is in the present and response is immediate ('now . . . now . . . now . . .').

Even at the very end when sister and brother are in the boat together, the triumph of Maggie's martyrdom over Tom's comes without commentary or interrogation: 'It came with so overpowering a force—it was such a new revelation to his spirit, of the depths in life, that had lain beyond his vision which he had fancied so keen and clear—that he was unable to ask a question.'

What is this new reality where actions are so intuitive and transparent that they need neither justification nor interpretation? A reality where all the premises of George Eliot's realism—that character is not destiny, that words cannot say what they mean, that motives are never simple—are in abeyance? Where the flood is immediately recognised as 'that awful visitation of God,' and where Maggie's whole being is directed towards a single end in 'a story of almost divinely-protected effort'? And where characters return to their primary roles of brother and sister, expressing their deepest feelings through simple nomination: 'It is I, Tom—Maggie.' To which Tom need only reply, 'Magsie!' It is, of course, the world of melodrama which has emerged finally from the complex hermeneutics of her fiction. Though it appears to share the logic of a dream, George Eliot is keen to contrast it with that other boating episode which was described in dream-like terms and where the self was passive. Here, Maggie rows strenuously against the tide to achieve fulfilment through self-sacrifice. What validates the action of the melodrama is myth, in this case the legend of St Ogg's, the foundation myth which the town has lost sight of. As Peter Brooks has suggested [in his *The Melodramatic Imagination: Balzac, Henry James, Melodrama, and the Mode of Excess,* 1976], melodrama is 'the repository of the fragmentary and desacralized remnants of sacred myth'. Maggie 'wakes back', not only into childhood to recover her unity with Tom, their atonement, but also into the mythic reality of the original social contract. Her action combines the two dreams which, separated and contradictory in the first boating episode, now coalesce: she responds, like Ogg, to human need as well as 'waking back' into her childhood with Tom. From this coalescence some critics choose to emphasise the former, some the latter. As in *Adam Bede,* the melodrama is a form of typology: there, Dinah's sermon and prayers defined the type which the final meeting in the prison fulfilled, while here the early account of St Ogg and his response to need is the type of which Maggie's and Tom's self-sacrifice is the antitype. In both cases, the novels present the long and circuitous process of hermeneutic restoration through which the world of transparent meaning returns. St Ogg's 'inherited a long past without thinking of it, and had no eyes for the spirits that walk the streets,' but these are now given substance again by Maggie and Tom in their mutual need and its fulfilment.

The first boating episode was so problematic because, dramatising Maggie's contradictory motives as it did, it frustrated all the hermeneutic codes applied to it. In this second episode her motives are intuitive, unified, and unquestioned: 'the threads of ordinary association were broken' and she is disentangled from the complications of the web-like circumstance of George Eliot's fictional realism. This, however, does not mean that the final action itself is without ambiguity, as generations of critics have reminded us. The flood, as its description makes clear, is simultaneously both destruction and creation, both that of Noah and of Genesis. Maggie's action is both the ekstasis she has been searching for and the culminating example of those adjournments of her conflict which have punctuated the novel. Each victory can still be seen as a defeat. It has even been suggested [by Nina Auerbach, "The Power of Hunger: Demonism and Maggie Tulliver," in *Romantic Imprisonment,* 1985] that Tom would have been safe if he had stayed in the mill—'the house stood firm'—and not been lured into the boat. And, though Tom and Maggie by accepting each other's renunciation 'wake back' to their childhood love before renunciation was necessary, they die and, as Maggie commented in recounting the story of the drowned witch—'what good would it do her then?' And, finally, though Tom and Maggie re-validate the myth of St Ogg's, it is in a severely reduced, demythologised form: a sister tries to rescue a brother before they both drown. Even their epitaph—'In their death they were not divided'—has different meanings depending on whether the emphasis falls on 'death' or 'divided'.

Such ambiguities should not surprise us as the pressure of the whole novel is working against any clear-cut moral. For while their motives are at the last clear to themselves—they incarnate them in their final embrace—the double martyrdom of Tom and Maggie is acted out in a world without generally shared beliefs which will make of the drowning what it will. Maggie cannot be suddenly transformed from scapegoat and witch into martyr, saint, and prodigal; nor, in his different way, can Tom. The ambiguities of the novel as a whole remain. But the final episode is written in a different mode from the fictional, that of story, in Walter Benjamin's terms, which descends from and is taken up into legend and which eschews motivation and explanation. The ambiguity and the tension rest finally between two kinds of narrative, that of the logic of cause-and-effect based on observation and past experience, and that of typology which looks to the future and is based on faith, hope, and vision. In the former, repetition can lead only to frustration and disillusionment: the final reunion of Tom and Maggie is, therefore, a defeated and incestuous regression to childhood. In the latter, repetition is a fulfilment of the apocalyptic promise to 'make all things new', a forward-looking vision of the possible: the final reunion is then a repetition of their earliest unity lifted to a mythical level. In *The Mill on the Floss* we have, as it were, both narrative logics so that the novel and its legendary, melodramatic ending remain in tension. The novel can be read as a long digression between the childhood union of Tom and Maggie, fleetingly hinted at the beginning, and its fulfilment in their death; or more sceptically, as a piece of fictional realism which casts doubt both on the pastoral unified world of childhood which predates the novel and on their ecstatic reunion after the novel proper has ended. As the history of its reception shows, it has not been easy to read *The Mill on the Floss* in both ways at the same time.

Alan W. Bellringer (essay date 1993)

SOURCE: "A Story of Nature: *The Mill on the Floss*," in *Modern Novelists: George Eliot,* St. Martin's Press, 1993, pp. 43-62.

[*Below, Bellringer contends that the conclusion of* The Mill on the Floss *is suitable to the story.*]

The Mill on the Floss (1860) followed rapidly on *Adam Bede,* an altogether darker companion-piece, the characters being on a lower level generally, and the environment less romantic,' as the author herself remarked.

Set thirty years on from her first novel, it leaves the fertile slopes of the Midland shires for the hazardous watery plains to the east, where the Ripple runs into the Floss south of the Mudport estuary, whose tide, 'the awful Eagre', checks the impetuous current, coming up against it in spring 'like a hungry monster'. The constant fear of the riparian population there is of drowning. Dependent on wharf, water-wheel and black boats, it takes risks and thrives, beaver-like, trading with its continental counterpart in Holland. The narrator, pronouncedly feminine this time, envying the ducks and 'in love with moistness', introduces into this liquid destructive element her two adolescents, Tom and Maggie Tulliver, whose roles are to struggle and be immersed. The germ of the novel was the idea of an impending flood. With the flooding goes feeling, feeling for young life swept away. The first appearance of Maggie Tulliver is as a little girl in a 'chill damp' season, standing 'at the edge of the water', but, dreamt of, not seen, by the narrator, whose 'really benumbed' arms had seemed to be resting 'on the cold stone', an omen of death, surely, and of the tombstone at the end. Even after finishing the novel, George Eliot was glad to get away from thinking about Maggie and the mill, 'for she and her sorrows have clung to me painfully'. She later admitted to 'having an unused stock of motherly tenderness, which sometimes overflows, but not without discrimination'. So when

in March 1860 Lewes told Herbert Spencer to go in and comfort George Eliot ('she is crying her eyes out over the death of her children') he had no need to explain that the children in question were fictional. She was terminating *The Mill on the Floss.*

Some of the tears suggest deploring. This whole novel has a contentious air, with the disputants more than likely to topple and be engulfed, as happens literally to the reconciled brother and sister in 'The Last Conflict'. There is a first conflict too, and many others. Families argue, generations quarrel, lovers separate, siblings nag, friends fight. There are feuds, boycotts, lawsuits, tiffs and hagglings. The seasons are divided, trees cloven, hills parted, bridges broken, dwellings ruined, dolls defaced, locks jaggedly snipped, and within the individual there are contending passions, contradictory impulses, split loyalties. If at the end the hero and heroine, like David and Jonathan, were not divided, in their life they increasingly were. As U. C. Knoepflmacher has noted. *The Mill on the Floss* is founded upon 'Collision' which was the original title of Book V; he says, 'fragmentation is inherent' in its unstable world, which is pluralistic and puzzling (it has been, as is repeatedly said, 'too many' for Mr Tulliver, . . . and really for nearly everyone in it). Observing the rifts, the narrator is less patient in tone that we might expect; her interventions are sometimes ominous, sometimes poignant, always problematic, and though ready to turn humorous at any moment, in fact *very* humorous, they are not I think, very good humoured. Life is actually too sad, too short, too complicated for much of the posturing of the emmet-like inhabitants of St Ogg's, whose 'oppressive narrowness' irritates the narrator. In *The Mill on the Floss,* then, most of the comedy is satiric, supplied by the narrator, or when attempted by the characters not shared by those against whom it is directed. Umbrage is taken too quickly for that. On the other hand, there are no outright villains in the story. The negligence, casualness, pettiness and rigidity that reveal themselves are regarded by the narrator with an annoyance that can moderate into forbearance and understanding; she warns the reader who is inclined to be severe on the mistaken characters to 'remember that the responsibility of tolerance lies with those who have the wider vision'.

It is the river which leads the attention to the width of the environment; the Floss 'links the small pulse of the old English town with the beatings of the world's mighty heart'. This Wordsworthian phrase does not, however, mean that for George Eliot nature never does betray the heart that loves her. The rich responses to nature in the descriptive passages of the novel are overshadowed by the more prominent recognition of the randomness and destructiveness of life on earth. Much of man's productive experience is also violent; grinding, pulverising, crushing, sawing, hooking, burning, liquefying, all go on, some unintended. It is a world where accidents of all magnitudes will happen. The narrator, though not moody herself, is both amused and sobered by the moodiness of the characters and their underestimating of nature. The two main themes of the novel, growing up and falling in love, lend themselves to amusement, but it is stunted growth and frustrated love that are emphasised. In both long episodes, the first stretching, appropriately enough, for five of the seven books into which *The Mill on the Floss* is divided, aspiration has to give way to disappointment, pleasure to suffering, excitement to dilemma; in both cases there are repeated small movements of this sort, before painful climaxes. It is an intricate, detailed kind of tragic development not dependent on any single moral flaw or initial error, but pervading all aspects of speech and thought, personal feelings and social relations, so that the final catastrophic drowning of the young hero and heroine cannot surprise us. The author's claim that she had looked forward to the concluding tragedy 'with much attention and premeditation from the beginning' is borne out by even a cursory reading.

The mill itself in its constant motion is capable of a hypnotic effect, but that is deceptive. With its rushing water and booming, unresting wheel, 'like a great curtain of sound, shutting one out from the world beyond', it seems to belong to an order of things where time stands still and the imagination can recycle past experience. It produces in the narrator a 'dreamy deafness', heightening peacefulness. To the child Maggie too the mill seems 'a little world apart', which engages her by its monotony: 'The resolute din, the unresting motion of the great stones, giving her a dim delicious awe as at the presence of an uncontrollable force—the meal for ever pouring, pouring—the fine white powder softening all surfaces'. Maggie is a story-teller, like the narrator, though not a writer; their longing for a different world with 'great spaces' seems sustained by their aesthetic response to steady material forces, like the river itself. But the world of normal consciousness with intimation of change and mortality inevitably obtrudes itself with a jolt that is both wry and sad. The mill is, after all, a lot more than an adjunct to a picturesque rural house. It is an example of early industry, a human artefact, which had replaced a half-timbered building damaged in the floods three generations back and with a malt-house added. Massively productive, it needs servicing and could still be improved, 'especially if steam were applied'. It can also be badly damaged by the elements; at the end part of it falls with the crash of trees and stones against it and hurries down the flooding Ripple in the form of 'heavy fragments'. Though the mill can survive its disintegration, its rebuilding is not a 'thorough repair' to those who have known it in the past. The human present does not grow seamlessly from the past, but is divided from it by change and loss.

The mill is also, as a piece of working capital, the occasion of human disputes and tensions. Mr Tulliver, a headstrong, emotional, prejudiced, ill-informed man, who is obstinately vindictive to some and generous to others, is obsessed with his personal ownership of the mill. Descended from one Ralph Tulliver, who had reputedly 'ruined himself', Maggie's father is proudly conscious that Dorlcote Mill has been in his family's hands for a century 'and better'. Yet he is not keen to see it pass into the control of his own son, Tom; 'he'd be expectin' to take to the Mill an' the land, an' a-hinting at me as it was time for me to lay by an' think o' my latter end. Nay, nay, I've

seen enough o' that wi' sons'. The implicit contradiction in this attitude to inheritance is characteristic of Mr Tulliver's mentality. The mill, situated near the sea and dependent on a lively tributary current for its power, is affected by agricultural schemes upstream, dams, weirs, 'dykes an' errigations', which could have brought Mr Tulliver useful compensation, but which he resists more and more uncompromisingly. His forays into litigation bring about his bankrupcy. Closely involved with these hostilities is his decision not to train Tom as a miller, but instead to give him an expensive secondary education which will qualify him to be 'a help to me wi' these lawsuits' as a surveyor, solicitor or 'smartish' entrepreneur, though in the last case it is to be in a 'business as he can go into without capital', whatever that could be ('all profits and no outlay', he enviously suggests). Such a groundless desideratum contradicts what Mr Tulliver knows about agriculture, since he has lent his brother-in-law Mr Moss, a tenant-farmer working poor soil, a capital sum without interest, though his own property is already mortgaged for two thousand pounds on the freehold, one half of which sum went to his sister on her marriage to Moss. Mr Tulliver believes, however, the general report about himself as a 'man of considerable substance' and imprudently fails to pay off any of the capital on his mortgage. Instead he borrows from his wife's sister, Mrs Glegg, with whom he quarrels vehemently when she reminds him of the fact, eventually returning the money to her when she does not want it back. These details of Mr Tulliver's financial mismanagement emerge from the dialogue and commentary in the early chapters. As they are above the children's heads, though, given time, they would both have sorted things out more sensibly themselves, an atmosphere of menace overhangs the childhood scenes. Despite her father's kindness to Maggie when others criticise her, he is not the responsible parent she needs. His decision to spare his sister Mrs Moss the consequences of his financial embarrassments is certainly honourable and is upheld by Tom after his father is incapacitated; it derives from the father's fear that Maggie might one day be as dependent on someone's generosity as his sister now is. The risks he takes are too dangerous, given the number of his dependents. He does nothing to encourage Maggie towards any kind of independence.

It is not only Mr Tulliver's impecuniousness when he loses the main lawsuit that is so damaging; it is his totally vindictive, unforgiving attitude to his opponent's lawyer, Wakem, and to this man's crippled artist-son, Philip Wakem. Ironically by sending Tom to Stelling's for the education which turns out to be so useless for the practical-minded boy, the miller brings first Tom and then Maggie into close contact with Philip and sows the seeds of further unhappiness and animosity. Mr Tulliver has attributed devilish qualities to Wakem, believing that 'rats, weevils, and lawyers were created by Old Harry'. This combative theology, referred to mockingly by the narrator as 'rampant Manichaeism', is the 'form of Protestantism unknown to Bossuet', little different from Pagan revenge, which appears in a later chapter title: Mr Tulliver presented the Christian doctrine of mercy with a 'very unreceptive' surface, on which it could not find a nidus.

His feuding bent is itself an object of disapproval by his wife's family, the Dodsons, who regard it as a form of rigidity, not rectitude. For them it lacks both respectability and foresight; 'It 'ud be a fine deal better for some people . . . if they'd let the lawyers alone,' remarks Mrs Glegg, certain that the Tulliver family is 'going headlong to ruin'. But Tom, unfortunately, tends to admire and later to replicate his father's inflexibility, with adverse effects on Maggie's personal life. He also adheres to Mr Tulliver's dying wish that he should try and get the Mill back again from Wakem whenever he could ('It was in his family for five generations'), and he finally works off the price. Tom's return to the mill in order to vindicate his father leads indirectly to the catastrophe, since it was to rescue him from there during the flood that Maggie, in spite of having been made aware of the danger of lethal collision in the confused currents, jeopardised and lost both their lives.

The series of mistakes and crises which spoil the Tulliver children's lives has another source, apart from ownership instinct, namely, sexism. Mr Tulliver, determined to be the boss in his own home, chose Bessy out of the Dodson sisters because 'she wasn't o'er cute . . . ; for I wasn't going to be told the rights o' things by my own fireside'. Mrs Tulliver's intellectual inferiority to her husband brings him unexpected disadvantages, however. She retains 'a facility of saying things which drove him in the opposite direction to the one she desired'; she piques his pride by getting her sister Mrs Pullet to intervene with Mrs Glegg about recalling her loan so that he now insists on repaying it when he can ill afford it, with the result that the family breach is made 'more difficult to mend'. Mr Tulliver also finds it convenient to deceive Mrs Tulliver on the bill of sale on their furniture, 'the possession of a wife conspicuously one's inferior in intellect' being like other high privileges 'attended with a few inconveniences'. Later, still more seriously, Mrs Tulliver quite off her own bat alerts Wakem inadvertently to the possibility that he might rub salt in her husband's wounds by acquiring the mill himself and employing Tulliver to run it. The imagery used in this episode, comparing Mrs Tulliver with a fly-fisher with unalluring bait or a hen unable to dissuade a farmer from wringing her neck, and then as Wakem's victim, with a man turned fortuitously into mincemeat by 'some fly-wheel or other' or a roach considered by a pike to be 'excellent good eating', is especially harsh and sardonic. The legal profession, as entrencher of male privilege, is given no quarter. Wakem is not above petty revenge when the opportunity offers, though he is no evil schemer; he merely 'always knew the stepping-stones that would carry him through very muddy bits of practice'. Mrs Tulliver too is ridiculed for her exaggeration of her own personal influence. The subservience forced on her by her husband and the law leaves her a fetishism over her household possessions, ornaments and clothes as her main outlet.

The mismatch between the Tulliver parents does not only exacerbate family tension; it has direct genetic results, 'like as if the world was turned topsy-turvy'. Tom's relative slow wittedness and purposive honesty are attribut-ed to his taking after his mother's side, whereas Maggie's high intelligence, darkness and impetuosity are seen as Tulliver traits. 'That's the worst on't wi' the crossing o' breeds: you can never justly calkilate what'll come out'. Maggie first enters the room, in the narrator's phrase, as 'this small mistake of nature'. It is the people around her who mistake her capacity rather than nature's mistaking it, of course, but it is true that some of her traits are unfortunate. Her dreaminess and forgetfulness sit ill with her sharpness of judgment and pride in her own erudition. Maggie would have benefited so much from a literary education that it is quite deplorable that one has to be bestowed fruitlessly on Tom, while she is left to fend culturally for herself. She is clearly handicapped unfairly by the prejudices of the older generation. Her father's belief that Maggie's cleverness will 'turn to trouble' is self-fulfilling, enforced by the family's inhibitions about her upbringing. As a girl Maggie is not envisaged as having any vocation beyond being married or becoming Tom's housekeeper, for whom his caring for her will not exclude punishment, 'when she did wrong'. Tom, of course, perpetuates the unfairness into adulthood. The reasons for his growing alienation from his sister are intimately probed: they outlast the reconciliations brought about by affectionate feeling, shared memories and mutual distress. Maggie, deprived of the prospect of independence, becomes psychologically adrift, acting 'like a gypsy', emotionally over-reliant on the males in her life and enthralled to a private world of fantasy in which her desire for harmony and self-fulfilment can find expression, closely linked to her intense aesthetic appreciation of sounds and sights. Many of Maggie's mistakes are obviously comic, like her pushing her head through Tom's kite 'all for nothing', as are the stories she makes up, like the one about a young earwig that falls into a 'hot copper', but their cumulative effect is quite sinister. The death of Tom's rabbits through her neglect is hardly pretty.

Tom continually asserts his superiority to Maggie in his boyish skills, as in building playing-cards into the 'wonderful pagoda', which she inadvertently upsets. Tom 'would never do anything cowardly' like hitting a girl, but Maggie has no code on which to found a similar restraint. When Tom, angry with her for spilling his cowslip wine, excludes her from the pleasures of the 'insurrectionary visit to the pond', Maggie pushes the favoured Lucy into the cow-trodden mud. Such incidents, though lacking, as the narrator points out, the magnitude required of a tragic action by Aristotle, are bitter at the time and clearly anticipate the rough treatment meted out by Maggie to Lucy in adult life, when she involves herself with Lucy's boy-friend without warning her. They derive, of course, from Maggie's sense of exclusion; there had been 'no room' for Maggie on the peninsula of dry grass where Lucy had been escorted by Tom. She is ever diffident about making room for herself. When incautiously or desperately she attempts it, as in her flight from her own shadow to the gypsies, the result invariably is to make matters worse. Maggie's capacity for shrewd observation and reasonable generalisation comes out delightfully in the conversations in which she is permitted to join as a child, yet she is always somehow snubbed. Tom, for example, when she notes that all women in her experience are crosser than men, reminds her that she will be a woman herself some day and probably a 'nasty conceited' one, whom everyone will hate for being 'disagreeable'. The requirement of compliance presses unfairly on Maggie.

Her view of older women as too prone to complain and disapprove is certainly borne out by the behaviour of her mother and aunts, the Dodson sisters. Though E. S. Dallas in *The Times* review of 1860 went too far in designating them a 'degraded species' of 'stingy, selfish wretches, who give no sympathy and require none', their defensive narrowness is prominently displayed in that tone of saddened comedy which is perhaps George Eliot's single most felicitous effect. Aunt Pullet's whispered pride, for example, in possessing 'the best bonnet in Garum Church, let the next best be whose it would', combines conventional piety and materialistic bad taste in an enjoyable amalgam, but when her fascination with illness is adduced the effect is subtler. She regards Mrs Glegg's preference for home remedies (like 'chewing turkey rhubarb') to going to the doctor as dreadful, as 'flying' i' the face o' Providence; for what are doctors for if we arn't to call em in? And when folks have got money to pay for a doctor, it isn't respectable, as I've told Jane many a time. I'm ashamed of acquaintance knowing it'. This well-meaning illogicality has overtones of anxiety. Critical candour within the Dodson clan goes with a coolness to all those outside it, who seem to include in-laws.

The idea that families continually disperse and re-form themselves is too disturbing to be acknowledged by the Dodsons; mere cloning would seem more suitable to the childless Mrs Glegg, who criticises Mr Tulliver for spoiling Maggie: 'My father niver brought his children up so, else we should ha' been a different sort o' family to what we are.' That there might have been gain as well as loss is again too disturbing to be admitted; not that Mrs Glegg has not a lot of valuable advice to give. But it is given too unsparingly. Her warning that Tom is being educated above his fortune being rebuffed by Mr Tulliver, she turns on Mrs Tulliver, 'very much with the feeling of a cur that seizes the opportunity of diverting his bark towards the man who carries no stick. "It's poor work, talking o'almonds and raisins"'. Mrs Glegg is staking a claim for women's equal status in the discussion of serious affairs, yet at the same time weakening her case by her own ill-temper. She is determined to survive in the world she knows. When her husband accuses her of going on 'biting and snapping like a mad dog', Mrs Glegg is quick to pick up his hint about leaving her 'with everything provided for her'. She now takes a more conciliatory view of the future, the narrator adding wittily, 'For if people are to quarrel often, it follows as a corollary that their quarrels cannot be protracted beyond certain limits'. Though R. Ebbatson [in *George Eliot: The Mill on the Floss,* 1985] may be right to refer the finely balanced tone here to the cunning combination of the narrator's 'highly educated syntax and diction' with the Gleggs' 'ignorant ideas and colloquial diction', Mrs Glegg, in spite of her quaint beliefs, does not lend herself easily to stereotyping.

Constricted to the sphere of the small investor rather than that of the independent businesswoman, she feels both the 'pleasure of property' and the importance of a reliable network of kin-relationships. The pride she takes in having all her cousins with money 'out at use' or owning 'some houses of their own, at the very least', is partly self-protective, but it is also related to impersonal principle, to the 'great fundamental fact of blood', which should ideally apply universally to all men and women, but is in provincial society limited to near-relatives. When Maggie all but loses her reputation, it is Mrs Glegg who insists on still attributing honour to her while she can, bursting forth in severe reproof of Tom's severity with, among others, the remark that 'fair-play was a jewel'. The narrator's analysis is especially cogent here; 'it was a case in which her hereditary rectitude and personal strength of character found a common channel along with her fundamental idea of clanship as they did in her life-long regard to equity in money matters'. The water-imagery suggests a positive, if confined, forward movement of limited benefit. The absence of irony is very noticeable.

Maggie's own conspicuous failure to get her act together in the more expansive conditions of her young adulthood is presented in terms of both blockage and uncontrolled impulse. Though she appears to be at one with the strong growths of nature, the branching ash, the dog-roses, the 'grand Scotch firs', Maggie's emotional involvement with the deformed artist, Philip Wakem, subjects her to all sorts of stress. One has a 'sense of opposing elements, of which a fierce collision is imminent', in observing her, as we are told. Her loyalty to Philip traps her into furtiveness, since the relationship, if known, would infuriate her father and, as it actually does, earn her brother's contempt. The 'urgent monotonous warning' voice of conscience comes athwart the harmonious voice of friendship. Philip sees himself as tending her mind, which is withering in its youth 'for want of the light and space it was formed to flourish in', but it must be said that he gives her little idea of equality or independence. His aim is to possess her by converting her 'sweet girlish tenderness' into eventual love. The 'certain dim background of relief' of which Maggie is conscious when Tom forces her separation from Philip probably, therefore, includes a suppressed repugnance to a personality which presses need without arousing a sexual response. The episode with Philip already belongs in its subtlety to the last part of the novel, which Joan Bennett [in *George Eliot,* 1948] sees as anticipating the 'new development' of psychological fiction seen through the lens of an observer, since the narrator gives the required perspective in comments and hints. Philip's culpability is, of course, admitted, while not regarded as gross.

Maggie's ultimate trial, her affair with Stephen Guest, Lucy's acknowledged young man, gains its extraordinary power because of the contrast with its predecessor. Maggie's physical passion is now awake, and Stephen's accompanies it; the process of self-discovery is shown effectively on both sides. Unfortunately, traces of moral cowardice and deviousness, notably in dealings with Lucy, accumulate until an unresolvable dilemma is reached. Maggie drifts into the position where she has, in effect, eloped with Stephen, but refuses his proposal of marriage, because of her wish not to injure Lucy and Philip. Even though the strong sexual attraction between Maggie and Stephen has invalidated the two relationships which it has supplanted, Maggie feels her honour would be compromised if she went on with Stephen. She is unlucky in giving her conduct the appearance of casualness without having the confidence to build on her own natural desire. It must be added that no one else is particularly helpful. The jealous Philip writes to Maggie that the strong attraction proceeded from only one side of her and Stephen's characters, 'belonging to that partial, divided action of our nature which makes half the tragedy of the human lot. I have felt the vibration of chords in your nature that I have continually felt the want of in his'. It may be true that nature as well as culture divides people in the way Philip means, that some and not others have an inherent disposition to sensitivity and aesthetic pleasure: he assumes that a gradual union based on cultural affinity is superior to a tempestuous affair based on physical passion. Stephen is certainly shown at first as following intellectual tastes rather than searching out truth for himself, but he speaks respectfully of Dr Kenn's views on taxation at one point and matures rapidly under Maggie's influence. She is led by Stephen's devotion to doubt 'the justice of her own resolve' in renouncing him; she has not the sense that she will succeed in her resolution without further falls and repentance. Philip's argument only adds to her confusion, making her doubt if her love for Stephen would have lasted.

Lucy, too, is less than perceptive when she spontaneously praises Maggie for her moral superiority in giving Stephen up. And Dr Kenn, in approving Maggie's following her conscience in giving priority to remembered loyalties, shows her no way forward: he abstains from advising Maggie that an ultimate marriage with Stephen would be the least evil in a situation where 'each immediate step was clogged with evil'. Each of these attitudes can be justified, but Tom's reaction is particularly forbidding. Limited in intelligence by nature and only superficially polished by his education, Tom feels hostility and repulsion, based on his observation of Maggie's past untrustworthiness, her habit of changing her perverse resolves into 'something equally perverse'. Unlike his aunt Glegg, he assumes the worst of Maggie and refuses to have her under his roof. Prejudiced and coldly inflexible in his sense of family disgrace, he expresses a loathing of her character and conduct. Maggie's secrecy in her relations with Stephen, sustained partly to avoid injury to Lucy, but in fact increasing the chance of it, touches Tom's pride in his uprightness and blinds him to his own interest in the affair. With Stephen's affections elsewhere engaged, Lucy might have come to entertain Tom's long-cherished feeling for herself with favour: she is aware that 'he always had that pleasant smile' when he looked at her. But instead of counselling caution, Tom reinforces Maggie's guilt, so that 'it seemed as if every sensitive fibre in her were too entirely preoccupied by pain ever to vibrate again

to another influence. Life stretched before her as one act of penitence'. It is mainly this exclusion from her brother's forgiveness which turns Maggie's alienation into despair.

At times Tom's and Maggie's characters seem split from a single personality. Had they been united into one, his prudence and self-command and her sensibility would have produced an integrated personality. But divided, they tend to clash unpredictably, leaving both vulnerable to accident and sudden pressures. Maggie's emotionality is not by itself tragic, the narrator insists. Though she is caught in conflicts between 'inward impulse and outward fact', internally her passionate sensibility can make 'her faults and virtues all merge in each other', giving to her impatience and vanity 'the poetry of ambition'; left communing with herself alone in her 'bright aerial world again', Maggie is able to enjoy piano-playing and music-theory, where her romantic and idealising qualities, associated with tenderness, forgetfulness and gentle remorse, can express themselves without harmful consequences. The narrator questions, in this connection, Novalis's dictum that character is destiny. Had Hamlet's close relatives not impinged on his life, his destiny would have been normal. Even the passion for Stephen which shocks Maggie with its 'invisible influence' is not in itself dangerous. There is no inherent reason why Philip's dream of an 'awful crash' at the foot of 'a glistening, green, slimy channel of a waterfall' should ever actually befall Maggie. The arbitrary nature of the flood which drowns her is, then, part of the design. Where character comes in is in the tendency to renunciation and passivity followed by impulses of affectionate loyalty, which makes Maggie vulnerable to misfortune; liable, but not predestined. Unable to make 'a world outside' herself as men do, she forces herself back from the affair with Stephen into isolation, searching, as Philip reminds her, for 'a mode of renunciation that will be an escape from pain'. The pain comes from her consciousness of the unhappiness and disapproval of others. It is in this state of restlessness that she is caught by the flood and reminded of her old home. She is impelled by an 'undefined sense of reconcilement with her brother'. His trust in her is likely to be restored by the 'primitive mortal needs' produced by the natural calamity. The dangerous mission of rescue is undertaken, then, in response to the emotional pull of home and family, and, when he is rescued by Maggie, Tom is duly awakened to a new sense of unsuspected 'depths in life' lying beyond his supposedly 'keen and clear' vision. The depths include the value of memory, mutual support in times of emergency and spontaneous courage. But under Maggie's temporary ascendancy as these influences are at play, Tom unquestioningly responds to Maggie's impulse to see Lucy, a highly risky undertaking with the cross-currents then at their fiercest. Tom's agreement to row vigorously to Tofton, where Lucy should be, is conditioned by 'a certain awe and humiliation' which he feels in contemplating his sister's intensity of life and effort at this crisis. His old boyish plan to have a well-stocked ark ready for the floods is forgotten. Tom's habitual caution, checking the Tulliver impetuousness, is now in suspense under Maggie's imperious foolhardiness. The consequenc-

George Henry Lewes in 1867.

es are fatal, since she ignores the 'distinct idea of danger' that had pressed on her in an agony of dread a little earlier. The interaction of the two personalities, traced with intricate patterning, thus contributes to the circumstances which surround their deaths, without controlling them.

The Mill on the Floss has, then, a consistent tragic technique throughout. It avoids suicide and murder (Maggie arrests her father's arm before he can flog Wakem to death with his 'riding whip'), it displays frightening error and accident, and it investigates causation as being highly subtle and intricate. The repeated references to death by drowning and dangerous waters suggest an environment which can move on without people, since people do not fully understand and control it. Mr Tulliver's head-scratchings over old Harry's role in this puzzling world, where if you drove your wagon in a hurry you might 'light on an awkward corner', his wife's awareness that people will believe in a Providential judgement upon herself for her having done 'summat wicked', Mrs Deane's view that trouble 'isn't sent without a cause' in an unpredictable world, or Luke's doctrine that God dislikes things 'out 'o

natur' such as lop-eared rabbits, are all untrained attributions of purpose and meaning to an environment, the implication of which is that human mentality is unfit for the world in which it is placed. Proper use is not made of accumulated information.

In Mrs Glegg's day, the St Ogg's mind 'did not look extensively before or after. It inherited a long past without thinking of it'. Since there had been no floods recently, people thought that the next day would be like the last, 'and the giant forces that used to shake the earth were forever laid to sleep'. Such ignorance or complacency is in its way as disturbing as metaphysical certainty, though it was 'received with all the honours in very good society'. The narrator with her 'large vision of relations' speaks from a vantage point of scientific study, where 'every single object suggests a large sum of conditions' but there are still no easy answers to physical or moral problems. The young people in *The Mill on the Floss* rise towards the level of understanding of the narrator above 'the mental level' of the previous generations, to whom they are nevertheless tied by heart-felt memories, filial loyalty and confused respect. Familial ties effect a kind of moral pattern, but they can reinforce unnecessary constraints and weaken the vigilance required if one is to avoid rash moves and accidents. Maggie is, therefore, not ready for the affair with Stephen Guest, which throws her off her feet and involves her in concealment. The flood puts even that in perspective, being so much vaster and more dangerous. It alone can be used to make sense of the novel's title, when in the unpredictable movements of water the river comes to the mill, which is normally on the Ripple, not on the Floss. No one takes any precaution against the flood though several characters have riverside homes. Even the resourceful Bob Jakin, who has invested his savings in pleasure-boats for hire, is swept away helplessly in his own boat 'far past the meeting current'. The heavy rains which bring on the flood are a variation of nature not unknown to the inhabitants, yet are too rare and irregular to be expected, occurring more frequently, indeed incessantly, elsewhere, in 'the counties higher up the Floss'. To Maggie the flood is 'that awful visitation of God which her father used to talk of'. The half-hearted recourse to theism, associating doctrine with the previous generation, highlights human vulnerability and ignorance in the face of a menacing environment, which is often deceptively calm. The flood can be aligned with innumerable other random events in the novel, major and minor, central and peripheral, on and off-stage, such as the accident which had crippled Philip Wakem 'in infancy', the turn of the tide which carries Maggie and Stephen past the point of no return at Luckreth, the fortuitous combination which goes to every individual conception and birth, destructive fires of various sorts, chance meetings and attractions, the lump in the throat which destroys Jap the dog, the illness which takes off Mrs Deane, the timing of Mr Tulliver's two strokes. In a world where cockatrices and wolves have not 'ceased to bite', aggression, ailments, coincidences and mistakes are interwoven in human experience. Maggie's grandmother, whom she resembles 'as two peas', died young, we are informed. The unhappy Jetsome, Wakem's illegitimate son, is 'pitched off his horse in a drunken fit'. Mr Tilt has 'got his mouth drawn all o' one side'. Poor Gratton shot his mother by accident. Aunt Pullet's constant harping on her own demise is a comically selfish version of the same theme of insecurity: 'I may go off sudden when I get home to-day—there's no telling'. Even her critics make similar assumptions. She is rebuked by her sister Mrs Glegg for lamenting the dropsical Mrs Sutton's death as much as if their cousin Abbott 'had died sudden without making his will.'

Less neurotic or calculating in her reaction to personal misfortune is the mill-hand Luke's mother, who fought sore against 'shortness o' breath when it fust come on', but afterwards 'made friends wi't'. That seems to be the best course when one of the 'thousand natural shocks that flesh is heir to' arrives, to try to get used to it. Special effort may be needed when larger adversity strikes, as when 'the rowers pulled anew' when the vision of St Ogg was seen during ancient floods, and yet there are no guarantees of security in the known world; the records of the past are themselves subject to mischance and misinterpretation. The narrator inclines to the briefest manuscript versions of the St Ogg legend since it is 'likely to contain the least falsehood'. Human motives are mixed and often casual, running parallel to the myriad coincidences of teeming natural life.

The Mill on the Floss seems especially concerned with tiny prolific life, especially insects; the entomological allusions seem to be questioning the significance while also asserting the claims of individual young people like Tom and Maggie Tulliver. Mr Glegg, inexhaustibly occupied with the caterpillars, slugs and insects in his garden, may be ridiculous in noticing 'remarkable coincidences between these zoological phenomenena and the great events of that time', such as the burning of York Minister. But the question of the scale of events, the interconnection between large and small, the vastness of the universe which dwarfs human concerns, both wittily and gloomily preoccupies the narrator. The flood which 'swept as sudden death over all smaller living things' threatens the novel's characters too, by this token. In nature's enormity, minute threats may be as important as huge ones, and similarly in social life. When Riley recommends Stelling to Mr Tulliver as Tom's tutor, with all the incalculable, bad consequences which the novel traces, the ingredients that go to the advice are not delicate scruples, but 'little dim ideas and complacencies' which make up the auctioneer's consciousness; the narrator explains ironically, 'One cannot be good-natured all round. Nature herself occasionally quarters an inconvenient parasite on an animal to whom she has otherwise no ill-will. What then? We admire her care for the parasite'. The personification of nature as a caring but inconsistent female is itself sharply ironic. Nature has evidently no will as such at all and cannot reasonably be admired in the way a caring person may be. We know that the parasite is as subject to adversity as the animal to irritation from the parasite. The 'superannuated bluebottle' which Tom punishes instead of Maggie, like the toad he tickles and cockchafers he desires to master, is an inferior creature subject to arbitrary

torment; it is noticed 'exposing its imbecility in the Spring sunshine, clearly against the views of Nature, who had provided Tom and the peas for the speedy destruction of this weak individual'. The erudite wit here not only mocks the boy's search for excuses, but also questions simplistic biological metaphysics. Nothing in the way of views or a destructive purpose can be attributed to nature. The relation of the bluebottle to the boy's aimless frustration is random. It is Tom's father's fault to 'interpret any chance-shot that grazed him as an attempt on his life'. All such rationalisations lead to confusion; every case must be examined sceptically on its merits; otherwise it will be misread like the indeterminately featured human faces which nature turns off 'by the gross' only to conceal the 'rigid, inflexible purposes' which underlie them, thus refuting simple people's 'confident prophecies'. Despite the overwhelming, pervasive stream of allusions to the dangers of nature in *The Mill on the Floss,* the narrator's own superb, intelligent, knowledgeable voice, embracing, in beautiful studied prose, geography, history, science, the arts and philosophy, by its even, patient, amused, female tone counteracts the pessimism with an implicit claim to advancement and survival.

The importance of education as a theme in the novel appertains to this narrator's voice; Maggie clearly could have become as learned, if not as astute, as the speaker. Why did she not? How far did she get? The novel continually poses these questions. The fact that she is excluded from the classical education provided for Tom is, as I have indicated, especially poignant, for she would have made a lot of it, perhaps even improved it. That type of education is itself rigid and unadapted. Indeed the Rev'd Stelling's educational practices resemble the automatic behaviour of animals which human intelligence is supposed to have superseded; like that of a beaver 'understood to be under the immediate teaching of nature', who instinctively builds a dam, even in captivity; 'the absence of water or of possible progeny was an accident for which he was not accountable'. This statement is ironically attributed to a beaver, but the unaccountability of people in the face of accidents is a theme of the novel. Stelling applies Euclidian geometry and Latin grammar to Tom, irrespective of Tom's circumstances and aptitude. He is compared (as a teacher) with an 'animal endowed with a power of boring a hole through a rock'. To Tom lessons provide a 'mill-like medium of uninteresting ideas'; he can no more understand their justification than 'an innocent shrew-mouse imprisoned in the split trunk of an ash-tree in order to cure lameness in cattle' can understand superstition. The torturer of small animals is now himself like a tortured small animal. George Eliot's powerful satire here does not exclude the idea that it may be difficult to tailor educational reform to individual needs like Tom's (Philip seems to have made more of Stelling's offerings), but it gains a special thrust from her acute awareness of the injustice suffered by girls in schooling. If education generally in those days 'was almost entirely a matter of luck—usually of ill-luck', with a father having no more certainty of selecting the right school for his son than someone taking a 'dice box' in his hands, for girls it was much worse. They came out of school untrained for life, with no other part of their 'inherited share in the hard-won treasure of thought . . . than shreds and patches of feeble literature and false history'. Maggie is thus ignorant of psychology and science, and of morality too in its deepest sense. Scott and Byron are not subtle and modern enough for her, not as regards women's problems certainly. Her mind withers in a 'vulgar level' of culture. Not being 'a thoroughly well-educated young lady with a perfectly balanced mind', Maggie has no framework of reference in which to find her bearings during her emotional entanglements with Philip and Stephen. The narrator's irony concerning contemporary perfectibility in female education (a bid for sympathy with her heroine) does not invalidate the point that Maggie is culturally disadvantaged. What strikes us most in her encounters with Stephen is her vulnerability. His fine bass voice and 'well-marked horizontal eyebrows' make her glance vibrate (the appeal of his masculinity is unmistakable), but she is unaware that he sings in 'a provincial amateur fashion'. The deficiencies in Stephen's culture are clearer to the reader than to Maggie. His easy exposition of one of the *Bridgewater Treaties on the Power, Wisdom, and Goodness of God, as manifested in the Creation* (1833-6) shows sincerity and a concern for topicality, but not the painful intellectual honesty of which Maggie is capable. By the time she has refused to elope with him, Stephen has learned the hard way that Providence is unreliable, though he persists against the odds in trying to make the best of a bad job. Maggie is too demoralised to match him here and languishes in a bewilderment not altogether unlike her father's, faced by a puzzling world. Her soul goes out to the 'Unseen Pity that would be with her to the end', a prevision of enduring religious consolation, which is ironic in view of the actual imminence of her end.

Maggie's end gives rise to mixed feelings precisely because it would be so natural for her to pray for it, given her state of self-despair, yet she does not. In some ways Tom's death is the more tragic of the two, since he had learned already what his capacities were and at the very end was beginning to learn about his limitations too. Tom picks up his business skills as he goes, helped by his uncle Deane, to whom a formal education such as Tom had received from Stelling is a 'raw material in which he had had no experience'. He picks up his investment skills from the packman Bob Jakin, who, if a bit of luck turns up, is always 'thinking if I can let Mr Tom have a pull at it'. Jakin's friendly support for his Tulliver friends is more than sentimentality; it is part of a general philosophy of observing the signs, recovering from adversity, insuring against loss, profiting from unexpected windfalls, which humanity needs if it is to progress. The untutored Jakin made his original nest-egg as a reward for his sharpness in dousing a fire at Torry's mill. Bob's opportunism includes the ability to take advantage of the presence of accidentally damaged goods and persuade others to overlook what may be superficial or negligible chance flaws. It is in this way that Aunt Glegg learns the 'breadth of his thumb.' Moth-holes and mildew, the effects of insects and dampness, two phenomena to which the novel continually draws our attention, are, in Bob Jakin's view, 'sent by Providence' to foster his trade in cheap woollen kerchiefs: 'it's took me a deal o' study to know the vallyu o' such articles'. Such un-ideal but useful commerce is regarded as comically benign by the narrator, who extends the metaphors from cloth-making, moisture and animal vitality into her accounts of Maggie's emotional experience, where there is no corresponding sense of confidence and ingenuity. Maggie's daily life is a woof, absorbing a 'tissue of vague dreams' and 'threads of thought and emotion', but here imperfections can have abysmal results. There are times when feeling can overwhelm restraints, 'can rise and leave flood-marks' never reached again; at such times speech is both 'sincere and deceptive'. The perception that language itself is not to be trusted as the expression of some inner truth, that consciousness is not necessarily coherent, but grabs at chance associations, presenting them as analogies, is a further, deeper scepticism present in *The Mill on the Floss*. At one point the narrator challenges Aristotle on this issue, regretting the fact that 'intelligence so rarely shows itself in speech without a metaphor—that we can so seldom declare what a thing is, except by saying it is something else'. Changing the metaphor not only alters one's conception of a thing (the metaphor here being the classics as culture or ploughing); it is a sign that human intelligence is frequently arbitrary and unreliable even at its most prestigious and committed.

To regard the flood and drowning as inevitable or conclusive or, conversely, to discover that they do not necessarily follow from the characters' actions is, therefore, to miss the point of *The Mill on the Floss* completely. Such a drastic use of nature to symbolise culpability or irresponsibility would have been regarded by George Eliot as fallacious. In a reported conversation with a Russian interviewer, who inquired how Maggie Tulliver would have dealt with her powerful passions had she not drowned, George Eliot replied, 'Have you not found that life, itself, often provides unexpected possibilities and resolutions through death? Indeed, for me it has often been the certitude of death that has given me the courage to live.' This Darwinian view of death as a means to more highly organised life does not diminish the tragedy of the loss of individuals, particularly of young, gifted individuals, whom we have come to know in detail in an extended work of fiction. But it shows death as a condition of Maggie's and Tom's lives (in a context of acknowledgement that such things occur) which is what *The Mill on the Floss* presents to us as at once terrible and possible.

It is a work in which hopes are successively dashed and memories of the 'primitive fellowship of kindred' revived to sustain a complex response to life's uncertainties. The supreme moment in which Tom and Maggie 'in an embrace never to be parted' live through again 'the days when they had clasped their little hands in love' is not, then, sentimental melodrama, but an assertion of the need for human mutual support, in spite of prejudice and error, in the face of nature itself. The finale, read with bated breath by generations of readers, seems to me properly integrated with the novel as a whole.

FURTHER READING

Bibliography

Fulmer, Constance Marie. *George Eliot: A Reference Guide.* Reference Guides in Literature, edited by Joseph Katz. Boston: G. K. Hall & Co., 1977, 247 p.

    A comprehensive annotated bibliography of published critical commentary on Eliot's life and works, 1858-1971.

Biography

Cross, J. W. *George Eliot's Life as Related in Her Letters and Journals.* New York: AMS Press, 1965, 646 p.

    Official biography, originally published in 1885. Cross, whom Eliot married shortly before her death, promoted the somber, sibylline image of his wife which dominated Eliot biography and ciriticism for many years.

Haight, Gordon S. *George Eliot: A Biography.* London: Oxford at the Clarendon Press, 1968, 616 p.

    The definitive biography.

Criticism

Carlisle, Janice. "The Mirror in *The Mill on the Floss*: Toward a Reading of Autobiography as Discourse." *Studies in the Literary Imagination* XXIII, No. 2 (Fall 1990): 177-96.

    Studies autobiographical references found in *The Mill on the Floss*.

Doyle, Mary Ellen. "*The Mill on the Floss*." In her *The Sympathetic Response: George Eliot's Fictional Rhetoric,* pp. 57-91. London: Associated University Presses, 1981.

    Emphasizes the character of Tom Tulliver as the "joint protagonist" of the novel, contending that "the repeated parallels and contrasts of Maggie and Tom all suggest that he is not merely her foil but is parallel to her in thematic and structural importance."

Drew, Elizabeth. "The Tragic Vision: George Eliot (1819-1880)— *The Mill on the Floss*." In her *The Novel: A Modern Guide to Fifteen English Masterpieces,* pp. 127-40. New York: Dell Publishing Co., 1963.

    Maintains that Eliot was the first sociological novelist, stating that "no one before George Eliot had established the close, organic relationship between the nature of the individual and the nature of the society in which the individual has developed and in which it has to function."

Emery, Laura Comer. "*The Mill on the Floss*." In her *George Eliot's Creative Conflict: The Other Side of Silence,* pp. 5-54. Berkeley: University of California Press, 1976.

    Offers a neo-Freudian interpretation of the perceived underlying fantasy as applied to the characters and to Eliot.

Higdon, David Leon. "Failure of Design in *The Mill on the Floss*." *The Journal of Narrative Technique* 3, No. 3 (September 1973): 183-92.

    Criticizes the ending of *The Mill on the Floss,* contending that no conclusion in nineteenth-century literature "has been considered less successful and less satisfactory."

Jones, R. T. "*The Mill on the Floss*." In his *George Eliot,* pp. 19-30. London: Cambridge University Press, 1970.

    Approves the lengthy treatment of Maggie Tulliver's childhood as important to the characterization of her as an adult.

Law, Jules. "Water Rights and the 'Crossing O' Breeds': Chiastic Exchange in *The Mill on the Floss*." In *Rewriting the Victorians: Theory, History, and the Politics of Gender,* edited by Linda M. Shires, pp. 52-69. New York: Routledge, 1992.

    Politicized analysis of both the symbolic value of the river and specific references within the novel to its material function in generating steam power and agricultural technology.

Leavis, F. R. "George Eliot: The Early Phase." In his *The Great Tradition: George Eliot, Henry James, Joseph Conrad,* pp. 42-64. Garden City, N. Y.: Doubleday & Company, 1954.

    Asserts that a weakness of *The Mill on the Floss* is the characterization of Stephen Guest and Maggie Tulliver's attraction to him.

Liddell, Robert. "*The Mill on the Floss*." In his *The Novels of George Eliot,* pp. 51-71. New York: St. Martin's Press, 1977.

    Contends that *The Mill on the Floss* "is rushed to its conclusion" and states that the faulty development of the latter part of the book is "largely referable to the author's self-identification with the heroine."

Moldstad, David. "*The Mill on the Floss* and *Antigone*." *PMLA* 85, No. 3 (May 1970): 527-31.

    Outlines "the conflict between the conventions of society and individual judgment" at the center of *The Mill on the Floss* and in *Antigone*.

Newton, K. M. "Memory and *The Mill on the Floss*." In his *George Eliot: Romantic Humanist, A Study of the Philosophical Structure of her Novels,* pp. 97-122. London: Macmillan, 1981.

    Studies the use of memory in *The Mill on the Floss* as a unifying factor between past and present and as a moral authority.

Rubin, Larry. "River Imagery as a Means of Foreshadowing in *The Mill on the Floss*." *Modern Language Notes* LXXI, No. 1 (January 1956): 18-22.

    Contends that the ending of *The Mill on the Floss* is alluded to throughout the novel, stating that "the author's long, deliberate preparation virtually makes the drowning artistically inevitable."

Skilton, David. Introduction to *The Mill on the Floss,* by George Eliot, pp. v-xii. London: J. M. Dent & Sons, Ltd., 1976.

    Suggests that the theme and subject of *The Mill on the Floss* was not unique to Eliot but was "in a sense typical of a whole phase in British intellectual and social history."

Smith, Jonathan. "The 'Wonderful Geological Story': Uniformitarianism and *The Mill on the Floss.*" *Papers on Language and Literature* 27, No. 4 (1991): 430-52.

    Focuses on the impact of contemporary evolutionary theory on the form and content of Eliot's novel.

Stewart, Garrett. "Transitions: The Brontës, Gaskell, Eliot, Thackeray, Hardy." In his *Death Sentences: Styles of Dying in British Fiction*, pp. 99-138. Cambridge: Harvard University Press, 1984.

Analyzes the ironic and metaphoric aspects of the double drowning in *The Mill on the Floss.*

Stump, Reva. "*The Mill on the Floss*: The Special Circumstances." In her *Movement and Vision in George Eliot's Novels,* pp. 67-109. Seattle: University of Washington Press, 1959.

    Examines the single "fairly direct line of personal positive movement which is held in constant tension by the more ponderous negative movement of a whole society."

Additional coverage of Eliot's life and career is contained in the following sources published by Gale Research: *Concise Dictionary of British Literary Biography,* **1832-1890;** *Dictionary of Literary Biography,* **Vols. 21, 35, 55;** *DISCovering Authors*; *Nineteenth-Century Literature Criticism,* **Vols. 4, 13, 23, 41;** and *World Literature Criticism.*

Alexander Hamilton

1755(?)-1804

American statesman and essayist.

INTRODUCTION

One of the Founding Fathers of the United States of America, Alexander Hamilton is best known as the principal author of the classic work on constitutional government, *The Federalist* (1787-88). However, his enduring influence on American matters of state lies equally with his reports to Congress on the financial affairs of the Federal government. Hamilton is chiefly responsible for the design and establishment of Federal institutions, and above all for the financial system which helped consolidate the states into a nation, and then put that nation on its path toward an industrial economy. Hamilton is often considered the rival of Thomas Jefferson, for while Jefferson promoted a democratic agrarian society, and sided with France in matters of foreign policy, Hamilton foresaw a manufacturing economy founded on secure financial principles, and he sought for the United States a government closer to the British model.

Biographical Information

Hamilton was born on the island of Nevis in 1755, the illegitimate son of Rachel Faucett Lavien and James Hamilton. Orphaned early, Hamilton worked for a merchant on the island of St. Croix. His precocity and business acumen were quickly noted, and he was sent to the American colonies to be educated. Hamilton enrolled at King's College in New York (now Columbia University) but his studies were cut short by war with the British; he was appointed captain of an artillery company, and in 1777 was appointed aide-de-camp to General George Washington. In 1782 Hamilton was admitted to the New York Bar and appointed a New York delegate to the Continental Congress. He attended the Federal Constitutional Convention of 1787, and his essay-writing campaign for ratification of the Constitution resulted in *The Federalist*, which also contained essays by John Jay and James Madison. Hamilton's appointment as Secretary of the Treasury in 1789 prompted the reports on finance and manufacturing which Jacob E. Cooke has called Hamilton's "enduring claim to fame." Following his resignation in 1795, Hamilton practised law in New York City and continued his interest in New York and national politics. His attacks on political rival Aaron Burr resulted in the latter's challenge to a duel. He reluctantly accepted, and he met Burr on the morning of July 11, 1804 in Weehauken, New Jersey. Hamilton was mortally wounded and died the following day.

Major Works

Hamilton's most enduring work is *The Federalist* (1788), the series of political essays he wrote with Madison and Jay. Hamilton was responsible for two thirds of the papers, which were written under the pseudonym "Publius" to support ratification of the Constitution, but now provide a contemporary commentary on the intentions of the Founders. Taken as a whole, *The Federalist* is considered a classic treatise on constitutional government; it provides a theoretical foundation for the United States Constitution. In addition, in his capacity as Secretary of the Treasury, Hamilton wrote a series of important and influential reports. His *Report on Manufactures* (1791) argued that only by establishing an industrial economy would the United States be free of reliance on foreign markets. This work, and others such as the *Report on a National Bank* (1790) and the *Report on the Public Credit* (1795), sought to expand the powers of central government. Throughout his life Hamilton was a prolific pamphleteer; under a variety of pseudonyms—Publius, Phocion, Catullus, Tully, Pacificus, Lucius Crassus—he used the press to engage in vigorous political argument. These essays, along with his legal writings, attest to Hamilton's faith in the written word as both a guarantor of civil order and a spur to action.

Critical Reception

Hamilton's writing sought and often resulted in political change. From the outset he engaged in a polemical dialog with his political rivals, and his ideas prompted strong partisan reactions of acceptance and rejection. Hamilton's success as a rhetorician is measured less in critical reviews than in the shape of American government during his lifetime and since, for the acceptance of his arguments brought on practical remedies. The success of Hamilton's ideas and the persuasiveness of his rhetoric determined, in large measure, the industrialized capitalist character of the United States, and spawned the judicial, governmental and financial institutions which sustain it. Hamilton's conservatism, his attachment to monarchy and aristocracy, and his claim that self-interest is a political constant have made him a clear target for criticism, but the widespread implementation of his ideas is testament to his capacity for compromise.

PRINCIPAL WORKS

The Federalist (essays) 1788
*The Mind of Alexander Hamilton (essays, speeches and letters) 1958
†*The Papers of Alexander Hamilton* 27 vols. (essays, letters, speeches and notebooks) 1961-1987
‡*Selected Writings and Speeches of Alexander Hamilton* (essays, speeches and letters) 1985

*These works were written between 1757 and 1804.
†These works were written between 1768 and 1802.
‡These works were written between 1775 and 1803.

CRITICISM

Thomas Jefferson (memoir date 1818)

SOURCE: "The Anas: Explanations of the 3 Volumes Bound in Marbled Paper," in *The Writings of Thomas Jefferson*, edited by Saul K. Padover, The Heritage Press, 1967, pp. 107-20.

[*The third president of the United States, Jefferson is best known as a respected statesman whose belief in natural rights, equality, individual liberties, and self-government found its fullest expression in the Declaration of Independence. During the early years of the American republic Jefferson, by his outspoken opposition to Federalist policies, became the leader of the Republican (now Democratic) Party. As such, he was a bitter opponent of the Federalists' chief spokesman, Hamilton. In the following excerpt from a portion of his memoirs originally published in 1818, Jefferson offers a contemptuous portrait of Hamilton.*]

Hamilton was not only a monarchist, but for a monarchy bottomed on corruption. In proof of this, I will relate an anecdote, for the truth of which I attest the God who made me. Before the President set out on his southern tour in April, 1791, he addressed a letter of the fourth of that month, from Mount Vernon, to the Secretaries of State, Treasury and War, desiring that if any serious and important cases should arise during his absence, they would consult and act on them. And he requested that the Vice-President should also be consulted. This was the only occasion on which that officer was ever requested to take part in a cabinet question. Some occasion for consultation arising, I invited those gentlemen (and the Attorney General, as well as I remember), to dine with me, in order to confer on the subject. After the cloth was removed, and our question agreed and dismissed, conversation began on other matters, and by some circumstance, was led to the British constitution, on which Mr. Adams observed, "Purge that constitution of its corruption, and give to its popular branch equality of representation, and it would be the most perfect constitution ever devised by the wit of man." Hamilton paused and said, "Purge it of its corruption, and give to its popular branch equality of representation, and it would become an *impracticable* government: as it stands at present, with all its supposed defects, it is the most perfect government which ever existed." And this was assuredly the exact line which separated the political creeds of these two gentlemen. The one was for two hereditary branches and an honest elective one: the other, for an hereditary King, with a House of Lords and Commons corrupted to his will, and standing between him and the people. Hamilton was, indeed, a singular character. Of acute understanding, disinterested, honest, and honorable in all private transactions, amiable in society, and duly valuing virtue in private life, yet so bewitched and perverted by the British example, as to be under thorough conviction that corruption was essential to the government of a nation. Mr. Adams had originally been a republican.

Henry Cabot Lodge (essay date 1882)

SOURCE: "Professional Life—Duel and Death," in *Alexander Hamilton,* 1882. Reprint by Houghton, Mifflin and Company, 1883, pp. 237-84.

[*Lodge was an American politician, historian, and author, who coedited the* North American Review *with Henry Adams from 1873 to 1876, and who later served as associate editor of the* International Review. *His works of American history and biography include* A Short History of the English Colonies in America *(1881),* Alexander Hamilton *(1882), and* Daniel Webster *(1883). In the excerpt below, from his biography of Hamilton, Lodge summarizes his subject's accomplishments in glowing terms.*]

Hamilton is one of the statesmen of creative minds who represent great ideas. It is for this reason that he left the deep mark of his personal influence upon our history. His principles of finance, of foreign affairs, of political economy, and of the powers and duties of government under the constitution may be found on every page of our history, and are full of vitality to-day. But Hamilton is identified with two other ideas which go far deeper, and which have been the moving forces in our national development. He did not believe in democracy as a system of government. He strove with all his energy to make the experiment of the constitution succeed, but he doubted its merit at the outset, and finally came to the conclusion that in its existing form it was doomed to failure. He believed in class influence and representation, in strong government, and in what, for want of a better phrase, may be called an aristocratic republic. Curiously enough, this theory was put in practice only in the South, where Hamilton had scarcely any followers.

The other great idea of which he was the embodiment, was that of nationality. No other man of that period, except Washington, was fully imbued with the national spirit. To Hamilton it was the very breath of his public life, the essence of his policy. To this grand principle many men, especially in later times, have rendered splendid services, and made noble sacrifices; but there is no single man to whom it owes more than to Hamilton. In a time when American nationality meant nothing, he alone grasped the great conception in all its fullness, and gave all he had of will and intellect to make its realization possible. He alone perceived the destiny which was in store for the republic. For this he declared that the United States must aim at an ascendant in the affairs of America. For this he planned the conquest of Louisiana and the Floridas, and, despite the frowns of his friends, rose above all party feelings and sustained Jefferson in his unhesitating seizure of the opportunity to acquire that vast territory by purchase. To these ends everything he did was directed, and in his task of founding a government he also founded a nation. It was a great work. Others contributed much to it, but Hamilton alone fully understood it. On the other side was Jefferson, also a man who represented ideas, that of democracy and that of a confederacy, with a weak general government and powerful states threatening secession. The ideas which these two men embodied have in their conflict made up the history of the United States. The democratic principles of Jefferson, and the national principles of Hamilton, have prevailed, and have sway to-day throughout the length and breadth of the land. But, if we go a step farther, we find that the great Federalist has the advantage. The democratic system of Jefferson is administered in the form and on the principles of Hamilton, and while the former went with the current and fell in with the dominant forces of the time, Hamilton established his now accepted principles, and carried his projects to completion in the face of a relentless opposition, and against the mistaken wishes of a large part of the people.

To attempt to measure the exact proportions of a great man is neither very easy nor perhaps very profitable. This biography has been written to little purpose if it has failed to show the influence of Hamilton upon our history, and this of itself is a title of the highest distinction. It is given to but few men to impress their individuality indelibly upon the history of a great nation. But Hamilton, as a man, achieved even more than this. His versatility was extraordinary. He was a great orator and lawyer, and he was also the ablest political and constitutional writer of his day, a good soldier, and possessed of a wonderful capacity for organization and practical administration. He was a master in every field that he entered, and however he may have erred in moments of passion, he never failed. Weakness and incompetency were not to be found in Hamilton. Comparisons are valueless, because points of difference between men are endless. John Marshal ranked Hamilton next to Washington, and with the judgment of their great chief justice Americans are wont to be content. But wherever he is placed, so long as the people of the United States form one nation, the name of Alexander Hamilton will be held in high and lasting honor, and even in the wreck of governments that great intellect would still command the homage of men.

L. H. Boutell (review date 1885)

SOURCE: "Alexander Hamilton," in *The Dial,* Chicago, Vol. VI, No. 61, May, 1885, pp. 5-7.

[In the excerpt below, Boutell provides a laudatory account of Hamilton's life and works.]

When New York ratified the Federal Constitution, the people of that State celebrated the event by a festival procession, in which was borne a flag with the portrait of Washington on one side and that of Hamilton on the other. The enthusiasm of the hour, which recognized these great men as foremost among the founders of the republic—as the men who knew how to build and save a State—has been justified by the political history of succeeding years, and especially by the fierce and bloody struggle of our own time. That we are to-day a united and powerful nation, and not the weak and hostile fragments of a once great republic, is owing to the triumph of those sentiments of nationality which Hamilton strove throughout his life to foster and strengthen.

To estimate aright Hamilton's greatness, we need to remember that while he was a many-sided man, and great in many different ways, as statesman, lawyer, financier, orator, writer and soldier, he was greatest in the successful solution of those difficult problems of civil government which most profoundly affect human welfare, but in respect to which men are most liable to err. While the science of political economy was in its infancy, he exhibited a mastery of its principles which placed him beside Adam Smith and Turgot. He saw, as with an unerring instinct, the kind of government best suited to the needs of a handful of people as they emerged from the war of Independence, and which would also prove adequate to the needs of the greatest of nations. Although he had never been in Europe, he was able to forecast the movements of European governments with a correctness that led Talleyrand to say of him, "He divined Europe."

In his lifetime, it was the fashion of his opponents, the State-rights men of that day, to call him a monarchist. His writings abundantly prove the falsity of this assertion. He was, above all things, a practical statesman, and never wasted an effort in attempts to establish a government unsuited to the genius of the people. But what he did believe in, and saw was essential to the very existence of the nation, was a strong central government, supreme in its own domain, springing from the people and acting directly upon them, and sufficiently expansive to meet the wants of a continental republic. To establish such a government, he exerted to the utmost all the powers of his richly-gifted nature. This was the great work of his life; and for this work he is entitled to rank, not merely among the greatest statesmen of his time, but among the great benefactors of the race.

No man ever labored more diligently to produce an enlightened public opinion. His tongue and pen were never idle. He had an abiding faith in the ability and disposition of the people to form correct judgments on public affairs when properly instructed. As a political controversialist, he had no equal. His bitterest enemy, Aaron Burr, said of him: "If you put yourself on paper with him, you are lost." Jefferson thought that Madison was the only person competent to measure swords with him. He was not a literary artist like Burke. His power as a writer consisted in the clearness of his statements and the strength of his arguments. He persuaded men, not by stirring their passions or charming their fancies, but by convincing their judgments.

No adequate report of Hamilton's speeches has been preserved, from which to judge of his powers as an orator; but from the testimony of the ablest of his contemporaries, and from the effect which his speeches produced, we know that he is entitled to rank among the great orators of the world. His greatest efforts as an orator were put forth in the Constitutional Convention at Poughkeepsie. When that convention of sixty-five members assembled, forty-six were opposed to the adoption of the Constitution, and only nineteen were in favor of it. The opposition to it was headed by Governor Clinton, one of the most astute and influential politicians of his time. Some of the ablest debaters in the State were arrayed on the same side, and at their head was Melancthon Smith, a most acute dialectitian. Day after day the great debate went on, the speeches of Hamilton filling men with wonder at their power, and melting them to tears with their pathos; but on the test votes the majority against the Federalists was always two to one. Finally, Melancthon Smith, overpowered by the arguments of Hamilton, gave up his opposition, and one after another of his followers joined the Federalists, till on the final vote there was a majority of three in favor of the Constitution. We know of no triumph of oratory in modern times surpassing this.

Although the specimens of Hamilton's oratory which are preserved to us are exceedingly meagre, it is not difficult to see what was the secret of his oratorical power. He had the requisite physical qualities—the charm of voice, of eye, of action. He had the requisite intellectual equipment—clearness of perception, argumentative power, and fullness of information. And in addition, he had the moral earnestness, the intensity of conviction and the force of will essential to arouse and sway an audience.

Hamilton's loyalty to his adopted country is one of the most interesting features of his character. His faith in its future greatness and his devotion to its welfare never wavered. And when the clouds of disaster were gathering thick and dark above it, he exclaimed, "If this Union were to be broken, it would break my heart." Opposition to slavery was no uncommon thing in these early days, but few expressed that opposition so strongly as Hamilton. "I consider," he said, "civil liberty, in a genuine, unadulterated sense, as the greatest of terrestrial blessings. I am convinced that the whole human race is entitled to it; and that it can be wrested from no part of them without the blackest and most aggravated guilt." His views on this subject, as on every other, took a practical form. On the 14th of March, 1779, he wrote a letter of introduction for his friend, Colonel Laurens, to the President of Congress, in which he advised the raising of negro troops in the South. After stating the reason why he thought the negroes would make good soldiers, and why such a plan seemed necessary for the safety of the South, he goes on to say:

> An essential part of the plan is to give them their freedom with their swords. This will secure their fidelity, animate their courage, and, I believe, will have a good influence on those who remain, by opening a door to their emancipation. This circumstance, I confess, has no small weight in inducing me to wish the success of the project; for the dictates of humanity and true policy equally interest me in favor of this unfortunate class of men.

The first two papers in the volume before us illustrate the precocity of Hamilton's genius. Very young men have exhibited marvellous skill in music and painting, in mathematics and the acquisition of languages. But we know of no other instance in which a boy in his eighteenth year has produced such essays on government as these papers on the rights of the colonies. His great admiration for the English Constitution at first inclined him to side with the mother country. But maturer reflection satisfied him that the colonies must be governed by laws of their own making, and be taxed by their own representatives, or lose forever the qualities that made England great. The case of the colonies against the mother country was never more ably stated than in these essays. On their first appearance they attracted universal attention, and so marked was their ability that they were attributed to the pen of John Jay. From this time on, Hamilton was constantly seeking, by letters, by pamphlets, and by newspaper articles, to impress others with his views of public affairs. And this he did, though his days and nights were full of the most arduous labors. Some of the papers in this volume were produced amid the confusion and excitement of the camp, others were the work of hurried moments snatched from the exacting labors of the law. An interesting anecdote, illustrative of Hamilton's habits in this respect, is related in the autobiography of Jeremiah Mason. Speaking of William Coleman, the editor of the New York "Evening Post," Mr. Mason says:

> His paper for several years gave the leading tone to the press of the Federal party. His acquaintances were

often surprised by the ability of some of his editorial articles, which were supposed to be beyond his depth. Having a convenient opportunity, I asked him who wrote, or aided in writing, these articles. He frankly answered that he made no secret of it; that his paper was set up under the auspices of General Hamilton, and that he assisted him. I then asked, "Does he write in your paper?" "Never a word." "How, then, does he assist?" His answer was, "Whenever anything occurs on which I feel the want of information. I state the matter to him, sometimes in a note. He appoints a time when I may see him, usually a late hour of the evening. He always keeps himself minutely informed on all political matters. As soon as I see him, he begins in a deliberate manner to dictate, and I to write down in short hand (he was a good stenographer); when he stops, my article is completed."

Hamilton's fame as a financier, as the creator of the national credit, is so great that we are apt to overlook his greatness in other respects. But as a lawyer he stood at the head of the New York bar, and his opinion on the constitutionality of the act creating the United States Bank has been a model for all succeeding arguments on the implied powers of the Constitution. The manner in which this argument was produced (it was in great part written in a single night) illustrates the rapidity with which his mind worked, even upon the greatest themes. The famous opinion of Chief-Justice Marshall on this subject was little more than a reproduction of Hamilton's arguments.

Hamilton began life as a soldier, and though his position as a staff-officer, after the first year of the war, gave him but little opportunity for the display of soldierly qualities, yet Washington was so impressed with his military abilities that, when placed for the second time in command of the army, he insisted that Hamilton should be the next to him in command. In his letter to President Adams on Hamilton's military qualifications, Washington said: "He is enterprising, quick in his perceptions, and his judgment is intuitively great; qualities essential to a military character." We have sometimes wondered, had we then gone to war with France, what new laurels Hamilton would have won in fighting the armies of Napoleon. To the close of his life, Hamilton kept himself ready to obey the call to arms. He never was free from the fear that at any time war might break out with foreign nations, or among these newly united but jealous States. That he might, in such an emergency, be prepared to command the armies of his country, he felt that he must keep his soldier's reputation without a stain. It was his solicitude for that reputation that led him to accept Burr's challenge. And so he perished, yielding to the requirements of a false code of honor, rather than have the suspicion of cowardice tarnish his soldier's fame.

Of all the great men of the Revolution, Hamilton deserves to stand nearest to Washington, for the importance of his services and for the unselfishness of his devotion to the country. He never sought public office. He declined the position of Chief-Justice of the Supreme Court of the United States. At a great personal sacrifice he accepted the most difficult and important place in Washington's

cabinet; and when he had organized the Treasury Department so perfectly that his methods have remained substantially unchanged to the present time, and had lifted the nation out of almost hopeless bankruptcy to a position of the highest financial credit, and had assisted in shaping that foreign policy which has kept us free from the complications of European politics, he returned to the practice of his profession so poor that little was left him besides his household furniture. After his retirement from office, he was constantly consulted by Washington on all important affairs, and he spared no pains in giving to every subject submitted to him the most thoughtful attention. So that, although nominally out of office, he never ceased to be in the public service. We may say of him as Burke said of his dead son: "He was made a public creature, and had no enjoyment whatever but in the performance of some duty."

Hamilton was a man of exceedingly generous and kindly disposition. While minutely exact in regard to all his pecuniary obligations, he was ever ready to lend a helping hand to others—especially to an old army comrade. He had no personal quarrel even with the man who killed him, and made quite an effort to relieve him from pecuniary embarrassment only a short time before the fatal duel. He died at the age of forty-seven. Had he lived to the allotted period of human life, what might he not have accomplished! His work as the leader of the party in power was over, for the government had passed into the hands of Jefferson and his followers, and was there to remain for the next twenty-one years. But had his life been spared he would have enriched our jurisprudence; and he would doubtless have given to the world some work on civil government, the fruit of life-long studies, and meditations, and experience in public affairs, which would have been a storehouse of political wisdom for all coming time.

A few months before Hamilton's death Chancellor Kent spent a night with him in his charming home. In the course of the conversation Hamilton spoke of a work on civil government which he had in contemplation. Referring to this, the Chancellor writes:

> I have very little doubt that if General Hamilton had lived twenty years longer he would have rivaled Socrates or Bacon, or any other of the sages of ancient or modern times, in researches after truth, and in benevolence to mankind. The active and profound statesman, the learned and eloquent lawyer, would probably have disappeared in a great degree before the character of the sage philosopher, instructing mankind by his wisdom, and elevating his country by his example.

The Atlantic Monthly (review date 1887)

SOURCE: "Alexander Hamilton," in *The Atlantic Monthly,* Vol. LIX, No. CCCLI, January, 1887, pp. 115-23.

[*The following is an approbatory overview of Hamilton's character and works.*]

As one reads the writings of Alexander Hamilton, it is impossible to escape a sense of regret that he was not born within the limits of the thirteen colonies in British America. The most distinguished statesman of the United States should have been a son of their soil, a product of their civilization, a result of their formative influences. It was a strange freak of chance or destiny which placed so magnificent an intellect in the head of a child to be born illegitimately, of obscure parentage, on the insignificant island of St. Kitt's. Many a mother, under the like embarrassing circumstances, would have so managed the infantile career of the unwelcome little waif that the world would have lost, nor have ever known it, one of the grandest and most useful brains of this hemisphere. One may fancy that Dame Nature, humorously inclining to amuse herself with a grotesque practical joke, devised the notion of dropping this overshadowing mind into this tiny, neglected, and remote nook. It was a perilous jest, which might easily have become a costly blunder; but, fortunately, matters were rectified by Hamilton himself, who, finding himself, as we know by his own boyish confession, troubled with a *"prevalent ambition"* at about the age at which children are more wont to be troubled with getting their permanent teeth, wisely established himself in New York. He had been there but a short time, and was getting well advanced in his "teens," when he published the earliest of those writings which have justly been deemed worthy of preservation as being of real historical value. Nor did many years elapse before he began to instruct his countrymen, indeed to illumine the coming generations, with some of the most profound treatises on government and finance, and some of the ablest state papers, which have ever been written in any age or country.

But though this brilliant and precocious fugitive from little St. Kitt's became one of ourselves only through the process of immigration, there was nothing more striking in his history than the rapidity and thoroughness with which he became Americanized. I do not remember to have seen this fact anywhere so brought out as it ought to be, for the utter transformation whereby this child of a French mother by a Scotch father, born and reared in a tropical settlement, became an integral part of an entirely different people was nothing less than wonderful. We recognize Washington, Franklin, Adams, Jefferson, Madison, Pickering, as distinctively American; all, save perhaps Washington, may be regarded as types quite as much as individuals; and while large numbers of their countrymen resembled one or another of them in moral and mental traits, it is obvious that they could have sprung from no other race, and could have found their special development amid no other surroundings or social influences. Lafayette was a young man when he came to this country, in a condition of extremely receptive enthusiasm; yet his perfect Frenchness was not even visibly modified here. Gallatin remained an Americanized Swiss all his life, and could never get rid of his foreign accent. But Hamilton was at once fully and absolutely an American, and almost as much a type as were those eminent men above named. He seems never to have thought of himself, nor to have been regarded by any one else, in any other light. His position, feelings, ideas, sympathies, all his habits of thought, his ways of considering questions, his points of view, could not have been more national if his ancestors had come over in the Mayflower. If we read his writings, especially all his correspondence, which is the best evidence on such a question, with an especial view to studying this aspect of nationality in mind and character, we cannot but be greatly struck by it. He feels, thinks, and speaks not as one who has cast in his lot with a people whom he admires and understands, but as himself being absolutely and in fact one of those people. Thus he always so regarded himself as an American that he felt no protestations necessary; he forgot, and made others forget, that he could have any other character. Every line in these eight volumes of his writings bears evidence of this perfect assimilation, extraordinary even in a country in which assimilation seems the order of nature. It is no contradiction of this to say that he probably owed to his French blood a vivacity and a power of making himself agreeable and attractive in society which few Americans enjoyed; neither to say that of all the Americans of his day he was far the most cosmopolitan. It may be added that he, Franklin, and Gouverneur Morris were the only Americans who were cosmopolitan at all. The trait did not mark our great men in that time. Even John Adams could not acquire it, though he had such extensive experiences on the Continent and in England, regions which Hamilton never in his life had the good fortune to visit. Nor could Jefferson get it, though half of his heart was always with France, and though he prided himself on the comprehensiveness of his knowledge, the scope of his sympathies, and the liberality of his views, which he conceived to embrace all civilized human kind. But Hamilton's cosmopolitanism was due to the expansiveness of his intellect and grasp of his mind, which were too large to accept the limitations established by the thoughts and ways of any one people. With him cosmopolitanism was a purely mental characteristic.

The quiet manner in which Hamilton laid entirely aside, far remote from sight or memory of himself or others, the fact that he was not sprung of old American stock, was not an autochthon of the North American colonies, is only one among several evidences of a peculiar trait in his character. In just the same way, his writings indicate that he neither spoke nor apparently thought at all of his social origin. Who he was, what he might be expected to be according to the principles of descent and heredity, were questions which he so tranquilly ignored that the few persons who ventured to ask or to answer them did so covertly, and whispering among themselves. He simply stepped into a position among those who were socially and intellectually the best and foremost people; and in doing so did not seem to be challenging a right, but only to be appearing where he naturally belonged. What he, in this easy and careless fashion, took for granted was granted, at once and by everybody. No one ever doubted that he belonged where he placed himself. He did not present as credentials the status of any ancestor, near or remote; he only easily offered himself, his own brains and his own breeding. No one ventured to say that these were not perfectly satisfactory. Almost, if not quite, his only remark concerning his father occurs in a paper wherein, in the course of some business arrangements, he had to speak of certain pecuniary assistance rendered to the old gentleman; he then says, "Though, as I am informed, a man of respectable connections in Scotland," etc. Was there ever shown a more utter indifference to the source of one's being,—to one's antecedents, as the phrase is? No man, not even Lord Thurlow, was ever more frankly ready to *start with himself,* so to speak; and Hamilton was a man of such force, such impressiveness, and in matters of detail so perfectly finished that the world let him start and stand as and where he chose, quite as a matter of course and without question or comment. In precisely the same way, when little more than a boy, he never seems to have thought that his juvenility was a matter of the slightest consequence, as in a certain sense it was not. He spoke and wrote what he thought, on the one hand without humility, and on the other hand equally without that conscious assumption which almost always marks the efforts even of the ablest youths. The value of his thoughts, opinions, and arguments was intrinsic in them, and had nothing whatsoever to do with the greater or less number of years during which he happened to have been in the world,—a matter which, as he never thought of it himself, so also other people generally seem to have forgotten, except in the way of occasional admiration. A striking instance of this is found in his temporary alienation from Washington. There is something imposing in the spectacle of this stripling indulging in a quarrel with the great and impressive commander in chief, and describing it in a letter, perfectly temperate and dignified in tone, as if it had been in every respect a falling out between persons equal in all else save the mere matter of military rank.

Since the first generation of citizens of the United States passed away, it has become a lamentable and growing habit of the country to breed small politicians with that exuberant fecundity with which tropical swamps beget noisome reptiles. Now and again a real statesman towers among the unwholesome and insignificant groups, like an oak loftily overtopping the expanse of stunted and too often noxious underbrush. At last, the henchman and the heeler, the wire-puller and the manipulator of primaries, have attained such consequence that they close around and destroy the statesman before he can develop his independent proportions, just as the poisonous ivy can strangle in its fatal embrace the young tree which might otherwise grow to noble size. A century ago these *dramatis personæ* were unknown among the villains upon the stage of public affairs. Then the political "machine" was uninvented, with the countless other more praiseworthy machines which restless Yankee ingenuity has since devised and carried to excellence approaching perfection. It is true that in those days even cabinet officers could conduct mean intrigues, and could slander and covertly backbite not only each other, but Washington himself. The times were not ideal, but the prizes of the public service were not sufficiently valuable to compensate for any great squandering of time, labor, or virtue. Even the public men most open to criticism in that earlier and simpler era, reversing the proportions of our day, devoted probably three fourths of their energy to advance what they deemed the public welfare, and allied their political fortunes with broad doctrines of policy and genuine principles of statecraft. Nor was it because a policy or principle seemed likely to be popular that they adopted it, but because they believed in it; so that their allegiance to political creeds grew out of and illustrated their intellectual constitution. If one seeks evidence of this, it may be found not alone in their public acts and writings, but in their private correspondence. Of Hamilton this statement is peculiarly true. If he was ambitious to rise, at least it was not by jostling and displacing others that he endeavored to get to the front. It was the prevalence of principles and policies in which he honestly had faith which he first sought to secure; his own power he regarded only as the natural and logical sequence of the success of these; and it was hostility to these, not hostility to himself personally, which he conceived to be a just cause for political antagonism upon his part. All his letters show a singular absence of the purely personal element in his valuation of men, and in his advice in matters of candidacy.

The student of history feels, then, as he studies the works of the men who were busied with the birth and childhood of our republic, that he is among great statesmen. They were so. The fact is beyond a question. They were men of large ability, generously developed by the rare responsibilities of the formative era in a country too young and too poor to have nourished selfishness; they were substantially honest; they were, for men in public life, exceptionally disinterested; they generally had honorable purposes and high aims. One has only to read their writings to be convinced upon these points. These writings, indeed, it may be supposed, are read much less than they ought to be; for in their respective sets of eight, ten, or a dozen clumsy octavos they look far from alluring. Yet, seriously, a large part of them will very well bear reading. Especially is this true of the Hamilton volumes and those of Jefferson. Beyond question Hamilton's are the most broadly valuable. We may read the others in order to gain a knowledge of the history of the times; we may read his not only for this purpose, but also to gather knowledge useful in all ages so long as modern civilization and modern habits of polity and of business shall endure. A large proportion of his public papers bear upon questions of finance, internal taxation, tariff, protection, encouragement of manufactures, commerce, national banking, a multitude of subjects not less important to-day than when they were freshly written; and these topics cannot now be discussed in satisfactory shape by any one of our publicists unless he is familiar with all that Hamilton had to say on the subject in hand. What Hamilton did say is liable to be undervalued now, because it will seem to many persons trite and familiar. So it is; for no small part of what he taught has entered into and informed the views of the American people upon matters of public policy; and such a criticism would be like that of the gentleman who went to see Hamlet played, and came away remarking that Shakespeare was a fellow of no originality, for the whole play was only a string of quotations. The Tables of Contents in these eight volumes [of *The Works of Alexander Hamilton,* edited by Henry Cabot Lodge] may rattle dryly on the ear, but the perusal of the pages themselves will be found surprisingly agreeable, even by the "general reader" who shall have the enterprise to undertake it. For those who do so Hamilton possesses one great advantage: he wrote admirable English, and had a style which is read with ease and pleasure. In this he excelled his contemporaries. Washington, if one could wish to speak unkindly of him, would narrowly escape being called illiterate; if we do not sneer at what he wrote, it is out of our great respect for what he did, and because he had the help of other men's pens in his lifetime, supplemented by the aid of very loyal and helpful editors and biographers since his death. Adams, when writing what he did not expect to publish, wrote like a plain man of sense, and readably enough; but no human being can now force a way through the stilted dullness and stale erudition of the lucubrations which he designed for the enlightenment of his much-to-be-pitied readers in his own generation. Jefferson is very agreeable, and more modern in some respects than were his contemporaries; yet he inundates his subject with such a torrent of words as deprives us of the pleasure to be derived from confidence in the accuracy of his statement or the soundness of his thinking. Madison, less open to direct criticism, is dry and tedious. But Hamilton is read with rapidity and pleasure. His style is vigorous and masculine, and but little defaced by the tiresome elaboration and propriety of the day. The singular clearness of his mind illumines his language; he neither wastes words nor leaves anything obscure. Many of his papers deserve study on rhetorical grounds, as examples of exposition and argument. He furnishes some of the finest specimens in existence of that most effective of all the forms of argument, the argument through statement. After he has arrayed his facts he seems to have left nothing further to be done; his mere statement of his position often embodies both its explanation and its defense. It was this faculty which made it impossible for Hamilton's opponents, numerous and industrious as they were, to prevail against the schemes which he proposed to Congress. He had such a way of enlisting reason in his service that discussion seemed superfluous. Perhaps it may be said that his arguments came disguised in the clothing of facts. In logic, in rhetoric, or in controversy, there is no higher art, no more formidable skill. It is a curious as well as a very useful and instructive study to compare his papers, in this especial point of view, with the documents of the other side, notably with those prepared, certainly with no slight eloquence and plausibility, by his arch opponent, Jefferson. Hamilton forces conviction to-day as he did in his own time.

Probably the student of Hamilton's writings will regard it as a fair judgment rather than an outgrowth of partiality to set him at the head of all statesmen of the United States, and among the few very greatest of the world. He had a native aptitude for the problems of statesmanship; it was the kind of work which his mind was created to do. By way of furnishing a scale to measure this, it may be said that it involved, as one department or faculty only among many, such a capacity for constitutional law that in this respect Marshall did not surpass him, though Marshall left a monumental reputation reared upon this sole basis. One has the consciousness of strength, of pow-

er, in his way of thinking; his brain seems to work in an atmosphere so clear that every fact and every argument must stand out in sharply cut outlines; there can be no distortion, neither any error in perspective, in relationship or proportion, where all is pure lucidity. There is also extraordinary grasp and breadth,—nothing is so remote as to escape just appreciation; there is fullness of knowledge which makes contradiction hopeless, and with this there comes as a detail a singular accuracy of information extending to every minute part of the business. He never seems ingenious or subtle, never surprises the reader by bringing him to an unexpected conclusion through by-roads. He is seen always to travel along the straight turnpike. What escape then remains from implicit confidence in the result? Such was and still is the state of mind in which Hamilton leaves his reader. Of all the men of that day, Jefferson alone can be compared with Hamilton in controversial ability or in skill with his pen, and Jefferson is only near enough to provoke comparison, not to profit by it. For he was less accurate, less clear, less honest in thought, and less simple in exposition; ingenious and sophistical when it serves his turn, he fails to give the impression of having grasped truth so surely. But he had what Hamilton lacked,—the capacity to attract and persuade the masses, to gather a devoted following among the people at large. Hamilton, in respect of sheer intellect, stands easily preëminent; but when he left state papers, financial and constitutional topics, he could not talk humanitarianism and so-called philosophy as Jefferson could. One conceives that he thought this style a trifle disingenuous, and too much interlarded with humbug. Suffrage substantially universal without universal intelligence established a condition of the constituent body by no means well adapted for Hamilton's success. Perhaps this lack of control over the people is to be regarded as a shortcoming in a statesman; if so, it was in Hamilton a serious defect.

There is one more observation which cannot be omitted in any remarks upon Hamilton's writings, and this is the noble tone which pervades them. The reader sees not only patriotism, not only political honesty and of course personal integrity, but he must be struck with a certain high spirit, a loftiness of aim, a pride of consciously pure purpose. Morally, these volumes are elevating. Hamilton was eminently human, a man of strong passions, not wholly devoid of prejudice, occasionally, though very slightly, suspicious. These traits led him into a few mistakes in his judgments of men, a few blunders in matters of policy. Yet amid times of great excitement and of bitter animosities there was only one instance in which he did anything that seems beneath the standard of a perfectly honorable and exceptionally highminded man. When it is frankly said that there is one such instance, it should also be said that probably few men holding public office in any country have had all their doings so fully known as were those of Hamilton. Obscurity never covered any act or word of his which could provoke criticism; it is undeniable that he had very singular ill-luck in this respect.

Hamilton had the imperious, or rather the imperial temper. There was about him the atmosphere of command.

One perceives it clearly throughout his correspondence, though it does not appear in an offensive way. He never addressed his political associates or followers in a dictatorial form; yet his letters none the less plainly emanate from the controlling mind. Clearly enough he is one giving advice to those who will take it, and who will do well in taking it. He did not conceal this fact by an intentional art of expression. It was a common understanding between himself and his correspondent that his knowledge was best, his counsel wisest, his insight deepest, and that his friends would recognize the palpable truth. So they generally did. If he could not lead the ignorant masses, at least he governed nine tenths of the intelligent and thinking people in the United States, and rarely did they question, and never revolt. Seldom did he fall into serious error; once only, in his behavior before the election of Jefferson, he lost his judgment unpardonably, and laid himself open to the criticism of the more independent thinkers of his party. Generally he was greatly wiser than the chief men among the Federalists, and notable instances of the sound influence which he endeavored to exercise may be noticed in his letter to Pickering of June 8, 1798, wherein he advises to "mete the same measure" to France and to England; and in his letter to Wolcott, a few days later, wherein he beseeches the party to go cautiously in the matter of the Alien and Sedition laws: "I hope sincerely the thing may not be hurried through. Let us not establish a tyranny. Energy is a very different thing from violence," etc. But these sage counsels, far above the level of Federalist intelligence, unfortunately proved of little avail.

Hamilton retired from public life at the age of thirty-eight years,—for his military service in Adams's administration was a nominal affair,—and died at the age of forty-seven years. Jefferson was in active public service until he was within a month of his sixty-seventh birthday; and Andrew Jackson left the presidency eleven days before he was seventy years old. Moreover, Jefferson and Jackson each had for eight years all the power attendant upon the highest office in the nation. The three have exercised greater authority in shaping the political customs and doctrines of the American people than have any other of our public men; and certainly neither long life nor high office placed either Jefferson or Jackson ahead of Hamilton in this regard. Jefferson gave shape and expression, coupled with a powerful party organization, to what may be called genuine American democracy. Open as he may be to criticism in matters of detail, he was a great statesman, he did good work, and he left the government and the national politics substantially in excellent condition. Jackson wielded the widest influence for harm that has ever been exercised in the country: he led and organized democratic ignorance as Jefferson had led and organized democratic intelligence; he inaugurated the "spoils system," which Jefferson, though with somewhat itching fingers, had refused to handle, at least with any real efficiency; he introduced the low and personal tone into politics, and made the politician succeed the statesman in public affairs. But Hamilton, whose day of power preceded that even of Jefferson, organized much more than a party or a political system: he organized the very government of the United States; he infused into that vast and complicated machinery so wonderful a combination of strength with smoothness of running that those who came after him could neither remodel it nor easily throw it out of gear. His was the constructive intellect, which fortunately came earliest in the order. The student of American history prior to the slavery and civil war period, who wishes to understand the principles of the government, the spirit of the politics, and the genius of the people of the United States, must study the works of Hamilton and of Jefferson and the doings of Jackson,—not his writings!—for the order of time between these three is the order of logical sequence in our history and in our political development. To borrow a simile from physics, it may be said that Hamilton, with most of the intelligence of the nation at his back, and Jefferson, with the bulk of the population behind him, came into collision; and the resultant of the two opposing forces sent the American people along the course upon which they have ever since been moving, subject only to such deflections as are attributable to an occasional Jacksonian, or other irruptive influence.

Vernon Louis Parrington (essay date 1927)

SOURCE: "Political Thinkers—The English Group," in *Main Currents in American Thought, An Interpretation of American Literature from the Beginnings to 1920: The Colonial Mind, 1620-1800*, Vol. I., 1927. Reprint by Harcourt Brace Jovanovich, 1955, pp. 297-326.

[*Parrington was an American historian, critic, and educator. He was awarded a Pulitzer Prize for the first two volumes of his influential* Main Currents in American Thought *(1927); the third volume remained unfinished at the time of his death. In the following excerpt, Parrington presents Hamilton as a key theorist of American industrial economy.*]

Of the disciplined forces that put to rout the disorganized party of agrarianism, the intellectual leader was Alexander Hamilton, the brilliant Anglo-French West Indian, then just entered upon his thirties. A man of quite remarkable ability, a lucid thinker, a great lawyer, a skillful executive, a masterly organizer, a statesman of broad comprehension and inflexible purpose, he originated and directed the main policies of the Federalist group, and brought them to successful issue. For this work he was singularly well equipped, for in addition to great qualities of mind and persuasive ways he was free to work unhampered by the narrow localisms and sectional prejudices that hampered native Americans. He was rather English than American, with a certain detachment that refused to permit his large plans to be thwarted by minor, vexatious details, or the perversity of stupid men. He was like the elder Pitt in the magnificence of his imperial outlook.

Such a man would think in terms of the nation rather than of the state. He would agree with Paine that the continental belt must be more securely buckled. The jealousies and rivalries that obstructed the creation of a centralized Federal government found no sympathy with him. He was annoyed beyond all patience with the dissensions of local home rule. In his political philosophy there was no place for "the political monster of an *imperium in imperio*"; he would destroy all lesser sovereignties and reduce the several common-wealths to a parish status. For town-meeting democracies and agrarian legislatures he had frank contempt. The American villager and farmer he never knew and never understood; his America was the America of landed gentlemen and wealthy merchants and prosperous professional men, the classes that were most bitterly anti-agrarian. And it was in association with this group of conservative representatives of business and society that he took his place as directing head in the work of reorganizing the loose confederation into a strong and cohesive union. When that work was accomplished his influence was commanding, and for a dozen years he directed the major policies of the Federalist party. His strategic position as Secretary of the Treasury enabled him to stamp his principles so deeply upon the national economy that in all the intervening years since he quitted his post they have not been permanently altered. That we still follow the broad principles of Hamilton in our financial policy is a remarkable testimony to the perspicacity of his mind and his understanding of the economic forces that control modern society. And hence, because the Hamiltonian principles lie at the core of the problem which has proved so difficult of solution by modern liberalism, the life and work of Hamilton are of particular significance in our democratic development.

Thomas Jefferson, Hamilton's longtime political antagonist.

Hamilton was our first great master of modern finance, of that finespun web of credit which holds together our industrial life; and because his policies opened opportunities of profit to some and entailed loss upon others, they have been debated with an acrimony such as few programs have endured. About the figure of the brilliant Federalist the mythmakers have industriously woven their tales, distorting the man into either a demigod or a monster. The individual has been merged in the system which he created, and later interpretation has been shot through with partisan feeling; political and economic prejudice has proved too strong for disinterested estimate. Any rational judgment of Hamilton is dependent upon an interpretation of the historical background that determined his career, and in particular of the state of post-Revolutionary economics; and over such vexing questions partisans have wrangled interminably. Thus Sumner, in his life of Hamilton, asserts dogmatically that Federalism was no other than the forces of law and order at war with the turbulent, anarchistic forces unloosed by the Revolution, and that the putting down of the scheme of repudiation was the necessary preliminary to the establishment of a great nation. In the light of such an interpretation, Hamilton the far-seeing, courageous and honest master of finance, was the savior of nationality, the one supreme figure rising above an envious group of lesser men. But, as has been sufficiently pointed out in preceding chapters, the historical facts are susceptible of quite other interpretation; and as our knowledge of the economic struggle then going on becomes more adequate, the falsity of such an explanation becomes patent. If, on the other hand, we concede that the crux of the political problem in 1787 was economic—the struggle waging between farmer and business groups for control of government—then the position of Hamilton becomes clear; he was the spokesman of the business economy. He thought in terms of nationality and espoused the economics of capitalism, because he discovered in them potentialities congenial to his imperialistic mind.

The career of Hamilton followed logically from the determining facts of temperament and experience. He came to New York an alien, without position or influence, ambitious to make a name and stir in the world; and in the America of his day there could be little doubt what doors opened widest to preferment. He made friends easily, and with his aristocratic tastes he preferred the rich and distinguished to plebeians. Endowed with charming manners and brilliant parts, he fascinated all whom he met; before he was of age he was intimate with all the Whig leaders, civil and military, on Washington's staff and elsewhere, lending his brains to the solution of knotty problems, prodding stupider minds with illuminating suggestions, providing himself the clearest thinker in whatever group he found himself. It was by sheer force of intellect that he gained distinction. Singularly precocious, he matured early; before his twenty-fifth year he seems to have developed every main principle of his political and economic philosophy, and thereafter he never hesitated or swerved from his path. He was tireless in propaganda, urging on the proposed Constitutional convention, discussing with Robert Morris his favorite project of a national bank, outlining various systems of funding, advocating tariffs as an aid to domestic manufacture, and sketching the plan of a political and economic system under which native commercialism could go forward. His reputation as an acute and trustworthy financial adviser was well established with influential men north and south, when the new government was set up, and Washington turned to him naturally for the Treasury post, to guide financial policies during the difficult days immediately ahead. But so able a man could not be restricted within a single portfolio, and during the larger part of Washington's two administrations Hamilton's was the directing mind and chief influence. He regarded himself as Prime Minister and rode roughshod over his colleagues. Major policies such as that of no entangling alliances must receive his careful scrutiny and approval before they were announced; and in consequence more credit belongs to Hamilton for the success of those first administrations than is commonly recognized.

But when we turn from the administrator and statesman to the creative thinker, there is another story to tell. The quickness of his perceptions, the largeness of his plans and efficacy of his methods—his clear brilliancy of understanding and execution—are enormously impressive; but they cannot conceal certain intellectual shortcomings. There was a lack of subtlety in the swift working of his mind, of shades and *nuances* in the background of his thought, that implied a lack of depth and richness in his intellectual accumulation. Something hard, almost brutal, lurks in his thought—a note of intellectual arrogance, of cynical contempt. He was utterly devoid of sentiment, and without a shred of idealism, unless a certain grandiose quality in his conceptions be accounted idealism. His absorbing interest in the rising system of credit and finance, his cool unconcern for the social consequences of his policies, reveal his weakness. In spite of his brilliancy Hamilton was circumscribed by the limitations of the practical man.

In consequence of such limitations Hamilton was not a political philosopher in the large meaning of the term. In knowledge of history he does not compare with John Adams; and as an open-minded student of politics he is immensely inferior to Jefferson. Outside the domain of the law, his knowledge does not always keep pace with his argument. He reasons adroitly from given premises, but he rarely pauses to examine the validity of those premises. The fundamentals of political theory he seems never to have questioned, and he lays down a major principle with the easy finality of a dogmatist. Compare his views on any important political principle with those of the greater thinkers of his time, and they are likely to prove factional if not reactionary. The two tests of eighteenth-century liberalism were the doctrine of individualism, and the doctrine of the minimized state; and Hamilton rejected both: the former in its larger social bearing, and the latter wholly. He was not even abreast of seventeenth-century liberalism, for that was strongly republican, and Hamilton detested republicanism only a little less than democracy. Harrington and Locke were no masters of his; much less were Bentham or Priestley or Godwin. He called

the French revolutionary writers "fanatics in political science"; to what extent he read them does not appear. The thinkers to whom he owed most seem to have been Hume, from whom he may have derived his cynical psychology, and Hobbes, whose absolute state was so congenial to his temperament. But political theory he subordinated to economic theory. He was much interested in economics. With the Physiocratic school and its agrarian and sociological bias he could have no sympathy, but with the rising English school that resulted from the development of the industrial revolution, he found himself in hearty accord. Capitalism with its credit system, its banks and debt-funding and money manipulation, was wholly congenial to his masterful temperament. He read Adam Smith with eagerness and *The Wealth of Nations* was a source book for many of his state papers. To create in America an English system of finance, and an English system of industrialism, seemed to him the surest means to the great end he had in view; a centralizing capitalism would be more than a match for a decentralizing agrarianism, and the power of the state would augment with the increase of liquid wealth.

But granted that he lacked the intellectual qualities of the philosopher, it does not follow that his significance diminishes. On the contrary his very independence of contemporary European theory enlarged his serviceableness to party. He was free to employ his intelligence on the practical difficulties of a new and unprecedented situation. English liberalism did not answer the needs of Federalism, if indeed it could answer the needs of the country at large. The time had come to decide whether the long movement of decentralization should go further, and confirm the future government as a loose confederacy of powerful states, or whether an attempt should be made to check that movement and establish a counter tendency towards centralized, organized control. If the former, it meant surrendering the country to a democratic *laissez faire*, and there was nothing in the history of political *laissez faire* as it had developed in America, that justified the principle to Hamilton. It had culminated in agrarianism with legislative majorities riding down all obstacles, denying the validity of any check upon its will, constitutional, legal or ethical. The property interests of the minority had been rendered insecure. There had been altogether too much *laissez faire;* what was needed was sharp control of legislative majorities; the will of the majority must be held within due metes and bounds. Even in the economic world the principle of *laissez faire* no longer satisfied the needs of the situation. Parliamentary enactments had aided British interests in their exploitation of America before the war; it was only common sense for an American government to assist American business. The new capitalism that was rising stood in need of governmental subsidies. Business was languishing; infant industries could not compete on even terms with the powerful British manufacturing interests, long established and with ample capital. From a realistic contemplation of these facts Hamilton deduced the guiding principle that has since been followed, namely, that governmental interference with economic laws is desirable when it aids business, but intolerable and unsound when it aims at business regulation or control, or when it assists agriculture or labor.

Throughout his career Hamilton was surprisingly consistent. His mind hardened early as it matured early, and he never saw cause to challenge the principles which he first espoused. He was what a friendly critic would call a political realist, and an enemy would pronounce a cynic. With the practical man's contempt for theorists and idealists, he took his stand on current fact. He looked to the past for guidance, trusting to the wisdom of experience; those principles which have worked satisfactorily heretofore may be expected to work satisfactorily in the future. Whoever aspires to become a sane political leader must remember that his business is not to construct Utopias, but to govern men; and if he would succeed in that difficult undertaking he must be wise in the knowledge of human nature. At the basis of Hamilton's political philosophy was the traditional Tory psychology. Failure to understand human nature, he believed, was the fatal weakness of all democratic theorists; they put into men's breeches altruistic beings fitted only for a Utopian existence. But when we consider men as they are, we discover that they are little other than beasts, who if unrestrained will turn every garden into a pigsty. Everywhere men are impelled by the primitive lust of aggression, and the political philosopher must adjust his system to this unhappy fact. He must not suffer the charge of cynicism to emasculate his philosophy; "the goodness of government consists in a vigorous execution," rather than in amiable intentions; it is the business of the practical man and not of the theorist.

It needs no very extensive reading in Hamilton to discover ample justification for such an interpretation of his political philosophy; the evidence lies scattered broadly through his pages. At the precocious age of seventeen he laid down the thesis, "A vast majority of mankind is entirely biassed by motives of self-interest"; and as political systems are determined by the raw material of the mass of the people, they must be conditioned by such egoism. A year later he discovered in Hume the central principle of his philosophy:

> Political writers, says a celebrated author, have established it as a maxim, that, in contriving any system of government, and fixing the several checks and controls of the constitution, *every man* ought to be supposed a *knave;* and to have no other end, in all his actions, but *private interest.* By this interest we must govern him; and, by means of it, *make him co-operate to public good,* notwithstanding his insatiable avarice and ambition. Without this, we shall in vain boast of the advantages of *any constitution.*

At the age of twenty-seven he reiterated the doctrine, "The safest reliance of every government, is on men's interests. This is a principle of human nature, on which all political speculation, to be just, must be founded." Obviously this was not a pose of youthful cynicism, but a sober judgment confirmed by observation and experience.

Accepting self-interest as the mainspring of human ambition, Hamilton accepted equally the principle of class domination. From his reading of history he discovered that the strong overcome the weak, and as they grasp power they coalesce into a master group. This master group will dominate, he believed, not only to further its interests, but to prevent the spread of anarchy which threatens every society split into factions and at the mercy of rival ambitions. In early days the master group was a military order, later it became a landed aristocracy, in modern times it is commercial; but always its power rests on property. "That power which holds the purse-strings absolutely, must rule," he stated unequivocally. The economic masters of society of necessity become the political masters. It is unthinkable that government should not reflect the wishes of property, that it should be permanently hostile to the greater economic interests; such hostility must destroy it, for no man or group of men will be ruled by those whom they can buy and sell. And in destroying itself it will give place to another government, more wisely responsive to the master group; for even a democratic people soon learns that any government is better than a condition of anarchy, and a commercial people understands that a government which serves the interests of men of property, serves the interests of all, for if capital will not invest how shall labor find employment? And if the economic masters do not organize society efficiently, how shall the common people escape ruin?

Such are the fundamental principles which lie at the base of Hamilton's philosophy. He was in accord with John Adams and James Madison and Noah Webster, in asserting the economic basis of government, with its corollary of the class struggle. He not only accepted the rule of property as inevitable, but as desirable. As an aristocrat he deliberately allied himself with the wealthy. That men divide into the rich and the poor, the wise and the foolish, he regarded as a common-place too evident to require argument. The explanation is to be sought in human nature and human capacities. For the common people, about whom Jefferson concerned himself with what seemed to Hamilton sheer demagoguery, he felt only contempt. Their virtues and capacities he had no faith in. "I am not much attached to the *majesty of the multitude,"* he said during the debate over the Constitution, "and waive all pretensions (founded on such conduct) to their countenance." His notorious comment—which the American democrat has never forgiven him, "The people!—the people is a great beast!"—was characteristically frank. Hamilton was no demagogue and nothing was plainer to his logic than the proposition that if the people possessed the capacity to rule, their weight of numbers would give them easy mastery; whereas their yielding to the domination of the gifted few proves their incapacity. A wise statesman, therefore, will consider the people no further than to determine how government may be least disturbed by their factional discontent, and kept free to pursue a logical program. Under a republican form good government is difficult to maintain, but not impossible. The people are easily deceived and turned aside from their purpose; like children they are diverted by toys; but if they become unruly they must be punished. Too much is at stake in government for them to be permitted to muddle policies.

It is sufficiently clear that in tastes and convictions Hamilton was a high Tory. The past to which he appealed was a Tory past, the psychology which he accepted was a Tory psychology, the law and order which he desired was a Tory law and order. His philosophy was not liked by republican America, and he knew that it was not liked. Practical business men accepted both his premises and conclusions, but republicans under the spell of revolutionary idealism, and agrarians suffering in their pocketbooks, would oppose them vigorously. He was at pains, therefore, as a practical statesman, to dress his views in a garb more seemly to plebeian prejudices, and like earlier Tories he paraded an ethical justification for his Toryism. The current Federalist dogma of the divine right of justice—*vox justiciae vox dei*—was at hand to serve his purpose and he made free use of it. But no ethical gilding could quite conceal a certain ruthlessness of purpose; in practice justice became synonymous with expediency, and expediency was curiously like sheer Tory will to power.

In certain of his principles Hamilton was a follower of Hobbes. His philosophy conducted logically to the leviathan state, highly centralized, coercive, efficient. But he was no idealist to exalt the state as the divine repository of authority, an enduring entity apart from the individual citizen and above him. He regarded the state as a highly useful instrument, which in the name of law and order would serve the interests of the powerful, and restrain the turbulence of the disinherited. For in every government founded on coercion rather than good will, the perennial unrest of those who are coerced is a grave menace; in the end the exploited will turn fiercely upon the exploiters. In such governments, therefore, self-interest requires that social unrest shall be covered with opprobium and put down by the police power; and the sufficient test of a strong state lies in its ability to protect the privileges of the minority against the anarchy of the majority. In his eloquent declamation against anarchy Hamilton was a conspicuous disciple of the law and order school. From the grave difficulties of post-Revolutionary times with their agrarian programs, he created a partisan argument for a leviathan state, which fell upon willing ears; and in the Constitutional convention, which, more than any other man, he was instrumental in assembling, he was the outstanding advocate of the coercive state.

In his plan of government presented to the Convention, the principle of centralized power was carried further than most would go, and his supporting speeches expressed doctrines that startled certain of his hearers. He was frankly a monarchist, and he urged the monarchical principle with Hobbesian logic. "The principle chiefly intended to be established is this—that there must be a permanent *will*." "There ought to be a principle in government capable of resisting the popular current."

> Gentlemen say we need to be rescued from the democracy. But what [are] the means proposed? A democratic assembly is to be checked by a democratic senate, and both these by a democratic chief magistrate. The end will not be answered, the means will not be equal to the object. It will, therefore, be feeble and inefficient.

The only effective way of keeping democratic factionalism within bounds, Hamilton was convinced, lay in the erection of a powerful chief magistrate, who "ought to be hereditary, and to have so much power, that it will not be his interest to risk much to acquire more," and who would therefore stand "above corruption." Failing to secure the acceptance of the monarchical principle, he devoted himself to the business of providing all possible checks upon the power of the democracy. He "acknowledged himself not to think favorably of republican government; but he addressed his remarks to those who did think favorably of it, in order to prevail on them to tone their government as high as possible." His argument was characteristic:

> All communities divide themselves into the few and the many. The first are the rich and well born, the other the mass of the people. The voice of the people has been said to be the voice of God; and, however generally this maxim has been quoted and believed, it is not true to fact. The people are turbulent and changing; they seldom judge or determine right. Give, therefore, to the first class a distinct, permanent share in the government. They will check the unsteadiness of the second; and as they cannot receive any advantage by a change, they therefore will ever maintain good government. Can a democratic assembly, who annually revolve in the mass of the people, be supposed steadily to pursue the public good? Nothing but a permanent body can check the imprudence of democracy. Their turbulent and uncontrollable disposition requires checks.

The argument scarcely needs refuting today, although curiously enough, it was rarely questioned by eighteenth-century gentlemen. It was the stock in trade of the Federalists, nevertheless Hamilton was too acute a thinker not to see its fallacy. It denied the fundamental premise of his political philosophy. If men are actuated by self-interest, how does it come about that this sovereign motive abdicates its rule among the rich and well born? Is there a magic in property that regenerates human nature? Do the wealthy betray no desire for greater power? Do the strong and powerful care more for good government than for class interests? Hamilton was found of appealing to the teaching of experience; but he had read history to little purpose if he believed such notions. How mercilessly he would have exposed the fallacy in the mouth of Jefferson! It was a class appeal, and he knew that it was a class appeal, just as he knew that success knows no ethics. He was confronted by a situation in practical politics, and in playing ignobly upon selfish fears he was seeking to force the convention towards the English model. He had no confidence in the Constitution as finally adopted, and spoke in contemptuous terms of its weakness; whereas for the British constitution he had only praise, going so far, according to Jefferson, as to defend the notorious corruption of parliament on the ground of expediency: "purge it of its corruption"—Jefferson reports him as saying—"and give to its popular branch equality of representation, and it would become an *impracticable* government; as it stands at present, with all its supposed defects, it is the most perfect government which ever existed." The argument savors of cynicism, but it is in keeping with his philosophy; the British constitution owed its excellence to the fact that in the name of the people it yielded control of the state to the landed aristocracy.

It was as a statesman that the brilliant qualities of Hamilton showed to fullest advantage. In developing his policies as Secretary of the Treasury he applied his favorite principle, that government and property must join in a close working alliance. The new government would remain weak and ineffective so long as it was hostile to capital; but let it show itself friendly to capital, and capital would make haste uphold the hands of government. Confidence was necessary to both, and it was a plant of slow growth, sensitive to cold winds. The key to the problem lay in the public finance, and the key to a strong system of finance lay in a great national bank. This, Hamilton's dearest project, was inspired by the example of the Bank of England. No other institution would so surely link the great merchants to government, he pointed out, for by being made partners in the undertaking they would share both the responsibility and the profits. It was notorious that during the Revolution men of wealth had forced down the continental currency for speculative purposes; was it not as certain that they would support an issue in which they were interested? The private resources of wealthy citizens would thus become an asset of government, for the bank would link "the interest of the State in an intimate connection with those of the rich individuals belonging to it." "The men of property in America are enlightened about their own interest, and would easily be brought to see the advantage of a good plan." Hence would arise stability and vigor of government.

Moreover, the bank would be of immense service in the pressing business of the public debt. In regard to this difficult matter Hamilton was early convinced that only one solution was possible: all outstanding obligations, state and national, must be assumed by the Federal government at face value, and funded. Anything short of that would amount to repudiation of a lawful contract, entered into in good faith by the purchaser; and such repudiation would destroy in the minds of the wealthy the confidence in the integrity of the new government that was vital to its success. It was true that speculators would reap great and unearned profits; but the speculators for the most part were the principal men of property whose support was so essential that any terms were justifiable, and nothing would bind them so closely to the government as the knowledge that it would deal generously with them. It was true also that thousands of small men would lose by such a transaction; but under any existing social economy the small man was at a disadvantage, and the present state of affairs was not such as to justify Utopian measures. To alienate the rich and powerful in order to conciliate the poor and inconsequential seemed to him sheer folly. The argument of expediency must prevail over abstract justice; the government must make terms with those in whose hands lay the success or failure of the venture.

His report on the public credit, of January 14, 1790, is one of the significant documents in the history of American finance. It is the first elaboration by an American statesman of the new system of capitalization and credit developed in eighteenth-century England, and it laid a broad foundation for later capitalistic development. To less daring financiers of the time the public debt was no more than a heavy obligation to be met; but to Hamilton it offered an opportunity for revivifying the whole financial life of the nation. Let the debts be consolidated and capitalized by a proper system of funding, and the augmented credit would multiply capital, lower the rate of interest, increase land values, and extend its benefits through all lines of industry and commerce. It was a bold plan and it encountered bitter opposition, which was not lessened by the heavy taxation that it called for. In his tax proposals Hamilton revealed his political philosophy so nakedly as almost to prove his undoing. His doctrine of the blessing of a national debt smacked rather too strongly of English Toryism for the American stomach.

> A national debt, if it be not excessive, will be to us a national blessing. It will be a powerful cement to our Union. It will also create a necessity for keeping up taxation to a degree which, without being oppressive, will be a spur to industry. . . . It were otherwise to be feared our popular maxims would incline us to too great parsimony and indulgence. We labor less now than any civilized nation of Europe; and a habit of labor in the people, is as essential to the health and vigor of their minds and bodies, as it is conductive to the welfare of the State.

A further struggle was encountered over the proposals of an internal revenue and a tariff. In his advocacy of the former Hamilton encountered the vigorous opposition of the backcountry. The total lack of adequate means of transportation rendered the problem of a grain market a chronic difficulty to the frontier farmers. The most convenient solution lay in distilling, and so whisky had become the chief commodity of the farmer that was transportable and brought a cash price. In placing a tax upon distilled liquors, therefore, Hamilton struck so directly at the economic interests of thousands of backwoodsmen, as to bring a rebellion upon the new administration. He knew what he was doing, but he calculated that it was safer to incur the enmity of farmers than of financiers; nevertheless the fierceness of the opposition surprised him, and aroused all the ruthlessness that lay in the background of his nature. He called for the strong arm of the military and when the rising was put down, he was angered at Washington's leniency in refusing to hang the convicted leaders. In his advocacy of a tariff he was on safer ground, for he was proposing a solution of the difficult situation confronting the manufacturers. Something must be done to revive industry so long stagnant. The old colonial machinery had been destroyed and new machinery must be provided. Industrial independence must follow political independence; and the easiest way lay in providing a tariff barrier behind which the infant industries of America might grow and become sufficient for domestic needs.

In his notable report on manufactures, submitted on December 5, 1791, Hamilton showed his characteristic intelligence in his grasp of the principles of the industrial

*Massachusetts Congressman Fisher Ames,
strong Federalist ally of Hamilton.*

revolution. Certainly no other man in America saw so clearly the significance of the change that was taking place in English industrialism, and what tremendous reservoirs of wealth the new order laid open to the country that tapped them. The productive possibilities that lay in the division of labor, factory organization, the substitution of the machine for the tool, appealed to his materialistic imagination, and he threw himself heart and soul into the cause of industrial development in America. He accepted frankly the principle of exploitation. He was convinced that the interests of the manufacturers were one with the national interests, and he proposed to put the paternal power of the government behind them. With the larger social effects—the consequences to the working classes, congestion of population, the certainty of a labor problem—he concerned himself no more than did contemporary English statesmen. He was contemptuous of Jefferson's concern over such things. He had no Physiocratic leanings towards agriculture; material greatness alone appealed to him; and he contemplated with satisfaction the increase in national wealth that would accrue from levying toll upon the weak and helpless.

> Besides this advantage of occasional employment to classes having different occupations, there is another, of a nature allied to it, and of a similar tendency. This is the employment of persons who would otherwise be idle, and in many cases, a burthen on the community, either from bias of temper, habit, infirmity of body, or some other cause, indisposing or disqualifying them

for the toils of the country. It is worthy of particular remark, that, in general, women and children are rendered more useful, and the latter more early useful, by manufacturing establishments, than they would otherwise be. Of the number of persons employed in the cotton manufactories of Great Britain, it is computed that four-sevenths, nearly, are women and children; of whom the greatest proportion are children, and many of them of a tender age.

If the material power and splendor of the state be the great end of statesmanship—as Hamilton believed—no just complaint can be lodged against such a policy; but if the well-being of the individual citizen be the chief end—as Jefferson maintained—a very different judgment must be returned.

Although the fame of Hamilton has been most closely associated with the principle of constitutional centralization, his truer significance is to be found in his relation to the early developments of our modern capitalistic order. In his understanding of credit finance and the factory economy, he grasped the meaning of the economic revolution which was to transform America from an agrarian to an industrial country; and in urging the government to further such development, he blazed the path that America has since followed. "A very great man," Woodrow Wilson has called him, "but not a great American." In the larger historical meaning of the term, in its democratic implications, that judgment is true; but in the light of our industrial history, with its corporate development and governmental subsidies, it does not seem so true. As the creative organizer of a political state answering the needs of a capitalistic order—a state destined to grow stronger as imperialistic ambitions mount—he seems the most modern and the most American of our eighteenth-century leaders, one to whom our industrialism owes a very great debt, but from whom our democratic liberalism has received nothing.

Frederick C. Prescott (essay date 1934)

SOURCE: An introduction to *Alexander Hamilton and Thomas Jefferson,* American Book Company, 1934, pp. xi-lxxii.

[*In the excerpt below, Prescott traces Hamilton's career as both a political theorist and participant in government.*]

Hamilton's interests of public concern were mainly political. His work as a lawyer was secondary; that as a financier and economist, as will appear, was subordinate to his political activity. We are here concerned, therefore, primarily with the development of his political theory and its applications.

When the outbreak of the Revolution converted Hamilton, at the age of nineteen, from a student to a soldier, his political views, as in spite of his precocity we might expect, were drawn not so much from his own mind as from his reading and from the revolutionary atmosphere of the time. A memorandum kept in 1776 contains a list of books indicating the quality of his reading. This ranges from *Orations—Demosthenes,* through many works political and financial—*Lex Mercatoria* and *Hobbes's Dialogues*—to *Smith's History of New York*; and is followed by serious notes and reflections. If we may trust his own statement, he had at first "strong prejudices" on the loyalist side—perhaps a significant admission—but was won over by "the superior force of the arguments in favor of the American claims."

What were the theories of government, inherited by Hamilton and his contemporaries, between which they might choose to find "arguments" fitted to support their "claims"? When Englishmen gave up the notion of rule by divine right, they attempted to solve their political difficulties by suiting government rationally to human needs. Reviving ideas that had come down to them from antiquity and the middle ages—the state of nature, the law of nature, natural rights, the social compact—they gave them new and vigorous discussion. From this emerged, in the seventeenth and eighteenth centuries, three main tendencies in government: first, the notion of an enlightened absolutism; secondly, that of a limited and responsible rule under a constitution; and finally, that of a democracy. The first is best represented by Hobbes in his *Leviathan* (1651). Having a poor opinion of men and believing them moved solely by their passions, Hobbes pictured them in a state of nature as equal and free indeed, but miserable indeed also—constantly at war, and their life "poor, nasty, brutish, and short." To escape anarchy they surrendered their natural rights to a sovereign, making an indefeasible contract. Henceforth the duty of the sovereign, after vigorously protecting his own sovereignty, was to promote the welfare of the people; the duty of the subject was entire obedience. This doctrine sets up a benevolent, but absolute and paternal government. Though Hobbes contemplates a monarchical sovereign, there is nothing in his theory to prevent the sovereign being an absolute parliament or congress. This theory was obviously not one to attract the American revolutionists; but in considering Hamilton we must keep it in mind and later revert to it.

Locke, who developed the second theory in his *Two Treatises on Government* (1690), and who fathered the ideas prevailing in the eighteenth century, had a better opinion of mankind. In a state of nature men lived tolerably, but finding it convenient in order to protect a certain precious portion of their natural rights—particularly that of property—they contracted to form a government, which, however, derived its powers from their consent. Not merely a theorist but also an apologist for the revolution of 1689, Locke took care to include in his theory the principle that if government disregarded the people's welfare, the contract was thereby broken and government dissolved. The third, the democratic theory, most Americans were not yet quite ready for. This of Locke, however, suited them exactly. Having lived under pioneer conditions, they were familiar with equality, freedom, and "natural rights"; they could interpret their characters as "social compacts"; and they were governed mainly by laws made with their own

consent. Above all, they could use the arguments by which Locke had justified one revolution to justify another. "If," says Locke, [In *Two Treatises on Government*] "a long train of abuses, prevarications, and artifices, all tending the same way, make the design [of tyranny] visible to the people . . . it is not to be wondered at that they should then rouse themselves." This theory supplied "the glittering generalities that became the political gospel of the American revolutionists." And with these "generalities" Hamilton, at first at any rate, was very much impressed. Later, with greater experience, he developed quite different views, as, if we take up his writings, we shall see.

As in 1774 the people of the New York colony were dividing themselves into Whigs and Tories, the "no-trade agreement," recently adopted by Congress, was warmly debated. A forcible pamphlet, by "A Westchester Farmer," attacking it, called forth many replies, among them *A **Full Vindication of the Measures of Congress*** (1774) and *The Farmer Refuted* (1775), from the pen of Hamilton, a student at King's College. These pamphlets, which exhibit their immaturity in a jocosity which fortunately he later abandoned, were able enough to give him reputation as he "Defender of Congress"; and being the only public expression of his political views before 1781, they deserve some examination. "All men," he declares in the first, "have one common original; they participate in one common nature, and consequently have one common right. . . . The pretensions of Parliament are contradictory to the law of nature, subversive of the British Constitution, and destructive of the faith of the most solemn compacts." Presently, however, he proceeds from abstract right to more realistic argument, and with some show of the information and thoroughness which are the sources of his later strength, he examines the consequences of interrupted trade. Here very early he hit upon one of his important ideas. One of these consequences will be the extension of American manufactures; and "if, by the necessity of the things, manufactures should once be established . . . they will pave the way still more to the future grandeur and glory of America; and by lessening its need for external commerce, will render it still securer against the encroachments of tyranny." This is almost a brief summary of the argument of his famous "Report on Manufactures."

The Farmer Refuted, though later by only a few weeks, marks a striking advance; its careful examination of colonial rights under the charters, for example, exhibits the research and acumen which made Hamilton a great lawyer. It is most interesting, however, as showing a conflict in his mind between what might roughly be called Lockian and Hobbesian principles. He begins by rehearsing the familiar arguments, appealing "more especially" to "the law of nature, and that *supreme law* of every society—*its own happiness*." He presently finds "the fundamental source of all the errors" of his opponent in "a total ignorance of the natural rights of mankind." Curiously, he detects a "strong similitude" between his opponent's low notions of man in the natural state and "those maintained by Mr. Hobbes." But after all, "the sacred rights of mankind are not to be rummaged for among old parchments or musty records. They are written, as with a sunbeam, in the whole volume of human nature, by the hand of divinity itself; and can never be erased or obscured by mortal power." Hamilton, however, was perhaps not as much of an anti-Hobbesian as he supposed. Elsewhere in this pamphlet, writing with less revolutionary enthusiasm but perhaps greater sincerity, he appears more realistic. Arguing shrewdly concerning the relations of the colonies to Europe, he finds these governed by anything but altruism. Americans cannot trust to the good will of England, which already discovers "a jealousy of our dawning splendor"; for "jealousy is a predominant passion of human nature." He cites from Hume, who held Hobbes's low opinion of human nature, a passage which perhaps colored all his later views. "Political writers," he quotes Hume as saying, "have established it as a maxim that, in contriving any system of government . . . *every man* ought to be supposed a *knave;* and to have no other end but *private interest*. By this interest we must govern him; and, by means of it, *make him coöperate to public good,* not withstanding his insatiable avarice and ambition." If such, politically, are the motives of mankind, it is vain to trust to the wisdom or justice of the British Parliament. "A fondness for power is implanted in most men, and it is natural to abuse it when acquired." Such abuse can be met only by forcible resistance. Natural rights are very fine, Hamilton now seems to say, but they belong to those who can obtain and defend them. Here, then, there are two strains of thought, two attitudes toward human nature and human rights, confused and unreconciled; the thought is not yet integrated. The second, as we shall see, indicates the direction in which Hamilton's thought eventually moved. We may note further that Hamilton closes by acknowledging himself, perhaps only formally, "a warm advocate for limited monarchy, and an unfeigned well-wisher of the royal family." However, in proposing that, though sovereignty should remain in a common monarch, coördinate legislatures should be provided for his English and American dominions, he is advocating the very principle of decentralization, or states' rights, which he spent his later life in combating. But experience, "the parent of wisdom," will clarify his views.

. . . . .

Thoughtful Americans of the 1770's realized, as Hamilton was wise enough to do very early, that the forces behind the Revolution might break down not only British domination but the ties of ordered government at home; that the prevailing notions of "natural right" and "consent of the people," carried too far, would lead to disintegration and anarchy. "The same state of the passions," Hamilton writes in 1775, "which fits the multitude . . . for opposition to tyranny and oppression, very naturally leads them to contempt and disregard of all authority. . . . When the minds [of the unthinking populace] are loosened from their attachment to ancient establishments and courses they . . . are apt more or less to run into anarchy." Troops, he recommends, should be stationed in New York to preserve order. Realization of this danger grew stronger with experience, and experience came rapidly. When in 1777, barely turned twenty, Hamilton was made an aide to Washington, he found himself in a position with many advantages. He was thrown into the very midst of momentous affairs, he was in intimate relations with the wisest statesman of his time, and he probably soon knew more about continental affairs than any one else, save Washington himself. He continued his study of finance and administration, not merely in books but in events. He matured his character and his views.

He soon found that men who had had too much of English government were determined to have as little as possible of their own. The jealousy of the states had been transferred from Parliament to a Congress, which, weak in its personnel, half legislative and half administrative in its functions, full of corruption and divergent interests, could act only on sufferance and was growing more and more inefficient. The result was failure in recruitment and supply, and disintegration of the finances. In 1780 he says of the army: "It is now a mob rather than an army; without clothing, without provision, without morals, without discipline." Nothing could have been more distressing to one of orderly temperament. Seeing these evils meant with Hamilton devising a remedy—even though he were as yet powerless to apply it. As usual he sought the underlying causes, and found one of these in a direction to which he had given much attention. "It is by introducing order into our finances—by restoring public credit—not by gaining battles, that we are finally to gain our object." He devotes two notable letters to this subject. The first, probably of 1779, contains this characteristic sentence: "A great source of error in disquisitions of this nature is the judging of events by abstract calculations; which, though geometrically true, are false as they relate to the concerns of beings governed more by passion and prejudice, than by an enlightened sense of their interests." Henceforth Hamilton is to be influenced mainly by practical considerations. After careful review of actual conditions he proposes a national bank, the earliest known project of that character in America. In the second letter, of the following year, to Robert Morris, he deals more fully with the finances. Utilizing the experience of other countries and then carefully calculating the possibilities of taxation, he concludes that the government must borrow, and he again proposes, as an instrument, a national bank, with a detailed plan for its establishment. "A national debt," he says, in words later turned against him, "if it is not excessive, will be a national blessing." His purpose, however, is not merely financial but also political, for he adds: "It will be a powerful cement of our Union."

Another letter, to James Duane, written between the dates of those just mentioned, ranking among the most significant of his papers, makes a landmark in the development of his theory. In this he is seeking "the defects of the present system, and the changes necessary to save us from ruin." One defect is "want of method and energy in the administration" due to the lack of "a proper executive." The revolutionary jealousy of strength in administration has trusted everything to the legislature. This might be remedied by separating the executive functions, and assigning them to single responsible ministers—of war, finance, etc. But "the fundamental defect is want of power in Congress," arising partly from "an excess of liberty in the states," partly from timidity and want of vigor in Congress itself. "Nothing appears more evident to me," he says, "than that we run much greater risk of having a weak and disunited federal government, than one which will be able to usurp the powers of the people." The danger is "that the common sovereign will not have power sufficient to unite the different members together, and direct the common forces to the interest and happiness of the whole." The goal, then, is national strength and unity. Congress, therefore, should "consider themselves vested with full power *to preserve the republic from harm,"*—that is, Congress should assume all powers necessary to the ends of government. If this be considered too bold, it should call a convention which may grant these powers. Those necessary he carefully enumerates, and, be it noted, they are, with minor exceptions, those granted under the Constitution in 1787. Let Congress, he concludes, assume an air of authority and confidence, for "men are governed by opinion; this opinion is as much influenced by appearances as by realities."

As a step toward action Hamilton attempted to place these ideas before the public in a series of papers, significantly entitled the ***Continentalist***. "The extreme jealousy of power . . . attendant on all popular revolutions" has fatally reduced the authority of Congress. But "in a government framed for durable liberty, not less regard must be paid to giving the magistrate a proper degree of authority to make and execute the laws with rigor, than to guard against encroachments upon the rights of the community; as too much power leads to despotism, too little leads to anarchy, and both eventually to the ruin of the people." In a federation, like the United States, the real danger is anarchy—with state discord and foreign interference. The only safety is in a strong central government. The government must have the "power of the purse," for "power without revenue . . . is a name"; and the power of regulating trade, for trade will not regulate itself and a regulation national in scope is necessary. From the contemptible actuality—"a number of petty states, with the appearance only of union, jarring, jealous, and perverse, without any determined direction, fluctuating and unhappy at home, weak and insignificant in the eyes of other nations"— from this he turns, in his often quoted conclusion, to the "noble and magnificent perspective of a great Federal Republic, closely linked in the pursuit of a common interest, tranquil and prosperous at home, and respectable abroad." Hamilton is already an architect of government; he has devised his essential plan, if not all of his specifications; he has, by publishing it, taken a step toward its adoption. He is in fact prepared to become one of the builders of the nation he has already in imagination conceived. In other words these papers, of 1779 to 1781, contain or imply the essential principles in Hamilton's political theory. His appeal is no longer to the abstractions of "natural right," but to "experience and reason"; he is no longer troubled by confusion and conflict; and he now speaks with entire conviction and confidence. From this time, 1781, his principles develop but they do not change.

The student of Hamilton is impressed by a remarkable agreement between his political thought, in its maturity, and his personal character. Life, career, and thought were unusually integrated. He was ambitious, as Washington said after long intimacy,—adding, however, that his ambition was "of that laudable kind that prompts a man to excel in whatever he takes in hand." He found it easy to excel, for he had, within his range, extraordinary ability. He had concentration of purpose and of will, which accounted largely for his strength; and this accorded with his idea of strength and unity in a sovereign state. He had courage and tireless energy; it was natural for him to conceive an equally bold and energetic government. He was scrupulously honest; and he had a strong sense of governmental and international obligation. He had a passion for order, and easily mastered details by ordering them; he was by temperament the foe of anarchy and the friend of ordered government. He was a born organizer and executive; and he was fond of comparing efficient government to a machine smoothly running under the control of its engineer. Coming to New York an alien and alone, he had neither the strength nor the weakness of local ties and sentimental attachments. He was thus fitted to take "continental" views. Though he was not without patriotism, and though he found in the new world a field favorable to his ambition and invention, he would perhaps have been equally at home had his lot fallen in another age or country—in the England of Pitt or the France of Colbert. He perhaps cared less for the people of his adopted country than for his appointed task of providing them with an efficient government. "His sympathies," says a friendly biographer, "were always aristocratic, and he was born with a reverence for tradition." He thought accordingly that government should be in the right hands, and that its conduct should command an honor and respect akin to that due to right behavior in a private gentleman. Though inventive and no slave of the past, he was fond of appealing to history, and especially to experience. He was a realist, not a visionary or a romantic,—not, in his own words, among those "enthusiasts who expect to see the halcyon scenes of the poetic or fabulous age realized in America." His deficiencies appear only when he is compared with the greatest men; he lacked the serene wisdom of Washington, the sympathy and humanity of Lincoln, and these deficiencies affected his policy.

As the Revolution closed Hamilton saw clearly not only the national need and the remedy, as we have seen, but also the difficulties, which were great. "Peace made," he wrote in 1782 to his friend Laurens, "a new scene opens. The object then will be to make our independence a blessing. To do this we must secure our Union on solid foundations—a herculean task—and to effect which mountains of prejudice must be leveled." To Washington he wrote a year later: "The centrifugal is much stronger than the centripetal force in these States; the seeds of disunion much more numerous than those of union." For five more years he saw the country slipping deeper into anarchy, into bankruptcy in its finances and reputation. Entering Congress in 1782 he had experience with its disability; he urged measures for strengthening the government, but had to abandon them, he says, for "lack of support." In a

Vindication of Congress (1783), he found the fault not in the personnel but in the system. "In these circumstances" he urged that all should unite "to direct the attention of the people to the true source of the public disorders—the want of an *efficient general government.*"

At last came an opportunity for effective action. Sent in 1786 as delegate to the Annapolis Convention, he framed an address which was unanimously adopted, recommending that Commissioners be appointed by the States to meet at Philadelphia, to devise such "provisions as shall appear to them necessary to render the Constitution of the Federal Government *adequate to the exigencies* of the Union." He was presently chosen as delegate to the Convention of 1787.

The problem confronting this famous body was formidable,—to provide a government. It was natural to seek precedents; for men of English race—provided they were not experimentalists or visionaries—to seek them in the English constitution. This had on the whole secured both stability and freedom; and this had already served as model for the colonial governments. Evidently, however, it must be modified to suit their purposes. Having got rid of one king, most of them did not wish another. They must transform their monarchical model into a republic. They knew, indeed, that modern examples of republican government had not met with reassuring success; they could not know that their own experiment would eventually furnish the most notable one. All was project and experiment. The essential question, however, was how far they should go in modifying their English model by the introduction of republican and democratic principles. The whole problem was further complicated by the difficulty of adjusting the relations of the already existing state governments to the proposed central one.

Though for well-known reasons Hamilton's share in the convention was not large, it discloses very interesting developments in his theory. He at once placed his views before the convention in a speech, submitting at the same time a draft for a constitution, and from time to time he made other speeches. Closed doors permitted him to express himself with the greatest frankness. In a word, he favored, first, as near an approach as possible to the English model; secondly, as complete a subordination as possible of the states to the federal government. His speech, however, must be briefly examined.

The only solution, he believes, is "one General Government" with "complete sovereignty," for "two sovereignties cannot exist within the same limits." Two objections indeed arise: first, the expense of such an all-embracing government,—which, however, will not be too great if the burden of the state governments is largely removed; and, secondly, the size of the country; he despairs of extending republican government over so great a territory. He hesitates about proposing any other form, but in his private opinion he has "no scruple in declaring that the British government is the best in the world"; and he "doubts whether anything short of it will do for America." In the words of Necker: "It is the only government

which unites public strength with individual security." In every community there will be a natural division into the *few* and the *many*. Each of these interests should have power, and they should be separated, one checking the other. The people should have their voice in an Assembly; but the voice of the people is not the voice of God; "the people are turbulent and changing. They seldom judge or determine right." Give, therefore, the few a distinct permanent share in government. The English House of Lords "is a most noble institution," a barrier against "pernicious innovation" attempted by either Crown or Commons. And so with the executive: you cannot have a good executive on the democratic plan; nothing short of the excellency of the British executive can be efficient. Accordingly he proposes an Assembly to be elected by the people for three years; a Senate and an Executive to be elected by electors chosen by the people, to hold office during life. Will this be a truly republican government? Yes, if all officers are chosen by the people, or by a process of election originating with the people. To give the general government full sovereignty the states must be, not extinguished indeed, but completely subordinated—reduced to "corporations for local purposes."

Hamilton then did not propose a monarchy or an oligarchy, though in his balanced constitution he gave great weight to the principles which those features in the English system represent. It should be especially noted, indeed, that he proposed an assembly chosen by universal manhood suffrage—an unheard-of innovation in that day when a property qualification was everywhere a requirement. In general, however, the provisions of his proposed constitution look toward unity, strength, stability, and conservatism.

It has been said by defenders of Hamilton against the charge of "monarchical principles" that he was here advocating a system beyond that in which he really believed, merely to counteract tendencies in an opposite direction. His record both before and after the Convention, indeed in the Convention itself, does not bear this out. He was perfectly frank and explicit. "He acknowledged himself not to think favorably of a republican government, but addressed his remarks to those who did think favorably of it, in order to prevail on them to tone their government as high as possible." He recalls the prevalent opinion that a republican form of government is dependent on the virtue of its citizens; and finds the prospect not reassuring. "The science of policy," he says, "is the knowledge of human nature. . . . Take mankind as they are, and what are they governed by? Their passions. There may in every government be a few choice spirits, who may act from more worthy motives. . . . Our prevailing passions are ambition and interest; and it will ever be the duty of a wise government to avail itself of the passions, in order to make them subservient to the public good." The English system, in its wisdom, recognizes and profits by the evil in human nature. Hume, he says, "pronounced that all the influence on the side of the crown which went under the name of corruption, was an essential part of the weight which maintained the equilibrium of the constitution."

In these speeches of 1787 Hamilton probably expressed more definitely and frankly than anywhere else his true policy of government. When, however, as he expected, the Convention adopted what seemed to him a weaker plan, he was too wise and too magnanimous to withhold his support. "No man's ideas," he said, "were more remote from the plan than his own were known to be; but is it possible to deliberate between anarchy and convulsion on the one side and the chance of good to be expected on the other?" He urged that all delegates should sign, and when the Constitution was submitted he became its most effective supporter.

The *Federalist* was so entirely conceived and planned, and so largely written by Hamilton, that it will always be thought of as his work. Of the compromise constitution now submitted, however, he must be regarded not as the author, but as the highly effective, if not quite wholehearted advocate. An expression in the first number is significant: "My motives must remain in the depository of my own breast. My arguments will be open to all. . . . They shall at least be offered in a spirit which will not disgrace the cause of truth." It is not hard in the *Federalist* to detect shiftings of position for the sake of more effective advocacy. Hamilton could now find, for instance, along with depravity, "other qualities in human nature which justify a certain portion of esteem and confidence." There was thus some hope even for a republic. Though he had before and probably still believed in "complete sovereignty," he could now turn a defect into a virtue: "the vigilance and weight" of the states will serve as an effective check against federal usurpations.

Fortunately, however, he could on the whole support the Constitution with sincerity. If a compromise, it was a compromise in the right direction, and the country had gone a long way toward meeting his views. In 1776 the leaders were intent on "dissolving bands"; now on forming at least a "*more* perfect union." The *Federalist,* therefore, carries over indeed, but does not dwell upon the ideas of '76—natural rights, the social compact, the necessary-evil theory of government; its argument is little related to them. Much more conspicuous is the idea that "the citizens of America have too much discernment to be argued into anarchy. . . . Experience has wrought a deep and solemn conviction in the public mind that greater energy of government is essential to the welfare of the community." The problem indeed is the perennial one,—of combining "stability and energy in government with the inviolable attention due to liberty and to the republican form." Liberty will not suffer, however, under a government deriving ultimately from the people, and provided with a most effective system of checks and balances. Even a Bill of Rights is unnecessary. It is the other principle of strength that is in danger of being slighted. Hamilton has been forced to compromise on the Constitution, but he has by no means modified his views.

In brief, his argument rests ultimately on principles with which we are now familiar. He has no use for "the reveries of those political doctors whose sagacity disdains the admonitions of experimental instruction." Experience has abundantly shown that the selfishness of man inevitably brings dissension and aggression—between individuals, states, nations. Let us not think that human nature has improved—even in an American republic. Alike to avoid domestic strife and foreign attack, a firm government is necessary; and only a government having powers adequate to its ends will ensure national stability and permanence. "These powers ought to exist without limitation, because it is impossible to foresee or define the extent and variety of national exigencies, or the correspondent extent and variety of the means which may be necessary to satisfy them." It is the plain duty, then, of the American people to ratify and establish such an authoritative government, and to give it their support. Only by so doing can they secure true freedom, threatened alike by tyranny on the one hand and anarchy on the other. Thus would Hamilton reconcile two apparently opposed principles; true liberty comes only from submission to a just, self-constituted authority. Thus might becomes right, because might secures right. The antagonisms are reconciled in the more inclusive conception of political justice.

Though the *Federalist* papers are said to have been written hurriedly—"in the cabin of a Hudson River sloop; by the dim candle of a country inn"—they represent Hamilton at his best. Their style has become classical in the sense that it has served as a model for later writings on the Constitution and for opinions of the Supreme Court. In no sense a man of letters, Hamilton made his way in life largely through the use of his pen. His boyish description of a West Indian hurricane won him an education; his reply to the *"Westchester Farmer"* led to a military secretaryship under Washington. Writing in this capacity countless letters, he learned even under pressure to write well. His skill was widely recognized. His friend Laurens thought he held the pen of Junius; his opponents, Callender and Jefferson, considered him the Burke of America, the "Colossus" of the Federalist party. To natural gift he added industry. He was tireless in investigating his subject, in seeking its governing principles, in tracing these principles in their remotest applications; and he could support his conclusions with complete confidence. If in the letters of Publius or Camillus his elaboration is sometimes excessive, he always carries his reader along by his logic, lucidity, and force.

Though too busy to formulate a theory, he occasionally indicated his notions of style. "Our communications," he says in 1796, "should be *calm, reasoning,* and *serious,* showing steady resolution more than feeling, having force in the idea rather than in the expression." And again, "Energy without asperity seems best to comport with the dignity of a national language."

He is here speaking of public communications, in which he is ordinarily severe,—without humor, figure, or ornament. In private letters he could be graceful. Hawthorne notes of one of these: "It gives the impression of high breeding and courtesy, as little to be mistaken as if we could see the writer's manner and hear his cultivated accents. . . . There is likewise a rare vigor of expression and pregnancy of meaning, such as only a man of habitual energy of thought could have conveyed into so commonplace a thing as an introductory letter."

Hamilton's style cannot be highly individual, else it would have given a clue to the authorship of the disputed letters in the *Federalist*. It approaches a common or standard style—formal but earnest and business-like—in which the statesmen of the period seem naturally to have expressed themselves. In the political writers of the Revolution and early Republic, who thought independently and maturely, and who felt too strongly to be insincere, America may be said to have come of age and to have made its first substantial contribution to literature. Among these Hamilton holds high rank.

In the writings already examined, particularly in those on the Constitution in 1787, we have Hamilton's political theory developed in virtual maturity and completeness; in the future it is only elaborated and applied. His work was now not to plan government but to execute it. Concerned here with his thought, we may therefore pass somewhat rapidly over the less formative, though more eventful, portion of his career. Appointed in 1789 Secretary of the Treasury, he found himself in a position of great influence. Having the support of Washington and of Congress, he became the directing mind in the new administration. For the first and only time he was in power, with practically a free hand to realize his notions of government. His business was to make the paper constitution work,—at the outset, and in the right way; in Madison's phrase, to *administration* it into efficiency; in his own words, to provide "additional buttresses to the Constitution, a fabric which can hardly be stationary, and which will retrograde if it cannot be made to advance." The task suited his love of power, his sense of public duty, his joy in difficulty to be overcome.

Wise politicians, he had noted in one of his earliest memoranda, ought to "march at the head of affairs," and "produce the *event*." How then produce the event? He had, if possible, to contrive measures which should be immediately and strikingly effective, and at the same time provide a basis for permanent development. The exigencies of the moment, however, were decisive. To restore the public credit was the first step toward buttressing the national government.

The measures Hamilton adopted, all directed to this one purpose, may be very briefly noted. In his *Report on Public Credit* (1790) he advocated full payment of public debts,—including those incurred by the States "as the sacred price of liberty." He would thus "cement the Union" by establishing the national credit, and by enlisting the support of all holders of public securities. In his *Report on a National Bank* (1790) he revived, in new form, the project of his Letter to Morris of 1781. He remembered how an English government, after a revolution, had chartered the Bank of England, in order to solve its financial difficulties, and at the same time to solidify the Whig mercantile interest in its support. By incorporating a similar syndicate he could accomplish the same purposes. He must of course draw upon the "implied powers"; he had

long since seen that only thus was it possible to meet the needs of government. In his famous *Report on Manufactures* (1791) he proposed government aid to "infant industries," in order to assure in war a "national supply," to establish economic along with political independence, and in general to develop the national resources. Contemplating a wise central management of the whole American estate, he foresaw local swallowed up by national interests in a country self-contained and self-sufficient.

In urging government interference to this end Hamilton was pursuing an economic policy entirely parallel to his political one. In both one notes a kinship with seventeenth-century thought. The old theory of mercantilism, favoring national regulation of trade, had in European countries gradually given way to one more in accord with modern ideas. In the economy of a state, as in other sciences, human and physical, philosophers had traced laws—the laws of nature and of reason; of God also, for "neither men nor governments *make* them nor *can* make them. They recognize them as conforming to the supreme reason which governs the universe." The true political economy, then, was to trust to nature's laws and abandon all foolish human interference. This philosophic position was reënforced by the growing power of the mercantile classes, now ready to profit by freedom. Thus was developed, first in France by the physiocrats, then in England by Adam Smith, the doctrine of *laissez faire*. Though before writing his report Hamilton had carefully read the *Wealth of Nations,* he was as little inclined, either by temperament or by his realistic view of American conditions, to adopt this abstract doctrine of economics as he was any of its congeners in politics. Here again he would trust not to a providential operation of the "laws of nature," but to the well-considered policy of a paternal government.

Especially in connection with these measures, all financial in character, there is danger of a misleading "economic interpretation of history,"—of finding their key in an economic purpose. A recent writer [V. L. Parrington, in *The Colonial Mind,* 1927] makes Hamilton the protagonist in a great struggle between capitalism and agrarianism, coolly devising a system favoring the privileged classes to which he belonged at the expense of the common people whom he despised. Mixed and human as his motives may have been, this view does not on the whole accord with his expressions, with his habit of thought, with the habit of thought of his time. He had indeed a keen sense of property rights; he might even have subscribed to Locke's dictum that "government has no other end but the preservation of property." His measures were on their face economic, and had large economic consequences in which he was by no means uninterested. Could he have foreseen the tremendous economic development of which he was laying the foundations he would doubtless have gloried in it. As far as the two can be separated, however, his ends both seemed to him, and actually were, political. He knew nothing of the modern science of *economics,* with its forces determining political events. Like other statesmen of his time he had read and thought upon *political* economy,—that is, on the business side of a political state. His interest was in business only as furthering the interests of the state.

A typical example may be found in the much discussed assumption of the state debts. For this there was little economic motive, the national government having quite debts enough of its own without assuming others. The true motive was political: "If all the public creditors receive their dues from one source . . . their interest will be the same. And having the same interests, they will unite in the support of the fiscal arrangements of the government." Furthermore, this measure would replace state by national tax-gatherers, and bring his government to every door. The final argument for every measure is the old one: "It will be a powerful cement for our Union."

To hold him responsible for building up Northern capitalism would be like holding his democratic states' rights opponents guilty of building up the slavery capitalism of the South. The true issue was not between capitalistic and agrarian interests, not even between aristocratic and democratic control, though both these conflicts were involved in the problem. The issue for Hamilton was where the older critics placed it: between ordered government and the disintegrating forces unloosed by the Revolution. He would increase national authority by drawing on every available source of interest or good will. He favored capitalism as a centralizing, opposed agrarianism as a decentralizing influence. It was blindness to ignore classes. One might temporarily suffer; another, employed as an instrument, might be temporarily advantaged. In the long run, he believed, his policy would benefit both, and the wise statesman considers the permanent welfare of the whole. Individuals, classes, interests, states, must be duly organized, according to their character and weight, into an ordered government.

Familiar now with Hamilton's principles, we shall have no difficulty with his foreign policy, directed to the same ends. The new American sovereignty, the first outside Europe, must be not merely recognized, but established and adjusted in its international relations. His ultimate purpose had been stated in the *Federalist*. "Let the thirteen States, bound together in a strict and indissoluble Union, concur in erecting one great American system, superior to the control of all transatlantic force or influence, and able to dictate the terms of the connection between the old and the new world." The key, at the outset, lay in non-interference and neutrality: "peace and trade with all nations, . . . political connection with none." Any other policy would be expensive, interfere with the development of the Constitution, and make the United States a football in the European struggle for empire. The new nation, still weak, must indeed proceed cautiously, for "America, if she attains to greatness, must *creep* to it." Its policy, however, must be entirely realistic. It must of course observe international obligation; but within the bounds of honesty and justice, it must be directed neither by friendship nor enmity, but solely by national interest.

The outbreak of European war in 1793 turned Hamilton's attention, with that of the country, sharply to international affairs. Peace and independence were threatened by both England and France. Hamilton, however, had only to apply, amid great difficulties and so far as conditions would permit, his established principles. American welfare should be the only guide. Gratitude to France and resentment against England, though natural fruits of the Revolution, are alike childish in foreign policy. "I would *mete* the same measure to both of them, though it should even furnish the extraordinary spectacle of a nation at war with two nations at war with each other." And again, with the significant word underlined: "We are laboring hard to establish in this country principles more and more *national,* and free from all foreign ingredients, so that we may be neither 'Greeks nor Trojans,' but truly Americans."

The proclamation of neutrality of April, 1793, probably the most important action of Washington's administration in foreign affairs, had Hamilton's entire support. It will hardly do to give him credit for thus establishing the Monroe principle, which, going beyond neutrality, undertook to exclude the "system" of the Holy Alliance from every "portion of this hemisphere"; this point Hamilton was never called upon to decide. His whole policy, however, was permanently embodied in Washington's Farewell Address, which he had a large share in preparing; here, it might be said, he joined Washington in warning the country against weakening the Union, against factional divisions, and against foreign entanglements.

After his resignation from the Treasury in 1795, as has been frequently noted, there was a lowering of Hamilton's behavior. He gave up to party, even to intrigue, what was meant for mankind. There is a corresponding loosening of his principles,—at least misapplication or exaggeration of them. The hidden forces of democracy, now marching against him, like Birnam Wood on Dunsinane; the poison of French revolutionary doctrines, covering the earth like a miasma,—these were enemies beyond the weapons which even Hamilton carried. One notes a change of tone. Already as he addresses the "pretended republicans" of the Whiskey Rebellion, in 1794, his firmness seems verging on a truculence which suggests alarm: "It is our intention," he says, "to begin by securing obedience to our authority, from those who have been bold enough to set it at defiance." These "pretended republicans" were only too closely related to those of France. From the beginning Hamilton had looked with suspicion on the French Revolution,—on its "mere speculatists" and "philosophic politicians." As it ran its course his feeling grew to foreboding, horror, detestation. In 1793 he thought the revolutionists butchers, atheists, and fanatics. In 1798, with the "despots of France" waging war against us, he was moved to solemn warning and adjuration: "Reverence to the Supreme Governor of the Universe enjoins us not to bow the knee to the modern Titans who erect their impious crests against him and vainly imagine they can subvert his eternal throne."

Now forsaking his previous policy of neutrality, he urged on a war with France which events soon proved avoidable. The motives of this change should be weighed carefully by the student of his statesmanship. He hoped to defend American shores against the enemies of liberty, religion, and ordered government. He probably hoped at last to discipline the people, concentrate the federal power, and discomfit its democratic enemies. It is even said that, forming ambitious plans of conquest, he hoped to lead an army into Louisiana and Mexico, and after acquiring by arms what was later got by purchase, to "return laurel-crowned, at the head of his victorious legion, to become the first citizen of America." He is thus represented as approaching in grandiose ambition, though not perhaps in perfidy, that final antagonist whom he so often styled the Cæsar or the Catiline of the Republic. That this view can be held, with or without conclusive evidence, by competent historians is significant.

In this connection we may note Hamilton's only memorable references to education and religion—in two letters to Bayard of Delaware. In the first, anxious to find a president for Columbia College, he states the requirements: "That he be a gentleman in his manners, as well as a sound and polite scholar," and so forth,—and lastly, "that his politics be of the right sort." In the second he proposes, as a cure for what he somewhere calls "Godwinism," the founding of a "Christian Constitutional Society . . . its objects to be: 1st. The support of the Christian Religion; 2d. The support of the Constitution of the United States." These letters, which both turn shortly to politics, show, among other things, the narrowness of his effective thought and its exclusively political character.

In a letter written near the end of his career Hamilton struck an unusual note of despondency. "Mine," he says, "is an odd destiny. Perhaps no man in the United States has sacrificed or done more for the present Constitution than myself; and contrary to all my anticipations of its fate, as you know from the very beginning, I am still laboring to prop the frail and worthless fabric. . . . Every day proves to me more and more that this American world was not made for me. . . . The time may ere long arrive," he adds, "when the minds of men will be prepared to make an effort to *recover* the Constitution, but . . . we must wait a while."

Hamilton was clearly undervaluing his own labors. If he seemed to fail, it was because he had gone too fast and had neglected elements of the problem which to the country seemed essential. In the further development of the Constitution it was necessary to go back and pick up principles which were the result of hard-won victories in the pre-constitutional period—local and individual rights, democratic participation in government—principles which he had passed over but which must now be incorporated with his work. He lacked sympathy and experience with the people, and underestimated their power. His character was, so to speak, completed in that of Lincoln, who, with equal devotion to the Union, had the humane understanding to give it a broader base. This lack perhaps led Woodrow Wilson to say that he was a great statesman, not a great American. The verdict is a harsh one, considering his great services to America—services too well known to be recounted here. The essential idea animating and

quickening his political activity throughout was that of a strong, united, and permanent American nation. "In a time when American nationality meant nothing, he alone grasped the great conception in all its fulness, and gave all he had of will and intellect to make its realization possible."

Hamilton's ideal conception of government was never realized, but it has perhaps made some contribution to the general theory of politics. By a recent writer it has been identified with that of Hobbes—the "leviathan state." With this indeed it has something in common—in its outlook, even in its principles. Hamilton believed in an undivided and indefeasible sovereignty, and in the subject's duty of disciplined obedience. He believed it the duty of the sovereign jealously to protect its own sovereignty, and to provide for the subject's welfare by well considered and strictly enforced laws. He believed in a wise and benevolent paternal government. Not, however, in an absolute one. Taking over the conception of the strong state as he found it in Hobbes and elsewhere, he modified it to suit his own purposes, by adapting it to American conditions, by attempting to make it at once strong and responsible. He clearly added to it a new element in combining it with universal manhood suffrage. He took care to introduce also other principles of representation and carefully devised safeguards on the popular will. Thus he sought to make his state not only powerful and permanent, but balanced and responsible—indeed the more permanent because balanced and responsible. He attempted to reconcile apparently conflicting, but, as he thought, essential principles by turning the leviathan state into a republic. Though not in its fulness realized, his conception has influenced the political thought not only of America but of Europe. . . .

Bertrand Russell (essay date 1934)

SOURCE: "Jeffersonian Democracy," in *Freedom and Organization: 1814-1914,* George Allen & Unwin Ltd, 1934, pp. 259-73.

[*A respected and prolific author, Russell was an English philosopher and mathematician known for his support of humanistic concerns. In the following excerpt, Russell compares the political philosophies of Jefferson and Hamilton, noting that the success of the Jeffersonian Republicans ironically led to the advent of Hamiltonian economic policies in the United States.*]

In the first Congress elected under the new Constitution, the business of using democratic machinery to make the rich richer was brilliantly inaugurated. During the War of Independence, the Government of the United States and the Governments of the several States had borrowed money, and had often given promises to pay to soldiers in place of cash. These debts had sunk to a small part of their nominal value, as there was great doubt whether they would ever be redeemed. Congress decided to redeem them at par. No pains were taken to prevent interested persons from obtaining knowledge in advance of this intention, with the consequence that rich speculators bought up the debts, very cheaply, from retired veterans in country places, who had not yet heard what was going on in Congress. There was an orgy of corruption, in which shrewd business men, most of whom had taken no part in the war, profited at the expense of old soldiers and other simple folk. There was much indignation, but it was powerless to influence the course of events.

The prime mover in these transactions was the Secretary of the Treasury, Alexander Hamilton, one of the ablest and most important men in history. There is no evidence that he was personally corrupt, indeed he left office a poor man. But he deliberately promoted corruption, which he considered desirable as giving due influence to the rich. What others defended only from self-interest, he defended disinterestedly; for instance, he advocated the growth of manufactures, partly because he thought child labour a good thing. "Women and children," he says, "are rendered more useful, and the latter more early useful, by manufacturing establishments, than they would otherwise be. Of the number of persons employed in the cotton manufactories of Great Britain, it is computed that four-sevenths, nearly, are women and children; of whom the greatest proportion are children, many of them of a tender age." He disliked democracy, and admired England. Throughout his career, he aimed at making America resemble England. He hoped that plutocracy would develop into aristocracy, and he rightly regarded corruption as the best method for causing plutocracy to prevail over democracy. . . .

He became the leader of the Federalists, and accomplished a great deal in the way of a wide interpretation of the powers of the Federal Government. He used the tariff to encourage manufactures. He consolidated financial, commercial, and industrial capital, and so built up a party which controlled America, except to some extent in foreign policy, from 1789 till Jefferson's accession to the Presidency in 1801.

From 1790 and 1794, both Hamilton and Jefferson were members of Washington's Cabinet. At first, on his return from France, Jefferson failed to apprehend the drift of Hamilton's policy, and helped him to secure the assumption of the States debts at par by the Federal Government—an action which he subsequently regretted. Before long, a bitter hostility developed between Jefferson and Hamilton, and they became the respective leaders of two violently hostile parties. No two men could have been more antithetical. Jefferson stood for democracy and agriculture, Hamilton for aristocracy and urban wealth. Jefferson, who had always been rich and prominent, believed men to be naturally virtuous; Hamilton, who had had to struggle against poverty and the irregularity of his birth, believed men to be fundamentally corrupt and only to be coerced into useful behaviour by governmental pressure. Jefferson, secure on his estates and among his cultivated friends, believed in the common man; Hamilton, who knew the common man, sought out the society of the socially prominent. Jefferson, whose multifarious interests made him happy and unambitious, was of a forgiving disposi-

James Madison, coauthor of The Federalist, *with Hamilton and John Jay.*

tion and high-minded in all his political campaigns; Hamilton, whose vanity needed the re-assurance of success, was venomous as an enemy and unscrupulous in controversy. Both in a measure succeeded, and both in a measure failed: Jefferson made America the home of democracy, Hamilton made it the home of the millionaire.

In politics, the victory went to Jefferson; in economics, to Hamilton. Hamilton's party went to pieces, largely because he lost his head, but it could not have controlled the government much longer than it did, however ably it had been led. The expansion of America westward increased the number of voters who believed in Jeffersonian democracy; so did the foreign immigration, particularly of the Irish, since Hamilton and his party were pro-English. Later developments, by increasing the area devoted to agriculture, only increased the hold of democracy on American politics. Politically, Hamilton's attempt was a forlorn hope.

From an economic point of view, the history of his policies has been very different. For various reasons, at first more or less accidental, American manufactures enjoyed a gradually increasing measure of protection; as the tariff was frequently an issue in elections, employers and employed in industry had the same economic interests. Consequently, in spite of some sporadic movements in the '30's, there was little proletarian politics, and industrial regions tended to be solidly conservative. Corruption, deliberately introduced into the body politic by Hamilton, found increasing opportunities in the development of the West, first in connection with the allotment of new lands, and then in the financing of railways. The West, while it struggled against the power of Eastern capital, was invariably defeated, partly by corruption, partly by its inability to formulate a programme. The Western farmer's own convictions, like the Constitution of his country, forbade disrespect for the rights of property, and these very rights secured his subjection to the banks. The rich in America grew richer than any men had ever been before, and acquired a degree of power far exceeding that of the monarchs of former times.

Agricultural democracy of the Jeffersonian type can succeed in a country like Denmark, which offers little opportunity for large-scale capitalistic developments. But in a vast region such as the United States, where the agriculturist is in essential dependence upon the railway, an agrarian liberalism cannot hope to succeed. To master the great forces of modern capitalism is not possible by means of an amiable go-as-you-please individualism. By fastening this now inadequate philosophy upon American progressives, Jefferson unintentionally made the victory of Hamiltonian economics more complete than it need have been.

The philosophies of which these two men were the protagonists dominated American life until the year 1933.

John Allen Krout (essay date 1957)

SOURCE: "Alexander Hamilton's Place in the Founding of the Nation," in *American Themes: Selected Essays and Addresses of John Allen Krout,* edited by Clifford Lord and Henry F. Graff, Columbia University Press, 1963, pp. 19-32.

[*In the following essay, originally a paper delivered before a meeting of the American Philosophical Society in 1957, Krout stresses Hamilton's importance as a pioneer American economist and advocate of centralized government.*]

Every successful nation-builder of modern times—Colbert in the seventeenth century, the elder Pitt in the eighteenth, Cavour and Bismarck in the nineteenth—understood the relation of economic strength to political power, and the links between each of these and national security. Alexander Hamilton was no exception. If he seems, at times, to tower above the others in that company of talented men who brought into being the United States of America, it is because he stated more precisely and more forcefully than most of his fellows the principles which would enable his generation to use economic policy as an instrument to achieve both national unification and national power. He was not concerned primarily with the development of a consistent theory or the formulation of an ideal system. His thinking about national power was strongly conditioned by two facts: first, that the young Republic was an almost insignificant weakling in the power politics of western Europe, and second, that despite the influence of the American Revolution and the immediate impact of Adam Smith's *Wealth of Nations,* the theories and practices of mercantilism still dominated the thought and action of those who wielded political power.

It is useless to speculate on the course which Hamilton might have taken, had conditions been different; but there is fascination in reading his eloquent exposition of the international advantages of free trade which appears in the opening paragraphs of his ***Report on Manufactures,*** submitted to the Congress in 1791. Here is no mercantilist brief, no slavish copying of British practices. It is a convincing demonstration of one of Hamilton's greatest sources of strength as a political realist—his courageous facing of the facts, however intricate, whenever he chose a plan of action.

Action, not theory, was the central theme of his entire career. There was little of the cloistered study about him. From his early years on St. Croix in the British West Indies to the hour he left Washington's Cabinet, he found himself trying to resolve increasingly complicated problems rather than to formulate logical theories. Even in little King's College, where the academic pace was much too leisurely for him, he became involved in public affairs. To be sure, he worked hard on the classics and moral philosophy; he read rapidly in Plutarch's *Lives,* Bacon's *Essays* and Hobbes's *Dialogues,* but nothing could keep him out of the momentous debate between colonies and mother country. His pen was soon active in the war of pamphlets, and so effective was his argument that he had established a reputation as one of the abler writers of his generation before the first shots were fired at Lexington and Concord.

For Hamilton the war years, in spite of his close association with Washington, were cruelly disappointing. His craving for military fame was never satisfied; yet his military service inspired, or at least did not seem to impede, his logical thinking about the problems that caught his imagination. His brilliant reports on army organization and administration, as well as his penetrating analysis of the business of raising money to fight a war, still make exciting reading. Notable as these contributions to our military annals were, they seem inconsequential compared to the essay, in the form of a letter addressed to Robert Morris, which he put into the post on the very day in 1781 that he resigned as Washington's aide.

This message to Morris, newly established in his position as Superintendent of Finances, looms larger the longer one contemplates it. Here Hamilton, just past his twenty-fourth birthday (or his twenty-sixth, if one accepts the most recent calculations of historical scholars), boldly stated the principles essential for the building of a strong nation. Some of his associates had heard his thesis in fragmentary form on other occasions; but he had never indicated so explicitly how he would use political power, if it ever came to him. His plan was much too bold for Morris, who was naturally cautious, in spite of his financial speculations, and at the moment uncertain of his own ability to lead. The Financier could not know that his young correspondent had actually provided him with a workable blueprint for the next decade—and for generations thereafter.

But nothing that Hamilton wrote in later years reveals any more clearly the shape of a nation in the making. Out of his awareness of local prejudices, provincial rivalries, and the clamor for state sovereignty came his insistence that the Republic, to which he was emotionally devoted, must begin to "think continentally." Out of his contempt for the vague and the visionary, he fashioned a plan that was difficult but possible, bold but not dangerous, furthering the self-interest of men of property but cleverly contrived to use that self-interest for the public good. He did not fall into the error of so many in his generation, who persisted in confusing the economy of the private household with the principles of public finance.

What the nation needed most, Hamilton argued, was a currency adequate to its business needs and financial credit sound enough to command international confidence. Both could be provided by a national bank under public auspices, but attractive to private capital. Such an institution would

> create a mass of credit that will supply the defect of moneyed capital, and answer all the purposes of cash; a plan which will offer adventurers immediate advantages, analogous to those they receive by employing their money in trade, and eventually greater advantages; a plan which will give them the greatest security the nature of the case will admit for what they lend; and which will not only advance their own and secure the independence of their country, but, in its progress, have the most beneficial influence upon its future commerce, and be a source of national wealth and strength.

Hamilton admitted that the "national wealth and strength" would be dependent upon the willingness of the government to borrow against its future and to pledge complete repayment of all its debts. He quickly tried to quiet the opposition of those who feared such a burden by characterizing a national debt as "a national blessing." "It will be a powerful cement of our union. It will also create a necessity for keeping up taxation to a degree, which, without being oppressive, will be a spur to industry." Probably no part of Hamilton's plan came closer to the English model, which he so greatly admired, and certainly no other feature was so violently attacked.

The financial proposals in the 1781 memorandum were less startling than the frank revelation of his political nationalism. On this theme his words were never to be "sicklied o'er" with moderation. The weaknesses of the Continental Congress, the lack of a strong central government, could not be corrected by the Articles of Confederation, which had just been ratified. A century and three-quarters after the event, one cannot read his words without being convinced of the genuineness of his alarm. "Disastrous dissolution" would be the fate of the Republic at its very beginning unless Congress was given "complete sovereignty in all but the mere municipal law of

each state." "I wish to see a convention of all the States, with full power to alter and amend, finally and irrevocably, the *present futile and senseless Confederation*." It is no exaggeration to regard this as the "first call" for the Constitutional Convention which finally met in May, 1787.

Almost forty years ago Henry Jones Ford insisted that the events of 1787 constituted for the young New Yorker his "wonderful year." And so it was. This was the time when Hamilton began to build on the blueprint of 1781. He had help in construction, but there is a large measure of truth in the assertion of some historians that we owe to Hamilton more than to any other person the fact that we have a federal constitution and that we are a union rather than a league of jealous and warring states. His was the determination, the fixed objective, the steady hand. Much has been made of his relatively minor role in the Philadelphia Convention, his dislike of both the New Jersey and the Virginia plans and his own futile proposal of a plan of government as close to the "English model as circumstances and the temper of the people would permit." "I have no scruple," he declared, "that the British government is the best in the world and I doubt much whether anything short of it will do in America."

Such a sentiment went against the silence with which the Convention treated his proposals, and his speedy departure for New York, seems to mark his complete failure at Philadelphia. But this is a superficial view. It was Hamilton, neither Washington nor Madison nor Jay nor Franklin, who had made the Constitutional Convention possible. He had moved from the feeble conference of Virginia and Maryland commissioners at Mount Vernon in 1785 to the unsuccessful convention a year later at Annapolis, attended by representatives of only five states. But with Madison's help he used failure at Annapolis as the sounding board against which to issue the call for a meeting in 1787 that was successful. Hamilton's departure from Philadelphia was not the act of a leader too stubborn to compromise, who sulks at the first rebuff. So it has been portrayed by some of his biographers; but they are mistaken. He used the weeks from June 30 until September 2, when he returned to Philadelphia, in trying to overcome hostility to the whole idea underlying the Convention and in preparing men's minds for whatever compromise the delegates might finally approve.

His persuasive efforts involved no speeches, no appearances before mass meetings, no appeals to the crowd. Hamilton's medium was the written word. As a political essayist, he was unsurpassed. His articles appeared in the press, his encouraging letters went to Washington and Rufus King in the Convention, to Jeremiah Wadsworth, David Humphreys, and other friends in New England, advising them how to answer the Convention's foes. It was a period of preparation for the defense of the Constitution that was to come. Indeed, some of the letters of this period may have been as influential as some of the essays that comprise *The Federalist*.

Anyone who reads widely in the incomparable *Federalist* essays, in which Madison and Jay joined Hamilton, will quickly realize what Thomas Jefferson meant when he said "in some parts it is discoverable that the author means only to say what may be best said in defense of opinions in which he did not concur." He could not have come closer to the mark, if he had known that he was really aiming at Hamilton, for the young New Yorker never tried to conceal his disagreement with many of the provisions of the Constitution—though he gladly signed it. It was the measure of his statesmanship—that he put his own opinions aside, overcame his personal prejudices, and accepted the document as the only safeguard against "disunion and anarchy." Having made that decision, he never wavered in his public support of the work of the Convention. He wrote the major portion of the *Federalist* essays, which Jefferson praised as "the best commentary on the principles of government which ever was written"; and no American voice has ever dissented from that appraisal.

Hamilton's contemporaries, as well as his biographers, have been in substantial agreement that his own effort was the deciding factor in persuading New York to ratify the proposed Constitution at the Poughkeepsie Convention in 1788. When the document became fundamental law the following year, his most important work was actually finished. He had made his great gift to his fellow countrymen. He had shown them how their slender resources might be marshaled effectively to provide the national defense and domestic tranquility which they so sorely needed. His whole fiscal and financial program, as Secretary of the Treasury, had been explicitly stated years before he entered Washington's cabinet. However remarkable the famous Reports of 1790 and 1791, they rest securely on political foundation stones which Hamilton had set a decade earlier: first, the business and propertied classes generally must be tied by bonds of self-interest to the national government; and second, public policy should be directed toward the encouragement of economic diversification—including manufacturing and commerce as well as agriculture—capable of creating an integrated national economy and a firm political union.

The translation of his policies into law was a major triumph for the Secretary of the Treasury, but it was less important for the young Republic than the imaginative formulation of the principles out of which the policies grew. Indeed, the years during which Congress accepted the financial program known as the "Hamiltonian System" were marred by the blunders of the man who had written the legislation. Hamilton was not content to serve merely as a Chancellor of the Exchequer. He never overcame his desire to be regarded as the Prime Minister. He gave Washington advice, even when the President had not requested it, on foreign policy, legal affairs, military problems, and matters of protocol. In the process he established precedents which are still followed, but he also alienated associates in the government whose support would have been invaluable.

Perhaps Hamilton's greatest weakness in the half dozen years of the apparent triumph of his fiscal and economic policies was his failure to understand how rapidly the political opinions of his fellow countrymen were changing. Between the inauguration of George Washington and the election of Thomas Jefferson in 1800 a process of education in democracy had been going forward steadily. Wherever Hamilton encountered this process, he was inclined either to oppose or to ignore it. He refused to see that the Jeffersonian doctrine of "the cherishment of the people" encouraged the greatest possible diffusion of political power among a progressively educated body of citizens. Instead, he regarded the Republicans, who carefully nurtured the Jeffersonian doctrine, as a group of fractional insurgents, too quick in their imitation of the French Jacobis. But the Republicans had sensed the temper of this generation. To their standard rather than to the symbols of the Federalist party, the new voters were drawn. As a result, Hamilton and his associates were able only to design and construct the new edifice of government; men motivated by a broader concept of their civic responsibility moved in and took over the completed structure.

They did not dare, however, to destroy Hamilton's design. Indeed, they modified but slightly the precedents which he had set. Federalist institutions, even Federalist policies, survived, surprisingly intact. The Bank and the public funds remained undisturbed. The military and naval establishments, though reduced in size, were not abolished. The hated excise tax was repealed and other internal revenue duties were modified; but the Republicans in Congress initiated no general assault on the powers of the central government, which Hamilton had done so much to create.

Many Americans today are inclined to regard the first Secretary of the Treasury as merely an adroit politician, brilliant and versatile, but no greater in his influence on later generations that the short-lived Federalist party to which he belonged. A partisan leader he was, and a determined one. Yet no strategy of his in the political arena, not even his triumph in persuading the First Congress to accept his fiscal plans, can compare with the persistent force of his economic ideas. His critics, as well as his friends, recognized that during his years of service in Washington's cabinet he seemed to do the thinking for the administration.

The leaven of Hamilton's thought in time brought action even within the ranks of the Jeffersonian Republicans. By 1815 the leaders of the faction, dubbed the "War Hawks," had accepted a nationalistic program highly imitative of the "Hamiltonian System." Though they had won no decisive victory over the British during the War of 1812, they had captured President Madison and persuaded him to accept their program. It was, therefore, James Madison, once Thomas Jefferson's chief lieutenant, who wrote the proposals of the economic nationalists into his presidential message of December, 1815. Josiah Quincy, Massachusetts Federalist, listening to that message, sarcastically remarked that the Republican party had "out-Federalized Federalism"; for Madison asked the Congress to approve (1) a liberal provision for national defense, (2) governmental aid for the construction of roads and canals, (3) encouragement to manufacturers by means of a protective tariff, and (4) the re-establishment of a National Bank. Though the words were Madison's, many in both House and Senate must have been thinking of Alexander Hamilton.

The response of the Congress was quick and enthusiastic. A committee of the House, headed by John C. Calhoun, reported a bill to establish a Bank of the United States, not unlike the First Bank which had ceased to exist with the expiration of its Charter in 1811. A few of the "Old Republicans," like John Taylor of Virginia, protested against this "surrender to the money power," but most of their Republican colleagues accepted the Bank as a necessary extension of the powers of the national government. Henry Clay, with a characteristically dramatic flourish, rose to confess that he had spoken vigorously against the recharter of the old Bank in 1811, but that he was now sacrificing consistency for the welfare of his country. The sense of high drama must have been heightened for those among his hearers who realized that his eloquent speech closely followed Hamilton's arguments in 1791, when he wrote for Washington a defense of the constitutionality of the first Bank bill.

Nor was Henry Clay the only leader in his generation who turned to the writings of Hamilton for inspiration, even for the effective phrasing of ideas. John Marshall, then brilliantly engaged in reenforcing the spirit of nationalism, presided over a Supreme Court that handed down a series of opinions calculated to strengthen the federal government and to give judicial sanction to the doctrine of the implied powers to be derived from the Constitution. Few decisions have had greater influence on the course of constitutional government in this country than Marshall's opinion in the case of *McCulloch vs. Maryland* in 1819. His vigorous argument, upholding the power of Congress to charter a bank, was actually a rephrasing, in somewhat more legalistic terms, of Hamilton's classic exposition of the doctrine of implied powers.

Though sectional rivalries and partisan politics thwarted the plans of these economic nationalists early in the nineteenth century, their followers in a later generation carried similar views into the Republican party. Young Abraham Lincoln in Illinois, a devoted supporter of Henry Clay and the American System, was but one of many whose imagination was quickened by the spirit of nationalism that pervades every public paper written by Alexander Hamilton. Consider, for example, Lincoln's first political speech. The report of it may be apocryphal; yet the tone is so characteristic of him that it almost compels acceptance. In announcing his candidacy for the Illinois state legislature early in 1832, he said:

> I presume you all know who I am. I am humble Abraham Lincoln. I have been solicited by many friends to become a candidate for the Legislature. My politics are short, and sweet, like the old woman's dance. I am in favor of a national bank. I am in favor of the internal improvement system, and a high protective tariff. These are my sentiments and political principles. If elected, I shall be thankful; if not, it will be all the same.

Though the personal mood is alien to Hamilton, the political program is his.

Surely it is not merely the eye of fancy that sees in the Congressional legislation of the Civil War years some of the greatest triumphs of the Hamiltonian philosophy. His ideas were but slightly modified by those who championed such laws as the protective tariffs of 1862 and 1864, the granting of federal lands to the Union Pacific and Central Pacific railroads, the establishment of a national banking system in 1863, and the passage of a contract labor law to stimulate European immigration. Every one of these measures received the approval of the Illinois "railsplitter" in the White House, who had dedicated his life to the preservation of the Union which Hamilton had done so much to build.

It is wise for us to remember that Hamilton, like every worthy statesman, spoke and wrote in context. His United States of America was a young and relatively insignificant republic in the great family of nations. His task was to give it energetic leadership in the uncertain years of its infancy. His loyalty transcended every parochialism and embraced the nation. His quest was for national strength, and he used skillfully whatever resources promised to be most effective. Among the founders of this nation none argued more eloquently than he for that combination of private enterprise and governmental policies which has made industrial America what it is today. And none succeeded so well in translating theory into action.

Schlesinger compares Hamilton with John Adams:

Adams was . . . more consistent than Hamilton in his belief in the knavery of men. Hamilton was ready to repose confidence in the "rich and well-born" on the ground that, "as they cannot receive any advantage by a change, they therefore will ever maintain good government." He believed that "no plan could succeed which did not unite the interest and credit of rich individuals with those of the state." Adams, on the other hand, found little to choose between the greedy rich and the hungry poor. "There is no reason," he wrote, "to believe the one much honester or wiser than the other"; in a homogenious system, "equal laws can never be expected. they will either be made by numbers, to plunder the few who are rich, or by influence, to fleece the many who are poor." . . .

They were sharply contrasting figures—the staunch, irasible, honest Yankee lawyer with his instinct for the past, and the ambitious, lucid, bold West Indian with his instinct for the future. And the contrast illuminates a chronic dilemma of American conservatism: does conservatism mean a belief in keeping things as they are? or does it mean a faith in the "rich and well-born" even if such faith may be a means of change? Adams' philosophy would have probably produced social responsibility but economic stagnation; Hamilton's has produced social irresponsibility but economic progress.

Arthur Schlesinger Jr., in The New Republic, *January 1, 1962.*

Gouverneur Morris's funeral oration for Hamilton, read July 14, 1804.

If on this sad, this solemn occasion, I should endeavor to move your commiseration, it would be doing injustice to that sensibility which has been so generally and so justly manifested. Far from attempting to excite your emotions, I must try to repress my own; and yet, I fear, that, instead of the language of a public speaker, you will hear only the lamentations of a wailing friend. But I will struggle with my bursting heart, to portray that heroic spirit, which has flown to the mansions of bliss.

Students of Columbia—he was in the ardent pursuit of knowledge in your academic shades when the first sound of the American war called him to the field. A young and unprotected volunteer, such was his zeal, and so brilliant his service, that we heard his name before we knew his person. It seemed as if God had called him suddenly into existence, that he might assist to save a world! The penetrating eye of Washington soon perceived the manly spirit which animated his youthful bosom. By this excellent judge of men he was selected as an aide, and thus he became early acquainted with, and was a principal actor in the more important scenes of our Revolution. At the siege of York, he pertinaciously insisted on and obtained the command of a Forlorn Hope. He stormed the redoubt; but let it be recorded that not one single man of the enemy perished. His gallant troops, emulating the heroism of their chief, checked the uplifted arm, and spared a foe no longer resisting. Here closed his military career.

Shortly after the war, your favor—no, your discernment, called him to public office. You sent him to the convention at Philadelphia; he there assisted in forming that constitution which is now the bond of our union, the shield of our defense, and the source of our prosperity. In signing the compact, he expressed his apprehension that it did not contain sufficient means of strength for its own preservation; and that in consequence we should share the fate of many other republics, and pass through anarchy to despotism. We hoped better things. We confided in the good sense of the American people; and, above all, we trusted in the protecting providence of the Almighty. On this important subject he never concealed his opinion. He disdained concealment. . . .

At the time when our government was organized, we were without funds, though not without resources. To call them into action, and establish order in the finances, Washington sought for splendid talents, for extensive information, and above all, he sought for sterling, incorruptible integrity. All these he found in Hamilton. The system then adopted, has been the subject of much animadversion. If it be not without a fault, let it be remembered that nothing human is perfect. Recollect the circumstances of the moment—recollect the conflict of opinion—and, above all, remember that a minister of a republic must bend to the will of the people. The administration which Washington formed was one of the most efficient, one of the best that any country was ever blessed with. And the result was a rapid advance in power and prosperity, of which there is no example in any other age or nation. The part which Hamilton bore is universally known.

Brethren of the Cincinnati—there lies our chief! Let him still be our model. Like him, after long and faithful public services, let us cheerfully perform the social duties of private life. Oh! he was mild and gentle. In him there was no offense; no guile. His generous hand and heart were open to all.

Gentlemen of the bar—you have lost your brightest ornament. Cherish and imitate his example. While like him, with justifiable and with laudable zeal, you pursue the interests of your clients, remember, like him, the eternal principle of justice.

Fellow citizens—you have long witnessed his professional conduct, and felt his unrivaled eloquence. You know how well he performed the duties of a citizen—you know that he never courted your favor by adulation or the sacrifice of his own judgment. You have seen him contending against you, and saving your dearest interests, as it were, in spite of yourselves. And you now feel and enjoy the benefits resulting from the firm energy of his conduct. Bear this testimony to the memory of my departed friend. I charge you to protect his fame. It is all he has left—all that these poor orphan children will inherit from their father. But, my countrymen, that fame may be a rich treasure to you also. Let it be the test by which to examine those who solicit your favor. Disregarding professions, view their conduct, and on a doubtful occasion ask, Would Hamilton have done this thing?

You all know how he perished. On this last scene I cannot, I must not dwell. It might excite emotions too strong for your better judgment. Suffer not your indignation to lead to an act which might again offend the insulted majesty of the laws. On this part, as from his lips, though with my voice—for his voice you will hear no more—let me entreat you to respect yourselves.

And now, ye ministers of the everlasting God, perform your holy office, and commit these ashes of our departed brother to the bosom of the grave.

Dumas Malone (essay date 1964)

SOURCE: "Jefferson, Hamilton, and the Constitution," in *Theory and Practice in American Politics,* edited by William H. Nelson with Francis L. Loewenham, The University of Chicago Press, 1964, pp. 13-23.

[*Malone wrote the definitive biography of Jefferson: the six-volume* Jefferson and His Time *(1948-1981). In the following essay, he explicates the respective roles of Jefferson and Hamilton in shaping the interpretation of Constitutional law and the role of government.*]

Jefferson and Hamilton had much to do with interpreting the Constitution, but little or nothing to do with its framing. Had Jefferson been available, he could hardly have failed to be a delegate from his state to the convention which met in Philadelphia in 1787, but he was then minister of the United States at the court of France; he did not return to his own country, in fact, until after the Constitution had been ratified and put into operation with George Washington as President. Hamilton was a delegate to the Convention from the state of New York, but, since they voted in the Convention by states and he was regularly outvoted by the other New York delegates, he soon withdrew, realizing that he was virtually without influence on the deliberations. From what he said, however, and from what he wrote out for incorporation in the record, we know that he favored a national government so strongly centralized, so consolidated, that it would have had no chance of adoption by the states of the Union if it had been submitted to them. He would have reduced these states to administrative provinces, the governors of which were appointed by the President, who would himself hold office for life; and he would have reduced popular control to a very low point, for he had no confidence in the wisdom of the people. No doubt he would have accepted something less, as of course he had to do, but these views could not command much favor. Since the deliberations of the Convention were secret, they did not need to be made public, which was fortunate for him.

One person who certainly knew about them and, in fact, knew more about these proceedings than anybody else was James Madison, the man who best deserves to be called the father of the Constitution. . . . Not only was he there all the time; he also kept careful notes on the proceedings. These were not published in his own lifetime, but it is safe to say that no man of his generation knew as much about what actually went on in the closed meetings in Philadelphia and about what the framers had in mind. His intimate knowledge was fully available to Jefferson after that gentleman returned from France, for these two had no secrets from each other. It is my own guess, however, that Jefferson did not take time to study the written notes carefully, and that he got his impressions chiefly from what Madison told him personally. This must have included some reference to the extreme views which Hamilton had expressed with respect to national consolidation.

Hamilton settled for considerably less in the ratification fight and performed magnificent service in that fight. Madison's

service in it was comparable, and these two men co-operated in writing the *Federalist* papers, a work which excited Jefferson's enthusiasm and which has been universally recognized as a classic interpretation of the American governmental system under the Constitution. Since the original purpose of this series of essays was to win votes for ratification, however, and it was written in great haste, both men said some things they afterward regretted. For this reason no doubt both of them were glad that the authorship of the individual essays was not revealed. Since we now know just who wrote what, we can perceive that the constitutional philosophies of the two men were not identical, but it is as indisputable that they stood shoulder to shoulder in this fight as that they afterward diverged.

The explanation of this later divergence most favored by Hamilton's partisans was that it was owing to the sinister influence on Madison of Jefferson, after he came back from France full of wild revolutionary ideas. One difficulty about that fanciful theory is that Madison began to diverge from Hamilton before Jefferson got back on the national scene. Furthermore, in constitutional matters at this stage and perhaps at most times, it is nearer the truth to say that Madison told Jefferson than that Jefferson told Madison. Finally, it may be seriously doubted whether Jefferson brought back from France any important ideas that he did not already have when he went there. A more plausible explanation, it seems to me, is that Madison concluded that Hamilton in office as Secretary of the Treasury was seeking a greater degree of consolidation than he had argued for in the ratification fight, that he was in fact moving toward the sort of government that, as his expressions in the Philadelphia convention showed, he really wanted. This is to oversimplify the matter, however. Economic considerations were involved, and political opinion in Virginia surely was. That is, this was not merely a matter of constitutional theory. Further explanation must be sought in the actualities of the political situation.

Let us now return to Jefferson, who had been relegated to the role of distant observer while he was in France. If the Constitution as framed was a less powerful instrument than Hamilton wanted, it was a more powerful one than Jefferson had expected or thought necessary, and at first glance he feared that it might be made into an instrument of oppression. Unlike Hamilton and Madison, he had seen despotism at first hand in Europe and had recoiled against it. One of his specific objections—of which there were really only two—was to the perpetual re-eligibility of the President, which seemed to leave the way open to the eventual establishment of a monarchy. He had a phobia about kings which now appears to have been unwarranted so far as his own country was concerned, but we must remember that he lived in a world in which kings were the rule and republics the very rare exception. He was determined that in America the clock should not be turned backward, that there should be no resort to the British example, no return to the political system from which the young American republic had so painfully emerged. In that context his talk about kings and monocrats in this period of history does not sound so unrealistic. He continued to be disturbed, throughout this period, by what he described as monocratic tendencies, but his immediate fear that there might be an American king was quieted by the reflection that George Washington would be the first president. Jefferson, who viewed the national hero with a respect bordering on reverence, never thought he would permit himself to be made king. (In passing we may remind ourselves that Washington started the two-term tradition, and that Jefferson confirmed it.)

The second specific objection was not, as some might suppose, that the Constitution went too far in curtailing the powers of the states. He was surprised that the states had yielded so much but was fully aware that their powers had been far too great, and as an official he had had abundant reason to recognize the imperative need of bolstering up the general government. No, his immediate fears were not of what might happen to states; they were of what might happen to individuals. This is a crucial point, I think. A good reason for not putting tags on people is that it is generally impossible to find a perfect fit, but if I had to designate this complicated man of diverse genius by a single term I would call him an individualist. We must remember also that, although in his own commonwealth of Virginia he had observed and been part of a mild government, he had seen nowhere a government which in a positive way could be truly called beneficent. There was nothing remotely suggesting the welfare state, which renders direct services and benefits to its individual citizens. He had insufficient reason to think of government as a positive good. He did not say that government is a necessary evil and I do not believe that his approach to it was as negative as has often been alleged, but unquestionably he believed that all sorts of governments tended to be repressive and that rulers tended to become tyrannical.

In other words, individuals needed to be protected against their rulers, against any rulers. Specifically, the American Constitution needed a bill of rights and he was shocked that it did not have one. His correspondence with Madison on that subject is most interesting and illuminating. It made an impress on Madison, who was himself a staunch friend of human rights but had been giving most of his thought lately to the creation of an effective federal government. It was Madison who introduced the Bill of Rights in the form of amendments to the Constitution in the first Congress. Indeed, the promise of some action of the sort was a virtual condition under which his state and other states ratified the Constitution, and we have always regarded the Bill of Rights as a part of the original document, thought it was not actually quite that. (Incidentally, it should be noted that Madison was particularly aware of the criticisms of the Constitution in the ratification fight, and of the explanations and assurances that were then given by its advocates. These bore chiefly on the limitation of centralized authority, and he took them so seriously that perhaps it may be said that he was now prepared to settle for less central power than he had advocated in the Federal Convention.)

Since Jefferson's major objections to the Constitution were met, he accepted it. He would never have assumed the secretaryship of state if he had not. The partisan charge of later years that he was against the Constitution meant nothing more than that in his interpretation of that document he did not agree with Hamilton. He was no antifederalist in the original meaning of the term, whatever his political enemies might say.

The two men did not disagree on all points, of course, and we must recognize the danger of exaggerating their differences and ignoring the very large area of agreement. They approached constitutional questions from opposite angles, however, and the gap between them widened in the actualities of successive political situations. Had situations been different it is certainly conceivable that the gap would never have become so wide. I regard it as exceedingly unfortunate that it became such a chasm. I am disposed to explain it on the ground of what appears to be virtually a law of history, namely, that excess tends to promote excess, that extremes on one side lead to extremes on the other. To be more specific, I do not believe that Jefferson would have gone as far as he did in interpreting the Constitution in this era if Hamilton had not pressed things so far and so hard, and in the duel with Jefferson which ensued, I regard Hamilton as the aggressor, even though he himself claimed just the opposite.

Some degree of conflict was probably inevitable, however, in view of their antithetical philosophies and incompatible personalities. The temptation to dwell on their personalities must be resisted, for this conflict went much deeper than that. But in this connection Hamilton's personality is of particular importance, because the reaction against his policies and the constitutional interpretation with which he supported them cannot be dissociated from the personal reaction against him. He had constructive talents of the first order and in the realm of government and finance may truly be described as creative. But he was an exceedingly aggressive man, inordinately ambitious, and undeniably arrogant. He was a hard man to like unless one agreed with him completely, and it was easy to believe that he was doing everything possible to increase his own power. He provoked resistance. That he wanted power for himself cannot be doubted, but he also wanted it for the nation. Indeed, that is the best way to describe his central purpose.

Hamilton's patriotism cannot be questioned, but one can ask what he wanted a powerful nation for. He himself gave one of the best answers in something he said later in this decade, at a time when he and his partisans would have liked to enter the international arena on the side of Great Britain and against France. He wrote Rufus King, then our minister in London: "I anticipate with you that this country will, ere long, assume an attitude correspondent with its great destinies—majestic, efficient and operative of great things. A noble career lies before it" Hamilton to Rufus King, Oct. 2, 1798 [*Works of Alexander Hamilton,* ed. H. C. Lodge, 1904]. He wanted it to play a great and active role in the world, and it is easy to see why Theodore Roosevelt admired him. In the perspective of history it seems that Hamilton's major service was in laying foundations of national power for the future, and for this we should be grateful, since we have had to enter the world arena. In his own time he seized every opportunity to extend the authority of the general government; indeed, he created opportunities. He wanted as much as possible to be done at the center; regarding the state governments as a good deal of a nuisance, he had no concern for state rights; and he was indifferent to, even contemptuous of, the ordinary individual.

His attitude toward ordinary individuals would not commend him to our democratic age, but in certain respects he was a notably prophetic figure. Indeed, he was far ahead of his time. The United States was not ready to play a great role in the world until the era of Theodore Roosevelt, and prior to our own century its major task was to open up its own land and develop its own resources. That sort of thing could not be well directed from the center. Jefferson correctly perceived that at this stage it was of the utmost importance to have local vitality, or, if you will, vitality at the grass roots; and he believed that men will do and dare most if they breathe the air of freedom. It can be argued, therefore, that after Hamilton's great financial measures, which served not only to make the nation solvent but also to widen the authority of the national government, centralization had gone far enough. He envisioned a more spacious governmental edifice than these times required. That was the way Jefferson and Madison felt about it anyway, and if they could not stop him one way they would try another.

They did not do too well when they sought to check him on constitutional grounds in the most important theoretical conflict (outside the field of foreign affairs) in Washington's administration, the one over the first Bank of the United States. In this, Hamilton had much the better of the argument. Here is an excellent example of the impingement of political considerations on constitutional interpretation. Madison and Jefferson opposed the creation of this bank for a good many reasons, including their own ignorance of banking. Their own state had benefited relatively little from Hamilton's financial system, of which he regarded the bank as the crown, and they saw this as another instance of federal encroachment. Madison opposed it in the House on its merits, but he was not at his best in the field of banking, and he fell back on the Constitution. He could find nothing in the Constitution which, in his opinion, empowered Congress to grant a charter to a corporation. The bill was passed nonetheless, but Washington hesitated to sign it, since he rightly had a very high opinion of Madison as an interpreter of the Constitution. He passed it on to the Attorney General, who agreed with Madison, and then to Jefferson. It is from the latter's argument that we generally date the doctrine of strict construction. We might date it from Madison's speech, which contained essentially the same arguments, though they sound stricter in Jefferson's paper.

The doctrine of strict construction is much easier to understand than the one with which Hamilton opposed it. It is simply that a document means just what it says—no more, no less. According to the Constitution the general,

or federal, government possesses only specifically enumerated powers, all the others belonging to the states. In none of these enumerated powers is there any reference to granting charters of incorporation. Accordingly one must have recourse to the general expressions—the necessary and proper clause, for example. This Jefferson construed with complete rigidity, as meaning in effect "absolutely necessary." At this point I begin to be somewhat repelled by his argument; it is too rigid; he is imposing too severe a test. And I wonder if he would have taken so stiff and unyielding a position if he had not had so many grounds for wanting to stop Hamilton. As for the general welfare clause, his discussion of that, while somewhat pedantic, makes a lot of sense. If that clause were construed too liberally, Congress could do anything it liked, and there would be no need to have in the Constitution a list of the things it could do. Like Parliament, the legislature would be omnipotent.

The forbidding rigidity he displayed in this argument is not at all like Jefferson when he was discussing science or religion, and does not sound like the man who had said that constitutions should be revised every twenty years or so. But he would stand for no trifling with law while it was still on the books, least of all with a constitution; he regarded basic law as a shield or fence for the protection of human beings against wrong; he distrusted rulers who might interpret law in their own way for their own purposes; and by now he deeply distrusted Hamilton. So he prepared a paper which, though narrow, was utterly logical and which upon its face looked unanswerable.

Hamilton's answer to it is, in my opinion, the greatest paper he ever drew. He had to prove that the Constitution meant more than it explicitly said, that no government could be effective if rigidly confined within a narrow framework, that latitude must be permitted in the interpretation of basic law. He did this by starting with the premise that the federal government has sovereign power within the field allotted to it, and by concluding that in the exercise of this it may reasonably employ any means not specifically prohibited. There is more to his argument than this, but the important thing to remember is that the dominant trend of constitutional interpretation in our country was here anticipated. And whatever else this meant, it surely meant that our constitutional system would not be static but would be allowed to grow and might become dynamic. The essence of the matter Hamilton himself stated in a passage which ought to be quoted more often than it is: "The moment the literal meaning is departed from, there is a chance of error and abuse. And yet an adherence to the letter of its powers would at once arrest the motions of government." If Jefferson's observations of government and of his colleague had not rendered him so distrustful, he might have fitted these words into his own philosophy of progress, for certainly he did not believe in a static society. There is more sweet reasonableness in Hamilton's words, however, than those who differed with him in policy had detected in his public conduct; and they may be pardoned for believing that he was interpreting and would continue to interpret the Constitution to suit himself. They did not give up the fight, and it is well they did not, for he was a man who had to be kept in bounds. He was always likely to overreach himself.

This conflict had been waged behind the scenes, not in public; and there is no reason to suppose that Hamilton's opinion was shown to Jefferson and Madison. They undoubtedly knew his general line, but they did not see his full argument and had no occasion to rebut it. They did not abandon strict construction, though I do not believe that they again used it in a form which was quite this rigid. It was a natural, almost inevitable line for them to take afterward as leaders of the opposition to a government which was exercising powers which they thought unwarranted and regarded as dangerous to human liberty. This was after Washington had relinquished the first office but when Hamilton was more powerful than ever. It was the time of the Alien and Sedition Acts.

(Some extremely interesting constitutional questions, relating to the powers of the House of Representatives with respect to treaties, came up in the long fight over Jay's treaty. Jefferson was then in retirement and Republican policy was determined by Madison, Gallatin, and others in Congress. The episode is an unusually good illustration of the effect of party policy on constitutional positions. Jefferson expressed himself freely on the subject in private, showing himself a complete Republican in this matter and taking a different position from the one he probably would have as Secretary of State. Since this subject is relatively technical, however, I shall not enter into it here.)

The situation created by the notorious Alien and Sedition Acts was far more dangerous to Jefferson's dearest interests than the one in which Hamilton successfully defended the Bank of the United States. That proved to be an excellent institution even though it did relatively little for the agricultural districts. These measures were adopted at a time of hysterical patriotism and fantastic fear of subversive foreign influences (especially French) the like of which our country has rarely seen, though our own generation can perceive a certain similarity to it in the madness we had to live through shortly after World War II, when some excited people saw subversives behind every bush. There was no single public figure in this earlier period of hysteria who can be properly compared to the late Senator Joseph McCarthy, who played a unique role as an inciter of suspicion and hatred, but on the whole I believe that the situation then was considerably worse. There was a concerted campaign, in the name of patriotism, against every form of criticism of the federal government, and against the very existence of political opposition. In short, freedom of opinion and speech was at stake, and the party of which Jefferson was the undisputed leader was threatened with destruction. By silencing its newspapers the party in power sought to deprive it of a voice. This was the policy of the extreme section of the party commonly described as High Federalists. Their acknowledged leader was not John Adams but Hamilton, who was not in office but whose influence was at its height. If I seem to ignore him in discussing this particular matter you may safely assumed that Jefferson and

Madison were battling against him, more than against any other man, and that he opposed them on all points.

All I have space for here is the response to this challenge which Jefferson and Madison made in the Kentucky and Virginia Resolutions. These were conceived in no vacuum, and the direction they took, though not necessarily the details, was determined by the actualities of the situation. The three branches of the general government—executive, legislative, and judicial—were united with respect to these detested laws. Hence Jefferson turned to the states because he had nothing else to turn to. He had said very little about the rights of states before he became fearful of Hamiltonian consolidation. Now, under the pressure of circumstances he found intolerable, he took the most extreme position of his entire life with respect to state rights.

The direct part he played in these events was not made public until long years afterward, by which time he had returned to a more moderate position and his own administration as President had been assailed on grounds of state rights by his political opponents. Not until after his retirement was it known that he drafted the Kentucky Resolutions. But they and their companion Virginia Resolutions, which Madison drew, became part of the public record. In later years these documents were often cited by upholders of the state-rights tradition—a tradition which our Southern forefathers naturally clung to as they passed into the minority, but in the name of which they took actions which proved disastrous. Many of these forefathers of ours misinterpreted Jefferson's position. Never again did he emphasize the theory of state rights as he did here, and not even here were these the prime consideration. What he did was to invoke state rights in defense of human rights, as a means and not an end. And it is as a champion of human rights that he should be best remembered.

This question has so many ramifications that I cannot possibly do justice to it in brief compass. For the purposes of the present discussion, I should remind you that the Alien and Sedition Acts have received virtually unanimous condemnation at the bar of history. Therefore, Jefferson was abundantly warranted in inducing the states of Kentucky and Virginia to protest against them. He sought to support his position, as the Republicans had already done in Congress, by arguing that these acts were unconstitutional. Without entering into these arguments I simply make the point that in a dangerous political situation he and his party resorted to the Constitution for defense. Naturally, they followed the line of strict construction and, against what they regarded as an unwarranted assumption of power by the federal government, they talked of the reserved rights of states. In the Kentucky Resolutions of 1798, Jefferson went to the dangerous extreme of asserting the right of a single state to declare unconstitutional an act of Congress which it judged to be in violation of the original compact, and in his draft he said that the nullification of such a law within a state's own borders was proper procedure. This proposal the Kentuckians left out of their first set of resolutions but they used it the next year in a second set which Jefferson did not write.

The South Carolinians resurrected the word "nullification" a generation later in a wholly different situation. They were then opposing a tariff which was obviously disadvantageous to them, but their protest, unlike Jefferson's, was not in the name of the universal human right to freedom. Madison in his resolutions did not claim the right of nullification by a single state. In the final document of this series, his magnificent Report of 1800, he refined away the original excesses and put the Republican party on defensible ground. Without implying that I now agree with everything he said, I can safely say that there is real validity in the doctrine of state rights as presented in this report. With all this Jefferson went along, showing increased moderation as dangers lessened. But the highest wave at the peak of the storm left its mark on the shore.

This episode provides a striking illustration of the intimate connection between constitutional interpretation and political situations. Indeed, we would do well to think of these historic resolutions primarily as political documents. We should certainly remember that Jefferson never attempted to put into practice the extreme theory he advanced at a time when he almost despaired of human liberty and the survival of his party. This was a theoretical matter altogether. It is far more important to remember what he fought against and what he fought for than a particular weapon which he never regarded as anything but a threat and which in fact he afterward discarded.

In dealing briefly with so complicated a subject as this, it is easy to create a confused impression. I hope that one impression at least is clear: namely, that people ought to know more about history. We have no right to expect highly detailed and special knowledge of many people, but surely we can ask that anybody who draws on ancient documents or doctrines to support a position he himself is taking should inform himself of the major circumstances which caused that document or doctrine to come into being. The only thing that can be safely quoted out of context is something that bears upon itself the mark of timelessness and universality. Constitutional interpretations do not do that, even when they are reiterated often enough to become doctrines, even when they harden into dogma. They cannot be divorced from circumstances. It is fortunate that this is so, for no constitution which cannot be adjusted to changing conditions can be expected to survive. One of the major reasons for the long survival and recognized success of our Constitution is that it has proved flexible. Judges have to consider all that has gone before, and they should anticipate as best they can what the future effects of their judgment may be, but, after all, they are addressing themselves to particular cases in specific situations.

In constitutional matters, as in theological, I regard the absolutist spirit as unfortunate. It is presumptuous to think that God is on one side or the other in a constitutional debate. The truth need not lie precisely in the middle, but in major controversies there are generally important conflicting interests which must somehow be reconciled. One of the major tasks of government is to reconcile them. To me it is regrettable that the two eminent men we have been talking about diverged so far, and I dislike the excesses of both, though I do not say that I dislike them equally. I can forgive Jefferson more because I tend to value freedom more than power, to be more fearful of power than of liberty. But if we now had as feeble a national government as he advocated a century and a half ago, our liberties would surely perish. So I must recognize that somehow we must reconcile ourselves to Hamilton. Indeed, I suppose that we have been reconciling the conflicting philosophies of these two men from their day to this as we have found ourselves in a succession of particular situations.

Albert Furtwangler (essay date 1979)

SOURCE: "Strategies of Candor in *The Federalist*," in *Early American Literature,* Vol. XIV, No. 1, Spring 1979, pp. 91-109.

[*In the following excerpt, Furtwangler provides a close analysis of language and rhetorical strategy in* The Federalist.]

In the course of the eighteenth century an important shift occurred in the usage of the word "candor," so that it came to mean what it does today: forthrightness, frankness, direct honesty. Corresponding with this shift was a perceptible turn in the way readers and authors regarded one another or looked at the writings that stood between them. When a writer early in the century asked his readers to be candid in accepting his productions, he relied on a kind of polite deference that was to disappear in the course of succeeding decades. Yet as late as 1788, we can find the authors of the **Federalist** papers appealing to this earlier mood of candor. In fact, Hamilton, Jay, and Madison went out of their way to make this mood a persistent theme of their work, referring to it at the beginning and end of the entire series and frequently recalling it in the midst of their most rigorous political reasonings. Why should they have done this and exactly how did they manage this appeal? The answers to this question provide us with a valuable way into the flavor of their constitutional arguments and into the structure not only of disparate papers but of the **Federalist** as a whole.

The history of "candor" and its meanings is briefly summarized in the *Oxford English Dictionary.* Five definitions of the word are listed there, but the first two need not detain us long. Both are obsolete and are valuable chiefly as root meanings from which later usages have developed. The first, "brilliant whiteness; brilliancy" was last recorded in 1692; the second, "stainlessness of character; purity, integrity, innocence," faded out around 1704.

The third definition, now marked obsolete or archaic in the *Shorter Oxford English Dictionary,* more directly affects later developments: "freedom from mental bias, openness of mind; fairness, impartiality, justice." It is first

John Jay, who cowrote The Federalist *with Hamilton and James Madison.*

recorded in a poem of Ben Jonson's dated 1637, and this usage is common throughout the eighteenth century. The remaining meanings trace a shift of attitudes toward such disinterestedness or freedom from bias.

The older attitude is given in the fourth definition: "freedom from malice, favourable disposition, kindliness," or in Dr. Johnson's words, "sweetness of temper, kindness." (Later editions of Johnson's dictionary defined "candid" as "free from malice; not desirous to find faults.") Two examples from the great lexicographer's writings precisely catch this meaning: "He shews himself sincere, but without candour" (1751) and "That bigotry which sets candour higher than truth" (1765). This is an old-fashioned, deferential sort of candor to be sure. The word fits in conveniently with eighteenth-century optimism and doctrines of benevolence, and with the good manners they have begotten. This usage arises around 1653 and passes away, or is last recorded, in 1802.

The fifth, modern, and only surviving definition turns from such good feeling and indulgence to a balder sort of disinterestedness, and even to an energetic challenge against presumed doubtfulness or secrecy: "freedom from reserve in one's statements; openness, frankness, ingenuousness, outspokenness." The first example is dated 1769 and comes from the *Letters of Junius:* "This writer, with all his boasted candour, has not told us the real cause of the evils."

Thus does the usage of a single word suggest a subtle change in the mental outlook of an age. And looking up from the dictionary for a moment, one may recall that that is just what this word does in that mid-century masterpiece, Voltaire's *Candide.* The protagonist of that little work is nothing if not free from malice, sweet of temper, and favorably disposed to all that he encounters. As the opening words explain, he is a perfect example of the trusting candor of the fourth definition: "un jeune garcon à qui la nature avait donné les moeurs les plus douces. Sa physionomie annonçait son âme. Il avait le jugement assez droit, avec l'esprit le plus simple; c'est, je crois, pour cette raison qu'on le nommait Candide." Yet the more modern candor of the author shows him up at every turn imaginable, revealing the limitations of such persistent and groundless optimism, and trying to penetrate to a deeper truth. In the end, both the character's name and the title of the book stand for a wisdom born of bitter experience rather than the easy hope of an innocent.

Looking further abroad into the writings of this period, we should also notice that an author's understanding of candor could condition the way he presented himself before the public. As long as old-fashioned candor could be trusted, he might appeal to a reader's good will and try out new experiments and propositions without personal risk. If the readers "bring not candor to the reading of this Discourse," says Walton in the earliest example of this usage, they shall "injure me . . . by too many criticisms." And, by implication, if the readers do bring candor, then they and the writer can build on a platform of mutual generosity. It would not be correct to say that the peculiar prose form of the eighteenth century, the anonymous or pseudonymous periodical essay, arose on this basis alone, but it was certainly nourished by a mood of candor. In the early and influential *Spectator,* for example, Addison was at pains to try out experiments in criticism and sustained argument from paper to paper. And at the outset of his most ambitious projects he adverted to this mood quite specifically. When he introduced a series of eighteen papers on *Paradise Lost,* he asked his readers to respond freely but gently. "If you have made any better Remarks of your own, communicate them with Candour; if not, make use of these I present you with." Later, he apologized for seeming picayune in criticizing Milton, recalling that "Ancient Criticks . . . who were acted by a Spirit of Candour, rather than that of Cavilling, invented certain figures of Speech, on purpose to palliate little Errors of this nature." Finally, when he reviewed his critical efforts and tried to sum them up in his papers on pleasures of the imagination, he appealed for polite indulgence: "As an Undertaking of this nature is entirely new, I question not but it will be receiv'd with Candour." A spirit of generous courtesy thus informed Addison's ideal relation with his readers, especially when he threatened to become censorious himself or embark on a risky venture. And his continuing importance as a moralist and essayist may well have promoted a century-long remembrance of this kindly decorum in public discourse.

Yet, in adopting Addison's essay form and perhaps by borrowing something of his prose style, the *Federalist* did not necessarily have to be kindly, generous, and sweet tempered. It could just as easily have been harsh, biting, mean, blunt, or aggressive—with good precedents from other more polemical essays of the age. Most writers on the proposed Constitution, to be sure, simply took up the standard device of persuasive anonymity and applied it to the urgent necessities of their situation. Furthermore, an appeal to the good name of candor became a well-worn debating maneuver in 1787. Richard Henry Lee, for example, opened his *Letters of a Federal Farmer* by promising to study the issues "so far as I am able, with candor and fairness; and leave you to decide upon the propriety of my opinions, the weight of my reasons, and how far my conclusions are well drawn." Governor George Clinton, in the first of his *Cato* letters, urged his readers to "deliberate . . . on this new national government with coolness; analyze it with criticism; and reflect on it with candor." And again: "Beware of those who wish to influence your passions . . . —personal invectives can never persuade, but they always fix prejudices, which candor might have removed." In other words, two senses of candor seem to have been widely used on this occasion. Anyone drawn into analyzing the new Constitution would want to seem disinterested. And a shrewd debater would also want to persuade readers that they were acting candidly—from pure and generous motives—in siding with him.

The *Federalist,* however, penetrated through these tactics to focus on a candor that went beyond disinterest or enlightened self-interest, a generous candor that became almost an end in itself. Its opening paper makes this attitude the central issue of a proper approach to the Constitution.

In a long central paragraph, Hamilton uses the word for the first time—not merely to warn readers away from the wild zeal of adversaries, but to generously admit that truth and motives for zeal can make strange combinations.

> I am well aware that it would be disingenuous to resolve indiscriminately the opposition of any set of men (merely because their situations might subject them to suspicion) into interested or ambitious views. Candor will oblige us to admit that even such men may be actuated by upright intentions; and it cannot be doubted that much of the opposition which has made its appearance, or may hereafter make its appearance, will spring from sources, blameless at least, if not respectable—the honest errors of minds led astray by preconceived jealousies and fears. So numerous indeed and so powerful are the causes which serve to give a false bias to the judgment, that we, upon many occasions, see wise and good men on the wrong as well as on the right side of questions of the first magnitude to society. This circumstance, if duly attended to, would furnish a lesson in moderation to those who are ever so much persuaded of their being in the right in any controversy. And a further reason for caution, in this respect, might be drawn from the reflection that we are not always sure that those who advocate the truth are influenced by purer principles than their antagonists.

Of course, Hamilton moves on promptly to suppose that truth and safety are most likely to be found among partisans of strong government; to frankly acknowledge that these papers "proceed from a source not unfriendly to the new Constitution"; and thus to set adversaries of the new plan under a shadow. But this fair-minded wavering at the outset is ample and generous, and it leads to a promise which Publius was scrupulous to observe: "My arguments will be open to all, and may be judged of by all. They shall at least be offered in a spirit which will not disgrace the cause of truth."

The reasons for this generous opening may lie partly in the immediate circumstances of the *Federalist*'s publication. In New York, the Constitution had been attacked in September in Clinton's *Cato* letters. Two virulent papers of counterattack, by "Caesar," soon followed. Whether or not these latter papers were by Hamilton, they set a precedent of intemperate squabbling from which the *Federalist* authors needed to distance themselves. But they also had better reasons for sustaining a more tolerant spirit—reasons that lay in the way this series was organized, the nature of its own argument, and the larger political situation it addressed. Each of these factors deserves some extended attention.

First of all, the *Federalist* aimed to meet *every* criticism that was likely to arise against the Constitution. This is stated quite specifically near the end of the first paper. "In the progress of this discussion I shall endeavor to give a satisfactory answer to all the objections which shall have made their appearance, that may seem to have any claim to your attention." The point is stressed again at the opening of No. 15. "If the road over which you will still have to pass should in some places appear to you tedious or irksome, you will recollect . . . that the difficulties of the journey have been unnecessarily increased by the mazes with which sophistry has beset the way. It will be my aim to remove the obstacles from your progress in as compendious a manner as it can be done, without sacrificing utility to despatch." This design of meeting and answering objections shows up in the structure of paper after paper, especially in the later stages of this work.

The consequences of such a plan are subtle and far-reaching. By setting out to meet objections, Publius immediately cast himself as a defender rather than an attacker in this debate—as a spokesman for positive action rather than captious criticism. He also committed himself to develop an extensive argument. The *Federalist* is longer than other contemporary essays on ratification; it does take in a "compendious" survey of Constitutional problems. Its purpose, moreover, was not only to survey these problems but to conclude discussion about them, "to give a satisfactory answer" that might silence the noise of a misleading opposition. In this way Publius could display a massive weight of authority. Hamilton and Madison had been leaders in the call for the Philadelphia convention, and the latter had been the most assiduous delegate there, recording and mastering the details of the long summer's debates. Now in the public forum of the periodical press of New York, these men had the chance to enlarge and settle the strength of their positions as constitutionalists. In appropriating the name "federalist" for their cause they tacitly absorbed the legitimacy of those who would preserve the old confederation, and so left their opponents in the position of useful antagonists, purveyors of objections to be met and fully answered. For all these reasons, they were well prepared to write amply and generously on the Constitution. In a word, they were better prepared than anyone else to write with full-bodied candor.

Some leading ideas in the *Federalist* also required a tone of assured good will. For example, the authors were prompt to develop the notion that the Philadelphia convention itself had been specially blessed by concord, respect, civility, and sober deliberation.

> This convention, composed of men who possessed the confidence of the people, and many of whom had become highly distinguished by their patriotism, virtue, and wisdom, in times which tried the minds and hearts of men, undertook the arduous task. In the mild season of peace, with minds unoccupied by other subjects, they passed many months in cool, uninterrupted, and daily consultation; and finally, without having been awed by power, or influenced by any passions except love for their country, they presented and recommended to the people the plan produced by their joint and very unanimous councils.

These words, taken alone, might seem a parody of filiopietistic historical writing. In fact they come directly from Jay's *Federalist* No. 2, and a steady chain of reasoning in favor of "that sedate and candid consideration which the magnitude and importance of the subject demand, and which it certainly ought to receive." Madison dwelt further on how important it was to catch the fleeting occasion for a stable constitution. In No. 49 he insists that constitutional questions are too ticklish to be brought often before the public.

> We are to recollect that all the existing [state] constitutions were formed in the midst of a danger which repressed the passions most unfriendly to order and concord; of an enthusiastic confidence of the people in their patriotic leaders, which stifled the ordinary diversity of opinions on great national questions; of a universal ardor for new and opposite forms, produced by a universal resentment and indignation against the ancient government; and whilst no spirit of party connected with the changes to be made, or the abuses to be reformed, could mingle its leaven in the operation. The future situations in which we must expect to be usually placed, do not present any equivalent security. . . .

Again, in discussing the compromise of popular representation in the House and state representation in the Senate, he ascribes it to "a spirit of amity, and that mutual deference and concession which the peculiarity of our political situation rendered indispensible" (No. 62).

A very sophisticated treatment of why men can so seldom agree on basic issues appears in Madison's celebrated paper on faction, No. 10. There he argues that "the latent causes of faction are . . . sown in the nature of man." The reason of man is fallible and subject to the pressures of passion and self-love. Men join together most naturally over partial or factional issues, which are "adverse to the rights of other citizens, or to the permanent and aggregate interests of the community." For this reason, society is constantly divided into fragments or short-sighted interest groups, and the chief task of modern legislation is to regulate these interfering interests, and direct their energies to the common good. Englightened statesmen, even if such rare talents happen to be in power, cannot overcome this situation by themselves. They must be aided and sustained by the structure of a constitutional republic. Only be entrusting power to delegates, and by drawing governmental officers from a large geographical territory, can a people hope to control the effects of faction. By this means, no faction can grow large or strong enough to impose its will on the nation. Thus, concludes Madison, "we behold a republican remedy for the diseases most incident to republican government." Pressed to its logical conclusion, however, this line of argument leads to an enormous new problem. For if disinterestedness is so rare among men in politics—if indeed its opposite, factional interest, provides the energy necessary to animate popular government—how can a wisely designed constitution arise and come to control the endless, chaotic struggles for power among local demagogues and partisan alliances?

This problem preyed on Madison's mind as he continued to reason his way through these papers. Looking to antiquity in No. 38, he saw that in every government which ruled by consent of the governed, the task of framing a constitution fell to a single wise, just statesman. The task was too delicate, the difficulties too large, to risk dissension among collaborators. And in the end even Solon and Lycurgus resorted to compromise and stratagem to complete their undertakings. There was no other way to bring their own disinterested wisdom within the grasp of ordinary men. Viewed in this light, the Philadelphia convention was a prodigy in history. Only a candid eye could see properly into its disinterested work and, further, into the hopeful balance of compromises it had reached. Ideal readers of the *Federalist,* Madison insisted, "will proceed to an examination of the plan submitted by the convention, not only without a disposition to find or to magnify faults; but will see the propriety of reflecting, that a faultless plan was not to be expected. Nor will they barely make allowances for the errors which may be chargeable on the fallibility to which the convention, as a body of men, were liable; but will keep in mind, that they themselves also are but men, and ought not to assume an infallibility in rejudging the fallible opinion of others" (No. 37). Later in the same paper, he plainly expresses the problem the convention faced in overcoming the impediments of faction. A variety of factional interests, "for reasons sufficiently explained in a former paper, may have a salutary influence on the administration of the government when formed, yet everyone must be sensible of the contrary influence, which must have been experienced in the task of forming it."

> The real wonder is that so many difficulties should have been surmounted, and surmounted with a

unanimity almost as unprecedented as it must have been unexpected. It is impossible for any man of candor to reflect on this circumstance without partaking of the astonishment. It is impossible for the man of pious reflection not to perceive in it a finger of that Almighty hand which has been so frequently and signally extended to our relief in the critical stages of the revolution.

If candor thus led to astonishment and even awe at the work of the convention, the same spirit might accomplish yet more in the moment at hand. A paper constitution had been completed at Philadelphia, but it was still to be established as the basis of American life. Ratification remained uncertain as the *Federalist* was being written, and beyond lay the difficulties of turning words into deeds, clauses into precedents, the consent of a majority into sustained acceptance by a nation. "'T is time only," wrote Hamilton, "that can mature and perfect so compound a system, can liquidate the meaning of all the parts, and can adjust them to each other in a harmonious and consistent WHOLE" (No. 82). In such a delicate political situation, it was essential to develop a national spirit of good will. The Constitution obviously had to survive the worst attacks generated in the struggle over ratification, but to carry authority it also had to rise above them. The *Federalist,* in turn, had to be more than trenchant, and its authors had to see further than the winning of a few grudged ballots or narrow majorities. They had to dispel doubt, elicit assent, and promote a lasting sense of confidence in the new framework of government.

Pressure toward candor must have become even firmer when they considered that their cause might well succeed. Then not only would the Constitution come into force, but the collected *Federalist* would become its earliest full commentary. It might see prolonged service in the establishment of early administrations. Its arguments could be repeated to settle nice questions of interpretation. Its tone could be scrutinized again as actual crises revived doubts about the propriety of some provisions. If it should somehow become known that Hamilton and Madison were the authors behind Publius, further questions might arise about interpretations from their hands. Such major provisions as the accommodations between large states and small, and the distinctions between national and state powers, could take on a different color, especially if tell-tale personal remarks could be found in these papers. The only way out of such a perplexity was to produce arguments that would wear well no matter who had written them, to survey and anticipate all major criticisms that might arise, and to approach the worst that adversaries might offer in a mood of clear-sighted conciliation.

Thus candor developed as a mood directed outward from Publius toward his readers and even toward his opponents. But Publius stood as an ethical model, too, for the conduct and attitudes readers should adopt in return. He worked to elicit feelings of candor not only toward himself, or the *Federalist* papers, but toward the work of the convention, the new Constitution, and the embryo nation that would grow from its ratification.

Let us now consider the actual strategies used to foster this mood and look first at the general arrangement of arguments in the *Federalist* and then at devices peculiar to certain arguments or sets of papers. The first paper provides a general outline of topics, which Publius carefully recalled as he marked his progress from stage to stage. We can use it to construct a table of topical divisions:

1. The utility of the Union to . . . political prosperity (Nos. 2-14);

2. The insufficiency of the present Confederation to preserve that Union (Nos. 15-22);

3. The necessity of a government at least equally energetic with the one proposed, to the attainment of this object (Nos. 23-36);

4. The conformity of the proposed Constitution to the true principles of republican government (Nos. 37-84);

5. Its analogy to your own State constitution (No. 85);

6. The additional security which its adoption will afford to the preservation of that species of government, to liberty, and to property (No. 85).

The uneven division of space here, however, makes clear that this scheme was worn out well before the end. In fact, any such topical outline obscures the rhetorical stress points in these papers. The greatest number consist of replies to attacks made against particular points in the Constitution. But the consistent use of this approach comes late, from No. 39 to the end. Earlier papers prepare the way for it by focusing on the need for union among the American states and on the weaknesses of the old Confederation. The rhythm of argument thus falls into three segments—favoring union (Nos. 2-14); analyzing needs beyond Confederation (Nos. 15-36); and defending the structure of the Constitution (Nos. 37-85). It also falls into two large movements: positive remarks on the necessities and resources of American government, and defense of the Constitution at just those points where attack was heaviest or confusion was most likely. It is worth noticing that both these major movements are prefaced by explicit appeals to candor. The first follows Hamilton's opening paper and Jay's paean to the providential powers that so far had fostered a spirit of confidence in American union. The second begins with Madison's Nos. 37 and 38, which No. 39 describes as "observations . . . meant to introduce a candid survey of the plan reported by the convention."

The opening strategy of the *Federalist,* then, is to stress positive advantages of union. The states should further the harmony that already subsists under Confederation, to avoid dangers of strife from without and within. A series of three papers by Jay (Nos. 3-5) describes how disunion could draw foreign powers into local broils and lead to continuous warfare. Hamilton continues by discussing grounds of irritation that by themselves could lead to sectional disputes. Madison's No. 10 describes the positive advantages of size for a republican government. And Hamilton then observes several economic advantages in union. Madison closes this section by repeating how suitable an extensive union is to particular American conditions. His peroration in No. 14 then urges his readers to shut their ears to the "unnatural voice" that would counsel a separation, to heed rather the blood ties of family and mutual sacrifice, and to perpetuate the progress toward stable government that has been made since the revolution.

The substance of this argument now seems specious, since union among the states was already accomplished and its loss was not a necessary consequence of rejecting the Constitution. Hamilton introduces the subject rather warily at the end of No. 1, and neither he nor the other writers proves here that disunion was really imminent. As an opening maneuver, however, this line of argument gives Publius two clear advantages. First, he can press for a more perfect union—with a stronger central government—very forcefully by detailing the palpable advantages of present union. Second, he can make common cause from the first with almost any patriot; he appeals to a point already "deeply engraved on the hearts of the people in every State." Actually the logic of this argument depends on what was to follow. *If* Confederation was no longer workable and *if* the Constitution were rejected, *then* separation into new confederacies might have been a possibility. But consider the consequences of stating the argument in this more "logical" form: confederation is outworn; union is necessary; the Constitution is therefore an alternative to chaos. This is to begin with an attack on things-as-they-are, to run against the grain of adversaries and patriots alike, to set oneself up for heavy counterattack. Instead, Publius not only escapes rejoinder here, he puts his adversaries in the weaker position. He stands for union, for strengthening common advantages, for the steady progression of stable government. Cutting two ways at once, Madison in No. 14 accuses others of standing for novelty—"the most alarming of all novelties . . . that of rending us in pieces"—while he moves with the manly spirit of American innovation, from revolution to Constitution.

At the next stage of argument, Publius could not be so completely positive. To describe the insufficiency of Confederation he had to engage in attack and criticism. Yet he still manages to argue his case by maintaining a tone of affirmation. The strategy here is to assert that principles beyond reasonable dispute are what matters. Candid (i.e., disinterested) reasoners all must agree that Confederation is too weak. "It may perhaps be asked what need there is of reasoning or proof to illustrate a position which is not either controverted or doubted, to which the understandings and feelings of all classes of men assent, and which in substance is admitted by the opponents as well as by the friends of the new Constitution" (No. 15). Therefore it remains only to explain the grounds of this weakness and thereby build a candid (i.e., tolerant, appreciative) attitude toward the newly proposed form of government. The argument here divides into two topics—"the insufficiency of the present Confederation to pre-

serve . . . Union" and "the necessity of a government at least equally energetic with the one proposed." For both topics, incontrovertible axioms of government are set forth and the individual papers are derived from them.

Federalist No. 15 opens the discussion of Confederation by emphasizing a general weakness: "The great and radical vice in the construction of the existing Confederation is in the principle of LEGISLATION for STATES or GOVERNMENTS, in their CORPORATE or COLLECTIVE CAPACITIES, and as contradistinguished from the INDIVIDUALS of which they consist." This central point about weakness in government is then developed through reference not only to the present union of American states, but also to major confederacies of the past: feudal alliances (No. 17), the leagues of ancient Greece (No. 18), Germany, Poland, and Switzerland (No. 19), and the United Netherlands (No. 20). It is only after this prolonged discussion of general and historical considerations that Hamilton moves on to detail specific weaknesses in the Articles of Confederation (Nos. 21 and 22).

The general principle behind the next section also appears in emphatic typography. National powers (in particular, powers over national defense) "ought to exist without limitation *because it is impossible to foresee or define the extent and variety of national exigencies, or the correspondent extent and variety of the means which may be necessary to satisfy them*" (No. 23). The justification for this point, Hamilton insists, is sheer self-evidence. "This is one of those truths which, to a correct and unprejudiced mind, carries its own evidence along with it; and may be obscured, but cannot be made plainer by argument or reasoning. It rests upon axioms as simple as they are universal; the *means* ought to be proportioned to the *end;* the persons, from whose agency the attainment of any *end* is expected, ought to possess the *means* by which it is to be attained." The issue at hand is not how much power should be granted, therefore, but what ends the federal government should pursue without limitation. In general, the papers that follow serve to define these major ends—common defense and public safety (Nos. 24-29) and control over national revenue (Nos. 30-36).

At this point in the *Federalist* some individual papers also make a conspicuous display of rigorous, incontrovertible reasoning. The survey of historical confederacies effects its "experimental instruction" with the weight of sheer fact. And Hamilton's later papers devote much precious space to repeating that primary truths can be found in ethics and politics as surely as in geometry (No. 31); or that there are propositions so necessarily implied in "the very act of constituting a federal government . . . that moderation itself can scarcely listen to the railings which have been so copiously vented against this part of the plan, without emotions that disturb its equanimity" (No. 33). Altogether these papers witness an intensive effort to make criticism appear as affirmation, or at least as the corollary of shining certainties.

Yet from No. 24 onward Hamilton had also organized some of his papers by noticing the objections of adversaries. As Madison moved on to discuss the main features of the Constitution, he too assumed this approach as his central mode of argument. He begins by generally and affirmatively surveying the Constitution as a whole under several general topics: the republican form of government that would be established (Nos. 39-40), the amount of power to be vested in the new government (Nos. 41-46), and the structure through which that power would be distributed (Nos. 47-51). On each of these topics, however, he immediately turns to questions raised by real or supposed adversaries, and develops his papers as replies.

The advantages of this third major strategy are plain enough. Earlier, the *Federalist* authors had been able to use materials they already had at hand. Hamilton had notes he had used in the longest speech given at the Constitutional Convention. Madison had prepared a set of "Notes of Ancient and Modern Confederacies" for use in Philadelphia, and his novel theory of extensive republics had gone through three written versions before the *Federalist* began. But this material was now exhausted. The demands of the printers continued at the rate of three or four papers a week. And Madison and Hamilton went on writing their papers in consecutive series, singlehandedly. "It frequently happened," Madison wrote later, "that, while the printer was putting into types parts of a number, the following parts were under the pen and had to be furnished in time for the press." Under these circumstances, the clamor of the opposition provided Publius with some welcome assistance. By taking up the chief arguments that had already been made on a subject, he could readily provide himself with a clear focus. Furthermore, he could shift the burden of his argument very conveniently, without sacrificing its continuous development. Earlier he had had to attack Confederation while seeming to affirm its basic principles of union and representative government. Now he had to explain the Constitution without reducing it too compactly into the controversial products of a rigorous theory. To deal with the Confederation he had had to be positive, asserting his own authority in interpreting a common experience. But the Constitution was not yet common to public knowledge, let alone experience. It was still being developed. As it stood, it went beyond the plans that Hamilton, Madison, or anyone else had brought to the convention. It still had to survive the test of nine or more ratifications. Even then it might be amended (with perhaps a bill of rights). And it would surely be modified by the precedents to be set in establishing an actual federal executive and judiciary. Its clauses now called for interpretation that would be clear but not rigid, precise but not narrow. Hamilton and Madison were exceptionally well prepared for detailed argument of just this sort. And if there was a danger of becoming too detailed, it was offset by the fact that there were to be more than thirty of these papers, progressing steadily through the sections of the Constitution on "the several parts of the government" (No. 52).

The "edge" of argument in these later papers thus arose from the antifederalists, to be smoothed by Publius. Candor was observed by blunting and absorbing attacks so that argument might end in justified agreement.

Publius began the reconciliation by looking beyond persons to issues, and drawing the latter into the full light of day. He practiced severe restraint toward particular adversaries, almost never mentioning names or otherwise calling attention to the exact source of any attack on the Constitution. Frequently he made arguments seem widely held by imputing them broadly to "the adversaries of the plan of the convention." He might take note that various (unspecified) groups objected to the same point for different reasons. (As Madison put it in No. 58, "most . . . objections against the Constitution . . . can only proceed from a partial view of the subject, or from a jealousy which discolors and disfigures every object which is beheld.") He might distinguish "the more respectable adversaries" (No. 47), "the most intelligent of those who have found fault" (No. 76), or even "the more candid opposers" (No. 61). But proper names are rare. I have found them raised in only five papers, and invoked there mainly to clarify some marginal observations.

To completely absorb attacks, Publius was careful, too, to state them fully and allow for the most contingent circumstances in which they might prove telling. An especially good example of this fullness can be found in No. 44. This paper faces the "necessary and proper" clause (Article I, section viii, clause 18), which seems to grant blanket powers beyond those enumerated in the same section of the Constitution. Madison denies that excessive powers are granted here, and the method of his answer is characteristic. First he appeals to the alternative means that might have been used to the same end. "There are four other possible methods which the Constitution might have taken on this subject." One by one he names them, and one by one he shows that each of them leads to impossible consequences. Then he goes further. What if Congress itself misconstrues this part of the Constitution? He describes a remedy for that in the separation of federal powers and in the balance between the states and the federal government. Then he goes further still, by noticing another similar provision—the "supreme law of the land" clause (Article VI, clause 2)—and giving three prompt arguments in its defense, too. In short, Publius not only returns a sufficient answer, but penetrates beyond the immediate objection into the depth of the problem that prompts it.

Even when an adversary's charges seem strained and farfetched we find Publius leaning out to catch and respond to them. "The only refuge left for those who prophesy the downfall of the State governments," reads No. 46, "is the visionary supposition that the federal government may previously accumulate a military force for the projects of ambition." Is this remark an out-of-hand dismissal of such prophets? No; their position is attacked here as absurd on its face, but the paragraph goes on to meet it even so. "Extravagant as the supposition is, let it however be made." The *Federalist* has a further answer ready in that case, too. Similar concessions can be found at the close of Nos. 40, 60, 63, and 64.

The most extraordinary involution of deference toward adversaries occurs, however, in No. 54, concerning the provision in Article I for counting slaves as three-fifths of "other persons" for purposes of taxation and representation. Madison begins by condensing the leading objection: "Slaves are considered as property, not as persons. They ought therefore to be comprehended in estimates of taxation which are founded on property, and to be excluded from representation which is regulated by a census of persons. This is the objection, as I understand it, stated in its full force." But to answer the objection, Publius invokes yet a further mask. "I shall be equally candid," he says, "in stating the reasoning which may be offered on the opposite side"; but that reasoning is presented as what "might" be observed by "one of our Southern brethen." This manifestly fictitious slaveholder is quoted through several paragraphs, and in the end Publius concludes that though such reasoning "may appear to be a little strained in some points, yet, on the whole, I must confess that it fully reconciles me to the scale of representation which the convention have established."

The light of later history makes this part of the *Federalist* seem ingenuous if not inhumane, in its compromised calculations of how much like a man a black slave could be. And all for the remote end of adjusting votes and taxes! But a closer look reveals Madison being conscious, steady, and principled here. If the convention had been strained to its limits, it had been so over questions of representation. And as Madison had noticed in the debates, if there were one great difference between regions it was the contrast between small, free states to the north, and large, slave states to the south. Constitutionalist James Madison of Philadelphia here holds slaveholder Madison of Virginia at arm's length, and acknowledges the weaknesses of the southern case. In fact, he forces the southern spokesman to admit from the first that slaves are persons and that "it is only under the pretext that the laws have transformed the negroes into subjects of property, that a place is disputed them in the computation of numbers; . . . if the laws were to restore the rights which have been taken away, the negroes could no longer be refused an equal share of representation with the other inhabitants." At the same time he catches northerners in the paradox of reproaching the South for the "barbarous policy" of considering "human brethen" as property, while arguing on the other hand that Negroes should not be represented. Publius thus upholds this provision by anatomizing the difficulties of any partisan approach to it. He interprets it by allowing that it is, and can only be, a strained compromise—one that he cannot defend on any principles of his own. Yet he shows, too, that no matter how anyone writhes around the point, a Negro has to be considered a man.

As the *Federalist* authors refined and nullified the objections they saw, they exposed the confusion of some critics and the misunderstandings of others. They also called into question the motives that might have lain behind some lines of opposition. Preaching candor themselves, they were quick to find and comment on others' lapses. In No. 24, for example, Hamilton asks us to follow the mental processes of "a stranger to our politics, who was to read our newspapers at the present juncture, without having previously inspected the plan reported by the convention." As this perfectly disinterested observer sought information about the controversy before him, he would find himself astonished at the groundless vehemence of attacks on certain points. And as he went on to gather complete information, "his astonishment would not only be increased, but would acquire a mixture of indignation." And if "he happened to be a man of calm and dispassionate feelings, he would indulge a sigh for the frailty of human nature, and would lament, that in a matter so interesting to the happiness of millions, the true merits of the question should be perplexed and entangled by expedients so unfriendly to an impartial and right determination." With remorseless logic, Madison likewise separated the critic from the unthinking supporter of the Constitution. Both types were wrong, he said in No. 37, but at least the latter was temperamentally in the right. And Jay began the only paper he contributed to the later *Federalist,* No. 64, by questioning "the motives of their conduct, who condemn the proposed Constitution in the aggregate, and treat with severity some of the most unexceptionable articles in it."

These considerations seem to justify the several shorter remarks tossed off here and there on the "rage for objection" that provokes one attack or the "insatiable avidity for censure" that has invented another. But counterattacks like these could go only so far before they violated candor in their turn.

Thus it is almost amusing to contemplate Hamilton's dilemma in *Federalist* No. 67. This paper begins his series on the presidency, the focus of centralized power, and it seems to touch Hamilton on a tender spot. Instead of opening with a broad consideration of the needs for a well-organized executive branch (as he does later, in No. 70), he immediately lashes out—and at the particular barb of a particular foe, the fifth letter of Governor Clinton's *Cato* series. The language of this *Federalist* is harsh; its imagery vivid; its central argument narrowly conceived. Cato had charged that the president would be like a monarch; Publius replies by hammering at one small point, that presidents cannot fill casual vacancies in the Senate. One can almost feel the heat glowing off Hamilton's cheeks here in a hand-to-hand struggle between the two mighty New Yorkers. But only "almost"—because even here he is at pains to acknowledge that the *Federalist* allows only so much. No part of the Constitution, he says, has been attacked with so little candor; and it is therefore necessary not only to meet adversity here, but to unmask it.

> In the execution of this task, there is no man who would not find it an arduous effort either to behold with moderation, or to treat with seriousness, the devices, not less weak than wicked, which have been contrived to pervert the public opinion in relation to the subject. They so far exceed the usual though unjustifiable licenses of party artifice, that even in a disposition the most candid and tolerant, they must force the sentiments which favor an indulgent construction of the conduct of political adversaries to give place to a voluntary and unreserved indignation.

Facsimile of Hamilton's commission as inspector general of the U.S. Army, signed by President John Adams.

At the end of the paper, he apologizes again: "Nor have I scrupled, in so flagrant a case, to allow myself a severity of animadversion little congenial with the general spirit of these papers." Even in anger, Hamilton preserves so much of Publius' decorum.

Throughout the *Federalist,* then, we find remarks about candor, arguments about how indispensable it is in this debate, and, more important, conscious perceptions of how intrinsic it is to republican government, matched by deliberate maneuvers and restraints in the rhetoric of all three authors and in the design underlying their collaboration.

Even so, a scrupulous reader may still feel uneasy about this term and its usage in this work. The *Federalist* authors may have toyed with the name of candor and even seen advantages in flaunting their own practice of the attitude. But generous candor, as it is defined here, is nothing if not an exercise in deference—a feeling that might well be encouraged by an authoritarian Hamilton or a well-born Madison. How better defend the indefensible than by insisting on the necessity for trust in matters too pressing for delay and too delicate for complete analysis? To modern readers, accustomed to the modern sense of candor—and to debates about the motives of the founders—a haunting question still lingers. Does the *Federalist* present genuine, forthright insights about the nature and promise of the Constitution, or does it not? The evidence we have reviewed here does not provide a sufficient answer.

But I have tried to make a different approach to such questions by looking at the *Federalist* as a whole and on its own terms. The generalized views of its several authors, or the secrets of their personal motivation, have thus been slighted here; so have the substantial issues and arguments of separate *Federalist* numbers. Instead I have tried to focus attention on one important line of coherence that can be traced throughout this composite text. If I still refrain from saying *whose* strategies of candor are at work in the *Federalist,* it is for this reason. To be candid myself, I believe that such strategies originated with neither a person nor a cabal, but may rather have been intrinsic to the nature of a full argument in favor of the Constitution. To pursue this matter further, one should explore how the demands of both form and argument drew Hamilton and Madison into areas of agreement they never knew before or after. This would involve detailed review of how each of them saw the Constitution through its several stages of creation and ratification. But it would also call for further searches into the coherence of these papers and the conventions of the essay-series in which they are cast. Such studies would end, I think, not in a vindication of anyone's sincerity, but in fuller discoveries of just how far we can ascribe integrity, consistency, or harmony to the writings of Publius.

Already we have seen how a commitment to candor checked and conditioned the answers Hamilton and Madison gave on issues that touched them closely. And we have found them avowing that the tone of these papers should count as much as their cold logic. In a perverse way, at least one major adversary acknowledged this point. Recall Madison's famous remark in No. 55: "As there is a degree of depravity in mankind which requires a certain degree of circumspection and distrust, so there are other qualities in human nature which justify a certain portion of esteem and confidence. Republican government presupposes the existence of these qualities in a higher degree than any other form." Or review the way Hamilton closes the whole series in No. 85, by adverting to "the spirit with which my endeavors should be conducted" and reminding his readers that the present moment can inspire awe: "The establishment of a Constitution, in time of profound peace, by the voluntary consent of a whole people, is a prodigy, to the completion of which I look forward with trembling anxiety." And now hear how Clinton closes the last of the *Cato* letters, for January 3, 1788. Reasonable confidence, he admits, has a proper place in government; "but such an unbounded one as the advocates and framers of this new system advise you to, would be dangerous to your liberties." There is only one sure bulwark against their appeal, prescribed by Demosthenes and echoed by Montesquieu: distrust. "There is, therefore, no other way of interrupting this insensible descent and warding off the evil as long as possible, than by establishing principles of distrust in your constituents, and cultivating it among yourselves." The price of liberty *is* eternal vigilance. But Cato seems not to understand that even vigilence in excess can become a yoke. His own pessimism reverberates in the dim prospect of merely "interrupting" and "warding off" inevitable evils. And he all but insists that the constitutionalists had a special potency on their side—not in what they propounded so much as in the positive faith with which they fostered it.

Forrest McDonald (essay date 1980)

SOURCE: "The Rhetoric of Alexander Hamilton" in *Rhetoric and American Statesmanship,* edited by Glen E. Thurow and Jeffrey D. Wallin, Carolina Academic Press and The Claremont Institute for the Study of Statesmanship and Political Philosophy, 1984, pp. 71-86.

[*In the following essay, originally a paper delivered at a conference in 1980, McDonald discusses Hamilton's language, his rhetorical strategies, and his literary style.*]

The political rhetoric of the Founders of the American Republic has received scant attention from scholars. The relative neglect is understandable. On the one hand, the very concept of rhetoric has, in modern times, all but lost its classical signification, and has come to mean empty verbosity or ornament. On the other, the political achievements of the Founders—the winning of independence, the establishment of a durable federal Union on republican principles, the creation of a system of government which is itself bound by law—were of such monumental proportions as to make their methods of persuasion seem of pedantic and picayune consequence. And thus, though every student of the epoch is at least vaguely aware that the general level of public discourse in late eighteenth-century America was extraordinarily high, perhaps unprecedentedly so, we tend to regard the way the Founders spoke and wrote as only incidental to what they did. I would contend, on the contrary, that it was their commitment to and practice of open, dispassionate, informed, and reasoned discussion of public questions which made their achievements possible. Their rhetoric, in other words, was not a mere by-product of their accomplishments: rather, their accomplishments were the product of their rhetorical interchange.

In the most general proper sense of the term, rhetoric is the art of persuasion through written or spoken language. In the classical and eighteenth-century usage, however, it meant persuasion according to certain formal rules. The Founding Fathers studied and practiced the art in accordance with the Aristotelian model, and . . . I shall begin by pointing out a couple of the implications inherent in that model.

First, Aristotle ruled out the relationship of rhetoric to pure knowledge, insisting instead that, since it was founded upon opinion rather than upon absolute truth, it was concerned only with matters of probability. I shall clarify that point later. For now, what is important is that consciousness of that limitation of the art was of immense value in the building of American republican institutions, for it meant that public discourse could not be conducted

in terms of ideological certainties of the sort that perverted the French Revolution and, indeed, most other revolutions. Instead, discussion of public questions was at its best a trial-and-error process of moving toward ever-greater probabilities of truth without succumbing to the fatal sin of gnosticism, the belief that one has arrived at absolute Truth.

Second, though the rules required that persuasion be based on reasoned argument, they permitted two additional forms of "proof" besides logical proof. These were ethical proof, which was designed to win from the audience a favorable attitude toward the author or speaker, and emotional proof, which was aimed at putting the audience in a receptive frame of mind. Given the Founding Fathers' understanding that men are governed by their passions—that is, drives for self-gratification—and by habits and sentiments, and that reason is normally the servant rather than the master of the passions, this meant that their rhetoric and their view of the nature of man could complement and reinforce one another. It also meant that they were enabled to (as they were obliged to) work toward raising the level of public sentiments as well as the level of public understanding. This was put simply and clearly by the celebrated author of the 1767 *Letters from a Farmer in Pennsylvania,* John Dickinson. In his seventh letter Dickinson quotes at length from speeches that Lord Camden and William Pitt had given in Parliament, praises the "generous zeal for the rights of mankind that glows in every sentence," and analyzes what it was that made their rhetoric so powerful: "Their reasoning is not only just—it is, as Mr. *Hume* says of the eloquence of Demosthenes, 've-hement.' It is disdain, anger, boldness, freedom, involved in a continual stream of argument."

Historians, in dealing with the Founding Fathers, have paid too much attention to the "justice of their reasoning" and not enough to their "vehemence." If a proper balance were brought to a study of the writings of the founders, I believe, the result would be an enormous contribution to our understanding of them. If I were outlining such a study, I would suggest a rhetorical analysis of a half-dozen patriotic tracts written between the 1760s and 1776: Dickinson's *Letters,* John Adams's *Novanglus Letters,* James Wilson's *Considerations on the . . . Authority of the British Parliament,* Thomas Jefferson's *Summary View of the Rights of British America,* Thomas Paine's *Common Sense,* and the *Declaration of Independence.*

I would also suggest that the student be sensitive to certain nuances of eighteenth-century political writing which have eluded most investigators. One concerns the meaning of words. The meaning of many crucial words has changed so radically that, without an *Oxford English Dictionary* at one's side, one is likely to commit grave errors of interpretation. In a moment I shall offer some fairly dramatic examples of the ways that meanings have changed; meanwhile, a related subtlety is that there were then, as there are now, a variety of code words in common currency. For instance, there was the phrase "Great Man." In one of my early books I missed entirely the connotations of the phrase: having noticed that it was frequently used to describe the financier of the Revolution, Robert Morris, I misread it to mean that even Morris's enemies viewed him with a touch of awe. Much later I learned that it had been used by English Oppositionists as a contemptuous description of Sir Robert Walpole, then applied to the corrupt and wealthy aristocrats who dominated English politics in mid-century. It was the Oppositionists' ideological heirs in America, anti-Federalists and Jeffersonian Republicans, who applied the term to Morris—as they did also to Hamilton and Washington—and they were using it as a form of condemnation. Finally, there are literary conventions which can sometimes be revealing. For example, pre-Revolutionary political tracts abounded in typographical variations—the use of italics, all capital letters, and extravagant punctuation—designed to achieve emphasis, indicating that the authors were thinking in terms of speech to small, tangible audiences. Upon the emergence of a truly national politics and the large, impersonal audience that that implied, typographical variations were abandoned, indicating that the writers now intended their words to be read rather than heard.

Enough of preaching: it is time to start practicing. I have been speaking of a study that someone should make; let us turn to one that I have made, of the rhetoric of Alexander Hamilton. As we do so, we immediately face three formidable obstacles, all of which arise from Hamilton's historical reputation. It is commonly alleged that Hamilton was contemptuous of public opinion; that he created a system based upon greed, in disdain of public spiritedness; and that he was hypocritical, saying one thing in private and another in public. These allegations, if true, would make analysis of his rhetoric pointless, save perhaps as an exercise in the study of duplicity. Each must therefore be considered before we proceed.

The first allegation rests mainly on a misreading of Hamilton's language. After the Whiskey Rebellion in 1794, Hamilton said in a letter to Washington that he had "long since . . . learnt to hold popular opinion of no value." If those words are read in their twentieth-century sense, they are pretty damning, and they seem conclusive; and that is the sense in which historians have read them. Richard K. Kohn, for instance, though usually a careful scholar, quotes Hamilton's remark, adds that President Washington "knew he could not govern on such principles," and cites with approval Secretary of State Edmund Randolph as saying that "Hamilton's ideas 'would heap curses upon the government. The strength of a government is the affection of the people'."

But let us consider Hamilton's language more carefully. The operative words are "popular" and "opinion." I do not have space here (even if I knew enough) to do full justice to the etymology of the word "popular" or to the historical distinction between it and the word "public," but I can summarize briefly. In its ancient forms and in its seventeenth and eighteenth century usage, "popular" comprehended everybody; in meaning, though not in its roots, it was akin to "common" or "vulgar." It also had a specific political connotation, namely left-wing (significantly, Hamilton's remark was apropos political attacks

in Philip Freneau's left-wing newspaper, *The National Gazette*). "Public," by contrast, was derived from the same root as the word public, meaning manhood; it referred individually to those who had attained the full status and responsibilities of manhood and referred collectively to the political society or body politic itself. Interestingly, "virtue"—which Montesquieu and others regarded as the actuating principle of a *republic*—was also derived from a root word meaning manhood. Thus the phrases "public virtue" and "republican virtue," which had considerable currency in eighteenth century America, were somewhat tautological, whereas "popular virtue" would have been a contradiction in terms, the component words being mutually exclusive. As for the word "opinion," it was used in at least three distinct ways in the eighteenth century. One was the Aristotelian usage, as a technical term associated with probability, with the assembly and the courts, and thus with rhetoric. More frequently, it was used in the present sense, meaning belief or prejudice. Still a third usage signified confidence, esteem, and high regard. Following an essay by David Hume, Hamilton had indicated in the Constitutional Convention that he used the term in the third sense. In other words, he was saying in 1794 that he held it of no value to be well-regarded by the rabble and by rabble-rousers—or, to phrase it differently, that statesmanship is not a popularity contest.

That is a far cry from expressing contempt for what the public thinks and believes. Hamilton made his meaning clearer in the rest of his letter to Washington: after saying that he had learned to hold popularity of no value, he added that his reward for service to the public would be in "the esteem of the discerning and in internal consciousness of zealous endeavours for the public good." Historians have somehow managed to omit that part of his letter, just as they have managed to ignore the fact that Hamilton probably expended more energy, thought, and words trying to create and guide an informed public opinion than did any of his contemporaries.

The second allegation, that Hamilton's policies represented an effort to build a political system on greed rather than on civic virtue, stemmed from more complex roots. It originated in the charges of his political enemies. Some (William Maclay, for example) were economically interested in discrediting Hamilton; others (Jefferson and Madison, for example) were politically interested in doing so; still others (John Taylor of Caroline, for example) were ideologically interested in doing so. But that view of Hamilton has also been expounded by an impressive array of modern scholars including E. James Ferguson, Gerald Stourzh, J. G. A. Pocock, and, most recently, Drew R. McCoy. The eighteenth century, as these historians have pointed out, witnessed the development of a school of political theory that espoused what Pocock calls "the movement from virtue to interest" as the activating principle of government: it began with Bernard de Mandeville's *Fable of the Bees* (1714), holding that private vice was the wellspring of public virtue, and ran through Adam Smith and his often-quoted passage which begins, "It is not from the benevolence of the butcher, the brewer or the baker that we expect our dinner, but from their regard of their own interest." According to McCoy, the "powerful, economically advanced modern state" which Hamilton envisaged "would stand squarely on the worldly foundations of 'corruption'" that Bernard Mandeville had spoken of.

The case is persuasive. Though Hamilton never read Mandeville, as far as I am aware, he did read and on several occasions quote from David Hume's essays in a similar vein, and he read and was influenced by Adam Smith. Moreover, in 1783 he clearly advocated the consolidation of national authority through appeals to the interests of public creditors and financial and commercial groups, and in 1784 he said flatly that "the safest reliance of every government is on men's interest." I myself have been guilty of writing that Hamilton's program as Secretary of the Treasury depended upon tying the interests of public creditors to the fate of his measures.

But I was wrong, and so are the others. Two things happened to Hamilton between 1783 and 1789 which radically altered his thinking on this subject: he learned from observing and participating in state politics that state governments could be more effective in employing avarice to win political support than could a national government, and he learned from study of the principles of natural law that morality, in the long run, was a more stable foundation for government than was economic self-interest. Despite the abundance of charges, there is no evidence whatsoever that Hamilton used the lure of personal gain in seeking congressional support for his measures. Moreover, he expressed himself clearly on the subject in a remarkable private document he wrote in 1795. In drafting his plan for assuming the state debts, he admitted, he had taken into account the tendency of assumption "to strengthen our infant Government by increasing the number of ligaments between the Government and the interests of Individuals. . . . Yet upon the whole it was the consideration upon which I relied least of all." Even on purely practical grounds, had this been "the weightiest motive to the measure, it would never have received my patronage." And, he added in a marginal note to himself, "such means are not to be resorted to but the good sense & virtue of the people."

The third common allegation against Hamilton, that he was hypocritical in his public utterances—and most particularly, that he spoke contemptuously of "the people" in private and sang a different tune for public consumption—is likewise without foundation. It is true that, in his youthful disillusionment with the way the Revolutionary War was going, he expressed his disgust with the people. In 1779 he wrote his intimate friend Henry Laurens that "the birth and education of these states has fitted their inhabitants for the chain, and . . . the only condition they sincerely desire is that it may be a golden one." The next year he wrote Laurens that "Our countrymen have all the folly of the ass and the passiveness of the sheep in their composition. . . . The whole is a mass of fools and knaves." In maturity, however, he arrived at a different and more balanced view and expressed it in public and private alike. I shall return to that later. Meanwhile, the measure of his

duplicity, or lack of it, is to be found in comparing his public writings, from *The Federalist Papers* through the 1790s, with his private correspondence. Such comparison reveals a record of virtually perfect consistency. The truth is that Hamilton was, as Fisher Ames said of him, "the most frank of men"; and, as he said of himself in a letter to an intimate friend, "what I would not promulge I would avoid . . . pride makes it part of my plan to *appear truly what I am*." Indeed, his passion for candor more than once led him to transcend the boundaries of prudence—as he did, for instance, in publishing the details of his sexual affair with Maria Reynolds so as to protect the integrity of the office he had filled.

Hamilton's rhetoric may be fruitfully examined by considering separately his employment of each of the Aristotelian forms of proof. Thorough analyses of two of his performances have been made along those lines: Bower Aly's study of Hamilton's speeches in the New York ratifying convention, published in 1941, and Larry Arnhart's study of the rhetoric of *The Federalist,* delivered before the Midwest Political Science Association in 1979, Some of what I have to say in the following pages draws on these two studies.

Logical proof, as opposed to ethical and emotional proof, carries the greatest portion of the burden in Hamilton's rhetoric. Let me pause here to say . . . that I shall try to keep this as simple as possible. Logical reasoning is of two broad kinds: deductive, which means reasoning from general propositions to arrive at particular conclusions, and inductive, which means reasoning from a number of particular observations to arrive at general propositions. The principal device of deductive reasoning is called a syllogism, and it is something we all employ even if we have never heard the word. A syllogism consists, in order, of 1) a major premise, 2) a minor premise, and 3) a conclusion, as in this example: 1) no man is immortal. 2) John Smith is a man, and 3) therefore John Smith is not immortal.

But deductive reasoning in rhetoric, though having the same structure as that in other forms of logic, is not quite the same in substance. In rhetorical reasoning, one uses a special kind of syllogism called an enthymeme. The main difference between a pure syllogism and an enthymeme is in the nature of the major premise. In a pure syllogism the major premise is absolutely true, as in "the square of the hypotenuse of a right triangle equals the sum of the squares of the other two sides." In an enthymeme, the major premise is based instead upon the reputable beliefs of the audience, which are only probably and relatively true, as in the statements "people are creatures of habit," or "honesty is the best policy."

Hamilton described the two kinds of premises, as well as deductive reasoning as he practiced it, in *"Federalist 31."* "In disputations of every kind," he said at the beginning of that essay, "there are certain primary truths or first principles upon which all subsequent reasonings must depend. These contain an internal evidence, which antecedent to all reflection or combination commands the assent of the mind. . . . Of this nature are the maxims in geometry, that 'the whole is greater than its part,'" and so on. "Of the same nature are those other maxims in ethics and politics, that there cannot be an effect without a cause; that the means ought to be proportioned to the end; that every power ought to be commensurate with its object; that there ought to be no limitation of a power destined to effect a purpose, which is itself incapable of limitation."

A couple of aspects of this description want special notice. One is that Hamilton tends, in the passage quoted, to treat the two kinds of premises as equally valid. Doing so was an effective rhetorical device as well as a reflection of his personality—he was nothing if not positive and forceful—but he knew the difference. The first kind was what, elsewhere, he called "geometrically true," the other what he called "morally certain." The second subtle aspect of the passage quoted is that there is a progression in his examples of "maxims in ethics and politics," from one which nobody would question to one that many members of his audience might challenge. The listing itself is almost a process of deduction. That, too, was both an effective rhetorical device and a reflection of his personality.

As for Hamilton's inductive reasoning—that is, reasoning from experience, observation, or example—he always employed it, his mixture of inductive and deductive varying with the audience. Temperamentally, he distrusted the deductive and preferred the inductive, "A great source of error," he wrote early in his career, "is the judging of events by abstract calculations, which though geometrically true are false as they relate to the concerns of beings governed more by passion and prejudice than by an enlightened sense of their interests." In *"Federalist 20,"* echoing a sentiment shared by most of the Founding Fathers, he and Madison said that "Experience is the oracle of truth; and where its responses are unequivocal, they ought to be conclusive and sacred." In any event, as Arnhart has pointed out, he made clear to his audience whether he was using one or the other or both by introducing his arguments with such phrases as "theory and practice conspire to prove."

I shall not go into a detailed analysis of all the rhetorical techniques Hamilton employed in his logical proof. Aly has done so at great length, in regard to speech after speech. Aly points out where Hamilton has employed dilemma, antecedent probability, analogy, exposure of inconsistency, reduction to absurdity, causal relation, turning the tables, and other devices. For those who are interested in pursuing the matter further. I recommend Aly's work heartily.

But there are three additional aspects of Hamilton's method of using rhetorical logic which, while compatible with the Aristotelian model, were unique to him. One was that his approach was always positive, never negative. As the editors of his law papers put it, "His habit of thought even when acting for the defense was affirmative; in other words, he was always carrying the war to the enemy." That habit reflected his personality, but it was also a deliberate choice of rhetorical strategy and tactics. In this regard, it is instructive to observe the brief notes Hamilton recorded from Demosthenes' Orations (which he studied while in the army). "'Where attack him, it will be said? Ah Athenians, war, war itself will discover to you his weak sides, if you will seek them.' Sublimely simple." And again, "As a general marches at the head of his troops, so ought wise politicians, if I dare to use the expression, to march at the head of affairs; insomuch that they ought not to await the *event,* to know what measures to take; but the measures which they have taken, ought to produce the *event.*" In addition to being effective, this positive style had a special advantage that is related to the inner logic of rhetorical reasoning. The speaker or writer is limited, in attempting to persuade his audience, by the fact that the premises from which he can argue are restricted to what the audience already accepts as an established truth. Hamilton's practice of seeking the enemy's weak sides and seizing the initiative "to produce the event" enabled him to broaden the range of acceptable premises, and thus to educate as well as to persuade his audiences.

The second of Hamilton's special qualities was an intuitive sense of the heart of a subject combined with an awesome capacity for mastering its details. As William Pierce wrote of him in the Constitutional Convention, "he enquires into every part of his subject with the searchings of philosophy . . . there is no skimming over the surface of a subject with him, he must sink to the bottom to see what foundation it rests on . . . and when he comes forward he comes highly charged with interesting matter." His speeches and writings were characteristically long, for he was rarely content to rely upon only one approach to an argument, even when he was confident of winning in a single stroke. His celebrated opinion on the constitutionality of the bank affords an excellent example. He disposes of Randolph's and Jefferson's arguments in six brief but devastating paragraphs—piercing immediately to the heart of their position, showing the false premise on which it rests, indicating the appropriate premise, and drawing from it the only reasonable conclusion. But then he goes on for another 15,000 words, ringing every imaginable change on the argument. The beauty of this technique is again its educational value: it goes beyond successful persuasion in the particular instance and establishes new foundations for further persuasion on the morrow.

Hamilton's third special quality is more difficult to describe. He was sensitive to the difference between the two nontechnical connotations of the word opinion: belief, judgment, prejudice on the one hand, approval, esteem, regard on the other. In conventional rhetorical theory, it was opinion in the first sense, belief, that supplied the premises for deductive logical proof; opinion in the second sense, approval, would fall under ethical proof, having to do with the audience's favorable view of the author or speaker. Hamilton perceived that in the circumstances in which he labored—the attempt to establish a durable republican system of government—the two were so interrelated as to be inseparable. Each supported the other: the tasks of winning belief and approval went hand in hand. As a statesman he was seeking to establish public "credit" in the broad sense of credibility or confidence as well as in the narrow financial sense; indeed, in some respects he viewed the latter as only a means of attaining the former. Moreover—and this is crucial—he understood that opinions derive as much from perceptions as they do from facts. "A degree of illusion mixes itself in all the affairs of society," he wrote; "The opinion of objects has more influence than their real nature." Or, as he said in his First Report on the Public Credit. "In nothing are appearances of greater moment, than in whatever regards credit. Opinion is the soul of it, and this is affected by appearances, as well as realities." There is an extremely subtle point here: one central aim of Hamilton's public life was to replace the prevailing law of contract, based upon the medieval concepts of just price and fair value, with a modern theory of contract based upon consent in a free market. Thus Hamilton's attention to the effect of appearances on opinion, like his other two special qualities, was an extension of the dimensions of logical proof, for it broadened the possible range of premises available within the rules of reasoning with enthymemes.

Most of the techniques I have been describing can be illustrated by a brief analysis of one of Hamilton's greatest performances, the *Report on Manufactures* presented to Congress in December, 1791. The rhetorical situation was different from what it had been when Hamilton had given his reports on the public credit and the bank. On the earlier occasions the audience agreed with the first premise, that it was imperative to establish a system of public credit; Hamilton's task of persuasion was to convince Congress that it was desirable to do so in a particular way. In regard to the *Report on Manufactures,* the body of beliefs shared by most members of the audience, which we may describe in shorthand as the agrarian ideal, was hostile to Hamilton's objective, the promotion of industry. His task of persuasion was to convince Congress that it was desirable to encourage manufacturing, whatever the means.

He began by isolating and attacking the enemy's weakest side. The agrarian ideal itself was an impregnable bastion of prejudice, but the economic theory used to justify it—the physiocrat's rather silly notion that land is the source of all wealth and that the labor of craftsmen adds nothing to the value of things—was highly vulnerable. Hamilton demolished the physiocratic theory by quoting and paraphrasing at length from Adam Smith's *Wealth of Nations,* a work whose free-trade doctrines the audience regarded with great respect. He was careful, however, not to draw any conclusions beyond what his argument demonstrated: all he claimed at that stage was that manufacturing could produce wealth, probably about equally with farming.

Hamilton's rhetorical strategy so far, that of using one body of acceptable premises to displace another, was effective, but it created a new rhetorical problem. The use of Smith's work had the advantage of establishing as premises for further argument, that the wealth of a nation could be increased. On the other hand, it also had a disadvantage, for Hamilton was advocating active government promotion of manufactures, and Smith had championed the doctrine of noninterference—the idea that hu-

man industry, "if left to itself, will naturally find its way to the most useful and profitable employment." To overcome that difficulty, Hamilton again sought the weakest sides of the argument. Smith, as Hamilton paraphrased him, had laid down seven new premises to prove that manufacturing could increase the wealth of a nation—the principle of the division of labor, the advantages of the use of machinery, the possibility of enlarging the labor pool by pulling normally idle people into it, and so on. As Hamilton developed each point, he corrected Smith by using inductive rather than deductive reasoning, which is to say by employing the awesome array of factual data which Hamilton had laboriously gathered for the purpose. By that means he transformed Smith's premises into his own. To put it another way, he had taken premises acceptable to the audience, from which it was not logically possible to conclude that governmental activism was desirable, and altered them in such a way that it could logically be shown that such activism was not only desirable but in fact necessary.

Now Hamilton brought the cumulative effects of previous argumentation into play. Given the proposition that manufacturing should be encouraged, the fact remained that the United States, as an undeveloped country, was woefully short of the necessary capital. That obstacle was readily overcome, Hamilton said, and he showed how by reviewing his reports on public credit, where he had demonstrated that the public debt could be institutionally manipulated in such a way that, with the support of public opinion, it would be turned into a great pool of liquid wealth or capital. From there to the end of the report, Hamilton had smooth sailing: all he had to do was propose a series of practical steps to be taken to bring about the desired ends.

I described the *Report on Manufactures* as one of Hamilton's greatest performances. The historians among you, however, will recall that Congress did not act on the report; and the rhetoricians, armed with that datum, will conclude that the performance was not a great one at all. Let me construct the enthymeme: excellent rhetoric persuades the audience, Hamilton's report failed to persuade the audience, and therefore the report was not excellent rhetoric. But Hamilton's audience did not consist exclusively of the members of the Second Congress. In his rhetoric as in his statesmanship, Hamilton was addressing posterity and building cumulatively toward the future. In the course of time, the nation would begin the active promotion of manufactures, and for more than a century Hamilton's report would provide the rhetorical foundation for such a policy. Indeed, the report itself became a first premise.

There remains the task of reviewing briefly Hamilton's use of ethical and emotional proof and, finally, his style. In regard to the first two I shall depend, for my theoretical underpinnings, largely on Arnhart, [in *"The Federalist* as Aristotelian Rhetoric"] for he has put the matter extremely well. For the last I shall return exclusively to my own analysis, for there is an important dimension to Hamilton's style which he and others have overlooked.

Since the time of John Locke, logicians and rhetoricians have tended to share Plato's suspicion of traditional rhetoric because of its admission of irrational appeals to the audience. If ethical and emotional proofs are made in adherence to Aristotle's standards, however, they can in fact contribute to rational discourse. As for ethical proof, Aristotle says that a speaker will be most persuasive if he shows himself to be possessed of prudence, virtue, and good will. The persuasiveness of a speaker's character, based upon those criteria, can scarcely be dismissed as irrational: it is obviously quite reasonable to judge the reliability of a writer or speaker as being proportionate to his prudence, his virtue, and his good will. Besides, the more an author or speaker establishes his own credentials on those foundations, the more he conditions the audience to expect and demand them of other authors and speakers—and thus contributes to raising the general level of the rationality of the audience, which in turn elevates the rational possibilities available to the author or speaker.

Hamilton's use of ethical proof was calculated to obtain just that end. His techniques varied with his audience, of course, as they necessarily must. In dealing with Washington, for instance, the appropriate tone was one of deference—not of flattery, which the president would instantly have regarded as showing an absence of character, but out of respect for the presidential office and for the president's own character. In other words, one gained Washington's respect by showing respect in a proper manner. Washington was a special case, but in a sense that was the way Hamilton employed ethical proofs in more conventional rhetorical situations. That is to say, Hamilton normally sought to establish his good character among the members of his audience not by reciting his own virtues but by appealing to theirs. He appealed to his audiences to judge his arguments dispassionately, openly, and in a spirit of moderation tempered by zealous concern for the happiness of their country. By urging them to be prudent, virtuous, and possessed of good will, he avoided the necessity of claiming to have those qualities himself; and to the extent that he succeeded, he actually instilled them in his audiences.

As for emotional proofs, they are legitimate in Aristotle's scheme of things only insofar as the passions with which they deal are rational ones. Now, passions are passions and reason is reason, to be sure; but passions can be short-sighted or prudent, biased or open, hastily formed or carefully considered. After all, there is such a thing as reasonable fear, and in some circumstances to be unafraid is to be unreasonable. Hamilton sometimes appealed to the fears of his audience, as when, in numerous of the *Federalist* essays, he declared that failure to adopt the Constitution would result in anarchy, tyranny, and war—and when, in essays on the French Revolution, he warned of the perils of emotional or ideological attachment to foreign powers. There are those of us who believe those fears were entirely reasonable. More characteristically, however, Hamilton's appeals were to noble and positive passions: pride, honor, love of liberty, love of country. There are those of us who believe that stimulation of those passions is likewise reasonable.

Lastly, there is the matter of Hamilton's literary style. His style changed and improved over the years, as one might expect (though few scholars seem to have noticed); but what is more significant is that it evolved in a direction. Whatever one thinks of the intellectual merits of his earliest political writings, the 1774-1775 polemics entitled *A Full Vindication of the Measures of Congress* and *The Farmer Refuted*—unlike most other Hamilton scholars, I regard them as extremely muddle-headed—one is struck by their sophomoric literary quality. *The Farmer Refuted,* especially, is studded with strained metaphors, pretentious words, latinisms, citations of authorities (many of whom young Hamilton had obviously not read), and other displays of affected erudition. By 1781-82, when he wrote *The Continentalist* essays, and 1784, when he wrote the *Letters from Phocian,* he had discarded most of that excess baggage, but there was still more than was necessary. By 1788, when he co-authored *The Federalist,* he had almost reached his mature form, but not quite: though he made far fewer classical allusions than Madison did, he was still making unnecessary ones, and though he rarely attempted a consciously ornate metaphor, his unconscious metaphors were sometimes mixed or strained. Thereafter, he had arrived: from 1790 until the end of his life his prose style was straightforward, clear, lean, hard, and energetic.

That course of evolution paralleled the growth of Hamilton's commitment to making a success of the American experiment in constitutional government. More than most of his countrymen, he doubted that the experiment could succeed; more than any of them, he was dedicated to making the effort. He perceived clearly that political rhetoric of the highest order was necessary to the attempt, for such is essential to statecraft in a republic. Now, we hear a great deal these days about the public's "right to know." That is a perversion of the truth, even as modern public relations, propaganda, and political blather are perversions of classical rhetoric. If the republic is to survive, the emphasis must be shifted from rights back to obligations. It is the obligation, not the right, of the citizen of a republic to be informed; it is the obligation of the public servant to inform him and simultaneously to raise his standards of judgment. In adapting his style to his audience, Hamilton was fulfilling his part of the obligation.

I would close with a postscript. Despite Hamilton's efforts, and despite the efforts of other patriotic souls, the level of public discourse degenerated rapidly in the late 1790s. A plague of unscrupulous scribblers infested the nation, spewing venom, scurrility, deception, and hysteria throughout the land. Hamilton himself was subjected to as much abuse as any man, and possibly more. But he remained true to his principles until the very end.

One of his last and most celebrated cases as a lawyer arose from the frenzied partisan propaganda warfare that had developed. Harry Croswell, editor of a small-town newspaper, published a report that Jefferson had paid the notorious pamphleteer J. T. Callender to slander Washington, Adams, and other public men. The charge against Jefferson was true; but the Jeffersonians, who had stoutly

Portrait of Aaron Burr, who fatally wounded Hamilton in a duel at Weehauken, New Jersey in 1804.

defended freedom of the press when in the opposition, thought a "few wholesome prosecutions" were in order once they came to power. The Jeffersonian attorney general of New York, Ambrose Spencer, brought proceedings against Croswell for libel. On conviction, he appealed, and Hamilton became his counsel in the arguments before the state supreme court.

The key point at issue was that the judge in the trial court had refused to admit testimony regarding the truth of the statement as defense. English common-law doctrine, to which Republicans adhered, held that truth was not a defense. Hamilton scored effectively with a bit of emotional proof, showing that the doctrine itself was questionable since it had originated not in common-law courts but in the odious Star Chamber, as a departure from older law. But he was particularly concerned with the suitability of the doctrine in a republic. Libel, he said, was "a slanderous or ridiculous writing, picture or sign, with a malicious or mischievous design or intent, towards government, magistrates, or individuals." Intent was crucial, and truth was relevant to determining intent. Truth was therefore a defense, though not an absolute one. If it were used "wantonly; if for the purpose of disturbing the peace of families; if for relating that which does not appertain to official conduct," it was not acceptable. "But that the truth cannot be material in any respect, is contrary to the nature of things. No tribunal, no codes, no systems can repeal or impair this law of God, for by his eternal laws

it is inherent in the nature of things. . . . It is evident that if you cannot apply this mitigated doctrine for which I speak, to the cases of libels here, you must for ever remain ignorant of what your rulers do. I never can think this ought to be; I never did think the truth was a crime; I am glad the day is come in which it is to be decided; for my soul has ever abhorred the thought, that a free man dared not speak the truth."

Russell Kirk (essay date 1986)

SOURCE: "John Adams and Liberty under Law: Alexander Hamilton," in *The Conservative Mind: From Burke to Eliot,* revised edition, Regnery Books, 1986, pp. 75-80.

[*An American historian, political theorist, novelist, journalist, and lecturer, Kirk was one of America's most eminent conservative intellectuals. His works have provided a major impetus to the conservative revival that has developed since the 1950s. In* The Conservative Mind, *Kirk traces the roots and canons of modern conservative thought to such important predecessors as Edmund Burke, John Adams, and Alexis de Tocqueville. In the following excerpt from the seventh (1986) edition of that work, Kirk discourses on Hamilton's thought and stature as a conservative statesman.*]

"In the commencement of a revolution, which received its birth from the usurpations of tyranny, nothing was more natural than that the public mind should be influenced by an extreme spirit of jealousy." So Alexander Hamilton spoke to the Convention of New York, in 1788. "To resist these encroachments, and to nourish this spirit, was the great object of all our public and private institutions. The zeal for liberty became predominant and excessive. In forming our Confederation, this passion alone seemed to actuate us, and we appear to have had no other view than to secure ourselves from despotism. . . . But there is another object, equally important, and which our enthusiasm rendered us little capable of regarding. I mean a principle of strength and stability in the organization of our government, and of vigor in its operations."

Both the virtue and the weakness of Hamilton as a conservative thinker may be detected in this brief passage. His political principles were simple: he distrusted popular and local impulses, and he believed that salvation from the consequence of levelling ideas lay in establishing invincible national authority. He would have liked a central government; perceiving this wholly unacceptable to America, he settled for a federal government, and became its most vigorous organizer and pamphleteer. To him, with Madison and Jay, the United States owe the adoption of their Constitution. Such was Hamilton's wisdom and such were his achievements, and they have kept his memory fresh even in this generation, celebrating the Constitution's bicentenary, which in many ways badly misunderstands Hamilton. But General Hamilton was not vouchsafed the gift of prophecy, the highest talent of Burke and (in a lesser degree) of Adams. It seems hardly to have occurred to Hamilton's mind that a consolidated nation might also be a levelling and innovating nation, though he had the example of Jacobin France right before him; and he does not appear to have reflected upon the possibility that force in government may be applied to other purposes than the maintenance of a conservative order. Even in political economy, he was a practicing financier rather than an economic thinker, and he ignored the probability that the industrialized nation he projected might conjure up not only conservative industrialists, but also radical factory-hands—the latter infinitely more numerous, and more inimical to Hamilton's old-fashioned idea of class and order than all the agrarians out of Jefferson's Virginia. Now Hamilton's scheme for stimulating American industry was neither narrow nor selfish, it ought to be said; he looked forward to benefits truly general. "Hamilton asked for protection, not to confer privilege on industry, or to swell its profits, but to bring the natural occupation of a free country, namely, agriculture, into the stream of cultural advance," writes C. R. Fay. Still, his splendid practical abilities had for their substratum a set of traditional assumptions almost naïve; and he rarely speculated upon what compound might result from mixing his prejudices with the elixir of American industrial vigor.

Vernon Parrington, though now and then guilty of using the terms "Tory" and "liberal" in a sense hardly discriminating, is accurate when he remarks that Hamilton was at bottom a Tory without a king, and that his teachers were Hume and Hobbes. All his revolutionary ardor notwithstanding, Hamilton loved English society as an English colonial adores it. His vision of the coming America was of another, stronger, richer eighteenth-century England. To the difficulties in the way of his dream, he was almost oblivious. American hostility to his proposal for a more powerful chief magistracy, preferably hereditary, grieved and rather surprised him, and with pain he relinquished this plan. As England was a single state, its sovereignty indivisible and its parliament omnicompetent, so should America be: he shrugged impatiently away those considerations of territorial extent, historical origin, and local prerogative which Burke would have been the first to recognize and approve.

"It is a known fact to human nature, that its affections are commonly weak in proportion to the distance or diffusiveness of the object," wrote this "bastard brat of a Scotch pedlar" (Adams' epithet) from Nevis; he had none of those local attachments of ancestry and nativity that caused leaders like Josiah Quincy and John Randolph to love their state with a passion beside which nationalism was a feeble infatuation. "Upon the same principle that a man is more attached to his family than to the community at large [he wrote in *The Federalist,* No. 17], the people of each State would be apt to feel a stronger bias toward their local governments than towards the government of the Union; unless the force of that principle should be destroyed by a much better administration of the latter." But Hamilton's very exoticism, which enabled his patriotism to ignore local distinctions, tended to conceal from him the obdurate resolution which was latent in the several state governments and local affections. Despite his remarks above, generally he mistook these profound impulses for mere transitory delusions; he thought they could be eradicated by the strong arm of national government— by the federal courts, the Congress, the tariff, the Bank, and his whole nationalizing program. In the long run, his instruments did indeed crush particularism to earth; but only by provoking a civil war which did more than all of Jefferson's speculations to dissipate the tranquil eighteenth-century aristocratic society that really was Hamilton's aspiration. Hamilton misunderstood both the tendency of the age (naturally toward consolidation, not localism, without much need of assistance from governmental policies deliberately pursued) and the dogged courage of his opponents. A political thinker of the first magnitude possesses greater prescience.

Similarly, that industrialization of America which Hamilton successfully promoted was burdened with consequences the haughty and forceful new aristocrat did not perceive. Commerce and manufactures, he believed, would produce a body of wealthy men whose interests would coincide with those of the national common-wealth. Probably he conceived of these pillars of society as being very like great English merchants—purchasing country estates, forming presently a stable class possessed of leisure, talent, and means, providing moral and political and intellectual leadership for the nation. The actual American businessman, generally speaking, has turned out to be a different sort of person: it is difficult to reproduce social classes from a model three thousand miles over the water. Modern captains of industry might surprise Hamilton, modern cities shock him, and the power of industrial labor frighten him: for Hamilton never quite understood the transmuting properties of social change, which in its operation is more miraculous than scientific. Like Dr. Faustus' manservant, Hamilton could evoke elementals; but once materialized, that new industrialism swept away from the control of eighteenth-century virtuosos like the masterful Secretary of the Treasury. Indeed, Hamilton was contemplating not so much the creation of a new industrialism, as the reproduction of European economic systems which the spirit of the age already was erasing:

> To preserve the balance of trade in favor of a nation ought to be a leading aim of its policy. The avarice of individuals may frequently find its account in pursuing channels of traffic prejudicial to that balance, to which the government may be able to oppose effectual impediments. There may, on the other hand, be a possibility of opening new sources, which though accompanied with great difficulties in the commencement, would in the event amply reward the trouble and expense of bringing them to perfection. The undertaking may often exceed the influence and capitals of individuals, and may require no small assistance, as well from the revenue as from the authority of the state.

This is mercantilism. Hamilton had read Adam Smith with attention, but his heart was in the seventeenth century. The influence of government, in his view, might properly be exerted to encourage and enrich particular classes and occupations; the natural consequence of this would be an ultimate benefiting of the nation in general. Had America left fallow what Hamilton took in hand, her industrial growth would have been slower, but no less sure; and the consequences might have been perceptibly less rough-hewn. Hamilton, however, was fascinated by the idea of a planned productivity: "We seem not to reflect that in human society there is scarcely any plan, however salutary to the whole and to every part, by the share each has in the common prosperity, but in one way, or another, will operate more to the benefit of some parts than of others [he wrote in 1782]. Unless we can overcome this narrow disposition and learn to estimate measures by their general tendencies, we shall never be a great or a happy people, if we remain a people at all." Burke—who, despite his reforming energy, would have delayed indefinitely any alteration if it menaced the lawful property and prerogative of a single tidewaiter—was extremely suspicious of such doctrines in their English form. To excuse present injustice by a plea of well-intentioned general tendency is treacherous ground for a conservative; and in this instance the argument is suggestive of how much more familiar Hamilton was with particularities than with principles.

For the rest, Hamilton gives small hint as to how this mercantilistic America is to be managed; he appears to have thought (since he had a thoroughgoing contempt for the people) that somehow, through political manipulation, through firm enforcement of the laws and national consolidation, the rich and well-born could keep their saddles and ride this imperial system like English squires. These are the hopes of a man who thinks in terms of the short run. Seven years before, the shrewd young John Quincy Adams had written from Europe to his father, "From the moment when the great mass of the nations in Europe were taught to inquire why is this or that man possessed of such or such an enjoyment at our expense, and of which we are deprived, the signal was given of a civil war in the social arrangements of Europe, which cannot finish but with the total ruin of their feudal constitutions." Those powers which Hamilton was so ready to bestow upon the state eventually would be diverted to ends at the the antipodes from Hamilton's; and the urban population that Hamilton's policies stimulated would be the forcing-ground of a newer radicalism. The conservative side of Jefferson's complex nature frowned against this arbitrary meddling with populations and occupations, and presently Randolph, and after him Calhoun, denounced with impotent fury the coming of the new industrial era, more hideous in their eyes than the old colonial condition. In several respects, they were sounder conservatives than Hamilton: for he was eminently a city-man, and veneration withers upon the pavements. "It is hard to learn to love the new gas-station," writes Walter Lippmann, "that stands where the wild honeysuckle grew." But Hamilton never penetrated far beneath the surface of politics to the mysteries of veneration and presumption.

For all that, one ought not to confuse Hamilton with the Utilitarians; if he erred, it was after the fashion of the old Tories, rather than that of the philosophic radicals. He remained a Christian, in the formal eighteenth-century way,

and wrote of the follies of the French Revolution, "The politician who loves liberty, sees them with regret as a gulf that may swallow up the liberty to which he is devoted. He knows that morality overthrown (and morality *must* fall with religion), the terrors of despotism can alone curb the impetuous passions of man, and confine him within the bounds of social duty." Burke's vaticinations had stirred him here, as they affected John Adams, J. Q. Adams, Randolph, and so many other Americans; but the influence of Burke went no deeper. Hamilton was a straggler behind his age, rather than the prophet of a new way. By a very curious coincidence, this old-fangled grand gentleman died from the bullet of Aaron Burr, friend and disciple of Bentham.

FURTHER READING

Biography

McDonald, Forrest. *Alexander Hamilton: A Biography.* New York: W. W. Norton & Co., 1979, 464 p.

> Complete biography and critical reading by one of the foremost modern authorities on the era of the Constitution's framing.

Miller, John C. *Alexander Hamilton: Portrait in Paradox.* New York: Harper & Brothers, 1959, 659 p.

> Focuses on Hamilton's political life, especially his dedication to American national unity.

Mitchell, Broadus. *Alexander Hamilton: Youth to Maturity, 1755-1788.* New York: Macmillan, 1957, 675 p. and *Alexander Hamilton: The National Adventure, 1788-1804.* New York: Macmillan, 1961, 807 p.

> Exhaustive two-volume study of Hamilton's life and work, with a bibliography.

Criticism

Aly, Bower. *The Rhetoric of Alexander Hamilton.* New York: Columbia University Press, 1941, 213 p.

> A critical and bibliographic overview of Hamilton scholarship, followed by a systematic examination of Hamilton's methods of argument.

Christman, Margaret C. S. *"The Spirit of Party": Hamilton & Jefferson at Odds.* Washington, D.C.: National Portrait Gallery (Smithsonian Institution), 1992, 64 p.

> Well-illustrated essay intended to present the views of Hamilton and Jefferson in tandem, "to suggest something of the nature of the political contest that raged in the final decade of the eighteenth century as these two powerful leaders and their followers contended for the leadership of the nation."

Cooke, Jacob E. Editor, *Alexander Hamilton: A Profile.* New York: Hill & Wang, 1967, 259 p.

> Selected essays on Hamilton's life and career, with an introductory essay and a brief bibliography.

Flaumenhaft, Harvey. *The Effective Republic: Administration and Constitution in the Thought of Alexander Hamilton.* Durham, N.C.: Duke University Press, 1992, 314 p.

> Draws on Hamilton's own words to explicate his thinking about the parts of government and their work. Flaumenhaft's aim is to examine what his subject said in his discussion of particular affairs, "to consider Hamilton's *principles.*"

Frisch, Morton J. *Alexander Hamilton and the Political Order.* Lanham, Md.: University Press of America, 1991, 118 p.

> Examines Hamilton's political thought and his contribution to constitutional government.

Lewis, Wyndham. "The Beauty and Polarity of Hamilton and Jefferson." In his *America and Cosmic Man,* pp. 119-30. Garden City, N.Y.: Doubleday & Co., 1949.

> Acerbic discourse comparing Hamilton with Jefferson: "two men who thought very differently. Lewis holds that "The issue that separated them so profoundly was that fundamental one of the 'Haves' and 'Have-nots'."

Rossiter, Clinton. *Alexander Hamilton and the Constitution.* New York: Harcourt, Brace & World, 1964, 372 p.

> Examines Hamilton's contributions to the Constitution and his political ideas, and assesses his place in history.

Additional coverage of Hamilton's life and career is contained in the following source published by Gale Research: *Dictionary of Literary Biography,* Vol. 37.

Higuchi Ichiyo

1872-1896

(Pseudonym of Higuchi Natsuko) Japanese novelist and short story writer.

INTRODUCTION

Higuchi is considered the first major woman writer of Japan's Meiji period (1868-1912). Her literary focus on the role of women in Japanese society, and in particular on the lives of the poor, represented a departure from most Japanese literature of her time, which focused on traditional gender roles in aristocratic society.

Biographical Information

Higuchi was born into a middle-class family in Tokyo. Although she was an excellent student, girls commonly received limited formal education in nineteenth-century Japan, and at the age of 11 her parents removed her from school. In 1886, when she was 14, she convinced her parents to allow her to study poetry at a private school. Her father's death in 1889 left Higuchi, the best-educated member of her family, responsible for their support. Wanting to write professionally, she solicited advice and assistance from the popular journalist and editor Nakarai Tosui. Higuchi's first published stories, "Yamizakura" ("Flowers at Dusk") and "Wakarejimo" ("The Last Frost of Spring") appeared in the literary magazine *Musashino,* edited by Tosui, in 1892. Ongoing financial hardship influenced Higuchi's writing: in her fiction she examined themes of poverty, social class, women's roles, and societal expectations. Higuchi earned fame as a writer but not financial security. She died of tuberculosis at the age of twenty-four.

Major Works

Higuchi's third published story, "Umoregi" (1892; "A Buried Life") explores the motivation of a potter dedicated to perfecting his craft. This story appeared in the prestigious literary journal *Miyako no hana* and was favorably reviewed by the critic and editor Hoshino Tenchi. He solicited further stories from Higuchi for his magazine *Bungakkai (The World of Literature),* including "Yuki no Hi" (1893; "A Snowy Day"), which examines the consequences of a relationship between a student and her teacher. Her most highly regarded work, the novel *Takekurabe (Child's Play)*, appeared serially in *Bungakkai* in 1895 and 1896. This coming-of-age novel examines the limited choices facing a group of self-sufficient adolescents living on the streets of a city's licensed "pleasure quarter." Subsequent works included the stories "Yuku Kumo" (1895; "Passing Clouds") and "Wakare-

Michi" (1896; "Separate Ways") and the novels *Nigorie* (1895; *Troubled Waters),* and *Jusan'ya* (1895; *The Thirteenth Night).* "Separate Ways" treats a poor woman who contemplates abandoning the drudgery of work as a laundress and seamstress to become the mistress of a wealthy man. While she regrets relinquishing her self-respect and ending longtime friendships with people who disapprove of her choice, she cannot resist the material comforts and financial security that will accompany life as a kept woman. *Troubled Waters* examines with insight and compassion the life of a young prostitute. *The Thirteenth Night* focuses on the social conventions that impede a young woman seeking to escape from an abusive marriage. Higuchi's diary, published after her death, describes in her lyrical prose style the motivation and inspiration for many of her works.

Critical Reception

Higuchi received much critical and popular attention during her brief career, which she believed was at least partly due to the fact that she was a professional author at a time when few women published regularly. The favorable review of "A Buried Life" by Tenchi lead to Higuchi's recruitment into Japanese literary society, and the distinguished author and critic Mori Ogai hailed *Growing Up* as a literary masterpiece. Modern critics consider Higuchi an important pivotal writer in Japanese literature. They acknowledge that while her prose style adhered to classical Japanese literary characteristics of lyricism, allusiveness, and elaborate wordplay, her works nevertheless exhibit a distinctly modern sensibility. Hailed during her lifetime as "the last woman writer of old Japan," she has been regarded since her death as the first modern Japanese woman writer.

PRINCIPAL WORKS

"Yamizakura" ["Flowers at Dusk"] (short story) 1892

"Wakarejimo" ["The Last Frost of Spring"] (short story) 1892

"Umoregi" ["A Buried Life"; also translated as "In Obscurity"] (short story) 1892

"Yuki no Hi" ["A Snowy Day"] (short story) 1893

Takekurabe [*Child's Play*; also translated as *Growing Up, Teenagers Vying for Tops,* and *They Compare Heights*] (novel) 1896

"Yuku Kumo" ["Passing Clouds"] (short story) 1895

Nigorie [*Troubled Waters;* also translated as *In the Gutter,* and *Muddy Bay*] (novel) 1895

Jusan'ya [*The Thirteenth Night*] (novel) 1895

"Wakare-Michi" ["Separate Ways"; also translated as "The Parting of the Ways"] (short story) 1896

CRITICISM

Hisako Tanaka (essay date 1956)

SOURCE: "Higuchi Ichiyo," in *Monumenta Nipponica,* Vol. XII, Nos. 3-4, October, 1956-January, 1957, pp. 3-26.

[*In the following essay, Tanaka discusses the relationships between events recorded in Higuchi's diary and themes in her short stories and novels.*]

With the beginning of the Meiji era Japan entered upon a new epoch of her history. The sudden impact of Western ideas made itself felt in many phases of life, and it took quite a time until the people had adjusted themselves to the changes which the restoration had brought to the nation.

This early Meiji era gave to Japan a woman writer, Higuchi Ichiyo (with her personal name called Natsu), who, during the short span of her life from 1872 to 1896, created a genre of stories which is unique in Japanese literature. Her life was full of suffering, part of which was shared by fellow men of her time. However, much of the agony she had to go through was personal in nature. The latter part of her life was constantly threatened by extreme financial insecurity. The gossip of her friends forced

her to give up her friendship with her teacher, Nakarai Tōsui. She had to struggle to keep alive, and to fight to conquer her passion, but because of all difficulties with which she had to contend she could write the stories for which she has become famous.

Ichiyō's own miseries had opened her eyes to see the pain of others. The people of the lower strata of society, women and children of the down-town sections of the capital are her heroes. She had so many things in common with the less privileged people that it was easy for her to understand what was going on in their hearts.

Her name will be remembered for her short novels, such as *Takekurabe* (*Comparing Heights*), *Nigorie* (*The Muddy Bay*), and *Jūsanya* (*The Thirteenth Night*), and also for her remarkable diary. In her lifetime she kept a diary without any intention of publishing it. There she expressed her uninhibited self and faithfully recorded the delicate shadings of her maiden heart. Although she tended to be rather subjective in her diary, it proves to be a valuable document, because it reflects, in part, the literary trend of her time. It furnishes important keys to unlock her outwardly reserved personality and provides clues to understand the process by which some of her literary works had been created.

In this brief study of Higuchi Ichiyō, I shall merely try to sketch her life adhering closely to her diary and briefly to touch upon her literary products, which are delicately interwoven with the mosaic of her own strenuous life.

Ichiyō wrote in her diary in the fall of 1895:

> Since the time I was a child of seven, I have had in my mind an ambition to write, and the fact that I am writing now is nothing more than a partial realization of my long cherished dreams. . . .

Earlier in August, 1893, she had already written:

> Since the time I was about nine years old, I began to feel resentful over the fact that I might end by being a mediocrity, and day in and day out, I used to yearn to excel others by a segment of a black bamboo. . . .

She certainly was an extraordinary individual for a woman of the middle Meiji period. Elementary schools were first organized in Tōkyō in 1873, when Ichiyō was about one year old, but in her days an education for women, at best, was intended for nothing more than making good wives and wise mothers. Although her parents came from the present Yamanashi prefecture, she was born in Tōkyō. While the metropolis was still called Edo, her ambitious parents had left their native place to attain the rank of samurai in the capital. Their ambition was realized just a year before the restoration of Meiji and, regrettably enough, soon their hard sought and newly attained rank was reduced to a mere name. However, as a daughter of a samurai, a fact in which she took considerable pride, Ichiyō received a strict family education after the fashion of the Confucian teachings. Under the new political regime, her father held a post in the metropolitan government, and with her two brothers and two sisters she had a relatively happy childhood.

Ichiyō was a bright child. Her father boasted about her, and her teachers preferred her to all other pupils. About her early interest in reading, she wrote in her diary:

> From the age of seven I was fond of illustrated story books, and I used to indulge in them forgetting all about playing with a ball or a battledore. Among the story books, what I liked best were biographies of great men and heroes. The deeds of chivalrous and righteous men seemed to penetrate deep into my mind, and I used to be thrilled over anything that was gallant and brilliant.

Her heroic outlook on life, which is often exhibited in her diary, must have had its roots in such yearnings for heroes in her childhood. As a result of her persistant habit of reading under insufficient light, she became very nearsighted. Before she reached her twelfth birthday, she completed six years of elementary school with highest honors. However, because of her mother's opposition, she had to discontinue school, although, Ichiyō said, it nearly meant death for her. Complying with her mother's wish, she began to pursue the ordinary routine of practicing sewing and other domestic arts, but she did not give up her nightly habit of sitting at her desk. Her father bought her an anthology of *waka* and other texts for her to read, and with a private tutor she studied *waka* for about half a year. In contrast to Ichiyō's mother, her father, who was well versed in the Chinese classics, was very much interested in giving his promising daughter a further education. Finally, in August, 1886, when she was fourteen years old, he made an arrangement through his friend for her to enter a private school called Hagi-no-ya operated by Nakajima Utako, where Ichiyō received instruction in *waka* and classic Japanese literature. In this school, she was trained in the orthodox school of *waka* called *Keienha,* or Kagawa Kageki's school, which adhered closely to the style of the *Kokinshū.*

Although her style of *waka* was rather outmoded, Utako was quite influential among society people, and young ladies from noble families were sent to Hagi-no-ya mainly to cultivate their taste for poetry. Among these gorgeously attired young ladies, the small statured, extremely nearsighted and thin-haired Ichiyō in her simple clothes could not be impressive. Soon she found friendship there with two other girls who happened to be daughters of commoners, and the three of them together, in a rather comical vein, called themselves *Heimin-gumi* (commoners' clique). Of course, Ichiyō was a daughter of a samurai, but it all goes to show that the kind of distinction her father enjoyed was nothing to compare with the standing of those who were sending their daughters to Hagi-no-ya in lacquered carriages.

If not in anything else, Ichiyō certainly excelled others in her studies. At this school she met Tanabe Tatsuko, later Miyake Kaho, a daughter of Tanabe Taiichi, who was a

diplomat and a great functionary of Japan. These two stood out from others in their lessons. In January, 1887, Ichiyō began to write her diary, and an entry was made of a ceremonial first meeting of the year held in February. On a grand occasion such as that, girls vied with one another in the exquisiteness of their kimonos and accessories. Naturally Ichiyō, from the modest family of a minor government official, could not think of competing with them. It was enough of a blessing perhaps for her to be able to continue her studies there, and already in her teens she learned to take a detached attitude toward such vanity of life. She wrote on 19 February of that year:

> Although I was terribly ashamed, I found my old clothes more precious than their damask and brocade, for I found in mine the unfathomable benevolence of my parents and was thoroughly pleased with them.

It must have been a harsh lesson to learn for the girl of fifteen, that there existed the high and the low in society, and that some could afford to adorn themselves sumptuously while others, through no fault of their own, had to do without the beautiful. However, Ichiyō found a compensating sense of value in the spiritual side of life, and although outwardly she might have appeared shabby, she possessed a proud heart which yielded to none.

When she was seventeen, she had to face a grave reality, her father's death. All of a sudden the family lost its sole support. Ichiyo's eldest brother had died, too, and her second brother had already established a family of his own; so Ichiyō was left with the obligation to look after her mother and her younger sister. Her father's death had occurred following his failure in some business enterprise; the widow and the two immature girls were, consequently, left in a helpless situation without means of support. For a while they went to live with Ichiyō's brother, but this arrangement did not work out satisfactorily, for the widow and her son constantly disagreed. In May of 1898, Ichiyō went to live with her teacher Utako at Hagi-no-ya. However, the family problems remained unsolved. Finally, in September she found a house for rent in Hongō, in which she started on the hard journey to maintain the household with her mother and sister. The family had no source of income except whatever the aged woman and the two girls could produce. All they could do was occasional sewing and washing which they took in from their neighbors and acquaintances. Her teacher Utako promised to find her a teaching position at a girls' school where she might teach *waka* or calligraphy, but, probably due to Ichiyō's insufficient formal education and her immature age, no such position was available for her.

About this time, she began seriously to consider writing novels. In 1877 her friend Tanabe Tatsuko, four years senior of Ichiyō, wrote her first novel *Yabu no Uguisu* after the fashion of *Tōsei Shosei Katagi* (Scenes from Modern Student Life) by Tsubouchi Shōyō. Tatsuko not only won popularity through this novel, but also was amply rewarded financially for her manuscript. Ichiyō, therefore, wished to follow the path of her friend. She turned to writing as a means of supporting her family.

The diary she had begun to write in January, 1887, was discontinued in April of the same year. Four years later, she started writing it again, this time with all seriousness, and she continued it until July, 1896, four months before her death. The day when she resumed her diary, 15 April, 1891, was an unforgettable day for her. Introduced by her sister's friend, she formally called upon Nakarai Tōsui with the purpose of asking for his guidance in writing. In her diary she wrote:

> As I am not yet accustomed to this sort of situation, my ears burned and lips became dry. I couldn't think of words and I didn't know what to say. All I could do was just to bow repeatedly. How foolish I must have appeared! I am ashamed of myself. . . .

Tōsui, born in 1860, was then a journalist and a popular novelist in his early thirties, who was connected with the Tōkyō Asahi Newspaper. While new writers equipped with the European technique of realistic writing had begun to establish their place among the critical readers of the time, Tōsui and others were gradually losing their ground.

When Ichiyō decided to be tutored by Tōsui, she was hardly aware of such a trend in her time. Until then her literary training consisted mainly in the study of *waka* and some classics. Professor Shioda has observed that, if she had read more of the literature of her time, and if she had been familiar with the general literary trend, she would not have chosen Tōsui, who belonged to the category of *gesakusha* (imaginative writers), as her teacher. However, her need was urgent, and just as her friend Tatsuko had the backing of Tsubouchi Shōyō for her first novel, Ichiyō felt the need of someone who could guide her in her new venture. She had no connection with anyone in literary circles. Just then, the individual who happened to come into her vista was Tōsui, and she immediately sought his aid without much reflection.

When she called on him again about a week after their first meeting, he commented on her story which she had left with him. He said that is was too long to be printed in the newspaper, and he further advised her to make her style more colloquial because hers was too classic.

She wrote of her second impression of him as follows:

> A person who is likable the first time may not necessarily be so the second time. However, in his case, I felt much more intimate toward him today than I did the last time, and I thought of him as a most unusual individual. . . .

Near the end of the same month, he sent her a letter telling her to come to see him. On the day of that visit, after giving her general instructions and hints for writing novels, he had this to tell her:

> Today I have something I'd like to tell you. It is nothing else but that I am not quite an old man yet. Besides you are a young lady just coming of age. I find it extremely difficult to associate with you. . . . Therefore I have thought up a device. It is this. When I see you, I am going to think of you as a young man, a close friend or comrade whom I have been associating with all along, and I will carry on our discussion on that basis. Similarly, on your part, rather than to think of me as a man, you must consider me as a girl in your own circle and treat me accordingly.

She herself had not been altogether free from such concerns, and, upon hearing this, she wrote that her face burned like fire and she didn't even know what to do with her hands. She was filled with embarrassment.

It was an extremely naive and unnatural device Tōsui had worked out, but in the Meiji twenties, it was exceptionally rare for a girl to meet a man in the manner Ichiyō had done. Her primary concern was to sell her manuscripts for the livelihood of her family. Her only hope, at a time like this, was to enlist the help of Tōsui who was connected with the influential newspaper. In order to accomplish her goal, she could not be hesitant about her means.

About this time, she commenced her frequent visits to the Ueno library to read modern and classic literature, and plunged into the serious struggle of producing creative writing of her own.

On 7 October of the same year she wrote:

> In the afternoon I sat at my desk and, somehow or other, I was engaged in writing. However, for various reasons I got disgusted. I have already torn up my manuscripts about ten times. It is really strange that I haven't even completed a story . . . I can't go on like this forever, and so I start writing anew thinking up another plot; but none is good enough. Every time I read famous tales and novels, both ancient and modern, I become distressed over my own writing, and finally I begin to feel like giving up. However, perverse as I am, I can't give it up quite so easily, and presumptuously enough I have started writing again. I must, by all means, complete it by day after tomorrow. I feel that I will die if I don't finish it. If people wish to laugh at my faint heart, let them laugh!

In the meantime, the financial situation of the family was not improving at all. Besides her desk work, Ichiyō and her sister had to sew for others for their living. However, at times she took rather a light and graceful attitude toward her poverty. For instance, she was even in the mood to compose *waka* allegorizing the patch work (*hagi*) on her kimono she had just finished sewing with the bush clover (*hagi*) in the field, and fortunately at times her brush flowed more smoothly than at other times. She wrote on the 27th of the same month:

> As of tonight my brush has begun to flow at my will, and I have worked till later than usual. I went to bed at one o'clock.

The following entry which she made in the following month reveals her mind at that time:

> It has been nearly one year since I began writing novels. I have published none yet, and none satisfies me. My mother and sister blame me repeatedly by saying that I am weak minded and always retrospective.... Even though I write for our livelihood, what is poorly done would seem poor to anyone's eyes. Once I have claimed myself a writer, I would dare not write anything that may be thrown into a waste basket after being read once, as is the case with the majority of writers. People today are frivolous, and what is welcomed today may be discarded tomorrow in a world like this, but if I appeal to the genuine feeling of the people, and if I depict genuine feeling, even if it may be a fictitious writing by Ichiyō, how could it be without value? I do not desire a brocade gown nor am I after a stately mansion. How could I ever stain my name which I wish to leave behind for a thousand years for the sake of temporary gain? I will rewrite even a short story three times, and then I will ask the world to pass judgment. In spite of that, should my efforts be lost as a mere waste of paper and brush, still I would take it as heaven's decree.

Although she was then an insignificant and obscure individual, she certainly entertained high aspirations. As one reads in her diary, one frequently encounters such spirited enthusiasm. Throughout the adversities of her life, it was this tenacious and unyielding spirit which sustained her.

Ichiyō welcomed the New Year in 1892 in a cheerful mood. On 14 February, she completed a story manuscript, having stayed up practically all night, and she felt extremely relieved as if a heavy load was off her shoulders. This was the manuscript of **"Yamizakura"** (**"Cherry Blossoms in a Moonless Night"**), which was read and somewhat retouched by Tōsui, before it was published in March in the first volume of *Musashino,* a literary magazine put out by him for his circle of young writers. This was the first story of hers to be published and for which she used her pen name Ichiyō for the first time. In the subsequent issues of *Musashino* a few of her early works were also printed. **"Yamizakura"** was a naive story of love between childhood friends, and like other stories she wrote in the early stage of her career it was rather crude. Her plots tended to be fanciful and unnatural, and she adhered to a classic style.

However, in these sorrowful love stories, it is discernable that she was, in one way or another, casting the shadow of her own suppressed self. Since the day she first met her teacher Tōsui, she was impressed with his manliness and generous heart. As the days passed, her tender passion toward him began to grow. Tōsui, being only a popular writer, naturally was limited in his capacity, beyond a certain degree, to coach Ichiyō in the art of story writing. But Tōsui exerted an immeasurable influence upon the heart of Ichiyō, sensitive and single-minded as she was, for, ever since the time of their first interview, her entire emotional life evolved around a vividly idealized image of Tōsui. Nevertheless, owing to her Confucian discipline, she was an individual of stern and strict mor-

als. Even if she loved anyone, she was not supposed to admit it. In the kind of society she was in, i.e. the Japan of the 1890's, it was considered especially disgraceful for a girl to assert her affection toward a man she loved.

In the summer of the same year (1892), her friend Itō Natsuko at Hagi-no-ya one day demanded, out of a clear blue sky, "Which do you consider more important, social obligations or your family name?" Puzzled, Ichiyō replied that she placed a particularly high importance on her social obligations and that she considered her obligation toward her family equally important. Staring straight into Ichiyō's face, Itō Natsuko continued, "Then, tell me whether you can sever your relationship with Nakarai (Tōsui) or not." Not only Itō Natsuko, but also Ichiyō's teacher, Nakajima Utako, and the girls in the Hagi-no-ya circle, all believed in the malicious rumors then widely in circulation that Tōsui and Ichiyō were as intimate as man and wife. Utako advised Ichiyō, "If there is nothing of the sort between you and Tōsui, it would be better for you not to associate with him any longer."

For one moment, Ichiyō was utterly dumbfounded, and in the next she was thoroughly shocked. She wrote that she even felt reproachful toward her teacher for not knowing her stupidly honest nature and her steadfast character after associating with her for some seven long years. She could not sleep that night because of her astonishment. Immediately she made up her mind to discontinue receiving guidance from Tōsui. About ten days later she called on him to bid him farewell. It was the only way left for her to prove her uprightness and integrity before her friends and especially before her teacher Utako. It would have been too much of a blow for Ichiyō to have been forsaken by Utako on grounds of an unfounded rumor, because Ichiyō then was drawing a salary, though small in amount, as an assistant teacher in Utako's school, and Ichiyō and her sister were also doing sewing for Utako for their living.

At that time, Tōsui was trying to arrange for Ichiyō to meet Ozaki Kōyō so as to open a way for her to sell her manuscripts, but Ichiyō also refused this kind offer of Tōsui. The fact was not of great regret for Ichiyō, because Kōyō would not have been able to give Ichiyō as much insight into literature as she herself attained later.

After she severed her connection with Tōsui and his *Musashino,* she was able, through her friend Miyake Kaho's effort, to have her story **"Umoregi"** (**"Bog-wood"**) printed in *Miyako no Hana* by November of that year. It was a story of a potter modeled after her brother, written under the definite influence of Kōda Rohan's novels on artisans, such as *Fūryūbutsu* (Romantic Saint), *Hitofuri Ken* (*The Superb Swordsman*), and *Gojū no Tō* (*Five-Storied Pagoda*). Her technique of writing this story was more realistic than in her earlier works, but still she had not completely grown out of the imitative stage of her development as a novelist. About the time she wrote **"Umoregi,"** she was consciously trying to grow out of Tōsui's method of fictitious writing, and her independent effort to improve herself as a writer, by assimilating whatever she could from the writers of her time, is worth noting.

By spring of the following year in 1893, again through the kind office of Miyake Kaho, she began to contribute her stories to a literary monthly called *Bungakkai* (The Literary Circle). The story which appeared in the March issue was entitled **"Yuki no Hi"** (**"Snowy Day"**), the scheme for which had been conceived about a year before on a snowy day on her way home from Tōsui's place. Her visit to him on that day was an exceptionally impressive one, and as she started on her way home from his house in a penetratingly cold and heavy snowstorm, she was overwhelmed by emotions welling up, and instantly an idea was formulated to write a novel entitled **"Snowy Day"**.

In fact, in her mind the association of the snowy day and the pleasant memory of the afternoon she had spent with Tōsui became so strong that ever since, as she relates in her diary, a snowy day always reminded her of him. On the 29th of January in 1893 she wrote, ". . . the snow scene gives me unbearable pains. . . ." Yuchi Takashi comments upon this story, "it is Ichiyō's dream itself which is narrated here. Tamako, who on a snowy day fled to a man who used to be her teacher as well as lover, probably was Ichiyō herself. Perhaps she was able to avoid the danger of being overtaken by her love, because she was composed enough and rational enough to write a novel like this . . . and, at the same time, was she not also compensating her dissatisfaction for not being able to pursue her love in reality, by realizing it in fiction?"

From about this time, young and ambitious men of letters began to call on Ichiyō one after another. Most of them were members of the *Bungakkai* coterie. Her vivacious and stimulating association with these men turned out to be valuable moments in her career as a novelist. There is no doubt that the enlightening contacts she had with them were in part conducive to the production of her splendid works.

Although Ichiyō received some money for her manuscripts which began to sell, the financial situation of the family was no better than before. She wrote in July 1893:

> Unless one has secure property, there is no secure mind. Even though I do not long for a life of luxurious living in idleness, I will not be able to live without salt and *miso* (bean paste). Moreover, I must not engage in literary work for the sake of my livelihood. If I ever should be writing, I ought to be able to do it as I please and as my fancy dictates. From now on, instead of writing for the sake of a bare livelihood, I am going [to set out] in the world counting on an abacus and with my sweat running down in beads (*tama*, a pun word with *soroban no tama* 'beads of abacus') by starting in business.

In order to raise funds for this new venture, the family had to sell whatever little they still had in their possession. Along with the relics of her deceased father, such as picture scrolls and art pieces, her best suit of kimono, which she had saved for the occasions of formal meetings at Hagi-no-ya, had to be sold. On 20 July, they moved into a three room house, the front room of which was to be used as their shop. It was situated in Ryūsenji-chō or commonly known as Daionji-mae in the neighborhood of the gay quarters of Yoshiwara.

In these totally strange surroundings Ichiyō had to try her best to adjust herself, and in her new house she still could not relinquish her longings for Tōsui:

> I have thus fallen low, and if I should rust away without ever rising above this, I will loose a chance of ever seeing him again in this world. I would be forgotten by him, completely forgotten by him, and my love would probably vanish in the sky yonder like a floating cloud! He has been to the house where I have lived until yesterday. On some occasions, if, rarely, indeed very rarely, he might recall the way my [former] house looked, and if only he remembers that there existed an individual like me, I would have something to live for!

As her thoughts wandered on, her heart ached with helplessness. About two weeks later, the family finally opened a small shop to sell cheap candies, toys, and small wares, such as needles, thread, soap, candles, paper and what not. Children in the neighborhood began to flow into the store. They were kept busy, but still the net profit of their hard labor was far from rewarding.

In the fall of the same year, after paying a visit to her teacher Nakajima Utako, a desire awakened within her to write once more and, struggling for many days, she produced a story **"Koto no Ne"** (**"The Tone of a Koto"**), in which she expressed her long suppressed yearnings for the beautiful. The influence of the romantic spirit of the *Bungakkai* circle is discernable in the pervading sentiment of this story.

When New Year came, Ichiyō did not have a proper outfit to wear for her call upon her teacher Utako. About then, a shop selling the same goods was opened across the street from theirs and created a stiff competition. The family became so hard pressed that, as a last resort, Ichiyō even began to think of speculating in order to raise money. Using a false name, she called in February on a man who practiced a kind of spiritualism. She wrote in her diary that she disburdened herself to him saying:

> . . . I have been having a difficult time even to let my mother have the simplest of meals, and this is the greatest cause of worry for my sister and me. I have lost all hope in this world. What am I good for if I live on? All I think of is about my mother. And so, by sacrificing myself and by taking a great risk, I would like to go into speculation. . . .

The man advised her against her plan, but Ichiyō at least felt a temporary relief during the afternoon she was engaged in a long conversation with him. However, obviously this man was not the kind of person who would extend a genuine helping hand. Later he made a conditional offer of financial aid, which she flatly declined. It was next to impossible for a woman to try to make a living by her slender means, especially under the early capitalistic regime of Meiji. Ichiyō was gasping for mere survival, trying to make the impossible possible. Gradually the mother and the two daughters began to realize that they were not suited to selling odds and ends. About this time, the mother even persuaded Ichiyō to go to see her former teacher Tōsui, clinging to the hope now that her daughter might still write and sell her stories to relieve the financial distress of the family. By April Ichiyō finally had come to the decision to close the shop, and on 1 May they moved again to Maruyama Fukuyama-chō in Hongō.

The ten months she had spent in Daionji-mae had been full of difficulties and financially unrewarding, but it was exactly the locality which she delineated as the setting of her later work *Takekurabe,* her masterpiece, and it was exactly the kind of little urchins to whom she sold less than a *sen* worth of candies or balloons, that she vividly depicted in the story. Her circumstances had been trying, but she transformed them into her creative writing, thus finding poetry in the midst of human sufferings.

It was in the summer of this year that the Sino-Japanese war broke out. The nation as a whole was thrown into a state of unrest. In the fall, Kunikida Doppo, serving as a correspondent for *Kokumin Shimbun,* started to write *Aitei Ts shin* (*Message to Beloved Brethren*) from the war front. In the midst of the bustle of the war, Ichiyō now shut herself into a life of almost complete seclusion. The plot of the story, modeled after the children of Daionji-mae, was gradually taking shape in her mind about then. By the end of the year she completed the original manuscript of *Takekurabe.* Starting in January 1895, the story was serialized irregularly in *Bungakkai* for about a year.

In the meantime, the financial situation of the family had grown worse than ever. On May 14, 1895, she wrote:

> . . . after eating our supper today, there is not even a grain of rice on hand. My mother grieves over it incessantly, and Kuniko keeps on grumbling. . . .

However, in the midst of their hardships, which accompanied them wherever they went, Ichiyō, who had been only Higuchi Natsu the summer before, now felt that she was another individual:

> It is just the beginning of summer now. We must change our clothes. Our *yukata* (summer dress) and most of our summer clothes are in the storehouse of Iseya (a pawnshop). . . . As I quietly ponder about this and that, numerous matters give me headaches. However, it was like Natsu of summer last year to be troubled by these matters, but Ichiyō of today ought not take the suffering on this earth as such. Living as we are, without any fixed property, it is natural for us to face this sort of hardship, and I am quite determined to accept it. . . .

When she moved to Daionji-mae about ten months before, her heart was still bleeding for Tōsui, but in the subsequent months she certainly had made a long stride in her effort to become master of herself, and finally her reason conquered her passion. On 3 June, 1895, an entry in her diary states that she had a chance to meet the man for whom she "went through all the agonies of life and gulped down many a sob," but by this time she was able to face him with serenity:

> I have completely outgrown my desire, and, not even for a moment, do I wish to enjoy my life with him in this world in the plain ordinary way. . . . All I hope is to carry on our former friendship. . . . As I gazed at him in this sort of frame of mind . . . he appeared to me like a real Buddha, and I was thoroughly filled with joy. . . .

It was only when she began to assume this transcendental outlook on life that was she able to write anything of worth. After abandoning everything on this earth, she realized that there was still something remaining. In pursuit of that which is eternal she began to grasp, in her own way, the essence of art. From the latter part of 1894 through 1895 she was at the peak of her activity as a writer. As if possessed by some spirit or having a premonition of her approaching end, she produced in succession, along with her *Takekurabe,* other stories of importance, such as *Nigorie* (*Bungei Kurabu,* September. 1895), *Jūsanya* (*Bungei Kurabu,* December, 1895), **"Wakaremichi"** ("Parting of the Way," supplement to *Kokumin no Tomo,* January, 1896), **"Otsugomori"** (New Year's Eve, *Bungakkai,* December, 1894, reprinted in *Taiyō,* February, 1896), and **"Ware kara"**, (From Myself, *Bungei Kurabu,* May, 1896). While *Takekurabe* ran serially in *Bungakkai,* it did not attract much attention from the general reading public, but once it was printed as a whole in *Bungei Kurabu* in April, 1896, it suddenly created a sensation.

In *Takekurabe* Ichiyō minutely depicted the life of teenage children scrambling for power in the neighborhood of the gay quarters. The heroine is Midori, a younger sister of a popular geisha and herself destined to follow the path of her elder sister. Love was beginning to awaken between Midori, who was approaching womanhood, and Shinnyo, the son of a Buddhist priest, but they had to part, because Shinnyo was to enter the training for the temple.

Mezamashigusa, a literary magazine, carried a series entitled *Sannin Jōgo* (Idle Talks by Three), an authoritative literary criticism of the time written jointly by Mori Ogai, Kōda Rohan, and Saitō Ryokuu. In the issue of April, 1896, a criticism of *Takekurabe* appeared, in which Mori Ogai praised Ichiyō's skill in describing vividly individual characters in a specific milieu and the eloquent manner with which she brought forth the local color of the gay quarters. He wrote:

> What is amazing is that the characters which appear in this story are not those beastlike human beings

frequently depicted by Zola and Ibsen, whose technique the naturalist writers tried to imitate to the utmost, but they are real human individuals who laugh and cry with us. . . . Even though I may be derided by the world for worshiping Ichiyō, I do not hesitate in conferring the title of 'real poet' upon this person. . . .

In the same section, Rohan complimented the story by saying:

> . . . I feel like making pills out of some words in this story and let a great number of critics and novelists of our day take them as a magical formula to improve their ability in writing. . . .

Among Ichiyō's representative works, *Takekurabe* is considered outstanding. Yuchi Takashi, agreeing with other Japanese critics, is of the opinion that among her representative works *Takekurabe* alone is absolutely and unconditionally excellent for the rare combination of dexterity in developing the plot, minuteness in delineation, and satisfying aftereffects. *Takekurabe* is unique in that it deftly treats the world of children. Ichiyō here displays superb skill in the portrayal of Midori, a partial projection of the author herself, in the delineation of delicate psychological changes that take place in her together with her physiological changes. About the time Ichiyō wrote *Takekurabe* she had almost completely grown out of imitative writing, and had developed a style of her own. This smooth and flowing style, a compromise between classic and colloquial Japanese, was a point worthy of note and certainly was a factor in enhancing the value of her story. *Takekurabe* is considered a masterpiece of Meiji literature in which Ichiyō consummated the realistic and exquisite manner of delineation and crystallization of her lyricism.

Nigorie and *Jūsanya,* in both of which she described the unfortunate lot of women, are next in importance among her novels. In *Nigorie* Ichiyō presents a barmaid Oriki and her patron. The appearance of Genshichi, Oriki's former lover, complicates the situation. Because of his infatuation with Oriki, Genshichi breaks up his own family, and in the end commits suicide after killing Oriki.

In this work, unlike most of her other works, Ichiyō depicts a woman in her full maturity. The ingenuity of Ichiyō's pen is devoted to the delineation of Oriki who had fallen, not out of her own volition, but because of her destitution. The model of Oriki is believed to have been a barmaid who lived next door to Ichiyō in Maruyama Fukuyama-chō, and the poverty stricken household of Genshichi may be that of a family Ichiyō's mother served as a wet-nurse before the Higuchis acquired their title of samurai. Baba Kochō also suggests a resemblance between Oriki's patron and Tōsui, and a glimpse of Ichiyō herself in the workings of Oriki's mind. As in most of her other stories, the male characters in this story are not treated with the same care and minuteness as the women.

The suffering of a woman in an unhappy marriage is the theme of *Jūsanya*. While *Nigorie* exemplifies Ichiyō's skill in realistic writing, this story is predominantly lyrical. The heroine Oseki is the mother of one son. She is unable to bear her husband's cruel treatment and makes up her mind to leave him. However, persuaded by her parents, she decides to return to him. On the way back to her husband, she encounters her former lover, but such a meeting means only added distress, for she has just determined to lead a life of complete renunciation. With a sympathetic touch, Ichiyō tells of the distressing lot of a woman of her day, but she does not go any further than to let the heroine resign herself to such a situation, without delving into the problem as a social issue.

"Wakaremichi" and "Ware kara," both of which were written toward the end of 1895, treat of women who deviate somewhat from the usual type of women she ordinarily described. The heroine Okyō in "Wakaremichi," having grown tired of earning her own living by taking in washing and sewing, decides to become the secret mistress of a wealthy man. In "Ware kara" Ichiyō depicts a married woman, whose dissatisfaction is caused mainly by the infidelity of her husband. As she becomes too attached to their houseboy, seeking an outlet for her dissatisfaction, her husband accuses her and orders her to leave at once the household, the house which she had inherited. In neither novel do we find such feminine qualities as modesty, extreme shyness, or complete passiveness, which often characterize women in Ichiyō's previous works. In the former story the heroine is about to defy the established code of ethics, and in the latter the author tacitly protests against the unfairness in judging a woman's conduct, since society which tolerates loose conduct on the part of a man does not allow it on the part of a woman.

"Otsugomori" was the only story of hers which dealt directly with poverty. In this story, a servant Omine, whose parents died in her childhood, steals money from her master's household in order to relieve her destitute uncle's family. Compared with her previous works, this story, written toward the end of 1894, achieved a high degree of realism. Having gone through the bitterness of poverty herself, Ichiyō was able to depict the heroine with all her sympathy. Perhaps out of her compassion, in spite of the immoral act on the part of the heroine, the story ends without having her crime exposed. Yuchi Takashi has pointed out the unnatural elements in the development of the plot of this story in spite of its relative success.

In the brief period of her literary activity which lasted only for four and a half years, Ichiyō wrote some twenty novels, the longest of which is *Takekurabe*. Her stories are characteristically short, and excepting *Takekurabe* and a few others, as far as the literary merit of her works is concerned, the rest of her stories, especially those produced in the earlier stage of her writing, are relatively insignificant.

Her career as a writer was preceded by her study of *waka,* but *waka* could never provide for her a proper means for expressing her inner self. *Waka* as stressed at Hagi-no-ya in particular was rather obsolete and too formalized for Ichiyō's needs, and, besides, her teacher Utako could not give her anything more than a general knowledge of classic literature related to the study of *waka*. Ichiyō composed some 4000 verses in her lifetime, but they do not represent the best of her work.

While she was groping in the dark, she resorted to Murasaki Shikibu, the author of the *Genji Monogatari,* and having sought out Saikaku as her model, she made his realistic technique of writing her own. She was eager to learn also from other writers of the Edo period, and among her contemporaries she held Kōda Rohan in high esteem and followed his example.

It was very fortunate for Ichiyō as a writer that she found an opportunity to associate with members of the *Bungakkai*. Her close contacts with them introduced her to the literary ideas of her time. Hirata Tokuboku, Baba Kochō, Togawa Shūkotsu, Ueda Ryūson (or Bin), and others began to frequent her place after the spring of 1893, and were often engaged in lively and stimulating literary discussions, as is evident from her diary. These young men, well versed in European literature, were enthusiastic idealists constantly in search of the beautiful and the noble, and their efforts noticeably brought about the romantic movement of Japan.

About the members of the *Bungakkai*, Sōma Gyofū wrote:

> They were not satisfied with the traditional view of life, nor did they submit themselves to conventional morals. Rather, they were after certain ideals. They considered love as primary in life, and tried to devote themselves to beauty in art. They were passionate individuals, in constant agony and pain. . . .

According to Gyofū, the romantic movement became articulate in the literary circle in 1893, the second year of Ichiyō's literary career. Of the general trend of literature in Ichiyō's time he has the following to say:

> . . . when Ichiyō first made her stories public, Kōyō and Rohan reigned in the literary circle. The general trend in novels was characterized by superficial realism and naive and fanciful idealism. In other words, it was the time when volatile literature was in full swing. . . .

At first, Ichiyō was not able to free herself completely from such a trend in writing, and in her earlier works there were definite traces of such influences. It would be reasonable to assume that *Takekurabe* and a few other outstanding stories of hers, all of which were written within the last two years of her life, were done under the influence of the romantic and vigorous spirit of the youthful members of the *Bungakkai*.

Accounting for the influence of the members of the *Bungakkai* upon Ichiyō, Miyamoto Yuriko wrote in *Fujin to Bungaku:*

> No matter how minutely Ichiyō might have observed and been familiar with Daionji-mae, the lyric beauty of *Takekurabe* would never have been born out of it, without the influence of the members of the *Bungakkai*. . . .

As for the unique position Ichiyō's literary works occupy in the development of Meiji literature, Katsumoto Seiichirō remarked in *Jiyū Fujin:*

> . . . as to whether to consider her position as an extension of the literary trend—a revival of Genroku literature—lead by Kōyō and Rohan, or to find her place in the rising movement of early romanticism . . . it might be proper to say that she occupied the middle point between the two. . . .

In the same essay, he pointed out the neutrality of her stand upon the main literary currents of her time, and that having arisen just when she did, she barely found her place in the literary history of Meiji:

> . . . if she had appeared a bit earlier or a bit later there would be no historical significance of her stand. If she had come earlier, she would not have been able to get away from the bounds of the literature of Kōyō and Rohan, and if later, her works would have been outmoded before *Wakanash* (Collection of Young Herbs) by Tōson and *Midaregami* (Dishevelled Hair) by Akiko.

Ichiyō, as a prose writer, thus occupies a significant place in Meiji literature. Along with her short novels, her diary is also considered an outstanding literary product. Wada Yoshie has pointed out the strong narrative nature of her diary and even suggested that "it may be considered as an 'I' story in the form of a diary." If it is a novel, unlike her other works, it is a full-length novel, covering a period of over five years of vicissitudes of an individual.

Although her works may be limited in scope, lacking the quality of grandeur such as found in long novels of Western origin, and short of philosophical content, one cannot help but be impressed by the genuineness and sincerity reflected in each of them. Ichiyō bent herself to the task of writing, confident that at least the expression of her genuine self in her work ought to be worth of attention.

In many respects, Ichiyō belonged to the old world. In many a crucial moment of her life, she acted as if she were a blind follower of the traditional ways of life, and at times even positively defended them. However, in her later works she depicted women who were not always submissive to tradition, and in one way or another showed resistance toward conventional ideals. It is this long hidden progressive side of Ichiyō which at present is beginning to receive attention in the critical study of her works.

Nevertheless, her way of life itself was rather unique and exceptional for a woman of Meiji, in that she at least tried to live a financially independent life, although she was unsuccessful in this respect until her death. Ichiyō lived a serious life, seriously loved and struggled, and took an equally serious attitude toward her writing. It is this earnestness, which is reflected in her art. For Ichiyō writing did not mean a mere task of producing fiction. In the words of Professor Shioda, "Her art was heightened to the point where it was a reflection of her own life: wherein lies the merit of her art."

Donald Keene (essay date 1984)

SOURCE: "Higuchi Ichiyo," in *Dawn to the West, Japanese Literature of the Modern Era: Fiction, Vol. 1,* Holt, Rinehart and Winston, 1984, pp. 165-85.

[*In this following excerpt, Keene chronicles Higuchi's literary career, discussing her influences and the critical reception of her work.*]

During the six centuries after the composition of *Izayoi Nikki* in 1280 hardly a single work by a woman left its imprint on Japanese literature. It is true that the court ladies continued to compose imitations of Heian tanka and fiction until well into the fifteenth century, and in the Tokugawa period a few women enjoyed reputations for their tanka, haiku, and even poetry in Chinese, but their works, with a few exceptions, were of minor interest. The Heian tradition of writing by women was broken when the court society itself lost its importance and when the position of women came to be threatened by the hostile attitudes of the feudal government.

Early in the Meiji period, however, the long-standing prejudices against education for women began to give way to more enlightened views, largely in response to Western influence. Girls were among the students sent abroad by the government, and they were admitted to the educational institutions founded at home; the first graduate of the national music school was a woman, a sister of Kōda Rohan. But the role of women in literature remained modest. The nun Otagaki Rengetsu (1791-1875), the best-known woman writer of the early Meiji era, is remembered today for a few tanka and for some paintings whose charm reflected little of the new epoch.

Although women writers became more prominent later in the period, the only one of consequence was Higuchi Ichiyō (1872-96); indeed, she ranks among the major authors of the time, despite the fewness of her works. Ichiyō's fiction, at once sensitive and realistic, earned her so high a place in modern literature that voluminous studies have appeared, painstakingly examining every detail of her short life in the hopes of discovering clues as to how a woman with so little formal education and initially, at least, so little contact with other writers (she belonged to no school) managed to attain such great distinction. Ichiyō's diaries are of importance not only for what they reveal about her life but because these autobiographical records of a woman's life, selectively and poetically related, restored to importance one of the oldest elements of Japanese literature.

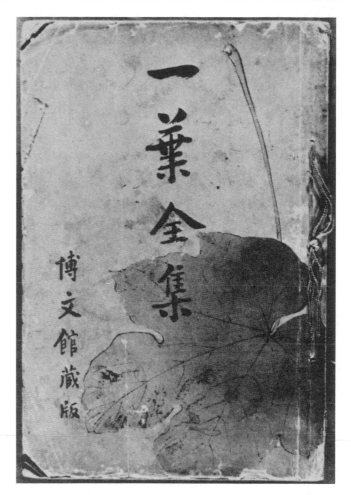

Cover of the first edition of Higuchi's collected short stories, 1897.

Ichiyō was the daughter of an ambitious farmer who had gone up to Edo from the country shortly before the Meiji Restoration and purchased status as a samurai. She was proud of this samurai "ancestry," dubious though it was, and liked to think of herself as an impoverished gentlewoman—one of the victims of the changes brought about by the Meiji Restoration. As long as her father was alive, Ichiyō and her family lived in reasonable comfort, but after the death of her elder brother in 1887 and her father in 1889, she, her mother, and her sister knew real poverty. Ichiyō's formal education had come to an end when she was eleven. This was not for lack of scholastic ability—she stood at the head of her class—nor even because of poverty, but because her parents, typically for the times, were sure that too much book learning was undesirable for a girl. Ichiyō was permitted, however, to study the tanka—an appropriate accomplishment for a young lady—and in 1886 she entered a private school called Hagino-ya (House of the Bush Clover) run by Nakajima Utako (1841-1903), a leading woman tanka poet. Not only did Ichiyō learn to write tanka in the faded style of the late Keien school, but she received instruction in such classics as the *Kokinshū, The Tale of Genji,* and *Essays in Idle-*

ness. These studies conspicuously affected her prose style, especially in her diaries—kept throughout in a classical Japanese reminiscent of the Heian period—despite the specifically Meiji content of the incidents described.

At the Hagi-no-ya Ichiyō became friends with Tanabe Kaho (1868-1943), the daughter of a distinguished statesman. Kaho had shown a precocious interest in gesaku fiction, and had later delved into the Heian classics, as well as into Saikaku and Washington Irving's *Sketch Book*. The rediscovery of Saikaku in the late 1880s directly influenced the style and manner of Kaho's "Yabu no Uguisu" (Nightingale in the Grove), the first noteworthy story by a Meiji woman writer.

"Nightingale in the Grove," revised and with an introduction by Tsubouchi Shōyō, was published in 1888. No doubt the eminence of Kaho's father helped her to find a publisher for the story, but it was generally praised, perhaps because it appeared just after the reaction had set in against the adulation of the West symbolized by the fancy-dress balls at the Rokumeikan. The heroine's superficial worship of the West—the story opens at a ball—leads to her downfall: she betrays her fiancé, a man of impeccable virtue, to take up with her tutor of English, a scoundrel interested only in her money. The construction of the story, hardly impressive by other standards, was condescendingly praised for being surprisingly complex (considering the author was a woman), and the style was deemed to be elegant and smooth-flowing. This style resembles Shōyō's in *The Characters of Modern Students*, combining dialogue in the contemporary colloquial with descriptions in classical Japanese.

The success of "Nightingale in the Grove," and especially the reports that Kaho had received thirty-three yen in royalties for her manuscript, aroused Ichiyō's envy and ambitions of doing the same. Her first literary compositions, written in 1890, were no doubt prompted by the financial crisis in her household precipitated by her father's death the year before. Throughout her career Ichiyō wrote fiction primarily in order to earn money to support herself and her family, and even her brief romances seemed to have been inspired, in part at least, by the same purpose.

In April 1891 Ichiyō paid a call on the journalist and hack novelist Nakarai Tōsui (1860-1926). She had apparently not read his novels, but sought him out anyway, probably because he was the one author accessible to her; a friend at the Hagi-no-ya knew Nakarai's sister and—if we can believe what Nakarai wrote years later—Ichiyō was at the time doing the laundry for the Nakarai family. Ichiyō described this visit in the first of her diaries:

> His greetings when we first met were friendly, but I was still such a novice at such encounters that I felt my ears grow hot and my lips become dry, and I couldn't remember what I had intended to say. Totally incapable of speech, all I could do was to bow profusely. It embarrasses me when I think what an idiot I would have seemed to an outsider!

> Mr. Nakarai must be about thirty. I realize it is unladylike for me to comment in detail about his figure and appearance, but I will set down my impressions exactly as they came to me. His coloring is excellent, and his features are composed. When he gave a little smile he really looked just like what they call "an innocent child of three." All the same, he is most impressive, no doubt because he is considerably taller than average and well built.

> He discussed at length the contemporary novel, remarking that other people did not like the books that he himself preferred, and unless books had general appeal, they did not enjoy much success. He wondered what he should write, considering the childish tastes of the Japanese readers, who do not appreciate serialized novels unless the author strings together the usual tales of plotters and bandits or else accounts of the doings of wicked women and prostitutes. The various novels he has recently been publishing were not written with any sense of pride. It was difficult for him to look scholars or men of discrimination in the face when they criticized or attacked his stories, but what was he to do? He wrote not in the hopes of fame but in order to feed and clothe his parents, brothers, and sisters. Of course he was prepared to be criticized, since what he wrote was dictated by the needs of his family, but if some day he ever had the chance to publish a novel after his own tastes, he would probably not accept criticism so readily. He concluded with a great laugh, and I thought he really had meant what he said.

Nakarai's remarks accurately conveyed the predicament of authors at this time. Unless they wrote fiction that would appeal to badly educated readers, they could not hope to earn a living, no matter how highly their works might be praised by the discriminating few (as Futabatei Shimei had learned). Nakarai was primarily a reporter—he became the first overseas correspondent for a Japanese newspaper, thanks to his dispatches from Korea in 1882 to the *Asahi Shimbun*—and wrote the novels he serialized in the newspaper as part of his job. Ichiyō went to him not in the hopes of emulating his literary success, but because she dreamed of earning enough money from her writing to give up sewing and washing clothes. She seems to have fallen in love with Nakarai at first sight, but her love never blinded her to his inadequacies as a writer, nor to the possibilities of using him to advance her career.

Nakarai agreed to read a manuscript by Ichiyō, and she left with him the first installment of a projected story. When she visited him again a few days later his only comments were to note that this installment was too long to be published in a single issue of a newspaper, and that the Heian flavor to Ichiyō's prose was somewhat excessive—she should write in a more colloquial style. Nakarai promised, however, to introduce her to various scholars. Far from being discouraged by Nakarai's apparent lack of enthusiasm for her work, Ichiyō was even more impressed by him than the first time. Nakarai, though friendly, seems not to have contemplated any romantic involvement with her.

Ichiyō visited Nakarai frequently during the following year, ostensibly for consultations about her writings, but seemingly more attracted by the man himself than by his literary pointers. Nakarai cautioned her that her visits were likely to arouse gossip, but Ichiyō paid no attention to this warning. In her diary she deplored her own forwardness, wondering how she, who had always been so timid, had become so brazen.

In February 1892 Nakarai disclosed his plans for starting a literary magazine, *Musashino,* which would publish only new writers. He urged Ichiyō to contribute a short work even though he could not promise any payment until the magazine had caught on with the public. Ichiyō at once set to work on the story **"Yamizakura"** (**"Flowers at Dusk"**), published in the first issue of *Musashino*. This is the inconsequential account of a boy of twenty-one and a girl of fifteen who have been childhood friends. The girl, Ochiyo, begins to feel romantic interest in the boy, Ryonosuke, but the boy, an ambitious student, thinks of her only as a younger sister. One day when they are walking together a friend knowingly comments on their intimacy. Ochiyo, ashamed to think that her secret love has revealed itself, falls into a wasting sickness. On her deathbed she calls for Ryōnosuke, gives him her ring as a memento of herself, then sends him away.

The main theme of the story suggests Ichiyō's own feelings toward Nakarai, who treated her like a younger sister, in the manner of Ryōnosuke; it also prefigures similar situations in her later works, especially the boy Nobu's embarrassed rejection of Midori's love in *Takekurabe* (*Growing Up*), Ichiyō's masterpiece. This and the other early stories are otherwise not of great interest, possibly because Ichiyō was too conscientiously attempting to follow Nakarai's suggestions. Nakarai apparently made many small corrections on the manuscript of **"Flowers at Dusk"**; even though he was by no means a distinguished stylist, he was able to help the inexperienced Ichiyō, especially with the dialogue spoken by the young man in the story. The manner of **"Flowers at Dusk,"** with its emphasis on twists of plot rather than on characterization, may be indicative not only of Ichiyō's immaturity as a writer but of Nakarai's influence, his own literary preferences lying in that direction.

Ichiyō's next stories, published in *Musashino* (which ceased publication after three issues) and in a minor newspaper, also bear the marks of Nakarai's suggestions, especially **"Wakerejimo"** (**"The Last Frost of Spring"**), which was directly inspired by him. In this story an unscrupulous merchant drives his former benefactor into bankruptcy, breaks the engagement of his daughter to the benefactor's son, and plans a more advantageous marriage for the girl. One snowy night the daughter accidentally gets into a rickshaw pulled by her former fiancé, now driven to this desperate expedient, and confesses that she still loves him. The two agree to commit suicide, but although the man succeeds in this plan, the girl is prevented. Seven years later she at last manages to escape from the house where she has been closely guarded and kills herself before her beloved's grave.

This overplotted story contains scenes that would appear in the later Ichiyō, especially the chance meeting of the girl, in affluent circumstances, with her lover, now a rickshaw puller, which was repeated in *Jūsanya* (*Two Nights before the Full Moon*). Snowy nights were also to be a favorite background for Ichiyō's dramatic scenes.

Although these stories did not reveal great talent, Nakarai confidently predicted that Ichiyō would become famous once they were published. Realizing perhaps that someone better placed than himself was needed to help her advance in her career, he promised to arrange a meeting with Ozaki Kōyō, then the literary editor of the *Yomiuri Shimbun,* the most important outlet for newspaper fiction; only with such a connection could Ichiyō hope to earn a regular income as a writer. But before the meeting with Kōyō could take place, Ichiyō, at a funeral service for Nakajima Utako's mother, was warned by a friend from the Hagi-no-ya that she must break with Nakarai if she valued her reputation. Ichiyō had earlier heard rumors about Nakarai's profligacy, but they seem not to have disturbed her; now, however, gossip had it that she herself was his mistress. Horrified, she swore she was innocent of any improper behavior. Two days later she went to see Nakajima Utako and learned from her that Nakarai had publicly referred to Ichiyō as his "wife." She declared her intention of breaking with him and said she would inform him of this the next day.

Ichiyō apparently could not muster the courage to tell Nakarai the news all at once. On her visit the following day she merely declined his offer of an introduction to Kōyō, and only a week later did she tell him of the rumors and of her painful decision not to see him for the time being. Nakarai admitted that he had discussed Ichiyō with friends and had stated that he would like to marry her if he were in a position to do so. (He had made a vow when his wife died never to remarry). No doubt this conversation had occasioned the gossip. He agreed to their separation, but hoped they would meet again when the rumors had died down.

Ichiyō's diary describing this period is so movingly written, despite the sometimes incongruous Heian language in which it is phrased, that it is easy to see why some critics have praised it as her finest work. Wada Yoshie, a specialist who devoted his life to the study of Ichiyō, suggested that the diary should be read not as truth but as autobiographical fiction. Commenting on the entries that narrate Ichiyō's decision to break with Nakarai Tōsui, he wrote:

> Ichiyō outspokenly described in her diary the rupture in the affections between Tōsui and herself. However, objectively viewed, all that happened was that she rejected Tōsui's help, having realized it was useless relying on him to sell her stories if she hoped to be able to live on the income from them, and decided to depend on Kaho instead. The result, then, was that Ichiyō utilized this scandal in order to establish ties with *Miyako no Hana*. If Tōsui could have helped her to make her début successfully, or if she could have received a steady allowance for living expenses from

him, Ichiyō would certainly not have made any formal break with Tōsui, no matter how much of a row people might have raised at the Hagi-no-ya. Tōsui, it might be argued, was a man in adverse circumstances betrayed by Ichiyō.

This harsh interpretation of Ichiyō's motives can be disputed, but Ichiyō's diary undoubtedly departed from the truth—or at any rate, gave only a partial account—when she described her relations with Nakarai and other men. She was not only reticent, as we might expect of a proper young lady of the Meiji period, but she had the writer's natural tendency to make even a diary into a work of literature; certainly the diary is far more interesting than the stories or the tanka Ichiyō was writing about the same time. Conversely, Ichiyō's diary was neglected during her last year, when her stories were finally recognized and acclaimed, perhaps because she no longer needed this outlet for thoughts and emotions too advanced for the conventional fiction she had been writing.

A few days before she broke with Nakarai, Ichiyō had been urged to submit a manuscript to *Miyako no Hana (The Flower of the Capital)*, a literary magazine founded in 1888 that had published Futabatei Shimei, Ozaki Kōyō, and many other important writers. Perhaps, as Wada suggested, this promise of new and important connections in the literary world emboldened Ichiyō to give up Nakarai and the help he could provide with her career. She completed the story **"Umoregi" ("A Buried Life")** in September 1892 and took it to Tanabe Kaho, who wrote a laudatory preface before delivering it to the editors of *Miyako no Hana*. When published in November it brought Ichiyōµ the first attention outside the small circle of Nakarai and his friends.

"A Buried Life" is unique among Ichiyō's stories in that the central character is a man, the potter Irie Raizō. Ichiyō seems to have modeled Raizō on her brother, Toranosuke, also a potter, and the description of Raizō's masterpieces, a pair of flower vases, was derived from two works Toranosuke executed for the Chicago Exposition of 1893. The theme of an artist's devotion to his craft immediately suggests the influence of Kōda Rohan (in such works as *The Buddha of Art* and *The Five-Storied Pagoda*), but it is obscured by complications revolving around the character Tatsuo, Raizō's apparent benefactor. Tatsuo encourages Raizō to create works of art that will redound to Japan's glory abroad. All goes well until Raizō, so sure of Tatsuo's friendship that he does not bother to knock when he enters his mansion, overhears Tatsuo describe how he is using Raizō and his sister, Ochō, to achieve nefarious purposes. Raizō, aghast, rushes home to discover that Ochō has gone, leaving behind a suicide note, which reveals that Tatsuo had asked her to give herself to a rich man. In despair Raizō smashes the two vases that were the culminating glory of his career.

"A Buried Life" is unconvincing and awkwardly constructed. The style throughout is irritatingly old-fashioned, even in the conversations, and the elaborate descriptive passages have the mannerisms of gesaku fiction. The

account of Raizō's devotion to his art is vitiated by the melodramatic ending, and the character Tatsuo, first described as building a hospital for the poor or anonymously bestowing alms on an unknown woman, then seen as an unrepentant criminal cold-bloodedly taking advantage of a trusting friend, is utterly implausible. **"A Buried Life"** was nevertheless favorably reviewed by the critic Hoshino Tenchi (1862-1950):

> I am delighted to have the honor to introduce a new woman writer. I refer to Ichiyō, whose story **"A Buried Life"** has appeared in *Miyako no Hana* since issue 95. According to the preface written by Kaho, she and Ichiyō studied together at the Hagi-no-ya under Nakajima Utako.
>
> The story describes the arduous efforts of a potter who lives in a lonely house near the Nyorai Temple in Takanawa. Moonflowers cling to his fence and mosquito incense hovers smokily by his eaves; he has neither friend, nor disciple, nor wife, and only his younger sister Ochō to keep him company. He leads a life of poverty, lamenting the decline in his art; not having any outlet for the original ideas in his breast, his hot tears well up and his entrails seethe. Not only is the conception unusual, but the style is so incisive it makes one doubt the work was written by a woman. I understand that she plans henceforth to devote herself to literature, and I hope therefore that her achievements will rise to ever greater heights.

Tenchi was a leading spirit in the group then planning to publish a new literary magazine called *Bungakkai (The World of Literature)*, which would have as one of its missions the promotion of writing by women. He was particularly impressed by Tanabe Kaho and Ichiyō, and requested contributions from each for the first issue. Ichiyō wrote **"Yuki no Hi" ("A Snowy Day")** in January 1893, but it did not appear until the third issue of *Bungakkai*, perhaps because Kaho was disappointed by this tentative story. The central figure, a girl in a provincial town, is an orphan, living with her aunt. She is attracted to a teacher from the city because of his learning and gentle ways, only for rumors to start about the nature of their relationship. The girl is warned by her aunt of the danger of besmirching the family name by becoming involved with the man, but one snowy day the girl, visiting the teacher, impetuously agrees to run off with him to Tokyo. Now, as she recalls these events, she bitterly regrets her action, which brought her only grief and resulted in the death of her aunt.

It is easy to trace autobiographical elements in **"A Snowy Day."** Ichiyō's visit to Nakarai—her teacher—on a snowy day in February of the previous year, together with the warning she received from her Hagi-no-ya friends about the gossip circulating concerning Nakarai and herself, provided most of the thematic material for the story. But the conclusion is disappointing: the girl, far from rejoicing over her liberation from the constricting gossip of the village and over her happiness with the man of her choice, bitterly regrets her imprudent and selfish act. This conclusion may have represented no more than a bow in the direction of the traditional morality; presumably it was not calculated to please the romantically inclined editors of *Bungakkai.*

Ichiyō subsequently published a half-dozen stories in *Bungakkai,* including two of her finest works, but she was never counted among the regular members of the group. Nevertheless, it was thanks to Hoshino Tenchi, Hirata Tokuboku, Baba Kochō, and the other *Bungakkai* regulars that she gained her first fame and eventually, in the year before her death, became the central figure of a literary salon. Ichiyō did not adopt the Romanticism associated with *Bungakkai,* but she was stimulated and excited to be even on the periphery of a group of writers so passionately devoted to literature—a far cry from the women poets of the Hagi-no-ya. Her diary entry for February 6, 1893, suggests how receptive she was to the literary speculations of the *Bungakkai* writers:

> I can't seem to get my story going as I want it. My head keeps aching, and every scrap of good sense has deserted me. All I keep dreaming of is creating a woman of complete and flawless beauty. I shut my eyes and face the wall. I cover my ears and lean against my desk. When I attempt to capture this ideal beauty in the realm of mystery (*yūgen*), heaven and earth alike become dark; neither the form of that lovely flower nor the voice of the bulbul finds any reflection in my mind. . . . Is the beauty I long for so difficult to discover in this world? Or is it my fate to have only the commonplace beauties of cherry blossoms and crimson maple leaves show themselves in my mind's eye? Or is it that there is no such thing as true beauty in heaven and earth? Or is it, perhaps, that what does not seem beautiful to my eyes is true beauty? . . . My mind, torn by these thoughts, raced over heaven and earth, and my body was bathed in the sweat of anguish.

Ichiyō's earlier conception of beauty had been precisely the cherry blossoms and crimson leaves she now derided. These speculations on the nature of beauty, many times echoed in her diary, were inspired by readings in the essays published by the *Bungakkai* writers. The admiration she expressed on reading Hirata Tokuboku's essay on Yoshida Kenkō suggested to one scholar that "her views on love, like Tokuboku's, were progressing in the direction of a rejection of the earthly and human." Her inconclusive romance with Nakarai Tōsui may have convinced her that a transcendental love would be less disappointing, and the writings in *Bungakkai* helped her to formulate her views in the vocabulary of Romanticism.

At the same time that Ichiyō was absorbing these influences, her rejection of her old mentor, Nakarai, grew more pronounced. On February 23 he suddenly paid a call with a copy of his new book, *Kosa Fuku Kaze (Winds Blowing a Northern Flute),* a long novel on a Korean subject, no doubt a product of his residence in that country. Ichiyō commented in her diary, "Tōsui's style has always been crude, lacking in any brilliance or depth. Moreover, he seems to make no attempt to improve it, but is interested only in achieving novel effects of plot and overall design. . . . The characters in the work do not move of their own,

but are merely creatures manipulated inside the author's mind. . . . It is certainly not a work of perfect beauty."

Ichiyō continued during 1893 to write for *Bungakkai.* At first she was the only paid contributor, perhaps because the editors tacitly recognized her dire poverty, but the income was insufficient for her and her family to live on, and she was forced to borrow money again and again. In August 1893 she opened a shop selling sundries and cheap candy near the Yoshiwara quarter. At first the shop did fairly well, even driving two competitors out of business, but in 1894 Ichiyō's shop was in turn threatened by a new shop opened just across the street. She resorted to desperate stratagems, even consulting a diviner on ways to make money. She encouraged the man when he showed an interest in her, but finally rejected his proposal to supply her with a regular income in return for becoming his mistress.

In April 1894 Ichiyō decided to give up the shop and moved again, this time to a district known for its drinking establishments. For a time she assisted Nakajima Utako at the Hagi-no-ya, even though she had come to question the place of the tanka in the modern world: "To follow the old style of writing poetry in thirty-one syllables is as indefensible as lazily riding along by oneself in an oxcart in this age of trains and steamships." This was precisely the time when Masaoka Shiki and Yosano Tekkan were calling for changes in the haiku and tanka, but Ichiyō probably was unacquainted with their criticisms; in any case, she continued to write much the same kind of tanka even in her last years, using the hackneyed old fixed epithets and the rest of the baggage of the conventional tanka without embarrassment. For all her doubts, she had apparently reached the conclusion that although the spirit of the new age could best be expressed in the poetry in the new style (*shintaishi*), the beauties of nature and the seasons were still the proper business of the tanka.

In December 1894 Ichiyō wrote **"Otsugomori" ("On the Last Day of the Year")** and published it in *Bungakkai* the same month. This was the first of the stories on which her reputation is based, though the plot and characterization are still immature. Omine, a servant in the rich Yamamura household, is an orphan who has been reared by an uncle. Toward the end of the year this bedridden and impoverished man asks her to borrow some money so that he can pay back a usurer and spend a cheerful New Year. He urges her to ask her employer to advance the money. But Mrs. Yamamura, a coldhearted and stingy woman, refuses the girl. Omine, desperately eager to help her uncle, is in the end driven into stealing two yen from a drawer. She supposes that no one has seen this act, but Ishinosuke, the dissolute son of the household, has observed her. Moved to pity by the girl's evident desperation—and perhaps revolting against a society in which he too has no place—Ishinosuke removes the rest of the money in the drawer, leaving behind a note saying he has "borrowed" it. Mrs. Yamamura, finding the note after he has left the house, disowned, does not suspect Omine's theft, and she is saved by this unimagined act of generosity.

"On the Last Day of the Year," particularly in the overingenious ending, suggests how much Ichiyō still had to learn as a writer, but the story comes alive, thanks to the realism of the details. Ichiyō's own poverty and the gulf she must have felt between herself and the rich young ladies she tutored at the Hagi-no-ya undoubtedly occasioned the contrasts she depicts between the poverty of the uncle's house and the affluence of the Yamamuras, or between the serving girl slaving in the kitchen and the daughter of the household frolicking in her New Year's finery. Ichiyō certainly had no political convictions—her diaries reveal an almost total lack of interest in the political events reported in the newspapers—and she offered no solutions to the problems she described. But the very fact that she treated material derived from her own experiences—unlike the fantasy of **"A Buried Life,"** for example—gives this story authenticity, and the involved, classical style still used in the descriptions is replaced in the dialogue by a vivid colloquial, making the story more immediate. Ichiyō, consciously or not, had moved closer to her contemporaries in her concern for an appropriate language in which to cast modern stories.

The first section of Ichiyō's next story, **Takekurabe (Growing Up),** was published in the January 1895 issue of *Bungakkai,* and subsequent sections appeared irregularly during the next twelve months. In the meantime, before the complete publication revealed a masterpiece had been created, Ichiyō was discovered by the literary world. She was asked to write a story for the Sunday supplement of the *Mainichi Shimbun,* and then for *Taiyō (The Sun),* a magazine founded in January 1895 that had quickly established itself as the outstanding periodical of the day. **"Yuku Kumo" ("Passing Clouds"),** published in *Taiyō,* was not one of Ichiyō's best works, but it brought her recognition with general readers and led to further requests for manuscripts from the major newspapers and magazines and to the re-publication of earlier stories that had appeared in *Musashino* and other magazines of limited circulation. **"Passing Clouds"** was highly praised by the critics; one of them declared, "If you showed this story to someone, concealing the author's name, he would probably never guess it was written by a woman."

As Ichiyō's reputation rose, her circle of acquaintances among the writers expanded, and some of her new friends attempted to interest her in Western literature. Hirata Tokuboku wrote, "She had never ventured beyond her training in *Genji,* Saikaku, and other works of Japanese literature, and it was truly remarkable that she could understand us—who were completely steeped in Western poetry and literature—so well, and could go forward in our company at the same pace with us." Ichiyō, who had hitherto avoided discussions on foreign literature, showed special interest in the work of Wakamatsu Shizuko (1864-1896), the celebrated translator of *Little Lord Fauntleroy* (published 1890-1892). About this time Ichiyō began to read not only the translations appearing in *Bungakkai,* but *Macbeth,* a life of Schiller, and *Crime and Punishment.* Her diary, skimpy by now, provides no clue as to what these readings in foreign literature might have meant to

her, and it is hard to find anything in her later works that reveals specific foreign influence. It is nevertheless tempting to attribute the remarkable development in Ichiyō's work at this time to such an influence. Like the members of the *Bungakkai* group, Ichiyō found herself at odds with the world around her, and she probably shared their interpretation of Raskolnikov as a rebel against the constricting regulations of society. The characters in Ichiyō's later stories do not suggest Dostoevski's, but their rebelliousness, as contrasted with the docility of, say, the tepid lovers of **"Passing Clouds,"** may have been occasioned by her readings. Perhaps too *Little Lord Fauntleroy,* for all its sentimentality, contributed to the realistically depicted world of children in **Growing Up.**

The writing of **Growing Up,** under the title "Hinadori" (Baby Chicks), apparently began in the autumn of 1894, after Ichiyō closed her shop outside the Yoshiwara gate. Many changes, mostly minor, exist between the two versions; for example, Midori's family background—her father, a samurai, caused the ruin of his household by his heavy drinking—is carefully described in "Baby Chicks," but hardly mentioned in **Growing Up.** A pruning of unnecessary detail is apparent also in the dialogue of the later version, which replaced the coarse, excessively realistic language of "Baby Chicks" with a more elegant, concise language that still seems colloquial. The title **Takekurabe** (literally **Comparing Heights**) was borrowed from the passage in *Tales of Ise* in which a young man and woman recall childhood days when they compared their heights against a well-curb—another indication of Ichiyō's desire to impart elegance to an otherwise realistic, contemporary story.

The style of **Growing Up** is reminiscent of Saikaku's, whose works Ichiyō first read in 1894, especially in the descriptive passages. She chose Saikaku not only because she admired his style, but because she wished to give her story greater depth by associating its incidents with the long traditions of the literature of the licensed quarters. Saikaku never suggested any doubts about the propriety of women selling their bodies to satisfy the appetites of men, but Ichiyō, even though she certainly never advocated closing the Yoshiwara quarter, saw the pity of children growing up in that world, and she recorded her observations without sentimentality.

Growing Up was acclaimed as a masterpiece, especially when the entire work was republished in a single issue of the popular magazine *Bungei Kurabu* in April 1896, Mori Ogai, Kōda Rohan, and Saitō Ryokuu, anonymously reviewing the story, lavishly praised its every feature:

> (ROHAN): The works of this author are never inconsequential, but the present work is especially notable, both in the beauty of the style and the profundity of the themes. It is true that some phrases have a slightly familiar ring, and it would not be impossible to discover flaws in the writing, but the skill of the whole is such as to dazzle the eyes and intoxicate the mind, leaving us at a loss for words. . . . One can appreciate the density of the texture of her writings from the fact that not one word can be omitted; this must be what they mean

when they say "take away one word and you destroy the sense." I would like to urge all the many critics and novelists who seem to think that a novel does not merit being called a serious work unless it applies a knife to people's bodies, strips away the skin and digs out the internal organs, swallow a dose of her language, five or six words at a time, as a miracle-working antidote guaranteed to improve their literary techniques. . . .

(OGAI): It is not especially remarkable that this author, a member of a literary circle in which the Naturalist school is said to be enjoying a vogue should have chosen to set her story in this place [the Yoshiwara district]. What *is* remarkable is that the characters who haunt this area are not the brute beasts in human form—the copies of Zola, Ibsen, and the rest—presented by the assiduous imitators of the so-called Naturalist school, but human beings with whom we can laugh and cry together . . . At the risk of being mocked as an Ichiyō-idolator, I do not hesitate to accord to her the name of "poet." It is more difficult to depict a person with individual characteristics than a stereotype, and far more difficult to depict an individual in a milieu than a special person all by himself. This author, who has painted the "local coloring" of Daionji-mae so effectively that one might say it has ceased to exist apart from *Growing Up,* without leaving any trace of the efforts such portraiture must have cost her, must truly be called a woman of rare ability.

The success of *Growing Up* can be measured historically in terms of the other fiction of the day, whether the lurid tales of grotesque and maimed people by Hirotsu Ryūrō, or the melodrama of the early Izumi Kyōka stories with their implausible dilemmas, or the farcicality of Saitō Ryokuu. *Growing Up* develops a theme at once peculiarly Japanese and universally intelligible; it describes the loss of innocence. The children of the story—the tomboyish Midori, the cheerful Shōta, the shy Shinnyo (Nobu), and the rest—are at the moment when they must surrender the privileges of childhood to accept their harsh destinies as adults. They will henceforth occupy the roles in life assigned them by society and their particular circumstances, not by their own choice. Their smooth faces will be marked by lines that time can only engrave deeper.

Midori, the day her hair is done up in an adult style, realizes she will soon become a prostitute like her sister. Shōta in the past had teasingly spoken of buying her favors when he grew up; but now, at the threshold of adulthood, he is about to become a moneylender, and no doubt he will in fact pay money to lie with his former playmate. Shinnyo, whose puritanical instincts make him turn against the worldliness of his father—a married priest with a taste for greasy eels—realizes that he and Midori must live in different worlds; the book concludes when Shinnyo, on the eve of his entering a seminary, leaves a paper daffodil at her door.

The pain of leaving childhood behind is so readily intelligible that it may not strike us at once how greatly Ichiyō's treatment differed from the typical stories of "growing up" in nineteenth-century European fiction. In Louisa May Alcott's *Little Women* (1868), for example, growing up is a promise, not a threat: the virtuous girl will be rewarded with a splendid husband. But there is no question of Midori's generosity or high spirits being rewarded with a husband of any kind; she can look forward only to passing customers. Not even the usual compensation for leaving childhood behind—first love—can compensate for the loss of freedom of sexless childhood. Certainly there are children in some Western novels who fear the world of adults—Peter Pan has become the epitome of the child who refuses to grow up. But Ichiyō, unlike Sir James Barrie, is totally unsentimental; her children are afraid not merely of losing their childish purity and beauty but of leading the lives of the adults surrounding them at Daionji-mae, just outside the Yoshiwara.

Growing Up is memorable also for its superb scenes. The best perhaps is the one in which Midori, seeing Shinnyo struggling to mend the broken thong of his *geta* with a piece of paper, throws him a scrap of silk, which he ignores, both children too proud to make the simple gesture of reconciliation needed for them to become friends again. The scrap of silk, brightly printed with a design of maple leaves, is left in the mud and rain.

Japanese scholars have painstakingly attempted to trace the sources of *Growing Up* in Ichiyō's diary, in the accounts of people who knew her when she ran her shop in Daionji-mae, and even in the works of the Kabuki stage, though nothing indicates she ever attended a performance. Such efforts may someday yield a few scraps of information about her literary techniques, but they are unlikely ever to answer the question of how Ichiyō came to create this single masterpiece.

Two other stories from her last period are still widely read, *Two Nights Before the Full Moon* and *Nigorie (Troubled Waters)*, both published in 1895. The former is in a vein familiar from other works, by Ichiyō and by other writers of the period: a girl who has married above her station is mistreated by her husband and returns to her family, hoping they will sympathize with her in her predicament, only to discover that her parents are unwilling to give up the advantages of having a rich son-in-law. They persuade the girl to return to her odious husband. She stops a passing rickshaw and soon discovers that the puller is a childhood friend, reduced by circumstances to menial labor. They part, each to his or her allotted unhappiness.

Troubled Waters, a more impressive work, has been ranked by some critics even above *Growing Up,* but their praise seems excessive. The central figure, the prostitute Oriki, is unable to forget a former customer, Genshichi, though his extravagance and neglect of his business have driven him and his family into grinding poverty. Oriki tells her story to another customer, who suggests that they marry, but she refuses, sure that this is not the fate awaiting anyone like herself. In the meantime life at home becomes intolerable for Genshichi, whose wife is insanely jealous. Finally—Ichiyō does not make it clear under what circumstances the act was committed—he kills Oriki and commits *seppuku* afterward.

If *"Growing Up"* recalls Saikaku, the model for *"Troubled Waters"* is Chikamatsu. The seamy side of the relationship between the prostitute and her customers, barely hinted at in *"Growing Up,"* becomes the focal point of interest, and Ichiyō treats her theme with compassion as well as realism. But the characters (as in some Chikamatsu plays) run to stereotypes, the plot is conventional, and the ending leaves the reader puzzled.

During the last months of Ichiyō's life, when she was too ill to write, a steady stream of visitors came to pay respects. In May 1896 Saitō Ryokuu, who would figure importantly in the disposition of Ichiyō's papers after her death, first visited her; Kōda Rohan came to ask for a manuscript; and Izumi Kyōka, another caller, was so impressed that he styled himself a disciple. Her illness, which first became noticeable in April of that year, grew steadily worse. In July she took to her sickbed, and four months later she died, at the height of her fame, not only the first woman writer of distinction for centuries but, thanks to *"Growing Up,"* the finest writer of her day.

Margaret Mitsutani (essay date 1985)

SOURCE: "Higuchi Ichiyo: A Literature of Her Own," in *Comparative Literature Studies,* Vol. 22, No. 1, Spring 1985, pp. 53-66.

[*In the following excerpt, Mitsutani examines Higuchi's place as a woman writer in Meiji period (1868-1912) literature and examines the evolution of her literary style.*]

At the close of his small book on one of the masterpieces of Heian literature, *The Pillow Book of Sei Shonagon,* Arthur Waley mentions Higuchi Ichiyō, drawing an analogy between her position in the literature of the Meiji era, and that of women writers such as Sei Shonagon and Murasaki Shikibu in the literature of Heian, approximately a thousand years before Ichiyō lived:

> While the energy of male writers was largely absorbed in acquiring a foreign culture, and their output was still too completely derivative to be of much significance, there arose a woman [Higuchi Ichiyō (1872-1896)] whose work, hitching straight on to the popular novelettes of the eighteenth century, has outlived the pseudo-European experimentations of her contemporaries.

In other words, at a time when convention required men to do most of their prose writing in Chinese, women such as Sei Shonagon and Murasaki Shikibu were producing, in the *kana* phonetic script, works that were later to be regarded as classics; by the same token Ichiyō, who was also a woman, was able to surpass her male contemporaries and create works now considered classics of Meiji literature by staying within the indigenous Japanese tradi-

tion. I am more concerned with Ichiyō's relation to her own time, and with what she wanted to say as a writer, both to her contemporaries and to us today, than with exploring her relationship to the past. Waley's analogy does, however, provide a starting point for a consideration of how the position of women writers changed during the thousand years that lie between the Heian and Meiji periods, and of Ichiyō's position in the Meiji literary scene.

The very fact that during the Heian period Chinese characters (*kan-ji*) were referred to as "men's letters" (*otoko-moji*), while the *kana* phonetic script was called "woman's hand" (*onna-de*), clearly indicates the extent to which the prose writing of the men and women of Heian was confined to separate spheres. While I have no intention of attempting to analyze the background of Heian court life that produced this situation, I would like to suggest that literary seclusion from the world of men provided Heian women writers with a certain freedom to develop a literature of their own, in their own space and time. Heian women writers had no need either to compete with or to imitate the writing of men, and in this sense, their writing in itself denies the charge made by John Stuart Mill in his essay "The Subjection of Women" (1869). Mill asserted that "If women lived in a different country from men, and had never read any of their writings, they would have a literature of their own;" this, unfortunately, not being the case, he concluded that they would always be imitators and never innovators.

The situation for Ichiyō and her contemporaries was, needless to say, vastly different. As Waley points out, many male writers were absorbed in imitating the modern novel, the most significant European literary genre to be imported into Meiji Japan. He did not, however, mention the fact that Meiji women writers began by imitating the men. *Yabu no Uguisu* (*A Songbird in the Grove,* 1888), the first novel to be produced by a woman in the Meiji era, was written by a twenty-year-old student named Tanabe Kahō (1868-1943).

Both Ichiyō and Kahō grew up reading the epic romances of the Edo period, such as Takizawa Bakin's *Hakkenden* (The Legend of Eight Dogs, 1814-41), and both received instruction in the classical literature of the Heian period, and in the composition of *waka,* one of the forms of classical Japanese poetry, at the private school of Nakajima Utako, one of the prominent women poets of the time. . . .

In a backhanded sort of way, fate seems to have favored Ichiyō the writer—she had neither the lack of dedication that put an end to Kahō's literary career, nor a husband to prohibit her from writing. Nevertheless, when she embarked on a career as a professional writer at the age of nineteen, Ichiyō was faced with an overwhelming obstacle—she was a young woman seeking entrance into a man's world. Her male mentor, Nakarai Tōsui, told her as much when they met for the first time. He tried to warn her of the many hardships she would encounter, and suggested that she look for some other kind of employment.

But Ichiyō was determined, and with good cause. She, her mother, and her sister were already engaged in what was virtually the only "other kind of employment" available to women at the time—taking in washing and sewing—and were having a hard time making ends meet.

At the height of her career, Ichiyō had long since left both Tōsui and Kahō behind. She had, in fact, succeeded in becoming that rarity of rarities—an artist who is recognized in her own time. When *Takekurabe* (*Growing Up*), her most widely read novel today, was published in complete form for the first time in the magazine *Bungeikurabu* (*The Literature Club*) in April, 1896, it was highly praised in a review written jointly by Mori Ogai, Kōda Rohan, and Saitō Ryoku-u, three of the most outstanding literary figures of the time. The review thrilled Ichiyō's young colleagues on the staff of *Bungakkai* (*The World of Literature*), the magazine in which *Growing Up* had previously been published in installment form. Aspiring young writers like themselves would be happy to die if they received such praise from Ogai, they told her.

The young men were almost delirious with you, but Ichiyō found herself unable to join in their rapture. She later reflected bitterly in her diary:

> Nine out of ten of the people who come to see me are delighted just to see a woman; they are drawn by the unusual. That's why even the merest scrap I produce sets them all aflutter, hailing me as today's Sei Shonagon or Murasaki, They're really just unthinking people with no depth; just seeing a woman is enough to keep them amused. And the vagueness of their reviews! There are faults in my writing, but they can't see them. Even the good points they don't bother to explain. It's all just "Ichiyo is wonderful. Ichiyo is great. Say nothing of women writers, even men should take their hats off to such skill." That's all, just "Ichiyo is wonderful, Ichiyo is great." Don't they have anything else to say? Surely they should be able to find some faults to point out. A strange state of affairs indeed.

The young men had given Ichiyō the nickname "cynic," and in this passage from her diary, she certainly seems to have earned it. Yet as Shigematsu Yasu has pointed out, the pessimism of this diary entry cannot wholly be discounted as the mere product of a cynical personality. To most of her readers, Ichiyō was, as a woman writer, little different from the popular female entertainers of the time. Even the intentions of such distinguished men of letters as Mori Ogai and Kōda Rohan are not completely above suspicion. Ogai, for example, sent his younger brother, Miki Takeji, along with Rohan to Ichiyō's house the summer before she died to request her participation in the writing of a "dramatic joint novel." The novel was to be written in letter or diary form, with each writer taking an assigned role, and Ichiyō was to be the "leading lady." While it might be argued that Ogai wanted Ichiyō to participate because he saw her as an equal, the jovial nature of the discussion of plans for the novel as recorded in Ichiyō's diary suggests that Miki Takeji and Kōda Rohan regarded the whole project as something of a sport, and were hoping that the presence of a female celebrity would

brighten it up a bit. Ichiyō did not enjoy the status of celebrity, for it made her the target of gossip and brought the antagonism of old friends. At the same time, however, it is probable that she sensed and resented the existence of a double standard in the criticism of men's and women's writing, and that this resentment was at least partially responsible for her cynicism.

She was, however, mistaken when she compared her fame to the ephemeral blossom of the morning glory (diary, May 2, 1896). Whether or not the double standard still exists is a moot point, but at any rate, Ichiyō's novels continue to be read and criticized, and she continues to be compared to Murasaki Shikibu and Sei Shonagon. Her best loved novel is still *Growing Up,* and her most criticized one, *Nigorie* (*Troubled Waters*). There is no doubt as to whether these two novels deserve the attention they have received. *Growing Up,* an elegiac portrayal of what growing up means to a group of children who live just outside the licensed quarter, in a world in which neither dreams nor freedom are permitted to exist, is a masterpiece. Oriki, the beautiful and complex heroine of *Troubled Waters,* who finally dies by the side of her lover, Genshichi, has with reason kept the critics puzzled since the novel was first published in 1895. Although it is these two works that have gained her an established place in the literary history of modern Japan, her last works show us that she had not said all she had to say when she died at the age of twenty-four.

Ichiyō's last completed story is about a beautiful but impoverished seamstress of mysterious origin named Okyō, and Kichizō, the defiant but lonely orphan who depends on her as his sole source of emotional support. Because of his small stature, Kichizō is often teased and has been nicknamed "Tom Thumb;" on the other hand quick to use his fists, he is also feared throughout the neighborhood as "a regular fire-ball." Teased or feared, Kichizō is totally isolated from those around him, and his isolation only strengthens his affection for the kindly Okyō, who is the only one willing to fully accept him. When Okyō decides to leave her life of poverty behind and become the mistress of a wealthy man, however, the two must part. The furious Kichizō rants and raves, but her mind is made up, and she refuses to listen. Her affection for him is nevertheless not dead and, pinioning his arms from behind, she tries one last time to make him realize it. Her effort is to no avail, however, and the story ends with Kichizō's words: "Okyō, please, take your hands off me."

"**Wakaremichi,**" the title of this story, has been translated both as "The Parting of the Ways," and "Separate Ways" As the story concerns the parting of two people, either translation is acceptable. However the fact that the original title contains the nuance of a fork in the road also suggests that the characters are not only parting from each other, but that each—Okyō in particular—is standing at a crossroads in life.

This is an element that is absent from all of Ichiyō's previous novels. Midori, the lively heroine of *Growing*

Up, is destined to follow in her older sister's footsteps and become a prostitute, and although she bemoans her fate at the close of the novel, she can do nothing to change it. In *Troubled Waters,* Oriki, the mainstay of the Kikuno-i, a low class brothel, dies with her lover, Genshichi, and although there is some contention as to whether or not she dies willingly, few would dispute that she was fated to do so. Oseki, the female protagonist of *Jusan'ya (On the Thirteenth Night),* is the daughter of a *shizoku* (samurai) family who have fallen on hard times. Her marriage to Harada Osamu, a wealthy politician, has brought financial help to her parents and employment for her brother; she is nevertheless unable to bear her husband's cruelty and, leaving her small son, comes back to her parents' home, determined never to return to him. Her father, however, convinces her that the family name is more important than her own personal happiness. They will all cry with her, he tells her, if she will cry as Harada's wife.

"Wakaremichi," her last completed story, marked a turning point for Ichiyō. Stylistically, the skillful use of dialogue replaced long, lyrical, descriptive passages peppered with allusions to Heian literature, producing a degree of restraint that she had never before achieved. More importantly, however, in Okyō, Ichiyō created a new kind of heroine. Unlike all of Ichiyō's previous heroines, Okyō is not overwhelmed by a force that comes from outside of herself. Albeit within an extremely limited range of possibilities, she herself makes the decision that will determine her fate.

For Ichiyō, writing was always a long and painful process, and for almost every story she completed, she left behind a series of fragments which show the development of the story from its conception to the finished product. An examination of the fragments which are thought to be direct predecessors of "Wakaremichi" reveals two types of women who were eventually to be united in the character of Okyō. One is a woman alone—an orphan who has been jilted by her lover. "You must be terribly lonely now," say the friends of Otae, the heroine of an untitled fragment, while the nameless heroine of another, entitled "Living Alone," weeps all day when her lover fails to appear. The other type is a young woman who, like Ichiyō herself, has a family to support. Okyō the hairdresser, the heroine of one fragment of which only a page or so remains, is a dutiful daughter who has always managed to keep her mother comfortably dressed. Ichiyō might have been indulging in wishful thinking when she added this detail, for she herself never managed to keep her own mother "comfortably dressed." Like Ichiyō herself, however, Okyō the hairdresser is the sole source of financial support for a fatherless family, and it therefore seems reasonable to assume that in this fragment Ichiyō was projecting her own situation, and her own responsibilities, onto a factitious character.

The most striking difference between Okyō the hairdresser and Okyō the seamstress is that Okyō the seamstress has been released from the burden of family responsibility which Ichiyō had previously projected onto Okyō the

hairdresser. Okyō the seamstress is, in fact, stripped of a past. Aside from the opening scene in which Kichizō reminds her that people say that she is of noble origin, the reader is not given the slightest hint as to how Okyō came to be living alone in a rundown tenement, supporting herself by taking in sewing. This is very unusual for Ichiyō, who sketched the origins of all her heroines preceding Okyō with painstaking care.

Okyō also differs from Otae in that, although alone, she is dependent on no one. As can be seen from the following passage, even when she *says* she is lonely, the force of her bright, outgoing personality is enough to eliminate any trace of the pathos we feel for a halpless creature like Otae, or the heroine of "Living Alone":

> Okyō, the seamstress, had moved into the tenement in the spring. Quick-witted and sensible, she got along well with everyone, and since the owner of the umbrella shop was her landlord, she was especially friendly to the boys who worked there.
>
> "Bring your mending to me," she told them, "there are so many of you, the owner's wife can't possibly have enough time to do it all herself. All I've got to do is sew all day, so it's really no trouble. I get lonely here all by myself, so come on over for a visit when you're free. I have no use for people who put on airs, so that rascal Kichizō suits me just fine. The next time you lose your temper, and think you want to pound the white dog over at the rice shop, come on over to my place—I'll give you the mallet and you can pound the fulling block instead. That way, no one will be angry at you, and it'll be a great help to me—we'll kill two birds with one stone."

Okyō is, in fact, the light to Kichizō's dark—the positive to his negative. Because of her extroverted personality, she has no need to cling to a single person, whereas Kichizō, who is totally alienated from his neighbors and fellow workers, expends most of his emotional energy in an endless search for one person who will be everything to him and him alone. When it appears that Okyō might actually be that person, he clings to her desperately, and when she decides to leave him, "comparing her to his own purity," he berates her for her dishonesty. There is an element of childlike purity in Kichizō's desire to cling to the dream that he and Okyō might live forever side by side, as brother and sister. At the same time, however, his possessiveness reveals the childish, narcissistic side of his nature.

As Kichizō's desire to keep Okyō by his side is a selfish one, so might Okyō's decision to leave behind Kichizō and her life of poverty be called selfish. Yet whereas Kichizō's selfishness is rooted in a childish wish to surround himself with a dream world which will protect him from the harsh reality of his isolation, Okyō's stems from a much more practical source—the will to survive.

"I'm tired of washing and mending," she tells Kichizō, "and I know things aren't going to get any better, so I'm ready to try anything—even life as a kept woman. I won't mind going through this world in a soiled kimono." In an essay on Ichiyoµ's work, a leading Meiji critic, after quoting these lines, wrote, "Is this not a voice of true desperation? . . . Is this not, indeed, the last voice to be raised by a woman of old Japan?" [Sōma Gyōfūn, *Waseda Bungaku,* January, 1910]. The situation of women in the Meiji era was indeed desperate. Many young girls like Midori were still being sold into prostitution by their parents, and the only avenue of escape from poverty for a woman like Okyō was to enter into a kind of modified prostitution. Behind the note of despair in Okyō's words, however, we hear the voice of a woman who has the strength to make her own decisions; to change, albeit in a small way, the course of her own fate.

Ichiyō ends the story with the following exchange between Okyō and Kichizō:

> "It's not a place where anyone would *want* to go, but my mind is made up, and I'm not going to change it now. Thanks for the advice, but I can't follow it." Kichizō had tears in his eyes. "Okyō, please take your hands off me."

As Okyō herself realizes, the decision she has made will not lead to a "happy" solution to the problem of poverty. Life as a kept woman will be, in many ways, as degrading as poverty itself. It is, nevertheless, the life that Okyō has chosen for herself, and she marches toward it with a graceful resignation that is perhaps the best expression of her personality. As an impoverished seamstress, her outgoing personality led her to turn her attention to those around her, rather than dwelling on her own problems; now that she has decided to leave that life behind, she turns toward the future and does not look back. Her decision has robbed Kichizō of his female mentor; he must reach the painful realization that Ichiyō herself reached near the end of her life—that all human beings are alone in this world, and that each must fend for himself.

In considering Okyō's place in the line of Ichiyō's heroines, it is important to note that her decision is entirely her own. Unlike Otama, the female protagonist of Mori Ogai's *Wild Geese* (1911-13), who is forced to become a kept woman in order to support her aging father, Okyō, who is stripped of a past, has no outside obligations. She is the first of Ichiyō's heroines to stand at a crossroads— to be offered, and take, a choice that can change her future. Before she died, Ichiyō was to attempt the depiction of another heroine who stands at a crossroads. In contrast to the world of poverty and prostitution that is usually associated with Ichiyō, Oritsu, the heroine of *Uramurasaki,* is a well-to-do wife whose material needs are more than satisfied, but who commits adultery in order to fulfill a purely emotional need. Although this story was left incomplete, its significance lies in the fact that it shows a final attempt on Ichiyō's part to leave the sphere in which the fate of her protagonists was determined by forces beyond their control, and enter a new stage, in which the protagonist has become aware of her own subjectivity, and must decide for herself what course she will take in life.

Oritsu tells her good-natured husband that she is going to see her sister, and sets out for the lodging house where her lover, a student named Yoshioka, lives. After leaving her house, however, she stops, and begins to consider the possible consequences of her adultery. Her husband is, after all, good to her, and her lover is still young—their relationship, if discovered, would ruin his future. At this point in the story, Oritsu is literally standing at a crossroads in life, and, "with an icy smile on her lips," chooses the road that leads to her lover.

The first chapter, which was all of *Uramurasaki* to be published in Ichiyō's lifetime, ends here. As Kawamura Sei-ichiro has pointed out, however, this fragment can be read as a complete work which depicts the psychology of a woman as she stops, wavers, then comes to a final decision. If this is so, then *Uramurasaki* has the added significance of showing that in her later works, Ichiyō's literary interest lay in the psychology of her characters, rather than "the story" itself. Be that as it may, it is clear that in these last two works, Ichiyō, no longer satisfied with telling the sad stories of women overwhelmed by fate, had begun to grapple with the problem of how a woman should live in the society of Meiji Japan. The problem was not an easy one (because of the nature of Meiji society, the possibilities were, as we have seen, extremely limited) and Ichiyō was not able to solve it in her own lifetime. The fact that just before her death she had begun to try, however, is in itself enough to warrant her being called the first modern woman writer of Japan.

As we have seen, Ichiyō's last heroines were women who are no longer left to be carried this way or that by the ill winds of fate. Having become aware of their own subjectivity, Okyō and Oritsu were each forced to make a decision that would determine the course of their lives. In these two heroines, we can see Ichiyō's final attempt to depict the awakening of a sense of self.

The impact that the idea of individualism, which first entered Japan by way of the English romantic poets and the American transcendentalists, had on Ichiyō's male contemporaries has been widely discussed. Through her association with Shimazaki Tōson (1872-1943) and other members of the staff of the magazine *Bungakkai,* who formed the nucleus of the romantic movement in Meiji literature, Ichiyō is thought to have had some vicarious exposure to Western literature. Yet it must be remembered that a complete lack of foreign languages barred Ichiyō from direct contact with foreign literature, and that, more importantly, having been trained (or rather self-taught) entirely in the Japanese classics, she had no means of developing a foundation upon which to accept foreign ideology. The awakening of the self that can be seen in her last heroines should therefore be seen not as the result of Western influence, but rather as something which grew out of her own experience.

The relationship between Ichiyō and her "mentor," Tōsui, has provided a focal point for much of the criticism on Ichiyō which has appeared to date. This first and last love affair was undoubtedly important for Ichiyō, not only because it formed the basis for her pessimistic view of love itself, but also because through it, she came to an awareness of feelings within herself that were not compatible with her "public" duties as heir to the Higuchi family. I believe that it was this conflict between personal emotion and public responsibility, which arose within Ichiyō when her love for Tōsui threatened to tarnish the family name, that made her aware, for the first time, of the existence of a self which was in direct opposition to the samurai morality that demanded sacrifice of the individual for the sake of the family.

In the end, Ichiyō rejected Tōsui and remained the dutiful daughter. The self which she was unable to express through her lifestyle, however, came to maturity along with her growing sense of herself as an artist. As an artist, she was able to attain the independence that was denied her on the level of everyday life. Thus, although the tender feelings she had for Tōsui never died, as an artist she thought nothing of passing judgement on his work, and her judgements were never favorable.

More importantly, however, is the fact that although she had embarked on a literary career as a means of supporting her family, she continued to write even after all hopes of achieving this initial goal were gone. Her mother, who had no understanding of the creative process, and who never lost sight of the initial monetary goal, chided her for her slowness, but writing for Ichiyō had long ceased to be a mere means of financial support. She neither could nor would "grind it out" as Tōsui did. Herein lies at least one reason why the *Bungakkai* group, some of whom were actually older than Ichiyō, tended to look upon her as an older sister. They were aspiring to be what she had already become—a mature artist with a literary world that was all her own.

Here I would like to call attention to the fact that the members of the *Bungakkai* group, when talking among themselves, often referred to Ichiyō as "Brontë." While this fact does not appear to be particularly significant in itself—the practice of "internationalizing" Japanese writers by comparing them to outstanding Western literary figures was, and still is, a popular one—some interesting parallels emerge when we consider the experience of Ichiyō and Brontë and her generation as women writers. There are, of course, great differences in genre and subject matter. The three-decker novel was an established form when the Brontë sisters began to write, and a comparison between *Jane Eyre* and a ten-page story like **"Wakaremichi"** would be meaningless. Nor would any Englishwoman of Brontë's generation have been able to deal as openly with the licensed quarter and the plight of the prostitutes who lived there as openly as Ichiyō did. Yet when she set out to become a writer, Ichiyō faced some of the same obstacles as women in Brontë's generation, and shared with them a similar seriousness about the task of writing itself.

The first of these obstacles was a lack of formal education. As Elaine Showalter has pointed out, nearly all of the Victorian women novelists were educated at home; in other words, they were self-taught, and in order to compensate for their lack of schooling, they struggled to master Latin and Greek. Although Ichiyō did receive an elementary education, her mother believed that too much time spent at school could only have a detrimental effect on a young girl. Her father was sympathetic to his daughter's eagerness to learn, but he was overruled, and Ichiyō's formal schooling came to an end when she was twelve. Like her Victorian counterparts, Ichiyō felt a need to compensate for her lack of education, and this she did through copious reading and frequent trips to the library, where she always found herself to be the only woman.

Although it has been convincingly argued that her immersion in the classics actually hobbled Ichiyō early in her career, just as the zeal of some Victorian women writers for Greek and Latin scholarship resulted in overly pedantic works, Ichiyō's diligence paid off in other ways. At the age of twenty-two, she was delivering lectures on *The Tale of Genji,* as well as tutoring male students—young men in the process of receiving the higher education of which she herself had been deprived—in the Japanese classics. In an essay entitled "Silly Novels by Lady Novelists" (1856), George Eliot expounded upon the need for diligence, responsibility, and "an appreciation of the sacredness of the writer's art." Had Ichiyō had the opportunity to read this essay, she certainly would have wholeheartedly agreed.

The second obstacle was the double standard in criticism of men's and women's writing. Ichiyō seems to have sensed this instinctively, and that is why she could not share in the innocent joy of the young *Bungakkai* group when they told her of the praise that Mori Ogai had bestowed on her novel ***Growing Up***. Unlike Charlotte Brontë, who was outspoken enough to write letters of protest to reviewers who discriminated against her because of sex, Ichiyō remained demure, keeping her protestations for the pages of her diary. The bitter cynicism she directed toward male critics who gushed with approval yet were unable to find anything to criticize in her work, and toward the public at large who regarded her as an entertainer rather than an artist, is nevertheless no less poignant than Brontë's openly expressed complaints.

Finally, as Showalter has pointed out, the Brontë sisters, George Eliot, and their generation of women writers were ". . . what sociologists call 'female role innovators;' they were breaking new ground and creating new possibilities?" [Elaine Showalter, *A Literature of their Own: British Women's Novelists from Brontë to Lessing,* 1977]. I believe that the same can be said of Ichiyō. There is, of course, an obvious difference here as well. The Victorian novelists were really "breaking new ground," and for them, writing created a need to transcend their feminine identity, as is evidenced by the appearance of the male pseudonym. Ichiyō, on the other hand, was backed by a long tradition of female literature, and was, in fact, hailed by critics as a new Murasaki or Sei Shōnagon. The novel was, nevertheless, a genre imported from the West, and Western learning was a realm reserved for the male elite. Only a few women were fortunate enough to get a taste of it at the mission and normal schools which were large-ly modeled on American schools for girls. It is significant that many women writers of Ichiyō's generation were grad-uates of these early girls' school; for some of them, like Tanabe Kahō, writing began as a process of imitation, and failed to mature into the status of a true vocation, whereas others, such as Wakamatsu Shizuko and Koganei Kimiko (1870-1956), the younger sister of Mori Ogai, became known for translations and adaptations, rather than for creative work.

As a mature artist, Ichiyō imitated no one. The writers from whom she learned the most were those of the Heian and Edo periods, and in this sense her writing does, to borrow Waley's phrase, "hitch straight on" to these indig-enous roots. Yet particularly in the portrayals of Okyō and Oritsu, in whom a sense of self has begun to emerge, there is a note of modernity that can still be heard today. Through her dedication to her art, Ichiyō succeeded in creating a literature of her own, thus paving the way for the generations of women writers who were to follow.

Yoshiko Enomoto (essay date 1987)

SOURCE: "Breaking Out of Despair: Higuchi Ichiyo and Charlotte Bronte," in *Comparative Literature Studies*, Vol. 24, No. 3, 1987, pp. 251-63.

[*In the following essay, Enomoto explores parallels as well as differences between the lives and works of Higu-chi Ichiyo and Charlotte Bronte, maintaining that both were motivated by a "sense of powerlessness and loneli-ness" as women writers.*]

This article will explore the striking similarities and dif-ferences between the lives and works of Higuchi Ichiyô and Charlotte Brontë, two leading women novelists of the nineteenth century. Ichiyô was often called "Brontë" by a contemporary Japanese critic, Hirata Tokuboku, and his friends in the *Bungakkai (Literary World)* group. The first and only work of Charlotte Brontë introduced to Japan during Ichiyô's lifetime was an abridged translation by Mizutani Futô of *Jane Eyre,* entitled *Risô Kajin (An Ideal Beauty,* 1896). While no evidence exists of Ichiyô's hav-ing read Brontë, Tokuboku noted one interesting affinity between the two. In an article entitled "Brontë and Kings-ley," he observed that Ichiyô and Brontë's character Jane Eyre both have "a strong sense of honor" and a "defiant passion." Moreover, he wrote, "In the depth of their hearts, the people of this kind have tender feelings and longings for love, but their cool, willfull and rational disposition resists it. This conflict creates terrible suffering" [Hirata Tokuboku, *Hirata Tokuboku Senshû (The Selected Works of Hirata Tokuboku)* Shimada Kinji, Takezawa Keiichirô, Ogawa Kazuo, eds., 1981]. Tokuboku was not only Ichiyô's contemporary but also her friend, so I believe that it is worthwhile pursuing the relation between these two writers. Here I would like to base my discussion on Ichiyô's **Nigorie** (Troubled Waters) and **"Wakaremichi"** (**"The Parting of the Ways"**) and Brontë's *Jane Eyre* and *Villete.*

Before examining their novels, however, I would like to consider some factors which may have contributed to the affinities between the writers. First, the two have numer-ous biographical similarities. Both were born into proud but impoverished families. Ichiyô's father was a govern-mental official who took pride in his past as a samurai; Brontë's father similarly took pride in being a clergyman of the Established Church of England. Both women had to support their families and tried to earn their living by writing. They also experienced unrequited love for their respective mentors, Nakarai Tôsui and Constantin Herg-er. Also notable are their physical similarities: delicate in health, both suffered from chronic insomnia and migraine, and both died rather young.

Another set of similarities is found in the social back-ground of their times. Ichiyô was born in 1872, eleven years after Brontë's death, at the age of thirty-eight. The societies of Meiji Japan (1868-1912) and Victorian En-gland (1837-1901) provided an oppressive environment for women, full of restrictions which confined them to their "proper sphere" and fixed roles. The twelve-year-old Ichiyô who was at the top of her class had to leave school because of her mother's firm belief: "Too much education spoils a young girl's future; she should learn sewing and help with the housework." In *Shirley,* Brontë has Reverend Helstone speak in a similar manner to his niece: "stick to the needle—learn shirt-making and gown-making, and piecrust-making, and you'll be a clever woman someday."

Ichiyô and Brontë both rebelled against this generally accepted trend, this ordinary, commonplace way of life. Early in their lives they became aware of their great po-tentials and fervently wished to fulfill them. Ichiyô con-fided in her diary: "Since I was about nine years old, I had loathed to live and die in obscurity. Day in day out, I wished to surpass others even by an inch."

Brontë had a similar aspiration. When she was nineteen years old, she wrote to Robert Southey, the Poet Lau-reate, with whom she had no previous acquaintance, and asked him to comment on her and her sister's poems. Southey admonished her not to have literary ambitions:

> Literature cannot be the business of a woman and it ought not to be. The more she is engaged in her proper duties, and the less leisure she will have for it, even as an accomplishment and recreation. To these duties you have not yet been called, and when you are you will be less eager for celebrity.

Bronte's disappointment is echoed in her first novel, *The Professor.* William Crimsworth, the protagonist, tells us that on the threshold of youth he was "lost in vague mental wandering, with many affections and few ob-jects, glowing aspirations and gloomy prospects, strong desires and slender hopes." Zoraïde Reuter, the head-mistress in *The Professor,* sums up the general reaction of Victorian society against intellectual ambitions in women:

It appears to me that ambition, literary ambition especially, is not a feeling to be cherished in the mind of a woman; would not Mlle. Henri be much safer and happier if taught to believe that in the quiet discharge of social duties consists her real vocation, than if stimulated to aspire after applause and publicity?

Despite such social pressures, however, family circumstances did not allow Ichiyô and Brontë to live like other ordinary women. They could not afford to wait for marriage in leisure, learning sewing and helping with the housework. Before opening a kitchenware and candy store in Ryûsenji, Ichiyô wrote in her diary that she had told Shibuya Saburô, her former fiancé, "when you come to see me next time, I don't know what I will be doing. I may be selling green beans or delivering newspapers." This remark reveals how little work was available for women at that time.

Similar misfortunes affected the life of Charlotte Brontë. She lost her mother early, and when her father's eye trouble worsened, she had to earn her living and take care of her younger brother and sisters. In Victorian England, job opportunities were similarly limited. The only openings were in "teaching, sewing, or washing," as Brontë's friend Mary Taylor complained. Brontë herself became a governess and her letters to her friends reveal how the poor employment conditions left her mentally and physically exhausted.

From these correspondences in the external circumstances of the two writers emerge some inner links that connect the two: they were constantly aware of their situation as women and felt overwhelmed by the sense of powerlessness and loneliness:

> Sitting at a writing desk with my cheeks on my hands and reflecting, I feel that if there is something I want to do, I don't know whether I should try to do it or not, because I am a woman. . . . As I cannot find anyone whom I can call my friend among the people whom I see day in day out, and as there is no one who really knows me, I feel as if I were born all alone in this world. I am a woman. If there is something I really want to do, I don't know if I should do it or not.

This passage from Ichiyô's diary expresses with deep pathos the grief and loneliness of being a woman, and in her diary the phrase "powerless woman" appears several times. Even after her novel received favorable review and her name came to be known, she remained pessimistic; she still felt that she was a woman:

> Nine out of ten of my visitors are delighted just to see a woman; they swarm to me to see the unusual. Therefore, even if I write a mere scrap, they hail me as today's Seishô Nagon or Lady Murasaki. They are really unthinking people without depth; they are amused to see me only because I am a woman.

Similarly, Brontë was keenly aware of the fact that she was a woman and felt profound concern for the position of women in society. In her novels, she made her heroines protest against the fixed, traditional sex roles. Jane Eyre cries out her aspirations as a human being: "Women are supposed to be very calm generally; but women feel just as men feel; they need exercise for their faculties, and a field for their efforts as much as their brothers do." In *Shirley*, Caroline wishes she were a boy: "I should like an occupation; and if I were a boy, it would not be so difficult to find one. I see such an easy, pleasant way of learning a business, and making my way in life." The view Brontë ultimately held, however, seems to have been pessimistic. In her letter referring to the "woman question," she reflected with resignation that there was no solution to the problem:

> One can see where the evil lies, but who can point out the remedy? When a woman has a little family to rear and educate and a household to conduct, her hands are full, her vocation is evident; when her destiny isolates her, I suppose she must do what she can, live as she can, complain as little, bear as much, work as well as possible.

She also suffered from loneliness as acutely as did Ichiyô. Brontë revealed the agony of her solitary life to her friend Ellen Nussey:

> I might indeed repeat over and over again that my life is a pale blank and often a very weary burden—and that the future sometimes appalls me. . . . The evils that now and then wring a groan from my heart—lie in position—not that I am a *single* woman and likely to remain a *single* woman—but because I am a *lonely* woman and likely to be *lonely*. But it cannot be helped, and therefore *imperatively must be borne*—and borne too with as few words about it as may be.

Both Ichiyô and Brontë are said to be subjective writers, and they do in fact often project themselves into the protagonists of their novels. Let us then consider how their sense of powerlessness and loneliness is reflected in their works.

Whether male or female, the protagonists of Brontë's novels are invariably orphans. William Crimsworth in *The Professor* has lost his parents early in youth. He works in his brother's office, but suffering from alienation and loneliness, he abandons his country and goes to Brussels to seek employment. Frances Henri, who is to be his wife, is also an impoverished orphan, and she teaches sewing and lace-mending in Mlle. Reuter's boarding school. At the beginning of *Jane Eyre*, the ten-year-old Jane is a poor, sensitive orphan, living in loneliness as a dependent of the Reed family. In *Shirley*, Caroline Helston has lost her father in childhood and scarcely remembers her mother's face. Her foil, Shirley Keeldar, is blessed with wealth, beauty, and privileges in everything, but she, too, is parentless. In *Villette*, Lucy Snowe appears as a fourteen-year-old orphan who is unable to express her feelings.

Ichiyô's works contain a number of short stories in which the leading characters are orphans. **"Kyôzukue"** (A Desk for Sutras), **"Akatsuki Zukuyo"** (Moonlight at Dawn), **"Yuki-no-hi"** (On a Snowy Day), **"Koto-no-ne"** (The Sound of the Koto), and **"Otsugomori"** (**"The Last Day of the Year"**). In **"Yuku Kumo"** (The Passing Clouds), Onui has lost her mother and endures the cruel treatment of her stepmother. Oriki in **Nigorie** becomes an orphan in childhood, while Kichizô in **"Wakaremichi"** is an abandoned child who does not even know the faces of his parents.

In *Villette,* thrown out alone in the world, Lucy Snowe likens the change in her circumstances to the change from "a bark slumbering through halcyon weather, in a harbour still as glass" to "the sole survivor of a shipwreck in the storm." In her diary, Ichiyô repeatedly compares her existence to "a boat drifting through the whirlpool of life." The orphaned protagonists of the two novelists have neither parents nor home, no anchor to support and sustain them. These characters are outsiders who keep drifting spiritually, straying from their homes, which are supposed to give them peace of mind and a sense of security.

The protagonists of their novels are not only orphaned but also placed in a suffocating situation with no exit. The best known example in Brontë's novels is Gateshead Hall, and especially "the red room," where young Jane is confined as a punishment and passes out in fright. William Crimsworth in *The Professor,* who works under his domineering and merciless brother, feels that he is "imprisoned" in his office. In *Shirley,* Caroline Helstone has no prospect of marriage and is not even allowed to go out into the world as a governess. For her, "the prison" may be her uncle's rectory, where she idles her time away: "What was I created for, I wonder: where is my place in the world?" Lucy Snowe in *Villette* likewise finds herself in confined situations, such as Miss Marchmont's hot, stifling rooms or the boarding school during the long vacations, where she is left alone with a deformed, mentally afflicted child.

In Ichiyô's **Nigorie,** the brothel where Oriki lives is another example of this kind of enclosed world, while many protagonists in other tales are similarly placed under confinement. Oran in **"Yamiyo"** ("A Dark Night") lives in a large, ruined house, cut off from the outer world, after her father's suicide and her fiancé's betrayal. Midori in *Takekurabe* (*Growing Up*) is an attractive girl brought up in the licensed quarters, Yoshiwara; she can never escape her destiny of becoming a prostitute. Oseki in *Jusan'ya* (*On the Thirteenth Night*) is fettered by the family system. She suffers from the cruel treatment of her husband, a wealthy politician. But she is doubly bound by her love of her child and concern for her parents and brother who receive material help from the politician. She cannot divorce him even though her married life is unbearable.

All of the men and women who live like "a plant growing in humid darkness out of the slimy walls of a well," excluded from "the sunshine of life", are in despair and loneliness, and they struggle to escape from it. Yet the protagonists of Ichiyô's and Brontë's novels reveal some differences in the ways in which they seek to escape. Here I would like to consider how each of the protagonists in **Nigorie,** **"Wakaremichi,"** *Jane Eyre,* and *Villette* acts when he or she is placed in a hopeless situation.

The brothel where Oriki in **Nigorie** lives is compared to *mugenjigoku,* the most tormenting of the Eight Hells. It looks gay, but it is really a living hell isolated from the outer world; whoever has fallen in there can never escape. The women of the amusement quarters appear to lead merry lives entertaining their customers, but in the depths of their hearts, all hide pain and sorrow. For example, a barmaid muses as she stands in front of a mirror with tears in her eyes:

> It is sad to be born as a woman. I cannot eke out a living by making match boxes, nor can I work as a kitchen maid, as I am not physically strong. This business is not pleasant either, but as it is not so trying for the body, I lead such a life. I am by no means frivolous, but my son will be sure to scorn me as a mother not worth mentioning. Today I am ashamed of my heavy coiffure which I don't mind at ordinary times.

Oriki, the most beautiful and strong-minded of the prostitutes, looks cheerful in appearance and betrays no weakness to others, but her nerves are just as sensitive as "a spider's thread which will break if one touches it." She works with the aid of a drink and has sad and dreadful things hidden in her heart. Her scholarly grandfather, who is well-versed in the Chinese classics, produced "a mere worthless scrap." When its publication was prohibited by the feudal government, however, he fasted to death in protest. Her father had a masterly skill as a metal worker, but too proud to be sociable, he died in extreme poverty.

Oriki, too, is painfully aware of the fatal discrepancy between what she is and what she ought to be. Her monologue after running out of the drinking bout in Chapter Five reveals the conflict within her mind. For Oriki, the place in which she lives, the amusement quarters, is a "dull, worthless, unpleasant, miserable, sad and hopeless" world which negates her pride and aspirations. She wants to escape from it, but on the other hand, she resigns herself to her fate: "Since I am in such a situation, doing such work, and having such a fate, I am not, to be sure, like other normal people no matter what I do, so it is no use troubling myself to think about normal things." She thinks that even if she longs to "rise in the world," she cannot fulfill her desire, and her resignation seems to be rooted in her fatalism. She believes that fate has governed her family for three generations. Both her grandfather and father died rejected by the world despite their high ideals, and she thinks that she, too, will have a similar fate: "Those who were born in a family such as mine can never become anybody. I can guess what will happen to me as well."

Since Oriki feels strongly that she is not placed where she should be and hates the world in which she lives, she wishes to escape. Her fatalism, however, represses her desire and drives her to crushing despair. Weary and irritated at the great gap between what she is and what she ought to be, Oriki faces the only means of escape left for her—madness or death. In **"Utsusemi" ("The Ephemeral Life")**, Ichiyô created a woman who tries to free herself from despair by way of madness. Yukiko, the female protagonist, distracted by a sense of guilt toward a man who fell in love with her and committed suicide, thinks "the inside of her house is a large field." Like her, Oriki feels as if "she were walking in a large, desolate, wintry field," when, in reality, she is walking on a brightly lit street which is alive with a row of stalls. A fear flashes through her mind—she may be going mad.

Oriki invokes death as well for her relief and deliverance. She ponders, "How can I go to an absolutely quiet place, where not a human voice, not a sound is heard—where everything including my mind is in a daze and I need not think of anything?" The quiet place where she longs to flee is the state of void, as desolate as "a large, wintry field." She can only go there by dying. In fact, she does escape from the amusement quarters through death, which is brought about byūgenshichi, one of her customers who was ruined by his love for her.

While *Nigorie* describes escape through death, **"Wakaremichi"** describes two people, one of whom escapes from confinement by other means, while the other remains in confinement. Ichiyô seems to project her two selves here: one into Kichizô, a boy who works in an umbrella shop; the other into Okyô, a beautiful but impoverished seamstress. Kichizô is a defiant but lonely orphan who is also physically handicapped: he is so short that he is nicknamed "Tom Thumb." The proprietress of the umbrella shop, Omatsu, saves him from the condition of a wandering street performer. When she dies, Kichizô continues to work at the shop. He does not like the present proprietor, but he has nowhere else to go. Kichizô is completely isolated from those around him because everyone teases him about his height, and he fights back with his fists. He can find no one to comfort him, and in the depths of his heart he thinks, "If there were someone who gave me a kind word, I would cling to him and never leave him." His sense of loneliness and alienation is so strong that he even thinks that he would rather "die now and be freed from care."

Okyô is the only person on whom Kichizô, craving for love, depends for emotional support. She holds him as dear as her own brother and encourages him to "rise in the world." But she herself finds the life of poverty in a tenement house unbearable. Finally, she decides to get out of this "barren, dull world" by becoming the mistress of a wealthy man. She declares to Kichizô, who entreats her to change her mind: "But I am tired of washing and mending! I no longer care about anything. I will even become a kept woman. Things are so dull anyway; I would rather go through the world in a soiled silk kimono." She has made a desperate decision to escape from her plight, but she knows that there is no future for a kept woman. In other words, her present life of poverty is hopeless, but the condition of a kept woman is just as hopeless, and degrading as well.

Like Oriki, Okyô, and Kichizô, the heroine of *Jane Eyre* is hopelessly confined in disagreeable circumstances at the beginning of the novel. The ten-year-old orphan, Jane, is an outsider in Gateshead Hall, despised by Mrs. Reed and her children as a dependent and rejected even by the servants because she is plain and unsociable. She is habitually tormented by "the mood of humiliation, self-doubt, forlorn depression." Her sense of alienation and despair is mirrored by the desolate wintry scenes outside Gateshead Hall and the illustrations of Bewick's *History of British Birds,* such as "the rock standing up alone in a sea of billow and spray," "the broken boat stranded on a desolate coast," and "the black, horned thing seated aloof on a rock, surveying a distant crowd surrounding a gallows."

Jane's sense of isolation and despair intensifies when she is literally imprisoned in "the red room" because she defended herself against bullying by her cousin, John Reed. The chilly, silent, dark room covered with crimson curtains and carpets is a spare bedroom which the family seldom uses. It is the room where Mr. Reed died, and so it is closely associated with death. Jane fears that she might be taken into the world of the dead. She then sees a strange light gleaming on the wall and is driven temporarily insane: "My heart beat thick, my head grew hot; a sound filled my ears, which I deemed the rushing of wings; something seemed near me; I was oppressed, suffocated: endurance broke down." She screams frantically and faints.

As critics have often noted, the fainting fit signifies temporary death in Brontë's novels, and those who have lost consciousness invariably awaken into a new state of being. Before she was locked up in "the red room," Jane was a timid and nervous child who tried to gain the favor of others, but while in the room, she examines the condition in which she is placed and asks herself why she is always unjustly accused and condemned. She finally decides to escape from "insupportable oppression" by some means, "by running away, or if that could not be effected, never eating or drinking more," and letting herself die. After awakening in "the red room," Jane is no longer a timid child, crushed by powerlessness. She no longer resignedly tolerates unfair treatment. She begins to assert herself; she fights off John's violence and tells Mrs. Reed what she thinks of her with sharp words. When Jane openly accuses her aunt, she feels that her "soul began to expand, to exult, with the strangest sense of freedom of triumph, I ever felt. it seemed as if an invisible bond had burst, and that I had struggled out into unhoped-for liberty." Shortly afterwards, in fact, she escapes from Gateshead and starts for Lowood, where new experiences await her.

The heroine of *Villette,* Lucy Snowe, undergoes a similar experience. In the small, closed world of Mme. Beck's boarding school, she tries to repress her feelings and lives with reason alone in the role of an efficient teacher. Sometimes, however, she feels not quite satisfied with her present life and longs for "something to fetch" her out of her present existence, and lead her "upwards and onwards."

When she is left alone in the deserted school with a physically and spiritually deformed child assigned to her care during a long vacation period, she faces a spiritual crisis.

Living with the unwanted child, Lucy feels as though she were "prisoned with some strange tameless animal." Deprived of the accustomed role of teacher in which she has buried herself, Lucy is forced to reflect upon her own life. Life seems to her "but a hopeless desert: tawny sands, with no green field, no palm-tree, no well in view," and she is often seized with "a despairing resignation to reach betimes the end of all things earthly." Like Oriki, she is attracted to death for deliverance and relief, and she succumbs to fatalism. She is convinced, "Fate was my permanent foe, never to be conciliated."

Even after her aunt takes away the deformed child, Lucy's sense of loneliness and despair increases, and she suffers from a strange fever, nightmares, and insomnia. At last it seems to her that the white beds in the long dormitory are "turning into spectres—the coronal of each became a death's head, huge and sunbleached." Unable to stand the strain any longer, she goes to a Catholic church, although she is a Protestant. She is comforted by just hearing the priest's voice and telling him how she feels. After leaving the church, Lucy loses her way and, battered by the rain and wind, swoons. But before losing consciousness, she becomes aware of the will to live within her: "My heart did not fail at all in this conflict; I only wished that I had wings and could ascend the gale, spread and repose my pinions on its strength, career in its course, sweep where it swept."

Here, as in *Jane Eyre,* the fainting fit signifies the end of the spiritual life which she has led up to that moment, and the experience makes her awaken into a new life. When she recovers her consciousness, she finds herself in the house of Mrs. Bretton, her godmother, who loved her in her childhood but who became estranged from her ten years ago. Lucy is to be under the care of the Brettons until she recovers from her illness, and the Brettons serve as the link between her peaceful childhood and her present hard life. The incident in the Catholic church and her subsequent fainting fit mark a turning point for Lucy. After these experiences, she realizes the importance of the feelings which she has repressed, and with the kind help of Mrs. Bretton and her son Graham, she finds "a new creed . . . a belief in happiness."

Thus, both Jane and Lucy are seized with a moment of madness or a regressive desire for death, and when they can no longer stand the strain of their circumstances, they even go through temporary death. Yet they are always brought to life from suffering and temporary death. When they awaken, they are already out of their spiritual crisis and are able to look at themselves and those around them in a new light, even though their circumstances have not much changed. The experience of suffering serves as a test of their inner worth, and the fainting fit prompts their psychological development.

In contrast to Jane and Lucy, Oriki and Okyô escape from the outer darkness where they actually live, but they are not freed from the inner darkness of their minds. As for Kichizô, he is left alone in despair and loneliness. Ichiyô feels constantly harried under the pressure of being the breadwinner of the Higuchi family, and she is obsessed with a sense of the powerlessness of being a woman. Suffering from tuberculosis, Ichiyô was also conscious of her approaching death. When she heard of the death of her cousin, Higuchi Kôsaku, she wrote in her diary, "A person near me came to a pitiable end. My own destiny, too, seems somehow doomed." The following passage from her diary reveals her ultimately pessimistic view of life: "It is enough for me if there is a good place to die in this weary world." Like the author, the protagonists of her novels cannot escape from their deep inner gloom.

Brontë, too, held a gloomy outlook on life. In *The Life of Charlotte Brontë,* Mrs. Gaskell writes that Brontë told her, "she believed some were appointed beforehand to sorrow and much disappointment. . . . and she was trying to school herself against ever anticipating any pleasure." Brontë, however, cherished strong longings for release and fulfillment; she wished to break out of her present sorrowful life and fly away to a wider world where she could lead a free, happy life. She wrote how she felt when she read a letter from Mary Taylor, an active feminist friend:

> I hardly knew what swelled to my throat as I read her letter—such a vehement impatience of restraint and steady work. Such a strong wish for wings—wings such as wealth can furnish—such an urgent thirst to see—to know—to learn—something internal seemed to expand boldly for a minute—I was tantalized with the consciousness of faculties unexercised. . . . These rebellious and absurd emotions were only momentary. I quelled them in five minutes.

Brontë had to suppress her "wish for wings" when she faced the bitter facts of her own life, but the protagonists of her novels escape from their predicament through the mysterious experience of death and spiritual rebirth. Brontë probably tried to realize her unfulfilled dreams and aspirations through her works.

Both Ichiyô and Brontë, then, were caught in the double bind of their gender and their social situation. Yet they struggled to realize their potential as human beings, despite the enormous limitations of their circumstances. In the enclosure-escape pattern of their novels, we can see their tenacious struggle against their plight.

FURTHER READING

Danly, Robert Lyons. *In the Shade of Spring Leaves: The Life and Writings of Higuchi Ichiyo, a Woman of Letters in Meiji Japan.* New Haven: Yale University Press, 1981, 335 p.

Critical biography focusing on Higuchi's short stories and diary. Danly maintains the importance of examining "the experiences and preoccupations out of which great literature grows. . . . If any writer gave her life the shape and meaning of a work of art it was Ichiyō—this was a central purpose of the diaries." The volume includes annotated translations of nine stories selected by Danly as representative.

Karl Lebrecht Immermann

1796-1840

German novelist, playwright, and poet.

INTRODUCTION

Best known as the author of *Münchhausen* (1839), Immermann is a transitional figure in his national literature, standing between the Romanticism of eighteenth- and early nineteenth-century German literature and the realistic novels of the later nineteenth century. Immermann wrote during a politically and culturally turbulent period in Germany, after the Napoleonic Wars. Many of his works are satirical attacks on what he saw as the dissolution of the traditional moral and spiritual values which he believed inhered in the monarchist system.

Biographical Information

Immermann was born in Magdeburg, into a family of Prussian civil servants. He enrolled at Halle University in 1813 to study law, but his education was almost immediately interrupted by the war with France. He entered military service that same year and fought at Waterloo in 1815, leaving the army a commissioned officer. Returning to Halle University, he became known for his public opposition to the nationalist student movements of the time. He wrote pamphlets against these groups and protested in person to the king—actions that alienated him from much of the German intellectual community, which was generally unsympathetic to the monarchy. After finishing his education, Immermann entered the Prussian civil service. He served as a judge in Magdeburg and then in Düsseldorf, where he died suddenly at the age of forty-four.

Major Works

Immermann wrote a number of plays that were indifferently received and have been assessed by Jeffrey Sammons as "of no more than antiquarian interest." He also wrote an epic in verse and was at work on his memoirs when he died. His best works are the novels *Münchhausen* and *Die Epigonen* (1836). The latter is his portrait of the disoriented character of his generation, overshadowed by the generation of Romantics that preceded them and fractured by the social and political dislocations that followed the Napoleonic Wars. The central character of *Die Epigonen* is a young man named Hermann who becomes entangled in a protracted struggle between a duke and an industrialist over the inheritance of an estate. In this work Immermann parodies aristocratic excesses, including an attempt to stage a medieval tournament. During the course of the often-convoluted plot Hermann becomes unwittingly involved with the nationalist student revolution.

Immermann continued his attack on the values of contemporary society in *Münchhausen.* Half the book is set in a castle, where Münchhausen mysteriously appears and begins narrating a series of incredible tales to an old baron and his daughter. The character of Münchhausen is generally considered a parody of the romantic artist—a fantastic visionary who cannot survive in the practical, modern world. The book is divided between this satirical portrait of an increasingly irrelevant aristocracy and a compassionate, detailed depiction of German agricultural society. Immermann moves back and forth between Münchhausen's accounts of his adventures and description of the life of the peasants around the castle.

Critical Reception

Münchhausen is so sharply divided between comic fantasy and social realism that some critics consider it two novels. Ferdinand Freiligrath has said the two halves are "rather connected by the thread of the bookbinder, than by a link springing from their nature." In fact, the village story was published separately as *Der Oberhof* (1863) after Immermann's death. Immermann's reputation has fluctuated since the nineteenth century. Critics who admire the ambitions of his satire have often been disappointed with his actual achievements, and many have noted his debt to Goethe, especially the influence of *Wilhelm Meister* on *Die Epigonen*. Immermann has been accused of a certain plodding seriousness, as if he were trying too hard, and Lee B. Jennings judges that "he lacks the saving grace of lightness as well as the unshakable certainty as to his own position." But most critics recognize the brilliance of individual passages in his works, and his novels are still widely read.

PRINCIPAL WORKS

Die Prinzen von Syrakus: Romantisches Lustspiel [first publication] (drama) 1821

Die Papierfenster des Eremiten (novel) 1822

König Periander und sein Haus (drama) 1823

Das Auge der Liebe (drama) 1824

Das Trauerspiel in Tyrol (drama) 1828; also published in revised form as *Andreas Hofer,* 1834

Der im Irrgarten der Metrik umhertaumelnde Kavalier (drama) 1829

Merlin [first publication] (drama) 1832

Tulifäntchen (drama) 1832

Karl Immermanns Schriften. 14 vols. (drama, novels, and poetry) 1835-1843

Die Epigonen: Familienmemoiren in neun Büchern (novel) 1836

Münchhausen: Eine Geschichte in arabesken (novel) 1839

Memorabilien (unfinished autobiography) 1843

Der Oberhof [*Der Oberhof: A Tale of Westphalian Life*] (novella) 1863

Werke. 5 vols. (drama, novels, and poetry)

CRITICISM

The Foreign Quarterly Review (essay date 1843)

SOURCE: "Immermann's New Münchhausen," in *The Foreign Quarterly Review,* Vol. XXXI, No. XLI, April, 1843, pp. 5-23.

[*In the following excerpt, the critic offers a general overview of* Münchhausen, *arguing that the novel can be divided into two parts: comedy and social realism.*]

The recent death of Immermann seems to have raised him to an importance in Germany which he did not enjoy during his lifetime; and if his productions were at one period less noticed than they deserved to be, they are now, if the little book at the head of this article is an index of national feeling, likely to be considerably over-rated. Under the superintendence of the poet Freiligrath, a number of enthusiastic admirers have contributed each his mite towards the immortalization of their favourite author; and scraps illustrative of Karl Immermann are collected with the care and earnestness which distinguish the collectors of materials towards the life of Göthe or of Schiller. One tells us what Immermann did at Weimar; Freiligrath himself furnishes a few letters which he received from the deceased; and two critical gentlemen, MM. Kinkel and Schucking, give us a couple of critiques on the **'Merlin,'** which, they inform us, is one of the most wonderful works that ever was penned; and hint pretty broadly, that although, from the time of its publication in 1832, it created no great sensation, it ought by rights to throw *Faust* into the shade. . . .

The most original genius cannot help straying into the paths in which some favourite author has already trodden; but in Immermann we can see that he laboriously essayed to follow. Even where we cannot detect a predecessor, we can perceive that nothing was done without toil; and in those places where the author affects to sport with the lightest recklessness, we feel that he is most seriously plodding.

Münchhausen, though from the variety of its contents it might be separated into fifty divisions, may readily be considered as containing two. One of these is a humoristic novel, of which Münchhausen, grandson of the great liar, is the hero, and which abounds in strange narratives, fantastical incidents, and literary satire: while the other exhibits the life of the peasants in Westphalia. These two parts of the tale are not formally separated, but, nevertheless, they are so distinct, not only in subject, but also in tone and treatment, that the work may almost be considered as two novels, united under one common title, and, as was said of a certain English history of German literature, rather connected by the thread of the bookbinder, than by a link springing from their nature. It is in the Münchhausen portion of the book that all the Shandyisms appear; and this portion, though it is enlivened with pictures and adventures of great humour, is certainly the weakest of the two, and often runs into mere dull absurdity. The Westphalian part, on the other hand, is only objectionable from its tediousness, since, on the whole, it is intrinsically good; and the author, if here, as in the other part, he is seen fagging hard, has at any rate solid material to work upon. Obvious labour does not appear so strange, when we find it employed in a sturdy portraiture of real life, as when we find it aping the tricks of spontaneous fancy.

The scene of the Münchhausen part is the old tumble-down castle of Schnick-Schnack-Schnurr, the property of an old baron, who hopes for the return of the times that existed before the French invasion, and his consequent elevation to the honourable post of privy councillor to a Prince, whose dominion, alas! has been destroyed by the latest partition of Germany. This wish is with him a sort of lunacy; and he has with him a daughter, an *old* young lady, who believes herself born for the same Prince, and who, likewise mad upon this point, expects from year's end to year's end the appearance of her noble lover. It is a melancholy place, the old castle:—the flag-stones that lead to it have been pulled up; the rails have been taken down to relieve the necessities of the family; a stone shepherd in the garden stands with hands and mouth formed for playing on the flute, but the flute is lost; a stone dolphin turns up its nose mournfully in a dry basin:—altogether it is a symbol of the dilapidated state, of the proud poverty of an old German baron, still adhering to the French fashion of the last century. The old baron cannot for ever amuse himself with hopes—what is he to do with himself?—as a last resource he takes to reading. A few dull books are in his library, but these will not satisfy him; so he belongs to a reading society, and becomes a student of journals.

> This amusement was quite to the old baron's taste. 'At last,' cried he, joyously, when he had made himself acquainted with the extent of the newly-discovered treasures,—'at last there is something in print, which instructs without fatiguing.' And indeed his mind was wonderfully enriched by the reading of journals. If one sheet gave him a short notice of the great poison-tree in India, which infects the atmosphere for a thousand paces round; the next told him how to keep potatoes from the frost during the winter. In one minute he read of Frederic the Great; in the next of the water-cure of Gräfenberg, at which, however, he did not stop long, as he went on at once to an account of the new discoveries in the moon. One quarter of an hour he was in Europe; then again, as if transported by the mantle of Faustus, under the palm-trees; sometimes he had a historical Redeemer, sometimes a mythical one, sometimes none at all. In the forenoon he attacked the ministers with the extreme *gauche;* in the afternoon he leaned towards absolutism; in the evening he did not know which way to turn; and at night he went to bed, as a *juste-milieu,* to dream of the juggler Janchen, of Amsterdam.

But even these varied enjoyments wear out after a while, and it is a real delight to the old baron, when a neighbouring school-master, who has become insane, and who has in consequence lost his school, comes to the castle, and boldly asks the owner to receive him as an inhabitant. The origin of the pedagogue's madness will be particularly diverting to those who are familiar with the aspect of a German philosophical grammar. . . .

The endeavour to learn has turned the poor schoolmaster's brain. He sighs for a land where learning was unknown, and where the subtleties of modern grammar never entered; he sighs for ancient Sparta; and converting his name 'Agesel' into 'Agesilaus,' he fancies himself a descendant of the Lacedœmonian king. The goodnatured Baron Schnurr, partly out of compassion, and partly to have a companion besides his wearisome sentimental daughter, allows the pedagogue to live in a little summer-house in the garden. There he dwells in an imaginary Sparta: wearing no garment but a cloak; calling the hillock upon which the summer-house stands Mount Tayge-tus, and a streamlet in the vicinity, the river Eurotas; and appeasing his appetite with a home-made imitation of the antique black broth. The monotony of the castle is for a

while interrupted. The baron can discuss with the school-master whether Brutus was right in killing Cæsar, and what would have happened if Frederick the Great and Napoleon had been contemporaries. But the subjects are soon exhausted, the three inhabitants of the castle become as weary as the two were before the arrival of the third, and the demon of *ennui* reigns once more in Schnick-Schnack-Schnurr. A new visiter is required to break the spell, and this visiter is the Baron Münchhausen.

This descendant of the great professor of marvels has so far a family likeness to his grandfather, that he indulges in the narration of improbable incidents; but he differs from him, inasmuch as almost all his legends have a definite purpose, and satirize some feature of the day. The state of the German stage, the vagaries of Pückler Muskau, the dreams of Justin Kerner at Weinsberg, the modern philosophy of Germany, the rage for projects and shares: all these, and more than these, receive severe sarcasm through the medium of Münchhausen. He is supposed to have an effect on his hearers almost magical. He entraps them into listening to one story, then runs that into another—and another—and another,—so that their brains are completely bewildered, and they follow him like an *ignis fatuus.* Some of the narratives are excellent, and some remarkable for their poverty; while of some perhaps it would scarcely be fair for a foreigner to judge, for a want of familiarity with the more trivial objects of the satire. The most amusing of them is his own life, in which it is impossible not to perceive that he has in a great measure followed Swift.

According to his own account of himself, his father and mother had a violent quarrel in his infancy, which ended in the former leaving his home, and setting off for Thessaly with the baby Münchhausen in his coat-pocket. The child is miserably uncomfortable in his position; he is annoyed at the presence of certain eatables, which the same pocket contains; he sighs for fresh air; and above all, he is annoyed at a habit in which his father is wont to indulge, namely, that of jumping about when he is in an ecstasy of delight, which has the effect of bumping the young gentleman against the calves of the paternal legs. He creeps out, and a vulture carries him off. An Englishman shoots the vulture, but leaves the child to starve, observing, in answer to a request to take him with him: "You would deprive me of my comfort." Dressed in the uniform of a Janizary, with a little turban, and a little tin sword, for such was the fancy of his father, who had expectations from the Turks, he finds himself alone in a desert place. He tastes of a spring—when lo! it is the Hippocrene—the eminence on which he stands being Mount Helicon. Instantly he is seized with a fit of poetic inspiration; he flings off his clothes, that he may rejoice in classic nakedness; and he ejaculates fragments of verses in all sorts of metres, these ebullitions being doubtless intended to satirize Count Platen, well known for the enthusiasm with which he regarded the *forms* of poetry, and his successful treatment of a variety of measures. Some benevolent goats of Mount Helicon find him exhausted, taking him for some miserable creature which has lost its skin, and by these he is adopted. Now we are introduced to the manners and customs of the goats, who are made rational creatures, and whose language the child understands. By their general wisdom and benevolence they remind us of the Houyhnhmns, and by their occasional weaknesses of the Laputans. The females have a project for relieving sick vermin, and the males for extending intellectual culture to inferior creatures, both of which projects turn out manifest failures. Gradually Münchhausen becomes more and more of a goat, having at last contracted the habit of ruminating; and he would lose his humanity altogether, did not an old Dutch traveller find him, and take him home as a curiosity. The Batavian had journeyed to Greece for the sake of his health, and Mount Helicon was the term of his pilgrimage. . . .

A capital fellow this Mynheer van Streef—this comfortable Dutchman, with his love of flat country, and navigable canals! He is one of the best specimens of Immermann's book, and we shall not yet let him go, but follow him home to the seat of his enjoyments: first recording that he has a temporary inspiration, from making his tea with the waters of the Hippocrene. To Holland he goes, taking with him his man-goat—for Münchhausen is already covered with hair, and more than half a beast—and thus he spends his peaceful days. . . .

There is a fine satire in the Dutchman, who is little more than a vegetable, compassionating the "senseless animals." The whole portrait is a masterpiece, the author having cleverly assumed a sort of monotony of style which admirably harmonizes with the monotony of life he is describing. We leave Mynheer with regret. His two neighbours each harbour a design against his curious beast, one wishing to steal and stuff it, and the other to have its likeness clandestinely taken by a painter on porcelain. Indignation at the notion of being stuffed rouses Münchhausen once more to manhood, and the hair of the goat falls from him. The porcelain painter turns out to be his father, and a happy meeting takes place.

This narrative, as we have said, is one of the most amusing in the book, but it is by no means amusing to the old baron, who is compelled to hear it. It is the destiny of the inhabitants of Schnick-Schnack-Schnurr to sink back into weariness, whatever temporary excitement they have felt, and Münchhausen himself, who when he at first introduced himself to them was hailed with delight, is at last voted a "bore." His entangled narratives, once drunk in with such eagerness by the old baron, who is particularly captivated by his knowledge respecting the *infusoria,* produce less and less effect; and in time his listener begins impatiently to cry out, "That's nothing!" after the most astounding marvels. Driven to the last resource, Münchhausen at last breaks out with a magnificent project of a society for petrifying air, and thus making an article for building purposes. The baron's interest is once more awakened for his eccentric guest, but the latter finds the eagerness after this project a little inconvenient, and therefore whenever the subject is started, he shirks it by forcing upon his questioner some long narrative. One of these is the imaginary history of his childhood, and another is

a description of Justin Kerner, and his residence among the spirits at Weinsberg, the chief humour of this consisting in the celebrated supernaturalist turning out to be an old woman in man's clothes.

The old baron's patience is again exhausted. He vows that if his guest does not immediately bring the air-scheme into operation he shall quit his house. But the provoking adventurer has a new expedient. He goes to bed and slumbers from day to day, merely waking to ask for his dinner to be sent in, and finally, when his unwary host is walking in the garden, he locks up the castle, and thus keeps out the lawful inhabitants. At this period all his admirers, who have met him in various parts, flock to the castle, and it seems that to nearly all of them he has appeared in a different character. While he is known to the old baron as Münchhausen, Semilasso (Pückler Muskau), who appears as a *dilettante* traveller in an oriental costume, contends that he is Dr. Reifenschläger, whom he has met among the pyramids, and who has a project for improving mankind by cross-breeding; a pedler swears that he is Captain Gooseberry, the head of an emigration scheme; and three brothers, a philosopher, statesman, and poet, who are called the three "discontented ones," declare that he is no other than Hegel himself. The declaration of the philosopher is so excellent of its kind as a sarcasm on the Hegelian tone, that we cannot resist giving it: though few, we fear, will appreciate it:

> I say this is the greatest man of the time, yet properly no man, but the pure *Begriff* (conception) of man, or the manly *Begriff*—perhaps even this expression is too concrete; to speak more abstractly, we must call him the *Begriff—griff—riff—iff—ff.* Oh would I could express myself abstractly enough! The pure *Begriff—riff—iff—ff,* which only apparently died of the cholera on the 14th November, 1831, was apparently buried in the churchyard before the gate; where in his coffin, instead of himself lies the nothing, which again is the something, continuing in fact to live, taking snuff, and playing whist; therefore not only concerned with the subjective feeling, opinion, and fancy, but real, and consequently rational; in one word, the great, immortal, eternal Hegel, who is the paraclete; that is to say, the spirit; promised in the fulness of time, with which begins the millennium, when the Hegelianer shall reign.

The latter part of this speech is evidently aimed at the bold declaration, ascribed to an enthusiastic Hegelianer, that Hegel was the third person in the Trinity. The truth of the anecdote is, however, very questionable.

To heighten the confusion occasioned by so many claimants of Münchhausen, Immermann himself, *in propriâ personâ,* joins the crowd; and indeed it is to his personal strength that all are indebted for their entrance into the castle, for he bursts the door open. Between the author and his hero, a curious Frankenstein dialogue ensues: the former telling the latter, that he is a mere creation of his own brain, and the latter claiming an independent existence. By this the perplexity of the tale is wound up to its highest pitch: the bounds which divide the actual from the fictitious being broken down, with a recklessness which reminds us of the comic dramas of Ludwig Tieck. But the old course of extravagance is not changed by this new event. The servant of Münchhausen, with whom the baron's daughter has fallen in love, madly taking him for her early flame, reveals the secret, that his master was never born in the regular way, but was artificially composed by his reputed father, out of certain chemical elements: while Münchhausen, to defend his claims to humanity against this new attack, daringly asserts that the chemical story is false, and that he is his own grandfather, the Old Liar, who is preserved and metamorphosed to meet the progress of the age. Shortly after this scene of confusion, Münchhausen disappears altogether; and whether he is a lying charlatan, or a supernatural being, or a phantasy existing in the brain of Immermann, is never cleared up. The best hypothesis concerning him is that uttered by a young count . . .

> In this bragger has heaven wished to enclose all the winds of the age, jest without mind, cold irony, heartless phantasy, rambling understanding; that when the rascal dies they may be kept quiet for a season. This ingenious satirist, liar, humoristically complicated buffoon, is the spirit of the time in personâ: not that spirit of time, or rather eternity, which carries on its secret work deep below in the silent hollows, but the motley buffoon whom that artful old spirit sends up among the witless multitude, that they, lured by carnival jests and sycophant declamations from him and his unfathomable labour, may not disturb the birth of the future, by their foolhardy peeping and meddling.

In other words, the author's notion of modern Germany is personified in this one picture of Münchhausen; who combines within himself the frenzy for travelling, the philosophy of Berlin, the tricks of the lyric poets, the rage for civilization, and above all, the frivolity of the 'Young Germany' school, with the witty irony which it acquired from the other side of the Rhine. Hence to understand his subtleties, his vagaries, and his ramblings, a considerable degree of familiarity with the most modern German literature is required; and those who have not made a point of watching the progress of that literature, will read most of his strange narrations with little interest.

Far different is it with the other portion of the tale, which exhibits the life of the Westphalian peasants, and which must charm all, initiate or uninitiate, as a vigorously chosen picture of a humanity, carefully finished by an artist who is glowing with a love of his subject. It is true that Immermann unfolds the low cunning and the narrow prejudices of the peasant life—it is true that he declares it is as much fettered by conventions as that of the most rigid aristocracy, and that freedom is to be found alone in the middle classes—but still it is easy to perceive that the author gladly flies from a state of ultra-civilization, from the region of pedantry and frivolity, to the society of the hardy tillers of the soil; and that with his love for masculine firmness, he even admires the pertinacity with which they cleave to their follies. The same spirit which drives Freiligrath from modern life into African deserts, and makes him sing so many a graphic song, drives Immermann to the fields of Westphalia, and makes him achieve a representation of a peculiar state of society, which would

be absolutely perfect, were it not blemished by the author's unconquerable vice—tediousness. These peasants are in the eye of Immermann the Germans *par excellence;* not the Germans of an age or a period, but the eternal Germans'; the Germans of Tacitus; the Germans of Charlemagne; still living under a patriarchal government, and still preserving that once formidable institution, the Vehmgericht, or secret tribunal. Whether there actually exist any vestiges of this tribunal among the Westphalian peasants, or whether it is but a fiction of Immermann's, we are not in a position to decide; but if it is an invention, it is one of a high artist, admirably adapted to enforce that impression of durability, which it is his purpose to convey. . . .

The principal figure in this portion of *Münchhausen* is the owner of the head farm of a Bauerschaft, who bears the title of Hofschulze, which, for want of a better word, may be translated 'Justice of the farm.' . . .

We close *Münchhausen* with a mixed feeling. It was certainly a toil to get through it; we often lamented the pertinacity with which the author wore threadbare the subjects he took in hand; we often grumbled as we proceeded: but still in the better portions there is such vigour of colouring, such a strong reality given to the characters, that we part from them like familiar friends, and quit old Westphalia as if it were a place in which we had spent a holiday, pleasant on the whole, though a few rainy days may have rendered it tedious. Before we quite leave Immermann, let us take a glance at the very spirited portrait which forms the frontispiece to the book edited by Freiligrath.

The face would never strike the spectator as that of a poet. There is to be sure a fine expansive forehead, but the expression of the features is rather that of hardened sense than of genius; the compressed lips exhibit sturdy resolution, with a slight touch of irony. And is not this the characteristic of the writings of Immermann? He seems to us as one in whom the fountain of genius did not spontaneously spring forth; but who, having chosen the sphere of poetry as his world, sturdily resolved to work his way through it. Magnificent as his crude notions might be, the high ideal seems to have been above his reach; but where, as in the best parts of his Münchhausen, he had a firm reality to grasp, he seized it with muscular strength, and the result was such a picture as—the Peasant Life of Westphalia.

Lee B. Jennings (essay date 1963)

SOURCE: "Immermann's Münchhausen and the Post-Romantic Predicament," in *Kentucky Foreign Language Quarterly,* Vol. X, No. 3, 1963, pp. 145-48.

[*In the following essay, Jennings qualifies the common critical conception that Immermann intended to parody German Romanticism in* Münchhausen.]

A common interpretation of Immermann's quixotic and mercurial protagonist Münchhausen (a distant relative, as he claims, of the old liar-baron) is that he is intended as a parody of the romantic artist, the subjective visionary and dreamer who can no longer persist in a prosaic age.

As is the case with most claims to an "overcoming" of romanticism, this interpretation represents a half-truth. The most obvious counter-argument is that Münchhausen's tales are not so much parodies or exaggerations of the romantic technique as they are travesties of the inane journalistic factualities that seemed to be taking the place of idealistic and imaginative literature. His "lies" are truths deprived of their essence, facts with no real meaning behind them, prosaic phantasms quite in keeping with the spirit of the modern age.

To be sure, some element of romanticism is also implied in Münchhausen's flair for creativity, his inspired proclivity for spinning yarns, his delight in play, and his very insubstantiality and occasional vagueness of identity. However, to say that this "romantic" aspect of Münchhausen is repudiated, or even disapproved of with any thoroughness, would be an exaggeration. The author's deep personal involvement in Münchhausen's tales is attested by the Rabelaisian relish with which they are presented. The arbitrary manipulation of language takes on a truly baroque flavor. We hear of the Apapurincasiquinitschchiquisaqua Indians (who weave huge straw bottles as receptacles for their own mortal remains); the various branches of the aristocratic Schnuck family, such as "Schnuck-Puckelig-Schimmel-sumpf, genannt aus der Rumpelkammer," or "Schnuck-Puckelig-Erbsen-scheucher in der Boccage zum Warzentrost"; enterprising industrial projects such as "Hühneraugenessenzbereitungsversuche"; and, if the spirit medium who provides it is to be trusted, there is even a specimen of the original language of mankind: "Rummeldebummeldefimmeldepippeldehusseldebusseldekimmeldelümmeldeschwips."

The joys of satire, of playing the creator and sending the light of one's wit into all the dark nooks and crannies of the age, are extolled by Münchhausen, and we cannot help feeling that the author shares his exuberance. To be sure, there are voices of discontent with regard to this point of view within the work. The so-called "wild hunter" Oswald is vehement and contemptuous in dismissing Münchhausen's tales as a smirking, niggling glorification of the rubbish heap whose very mention credits them with too much importance. These "grotesque" inventions, he says, do not spring from a constructive desire for betterment or from the zeal of the reformer—they are the misshapen products of a soul whose very fabric of existence is the perverse. Even Münchhausen compares himself to a Don Juan who goes about fathering monstrosities. Oswald, on the other hand, claims to cling to "the positive," to inspiration and love as the "only worthy nourishment of noble souls."

It is important to understand, however, that both Münchhausen and his denouncer Oswald are projections of Immermann himself. He, too, in his correspondence, claims to be of a highly "positive" nature and attempts to eschew the "cold mockery" formerly evident in his character. At times he avows a conventional religious belief that he hopes will lay the ghost of his former sensuality—a dangerous tendency, since, like all pronounced joy in life, this sensuality carried with it a terrible awareness of nothingness. At other times he favors the more sophisticated view that heaven must be realized on earth, the infinite grasped in the fleeting moment. A very curious feature of these attempts to gain peace of mind is that the imagination is anxiously excluded from the contemplation of ultimate things. Immermann even goes so far as to assert that everything deep and genuine in human nature takes place without fantasy—a strangely unpoetic view.

There is, to be sure, some reason for Immermann to repudiate the pronounced exercise of fancy and the literary movement which favored it. As a student he underwent a crisis as the result of reading works of Fouqué, Arnim, and Brentano and brooding about them; he says that he was afraid of ghosts in broad daylight and envisioned a hodge-podge of rampant witches, devils, and specters reminiscent of a picture by Callot.

The ostensibly satirical novel *Münchhausen* is in part a "last fling" of highly imaginative, hence (perhaps) "romantic" art; at the same time it is a purgation, through expression, of that fancy held to be unhealthy. It is well known that the "Oberhof" sequences represent Immermann's attempts to find a lasting basis for human strivings, a valid framework of existence, in the wholesome and relatively uncorrupted life of the peasant. As a locale in the novel, the "Oberhof" world of the village alternates with the moribund, chaotic, and shadowy realm of castle Schnick-Schnack-Schnurr and its addled occupants. Taken together, the two realms might seem to form a stratified picture of the world, a worth-while, ordered realm being placed above a chaotic realm of disorientation. Actually, however, there is too little connection between the two spheres for this to be the case, and we do not get the impression that they are different levels of the same reality, but rather that they are wholly autonomous domains. Satirical purposes complicate the picture; Schnick-Schnack-Schnurr not only represents a vicious caricature of the decaying aristocracy, but also provides a fitting atmosphere of decay and futility for the bloodless virtuosity of Münchhausen. Furthermore, Immermann's espousal of order is always hindered by his conviction that chaos in an inherent and prominent part of any sort of vital existence.

It is fairly clear in any case that the air of decay surrounding both Münchhausen and his sphere of operation goes beyond the demands of satire. Aside from the phenomena of decay observed in the aristocratic figures, we might consider, for example, Münchhausen's peculiarity of turning green instead of blushing; his alleged transformation into a goatlike creature when among the goats on Mt. Helicon, and his resultant fear of being stuffed and thus taking on a chemical mock-immortality; and finally, his mysterious disappearance in the crypt of a church amidst remarks on the nothingness whence we come and whither we shall return. Some of these phenomena are cleverly allied with satirical targets as widely varying as Prince

Pückler-Muskau, Platen, and watered-down neo-Hellenism, but in all of them we can also glimpse that sense of the futility of everything which Immermann sometimes confesses harboring in spite of all "positive" tendencies and which obviously underlies his reluctance to allow his fancy free rein. In creating the figure of Münchhausen he purges himself of this preoccupation with decay while indulging in the most outrageous flights of fancy. Münchhausen is the cold, Mephistophelean side of Immermann's being. Seen in this light, the confrontation of author and character within the novel takes on subtleties of meaning above and beyond the "romantic irony" usually mentioned in connection with it.

The fact that the display of fantasy resulting from this self-expression and purgation can take place only in a coldly intellectual manner, divorced from any real sense of purpose, probably represents a personal problem of the author. As so often happens, however, it is also a problem of the age. As the character Oswald puts it, the modern wanderer has only two paths before him, one leading to the insane asylum and the other to the insipid life of the Philistine. The free play of the imagination has been discredited since—and to some extent because of—the extremes of romanticism. The danger of complete disorientation, of rousing the sleeping lion of the demonic, has become evident, but so have the more subtle pitfall of triviality, the senseless jumble, and the private joke.

The vanishing of Münchhausen has been regarded as symbolic of the fading of romanticism before a new age, as no doubt it is in part. Romanticism has become nihilism, since there has been a drastic diminution of the faith in a higher scheme of things which it presupposed in perturbing the affairs and institutions of this world. This is not to say, however, that Immermann enthusiastically embraces the new age. It has its own nihilism, namely the obliteration of real meaning in all spheres of life by the glorification of superficial and prosaic things.

Immermann walks a tightrope between two nihilisms, and his rather frantic search for "roots" and for a wholesome mode of life must be understood in this light. His attitude toward Münchhausen, a figure representing the nihilism of both ages and the nihilism within himself, understandably falls short of adoration, but neither is it altogether one of repudiation. The empty intellectual pyrotechnics of this personage represent a deeply ingrained part of the author objectified in drastic caricature, and Immermann's search for stable values can be regarded as the desperate measure of a man for whom a beguiling nothingness beckons in the form of an alter ego.

As often proves to be the case in this perplexing period, we can not speak of a simple overcoming of romanticism. The phenomenon Münchhausen is a "last fling" of subjective spirit, but a deeply satisfying as well as an abhorrent one, the harbinger of sinister, nihilistic romanticisms more proper to a materialistic age. We know from the works of other authors that Fate, as the threat of hostile demons, is, in the post-romantic era, in the process of being converted into the idea of one's random determina-

tion by material, historical, and psychological forces, a state of affairs actually constituting no fate at all and worthy of representation by its own demons. The threat of Hell has become the threat of nothingness; yet the symbols used to portray the two spheres may remain the same. The figure of Münchhausen is likewise a transitional symbol; in him the bugbears of overactive fancy and demonic attack are shown being replaced by those of futility and nothingness. He embodies not only the private conflict of an author, but also the central problem of an age.

Lee B. Jennings (essay date 1964)

SOURCE: "The Dance of Life and Death in Heine and Immermann," in *German Life & Letters,* Vol. 18, 1964-1965, pp. 130-35.

[*In the following essay, Jennings provides a detailed comparison of parallel scenes in Immermann's* Die Epigonen *and Heine's* Florentinische Nächte.]

As a poet, Heine is deeply concerned with a theme both profound and simple: the struggle of beauty with the forces of death and decay. As a satirical journalist he was concerned with a number of more contemporary matters which have received a good deal of critical attention and will not be discussed here. The threatened effacement of beauty, however, obviously underlies even such a seemingly innocuous poem as the familiar 'Du bist wie eine Blume', and it is probably one of the few things about which Heine is sincere beyond all question. It is also a point with respect to which both his affinity for and his departure from Romanticism can be made plain. Heine is Romantic in his aestheticism, his glorification of an almost unearthly beauty, but highly unromantic in that this beauty is firmly anchored in this world and will be destroyed rather than liberated by the casting off of earthly shackles. At times there is, to be sure, an alliance of beauty with death to produce a weird dream world of lotus blossoms and nightingales; but there is not, as with Novalis, the feeling that this is a better or more complete world lying beyond the familiar world of the senses or coming after our sojourn upon Earth. He yields to death as to a dream from which there is no awakening, perhaps even pleasant, at least in its preliminary stage, as a realm in which time is suspended and the senses seem to achieve a satiety impossible during fully conscious life. This lotus and morphine world, however, is recognized as an inferior grade of reality, not a superior one, a realm of illusion and impermanence. As regards personal immortality, there is nothing to indicate that the grave misgivings he expresses in the poem 'Der Abgekühlte' do not represent his well-considered and final view on the subject: 'Ja, ich bin bang, das Auferstehen/ Wird nicht so schnell von Statten gehen.' It is to Heine's credit that he never accepts a comforting solution nor seeks to make of life more than it is. Even his professed return to the belief in a personal God (in the epilogue to the *Romanzero*) in no way detracts from his basic conviction that a life apart from physicality and sense experience, and one not subject to death, cannot be conceived. The dismal conclusion of the poem 'Morphine'—that death is better than sleep but the best thing would be never to have been born at all—escapes banality as a philosophical pronouncement (however heartfelt the despair that gave rise to it) by virtue of its implication that the problem-free, ideal state belongs to a realm of non-existence that we cannot even conceive of. On the other hand, it is to Heine's credit that, despite his despair at finding no answer to his questions about life (other than a mouthful of earth, which he rightly finds inadequate, in the poem 'Lass die heilgen Parabolen'), he progressively abandons the non-metaphysical humanistic ideologies that seek to develop the meaning of life from within life and human society itself. It is evident, again in the epilogue to his Romanzero, that he is instinctively aware of the pitfall of such undertakings: the creation of new religious (and less attractive ones at that) in the belief that one is abolishing religion. Meaning is usually imposed from without, and Heine realizes that this process is ultimately self-defeating, and, as expressed in the poem 'Fragen', only a fool will expect the riddle of life to be solved.

Thus, in his mature appraisal of life, Heine arrives at an honesty almost unique among his contemporaries. He avoids all easy solutions, whether idealistic or materialistic in nature. He sees death neither as the curtain separating us from a better world nor as the incidental cessation of a meaningful life. One can surrender to it or abhor and combat it, but one cannot pretend it is not there, nor conceive of life without it. This is not to say that life thereby becomes more meaningful; it merely becomes more precious, whereas its ultimate meaning, if there is one, still remains inaccessible. Though Heine can frequently be said to affirm life in his later years, the striking thing is the degree of despair which persists alongside the affirmation, and the lighthearted tone which is nevertheless maintained.

Although, as noted, a realm of beauty-in-death cannot be overlooked in Heine's poetic world, the more typical situation is one in which beauty is equated with vitality and is indeed seen as the essence of life. Even before Heine's confinement to the 'Matratzengruft', the validity of beauty lies precisely in its fleeting, earth-bound quality. When, in *Florentinische Nächte* (1837), he writes of party-going Parisiennes who, like wraiths of doomed brides dancing on their graves, greedily indulge in the pleasures of the world before icy death can claim them, we may take this as a valid expression at least of one phase of the general pattern of Heine's poetic outlook. Though there are overtones of Saint-Simon's doctrine of rehabilitation of the flesh, perhaps, too, of a fashionable decadence and 'Weltschmerz', the passage is typical of Heine's fascination with a beauty robbed of its idealistic foundation and hence vulnerable to decay. Though Heine's experience is personal and intense, the problem is one engendered by the literary and intellectual scene in Germany in the post-Romantic and post-Classical years.

The 'frame' situation of this intentionally rambling poetic prose work is macabre enough: the narrator, Maximilian,

tells stories to the beautiful but doomed Maria to while away her last days. Although this invention smacks of calculated pathos (while at the same time mildly lampooning this very tendency), its sombre realization that frivolity may at times involve quite urgent matters is shared by as distinguished a forebear as Boccaccio (whose plague, to be sure, is less imminent and inexorable than Maria's malady).

The central episode of *Florentinische Nächte* is the narrator's encounter, in England, with Mlle Laurence, a street carnival performer who dances amidst a small freakish entourage: a red-faced woman with a tiny head and huge abdomen, who resolutely beats the drum; the wizened, spindly-legged, largeheaded dwarf Türlütü who periodically crows like a rooster (he is later to die in a cradle); and a learned dog who rounds off the motley group. This weird assemblage, abnormal as it seems, is typical of Heine's usual depiction of human society in general; he sometimes approaches paranoia in his insistence upon a widespread conspiracy of prosaic persons given over to practical routine ('Philister') against the man of poetic sensibilities. It is the ludicrous, yet grisly, carnival of life, the summation of the absurd and futile doings which we pompously assume to be important and real.

Mlle Laurence, on the other hand, moves in the sphere of true poetic reality, not that of the mock reality of Philistines. Her dance, not the risqué tale of amorous conquest that follows, is the important thing, for the conquest is really an attempt to grasp and explain the phenomenon. It is an enigma to Maximilian, accustomed as he is to solving riddles; it seems to speak in a language of its own and to say something horrible and painful.

Mlle Laurence dances as nature bids man dance; her whole being is engaged. There is nothing rigidly classical and nothing Romantic, macabre, deformed, or medieval here; so the narrator would have us believe. Yet, towards the end of the dance it is described as 'fatalistic' and acquires a distinctly eerie air. The dancer trembles, inclines her ear towards the ground, makes mad, abandoned leaps, listens again, grows rigid, and finally makes compulsive handwashing motions.

Later the mystery is solved to some extent. Mlle Laurence was born in the coffin of a mother only believed dead (who, however, died soon afterwards). As a result, she is known as a child of the dead ('Totenkind'). Her foster father, an unscrupulous ventriloquist, made her believe that the voice of her dead mother issued from the ground. It is this voice, traumatically ingrained as a recurring auditory hallucination, that she listens to in the midst of her dance.

It is, in short, a dance of life and death that we have before us, a graphic representation of vitality faced with extinction. The enigma is as simple and as complex as this. When the narrator seeks to decipher the symbolism (as he calls it) of his beloved's features and movements, he pays homage to the Romantic belief that a higher meaning shines through such earthly symbols; yet the voice to which she harkens is from below, not from above. It is the voice of nothingness, not of the Absolute. For this 'Totenkind' birth and death are peculiarly compressed, and the most intense life and the most moving beauty occur when the presence of the Destroyer is most strongly perceived. We feel that the core of Heine's poetic work is presented here in pure form, and that he himself stands in some awe of his creation. He is puzzled as to its supposed ulterior meaning and is perhaps reluctant to admit the tragic secret which one may continually grasp and expound only to be confounded anew by it: that there is no beauty without death. Like his heroine, he washes his hands of the knowledge.

In his pondering over a possible higher meaning, Heine is Romantic; in his failure to solve the riddle or to discover any secrets, he belongs to a later age. The deformed performers appear again as ghosts in Mlle Laurence's boudoir, and she arises entranced to dance to their tune; but these figures are not so much emissaries of a spirit world as shadowy remnants of the world we know, which is itself shadowy and fleeting enough.

The music provided by the freakish performers, it is interesting to note, has some of the essential features of Heine's own work, to judge by his description. It is ungainly yet titillating, melancholy, impudent, bizarre, yet characterized by a singular simplicity. The last feature we may readily believe, since Heine repeatedly insists that it is produced by a triangle and a drum.

Karl Immermann, though at times almost feverishly satirical and as fantastically inclined as is consistent with the prosaic spirit of the times which he finds so oppressive, lacks the saving grace of lightness as well as the unshakable certainty as to his own position and the incisive eye for foibles and weaknesses that lends perennial freshness to Heine's work. The two authors were born within one or three years of each other (depending on which of Heine's birth dates is authentic), and both recognize the waning of purely abstract and idealistic art. Immermann is, if anything, more successful in eschewing the paraphernalia of Romanticism. Heine, in fact, displays few compunctions in borrowing the most effective techniques from Romantic authors while denouncing these slightly older contemporaries as reactionary and backward-looking; but, since he delights in playing the literary rogue, our criticism of such procedures is disarmed from the outset.

The significance of a similar motif in the work of such temperamentally dissimilar authors might be questioned; it seems more probable, however, that the dissimilarity of the authors actually strengthens the argument that a trend significant for the age is involved. The grim, yet hopeful, import of Immermann's corresponding dance scene is, in any case, nearly identical with that of Heine's.

The dancer is Fiammetta, or Flämmchen, of **Die Epigonen,** a Mignon-like character and curiously modern-sounding exponent of *la dolce vita* who is clearly intended to represent nature in all its vitality and chaotic intractability.

In one episode she disrupts a play by singing a nonsense song with her face painted in all imaginable colours. She mourns her husband in red and yellow garb and favours flame-red stockings, gaily flying ribbons and golden shoes. Her only belief is in 'sweet flesh and blood'. Her vitality is that of the flame—a consumption of vital fluid continually on the verge of extinction, continually reborn.

Flämmchen's late husband and his eccentric legacy deserve some comment. One room of the villa he has left behind houses his agglomeration of natural specimens, representing the meaningless variety of nature. A blue, empty room is meant to represent infinity, which, even in 1835, bears a suspicious resemblance to nothingness. A third room, intended to contain a representation of God, is occupied instead by the mummified corpse of the husband himself. It is before this singular specimen of misdirected religiosity, and in terror of it, that Flämmchen's dance takes place. She begins in a terrifying trance-like state of expanded consciousness. The music is provided by an uncanny old hag, actually her mother, who is inclined towards devil worship and has unsettling views about the hereafter; after death, she thinks, decay proceeds even in the spiritual realm, until the decomposed souls flutter aimlessly in the air. Flämmchen, correspondingly, seems to become a lemur-like, wispy figure dissolving into the air in the more wild and disjointed phases of her dance. At other times she grows stonily rigid, and her typical aspect (as Immermann observes with rather ponderous rhetoric) is that of a dying Magdalene, whose sweet flesh is already attacked by the grim foe of joy.

Immermann's scene is quite seriously presented, with all the horror and pathos due it; Heine is facetious, risqué, and morbid in a way that invites the suspicion of a modish indulgence in 'Weltschmerz' and 'Zerrissenheit' after the manner of Byron. Both, however, portray a charming and vital creature hovering on the threshold of another realm: not a harmonious All, but rather the void. The threat of extinction is of course present in all ages, but one period of more intense awareness of the presence results from the collapse, around 1800, of the orderly and benevolent cosmic scheme posited by the Enlightenment and frantically reaffirmed by Romanticism, already with noticeable lapses. The nihilistic strain running from the 'Sturm und Drang' through Jean Paul, the early Tieck and some other Romantic writers and culminating in the odd and monstrous anonymous *Nachtwachen des Bonaventura* remains to be clearly identified and traced. Both of our authors, however, sense its presence and seek to combat it with a representation of intense vitality in the form of the dance—a type of activity curiously suited to the portrayal both of exuberant life and lugubrious decay. Heine purports to have no qualms about a *carpe diem* outlook, though he eventually settles for a form of quasi-Romanticism, poignant in its hints of a supernal realm which, in the end, cannot be realized. Immermann, on the other hand, is troubled by the bugbear of sensuality and, when not preaching a pious doctrine of wholesomeness, finds himself torn between the chaotic abundance of colourful nature and the colourless emptiness of attenuated spirit—between bleakness and inanity and the intense vitality that leads to dissoluteness and dissolution. It sometimes seems to him, as it does to his aforementioned uncanny hag, that the Devil is responsible for vital things and God only for the realm of sameness, that is, of nothingness.

Our authors, at any rate, seem almost puzzled and disconcerted by the charming images of bold but vulnerable life that they have conjured up. Heine, though more willing than Immermann to condone animal exuberance as a way of life, likewise seems happier in the role of pensive spectator. The ultimate aim of both authors is the same: the establishment of a meaning in life which does not presuppose some realm beyond life as its source. They envisage a life bearing its fullness within itself, lending an ear to the voice of gravity and gloom the better to defy it. The resulting gyrations anticipate Nietzsche's madly triumphant dancing over the abyss and dramatically bear witness to the need for eschewing the prevalent glorification of grey abstraction. The battle of vitality and decay can never be won; but these colourful images do much to dramatize the import of the battle.

Gunther J. Holst (essay date 1979)

SOURCE: "Karl Immermann and the Romantic Fairy Tale: Between Two Literary Poles," in *Vistas and Vectors: Essays Honoring the Memory of Helmut Rehder,* edited by Lee B. Jennings and George Schulz-Behrend, University of Texas at Austin, 1979, pp. 152-156.

[*In the following excerpt, Holst uses a fairy tale retold in* Münchhausen *to discuss Immermann's relation to German Romanticism.*]

For almost half a century Karl Immermann was threatened by near obscurity or at best, remembered as the author of *Oberhof,* a fragment taken capriciously from the torso of his greatest novel and published separately as an impressive depiction of village life in the early nineteenth century. But of late this impressive literary and intellectual personality from the German Restoration period has been accorded renewed critical attention. Of the more recent endeavors, two works are particularly outstanding: Manfred Windfuhr's monograph and Benno von Wiese's life which constitutes the introductory volume of his critical edition of the works of Immermann.

One might still agree with Boxberger's devastating judgment that our great respect is due "mehr dem Streben als den Leistungen des Mannes." This statement, however, applies at best to Immermann's many ultimately unsuccessful dramatic and lyrical experiments. Quite another matter are his novels: the comprehensive depiction of his generation, *Die Epigonen,* and the far ranging satire, *Münchhausen*. To be sure, the social and political climate which Immermann described, was antagonistic toward serious literary production. It is not this fact, however, that lifts the two novels out of the realm of the ordinary, but rather the incisive way in which Immermann perceives and depicts the times and mores of the

Epigonenzeit. This permits us to call the above-mentioned works genuine achievements of a high order. Especially impressive is Immermann's struggle for a new method of presentation through which he attempted to express a more realistic world view and thereby to divorce himself from the intellectual and literary heritage both of Goethe and the Romantics. A comparison of two interpolated fairy tales may help to establish Immermann's position vis à vis Romanticism.

In each of Immermann's novels there is an interpolated fairy tale. In the *Epigonen,* it is the entirely unanticipated "Mondscheinmärchen." This is a narrative in itself, but relative to the novel as a whole it lacks the expected function of integration and completion. Basically it is no more than a poetically embellished cosmogony, a theme encountered repeatedly in Immermann's works; and it shows little of his attitude toward Romanticism. This posture can be determined much more clearly from his later fairy tale "Die Wunder im Spessart" in the fifth book of *Münchhausen*.

In interpolating fairy tales, Immermann, of course, followed a favorite literary technique of his day. Various types of interpolations were consistent with the attitude of the Romantics, who wanted to create in their works a new unification of genres and forms. The fairly tale was the most appropriate expression of Romantic endeavor, for no other form accorded the poet such an unlimited range of his imagination. Novalis conceived of the fairy tale as the most suitable means for a deliberate poeticizing of the whole world. Its powerful imagery enabled him to make accessible all of the finite and infinite world by breaching reality, experience, and casuality and dissolving time and space. Thus the fairy tale placed in an insubstantial medieval setting became a symbol of undistilled longing for the transcendent. The return to a distant past made possible "der verworrenen Gegenwartswelt des Romans in der Einlage eine heile Vorzeit als Massstab und Leitbild gegenüberzustellen." Closely connected to this implied criticism of the present is the role of the forest as the predominant place of action. In no other body of fairy tales does the forest have such an essentially deictic function as in German, where it is distinctly identified with an untamed primordial state. As the wild part of an otherwise cultivated nature, it is precisely the forest that can become the main scene of enchantment.

Among the individual authors of Romanticism, however, fairy tales do point to essential differences in their respective attitudes toward nature though in every case nature is viewed in an intimate connection with the hero. Tieck emphasizes nature's demonic, hostile character; while in the case of Eichendorff, at least for those of his heroes who have faith in God, the more benevolent aspects of nature predominate. Both poets succeed in creating a truly magical mood in elevating the ideal content of their fairy tales to the symbolic plane.

In Eichendorff's "Märchen vom Wassermann" (chapter 5 of Ahnung und Gegenwart) Erika Voerster finds an important shift in the significance of the interpolated fairy tale. It no longer has the character of a Golden Era, of an ideally harmonious, original state. Instead it is just as problematic and as much subject to crises as is the real world. Thus it is no longer the model and goal for the action and development of the novel. As a result, the claims made upon the hero have changed as well. According to Mimi Jehle's comprehensive investigation of the *Kunstmärchen,* Eichendorff's fairy tales challenge man to act and strive within the real world. Consequently the end of *Das Marmorbild* returns to reality, for Eichendorff ultimately rejects the world of moonlight and dreams and acknowledges that of bright daylight, even if the latter is still colored in a romantic way. In the second of the interpolated fairy tales of *Dichter und ihre Gesellen* ("Kasperl und Annerl") all is daylight. Contrary to Novalis's "Hyazinth und Rosenblüte," for example, there is none of what Jehle calls "Suchen nach letzter Erkenntnis, von dämmernden Zuständen and Halbentschlossenem. Bei aller Phantasterei ist Eichendorffs Märchen der Wirklichkeit näher. Seine grossse Kunst besteht darin, das wirkliche Leben so zu veredeln, dass es dem Märchen nahekommt." It is precisely in the aspect of *Wirklichkeitsnähe* that Immermann's tendency can be perceived. But before a detailed analysis of the *Waldmärchen* "Die Wunder im Spessart" is undertaken, its content should be sketched.

The setting is the Middle Ages. Konrad, a young knight in colorful garb, encounters Petrus, a scholar clad completely in black. While sharing a meal, they recognize each other as former playmates. Their characters are as opposite as their clothes. Konrad is vivacious, dedicated to knightly skills and fleeting pleasures. Petrus is quiet and pensive; as a disciple of the famous Albertus Magnus he is dedicated to the sciences and the secret arts by means of which he wants to penetrate the innermost core of nature. Konrad tries in vain to persuade his friend to accompany him to a joust. They separate; and Petrus, following an irresistible urge, walks deep into the forest. There he pronounces the magic word which enables him to understand the language of animals. He encounters a princess who—according to what the magpie says—has been put to sleep by the evil canker king. The magpie tells him that in order to release her from the spell, he must get the twig of a yew tree from the wise old man who lives in the ravine and touch the princess with it. Then she will be his. By way of recompense Petrus has to plug all the cracks in the cave which the old man inhabits. While he works at this, the years fly by. One day, when the sleeping princess appears to him in a vision, he finally seizes the twig of the yew. With a mighty thunderclap, nature reverts to its earlier state. But Petrus finds himself an old man. At the edge of the forest he meets his friend Konrad and the beautiful princess when Konrad has awakened with a kiss—not from a spell but merely from a natural slumber.

Many of the former fairy tale elements resemble those of the Romantics, such as the contrast of reality and phantasy, the real world and the hidden one. In addition, there are the youths' quest for adventure and Petrus's character

as a dreamer searching for the ultimate wisdom. Dreamlike states, subconscious action, a transformation into an old man, and the atmosphere of the forest are also found. But an unusual element in Immermann's fairy tale is the occurrence of two heroes, both of whom are in love with the princess. Thus, even in its basic structure this fairy tale is set apart from most. Petrus and Konrad are as different from each other as they can be. Petrus is a night person, singlemindedly devoted to the intellect, to phantasy, and to the pursuit of magic in the hidden world. Konrad, on the other hand, prefers sunlight; he is energetic, impervious to moods, devoted to reality and the pleasures of this world. The princess can belong only to one of them. Eichendorff, to be sure, has Florio start out as a dreamer; but Florio changes. He acknowledges the real, workaday world and returns to it. Petrus is unable to do this. Consequently, the princess goes to the lighthearted, vivacious Konrad, the man of action, who perceives in her no more and no less than a desirable, beautiful woman instead of a bewitched being. He proceeds to marry his Emma and, like a good bourgeois, expects of her a happy household and many handsome children. Petrus, the man of reflection, remains behind, a wretched fool, a victim of his imagination.

In contrast to the symbolically enhanced narratives of Tieck and Eichendorff, Immermann's *Waldmärchen* is clearly an allegory. The sylvan atmosphere which Tieck creates by way of suggestion, euphony, and emphasis of the typical is in Immermann's case precise, definite, and graphic. As a matter of fact, there exist actual impressions which Immermann recorded in his diary during his *Fränkische Reise* and which he subsequently embellished poetically. Moreover, the mood is frequently broken by reflections and explanations. It could be maintained that he chose the form of an allegorical fairy tale in keeping with the character of his novel, for the whole of ***Münchhausen*** gives the impression of being an allegory.

In regard to Immermann's attitude toward nature Harry Maync remarks: "Aus dem Schosse der wahren Natur und der unmittelbaren Gegenwart wächst ihm alles Erstrebenswerte hervor." The text will support this observation. The fairly tale is unexpectedly inserted at the end of the fifth book instead of being attached to the love scene ten pages earlier, where it is reported that Oswald is telling it to Lisbeth. But well before the reader himself is privy to it, the two discuss its pros and cons.

> Als er auserzählt hatte und sie nichts sagte, fragte er sie wie es ihr gefallen habe.—"Ja, sieh," erwiderte sie schüchetern, "es ging mir eigen mit deinen Wundern im Spessart. Ich glaube, ich hätte sie in der Stube hören müssen, da würde ich mir den Wald hinzugedacht haben, aber hier unter den grünen Blättern, bei den wehenden Winden und dem fliessenden Wasser kam mir alles so unnatürlich vor, und ich konnte nicht recht daran glauben."

> Die Antwort machte ihn froh, als habe er das begeistertste Lob vernommen.

This passage shows that the actual and objective is preferable to that which is merely described, no matter how wondrous the latter might be. Thus Immermann prepares the way for the reader to understand the fairy tale which follows, seemingly without an immediate plot connection.

Petrus, the apprentice magician, wants to be master of the mysterious forces of nature. He thinks: "Gott wirkt zwar in der Natur, aber die Natur wirkt auch für sich, und wer der rechten Kräfte Meister ist, der kann ihr eigenes und selbständiges Leben hervorrufen, dass ihre sonst in Gott gebundenen Glieder sich zu ganz neuen Regungen entfalten". But his aspiration turns out to be sacrilege. Petrus utters the magic word and immediately finds himself in a horrifying nightmare. Although he can understand the language of the animals and look into the interior of plants, he remains helpless in a world of nature that holds only chaos and horror. Space and time are monstrously distorted. In the actual duration of one hour he turns from a youth into an old man as punishment for his sacrilege. While it is true that in the writing of poets who are unequivocally part of the romantic scene, destruction, physical and mental, does occur; nevertheless, the *Ahndung* of nature in its transcendence generally retains its attractive powers. For Immermann, however, "wird die Hingabe an das Dämonische der Natur zu einem blossen Verfehlen, sie gehört in den Bereich des menschlichen Wahns und des Fixiertseins an eine 'Idealität,' die in Wahrheit gar keine ist." Thus Petrus realizes in the end: "War Gott versucht und die Natur, über den stürzen Gesichte, an denen er rasch verwittert".

The supreme law is that God is at work in nature; only He is "der rechten Kräfte Meister." Contrary to Petrus's assumption, nature does not possess a life based on inherent inner laws into which man is able to gain insight by virtue of his intellectual powers. That attempt leads to terrifying *Gesichte,* that is, phantomlike figments of the imagination. The *Waldmärchen* thus incorporates as well a contrast between intellect and emotion. Petrus is searching for the ultimate sense of things in the realm of *Wissen.* He keeps apart from others and his environment; he knows no other street than the one that takes him to the monastery. Only the search for the treasures of the intellect, the dialectic idea, and ultimate comprehension occupies him. When Konrad points out to Petrus how pale he is, the latter answers; "Nicht der Sprung des Blutes macht das Leben aus; weiss ist der Marmor, und Marmorwähde pflegen die Räume einzuschliessen, in welchen Götterbilder aufgerichtet stehen". This reply reveals the onesidedness of a mind as cold as splendid marble which negates the pulse of life and confuses in tragic misjudgment *Gott* and *Götterbilder.*

As Lisbeth says, nature is "der Mantel Gottes"; it is an eternal divine cloak that cannot be stripped off by a magic word. For someone alienated from life it is ultimately as empty as the pockets of Petrus's black overcoat, as meaningless as the jumbled chatter of the animals which he imagines he hears, as transient as the savings, "deren keiner aufbehalten geblieben ist," which, with sightless eyes, he

mumbles to himself. But for one who can feel deeply, nature is the final essence; forest and flowers are eventual reality, in whose beauty one delights, whose colors—red, yellow, and green—are the expression of vitality. For him "die grünen, gelben und roten Zeichen" join to form a complete image instead of breaking apart as they do for Petrus. Beings such as Oswald, Lisbeth, and Konrad both see and feel the innermost character, the essence of nature simply in the way it is, in its beauty yet also in its productive interchange between man, animal, and insect. For them, nature is not a secret that needs to be unraveled; the owl is no wise old man; a woman's veil no magic spiderweb cast by the canker king; a sleeping girl no enchanted princess. Any attempt to perceive something unreal behind all these is an exercise in futility. This is signified by Petrus's "unending" endeavor to seal off from the light of day the cave of the supposed wise old man, a task akin to that of Sisyphus; for Petrus has hardly filled one chink when the moss he uses falls out again. In the last analysis, his undertaking is nothing but a tragic flight into darkness rather than into enlightenment.

For Immermann, the mere supposition of any sort of supernatural feature in nature should be relegated to the province of erroneous human fancy. The actual miracle of the Spessart is the coincidence which allows Konrad to find his lady love in the forest. Emma is for him "holdseliges Wunder dieses Forstes," his *Seligkeit* blossoming forth "wie ein goldenes Märchen" (p. 104). With a firm belief in God, his consciousness—quite like that of Lisbeth when she listens to Oswald's tale—is open to the objective beauty of nature and life. This oppenness vis à vis den Dingen is for Immermann the essential core of a "sensible" attitude toward life. Related to this—in a parallel to Eichendorff—is also the zestful Sicheinlassen with the objects in and of life, with actual existence. In Immermann's "Waldmärchen," too, the frame of the past is no longer the measure of an harmonious original condition. *Die Dinge* are in themselves the ground of being, as Immermann indicates in one of his "Chiliastische Sonnette." When Lisbeth then calls nature the *Mantel Gottes* which no magic word can strip off, it means that the innermost core of nature is God Himself. Trying to intrude into the essence of God by means of magic is sheer delusion.

Thus the fairy tale, with which Novalis wanted to poeticize the world, serves Immermann as a means to disenchant an artificially conceived construct of nature. In its place, he sets the natural magic which emanates from the things themselves as the essence of God. This attitude removes Immermann from the magic idealism of Novalis which—as he says in the ***Memorabilien***—has arisen "aus der Sehnsucht nach einem Nichtdaseienden." Instead he considers as requisite the task of passing through the Romantic "in das realistisch-pragmatische Element." His interpolated fairy tale "Die Wunder im Spessart" distinctly reveals not only the break between the romantic and realistic attitude, but also a whole new orientation based on an instinctive embracing of reality. Thus form and ethos of the *Waldmärchen* clearly show Immermann as a precursor of realism.

Michael Minden (essay date 1985)

SOURCE: "Problems of Realism in Immermann's *Die Epigonen*," in *Oxford German Studies,* Vol. 16, 1985, pp. 66-80.

[*In the following excerpt, Minden analyzes some of the literary devices Immermann employed in* Die Epigonen *to depict German culture in the 1820s.*]

Die Epigonen (1836) cannot refer to the validating authority that the notion of realism was later to come to offer the genre of the novel. The absence of a stable mimetic focus is one of the most striking things about it . . . Sammons [in *Six Essays on The Young German Novel*] rightly observes: 'Every world that Immermann constructs, houses the potential of grotesque catastrophe.' The novel slips from register to register, or from language to language, so that each mode of discourse relativises the others. Indeed, as critics from Lauschus to Sengle have pointed out, this is one of the novel's greatest stylistic virtues. At the same time, because it is a novel, it cannot refer to the validating authority that resides in literary convention either. For Immermann, as for everybody else in German letters in the 1820s and 1830s, the novel was (despite the various advances made in different directions by Goethe and Sir Walter Scott) still to be counted amongst the 'an und für sich . . . niedere oder gemischte Genres.' . . .

The novel's most obvious literary debts are to Goethe's *Wilhelm Meister* novels. The main points to bear in mind in the present context are that Immermann's protagonist (Hermann) is a rather shadowy figure, whose function is less to offer a paradigm of development than to be a link between the various episodes. In this, Immermann is moving towards the *Wanderjahre* model which he admired. Immermann is concerned with giving a picture of the times more than with giving one of an individual character. But it would be misleading to cite Goethe as an authoritative reference point, because the dominance of Goethe, and the hopelessness of emulating him, play an important part in the sense of *Epigonentum* which Immermann is defining. At the same time, Goethe's models were widely felt, by Immermann as much as by many of his contemporaries (and arguably somewhat unjustly) to offer insufficient guidance as to how to represent contemporary reality. The lack of suitable models and the surfeit of unsuitable ones are the very problems with which Immermann grapples.

The reason Immermann had recourse to an array of mutually relativising modes of discourse was that he considered such cacophony to be characteristic of the period of *Epigonentum* in the 1820s which he wished to represent. 'Alle Ansichten abrupt—einander ablösend', he noted as part of a description of the projected character his novel should take. But he did not wish his novel as a whole to be as trivial as the various attitudes it pilloried and satirised. Thus, because the novel form did not hold in itself any automatic standing either as 'realism' or as 'serious literature', he had to devise ways in the organisation of the novel itself of correcting the sense of 'moral seasickness' which he is so successful at conveying.

What follows is an attempt to offer a fresh analysis, and assess the importance, of these strategies.

The most prominent attempt to create a single perspective on the panorama of styles and attitudes occurs in Book 8. Immermann's basic strategy is an appeal to history. The epoch of confusions, the 1820s, is over, and in Book 8 (dated 1835), we are looking back from the present upon a time of disorder which has fallen into perspective. It is not surprising that Immermann should look for meaning in history as a concept, writing as he was at a time deeply fascinated by all issues related to history and its philosophy. Yet the terms in which Immermann invokes history to seek an anchor in the storms of *Epigonentum* need to be scrutinised in context, if we are to understand his method of establishing authority over his disparate materials.

The *Herausgeber* of Book 8 is a familiar novelistic device, used by Immermann to enable him to present his own credentials as a novelist rather than an historian, but a novelist who nevertheless wishes to offer an authentic representation of the time. . . . This editor is provided with a correspondent plucked from the relativising morass of the 1820s. In the mainstream of events, this character (known only as 'Der Arzt'), had been as much prone to relativisation as anyone else. . . . Now, in Book 8, he and the editor combine to offer an objective assessment of the tangle of events and plots in the past. In a sense, they make history of it.

The doctor's credentials for helping in the task of establishing a perspective upon a difficult historical flux, are, first, his advancement from a role as a house surgeon in a small court to Prussian state service (reflecting social change), and, secondly, a religious conversion which has rescued him in the meantime from a laming feeling of fragmentation (he speaks of his experience as having formerly been made up of 'ein lockres Aggregat problematischer Einzelheiten, welchen der eigentliche Mittelpunkt fehlte', and given him a sense of higher coherence). Just as the editor represents Immermann via his views on the novel and history, so the doctor represents Immermann too, for the conversion attributed to the doctor is an experience of the novelist's own, described in partially identical words.

The characteristics of the authority displayed in Book 8 are thus: that it comes from a safe perspective after the main events of the novel; that it is administered by males; that it has recourse both to historical thought, and to transcendent religious experience, for this is the point of the specific team Immermann puts together; and that it is more or less frank about its own provenance: this is *Immermann's* attempt to write a significant story, a serious novel, a discourse both of the times and universal.

There is a corresponding source of truth on the level of the characters, a figure who, like the two men who guarantee the narrative perspective from above, guarantees the stability of the world on the ground, as it were. This is the character Cornelie.

Whilst Hermann changes with the seasons, circumstances and episodes, his eventual union is anticipated in Book 1. This union is 'keimhaft angelegt' in Hermann just as is Wilhelm Meister's with Natalie in the *Lehrjahre*. Cornelie is *the* woman for Hermann, she is his destiny, his content and meaning. . . . Hermann is a device without substance in the service of an historical panorama. Cornelie gives him a content, . . . so that by these means the threat of emptiness is overcome; again, a truth is discerned where before there had appeared to be only a succession of disastrous errors.

If the novel consists of a series of discrete scenes linked inorganically by a directionless male protagonist, then the two editor-narrator figures render the scenes coherent, while Cornelie functions as an organic justification of Hermann's existence.

A simple symmetry connects Cornelie with another prominent figure in the novel, Flämmchen, a mixture of Mignon and Philine with Romantic connections. As a structural element, this symmetry works against the mutually relativising contrasts, but it also leads back to that unstable and unstructured series. This is because Flämmchen interacts with the various poses and attitudes of the main narrative, while Cornelie does not, remaining instead stable and withdrawn until her time comes to shine forth. Cornelie and Flämmchen are symmetrically paired because they both represent erotic, but often ill-defined, attractions for Hermann. . . .

These two characters are identified as standard projections of contemporary male fantasy by their property of sexual ambivalence, familiar in nineteenth-century literature from authors as different as Stifter and Storm and Lewis Carroll. The difference between them lies in the predominance of innocence in the first instance, and that of sensuality in the second.

Cornelie is characterised by her sexual inaccessibility, and in this role, broadly speaking, keeps the story going. As she is Hermann's social, moral, erotic and natural partner, union with her will mark the end of the story and its deferment will facilitate its extension, otherwise known as the plot. Hence, at important moments, Cornelie more or less unaccountably withdraws from Hermann (the passage just cited; the end of Book 3; Book 7, Chapter 5; the final chapter), only to be united with him in the closing tableau.

Flämmchen, on the other hand, is characterised by her erotic overavailability. She represents a surfeit of sexuality which is related to the 'Überfluss' of forms and styles of representation which is the distinguishing mark not only of the novel's idiom, but of the phenomenon of *Epigonentum* itself, in Manfred Windfuhr's definition. This relation can be seen in the habit she has of destroying theatrical illusions. In these instances an unruly sexuality

disrupts disguises. . . . But she will also instigate confusion in order to facilitate the long-desired sexual union with Hermann (by pretending to be Johanna). It is not by accident that this seduction takes place as the culmination of a mad party during which Hermann's mood is described as follows: 'Seinen durch Tanz und Wein aufgeregten Geist hatten im Verlauf einer Stunde die fremdesten Gegensätze berührt'. This background of 'fremdeste Gegensätze' is the appropriate setting for the incestuous transgression which leads to the temporary dislocation of Hermann's personality. (The act of incest itself turns out of course to be no such thing, to be a false appearance, a Romantic excess, too.) The point is that Flämmchen, let loose, encourages a disorder which ultimately threatens to shatter male personality completely. In this too she is the antithesis of Cornelie.

This symmetry between two sexually ambiguous figures, which are both embodiments of different aspects of male fantasy, indicates alternative, contrasted literary-novelistic ways of dealing with the sexual. In Cornelie an attempt is made to visualise the sexual contained within social and moral orders, themselves enveloped in a nature in which the sexual is not in any way a problem or force for disruption, but the guarantee of direction and fulfilment (as such she is a typical and indispensable component of the *Bildungsroman,* and, insofar as she is the fuel of the plot, of the nineteenth-century novel in general).

Flämmchen, by contrast, who has read too much E. T. A. Hoffmann, and is a living (if that is the right word) allusion to the *Lehrjahre* (as a blend of Mignon and Philine), an embodiment of 'das Phantastische', represents the energy of sexuality rampantly on the loose outside the constraining simple, natural, moral harmony which defines Cornelie and vice versa. Outside this postulation of serene truth, what else can this energy do, but become ensnarled with all the props and flats which clutter up the contemporary stage of human activity, and from the oppressive presence of which there appears to be no escape?

Both figures, as women, are related to nature. So Cornelie, whose sexuality is contained within a naturally harmonious order, is most often depicted in rural settings. Flämmchen's sexuality is a natural force which has somehow become estranged from itself, and is only manifest in the violence and disruptiveness with which it possesses whatever forms of expression, means to fulfilment, sets of ideas or attitudes, come to hand. Hence, whilst Cornelie is virtually invisible except as an obscure object of desire, Flämmchen is a bundle of literary stereotypes in her very constitution.

The specific relation to nature which Flämmchen represents is especially clear in a rather wearisomely symbolic dancing scene in Book 4 Chapter 5. It is fascinating to observe how Flämmchen encounters nature (in its narrow sense), and how an awkward theatricality results which evokes the state of the world and its pervasive inauthenticity in the age of the epigone. . . .

'Sie spielt Komödie wie keine andere . . . ', the character Wilhelmi has already said about the epoch in which they live, and here we have an extraordinary enactment of a meeting between unruly sexuality and nature, resulting in visible forms of response, which, in their awkwardness and lifelessness ('erstarrt'; 'Konvulsionen'), typify with special clarity and unexpectedness the unnatural forms of accommodation the age has to offer, and the inauthentic and redundant discourses with which the book plays.

What one might call Immermann's 'pre-realist' idiom can make great use of this riotous disorder, for it directs and jumbles his material in the way he needs. (Witness the way Flämmchen disrupts Wilhelmi's sensitive *Zeitanalyse* in Book 1 Chapter 10, or the sequences in Book 7, Chapters 11-14, involving the Domherr's estate.) But how will Immermann bring this riot to order once the time comes to establish authority over his materials in the name of a stable view of things, as we have seen him doing in the cases of Book 8 and Cornelie?

This resolution comes, or is attempted, in a curious scene in Book 9, Chapter 2. Hermann and Flämmchen's child has died at birth and the infant's body been buried. The composition of the soil is such as to have preserved the skeleton of the baby, while stripping it completely bare of all flesh. This strange relic, struck by the light in a certain way, has an appearance of beauty, which gives rise to a sense of reverence in those who have discovered it. It is worth dwelling on this episode for a moment.

Here, Immermann is resolving a theme by the stylistic means of symbolism. . . .

In other words, symbolism fulfils the function fulfilled elsewhere by the two editing correspondents and Cornelie. But this *stylistic* solution is more problematic than the other two. The book is largely about the problems involved with finding adequate symbolic expression for contemporary experience.

Elsewhere in **Die Epigonen** Immermann pokes fun at the pitfalls of elaborate symbolism. For instance, the ridiculous character called the Domherr has had two rooms in his mansion especially decorated. . . .

Far from representing the true relationship between the complex circumstantiality of nature and eternal truth, the allegory becomes subjective: where God was to have been, there now lies the mummified corpse of the canon himself, because there is nowhere else for it to go. The point would appear to be that one is trapped within one's own grandiose efforts to make sense (and to make it visible). Immermann saw Goethe as supremely subjective and the Egyptian trappings which surround the canon's lying in state underline the ironic allusion to the 'Saal der Vergangenheit' in *Wilhelm Meisters Lehrjahre,* and its more or less secularised forms of reverence. This is all part of the exposition of *Epigonentum.*

Yet Immermann is left with the problem of making his own meaning clear and visible; which is another way of saying that he must find a *style* for the expression of what he means to say. The Hermann-Flämmchen theme demands a serious resolution, for it touches upon basic questions about human life; upon sex, mortality, the role of adventure, disorder, chance, in the otherwise necessarily ordered and predictable life of civilised society (and civilised literature).

The solution he hits upon is to have *nature* produce a symbolic token in such a way as to transform a chance occurence into a natural-religious epiphany: 'Der Oheim wollte die Hand nach den *von der Natur geweihten Resten* ausstrecken, zog sie aber zurück und sagte: 'Nein! dies ist zu schön, als dass man es nicht, so wie es ist, lassen müsste'.' (my emphasis); '"so hält die Natur in ihrer regelrechten Tätigkeit zu jeder Zeit die frischesten Wunder in Bereitschaft"'.

A further complication emerges when we consider the context of the uncle's remarks just quoted. Here is a man who is presented as being rather too self-consciously in search of religious certainty. Five pages earlier he has been warned that 'die böse Täuschung, dem Göttlichen durch geheime Zeichen und eine willkürliche Allegorie beikommen zu können, fortwuchern wird, so lange es ein Christentum gibt', and here he is attributing metaphysical significance to something which is as likely to be arbitrary as it is to be a genuine revelation. Whether or not the natural miracle comes from God or from chance, moreover, the uncle's misguidedness in the matter of visibly expressing spiritual values becomes amply evident before the end of the novel.

The awkward symbol of the preserved skeleton is both a thematic necessity and an obvious piece of staging. For the uncle it has personal religious significance (' . . . etwas, was meiner Sinnesart die ihr gemässe religiöse Erhebung gab'), and for the book as a whole it has a clear-cut literary function as a symbolic resolution of a theme involving ultimate questions (' "Der Mensch bedarf solcher symbolischer Handlungen . . . " ', says Wilhelmi after Hermann has thrown his ring into the infant's grave.) It brings natural and religious imponderables into a stable position with reference to one another. It puts natural and religious themes and illegal sex into a symbol, that is to say, it puts them all into something advertising itself as 'poetry', not prose, but something nevertheless imagined and presented as growing out of the prose of natural (scientific) reality, being continuous with it and not metaphorical or supernatural.

Put into the appropriate context of the thematic history of the *Bildungsroman,* this transition from life to poetry amounts to an assassination, for it is the murder of Wilhelm Meister's son Felix, who is here turned into a rather tawdry piece of poetic decoration, an embarrassed mixture of prose and poetry which makes a poor substitute for the life and hope embodied in the figure of Wilhelm Meister's illegitimate son in the two *Meister* novels.

Immermann has come up with a style in which the symbol must do the work of subsuming the unassimilable under the heading of poetry, without leaving the realm of the natural. Representation of the natural is asked to do more than it is well suited for, and consequently rings untrue. This may be something to do with Immermann's limitations as a novelist. But he was both a man of very high literary culture, and someone who had a differentiated and perceptive sense of his own epoch, and therefore it is not unreasonable to suppose that this awkwardness is also intimately bound up with the situation of German literature and its possibilities in the earlier decades of the nineteenth century.

Such symbols are not compelling in the sense a religious symbol would be, for they are just monuments to uncertainty (like so many of the ill-founded and collapsing monuments of the novel's plot). Nor are they convincing as literary symbols, for they lack all authority. Yet, in another way, they are compelling, because they bear the trace of their own emptiness. Their melancholy is not an evocative or genuinely literary awareness of realms beyond precise expression. It is rather that of a style which knows of its own inadequacy. The symbols thrown up, hastily erected, in the intention of fixing meaning, bear the imprint of their own redundancy. How else can one read the ambiguity with which Immermann offers the symbol of the skeleton; as simultaneously the upholder of a clinching meaning in the economy of the work as a whole, and the arbitrary and personal symbol of a man, driven by a lack of religious conviction and satisfying religious forms, to seek such symbols?

'"Ich ehre die Religion, das weisst du, ich fühle, dass sie manchem Ermatteten Stab, manchem Verschmachtenden Erquickung ist. Nur—kann sie denn das einem jeden sein?"' says Werther. It can be no coincidence that at the same time he becomes aware of a certain 'Erstarrung' that can arise when one's image of nature is detached from a coherent context and becomes grotesque instead of life-enhancing: ' "O! wenn da diese herrliche Natur so starr vor mir steht wie ein lackiertes Bildchen . . . ."'

The realism of *Werther* is of a different order to that of Immermann, but Werther's horror at the inauthentic image is not irrelevant in our context. It is an early point in a line of tribulations suffered by symbolic and realist representations which carries on prominently through *Die Wahlverwandtschaften* and further to the style we know as Poetic Realism. And the circumstances giving rise to these tribulations are well illuminated in Immermann's style as we have just scrutinised it. We see him situated between an acute awareness of the by now pervasive presence of 'lackierte Bildchen' (the novel delights in them), and the unremitting necessity to fix compelling meaning in *some* form that will do it justice (the novel grapples with the problem of fixing authority).

Immermann also runs into revealing difficulties when he explores the relationship between the two sorts of authority analysed earlier (the editing males and the welcoming female). These difficulties involve his important and innovative attempt to write an historically aware novel.

Book 8 effectively offers a model for perception, a way in which the knowledge of the editor and the truth held by the characters can be brought together (so that a conscious, organised discourse, that of the editor and the doctor, will once again be joined to essential truth, and the moral seasickness will have an end). The doctor is promoted an epistemological rung and allies himself with the editor, thus leaving the bulk of what needs to be revealed in the hands of two women characters, a character known only as 'die Herzogin' and Johanna. This model is fundamentally voyeuristic. The doctor speaking from his new vantage-point explains this to the editor in the course of a simile concerning a beehive with a glass side: 'So haben Sie uns verstohlen betrachtet, freilich mit Vorsicht, sonst würden wir die Scheibe zu verkleben gewusst haben'.

The doctor acts as a mediator and arranges for depositions from both women. Thus *secrets* are revealed, the secrets of women, the content of the book, disclosed by the motivating force of its style (the editor's organising curiosity, the *desire* to know and show). 'Grosser Gott, wie soll es eine arme Frau anfangen, ihr Innres vor anderen zu enthüllen?'; 'mit welcher Scham schreibe ich dieses nieder!'—these exclamations of the duchess convey well the sense of delighted discovery experienced by their author, a sort of erotic pleasure in the very delivery of truth. The fundamentally voyeuristic disposition of the novel is demonstrated in the following description of Cornelie in distress: 'Ihr Innres war wider ihren Willen an das grelle Tageslicht herausgekehrt worden, sie empfand eine innige Scham über die Entweihung des Heimlichsten . . . '. Hermann too displays this kind of pleasure in his attitude to the women he encounters in the main course of the action. Here he is scrutinising the duchess's room in her absence (we are reminded of the parallel scene of Faust in Gretchen's room): 'Hermann warf seine verlangenden Blicke umher, und empfand ganz den süssen Schauder, der uns ergreift, wenn wir für uns die stillen Umgebungen der Frauen mustern dürfen', or else there is the scene in which he watches Cornelie going unobserved about her work, and which begins 'er sass in einer beschatteten Ecke, so dass sie ihn nicht bemerkte'.

The novel derives an important dynamic from the model of erotic looking, which involves the roles of watcher and watched. The first is played by the historical intelligence and the second by the women characters, so that the male principle of analytical intelligence enjoys a safe dominance over 'nature' represented in women figures, upon whom it is nevertheless dependent for its justification and pleasure.

The specific relation between nature and history (between *Bildungsroman* and *Zeitroman,* to use the literary-historical terms appropriate to **Die Epigonen**) receives its clearest definition in the way the figure of Johanna is presented. Johanna is a more substantial figure than the other women in the book, her secrets are altogether weightier and more worth knowing. In this, in her circumstantial involvement with other people, in her political involvement, in her emancipated views according to which she acts and in the name of which she suffers, in all these qualities she approaches the kind of realised fictional character one would more readily associate with full-blown realism of the French or Russian type.

The editor at one point becomes considerably heated about his pleasure in having uncovered and been able to survey the figure of Johanna. The precise terms of his excitement are worthy of attention. . . .

Here the desire to narrate, to edit and organise, is fastened upon an object which combines nature and history, sees them fused as a desired object of attraction. These terms—the attractive woman *and* the weapons of war, the fine dainty hands *and* the rough implements of politics and history—present, in a privileged position in Book 8, almost a formula for the kind of novel we understand as Realist, in which the pleasure of the plot has the ability to manifest itself in its movement through social and historical realities. The creation of a genuine German Realism is at hand.

What actually happens, however, is something different. Johanna's flirtation with the weapons of war proves to have been a mistake. The impossible configuration, which had seemed possible for a moment, is dissolved. Similarly, it turns out that it is not Johanna, but Flämmchen with whom Hermann has spent the fateful night. Because it transpires that Johanna is Hermann's sister (this is her main 'secret'), this means that the adventure beyond the taboo, whether it be incest or a proscribed intimacy between art and politics, is prominently avoided. The sense of last-minute withdrawal from an advanced position is also present in Johanna's fate: after an alliance with the anarchist activist Medon (based in part on the radical, Karl Follen), she survives his disgrace and is rendered safe in a marriage to a retired general, old enough to be her father.

Now, all this appears to be a victory for the male historical and analytical intelligence, which, in Book 8, has sorted out not only the rationale of the narrative and its historical and philosophical legitimacy, but has also uncovered the secrets of the women and put them into their proper place (which for the conservative Immermann was as administrators of 'häusliches Behagen', for their menfolk). In short, the men appear to have asserted themselves as writers of the true order and meaning: 'Ihr Wunsch ist erfült', writes the doctor to the editor announcing the duchess' confessions ' . . . freilich mit Widerstreben, indessen haben Sie Ihren Willen, den die Schriftsteller überhaupt in der Regel durchzusetzen wissen'. After this, gentle but firm, imposition of male 'system' upon the desirable but resistant stuff of 'nature', the editor has ended Book 8 with a quotation from Lamartine, most apt, both in the matter of its author and in itself, for announcing a fruitful union between poetry and politics.

Yet the end of Book 8 is not the end of the novel, and the motto of the final book (which is revealingly entitled 'Cornelie') is 'Über allem Zauber Liebe!' Stylistically,

the novel can find no image to represent itself in the terms in which it had set out to exist, 'Amor mit den Waffen des Mars spielend' has, after all, been disarmed. Instead we have the triumph of nature over history, and not a fraught but vibrant conjunction of the two, such as we find, for instance, in Stendhal's chronicles of the same period. The greatest novel stereotype of all—the ending in marriage—subsumes the whole panorama of specific historical reference. The banal erotic motivation wins out and outwits all the men's history. We are left with a vague and unconvincing concept of stewardship against a better future, which appears a secondary consideration after the fulfilment of the desired union with Cornelie, the feminine ending.

Where Goethe, in the *Lehrjahre,* had commandeered this banal conclusion for his own stylistic and thematic purposes, thereby turning it into a symbol with some strength, Immermann turns it right back into a cliché again. We have the same 'Erstarrung' of symbolic means as we saw in the case of the 'naturally' preserved infant, where once Felix had been.

The point can be made most clearly by quoting the closing tableau of the novel itself:

> Ich bin es, mein Bruder, und bringe dir die Braut!' rief Johanna, in Seligkeit blühend. Sprachlos fiel er in die geöffneten Arme Corneliens und dann an die Brust der hohen Schwester. So ruhte er zwischen den beiden, die seine Seele liebte. Zärtlich hielten sie ihn umschlungen. Wilhelmi blickte mit gefaltnen Händen nach den Vereinigten hin. Der General stand, auf sein Schwert gestützt, und sah, eine Rührung bekämpfend, vor sich nieder. In dieser Gruppe, über welche das Abendrot sein Licht goss, wollen wir von unsern Freunden Abschied nehmen.

'Nichts lässt auf eine versteckte Ironie schliessen', writes Halm [in *Formen der Narrheit in Immermanns Prosa*] in his perceptive study of the scene, and one must sadly agree with him. The tableau is genuinely awful; one only has to visualise the manly emotion of the retired general to see the point. There is the same unwholesome feel about this 'resolution' as there had been about the infant preserved in limestone; seemingly inevitably, they are touched by the same evening sun, how else can one signal the presence of simple but profound 'point'? They are both examples of the 'lackiertes Bildchen', not as a psychological experience, but 'in place' as an element of style. These are the awkward distortions of nature familiar from Flämmchen's dance.

It is unsettling to observe, incidentally, how the threat of incest, so laboriously overcome by the plot, has re-established itself at the heart of this 'tableau vivant' (or should one say 'mort'?) in the gesture of the sister *presenting* the bride to her brother—'zärtlich hielten sie ihn umschlungen'—so that they tend to merge. There is nothing accidental about this involuntary subversion. It is simply what happens when one tries to imagine (and represent) 'innocent' desire: one becomes ensnarled in a more serious taboo than frankness about sexuality might infringe. To assure oneself of the continued danger of this trap in the serious German novel, one need only examine the relationship between Natalie and Heinrich Drendorf's sister in *Der Nachsommer*.

These two moments of symbolic embarrassment display an eery sense of 'something missing'. In the earlier case what was missing was a compelling religious frame of reference, so that nature congealed grotesquely in the author's hands. In the closing tableau we are dealing with a sense of that 'defeat' of history, in favour of a banal oedipal wish-fulfilment, of which we have been speaking.

Immermann strove to fix and define his fiction in religious and historical terms (this is the point of Book 8), but his efforts are subject to a stylistic subversion. Although he perceives so clearly how the erotic journey of narrative might combine with the specifics and circumstances of an historical time (in the image of Johanna), his yearning for 'nature' as a final term subverts the attempt. 'Nature' in the novel is too easily equated with preferred male representations of women ('die grüne Erde, welche alles zuletzt mütterlich verhüllt'), so that one is left with the kind of stylistic short-circuits we have been discussing, when it comes to making a bid for stable meaning. Underlying stereotypes become discernible behind the ephemeral ones which Immermann exposes with such percipience and humour.

In terms of German Realism, or the history of the serious German novel from Goethe onwards, we are dealing with what one might call the problem of the over-worked symbol. Too much comes to be expected from symbols from nature; the gaps they must both signify and fill are too large for them. As Jürgen Kolbe pointed out, Immermann's closing tableau recalls, within the wider context of contemporary taste, the ending of *Die Wahlverwandtschaften*. But . . . one could also argue that the full resonance of Goethe's image can only be understood as including a

revolutionary awareness of its own emptiness as symbolism, and that, and specifically within that dominant field of taste, it is this sense of emptiness, fixed in a stylistic difficulty, which Immermann picks up and exhibits. After all, having perceived so well the pervasiveness of bogus representations, it is unlikely that Immermann will be able to outwit his own insight, and certain that he will be unable to prevent the relativising tide of the bulk of his novel from engulfing the tiny patch of stable ground he tries to stake out.

FURTHER READING

"The *Bildungsroman* and Social Forms: Immermann's *Die Epigonen*," *Ideas and Production* 2 (1984): 10-27.
> Argues that Immermann's *Die Epigonen* was extensively influenced by Goethe's *Wilhelm Meister*.

Kohn-Bramstead, Ernst. "The Change in Economic Equilibrium: 1830-1848." In his *Aristocracy and the Middle-Classes in Germany: Social Types in German Literature, 1830-1900*, pp. 44-67. London: P. S. King & Son, 1937.
> Includes discussion of Immermann's portrayal of relations between the aristocracy and the bourgeoisie in his novels.

Porterfield, Allen Wilson. *Karl Lebrecht Immermann: A Study in German Romanticism*. New York: Columbia University Press, 1911, 153 p.
> Analyses Immermann in relation to German Romanticism.

Sagarra, Eda. "The Beidermeier Writers: 1820-50." In *Tradition and Revolution: German Literature and Society, 1830-1890*, pp. 86-114. New York: Basic Books, 1971.
> Examines Immermann's portrayal of social and political upheaval in his novels *Die Epigonen* and *Münchhausen*.

Additional coverage of Immermann's life and career is contained in the following source published by Gale Research: *Nineteenth-Century Literature Criticism, Volume 4.*

"Bartleby, the Scrivener"

Herman Melville

The following entry presents criticism of Melville's short story, "Bartleby, the Scrivener: A Story of Wall-Street" (1853). For information on Melville's complete career, see *NCLC,* Volume 3; for criticism devoted to his novels *Moby-Dick, Billy Budd,* and *Typee,* see *NCLC,* Volumes 12, 29, and 45, respectively.

INTRODUCTION

The account of a young man's inability to conform to business life on Wall Street in the mid-nineteenth century, "Bartleby, the Scrivener" is hailed by some scholars as the first modern American short story for its break with the dense moralizing, overt allegorizing, romantic characterization, and strict form of more traditional tales. The symbolic suggestiveness and narrative ambiguity of "Bartleby" has garnered it more critical attention than any of Melville's other short stories.

Plot and Major Characters

"Bartleby, the Scrivener" is narrated by a Wall Street lawyer who deals in investment opportunities for wealthy clients. The narrator hires a man named Bartleby as a scrivener, a clerk who copies legal documents. Bartleby works diligently at first but gradually begins to decline his responsibilities with the statement "I would prefer not to." Bartleby eventually stops working entirely and stares at the wall immediately outside of a window in the law office. Only when clients are unnerved by Bartleby's idiosyncratic behavior does the narrator take significant action; he moves his business to another building rather than forcefully remove Bartleby, who "would prefer not to" quit the lawyer's service. Bartleby then refuses to leave the vacated building and is consequently jailed for vagrancy. The narrator, feeling somehow responsible for Bartleby's condition and incarceration, visits Bartleby, whom he finds dead from self-imposed starvation. At the conclusion of the story, the narrator relates a rumor about Bartleby's previous occupation: employment in the postal service's dead-letter office, the final repository of lost or otherwise undeliverable mail.

Major Themes

Much of the story's complexity originates from the limited perspective of the narrator, who reveals much about himself while he relates the few facts known about Bartleby. As a result, differing and sometimes conflicting interpretations have been advanced. Some critics focus on the narrator, variously characterizing him as self-serv-

ing or well-meaning. Others have examined Bartleby, who they perceive as comical, nihilistic, Christ-like, or devoid of a social persona. Bartleby is most commonly identified as emblematic/symbolic of the writer alienated by society for his refusal to "copy" the formulas of popular fiction; many critics contend that Melville intended "Bartleby" to be autobiographical in this respect. Other commentators, focusing on the bleak mood and tragic conclusion of the story, consider the story a condemnation of capitalist society or a disheartening existentialist commentary. Others interpret the story as a satire of specific individuals, a parable about failed Christian charity, or an explication of contemporary philosophies. Another influential school of critics approach "Bartleby" from a psychoanalytic perspective, diagnosing Bartleby as schizophrenic, compulsive neurotic, manic depressive, or autistic.

Critical Reception

"Bartleby, the Scrivener" was Melville's first published short story. Out of financial need, he contributed stories and sketches to popular magazines throughout the mid-

1850s; his previously published novels, including *Moby-Dick* and *Pierre,* were favorably reviewed but earned him little income. Melville's short fiction received scant critical or popular attention until the novella *Billy Budd,* left in manuscript at his death, was published in 1924. Its appearance sparked critical attention that revived interest in the Melville canon. Since then, "Bartleby" has attracted a particularly extensive collection of criticism.

CRITICISM

Mordecai Marcus (essay date 1962)

SOURCE: "Melville's Bartleby as Psychological Double," in *College English,* Vol. 23, No. 5, February, 1962, pp. 365-68.

[*Marcus is an American poet, critic, and educator who has written extensively on nineteenth-century American writers. In the following essay, Marcus insists that Bartleby represents the narrator's own protests against the impersonality of Wall Street.*]

Most interpreters of Melville's haunting story **"Bartleby the Scrivener"** (1853) have seen it as a somewhat allegorical comment on Melville's plight as a writer after the publication of *Moby-Dick* and *Pierre.*

Others have suggested that the story dramatizes the conflict between absolutism and free will in its protagonist, that it shows the destructive power of irrationality or that it criticizes the sterility and impersonality of a business society. The last of these interpretations seems to me the most accurate, and the others suffer either from an inability to adjust the parts of the story to Melville's experience (or that of any serious writer), or to adjust the parts to one another.

I believe that the character of Bartleby is a psychological double for the story's nameless lawyer-narrator, and that the story's criticism of a sterile and impersonal society can best be clarified by investigation of this role. Melville's use of psychological doubles in *Mardi, Moby-Dick,* and *Pierre* has been widely and convincingly discussed. Probably Melville's most effective double is Fedallah, Ahab's shadowy, compulsive, and despairing counterpart. Bartleby's role and significance as a double remain less evident than Fedallah's, for the lawyer is less clearly a divided person than is Ahab, and Bartleby's role as double involves a complex ambiguity. Bartleby appears to the lawyer chiefly to remind him of the inadequacies, the sterile routine, of his world.

Evidence that Bartleby is a psychological double for the lawyer-narrator is diffused throughout the story, in details about Bartleby and in the lawyer's obsessive concern with and for Bartleby. The fact that Bartleby has no history, as we learn at the beginning of the story and in a later dialogue, suggests that he has emerged from the lawyer's mind. He never leaves the lawyer's offices and he subsists on virtually nothing. After he refuses to work any longer, he becomes a kind of parasite on the lawyer, but the exact nature of his dependence on the lawyer remains mysteriously vague. His persistent refusal to leave despite all inducements and threats implies that he cannot leave, that it is his role in life not to leave the lawyer's establishment. Bartleby's compulsive way of life, calm determination, and otherwise inexplicable tenacity suggest that he is an embodiment of the kind of perverse determination we might expect to flower in the rather gentle and humane lawyer should he give over to an unyielding passivity as a protest against his way of life.

The behavior of the lawyer gives stronger evidence that Bartleby is his psychological double. The screen which the lawyer places around Bartleby's desk to "isolate Bartleby from my sight, though not remove him from my voice" so that "privacy and society were conjoined" symbolizes the lawyer's compartmentalization of the unconscious forces which Bartleby represents. Nevertheless, Bartleby's power over the lawyer quickly grows as the story progresses, and it grows at least partially in proportion to Bartleby's increasingly infuriating behavior. Towards the beginning of the story the lawyer feels vaguely that "all the justice and all the reason" may lie with Bartleby's astonishing refusal to check his copy. Later the lawyer confesses to being "almost sorry for my brilliant success" when he thinks he has succeeded in evicting the now wholly passive Bartleby; and when he finds that he is mistaken, he admits that Bartleby has a "wondrous ascendancy" over him. Growing used to Bartleby's amazing tenacity, he feels that Bartleby has been "billeted upon me for some mysterious purpose of an all-wise Providence," and he muses about Bartleby: "I never feel so private as when I know you are here."

The lawyer finally accepts Bartleby's presence as a natural part of his world, and he admits that without outside interference their strange relationship might have continued indefinitely. But the crisis of the story arrives when his professional friends criticize him for harboring Bartleby and thus lead him to his various struggles to be rid of him. The professional friends represent the rationality of the "normal" social world, an external force which recalls the lawyer from his tentative acceptance of the voice of apparent unreason represented by Bartleby. When he finally resorts to moving out of his offices in order to leave Bartleby behind, he declares "Strange to say—I tore myself from him whom I had so longed to be rid of."

The lawyer's intermittently vindictive responses to Bartleby's passivity, which are combined with acceptance of and submission to Bartleby, suggest an anger against a force which has invaded himself. The last action which suggests identification of the two occurs when in the prison yard Bartleby behaves as if the lawyer is responsible for his imprisonment and perhaps for his hopeless human situation as well.

Bartleby's role as a psychological double is to criticize the sterility, impersonality, and mechanical adjustments of the world which the lawyer inhabits. The setting on Wall Street indicates that the characters are in a kind of prison, walled off from the world. The lawyer's position as Master of Chancery suggests the endless routine of courts of equity and the difficulty of finding equity in life. The lawyer's easygoing detachment—he calls himself an "eminently safe man"—represents an attempt at a calm adjustment to the Wall Street world, an adjustment which is threatened by Bartleby's implicit, and also calm, criticism of its endless and sterile routine. Although the humaneness of the lawyer may weaken his symbolic role as a man of Wall Street, it does make him a person to whom the unconscious insights represented by Bartleby might arrive, and who would sympathize with and almost, in a limited sense, yield to Bartleby.

The frustrating sterility and monotony of the world which Bartleby enters is further shown in the portraits of the lawyer's two eccentric scriveners, Turkey and Nippers. These men display grotesque adjustments to and comically eccentric protests against the Wall Street world. Both of them are frustrated by their existences. Turkey spends most of his money for liquor, imbibing heavily at lunchtime, presumably to induce a false blaze of life which will help him to endure but which makes him useless for work during each afternoon. Nippers, on the other hand, needs no artificial stimulant; he possesses a crude radiance of his own, and in the mornings is "charged . . . with an irritable brandy-like disposition," but at this time of day his work is poor. Nippers can get through life in the office only with the aid of endless re-adjustments of his writing table; no matter how he places it, he is still uncomfortable. Both of these men are least serviceable when they are, in a sense, most alive. Turkey and Nippers combine automaton behavior, self-narcosis, and awkward attempts to preserve their individuality.

Entering this world of mildly smug self-satisfaction and mechanical behavior, Bartleby begins his work eagerly, "as if long famishing for something to copy." This action probably represents both a hunger for life and a desperate attempt to deaden his sensibilities among such sterile surroundings. Very soon, however, Bartleby evinces the first of his many refusals: he will not help to verify his copy against the original. Apparently Bartleby is willing to act within the lawyer's world, but he refuses all personal contact because it is spurious. His refusal is paradoxical, for he rejects the illusion of personality in an impersonal world by retreating to another kind of impersonality which alone makes that world endurable. His insistence that he "prefers not" to conform reflects both his gentleness and the profundity of his rejection of impersonality masking itself as personal contact. As such, it appropriately represents a voice deep within the lawyer himself, a desire to give over his mode of life. As the story progresses, Bartleby rejects all activity and refuses to leave; he has discovered that impersonality is not enough to help him endure this world. Bartleby clings to the lawyer because he represents a continuing protest within the lawyer's mind, whom he makes "stagger in his own plainest faith."

As Bartleby's passivity picks up momentum, he moves from the impersonality of copying to the impersonality of contemplating the dead, blind wall which fronts the window near his desk. This wall, and the prison walls "of amazing thickness" at the base of which Bartleby finally lies dead, parallel the images of the whale as "that wall shoved near to me" (Chapter 36) and of the whale's head as a "dead, blind wall" (Chapters 76 and 125) in *Moby-Dick*. Noting this parallel [in his "Melville's Parable of the Walls"], Leo Marx takes these images to represent the wall of death. I believe, however, that in both story and novel, they represent chiefly the terror and implacability of existence, against which Ahab actively and Bartleby passively revolt. Both men suggest that, in Ahab's words, "The dead, blind wall butts all inquiring heads at last" (Chapter 125). The wall may also symbolize those limitations which give every individual his personal identity, for Ahab's unwillingness to accept his limitations as a suffering man motivates his vindictive drive to pierce the wall.

The parallel between another image in **"Bartleby"** and a significant symbol in *Moby-Dick* adds to the likelihood that Bartleby represents a force in the lawyer's unconscious mind: Bartleby, "like the last column of some ruined temple . . . remained standing mute and solitary in the middle of the otherwise deserted room." This passage resembles a series of remarkable images which symbolize the unconscious part of Ahab: "those vast Roman halls of Thermes," where man's "awful essence sits . . . like a Caryatid . . . upholding on his frozen brow the piled entablature of ages" (Chapter 41).

The wall in **"Bartleby"** symbolizes the human condition in the society within which Bartleby feels trapped, and by extension the burden of his own identity within the limitations of such a society. The lawyer's establishment on Wall Street, and the wall which is ten feet from his window (Bartleby's is three feet from his), suggest his slighter awareness of his trapped human condition. When at the end Bartleby lies dead within the prison walls "of amazing thickness," he has succumbed to the impersonality of his society and to his inability to resist it actively. His assuming the foetal position in death, "his knees drawn up, and lying on his side, his head touching the cold stones," suggesting a passive retreat to the womb, seems the opposite of Ahab's desire to be a superman who will pierce the wall of limitations and identity.

However, the symbol of the prison walls is complicated by the appearance within them of a green turf and by the lawyer's exclamation to Bartleby, within the prison, "There is the sky, and here is the grass." These images of grass symbolize the creative possibilities of life. Bartleby's response to the lawyer's declaration is, "I know where I am," which is an accusation that the lawyer is responsible for Bartleby's incarceration in the prison of the world. The lawyer's sensitivity to both the validity of Bartleby's general protest and to the creative possibilities which it neglects indicates, I believe, that Bartleby represents a protest within the lawyer which has at least partially taken the form of a death drive. Parallel to this paradox is the fact that Bartleby's protest also resembles the protests of Turkey and Nippers, who combine self-effacement, self-assertion, and self-narcosis.

The concluding section of the story in which the lawyer seeks for a rational explanation of Bartleby's actions by reporting a rumor that he had worked in the dead letter office in Washington and so had become obsessed with human loneliness seems to me an artificial conclusion tacked on as a concession to popular taste. The lawyer's otherwise final statement that Bartleby lies asleep "with kings and counselors" is probably the story's authentic conclusion, for—despite the hopelessness of Bartleby's position—it attributes profundity and dignity to Bartleby's protest against the sterility of a spiritless society.

Melville, however, appears to intend further metaphysical speculation. The embodiment of a protest against sterility and impersonality in the passive and finally death-seeking Bartleby may suggest that man is hopelessly trapped by the human condition in an acquisitive society. Thus the lawyer may feel wisdom in Bartleby's final resignation as well as in his protest. The situation, however, is

---

On the Inscrutability of "Bartleby":

It is interesting to imagine what the response of the average reader of *Putnam's Magazine* must have been when he read Herman Melville's "Bartleby the Scrivener" in the November and December issues of 1853. He had little preparation for it, as it is a piece of fiction unlike any other he was likely to read in the contemporary periodicals. . . . It is one of those few stories in English, or any other language, which will continue to defy any definitive or generally satisfactory explication, and this may finally be its theme, of course—that the inscrutable does not yield one iota to the rational categories of existence.

. . . . .

My guess is that there will be no last word on this minor masterpiece, because Bartleby will continue to affirm his negative preference for another 125 years in the face of all efforts to fix him in a formulated phrase.

M. Thomas Inge, in a preface to Bartleby the Inscrutable: A Collection of Commentary on Herman Melville's Tale "Bartleby the Scrivener," *Archon Books, 1979.*

---

complicated by the likelihood that Bartleby appears as a protest within the lawyer's mind against his way of life, but this protest leads to death, and only the lawyer perceives the creative possibilities that Bartleby ignores.

I do not believe, however, that Melville was suggesting that the lawyer's way of life contained promises of creativity which Bartleby could not see. Rather he was suggesting the negative course which impulses represented by Bartleby might take, particularly when they emerge in a rather thoroughly sterile environment. Thus the story lacks a thematic resolution. Its conclusion creates not so

much a counter-criticism of Bartleby's passivity as an expression of quiet despair about the human predicament. The lawyer is not visibly changed after a struggle with his double, as are Dostoyevsky's Raskolnikov or Conrad's young sea captain in "The Secret Sharer." Neither does he succumb to an intense and destructive despair, although Bartleby has partially represented a subliminal death drive within him. However, the standstill to which the lawyer's insights have brought him does show Melville's imagination moving in the direction of the intense despair found in much contemporary literature.

Harold Kaplan (essay date 1972)

SOURCE: "Melville: 'One Royal Mantle of Humanity'," in *Democratic Humanism and American Literature,* The University of Chicago Press, 1972, pp. 159-97.

[*Kaplan is an American poet and critic. In the following excerpt, Kaplan explores the metaphysical implications of "Bartleby" by comparing Bartleby and* Moby Dick*'s Captain Ahab.*]

It would be plausible to read **"Bartleby the Scrivener"** as social criticism; the setting is Wall Street and the man is the palest of the imprisoned office clerks who could symbolize human alienation in modern bureaucratic and technological society. But most would agree that this would be as limited a reading as the same emphasis would be for Kafka. It has been reported by several critics, chief among them Lionel Trilling and Richard Chase, that American writers of the classic period had little interest in social realism, the depiction of life styles and manners, the analysis of specific social conflicts. The mistake, as I have said elsewhere, is to extend this judgment too far, in suggesting that the theme of their work is not man in society. This is precisely the most actively considered theme of Emerson, Thoreau, Hawthorne, Melville, and Whitman, but they write in terms of the *first* questions which associate with this theme and not the last. That is to say they write as if the problem of living in society had just been offered to men who were otherwise morally and intellectually complete. These were the men of the myth of America, stepping onto the soil of a new continent and preparing to establish a new society. As such they had no social experiences to describe but they did indeed have the most intense interest in the first principles of social relationships.

In this respect **"Bartleby"** is as much a legend for the primordial stages of human intercourse as **Moby Dick,** and as much as the latter its "social" theme is deeply intermixed with the metaphysical. This is true despite the fact that the scene is not the high seas and the personages are not the great beasts of nature and man in an atavistic contest with them. Bartleby is best understood as an inverted Captain Ahab; crushed into a small office space and now entirely deprived of either the will or the freedom to act, he nevertheless faces the same metaphysical wall or barrier to human freedom. Bartleby has lost more than a leg; he is barely left alive, but he is still capable of a muted, frozen rebellion. His inertia is as stubborn as Ahab's exertion; he won't be moved, he won't work, he won't be helped. "I would prefer not to," replaces "I'd strike the sun if it insulted me," but it is reasonable to see the parallel.

Bartleby is best understood as an inverted Captain Ahab; crushed into a small office space and now entirely deprived of either the will or the freedom to act, he nevertheless faces the same metaphysical wall or barrier to human freedom.

— *Harold Kaplan*

Certainly Ahab, after his address to the "Carpenter-God," would understand the hints of a grim education which Bartleby received working for the Dead-Letter Office. Those letters which never reach their destination are the chorus for another Job-like reproach, and Bartleby makes it, facing the wall outside the office window, and the wall of his prison as he dies. The prison is almost a melodramatic postscript to a life whose main feature is empty and pointless routine. Bartleby's world seems to have been ordained by a master whose intentions or interests are best characterized by the dry unreadable jargonized legal documents which Bartleby has been set to *copy* for the duration of his life. His home, it appears, is only that barren office in which his duties are performed. Anticipating his use of Captain Vere in *Billy Budd,* Melville puts special significance into the role of Bartleby's employer, the lawyer and original author of the documents. Like Vere he is a kind of surrogate god or providence who is nonplussed by his own creature, man. He says now and then, to cover his confusion and his random sense of guilt, that despite this or despite that, he found Bartleby "a useful man to me." That remains until Bartleby's refusals are complete and he must forcibly evict him. (It is characteristic for Melville to add another touch. The lawyer is a Master of Chancery, a sinecure position with no meaning or function, but he is quite resentful because it is about to be abolished.)

When Bartleby's refusals begin, it is with the small step of refusing to read what he has written. This actually may be the crucial point of his rebellion for he is thus exposing the possibility that the world's document is meaningless. Copying it would be something like an act of automatic life, like breathing or eating, but it does not pay much honor to the draft.

The subtlety of Bartleby's defiance lies in the effect of indicting his master and his fate. He will die in the principle by which he has been forced to live. Life faces a dead wall; he will do so. Man is a mechanically driven creature; he will be so. And yet finally he must say no,

like Ahab. Again he is more subtle than Ahab. "I would prefer not to" is a reduction of the will past hopelessness to inarticulate passive resistance. "He was a man of preferences rather than assumptions."

In the walled space of his existence, Bartleby, like Ahab, preserves a salient dignity. When the lawyer interrupts him in the early morning, he sends him away until he can dress and put away the meager personal articles in the bedroom-office. "I am occupied," he says. In his silence as well as his refusals, he keeps his independent though empty being.

But yet he does cling to the lawyer's premises, and he must in the end be pulled from the scene of his desiccated life and work. He dies finally before another wall, in the New York Tombs. Even as this is said the implications are clear. So other men live in their prison of life and the inhospitable universe. But more directly he means to haunt the lawyer's remorse. His protesting spirit seems to demand something from men and God, the more terribly as it seems unreasonable, silent, and stubborn. He has already understood the negatives of the Dead-Letter Office, but still he remains in his metaphysical prison, like the shadow in some universal conscience. "I know where I am," he says finally, peered at, from the jail windows, by "murderers and thieves."

"He's asleep, ain't he?"

"With kings and counselors."

"Bartleby" has a major role to play in the understanding of Melville's richest, sustained theme. Reflection at this point would show the sharp contrast but also the significant affinity with the later portrait of Billy Budd, as this in turn relates to Ahab. The pantheon in Melville's mind became complete; he had created three demigods of his fictional imagination. If we search for the stimulus we may find it in the image of "a certain tragic phase of humanity" that he found in Hawthorne's work and which he described [in a letter] as follows.

We mean the apprehension of the absolute condition of present things as they strike the eye of the man who fears them not, though they do their worst to him,— the man who, like Russia or the British Empire, declares himself a sovereign nature (in himself) amid the powers of heaven, hell, and earth. He may perish; but so long as he exists he insists upon treating with all Powers upon an equal basis. If any of those other Powers choose to withhold certain secrets, let them; that does not impair my sovereignty in myself; that does not make me tributary. And perhaps, after all, there is *no* secret.

These sentences, I believe, describe what was strongest in Melville's inspiration to write. With Ahab, Bartleby, and Billy Budd the sovereignty of a man is asserted against those rival powers and their secrets, and progressively in each case the secret diminishes in proportion to the increasing weight and significance of the man, until we are left finally with that sovereignty and no other.

Daniel Stempel and Bruce M. Stillians (essay date 1972-1973)

SOURCE: "*Bartleby the Scrivener:* A Parable of Pessimism," in *Nineteenth-Century Fiction,* Vol. 27, No. 1, 1972-73, pp. 268-82.

[*In the following essay, Stempel and Stillians consider "Bartleby" to be the result of Melville's interest in Schopenhauer.*]

In October 1853 a troubled Matthew Arnold explained why he had chosen to drop *Empedocles on Etna* from his new collection of poems. Certain situations, Arnold suggested, are intrinsically devoid of the power to provide "poetical enjoyment": "those in which the suffering finds no vent in action; in which a continuous state of mental distress is prolonged, unrelieved by incident, hope, or resistance; in which there is everything to be endured, nothing to be done. In such situations there is inevitably something morbid, in the description of them something monotonous" [*Poetical Works*]. And so, Empedocles, having chosen to leap into the crater of Etna in a fit of weltschmerz, was banished by the stern Victorian conscience of his creator. But the romantic pessimism which is as much a part of nineteenth-century literature as the optimistic faith in progress was not to be exorcised so easily, either from Arnold's poetry or from the work of his contemporaries.

Shortly after Arnold wrote this condemnation of the literature of futility, **"Bartleby the Scrivener"** appeared in two installments in *Putnam's Monthly Magazine* (November-December, 1853). Through one of the ironic coincidences of literary history, Melville's story exemplifies every one of the gloomy traits which Arnold had listed as fatal to "poetic enjoyment," but nevertheless survives as a masterpiece of what Unamuno has called "the tragic sense of life." It remains an enigmatic fable, an allegory with infinite reverberations, like one of Kafka's disturbingly matter-of-fact nightmares. And, like a Kafka narrative, it seems to elude all efforts to isolate the hidden frames of reference to which the play of symbols is linked by fragmentary allusions. But the task, if difficult, is not hopeless; one can at least begin with the most relevant data of sources, milieu, and biography, and chart the structure of the allegory by working from the known to the unknown. The historical approach cannot provide an "explanation" but it can give us a point of departure for a meaningful and focused discussion. In this instance, the fact that some months before the writing of **"Bartleby"** the first summary of Schopenhauer's philosophy in English was published in a periodical which was readily available to Melville forces us to consider the possibility that his acquaintance with Schopenhauer's pessimism began long before he bought Schopenhauer's works in the last years of his life.

On 1 April 1853, the *Westminster Review and Foreign Quarterly Review* published a survey of Schopenhauer's works under the title of "Iconoclasm in German Philosophy." This article, written by John Oxenford, was des-tined to become one of the landmarks of nineteenth-century intellectual history. Not only did it introduce Schopenhauer to the English-speaking world, it also catapulted the hitherto obscure philosopher into fame in his own country. Within a month the article was translated into German and published in the *Vossische Zeitung* (Berlin). Schopenhauer, whose command of English was excellent, praised Oxenford for the fidelity of his translations of excerpts from his works and in general was delighted by the article, which attacked the German academicians for failing to recognize the genius of a philosopher who was not a professor.

The *Westminster Review,* as Hugh W. Hetherington has pointed out [in his *Melville's Reviewers*], was one of a number of British magazines which were widely circulated in the United States, often arriving by fast steamer after a two-week crossing. Melville was an avid reader of the periodical press, and it is likely that he read the *Westminster Review,* if only to see whether his books had been included in the regular survey of American writing. The *Review* had printed a brief but favorable reference to Melville's work in 1852. It is not possible to determine exactly where and when Melville picked up the April issue because the opportunities were omnipresent. In May he was in New York to see his father-in-law off to Europe and it was his custom to go to the reading room of the New York Society Library and scan the latest periodicals. Further, he could have read the April issue in Boston at the Athenaeum or even in Pittsfield.

Granted the opportunity, what about the interest? Here the evidence is so strong as to rule out the possibility that he might have simply ignored the article. On his trip to Europe in 1849 Melville traveled with George J. Adler, professor of German at New York University. Adler, whom Melville described as "Coleridgean," was an enthusiastic student of German philosophy and lost no time in initiating his traveling companion into the mysteries of transcendental metaphysics, "Hegel, Schlegel, Kant, & c." [*Journal of a Visit to London and the Continent*]. And Melville was a far from unwilling listener as they strolled the deck talking of his favorite topics, "Fixed Fate, Free will, foreknowledge absolute" [*Journal*]. Nor did this interest wane when he returned and settled at Arrowhead. J. E. A. Smith of Pittsfield noted that after his day's work was finished Melville would join his family for "light reading—which was not so very light; as it included much less of what we commonly call 'light literature' than it did of profound reviews, abstruse philosophy in prose or verse, and the like."

In the spring and summer of 1853 Melville's personal circumstances perhaps made him more than usually receptive to any pessimistic evaluation of life. He was seeking desperately for an escape from the pressures of a career as a professional writer and finding it almost impossible to continue because of failing sight and mental strain. We can imagine, then, the strong impression which Oxenford's article must have made as Melville found his own intimations of a malignity inherent in the fabric of creation supported by Schopenhauer's metaphysics of an evil will as Kant's thing-in-itself. Even more important, Schopenhauer left one gate open in the gloomy prison of his system—he taught an ethic of total disengagement from life and its obligations, similar to that which Ishmael had sought at sea, but in Schopenhauer's philosophy carried to its ultimate and logical extreme.

Every reader of **"Bartleby the Scrivener"** is immediately struck by the obvious fact that Bartleby consistently avoids the use of the verb "to will" and substitutes "prefer." This eccentricity of speech first excites the curiosity of his employer and his fellow scriveners, then their wrath, and, finally, like an insidious contagion, infects their speech as well. It is the verbal symbol of that calm negation of which his employer sagely remarks, "nothing so aggravates an earnest person as a passive resistance." When the narrator, testing this strange phenomenon of denial, which is totally at odds with his own experience of the relationship between master and man, asks him to go to the post office, Bartleby replies, "I would prefer not to." His employer probes for the exact meaning of this baffling statement: "You *will* not?" and receives the equally emphatic reply, "I *prefer* not." Bartleby wills nothing—he merely prefers and this is the key to his enigmatic character.

In his discussion of Schopenhauer's ethical system Oxenford points out that his scale of values culminates in an ideal individual higher than the just or good man:

> Just as ignorant persons, who have a smattering knowledge of Berkeley, think that the good bishop regarded the whole world as a creation of the fancy, and that they can refute his disciples by giving them as actual (not metaphorical) rap on the knuckles, so doubtless there may be wiseacres, who will fancy that as Schopenhauer has declared the will to be the real essence of the world, and every human being a manifestation of that will, every human being is in a state of the most perfect freedom. Quite the reverse! With respect to the individual will, Schopenhauer is an absolute necessitarian, holding that the action of a certain motive on a certain character is as sure of producing a certain result, as an operation of agent upon patient in the sphere of mechanics. What may be a motive to one person may not be a motive to another, for the characters may be different; but given the character and the motive, the result is infallible. The absolute will, which lay beyond the jurisdiction of causality, has forced itself into the world of phenomena in an individual shape, and it must take the consequences, that is to say, a subjugation to that law of cause and effect by which the whole world of phenomena is governed, and which is equally potent in the discharge of a pistol and the performance of a virtuous action. The "character," which is the Idea of the human individual, just as gravitation is one of the Ideas of matter, is born with him, and cannot be altered. The knowledge of the individual may be enlarged, and consequently he may be put in a better track, by learning that his natural desires will be more gratified if he obeys the laws of society, than if he rises against them; but the character remains the same, although the cupidity which would have made a gamester or a highwayman, may become a constituent element in an honest tradesman. Thus every man brings his own depravity into the world with him, and this is the great doctrine of original sin, as set forth by Augustine, expounded by Luther and Calvin, and applauded by Schopenhauer, who, though a free-thinker in the most complete sense of the word, is absolutely delighted with the fathers and the reformers, when they bear witness to human degradation. The world of phenomena is a delusion—a mockery; and the fact of being born into such a world is in itself an evil.

> And now we may introduce Schopenhauer's ideal. The artist comes in for a large share of his respect, for he, without regard to selfish motives, contemplates the ideas which form the substrata of the world of phenomena, and reproduces them as the beautiful and the sublime. The good man, with his huge sympathy, is another estimable being; but higher still is he, who, convinced of the illusion of the world, is resolved to destroy it, as far as he is concerned, by extinguishing the will to live. Suicide will not answer this purpose. Suicide is a dislike of a particular chain of circumstances, which it endeavours to break through, but it is no alienation of the individual desires from life in general. Asceticism, that gradual extinction of all feelings that connect us with the visible world—the life of the anchorite in the Egyptian desert—of the Quietist of the time of Louis XIV,—of the Indian Fakeer, who goes through years of self-torture,—this is the perfection of Schopenhauer. The particular theological creed under which these saints performed their austerities is a matter of trivial importance,—they are all alike in the one grand qualification of holiness; they receded from the visible world and gradually extinguished the "will to live," till death, commonly so called, came as the completion of their wishes.

> In this asceticism consists the only possible freedom of the will. While acting in the world of phenomena the will becomes entangled in the law of causality, but now it recedes back to a region where that law can operate no more, and where it is consequently free. The freedom of the will is, in a word, annihilation, and this is the greatest boon that can be desired.

When Bartleby first appears, he already exhibits the stigmata of one of Schopenhauer's ascetic saints: "I can see that figure now—pallidly neat, pitiably respectable, incurably forlorn! It was Bartleby." There is an aura of holiness about him which impresses his employer, if not his fellow clerks. And it is precisely because there is no "particular theological creed" to provide an external frame of values that the story becomes an absurd parable. The passion of Bartleby is played out against a background of comic Dickensian clerks, pompous lawyers, and all the money changers of Wall Street. His passing affects no one except himself and the narrator. The world goes on, pursuing its illusions, but Bartleby is no longer part of it, and his employer, shaken by his brief glimpse of the real nature of things, is left a much sadder and a somewhat wiser man. Thus, the structure of the tale is developed from the interaction of the narrator, the smug and comfortable attorney, and the "forlorn" Bartleby.

In the opening paragraph the narrator makes it clear that all that we can know of Bartleby is what he knows: "What my own astonished eyes saw of Bartleby, *that* is all I know of him, except, indeed, one vague report, which will appear in the sequel." As a result of this deliberate restriction of viewpoint, if Bartleby is a Schopenhauerian saint, we must remember that we are looking at him through the wrong end of the telescope, through the eyes of a man to whom he is a strangely magnetic riddle of obscure motivations—at best, eccentric; at worst, mad; in any event, incomprehensible. The complacent storyteller begins by congratulating himself on his estimable character and circumstances and unknowingly reveals that he is certainly the opposite of an ascetic. He has always acted on the belief that "the easiest way of life is the best." Without too much effort, he has managed to do a "snug business" and is known as a "safe" man, prudent and methodical. He is interested only in questions of legality, not morality, as he reveals when he bemoans the abolition of the office of Master in Chancery, which he has held: "It was not a very arduous office, but very pleasantly remunerative." He makes no mention of the fact that the remuneration usually comes from the property left to widows and orphans. In short, at the beginning of his story, the lawyer is what Oxenford describes as Schopenhauer's just man: "The just man, who is just, and nothing more, stands higher in the moral scale than the bad man, but he has not reached Schopenhauer's idea of virtue. He so far shows a sympathy with his fellow-creatures that he does not encroach upon their rights, but he is equally unwilling to go out of his way to do them any substantial good. He is a sort of man who pays his taxes and his church-rates, keeps clear of the Court of Requests and is only charitable when he has an equivalent in the shape of an honourable place in a subscription list."

When Bartleby enters the office, he is assigned a place in his employer's room behind a folding screen. His desk is close to a small window which opens on a brick wall three feet away. In this confined space, Bartleby does "an extraordinary quantity of writing," day and night, but he does it "silently, palely, mechanically," with no evidence of cheerfulness or vitality. In contrast, the copyists in the outer office are both so energetic in their own eccentric way that they seem to be driven by some demonic inner force—as indeed they are, from Schopenhauer's standpoint. After his noon meal, Turkey the Englishman becomes "altogether too energetic," is noisy, blots his pages, and exhibits "a strange, inflamed, flurried, flighty recklessness of activity." Nippers, his American colleague, is the "victim of two evil powers—ambition and indigestion." He is possessed by another form of generalized violence—grinds his teeth, constantly adjusts his desk, and mutters maledictions under his breath.

But Bartleby copies documents—and that is all he will do. When he is asked to verify his copies, he refuses in "a singularly mild, firm voice": "I would prefer not to." He repeats this formula three times, without offering any reasons, yet maintaining his composure. His employer is at a loss: "Had there been the least uneasiness, anger, impatience or impertinence in his manner; in other words,

had there been anything ordinarily human about him, doubtless I should have dismissed him from the premises. But as it was, I should have as soon thought of turning my pale plaster-of-paris bust of Cicero out of doors." He senses that Bartleby is not like other men, that there is something unmoved and unmoving in Bartleby, like the pallid bust of the old Roman. In a second encounter he receives the same answer, and again the strange charisma of Bartleby restrains his employer: "With any other man I should have flown outright into a dreadful passion, scorned all further words, and thrust him ignominiously from my presence. But there was something about Bartleby that not only strangely disarmed me, but, in a wonderful manner, touched and disconcerted me." The lawyer grasps the fact that this is not some arbitrary caprice, that while Bartleby feels the request is quite reasonable, he has some "paramount consideration" that takes precedence. Although he appeals to common sense by enlisting the support of other clerks, this has no more effect than his appeal to reason. Bartleby returns to his little niche, his "hermitage," as his employer now has unconsciously fallen into the habit of referring to it. He is, to use Oxenford's descriptive phrase, like "the anchorite in the Egyptian desert," an ascetic who is gradually contracting the span of his activity, withdrawing from the visible world.

Unable to cope with the remarkable behavior of Bartleby, the narrator is forced to rationalize his own inexplicable reaction in terms of his quid pro quo philosophy, the ethic of the just man. He pities Bartleby as an involuntary eccentric and consoles himself with the thought that his generosity will be rewarded by "laying up in my soul what will eventually prove to be a sweet morsel for my conscience." The conditions laid down by Bartleby are tacitly accepted: he copies documents, but he prefers not to do anything else, even the smallest errand. And so, for the moment, he remains secure in his hermitage.

The next crucial incident in the relationship between master and clerk comes on a Sunday morning, when the lawyer, on his way to Trinity Church, stops at his office and finds himself locked out by Bartleby. The locking out is symbolic as well as literal—what the lawyer discovers in his office will mark his passage from self-satisfaction and unconcern to a new compassion. In his usual mild-mannered way Bartleby asks his master to return after walking around the block two or three times, since he is busy and prefers not to admit him. When he returns, he discovers that Bartleby has gone, and, investigating his hermitage, he concludes that Bartleby has been living in his little corner. It is not Bartleby's apparent poverty that strikes him with sudden horror, it is the thought of the dreadful solitude of Wall Street on a Sunday morning or at night—"an emptiness."

At this point, the just man begins to experience the unfamiliar pangs that mark the birth of a new consciousness of suffering: "For the first time in my life a feeling of overpowering stinging melancholy seized me." The source of this new awareness is simply compassion: "The bonds of a common humanity drew me irresistibly to gloom. A fraternal melancholy! For both I and Bartleby were sons of Adam." The just man has now reached that stage of enlightenment where he can broaden his sensibility to include all mankind—he has become a good man, in the sense in which Oxenford describes him: "The good man . . . is he whose heart beats with sympathy for all creatures around him, practically if not theoretically acknowledging them as manifestations of the same great Will as himself. He loves every living being, from his neighbour down to a turtle-dove. . . ." The lawyer now sees that there is as much misery as happiness in the world and has "presentiments of strange discoveries." He seems to see Bartleby dead, "laid out, among uncaring strangers." Much as he may wish to pass off this new mood as "sad fancyings" of a "sick and silly brain," the fact remains that he, at least, can no longer play the role of an "uncaring stranger."

Opening Bartleby's desk, he finds a savings bank, knotted up in a handkerchief. This removes the one motive that, to his methodical mind, might have justified Bartleby's behavior—poverty. And the lawyer reviews that behavior: Bartleby's silence, never voluntarily broken; his long reveries before the blank wall opposite his window; his self-imprisonment in his hermitage; and his "pallid haughtiness," that totally self-possessed and deliberate withdrawal from life which not merely disarms but "awes" his employer into "a tame compliance with his eccentricities." The result of this meditation is what the narrator calls "a prudential feeling"—we remember that he has boasted that his first "grand point" is prudence. Melville's lawyer instinctively reacts as Arnold reacted in his preface to the contemplation of a situation "in which a continuous state of mental distress is prolonged, unrelieved by incident, hope, or resistance." Like Arnold, he feels that the absolute "forlornness" of Bartleby is simply painful, not tragic:

> So true it is, and so terrible, too, that up to a certain point the thought or sight of misery enlists our best affections; but, in certain special cases, beyond that point it does not. They err who would assert that this is owing to the inherent selfishness of the human heart. It rather proceeds from a certain hopelessness of remedying excessive and organic ill. To a sensitive being, pity is not seldom pain. And when at last it is perceived that such pity cannot lead to effectual succor, common sense bids the soul be rid of it. What I saw that morning convinced me that the scrivener was the victim of innate and incurable disorder. I might give alms to his body; but his body did not pain him; it was his soul that suffered, and his soul I could not reach.

While this passage is an acute and perceptive intuition of the nature of Bartleby's malady, which is metaphysical, not physical, we must keep in mind the fact that it is Bartleby who is enlightened, not his master. He has had a brief glimpse of the unbearable truth which, for the protection of ordinary men like himself, is veiled by the illusions that are necessary for the conduct of daily living. As John Oxenford remarks,

> All that the liberal mind looks forward to with hope, if not with confidence—the extension of political rights,

the spread of education, the brotherhood of nations, the discovery of new means of subduing stubborn nature—must be given up as a vain dream, if ever Schopenhauer's doctrine be accepted. In a word, he is a professed "Pessimist"; it is his grand result, that this is the worst of all possible worlds; nay, so utterly unsusceptible of improvement, that the best thing we can do is to get rid of it altogether, by a process which he very clearly sets forth.

Bartleby has already made the choice which initiates this process, the single free act of which man is capable, and then only through the refining process of great suffering: the denial of the will to live. This is the incurable and innate "disorder" which reflects the unspoken "paramount consideration" that inspires Bartleby's negative preferences. It opposes and negates every value which the Master in Chancery, that cheerful lover of life, cherishes. Thus, even the mere contemplation of Bartleby's passive but unfaltering withdrawal from the world stuns and repels him; it points toward a conclusion which, for him, is literally unthinkable, like the "horror" of Conrad's dying Kurtz. That morning the lawyer does not go to church: "Somehow the things I had seen disqualified me for the time for church-going."

Bartleby remains in the office, preferring to do nothing but his copying, and his employer continues to seek for new methods of drawing him back into the stream of life. But it is Bartleby who dominates the office, not his employer, who, to his dismay, finds that he and his staff are falling into the habit of using "prefer."

The lawyer resolves once more to dismiss Bartleby, but a new development offers him an opportunity to diagnose Bartleby's malady as a physical disorder, causally explicable, and therefore quite forgivable. Bartleby announces that he has "given up copying" and the lawyer, seeing that his eyes appear "dull and glazed," jumps to the conclusion that he has impaired his vision by working in poor light. Now Bartleby does nothing at all, and his presence becomes even more irritating, especially since it soon becomes obvious that his reason for giving up copying has nothing to do with his health. He is given six days notice, but mutely rejects all proposals, threats, or bribes, and remains "like the last column of some ruined temple . . . standing mute and solitary in the middle of the otherwise deserted room."

The narrator, becoming more and more disturbed, is at the same time experiencing an expansion of knowledge which opens up new vistas of his own character as well as Bartleby's. He has lived in a world of reassuringly predictable cause and effect. His clerks change their moods regularly according to the clock which measures their working day. He seeks for explanations that will fit this familiar pattern of causality and is driven to metaphysical musings on predestination and free will, pondering the relationship between guilt and responsibility. He feels that like the "hapless Colt," he is capable of murdering his tormentor. "But," he goes on, "when this old Adam of resentment rose in me and tempted me concerning Bartleby, I grappled and threw him. How? Why, by simply recalling the divine injunction: 'A new commandment give I unto you, that ye love one another.' Yes, it was this that saved me." His motive may be the same as Colt's but his character is different. Although he still comforts himself with the just man's maxims of enlightened self-interest, it is clear that he is, at heart, a good man, and that Bartleby's "holiness" has touched him deeply, bringing to the surface that deep love for others which is characteristic of this ethical genotype.

Nevertheless, as an "eminently safe man," the narrator finds comfort in reading explanations that stress strict causality and deny human freedom, "Edwards on the Will" and "Priestley on Necessity," and comes to the conclusion that all of this has been fated by an "all-wise Providence" and that to shelter Bartleby is "the predestined purpose of my life." Between the narrator and Bartleby lies the insurmountable barrier that divides necessity from freedom, illusion from reality. Edwards specifically refutes Locke's distinction between "prefer" and "will"; Joseph Priestley uses the two words without noting any difference. Both insist on absolute determinism; they deny that the chain of cause and effect can be broken by any act of the will. Schopenhauer, however, as Oxenford points out, teaches that there is one free decision, limited to those few who can understand the nature of life and renounce it: "In this asceticism consists the only possible freedom of the will." Bartleby's negative preferences are not acts of willing—they are acts of not-willing.

As in a medieval morality play, the narrator is torn between good and evil impulses; his compassion for Bartleby conflicts with his attachment to the world of illusion, Wall Street. He cannot oust Bartleby, for that is a cruelty that he will not inflict on a "helpless creature," and yet he cannot let him remain in his office and ruin his professional reputation. He resolves to leave Bartleby where he is and move his office elsewhere, but, curiously, he finds it difficult to part from the man whom he is fleeing.

Having shifted the responsibility for Bartleby's shelter to someone less tenderhearted, he finds that Bartleby has indeed been evicted from his hermitage, but haunts the building day and night. Finally confronting Bartleby he reduces the situation to its bare logical bones: "Now one of two things must take place. Either you must do something or something must be done to you." He suggests a number of possible occupations to all of which Bartleby is indifferent. Baffled, he even offers to take Bartleby to his home until he can arrive at some decision, but Bartleby replies, "No, at present I would prefer not to make any change at all." This answer, which defies all the logic of law and hardheaded finance, the courts and Wall Street, causes the narrator to flee again, fearing the anger of the landlord and the new tenants. But Bartleby in his own fashion is quite consistent; he is narrowing down the circle of his actions until he reaches the center, the "still point of the turning world," and ceases to exist.

Melville's parable of the Schopenhauerian saint in a depraved world reaches its climax in the Tombs, the prison in which Bartleby is confined after being arrested for vagrancy. His former employer, who has not deserted him after all, finds him in his usual position, his face turned toward a high wall in complete indifference, "while all around, from the narrow slits of the jail windows, I thought I saw peering out upon him the eyes of murderers and thieves." It is in this symbolic isolation that Bartleby states his last negative preference, "I prefer not to dine today," and slips away quietly from life into "annihilation," free of all will and all pain.

The epilogue to the tale is that "vague report" which the narrator mentions in his opening paragraph. Bartleby, it seems, was a clerk in the Dead Letter Office, and his employer muses over the possibility that, given Bartleby's character, "by nature and misfortune prone to a pallid hopelessness," nothing could have been worse for him than the opening and destruction of letters which have not been delivered but "on errands of life . . . speed to death."

But this epilogue, supplied as an "explanation" of Bartleby's tragic decline, fails like every other rational explanation offered by the narrator. It tells us nothing of real importance about Bartleby, but it does indicate that a deep and irreversible change has taken place in the narrator. Actually, the safe man, the successful lawyer, is far more complex than the enigmatic Bartleby. When one grasps the significance of the end toward which Bartleby is moving, his course appears ruthlessly linear. Having made the one free decision of which any man is capable, the choice of the extinction of the will to live, he allows nothing to turn him aside. In contrast, the narrator wavers, torn by an inner conflict. For him Bartleby represents a negation of values which he has never questioned, the values of his social group, and, more important, the value of existence itself. On the one side, native shrewdness and a prudent selfishness counsel that there must be a reasonable explanation for Bartleby's martyrdom; on the other, a still small voice cries out from the depths that suffering and existence are one and the same, that all men share Bartleby's pain, if not his wisdom.

The symbol of the dead letters is ambivalent precisely because it serves as the focus for this inner conflict in the closing paragraphs. What can be more depressing, the narrator wonders, than to open these letters which bring hope and relief and have never reached their destinations? This seems reasonable until the reader asks why, to be completely rational about the matter, the narrator does not seem to be aware that dead letters may contain bad news as well as good and that a clerk in the Dead Letter Office might spend much of his time disposing of unpaid bills! It is evident that Melville has deliberately emphasized one aspect of his analogy and suppressed the other in order to move the symbol of the dead letter out of the realm of normal everyday probability and into the realm of theology—or atheology. These letters, like the long-awaited blessing of grace which releases man from the slavery of his own will, never arrive. And so, despite his turning up of a "reason" for Bartleby's defection from life, the narrator concludes his story with a double sigh, "Ah, Bartleby! Ah, humanity!" That deep intuitive compassion which Bartleby has stirred in him testifies against all reason that Bartleby's fate is man's fate.

In 1856 Melville visited Hawthorne in England and spent several days with him at Southport. "Melville," Hawthorne noted in his journal, "as he always does, began to reason of Providence and futurity, and of everything that lies beyond human ken, and informed me that he had 'pretty much made up his mind to be annihilated'; but still he does not seem to rest in that anticipation; and, I think, will never rest until he gets hold of a definite belief." Hawthorne also noted that Melville had been afflicted with neuralgic complaints in the head and limbs and that "his writings, for a long while past, have indicated a morbid state of mind." He seemed to Hawthorne "a little paler and a little sadder."

Perhaps **"Bartleby the Scrivener"** was the journal of a descent into that valley of the shadow which Schopenhauer had charted for the nineteenth century, a metaphysical desert in which so many perished. "It is strange how he persists," Hawthorne mused, "and has persisted ever since I knew him, and probably long before—in wandering to-and-fro over these deserts as dismal and monotonous as the sand hills amid which we were sitting."

Morton Kaplan and Robert Kloss (essay date 1973)

SOURCE: "Fantasy of Passivity: Melville's *Bartleby the Scrivener*," in *The Unspoken Motive: A Guide to Psychoanalytic Literary Criticism,* The Free Press, 1973, pp. 63-79.

[*In the following excerpt, Kaplan and Kloss insist that Bartleby exhibits symptoms of manic-depression, and contend that the narrator's veneer of passivity is a neurotic attempt to repress underlying impulses toward aggression and violence.*]

Melville's **"Bartleby the Scrivener"** is a work of comic irony comparable to such novels as Ford's *The Good Soldier* or Durrell's *Justine,* both of which use the device of fallible narrator. In *The Good Soldier,* for instance, Dowell is an unperceptive, sentimental, sexually impotent man, married to an immoral sensualist. The focus of the novel is not the inevitable failure of the marriage, but the very efforts of this man—who has never felt toward his wife "the beginnings of a trace of what is called the sex instinct"—to comprehend and describe that failure. So long as he cannot acknowledge the importance of sexuality in human relationships his narrative vision is corrupted, and that is the whole point of the story. . . .

Melville's narrator is no less enmeshed in an effort to explain events beyond his comprehension. And the manner in which the author enables us to understand both the causes and the extent of that limitation rivals the full artistry of Ford's achievement.

"I am," this narrator writes, "a man who, from his youth upwards, has been filled with a profound conviction that the easiest way of life is the best." This belief, he tells us, has made him a certain kind of unambitious lawyer, one who can "in the cool tranquility of a snug retreat, do a snug business among rich men's bonds." And for thirty years he allows nothing to invade this peace—until he hires the scrivener Bartleby. The conflict which follows seems on the surface no more than an obscure antagonism in a Wall Street office, between the narrator and an employee who will not work. But in fact they collide with a force as intense as any which may bedevil two men. With precise accuracy, Bartleby undermines the tenuous code by which this lawyer has lived. The narrator's passivity, prudence, and life-long obsession with safety are all challenged with uncanny success. And as he continues to describe these events, he never suspects the nature of the role he himself has played.

The main character of the story (or so the narrator believes) is Bartleby, a pale, silent scrivener who comes in to his employ. At first Bartleby does an extraordinary amount of writing, but he refuses to do any other work, objecting each time with the incongruous remark that he "would prefer not to." Angry and astonished at this challenge to his authority, the narrator nevertheless allows Bartleby to remain, because of his ceaseless industry as copyist. But as the days follow, the complete oddity of the man becomes apparent. He lives at night in the office, associates with no one, never speaks except to answer (and not always then), never leaves the office, eats nothing but ginger nuts, and with increasing frequency stands unmoving, either in the center of the room or looking out the window at a "dead brick wall." At last the scrivener declares he will do no further work of any kind. When the narrator concludes that Bartleby is the victim of an incurable disorder and fires him at last, he finds that Bartleby would prefer not to be dismissed and would prefer not to leave the office.

Even under these conditions, the narrator allows Bartleby to remain, thinking that to do so is an act of charity and a service to God. But when his clients and colleagues all begin to talk about the strange, immobile apparition in his office, the narrator can tolerate Bartleby no longer. Unable to simply put him out, the lawyer himself moves, locating his office elsewhere. For a time Bartleby is still successful in refusing to change his life. Turned out of the office by the landlord and the new tenant, he haunts the building, "sitting upon the banisters of the stairs by day, and sleeping in the entry by night." In order to avoid any publicity, the narrator now tries to persuade the scrivener to find a new job, and even to come home with him until a job can be found. But Bartleby refuses in his usual manner, and at last is taken to prison as a vagrant. There, emaciated by his refusal to eat, he stares at a dead-wall in the yard, and finally dies in a foetal position at its base.

The narrator ends his story with what he calls a "suggestive rumor," that Bartleby once worked in a dead-letter office. "Conceive a man by nature and misfortune prone to a pallid hopelessness," he concludes, "can any business seem more fitted to heighten it than that of continually handling these dead letters, and assorting them for the flames?" But this is a maudlin view of Bartleby's character. The thought that there is a faulty communication among men may cause distress, but not madness. The world is full of grave-diggers, hangmen, and asylum attendants, who do not become Bartlebys. The narrator errs, and ascribes a factitious cause to Bartleby's derangement, because he fails to see the motivation behind such bizarre and self-destructive behavior. We can well understand why it is difficult enough to perceive the motivation implicit in *neurotic* behavior; and Bartleby's derangement, by almost any standards a psychosis, all the more completely masks the underlying motivation which directs him to his dead-wall reveries. The narrator has, in addition, his own reasons for misconstruing Bartleby's purposes. But if we take our cue from the psychoanalytic view, specifically of a manic-depressive psychosis, much in the text will support this understanding of the man.

Bartleby's disorder may be termed a psychosis because his surrender to symptoms is so complete that he breaks with reality. He makes no effort whatever to communicate with others, to end his depression, or break out of his immobile stupor—in short, no effort to comply with basic needs, including the need to eat. So complete is his submission that we have no reason to believe he is aware that anything is wrong. His comment, that he would prefer not to work, is like a later remark, when he is emaciated to the point of death, that he would prefer not to eat dinners. The language is rationally put, but the sense is bizarre and alien to rational goals. He speaks of "preferences," but no alternatives seem possible to him. Such behavior conforms with that of the manic-depressive. [In his "Manic-depressive Psychosis",] Silvano Arieti's description of the depressive stupor of this disorder seems almost to have been written as a portrait of Bartleby:

> Depressive stupor is the most pronounced form of depression. Here there is more than retardation: the movements are definitely inhibited or suppressed. The patients are so absorbed in their own pervading feeling of depression that they cannot focus their attention on their surroundings. They do not seem to hear; they do not respond. They are mute, with the exception of some occasional utterances. Since they cannot focus on anything, they give the impression of being apathetic, whereas they are actually the prey of a deep, disturbing emotion. These patients cannot take care of themselves. Generally, they lie in bed mute, and have to be spoon-fed.

> Unless they are successfully treated during the attack, physical health may suffer severely. They lose up to a hundred pounds in certain cases. . . .

This description accords well with Bartleby's immobility, apathy, and helplessness. But the only clue it offers to the inner motivation of the man is the comment that beneath the depression is disturbing emotion. But, we may ask, what is the nature of an emotion so uncompromising that it renders him incapable of both sanity and life? The basis for an answer is given in various ways by the story itself. Bartleby, after all, has an extraordinary effect on the small

world in which he lives. If we dismiss his passivity as simply a crazed negation of life, we miss the fact that in his own bizarre fashion he achieves a great deal. If we look, in fact, with a disinterested eye at the towering strength with which he refuses to comply with the demands of his world, and at the shattering effect he has on the man who represents that world to him, we will find he achieves an absolute "adjustment" on his own terms. Like a fallen Satan, Bartleby gives up one world to reign in another. The choice may be an insane one, but it is not without its own motivation.

The keynote to Bartleby's psychology is given in a superb description of the underlying dynamics of depressive behavior, by Walter Bonime. Dr. Bonime writes out of a psychoanalytic practice with depressives and with a theoretical orientation well-defined and fruitful. He points out that the psychotic person exhibits crucial attributes also found in the neurotic—specifically, that both are engaged in purposive behavior and that those purposes are best understood in the context of their social action. [In his "The Psychodynamics of Neurotic Depression,"] he offers a description of the depressive individual that brings us directly to the motives of the scrivener:

> . . . the depressive is an extremely manipulative individual who, by helplessness, sadness, seductiveness, and other means, maneuvers people toward the fulfillment of demands for various forms of emotionally comforting response. The emotional and behavioral corollary to this extreme manipulativeness is an almost allergic sensitivity to being influenced; this engenders forms of elusiveness manifested in helplessness, withdrawal, physical and mental retardation, manic behavior, stubbornness, irresponsibility, unproductive preoccupying activities, and various types of failure and self-destruction.

The manipulativeness of the depressive is the most significant fact of this description. Behind apparent apathy there is purposive action. The man who "would prefer" to do nothing, on the contrary, indulges in the power to frustrate. It is a grim battle in which the depressive spares himself least of all. Dr. Bonime vividly describes this tenacity in terms which again bring Bartleby directly to mind:

> The depressive is determined to prevail, to win in every interpersonal encounter. For him life is a battle—with individuals and with fate. He is going to get what he wants, and he is not going to be forced to exert himself responsibly in pursuit of a more realistic goal. . . . He will sacrifice some or all of his potentials for living, but in his subjective, distorted, competitive emotional orientation he will nevertheless be victorious.

> In the competitive world of the depressive, this rebellion is a living declaration that "Nobody's going to make me do anything, nobody can force me to respond." The depressive even carries this out by escape into psychosis or suicide, in which extreme instances the process may be a charade of "You can't make me live on your terms," or "at all."

This description of the uncompromising depressive is the criterion by which to judge Bartleby. To understand how successful he is in these terms, however, we must look again at the narrator. It is in the interaction between them that Bartleby's victory is enacted. And behind the self-deceptions of the narrator's story, the force of that victory is unmistakable.

Bartleby enacts his depression in the company of an antagonist exquisitely picked. There could hardly be imagined an interlocking of disorders greater than that which exists between the narrator and his scrivener. They are as intricately joined by nature and temperament as Othello to Iago, or Mario to the magician Cipolla. The narrator has lived all his life out of the reach of conflict, evidently with amazing success. He is now confronted in Bartleby with a man who must not only be fired, but forcibly taken from his office—if not directly by him, then by the police at his command. This would seem to be a not very difficult task, even for a peaceable man. He has, after all, no other rational choice, and morality and the law are on his side. But the difficulty of the task should not be judged solely on the basis of external obstacles. One is reminded of Hamlet, the man with no compunctions about killing and with all the motivation and opportunity he needs to kill, who yet delays so long he must at last exclaim:

> I do not know
> Why yet I live to say "This thing's to do,"
> Sith I have cause, and will, and strength, and
>   means
> To do't.

As the story gradually makes clear, the difficulty for Melville's narrator, as much as for Hamlet, is within the mind.

The first confrontation takes place shortly after Bartleby is hired. The scrivener has already indicated manic-depressive behavior, in the unnatural intensity of his diligence: the narrator tells us that "he did an extraordinary quantity of writing. As if long famishing for something to copy, he seemed to gorge himself on my documents. There was no pause for digestion. He ran a day and night line, copying by sun-light and by candle-light." And we see something of the melancholia which underlies the mania, in the narrator's observation that Bartleby "wrote on silently, palely, mechanically." But when Bartleby is asked to proofread documents—a standard part of any clerk's duties—he replies, as he invariably will, that he would prefer not to. His employer sits for a time in "perfect silence, rallying [his] stunned faculties." Understandably, and almost the last time his response to Bartleby will be so rational, he decides that either Bartleby misheard him or he misheard the reply.

He repeats his request, but Bartleby, in his unvarying way, states that he "would prefer not to." "Are you moon-struck?" the narrator asks in high excitement, striding across the room. "Moon-struck" is a fair enough appraisal of the scrivener, but the narrator has merely put the question rhetorically. It will be a considerable time, a reveal-ingly long time, before he considers again the question of Bartleby's sanity. On this occasion, when the scrivener voices again his refusal, the lawyer returns to his desk. Now he tells himself that he would have "violently dismissed" Bartleby from the premises, were it not for his peaceable manner. He writes that he would have "as soon thought of turning my pale plaster-of-paris bust of Cicero out of doors," and concludes that he is too hurried by business to take any corrective action.

There is something odd in all of this. The refusal of an employee to do his job should be equally objectionable in any tone of voice. And when the narrator concludes that he is hurried by business, he has in fact already retreated from Bartleby across the room to his desk. Equating his clerk with a plaster-of-paris bust of Cicero is perhaps understandable, given the scrivener's pale, inexpressive face. But to justify inaction on the basis of this resemblance seems far-fetched, even bizarre. Most curious is his comment that he would have *violently* dismissed Bartleby if the scrivener had been an ordinary man. An ordinary man can be simply told to go. If he wishes to save face because of his own passivity, we would expect him to refer to an *immediate,* not violent, dismissal.

On the second occasion that the scrivener is asked, and refuses, to proofread, the narrator responds in much the same way. He writes that he is "momentarily turned into a pillar of salt," and that with "any other man I should have flown outright into a dreadful passion, scorned all further words, and thrust him ignominiously from my presence. But there was something about Bartleby that not only strangely disarmed me, but in a wonderful manner, touched and disconcerted me." We note that he still imagines violence, which he refers to now as a "dreadful passion," as his only alternative to inaction. There is, in this repeated association to violence, the suggestion that he is passive with Bartleby because, for him, *any* action implies getting violent. We may recall that he has carefully shunned conflict all his life, made himself an eminently safe and prudent man and, as he puts it, suffered nothing ever to invade his peace. One wonders why such a design for living has been necessary. Perhaps, we can begin to infer, the overriding motive of his life has been a struggle to contain violence latent within him, violence needing only the smallest conflict to set it off.

If this is the case, if the "cool tranquility" of his "snug retreat" is a defense against his own murderous aggression, it becomes clear why he should so weakly suffer a clerk's challenge to his authority and why he works so hard to sustain his passivity with rationalizations. He must have the idea, however unconsciously, that were he to act in anger, he might kill the scrivener. There is a subtle measure of support for this view in his allusion to Lot's wife. He may choose the metaphor with the thought that he is himself as inert as a pillar of salt. But there is the suggestion, too, that he is paralyzed by the sight of destructive rage—not God's, but his own. He seems to sense the presence of this unconscious motivation with his comment that he is "strangely disarmed" in a "wonderful manner." "Strange" and "wonderful" often imply, as we have seen elsewhere, a sense of unconscious motivation. And the term "disarmed" itself suggests the prevention of violence.

The theme of passivity as a defense is underscored by what follows. He turns to his other employees for support, which they readily give. One of them thinks it perfectly right that Bartleby should be asked to proofread, another declares the scrivener should be "kicked" from the office, and a third thinks the scrivener is a "luny." Theirs is the realistic and normal response, reached without effort. We see how simply the problem can be solved when no unconscious inhibition intervenes. It is revealing enough that the narrator should need their guidance in the first place, and even more so that he now ignores it, concluding once again that he is too busy to face the problem.

And so, in the following scenes, we have the picture of a man who only partially suspects the extent of his ambivalence and who alternates between extremes of anger and abject surrender. Each time he surrenders, he offers himself new grounds to justify doing so. He decides that Bartleby "means no mischief" and "intends no insolence"; that his "eccentricities are involuntary"; that with a less indulgent employer Bartleby might be "driven forth miserably to starve"; and that in consequence he can get along with Bartleby notwithstanding his behavior. Finally, and by this time not surprisingly, Bartleby is permanently excused from anything he would prefer not to do—which is to say, everything but the work of copying. As the narrator tells us:

> His steadiness, his freedom from all dissipation, his incessant industry (except when he chose to throw himself into a standing revery behind his screen), his great stillness, his unalterableness of demeanor under all circumstances, make him a valuable acquisition.

In short, he converts a depressed and recalcitrant clerk with tendencies to catatonic stupor into a fortunate gain for the office; a piece of legerdemain designed solely to persuade himself. His argument leaves conveniently out of account what a painful experience for him surrender has been. For instance, he writes that he "could not, for the very soul of me, avoid falling into sudden spasmodic passions with him. For it was difficult to bear in mind all the time those strange peculiarities, privileges, and unheard of exemptions . . .". And, although he cannot let himself get angry, his repressed anger forces him back again and again to new confrontation. We read that "the passiveness of Bartleby sometimes irritated me. I felt strangely goaded on to encounter him in new opposition— to elicit some angry spark from him answerable to my own." He is caught between an anger he can neither effectively repress nor translate into action, so that each time he must be humiliated by the very encounter he has brought about. As he writes on one such occasion:

> I staggered to my desk, and sat there in a deep study. My blind inveteracy returned. Was there any other

thing in which I could procure myself to be ignominiously repulsed by this lean, penniless wight?— my hired clerk? What added thing is there, perfectly reasonable, that he will be sure to refuse to do?

That "added thing" is Bartleby's refusal, one Sunday morning, even to admit his employer into the office (Bartleby has been living there and is not yet ready to open the door). It is the ultimate degradation for the narrator, who "slinks away," in spite of "sundry twinges of impotent rebellion." He keeps repeating to himself, as he goes, that his inaction is the result of Bartleby's "wonderful mildness," but this explanation, as usual, begs the question. He never examines *why* this mildness should have such an effect on him. Even the language he uses beclouds the issue. For instance, he writes that he is "awed into a tame compliance" by the "austere reserve," of his clerk's "eccentricities." Were he to describe Bartleby's behavior more accurately as crazed and now criminal, his own situation would become intolerable. He would have to end his passivity, something he cannot do, or begin to question his own sanity, something he does not wish to do.

The insistence that it is Bartleby's mildness which is the narrator's undoing is not, however, without an element of truth. Walter Bonime's central point about the psychodynamics of depression is worth recalling in this connection: that it is a passive means to defy, manipulate, and defeat the world. The virtue of passivity is that it masks aggression under the guise of helpless suffering—a mask useful not only to prevent retaliation by the world, but to conceal from oneself, in order to allay guilt, the nature of this aggression. Bartleby's verbal formula for refusing to work is, in this light, a perfect extension of such a strategy. He uses the conciliatory word for the obstinate action.

It is one of the ironies of the story that such a transparent formula, so unlikely of success, should in fact so often succeed. Of course, this is so only because the narrator is the perfect victim, one whose inhibitions prevent him from identifying the aggression behind the mask of his clerk's passivity. He does, on one occasion, struggle with Bartleby to make him say "will not," rather than "prefer not," as though that change alone would end the ascendancy the clerk has over him. But Bartleby wins that struggle, too, as he wins all the others. Eventually, the narrator even tries to identify with his victorious clerk, as though that might erase his own ignominy. In perhaps the only comic scene in the story, however grim it may also be, the narrator catches himself using the same expression. He tells us that "somehow, of late, I had got into the way of involuntarily using this word 'prefer' upon all sorts of not exactly suitable occasions." Bartleby's formula for domination has not been lost on the other employees, either; and the lawyer finds that they too are, quite unconsciously, using the expression themselves. For instance, with the employee named "Turkey":

> "Oh, *prefer?* oh yes—queer word. I never use it myself. But, sir, as I was saying, if he would but prefer—"

"Turkey," interrupted I, "you will please withdraw."

"Oh certainly, sir, if you prefer that I should."

They identify with Bartleby, not for his depressions, the emptiness of his life, or his isolation from the world, but because of their intuitive sense that it is all a purposeful struggle for power, a struggle they see Bartleby win each day in the office. They rightly understand he is the aggressor who seems never to get caught.

Up to now, Melville has preserved a certain dramatic ambiguity. His narrator, for all the transparency of his rationalizations, has not been without at least some measure of justification for his inaction. His clerk has done good work in copying. And we can almost sympathize with the lawyer's continued sense that so mild a man can be tolerated and, perhaps in time, even reasoned with. (Bartleby's passive suffering has its demoralizing effect on the reader, too.) In addition, the narrator often takes his submission with a light heart. There is almost something comic about the way thoughts of decisive action (by "intimating the unalterable purpose of some terrible retribution very close at hand"), are immediately reversed ("I half intended something of the kind. But upon the whole, as it was drawing towards my dinner-hour, I thought it best to put on my hat and walk home for the day"). We might almost think that some comic resolution of the conflict is also at hand.

What does happen, however, is not in the least bit comic. The narrator recognizes, however slowly, how deranged his clerk is, with his catatonic depressions, his emaciation, his unending obstinacy. Concluding that Bartleby is the "victim of innate and incurable disorder," he decides at last to tell him that his "services were no longer required." On his first attempt, he makes the mistake of trying to reason with Bartleby, forgetting that one cannot reason with an incurable disorder. But when he has failed to voice the dismissal, he achieves his clearest sense that the problem is within himself. He tells us that "I strangely felt something superstitious knocking at my heart, and forbidding me to carry out my purpose, and denouncing me for a villain if I dared to breathe one bitter word. . . ." The old inhibition is still in force, not permitting a word in anger. Bartleby, however, as though sensing the imminence of dismissal, fights back with his own peculiar weapons. He declares that, henceforth, he will do no further work of any kind. It would appear that this is too much, even for the narrator. As politely as possible, he tells him at last to go. True, he gives the clerk six days' notice, not the usual thing with employees who will do no work whatever. But the termination, he says, is "unconditional." The struggle, for these men, may be more against inner forces than against each other, but it is as grim and ruthless, in its way, as the shedding of blood.

When the time is up, Bartleby is, of course, still there, standing in his corner motionless. Surely something now must give, we think. There is nothing more for the clerk to refuse to do, no more threats left for the lawyer to make. Something does give, and it is that which has been

increasingly compromised from the beginning—the narrator's sanity. He was able to persuade himself, once before, that Bartleby was a valuable acquisition. Now he takes one further step out of reality. He gives Bartleby severance pay, gives him instructions for locking the office and leaving the key, bids him goodby and farewell, and walks home "pluming" himself on his "masterly management in getting rid of Bartleby." In short, he concludes the clerk will go because he, the narrator, assumes it. As he tells us, "I *assumed* the ground that depart he must; and upon that assumption built all I had to say." This is infantile belief in the omnipotence of thought, to think something will happen because one has assumed it will. But at least it is madness with a method, since he has controlled his violence—that is, the greater problem, for him, than even Bartleby. This he has achieved, and he takes consolation in it: "The beauty of my procedure," he writes, "seemed to consist in its perfect quietness. There was no vulgar bullying, no bravado of any sort, no choleric hectoring, and striding to and fro across the apartment, jerking out vehement commands. . . ."

The next morning, however, having "slept off the fumes of vanity," he is realistic enough to wonder if his clerk has really gone. When he finds Bartleby still in the office, he is reluctant to give up his "doctrine of assumptions," as he calls it. He momentarily imagines acting as though Bartleby has really gone, pretending not to see him, and walking "straight against him as if he were air." It is crazy thinking, and he recoils from it. As if to recover his sanity, his freedom of action, and his rightful authority all at one stroke, he finally gives expression to his anger and advances on Bartleby "in a sudden passion." When Bartleby replies, as dispassionately as ever, that he would prefer not to leave, the violence which has begun to leak out can no longer be kept from consciousness, although the lawyer is still not without his defenses. He thinks of a murder committed in a business office, one which involved others, not Bartleby and himself: "I remembered the tragedy of the unfortunate Adams and the still more unfortunate Colt in the solitary office of the latter; and how poor Colt, being dreadfully incensed by Adams, and imprudently permitted himself to get wildly excited, was at unawares hurried into the fatal act. . . ." The idea of killing is there, but the names have been changed. It is a good example of how "free" association, like dreams, reveals more than one knows.

Nothing, however, has changed. Bartleby is still there, and the narrator tries to "fancy, that in the course of the morning, at such time as might prove agreeable to him, Bartleby, of his own free accord, would emerge from his hermitage, and take up some decided line of march in the direction of the door." As usual, the narrator's language is the rhetoric of the lawyer, blurring the outlines of his own thinking. He is, to put it bluntly, reduced to the point of merely wishing that his clerk would prefer to go. The situation is as intolerable as ever; another defense against his own anger must now be found and another step taken out of the real world. He adopts a fantasy, less rational even than the magical thinking of his "doctrine of assumptions." He decides that he has a mission, predestined from eternity, to keep and care for Bartleby! Thus he converts the ignominy of defeat into the exalted idea of a divine purpose. The humiliation of defeat, which he cannot erase at the risk of murderous violence, he dispels with a delusion of grandeur.

Such a retreat from reality is shocking and gives the full measure of how costly his inhibition has become. He writes that "gradually I slid into the persuasion that these troubles of mine, touching the scrivener, had been all predestined from eternity, and Bartleby was billeted upon me for some mysterious purpose of an allwise Providence. . . . At last I see it. I feel it; I penetrated to the predestinated purpose of my life. I am content." This is the contentment of an all-but psychotic delusion. We have a vivid illustration of the premise that the line between neurosis and psychosis can often not be clearly drawn. The narrator is not psychotic, but this delusion is. And we have, too, an example of how the bizarre elements of psychosis may be themselves part of the individual's efforts to save himself and his integration in the world. With this delusion, the narrator at least escapes from a hell in which he can no longer live. And he is able to conclude, with no sense of humiliation or despair: "Yes, Bartleby, stay there behind your screen. . . . I shall persecute you no more. . . ."

The narrator has not run from the world altogether, and his sense of reality helps to determine his next move. He becomes worried by the fact that his professional colleagues and acquaintances begin talking about the strange creature, the apparition, standing immovable in the middle of his office. The narrator's divine purpose has not been revealed to *them,* and the lawyer's reputation and practice is threatened. The narrator also has the queer idea that Bartleby will outlive him and so gain final possession of the office! This idea we can perhaps ascribe to his inveterate equating of conflict with murderous violence. Children often have murderous thoughts against their parents with the gratifying, and seemingly innocent, thought that they will "one day" outlive them. There is no reason for the narrator to care who possesses the premises when he is dead and gone. But the fear makes sense as another defense against his own murderous wishes. We can presume that, on the point of losing his profession, his violent wishes must be at their most intense. And so he projects them onto Bartleby, and imagines the clerk will outlive him (that is, might kill him). In any case, the narrator, as is the case with any neurotic, must decide how sick he is going to be. To put it differently, he must decide how much loss of adjustment in the external world he will tolerate in the interests of resolving inner problems. The choice is not always a conscious one, but it must always be made. Deciding he will not give up his profession, he does the only thing left to do. Unable to force Bartleby to go, he packs his own bags and moves his office elsewhere.

There is an utterly poignant moment when everything is moved, and Bartleby is left motionless in the middle of the naked room. Although their lives are highly disparate, each is pursuing the dictates of inner necessity. Bartleby remains uncompromising, although now he is left with

nothing, while the narrator runs from conflict, but hangs on to his profession. Bartleby, of course, is the more forlorn figure, and the lawyer, even now, feels sympathy and self-reproach for leaving. The reader, too, is likely to feel more compassion for the scrivener. But one must beware the tactics of depression. The lawyer seems to have learned the lesson, and he goes.

The remainder of the story illustrates one last fact about the neurotic. Reality sometimes protects them from realizing the full proportions of their own malady. When the new tenants find Bartleby "haunting the building generally, sitting upon the banisters of the stairs by day, and sleeping in the entry at night," the narrator is appealed to as the person responsible for having left him there. He agrees to speak to Bartleby because, as he tells himself, he might otherwise be "exposed" in the newspapers. What it is that he might be exposed for, he does not go into. It is, presumably, the old guilt born of latent violence which makes him vulnerable to intimidation. Back he goes to the old office and to more "reasoning" with Bartleby. At this point a most extraordinary thing happens, more bizarre and incomprehensible than anything that has gone before. After failing to persuade Bartleby to leave the office (as though that were ever possible) and failing to persuade him to take up some other profession (as though that were ever the problem), the narrator invites Bartleby to come home with him: "'Bartleby,' said I, in the kindest tone I could assume under such exciting circumstances, 'will you go home with me now—not to my office, but my dwelling—and remain there till we can conclude upon some convenient arrangement for you at our leisure? Come, let us start now, right away.'"

Nothing is more certain than that, once lodged with the narrator, Bartleby will prefer to remain. And in light of his failures with the scrivener to date, he could hardly expect to have the strength to then force him to leave. Yet he tells us that this invitation is one "which had not been wholly unindulged before." One hardly knows at first what to make of this folly. It is comprehensible only as the last and most extreme gesture of defense. His leaving the office has not worked; he is back and responsible for the clerk all over again. Trapped by an unconscious guilt which makes him fear "exposure," there is nothing else to do except take up the association; but at least in the privacy of his home, away from the prying eyes of the world. And the scrivener's demented strategy of passive and depressed suffering has always had its effect on the narrator. Fortunately for the narrator, Bartleby replies: "'No: at present I would prefer not to make any change at all.'"

This obstinacy has its measure of grandeur, too. One finds such uncompromising stubbornness in the rages of the infant, where Bartleby's malady may indeed have had its origin. In any case, we shall never know the full extent of the narrator's capacity for neurotic accommodation, since, through no doing of his (he would say through no fault of his,) Bartleby is led unprotesting to the tombs. The lawyer visits him there, and finds him "standing all alone in the quietest of the yards, his face towards a high wall." The narrator has another one of his revealing free-associ-

Melville, circa 1847.

ations, imagining that "all around, from the narrow slits of the jail windows, I thought I saw peering out upon him the eyes of murderers and thieves." It takes little analysis, at this point, to perceive that he has projected again his own guilt. It is the guilt which prevented him from sending the scrivener to prison in the first place, and which now makes him feel responsible for his being there.

Bartleby, now that he is in prison, declares that he "prefers not to dine today." He always has new measures of obstinacy to refute the world. And so, when the narrator finds him later at his wall, he is "strangely huddled at the base . . . , his knees drawn up, and lying on his side, his head touching the stones." In death, his foetal position links him again to the infant. This equation between depressed obstinacy and the infant is an explanation for the sympathy and compliance such men can extort from the world. All suffering children are victims, since they have not yet the freedom to create their own problems. And so it is difficult for the reader to break the spell with the thought that Bartleby has killed himself, and with as much freedom to do otherwise as any of us possesses.

The narrator seeks at the end to explain the scrivener as the victim of his previous work in a dead letter office, which occupation fatally intensified an already "pallid hopelessness." The irony of the story is sharpest at its conclusion. At the beginning, the narrator had said that a

description of himself was necessary for "an adequate understanding of the chief character about to be presented." But he has never understood the scrivener, beyond the dim sense that he is a "bit deranged." And attributing derangement to the effects of a dead-letter office is sentimental, and simplistic. But, above all, he does not understand that for the greater dramatization of his own inner conflicts, for his own perilous touch of madness, he himself has been the chief character. He can live in the world only as long as a passive avoidance of conflict is allowed him, and as long as anything which in the least disturbs the violence within him is kept away. Such neurotics are not often spared through an entire lifetime all conflict except the passivity of an obstinate clerk.

Marvin Fisher (essay date 1974)

SOURCE: "'Bartleby,' Melville's Circumscribed Scrivener," in *The Southern Review,* Louisiana State University, Vol. X, No. 1, Winter, 1974, pp. 59-79.

[*Fisher is an American educator whose books include* Going Under: Melville's Short Fiction and the American 1850's *(1977). In the following essay, Fisher provides an overview of several critical approaches to "Bartleby," and insists that Melville intended Bartleby to be representative of humankind generally.*]

"Bartleby" is certainly the most familiar of Melville's short stories, reprinted in dozens of anthologies and analyzed by scores of critics. It would be hard to say something new about this early study of alienation, frustration, and catatonic withdrawal, and the surest guard against originality, I suspect, would be to take account of every commentary on the story. It would be more foolish, however, to try to clear one's mind completely of what others have written about Melville's pitiable and peculiar clerk and the initially complacent but ultimately vulnerable lawyer who narrates the tale.

This was Melville's first published short story and constitutes a remarkable attempt at a new genre and a considerable recovery from his disappointment over the public reception of *Pierre*. It was a greater recovery in terms of technical virtuosity than in the expression of a more positive outlook, especially in regard to the title character, who, we have been frequently told, confronts the dismal prospects of the aspiring American artist or writer. It was a subject which, quite understandably, never ceased to interest, attract, and challenge Melville—whether in the general terms of the nature of art, the strengths and liabilities of the artist, or the particular circumstances of the American scene. One or more phases of this complex issue are present in *Typee, Mardi, Redburn, White-Jacket, Moby Dick, Pierre, The Confidence-Man,* and at least one-third of the short stories. The height of Melville's faith in what the serious writer could accomplish in America occurred in his enthusiastic review of Hawthorne's *Mosses,* but he reached the depths in *Pierre* and the two short works that followed in the early 1850s— **"Bartleby"** and **"Cock-a-Doodle-Doo!"**

To approach **"Bartleby"** only as an analogue of the alienated artist in an insensitive society is to ignore a great deal of the contextual richness or symbolic suggestiveness of the story. The stony impersonality of urban America so prominent in the latter part of *Pierre* is compressed into the Wall Street law office setting of **"Bartleby"** and both stories end with the death of the title character in the steel and granite isolation of the Tombs—the would-be writer crushed by the ponderous judgments of a matter-of-fact society. In each case the title character's pathetic end is a compound of his personality (ideals, expectations, delusions, and compulsions) and the pressures of a pragmatic, profit-oriented, and apparently unsympathetic society. And in each case also, the character's psychological demise and ultimate death follows a breakdown in communication between himself and his society.

When **"Bartleby"** first appeared (in two installments of *Putnam's Monthly* in late 1853), the title read **"Bartleby, the Scrivener. A Story of Wall-Street."** The shorter form adopted later was very likely the result of typographical considerations in listing the contents of Melville's *Piazza Tales,* where all the titles are brief; and since the *Piazza Tales* has been the source of most subsequent republications of the story, the shorter title has become the more familiar. This circumstance is unfortunate because it plays down the social and economic connotations of "Wall-Street" and the degree to which Bartleby was described or identified by his employment in the original title. Melville's intention, it seems likely, was to use the extended title to emphasize the highly dramatic, actually expressionistic, Wall Street setting—a law office where the four employees are literally and figuratively *walled in* by the circumstances of their employment and by the social assumptions embodied in their employer and *walled off* from any hope of mobility or self-fulfillment by the same concept of class structure.

In a less obvious sense than in *White-Jacket,* where the United States ship *Neversink* was a man-of-war representation of an overwhelmingly hierarchical society with distinct class and caste divisions, the Wall Street office is a microcosmic representation of a simpler but similarly structured segment of American society. To Bartleby—who secures employment as a legal copyist, a sort of animated Xerox machine duplicating the documents that reinforce and perpetuate the *status quo*—the office seems a dead-end existence, denying his unique human individuality, curtailing his freedom of choice, and corroborating his hopelessness. His withdrawal from what his employer would judge to be socially productive activity into his "dead-wall revery" is Bartleby's resentful confirmation of the gross inequities and subtle iniquities of an existence that is servile at best and imprisoning at worst. Although he somehow obtains a key to the office, Bartleby chooses to remain permanently within an enclosure with no exit, a prisoner who is also his own jailer, so that when he is imprisoned in the Tombs and surrounded by the massive walls, his condition seems changed hardly at all. To his own satisfaction—or more accurately, dissatisfaction—he has proved that democratic theory masks despotic practice, that the supposedly open society can easily be closed

off by those in power, and that Christian principle can be stretched to cover exploitative sham. But Melville grants Bartleby only a measure of truth and more than a modicum of distortion and delusion. He is a character akin to Kafka's Josef K. or Gregor Samsa, but his story is not as simple as one of Kafka's grotesque allegories. Disenchanted as he often was, Melville did not yet view American society as the Amerika of some present-day critics.

Technically **"Cock-a-Doodle-Doo!"** is a more Kafkaesque story than **"Bartleby."** For one thing the narrator in the former story becomes more and more subject to his hallucinatory perception of reality; whereas the narrator in **"Bartleby"** suffers the loss of his comforting preconceptions and brushes against an aspect of reality he could not earlier have imagined. More important perhaps, is the fact that we see nothing from Bartleby's point of view and have to guess at what ails him, both aided and hindered by the narrator's perception of Bartleby's symptoms and his interpretation of Bartleby's actions. As the narrator says in the opening paragraph, "Bartleby was one of those beings of whom nothing is ascertainable, except from the original sources, and, in his case, those are very small." Despite the scarcity of sources, we are given an extensive case history of Bartleby's last days. It is provided entirely by the narrator, who is a very unlikely and somewhat unwilling evangelist. His account thus has its inherent limitations, but it is the only gospel we have and it will have to suffice.

Melville's handling of the point of view in this story is a conscious and sustained artistic achievement, an exercise in irony unprecedented in American literature. Without apparent strain he manipulated his narrator so that this well-heeled, self-satisfied source both reveals and obscures the meaning of his troubling experiences. Not by any means an entirely unreliable narrator, this representative of conservative business interests is a man of realistically limited perception but capable of considerable moral growth. Melville's most telling tactic, much like that of Mark Twain in *Huckleberry Finn* but more subtle, is to make the narrator's language suggest far more than the character consciously realizes. Thus his attitudes, his actions and reactions, but more importantly his vocabulary, mark the meanings that his mind cannot reach and establish the three dimensions of the story.

Melville's handling of the point of view in this story is a conscious and sustained artistic achievement, an exercise in irony unprecedented in American literature. Without apparent strain he manipulated his narrator so that this well-heeled, self-satisfied source both reveals and obscures the meaning of his troubling experiences.

—*Marvin Fisher*

To understand those dimensions, we are required to approach them, at least in part, from Bartleby's point of view, to approximate his perspective. The first dimension (or direction of implicative meaning) involves the concept of *community*—an ideal that is social, political, and economic. The second involves the concept of *communication,* which extends the social function into areas of literary or artistic implication. And the third involves the concept of *communion,* the significance of which is obviously spiritual or religious. These dimensions are related and partially overlap while still being distinguishable. Yet from our growing intuition of Bartleby's point of view, each seems to have held forth a glowing possibility only to have it disproved by some inpenetrable obstacle—physical, social, or metaphysical. The various walls, tangibly representing the obstacles Bartleby has found in his experience, inevitably shape his perspective and deny him any further prospect.

In American society, where promise is so great and expectation so high, Bartleby finds no place to go and no fulfillment in life. He lapses into lethargy; flouts the obligations of a work-money-property-oriented society; stubbornly asserts the negative aspects of his freedom of will; and in withdrawing from the world of social affairs and human relationships, seems to will his withdrawal from life itself. There is no clear diagnosis of what Bartleby suffers from, but there is enough evidence to construct a complex pathology, demonstrating that Melville found the sources of this condition in the character of the existing society and in the peculiar susceptibilities of the sensitive individual.

The main dimension of the story is concerned with the idea of *community,* or rather the lack of it, within the physical and social divisions of the Wall Street office. The narrator's estimate of himself and his relationship to his subordinates tells us a great deal. The possessive pronoun is prominent as he tells about "myself, my *employés,* my business, my chambers." Like the complacent lawyers in **"The Paradise of Bachelors,"** men insulated from the troubling trials of life who used the law to right no wrongs, the narrator has sought "the cool tranquility of a snug retreat" where he can "do a snug business among rich men's bonds, and mortgages, and title-deeds." He prides himself for being known as a "safe" man and for possessing such virtues as "prudence" and "method." Morality, justice, sympathy, or passion are outside his value system. He unashamedly loves money and venerates "the late John Jacob Astor," whose name becomes part of the narrator's litany "for it hath a rounded and orbicular sound to it, and rings like unto bullion." Connotatively "Astor" suggests not only wealth but in combination with "orbicular" it also suggests a heavenly sphere in which the financial luminary "Astor" is the source of light and emotive power. And the narrator is not merely a well-to-do American or a spokesman for Wall Street, he is unabashedly an idolater of the golden bull—now become the almighty dollar. His priesthood of profit and his proprietary air shape his attitude toward the men who work for him. "My *employés*" could be a way of speaking, or it could mean that they have value as means to serve my financial ends.

This tendency of the narrator to judge others by their utility to him seems to make him more tolerant of human weakness or eccentricity, but in a very damaging way it mocks the possibility of men joining in a common enterprise founded on self-respect and sympathy. He is a benevolent master of his men and an enlightened employer-exploiter. He can put up with Turkey's excessive drinking, irritability, and carelessness if the elderly clerk remains useful and productive for a predictable part of the day. (Since he pays his copyists on a piecework rate rather than a salary, he can be more tolerant of their unproductive periods). Turkey cannot be relied on in the afternoon but Nippers, the other copyist, could be counted on to do his best work then. So between them these two employees (identified like Ginger Nut, the office boy, only by the demeaning nicknames which turn them into things) produced a good day's work—a situation which the narrator accepts as "a good natural arrangement, under the circumstances." Their greatest value, their existential purpose, is their service as distinct instrumentalities and not as individual human beings.

Of the two clerks, Nippers is easily the more ambitious, impatient at the routine and menial aspects of his employment and anxious to "be rid of a scrivener's table altogether." But instead of admiring Nippers for his enterprise, the narrator calls it "his diseased ambition"; instead of praising his attempts to raise his social position, the narrator charges him with "a continual discontent." From the employer's point of view, Nippers is too uppity: he ought to know his place and accept it more graciously. Instead, he envies and in some small way assumes a few perquisites of power. These traits make him seem to his employer an insidious and even at times a satanic threat to system and authority. Yet because Nippers' eccentricities were evident only when Turkey's were not, both men remained tolerably useful to their employer.

The narrator's essentially selfish standards and the superficial values of Wall Street society underlie his description of his employees' appearances and the acceptability of their dress. He can, for example, more easily overlook Nippers' shortcomings because "he always dressed in a gentlemanly sort of way; and so, incidentally, reflected credit upon my chambers." Turkey's clothes, however, were more apt to be messy and ill-fitting, and so the narrator, in an act of self-serving charity, gave him one of his own more "respectable-looking" coats, assuming that Turkey would show his appreciation by curbing his afternoon rashness. Instead of being useful and productive and a greater credit to his employer's establishment, Turkey reacted resentfully to what his employer cannot recognize as a demeaning form of charity; and the narrator's explanation further degrades his employee: "too much oats are bad for horses . . . [and] precisely as a rash, restive horse is said to feel his oats, so Turkey felt his coat. It made him insolent. He was a man whom prosperity harmed." The attitude underlying the narrator's remarks is extremely class (or caste) oriented and Turkey, like Nippers, is guilty of not knowing his place and not responding properly to what his employer has so graciously bestowed on him. The narrator's reasons for hiring Bartleby so quickly, after merely "a few words touching his qualifications," have to do largely with his appearance and dress—"singularly sedate," "pallidly neat, pitiably respectable"—and the hope that he would be a steadying influence on the uneven tempers of Nippers and Turkey, a model of the neatness, servility, dependence, obedience, gratitude, and contentment the master wants in his scriveners.

The narrator's supreme position in this social microcosm is understood by his employees' normally deferential attitudes, prefacing their statements with phrases like "with submission, sir" or "excuse me," very much as verbal communication with a reigning monarch would be prefaced with "by your grace." (In marked contrast, however, is Bartleby's "I prefer not to"—a subtly scaled down or understated "non serviam.") The need for a third clerk is occasioned by the increased business resulting from what the narrator terms "receiving the Master's office." It is a conveniently abbreviated way of referring to his position as a Master in Chancery, but it further stresses the social, economic, and psychological relationship between the narrator and his clerks. The appointment to this office was not only a very lucrative circumstance, as the narrator points out, but it also conveyed considerable quasi-judicial power. A Master in Chancery rendered decisions in those matters of equity which the common law did not cover and the courts were not constituted to settle. There is irony, of course, in the narrator's being responsible for determining matters of equity—what is fair, just, and impartial—when his Wall Street ways are so fraught with inequities. And there is further irony in the legal definition of *equity* which would apply the dictates of conscience or principles of natural justice to settle controversies. Needless to say, the partiality and self-interest of the narrator are never in doubt and his conscience is merely the internalized dictates of Wall Street. Melville may have had still more in mind in calling such considerable attention to "the Master's office," for *chancery* can refer to "a wrestling hold that imprisons the head or encircles the neck," and in legal usage the phrase *in chancery* can mean "in a helpless, hopeless, or embarrassing position." It would not have been beyond Melville to use such legalistic and lexicographical puns to stress the subjugation of Wall Street's white-collar proletariat. He could be even more blatant on this score in his indictment of socially respectable white slavery in **"The Tartarus of Maids."**

The divisions and confinements that underlie the social relationships are more tangibly embodied in the physical arrangements of the office. It becomes "a house divided" because such an arrangement fulfills the narrator's conception of propriety, proprietorship, and utility. It easily could be the stage setting for a work of twentieth-century expressionism:

> Ground-glass folding-doors divided my premises into two parts, one of which was occupied by my scriveners, the other by myself. According to my humor, I threw open these doors, or closed them. I resolved to assign Bartleby a corner by the folding doors, but on my side of them so as to have this quiet man within easy call, in case any trifling thing was to be done. I placed his desk close up to a small side-window . . . Within three feet of the panes was a wall, and light came down from far above, between two lofty buildings, as from a very small opening in a dome. Still further to a satisfactory arrangement, I procured a high green folding screen, which might entirely isolate Bartleby from my sight, though not remove him from my voice. And thus, in a manner, privacy and society were conjoined.

In these circumstances Bartleby, at least initially, "did an extraordinary quantity of writing," copying through the night as well as day. But it was writing done on command, with as much originality as a machine could muster. When the narrator wants Bartleby to aid in proofreading, he calls with the "natural expectancy of instant compliance," and instead of compliance, Bartleby issues his first "I would prefer not to." The narrator sits stunned and unbelieving, as Bartleby's assertion of autonomy throws into turmoil the carefully controlled network of assumptions, expectations, and relationships.

In his quiet way Bartleby terrorizes the Wall Street establishment. His understated parody of Satan's refusal implies a greater threat than Nippers' acts of resentment, but only in the dubious light of the Wall Street establishment, which he will not serve, does Bartleby appear a satanic character. From a different perspective there might be a noble madness in the stubborn obstructiveness and passive withdrawal which constitute the developing strategy of his peculiar and paradoxical insurrection.

In one sense it is merely that Bartleby knows his place and will not leave it; in another sense his immobilized behavior seems an act of gross contempt for the conventions of a property-and-profit-oriented society. His appropriation of private property for personal use—first sleeping in the office and then staging a passive sit-in when directed to leave—strikes at the heart of the system. It also hits the narrator where he lives, as it were: he first feels "disarmed" by Bartleby's quiet rebellion and ultimately feels "unmanned" by the threat to his authority.

However weakened he personally feels, the narrator finds his role forced on him and his will stiffened by the Wall Street society that has served him so well. He must now serve that society and not Bartleby's crippling eccentricity. By the standards of that society Bartleby is a perverse nut, and for the narrator to continue to tolerate him would be sheer insanity. He is caught between the attitude of blandly benign accommodation, which has enabled him to turn so many circumstances to his own benefit, and the social rigidities and conformist practices of Wall Street, which will permit no such perversity or eccentricity as Bartleby's. His decision to oust Bartleby reflects the pressure of the business community which determines substantially his status and identity, and his rather bland, apologetic explanation is that "necessities connected with my business tyrannized over all other considerations." On Wall Street, apparently, good form, conformity, and business forms are the essential means of communication; thus the narrator's hoped for farewell to Bartleby (after giving him an amount in excess of wages due) concludes with phraseology taken directly from the form of business correspondence: "If, hereafter, in your new place of abode, I can be of any service to you, do not fail to advise me by letter." The message and the gift preceding it are a form of literal generosity but clearly lacking the spirit of genuine charity, and in their formality both gift and message discourage further communication and deny any idea of community.

When Bartleby fails to leave the premises as he has been directed, the narrator, with unconscious irony, puts the matter on a basis of business law, asking first, "What earthly right have you to stay here?"—not realizing that something more than "earthly right" might be involved. Then he follows with questions that again stress the profit-property nexus of Wall Street and of the culture at large: "Do you pay any rent? Do you pay my taxes? Or is this property yours." Bartleby remains silent; these are not *his* questions, and his seemingly contemptuous withdrawal infuriates the narrator. In trying prudently to check his anger, he begins to recognize the lack of communal attachments in circumstances like those of his office. He recalls a recent murder case that must have been of note to the New York business community and wonders whether "the circumstance of being alone in a solitary office, upstairs, of a building entirely unhallowed by humanizing domestic associations" did not help trigger the act.

His innate prudence makes him seek an alternative to anger toward Bartleby, one that will soothe his sensibilities without offending his practical businessman's principles. His first refuge is a form of prudential charity but predicated on self-interest. His second is a kind of pragmatic predestination that glosses his providential relationship to Bartleby. But neither of these theological or philosophical rationalizations enables him to withstand the continuing pressure from his professional peers, and his conscience—more properly his malleable conscientiousness—cave in. Yet thrust Bartleby into the street, he cannot; so he takes the unlikely course of moving his offices to another location, leaving Bartleby behind, breaking any possible connection, denying any further responsibility.

While Melville, through artfully constructed narrative, conveys a strong sense of the obstacles to community and the barriers to communication, he also drops hints of further enclosure, separation, or division. For one thing the narrator's description of his own power and authority melds into a supremacy that is more than social or economic. In describing Turkey's daily rhythm, he praises him for being "the blandest and most *reverential* of men in the morning," especially, "valuing his morning *services*" and resenting "his afternoon *devotions*" (when he is rash and excessively spirited). This deference and reverence is, of course, directed toward the narrator, who refers to himself as "a *man of peace*." These italicized terms might be merely a mildly humorous sort of irony were it not for the kind of vocabulary used in reference to Bartleby, or as a consequence of Bartleby. His first appearance is referred to as his "advent." He is "this forlornest of mankind"; and for the puzzled and troubled narrator, he is "not only useless as a necklace, but afflictive to

bear." Several apparently unconscious puns on the word "assumption" spin off the narrator's reaction to Bartleby, and the narrator also speaks of Bartleby's "cadaverous triumph" and his "ascendency." Such a "string" of linked multiple meanings cannot be accidental, and most readers will recognize that these terms have special application in Christian worship.

Moreover, Bartleby is described repeatedly in terms that stress his lack of coloration, his silence, his omnipresence, and his seeming perpetuity—all of which give him a supernatural cast. He is "pallidly neat" upon his first appearance, and later the narrator is "awed into . . . tame compliance" by Bartleby's "pallid haughtiness." All told, the words *pallid, pale, pallor,* or some similar variation, are used fifteen times and *white* and *gray* once each in reference to Bartleby. Words that stress his silence—*quiet, calm, mute, still, noiseless,* as well as *silent* and other synonyms—appear more than twenty times. The emphasis on these attributes is important because of Melville's tendency to associate them with larger-than-life, awe-inspiring forces. To the narrator Bartleby also appears variously as an "apparition," "strange creature," "incubus," "ghost," or "haunt." Unlike other men, he never reads, never drinks beer, tea, or coffee, and seems to eat rarely and then only the spiced wafers called ginger nuts. In what seems an ironic commentary on the sacrament of communion, Bartleby dines on these wafers in solitude. Mystery surrounds his past; and his silence regarding his origins, family, motives, or complaints—Bartleby's own refusal to communicate—pushes the mystery into the present.

But before concluding that Bartleby is Christ (as Bruce Franklin, drawing heavily from the explication of Christian charity in Matthew 25, has done [in *The Wake of the Gods: Melville's Mythology*]), I would like to suggest that Melville has left room for a natural explanation as well as a supernatural one. Bartleby's symptoms could substantiate a diagnosis of severe mental illness; that is, his condition could be that of a man who is suffering from the delusion that he is Christ and reacting to the indifference, self-absorption, or ridicule of mid-nineteenth-century American society. Or even without the presence of such a delusion, Bartleby's condition could be the consequence of a sensitive individual's reaction to the insensitivity of his surroundings, and a present-day psychoanalyst would find the symptoms forming a familiar composite.

[In C. Peter Rosenbaum's *The Meaning of Madness: Symptomatology, Sociology, Biology, and Therapy of the Schizophrenias*] for example, we find the following symptoms for the type of catatonia which is characterized by stupor, with "an apparent, but not real, diminution of consciousness":

  i. Negativism, echolalia

  ii. Automatism, dreaminess, grimacing

  iii. Immobility, waxy flexibility

  iv. Refusal to eat

Bartleby's negativism permeates every phase of his behavior, but it can be viewed as a distorted form of autonomy, an attempt at affirming the "I," a passive protest at depersonalization. And his repeated response "I prefer not to" differs from the typical echolalia, in which the affected individual repeats the interviewer's or therapist's statements. Bartleby echoes and thereby asserts only himself. Automatism, of course, characterized his action before and after his refusal to work. First he worked day and night, copying "silently, palely, mechanically," then withdrew behind his screen into the dreamy, immobile state that the narrator terms "his dead-wall revery." The narrator compares Bartleby to a "pale plaster-of-paris bust of Cicero." Dr. Rosenbaum, describing schizophrenic patients in a catatonic stupor, writes that they "adopt strange, uncomfortable-looking, statuelike postures which they maintain for minutes or hours at a time." The narrator supposes that Bartleby's immobility and refusal to work are due to eye strain, "for his eyes looked dull and glazed." Rosenbaum explains that in this catatonic condition patients' "faces may portray dreaminess, grimacing, or tics, and frequently one has the impression that they are locked into contact with hallucinations to which . . . they cannot respond." The narrator is depressed by the thought of Bartleby's meager diet and after his removal to the tombs tries to provide more amply, but Bartleby refuses to eat and dies "huddled" and "wasted" on the stones "at the base of the wall." Dr. Rosenbaum concludes his description, observing that "such patients may frequently be so immobilized that they neither eat nor maintain sphincter control" and adding that "tube feedings may be necessary to avoid death through inanition." The symptomatology is remarkably similar in these instances, and the similarity is probably more than a matter of coincidence. Perhaps Melville offered a serious diagnosis when he had the twelve-year-old office boy in the story say of Bartleby, "I think, sir, he's a little *luny*."

But Melville's story is much more than a case history, and my purpose is not to force such a conjectural psychoanalysis of a fictional figure whose author, many will hasten to say, antedated the concepts and classifications of contemporary psychoanalysis. (There are too many instances when Melville's imagination led him to treat symbolically what social or behavioral science had not yet articulated for anyone to be long troubled by the thought that Melville could not have known such things. The serious artist is often surrogate psychoanalyst and vicarious victim in one.) My purpose here is to propose that Melville could have meant the natural explanation and the supernatural suggestions of Bartleby's behavior to reinforce each other in a more complex way than his friend Hawthorne had done in offering natural and supernatural alternatives.

To put it most simply, Bartleby is incapacitated by having internalized the schism that frustrates authentic community, intellectual and emotional communication, and spiritual communion. He has become a divided self, a kind of symbolic embodiment of what ails man and society. Obsessed by the imperfection around him, he is also affronted by such inadequate measures to make things right as

having to verify copy. There is far more that cannot be made right in the human relationships that exist, in the lack of recognition or reinforcement for individual members of this false community on Wall Street. Having concluded, apparently, that in the kind of existence where vital reinforcement is unavailable, frustration is inevitable, Bartleby has no faith in what might possibly sustain him and opts out.

To put it most simply, Bartleby is incapacitated by having internalized the schism that frustrates authentic community, intellectual and emotional communication, and spiritual communion. He has become a divided self, a kind of symbolic embodiment of what ails man and society.

—*Marvin Fisher*

In requiring the reader to approximate Bartleby's vantage point even as the events are recounted by his establishment-oriented employer, Melville has anticipated the sort of challenge that R. D. Laing has issued to traditional psychoanalysis. His approach is not to classify psychotic patients as examples of disease but, by approximating the point of view of the patient in his particular environmental circumstances, to show how apparently odd or irrelevant behavior can be meaningful and appropriate. Schizophrenia thus appears a psychological strategy devised to defend the victim's humanity in the midst of threatening circumstances, and even his most bizarre behavior can be seen as a comprehensible response to his immediate situation. The parallel to Melville's story is quite remarkable as Laing seeks to anchor the explanation of psychotic symptoms in the social setting of the patient. . . .

Ironically, Bartleby has had an effect and both minor and major changes are in process. Nippers and Turkey, as well as the narrator, come to use the word "prefer" with increasing frequency (while unaware that they use it at all) and thereby show the subtle impact of Bartleby, who also remains unaware of his power to make involuntary converts even among those who oppose him or make him the target of their separate hostilities. He also seems unaware that an important personality change is in process in his employer whose efforts at charity, at first so prudential and pragmatic, become increasingly suffused with a sense of humanity and compassion. Although he never completely breaks free from his Wall Street proprieties, he shows less need to rationalize his actions or find a utilitarian justification for them. His private reflections reveal not only the growth of tolerance and sympathy, but also the greater profundity of a spiritual conversion:

> For the first time in my life a feeling of overpowering stinging melancholy seized me. Before, I had never experienced aught but a not unpleasing sadness. The

bond of a common humanity now drew me irresistibly to gloom. A fraternal melancholy! For both I and Bartleby were sons of Adam. I remembered the bright silks and sparkling faces I had seen that day, . . . and I contrasted them with the pallid copyist, and thought to myself, Ah, happiness courts the light, so we deem that misery there is none. These sad fancyings . . . led on to other and more special thoughts, concerning the eccentricities of Bartleby. Presentiments of strange discoveries hovered around me. The scrivener's pale form appeared to me laid out, among uncaring strangers, in its shivering winding-sheet.

"The bond of a common humanity," upon which the ideal of community and the concept of communion both depend, is not constant in the narrator's consciousness. The pressure of his Wall Street peers is still there, affecting him both before and after his move to new quarters. The new tenant who finds Bartleby is no more successful in getting him to work or to leave and when he seeks out the narrator to question him about his former employee, the narrator admits to no personal knowledge of or responsibility for Bartleby. In fact he denies Bartleby three times publicly before returning to his old quarters in a final effort to oust him. Bartleby, however, shows no interest in any other possible employment and refuses the narrator's remarkably generous offer to take him into his own home.

He has seen something more in the offer than generosity and his refusal indicates his unwillingness to expose himself further to the kind of situation that has repeatedly victimized him. The situation has all the characteristics of what Gregory Bateson and his associates first formulated as the "double-bind." In *Self and Others,* Laing summarizes the concept and offers his view of its sequential ingredients: (I) two or more persons, one of whom can be designated the "victim"; (2) a repeated pattern that comes to be a habitual expectation in the victim's experience; (3) a negative injunction, such as the narrator's "if you do not go away from these premises . . . , I shall feel bound—indeed, I *am* bound . . . ," followed by a threat of abandonment. (4) a secondary injunction conflicting with the first, communicated by either verbal or nonverbal means, and absolving the narrator from responsibility for whatever punishment follows, as in the narrator's offer to take Bartleby into his home with the unspoken injunction that Bartleby will subsequently have to do his part; and (5) a further injunction prohibiting the victim from escaping, sealing him into the situation, as the symbolic walls or the narrator's reacting to Bartleby's immobility with "stationary you shall be, then," seem to have done. Once an individual has come to perceive his relationship in double-bind patterns, almost any part of the expected sequence can be enough to precipitate the end result. For Bartleby, who has learned to expect this kind of entrapment, any attempt at communication invites catastrophe, existence becomes increasingly circumscribed, the walls more rigid, permanent, and inescapable.

In a scene that must be an ironic reversal of Christ driving the money-men from the Temple, Wall Street landlords and city authorities with considerable difficulty,

remove Bartleby from the Wall Street office, arrest him as a vagrant, and lock him in the Tombs. When the narrator visits him there, he can stimulate in Bartleby no will to live, and Bartleby's last words to the narrator, who has tried to indicate what encouragement exists even in this environment are, appropriately enough, "I know where I am," and indeed this place of total enclosure is not unfamiliar—the same encircling walls, the same repressive and punitive normality, and the same stony embodiment of antihuman institutions. The narrator imagines Bartleby spending his last days amid "murderers and thieves," tries unsuccessfully to provide him with food, and describes him, after he has died, as asleep "with kings and counselors." The phraseology is extraordinarily portentous, yet somehow appropriate to "this forlornest of mankind."

Appended to the story is an unconfirmed rumor about Bartleby's previous employment as "a subordinate clerk in the Dead Letter Office at Washington." Its position compels us to consider the paragraph even more carefully than the narrator does for its relevance to the preceding account. He sees it as a possible seed bed for Bartleby's negativism and a more certain source of his depression:

> Dead letters! does it not sound like dead men? Conceive a man by nature and misfortune prone to a pallid hopelessness, can any business seem more fitted to heighten it than that of continually handling these dead letters, and assorting them for the flames?

His question is not merely rhetorical, and to some extent he answers it himself. But the question is also a challenge to the reader who has been led through an account of Bartleby's last days in a somewhat stultifying law office in the heart of New York's financial district, where he labored in the service of a man who did "a snug business among rich men's bonds, and mortgages, and title-deeds." Thus part of the answer points to a society where the business of life is business and not life, and to the example of a man who chose the quietest alternative to such a desperate business.

The narrator's answer points to something else, too. Considering those undeliverable letters, he continues:

> For by the cart-load they are annually burned. Sometimes from out the folded paper the pale clerk takes a ring—the finger it was meant for, perhaps, moulders in the grave; a bank-note sent in swiftest charity—he whom it would relieve, nor eats nor hungers any more; pardon for those who died despairing; hope for those who died unhoping; good tidings for those who died stifled by unrelieved calamities. On errands of life, these letters speed to death.

> Ah, Bartleby! Ah, humanity!

Undeniably, the narrator's words tend toward the sentimental and the melodramatic, but they are not banal. He has come a long way and has been drawn into a human problem for which there is no neat legal solution. In the only terms he could employ to express his tragic insight, he has called our attention again to the major areas of concern in the story—the frustration of timely communication, the distances between or the barriers to productive human union, the utter despair of those who die still looking for answers, and the essential inhumanity of a society that treats these poignant records of human experience as so much waste for the incinerator. From his earlier perspective he could insist that while there is life there is hope, a way out of any disturbing situation; the sad, concluding sentences of the story offer another view of the human condition: where there is life there is death, the most totally binding and inescapable aspect of existence.

The narrator had begun as a strong proponent of his own ethic of personal enrichment, a gospel of wealth for its own sake, and unexpectedly confronted a mysterious individual who, in an actual or in an ironic sense, represented "the truth that would make men free" and who died in prison himself. But instead of merely re-creating a basic pattern of Christian faith, Melville gives it compelling contemporary relevance by implying that the money-worshiper's utilitarian and demeaning view of men as commodity or chattel is "deicidal" because it is essentially "homicidal." It had cost Nippers and Turkey their full manhood, even before the "advent" of Bartleby. But paradoxically the lawyer-employer-master, who had been instrumental in stifling the human spirit and thereby denying God, is himself a slave to his Wall Street preconceptions. He seems to realize this at the end, but we do not know whether his insight will make him free. Like Emerson in his "Divinity School Address," Melville seems to be saying that any man can be his own Christ, not, however, in the role of serving as his own savior as Emerson insisted, but rather of realizing his own torment, abandonment, and martyrdom.

Despite the religious imagery in the story, there is little sense that death is Bartleby's liberation, somewhat more reason, perhaps, to believe in the narrator's redemption. He has had to serve as a not very willing or successful therapist in a relationship where the victim views his treatment as further persecution and where the narrator-therapist is forced to recognize in the victim an extreme example of what all men are heir to. Having lived as if he were already a prisoner, Bartleby precipitated a sort of self-fulfilling prophecy. Dying in the Halls of Justice, he confirms the metaphors by which he had lived—that the condition of life in human society is as circumscribed as that in a prison, and that a stony refusal is the most telling strategy against surrounding insensitivity.

R. D. Laing has used the term "petrification" to describe the kind of defensive network Bartleby employs. He suggests that an individual who dreads the possibility of being turned into an inanimate object, a machine, or an automaton, and deprived of personal autonomy, may fight back by negating the other person's autonomy, ignoring his feelings, and thereby depersonalizing him—as Bartleby does repeatedly, the last time being his answer to the narrator who has come to the Tombs, seen him, and called his name. Without turning around, Bartleby says, "I know

you . . . and I want nothing to say to you." According to Laing, such a contemptuous effort to turn the other person into a thing is a strategy of "nullifying any danger to himself by secretly totally disarming the enemy." Hence there is deep psychological trauma as well as social and economic threat in the circumstances which impel the narrator to refer to himself twice as "disarmed" and twice more as "unmanned." And those circumstances, beginning with Bartleby's first stony refusal, illustrate Laing's reciprocal dynamic of "petrification." The narrator describes his initial reaction in terms of stony transformation: "I was turned into a *pillar* of salt, standing at the head of my seated *column* of clerks," but he simultaneously reveals his own earlier depersonalization of his clerks. Melville actually seems to have been using this imagery of petrification consciously, for not only is Bartleby early compared to a piece of statuary, he seems, when the narrator gives him money and orders him to leave, "like the last column of some ruined temple." Laing's view, borne out by Melville's story, is that the petrification process "involves a vicious circle. The more one attempts to preserve one's autonomy and identity by nullifying the specific human individuality of the other, the more it is felt to be necessary to continue to do so, because with each denial of the other person's ontological status, one's own ontological security is decreased, the threat to the self from the other is potentiated and hence has to be even more desperately negated."

Bartleby's stony behavior thus could be viewed as an attempt to forestall the threat of being turned into an inanimate thing by his employer, a defensive strategy to avoid being sucked into or engulfed by the narrator's Wall Street whirlpool. To prevent his becoming an object and drawn into his employer's world, Bartleby turns himself into a stubborn and steadfast stone. His function is far more limited than before; he is either an opaque immobility that puzzles and offends his employer or a reflector turning back the other's gaze. Frustrated by the fraudulent communication he has had to participate in, he becomes a silence or an echo—the only communication one gets from a stone.

The narrator's last words express in part his realization of what Bartleby has exemplified and the general susceptibility of humanity to such a view. Not only has Bartleby been physically and psychologically crippled by the pattern of double-binds in his life, but the narrator has recognized his own involvement in the pattern, initially as master and ultimately as victim. Like the therapist who may be drawn into the psychosis of his patient or the lawyer who may participate vicariously in the criminality of his client, the narrator also recognizes that he has furthered the frequently unfair laws of the dominant society. In this sense of a shared fate he has become Bartleby's double, and his account might even be suggesting the universal applicability of such an appalling conclusion. At least he has grasped the general lesson that Bartleby never fully articulated, but we don't know whether he will act on any of its more immediate corollaries, such as the somber irony that there is as much justice in the Tombs as there is equity in the Wall Street law office.

There is no hint of a physical resurrection in the story; Bartleby does not rise from the Tombs, even though some tufts of new grass grow underfoot. But there is a possibility that the narrator has accomplished in his record of mind, memory, and conscience the only immortality Bartleby was to have. Or to put it differently, Melville, in the artfully re-created conscience of his narrator, has ambiguously reaffirmed Bartleby's "cadaverous triumph" and his ultimate "ascendency." And in this sense the narrator's lament for Bartleby and for humanity is prompted by his recognition that for the greater number of persons now alive or yet to be born Bartleby can appear only an unredeemable fool, his contempt for the world an unholy madness, his attempt at social insurrection an abortive failure, and his resurrection out of the question. In Melville's dimly lit theater of hope, life is too often a surrealistic allegory; and art, which could reverse the conventional view of the world and invert the more typical judgments of society, is our feeble means of redemption.

Christopher Bollas (essay date 1974)

SOURCE: "Melville's Lost Self: *Bartleby*," in *American Imago*, Vol. 31, No. 4, Winter, 1974, pp. 401-11.

[*In the following essay, Bollas argues that a psychological interpretation of "Bartleby" demonstrates the value of psychoanalysis to literary criticism.*]

Herman Melville's short novel **"Bartleby"** is, a tale about a "pallidly neat, pitiably respectable, incurably forlorn" young man who answers an advertisement for a position as a scrivener. He is accepted for employment, disrupts the routine of his new environment when he "prefers not to" engage in certain assigned tasks, forces the employer to feel a resourcelessness that compels him to move his office. It ends in Bartleby's pathetic death after he has been hustled off to prison.

I believe that Bartleby's arrival at the office and his subsequent breakdown into negativity is a mimetic representation of a need to find a nurturant space where he can regress toward the healing of a "basic fault" in the self. I want to focus on **"Bartleby"** as a transitional moment in Melville's fiction when his central heroic type (Ahab, Ishmael, Taji, Pierre) shifts from searching to being found, where Bartleby's search for the employer becomes a move toward discovery, his existential ambience that of throwing out a deeply dissociated self state. **"Bartleby"** provides us with an opportunity to study a subject's expression of his autism, where relinquishing of the self's executant ego functions becomes a lingual invitation to the other to fill the absence of function with the nurture of care, to cradle in supporting arms the dissolving self in its unintegrated muteness, as the other is induced, without words, to create the ambience desired by a self dying in order to be reborn. **"Bartleby"** is uniquely suited for study of several central concerns in contemporary psychoanalysis, and because it can provide the literary critic with an appreciation of the contribution current psychoanalytic studies of the self can make to literary studies.

The narrator begins the story by describing himself as a "rather elderly man, . . . a man who, from his youth upwards has been filled with a profound conviction that the easiest way of life is the best," made easier by "the cool tranquility of a snug retreat" where he does a "snug business among rich men's bonds, and mortgages and titledeeds." "All who know me," he tells us, "consider me an eminently *safe* man." Indeed, it is lucky for his employees, Turkey, Nippers, and Ginger Nut, that he is such a gentle man. For in the "snug retreat" of their office space, these workers—whose names have been mutually conferred as embodying their characteristics—regularly complement one another in the dripping of ink, knocking over of chairs, spilling of sandboxes, breaking of pens, and hoarding of food. In their kaleidoscopic world, these workers incarnate the instincts: oral; in their food names, their teeth grinding, hoarding and spilling of food; anal, in the spilling of ink, of sand, and waste of food remains; phallic, in the comic erections of self (i.e. when Turkey is up, Nippers is down). Despite the kindergarten atmosphere, the narrator values each of his helpers, and by dividing his space from theirs by a folding glass door, he indicates a distance between their embodiment of instinct and his own function as the executant self.

Then Bartleby arrives. The employer-narrator hires him and provides him with a special space on his side of the sliding doors, facing a wall some three feet away. "Still further to a satisfactory arrangement," he says "I procured a high green folding screen, which might entirely isolate Bartleby from my sight, though not remove him from my voice. And thus, in a manner, privacy and society were conjoined." In setting up this "necessary arrangement," the narrator continues his function as the facilitating agent in providing for others, his arranged space for Turkey, Nippers, and Ginger Nut already termed a "good natural arrangement, under the circumstances."

Readers of Melville's novel *Pierre,* which preceded this short novel by less than a year, may note the similarity between Bartleby's arranged space and Pierre's closet where the latter lapsed into reverential time before a portrait of his idealized dead father. Pierre's ritual withdrawal to his closet is vital to our knowledge of Bartleby and to the *meconnaisance* between the narrator and his curious employee. Disillusioned by the shattering news of his father's illegitimate siring of a daughter, Pierre rips his father's portrait from the wall of his closet. This collapse in the *image* of the idealized father precipitates a violent and more troubling rift with his mother, who casts him out of her home. Pierre flees to New York with his new wife, none other than his illegitimate sister. Above all, it seems to me, *Pierre* is a novel about the collapse of illusion—metaphorically stated, in the mimesis of Pierre's removal of his father's portrait—and in a youth's incapacity to rescue himself from catastrophic disillusion. As Pierre wanders through an art gallery not long before his violent death, he muses: "All the walls of the world seemed thickly hung with the empty and impotent scope of pictures, grandly outlined, but miserably filled." Walls no longer hold ideal images on their surface and in Melville's fiction, I believe, this signifies the absence of generative illusion, so that Bartleby's disfunctional autism is a psychosomatic communication, a use of the self as signifier, where the signified broadly represents the loss of generative illusion, and specifically, the loss of the paternal and maternal imagos. As we learn at the end of the story, Bartleby has come to this work after being fired from his post in the Dead Letter Office at Washington, a job that compels the narrator to reflect aptly: "Dead Letters! does it not sound like dead men?" "On errands of life," he ponders, "these letters speed to death," and Bartleby's former work signifies, I think, his retreat after his failure to find a voice in the Word to speak his pain, dead letters signifying the death of the Word.

The narrator senses Bartleby's needs by providing him with a private space, alongside of a protective other. "At first, Bartleby did an extraordinary quantity of writing. As if long famishing for something to copy, he seemed to gorge himself on my documents." But the feeding fails to nurture the novice scrivener, who writes "silently, palely, mechanically," his craft pointing to the absence of any internal creative potential. A man who has sorted dead letters now writes in a dead manner, his copying an empty gesture marking the absence of language. Copying of the Word leads not to an identification with the other (as a child's learning of language sponsors an identification with his parents), but to a truncated isolation from the fruits of grasping the Word. Embryonic in his enclosed space, the young scrivener resorts to the Word—spoken in neutral and economic tones—only to ward off the other. When asked to join in the varied routines of collective tasks, he refuses:

> "I would prefer not to," he said. I looked at him steadfastly. His face was leanly composed; his grey eyes dimly calm. Not a wrinkle of agitation rippled him. Had there been the least uneasiness, anger, impatience or impertinence in his manner; in other words, had there been anything ordinarily human about him, doubtless I should have violently dismissed him from the premises. But as it was, I should have as soon thought of turning my pale plaster-of-paris bust of Cicero out of doors.

At first outraged and perplexed by Bartleby's uncommon reply, the narrator shifts his response when he grasps that his new employee's resistance is unintended as rebellion, indeed, he feels himself drawn into "a bond of common humanity" with his strange office fellow. So, when he learns that Bartleby lives in the office, the narrator is plunged into sharing a sense of Bartleby's homelessness: "It is evident enough that Bartleby has been making his home here, keeping bachelor's hall all by himself. Immediately then the thought came sweeping across me, what miserable friendlessness and loneliness are here revealed! His poverty is great; but his solitude, how horrible!" He reflects on his new employee's habit of gazing in perfect solitude on "the dead brick wall," a phenomenon he describes as "dead-wall reveries." Feeling the new scrivener to be a "victim of an innate and incurable disorder," he says: "I might give alms to his body; but his body did not pain him; it was his soul that suffered, and his soul I

could not reach." With the others he has found viable interplay between his function as director (executant ego) and their rhythmic expression of instinct; but Bartleby brings to him a deep absence in the self, a subject prior to the reflexive experience of instincts. This vacant quality in the new employee threatens the narrator's moderately compulsive defenses and leaves him with the uncertain feeling that he is incapable of doing anything for Bartleby.

Matters worsen. As if sensing the narrator's recognition of his own helplessness, Bartleby gives up working altogether. The employer tries unsuccessfully to fire him, but fails because Bartleby remains unresponsive to demand. Once again, Bartleby's presence creates an alien feeling in the narrator: "I might enter my office in a great hurry, and pretending not to see Bartleby at all, walk straight against him as if he were air." Again he accommodates, in fact, finds solace simply in Bartleby's presence. "I never feel so private as when I know you are here," he muses and adds humorously, "my mission in this world, Bartleby, is to furnish you with office-room for such period as you may see fit to remain." He considers acting as if his existence were to serve his strange companion, but this reflection is never actualized because his colleagues' reaction to his eccentric employee compels him to acknowledge reality. Unable to budge Bartleby, the narrator goes to the extreme of moving his office ("Strange to say—I tore myself from him whom I had so longed to be rid of") but is later called upon by the legal counsel of the building's new occupant—who is faced with the same dilemma—to remove this strangely unresponsive character who now says: "I like to be stationary."

As the story comes to its enigmatically tragic end, Bartleby is hustled off to the Tombs by an irate crowd and a furious landlord. After a while, the narrator comes to visit him in the prison, and discovers that because of Bartleby's serenity and apparent harmlessness, the prison authorities have allowed him to freely wander about the prison. The narrator finds him "standing all alone in the quietest of the yards, his face towards a high wall." As he approaches, Bartleby replies: "I know you . . . and I want nothing to say to you." Once again, unable to get through to Bartleby, the narrator takes his leave, but returns several days later to find that he has refused to eat. Told by a guard that Bartleby is asleep, he approaches his friend's space.

> Strangely huddled at the base of the wall, his knees drawn up, and lying on his side, his head touching the cold stones, I saw the wasted Bartleby. But nothing stirred. I paused; then went close up to him; stooped over, and saw that his dim eyes were open; otherwise he seemed profoundly sleeping. Something prompted me to touch him. I felt his hand, when a tingling shiver ran up my arm and down my spine to my feet.
>
> The round face of the grub-man peered upon me now.
>
> "His dinner is ready. Won't he dine to-day, either? Or does he live without dining?"
>
> "Lives without dining," said I, and closed the eyes.

Bartleby, to my mind, is Ahab or Pierre come in out of the cold. The counterphobic search, the manic heroic *quest* is over, the true self finally existentially revealed in its condition of absolute need for the other is Melville's subject, in this, the saddest of his works. In **"Bartleby,"** the split in Melville's characters (Ahab/Ishmael) is fused temporarily in an isolated figure whose heroic passivity is both an active thrust against the narrator and an evocation of a desire to be provided for, permitting a complete shutting down of the self, willed into, and like Ahab, against existence. Unable to speak, except to use language against itself, Bartleby's loss of a creative use of the Word signifies a final stage in this character's renunciation of culture, begun with Pierre's disillusion with the image of an ideal father. But such withdrawal, like the artist's seclusion from what Heiddegger terms the world of "They," may be a falling into one's privacy in order to intensify the value of "They," to find in one's privacy a way back toward living. Michael Balint terms this a "regression for the sake of progression," a collapse in ego maintenance as the subject falls toward the "basic fault" in the self, in order to constitute a "new beginning." Bartleby falls into the "necessary arrangement" provided by the nurturant narrator, and after an intense satiation of rigid activity, he lapses into dead-wall reveries, in such deep regression that he can no longer work, nor respond to the narrator's exhortations to try.

It seems to me that the narrator, like the reader of this story, waits for something to happen, to materialize like the phoenix from Bartleby's ashen vacancy. Indeed, Bartleby hints at least once that his extraordinary privacy may be temporary when to the narrator's pleas for more information about himself he replies: "At present I prefer to give no answer." Will he, at some future date, finally tell? Melville's tale suggests to me an answer. In the culture of the 1850's, there is no generative space or time to permit a shutting down of the executant function of the self. Bartleby's only hope is to find some capacity to use the Word. The narrator's placement of his new employee, secluded in private, yet joined to a facilitating other, sequestered before the Word that he must copy if he is to live, is an instinctive and "necessary arrangement" for Bartleby's survival. The first step in this new beginning will be imitation (copying), like the child's imitating his mother's tongue, a preliminary to the child's creative use of his own Word. But Bartleby's copying of the Word does not revivify the dead letters, and failing to find a transformational grammar, he can only repeat an empty phrase that signifies his incapacity to symbolize his needs. In the America of the 1850's, there is no space but a prison for someone so desperately ill.

On one level, as I have argued, Bartleby's *presence* sponsors a series of actions by the narrator, responses to an *absence* in Bartleby, that in the dialectical rhythm of presence of the subject, signifying an absence in the subject eliciting a presence in the other, mimetically recreates the need of the lonely scrivener to have his pain held by the other. This mimesis—sponsored by the dialectical interplay of presence/absence/ presence—is Bartleby's language, his way of in-forming the other's response. With scant information about Bartleby through verbal language, the narrator comes to know his new friend by allowing himself to be manipulated (used as Bartleby's object), and by sensing the other through internal psychic and affective presences in himself. Like the narrator, we discover Bartleby as he exists inside the narrator. Indeed, Melville's story is primarily concerned with how Bartleby sponsors affective states in the narrator who feels compassionate, nurturant, helpless, resourceless, anxious, dispossesed, enraged, humiliated, abused, playful, pleaful, and guilty, and who tries to defend himself by compliance, compulsive boundary setting, avoidance, denial, exorcism, and finally flight. This phenomenology of affect and defense is a phantom reflection of the silent scrivener, an affect language not spoken to the narrator, but thrown into and then lived out by him.

It seems to me, after some reflection, that Bartleby embodies an absence in the self of this blithely cheerful narrator, a psychic double who represents the dramatic and aggravating presence of a repudiated true self: the internal other in the personality that is a collage of psychically, familially, and culturally disowned instincts and ego states that are never realized in the active life of the subject. Never actualized because they are sequestered through repression or splitting from being lived out, they are known to the executant self by the energy and style of the defenses organized against this true self. Ironically then, the presence of the true self is known primarily by the defenses that signify its absence. Bartleby, however, assaults the narrator's defensive style, forcing the narrator to feel the pain of the true self, to meet its needs, and to acknowledge its absence as a horrid personal loss. Gradually, the force of the true self threatens the executant self as the latter (personalized in the narrator) feels itself merging with the true self (personalized in Bartleby).

> Somehow, of late, I had got into the way of involuntarily using this word "prefer" upon all sorts of not exactly suitable occasions. And I trembled to think that my contact with the scrivener had already and seriously affected me in a mental way. And what further and deeper aberration might it not yet produce? This apprehension had not been without efficacy in determining me to summary measures.

It is when the narrator begins to merge with Bartleby— by adopting his habit of mind—that he is prompted by his anxiety to dissociate himself from Bartleby, the latter's state of being compelling the former toward a series of actions (doing) designed to protect the executant self (the doing self) against the true self (in Melville, the self in inert being). Indeed, the more the narrator is compelled toward doing, the more isolated is the being of Bartleby, until finally action becomes a psychic repudiation of being that leads to ultimate social dissociation (prison) and death.

Bartleby mimes the insistent presence of the unknowable and unspeakable. (Since the ultimate dissociation is separation from the Word, then the true self's vital depen-

> **On Bartleby's representativeness:**
>
> The narrator's realization that Bartleby's condition represents the human condition, that his relationship with the scrivener is symbolic, is the final and most profound irony of this ironic tale. Preternaturally and pathologically withdrawn, what more unlikely person could be found as a symbol for all humanity than this scrivener? Lacking in qualities "ordinarily human," the "forlornest of mankind," "A bit of wreck in the mid-Atlantic," "deranged," "inscrutable"—these are the terms the narrator has used to describe Bartleby, the terms we must recall fully to understand the depth of irony contained in the final revelation. The bond of common humanity the narrator finally sees, is not that of a comfortable Christian piety which enjoins love, compassion, and generosity; it is the strange and disconcerting bond of isolation which does not oppose but simply makes irrelevant the conventional pieties that have guided the narrator's life. This insight turns the mystery of Bartleby into an appalling revelation.
>
> *Richard Abcarian, in "The World of Love and the Spheres of Fright: Melville's 'Bartleby the Scrivener',"* Studies in Short Fiction, *Vol. 1, No. 3, Spring 1964, pp. 207-15.*

dency on the executant self's capacity to speak from it is lost). But this is not a story about the repudiation of a troubling and troubled presence as in *Moby Dick* (perhaps, a final exorcism of Ahab), for the narrator is made to mourn the loss of Bartleby. "For the first time in my life," he says "a feeling of overpowering stinging melancholy seized me. Before, I had never experienced aught but a not unpleasing sadness." The overpowering melancholy draws him toward his friend even after he has been removed from him: "the bond of a common humanity now drew me irresistibily to gloom. A fraternal melancholy."

So Bartleby does make the heretofore smooth running executant self feel the pain of grief for the first time in his life, a sadness sponsored by the unmet needs and desperate isolation of a double, a figure "out there" who embodies an internal absence. When this internal vacant self confronts the blithely cheerful narrator in his old age, he tries to provide for it, nurture it in his own way toward a lively integration with the natural order of things: the culture of his office. All his efforts fail to vitalize an absence in his being. For Bartleby is, finally, like the damaged true self, an internal presence that is *unconsolable*. All that is left to the grieving narrator is a profound recognition and sense that something terribly needy, horribly isolated, "incurably forlorn" is lost forever.

All of Melville's heroes feel this internal haunting other in themselves, whether it is the mysterious stranger that lives inside Babbalanja or the gnawing presence in Ahab. Sometimes, the other is projected outside, writ large upon the landscape and encountered by the executant self as with Ahab and the whale. I believe this aggravated and mysterious other is also in the author of all these stories, an absent presence in Melville who tries in his fiction to

throw it out into imaginary characters, but whose novels signify its mysterious isolation. Failing to exorcize this other in *Moby Dick,* to marry it in *Pierre,* or to revivify it in "Bartleby," Melville turns in *The Confidence Man* to an apparently bitter expostulation of the sorcery—the compensatory cleverness—of the false self (the executant self uninformed by the true self). In the *Confidence Man,* illusion manipulation becomes the tool of the con man who metamorphoses himself into multiple false selves, and Melville signifies in this novel the end of his effort to give voice to the unknown interior self by fashioning an illusionist who, like the artist, can obscure the existence of an interior presence by sheer artifice. If the Confidence Man is born of despair and failure, if it is a magical evocation of the art of deceit, it is still a curious celebration of Melville's talent for fashioning illusion, a sweet bitterness before the long years of silence and absence.

R. K. Gupta (essay date 1974)

SOURCE: "'Bartleby': Melville's Critique of Reason," in *Indian Journal of American Studies,* Vol. 4, Nos. 1-2, June and December, 1974, pp. 66-71.

[*In the following excerpt, Gupta insists that the narrator of "Bartleby" represents reason, and that Bartleby, in confounding the narrator, emphasizes the inability of pure reason to negotiate human behavior.*]

> "Say now, that in a day or two you will begin to be a little reasonable:—say so, Bartleby."
>
> "At present I would prefer not to be a little reasonable," was his mildly cadaverous reply.

The unnamed narrator of **"Bartleby"** is an apostle of reason. His outlook on life is clear, unambiguous, and uncluttered by mysticism or imagination. Reason and common sense are his deities, and he looks upon them as infallible guides to human conduct.

All goes well with the narrator until he decides to engage as his new scrivener an inscrutable and "motionless" young man named Bartleby. For two days, Bartleby diligently does "an extraordinary quantity of writing." But on the third day, when the narrator calls him to compare a copy sheet, Bartleby, "in a singularly mild, firm voice," replies: "I would prefer not to." The narrator is stunned by what he considers to be the unreasonableness of Bartleby's conduct and briefly argues with him. But Bartleby remains unmoved.

A few days later, the narrator again solicits Bartleby's help, and Bartleby again replies: "I would prefer not to." This time, the narrator is so amazed at Bartleby's intransigence that for a few moments he is "turned into a pillar of salt." The first thing he does on recovering his composure is to ask the "reason" for it: *"Why* do you refuse?" (italics Melville's). When Bartleby simply repeats the refrain: "I would prefer not to," the narrator begins to "reason with him." His appeal is to "common usage and common sense." But even this appeal goes unheeded and Bartleby tells him that his decision—or shall I say preference—is irreversible. This greatly upsets the narrator, particularly because Bartleby's refusal is "unprecedented" and "unreasonable."

Several days pass. But Bartleby shows no sign of relenting, and continues in his course of passive resistance. Again and again, the narrator asks him to do something "perfectly reasonable," and again and again his only reply is: "I would prefer not to." The narrator is not so much annoyed at the inconvenience that Bartleby's conduct causes him as he is flabbergasted by its "perverseness" and "unreasonableness." He has spent his whole life shutting out whatever is unpleasant or inconvenient. His mind has, therefore, fallen into a groove it cannot easily get out of. Bartleby's advent, however, creates a situation with which he can cope effectively only if he can break out of his routine and think in unaccustomed ways. Since nothing in his life and experience has prepared him for such an eventuality, he feels helpless and lost. The story dramatizes how tragically the narrator fails to deal with Bartleby in an effective manner and how Bartleby's steady and compulsive refusal gradually undermines the norms by which he has lived so far.

In course of time, the narrator becomes sufficiently interested in Bartleby to want to know the details of his life and the source of his malady. But even here he is frustrated, and Bartleby prefers not to tell him anything about himself. The narrator is now completely nonplussed: what "reasonable objection," he wonders, can Bartleby have to speak to him. After all, he feels "friendly" towards him. Even now, he clings tenaciously, although somewhat precariously, to his hope that given time, Bartleby may be brought round to see reason, and in a highly significant scene, he addresses Bartleby thus:

> "Bartleby, never mind, then, about revealing your history; but let me entreat you, as a friend, to comply as far as may be with the usages of this office. Say now you will help to examine papers to-morrow or next day: in short, say now that in a day or two you will begin to be a little reasonable—say so, Bartleby."

> "At present I would prefer not to be a little reasonable," was his mildly cadaverous reply.

Critics have shown great ingenuity trying to determine the cause of Bartleby's malady. But to look for a rational explanation of Bartleby's conduct is to repeat the narrator's mistake and to miss the whole point of the story. The most significant aspect of Bartleby's behavior is that it is not only unexplained but also inexplicable, and that it is therefore futile to invoke reason and common sense in dealing with it or in trying to understand it. Melville carefully refrains from identifying the source of Bartleby's problem, because Bartleby's very irrationality is the point of his story. In **"Bartleby"** Melville clearly suggests what is confirmed by modern psychology: that men are not primarily creatures of reason, but are controlled by dimly perceived instinctual drives and obscure impul-

sions, and that this being so, one needs much more than reason and common sense to deal effectively with human problems.

Herein, I think, lies the failure—or should we call it the limitation of the narrator. He pitches reason's claims exceptionally high and over-estimates the range of the results that can be achieved by an exclusive reliance on it. He has too much confidence in the efficacy of intellectual processes. Unaware of the merits of unreflecting spontaneity, he has committed himself to the slow pace, the qualifications and hedging of rational thought. For a long time, critics have debated what the narrator could or should have done, and some have gone to the extent of showing annoyance with Bartleby and considerable respect for the narrator. That the narrator is benevolent and well-intentioned is undoubtedly true, but it is also completely irrelevant. What is relevant is his flatulence and evasion, and his application of only compromises and half-measures to what is an extreme malady—"innate and incurable disorder" as he himself calls it. But the "disorder" is "incurable" only in terms of the palliatives that the narrator, with his limited vision, can think of. Because he has boundless faith in the efficacy of unaided reason as an instrument of action, he is totally helpless when exposed to a reason-defying situation. When faced with Bartleby's unreasonable wilfulness, the best that he can do is to try to reason him out of it through appeals to tradition, authority, and common usage. . . . But the situation calls for more than reason; it calls for intuition and imagination, which the narrator has eschewed all his life. Henri Bergson remarks that the surest way to attain the truth is by perception and intuition, by reasoning to a certain point, then by taking a "mortal leap." The narrator, however, can go only so far as reason takes him. Not being gifted with imagination and intuition, he is incapable of taking the "mortal leap" that might have enabled him to cope with his problem successfully.

From the standpoint of conventional morality, of course, no guilt attaches to the narrator. His guilt, as Maurice Friedman points out [in his "'Bartleby' and the Modern Exile"], is "existential guilt," the guilt of "human existence itself, the guilt that every man feels when his responsibility for another is unlimited while his resources are limited." He is, to be sure, more tolerant than most people would have been in his situation, and he was constitutionally incapable of the kind of sympathy that was required. But the narrator in "Bartleby" is not judged from the viewpoint of conventional morality. He is judged from the viewpoint of idealistic Christian morality, from standards which, to use Plotinus Plinlimmon's phrase in *Pierre,* are "chronometrical" rather than "horological." The attorney in Murray's ["'Bartleby' and I"] complains thus:

> But my profoundest, all-embracing grievance comes from an uneasy feeling, or suspicion, that Mr. Melville was out to flog me with the Sermon on the Mount, as if to say, you should have given the full measure of your love to Bartleby, all of it, every atom's atom of it, without reservations, qualifications, or reflections as to the consequences of so selfless a commitment of

compasion. You should have sacrificed your profession, deserted your clients, set aside your duties to the High Court of Chancery, and taken Bartleby to live with you at home. Is not the author implying this and nothing less? If he is, I'd like to ask, what right has he to judge me from that unearthly and inhuman pinnacle of ethics?

The narrator's morality, however, is firmly rooted in expediency, and his self-interest tends to supplant altruistic considerations. Even his kindness is not entirely a product of compassion but is often motivated by prudence. When faced with spiritual crises, he responds with his usual stance of reason and common sense, a stance admirably suited to his own utilitarian world, but hopelessly ineffectual in relation to Bartleby's situation. As an apostle of reason, he so desperately seeks rational explanations for Bartleby's conduct that he is driven to read "Edwards on the Will" and "Priestley on Necessity" in the vain hope that these writers might shed light on it. The rumored explanation of Bartleby's conduct that he offers in the epilogue is again an attempt on his part to account in a tidy and rational manner, for what is essentially above and beyond reason. Even after having undergone the experience, the narrator has not understood its full purport. Although he has had glimpses into hitherto unexplored aspects of life, he has not assimilated his experience fully. In fact, he is still bewildered by it, and his recounting of the experience might well be the result of his compulsive need to rationalize it, and thus to exorcise it out of his system where it has for long festered as a sore, upsetting his precise and measured ways of life.

In the final analysis then, the story focuses on the narrator's failure of perception and judgment. His unswerving faith in reason and common sense renders him unfit for dealing effectively with Bartleby's situation. He tries to cure Bartleby's spiritual paralysis by tentative acts of charity, and fails to realize that Bartleby's problem could not be fathomed by logic but only by imaginative understanding. He is thus one of those mundane men who reduce everything to what Carlyle's Teufelsdrockh calls "Attorney-Logic." Spiritual insight is not granted to such as he. Ministering utilitarian solutions to spiritual problems, he becomes what Tuefelsdrockh calls a "sandblind pedant":

> whoso recognizes the unfathomable, all-pervading domain of Mystery, which is everywhere under out feet and among our hands; to whom the Universe is an Oracle and Temple, as well as a Kitchen and Cattle stall,—he shall be a delirious Mystic; to him thou with sniffing charity, wilt protrusively proffer thy hand-lamp, and shriek, as one injured, when he kicks his foot through it—*Armer Teufel* . . . Retire into private places with thy foolish cackle; or what were better, give it up, and weep, not that thy reign of wonder is done, and God's world all disembellished and prosaic, but that thou hitherto art a Dilletante and sandblind pedant.

Thus in **"Bartleby"** Melville brings out the limits of reason as a guide to human conduct and as a controlling

factor in human behavior and stresses the need for understanding and imagination. He shows in unmistakable terms that intellectual and analytical processes are not the most decisive determinants of the beliefs and conduct of men, and that human behavior, therefore, cannot be fully grasped by reason but only by imagination. Although Melville did not share the Transcendentalist belief in the supremacy and infallibility of intuition, he recognized its need and its value in establishing meaningful human relationships. The need for human interdependence is, after all, a recurrent theme in Melville's fiction, and in **"Bartleby"** Melville shows a full awareness of how lack of insight and intuition and an exclusive reliance on reason can block channels of communication. No wonder, then, that the story should seem teasingly modern in rhythm, idiom, and controlling vision, and that critics should seek—and find—its analogues, not in Melville's contemporaries, but in such Russian masters as Gogol, Goncharov, and Dostoievsky, and in the modern existentialists such a Sartre, Camus, and Kafka.

Ted Billy (essay date 1975)

SOURCE: "Eros and Thanatos in 'Bartleby'," in *Arizona Quarterly*, Vol. 31, No. 1, Spring, 1975, pp. 21-32.

[*In the following essay, Billy interprets the narrator and Bartleby, respectively, as fictional projections of eros and thanatos principles in Melville's own psyche, and considers "Bartleby" a portrait of psychological conflict between the life and death instincts.*]

The final comment of Melville's narrator in **"Bartleby the Scrivener"** ("Ah, Bartleby! Ah, humanity!") acts as a synecdoche for the irreconcilable struggle that animates the novella. This brief statement of commiseration does more than merely link Bartleby's predicament to the universal human situation. It pinpoints the root of the conflict—the antagonism between the isolated individual and the whole of society. Melville chooses as his theme the tragic fragmentation of the human sensibility. This fragmentation in man's psyche stems from the loss of the intrinsic interaction between the human organism and his immediate physical environment. **"Bartleby"** serves as the literary objectification of Melville's intense awareness of the psychological trauma of fragmentation, anxiety, and alienation. And behind it all lies the source of psychic disequilibrium—a dead, blank wall—the void of nothingness.

The narrator and Bartleby are fictional projections of the eros and thanatos principles in Melville's divided self. Bartleby embodies the death instinct, separateness, negation, the futility of existence, masochism, and the desolation of human mortality. But the pathetic scrivener also signifies the impulse toward self-preservation through the isolating independence of the individual life, which utterly rejects the collectivity of the human species. The narrator represents eros, the life instinct, the desire for communion among the collective unconscious of mankind. In this respect, he is Melville's fictional representative of the love impulse (specifically charity) which seeks union and interdependence to promote the survival of the human species. The narrator's various attempts to empathize with Bartleby and offer the morose scrivener the community of his own home are expressions of the human need for the life instinct to attain unification with its opposite, the death instinct. For man can never be free of paralyzing anxiety until he accepts the nothingness of death.

This antagonistic dualism of eros and thanatos really oversimplifies a perennial and complex problem. Yet this conflict remains the basis for all human neuroses and discontent. For man's entrance into self-consciousness is a fall "from a condition of undifferentiated primal unity within himself and with nature" into a state of anxiety and alienation in which human individuality is promoted through differentiation and antagonism within the self and with his physical environment [Norman O. Brown, *Life Against Death*]. Self-consciousness shatters the primal unity between individual and species, independence and interdependence, union and isolation, and the end result of this division is anxiety. As the ultimate cause of repression and neurosis, anxiety thrives as the human response to separateness, individuality, and death. Anxiety builds up in that part of man which refuses to accept the insulation of individuality and rejects the finality of death.

This fragmentation of human nature breeds free-floating anxiety and nourishes man's estrangement from being. The ego or conscious will should be considered a social convention, not a psychological entity. The ego is an imaginary, socially fabricated self working against the whole organism, the biologically grown self. Isolation of the conscious will from the total organism spawns alienation. Thus, man lives in the symbolic self-image that he projects artificially rather than in the real self which is housed in his total organism. The attempt to adapt to life in an artificial way further separates him from his essential grounds of motivation. This fragmentation of man's functional processes distorts the individual's relation to his physical environment. As Norman O. Brown describes it, "civilized objectivity is non-participating consciousness, consciousness as separation, as dualism, distance, definition, as property and prison: consciousness ruled by negation, which is from the death instinct" [*Love's Body*].

Bartleby's consciousness is ruled by negation, a manifestation of the death instinct. His behavioral pattern involves passive resistance to everything. By refusing to act at all, for good or ill, Bartleby negates his reason for being. In existential terms, he *is* nothing (the sum of his actions), for he prefers to endure his suffering, without hope and without choice. By negating all alternatives, Bartleby abandons himself to a suicide of the will. He dies as a martyr to the futility of existence.

Bartleby's negation of the will is a kind of perversion of the Oriental doctrine of nonaction. This doctrine derives its substance from the belief that the self is merely an illusory fabrication which, when properly understood, dissolves into the maya of nonexistence. Thus, since the self doesn't really exist, action is an exercise in foolishness, and nonaction (contemplation) is the highest activity. But Bartleby's nonaction is the response of a diseased organism, a dying man. Freud's assertion that "a negative judgment is the intellectual substitute for repression" can be applied to the scrivener's everlasting *NO*.

Bartleby represents a fictional manifestation of the thanatos principle in Melville's consciousness. Throughout the narrative, Bartleby's passive resistance, absolute resignation, and specterlike appearance mark him as a tragic figure embodying the artist's submerged death wish. This is further illuminated by the biblical phrase which the narrator quotes over the prostrate form of the dead scrivener in the Tombs. Bartleby is indeed asleep "with kings and counsellors." Melville alludes to the Book of Job, specifically to Job's plaint, one of the most powerful poetic statements, rich in existential impact, in the Old Testament. An examination of the full text of Job's plaint significantly broadens the psychological horizons surrounding Melville's creation of Bartleby.

Job, unlike Bartleby, possesses a deeply moving lyrical voice to articulate the despair inflicted upon him by his manifold sorrows. Job wishes that the day of his birth would be annihilated. He asks for blackness, gloom, and darkness to obliterate its intolerable reality. He implores the night to be barren and joyless, and he wishes that he had perished upon emerging from the womb. Job bitterly expresses the death impulse when he desires that his existence had been stillborn or else aborted prior to his birth. He regards the dismal atmosphere of Sheol (the Hebrew version of hell) to be preferable to all the maladies of earthly life.

> For now should I have lain still and been quiet, I should have slept; then had I been at rest,
>
> With kings and counsellors of the earth, which built desolate places for themselves;
>
> Job 3.13-14

Sheol's morbid monotony at least gives rest to the weary and means the cessation of all trouble for even the most wicked sinners. Job identifies himself with those who wait in agony for death and rejoice when they finally reach the tomb. Job begs for ease, peace, and a final rest, but he is denied all this.

> For my sighing cometh before I eat, and my roarings are poured out like the waters.
>
> For the thing which I feared is come upon me, and that which I was afraid of is come unto me.
>
> I was not in safety, neither had I rest, neither was I quiet; yet trouble came.
>
> Job 3.24-26

The Book of Job concerns the problem of evil in the world. Job demands that God reveal the reason behind unjust human suffering. This is a thoroughly reasonable request. The dialectic of the Book of Job resolves itself solely through divine intervention. God cannot provide Job with a rational explanation of the problem of evil. But the fact that Job can see and hear the Lord saves him from the abyss of nothingness, and only because of this, he is willing to repent in dust and ashes before God. The experience of nothingness, rather than the problem of evil or unjust misery, is the true cause of despair. Because Job can substitute an inscrutable God for an impenetrable emptiness, he escapes the anxiety and alienation that overwhelms Bartleby.

The experience of nothingness, not the problem of evil, looms as the central issue in **"Bartleby."** It is not the power of blackness so much as the power of blankness that Melville depicts in his novella. Melville's chief symbol for the emptiness of existence is the series of dead, blank walls that enclose the scrivener within a repressive atmosphere throughout the tale. Melville relies upon architectural details and other physical references to convey his metaphysical observations. The Wall Street offices exhibit mute white walls in the interior and Bartleby's small side-window faces "a lofty brick wall, black by age and everlasting shade." The high green folding screen which the narrator employs to isolate Bartleby from his sight is another blank barrier prohibiting the free flow of life. Melville uses the expressionless impersonality of walls as graphic emblems of the forces that isolate and imprison man.

Melville forges a direct relationship between Bartleby's visual perception of the vacancy of existence and the constant anxiety that paralyzes his will. When the narrator finds Bartleby transfixed in a dead-wall reverie and preferring not to copy, the cursory reader may tend to overlook the scrivener's curious explanation—"Do you not see the reason for yourself?" Bartleby asks the narrator to open his eyes to the realization that the sensible world is only a panorama of illusions and therefore void of meaning. All organic life is enmeshed in a process of dying and decaying. This is the fundamental reality behind Bartleby's fixation on dead-wall vistas. Another glimpse of this concrete nihilistic vision occurs when the narrator tries to console the incarcerated Bartleby in the Tombs. The narrator assures him that the present moment is not unbearable and the future can be better. But Bartleby deflates all hope with his chilling remark: "I know where I am." The scrivener declines to transcend the rock-bottom reality of his human situation. He stands face to face with nothingness. The illusion of freedom is circumscribed and his doom is inevitable. Bartleby sees the world as a prison that can only be escaped through the pangs of death. Any hope for eternal life only begins a new round of meaningless illusions. Engulfed by anxiety and estrangement, Bartleby forlornly renounces his will to live.

Bartleby's conduct neutralizes his freedom of choice. He is a silent spectator, not an active participant, in the life he perpetually denies. Behind his green barrier, Bartleby barely exists—quietly, without external agitation, "oblivious to everything." "He was a perpetual sentry in the corner." The narrator considers Bartleby's plight an incurable disorder of the soul. The prolonged dead-wall reveries are transfixed emblems of hopeless spiritual suffering. Bartleby "prefers" to be stationary, an organic fixture sullenly composed behind his screen. "He seemed alone, absolutely alone in the universe. A bit of wreck in the mid-Atlantic." Even as his tragic existence approaches its end, Bartleby still clings to his hopeless doctrine of nonaction. "The poor scrivener, when told that he must be conducted to the Tombs, offered not the slightest obstacle, but, in his pale, unmoving way, silently acquiesced." Ultimately, Bartleby does lie down forever "with kings and counsellors."

Like Goethe's Mephistopheles, Bartleby is a "spirit that negates." His stolid "I would prefer not to" is completely divorced from the normal realm of human emotions. It's the muffled outcry of a pathetic victim—"pallidly neat, pitiably respectable, incurably forlorn"—who prefers to dwell silently in his hermitage, oblivious to all but his own anguish. Bartleby is not only alienated from the barren world around him but also from the internal void of his existence. He is so estranged from his own being that "he had declined telling who he was, or whence he came, or whether he had any relatives in the world." To the narrator, Bartleby is the "sole spectator of a solitude"—a sort of "transformed Marius brooding among the ruins of Carthage!" Melville's reference to ruins in his story, especially when he likens the Tombs to Egyptian pyramids, again suggests the "waste places" of kings and counselors in the Book of Job. "Like the last column of some ruined temple, he remained standing mute and solitary in the middle of the otherwise deserted room." In this respect, Bartleby is a kind of inverted Ozymandias figure, silently protesting the ephemeral quality of man's life and works.

There is a double irony implicit in the humorous scene in which the narrator suggests an assortment of alternative occupations for Bartleby. Melville displays light comedy when the scrivener proclaims "I am not particular" three times after he refuses the series of choices. Bartleby's obstinate behavior contradicts the apathy of his assertion. But the scrivener's "I am not particular" also contradicts Bartleby's individuality, the disease of unnatural separation from the total organic life that afflicts him throughout the novella. It is because Bartleby *is* "particular" that he cannot be reintegrated into his physical environment. Bartleby's particularity is the result of the fragmentation, anxiety, and alienation which isolate him from the collective whole of humanity and annihilates his will to resist disintegration. For this reason, his reiterated response ("I am not particular") is doubly ironic.

On one level of interpretation, Bartleby stands as a fatalistic victim of the basic human predicament: individualized man confronted with nothingness and devastated by fragmentation, anxiety, and estrangement. But on another level of meaning, Bartleby and the narrator function as fictional projections that mirror the interior landscape of Melville's psyche—the debilitating tension between the death and life instincts.

Melville's language firmly establishes Bartleby as the personification of death. The scrivener is described as "motionless," "pallidly neat," "dismantled," "immovable," "haunting," "cadaverous"—all suggesting a corpselike appearance. As the narrator observes, "the scrivener's pale form appeared to me laid out, among uncaring strangers, in its shivering winding-sheet." Often portrayed as an "apparition" and "ghost," Bartleby casts a spectral shadow of gloom on the dead blank wall of Melville's stage. In the Tombs, Bartleby's corpse is a "wasted" prostrate body. The stifling atmosphere of the Tombs only intensifies the funereal character of Bartleby. "The Egyptian character of the masonry weighed upon me with its gloom. But a soft imprisoned turf grew under foot. The heart of the eternal pyramids, it seemed." It is indeed a heart of darkness: dead in the center.

Just as Bartleby embodies thanatos, separation, the death instinct, Melville's narrator represents eros, the impulse toward unification, the life instinct in the author's psyche. The "life instinct also demands a union with others and with the world around us based not on anxiety and aggression" but on love, freedom, and the release of nervous tensions. "The principle of unification or interdependence sustains the immortal life of the species and the mortal life of the individual; the principle of separation or independence gives the individual his individuality and ensures his death" [Brown]. In this regard, the narrator acts as the agent of the life impulse to react against the death drive of Bartleby in Melville's literary dialectic.

Eros operates through the narrator's personality chiefly in the guise of Christian compassion. The theoretical Christian concern for the community of souls is diametrically opposed to Bartleby's heightened individuality and the diseased consciousness it engenders. The greatest example of love for Melville, as it is for St. Paul, is the act of charity. Surely charity is the predominant virtue in the narrator's character. Time after time he offers substantial financial help to the morose scrivener with the promise of further aid. The narrator visits him in prison and sees to it that Bartleby will receive good treatment, should he "prefer" to accept it. The narrator exhibits generosity and selflessness in reaction to Bartleby's eccentricities. " . . . when this old Adam of resentment rose in me and tempted me concerning Bartleby, I grappled him and threw him. . . . simply by recalling the divine injunction: 'A new commandment give I unto you, that ye love one another.' . . . charity often operates as a vastly wise and prudent principle—a great safeguard to its possessor. . . . no man, that ever I heard of, ever committed a diabolical murder for sweet charity's sake. Mere self-interest, then, if no better motive can be enlisted, should . . . prompt all beings to charity and philanthropy."

There is only one thing wrong with the narrator's charitable behavior toward Bartleby—it doesn't work. No amount of well-meaning humanitarianism can unravel the knot of tension built into the conflict of eros and thanatos in human nature. The narrator is most vulnerable to appeals to the bond of "fellow-feeling." He finds it difficult to divorce himself from Bartleby's plight. "The bond of

a common humanity now drew me irresistibly to gloom. A fraternal melancholy! For both I and Bartleby were sons of Adam." Bartleby's corrosive individuality would not permit him to share this sentiment. His self is severed from its natural relation to life.

The narrator's original feeling of pity turns to repulsion when Bartleby's pervasive despair infects him with the hopelessness of ever relieving the scrivener's anguish. "Disarmed" and "unmanned" by Bartleby's fatalistic resignation, the narrator feels "sundry twinges of impotent rebellion" in the antagonism. Despite the constant sympathy he expresses for the scrivener, the narrator is overburdened by the afflictive "millstone" of Bartleby on his conscience. The cross is too heavy for this Christian to bear. "The scrivener was the victim of innate and incurable disorder. I might give alms to his body; but his body did not pain him; it was his soul that suffered, and his soul I could not reach."

The narrator recognizes that Bartleby's pathetic condition is the cruel result of an existence "unhallowed by humanising domestic associations." He wants to draw Bartleby into his own sphere of interdependency, to meld together into a collective whole the scattered, fractured fragments of Bartleby's malignant consciousness. Yet reason tells him that the man he has abandoned should mean nothing to him. The narrator's gnawing sense of responsibility to the scrivener, which extends to the hour of Bartleby's death, is proof of the irreconcilably contrary forces of the life and death instincts at war in the human personality.

"Bartleby" is by no means an isolated nihilistic chronicle in the Melville canon. As early as 1849 Melville was preoccupied with the themes of alienation, nothingness, and self-annihilation. The author concludes *Mardi,* a probe into the validity of man's search for meaning, with a dithyrambic self-destruction of his questor-hero Taji: "Now I am my own soul's emperor; and my first act is abdication! Hail, realm of shades!" In *Moby-Dick,* Ishmael, the only survivor of Ahab's Faustian assault on the power of blankness, is saved ironically by a coffin life buoy, after he has been spinning around in a slowly wheeling circle of water that suggests the spirals of Dante's Inferno. Melville compares Ishmael to Ixion, whose punishment was to slowly revolve on a wheel of fire in Tartarus for eternity. For Melville, the wheel of life rolls only to death and oblivion. *Pierre,* too, ends on a grotesque suicidal note in a dank prison where virtue goes unrewarded and all values devaluate into nullity.

The years following the controversial publication of *Moby-Dick* and *Pierre* were dominated by an intense artistic and intellectual crisis in Melville's career. A period of deep dejection followed the critical attack on *Pierre.* Melville was plagued by a nagging sense of failure and many of the stories he wrote between 1853 and 1856 are tales of passive suffering, stoic endurance, renunciation, and defeat. **"Bartleby"** is chronologically the first of these stories, but was preceded by an impulsive burning of some of Melville's unsuccessful fictional works.

Three years after the publication of **"Bartleby,"** Hawthorne records a revealing historical meeting with Melville in his *English Notebooks* on November 20, 1856. He observes:

> Melville, as he always does, began to reason of Providence and futurity, and of everything that lies beyond human ken, and informed me that he had "pretty much made up his mind to be annihilated"; but still he does not seem to rest in that anticipation; and, I think, will never rest until he gets hold of a definite belief. It is strange how he persists—and has persisted ever since I knew him, and probably long before—in wandering to-and-fro over these deserts, as dismal and monotonous as the sand hills amid which we were sitting. He can neither believe, nor be comfortable in his unbelief; and he is too honest and courageous not to try to do one or the other.

Melville was caught in the self-torturing oscillations of his eros and thanatos impulses. The year after his despondent "annihilation" remark to Hawthorne, he wrote *The Confidence-Man,* the last work of prose fiction to be published in his lifetime. The final paragraph in this multifaceted novel is an inversion of the "Let it be" act of creation, as a solar lamp is extinguished—enshrouding *Fidèle* (the ship of the world) in darkness—the final event in Melville's cosmological negation.

Melville ultimately recognized that his philosophic dilemma could not be resolved, but only endured. However, he did commit a kind of symbolic self-annihilation after 1857. For almost three decades he abandoned prose fiction rather than compromise his talent by producing potboilers to appease the demands of the public.

Melville's declining stature as a man of letters and the burning of some of his literary failures are partially reflected in the narrator's account of Bartleby's routine in the Dead Letter Office:

> Dead letters! does it not sound like dead men? Conceive a man by nature and misfortune prone to a pallid hopelessness, can any business seem more fitted to heighten it than that of continually handling these dead letters, and assorting them for the flames? For by the cart-load they are annually burned. Sometimes from out the folded paper the pale clerk takes a ring—the finger it was meant for, perhaps, moulders in the grave; a bank-note sent in swiftest charity—he whom it would relieve, nor eats nor hungers any more; pardon for those who died despairing; hope for those who died unhoping; good tidings for those who died stifled by unrelieved calamities. On errands of life, these letters speed to death.

"Bartleby" is the creation of a man who believed himself speeding toward certain annihilation. Melville's novella is a literary last resort to blunt the impact of his nihilistic vision. Enacting the tragic conflict between eros and thanatos in the human psyche, the two major characters in the story dramatize the modern predicament of the fragmentation, anxiety, and alienation of life. In the midst of his despair, Melville sensed his heightened artistic awareness in conflict with his bitter feeling of personal failure. Bartleby, the man who *is* nothing, emerges as a sullen sentinel to announce that Melville "would prefer not to" exist merely as a man of "dead letters."

Milton Kornfeld (essay date 1975)

SOURCE: "Bartleby and the Presentation of Self in Everyday Life," in *Arizona Quarterly,* Vol. 31, No. 1, Spring, 1975, pp. 51-6.

[*In the following essay, Kornfeld claims that Bartleby is distinguished by his refusal to correspond to social roles.*]

Melville's **"Bartleby the Scrivener"** has been read as an attack on capitalism, an allegory of the frustrated artist in a commercial society, a study of passive resistance, an expression of melancholy, the absurd, the perverse, the irrational—the catalog is exhausting and seemingly endless. Some of this is helpful in elucidating the story, even useful from the teacher's perspective since **"Bartleby"** is a perennial favorite of anthologizers. But a problem of many of the interpretations is a tendency toward the inverted reification of Bartleby as a character. The difficulty and the temptation of trying to explain him subtly enough reinforce the habit of treating him as an abstraction. Thus Newton Arvin sees Bartleby as the "irreducibly irrational in human existence . . . the bitter metaphysical pathos of the human situation itself" [*Herman Melville*], and Kingsley Widmer has called the story an expression of the "metaphysical inadequacy of the liberal rationalist," with Bartleby as the "forlorn negation and as the obsession of the benevolent rationalist's consciousness" ["The Negative Affirmation: Melville's 'Bartleby'"]. Indeed, both may be right, but imagine the consternation of a freshman or sophomore student as he tries to scale these verbal Everests, or the glassy-eyed stare with which he meets this abstract wisdom.

To restore the story to students and the general reader Bartleby must be confronted in his elusive yet concrete actuality. Widmer is correct, "Bartleby *is*" [*The Ways of Nihilism: A Study of Melville's Short Novels*], but what he hasn't elaborated is the actual way in which Bartleby *is* and *is not.*

In *The Presentation of Self in Everyday Life,* sociologist Erving Goffman presents a very useful theory of social interaction based on impression management. Simply stated, various contexts demand different kinds of behavior, different roles, and in most social situations performers as well as audiences are generally aware of these roles and their limitations. "When an individual appears before others, he knowingly and unwittingly projects a definition of the situation, of which a conception of himself is an important part." Anyone who has read the mad scene in *Hamlet* must be aware of this; Jane Austen was aware of it; any writer of stature has dealt with it at one time or another. Goffman continues: "When an event occurs which is expressively incompatible with this fostered impression, significant consequences are . . . felt," and it is here that Bartleby's behavior becomes interesting.

Goffman theorizes that in society people sometimes adopt "dramaturgical strategies," play roles, and the role of Bartleby is *to play no role at all*. Like John Marcher in Henry James's "The Beast in the Jungle," who was "*the* man, to whom nothing on earth was to have happened," Bartleby is *the* man to whom no role was to accrue. He may be motivated by a desire to express the "metaphysical pathos of the human situation" or the absurd, to preserve his integrity, he may have any number of motives (hence the incredible range of interpretations the story has fostered), but exploring Bartleby's motives seems only to lead us away from the story into metaphysics. The problem in presenting Bartleby to students is to help them to see him as he *is*. By refusing to participate, by employing a "dramaturgical strategy" which none of the inhabitants of his world can understand or empathically relate to, Bartleby does seem to be the occupant of a "cosmic madhouse" [Arvin]. The results of this refusal to adopt a role are precisely those predicted by Goffman.

> First, the social interaction, treated here as a dialogue between two teams, may come to an embarrassed and confused halt; the situation may cease to be defined, previous positions may become no longer tenable, and participants may find themselves without a charted course of action. The participants typically sense a false note in the situation and come to feel awkward, flustered, and, literally, out of countenance. In other words, the minute social system created and sustained by orderly social interaction becomes disorganized.

Clearly, the lawyer and his clerks react in just such a manner; as the situation ceases to be defined they find themselves confronted with an ambiguity, a void, a presence of absence. It is as if Bartleby were the human incarnation of the whiteness of the whale "as in essence whiteness is not so much a color as the visible absence of color." Bartleby is not so much a character as the *visible absence* of character, and by his indefiniteness he "shadows forth the heartless voids and immensities of the universe." In *Moby-Dick* ghostly whiteness "imparts . . . an abhorrent mildness" to the polar bear and the shark, but to the relatively unmetaphysical narrator of "Bartleby," the scrivener's "mildness" is a "wonderful mildness . . . which not only disarmed me, but unmanned me as it were." There is something peculiar at work in Melville's use of adjectives in these two quotations. In *Moby-Dick* the shark and polar bear are clearly abhorrent, but in **"Bartleby"** the lawyer perceives the scrivener's mildness as wonderful; yet this mildness leads to his being disarmed and unmanned, essentially the same consequences suffered by Ahab at the jaws of the abhorrent white whale. The lawyer's use of "wonderful" conceals an anger and an unintended irony many fathoms below the surface.

In choosing not to choose a role the "motionless young man" confounds the expectations of his audience. To the simple-minded Ginger Nut, Bartleby is "a little *luny*," and to the irascible Nippers he is a "stubborn mule," and from their limited perspectives, like the readers of the doubloon in *Moby-Dick,* they are right. Refusing to do as he

is asked, to copy, to read proof, to divulge any biographical information about himself, and finally to eat, Bartleby steadfastly remains roleless and in ordinary clinical parlance assumes the characteristics of catatonic madness. If Bartleby's condition were so neatly clinical, however, the story would have lost its appeal long ago. The lawyer's perception that Bartleby seemed "alone, absolutely alone in the universe. A bit of wreck in the mid-Atlantic," allows the story to carry a great deal of metaphysical freight. Like Pip who fell overboard in *Moby-Dick* and in his solitary swim saw "God's foot upon the treadle of the loom," Bartleby's dead-wall stare seems fixed on more than bricks.

What makes this role-playing hypothesis such an interesting one is the way it dovetails with the rest of the story. Not only do the other characters come under its rubric, but it helps explain a comic and heretofore unexplained paragraph toward the end of the story which balances the lugubrious and often criticized last paragraph.

The difficulty Bartleby presents to his audience, what makes them feel so "awkward, flustered, and, literally, out of contenance" [Goffman], results from their being such expert role players, and hence unequipped to deal with someone who plays no role at all. The lawyer, who deals among "rich men's bonds, and mortgages, and title-deeds," is an "eminently *safe* man." He is conservative, trustworthy, a man whose character can be easily read and relied upon to remain the same. His disapproval of change, his commitment to the *status quo* and a unified role is evident at the very outset of the story in his display of grief at the "abrogation of the office of Master in Chancery," a sinecure (role) he expected to hold (play) for the rest of his life.

As a solid citizen deeply entrenched in his role, he is the very last person who could understand someone who has no role at all, and his efforts to force Bartleby into some definable position are evidence of the anxiety this confrontation with his inverted mirror image causes. His is the frustration of the achievement-oriented upper-middle-class parent confronted by his child the "drop out," whose plans for the future are to do nothing, have no role and experience life for a while as a free-form polymorph. Even when the lawyer does change, when his compassion and humanity are enlarged, his change is surreptitious. He doesn't want to do anything to disrupt his practice since "necessities connected with my business tyrannised over all other considerations."

Between the poles of Bartleby and the lawyer are Nippers and Turkey:

> It was fortunate for me that, owing to its peculiar cause—indigestion—the irritability and consequent nervousness of Nippers were mainly observable in the morning, while in the afternoon he was comparatively mild. So that, Turkey's paroxysms only coming on about twelve o'clock, I never had to do with their eccentricities at one time. Their fits relieved each other, like guards. When Nipper's was on, Turkey's was off; and *vice versa*.

These chameleon antics are only tolerable because they balance each other and because, in Goffman's terms, their predictability allows the lawyer to make the necessary accommodations in his perceptions of social reality. Bizarre as they may be, Nippers and Turkey still play definable and useful roles. But like the Cyclops who is fooled by Ulysses's trick of calling himself No-man, the lawyer, figuratively, cannot perceive or comprehend a man who has no role.

Melville's final comment on Bartleby's role-playing comes in a comic aside when the lawyer is talking to the grub man in the Tombs. In response to the lawyer's suggestion that Bartleby might be deranged, the grub man says:

> "Deranged? deranged is it? Well, now, upon my word, I thought that friend of yourn was a gentleman forger; they are always pale and genteel-like, them forgers. I can't help pity 'em—can't help it, sir. Did you know Monroe Edwards?" he added touchingly, and paused. Then laying his hand piteously on my shoulder, sighed, "he died of consumption at Sing-Sing. So you weren't acquainted with Monroe?"

Aside from expressing a degree of spontaneous pity in contrast to the lawyer's restrained feelings, why should the grub man think Bartleby a "gentleman forger" (forger of gentlemen?) instead of a thief, for instance? Could Melville be grimly punning at this point as Shakespeare has Hamlet do in the cemetery? Monroe Edwards died of

Melville in 1885.

consumption, of overdoing it as a forger, otherwise he wouldn't have been caught; and Bartleby dies of underconsumption, of refusing to eat, of refusing to forge any roles, in the manner of Kafka's Hunger Artist. In a world in which role-playing and reality are coextensive, refusing to play roles is a repudiation of what passes for reality, and those of us who refuse to play are relegated to the Tombs.

I have not tried to alter the metaphysics of Melville's tale; in fact the reverberations from *Moby-Dick* actually reinforce that dimension of the story. Instead, this is an attempt to provide an explanation of **"Bartleby"** which is descriptive, cross-disciplinary, and in touch with the strange dramatic fluctuations in the story.

Allan Moore Emery (essay date 1976)

SOURCE: "The Alternatives of Melville's 'Bartleby'," in *Nineteenth-Century Fiction,* Vol. 31, No. 2, September, 1976, pp. 170-87.

[*In the following essay, Emery explores themes of freedom and limitation in "Bartleby," particularly emphasizing the doctrines of Jonathan Edwards and Joseph Priestly.*]

In recent years Herman Melville's **"Bartleby, the Scrivener"** has attracted its share of critics, many of whom have rightly proclaimed the tale to be an ingenious treatment of the theme of freedom and limitation. Nevertheless, two questions of preeminent importance remain unanswered: What is the precise nature of Bartleby's revolt? And how ought we to characterize the narrator's response to his mysterious clerk?

It seems to me that we can most easily answer these questions if we approach Melville's tale contextually. The Herman Melville of 1853 was, after all, hardly an illiterate sailor; and no small portion of his knowledge of philosophy, theology, and literature appears to have gone into the making of **"Bartleby."** If we disregard this knowledge and slight the tale's intellectual roots, we shall inevitably miss much of the author's meaning; in fact, however diligently we may examine the story's surface, we shall continue, I think, to muddle through **"Bartleby"** as readers and to lapse into an embarrassing vagueness as critics. To be sure, a handful of scholars have endeavored to explore the tale's context. Yet those who have investigated the philosophical backgrounds—those backgrounds to be treated here—have failed thus far to recognize the care with which Melville read his sources and the precision with which he used them in **"Bartleby."** To understand the contextual basis of Melville's tale is only to make a beginning: we must be prepared to devote a good deal of attention to what may at first seem thoroughly irrelevant and obscure materials if our scholarship is to aid us in interpreting **"Bartleby."** But happily the critical payoffs are there: a brief consideration of Melville's sources not only sheds immediate light on his creative intentions and enhances our enjoyment of his tale, but also enables us to recognize **"Bartleby"** for what it clearly is—one of the most impressive achievements in the history of short fiction.

Jonathan Edwards, Puritan minister and theologian, and Joseph Priestley, chemist and free-thinking Unitarian, had little in common, but they agreed, nevertheless, in assaulting the notion of man's "free will." Edwards' *Freedom of the Will* and Priestley's *Doctrine of Philosophical Necessity Illustrated* argued, quite similarly in fact, that "free will," instead of being a concept readily understood and clearly exemplified by everyday human decision-making, was an absurd idea, impossible either to comprehend or define. One might briefly paraphrase the argument of the two philosophers this way. (1) For the will to be absolutely free would require its perfect isolation at any moment of decision—its separation from all such mental "determinants" as emotions, habits, dispositions, and general behavioral principles. Since these things are quite vulnerable to the influences of the physical body, external nature, and other people, they would, if allowed to affect decisions, make those decisions "determined"—caused by something outside the will. (2) But if the will were separated from the rest of the mind at all moments of decision, it would inevitably then be separated as well from the grounds upon which decisions ought to rest; thus if the will were indeed "self-determining," it would be given over, in effect, to a random, indeterminate, and essentially uncontrollable procedure.

Although the advocates of "free will" claimed to be espousing an intermediate position between the supposedly stifling "Determinism" and "Necessity" of Edwards and Priestley, on the one hand, and a chaotic indeterminism on the other, Edwards and Priestley insisted that no such position was possible. Either, they suggested, the will could be influenced by emotions, habits, and so on, in which case it was most certainly not "free," or else it could be influenced by nothing other than itself, in which case it was indeed "free," but only in the unpleasant sense of being a tiny nugget of indeterminate chance in the core of the mind. Edwards and Priestley insisted, in short, that the man without "free will" was the sort of man one saw everywhere; while the man with "free will" would have been for them "a creature that had no resemblance to the human race . . . a most bizarre and unaccountable being, a mere absurdity in nature."

The narrator of **"Bartleby"** is acquainted with the treatises of Edwards and Priestley. In fact, he "looks into" them at one point in the story and takes comfort in knowing that his difficulties with Bartleby have been "predestinated from eternity." Had the narrator looked into the treatises a little more closely, however, he would surely have discovered something else: he would have seen that in their energetic description of the absurdities of "free will," Edwards and Priestley were predicting the absurdities of precisely such a being as Bartleby. The reference to Edwards and Priestley is, as it turns out, a vital clue to the philosophical context within which Melville meant his tale to be read.

Bartleby, we recall, is a peculiarly enigmatic character. His past, if we disregard the "Dead Letter Office" rumor, is forever hidden; his emotions remain concealed; his general motivations go undivulged. Yet if we cannot uncover Bartleby's secrets, we can see, superficially at least, why he persists in being a mystery: when questioned by the narrator or when asked to perform some action Bartleby customarily responds simply with an expression of "preference," for which word, after referring to the opening of Edwards' treatise, we can legitimately substitute "will."

Bartleby is, in fact, an exceedingly willful individual; yet his powerful will seems completely inexpressive of the remainder of his mind. That he has memories, emotional responses, and general motivations is possible; but if so, we have no reason ever to believe that these influence his "preferences." Indeed, Bartleby seems to prefer a thing simply because he prefers it; his will, that is, seems "self-determined"; and hence he appears to be just that sort of incredible "creature" envisioned by Edwards and Priestley—a man whose will is free of the mental "determinants" which those philosophers insisted were a factor in the decision-making of every human being.

We recall that Melville's narrator has great problems in managing Bartleby and is forced to employ numerous arguments with him—arguments of custom, duty, "reasonableness," and legality, to name a few. But as the narrator laments at one point: "It seemed to me that, while I [was] addressing him, he carefully revolved every statement that I made; fully comprehended the meaning; could not gainsay the irresistible conclusion; but, at the same time, some paramount consideration prevailed with him to reply as he did." Bartleby's reason appears then to acquiesce in the face of the narrator's arguments; yet strangely enough, his perverse "preferences" continue. This, however, ought not to surprise us. The "paramount consideration" which lies behind Bartleby's refusals is evidently, as suggested earlier, a desire, previously fixed upon, to free his will from *everything* external to it, including all other motivations, and including his reason. One can then convince Bartleby's reason and have no consequent effect upon his "preferences"; for in order to establish the freedom of his will, Bartleby must prefer not to be normal, dutiful, reasonable, law-abiding, and anything else that would require his will to knuckle under to some "determining" consideration. Indeed, one suspects that when Bartleby seems to disregard his self-interest in rejecting first the narrator's offers of assistance and later the grubman's "dinners," it is because not even a concern for his own welfare can be allowed to influence his will.

The narrator does have a problem on his hands, as the following conversation demonstrates:

> "[Bartleby,] would you like to re-engage in copying for some one?"
>
> "No; I would prefer not to make any change."
>
> "Would you like a clerkship in a dry-goods store?"

"There is too much confinement about that. No, I would not like a clerkship; but I am not particular."

"Too much confinement," I cried, "why you keep yourself confined all the time!"

"I would prefer not to take a clerkship," he rejoined. . . .

"How would a bar-tender's business suit you?" . . .

"I would not like it at all; though, as I said before, I am not particular."

. . . "How, then, would going as a companion to Europe, to entertain some young gentleman with your conversation—how would that suit you?"

"Not at all. It does not strike me that there is anything definite about that. I like to be stationary. But I am not particular."

The best gloss on this perplexing bit of dialogue seems to be the following passage from Edwards' treatise on the will:

> Now the question is, whether ever the soul of man puts forth an act of Will, while it yet remains in a state of Liberty. . . . For how ridiculous would it be for any body to insist, that the soul chooses one thing before another, when at the very same instant it is perfectly indifferent with respect to each! This is the same thing as to say, the soul prefers one thing to another, at the very same time that it has no preference.

Edwards argued that if the definition of "free will" required the will to be isolated at the moment of decision, if it insisted, in other words, that the will be "indifferent" in that moment with respect to its alternative choices, then the definition was absurd—since an indifferent will could clearly never come to a decision. The "free" Bartleby, we notice, denies repeatedly his "particularity" of opinion, yet proves to be highly particular with respect to his occupational possibilities. He is simultaneously indifferent and not indifferent; and this paradox seems to result from the paradox inherent in "free will" (as Edwards and Priestley defined it): the decisions of the "free" will had to issue out of a state of perfect indecision. Thus in the conversation just cited, Bartleby may appear to exhibit reasons for his preferences, but these "reasons" are merely momentarily significant, at times contradictory, and certainly not expressive of any sort of *general* motivation or behavioral determinant. Despite his preferences, Bartleby's only "determination" is to remain "not particular"—for he must remain so in order to be "free."

There is more to be said, however, on the subject of Bartleby's intractability. Edwards and Priestley were aware of the objection most frequently urged against their "deterministic" psychological models—namely, that these models seemed to eliminate human moral responsibility. If all a man's actions were determined through the natural causal chains which Edwards and Priestley thought to be operating, then was it not improper, the proponents of "free will" asked, either to reward or punish a man for a decision in which he participated only as a causal link and not as a "free" initiator? Edwards and Priestley answered that only a determined act could properly be labeled "moral" or "immoral." They pointed out that it was man's long-standing custom to punish those who had evil motives, habits, and dispositions rather than those who for no apparent reason performed evil acts, which seemed to suggest that the common notion of morality was heavily dependent upon the idea of mental "determinants." Moreover, turning the logic of the free-willers upside down, Edwards and Priestley went on to insist that "free will," if it were achieved, would make its possessor morally *ir*responsible for his actions, since these would then be "decided upon" not by his whole mind but by chance.

Priestley treated the problem of moral responsibility by imagining that he were a father desirous of morally evaluating and educating two hypothetical sons. With the first, "son A," whose will was not "free," and who could thus be influenced in his behavior and decision-making by considerations of self-interest, affection for others, fear of punishment, and so on, Priestley had no problem; but with his second hypothetical child, equipped with "free will," there were difficulties:

> In my son B I have to do with a creature of quite another make. . . . In all cases where the principle of *freedom from the certain influence of motives* takes place, it is exactly an equal chance whether . . . my promises or threatenings, my rewards or punishments determine his actions or not. The *self-determining power* is . . . a thing with respect to which I can make no sort of calculation. . . . When I . . . praise my son A, [I] tell him [I] admire his *excellent disposition*, in consequence of which all good motives have a . . . never-failing influence upon his mind . . . his conduct is not directed by mere *will*. . . . Let us now suppose that B does the very same thing [as A]; but let it be fully understood, that the *cause* of his right determination was not any bias or *disposition of mind* in favour of virtue, or because a good *motive* influenced him to do it; but that his determination was produced by . . . a mere *arbitrary pleasure*, without any reason whatever . . . and I apprehend he would no more be thought a proper subject of praise . . . than the dice, which, by a fortunate throw, should give a man an estate. It is true that the action was right, but there was not the *proper principle*, and *motive*, which are the only just foundations of praise.

Priestley's situation becomes even more interesting, however, when both sons are guilty of misconduct. After having successfully disciplined "son A," Priestley notes:

> If son B has acted the same part [as A], the language which I addressed to A will not apply to [B]. It is true that he has done what is wrong . . . but it was not from any bad *disposition of mind*. . . . No, his determination . . . was a choice directed by *no bad motive whatever*, but a mere *will*. . . . My blame or reproaches, therefore, being ill founded, and incapable of having any effect, it is my wisdom to withhold them, and wait the uncertain issue with patience.

On "Bartleby" as social commentary:

The plain figure of Bartleby, considered dispassionately, is absurd enough; but in his context he is so disruptive of all normally-accepted conventions that the emotional power and sanction of such a steady refusal as his must be regarded as one of Melville's most original discoveries. The insidious webs that the complexity of Society was spinning round the individual were being steadily multiplied in the fifties of the last century. . . .

In **"Bartleby"** the stoic conclusion was faced, in a compressed and haunting prose piece containing as much of pity as of horror: that the courageous way out of the fatal dilemmas was independence, and that independence led to death. Bartleby the scrivener finds peace only in the grave—with the attendant consolation that he rests with kings and counsellors. Yet somehow Bartleby emerges from his own tragedy as the victor; he creates, but does not participate in, the spiritual disturbance which has quickened the imagination of the mediocrities he encounters. He becomes the still point about which their unstable world turns. The paradox of Bartleby is that although his principles destroy him, it is the preservation of those principles alone which can save the world that rejects him.

Ronald Mason, in The Spirit Above the Dust: A Study of Herman Melville, *John Lehmann, 1951.*

Bartleby is quite clearly, I think, a version of "son B." We remember that his ability to perform his duties varies remarkably. Upon entering the office, he works furiously, although "silently, palely, mechanically." The narrator remarks that he would have been "delighted" with Bartleby had the latter's dedication been the behavioral expression of a cheery or industrious disposition; but Bartleby simply works on, giving no evidence of any disposition at all. Then he begins to "prefer not," augmenting his refusals little by little, until finally he stops work altogether. But just as the narrator had previously found it strangely difficult to praise the eminently busy, but oddly unmotivated Bartleby, so he now finds it hard to punish him:

I looked at him steadfastly. His face was leanly composed; his gray eye dimly calm. Not a wrinkle of agitation rippled him. Had there been the least uneasiness, anger, impatience or impertinence in his manner; in other words, had there been any thing ordinarily human about him, doubtless I should have violently dismissed him from the premises. But as it was . . . I stood gazing at him awhile, as he went on with his own writing, and then reseated myself at my desk. This is very strange, thought I. What had one best do?

The narrator's predicament is precisely that of Priestley in the face of the contrariness of "son B"; for neither Bartleby's initial good behavior nor his later recalcitrance appears to originate in any motive or disposition (other than, as we have come to suspect, the "disposition" to be "unmotivated"). Like Priestley, the narrator finds it both oddly improper and decidedly ineffectual to reward or punish his employ-

ee; like Priestley, he can do nothing but postpone a decision on the matter and patiently "wait the uncertain issue."

The narrator might recall, by the way, that he did not have such difficulties with his three original employees—Turkey, Nippers, and Ginger Nut—whose most essential characteristic is their clear difference from Bartleby with respect to *will*. Turkey, who regularly becomes irascible in the afternoon, Nippers, whose unfortunate mornings the narrator attributes to a combination of "ambition and indigestion," and Ginger Nut, a boy remarkable only for his craving for nuts, are clear examples of what Priestley would have called "type-A" humanity; for their behavior is noted for its great dependence on disposition. These are human beings whose physical bodies, for instance, frequently influence their wills, whereas Bartleby's body has no known effect upon his "preferences." Like Priestley's "son A" the three perform predictably, so predictably that although their performance may at times fail to measure up to the standards set by their employer, the latter, confident in the consistency of their behavior, can discipline them amiably and effectively. [In his "Melville's **'Bartleby'**: Absolutism, Predestination, and Free Will,] Richard Harter Fogle is quite right then: the three do seem reminiscent of Dickensian "humors characters"—but only because Melville intended their wills to be clearly determined by dispositions, habits, and, if you like, "humors," and not by the self-determinative process we see at work in the case of Bartleby's paradoxical will.

Both Bartleby's eccentricity and his unmanageability then can be traced to his "free" will; but certain questions remain. If Bartleby has "free will" and Edwards and Priestley insisted that it could not exist, then why does Bartleby? Is Melville's tale merely the surrealistic dramatization of an incoherent philosophical postulate? The answer is clearly "No." Although Bartleby himself is absurd, just as Edwards and Priestley predicted, his desire is, after all, simply to maximize his freedom of mind; and thus he can be interpreted as the surrealistic representative of a great number of quite real rebels. Indeed, Melville seems to have meant the psychological cul-de-sac into which Bartleby strays to exemplify the ineffectual and distinctly risky nature of all intellectual rebellion.

For what does Bartleby's ill-fated career teach us? It suggests that the rebel who seeks to achieve a greater freedom of mind is, in effect, imposing upon himself a kind of mental paralysis; for in disengaging his will from even one of the emotions, dispositions, and habits that ordinarily influence it, the rebel, any rebel, must, like Bartleby, sever one of the causal connections by which his will is energized. Moreover, the rebel can maintain his freedom only so long as he continues to reject as potentially "determining" all behavioral motives, "reasonable" or otherwise; but ironically enough, having refused to obey the dictates of any particular motive, the rebel discovers to his chagrin that his will is now *less* free (by one alternative) than it was before.

This then is the paradoxical moral of Melville's tale: the rebel's quest for freedom of mind must inevitably involve him in a life of ever-increasing limitations. By the end of our story, Bartleby, for all his humorous absurdity, has come to a not very humorous end. Total freedom of mind can apparently be attained only at the cost of life itself—and any rebel, Melville implies, is somewhere on the road to Bartleby's unfortunate destination.

Melville may have derived Bartleby's negative preferences form John Locke, Edwards' chief foe in *Freedom of the Will,* who sought to locate man's liberty in his "freedom to prefer"; or they may have come from Arthur Schopenhauer's theory of the "freedom of not-willing," as Daniel Stempel and Bruce M. Stillians have suggested [in their "'**Bartleby the Scrivener**': A Parable of Pessimism"]. But in either case, it is Edwards' and Priestley's sense of the absurdity of absolute freedom of mind and Melville's own recognition of the psychological dangers involved in the quest for it that seem to have dominated Melville's attitude toward his protagonist. And whether Bartleby is meant to stand for the Byronic hero, whom he resembles in his solitary, brooding pessimism, and with whom he is subtly compared at one point; whether he is meant to represent the contemplative mystic, as H. Bruce Franklin has asserted [in his *The Wake of the Gods: Melville's Mythology*]; whether he is intended to be Melville himself, perhaps conscious of too "freely" pondering certain disagreeable facts of human existence; or whether, as seems to me most likely, Bartleby is capacious enough to stand for all of these; in any case, his rebellion can clearly end for Melville only in philosophical confusion and psychological disaster.

To say this of "**Bartleby**" is not to say enough, however. The catastrophe that abruptly ends the monomaniacal career of Ahab in *Moby-Dick* demonstrates in a powerful fashion the essential futility of Ahab's quest; yet the comfortable way of the "**Lee Shore**" remains for Melville an unsatisfactory alternative to that quest. And similarly, if half the ironic artillery of "**Bartleby**" is aimed and fired at the protagonist, the quester for an absolute freedom of mind, there is an equally potent attack launched squarely in the opposite direction—at the "comfortable" alternative to Bartleby, the narrator of the tale.

The physical walls within which Bartleby's story happens, those walls which so bother and bewilder Bartleby, have become so natural a part of the narrator's world that he is scarcely conscious of their existence. And this is a sign of something more significant; for after having glanced at the treatises of Edwards and Priestley, the narrator remarks:

> Under the circumstances, those books induced a salutary feeling. Gradually I slid into the persuasion that these troubles of mine, touching the scrivener, had been all predestinated from eternity, and Bartleby was billeted upon me for some mysterious purpose of an allwise Providence, which it was not for a mere mortal like me to fathom. Yes, Bartleby, stay there behind your screen, thought I. . . . At last, I see it, I feel it; I penetrate to the predestinated purpose of my life. I am content.

With his beliefs in Providence and predestination the narrator places himself philosophically in the camp of Edwards and Priestley; but more importantly, his cheery response to the limits imposed upon him by his philosophy, his reveling in the deterministic "walls" which limit both his freedom and his vision, suggests to us the equally cheery response of those philosophers. Keeping the narrator's declaration of contentedness in mind, let us listen for a moment to Priestley, for instance:

> We ourselves, complex as the structure of our minds, and our principles of action are, are links in a great connected chain, parts of an immense whole, a very little of which only we are as yet permitted to see, but from which we collect evidence enough, that the whole system . . . is under unerring direction, and that the final result will be most glorious and happy. . . .

> And when our will and our wishes shall . . . perfectly coincide with those of the sovereign Disposer of [that system] . . . we shall, in fact, attain the summit of perfection and happiness.

This is the blithe sort of attitude which Melville apparently intended to satirize in creating "**Bartleby**"'s narrator. While Melville found himself siding with Edwards and Priestley in their insistence upon the difficulties of "free will," he could not understand, it seems, their ability to rejoice in their deterministic bonds. A rigorously determined world did not seem to Melville an environment particularly conducive to "perfection and happiness"; in fact, in creating "**Bartleby**" he chose to depict Priestley's glorious necessitarian "system" as a labyrinth of bleak and claustrophobic walls. Perhaps the limitations of mental necessity were inescapable; but Melville, as pessimistic realist, as a man deeply aware of certain hints of ineptitude in the "unerring direction" of the universe, and as something of a rebel himself, could not help but sympathize strongly, I imagine, with a Bartleby who attempted to break the shackles of his mental confinement—one who questioned life even if no answers were forthcoming, one who sought to pass beyond the walls of his mind rather than bask ignorantly like our narrator in the blissful nonvision of an incomprehensible Providence.

Thus while Bartleby's flaw is his radical refusal to undergo the imposition of psychological limits, the narrator's unattractiveness stems from his readiness to accept them. Yet there is a good deal more wrong with the narrator than his philosophical stance: in his case, a dead-wall epistemology is bonded to a particularly subtle (and hence pernicious) form of immorality. Despite the narrator's frequent recourse to benevolent rhetoric and despite the common critical view which has characterized him as a somewhat befuddled but thoroughly sincere exponent of Christian charity, the alert reader of "**Bartleby**" must quickly recognize that the narrator's heart is no more right than his head.

In portraying the narrator's moral sense Melville seems to have relied heavily upon the moral theory of Jonathan Edwards, with whom the narrator was already linked philosophically. In his [*The Nature of True Virtue*] Edwards argued that "natural virtue" (based in man's love for himself), like "true virtue" (arising out of the redemptive effects of God's grace), was capable of producing good behavior; in fact, self-love, in Edwards' view, was not the bane of mankind some moralists thought it to be. Edwards wrote:

> A man may, from self-love, disapprove the vices of malice, envy, and others of that sort, which naturally tend to the hurt of mankind. . . . May he not from the same principle approve the contrary virtues of meekness, peaceableness, benevolence, charity, generosity, justice, and the social virtues in general. . . . It is undoubtedly true that some have a love to these virtues from a higher principle. But yet I think it as certainly true that there is generally in mankind a sort of approbation of them, which arises from self-love.

The narrator of "**Bartleby**" could well be thinking of that particular passage when, after fearing momentarily one afternoon that he might murder Bartleby out of frustration, he remembers the biblical injunction which exhorts men to "love one another" and remarks:

> Aside from higher considerations, charity often operates as a vastly wise and prudent principle—a great safeguard to its possessor. Men have committed murder for jealousy's sake, and anger's sake, and hatred's sake, and selfishness' sake, and spiritual pride's sake; but no man, that ever I heard of, ever committed a diabolical murder for sweet charity's sake. Mere self-interest, then, if no better motive can be enlisted, should, especially with high-tempered men, prompt all beings to charity and philanthropy.

The narrator clearly knows his Edwards—but perhaps not so well as he might; for although Edwards did admit that in the absence of better motives, self-interest might induce a "sort of approbation" of virtue, he quickly went on to say this:

> [Nothing] wherein consists the sense of moral good and evil which there is in natural conscience, is of the nature of a truly virtuous taste. . . .

> [For it] is approved . . . in the same manner as men . . . like those things with which they habitually connect the ideas of profit, pleasantness, comfortableness, etc. This sort of approbation . . . is easily mistaken for true virtue . . . [but] the difference [lies] in this, that it is not from love to Being in general, but from self-love.

Melville's narrator, however, goes so far as to suggest that "sweet charity" can issue out of self-love—or, more precisely, that a love for others can be founded, in his own case, upon the self-interested "prudence" which, we have been assured, is one of his strong points. We might well ask, with Edwards, if this brand of "charity" be not somewhat *too* sweet; and certainly Melville had no difficulty in locating the snake hidden within the profusion of the narrator's moralistic rhetoric. Self-interest could per-

haps produce an easy sort of benevolence; but like Edwards, Melville seems to have felt that only a "higher principle" could promote an honest sympathy for other people. A love rooted in self-interest was apparently for Melville hardly a love at all.

Thus we begin to understand more fully Bartleby's sullen unresponsiveness in the face of the narrator's persistent offers of friendship: these offers are motivated, as Bartleby seems instinctively able to recognize, by selfishness masquerading as "charity." The following self-serving reflection on the part of the narrator is typical:

> I regarded Bartleby and his ways. Poor fellow! thought I, he means no mischief; it is plain he intends no insolence. . . . He is useful to me. I can get along with him. If I turn him away, the chances are he will fall in with some less-indulgent employer, and then he will be rudely treated, and perhaps driven forth miserably to starve. Yes. Here I can cheaply purchase a delicious self-approval. To befriend Bartleby . . . will cost me little or nothing, while I lay up in my soul what will eventually prove a sweet morsel for my conscience.

The narrator is by no means the incarnation of outrageous cruelty or greed: at times he seems to achieve a certain degree of concern for Bartleby. But unfortunately his is always that tepid love, that oh-so-practical love, that always prudent love which Bartleby quite rightly views as dubious.

What does the narrator *lack* morally? His bust of Cicero is perhaps the best clue to that:

> The next morning came. . . .

> "Bartleby," said I . . . "come here; I am not going to ask you to do anything you would prefer not to do—I simply wish to speak to you."

> Upon this he noiselessly slid into view.

> "Will you tell me, Bartleby, where you were born?"

> "I would prefer not to."

> "Will you tell me *anything* about yourself?"

> "I would prefer not to."

> "But what reasonable objection can you have to speak to me? I feel friendly towards you."

> He did not look at me while I spoke, but kept his glance fixed upon my bust of Cicero, which, as I then sat, was directly behind me, some six inches above my head.

Since Cicero was himself an eminent barrister, it is not surprising that the narrator possesses a bust of him. Yet that bust is, in one sense, grossly out of place in the narrator's office; for Cicero (in his treatise on moral duties, his [*Three Books of Offices or Moral Duties*]) wrote as follows:

> If a man should lay down as the chief good, that which has no connexion with virtue, and measure [virtue] by his own interests, and not according to its moral merit; if such a man shall act consistently with his own principles, [but] is not sometimes influenced by the goodness of his heart, he can cultivate neither friendship, justice, nor generosity.

Unlike Edwards, Cicero maintained, in fact, that without a measure of fellow feeling unadulterated with self-love there could be no virtue of *any* kind. Hence Bartleby's meaningful glance at Cicero seems to be both Melville's way of endorsing Cicero's objection to the sort of "virtue" Edwards would later call "natural" and Bartleby's stubborn way of insisting that the self-interested narrator, "friendly" as he is, lacks the essence of "sweet charity"— a sympathetic heart.

But now we come to a crucial question. Does the narrator's encounter with Bartleby bring him to a state of increased awareness? Does Bartleby, in other words, make a better man out of the narrator? The affirmative case has been frequently argued, with the following remarks, made by the narrator in the course of examining the contents of Bartleby's desk, usually cited as proof:

> What miserable friendlessness and loneliness are here revealed! [Bartleby's] poverty is great; but his solitude, how horrible! Think of it. Of a Sunday, Wall-Street is deserted as Petra; and every night of every day it is an emptiness. . . . And here Bartleby makes his home. . . . For the first time in my life a feeling of overpowering stinging melancholy seized me. Before, I had never experienced aught but a not unpleasing sadness. The bond of a common humanity now drew me irresistibly to gloom. A fraternal melancholy! For both I and Bartleby were sons of Adam. I remembered the bright silks and sparkling faces I had seen that day, in gala trim, swan-like sailing down the Mississippi of Broadway; and I contrasted them with the pallid copyist, and thought to myself, Ah, happiness courts the light, so we deem the world is gay; but misery hides aloof, so we deem that misery there is none. These sad fancyings—chimeras, doubtless, of a sick and silly brain—led on to other and more special thoughts, concerning the eccentricities of Bartleby. Presentiments of strange discoveries hovered round me. The scrivener's pale form appeared to me laid out, among uncaring strangers, in its shivering winding sheet.

To be sure, there are clear signs here that Bartleby has had some effect upon his employer: the narrator is, in fact, glimpsing "for the first time in his life" what Melville liked to call the "dark" side of human existence. But glimmerings of awareness are only glimmerings—and ought not to be confused with epistemological or moral rejuvenation. Both the narrator's comfortable glance at Edwards and Priestley and his statement in praise of self-interest are, we recall, still to come; and even here, at his best, the narrator cannot quite rid his benevolence of sentimental-

ity; nor focus his wandering attention on possible ways of improving Bartleby's unfortunate situation; nor pass beyond "sad fancyings" and gothic imaginings into the more warm-blooded, though sometimes painful realm of genuine human feeling. And if, by the end of Melville's tale, we continue to cherish the notion that the perplexing confrontations with his mysterious clerk have managed to produce a significant dent in the narrator's obtuseness, we are doomed to disappointment; for the narrator attains new heights of vague sentimentality rather than a peak of awareness in his climactic and highly revealing sigh: "Ah, Bartleby! Ah, humanity!" Morally and epistemologically speaking, "strange discoveries" have indeed "hovered round" the narrator at times; but his chances for permanent improvement are apparently laid to rest forever in Bartleby's grave.

Who then is Melville's narrator? He is that sort of man one tends to find in high places: the snug man whose worldly success has convinced him that this is the "best of all possible worlds," and whose virtues cluster around a "prudential" concern for maintaining his own station. The narrator can never fully understand or truly befriend Bartleby because the narrator is simply too complacent, both philosophically and morally, to sympathize with human dissatisfaction and despair. Hence he is, as Melville well knew, precisely the sort of individual next to whom a Bartleby, however deranged and doomed, appears to us most admirable, most nearly heroic.

"Bartleby" is preeminently, then, a story of psychological polarities, of two views of life, unsatisfactory in themselves (though for very different reasons) and forever incapable of synthesis. And thus, in one important respect, "Bartleby" manifests a greater pessimism than does *Moby-Dick:* it may display a "Dickensian" mildness of tone and a web of humorous ironies that the "Shakespearian" tragedy of Ahab seems to lack; but it has, nevertheless, no Ishmael. From out of the wreck of Bartleby's quest, no one "steps forth"; the only survivor of Bartleby's catastrophe is the narrator, placid and uncomprehending to the end, firmly entrenched on the "Lee Shore." In "Bartleby" Edwards and Priestley, Melville and we his readers are fashioned into two representative individuals—a comfortable lawyer and his uncomfortable clerk— who meet, disturb each other for a time, and go their widely separate ways. Obliviousness or oblivion—those are the alternatives of "Bartleby."

Robert E. Abrams (essay date 1978)

SOURCE: "'Bartleby' and the Fragile Pageantry of the Ego," in *ELH,* Vol. 45, No. 3, Fall, 1978, pp. 488-500.

[*In the following essay, Abrams contrasts Bartleby's acceptance of his involuntary and subconscious motivation with the social and "willful hypocrisies" of the narrator.*]

Probing the "mysterious" wellsprings of preference and motive, Melville observes in *Pierre* that "no mere mortal who has . . . gone down into himself will ever pretend that his slightest . . . act originates in his own defined identity." An innocuous but involuntary habit, for example, can sneak up on one unawares. Man's "texture," writes Melville, "is very porous, and things assumed upon the surface, at last strike in" and become his own; "insensibly" his mind is "disposed" to perform them. More importantly, the mind itself, with its peculiar tendencies and processes "independent of me" and yet "going on in me," subliminally orchestrates conscious intentions and deliberations from within. As Warrick Wadlington writes of the paradox of identity in Melville, the "motivating" tendencies in the psyche "are so far below . . . conscious will that when we are somehow made aware of them, they seem to constitute an alien being."

In the dream state, the "alien" orchestrations of this *moi intérieur,* so fundamental to the unfolding of character in Melville's fiction, are perhaps most nakedly perceptible. For the dreamer sometimes finds himself performing the most preposterous actions and, half-detached from them, looks upon them almost from outside. In such dreams, the mind's conversions of the involuntary into the voluntary are caught, so to speak, in an illuminating state of incompletion. The half-willed remains half-estranged. But even the most passionately willed dramas of life itself, Melville suggests in his fiction, tend to develop out of roots as alien and obscure as those of dreaming. Man's suspicion that he may be something of a helpless dream-figure even at his most wide-awake proves more than merely rhetorical. Many of the unsettling tableaux in *The Confidence-Man* teach this very lesson. The Merchant, for example, begins to blurt out fervently that deep down he is mistrustful of the ways of Providence, however trusting of God and of humanity he has just appeared to be. And then he stops, "almost as . . . surprised as his companion" at what has "escaped him." It has popped "out of him unbidden." He is startled at his "mad disclosure." And yet, in a fervent "rhapsody," he himself has made that disclosure.

What is spontaneously blurted out, then, is paradoxically disowned. The self-vigilant personality shrinks back queasily from such "unbidden" and unpremeditated behavior, shrinking back from itself. And it is fundamentally such a revolt of the self from unpremeditated, automatic tendencies in itself that is enacted in **"Bartleby the Scrivener,"** albeit by detour and with a tinge of ambivalence, since the attorney beholds in his "copyist"—and draws nervously back from—a blind, instinctual core of being, irrationally fulfilling its own imperatives, that ultimately haunts and woos him in his own proper person. Freud initially defined "uncanniness" as the subliminal recognition of the intimate (but shunned) in the macabre, and what is subliminally intimate about macabre Bartleby is a certain unswerving deafness, dreamlike and beyond deflection, in his manner. His withdrawal from all normal activity may appear preposterous to common sense, but he seems eerily unalterable and mild in his preposterousness. That is to say, he never truly conveys the impression of being detached from, concerned for, and amazed at himself—and thus of being susceptible to rage or to derision. He lapses into an unblinking lack of self-wonder

and self-concern such as the attorney might himself lapse into only in the automatism of deepest dream life. For in the aloneness of dream the need for the self's watchful direction of itself begins to fade, and what to waking consciousness might seem outrageous then becomes unblinkingly and mildly accepted over long stretches. Bartleby exhibits the equanimity of a dreamer amidst the outrageousness of his acts even in broad, bustling day. Precisely because the scrivener is so serene in his preposterousness, dreamily in the world but not of the world, the attorney, through all his pretenses and inhibitions, feels more "private" near this copyist than near anyone else. The world demands signs of self-vigilance—evidence that we are looking in on ourselves at least partly from *its* perspective. It demands that we try to accommodate ourselves to its ways and, if we do not, that we at least offer, by way of anxious propitiation, lucid and opherent explanations of our conduct. But the queer heart of man sometimes moves of its own accord—or prefers not to budge at all—in a way neither fathomed nor governed by the socialized, deliberative mind: "It seemed to me that . . . he . . . revolved every statement that I made; . . . could not gainsay the . . . conclusion; but, at the same time, some paramount consideration prevailed." In Bartleby the logical—even in broad daylight—overtly yields to the psychological. Forced into speech, the scrivener simply confirms this:

> . . . I . . . demanded the reason for such extraordinary conduct.
>
> "*Why* do you refuse?"
>
> "I would prefer not to."

"You *will* not?" the attorney later queries. But to "will," ostensibly, is to choose, whereas one tends simply to have one's preferences in all their absurdity and inevitability. "I *prefer* not," answers Bartleby. The lawyer comes closest to comprehending what he is up against not when he is trying to reason his way into it, but, rather, when he looks "a little into 'Edwards on the Will' and 'Priestly on Necessity'."

With plantlike grace, Bartleby folds mildly and joylessly into himself behind a "green folding screen." Even in motion he resembles some deaf, joyless plant, copying without "pause" by "sun-light and by candlelight," writing "silently, . . . mechanically." But eventually he withdraws into an inert, total, behind-the-green-screen motionlessness, as if impelled by some tropism seeking ever simpler stages of being. Looking into his copyist's "dimly calm" eyes, the attorney finds nothing "ordinarily human" in them, but, rather, a mild presence beyond "uneasiness, anger, impatience, or impertinence," and he is both mesmerized and appalled.

Significantly, Freud mentions the uncanny fascination of deaf, aloof, and undeliberative human presence near the outset of his essay on "The 'Uncanny'." He quickly goes on to investigate other modes of the macabre, however, however, and his exploration of this particular motif is not especially thorough. Referring to Ernst Jenstch's earlier inquiry into the psychology of uncanny horror, and into the conditions which arouse it in works of art, Freud summarizes Jenstch's hypothesis that an uncanny feeling is sometimes evoked by the perception of deaf-and-dumb aloofness in the human. Or, conversely, such a feeling can be evoked by a suggestion of personality and awareness in the inanimate, as in the case of "wax-work figures" so artfully sculpted, dressed, and posed that they can almost be mistaken for living ones. "Epileptic seizures and the manifestations of insanity" can furthermore be added to this special category of the frightening, for "these" similarly "excite in the spectator the feeling" that "mechanical," deaf-and-dumb "processes are at work, concealed beneath the ordinary appearance of animation." In their equivocating dissonance, such images and forms of behavior tend to become uncanny. Freud emphasizes that he is summarizing Jenstch's hypothesis "without entirely accepting" it. But herein, I would suggest, is a promising *point d'appui* from which to explore the ambivalent figure of Bartleby.

Just how ambivalent a motif Melville is exploiting is suggested by Henri Bergson's hypothesis, in his complex study of laughter, that the discovery of the oblivious, unpremeditated, and deaf in a human figure is the foundation of the comic. "The laughable element" in a situation, Bergson writes, consists of "automatism" emerging just where "one would expect to find the wideawake . . . pliableness of a human being." The "suggestion must . . . be" somewhat "subtle," he adds, for if "the element of automatism" is allowed to obliterate utterly the impression of animation and personality in a human figure, the comic dissonance of automatism *within* the human is lost. Since automatism intermingles coolly and mildly with human form in **"Bartleby,"** one might well ask: in what way does Melville's tale differ from such comedy? How does Bartleby, alive and yet unreachable through glazed eyes and deadpan, shell-shocked looks, differ from, say, a Chaplinesque hero, similarly moving in an aloof, autistic daze through the perils and "roaring thoroughfares" of modern times?

The question is difficult to answer partly because the comic and the grotesque are in practice so related that they often fade in and out of each other. Incongruous, sudden fluctuations of the laughable into the nightmarish certainly occur in works by Poe and Hawthorne, by Kafka and Nathanael West, and Melville's tale as well traffics ambivalently in both the humorous and the macabre. Bergsonian comedy, arising from a perception of automatism in the human, is flirted with in the very midst of uncanny effects. Sometimes, to be sure, the comedy seems simply comedy; a hint of blind automatism, creeping into the otherwise vigilant and alert personality, evokes untroubled laughter. Turkey and Nippers, for example, the one predictably "on" in the morning and "off" in the afternoon, the other predictably the reverse, seem comically puppet-like and less than human as they relieve "each other, like guards," but they do not seem grotesque. Their clockwork behavior is manageable, follows a predictable routine, and does not threaten. Somewhat more macabre,

however, is Turkey's obliviousness to the automatism of his speech in his conversation with the attorney:

> "With submission, sir," said he, "yesterday I was thinking about Bartleby here, and I think that if he would prefer. . . ."
>
> "So you have got the word too," said I, slightly excited.
>
> "With submission, what word, sir," asked Turkey. . . .
>
> ". . . prefer . . ." . . .
>
> "Oh, *prefer?* oh yes—queer word. I never use it myself. But, sir, as I was saying, if he would but prefer—"

Such automatism, although comic, nevertheless begins to unsettle, for it hints of involuntary behavior following its own oblivious course in spite of the alert, self-vigilant personality—Turkey unaware of Turkey. Moreover, unlike the two clerks relieving each other like clockwork, this version of automatism cannot be incorporated into and made part and parcel of the smooth-running routine of the office. It stands out nakedly as intrusive and intractable behavior welling up deafly from within. Significantly, the attorney himself does not laugh in this episode. That a word may have "involuntarily rolled" from a human "tongue" makes him feel somewhat queasy. He has built his world on the premise that people act voluntarily and so can be appealed to and reasoned into productive forms of behavior. But the tale raises an unsettling question: how far can voluntary and self-conscious enactments of the self actually be taken for the self? To what extent is the voluntarily proffered personality—". . . *prefer?* . . . —a queer word. I never use it myself"—trustworthy? As automatism blindly creeps into the speech of his clerk in spite of his clerk, the attorney discovers his illusion of control over another shattered. His ability to cajole through skillful exhortation and appeal, the very foundation of his profession, is undermined by a deafly impersonal, deafly intractable process even in a self who would consciously oblige.

Bartleby raises this same spectre of unreachable, deaf process usurping the personality, only in a much more intensified and radical form. The "eccentricities" of this cadaverous figure appear to be "involuntary"; his "disorder" seems "innate and incurable"; his "glazed" eyes seem blindly beyond appeal. Bergson has explored the way society, through derisive and embarrasing laughter, strives to "humiliate" an oblivious figure out modes of subhuman, absentminded behavior—a tendency to daydream in public, perhaps, or to speak in malapropisms and tautologies, or to fall asleep at the opera or at the ballet. But such laughter proves powerless over a remote incommunicado such as Bartleby, in whom a responsive, socially engageable ego is all but missing. Bergson writes of such laughter:

> It begins . . . with what might be called *a growing callousness to social life*. Any individual is comic who automatically goes his own way without . . . getting in

touch with . . . his fellow-beings. It is the part of laughter to reprove his absentmindedness and wake him out of his dream. . . . Society holds suspended over each individual . . . a snubbing, which, although . . . slight, is none the less dreaded.

But Bartleby, in "cadaverously gentlemanly nonchalance," seems aloofly closed in upon himself, hollow to the knock, and deaf to derisive laughter. It is true that the Chaplinesque or Buster Keaton automaton exhibits a somewhat similar deafness, as does the deadpan, Mark Twain innocent. But these figures belong to the staged, contrived, and dreamlike universe of farce, where the grotesque and the repugnant become half-converted into the wished. That is to say, from within a fantasy world immune to serious dangers, such dazed, autistic figures invite an audience to half-laugh at—but also to take a certain laughing pleasure in—a childlike obliviousness to the rules of logic, or to careening automobiles, normally forbidden to an alert, vigilant humanity. In such grotesque anesthetizations of the self—Buster Keaton wandering through exploding shells and craters without blinking—lurks a narcotic charm. Melville, inserting his figure of "cadaverously gentlemanly nonchalance" into the dense realism of **"A Story of Wall-Street,"** focuses on the nightmarish aspect of the very same obliviousness which does not threaten, and even, in its radical innocence, appeals, in the Mark Twain naif and in the catatonic of silent, flickering movies. And even in Bartleby, as the attorney's enchantment-in-repugnance indicates, a tinge of uncanny appeal remains.

The uncanniness of Bartlebyian horror, then—the hint of something subliminally intimate and wished for in the grotesque—becomes more fully explicable once comic variations of the catatonic innocent are explored. The remote figure of Bartleby, however macabre, is a close cousin of the silent movie automation, and like him half-exercises the charm of the anesthetized self: ". . . his . . . mildness . . . not only disarmed me, but unmanned me"; ". . . and then—strange to say—I tore myself from him whom I had so longed to be rid of." Bartleby, in his snowy "nonchalance," breaks rules, stands silently in the middle of rooms while others "state," but remains "cadaverously" immune to derision and shame. The appeal of such a figure is acknowledged. But the horror of "glazed," torpid eyes is not exorcised out of this ambivalent version of an often purely comic motif. Innocence is nowhere more characteristically Melvillian—nowhere more seductive and terrifying both—than in **"Bartleby."** The scrivener's final withdrawal into a fetal oblivion, "knees drawn up," eyes "dim," in a womb-tomb of "surrounding walls," confirms that the dreamy charm of deadpan innocence is ultimately a call to mummified peace, enwombed or entombed.

The figure of the deadpan innocent, then, becomes a source both of horror and of pleasure as he moves in his pale, anesthetized way through an anxious and revved-up world. Precisely because he "automatically" follows his own course without bothering to get "in touch," he appeals even as he threatens. The deepest loyalty of the subconscious is with such a blind, instinctual figure, for whom blind instinct alone exists, as unaccommodating and "oblivious to everything" but its own "peculiar business" as an illogical twitching of the body or a recurring nightmare or dream.

Significantly, the deadpan innocent, dreamlike and aloof, does not truly reach out of himself and gesture. The alert movements of eye, lip, and limb through which humanity projects and perceives itself become strangely mechanized in such a figure, or sometimes are utterly missing, leaving a human shell: "I felt . . . goaded on to encounter him in new opposition—to elicit some angry spark. . . . But . . . I might as well have essayed to strike fire with my knuckles against a bit of Windsor soap." This same tar-baby routine between earnest gesticulator and autistic incommunicado, lost in an unruffled and undisturbed dream, can be comic on the vaudevillian stage. For in raw vaudevillian comedy events do not strive to be too credible and lifelike, and subconscious loyalties, accordingly, are freer to surface and to work themselves out. Melville's tale, acknowledging the conflicting validities of both social obligation and deepest instinctual wish, invites a more ambivalent response, but raw vaudevillian laughter illustrates the way the dice are loaded—at least in the most primitive and spontaneous recesses of being—against an anxious figure such as the attorney. On the revealing vaudevillian stage (and it is through such comedy that the subliminally attractive underside of this macabre motif most nakedly surfaces), the figure of the earnest gesticulator—flattering, begging, worrying, falling all over himself in a pageantry of chagrin—obligingly metamorphoses into a fool before our eyes. The deaf-and-dumb dreamer, in his unruffled grace, obliviously triumphs. And the laughter that erupts surely signals, at least in part, our own spontaneous pleasure in his cool and unruffled triumph. "My profoundest sense of being," Melville emphasizes to Hawthorne, is "irresponsibility," and the laughing repudiation of tense, worried figures is one avenue to such a state, which is no doubt why Hawthorne regarded laughter as "the most terrible modulation of the human voice"—when "out of place." Such laughter, however, is a returning or, more generally, a half-returning to the full innocence of instinctual being from an anxious and vigilant point of departure, and is not instinctual being in and of itself. It is hitherto tense, bottled-up energy becoming unfettered and unchained; its precondition is a tightly sealed lid. Significantly, the liberatingly comic aspect of naive, oblivious behavior, emphasizes Freud, exists only in "the apprehension" of "the person . . . with inhibitions." And one might say the same of the terror and shame such behavior sometimes provokes. The naif himself is dreamily and facilely oblivious to the fuss he is raising. He causes laughter or horror but is himself deaf to it, like pure white light coloring everything else.

His overt deafness, Melville illustrates, is humanity's covert deafness, for a residue of purely naive and oblivious behavior survives in even the most vigilant and guarded personality, working its own deaf-and-dumb way through the most deliberate gestures and acts: "*Prefer?* . . . —queer word. I never use it myself. But, sir, as I was saying, if he would but prefer. . . ." It is from the perspective of situations such as this that sincerity and purity of motive should be judged in Melville's tale. The Janus-faced personality tends to be partially oblivious to itself in what it thinks are its most earnest and committed gestures. Herein, to a certain extent, lies the "universal lurking insincerity" in human thought and word mentioned in *Pierre,* and a charity cognizant of this principle, when turned on Melville's attorney, would be most charitable indeed. Often, to be sure, the attorney is merely self-serving and complacent. But even when he tries to be authentically kind to Bartleby and to others, the cards are metaphysically stacked, so to speak, against mere trying to be kind, and, indeed, against mere trying in general in the queer madhouse-universe envisaged by Melville:

> "Mr. Nippers," said I, "I'd prefer that you withdraw for the present."
>
> Somehow, of late, I had got into the way of involuntarily using this word "prefer" upon all sorts of not exactly suitable occasions. . . .

One might argue that from this same preferring force, "involuntarily" moving and shifting within, a pure and unfettered mercy for Bartleby, hazarding all it has, might spontaneously surface of its own accord if the attorney would but let it. For true mercy, lived by the spirit and not by the letter, is not strained and flows generously outward. But, as Melville writes to Hawthorne, his closest and most intimate friend: "In me divine magnaminities are spontaneous and instantaneous—catch them while you can. The world goes round, and the other side comes up. So now I can't write what I felt." Moreover, "deepest . . . being"—what Pip tastes of when he becomes a castaway in the Pacific—is "uncompromised, indifferent as . . . God," and sees all gesture, caring, and chagrin in the third person. However intimate Pip may eventually become with Ahab, "Pip's missing," says Pip of Pip in the purest stage of his "insanity [,] . . . heaven's sense." The world, then, "goes round"; feeling divorced from willed, artificial consistency is capricious and unstable; love wanes and other feelings wax; and the primitive core of being, moreover, is as faceless and instinctual as the figure of Bartleby, and if Bartleby is to be forgiven in his purity and innocent "nonchalance," the attorney, surely, should be all the more forgiven, and all the more pitied, in his guilt, complexity, and ambivalent trying.

Insincerity-in-sincerity in Melville's tale, of course, is finally a matter of mediating inadequacies never to be fully transcended. Probing the cognitive foundations of empathy—the fragile paradigms through which human figures strive to reach out of their walled-in amorphousness and solitude—Melville lays bare an inevitable disjuncture between gesture and inmost being. The living human image tends to exist through and according to gesticulations, facial expressions, and roles. But these fluctuate markedly from culture to culture, from age to age, and the "copyist" who fails to "copy" gestures of eye, lip, and limb illustrates an unsettling epistemological principle: translucent, empathically "open" forms of human-ness, normally mimicked and gestured back and forth between figure and figure, are nevertheless configurations and images of human-ness ultimately severable from the self-in-itself. In an analysis of "dehumanization" in cubism and other modernist art forms, Ortega y Gasset explores the distillation of seemingly living and physiognomic shapes into "pure patterns" of cognition. And Melville as well, no doubt influenced by traumatic experiences of culture shock in the South Seas, severs the shifting iconography of the human form from fundamental being. The "beauty" in a Typee's tatooed face, for example, perceptible and attractive to the Typee, proves as uninterpretable to Tom's Western eyes as ancient, undecoded scripture. Forms of beauty, enticement, and gesture, like forms of writing, are translucent or opaque depending upon perspective, and Bartleby the non-copying copyist mimics none of these, receding into an impoverished timelessness beyond the shifting iconographies of social presence. Again and again he is pictured standing mutely amid ruins, silent and Adamic. Only through time-bound, historically compromising mimicries can the spirit in some oblique sense reach out of itself.

The mimicry of abstract icons of personality, of course, can be overdone as well as underdone. "Attorney" blithely informs "grub-man" that he has never been "socially acquainted with any forgers," but the tale itself is a study in overly forged and mimicked social presence, from Turkey's oratorial "With submission, sir," to the grub-man's clumsy simulations of "genteel" breeding—"Then, laying his hand piteously on my shoulder, [he] sighed"— to the attorney's initial introduction of himself: "Imprimis: I am . . . one of those unambitious lawyers who never addresses a jury, or in any way draws down public applause; but, in the cool tranquility or a snug retreat, do a snug business among rich men's bonds." Through such paradigms, as stylized as the attitudes, gestures, and stances on an ancient urn, Melville's characters struggle into variations of a presiding social iconography. It is mutual theater. And to a degree it is necessary. But it is so overdone in Melville's **"Story of Wall-Street"**—so engaged in without irony towards the speciousness of mere form as form—that the very paradigms in and around and through which the self might obliquely squirm into view become over-earnest, and, hence, become opaque.

Social paradigms become opaque; subjective being is hazed over; but its influence remains profound. And this continuing, if unaccountable, influence of the socially hazed over is largely what gives Melville's tale its Kafkaesque ring. Beyond—and in spite of—the rigidities of social presence, "I strangely felt something superstitious knocking at my heart," acknowledges the attorney. Or "a certain squeamishness, of I know not what, witheld me." Again and again one is left hovering between seizable, simplifying metaphors of selfhood and a lacuna in the perception of self—"something from within"—which in its very vagueness draws attention. Mysterious, the essence of being in its depths, it is, moreover, involuntary—"I strangely felt something . . . forbidding me to carry out my purpose"—and personality in the tale, albeit in acts of referential inadequacy, strives to sustain public guises of voluntary, approachable, and deliberative behavior. In attempted transcendence of blind and faceless forces within itself, and often in overt, willful hypocrisies gratefully accepted *because* struggling against the suspected tug of the inwardly preferred, the personality reaches out of itself in acts of social theater: "'Your sarvant, sir, your sarvant,' said the grub-man, making a low saluation with his apron." The grub-man, serving up both grub and a public face, performs, though rather grubbily, what is fundamental to social survival, and what Bartleby fails to perform. Somewhere between the overly willed behavior of a grub-man, however, and the absurd and fatal grace of a Bartleby, preposterous and yet as inevitable as a dream, a work of art tends to reach its own ambivalent equilibrium, and images and words become candid in that very ambivalence. The attorney is a loquacious and smooth talker. But he talks best when he talks just beyond himself. When "sad fancyings—chimeras, doubtless, of a sick and silly brain," involuntarily lead him "on to other and more special thoughts," when he begins to "stagger" in his "plainest faith" and confesses to being "browbeaten," when he admits to perplexity and ambivalence—"And then—strange to say—I tore myself from him whom I had so longed to be rid of"—he emerges at his most trustworthy and intimate, and the walls between him and us seem less thick, if more obscure.

Robert N. Mollinger (essay date 1981)

SOURCE: "The Literary Work: Herman Melville's 'Bartleby the Scrivener: A Story of Wall Street'," in *Psychoanalysis and Literature: An Introduction,* Nelson-Hall, 1981, pp. 85-96.

[*Mollinger is an English scholar with extensive training in psychoanalysis. In the following excerpt, Mollinger considers "Bartleby" to be a portrayal of basic human, psychological needs, focusing especially on Melville's portrayal of oral fixations.*]

In Melville's **"Bartleby the Scrivener: A Story of Wall Street"** Bartleby's lack of motivation to work, his employer's motivation for putting up with him, the imagery, and even the actual subject of the story have yet to be fully clarified. The characters have been seen either as doubles of each other or as opposites, while the theme has been looked at from a social perspective or related to the biography of the author. A study of the story's imagery clarifies both the personalities of the characters and the theme. The characters' personal and interpersonal dynamics show us the subject of the story which is a unified literary work displaying a complex intertwining of theme, character, and imagery.

To eat or not to eat is the question which reverberates throughout the story and in the minds of the characters. **"Bartleby the Scrivener"** is a feast of food in which all the characters partake. Smelling of eating-houses and spending his money on drink, the lawyer's old helper, Turkey, is described by metaphors of food: as a horse

feels his oats, Turkey feels the coat that the lawyer had given him, and it makes him rash and restive. The younger helper, Nippers, is equally self-indulgent with food. Always suffering from indigestion, he nevertheless continues to feed himself gingernuts, cakes, and apples. He does not need to drink, as Turkey does, because "nature herself seemed to have been his vintner, and at his birth charged him so thoroughly with an irritable, brandy-like disposition, that all subsequent potations were needless." Ginger Nut, the twelve-year-old boy, not only brings back food for the others but supplies himself with various sorts of nuts. It is clear that all three helpers are involved with food, so much so that they *are* food, as their names tell us: Turkey, Nippers (as in, to take a nip), and Ginger Nut.

Just as their mouths are their most important bodily part, "my two scriveners were fain to moisten their mouths very often with Spitzenbergs," the narrator-lawyer, their employer, is a man of the mouth. Instead of food, he digests words:

> I was not unemployed in my profession by the late John Jacob Astor; a name which, I admit, I love to repeat, for it hath a rounded and orbicular sound to it, and rings like unto bullion.

Though not with Spitzenbergs, he too moistens his mouth, nor does he hesitate to interrupt his work for his dinner hour.

Whereas Turkey, Nippers, Ginger Nut, and the lawyer are all well fed, some to the point of indigestion, Bartleby is not. The lawyer notices that Bartleby never goes to dinner and, in fact, barely eats or drinks.

> I was quite sure he never visited any refectory or eating-house; while his pale face clearly indicated that he never drank beer like Turkey, or tea and coffee even, like other men. . . .

In the end he dies from starvation, even though the suitably named prison grubman, Mr. Cutlets, attempts futilely to feed him.

The continual emphasis on food and eating indicates that this story is not just about life on Wall Street but is also about something much more basic. So, too, do the names of the characters: Turkey, Nippers, Ginger Nut, Mr. Cutlets, and even Bartleby, which [Henry A.] Murray [in his "Bartleby and I"] suggests refers to "bottle baby." In fact, food submerges, and merges with the work being done in the law office. Turkey seals a mortgage with a ginger cake, and Ginger Nut's perspective on his job is similarly confused with food, especially his collection of nuts. "Indeed, to this quick-witted youth the whole noble science of the law was contained in a nut-shell." The work routine of the law office was organized around the assistants' eating habits. Nippers, suffering from indigestion, does not do much work in the morning, but he recovers enough by the afternoon to do some labor. Turkey works well in the morning but, after dining and drinking at noon, accomplishes no work later. For Bartleby too, working and eating are confused. Upon being hired, he immediately and enthusiastically dives into copying.

> At first Bartleby did an extraordinary quantity of writing. As if long famished for something to copy, he seemed to gorge himself on my documents. There was no pause for digestion.

Hungry for work, he almost uncontrollably stuffs it in.

Life, then, on Wall Street becomes eating on Wall Street, and the story no longer seems to be just sociological but also psychological. The characters in the story are hungry; this fact gives meaning to their relationships which draw on a psychological, developmental stage of early childhood.

At this early childhood level, as [Erik H.] Erikson [in his *Childhood and Society*] puts it, one lives through and loves (as well as hates) with his mouth. In terms of the child's relationship with another person, the child experiences the other person as a fulfiller of needs like his mother. The mother has no separate life of her own and exists only to feed him.

If one accepts that the characters in **"Bartleby the Scrivener"** evidence a peculiar amount of interest in food, it should not be surprising to find that what interests them most is the satisfaction of their needs. Turkey, indisposed after eating his dinner, not only does not work well for his employer in the afternoon but actually ruins much of what he does work on. Asked to take the afternoons off by the lawyer, he refuses and insists on staying, regardless of his employer's wishes. Nippers only puts in a half day's good work for a full day's pay and even usurps some of the lawyer's professional affairs.

Both of them are symbiotically "living off" the lawyer; he feeds them full pay, while they give back much less—and, in fact, "giving and taking" is the essence of all relationships in the story. The lawyer gives Turkey an old coat, while Turkey defends the status of their relationship by nothing that he has supplied his employer some stationery. "With submission, sir, it was generous of me to find you in stationery on my own account." Described as a "piratical looking young man," his fellow worker Nippers is one who appears to take if not to steal. Ginger Nut functions as a fulfiller of needs, especially in "his duty as cake and apple purveyor for Turkey and Nippers."

Since his approach to life is basically the same, the lawyer wants his needs gratified in the easiest way. This attitude affects his life, as well as his job. "I am a man who, from his youth upward, has been filled with a profound conviction that the easiest way of life is the best." Being unambitious, the lawyer is only looking for work enough to feed him and make it easier for him to live. Counting on his appointment as a Master in Chancery to provide him eternal funds, he wanted to literally live off the appointment. "I had counted upon a life-lease of the profits." He views other people only in terms of what they can do for him and sees both Nippers and Turkey as "useful" to him. Upon first seeing Bartleby, he calls him a "valuable acquisition."

Although the lawyer does take from others, as they do from him, he functions mainly to feed others. He gives Turkey the coat; he continually hands money to Bartleby. His relationship to Bartleby becomes almost parental. The lawyer supports him monetarily, gives him a place to live, tries to protect him from others, feeds him through the grub-man, and even offers to take him home. The lawyer, half-seriously, begins to believe that his only role in life is to fulfill Bartleby's needs.

> Gradually I slid into the persuasion that these troubles of mine, touching the scrivener, had been all predestined from eternity, and Bartleby was billeted upon me for some mysterious purpose of an all-wise Providence. . . . Others may have loftier parts to enact; but my mission in this world, Bartleby, is to furnish you with office room for such period as you may see fit to remain.

The lawyer is here, functioning as the good mother who supplies what is needed, exactly the kind of relationship that Bartleby wants.

Pallid, sedate, forlorn, and melancholy, Bartleby is depressed, depressed from lack of food. First attacking his new job because he is famished, he then attempts to manipulate people to meet his needs. Ginger Nut brings him cakes, but that is not enough. Soon the lawyer is expected to provide him with room and board. Bartleby wants to be allowed to stay in the law office, or rather live in the law office, without doing any work. After all, a baby is not expected to work in order to be fed by his mother. Bartleby prefers to be taken care of, prefers to not work for love, prefers to have a loving parent catering to his needs. Realizing this, the lawyer notes that "he prefers to cling. . . ."

Unfortunately, having been starved for so long, Bartleby can no longer be nourished by what he eats. Gorging himself on his work does not sustain him. In the end, giving up copying, he stops working altogether. Soon real food nourishes him as little as symbolic food. Never dining, "I am unused to dinners," Bartleby "eats nothing but ginger nuts," but even these are worthless. "Ginger, then, had no effect upon Bartleby." For Bartleby, it really made no sense to take money from the lawyer, food from the grub-man, Mr. Cutlets, or to go home with the lawyer. Wanting to be fed, Bartleby is in hopeless despair of ever receiving anything nourishing. Seeking the good mother, he finds only the bad, a predicament symbolized by his previous job in the Dead Letter office:

> Dead letters! does it not sound like dead men? Conceive a man by nature and misfortune prone to a pallid hopelessness: can any business seem more fitted to heighten it than that of continually handling these dead letters, and assorting them for the flames? For by the cartload they are annually burned. Sometimes from out the folded paper the pale clerk takes a ring: the finger it was meant for, perhaps, moulders in the grave; a banknote sent in swiftest charity:—he whom it would relieve, nor eats nor hungers any more; pardon for those who died despairing. . . .

Despair for food leads to a hopeless "dead" man.

As well as being depressed, Bartleby is also angry, angry at being deprived. In part, his anger comes out in an oral way in his giving everyone the "silent treatment." "I remembered that he never spoke but to answer." It shows, too, in his negativity; when he does answer, it is always with a "no" or a "I'd prefer not to." Continually repeating this statement, Bartleby is appropriately referred to as "mulish" and stubborn by the others. They also see him as full of disdain and haughtiness. Though Bartleby does not realize how provocative he is, the others are indeed provoked. Turkey, for example, wants to fight him physically. It is the lawyer who is most affected by feeling the impact of Bartleby's maneuvers. "Nothing so aggravates an earnest person as a passive resistance." Feeling "twinges of an impotent rebellion" and "disarmed," the lawyer is castrated by Bartleby, "For I consider that one, for the time, is in a way unmanned when he tranquilly permits his hired clerk to dictate to him, and order him away from his own premises."

Bartleby's aggression is not only a way to coerce the gratification he longs for, it is also a reaction to the deprivation of that gratification. Thinking of Bartleby's melancholy, the lawyer realizes that "the scrivener's pale form appeared to me laid out, among uncaring strangers, in its shivering winding sheet," and he wants to protect him, shield him from "rude persecution." Uncared for, Bartleby is dead, first symbolically and then actually; yet, Bartleby is also suicidal. Hating the depriving other, he kills himself to make the other person suffer. The lawyer, who is continually upset about him, is provoked to do more and more for him even in the face of rejection. Finally taken to the tombs, Bartleby blames the lawyer and angrily distrusts him. Since trust in the world develops from

trust in the mother to feed one, and since this is a trust which Bartleby does not have, he turns on the lawyer. "'I know you,' he said, without looking round,—'and I want nothing to say to you.'" Bartleby, betrayed by being uncared for, angrily and suicidally rejects all help and starves himself to death.

The other characters experience that anger which is intimately connected to the need-fulfilling relationships they have established. This anger comes from needing someone, from being frustrated, or from having to appease the other person to receive from him. "Disposed, upon provocation, to be slightly rash with his tongue," Turkey, from the lawyer's perspective, feeds himself, or has been fed, too much. Rash with his tongue after his meal, he becomes even more insolent on receiving a gift, a coat from the lawyer:

> One winter day I presented Turkey with a highly-respectable looking coat. . . . I thought Turkey would appreciate the favour, and abate his rashness and obstreperousness of afternoons. But no. I verily believe that buttoning himself up in so downy and blanket-like a coat had a pernicious effect upon him; upon the same principle that too much oats are bad for horses. In fact, precisely as a rash, restive horse is said to feel his oats, so Turkey felt his coat. It made him insolent. He was a man whom prosperity harmed.

Thinking that feeding Turkey will mellow him, the lawyer discovers the opposite: like an overfed horse, Turkey becomes irritable. For Turkey, it seems that too much food is an intrusion to be fought off; he is "pugilistic" and images himself a military leader attacking the documents he works on.

Nippers' aggression also comes out of his mouth and is apparently caused by indigestion:

> The indigestion seemed betokened in an occasional nervous testiness and grinning irritability, causing the teeth to audibly grind together over mistakes committed in copying; unnecessary maledictions, hissed, rather than spoken, in the heat of business. . . .

Whereas Turkey becomes combative after drinking, Nippers, with his brandy-like disposition, well fed by the vintner Nature at birth, does not need any further drink to be irritable and curse.

Whereas both Turkey and Nippers become orally aggressive after having been well fed, the lawyer's aggression is related to food in a different way. Telling us that he seldom loses his temper and that he is a "man of peace," he prides himself on the fact that he engages in "no vulgar bullying, no bravado of any sort, no choleric hectoring. . . ." However, he does become resentful and angry when his needs are not being met. He becomes rash when he discovers that he will not have a life-long income for the Chancery to live off. He wants to expel Turkey because he does not work well in the afternoon. When Bartleby stops contributing to the office, the lawyer becomes more and more resentful and desires to eliminate him. His rage seems to operate on the principle "if you will not give to me, I will remove you." He wants to "thrust [Bartleby] ignominiously from my presence" and "violently . . . from the premises." Trying always to control this anger, he forgets the matter or, having fantasies of murder, he strives "to drown my exasperated feelings toward the scrivener by benevolently construing his conduct."

Again, this is a particularly oral rage, a rage at not being fed, at not having needs met, which comes out in the lawyer's continual ironic tone and in his fantasies of cursing at Bartleby. More importantly, it is the way the lawyer holds in his aggression: he feeds himself. After being disobeyed again, the lawyer begins to become angry.

> "Very good, Bartleby," said I, in a quiet sort of serenely severe self-possessed tone, intimating the unalterable purpose of some terrible retribution very close at hand. At the moment I half intended something of the kind. But upon the whole, as it was drawing towards my dinner-hour, I thought it best to put on my hat and walk home for the day. . . .

His dinner puts a stop to acting out his aggressive feelings. Here we see how the ingestion of food works in an opposite direction than it does with Turkey and Nippers. They become more distempered after eating and drinking. The lawyer's aggression is similar to Bartleby's; both become angry over deprivation. The lawyer, however, knows how to feed himself, while Bartleby starves himself even more. He joins the depriver by depriving himself.

In such symbiotic need-fulfilling relationships, there are usually attempts at separation. For, even though one has his needs satisfied, when one is merged with another person, one loses self-identity, or the sense of self. To have a complete self, one must function independently. Turkey and Nippers, both well fed, if not overfed, spend half the day having their desires gratified and fulfilling the employer's needs. The other half a day, they are themselves—aggressive (Turkey) and ambitious (Nippers). They have partially separated from a symbiotic relationship in the direction of their individual development. Bartleby, because his need is so great, cannot separate at all. While his extreme hunger leads him to gorge himself, his extreme distrust prevents him from finding nourishment. He is caught in the dilemma of forever seeking and never finding, he wants help but cannot accept it. To be on his own is dangerous, since his is a world of uncaring strangers and rude persecution: "I thought I saw peering out upon him the eyes of murderers and thieves."

The lawyer's dilemma is different. Wanting to be rid of Bartleby, that is, to be on his own, he also wants to be with Bartleby, that is, symbiotically together. He fantasizes throwing the scrivener out; he moves his office away from him; he deserts him at the end. The lawyer has difficulty in even having fantasies about leaving Bartleby; he must constantly fight himself to create them. Thinking

of confronting Bartleby, he feels that he is indulging an "evil impulse." Becoming resentful, he recalls the divine injunction "that ye love one another." For the lawyer, hate and separation are evil and forbidden.

The lawyer's negative view of separation, seeing it as an immoral abandonment of another human being, partially explains his difficulty in kicking the nonworking scrivener out. In addition, the lawyer benefits from his bond with Bartleby, for, as he says, Bartleby is useful and valuable to him. Though Bartleby is a "millstone," an affliction, a haunting apparition which produces melancholy in the lawyer, it is a "fraternal melancholy" caused in both of them by a deprivation of needs. It is the lawyer's own need which causes him to allow Bartleby to cling to him. In mothering, feeding, and caring for the scrivener, the lawyer is mothering himself. For all his rationalizations, he identifies with Bartleby and feeds him as he himself wishes to be fed:

> He is useful to me. I can get along with him. If I turn him away, the chances are he will fall in with some less indulgent employer, and then he will be rudely treated, and perhaps driven forth miserably to starve. Yes. Here I can cheaply purchase a delicious self-approval. To befriend Bartleby; to humour him in his strange wilfulness, will cost me little or nothing, while I lay up in my soul what will eventually prove a sweet morsel for my conscience.

The image of food, that delicious, sweet morsel, is revealing: in feeding the other person, he feeds himself. The lawyer is almost as involved in the symbiotic need-fulfilling relationship as Bartleby is. This is why he has such difficulty in breaking it up, a difficulty foreshadowed by his futile attempt to make Turkey take the afternoons off. Unfortunately, by fooling himself into thinking that the cost of these attachments is small, the lawyer sacrifices his identity. He becomes the victim of his surroundings. His colleagues laugh at him and gossip about him; he is driven from his office, and his employees rebel.

Since most of the characters are ambivalent over their needs, their other attributes are defenses against these symbiotic relationships. Describing himself as a safe, prudent man who keeps away from people, the lawyer never addresses a jury, never seeks public applause. Rather, he hides himself away among legal documents, "in the cool tranquility of a snug retreat, do a snug business among rich men's bonds and mortgages and title-deeds." Emotionally aloof, he chats about sentimental stories and admits that his first experience of melancholy, in sixty years of life, was caused by Bartleby. His organizational thoroughness and his capacity to distance himself and objectify himself results in him thinking of himself as a legal document. "*Imprimus:* I am a man who. . . ." This aloofness and distancing are meant to avoid invasions of himself. Speaking of the turbulence of the law profession, he states "yet nothing of that sort have I ever suffered to invade my peace." Yet, when Bartleby arrives his peace is invaded, first by Bartleby's symbiotic clinging and angry rebellion and then by the lawyer's own needs to mother

Melville's headstone, Woodlawn Cemetery, New York City.

and cling. Bartleby has such a strong effect on the lawyer because he has forced him after sixty years to experience needs and frustrations the lawyer has avoided throughout his whole life. When in his closing statement the lawyer speaks of starvation and despair and sighs "Ah Bartleby! Ah humanity!" he actually means "poor Bartleby and poor me."

Bartleby is even more aloof. Seeking solitude, Bartleby is constantly in his "hermitage," his work area. By neither eating, talking, working, looking at the lawyer, nor giving, he refuses to relate to others. Declining to join the group of Turkey, Nippers, Ginger Nut, and the lawyer, he symbolically makes clear his refusal to join humanity. The lawyer concludes that there is nothing "ordinarily human about him. . . ." Almost autistic, Bartleby's withdrawal from others is more severe than the lawyer's. he stares at the wall and day-dreams in his hermitage. Later, in the Tombs, he faces the "dead-wall" until he dies in a fetal position, the ultimate snug retreat. Like the lawyer, he, too, is attempting to prevent the invasion of his self by others, with all the emotional involvement that entails. He stands as "a perpetual sentry in the corner" forever, "without moving from his privacy." His first refusal to work is to fend off a demand which intrudes upon this privacy, but Bartleby's withdrawal is also a denial of his own needs. Not unexpectedly, this results in his death.

In summary, we have moved from an examination of the predominant oral imagery in the story to an understand-ing of the interpersonal dynamics of the characters. We are presented with a continuum of characters all involved in symbiotic, need-gratifying relationships. These relation-ships are founded on basic wishes, as Bartleby's favorite word "prefer" indicates. At one end of the continuum are Turkey and Nippers, who have been well nurtured, per-haps too well nurtured, and for whom more food means engulfment by the world. For at least half the day, they attempt to move on and develop their own selves, Turkey by being aggressive and Nippers by being ambitious. At the other end of the continuum are the lawyer and Bartle-by. Still longing for nurturance, the life-lease of easy gratification, the lawyer attempts to deny this desire by staying aloof from others and by controlling his emo-tions. When he does become involved, he denies his need by fulfilling it vicariously—he mothers instead of being mothered. Whereas the lawyer has at least partially found the easy way of life, Bartleby has never found it. Appar-ently never having been fed, he is famished. Since he cannot trust what is given to him, he autistically with-draws and creates his own world. In this ultimate despair, and angry because of betrayal by others, he gives up and kills himself.

Given the similarities in their characters, it is no wonder that critics vacillate between considering the lawyer or Bartleby more important. As some have pointed out, they are "doubles" of each other, and so indeed in their need, their anger, and their "fraternal melancholy," they are. In symbiotic relationships, there is no clear distinction be-tween the self and the other person. There is rather a fusion of the internal images of the self and the other person. Only when one has become one's self is there differentiation. The story certainly is not just about Wall Street. It is about basic needs, the symbiotic ways these needs are fulfilled, and the anger, distrust, and despair which results when they are not met. It concerns depen-dence on others for gratification, the loss of the self in such dependent relationships, the quest for the self in independence, and the defenses used to avoid acknowl-edging these complex feelings.

Dennis R. Perry (essay date 1987)

SOURCE: "'Ah, Humanity': Compulsion Neuroses in Melville's 'Bartleby'," in *Studies in Short Fiction*, Vol. 24, No. 4, Fall, 1987, pp. 407-15.

[In the following essay, Perry contends that the character of Bartleby is not schizophrenic, but neurotic.]

Psychoanalytic critics of Melville's **"Bartleby"** have been remarkably consistent in their diagnoses of the enigmatic scrivener as schizophrenic. Along with the tale's near-sighted narrator, they have isolated Bartleby as a fascinat-ing case study while overlooking the importance of his relationship to the other characters in the tale. The prob-lem with such readings is that, in isolating Bartleby as a psychological aberration, these critics have missed Melville's broader concerns. As we begin on the assump-tion that Melville constructs a coherent tale in which each character must be understood in the context of the others, it becomes possible to see their common compulsion neuroses. This more inclusive perspective reveals that the tale's structure is based on a continuum of the ego defenses each character erects against its compulsions and obsessions. It is the helplessness of all of Melville's characters and their common confinement, in what Newton Arvin called a "cosmic madhouse," that turn the activities of a Wall-Street law office into a shattering vision of modern times.

Though terms associated with Freud's definition of the mind have been criticized for reducing the complexities of literature, I use them here because they provide both a useful means to distinguish character psychology and a common vocabulary by which to respond to earlier studies. However, I use these terms without assuming their practical psychoanalytic value. As Harold Bloom notes, "Freud's universal and comprehensive theory of the mind probably will outlive the psychoanalytical therapy. . . ." While previous psychoanalytic critics have proceeded as if Bartleby were really insane—as if Melville were trying to realistically portray an interesting psychotic—I find Freud's terms most helpful as a means to define subtleties of character behavior. The characters in **"Bartleby,"** like those in "Ligeia," are not important as real people so much as emblematic of ideas associated with the plight of all people.

Because I rely heavily on Freud's definition of how the mind functions, a quick review of specifics is, perhaps, in order. In Freud's definition of the mind, the ego functions to mediate between the natural impulses of the id and external reality. Thus, in its attempts to physically and psychologically preserve the self, the ego pursues pleasure by adapting to, running from, or modifying the external world. Problems arise when the id attempts to force its way through the protective barriers erected by the ego. Otto Fenichel explains [in his *The Psychoanalytic Theory of Neurosis*] what happens when the id succeeds:

> In all psychoneuroses the control of the ego has become relatively insufficient. In conversion symptoms, the ego is simply overthrown; actions occur that are not intended by the ego. In compulsions and obsessions, the fact that the ego governs motility is not changed, but the ego does not feel free in using this governing power.

In **"Bartleby"** all of the major characters vainly attempt to use ego defense mechanisms to reduce the anxiety produced by the sterile activity of the law office. These mechanisms, discernible along a continuum, are most clearly manifested in the characters' compulsive behavior, the tale documenting the way they ultimately fail to wall out the natural impulses of the id with the artificial social conventions erected by the ego.

The lawyer, whose id seems nearly totally suppressed when we first meet him, represents the extreme right along the ego continuum of responses to Wall-Street's values. His ego's total endorsement of the "safe" and "prudent" life

of the material status quo, however, thinly disguises primitive impulses of his id. These impulses are manifested as compulsion neuroses, reaction formations of his ego designed to reroute his anti-social tendencies. Revealing themselves as obsessions with orderliness and money, his primitive impulses suggest that he is, as Freud suggests, one whose "instinctual life is anally oriented." His orderliness—abundantly evident in his careful structuring of his tale, the sectioning of his offices, his attempts to control his emotions, and his profession as a lawyer—points to his "obedience to . . . environmental requirements covering the regulation of excretory functions." Reflecting his frugality, even the sound of money gives the lawyer pleasure as he expresses his enjoyment of John Jacob Astor's name because its "rounded and orbicular sound . . . rings like unto bullion." In addition, he finds "snug" comfort in handling "rich men's bonds, and mortgages, and title-deeds." His obsessions with money and orderliness, then, are his ego's means of socializing and sublimating the primitive impulses of his id.

The obsession defenses of the lawyer's ego are visually reinforced by the ground-glass doors that protect him from the disorderly and threatening world of his scriveners, also reflecting his limited self-perception. In order to enjoy the social benefits of his status on Wall Street, he adopts its social class system and isolates himself from his scriveners in two ways. First, he walls them off physically with doors, and in Bartleby's case, with a screen. Second, he denies their behavior's legitimate motivation by characterizing them in comic terms. Because their unconventional and enigmatic patterns of behavior are reminders of the irrational desires of his own id, he attributes them to the convenient external causes of intemperance and indigestion. Moreover, he feels threatened by his inability to deal effectively with the copyists, undermining his Astorian self-image as an efficient and "prudent" business man. His lame attempt to reduce Turkey to part-time duties at one point presents him with further unwanted revelations of irresolution. In order to deny, or at least suppress, the outrageous "fits" of his employees and his own willingness to sanction their financially unproductive behavior, the lawyer resorts to rationalization: "It was fortunate for me that . . . their fits relieved each other, like guards. When Nippers' was on, Turkey's was off; and *vice versa*. This was a good natural arrangement, under the circumstances."

The central action of the tale is, of course, the lawyer's confrontation with the inscrutable Bartleby. Bartleby, even more than the other copyists, forces the lawyer to face the fragility of his ego's defenses. The confrontation between the two seems a dramatization of what Anna Freud calls the system of attacks, counter-attacks, and defenses between the id and the ego. The lawyer's inept responses to Bartleby's irrational behavior is his ego's denial of the Bartleby enigma. The lawyer, in fact, repeatedly delays any response at all to the scrivener's inexplicable behavior. When Bartleby "prefers not" to check his own copy, for example, the lawyer assumes that "my ears had deceived me." Later, upon Bartleby's refusal to copy, the lawyer denies the refusal by believing that the scrivener "might have temporarily impaired his vision." The lawyer's illusory world of ego screens and ground-glass metaphysics continues to break down as Bartleby's unconventional behavior causes the lawyer to doubt his own most basic assumptions: "When a man is brow beaten in some unprecedented and violently unreasonable way, he begins to stagger in his own plainest faith."

The real weakness of the lawyer's ego defenses are apparent in his vascillating emotional responses to Bartleby. On one occasion, after telling Bartleby that he feels "friendly" towards him, he confesses to the reader that he became "nettled" by Bartleby's refusal to cooperate. Soon, finding himself in a state of "nervous resentment" following Bartleby's refusal to do anything, the lawyer has to check himself "from further demonstrations." His subsequent revery on murder suggests the frenzied state of his feelings, which he checks with a burst of charity: "Men have committed murder for jealousy's sake, and anger's sake, and hatred's sake, and selfishness' sake, and spiritual pride's sake; but no man, that ever I heard of, ever committed a diabolical murder for sweet charity's sake." Such struggles between his id-inspired hatred of Bartleby and his ego-inspired reaction formation of pity and patience reappear as the lawyer leaves Bartleby alone in the deserted offices: "strange to say—I tore myself from him whom I had so longed to be rid of."

After these confrontations with Bartleby in which he uses the doctrine of assumptions (ego) to circumvent the preferences (id) of the scrivener, the lawyer is again forced, upon the entreaties of his old offices' new inmates, to confront Bartleby and his own fears. Following the scrivener's wall of incomprehensible rejections to new career suggestions, the lawyer lapses into complete incoherency and despair. The confounded lawyer's rationality—one of the ego's methods for self-preservation—finally snaps: "If you do not go away from these premises before night, I shall feel bound—indeed, I am bound—to—to—to quit the premises myself." With no verbal recourse available to modify his environment, his rhetorical strategies as bankrupt as Bartleby's, the lawyer must flee external reality. Faced with his own rational fall and the cumulative realization of the futility of his irrationalizations as well as his other rhetorical strategies to maintain a consistent Wall-Street image, he flees to Broadway to find temporary asylum. Significantly, his desire to be "carefree and quiescent" is his recognition of the futility of rational thought to solve his dilemma with Bartleby. He must, therefore, find his peace on Broadway, where imagination and emotion rather than the rationality of Wall Street rule. Thus his ego has temporarily broken down and seeks the state of the "ideal ego," wherein the id and ego are in harmony [Leland E. Hinsie and Robert Jean Campbell, *Psychiatric Dictionary*]. One characteristic of the "ideal ego" is the fantasy of returning to the womb, a regression that seems apparent in the lawyer's huddling in a rockaway.

In contrast to the lawyer who, until his climactic confrontation with Bartleby, uses language effectively to deny the impulses of the id, Turkey and Nippers are between the extremes of the lawyer and Bartleby on the Wall-Street continuum. Each of the scriveners is only able to deny his id's impulses half of each day. While both recognize the need to accept Wall-Street values for professional preservation, neither is able to do so fully. Freud called this condition a split in the ego, in which "an unpleasant knowledge is kept isolated from the rest of the personality." Freud describes the neurotic "split in the ego" as if he had Turkey and Nippers in mind:

> It is indeed a universal characteristic of the neuroses that there are present in the subject's mental life, as regards some particular behavior, two different attitudes, contrary to each other and independent of each other; in that case, however, one of them belongs to the ego and the opposing one, which is repressed, belongs to the id. [*An Outline of Psychoanalysis*]

In the case of both scriveners, the tedium and socially demeaning nature of law copying, being incompatible with their ambitions, must be partially denied by the ego. Consequently, both utilize fantasy as a means of denial, and their equal inability to maintain such fantasies more than half a day coincides with the difficulty of perpetuating that defense mechanism. Anna Freud suggests that in adults

> there is a greater degree of reality testing and intolerance of opposites. Fantasy is not so highly prized, but if there is considerable investment in fantasy, it can become incompatible with reality. [Anna Freud, summarized in Joseph Sandler's *The Analysis of Defense*]

Their unconventional "fits" are a release from Wall Street's repressive atmosphere, becoming vehicles for self-expression beyond copying others' words. Law copying itself reflects the processes of the ego copying and maintaining the conventions of an external source. To maintain the fiction of worth in the Wall-Street world, each creates a rhetorical strategy during his fit that enables him to deny his status as a mere copyist. Part of the humor of the tale, in fact, is in the grotesque forms their denials take, not quite elevating them to their desired status levels.

Turkey's id successfully attacks his ego's defenses each noon as he drinks his lunch at the local saloon. While he is an efficient and quiet copyist during the morning, adapting himself to the demands of his external environment, he displays his fundamental hatred of his position in the afternoon. In his subsequent drunkenness, he rhetorically substitutes the persona of cavalier gentleman for that of mere copyist. In this way his childish id creates a fantasy persona that, together with the alcohol, overwhelms the restraints of his ego. He displays this side of his personality as he explains to the lawyer his attitude towards copying in the afternoons: "'In the morning I but marshal and deploy my columns; but in the afternoon I put myself at their head, and gallantly charge the foe, thus—,'" which he declares "oratorically" while "gesticulating with a long ruler." His use of this military imagery expresses his desire for a more strategic role than his status as a copyist permits him. As in Anna Freud's example in children, only as Turkey "transforms reality by denying it by means of fantasy . . . could he accept it" [*The Analysis of Defense*]. Turkey's frustration is most clearly represented in a gesture that reflects his cavalier rhetoric and ironic social indignity: "Rashest of all the fiery afternoon blunders and flurried rashnesses of Turkey, was his once moistening a ginger-cake between his lips, and clapping it on to a mortgage, for a seal."

Like Turkey, Nippers also attempts to deny his station as mere copyist, a denial the lawyer interprets as a "diseased ambition." Nippers' ego and id also enjoy alternate ascendancy, making him feisty and restive in the morning while contentedly passive in the afternoon. When his ambitious id takes on a "grand air," Nippers imagines himself to be an autonomous man of affairs. In such states Nippers tries to deceive the skeptical lawyer:

> Among the manifestations of his diseased ambition was a fondness he had for receiving visits from certain ambiguous-looking fellows in seedy coats, whom he called his clients. . . . I have good reason to believe, however, that one individual who called upon him at my chambers, and who with a grand air, he insisted was his client, was no other than a dun, and the alleged title-deed, a bill.

Nippers reinforces his desire to be other than a copyist of law documents with a "gentlemanly sort of deportment," ambitiously dressing in a "gentlemanly sort of way." While his ego civilizes his ambition into identification with the lawyer in the afternoon, his id more clearly articulates his frustration in the morning, leading him to grind his teeth together in "maledictions hissed, rather than spoken." Even the fact that he hisses his curses upon life rather than speaks them is a rebellion against the verbal restrictions imposed upon him as a copyist of law documents. Like the lawyer's whose vascillating ego defenses surface in his changing responses to Bartleby, Nippers' psychomachia displays itself in his inability to comfortably adjust his desk height. In a rare burst of insight the lawyer declares that "the truth of the matter was, Nippers knew not what he wanted." Thus, like Turkey and his drinking ale and crunching ginger cakes, and the lawyer with his orderliness and money, Nippers illustrates the result of a conflict between the id and the ego as a compulsion neurosis. In Nippers' case, his constant adjustment of his desk is a "displacement onto a small detail" [*The Psychoanalytic Theory of Neurosis*], of his ego's inability to find pleasure within the narrow limits of his Wall-Street world.

On the far left of the Wall-Street ego continuum is Bartleby. More precisely stated, in the course of the tale he moves to that extreme. While Turkey and Nippers have reached a kind of metaphysical stasis between discontent (id) and resignation (ego), Bartleby's behavior reflects the diminishing ability of his ego to sustain the external conventions of the Wall-Street world. However, the usually overlooked fact that he seeks a job at the lawyer's offices indicates that at the tale's beginning he is not ready or able to forsake all of Wall Street's conventions or to give in fully to the impulses of the id. Our first glimpses of Bartleby indicate the degree of his ego's deterioration. Like the other copyists, Bartleby's appearance suggests traces of the gentlemanly Wall-Street conventions, but the "pallidly neat" and "pitiably respectable" condition of his appearance reflects the increasing inability of his ego to feign those conventions. Another suggestive contrast between Bartleby and the other copyists is in their similarly erratic work habits. While Turkey's and Nippers' conflicting impulses are in symmetrical check, allowing them to meet the lawyer's minimum professional expectations at least half of each day, Bartleby's id continually breaks down his ego's defenses until the lawyer is strained even beyond his ability to rationalize Bartleby's antisocial behavior. As Bartleby successively refuses to check copy, to copy documents, to move, to talk, and finally to eat, we see a deeper manifestation of—in fact an extension of—the neuroses of the other two copyists.

In the process of his id taking control from his ego, Bartleby actually negates his ego by making the lawyer a "negative ruler of the soul" [*Psychiatric Dictionary*]. Thus, in identifying with and then differentiating himself completely from the lawyer, Bartleby becomes compelled to do the opposite of the lawyer, or the opposite of what the lawyer would like him to do. This is clearly illustrated in Bartleby's galling refusal to be cooperative: "At present I would prefer not to be a little reasonable." Also, Bartleby's nonsensical rejections of the potential career ideas the lawyer gives him—"I am not particular"—seem calculated to needle the lawyer.

Melville's shattering message, finally, is the impossibility of language—the external and ultimate convention of the ego—to penetrate the dead-blind wall of reality in the modern world.

—*Dennis R. Perry*

Bartleby increasingly becomes aware of and resigned to the sterile life on Wall Street, and rather than trying to deny that reality by the creation of a false rhetoric as do Nippers and Turkey. Bartleby adopts a rhetoric that mimics the speech of the documents he copies. Ironically, by using copy-speech, Bartleby unconsciously re-creates himself in Wall Street's image. This response is a counterphobic reaction, relieving the anxiety he experiences with the struggle between his id and ego. The basic similarity between this response and the behavior patterns of the other characters is indicated humorously in the infectiousness of Bartleby's copy-speech on his fellow scriveners and on the lawyer himself: "Somehow, of late, I had got into the way of involuntarily using this word 'prefer' upon all sorts of not exactly suitable occasions." Bartleby is related intimately to the other scriveners, then, as one who reacts to the artificiality of the Wall-Street world. In any case, the lawyer, like his scriveners, is affected by

Bartleby, and Melville's comic tale darkens as it records the lawyer's and Bartleby's movement along the Wall-Street continuum—a simultaneous movement that epitomizes the inevitable fate of all humanity trapped in its own decaying systems of arbitrary conventions and linguistic clichés.

In effect, as his id begins to dominate, Bartleby's development becomes the reverse of the socialization process. This is what places him on the opposite end of the Wall-Street continuum from the lawyer whose ego is the most powerfully developed throughout most of the story. While people normally develop and mature as the ego learns to control the id, Bartleby's id has reestablished psychological control and the tale is his desocialization into the quiescence of childhood. Even his limited speech, which mimics copy-speech, is the speech of a child taking familiar words and repeating them sparingly. And, like a child, Bartleby does what he "prefers" to do, not what social convention and the ego would have him do. While Turkey and Nippers adopt the childish ability to fantasize—the id's way of pretending to socialize—Bartleby's return is to pre-fantasy infancy. Without a knowledge of convention one cannot fantasize. Also like an infant, Bartleby becomes more and more helpless, unable to move or take care of himself. His id has none of the ego's instinct for self-preservation. Significantly, our last image of Bartleby is as a fetus, curled helplessly before the prison wall.

While Bartleby represents the limits of modern neuroses, his response to Wall Street can only be understood in the context of the neuroses of the other characters. Together they suggest the ways the ego and id struggle to define the self in the crisis state of a Wall-Street world. Thus, the tale's power derives from the fact that Bartleby is not an isolated case, a freak who alone cannot handle modern life. Rather, what disturbs us is that the "normal" characters are intimately related to him and fight the same neurotic battles. The lawyer's story of his scriveners becomes, finally, a test of his and our comfortable rhetorical strategies that insulate from the incursions of the id, devices of the ego to make sense of experience. Fenichel notes that "the compulsion neurotic . . . flees from the macrocosm of things to the microcosm of words." The narration process, therefore, allows the lawyer to achieve mastery over the events themselves, his attempt to resurrect what Bartleby's words had killed. Melville's shattering message, finally, is the impossibility of language—the external and ultimate convention of the ego—to penetrate the dead-blind wall of reality in the modern world.

FURTHER READING

Bibliography

Bebb, Bruce. "'Bartleby': An Annotated Checklist of Criticism." In *Bartleby the Inscrutable: A Collection of Commentary on Herman Melville's Tale "Bartleby the Scrivener,"* edited by M. Thomas Inge, pp. 199-238. Hamden, Conn.: Archon Books, 1979.

Catalogue of criticism organized chronologically by publication date.

Newman, Lea Bertani Vozar. "Bartleby, the Scrivener." In *A Reader's Guide to the Short Stories of Herman Melville,* pp. 19-78. Boston: G. K. Hall, 1986.

Overview of critical perspectives accompanied by an extensive list of essays and books about "Bartleby."

Biography

Arvin, Newton. *Herman Melville.* New York: Sloane, 1950, 316 p.

Study of Melville's life and career, with extensive critical discussions of his oeuvre.

Leyda, Jay. *The Melville Log: A Documentary Life of Herman Melville, 1819-1891.* 2 vols. 1951. Reprint. New York: Gordian, 1969.

Thorough bibliography of Melville.

Mumford, Lewis. *Herman Melville: A Study of His Life and Vision.* 1929. Revised. New York: Harcourt, Brace & World, 1962, 256 p.

Biographical and critical discussion of Melville and his oeuvre, particularly focusing on the philosophies embedded in Melville's writings.

Criticism

Anderson, Walter E. "Form and Meaning in 'Bartleby the Scrivener'." *Studies in Short Fiction* 18, No. 4 (Fall 1981): 383-93.

Explains "Bartleby" as a Christian parable, according to which the lawyer is typical of humanity generally, who, given the same set of circumstances, also would fail to meet its moral obligation to Bartleby.

Barber, Patricia. "What If Bartleby Were a Woman?" In *The Authority of Experience: Essays in Feminist Criticism,* edited by Arlyn Diamond and Lee R. Edwards, pp. 212-223. Amherst: University of Massachusetts Press, 1977.

Explores what Barber perceives as an underlying homoerotic element of "Bartleby."

Bickley, R. Bruce, Jr. "'Bartleby' as Paradigm." In *The Method of Melville's Short Fiction,* pp. 26-44. Durham, N.C.: Duke University Press, 1975.

Delineates the influences of Washington Irving and Nathaniel Hawthorne on the style, structure, and themes of "Bartleby."

Bigelow, Gordon E. "The Problem of Symbolist Form in Melville's 'Bartleby the Scrivener'." *Modern Language Quarterly* 31 (1970): 345-58.

Argues that the symbolism in "Bartleby" is too rich to be reduced to a single, definitive interpretation.

Eliot, Alexander. "Melville and Bartleby." *Furioso* (Fall 1947): 11-21.

Asserts that "Bartleby" is Melville's portrayal of himself as tortured artist.

Forst, Graham Nicol. "Up Wall Street Towards Broadway: The Narrator's Pilgrimage in Melville's 'Bartleby the Scrivener'." *Studies in Short Fiction* 24, No. 3 (Summer 1987): 263-70.

> Contends that "Bartleby" records the narrator's spiritual awakening.

Franklin, H. Bruce. "Worldly Safety and Other-worldly Saviors." In *The Wake of the Gods: Melville's Mythology*, pp. 126-52. Stanford, Cal.: Stanford University Press, 1963.

> Interprets "Bartleby" as a religious allegory, with a particular emphasis on Christian and Hindu motifs.

Inge, M. Thomas, ed. *Bartleby the Inscrutable: A Collection of Commentary on Herman Melville's Tale "Bartleby the Scrivener."* Hamden, Conn.: Archon Books, 1979, 238 p.

> Anthology of important criticism, including written responses by Melville's contemporaries, several seminal essays, and four articles commissioned especially for the book.

Lacy, Patricia. "The Agatha Theme in Melville's Stories." *The University of Texas Studies in English* XXXV (1956): 96-105.

> Describes the effect of the Agatha story on Melville's metaphysics of good and evil, with special reference to "Bartleby, the Scrivener" "Cock-a-Doodle-Doo!," and the eighth sketch of "The Encantadas."

Marler, Robert F. "'Bartleby, the Scrivener' and the American Short Story." *Genre* VI, No. 4 (December 1973): 428-47.

> Contends that "Bartleby" is the first modern American short story because it avoids the overt moralism, allegory, and romantic characterization of its predecessors.

Marx, Leo. "Melville's Parable of the Walls." *The Sewanee Review* LXI, No. 4 (Autumn 1953): 602-27.

> Seminal examination of "Bartleby" as Melville's autobiographical depiction of the artist in society, focusing especially on the symbolic function of the walls.

McCall, Dan. *The Silence of Bartleby*. Ithaca, N.Y.: Cornell University Press, 1989, 206 p.

> Book-length study that approaches "Bartleby" from several critical perspectives.

Miller, Lewis H., Jr. "'Bartleby' and the Dead Letter." *Studies in American Fiction* 8, No. 1 (Spring 1980): 1-12.

> Argues that the language in "Bartleby" belies the narrator's assessment of the events related by him.

Murray, Henry A. "Bartleby and I." In *Melville Annual 1965, a Symposium: "Bartleby the Scrivener,"* edited by Howard P. Vincent, pp. 3-24. Kent: Kent State University Press, 1966.

Surveys several critical approaches to "Bartleby," with special emphasis on Melville and his psychological character portrayals.

Pinsker, Sanford. "'Bartleby the Scrivener': Language as Wall." *College Literature* II, No. 1 (Winter 1975): 17-27.

> Insists that "Bartleby" comments on the inability of language to fully circumscribe human experience.

Pribek, Thomas. "Melville's Copyists: The 'Bar-tenders' of Wall Street." *Papers on Language and Literature* 22, No. 2 (Spring 1986): 176-86.

> Considers the inequality, disillusionment, and discontentment of "Bartleby" to be a by-product of commercial society.

Reinert, Otto. "Bartleby the Inscrutable: Notes on a Melville Motif." In *Americana Norvegica: Norwegian Contributions to American Studies*, Vol. I, edited by Sigmund Skard and Henry H. Wasser, pp. 180-205. Philadelphia: University of Pennsylvania Press, 1966.

> Focuses on the existentialist dimension of "Bartleby," especially in relation to Melville's other works.

Roundy, Nancy. "'*That* is All I Know of Him . . .': Epistemology and Art in Melville's 'Bartleby.'" *Essays in Arts and Sciences* IX, No. 1 (May 1980): 33-43.

> Presents the narrator of "Bartleby" as an artist who, during the course of the story, is improved by his own storytelling.

Trilling, Lionel. "Bartleby the Scrivener: A Story of Wall Street," in his preface to *The Experience of Literature*, pp. 74-8, New York: Harcourt Brace Jovanovich, 1979.

> Describes Bartleby as an individual alienated by the capitalist system.

Vincent, Howard P., ed. *Melville Annual 1965, a Symposium: "Bartleby the Scrivener."* Kent, Ohio: Kent State University Press, 199 p.

> Collection of diverse essays on "Bartleby." A secondary bibliography and a facsimile reprinting of "Bartleby" are included.

Widmer, Kingsley. "The Negative Affirmation: Melville's 'Bartleby.'" *Modern Fiction Studies* VIII, No. 3 (Autumn 1962): 276-86.

> Argues that "Bartleby" portrays the inability of the narrator's rational perspective to contend with Bartleby's irrationality and nihilism.

Wilson, James C. "'Bartleby': The Walls of Wall Street." *Arizona Quarterly* 37, No. 4 (Winter 1981): 335-46.

> Argues that "Bartleby" indicts capitalism's reduction of Bartleby from human being to abstract concept.

Nineteenth-Century
Literature Criticism
Cumulative Indexes
Volumes 1-49

How to Use This Index

The main references

Calvino, Italo
1923-1985.....CLC 5, 8, 11, 22, 33, 39,
73; SSC 3

list all author entries in the following Gale Literary Criticism series:

BLC = *Black Literature Criticism*
CLC = *Contemporary Literary Criticism*
CLR = *Children's Literature Review*
CMLC = *Classical and Medieval Literature Criticism*
DA = *DISCovering Authors*
DC = *Drama Criticism*
HLC = *Hispanic Literature Criticism*
LC = *Literature Criticism from 1400 to 1800*
NCLC = *Nineteenth-Century Literature Criticism*
PC = *Poetry Criticism*
SSC = *Short Story Criticism*
TCLC = *Twentieth-Century Literary Criticism*
WLC = *World Literature Criticism, 1500 to the Present*

The cross-references

See also CANR 23; CA 85-88;
obituary CA 116

list all author entries in the following Gale biographical and literary sources:

AAYA = *Authors & Artists for Young Adults*
AITN = *Authors in the News*
BEST = *Bestsellers*
BW = *Black Writers*
CA = *Contemporary Authors*
CAAS = *Contemporary Authors Autobiography Series*
CABS = *Contemporary Authors Bibliographical Series*
CANR = *Contemporary Authors New Revision Series*
CAP = *Contemporary Authors Permanent Series*
CDALB = *Concise Dictionary of American Literary Biography*
CDBLB = *Concise Dictionary of British Literary Biography*
DLB = *Dictionary of Literary Biography*
DLBD = *Dictionary of Literary Biography Documentary Series*
DLBY = *Dictionary of Literary Biography Yearbook*
HW = *Hispanic Writers*
JRDA = *Junior DISCovering Authors*
MAICYA = *Major Authors and Illustrators for Children and Young Adults*
MTCW = *Major 20th-Century Writers*
NNAL = *Native North American Literature*
SAAS = *Something about the Author Autobiography Series*
SATA = *Something about the Author*
YABC = *Yesterday's Authors of Books for Children*

Literary Criticism Series
Cumulative Author Index

Aldiss, Brian W(ilson)
1925- .... CLC **5, 14, 40**
See also CA 5-8R; CAAS 2; CANR 5, 28;
DLB 14; MTCW; SATA 34

Alegria, Claribel 1924-........... CLC **75**
See also CA 131; CAAS 15; DLB 145; HW

Alegria, Fernando 1918-.......... CLC **57**
See also CA 9-12R; CANR 5, 32; HW

Aleichem, Sholom .... TCLC **1, 35**
See also Rabinovitch, Sholem

Aleixandre, Vicente 1898-1984 ... CLC **9, 36**
See also CA 85-88; 114; CANR 26;
DLB 108; HW; MTCW

Alepoudelis, Odysseus
See Elytis, Odysseus

Aleshkovsky, Joseph 1929-
See Aleshkovsky, Yuz
See also CA 121; 128

Aleshkovsky, Yuz .... CLC **44**
See also Aleshkovsky, Joseph

Alexander, Lloyd (Chudley) 1924- .. CLC **35**
See also AAYA 1; CA 1-4R; CANR 1, 24,
38; CLR 1, 5; DLB 52; JRDA; MAICYA;
MTCW; SAAS 19; SATA 3, 49, 81

Alfau, Felipe 1902-.............. CLC **66**
See also CA 137

Alger, Horatio, Jr. 1832-1899..... NCLC **8**
See also DLB 42; SATA 16

Algren, Nelson 1909-1981 .... CLC **4, 10, 33**
See also CA 13-16R; 103; CANR 20;
CDALB 1941-1968; DLB 9; DLBY 81,
82; MTCW

Ali, Ahmed 1910-................ CLC **69**
See also CA 25-28R; CANR 15, 34

Alighieri, Dante 1265-1321 .... CMLC **3**

Allan, John B.
See Westlake, Donald E(dwin)

Allen, Edward 1948-.............. CLC **59**

Allen, Paula Gunn 1939-.......... CLC **84**
See also CA 112; 143; NNAL

Allen, Roland
See Ayckbourn, Alan

Allen, Sarah A.
See Hopkins, Pauline Elizabeth

Allen, Woody 1935-........... CLC **16, 52**
See also AAYA 10; CA 33-36R; CANR 27,
38; DLB 44; MTCW

Allende, Isabel 1942- .... CLC **39, 57; HLC**
See also CA 125; 130; DLB 145; HW;
MTCW

Alleyn, Ellen
See Rossetti, Christina (Georgina)

Allingham, Margery (Louise)
1904-1966 .... CLC **19**
See also CA 5-8R; 25-28R; CANR 4;
DLB 77; MTCW

Allingham, William 1824-1889 ... NCLC **25**
See also DLB 35

Allison, Dorothy E. 1949-......... CLC **78**
See also CA 140

Allston, Washington 1779-1843.... NCLC **2**
See also DLB 1

Almedingen, E. M. .... CLC **12**
See also Almedingen, Martha Edith von
See also SATA 3

Almedingen, Martha Edith von 1898-1971
See Almedingen, E. M.
See also CA 1-4R; CANR 1

Almqvist, Carl Jonas Love
1793-1866 .... NCLC **42**

Alonso, Damaso 1898-1990 .... CLC **14**
See also CA 110; 131; 130; DLB 108; HW

Alov
See Gogol, Nikolai (Vasilyevich)

Alta 1942-..................... CLC **19**
See also CA 57-60

Alter, Robert B(ernard) 1935-...... CLC **34**
See also CA 49-52; CANR 1, 47

Alther, Lisa 1944-.............. CLC **7, 41**
See also CA 65-68; CANR 12, 30; MTCW

Altman, Robert 1925-............. CLC **16**
See also CA 73-76; CANR 43

Alvarez, A(lfred) 1929-.......... CLC **5, 13**
See also CA 1-4R; CANR 3, 33; DLB 14,
40

Alvarez, Alejandro Rodriguez 1903-1965
See Casona, Alejandro
See also CA 131; 93-96; HW

Amado, Jorge 1912-..... CLC **13, 40; HLC**
See also CA 77-80; CANR 35; DLB 113;
MTCW

Ambler, Eric 1909-............ CLC **4, 6, 9**
See also CA 9-12R; CANR 7, 38; DLB 77;
MTCW

Amichai, Yehuda 1924- ...... CLC **9, 22, 57**
See also CA 85-88; CANR 46; MTCW

Amiel, Henri Frederic 1821-1881 .. NCLC **4**

Amis, Kingsley (William)
1922- .. CLC **1, 2, 3, 5, 8, 13, 40, 44; DA**
See also AITN 2; CA 9-12R; CANR 8, 28;
CDBLB 1945-1960; DLB 15, 27, 100, 139;
MTCW

Amis, Martin (Louis)
1949- .... CLC **4, 9, 38, 62**
See also BEST 90:3; CA 65-68; CANR 8,
27; DLB 14

Ammons, A(rchie) R(andolph)
1926- .... CLC **2, 3, 5, 8, 9, 25, 57**
See also AITN 1; CA 9-12R; CANR 6, 36;
DLB 5; MTCW

Amo, Tauraatua i
See Adams, Henry (Brooks)

Anand, Mulk Raj 1905-........... CLC **23**
See also CA 65-68; CANR 32; MTCW

Anatol
See Schnitzler, Arthur

Anaya, Rudolfo A(lfonso)
1937- .... CLC **23; HLC**
See also CA 45-48; CAAS 4; CANR 1, 32;
DLB 82; HW 1; MTCW

Andersen, Hans Christian
1805-1875 .. NCLC **7; DA; SSC 6; WLC**
See also CLR 6; MAICYA; YABC 1

Anderson, C. Farley
See Mencken, H(enry) L(ouis); Nathan,
George Jean

Anderson, Jessica (Margaret) Queale
.... CLC **37**
See also CA 9-12R; CANR 4

Anderson, Jon (Victor) 1940- .... CLC **9**
See also CA 25-28R; CANR 20

Anderson, Lindsay (Gordon)
1923-1994 .... CLC **20**
See also CA 125; 128; 146

Anderson, Maxwell 1888-1959 ..... TCLC **2**
See also CA 105; DLB 7

Anderson, Poul (William) 1926- .... CLC **15**
See also AAYA 5; CA 1-4R; CAAS 2;
CANR 2, 15, 34; DLB 8; MTCW;
SATA-Brief 39

Anderson, Robert (Woodruff)
1917- .... CLC **23**
See also AITN 1; CA 21-24R; CANR 32;
DLB 7

Anderson, Sherwood
1876-1941 .... TCLC **1, 10, 24; DA;
SSC 1; WLC**
See also CA 104; 121; CDALB 1917-1929;
DLB 4, 9, 86; DLBD 1; MTCW

Andouard
See Giraudoux, (Hippolyte) Jean

Andrade, Carlos Drummond de ...... CLC **18**
See also Drummond de Andrade, Carlos

Andrade, Mario de 1893-1945..... TCLC **43**

Andreas-Salome, Lou 1861-1937... TCLC **56**
See also DLB 66

Andrewes, Lancelot 1555-1626 .... LC **5**

Andrews, Cicily Fairfield
See West, Rebecca

Andrews, Elton V.
See Pohl, Frederik

Andreyev, Leonid (Nikolaevich)
1871-1919 .... TCLC **3**
See also CA 104

Andric, Ivo 1892-1975 .... CLC **8**
See also CA 81-84; 57-60; CANR 43;
DLB 147; MTCW

Angelique, Pierre
See Bataille, Georges

Angell, Roger 1920-.............. CLC **26**
See also CA 57-60; CANR 13, 44

Angelou, Maya
1928- .... CLC **12, 35, 64, 77; BLC; DA**
See also AAYA 7; BW 2; CA 65-68;
CANR 19, 42; DLB 38; MTCW;
SATA 49

Annensky, Innokenty Fyodorovich
1856-1909 .... TCLC **14**
See also CA 110

Anon, Charles Robert
See Pessoa, Fernando (Antonio Nogueira)

Anouilh, Jean (Marie Lucien Pierre)
1910-1987 ...... CLC **1, 3, 8, 13, 40, 50**
See also CA 17-20R; 123; CANR 32;
MTCW

Anthony, Florence
See Ai

Anthony, John
See Ciardi, John (Anthony)

Anthony, Peter
   See Shaffer, Anthony (Joshua); Shaffer,
   Peter (Levin)

Anthony, Piers 1934- . . . . **CLC 35**
   See also AAYA 11; CA 21-24R; CANR 28;
   DLB 8; MTCW

Antoine, Marc
   See Proust, (Valentin-Louis-George-Eugene-)
   Marcel

Antoninus, Brother
   See Everson, William (Oliver)

Antonioni, Michelangelo 1912- . . . . . **CLC 20**
   See also CA 73-76; CANR 45

Antschel, Paul 1920-1970
   See Celan, Paul
   See also CA 85-88; CANR 33; MTCW

Anwar, Chairil 1922-1949 . . . . **TCLC 22**
   See also CA 121

Apollinaire, Guillaume . . **TCLC 3, 8, 51; PC 7**
   See also Kostrowitzki, Wilhelm Apollinaris
   de

Appelfeld, Aharon 1932- . . . . **CLC 23, 47**
   See also CA 112; 133

Apple, Max (Isaac) 1941- . . . . **CLC 9, 33**
   See also CA 81-84; CANR 19; DLB 130

Appleman, Philip (Dean) 1926- . . . . . **CLC 51**
   See also CA 13-16R; CAAS 18; CANR 6,
   29

Appleton, Lawrence
   See Lovecraft, H(oward) P(hillips)

Apteryx
   See Eliot, T(homas) S(tearns)

Apuleius, (Lucius Madaurensis)
   125(?)-175(?) . . . . **CMLC 1**

Aquin, Hubert 1929-1977 . . . . **CLC 15**
   See also CA 105; DLB 53

Aragon, Louis 1897-1982 . . . . **CLC 3, 22**
   See also CA 69-72; 108; CANR 28;
   DLB 72; MTCW

Arany, Janos 1817-1882 . . . . **NCLC 34**

Arbuthnot, John 1667-1735 . . . . **LC 1**
   See also DLB 101

Archer, Herbert Winslow
   See Mencken, H(enry) L(ouis)

Archer, Jeffrey (Howard) 1940- . . . . **CLC 28**
   See also BEST 89:3; CA 77-80; CANR 22

Archer, Jules 1915- . . . . **CLC 12**
   See also CA 9-12R; CANR 6; SAAS 5;
   SATA 4

Archer, Lee
   See Ellison, Harlan (Jay)

Arden, John 1930- . . . . **CLC 6, 13, 15**
   See also CA 13-16R; CAAS 4; CANR 31;
   DLB 13; MTCW

Arenas, Reinaldo
   1943-1990 . . . . **CLC 41; HLC**
   See also CA 124; 128; 133; DLB 145; HW

Arendt, Hannah 1906-1975 . . . . **CLC 66**
   See also CA 17-20R; 61-64; CANR 26;
   MTCW

Aretino, Pietro 1492-1556 . . . . **LC 12**

Arghezi, Tudor . . . . **CLC 80**
   See also Theodorescu, Ion N.

Arguedas, Jose Maria
   1911-1969 . . . . **CLC 10, 18**
   See also CA 89-92; DLB 113; HW

Argueta, Manlio 1936- . . . . **CLC 31**
   See also CA 131; DLB 145; HW

Ariosto, Ludovico 1474-1533 . . . . **LC 6**

Aristides
   See Epstein, Joseph

Aristophanes
   450B.C.-385B.C. . . . . **CMLC 4; DA; DC 2**

Arlt, Roberto (Godofredo Christophersen)
   1900-1942 . . . . **TCLC 29; HLC**
   See also CA 123; 131; HW

Armah, Ayi Kwei 1939- . . . . **CLC 5, 33; BLC**
   See also BW 1; CA 61-64; CANR 21;
   DLB 117; MTCW

Armatrading, Joan 1950- . . . . **CLC 17**
   See also CA 114

Arnette, Robert
   See Silverberg, Robert

Arnim, Achim von (Ludwig Joachim von
   Arnim) 1781-1831 . . . . **NCLC 5**
   See also DLB 90

Arnim, Bettina von 1785-1859 . . . . **NCLC 38**
   See also DLB 90

Arnold, Matthew
   1822-1888 . . . . . **NCLC 6, 29; DA; PC 5;**
                                                WLC
   See also CDBLB 1832-1890; DLB 32, 57

Arnold, Thomas 1795-1842 . . . . . **NCLC 18**
   See also DLB 55

Arnow, Harriette (Louisa) Simpson
   1908-1986 . . . . **CLC 2, 7, 18**
   See also CA 9-12R; 118; CANR 14; DLB 6;
   MTCW; SATA 42; SATA-Obit 47

Arp, Hans
   See Arp, Jean

Arp, Jean 1887-1966 . . . . **CLC 5**
   See also CA 81-84; 25-28R; CANR 42

Arrabal
   See Arrabal, Fernando

Arrabal, Fernando 1932- . . **CLC 2, 9, 18, 58**
   See also CA 9-12R; CANR 15

Arrick, Fran . . . . **CLC 30**

Artaud, Antonin 1896-1948 . . . . . **TCLC 3, 36**
   See also CA 104

Arthur, Ruth M(abel) 1905-1979 . . . . **CLC 12**
   See also CA 9-12R; 85-88; CANR 4;
   SATA 7, 26

Artsybashev, Mikhail (Petrovich)
   1878-1927 . . . . **TCLC 31**

Arundel, Honor (Morfydd)
   1919-1973 . . . . **CLC 17**
   See also CA 21-22; 41-44R; CAP 2;
   CLR 35; SATA 4; SATA-Obit 24

Asch, Sholem 1880-1957 . . . . **TCLC 3**
   See also CA 105

Ash, Shalom
   See Asch, Sholem

Ashbery, John (Lawrence)
   1927- . . . . . . **CLC 2, 3, 4, 6, 9, 13, 15, 25,**
                                                41, 77
   See also CA 5-8R; CANR 9, 37; DLB 5;
   DLBY 81; MTCW

Ashdown, Clifford
   See Freeman, R(ichard) Austin

Ashe, Gordon
   See Creasey, John

Ashton-Warner, Sylvia (Constance)
   1908-1984 . . . . **CLC 19**
   See also CA 69-72; 112; CANR 29; MTCW

Asimov, Isaac
   1920-1992 . . . . . . **CLC 1, 3, 9, 19, 26, 76**
   See also AAYA 13; BEST 90:2; CA 1-4R;
   137; CANR 2, 19, 36; CLR 12; DLB 8;
   DLBY 92; JRDA; MAICYA; MTCW;
   SATA 1, 26, 74

Astley, Thea (Beatrice May)
   1925- . . . . **CLC 41**
   See also CA 65-68; CANR 11, 43

Aston, James
   See White, T(erence) H(anbury)

Asturias, Miguel Angel
   1899-1974 . . . . **CLC 3, 8, 13; HLC**
   See also CA 25-28; 49-52; CANR 32;
   CAP 2; DLB 113; HW; MTCW

Atares, Carlos Saura
   See Saura (Atares), Carlos

Atheling, William
   See Pound, Ezra (Weston Loomis)

Atheling, William, Jr.
   See Blish, James (Benjamin)

Atherton, Gertrude (Franklin Horn)
   1857-1948 . . . . **TCLC 2**
   See also CA 104; DLB 9, 78

Atherton, Lucius
   See Masters, Edgar Lee

Atkins, Jack
   See Harris, Mark

Atticus
   See Fleming, Ian (Lancaster)

Atwood, Margaret (Eleanor)
   1939- . . . . . **CLC 2, 3, 4, 8, 13, 15, 25, 44,**
                                    84; DA; PC 8; SSC 2; WLC
   See also AAYA 12; BEST 89:2; CA 49-52;
   CANR 3, 24, 33; DLB 53; MTCW;
   SATA 50

Aubigny, Pierre d'
   See Mencken, H(enry) L(ouis)

Aubin, Penelope 1685-1731(?) . . . . **LC 9**
   See also DLB 39

Auchincloss, Louis (Stanton)
   1917- . . . . **CLC 4, 6, 9, 18, 45**
   See also CA 1-4R; CANR 6, 29; DLB 2;
   DLBY 80; MTCW

Auden, W(ystan) H(ugh)
   1907-1973 . . . . . . **CLC 1, 2, 3, 4, 6, 9, 11,**
                                    14, 43; DA; PC 1; WLC
   See also CA 9-12R; 45-48; CANR 5;
   CDBLB 1914-1945; DLB 10, 20; MTCW

Audiberti, Jacques 1900-1965 . . . . . . **CLC 38**
   See also CA 25-28R

Audubon, John James
   1785-1851 . . . . **NCLC 47**

Auel, Jean M(arie) 1936- . . . . **CLC 31**
   See also AAYA 7; BEST 90:4; CA 103;
   CANR 21

Auerbach, Erich 1892-1957 . . . . **TCLC 43**
   See also CA 118

Augier, Emile 1820-1889 . . . . NCLC 31

August, John
See De Voto, Bernard (Augustine)

Augustine, St. 354-430 . . . . CMLC 6

Aurelius
See Bourne, Randolph S(illiman)

Austen, Jane
1775-1817 . . . . NCLC 1, 13, 19, 33; DA;
WLC
See also CDBLB 1789-1832; DLB 116

Auster, Paul 1947- . . . . CLC 47
See also CA 69-72; CANR 23

Austin, Frank
See Faust, Frederick (Schiller)

Austin, Mary (Hunter)
1868-1934 . . . . TCLC 25
See also CA 109; DLB 9, 78

Autran Dourado, Waldomiro
See Dourado, (Waldomiro Freitas) Autran

Averroes 1126-1198 . . . . CMLC 7
See also DLB 115

Avison, Margaret 1918- . . . . CLC 2, 4
See also CA 17-20R; DLB 53; MTCW

Axton, David
See Koontz, Dean R(ay)

Ayckbourn, Alan
1939- . . . . CLC 5, 8, 18, 33, 74
See also CA 21-24R; CANR 31; DLB 13;
MTCW

Aydy, Catherine
See Tennant, Emma (Christina)

Ayme, Marcel (Andre) 1902-1967 . . . CLC 11
See also CA 89-92; CLR 25; DLB 72

Ayrton, Michael 1921-1975 . . . . CLC 7
See also CA 5-8R; 61-64; CANR 9, 21

Azorin . . . . CLC 11
See also Martinez Ruiz, Jose

Azuela, Mariano
1873-1952 . . . . TCLC 3; HLC
See also CA 104; 131; HW; MTCW

Baastad, Babbis Friis
See Friis-Baastad, Babbis Ellinor

Bab
See Gilbert, W(illiam) S(chwenck)

Babbis, Eleanor
See Friis-Baastad, Babbis Ellinor

Babel, Isaak (Emmanuilovich)
1894-1941(?) . . . . . . TCLC 2, 13; SSC 16
See also CA 104

Babits, Mihaly 1883-1941 . . . . TCLC 14
See also CA 114

Babur 1483-1530 . . . . LC 18

Bacchelli, Riccardo 1891-1985 . . . . . CLC 19
See also CA 29-32R; 117

Bach, Richard (David) 1936- . . . . CLC 14
See also AITN 1; BEST 89:2; CA 9-12R;
CANR 18; MTCW; SATA 13

Bachman, Richard
See King, Stephen (Edwin)

Bachmann, Ingeborg 1926-1973 . . . . . CLC 69
See also CA 93-96; 45-48; DLB 85

Bacon, Francis 1561-1626 . . . . LC 18
See also CDBLB Before 1660

Bacon, Roger 1214(?)-1292 . . . . . . CMLC 14
See also DLB 115

Bacovia, George . . . . TCLC 24
See also Vasiliu, Gheorghe

Badanes, Jerome 1937- . . . . CLC 59

Bagehot, Walter 1826-1877 . . . . . . NCLC 10
See also DLB 55

Bagnold, Enid 1889-1981 . . . . CLC 25
See also CA 5-8R; 103; CANR 5, 40;
DLB 13; MAICYA; SATA 1, 25

Bagrjana, Elisaveta
See Belcheva, Elisaveta

Bagryana, Elisaveta
See Belcheva, Elisaveta
See also DLB 147

Bailey, Paul 1937- . . . . CLC 45
See also CA 21-24R; CANR 16; DLB 14

Baillie, Joanna 1762-1851 . . . . NCLC 2
See also DLB 93

Bainbridge, Beryl (Margaret)
1933- . . . . CLC 4, 5, 8, 10, 14, 18, 22, 62
See also CA 21-24R; CANR 24; DLB 14;
MTCW

Baker, Elliott 1922- . . . . CLC 8
See also CA 45-48; CANR 2

Baker, Nicholson 1957- . . . . CLC 61
See also CA 135

Baker, Ray Stannard 1870-1946 . . . TCLC 47
See also CA 118

Baker, Russell (Wayne) 1925- . . . . . . CLC 31
See also BEST 89:4; CA 57-60; CANR 11,
41; MTCW

Bakhtin, M.
See Bakhtin, Mikhail Mikhailovich

Bakhtin, M. M.
See Bakhtin, Mikhail Mikhailovich

Bakhtin, Mikhail
See Bakhtin, Mikhail Mikhailovich

Bakhtin, Mikhail Mikhailovich
1895-1975 . . . . CLC 83
See also CA 128; 113

Bakshi, Ralph 1938(?)- . . . . CLC 26
See also CA 112; 138

Bakunin, Mikhail (Alexandrovich)
1814-1876 . . . . NCLC 25

Baldwin, James (Arthur)
1924-1987 . . . . . . CLC 1, 2, 3, 4, 5, 8, 13,
15, 17, 42, 50, 67; BLC; DA; DC 1;
SSC 10; WLC
See also AAYA 4; BW 1; CA 1-4R; 124;
CABS 1; CANR 3, 24;
CDALB 1941-1968; DLB 2, 7, 33;
DLBY 87; MTCW; SATA 9;
SATA-Obit 54

Ballard, J(ames) G(raham)
1930- . . . . . . CLC 3, 6, 14, 36; SSC 1
See also AAYA 3; CA 5-8R; CANR 15, 39;
DLB 14; MTCW

Balmont, Konstantin (Dmitriyevich)
1867-1943 . . . . TCLC 11
See also CA 109

Balzac, Honore de
1799-1850 . . . . NCLC 5, 35; DA; SSC 5;
WLC
See also DLB 119

Bambara, Toni Cade
1939- . . . . CLC 19; BLC; DA
See also AAYA 5; BW 2; CA 29-32R;
CANR 24; DLB 38; MTCW

Bamdad, A.
See Shamlu, Ahmad

Banat, D. R.
See Bradbury, Ray (Douglas)

Bancroft, Laura
See Baum, L(yman) Frank

Banim, John 1798-1842 . . . . NCLC 13
See also DLB 116

Banim, Michael 1796-1874 . . . . . . NCLC 13

Banks, Iain
See Banks, Iain M(enzies)

Banks, Iain M(enzies) 1954- . . . . CLC 34
See also CA 123; 128

Banks, Lynne Reid . . . . CLC 23
See also Reid Banks, Lynne
See also AAYA 6

Banks, Russell 1940- . . . . CLC 37, 72
See also CA 65-68; CAAS 15; CANR 19;
DLB 130

Banville, John 1945- . . . . CLC 46
See also CA 117; 128; DLB 14

Banville, Theodore (Faullain) de
1832-1891 . . . . NCLC 9

Baraka, Amiri
1934- . . . . CLC 1, 2, 3, 5, 10, 14, 33;
BLC; DA; PC 4
See also Jones, LeRoi
See also BW 2; CA 21-24R; CABS 3;
CANR 27, 38; CDALB 1941-1968;
DLB 5, 7, 16, 38; DLBD 8; MTCW

Barbellion, W. N. P. . . . . TCLC 24
See also Cummings, Bruce F(rederick)

Barbera, Jack (Vincent) 1945- . . . . . . CLC 44
See also CA 110; CANR 45

Barbey d'Aurevilly, Jules Amedee
1808-1889 . . . . NCLC 1; SSC 17
See also DLB 119

Barbusse, Henri 1873-1935 . . . . TCLC 5
See also CA 105; DLB 65

Barclay, Bill
See Moorcock, Michael (John)

Barclay, William Ewert
See Moorcock, Michael (John)

Barea, Arturo 1897-1957 . . . . TCLC 14
See also CA 111

Barfoot, Joan 1946- . . . . CLC 18
See also CA 105

Baring, Maurice 1874-1945 . . . . TCLC 8
See also CA 105; DLB 34

Barker, Clive 1952- . . . . CLC 52
See also AAYA 10; BEST 90:3; CA 121;
129; MTCW

Barker, George Granville
1913-1991 . . . . CLC 8, 48
See also CA 9-12R; 135; CANR 7, 38;
DLB 20; MTCW

Barker, Harley Granville
See Granville-Barker, Harley
See also DLB 10

Barker, Howard 1946- . . . . **CLC 37**
See also CA 102; DLB 13

Barker, Pat 1943- . . . . **CLC 32**
See also CA 117; 122

Barlow, Joel 1754-1812 . . . . **NCLC 23**
See also DLB 37

Barnard, Mary (Ethel) 1909- . . . . **CLC 48**
See also CA 21-22; CAP 2

Barnes, Djuna
1892-1982 . . . **CLC 3, 4, 8, 11, 29; SSC 3**
See also CA 9-12R; 107; CANR 16; DLB 4,
9, 45; MTCW

Barnes, Julian 1946- . . . . **CLC 42**
See also CA 102; CANR 19; DLBY 93

Barnes, Peter 1931- . . . . **CLC 5, 56**
See also CA 65-68; CAAS 12; CANR 33,
34; DLB 13; MTCW

Baroja (y Nessi), Pio
1872-1956 . . . . **TCLC 8; HLC**
See also CA 104

Baron, David
See Pinter, Harold

Baron Corvo
See Rolfe, Frederick (William Serafino
Austin Lewis Mary)

Barondess, Sue K(aufman)
1926-1977 . . . . **CLC 8**
See also Kaufman, Sue
See also CA 1-4R; 69-72; CANR 1

Baron de Teive
See Pessoa, Fernando (Antonio Nogueira)

Barres, Maurice 1862-1923 . . . . **TCLC 47**
See also DLB 123

Barreto, Afonso Henrique de Lima
See Lima Barreto, Afonso Henrique de

Barrett, (Roger) Syd 1946- . . . . **CLC 35**

Barrett, William (Christopher)
1913-1992 . . . . **CLC 27**
See also CA 13-16R; 139; CANR 11

Barrie, J(ames) M(atthew)
1860-1937 . . . . **TCLC 2**
See also CA 104; 136; CDBLB 1890-1914;
CLR 16; DLB 10, 141; MAICYA;
YABC 1

Barrington, Michael
See Moorcock, Michael (John)

Barrol, Grady
See Bograd, Larry

Barry, Mike
See Malzberg, Barry N(athaniel)

Barry, Philip 1896-1949 . . . . **TCLC 11**
See also CA 109; DLB 7

Bart, Andre Schwarz
See Schwarz-Bart, Andre

Barth, John (Simmons)
1930- . . . . . . **CLC 1, 2, 3, 5, 7, 9, 10, 14,
27, 51; SSC 10**
See also AITN 1, 2; CA 1-4R; CABS 1;
CANR 5, 23; DLB 2; MTCW

Barthelme, Donald
1931-1989 . . . . . . **CLC 1, 2, 3, 5, 6, 8, 13,
23, 46, 59; SSC 2**
See also CA 21-24R; 129; CANR 20;
DLB 2; DLBY 80, 89; MTCW; SATA 7;
SATA-Obit 62

Barthelme, Frederick 1943- . . . . **CLC 36**
See also CA 114; 122; DLBY 85

Barthes, Roland (Gerard)
1915-1980 . . . . **CLC 24, 83**
See also CA 130; 97-100; MTCW

Barzun, Jacques (Martin) 1907- . . . . **CLC 51**
See also CA 61-64; CANR 22

Bashevis, Isaac
See Singer, Isaac Bashevis

Bashkirtseff, Marie 1859-1884 . . . **NCLC 27**

Basho
See Matsuo Basho

Bass, Kingsley B., Jr.
See Bullins, Ed

Bass, Rick 1958- . . . . **CLC 79**
See also CA 126

Bassani, Giorgio 1916- . . . . **CLC 9**
See also CA 65-68; CANR 33; DLB 128;
MTCW

Bastos, Augusto (Antonio) Roa
See Roa Bastos, Augusto (Antonio)

Bataille, Georges 1897-1962 . . . . **CLC 29**
See also CA 101; 89-92

Bates, H(erbert) E(rnest)
1905-1974 . . . . **CLC 46; SSC 10**
See also CA 93-96; 45-48; CANR 34;
MTCW

Bauchart
See Camus, Albert

Baudelaire, Charles
1821-1867 . . . . . **NCLC 6, 29; DA; PC 1;
SSC 18; WLC**

Baudrillard, Jean 1929- . . . . **CLC 60**

Baum, L(yman) Frank 1856-1919 . . . **TCLC 7**
See also CA 108; 133; CLR 15; DLB 22;
JRDA; MAICYA; MTCW; SATA 18

Baum, Louis F.
See Baum, L(yman) Frank

Baumbach, Jonathan 1933- . . . . **CLC 6, 23**
See also CA 13-16R; CAAS 5; CANR 12;
DLBY 80; MTCW

Bausch, Richard (Carl) 1945- . . . . . . **CLC 51**
See also CA 101; CAAS 14; CANR 43;
DLB 130

Baxter, Charles 1947- . . . . **CLC 45, 78**
See also CA 57-60; CANR 40; DLB 130

Baxter, George Owen
See Faust, Frederick (Schiller)

Baxter, James K(eir) 1926-1972 . . . . **CLC 14**
See also CA 77-80

Baxter, John
See Hunt, E(verette) Howard, (Jr.)

Bayer, Sylvia
See Glassco, John

Baynton, Barbara 1857-1929 . . . . . . **TCLC 57**

Beagle, Peter S(oyer) 1939- . . . . **CLC 7**
See also CA 9-12R; CANR 4; DLBY 80;
SATA 60

Bean, Normal
See Burroughs, Edgar Rice

Beard, Charles A(ustin)
1874-1948 . . . . **TCLC 15**
See also CA 115; DLB 17; SATA 18

Beardsley, Aubrey 1872-1898 . . . . . **NCLC 6**

Beattie, Ann
1947- . . . . **CLC 8, 13, 18, 40, 63; SSC 11**
See also BEST 90:2; CA 81-84; DLBY 82;
MTCW

Beattie, James 1735-1803 . . . . **NCLC 25**
See also DLB 109

Beauchamp, Kathleen Mansfield 1888-1923
See Mansfield, Katherine
See also CA 104; 134; DA

Beaumarchais, Pierre-Augustin Caron de
1732-1799 . . . . **DC 4**

**Beauvoir, Simone (Lucie Ernestine Marie
Bertrand) de**
1908-1986 . . . . **CLC 1, 2, 4, 8, 14, 31, 44,
50, 71; DA; WLC**
See also CA 9-12R; 118; CANR 28;
DLB 72; DLBY 86; MTCW

Becker, Jurek 1937- . . . . **CLC 7, 19**
See also CA 85-88; DLB 75

Becker, Walter 1950- . . . . **CLC 26**

Beckett, Samuel (Barclay)
1906-1989 . . . . . . **CLC 1, 2, 3, 4, 6, 9, 10,
11, 14, 18, 29, 57, 59, 83; DA; SSC 16;
WLC**
See also CA 5-8R; 130; CANR 33;
CDBLB 1945-1960; DLB 13, 15;
DLBY 90; MTCW

Beckford, William 1760-1844 . . . . **NCLC 16**
See also DLB 39

Beckman, Gunnel 1910- . . . . **CLC 26**
See also CA 33-36R; CANR 15; CLR 25;
MAICYA; SAAS 9; SATA 6

Becque, Henri 1837-1899 . . . . **NCLC 3**

Beddoes, Thomas Lovell
1803-1849 . . . . **NCLC 3**
See also DLB 96

Bedford, Donald F.
See Fearing, Kenneth (Flexner)

Beecher, Catharine Esther
1800-1878 . . . . **NCLC 30**
See also DLB 1

Beecher, John 1904-1980 . . . . **CLC 6**
See also AITN 1; CA 5-8R; 105; CANR 8

Beer, Johann 1655-1700 . . . . **LC 5**

Beer, Patricia 1924- . . . . **CLC 58**
See also CA 61-64; CANR 13, 46; DLB 40

Beerbohm, Henry Maximilian
1872-1956 . . . . **TCLC 1, 24**
See also CA 104; DLB 34, 100

Beerbohm, Max
See Beerbohm, Henry Maximilian

Begiebing, Robert J(ohn) 1946- . . . . . **CLC 70**
See also CA 122; CANR 40

Behan, Brendan
1923-1964 . . . . **CLC 1, 8, 11, 15, 79**
See also CA 73-76; CANR 33;
CDBLB 1945-1960; DLB 13; MTCW

Behn, Aphra
1640(?)-1689 . . . . **LC 1; DA; DC 4;
PC 12; WLC**
See also DLB 39, 80, 131

Behrman, S(amuel) N(athaniel)
1893-1973 . . . . CLC 40
See also CA 13-16; 45-48; CAP 1; DLB 7,
44

Belasco, David 1853-1931 . . . . TCLC 3
See also CA 104; DLB 7

Belcheva, Elisaveta 1893- . . . . CLC 10
See also Bagryana, Elisaveta

Beldone, Phil "Cheech"
See Ellison, Harlan (Jay)

Beleno
See Azuela, Mariano

Belinski, Vissarion Grigoryevich
1811-1848 . . . . NCLC 5

Belitt, Ben 1911- . . . . CLC 22
See also CA 13-16R; CAAS 4; CANR 7;
DLB 5

Bell, James Madison
1826-1902 . . . . TCLC 43; BLC
See also BW 1; CA 122; 124; DLB 50

Bell, Madison (Smartt) 1957- . . . . . . CLC 41
See also CA 111; CANR 28

Bell, Marvin (Hartley) 1937- . . . . . CLC 8, 31
See also CA 21-24R; CAAS 14; DLB 5;
MTCW

Bell, W. L. D.
See Mencken, H(enry) L(ouis)

Bellamy, Atwood C.
See Mencken, H(enry) L(ouis)

Bellamy, Edward 1850-1898 . . . . . . NCLC 4
See also DLB 12

Bellin, Edward J.
See Kuttner, Henry

Belloc, (Joseph) Hilaire (Pierre)
1870-1953 . . . . TCLC 7, 18
See also CA 106; DLB 19, 100, 141;
YABC 1

Belloc, Joseph Peter Rene Hilaire
See Belloc, (Joseph) Hilaire (Pierre)

Belloc, Joseph Pierre Hilaire
See Belloc, (Joseph) Hilaire (Pierre)

Belloc, M. A.
See Lowndes, Marie Adelaide (Belloc)

Bellow, Saul
1915- . . . . . . CLC 1, 2, 3, 6, 8, 10, 13, 15,
25, 33, 34, 63, 79; DA; SSC 14; WLC
See also AITN 2; BEST 89:3; CA 5-8R;
CABS 1; CANR 29; CDALB 1941-1968;
DLB 2, 28; DLBD 3; DLBY 82; MTCW

Bely, Andrey . . . . TCLC 7; PC 11
See also Bugayev, Boris Nikolayevich

Benary, Margot
See Benary-Isbert, Margot

Benary-Isbert, Margot 1889-1979 . . . CLC 12
See also CA 5-8R; 89-92; CANR 4;
CLR 12; MAICYA; SATA 2;
SATA-Obit 21

Benavente (y Martinez), Jacinto
1866-1954 . . . . TCLC 3
See also CA 106; 131; HW; MTCW

Benchley, Peter (Bradford)
1940- . . . . CLC 4, 8
See also AAYA 14; AITN 2; CA 17-20R;
CANR 12, 35; MTCW; SATA 3

Benchley, Robert (Charles)
1889-1945 . . . . TCLC 1, 55
See also CA 105; DLB 11

Benedikt, Michael 1935- . . . . CLC 4, 14
See also CA 13-16R; CANR 7; DLB 5

Benet, Juan 1927- . . . . CLC 28
See also CA 143

Benet, Stephen Vincent
1898-1943 . . . . TCLC 7; SSC 10
See also CA 104; DLB 4, 48, 102; YABC 1

Benet, William Rose 1886-1950 . . . TCLC 28
See also CA 118; DLB 45

Benford, Gregory (Albert) 1941- . . . . CLC 52
See also CA 69-72; CANR 12, 24;
DLBY 82

Bengtsson, Frans (Gunnar)
1894-1954 . . . . TCLC 48

Benjamin, David
See Slavitt, David R(ytman)

Benjamin, Lois
See Gould, Lois

Benjamin, Walter 1892-1940 . . . . . TCLC 39

Benn, Gottfried 1886-1956 . . . . TCLC 3
See also CA 106; DLB 56

Bennett, Alan 1934- . . . . CLC 45, 77
See also CA 103; CANR 35; MTCW

Bennett, (Enoch) Arnold
1867-1931 . . . . TCLC 5, 20
See also CA 106; CDBLB 1890-1914;
DLB 10, 34, 98

Bennett, Elizabeth
See Mitchell, Margaret (Munnerlyn)

Bennett, George Harold 1930-
See Bennett, Hal
See also BW 1; CA 97-100

Bennett, Hal . . . . CLC 5
See also Bennett, George Harold
See also DLB 33

Bennett, Jay 1912- . . . . CLC 35
See also AAYA 10; CA 69-72; CANR 11,
42; JRDA; SAAS 4; SATA 41;
SATA-Brief 27

Bennett, Louise (Simone)
1919- . . . . CLC 28; BLC
See also BW 2; DLB 117

Benson, E(dward) F(rederic)
1867-1940 . . . . TCLC 27
See also CA 114; DLB 135

Benson, Jackson J. 1930- . . . . CLC 34
See also CA 25-28R; DLB 111

Benson, Sally 1900-1972 . . . . CLC 17
See also CA 19-20; 37-40R; CAP 1;
SATA 1, 35; SATA-Obit 27

Benson, Stella 1892-1933 . . . . TCLC 17
See also CA 117; DLB 36

Bentham, Jeremy 1748-1832 . . . . . NCLC 38
See also DLB 107

Bentley, E(dmund) C(lerihew)
1875-1956 . . . . TCLC 12
See also CA 108; DLB 70

Bentley, Eric (Russell) 1916- . . . . CLC 24
See also CA 5-8R; CANR 6

Beranger, Pierre Jean de
1780-1857 . . . . NCLC 34

Berendt, John (Lawrence) 1939- . . . . CLC 86
See also CA 146

Berger, Colonel
See Malraux, (Georges-)Andre

Berger, John (Peter) 1926- . . . . . . CLC 2, 19
See also CA 81-84; DLB 14

Berger, Melvin H. 1927- . . . . CLC 12
See also CA 5-8R; CANR 4; CLR 32;
SAAS 2; SATA 5

Berger, Thomas (Louis)
1924- . . . . CLC 3, 5, 8, 11, 18, 38
See also CA 1-4R; CANR 5, 28; DLB 2;
DLBY 80; MTCW

Bergman, (Ernst) Ingmar
1918- . . . . CLC 16, 72
See also CA 81-84; CANR 33

Bergson, Henri 1859-1941 . . . . TCLC 32

Bergstein, Eleanor 1938- . . . . CLC 4
See also CA 53-56; CANR 5

Berkoff, Steven 1937- . . . . CLC 56
See also CA 104

Bermant, Chaim (Icyk) 1929- . . . . . . CLC 40
See also CA 57-60; CANR 6, 31

Bern, Victoria
See Fisher, M(ary) F(rances) K(ennedy)

Bernanos, (Paul Louis) Georges
1888-1948 . . . . TCLC 3
See also CA 104; 130; DLB 72

Bernard, April 1956- . . . . CLC 59
See also CA 131

Berne, Victoria
See Fisher, M(ary) F(rances) K(ennedy)

Bernhard, Thomas
1931-1989 . . . . CLC 3, 32, 61
See also CA 85-88; 127; CANR 32;
DLB 85, 124; MTCW

Berriault, Gina 1926- . . . . CLC 54
See also CA 116; 129; DLB 130

Berrigan, Daniel 1921- . . . . CLC 4
See also CA 33-36R; CAAS 1; CANR 11,
43; DLB 5

Berrigan, Edmund Joseph Michael, Jr.
1934-1983
See Berrigan, Ted
See also CA 61-64; 110; CANR 14

Berrigan, Ted . . . . CLC 37
See also Berrigan, Edmund Joseph Michael,
Jr.
See also DLB 5

Berry, Charles Edward Anderson 1931-
See Berry, Chuck
See also CA 115

Berry, Chuck . . . . CLC 17
See also Berry, Charles Edward Anderson

Berry, Jonas
See Ashbery, John (Lawrence)

Berry, Wendell (Erdman)
1934- . . . . CLC 4, 6, 8, 27, 46
See also AITN 1; CA 73-76; DLB 5, 6

Berryman, John
1914-1972 . . . . . . CLC 1, 2, 3, 4, 6, 8, 10,
13, 25, 62
See also CA 13-16; 33-36R; CABS 2;
CANR 35; CAP 1; CDALB 1941-1968;
DLB 48; MTCW

Boethius 480(?)-524(?) . . . . **CMLC 15:**
See also DLB 115

Bogan, Louise
1897-1970 . . . . . . **CLC 4, 39, 46; PC 12**
See also CA 73-76; 25-28R; CANR 33;
DLB 45; MTCW

Bogarde, Dirk . . . . **CLC 19**
See also Van Den Bogarde, Derek Jules
Gaspard Ulric Niven
See also DLB 14

Bogosian, Eric 1953- . . . . **CLC 45**
See also CA 138

Bograd, Larry 1953- . . . . **CLC 35**
See also CA 93-96; SATA 33

Boiardo, Matteo Maria 1441-1494 . . . . **LC 6**

Boileau-Despreaux, Nicolas
1636-1711 . . . . **LC 3**

Boland, Eavan (Aisling) 1944- . . . **CLC 40, 67**
See also CA 143; DLB 40

Bolt, Lee
See Faust, Frederick (Schiller)

Bolt, Robert (Oxton) 1924- . . . . **CLC 14**
See also CA 17-20R; CANR 35; DLB 13;
MTCW

Bombet, Louis-Alexandre-Cesar
See Stendhal

Bomkauf
See Kaufman, Bob (Garnell)

Bonaventura . . . . **NCLC 35**
See also DLB 90

Bond, Edward 1934- . . . . **CLC 4, 6, 13, 23**
See also CA 25-28R; CANR 38; DLB 13;
MTCW

Bonham, Frank 1914-1989 . . . . **CLC 12**
See also AAYA 1; CA 9-12R; CANR 4, 36;
JRDA; MAICYA; SAAS 3; SATA 1, 49;
SATA-Obit 62

Bonnefoy, Yves 1923- . . . . **CLC 9, 15, 58**
See also CA 85-88; CANR 33; MTCW

Bontemps, Arna(ud Wendell)
1902-1973 . . . . **CLC 1, 18; BLC**
See also BW 1; CA 1-4R; 41-44R; CANR 4,
35; CLR 6; DLB 48, 51; JRDA;
MAICYA; MTCW; SATA 2, 44;
SATA-Obit 24

Booth, Martin 1944- . . . . **CLC 13**
See also CA 93-96; CAAS 2

Booth, Philip 1925- . . . . **CLC 23**
See also CA 5-8R; CANR 5; DLBY 82

Booth, Wayne C(layson) 1921- . . . . . **CLC 24**
See also CA 1-4R; CAAS 5; CANR 3, 43;
DLB 67

Borchert, Wolfgang 1921-1947 . . . . . **TCLC 5**
See also CA 104; DLB 69, 124

Borel, Petrus 1809-1859 . . . . **NCLC 41**

Borges, Jorge Luis
1899-1986 . . . **CLC 1, 2, 3, 4, 6, 8, 9, 10,
13, 19, 44, 48, 83; DA; HLC; SSC 4;
WLC**
See also CA 21-24R; CANR 19, 33;
DLB 113; DLBY 86; HW; MTCW

Borowski, Tadeusz 1922-1951 . . . . . . **TCLC 9**
See also CA 106

Borrow, George (Henry)
1803-1881 . . . . **NCLC 9**
See also DLB 21, 55

Bosman, Herman Charles
1905-1951 . . . . **TCLC 49**

Bosschere, Jean de 1878(?)-1953 . . . **TCLC 19**
See also CA 115

Boswell, James
1740-1795 . . . . **LC 4; DA; WLC**
See also CDBLB 1660-1789; DLB 104, 142

Bottoms, David 1949- . . . . **CLC 53**
See also CA 105; CANR 22; DLB 120;
DLBY 83

Boucicault, Dion 1820-1890 . . . . . . **NCLC 41**

Boucolon, Maryse 1937-
See Conde, Maryse
See also CA 110; CANR 30

Bourget, Paul (Charles Joseph)
1852-1935 . . . . **TCLC 12**
See also CA 107; DLB 123

Bourjaily, Vance (Nye) 1922- . . . . **CLC 8, 62**
See also CA 1-4R; CAAS 1; CANR 2;
DLB 2, 143

Bourne, Randolph S(illiman)
1886-1918 . . . . **TCLC 16**
See also CA 117; DLB 63

Bova, Ben(jamin William) 1932- . . . . **CLC 45**
See also CA 5-8R; CAAS 18; CANR 11;
CLR 3; DLBY 81; MAICYA; MTCW;
SATA 6, 68

Bowen, Elizabeth (Dorothea Cole)
1899-1973 . . . . . . **CLC 1, 3, 6, 11, 15, 22;
SSC 3**
See also CA 17-18; 41-44R; CANR 35;
CAP 2; CDBLB 1945-1960; DLB 15;
MTCW

Bowering, George 1935- . . . . **CLC 15, 47**
See also CA 21-24R; CAAS 16; CANR 10;
DLB 53

Bowering, Marilyn R(uthe) 1949- . . . **CLC 32**
See also CA 101

Bowers, Edgar 1924- . . . . **CLC 9**
See also CA 5-8R; CANR 24; DLB 5

Bowie, David . . . . **CLC 17**
See also Jones, David Robert

Bowles, Jane (Sydney)
1917-1973 . . . . **CLC 3, 68**
See also CA 19-20; 41-44R; CAP 2

Bowles, Paul (Frederick)
1910- . . . . **CLC 1, 2, 19, 53; SSC 3**
See also CA 1-4R; CAAS 1; CANR 1, 19;
DLB 5, 6; MTCW

Box, Edgar
See Vidal, Gore

Boyd, Nancy
See Millay, Edna St. Vincent

Boyd, William 1952- . . . . **CLC 28, 53, 70**
See also CA 114; 120

Boyle, Kay
1902-1992 . . . . . **CLC 1, 5, 19, 58; SSC 5**
See also CA 13-16R; 140; CAAS 1;
CANR 29; DLB 4, 9, 48, 86; DLBY 93;
MTCW

Boyle, Mark
See Kienzle, William X(avier)

Boyle, Patrick 1905-1982 . . . . **CLC 19**
See also CA 127

Boyle, T. C.
See Boyle, T(homas) Coraghessan

Boyle, T(homas) Coraghessan
1948- . . . . **CLC 36, 55; SSC 16**
See also BEST 90:4; CA 120; CANR 44;
DLBY 86

Boz
See Dickens, Charles (John Huffam)

Brackenridge, Hugh Henry
1748-1816 . . . . **NCLC 7**
See also DLB 11, 37

Bradbury, Edward P.
See Moorcock, Michael (John)

Bradbury, Malcolm (Stanley)
1932- . . . . **CLC 32, 61**
See also CA 1-4R; CANR 1, 33; DLB 14;
MTCW

Bradbury, Ray (Douglas)
1920- . . . **CLC 1, 3, 10, 15, 42; DA; WLC**
See also AITN 1, 2; CA 1-4R; CANR 2, 30;
CDALB 1968-1988; DLB 2, 8; MTCW;
SATA 11, 64

Bradford, Gamaliel 1863-1932 . . . . . **TCLC 36**
See also DLB 17

Bradley, David (Henry, Jr.)
1950- . . . . **CLC 23; BLC**
See also BW 1; CA 104; CANR 26; DLB 33

Bradley, John Ed(mund, Jr.)
1958- . . . . **CLC 55**
See also CA 139

Bradley, Marion Zimmer 1930- . . . . . **CLC 30**
See also AAYA 9; CA 57-60; CAAS 10;
CANR 7, 31; DLB 8; MTCW

Bradstreet, Anne
1612(?)-1672 . . . . **LC 4; DA; PC 10**
See also CDALB 1640-1865; DLB 24

Brady, Joan 1939- . . . . **CLC 86**
See also CA 141

Bragg, Melvyn 1939- . . . . **CLC 10**
See also BEST 89:3; CA 57-60; CANR 10;
DLB 14

Braine, John (Gerard)
1922-1986 . . . . **CLC 1, 3, 41**
See also CA 1-4R; 120; CANR 1, 33;
CDBLB 1945-1960; DLB 15; DLBY 86;
MTCW

Brammer, William 1930(?)-1978 . . . . **CLC 31**
See also CA 77-80

Brancati, Vitaliano 1907-1954 . . . . . **TCLC 12**
See also CA 109

Brancato, Robin F(idler) 1936- . . . . . **CLC 35**
See also AAYA 9; CA 69-72; CANR 11,
45; CLR 32; JRDA; SAAS 9; SATA 23

Brand, Max
See Faust, Frederick (Schiller)

Brand, Millen 1906-1980 . . . . **CLC 7**
See also CA 21-24R; 97-100

Branden, Barbara . . . . **CLC 44**

Brandes, Georg (Morris Cohen)
1842-1927 . . . . **TCLC 10**
See also CA 105

Brandys, Kazimierz 1916- . . . . **CLC 62**

Branley, Franklyn M(ansfield)
1915- . . . . **CLC 21**
See also CA 33-36R; CANR 14, 39;
CLR 13; MAICYA; SAAS 16; SATA 4,
68

Brathwaite, Edward Kamau 1930-. . . **CLC 11**
See also BW 2; CA 25-28R; CANR 11, 26,
47; DLB 125

Brautigan, Richard (Gary)
1935-1984 . . . . **CLC 1, 3, 5, 9, 12, 34, 42**
See also CA 53-56; 113; CANR 34; DLB 2,
5; DLBY 80, 84; MTCW; SATA 56

Braverman, Kate 1950- . . . . **CLC 67**
See also CA 89-92

Brecht, Bertolt
1898-1956 . . . . . . **TCLC 1, 6, 13, 35; DA;**
DC 3; WLC
See also CA 104; 133; DLB 56, 124; MTCW

Brecht, Eugen Berthold Friedrich
See Brecht, Bertolt

Bremer, Fredrika 1801-1865 . . . . . **NCLC 11**

Brennan, Christopher John
1870-1932 . . . . **TCLC 17**
See also CA 117

Brennan, Maeve 1917-. . . . . **CLC 5**
See also CA 81-84

Brentano, Clemens (Maria)
1778-1842 . . . . **NCLC 1**
See also DLB 90

Brent of Bin Bin
See Franklin, (Stella Maraia Sarah) Miles

Brenton, Howard 1942- . . . . **CLC 31**
See also CA 69-72; CANR 33; DLB 13;
MTCW

Breslin, James 1930-
See Breslin, Jimmy
See also CA 73-76; CANR 31; MTCW

Breslin, Jimmy . . . . **CLC 4, 43**
See also Breslin, James
See also AITN 1

Bresson, Robert 1907- . . . . **CLC 16**
See also CA 110

Breton, Andre 1896-1966. . . **CLC 2, 9, 15, 54**
See also CA 19-20; 25-28R; CANR 40;
CAP 2; DLB 65; MTCW

Breytenbach, Breyten 1939(?)- . . **CLC 23, 37**
See also CA 113; 129

Bridgers, Sue Ellen 1942- . . . . **CLC 26**
See also AAYA 8; CA 65-68; CANR 11,
36; CLR 18; DLB 52; JRDA; MAICYA;
SAAS 1; SATA 22

Bridges, Robert (Seymour)
1844-1930 . . . . **TCLC 1**
See also CA 104; CDBLB 1890-1914;
DLB 19, 98

Bridie, James. . . . . **TCLC 3**
See also Mavor, Osborne Henry
See also DLB 10

Brin, David 1950-. . . . . **CLC 34**
See also CA 102; CANR 24; SATA 65

Brink, Andre (Philippus)
1935- . . . . **CLC 18, 36**
See also CA 104; CANR 39; MTCW

Brinsmead, H(esba) F(ay) 1922- . . . . **CLC 21**
See also CA 21-24R; CANR 10; MAICYA;
SAAS 5; SATA 18, 78

Brittain, Vera (Mary)
1893(?)-1970 . . . . **CLC 23**
See also CA 13-16; 25-28R; CAP 1; MTCW

Broch, Hermann 1886-1951. . . . . . **TCLC 20**
See also CA 117; DLB 85, 124

Brock, Rose
See Hansen, Joseph

Brodkey, Harold 1930-. . . . . **CLC 56**
See also CA 111; DLB 130

Brodsky, Iosif Alexandrovich 1940-
See Brodsky, Joseph
See also AITN 1; CA 41-44R; CANR 37;
MTCW

Brodsky, Joseph . . **CLC 4, 6, 13, 36, 50; PC 9**
See also Brodsky, Iosif Alexandrovich

Brodsky, Michael Mark 1948- . . . . . **CLC 19**
See also CA 102; CANR 18, 41

Bromell, Henry 1947-. . . . . **CLC 5**
See also CA 53-56; CANR 9

Bromfield, Louis (Brucker)
1896-1956 . . . . **TCLC 11**
See also CA 107; DLB 4, 9, 86

Broner, E(sther) M(asserman)
1930- . . . . **CLC 19**
See also CA 17-20R; CANR 8, 25; DLB 28

Bronk, William 1918-. . . . . **CLC 10**
See also CA 89-92; CANR 23

Bronstein, Lev Davidovich
See Trotsky, Leon

Bronte, Anne 1820-1849. . . . . **NCLC 4**
See also DLB 21

Bronte, Charlotte
1816-1855 . . . **NCLC 3, 8, 33; DA; WLC**
See also CDBLB 1832-1890; DLB 21

Bronte, (Jane) Emily
1818-1848 . . . . **NCLC 16, 35; DA; PC 8;**
WLC
See also CDBLB 1832-1890; DLB 21, 32

Brooke, Frances 1724-1789 . . . . **LC 6**
See also DLB 39, 99

Brooke, Henry 1703(?)-1783 . . . . **LC 1**
See also DLB 39

Brooke, Rupert (Chawner)
1887-1915 . . . . **TCLC 2, 7; DA; WLC**
See also CA 104; 132; CDBLB 1914-1945;
DLB 19; MTCW

Brooke-Haven, P.
See Wodehouse, P(elham) G(renville)

Brooke-Rose, Christine 1926- . . . . . . **CLC 40**
See also CA 13-16R; DLB 14

Brookner, Anita 1928- . . . . . . **CLC 32, 34, 51**
See also CA 114; 120; CANR 37; DLBY 87;
MTCW

Brooks, Cleanth 1906-1994 . . . . . **CLC 24, 86**
See also CA 17-20R; 145; CANR 33, 35;
DLB 63; MTCW

Brooks, George
See Baum, L(yman) Frank

Brooks, Gwendolyn
1917- . . . . . . **CLC 1, 2, 4, 5, 15, 49; BLC;**
DA; PC 7; WLC
See also AITN 1; BW 2; CA 1-4R;
CANR 1, 27; CDALB 1941-1968;
CLR 27; DLB 5, 76; MTCW; SATA 6

Brooks, Mel. . . . . **CLC 12**
See also Kaminsky, Melvin
See also AAYA 13; DLB 26

Brooks, Peter 1938-. . . . . **CLC 34**
See also CA 45-48; CANR 1

Brooks, Van Wyck 1886-1963. . . . . . **CLC 29**
See also CA 1-4R; CANR 6; DLB 45, 63,
103

Brophy, Brigid (Antonia)
1929- . . . . **CLC 6, 11, 29**
See also CA 5-8R; CAAS 4; CANR 25;
DLB 14; MTCW

Brosman, Catharine Savage 1934-. . . . **CLC 9**
See also CA 61-64; CANR 21, 46

Brother Antoninus
See Everson, William (Oliver)

Broughton, T(homas) Alan 1936- . . . **CLC 19**
See also CA 45-48; CANR 2, 23

Broumas, Olga 1949- . . . . **CLC 10, 73**
See also CA 85-88; CANR 20

Brown, Charles Brockden
1771-1810 . . . . **NCLC 22**
See also CDALB 1640-1865; DLB 37, 59,
73

Brown, Christy 1932-1981 . . . . **CLC 63**
See also CA 105; 104; DLB 14

Brown, Claude 1937- . . . . **CLC 30; BLC**
See also AAYA 7; BW 1; CA 73-76

Brown, Dee (Alexander) 1908- . . **CLC 18, 47**
See also CA 13-16R; CAAS 6; CANR 11,
45; DLBY 80; MTCW; SATA 5

Brown, George
See Wertmueller, Lina

Brown, George Douglas
1869-1902 . . . . **TCLC 28**

Brown, George Mackay 1921-. . . . **CLC 5, 48**
See also CA 21-24R; CAAS 6; CANR 12,
37; DLB 14, 27, 139; MTCW; SATA 35

Brown, (William) Larry 1951-. . . . . . **CLC 73**
See also CA 130; 134

Brown, Moses
See Barrett, William (Christopher)

Brown, Rita Mae 1944-. . . . . . **CLC 18, 43, 79**
See also CA 45-48; CANR 2, 11, 35;
MTCW

Brown, Roderick (Langmere) Haig-
See Haig-Brown, Roderick (Langmere)

Brown, Rosellen 1939-. . . . . **CLC 32**
See also CA 77-80; CAAS 10; CANR 14, 44

Brown, Sterling Allen
1901-1989 . . . . **CLC 1, 23, 59; BLC**
See also BW 1; CA 85-88; 127; CANR 26;
DLB 48, 51, 63; MTCW

Brown, Will
See Ainsworth, William Harrison

Brown, William Wells
1813-1884 . . . . **NCLC 2; BLC; DC 1**
See also DLB 3, 50

Browne, (Clyde) Jackson   1948(?)-... **CLC 21**
See also CA 120

Browning, Elizabeth Barrett
     1806-1861 ..... **NCLC 1, 16; DA; PC 6;**
                                               WLC
See also CDBLB 1832-1890; DLB 32

Browning, Robert
     1812-1889 .... **NCLC 19; DA; PC 2**
See also CDBLB 1832-1890; DLB 32;
     YABC 1

Browning, Tod   1882-1962 .... **CLC 16**
See also CA 141; 117

Bruccoli, Matthew J(oseph)   1931-.. **CLC 34**
See also CA 9-12R; CANR 7; DLB 103

Bruce, Lenny .... **CLC 21**
See also Schneider, Leonard Alfred

Bruin, John
See Brutus, Dennis

Brulard, Henri
See Stendhal

Brulls, Christian
See Simenon, Georges (Jacques Christian)

Brunner, John (Kilian Houston)
     1934- .... **CLC 8, 10**
See also CA 1-4R; CAAS 8; CANR 2, 37;
     MTCW

Bruno, Giordano   1548-1600........ **LC 27**

Brutus, Dennis   1924- .... **CLC 43; BLC**
See also BW 2; CA 49-52; CAAS 14;
     CANR 2, 27, 42; DLB 117

Bryan, C(ourtlandt) D(ixon) B(arnes)
     1936- .... **CLC 29**
See also CA 73-76; CANR 13

Bryan, Michael
See Moore, Brian

Bryant, William Cullen
     1794-1878 .... **NCLC 6, 46; DA**
See also CDALB 1640-1865; DLB 3, 43, 59

Bryusov, Valery Yakovlevich
     1873-1924 .... **TCLC 10**
See also CA 107

Buchan, John   1875-1940 .... **TCLC 41**
See also CA 108; 145; DLB 34, 70; YABC 2

Buchanan, George   1506-1582 .... **LC 4**

Buchheim, Lothar-Guenther   1918-... **CLC 6**
See also CA 85-88

Buchner, (Karl) Georg
     1813-1837 .... **NCLC 26**

Buchwald, Art(hur)   1925-......... **CLC 33**
See also AITN 1; CA 5-8R; CANR 21;
     MTCW; SATA 10

Buck, Pearl S(ydenstricker)
     1892-1973 .... **CLC 7, 11, 18; DA**
See also AITN 1; CA 1-4R; 41-44R;
     CANR 1, 34; DLB 9, 102; MTCW;
     SATA 1, 25

Buckler, Ernest   1908-1984......... **CLC 13**
See also CA 11-12; 114; CAP 1; DLB 68;
     SATA 47

Buckley, Vincent (Thomas)
     1925-1988 .... **CLC 57**
See also CA 101

Buckley, William F(rank), Jr.
     1925- .... **CLC 7, 18, 37**
See also AITN 1; CA 1-4R; CANR 1, 24;
     DLB 137; DLBY 80; MTCW

Buechner, (Carl) Frederick
     1926- .... **CLC 2, 4, 6, 9**
See also CA 13-16R; CANR 11, 39;
     DLBY 80; MTCW

Buell, John (Edward)   1927-........ **CLC 10**
See also CA 1-4R; DLB 53

Buero Vallejo, Antonio   1916-... **CLC 15, 46**
See also CA 106; CANR 24; HW; MTCW

Bufalino, Gesualdo   1920(?)-........ **CLC 74**

Bugayev, Boris Nikolayevich   1880-1934
See Bely, Andrey
See also CA 104

Bukowski, Charles
     1920-1994 .... **CLC 2, 5, 9, 41, 82**
See also CA 17-20R; 144; CANR 40;
     DLB 5, 130; MTCW

Bulgakov, Mikhail (Afanas'evich)
     1891-1940 .... **TCLC 2, 16; SSC 18**
See also CA 105

Bulgya, Alexander Alexandrovich
     1901-1956 .... **TCLC 53**
See also Fadeyev, Alexander
See also CA 117

Bullins, Ed   1935- .... **CLC 1, 5, 7; BLC**
See also BW 2; CA 49-52; CAAS 16;
     CANR 24, 46; DLB 7, 38; MTCW

Bulwer-Lytton, Edward (George Earle Lytton)
     1803-1873 .... **NCLC 1, 45**
See also DLB 21

Bunin, Ivan Alexeyevich
     1870-1953 .... **TCLC 6; SSC 5**
See also CA 104

Bunting, Basil   1900-1985.... **CLC 10, 39, 47**
See also CA 53-56; 115; CANR 7; DLB 20

Bunuel, Luis   1900-1983 .. **CLC 16, 80; HLC**
See also CA 101; 110; CANR 32; HW

Bunyan, John   1628-1688 .. **LC 4; DA; WLC**
See also CDBLB 1660-1789; DLB 39

Burckhardt, Jacob (Christoph)
     1818-1897 .... **NCLC 49**

Burford, Eleanor
See Hibbert, Eleanor Alice Burford

Burgess, Anthony
     . **CLC 1, 2, 4, 5, 8, 10, 13, 15, 22, 40, 62,**
                                                        81
See also Wilson, John (Anthony) Burgess
See also AITN 1; CDBLB 1960 to Present;
     DLB 14

Burke, Edmund
     1729(?)-1797 .... **LC 7; DA; WLC**
See also DLB 104

Burke, Kenneth (Duva)
     1897-1993 .... **CLC 2, 24**
See also CA 5-8R; 143; CANR 39; DLB 45,
     63; MTCW

Burke, Leda
See Garnett, David

Burke, Ralph
See Silverberg, Robert

Burney, Fanny   1752-1840 .... **NCLC 12**
See also DLB 39

Burns, Robert
     1759-1796 ...... **LC 3; DA; PC 6; WLC**
See also CDBLB 1789-1832; DLB 109

Burns, Tex
See L'Amour, Louis (Dearborn)

Burnshaw, Stanley   1906-..... **CLC 3, 13, 44**
See also CA 9-12R; DLB 48

Burr, Anne   1937- .... **CLC 6**
See also CA 25-28R

Burroughs, Edgar Rice
     1875-1950 .... **TCLC 2, 32**
See also AAYA 11; CA 104; 132; DLB 8;
     MTCW; SATA 41

Burroughs, William S(eward)
     1914- .... **CLC 1, 2, 5, 15, 22, 42, 75;**
                                               DA; WLC
See also AITN 2; CA 9-12R; CANR 20;
     DLB 2, 8, 16; DLBY 81; MTCW

Burton, Richard F.   1821-1890.... **NCLC 42**
See also DLB 55

Busch, Frederick   1941-... **CLC 7, 10, 18, 47**
See also CA 33-36R; CAAS 1; CANR 45;
     DLB 6

Bush, Ronald   1946- .... **CLC 34**
See also CA 136

Bustos, F(rancisco)
See Borges, Jorge Luis

Bustos Domecq, H(onorio)
See Bioy Casares, Adolfo; Borges, Jorge
     Luis

Butler, Octavia E(stelle)   1947- ..... **CLC 38**
See also BW 2; CA 73-76; CANR 12, 24,
     38; DLB 33; MTCW

Butler, Robert Olen (Jr.)   1945-..... **CLC 81**
See also CA 112

Butler, Samuel   1612-1680 .... **LC 16**
See also DLB 101, 126

Butler, Samuel
     1835-1902 ...... **TCLC 1, 33; DA; WLC**
See also CA 143; CDBLB 1890-1914;
     DLB 18, 57

Butler, Walter C.
See Faust, Frederick (Schiller)

Butor, Michel (Marie Francois)
     1926- .... **CLC 1, 3, 8, 11, 15**
See also CA 9-12R; CANR 33; DLB 83;
     MTCW

Buzo, Alexander (John)   1944-...... **CLC 61**
See also CA 97-100; CANR 17, 39

Buzzati, Dino   1906-1972 .... **CLC 36**
See also CA 33-36R

Byars, Betsy (Cromer)   1928-....... **CLC 35**
See also CA 33-36R; CANR 18, 36; CLR 1,
     16; DLB 52; JRDA; MAICYA; MTCW;
     SAAS 1; SATA 4, 46, 80

Byatt, A(ntonia) S(usan Drabble)
     1936- .... **CLC 19, 65**
See also CA 13-16R; CANR 13, 33;
     DLB 14; MTCW

Byrne, David   1952-............... **CLC 26**
See also CA 127

Byrne, John Keyes   1926-
See Leonard, Hugh
See also CA 102

Byron, George Gordon (Noel)
1788-1824 ...... **NCLC 2, 12; DA; WLC**
See also CDBLB 1789-1832; DLB 96, 110

C. 3. 3.
See Wilde, Oscar (Fingal O'Flahertie Wills)

Caballero, Fernan 1796-1877..... **NCLC 10**

Cabell, James Branch 1879-1958 ... **TCLC 6**
See also CA 105; DLB 9, 78

Cable, George Washington
1844-1925 .... **TCLC 4; SSC 4**
See also CA 104; DLB 12, 74

Cabral de Melo Neto, Joao 1920-... **CLC 76**

Cabrera Infante, G(uillermo)
1929- .... **CLC 5, 25, 45; HLC**
See also CA 85-88; CANR 29; DLB 113;
HW; MTCW

Cade, Toni
See Bambara, Toni Cade

Cadmus and Harmonia
See Buchan, John

Caedmon fl. 658-680............. **CMLC 7**
See also DLB 146

Caeiro, Alberto
See Pessoa, Fernando (Antonio Nogueira)

Cage, John (Milton, Jr.) 1912- ..... **CLC 41**
See also CA 13-16R; CANR 9

Cain, G.
See Cabrera Infante, G(uillermo)

Cain, Guillermo
See Cabrera Infante, G(uillermo)

Cain, James M(allahan)
1892-1977 .... **CLC 3, 11, 28**
See also AITN 1; CA 17-20R; 73-76;
CANR 8, 34; MTCW

Caine, Mark
See Raphael, Frederic (Michael)

Calasso, Roberto 1941- .... **CLC 81**
See also CA 143

Calderon de la Barca, Pedro
1600-1681 .... **LC 23; DC 3**

Caldwell, Erskine (Preston)
1903-1987 .... **CLC 1, 8, 14, 50, 60**
See also AITN 1; CA 1-4R; 121; CAAS 1;
CANR 2, 33; DLB 9, 86; MTCW

Caldwell, (Janet Miriam) Taylor (Holland)
1900-1985 .... **CLC 2, 28, 39**
See also CA 5-8R; 116; CANR 5

Calhoun, John Caldwell
1782-1850 .... **NCLC 15**
See also DLB 3

Calisher, Hortense
1911- .... **CLC 2, 4, 8, 38; SSC 15**
See also CA 1-4R; CANR 1, 22; DLB 2;
MTCW

Callaghan, Morley Edward
1903-1990 ....**CLC 3, 14, 41, 65**
See also CA 9-12R; 132; CANR 33;
DLB 68; MTCW

Calvino, Italo
1923-1985 ..... **CLC 5, 8, 11, 22, 33, 39,
73; SSC 3**
See also CA 85-88; 116; CANR 23; MTCW

Cameron, Carey 1952- .... **CLC 59**
See also CA 135

Cameron, Peter 1959-............. **CLC 44**
See also CA 125

Campana, Dino 1885-1932........ **TCLC 20**
See also CA 117; DLB 114

Campbell, John W(ood, Jr.)
1910-1971 .... **CLC 32**
See also CA 21-22; 29-32R; CANR 34;
CAP 2; DLB 8; MTCW

Campbell, Joseph 1904-1987 .... **CLC 69**
See also AAYA 3; BEST 89:2; CA 1-4R;
124; CANR 3, 28; MTCW

Campbell, Maria 1940-........... **CLC 85**
See also CA 102; NNAL

Campbell, (John) Ramsey 1946- .... **CLC 42**
See also CA 57-60; CANR 7

Campbell, (Ignatius) Roy (Dunnachie)
1901-1957 .... **TCLC 5**
See also CA 104; DLB 20

Campbell, Thomas 1777-1844 .... **NCLC 19**
See also DLB 93; 144

Campbell, Wilfred .... **TCLC 9**
See also Campbell, William

Campbell, William 1858(?)-1918
See Campbell, Wilfred
See also CA 106; DLB 92

Campos, Alvaro de
See Pessoa, Fernando (Antonio Nogueira)

Camus, Albert
1913-1960 .... **CLC 1, 2, 4, 9, 11, 14, 32,
63, 69; DA; DC 2; SSC 9; WLC**
See also CA 89-92; DLB 72; MTCW

Canby, Vincent 1924-............. **CLC 13**
See also CA 81-84

Cancale
See Desnos, Robert

Canetti, Elias
1905-1994 .... **CLC 3, 14, 25, 75, 86**
See also CA 21-24R; 146; CANR 23;
DLB 85, 124; MTCW

Canin, Ethan 1960-.............. **CLC 55**
See also CA 131; 135

Cannon, Curt
See Hunter, Evan

Cape, Judith
See Page, P(atricia) K(athleen)

Capek, Karel
1890-1938 ..... **TCLC 6, 37; DA; DC 1;
WLC**
See also CA 104; 140

Capote, Truman
1924-1984 ...... **CLC 1, 3, 8, 13, 19, 34,
38, 58; DA; SSC 2; WLC**
See also CA 5-8R; 113; CANR 18;
CDALB 1941-1968; DLB 2; DLBY 80,
84; MTCW

Capra, Frank 1897-1991.......... **CLC 16**
See also CA 61-64; 135

Caputo, Philip 1941-............. **CLC 32**
See also CA 73-76; CANR 40

Card, Orson Scott 1951- .... **CLC 44, 47, 50**
See also AAYA 11; CA 102; CANR 27, 47;
MTCW

Cardenal (Martinez), Ernesto
1925- .... **CLC 31; HLC**
See also CA 49-52; CANR 2, 32; HW;
MTCW

Carducci, Giosue 1835-1907...... **TCLC 32**

Carew, Thomas 1595(?)-1640........ **LC 13**
See also DLB 126

Carey, Ernestine Gilbreth 1908- .... **CLC 17**
See also CA 5-8R; SATA 2

Carey, Peter 1943-........... **CLC 40, 55**
See also CA 123; 127; MTCW

Carleton, William 1794-1869...... **NCLC 3**

Carlisle, Henry (Coffin) 1926-...... **CLC 33**
See also CA 13-16R; CANR 15

Carlsen, Chris
See Holdstock, Robert P.

Carlson, Ron(ald F.) 1947-........ **CLC 54**
See also CA 105; CANR 27

Carlyle, Thomas 1795-1881... **NCLC 22; DA**
See also CDBLB 1789-1832; DLB 55; 144

Carman, (William) Bliss
1861-1929 .... **TCLC 7**
See also CA 104; DLB 92

Carnegie, Dale 1888-1955 .... **TCLC 53**

Carossa, Hans 1878-1956........ **TCLC 48**
See also DLB 66

Carpenter, Don(ald Richard)
1931- .... **CLC 41**
See also CA 45-48; CANR 1

Carpentier (y Valmont), Alejo
1904-1980 .... **CLC 8, 11, 38; HLC**
See also CA 65-68; 97-100; CANR 11;
DLB 113; HW

Carr, Caleb 1955(?)-.............. **CLC 86**

Carr, Emily 1871-1945........... **TCLC 32**
See also DLB 68

Carr, John Dickson 1906-1977 ...... **CLC 3**
See also CA 49-52; 69-72; CANR 3, 33;
MTCW

Carr, Philippa
See Hibbert, Eleanor Alice Burford

Carr, Virginia Spencer 1929-...... **CLC 34**
See also CA 61-64; DLB 111

Carrier, Roch 1937-........... **CLC 13, 78**
See also CA 130; DLB 53

Carroll, James P. 1943(?)-........ **CLC 38**
See also CA 81-84

Carroll, Jim 1951- .... **CLC 35**
See also CA 45-48; CANR 42

Carroll, Lewis .... **NCLC 2; WLC**
See Dodgson, Charles Lutwidge
See also CDBLB 1832-1890; CLR 2, 18;
DLB 18; JRDA

Carroll, Paul Vincent 1900-1968.... **CLC 10**
See also CA 9-12R; 25-28R; DLB 10

Carruth, Hayden
1921- ...... **CLC 4, 7, 10, 18, 84; PC 10**
See also CA 9-12R; CANR 4, 38; DLB 5;
MTCW; SATA 47

Carson, Rachel Louise 1907-1964... **CLC 71**
See also CA 77-80; CANR 35; MTCW;
SATA 23

Carter, Angela (Olive)
    1940-1992 . . . . . . CLC 5, 41, 76; SSC 13
    See also CA 53-56; 136; CANR 12, 36;
    DLB 14; MTCW; SATA 66;
    SATA-Obit 70

Carter, Nick
    See Smith, Martin Cruz

Carver, Raymond
    1938-1988 . . . CLC 22, 36, 53, 55; SSC 8
    See also CA 33-36R; 126; CANR 17, 34;
    DLB 130; DLBY 84, 88; MTCW

Cary, (Arthur) Joyce (Lunel)
    1888-1957 . . . . TCLC 1, 29
    See also CA 104; CDBLB 1914-1945;
    DLB 15, 100

Casanova de Seingalt, Giovanni Jacopo
    1725-1798 . . . . LC 13

Casares, Adolfo Bioy
    See Bioy Casares, Adolfo

Casely-Hayford, J(oseph) E(phraim)
    1866-1930 . . . . TCLC 24; BLC
    See also BW 2; CA 123

Casey, John (Dudley)   1939- . . . . CLC 59
    See also BEST 90:2; CA 69-72; CANR 23

Casey, Michael   1947- . . . . CLC 2
    See also CA 65-68; DLB 5

Casey, Patrick
    See Thurman, Wallace (Henry)

Casey, Warren (Peter)   1935-1988 . . . CLC 12
    See also CA 101; 127

Casona, Alejandro . . . . CLC 49
    See also Alvarez, Alejandro Rodriguez

Cassavetes, John   1929-1989 . . . . CLC 20
    See also CA 85-88; 127

Cassill, R(onald) V(erlin)   1919- . . . CLC 4, 23
    See also CA 9-12R; CAAS 1; CANR 7, 45;
    DLB 6

Cassity, (Allen) Turner   1929- . . . . CLC 6, 42
    See also CA 17-20R; CAAS 8; CANR 11;
    DLB 105

Castaneda, Carlos   1931(?)- . . . . CLC 12
    See also CA 25-28R; CANR 32; HW;
    MTCW

Castedo, Elena   1937- . . . . CLC 65
    See also CA 132

Castedo-Ellerman, Elena
    See Castedo, Elena

Castellanos, Rosario
    1925-1974 . . . . CLC 66; HLC
    See also CA 131; 53-56; DLB 113; HW

Castelvetro, Lodovico   1505-1571 . . . . . LC 12

Castiglione, Baldassare   1478-1529 . . . LC 12

Castle, Robert
    See Hamilton, Edmond

Castro, Guillen de   1569-1631 . . . . LC 19

Castro, Rosalia de   1837-1885 . . . . . NCLC 3

Cather, Willa
    See Cather, Willa Sibert

Cather, Willa Sibert
    1873-1947 . . . . TCLC 1, 11, 31; DA;
                                   SSC 2; WLC
    See also CA 104; 128; CDALB 1865-1917;
    DLB 9, 54, 78; DLBD 1; MTCW;
    SATA 30

Catton, (Charles) Bruce
    1899-1978 . . . . CLC 35
    See also AITN 1; CA 5-8R; 81-84;
    CANR 7; DLB 17; SATA 2;
    SATA-Obit 24

Cauldwell, Frank
    See King, Francis (Henry)

Caunitz, William J.   1933- . . . . CLC 34
    See also BEST 89:3; CA 125; 130

Causley, Charles (Stanley)   1917- . . . . . CLC 7
    See also CA 9-12R; CANR 5, 35; CLR 30;
    DLB 27; MTCW; SATA 3, 66

Caute, David   1936- . . . . CLC 29
    See also CA 1-4R; CAAS 4; CANR 1, 33;
    DLB 14

Cavafy, C(onstantine) P(eter) . . . . . . TCLC 2, 7
    See also Kavafis, Konstantinos Petrou

Cavallo, Evelyn
    See Spark, Muriel (Sarah)

Cavanna, Betty . . . . CLC 12
    See also Harrison, Elizabeth Cavanna
    See also JRDA; MAICYA; SAAS 4;
    SATA 1, 30

Caxton, William   1421(?)-1491(?) . . . . . LC 17

Cayrol, Jean   1911- . . . . CLC 11
    See also CA 89-92; DLB 83

Cela, Camilo Jose
    1916- . . . . CLC 4, 13, 59; HLC
    See also BEST 90:2; CA 21-24R; CAAS 10;
    CANR 21, 32; DLBY 89; HW; MTCW

Celan, Paul . . . . . . CLC 10, 19, 53, 82; PC 10
    See also Antschel, Paul
    See also DLB 69

Celine, Louis-Ferdinand
    . . . . CLC 1, 3, 4, 7, 9, 15, 47
    See also Destouches, Louis-Ferdinand
    See also DLB 72

Cellini, Benvenuto   1500-1571 . . . . LC 7

Cendrars, Blaise
    See Sauser-Hall, Frederic

Cernuda (y Bidon), Luis
    1902-1963 . . . . CLC 54
    See also CA 131; 89-92; DLB 134; HW

Cervantes (Saavedra), Miguel de
    1547-1616 . . . . . . LC 6, 23; DA; SSC 12;
                                               WLC

Cesaire, Aime (Fernand)
    1913- . . . . CLC 19, 32; BLC
    See also BW 2; CA 65-68; CANR 24, 43;
    MTCW

Chabon, Michael   1965(?)- . . . . CLC 55
    See also CA 139

Chabrol, Claude   1930- . . . . CLC 16
    See also CA 110

Challans, Mary   1905-1983
    See Renault, Mary
    See also CA 81-84; 111; SATA 23;
    SATA-Obit 36

Challis, George
    See Faust, Frederick (Schiller)

Chambers, Aidan   1934- . . . . CLC 35
    See also CA 25-28R; CANR 12, 31; JRDA;
    MAICYA; SAAS 12; SATA 1, 69

Chambers, James   1948-
    See Cliff, Jimmy
    See also CA 124

Chambers, Jessie
    See Lawrence, D(avid) H(erbert Richards)

Chambers, Robert W.   1865-1933. . . TCLC 41

Chandler, Raymond (Thornton)
    1888-1959 . . . . TCLC 1, 7
    See also CA 104; 129; CDALB 1929-1941;
    DLBD 6; MTCW

Chang, Jung   1952- . . . . CLC 71
    See also CA 142

Channing, William Ellery
    1780-1842 . . . . NCLC 17
    See also DLB 1, 59

Chaplin, Charles Spencer
    1889-1977 . . . . CLC 16
    See also Chaplin, Charlie
    See also CA 81-84; 73-76

Chaplin, Charlie
    See Chaplin, Charles Spencer
    See also DLB 44

Chapman, George   1559(?)-1634 . . . . . . LC 22
    See also DLB 62, 121

Chapman, Graham   1941-1989 . . . . . . CLC 21
    See also Monty Python
    See also CA 116; 129; CANR 35

Chapman, John Jay   1862-1933 . . . . . TCLC 7
    See also CA 104

Chapman, Walker
    See Silverberg, Robert

Chappell, Fred (Davis)   1936- . . . . CLC 40, 78
    See also CA 5-8R; CAAS 4; CANR 8, 33;
    DLB 6, 105

Char, Rene(-Emile)
    1907-1988 . . . . CLC 9, 11, 14, 55
    See also CA 13-16R; 124; CANR 32;
    MTCW

Charby, Jay
    See Ellison, Harlan (Jay)

Chardin, Pierre Teilhard de
    See Teilhard de Chardin, (Marie Joseph)
    Pierre

Charles I   1600-1649 . . . . LC 13

Charyn, Jerome   1937- . . . . CLC 5, 8, 18
    See also CA 5-8R; CAAS 1; CANR 7;
    DLBY 83; MTCW

Chase, Mary (Coyle)   1907-1981 . . . . . . DC 1
    See also CA 77-80; 105; SATA 17;
    SATA-Obit 29

Chase, Mary Ellen   1887-1973 . . . . CLC 2
    See also CA 13-16; 41-44R; CAP 1;
    SATA 10

Chase, Nicholas
    See Hyde, Anthony

Chateaubriand, Francois Rene de
    1768-1848 . . . . NCLC 3
    See also DLB 119

Chatterje, Sarat Chandra   1876-1936(?)
    See Chatterji, Saratchandra
    See also CA 109

Chatterji, Bankim Chandra
    1838-1894 . . . . NCLC 19

Clavell, James (duMaresq)
1925-1994 .... CLC 6, 25, 87
See also CA 25-28R; 146; CANR 26;
MTCW

Cleaver, (Leroy) Eldridge
1935- .... CLC 30; BLC
See also BW 1; CA 21-24R; CANR 16

Cleese, John (Marwood) 1939- ..... CLC 21
See also Monty Python
See also CA 112; 116; CANR 35; MTCW

Cleishbotham, Jebediah
See Scott, Walter

Cleland, John 1710-1789 .... LC 2
See also DLB 39

Clemens, Samuel Langhorne 1835-1910
See Twain, Mark
See also CA 104; 135; CDALB 1865-1917;
DA; DLB 11, 12, 23, 64, 74; JRDA;
MAICYA; YABC 2

Cleophil
See Congreve, William

Clerihew, E.
See Bentley, E(dmund) C(lerihew)

Clerk, N. W.
See Lewis, C(live) S(taples)

Cliff, Jimmy...................... CLC 21
See also Chambers, James

Clifton, (Thelma) Lucille
1936- .... CLC 19, 66; BLC
See also BW 2; CA 49-52; CANR 2, 24, 42;
CLR 5; DLB 5, 41; MAICYA; MTCW;
SATA 20, 69

Clinton, Dirk
See Silverberg, Robert

Clough, Arthur Hugh 1819-1861.. NCLC 27
See also DLB 32

Clutha, Janet Paterson Frame 1924-
See Frame, Janet
See also CA 1-4R; CANR 2, 36; MTCW

Clyne, Terence
See Blatty, William Peter

Cobalt, Martin
See Mayne, William (James Carter)

Cobbett, William 1763-1835 ..... NCLC 49
See also DLB 43, 107

Coburn, D(onald) L(ee) 1938- ...... CLC 10
See also CA 89-92

Cocteau, Jean (Maurice Eugene Clement)
1889-1963 .... CLC 1, 8, 15, 16, 43; DA;
WLC
See also CA 25-28; CANR 40; CAP 2;
DLB 65; MTCW

Codrescu, Andrei 1946- .... CLC 46
See also CA 33-36R; CAAS 19; CANR 13,
34

Coe, Max
See Bourne, Randolph S(illiman)

Coe, Tucker
See Westlake, Donald E(dwin)

Coetzee, J(ohn) M(ichael)
1940- .... CLC 23, 33, 66
See also CA 77-80; CANR 41; MTCW

Coffey, Brian
See Koontz, Dean R(ay)

Cohen, Arthur A(llen)
1928-1986 .... CLC 7, 31
See also CA 1-4R; 120; CANR 1, 17, 42;
DLB 28

Cohen, Leonard (Norman)
1934- .... CLC 3, 38
See also CA 21-24R; CANR 14; DLB 53;
MTCW

Cohen, Matt 1942-................ CLC 19
See also CA 61-64; CAAS 18; CANR 40;
DLB 53

Cohen-Solal, Annie 19(?)- .... CLC 50

Colegate, Isabel 1931- .... CLC 36
See also CA 17-20R; CANR 8, 22; DLB 14;
MTCW

Coleman, Emmett
See Reed, Ishmael

Coleridge, Samuel Taylor
1772-1834 .. NCLC 9; DA; PC 11; WLC
See also CDBLB 1789-1832; DLB 93, 107

Coleridge, Sara 1802-1852....... NCLC 31

Coles, Don 1928- .... CLC 46
See also CA 115; CANR 38

Colette, (Sidonie-Gabrielle)
1873-1954 ...... TCLC 1, 5, 16; SSC 10
See also CA 104; 131; DLB 65; MTCW

Collett, (Jacobine) Camilla (Wergeland)
1813-1895 .... NCLC 22

Collier, Christopher 1930-........ CLC 30
See also AAYA 13; CA 33-36R; CANR 13,
33; JRDA; MAICYA; SATA 16, 70

Collier, James L(incoln) 1928- ..... CLC 30
See also AAYA 13; CA 9-12R; CANR 4,
33; CLR 3; JRDA; MAICYA; SATA 8,
70

Collier, Jeremy 1650-1726.......... LC 6

Collins, Hunt
See Hunter, Evan

Collins, Linda 1931-.............. CLC 44
See also CA 125

Collins, (William) Wilkie
1824-1889 .... NCLC 1, 18
See also CDBLB 1832-1890; DLB 18, 70

Collins, William 1721-1759 .... LC 4
See also DLB 109

Colman, George
See Glassco, John

Colt, Winchester Remington
See Hubbard, L(afayette) Ron(ald)

Colter, Cyrus 1910- .... CLC 58
See also BW 1; CA 65-68; CANR 10;
DLB 33

Colton, James
See Hansen, Joseph

Colum, Padraic 1881-1972........ CLC 28
See also CA 73-76; 33-36R; CANR 35;
CLR 36; MAICYA; MTCW; SATA 15

Colvin, James
See Moorcock, Michael (John)

Colwin, Laurie (E.)
1944-1992 .... CLC 5, 13, 23, 84
See also CA 89-92; 139; CANR 20, 46;
DLBY 80; MTCW

Comfort, Alex(ander) 1920-........ CLC 7
See also CA 1-4R; CANR 1, 45

Comfort, Montgomery
See Campbell, (John) Ramsey

Compton-Burnett, I(vy)
1884(?)-1969 ...... CLC 1, 3, 10, 15, 34
See also CA 1-4R; 25-28R; CANR 4;
DLB 36; MTCW

Comstock, Anthony 1844-1915 .... TCLC 13
See also CA 110

Conan Doyle, Arthur
See Doyle, Arthur Conan

Conde, Maryse 1937-............. CLC 52
See also Boucolon, Maryse
See also BW 2

Condillac, Etienne Bonnot de
1714-1780 .... LC 26

Condon, Richard (Thomas)
1915- .... CLC 4, 6, 8, 10, 45
See also BEST 90:3; CA 1-4R; CAAS 1;
CANR 2, 23; MTCW

Congreve, William
1670-1729 ... LC 5, 21; DA; DC 2; WLC
See also CDBLB 1660-1789; DLB 39, 84

Connell, Evan S(helby), Jr.
1924- .... CLC 4, 6, 45
See also AAYA 7; CA 1-4R; CAAS 2;
CANR 2, 39; DLB 2; DLBY 81; MTCW

Connelly, Marc(us Cook)
1890-1980 .... CLC 7
See also CA 85-88; 102; CANR 30; DLB 7;
DLBY 80; SATA-Obit 25

Connor, Ralph .... TCLC 31
See also Gordon, Charles William
See also DLB 92

Conrad, Joseph
1857-1924 .... TCLC 1, 6, 13, 25, 43, 57;
DA; SSC 9; WLC
See also CA 104; 131; CDBLB 1890-1914;
DLB 10, 34, 98; MTCW; SATA 27

Conrad, Robert Arnold
See Hart, Moss

Conroy, Pat 1945-............. CLC 30, 74
See also AAYA 8; AITN 1; CA 85-88;
CANR 24; DLB 6; MTCW

Constant (de Rebecque), (Henri) Benjamin
1767-1830 .... NCLC 6
See also DLB 119

Conybeare, Charles Augustus
See Eliot, T(homas) S(tearns)

Cook, Michael 1933- .... CLC 58
See also CA 93-96; DLB 53

Cook, Robin 1940-............... CLC 14
See also BEST 90:2; CA 108; 111;
CANR 41

Cook, Roy
See Silverberg, Robert

Cooke, Elizabeth 1948- .... CLC 55
See also CA 129

Cooke, John Esten 1830-1886..... NCLC 5
See also DLB 3

Cooke, John Estes
See Baum, L(yman) Frank

Cooke, M. E.
See Creasey, John

Cooke, Margaret
See Creasey, John

Cooney, Ray .... **CLC 62**

Cooper, Douglas 1960- .... **CLC 86**

Cooper, Henry St. John
See Creasey, John

Cooper, J. California .... **CLC 56**
See also AAYA 12; BW 1; CA 125

Cooper, James Fenimore
1789-1851 .... **NCLC 1, 27**
See also CDALB 1640-1865; DLB 3;
SATA 19

Coover, Robert (Lowell)
1932- .. **CLC 3, 7, 15, 32, 46, 87; SSC 15**
See also CA 45-48; CANR 3, 37; DLB 2;
DLBY 81; MTCW

Copeland, Stewart (Armstrong)
1952- .... **CLC 26**

Coppard, A(lfred) E(dgar)
1878-1957 .... **TCLC 5**
See also CA 114; YABC 1

Coppee, Francois 1842-1908 ..... **TCLC 25**

Coppola, Francis Ford 1939- ...... **CLC 16**
See also CA 77-80; CANR 40; DLB 44

Corbiere, Tristan 1845-1875 ..... **NCLC 43**

Corcoran, Barbara 1911- .... **CLC 17**
See also AAYA 14; CA 21-24R; CAAS 2;
CANR 11, 28; DLB 52; JRDA; SATA 3,
77

Cordelier, Maurice
See Giraudoux, (Hippolyte) Jean

Corelli, Marie 1855-1924 .... **TCLC 51**
See also Mackay, Mary
See also DLB 34

Corman, Cid .... **CLC 9**
See also Corman, Sidney
See also CAAS 2; DLB 5

Corman, Sidney 1924-
See Corman, Cid
See also CA 85-88; CANR 44

Cormier, Robert (Edmund)
1925- .... **CLC 12, 30; DA**
See also AAYA 3; CA 1-4R; CANR 5, 23;
CDALB 1968-1988; CLR 12; DLB 52;
JRDA; MAICYA; MTCW; SATA 10, 45

Corn, Alfred (DeWitt III) 1943- .... **CLC 33**
See also CA 104; CANR 44; DLB 120;
DLBY 80

Corneille, Pierre 1606-1684 .... **LC 28**

Cornwell, David (John Moore)
1931- .... **CLC 9, 15**
See also le Carre, John
See also CA 5-8R; CANR 13, 33; MTCW

Corso, (Nunzio) Gregory 1930- ... **CLC 1, 11**
See also CA 5-8R; CANR 41; DLB 5, 16;
MTCW

Cortazar, Julio
1914-1984 ...... **CLC 2, 3, 5, 10, 13, 15,
33, 34; HLC; SSC 7**
See also CA 21-24R; CANR 12, 32;
DLB 113; HW; MTCW

Corwin, Cecil
See Kornbluth, C(yril) M.

Cosic, Dobrica 1921- .... **CLC 14**
See also CA 122; 138

Costain, Thomas B(ertram)
1885-1965 .... **CLC 30**
See also CA 5-8R; 25-28R; DLB 9

Costantini, Humberto
1924(?)-1987 .... **CLC 49**
See also CA 131; 122; HW

Costello, Elvis 1955- .... **CLC 21**

Cotter, Joseph Seamon Sr.
1861-1949 .... **TCLC 28; BLC**
See also BW 1; CA 124; DLB 50

Couch, Arthur Thomas Quiller
See Quiller-Couch, Arthur Thomas

Coulton, James
See Hansen, Joseph

Couperus, Louis (Marie Anne)
1863-1923 .... **TCLC 15**
See also CA 115

Coupland, Douglas 1961- .... **CLC 85**
See also CA 142

Court, Wesli
See Turco, Lewis (Putnam)

Courtenay, Bryce 1933- .... **CLC 59**
See also CA 138

Courtney, Robert
See Ellison, Harlan (Jay)

Cousteau, Jacques-Yves 1910- ...... **CLC 30**
See also CA 65-68; CANR 15; MTCW;
SATA 38

Coward, Noel (Peirce)
1899-1973 .... **CLC 1, 9, 29, 51**
See also AITN 1; CA 17-18; 41-44R;
CANR 35; CAP 2; CDBLB 1914-1945;
DLB 10; MTCW

Cowley, Malcolm 1898-1989 .... **CLC 39**
See also CA 5-8R; 128; CANR 3; DLB 4,
48; DLBY 81, 89; MTCW

Cowper, William 1731-1800 .... **NCLC 8**
See also DLB 104, 109

Cox, William Trevor 1928- ... **CLC 9, 14, 71**
See also Trevor, William
See also CA 9-12R; CANR 4, 37; DLB 14;
MTCW

Coyne, P. J.
See Masters, Hilary

Cozzens, James Gould
1903-1978 .... **CLC 1, 4, 11**
See also CA 9-12R; 81-84; CANR 19;
CDALB 1941-1968; DLB 9; DLBD 2;
DLBY 84; MTCW

Crabbe, George 1754-1832 .... **NCLC 26**
See also DLB 93

Craig, A. A.
See Anderson, Poul (William)

Craik, Dinah Maria (Mulock)
1826-1887 .... **NCLC 38**
See also DLB 35; MAICYA; SATA 34

Cram, Ralph Adams 1863-1942 .... **TCLC 45**

Crane, (Harold) Hart
1899-1932 .... **TCLC 2, 5; DA; PC 3;
WLC**
See also CA 104; 127; CDALB 1917-1929;
DLB 4, 48; MTCW

Crane, R(onald) S(almon)
1886-1967 .... **CLC 27**
See also CA 85-88; DLB 63

Crane, Stephen (Townley)
1871-1900 .... **TCLC 11, 17, 32; DA;
SSC 7; WLC**
See also CA 109; 140; CDALB 1865-1917;
DLB 12, 54, 78; YABC 2

Crase, Douglas 1944- .... **CLC 58**
See also CA 106

Crashaw, Richard 1612(?)-1649 ...... **LC 24**
See also DLB 126

Craven, Margaret 1901-1980 .... **CLC 17**
See also CA 103

Crawford, F(rancis) Marion
1854-1909 .... **TCLC 10**
See also CA 107; DLB 71

Crawford, Isabella Valancy
1850-1887 .... **NCLC 12**
See also DLB 92

Crayon, Geoffrey
See Irving, Washington

Creasey, John 1908-1973 .... **CLC 11**
See also CA 5-8R; 41-44R; CANR 8;
DLB 77, MTCW

Crebillon, Claude Prosper Jolyot de (fils)
1707-1777 .... **LC 28**

Credo
See Creasey, John

Creeley, Robert (White)
1926- ..... **CLC 1, 2, 4, 8, 11, 15, 36, 78**
See also CA 1-4R; CAAS 10; CANR 23, 43;
DLB 5, 16; MTCW

Crews, Harry (Eugene)
1935- .... **CLC 6, 23, 49**
See also AITN 1; CA 25-28R; CANR 20;
DLB 6, 143; MTCW

Crichton, (John) Michael
1942- .... **CLC 2, 6, 54**
See also AAYA 10; AITN 2; CA 25-28R;
CANR 13, 40; DLBY 81; JRDA;
MTCW; SATA 9

Crispin, Edmund .... **CLC 22**
See also Montgomery, (Robert) Bruce
See also DLB 87

Cristofer, Michael 1945(?)- .... **CLC 28**
See also CA 110; DLB 7

Croce, Benedetto 1866-1952 ...... **TCLC 37**
See also CA 120

Crockett, David 1786-1836 .... **NCLC 8**
See also DLB 3, 11

Crockett, Davy
See Crockett, David

Crofts, Freeman Wills
1879-1957 .... **TCLC 55**
See also CA 115; DLB 77

Croker, John Wilson 1780-1857 .. **NCLC 10**
See also DLB 110

Crommelynck, Fernand 1885-1970 .. **CLC 75**
See also CA 89-92

Cronin, A(rchibald) J(oseph)
1896-1981 .... **CLC 32**
See also CA 1-4R; 102; CANR 5; SATA 47;
SATA-Obit 25

Davison, Lawrence H.
See Lawrence, D(avid) H(erbert Richards)

Davison, Peter (Hubert) 1928- ..... **CLC 28**
See also CA 9-12R; CAAS 4; CANR 3, 43;
DLB 5

Davys, Mary 1674-1732............. **LC 1**
See also DLB 39

Dawson, Fielding 1930- .... **CLC 6**
See also CA 85-88; DLB 130

Dawson, Peter
See Faust, Frederick (Schiller)

Day, Clarence (Shepard, Jr.)
1874-1935 .... **TCLC 25**
See also CA 108; DLB 11

Day, Thomas 1748-1789............. **LC 1**
See also DLB 39; YABC 1

Day Lewis, C(ecil)
1904-1972 .... **CLC 1, 6, 10; PC 11**
See also Blake, Nicholas
See also CA 13-16; 33-36R; CANR 34;
CAP 1; DLB 15, 20; MTCW

Dazai, Osamu .... **TCLC 11**
See also Tsushima, Shuji

de Andrade, Carlos Drummond
See Drummond de Andrade, Carlos

Deane, Norman
See Creasey, John

**de Beauvoir, Simone (Lucie Ernestine Marie
Bertrand)**
See Beauvoir, Simone (Lucie Ernestine
Marie Bertrand) de

de Brissac, Malcolm
See Dickinson, Peter (Malcolm)

de Chardin, Pierre Teilhard
See Teilhard de Chardin, (Marie Joseph)
Pierre

Dee, John 1527-1608 .... **LC 20**

Deer, Sandra 1940-............... **CLC 45**

De Ferrari, Gabriella .... **CLC 65**

Defoe, Daniel
1660(?)-1731 .... **LC 1; DA; WLC**
See also CDBLB 1660-1789; DLB 39, 95,
101; JRDA; MAICYA; SATA 22

de Gourmont, Remy
See Gourmont, Remy de

de Hartog, Jan 1914-............. **CLC 19**
See also CA 1-4R; CANR 1

de Hostos, E. M.
See Hostos (y Bonilla), Eugenio Maria de

de Hostos, Eugenio M.
See Hostos (y Bonilla), Eugenio Maria de

Deighton, Len .... **CLC 4, 7, 22, 46**
See also Deighton, Leonard Cyril
See also AAYA 6; BEST 89:2;
CDBLB 1960 to Present; DLB 87

Deighton, Leonard Cyril 1929-
See Deighton, Len
See also CA 9-12R; CANR 19, 33; MTCW

Dekker, Thomas 1572(?)-1632...... **LC 22**
See also CDBLB Before 1660; DLB 62

de la Mare, Walter (John)
1873-1956 .. **TCLC 4, 53; SSC 14; WLC**
See also CDBLB 1914-1945; CLR 23;
DLB 19; SATA 16

Delaney, Franey
See O'Hara, John (Henry)

Delaney, Shelagh 1939-........... **CLC 29**
See also CA 17-20R; CANR 30;
CDBLB 1960 to Present; DLB 13;
MTCW

Delany, Mary (Granville Pendarves)
1700-1788 .... **LC 12**

Delany, Samuel R(ay, Jr.)
1942- .... **CLC 8, 14, 38; BLC**
See also BW 2; CA 81-84; CANR 27, 43;
DLB 8, 33; MTCW

De La Ramee, (Marie) Louise 1839-1908
See Ouida
See also SATA 20

de la Roche, Mazo 1879-1961 ...... **CLC 14**
See also CA 85-88; CANR 30; DLB 68;
SATA 64

Delbanco, Nicholas (Franklin)
1942- .... **CLC 6, 13**
See also CA 17-20R; CAAS 2, CANR 29,
DLB 6

del Castillo, Michel 1933- .... **CLC 38**
See also CA 109

Deledda, Grazia (Cosima)
1875(?)-1936 .... **TCLC 23**
See also CA 123

Delibes, Miguel .... **CLC 8, 18**
See also Delibes Setien, Miguel

Delibes Setien, Miguel 1920-
See Delibes, Miguel
See also CA 45-48; CANR 1, 32; HW;
MTCW

DeLillo, Don
1936- ..... **CLC 8, 10, 13, 27, 39, 54, 76**
See also BEST 89:1; CA 81-84; CANR 21;
DLB 6; MTCW

de Lisser, H. G.
See De Lisser, Herbert George
See also DLB 117

De Lisser, Herbert George
1878-1944 .... **TCLC 12**
See also de Lisser, H. G.
See also BW 2; CA 109

Deloria, Vine (Victor), Jr. 1933-.... **CLC 21**
See also CA 53-56; CANR 5, 20; MTCW;
NNAL; SATA 21

Del Vecchio, John M(ichael)
1947- .... **CLC 29**
See also CA 110; DLBD 9

de Man, Paul (Adolph Michel)
1919-1983 .... **CLC 55**
See also CA 128; 111; DLB 67; MTCW

De Marinis, Rick 1934-........... **CLC 54**
See also CA 57-60; CANR 9, 25

Demby, William 1922-....... **CLC 53; BLC**
See also BW 1; CA 81-84; DLB 33

Demijohn, Thom
See Disch, Thomas M(ichael)

de Montherlant, Henry (Milon)
See Montherlant, Henry (Milon) de

Demosthenes 384B.C.-322B.C. ... **CMLC 13**

de Natale, Francine
See Malzberg, Barry N(athaniel)

Denby, Edwin (Orr) 1903-1983..... **CLC 48**
See also CA 138; 110

Denis, Julio
See Cortazar, Julio

Denmark, Harrison
See Zelazny, Roger (Joseph)

Dennis, John 1658-1734............ **LC 11**
See also DLB 101

Dennis, Nigel (Forbes) 1912-1989.... **CLC 8**
See also CA 25-28R; 129; DLB 13, 15;
MTCW

De Palma, Brian (Russell) 1940-.... **CLC 20**
See also CA 109

De Quincey, Thomas 1785-1859 ... **NCLC 4**
See also CDBLB 1789-1832; DLB 110; 144

Deren, Eleanora 1908(?)-1961
See Deren, Maya
See also CA 111

Deren, Maya .... **CLC 16**
See also Deren, Eleanora

Derleth, August (William)
1909-1971 .... **CLC 31**
See also CA 1-4R; 29-32R; CANR 4;
DLB 9; SATA 5

Der Nister 1884-1950............ **TCLC 56**

de Routisie, Albert
See Aragon, Louis

Derrida, Jacques 1930-......... **CLC 24, 87**
See also CA 124; 127

Derry Down Derry
See Lear, Edward

Dersonnes, Jacques
See Simenon, Georges (Jacques Christian)

Desai, Anita 1937-............. **CLC 19, 37**
See also CA 81-84; CANR 33; MTCW;
SATA 63

de Saint-Luc, Jean
See Glassco, John

de Saint Roman, Arnaud
See Aragon, Louis

Descartes, Rene 1596-1650 .... **LC 20**

De Sica, Vittorio 1901(?)-1974 ..... **CLC 20**
See also CA 117

Desnos, Robert 1900-1945........ **TCLC 22**
See also CA 121

Destouches, Louis-Ferdinand
1894-1961 .... **CLC 9, 15**
See also Celine, Louis-Ferdinand
See also CA 85-88; CANR 28; MTCW

Deutsch, Babette 1895-1982 .... **CLC 18**
See also CA 1-4R; 108; CANR 4; DLB 45;
SATA 1; SATA-Obit 33

Devenant, William 1606-1649 .... **LC 13**

Devkota, Laxmiprasad
1909-1959 .... **TCLC 23**
See also CA 123

De Voto, Bernard (Augustine)
1897-1955 .... **TCLC 29**
See also CA 113; DLB 9

De Vries, Peter
1910-1993 .... **CLC 1, 2, 3, 7, 10, 28, 46**
See also CA 17-20R; 142; CANR 41;
DLB 6; DLBY 82; MTCW

Dexter, Martin
See Faust, Frederick (Schiller)

Dexter, Pete 1943- .... **CLC 34, 55**
See also BEST 89:2; CA 127; 131; MTCW

Diamano, Silmang
See Senghor, Leopold Sedar

Diamond, Neil 1941- .... **CLC 30**
See also CA 108

di Bassetto, Corno
See Shaw, George Bernard

Dick, Philip K(indred)
1928-1982 .... **CLC 10, 30, 72**
See also CA 49-52; 106; CANR 2, 16;
DLB 8; MTCW

Dickens, Charles (John Huffam)
1812-1870 ...... **NCLC 3, 8, 18, 26, 37;**
DA; SSC 17; WLC
See also CDBLB 1832-1890; DLB 21, 55,
70; JRDA; MAICYA; SATA 15

Dickey, James (Lafayette)
1923- .... **CLC 1, 2, 4, 7, 10, 15, 47**
See also AITN 1, 2; CA 9-12R; CABS 2;
CANR 10; CDALB 1968-1988; DLB 5;
DLBD 7; DLBY 82, 93; MTCW

Dickey, William 1928-1994 ..... **CLC 3, 28**
See also CA 9-12R; 145; CANR 24; DLB 5

Dickinson, Charles 1951- .... **CLC 49**
See also CA 128

Dickinson, Emily (Elizabeth)
1830-1886 .. **NCLC 21; DA; PC 1; WLC**
See also CDALB 1865-1917; DLB 1;
SATA 29

Dickinson, Peter (Malcolm)
1927- .... **CLC 12, 35**
See also AAYA 9; CA 41-44R; CANR 31;
CLR 29; DLB 87; JRDA; MAICYA;
SATA 5, 62

Dickson, Carr
See Carr, John Dickson

Dickson, Carter
See Carr, John Dickson

Diderot, Denis 1713-1784 .... **LC 26**

Didion, Joan 1934- ..... **CLC 1, 3, 8, 14, 32**
See also AITN 1; CA 5-8R; CANR 14;
CDALB 1968-1988; DLB 2; DLBY 81,
86; MTCW

Dietrich, Robert
See Hunt, E(verette) Howard, (Jr.)

Dillard, Annie 1945- .... **CLC 9, 60**
See also AAYA 6; CA 49-52; CANR 3, 43;
DLBY 80; MTCW; SATA 10

Dillard, R(ichard) H(enry) W(ilde)
1937- .... **CLC 5**
See also CA 21-24R; CAAS 7; CANR 10;
DLB 5

Dillon, Eilis 1920- .... **CLC 17**
See also CA 9-12R; CAAS 3; CANR 4, 38;
CLR 26; MAICYA; SATA 2, 74

Dimont, Penelope
See Mortimer, Penelope (Ruth)

Dinesen, Isak .... **CLC 10, 29; SSC 7**
See also Blixen, Karen (Christentze
Dinesen)

Ding Ling .... **CLC 68**
See also Chiang Pin-chin

Disch, Thomas M(ichael) 1940-... **CLC 7, 36**
See also CA 21-24R; CAAS 4; CANR 17,
36; CLR 18; DLB 8; MAICYA; MTCW;
SAAS 15; SATA 54

Disch, Tom
See Disch, Thomas M(ichael)

d'Isly, Georges
See Simenon, Georges (Jacques Christian)

Disraeli, Benjamin 1804-1881 .. **NCLC 2, 39**
See also DLB 21, 55

Ditcum, Steve
See Crumb, R(obert)

Dixon, Paige
See Corcoran, Barbara

Dixon, Stephen 1936-..... **CLC 52; SSC 16**
See also CA 89-92; CANR 17, 40; DLB 130

Dobell, Sydney Thompson
1824-1874 .... **NCLC 43**
See also DLB 32

Doblin, Alfred .... **TCLC 13**
See also Doeblin, Alfred

Dobrolyubov, Nikolai Alexandrovich
1836-1861 .... **NCLC 5**

Dobyns, Stephen 1941-............ **CLC 37**
See also CA 45-48; CANR 2, 18

Doctorow, E(dgar) L(aurence)
1931- ..... **CLC 6, 11, 15, 18, 37, 44, 65**
See also AITN 2; BEST 89:3; CA 45-48;
CANR 2, 33; CDALB 1968-1988; DLB 2,
28; DLBY 80; MTCW

Dodgson, Charles Lutwidge 1832-1898
See Carroll, Lewis
See also CLR 2; DA; MAICYA; YABC 2

Dodson, Owen (Vincent)
1914-1983 .... **CLC 79; BLC**
See also BW 1; CA 65-68; 110; CANR 24;
DLB 76

Doeblin, Alfred 1878-1957....... **TCLC 13**
See also Doblin, Alfred
See also CA 110; 141; DLB 66

Doerr, Harriet 1910- .... **CLC 34**
See also CA 117; 122; CANR 47

Domecq, H(onorio) Bustos
See Bioy Casares, Adolfo; Borges, Jorge
Luis

Domini, Rey
See Lorde, Audre (Geraldine)

Dominique
See Proust, (Valentin-Louis-George-Eugene-)
Marcel

Don, A
See Stephen, Leslie

Donaldson, Stephen R. 1947-....... **CLC 46**
See also CA 89-92; CANR 13

Donleavy, J(ames) P(atrick)
1926- .... **CLC 1, 4, 6, 10, 45**
See also AITN 2; CA 9-12R; CANR 24;
DLB 6; MTCW

Donne, John
1572-1631 .... **LC 10, 24; DA; PC 1**
See also CDBLB Before 1660; DLB 121

Donnell, David 1939(?)-........... **CLC 34**

Donoghue, P. S.
See Hunt, E(verette) Howard, (Jr.)

Donoso (Yanez), Jose
1924- .... **CLC 4, 8, 11, 32; HLC**
See also CA 81-84; CANR 32; DLB 113;
HW; MTCW

Donovan, John 1928-1992 .... **CLC 35**
See also CA 97-100; 137; CLR 3;
MAICYA; SATA 72; SATA-Brief 29

Don Roberto
See Cunninghame Graham, R(obert)
B(ontine)

Doolittle, Hilda
1886-1961 ..... **CLC 3, 8, 14, 31, 34, 73;**
DA; PC 5; WLC
See also H. D.
See also CA 97-100; CANR 35; DLB 4, 45;
MTCW

Dorfman, Ariel 1942-.... **CLC 48, 77; HLC**
See also CA 124; 130; HW

Dorn, Edward (Merton) 1929-... **CLC 10, 18**
See also CA 93-96; CANR 42; DLB 5

Dorsan, Luc
See Simenon, Georges (Jacques Christian)

Dorsange, Jean
See Simenon, Georges (Jacques Christian)

Dos Passos, John (Roderigo)
1896-1970 ...... **CLC 1, 4, 8, 11, 15, 25,**
34, 82; DA; WLC
See also CA 1-4R; 29-32R; CANR 3;
CDALB 1929-1941; DLB 4, 9; DLBD 1;
MTCW

Dossage, Jean
See Simenon, Georges (Jacques Christian)

Dostoevsky, Fedor Mikhailovich
1821-1881 ...... **NCLC 2, 7, 21, 33, 43;**
DA; SSC 2; WLC

Doughty, Charles M(ontagu)
1843-1926 .... **TCLC 27**
See also CA 115; DLB 19, 57

Douglas, Ellen .... **CLC 73**
See also Haxton, Josephine Ayres;
Williamson, Ellen Douglas

Douglas, Gavin 1475(?)-1522....... **LC 20**

Douglas, Keith 1920-1944 .... **TCLC 40**
See also DLB 27

Douglas, Leonard
See Bradbury, Ray (Douglas)

Douglas, Michael
See Crichton, (John) Michael

Douglass, Frederick
1817(?)-1895 .... **NCLC 7; BLC; DA;**
WLC
See also CDALB 1640-1865; DLB 1, 43, 50,
79; SATA 29

Dourado, (Waldomiro Freitas) Autran
1926- .... **CLC 23, 60**
See also CA 25-28R; CANR 34

Dourado, Waldomiro Autran
See Dourado, (Waldomiro Freitas) Autran

Dove, Rita (Frances)
1952- .... **CLC 50, 81; PC 6**
See also BW 2; CA 109; CAAS 19;
CANR 27, 42; DLB 120

Dowell, Coleman 1925-1985........ **CLC 60**
See also CA 25-28R; 117; CANR 10;
DLB 130

Dowson, Ernest Christopher
    1867-1900 .... **TCLC 4**
    See also CA 105; DLB 19, 135

Doyle, A. Conan
    See Doyle, Arthur Conan

Doyle, Arthur Conan
    1859-1930 .... **TCLC 7; DA; SSC 12;**
                                            WLC
    See also AAYA 14; CA 104; 122;
        CDBLB 1890-1914; DLB 18, 70; MTCW;
        SATA 24

Doyle, Conan
    See Doyle, Arthur Conan

Doyle, John
    See Graves, Robert (von Ranke)

Doyle, Roddy 1958(?)- .... **CLC 81**
    See also AAYA 14; CA 143

Doyle, Sir A. Conan
    See Doyle, Arthur Conan

Doyle, Sir Arthur Conan
    See Doyle, Arthur Conan

Dr. A
    See Asimov, Isaac; Silverstein, Alvin

Drabble, Margaret
    1939- .... **CLC 2, 3, 5, 8, 10, 22, 53**
    See also CA 13-16R; CANR 18, 35;
        CDBLB 1960 to Present; DLB 14;
        MTCW; SATA 48

Drapier, M. B.
    See Swift, Jonathan

Drayham, James
    See Mencken, H(enry) L(ouis)

Drayton, Michael 1563-1631......... **LC 8**

Dreadstone, Carl
    See Campbell, (John) Ramsey

Dreiser, Theodore (Herman Albert)
    1871-1945 ...... **TCLC 10, 18, 35; DA;**
                                            WLC
    See also CA 106; 132; CDALB 1865-1917;
        DLB 9, 12, 102, 137; DLBD 1; MTCW

Drexler, Rosalyn 1926- .... **CLC 2, 6**
    See also CA 81-84

Dreyer, Carl Theodor 1889-1968.... **CLC 16**
    See also CA 116

Drieu la Rochelle, Pierre(-Eugene)
    1893-1945 .... **TCLC 21**
    See also CA 117; DLB 72

Drinkwater, John 1882-1937...... **TCLC 57**
    See also CA 109; DLB 10, 19

Drop Shot
    See Cable, George Washington

Droste-Hulshoff, Annette Freiin von
    1797-1848 .... **NCLC 3**
    See also DLB 133

Drummond, Walter
    See Silverberg, Robert

Drummond, William Henry
    1854-1907 .... **TCLC 25**
    See also DLB 92

Drummond de Andrade, Carlos
    1902-1987 .... **CLC 18**
    See also Andrade, Carlos Drummond de
    See also CA 132; 123

Drury, Allen (Stuart) 1918-........ **CLC 37**
    See also CA 57-60; CANR 18

Dryden, John
    1631-1700 ... **LC 3, 21; DA; DC 3; WLC**
    See also CDBLB 1660-1789; DLB 80, 101,
        131

Duberman, Martin 1930-.......... **CLC 8**
    See also CA 1-4R; CANR 2

Dubie, Norman (Evans) 1945-...... **CLC 36**
    See also CA 69-72; CANR 12; DLB 120

Du Bois, W(illiam) E(dward) B(urghardt)
    1868-1963 ...... **CLC 1, 2, 13, 64; BLC;**
                                            DA; WLC
    See also BW 1; CA 85-88; CANR 34;
        CDALB 1865-1917; DLB 47, 50, 91;
        MTCW; SATA 42

Dubus, Andre 1936-... **CLC 13, 36; SSC 15**
    See also CA 21-24R; CANR 17; DLB 130

Duca Minimo
    See D'Annunzio, Gabriele

Ducharme, Rejean 1941- .... **CLC 74**
    See also DLB 60

Duclos, Charles Pinot 1704-1772 ..... **LC 1**

Dudek, Louis 1918- .... **CLC 11, 19**
    See also CA 45-48; CAAS 14; CANR 1;
        DLB 88

Duerrenmatt, Friedrich
    1921-1990 ...... **CLC 1, 4, 8, 11, 15, 43**
    See also CA 17-20R; CANR 33; DLB 69,
        124; MTCW

Duffy, Bruce (?)-................. **CLC 50**

Duffy, Maureen 1933-............ **CLC 37**
    See also CA 25-28R; CANR 33; DLB 14;
        MTCW

Dugan, Alan 1923- .... **CLC 2, 6**
    See also CA 81-84; DLB 5

du Gard, Roger Martin
    See Martin du Gard, Roger

Duhamel, Georges 1884-1966 .... **CLC 8**
    See also CA 81-84; 25-28R; CANR 35;
        DLB 65; MTCW

Dujardin, Edouard (Emile Louis)
    1861-1949 .... **TCLC 13**
    See also CA 109; DLB 123

Dumas, Alexandre (Davy de la Pailleterie)
    1802-1870 .... **NCLC 11; DA; WLC**
    See also DLB 119; SATA 18

Dumas, Alexandre
    1824-1895 .... **NCLC 9; DC 1**

Dumas, Claudine
    See Malzberg, Barry N(athaniel)

Dumas, Henry L. 1934-1968 ..... **CLC 6, 62**
    See also BW 1; CA 85-88; DLB 41

du Maurier, Daphne
    1907-1989 ...... **CLC 6, 11, 59; SSC 18**
    See also CA 5-8R; 128; CANR 6; MTCW;
        SATA 27; SATA-Obit 60

Dunbar, Paul Laurence
    1872-1906 ...... **TCLC 2, 12; BLC; DA;**
                                PC 5; SSC 8; WLC
    See also BW 1; CA 104; 124;
        CDALB 1865-1917; DLB 50, 54, 78;
        SATA 34

Dunbar, William 1460(?)-1530(?) .... **LC 20**
    See also DLB 132, 146

Duncan, Lois 1934-.............. **CLC 26**
    See also AAYA 4; CA 1-4R; CANR 2, 23,
        36; CLR 29; JRDA; MAICYA; SAAS 2;
        SATA 1, 36, 75

Duncan, Robert (Edward)
    1919-1988 .... **CLC 1, 2, 4, 7, 15, 41, 55;**
                                            PC 2
    See also CA 9-12R; 124; CANR 28; DLB 5,
        16; MTCW

Dunlap, William 1766-1839....... **NCLC 2**
    See also DLB 30, 37, 59

Dunn, Douglas (Eaglesham)
    1942- .... **CLC 6, 40**
    See also CA 45-48; CANR 2, 33; DLB 40;
        MTCW

Dunn, Katherine (Karen) 1945-..... **CLC 71**
    See also CA 33-36R

Dunn, Stephen 1939- .... **CLC 36**
    See also CA 33-36R; CANR 12; DLB 105

Dunne, Finley Peter 1867-1936 .... **TCLC 28**
    See also CA 108; DLB 11, 23

Dunne, John Gregory 1932-........ **CLC 28**
    See also CA 25-28R; CANR 14; DLBY 80

Dunsany, Edward John Moreton Drax
        Plunkett 1878-1957
    See Dunsany, Lord
    See also CA 104; DLB 10

Dunsany, Lord................. **TCLC 2, 59**
    See also Dunsany, Edward John Moreton
        Drax Plunkett
    See also DLB 77

du Perry, Jean
    See Simenon, Georges (Jacques Christian)

Durang, Christopher (Ferdinand)
    1949- .... **CLC 27, 38**
    See also CA 105

Duras, Marguerite
    1914- ...... **CLC 3, 6, 11, 20, 34, 40, 68**
    See also CA 25-28R; DLB 83; MTCW

Durban, (Rosa) Pam 1947-........ **CLC 39**
    See also CA 123

Durcan, Paul 1944-............. **CLC 43, 70**
    See also CA 134

Durkheim, Emile 1858-1917 ...... **TCLC 55**

Durrell, Lawrence (George)
    1912-1990 .... **CLC 1, 4, 6, 8, 13, 27, 41**
    See also CA 9-12R; 132; CANR 40;
        CDBLB 1945-1960; DLB 15, 27;
        DLBY 90; MTCW

Durrenmatt, Friedrich
    See Duerrenmatt, Friedrich

Dutt, Toru 1856-1877.......... **NCLC 29**

Dwight, Timothy 1752-1817...... **NCLC 13**
    See also DLB 37

Dworkin, Andrea 1946- .... **CLC 43**
    See also CA 77-80; CANR 16, 39; MTCW

Dwyer, Deanna
    See Koontz, Dean R(ay)

Dwyer, K. R.
    See Koontz, Dean R(ay)

Dylan, Bob 1941-...... **CLC 3, 4, 6, 12, 77**
    See also CA 41-44R; DLB 16

Eagleton, Terence (Francis)   1943-
See Eagleton, Terry
See also CA 57-60; CANR 7, 23; MTCW

Eagleton, Terry . . . . CLC 63
See also Eagleton, Terence (Francis)

Early, Jack
See Scoppettone, Sandra

East, Michael
See West, Morris L(anglo)

Eastaway, Edward
See Thomas, (Philip) Edward

Eastlake, William (Derry)   1917- . . . . . CLC 8
See also CA 5-8R; CAAS 1; CANR 5;
DLB 6

Eastman, Charles A(lexander)
1858-1939 . . . . TCLC 55
See also NNAL; YABC 1

Eberhart, Richard (Ghormley)
1904- . . . . CLC 3, 11, 19, 56
See also CA 1-4R; CANR 2;
CDALB 1941-1968; DLB 48; MTCW

Eberstadt, Fernanda   1960- . . . . CLC 39
See also CA 136

Echegaray (y Eizaguirre), Jose (Maria Waldo)
1832-1916 . . . . TCLC 4
See also CA 104; CANR 32; HW; MTCW

Echeverria, (Jose) Esteban (Antonino)
1805-1851 . . . . NCLC 18

Echo
See Proust, (Valentin-Louis-George-Eugene-)
Marcel

Eckert, Allan W.   1931- . . . . CLC 17
See also CA 13-16R; CANR 14, 45;
SATA 29; SATA-Brief 27

Eckhart, Meister   1260(?)-1328(?) . . CMLC 9
See also DLB 115

Eckmar, F. R.
See de Hartog, Jan

Eco, Umberto   1932- . . . . CLC 28, 60
See also BEST 90:1; CA 77-80; CANR 12,
33; MTCW

Eddison, E(ric) R(ucker)
1882-1945 . . . . TCLC 15
See also CA 109

Edel, (Joseph) Leon   1907- . . . . . . CLC 29, 34
See also CA 1-4R; CANR 1, 22; DLB 103

Eden, Emily   1797-1869 . . . . NCLC 10

Edgar, David   1948- . . . . CLC 42
See also CA 57-60; CANR 12; DLB 13;
MTCW

Edgerton, Clyde (Carlyle)   1944- . . . . CLC 39
See also CA 118; 134

Edgeworth, Maria   1767-1849 . . . . . . NCLC 1
See also DLB 116; SATA 21

Edmonds, Paul
See Kuttner, Henry

Edmonds, Walter D(umaux)   1903- . . CLC 35
See also CA 5-8R; CANR 2; DLB 9;
MAICYA; SAAS 4; SATA 1, 27

Edmondson, Wallace
See Ellison, Harlan (Jay)

Edson, Russell . . . . CLC 13
See also CA 33-36R

Edwards, Bronwen Elizabeth
See Rose, Wendy

Edwards, G(erald) B(asil)
1899-1976 . . . . CLC 25
See also CA 110

Edwards, Gus   1939- . . . . CLC 43
See also CA 108

Edwards, Jonathan   1703-1758 . . . . LC 7; DA
See also DLB 24

Efron, Marina Ivanovna Tsvetaeva
See Tsvetaeva (Efron), Marina (Ivanovna)

Ehle, John (Marsden, Jr.)   1925- . . . . CLC 27
See also CA 9-12R

Ehrenbourg, Ilya (Grigoryevich)
See Ehrenburg, Ilya (Grigoryevich)

Ehrenburg, Ilya (Grigoryevich)
1891-1967 . . . . CLC 18, 34, 62
See also CA 102; 25-28R

Ehrenburg, Ilyo (Grigoryevich)
See Ehrenburg, Ilya (Grigoryevich)

Eich, Guenter   1907-1972 . . . . CLC 15
See also CA 111; 93-96; DLB 69, 124

Eichendorff, Joseph Freiherr von
1788-1857 . . . . NCLC 8
See also DLB 90

Eigner, Larry . . . . CLC 9
See also Eigner, Laurence (Joel)
See also DLB 5

Eigner, Laurence (Joel)   1927-
See Eigner, Larry
See also CA 9-12R; CANR 6

Eiseley, Loren Corey   1907-1977 . . . . . CLC 7
See also AAYA 5; CA 1-4R; 73-76;
CANR 6

Eisenstadt, Jill   1963- . . . . CLC 50
See also CA 140

Eisenstein, Sergei (Mikhailovich)
1898-1948 . . . . TCLC 57
See also CA 114

Eisner, Simon
See Kornbluth, C(yril) M.

Ekeloef, (Bengt) Gunnar
1907-1968 . . . . CLC 27
See also CA 123; 25-28R

Ekelof, (Bengt) Gunnar
See Ekeloef, (Bengt) Gunnar

Ekwensi, C. O. D.
See Ekwensi, Cyprian (Odiatu Duaka)

Ekwensi, Cyprian (Odiatu Duaka)
1921- . . . . CLC 4; BLC
See also BW 2; CA 29-32R; CANR 18, 42;
DLB 117; MTCW; SATA 66

Elaine . . . . TCLC 18
See also Leverson, Ada

El Crummo
See Crumb, R(obert)

Elia
See Lamb, Charles

Eliade, Mircea   1907-1986 . . . . CLC 19
See also CA 65-68; 119; CANR 30; MTCW

Eliot, A. D.
See Jewett, (Theodora) Sarah Orne

Eliot, Alice
See Jewett, (Theodora) Sarah Orne

Eliot, Dan
See Silverberg, Robert

Eliot, George
1819-1880 . . . . . NCLC 4, 13, 23, 41, 49;
DA; WLC
See also CDBLB 1832-1890; DLB 21, 35, 55

Eliot, John   1604-1690 . . . . LC 5
See also DLB 24

Eliot, T(homas) S(tearns)
1888-1965 . . . . . CLC 1, 2, 3, 6, 9, 10, 13,
15, 24, 34, 41, 55, 57; DA; PC 5; WLC 2
See also CA 5-8R; 25-28R; CANR 41;
CDALB 1929-1941; DLB 7, 10, 45, 63;
DLBY 88; MTCW

Elizabeth   1866-1941 . . . . TCLC 41

Elkin, Stanley L(awrence)
1930- . . . CLC 4, 6, 9, 14, 27, 51; SSC 12
See also CA 9-12R; CANR 8, 46; DLB 2,
28; DLBY 80; MTCW

Elledge, Scott . . . . CLC 34

Elliott, Don
See Silverberg, Robert

Elliott, George P(aul)   1918-1980 . . . . . CLC 2
See also CA 1-4R; 97-100; CANR 2

Elliott, Janice   1931- . . . . CLC 47
See also CA 13-16R; CANR 8, 29; DLB 14

Elliott, Sumner Locke   1917-1991 . . . CLC 38
See also CA 5-8R; 134; CANR 2, 21

Elliott, William
See Bradbury, Ray (Douglas)

Ellis, A. E. . . . . CLC 7

Ellis, Alice Thomas . . . . CLC 40
See also Haycraft, Anna

Ellis, Bret Easton   1964- . . . . CLC 39, 71
See also AAYA 2; CA 118; 123

Ellis, (Henry) Havelock
1859-1939 . . . . TCLC 14
See also CA 109

Ellis, Landon
See Ellison, Harlan (Jay)

Ellis, Trey   1962- . . . . CLC 55

Ellison, Harlan (Jay)
1934- . . . . CLC 1, 13, 42; SSC 14
See also CA 5-8R; CANR 5, 46; DLB 8;
MTCW

Ellison, Ralph (Waldo)
1914-1994 . . . . CLC 1, 3, 11, 54, 86;
BLC; DA; WLC
See also BW 1; CA 9-12R; 145; CANR 24;
CDALB 1941-1968; DLB 2, 76; MTCW

Ellmann, Lucy (Elizabeth)   1956- . . . . CLC 61
See also CA 128

Ellmann, Richard (David)
1918-1987 . . . . CLC 50
See also BEST 89:2; CA 1-4R; 122;
CANR 2, 28; DLB 103; DLBY 87;
MTCW

Elman, Richard   1934- . . . . CLC 19
See also CA 17-20R; CAAS 3; CANR 47

Elron
See Hubbard, L(afayette) Ron(ald)

Eluard, Paul . . . . TCLC 7, 41
See also Grindel, Eugene

Elyot, Sir Thomas   1490(?)-1546 . . . . . LC 11

Folke, Will
See Bloch, Robert (Albert)

Follett, Ken(neth Martin) 1949- .... **CLC 18**
See also AAYA 6; BEST 89:4; CA 81-84;
CANR 13, 33; DLB 87; DLBY 81;
MTCW

Fontane, Theodor 1819-1898..... **NCLC 26**
See also DLB 129

Foote, Horton 1916-.............. **CLC 51**
See also CA 73-76; CANR 34; DLB 26

Foote, Shelby 1916- .... **CLC 75**
See also CA 5-8R; CANR 3, 45; DLB 2, 17

Forbes, Esther 1891-1967.......... **CLC 12**
See also CA 13-14; 25-28R; CAP 1;
CLR 27; DLB 22; JRDA; MAICYA;
SATA 2

Forche, Carolyn (Louise)
1950- .... **CLC 25, 83, 86; PC 10**
See also CA 109; 117; DLB 5

Ford, Elbur
See Hibbert, Eleanor Alice Burford

Ford, Ford Madox
1873-1939 .... **TCLC 1, 15, 39, 57**
See also CA 104; 132; CDBLB 1914-1945;
DLB 34, 98; MTCW

Ford, John 1895-1973............. **CLC 16**
See also CA 45-48

Ford, Richard 1944-.............. **CLC 46**
See also CA 69-72; CANR 11, 47

Ford, Webster
See Masters, Edgar Lee

Foreman, Richard 1937-.......... **CLC 50**
See also CA 65-68; CANR 32

Forester, C(ecil) S(cott)
1899-1966 .... **CLC 35**
See also CA 73-76; 25-28R; SATA 13

Forez
See Mauriac, Francois (Charles)

Forman, James Douglas 1932-..... **CLC 21**
See also CA 9-12R; CANR 4, 19, 42;
JRDA; MAICYA; SATA 8, 70

Fornes, Maria Irene 1930-...... **CLC 39, 61**
See also CA 25-28R; CANR 28; DLB 7;
HW; MTCW

Forrest, Leon 1937- .... **CLC 4**
See also BW 2; CA 89-92; CAAS 7;
CANR 25; DLB 33

Forster, E(dward) M(organ)
1879-1970 ..... **CLC 1, 2, 3, 4, 9, 10, 13,
15, 22, 45, 77; DA; WLC**
See also AAYA 2; CA 13-14; 25-28R;
CANR 45; CAP 1; CDBLB 1914-1945;
DLB 34, 98; DLBD 10; MTCW;
SATA 57

Forster, John 1812-1876 .... **NCLC 11**
See also DLB 144

Forsyth, Frederick 1938-...... **CLC 2, 5, 36**
See also BEST 89:4; CA 85-88; CANR 38;
DLB 87; MTCW

Forten, Charlotte L. .... **TCLC 16; BLC**
See also Grimke, Charlotte L(ottie) Forten
See also DLB 50

Foscolo, Ugo 1778-1827.......... **NCLC 8**

Fosse, Bob .... **CLC 20**
See also Fosse, Robert Louis

Fosse, Robert Louis 1927-1987
See Fosse, Bob
See also CA 110; 123

Foster, Stephen Collins
1826-1864 .... **NCLC 26**

Foucault, Michel
1926-1984 .... **CLC 31, 34, 69**
See also CA 105; 113; CANR 34; MTCW

Fouque, Friedrich (Heinrich Karl) de la Motte
1777-1843 .... **NCLC 2**
See also DLB 90

Fournier, Henri Alban 1886-1914
See Alain-Fournier
See also CA 104

Fournier, Pierre 1916-............ **CLC 11**
See also Gascar, Pierre
See also CA 89-92; CANR 16, 40

Fowles, John
1926- ...... **CLC 1, 2, 3, 4, 6, 9, 10, 15,
33, 87**
See also CA 5-8R; CANR 25; CDBLB 1960
to Present; DLB 14, 139; MTCW;
SATA 22

Fox, Paula 1923-................. **CLC 2, 8**
See also AAYA 3; CA 73-76; CANR 20,
36; CLR 1; DLB 52; JRDA; MAICYA;
MTCW; SATA 17, 60

Fox, William Price (Jr.) 1926- ..... **CLC 22**
See also CA 17-20R; CAAS 19; CANR 11;
DLB 2; DLBY 81

Foxe, John 1516(?)-1587 .... **LC 14**

Frame, Janet .... **CLC 2, 3, 6, 22, 66**
See also Clutha, Janet Paterson Frame

France, Anatole .... **TCLC 9**
See also Thibault, Jacques Anatole Francois
See also DLB 123

Francis, Claude 19(?)- .... **CLC 50**

Francis, Dick 1920- .... **CLC 2, 22, 42**
See also AAYA 5; BEST 89:3; CA 5-8R;
CANR 9, 42; CDBLB 1960 to Present;
DLB 87; MTCW

Francis, Robert (Churchill)
1901-1987 .... **CLC 15**
See also CA 1-4R; 123; CANR 1

Frank, Anne(lies Marie)
1929-1945 .... **TCLC 17; DA; WLC**
See also AAYA 12; CA 113; 133; MTCW;
SATA-Brief 42

Frank, Elizabeth 1945-........... **CLC 39**
See also CA 121; 126

Franklin, Benjamin
See Hasek, Jaroslav (Matej Frantisek)

Franklin, Benjamin 1706-1790... **LC 25; DA**
See also CDALB 1640-1865; DLB 24, 43,
73

Franklin, (Stella Maraia Sarah) Miles
1879-1954 .... **TCLC 7**
See also CA 104

Fraser, (Lady) Antonia (Pakenham)
1932- .... **CLC 32**
See also CA 85-88; CANR 44; MTCW;
SATA-Brief 32

Fraser, George MacDonald 1925-.... **CLC 7**
See also CA 45-48; CANR 2

Fraser, Sylvia 1935-.............. **CLC 64**
See also CA 45-48; CANR 1, 16

Frayn, Michael 1933-...... **CLC 3, 7, 31, 47**
See also CA 5-8R; CANR 30; DLB 13, 14;
MTCW

Fraze, Candida (Merrill) 1945-..... **CLC 50**
See also CA 126

Frazer, J(ames) G(eorge)
1854-1941 .... **TCLC 32**
See also CA 118

Frazer, Robert Caine
See Creasey, John

Frazer, Sir James George
See Frazer, J(ames) G(eorge)

Frazier, Ian 1951-................ **CLC 46**
See also CA 130

Frederic, Harold 1856-1898...... **NCLC 10**
See also DLB 12, 23

Frederick, John
See Faust, Frederick (Schiller)

Frederick the Great 1712-1786...... **LC 14**

Fredro, Aleksander 1793-1876..... **NCLC 8**

Freeling, Nicolas 1927- .... **CLC 38**
See also CA 49-52; CAAS 12; CANR 1, 17;
DLB 87

Freeman, Douglas Southall
1886-1953 .... **TCLC 11**
See also CA 109; DLB 17

Freeman, Judith 1946-............ **CLC 55**

Freeman, Mary Eleanor Wilkins
1852-1930 .... **TCLC 9; SSC 1**
See also CA 106; DLB 12, 78

Freeman, R(ichard) Austin
1862-1943 .... **TCLC 21**
See also CA 113; DLB 70

French, Albert 1943- .... **CLC 86**

French, Marilyn 1929-...... **CLC 10, 18, 60**
See also CA 69-72; CANR 3, 31; MTCW

French, Paul
See Asimov, Isaac

Freneau, Philip Morin 1752-1832.. **NCLC 1**
See also DLB 37, 43

Freud, Sigmund 1856-1939 .... **TCLC 52**
See also CA 115; 133; MTCW

Friedan, Betty (Naomi) 1921-...... **CLC 74**
See also CA 65-68; CANR 18, 45; MTCW

Friedman, B(ernard) H(arper)
1926-.................... **CLC 7**
See also CA 1-4R; CANR 3

Friedman, Bruce Jay 1930-.... **CLC 3, 5, 56**
See also CA 9-12R; CANR 25; DLB 2, 28

Friel, Brian 1929-............ **CLC 5, 42, 59**
See also CA 21-24R; CANR 33; DLB 13;
MTCW

Friis-Baastad, Babbis Ellinor
1921-1970 .... **CLC 12**
See also CA 17-20R; 134; SATA 7

Frisch, Max (Rudolf)
1911-1991 ..... **CLC 3, 9, 14, 18, 32, 44**
See also CA 85-88; 134; CANR 32;
DLB 69, 124; MTCW

Fromentin, Eugene (Samuel Auguste)
1820-1876 .... NCLC **10**
See also DLB 123

Frost, Frederick
See Faust, Frederick (Schiller)

Frost, Robert (Lee)
1874-1963 .... CLC **1, 3, 4, 9, 10, 13, 15,
26, 34, 44; DA; PC 1; WLC**
See also CA 89-92; CANR 33;
CDALB 1917-1929; DLB 54; DLBD 7;
MTCW; SATA 14

Froude, James Anthony
1818-1894 .... NCLC **43**
See also DLB 18, 57, 144

Froy, Herald
See Waterhouse, Keith (Spencer)

Fry, Christopher 1907- .... CLC **2, 10, 14**
See also CA 17-20R; CANR 9, 30; DLB 13;
MTCW; SATA 66

Frye, (Herman) Northrop
1912-1991 .... CLC **24, 70**
See also CA 5-8R; 133; CANR 8, 37;
DLB 67, 68; MTCW

Fuchs, Daniel 1909-1993 .... CLC **8, 22**
See also CA 81-84; 142; CAAS 5;
CANR 40; DLB 9, 26, 28; DLBY 93

Fuchs, Daniel 1934- .... CLC **34**
See also CA 37-40R; CANR 14

Fuentes, Carlos
1928- ...... CLC **3, 8, 10, 13, 22, 41, 60;
DA; HLC; WLC**
See also AAYA 4; AITN 2; CA 69-72;
CANR 10, 32; DLB 113; HW; MTCW

Fuentes, Gregorio Lopez y
See Lopez y Fuentes, Gregorio

Fugard, (Harold) Athol
1932- ... CLC **5, 9, 14, 25, 40, 80; DC 3**
See also CA 85-88; CANR 32; MTCW

Fugard, Sheila 1932- .... CLC **48**
See also CA 125

Fuller, Charles (H., Jr.)
1939- .... CLC **25; BLC; DC 1**
See also BW 2; CA 108; 112; DLB 38;
MTCW

Fuller, John (Leopold) 1937- .... CLC **62**
See also CA 21-24R; CANR 9, 44; DLB 40

Fuller, Margaret .... NCLC **5**
See also Ossoli, Sarah Margaret (Fuller
marchesa d')

Fuller, Roy (Broadbent)
1912-1991 .... CLC **4, 28**
See also CA 5-8R; 135; CAAS 10; DLB 15,
20

Fulton, Alice 1952- .... CLC **52**
See also CA 116

Furphy, Joseph 1843-1912 .... TCLC **25**

Fussell, Paul 1924- .... CLC **74**
See also BEST 90:1; CA 17-20R; CANR 8,
21, 35; MTCW

Futabatei, Shimei 1864-1909 ...... TCLC **44**

Futrelle, Jacques 1875-1912 ...... TCLC **19**
See also CA 113

Gaboriau, Emile 1835-1873 ...... NCLC **14**

Gadda, Carlo Emilio 1893-1973 .... CLC **11**
See also CA 89-92

Gaddis, William
1922- ..... CLC **1, 3, 6, 8, 10, 19, 43, 86**
See also CA 17-20R; CANR 21; DLB 2;
MTCW

Gaines, Ernest J(ames)
1933- .... CLC **3, 11, 18, 86; BLC**
See also AITN 1; BW 2; CA 9-12R;
CANR 6, 24, 42; CDALB 1968-1988;
DLB 2, 33; DLBY 80; MTCW

Gaitskill, Mary 1954- .... CLC **69**
See also CA 128

Galdos, Benito Perez
See Perez Galdos, Benito

Gale, Zona 1874-1938 .... TCLC **7**
See also CA 105; DLB 9, 78

Galeano, Eduardo (Hughes) 1940- ... CLC **72**
See also CA 29-32R; CANR 13, 32; HW

Galiano, Juan Valera y Alcala
See Valera y Alcala-Galiano, Juan

Gallagher, Tess 1943- .... CLC **18, 63; PC 9**
See also CA 106; DLB 120

Gallant, Mavis
1922- .... CLC **7, 18, 38; SSC 5**
See also CA 69-72; CANR 29; DLB 53;
MTCW

Gallant, Roy A(rthur) 1924- .... CLC **17**
See also CA 5-8R; CANR 4, 29; CLR 30;
MAICYA; SATA 4, 68

Gallico, Paul (William) 1897-1976 ... CLC **2**
See also AITN 1; CA 5-8R; 69-72;
CANR 23; DLB 9; MAICYA; SATA 13

Gallup, Ralph
See Whitemore, Hugh (John)

Galsworthy, John
1867-1933 .... TCLC **1, 45; DA; WLC 2**
See also CA 104; 141; CDBLB 1890-1914;
DLB 10, 34, 98

Galt, John 1779-1839 .... NCLC **1**
See also DLB 99, 116

Galvin, James 1951- .... CLC **38**
See also CA 108; CANR 26

Gamboa, Federico 1864-1939 ...... TCLC **36**

Gandhi, M. K.
See Gandhi, Mohandas Karamchand

Gandhi, Mahatma
See Gandhi, Mohandas Karamchand

Gandhi, Mohandas Karamchand
1869-1948 .... TCLC **59**
See also CA 121; 132; MTCW

Gann, Ernest Kellogg 1910-1991 .... CLC **23**
See also AITN 1; CA 1-4R; 136; CANR 1

Garcia, Cristina 1958- .... CLC **76**
See also CA 141

Garcia Lorca, Federico
1898-1936 .... TCLC **1, 7, 49; DA;
DC 2; HLC; PC 3; WLC**
See also CA 104; 131; DLB 108; HW;
MTCW

Garcia Marquez, Gabriel (Jose)
1928- .... CLC **2, 3, 8, 10, 15, 27, 47, 55,
68; DA; HLC; SSC 8; WLC**
See also AAYA 3; BEST 89:1, 90:4;
CA 33-36R; CANR 10, 28; DLB 113;
HW; MTCW

Gard, Janice
See Latham, Jean Lee

Gard, Roger Martin du
See Martin du Gard, Roger

Gardam, Jane 1928- .... CLC **43**
See also CA 49-52; CANR 2, 18, 33;
CLR 12; DLB 14; MAICYA; MTCW;
SAAS 9; SATA 39, 76; SATA-Brief 28

Gardner, Herb .... CLC **44**

Gardner, John (Champlin), Jr.
1933-1982 ..... CLC **2, 3, 5, 7, 8, 10, 18,
28, 34; SSC 7**
See also AITN 1; CA 65-68; 107;
CANR 33; DLB 2; DLBY 82; MTCW;
SATA 40; SATA-Obit 31

Gardner, John (Edmund) 1926- ..... CLC **30**
See also CA 103; CANR 15; MTCW

Gardner, Noel
See Kuttner, Henry

Gardons, S. S.
See Snodgrass, W(illiam) D(e Witt)

Garfield, Leon 1921- .... CLC **12**
See also AAYA 8; CA 17-20R; CANR 38,
41; CLR 21; JRDA; MAICYA; SATA 1,
32, 76

Garland, (Hannibal) Hamlin
1860-1940 .... TCLC **3; SSC 18**
See also CA 104; DLB 12, 71, 78

Garneau, (Hector de) Saint-Denys
1912-1943 .... TCLC **13**
See also CA 111; DLB 88

Garner, Alan 1934- .... CLC **17**
See also CA 73-76; CANR 15; CLR 20;
MAICYA; MTCW; SATA 18, 69

Garner, Hugh 1913-1979 .... CLC **13**
See also CA 69-72; CANR 31; DLB 68

Garnett, David 1892-1981 .... CLC **3**
See also CA 5-8R; 103; CANR 17; DLB 34

Garos, Stephanie
See Katz, Steve

Garrett, George (Palmer)
1929- .... CLC **3, 11, 51**
See also CA 1-4R; CAAS 5; CANR 1, 42;
DLB 2, 5, 130; DLBY 83

Garrick, David 1717-1779 .... LC **15**
See also DLB 84

Garrigue, Jean 1914-1972 .... CLC **2, 8**
See also CA 5-8R; 37-40R; CANR 20

Garrison, Frederick
See Sinclair, Upton (Beall)

Garth, Will
See Hamilton, Edmond; Kuttner, Henry

Garvey, Marcus (Moziah, Jr.)
1887-1940 .... TCLC **41; BLC**
See also BW 1; CA 120; 124

Gary, Romain .... CLC **25**
See also Kacew, Romain
See also DLB 83

Gascar, Pierre .... CLC **11**
See also Fournier, Pierre

Gascoyne, David (Emery) 1916- .... CLC **45**
See also CA 65-68; CANR 10, 28; DLB 20;
MTCW

Gaskell, Elizabeth Cleghorn
   1810-1865 .... NCLC 5
   See also CDBLB 1832-1890; DLB 21, 144
Gass, William H(oward)
   1924- ... CLC 1, 2, 8, 11, 15, 39; SSC 12
   See also CA 17-20R; CANR 30; DLB 2;
   MTCW
Gasset, Jose Ortega y
   See Ortega y Gasset, Jose
Gates, Henry Louis, Jr.   1950- ...... CLC 65
   See also BW 2; CA 109; CANR 25; DLB 67
Gautier, Theophile   1811-1872 ..... NCLC 1
   See also DLB 119
Gawsworth, John
   See Bates, H(erbert) E(rnest)
Gaye, Marvin (Penze)   1939-1984 ... CLC 26
   See also CA 112
Gebler, Carlo (Ernest)   1954- .... CLC 39
   See also CA 119; 133
Gee, Maggle (Mary)   1948- .... CLC 57
   See also CA 130
Gee, Maurice (Gough)   1931- ...... CLC 29
   See also CA 97-100; SATA 46
Gelbart, Larry (Simon)   1923- ... CLC 21, 61
   See also CA 73-76; CANR 45
Gelber, Jack   1932- .... CLC 1, 6, 14, 79
   See also CA 1-4R; CANR 2; DLB 7
Gellhorn, Martha (Ellis)   1908- ... CLC 14, 60
   See also CA 77-80; CANR 44; DLBY 82
Genet, Jean
   1910-1986 ... CLC 1, 2, 5, 10, 14, 44, 46
   See also CA 13-16R; CANR 18; DLB 72;
   DLBY 86; MTCW
Gent, Peter   1942- .... CLC 29
   See also AITN 1; CA 89-92; DLBY 82
Gentlewoman in New England, A
   See Bradstreet, Anne
Gentlewoman in Those Parts, A
   See Bradstreet, Anne
George, Jean Craighead   1919- ...... CLC 35
   See also AAYA 8; CA 5-8R; CANR 25;
   CLR 1; DLB 52; JRDA; MAICYA;
   SATA 2, 68
George, Stefan (Anton)
   1868-1933 .... TCLC 2, 14
   See also CA 104
Georges, Georges Martin
   See Simenon, Georges (Jacques Christian)
Gerhardi, William Alexander
   See Gerhardie, William Alexander
Gerhardie, William Alexander
   1895-1977 .... CLC 5
   See also CA 25-28R; 73-76; CANR 18;
   DLB 36
Gerstler, Amy   1956- .... CLC 70
Gertler, T. .... CLC 34
   See also CA 116; 121
Ghalib   1797-1869 .... NCLC 39
Ghelderode, Michel de
   1898-1962 .... CLC 6, 11
   See also CA 85-88; CANR 40
Ghiselin, Brewster   1903- .... CLC 23
   See also CA 13-16R; CAAS 10; CANR 13

Ghose, Zulfikar   1935- .... CLC 42
   See also CA 65-68
Ghosh, Amitav   1956- .... CLC 44
Giacosa, Giuseppe   1847-1906 ...... TCLC 7
   See also CA 104
Gibb, Lee
   See Waterhouse, Keith (Spencer)
Gibbon, Lewis Grassic .... TCLC 4
   See also Mitchell, James Leslie
Gibbons, Kaye   1960- .... CLC 50
Gibran, Kahlil
   1883-1931 .... TCLC 1, 9; PC 9
   See also CA 104
Gibson, William   1914- .... CLC 23; DA
   See also CA 9-12R; CANR 9, 42; DLB 7;
   SATA 66
Gibson, William (Ford)   1948- ... CLC 39, 63
   See also AAYA 12; CA 126; 133
Gide, Andre (Paul Guillaume)
   1869-1951 .... TCLC 5, 12, 36; DA;
                              SSC 13; WLC
   See also CA 104; 124; DLB 65; MTCW
Gifford, Barry (Colby)   1946- .... CLC 34
   See also CA 65-68; CANR 9, 30, 40
Gilbert, W(illiam) S(chwenck)
   1836-1911 .... TCLC 3
   See also CA 104; SATA 36
Gilbreth, Frank B., Jr.   1911- ...... CLC 17
   See also CA 9-12R; SATA 2
Gilchrist, Ellen   1935- .. CLC 34, 48; SSC 14
   See also CA 113; 116; CANR 41; DLB 130;
   MTCW
Giles, Molly   1942- .... CLC 39
   See also CA 126
Gill, Patrick
   See Creasey, John
Gilliam, Terry (Vance)   1940- .... CLC 21
   See also Monty Python
   See also CA 108; 113; CANR 35
Gillian, Jerry
   See Gilliam, Terry (Vance)
Gilliatt, Penelope (Ann Douglass)
   1932-1993 .... CLC 2, 10, 13, 53
   See also AITN 2; CA 13-16R; 141; DLB 14
Gilman, Charlotte (Anna) Perkins (Stetson)
   1860-1935 .... TCLC 9, 37; SSC 13
   See also CA 106
Gilmour, David   1949- .... CLC 35
   See also CA 138
Gilpin, William   1724-1804 .... NCLC 30
Gilray, J. D.
   See Mencken, H(enry) L(ouis)
Gilroy, Frank D(aniel)   1925- .... CLC 2
   See also CA 81-84; CANR 32; DLB 7
Ginsberg, Allen
   1926- ...... CLC 1, 2, 3, 4, 6, 13, 36, 69;
                              DA; PC 4; WLC 3
   See also AITN 1; CA 1-4R; CANR 2, 41;
   CDALB 1941-1968; DLB 5, 16; MTCW
Ginzburg, Natalia
   1916-1991 .... CLC 5, 11, 54, 70
   See also CA 85-88; 135; CANR 33; MTCW

Giono, Jean   1895-1970......... CLC 4, 11
   See also CA 45-48; 29-32R; CANR 2, 35;
   DLB 72; MTCW
Giovanni, Nikki
   1943- ...... CLC 2, 4, 19, 64; BLC; DA
   See also AITN 1; BW 2; CA 29-32R;
   CAAS 6; CANR 18, 41; CLR 6; DLB 5,
   41; MAICYA; MTCW; SATA 24
Giovene, Andrea   1904- .... CLC 7
   See also CA 85-88
Gippius, Zinaida (Nikolayevna)   1869-1945
   See Hippius, Zinaida
   See also CA 106
Giraudoux, (Hippolyte) Jean
   1882-1944 .... TCLC 2, 7
   See also CA 104; DLB 65
Gironella, Jose Maria   1917- .... CLC 11
   See also CA 101
Gissing, George (Robert)
   1857-1903 .... TCLC 3, 24, 47
   See also CA 105; DLB 18, 135
Giurlani, Aldo
   See Palazzeschi, Aldo
Gladkov, Fyodor (Vasilyevich)
   1883-1958 .... TCLC 27
Glanville, Brian (Lester)   1931- ...... CLC 6
   See also CA 5-8R; CAAS 9; CANR 3;
   DLB 15, 139; SATA 42
Glasgow, Ellen (Anderson Gholson)
   1873(?)-1945 .... TCLC 2, 7
   See also CA 104; DLB 9, 12
Glaspell, Susan (Keating)
   1882(?)-1948 .... TCLC 55
   See also CA 110; DLB 7, 9, 78; YABC 2
Glassco, John   1909-1981 .... CLC 9
   See also CA 13-16R; 102; CANR 15;
   DLB 68
Glasscock, Amnesia
   See Steinbeck, John (Ernst)
Glasser, Ronald J.   1940(?)- .... CLC 37
Glassman, Joyce
   See Johnson, Joyce
Glendinning, Victoria   1937- .... CLC 50
   See also CA 120; 127
Glissant, Edouard   1928- .... CLC 10, 68
Gloag, Julian   1930- .... CLC 40
   See also AITN 1; CA 65-68; CANR 10
Glowacki, Aleksander
   See Prus, Boleslaw
Glueck, Louise (Elisabeth)
   1943- .... CLC 7, 22, 44, 81
   See also CA 33-36R; CANR 40; DLB 5
Gobineau, Joseph Arthur (Comte) de
   1816-1882 .... NCLC 17
   See also DLB 123
Godard, Jean-Luc   1930-.......... CLC 20
   See also CA 93-96
Godden, (Margaret) Rumer   1907- ... CLC 53
   See also AAYA 6; CA 5-8R; CANR 4, 27,
   36; CLR 20; MAICYA; SAAS 12;
   SATA 3, 36
Godoy Alcayaga, Lucila   1889-1957
   See Mistral, Gabriela
   See also BW 2; CA 104; 131; HW; MTCW

Godwin, Gail (Kathleen)
1937- . . . . CLC 5, 8, 22, 31, 69
See also CA 29-32R; CANR 15, 43; DLB 6;
MTCW

Godwin, William 1756-1836 . . . . . . NCLC 14
See also CDBLB 1789-1832; DLB 39, 104,
142

Goethe, Johann Wolfgang von
1749-1832 . . . . NCLC 4, 22, 34; DA;
PC 5; WLC 3
See also DLB 94

Gogarty, Oliver St. John
1878-1957 . . . . TCLC 15
See also CA 109; DLB 15, 19

Gogol, Nikolai (Vasilyevich)
1809-1852 . . . . NCLC 5, 15, 31; DA;
DC 1; SSC 4; WLC

Goines, Donald
1937(?)-1974 . . . . CLC 80; BLC
See also AITN 1; BW 1; CA 124; 114;
DLB 33

Gold, Herbert 1924- . . . . CLC 4, 7, 14, 42
See also CA 9-12R; CANR 17, 45; DLB 2;
DLBY 81

Goldbarth, Albert 1948- . . . . CLC 5, 38
See also CA 53-56; CANR 6, 40; DLB 120

Goldberg, Anatol 1910-1982 . . . . CLC 34
See also CA 131; 117

Goldemberg, Isaac 1945- . . . . CLC 52
See also CA 69-72; CAAS 12; CANR 11,
32; HW

Golding, William (Gerald)
1911-1993 . . . . CLC 1, 2, 3, 8, 10, 17, 27,
58, 81; DA; WLC
See also AAYA 5; CA 5-8R; 141;
CANR 13, 33; CDBLB 1945-1960;
DLB 15, 100; MTCW

Goldman, Emma 1869-1940 . . . . TCLC 13
See also CA 110

Goldman, Francisco 1955- . . . . CLC 76

Goldman, William (W.) 1931- . . . . CLC 1, 48
See also CA 9-12R; CANR 29; DLB 44

Goldmann, Lucien 1913-1970 . . . . . . CLC 24
See also CA 25-28; CAP 2

Goldoni, Carlo 1707-1793 . . . . LC 4

Goldsberry, Steven 1949- . . . . CLC 34
See also CA 131

Goldsmith, Oliver
1728-1774 . . . . LC 2; DA; WLC
See also CDBLB 1660-1789; DLB 39, 89,
104, 109, 142; SATA 26

Goldsmith, Peter
See Priestley, J(ohn) B(oynton)

Gombrowicz, Witold
1904-1969 . . . . CLC 4, 7, 11, 49
See also CA 19-20; 25-28R; CAP 2

Gomez de la Serna, Ramon
1888-1963 . . . . CLC 9
See also CA 116; HW

Goncharov, Ivan Alexandrovich
1812-1891 . . . . NCLC 1

Goncourt, Edmond (Louis Antoine Huot) de
1822-1896 . . . . NCLC 7
See also DLB 123

Goncourt, Jules (Alfred Huot) de
1830-1870 . . . . NCLC 7
See also DLB 123

Gontier, Fernande 19(?)- . . . . CLC 50

Goodman, Paul 1911-1972 . . . . CLC 1, 2, 4, 7
See also CA 19-20; 37-40R; CANR 34;
CAP 2; DLB 130; MTCW

Gordimer, Nadine
1923- . . . . CLC 3, 5, 7, 10, 18, 33, 51, 70;
DA; SSC 17
See also CA 5-8R; CANR 3, 28; MTCW

Gordon, Adam Lindsay
1833-1870 . . . . NCLC 21

Gordon, Caroline
1895-1981 . . . CLC 6, 13, 29, 83; SSC 15
See also CA 11-12; 103; CANR 36; CAP 1;
DLB 4, 9, 102; DLBY 81; MTCW

Gordon, Charles William 1860-1937
See Connor, Ralph
See also CA 109

Gordon, Mary (Catherine)
1949- . . . . CLC 13, 22
See also CA 102; CANR 44; DLB 6;
DLBY 81; MTCW

Gordon, Sol 1923- . . . . CLC 26
See also CA 53-56; CANR 4; SATA 11

Gordone, Charles 1925- . . . . CLC 1, 4
See also BW 1; CA 93-96; DLB 7; MTCW

Gorenko, Anna Andreevna
See Akhmatova, Anna

Gorky, Maxim . . . . TCLC 8; WLC
See also Peshkov, Alexei Maximovich

Goryan, Sirak
See Saroyan, William

Gosse, Edmund (William)
1849-1928 . . . . TCLC 28
See also CA 117; DLB 57, 144

Gotlieb, Phyllis Fay (Bloom)
1926- . . . . CLC 18
See also CA 13-16R; CANR 7; DLB 88

Gottesman, S. D.
See Kornbluth, C(yril) M.; Pohl, Frederik

Gottfried von Strassburg
fl. c. 1210- . . . . CMLC 10
See also DLB 138

Gould, Lois . . . . CLC 4, 10
See also CA 77-80; CANR 29; MTCW

Gourmont, Remy de 1858-1915 . . . . TCLC 17
See also CA 109

Govier, Katherine 1948- . . . . CLC 51
See also CA 101; CANR 18, 40

Goyen, (Charles) William
1915-1983 . . . . CLC 5, 8, 14, 40
See also AITN 2; CA 5-8R; 110; CANR 6;
DLB 2; DLBY 83

Goytisolo, Juan
1931- . . . . CLC 5, 10, 23; HLC
See also CA 85-88; CANR 32; HW; MTCW

Gozzano, Guido 1883-1916 . . . . PC 10
See also DLB 114

Gozzi, (Conte) Carlo 1720-1806 . . NCLC 23

Grabbe, Christian Dietrich
1801-1836 . . . . NCLC 2
See also DLB 133

Grace, Patricia 1937- . . . . CLC 56

Gracian y Morales, Baltasar
1601-1658 . . . . LC 15

Gracq, Julien . . . . CLC 11, 48
See also Poirier, Louis
See also DLB 83

Grade, Chaim 1910-1982 . . . . CLC 10
See also CA 93-96; 107

Graduate of Oxford, A
See Ruskin, John

Graham, John
See Phillips, David Graham

Graham, Jorie 1951- . . . . CLC 48
See also CA 111; DLB 120

Graham, R(obert) B(ontine) Cunninghame
See Cunninghame Graham, R(obert)
B(ontine)
See also DLB 98, 135

Graham, Robert
See Haldeman, Joe (William)

Graham, Tom
See Lewis, (Harry) Sinclair

Graham, W(illiam) S(ydney)
1918-1986 . . . . CLC 29
See also CA 73-76; 118; DLB 20

Graham, Winston (Mawdsley)
1910- . . . . CLC 23
See also CA 49-52; CANR 2, 22, 45;
DLB 77

Grant, Skeeter
See Spiegelman, Art

Granville-Barker, Harley
1877-1946 . . . . TCLC 2
See also Barker, Harley Granville
See also CA 104

Grass, Guenter (Wilhelm)
1927- . . . . . CLC 1, 2, 4, 6, 11, 15, 22, 32,
49; DA; WLC
See also CA 13-16R; CANR 20; DLB 75,
124; MTCW

Gratton, Thomas
See Hulme, T(homas) E(rnest)

Grau, Shirley Ann
1929- . . . . CLC 4, 9; SSC 15
See also CA 89-92; CANR 22; DLB 2;
MTCW

Gravel, Fern
See Hall, James Norman

Graver, Elizabeth 1964- . . . . CLC 70
See also CA 135

Graves, Richard Perceval 1945- . . . . CLC 44
See also CA 65-68; CANR 9, 26

Graves, Robert (von Ranke)
1895-1985 . . . . . . CLC 1, 2, 6, 11, 39, 44,
45; PC 6
See also CA 5-8R; 117; CANR 5, 36;
CDBLB 1914-1945; DLB 20, 100;
DLBY 85; MTCW; SATA 45

Gray, Alasdair (James) 1934- . . . . . . CLC 41
See also CA 126; CANR 47; MTCW

Gray, Amlin 1946- . . . . CLC 29
See also CA 138

Gray, Francine du Plessix 1930- . . . . CLC 22
See also BEST 90:3; CA 61-64; CAAS 2;
CANR 11, 33; MTCW

Gray, John (Henry) 1866-1934 . . . . **TCLC 19**
See also CA 119

Gray, Simon (James Holliday)
1936- . . . . **CLC 9, 14, 36**
See also AITN 1; CA 21-24R; CAAS 3;
CANR 32; DLB 13; MTCW

Gray, Spalding 1941- . . . . **CLC 49**
See also CA 128

Gray, Thomas
1716-1771 . . . . . . **LC 4; DA; PC 2; WLC**
See also CDBLB 1660-1789; DLB 109

Grayson, David
See Baker, Ray Stannard

Grayson, Richard (A.) 1951- . . . . **CLC 38**
See also CA 85-88; CANR 14, 31

Greeley, Andrew M(oran) 1928- . . . . **CLC 28**
See also CA 5-8R; CAAS 7; CANR 7, 43;
MTCW

Green, Brian
See Card, Orson Scott

Green, Hannah
See Greenberg, Joanne (Goldenberg)

Green, Hannah . . . . **CLC 3**
See also CA 73-76

Green, Henry . . . . **CLC 2, 13**
See also Yorke, Henry Vincent
See also DLB 15

Green, Julian (Hartridge) 1900-
See Green, Julien
See also CA 21-24R; CANR 33; DLB 4, 72;
MTCW

Green, Julien . . . . **CLC 3, 11, 77**
See also Green, Julian (Hartridge)

Green, Paul (Eliot) 1894-1981 . . . . . . **CLC 25**
See also AITN 1; CA 5-8R; 103; CANR 3;
DLB 7, 9; DLBY 81

Greenberg, Ivan 1908-1973
See Rahv, Philip
See also CA 85-88

Greenberg, Joanne (Goldenberg)
1932- . . . . **CLC 7, 30**
See also AAYA 12; CA 5-8R; CANR 14,
32; SATA 25

Greenberg, Richard 1959(?)- . . . . **CLC 57**
See also CA 138

Greene, Bette 1934- . . . . **CLC 30**
See also AAYA 7; CA 53-56; CANR 4;
CLR 2; JRDA; MAICYA; SAAS 16;
SATA 8

Greene, Gael . . . . **CLC 8**
See also CA 13-16R; CANR 10

Greene, Graham
1904-1991 . . . . **CLC 1, 3, 6, 9, 14, 18, 27,
37, 70, 72; DA; WLC**
See also AITN 2; CA 13-16R; 133;
CANR 35; CDBLB 1945-1960; DLB 13,
15, 77, 100; DLBY 91; MTCW; SATA 20

Greer, Richard
See Silverberg, Robert

Greer, Richard
See Silverberg, Robert

Gregor, Arthur 1923- . . . . **CLC 9**
See also CA 25-28R; CAAS 10; CANR 11;
SATA 36

Gregor, Lee
See Pohl, Frederik

Gregory, Isabella Augusta (Persse)
1852-1932 . . . . **TCLC 1**
See also CA 104; DLB 10

Gregory, J. Dennis
See Williams, John A(lfred)

Grendon, Stephen
See Derleth, August (William)

Grenville, Kate 1950- . . . . **CLC 61**
See also CA 118

Grenville, Pelham
See Wodehouse, P(elham) G(renville)

Greve, Felix Paul (Berthold Friedrich)
1879-1948
See Grove, Frederick Philip
See also CA 104; 141

Grey, Zane 1872-1939 . . . . **TCLC 6**
See also CA 104; 132; DLB 9; MTCW

Grieg, (Johan) Nordahl (Brun)
1902-1943 . . . . **TCLC 10**
See also CA 107

Grieve, C(hristopher) M(urray)
1892-1978 . . . . **CLC 11, 19**
See also MacDiarmid, Hugh
See also CA 5-8R; 85-88; CANR 33;
MTCW

Griffin, Gerald 1803-1840 . . . . **NCLC 7**

Griffin, John Howard 1920-1980 . . . . **CLC 68**
See also AITN 1; CA 1-4R; 101; CANR 2

Griffin, Peter 1942- . . . . **CLC 39**
See also CA 136

Griffiths, Trevor 1935- . . . . **CLC 13, 52**
See also CA 97-100; CANR 45; DLB 13

Grigson, Geoffrey (Edward Harvey)
1905-1985 . . . . **CLC 7, 39**
See also CA 25-28R; 118; CANR 20, 33;
DLB 27; MTCW

Grillparzer, Franz 1791-1872 . . . . . . **NCLC 1**
See also DLB 133

Grimble, Reverend Charles James
See Eliot, T(homas) S(tearns)

Grimke, Charlotte L(ottie) Forten
1837(?)-1914
See Forten, Charlotte L.
See also BW 1; CA 117; 124

Grimm, Jacob Ludwig Karl
1785-1863 . . . . **NCLC 3**
See also DLB 90; MAICYA; SATA 22

Grimm, Wilhelm Karl 1786-1859 . . **NCLC 3**
See also DLB 90; MAICYA; SATA 22

Grimmelshausen, Johann Jakob Christoffel
von 1621-1676 . . . . **LC 6**

Grindel, Eugene 1895-1952
See Eluard, Paul
See also CA 104

Grisham, John 1955- . . . . **CLC 84**
See also AAYA 14; CA 138; CANR 47

Grossman, David 1954- . . . . **CLC 67**
See also CA 138

Grossman, Vasily (Semenovich)
1905-1964 . . . . **CLC 41**
See also CA 124; 130; MTCW

Grove, Frederick Philip . . . . **TCLC 4**
See also Greve, Felix Paul (Berthold
Friedrich)
See also DLB 92

Grubb
See Crumb, R(obert)

Grumbach, Doris (Isaac)
1918- . . . . **CLC 13, 22, 64**
See also CA 5-8R; CAAS 2; CANR 9, 42

Grundtvig, Nicolai Frederik Severin
1783-1872 . . . . **NCLC 1**

Grunge
See Crumb, R(obert)

Grunwald, Lisa 1959- . . . . **CLC 44**
See also CA 120

Guare, John 1938- . . . . **CLC 8, 14, 29, 67**
See also CA 73-76; CANR 21; DLB 7;
MTCW

Gudjonsson, Halldor Kiljan 1902-
See Laxness, Halldor
See also CA 103

Guenter, Erich
See Eich, Guenter

Guest, Barbara 1920- . . . . **CLC 34**
See also CA 25-28R; CANR 11, 44; DLB 5

Guest, Judith (Ann) 1936- . . . . **CLC 8, 30**
See also AAYA 7; CA 77-80; CANR 15;
MTCW

Guevara, Che . . . . **CLC 87; HLC**
See also Guevara (Serna), Ernesto

Guevara (Serna), Ernesto 1928-1967
See Guevara, Che
See also CA 127; 111; HW

Guild, Nicholas M. 1944- . . . . **CLC 33**
See also CA 93-96

Guillemin, Jacques
See Sartre, Jean-Paul

Guillen, Jorge 1893-1984 . . . . **CLC 11**
See also CA 89-92; 112; DLB 108; HW

Guillen (y Batista), Nicolas (Cristobal)
1902-1989 . . . . . **CLC 48, 79; BLC; HLC**
See also BW 2; CA 116; 125; 129; HW

Guillevic, (Eugene) 1907- . . . . **CLC 33**
See also CA 93-96

Guillois
See Desnos, Robert

Guiney, Louise Imogen
1861-1920 . . . . **TCLC 41**
See also DLB 54

Guiraldes, Ricardo (Guillermo)
1886-1927 . . . . **TCLC 39**
See also CA 131; HW; MTCW

Gunn, Bill . . . . **CLC 5**
See also Gunn, William Harrison
See also DLB 38

Gunn, Thom(son William)
1929- . . . . **CLC 3, 6, 18, 32, 81**
See also CA 17-20R; CANR 9, 33;
CDBLB 1960 to Present; DLB 27;
MTCW

Gunn, William Harrison 1934(?)-1989
See Gunn, Bill
See also AITN 1; BW 1; CA 13-16R; 128;
CANR 12, 25

Gunnars, Kristjana 1948-......... **CLC 69**
See also CA 113; DLB 60

Gurganus, Allan 1947-............ **CLC 70**
See also BEST 90:1; CA 135

Gurney, A(lbert) R(amsdell), Jr.
1930-................ **CLC 32, 50, 54**
See also CA 77-80; CANR 32

Gurney, Ivor (Bertie) 1890-1937... **TCLC 33**

Gurney, Peter
See Gurney, A(lbert) R(amsdell), Jr.

Guro, Elena 1877-1913.......... **TCLC 56**

Gustafson, Ralph (Barker) 1909-.... **CLC 36**
See also CA 21-24R; CANR 8, 45; DLB 88

Gut, Gom
See Simenon, Georges (Jacques Christian)

Guthrie, A(lfred) B(ertram), Jr.
1901-1991 .... **CLC 23**
See also CA 57-60; 134; CANR 24; DLB 6;
SATA 62; SATA-Obit 67

Guthrie, Isobel
See Grieve, C(hristopher) M(urray)

Guthrie, Woodrow Wilson 1912-1967
See Guthrie, Woody
See also CA 113; 93-96

Guthrie, Woody................... **CLC 35**
See also Guthrie, Woodrow Wilson

Guy, Rosa (Cuthbert) 1928-........ **CLC 26**
See also AAYA 4; BW 2; CA 17-20R;
CANR 14, 34; CLR 13; DLB 33; JRDA;
MAICYA; SATA 14, 62

Gwendolyn
See Bennett, (Enoch) Arnold

H. D. .... **CLC 3, 8, 14, 31, 34, 73; PC 5**
See also Doolittle, Hilda

H. de V.
See Buchan, John

Haavikko, Paavo Juhani
1931-..................... **CLC 18, 34**
See also CA 106

Habbema, Koos
See Heijermans, Herman

Hacker, Marilyn 1942- .... **CLC 5, 9, 23, 72**
See also CA 77-80; DLB 120

Haggard, H(enry) Rider
1856-1925 .... **TCLC 11**
See also CA 108; DLB 70; SATA 16

Haig, Fenil
See Ford, Ford Madox

Haig-Brown, Roderick (Langmere)
1908-1976 .... **CLC 21**
See also CA 5-8R; 69-72; CANR 4, 38;
CLR 31; DLB 88; MAICYA; SATA 12

Hailey, Arthur 1920- .... **CLC 5**
See also AITN 2; BEST 90:3; CA 1-4R;
CANR 2, 36; DLB 88; DLBY 82; MTCW

Hailey, Elizabeth Forsythe 1938-... **CLC 40**
See also CA 93-96; CAAS 1; CANR 15

Haines, John (Meade) 1924-....... **CLC 58**
See also CA 17-20R; CANR 13, 34; DLB 5

Haldeman, Joe (William) 1943-..... **CLC 61**
See also CA 53-56; CANR 6; DLB 8

Haley, Alex(ander Murray Palmer)
1921-1992 .... **CLC 8, 12, 76; BLC; DA**
See also BW 2; CA 77-80; 136; DLB 38;
MTCW

Haliburton, Thomas Chandler
1796-1865 .... **NCLC 15**
See also DLB 11, 99

Hall, Donald (Andrew, Jr.)
1928-.............. **CLC 1, 13, 37, 59**
See also CA 5-8R; CAAS 7; CANR 2, 44;
DLB 5; SATA 23

Hall, Frederic Sauser
See Sauser-Hall, Frederic

Hall, James
See Kuttner, Henry

Hall, James Norman 1887-1951 ... **TCLC 23**
See also CA 123; SATA 21

Hall, (Marguerite) Radclyffe
1886(?)-1943 .... **TCLC 12**
See also CA 110

Hall, Rodney 1935- .... **CLC 51**
See also CA 109

Halleck, Fitz-Greene 1790-1867 .. **NCLC 47**
See also DLB 3

Halliday, Michael
See Creasey, John

Halpern, Daniel 1945- .... **CLC 14**
See also CA 33-36R

Hamburger, Michael (Peter Leopold)
1924-..................... **CLC 5, 14**
See also CA 5-8R; CAAS 4; CANR 2, 47;
DLB 27

Hamill, Pete 1935-............... **CLC 10**
See also CA 25-28R; CANR 18

Hamilton, Alexander
1755(?)-1804 .... **NCLC 49**
See also DLB 37

Hamilton, Clive
See Lewis, C(live) S(taples)

Hamilton, Edmond 1904-1977....... **CLC 1**
See also CA 1-4R; CANR 3; DLB 8

Hamilton, Eugene (Jacob) Lee
See Lee-Hamilton, Eugene (Jacob)

Hamilton, Franklin
See Silverberg, Robert

Hamilton, Gail
See Corcoran, Barbara

Hamilton, Mollie
See Kaye, M(ary) M(argaret)

Hamilton, (Anthony Walter) Patrick
1904-1962 .... **CLC 51**
See also CA 113; DLB 10

Hamilton, Virginia 1936-........ **CLC 26**
See also AAYA 2; BW 2; CA 25-28R;
CANR 20, 37; CLR 1, 11; DLB 33, 52;
JRDA; MAICYA; MTCW; SATA 4, 56,
79

Hammett, (Samuel) Dashiell
1894-1961 .... **CLC 3, 5, 10, 19, 47;
SSC 17**
See also AITN 1; CA 81-84; CANR 42;
CDALB 1929-1941; DLBD 6; MTCW

Hammon, Jupiter
1711(?)-1800(?) .... **NCLC 5; BLC**
See also DLB 31, 50

Hammond, Keith
See Kuttner, Henry

Hamner, Earl (Henry), Jr. 1923- ... **CLC 12**
See also AITN 2; CA 73-76; DLB 6

Hampton, Christopher (James)
1946-........................ **CLC 4**
See also CA 25-28R; DLB 13; MTCW

Hamsun, Knut.............. **TCLC 2, 14, 49**
See also Pedersen, Knut

Handke, Peter 1942- .. **CLC 5, 8, 10, 15, 38**
See also CA 77-80; CANR 33; DLB 85,
124; MTCW

Hanley, James 1901-1985 ... **CLC 3, 5, 8, 13**
See also CA 73-76; 117; CANR 36; MTCW

Hannah, Barry 1942-.......... **CLC 23, 38**
See also CA 108; 110; CANR 43; DLB 6;
MTCW

Hannon, Ezra
See Hunter, Evan

Hansberry, Lorraine (Vivian)
1930-1965 ...... **CLC 17, 62; BLC; DA;
DC 2**
See also BW 1; CA 109; 25-28R; CABS 3;
CDALB 1941-1968; DLB 7, 38; MTCW

Hansen, Joseph 1923-............. **CLC 38**
See also CA 29-32R; CAAS 17; CANR 16,
44

Hansen, Martin A. 1909-1955..... **TCLC 32**

Hanson, Kenneth O(stlin) 1922- .... **CLC 13**
See also CA 53-56; CANR 7

Hardwick, Elizabeth 1916- .... **CLC 13**
See also CA 5-8R; CANR 3, 32; DLB 6;
MTCW

Hardy, Thomas
1840-1928 ...... **TCLC 4, 10, 18, 32, 48,
53; DA; PC 8; SSC 2; WLC**
See also CA 104; 123; CDBLB 1890-1914;
DLB 18, 19, 135; MTCW

Hare, David 1947- .... **CLC 29, 58**
See also CA 97-100; CANR 39; DLB 13;
MTCW

Harford, Henry
See Hudson, W(illiam) H(enry)

Hargrave, Leonie
See Disch, Thomas M(ichael)

Harjo, Joy 1951- .... **CLC 83**
See also CA 114; CANR 35; DLB 120;
NNAL

Harlan, Louis R(udolph) 1922-..... **CLC 34**
See also CA 21-24R; CANR 25

Harling, Robert 1951(?)- .... **CLC 53**

Harmon, William (Ruth) 1938-..... **CLC 38**
See also CA 33-36R; CANR 14, 32, 35;
SATA 65

Harper, F. E. W.
See Harper, Frances Ellen Watkins

Harper, Frances E. W.
See Harper, Frances Ellen Watkins

Harper, Frances E. Watkins
See Harper, Frances Ellen Watkins

Harper, Frances Ellen
See Harper, Frances Ellen Watkins

Harper, Frances Ellen Watkins
1825-1911 . . . . **TCLC 14; BLC**
See also BW 1; CA 111; 125; DLB 50

Harper, Michael S(teven) 1938- . . **CLC 7, 22**
See also BW 1; CA 33-36R; CANR 24;
DLB 41

Harper, Mrs. F. E. W.
See Harper, Frances Ellen Watkins

Harris, Christie (Lucy) Irwin
1907- . . . . **CLC 12**
See also CA 5-8R; CANR 6; DLB 88;
JRDA; MAICYA; SAAS 10; SATA 6, 74

Harris, Frank 1856(?)-1931 . . . . **TCLC 24**
See also CA 109

Harris, George Washington
1814-1869 . . . . **NCLC 23**
See also DLB 3, 11

Harris, Joel Chandler 1848-1908 . . . **TCLC 2**
See also CA 104; 137; DLB 11, 23, 42, 78,
91; MAICYA; YABC 1

Harris, John (Wyndham Parkes Lucas)
Beynon 1903-1969
See Wyndham, John
See also CA 102; 89-92

Harris, MacDonald . . . . **CLC 9**
See also Heiney, Donald (William)

Harris, Mark 1922- . . . . **CLC 19**
See also CA 5-8R; CAAS 3; CANR 2;
DLB 2; DLBY 80

Harris, (Theodore) Wilson 1921- . . . . **CLC 25**
See also BW 2; CA 65-68; CAAS 16;
CANR 11, 27; DLB 117; MTCW

Harrison, Elizabeth Cavanna 1909-
See Cavanna, Betty
See also CA 9-12R; CANR 6, 27

Harrison, Harry (Max) 1925- . . . . . . **CLC 42**
See also CA 1-4R; CANR 5, 21; DLB 8;
SATA 4

Harrison, James (Thomas)
1937- . . . . **CLC 6, 14, 33, 66**
See also CA 13-16R; CANR 8; DLBY 82

Harrison, Jim
See Harrison, James (Thomas)

Harrison, Kathryn 1961- . . . . **CLC 70**
See also CA 144

Harrison, Tony 1937- . . . . **CLC 43**
See also CA 65-68; CANR 44; DLB 40;
MTCW

Harriss, Will(ard Irvin) 1922- . . . . . . **CLC 34**
See also CA 111

Harson, Sley
See Ellison, Harlan (Jay)

Hart, Ellis
See Ellison, Harlan (Jay)

Hart, Josephine 1942(?)- . . . . **CLC 70**
See also CA 138

Hart, Moss 1904-1961 . . . . **CLC 66**
See also CA 109; 89-92; DLB 7

Harte, (Francis) Bret(t)
1836(?)-1902 . . . . **TCLC 1, 25; DA;**
SSC 8; WLC
See also CA 104; 140; CDALB 1865-1917;
DLB 12, 64, 74, 79; SATA 26

Hartley, L(eslie) P(oles)
1895-1972 . . . . **CLC 2, 22**
See also CA 45-48; 37-40R; CANR 33;
DLB 15, 139; MTCW

Hartman, Geoffrey H. 1929- . . . . **CLC 27**
See also CA 117; 125; DLB 67

Haruf, Kent 19(?)- . . . . **CLC 34**

Harwood, Ronald 1934- . . . . **CLC 32**
See also CA 1-4R; CANR 4; DLB 13

Hasek, Jaroslav (Matej Frantisek)
1883-1923 . . . . **TCLC 4**
See also CA 104; 129; MTCW

Hass, Robert 1941- . . . . **CLC 18, 39**
See also CA 111; CANR 30; DLB 105

Hastings, Hudson
See Kuttner, Henry

Hastings, Selina . . . . **CLC 44**

Hatteras, Amelia
See Mencken, H(enry) L(ouis)

Hatteras, Owen . . . . **TCLC 18**
See also Mencken, H(enry) L(ouis); Nathan,
George Jean

Hauptmann, Gerhart (Johann Robert)
1862-1946 . . . . **TCLC 4**
See also CA 104; DLB 66, 118

Havel, Vaclav 1936- . . . . **CLC 25, 58, 65**
See also CA 104; CANR 36; MTCW

Haviaras, Stratis . . . . **CLC 33**
See also Chaviaras, Strates

Hawes, Stephen 1475(?)-1523(?) . . . . . **LC 17**

Hawkes, John (Clendennin Burne, Jr.)
1925- . . . . . . **CLC 1, 2, 3, 4, 7, 9, 14, 15,**
27, 49
See also CA 1-4R; CANR 2, 47; DLB 2, 7;
DLBY 80; MTCW

Hawking, S. W.
See Hawking, Stephen W(illiam)

Hawking, Stephen W(illiam)
1942- . . . . **CLC 63**
See also AAYA 13; BEST 89:1; CA 126;
129

Hawthorne, Julian 1846-1934 . . . . . **TCLC 25**

Hawthorne, Nathaniel
1804-1864 . . . . . . **NCLC 39; DA; SSC 3;**
WLC
See also CDALB 1640-1865; DLB 1, 74;
YABC 2

Haxton, Josephine Ayres 1921-
See Douglas, Ellen
See also CA 115; CANR 41

Hayaseca y Eizaguirre, Jorge
See Echegaray (y Eizaguirre), Jose (Maria
Waldo)

Hayashi Fumiko 1904-1951 . . . . . . **TCLC 27**

Haycraft, Anna
See Ellis, Alice Thomas
See also CA 122

Hayden, Robert E(arl)
1913-1980 . . . . . . **CLC 5, 9, 14, 37; BLC;**
DA; PC 6
See also BW 1; CA 69-72; 97-100; CABS 2;
CANR 24; CDALB 1941-1968; DLB 5,
76; MTCW; SATA 19; SATA-Obit 26

Hayford, J(oseph) E(phraim) Casely
See Casely-Hayford, J(oseph) E(phraim)

Hayman, Ronald 1932- . . . . **CLC 44**
See also CA 25-28R; CANR 18

Haywood, Eliza (Fowler)
1693(?)-1756 . . . . **LC 1**

Hazlitt, William 1778-1830 . . . . . **NCLC 29**
See also DLB 110

Hazzard, Shirley 1931- . . . . **CLC 18**
See also CA 9-12R; CANR 4; DLBY 82;
MTCW

Head, Bessie 1937-1986 . . . **CLC 25, 67; BLC**
See also BW 2; CA 29-32R; 119; CANR 25;
DLB 117; MTCW

Headon, (Nicky) Topper 1956(?)- . . . **CLC 30**

Heaney, Seamus (Justin)
1939- . . . . **CLC 5, 7, 14, 25, 37, 74**
See also CA 85-88; CANR 25;
CDBLB 1960 to Present; DLB 40;
MTCW

Hearn, (Patricio) Lafcadio (Tessima Carlos)
1850-1904 . . . . **TCLC 9**
See also CA 105; DLB 12, 78

Hearne, Vicki 1946- . . . . **CLC 56**
See also CA 139

Hearon, Shelby 1931- . . . . **CLC 63**
See also AITN 2; CA 25-28R; CANR 18

Heat-Moon, William Least . . . . **CLC 29**
See also Trogdon, William (Lewis)
See also AAYA 9

Hebbel, Friedrich 1813-1863 . . . . . **NCLC 43**
See also DLB 129

Hebert, Anne 1916- . . . . **CLC 4, 13, 29**
See also CA 85-88; DLB 68; MTCW

Hecht, Anthony (Evan)
1923- . . . . **CLC 8, 13, 19**
See also CA 9-12R; CANR 6; DLB 5

Hecht, Ben 1894-1964 . . . . **CLC 8**
See also CA 85-88; DLB 7, 9, 25, 26, 28, 86

Hedayat, Sadeq 1903-1951 . . . . **TCLC 21**
See also CA 120

Hegel, Georg Wilhelm Friedrich
1770-1831 . . . . **NCLC 46**
See also DLB 90

Heidegger, Martin 1889-1976 . . . . . . **CLC 24**
See also CA 81-84; 65-68; CANR 34;
MTCW

Heidenstam, (Carl Gustaf) Verner von
1859-1940 . . . . **TCLC 5**
See also CA 104

Heifner, Jack 1946- . . . . **CLC 11**
See also CA 105; CANR 47

Heijermans, Herman 1864-1924 . . . **TCLC 24**
See also CA 123

Heilbrun, Carolyn G(old) 1926- . . . . . **CLC 25**
See also CA 45-48; CANR 1, 28

Heine, Heinrich 1797-1856 . . . . **NCLC 4**
See also DLB 90

Heinemann, Larry (Curtiss) 1944- . . **CLC 50**
See also CA 110; CANR 31; DLBD 9

Heiney, Donald (William) 1921-1993
See Harris, MacDonald
See also CA 1-4R; 142; CANR 3

Heinlein, Robert A(nson)
1907-1988 . . . . . . **CLC 1, 3, 8, 14, 26, 55**
See also CA 1-4R; 125; CANR 1, 20;
DLB 8; JRDA; MAICYA; MTCW;
SATA 9, 69; SATA-Obit 56

Helforth, John
See Doolittle, Hilda

Hellenhofferu, Vojtech Kapristian z
See Hasek, Jaroslav (Matej Frantisek)

Heller, Joseph
1923- . . . . **CLC 1, 3, 5, 8, 11, 36, 63; DA;**
WLC
See also AITN 1; CA 5-8R; CABS 1;
CANR 8, 42; DLB 2, 28; DLBY 80;
MTCW

Hellman, Lillian (Florence)
1906-1984 . . . . . . **CLC 2, 4, 8, 14, 18, 34,**
44, 52; DC 1
See also AITN 1, 2; CA 13-16R; 112;
CANR 33; DLB 7; DLBY 84; MTCW

Helprin, Mark 1947- . . . . . **CLC 7, 10, 22, 32**
See also CA 81-84; CANR 47; DLBY 85;
MTCW

Helvetius, Claude-Adrien
1715-1771 . . . . **LC 26**

Helyar, Jane Penelope Josephine 1933-
See Poole, Josephine
See also CA 21-24R; CANR 10, 26

Hemans, Felicia 1793-1835 . . . . . . **NCLC 29**
See also DLB 96

Hemingway, Ernest (Miller)
1899-1961 . . . . **CLC 1, 3, 6, 8, 10, 13, 19,**
30, 34, 39, 41, 44, 50, 61, 80; DA; SSC 1;
WLC
See also CA 77-80; CANR 34;
CDALB 1917-1929; DLB 4, 9, 102;
DLBD 1; DLBY 81, 87; MTCW

Hempel, Amy 1951- . . . . **CLC 39**
See also CA 118; 137

Henderson, F. C.
See Mencken, H(enry) L(ouis)

Henderson, Sylvia
See Ashton-Warner, Sylvia (Constance)

Henley, Beth . . . . **CLC 23**
See also Henley, Elizabeth Becker
See also CABS 3; DLBY 86

Henley, Elizabeth Becker 1952-
See Henley, Beth
See also CA 107; CANR 32; MTCW

Henley, William Ernest
1849-1903 . . . . **TCLC 8**
See also CA 105; DLB 19

Hennissart, Martha
See Lathen, Emma
See also CA 85-88

Henry, O. . . . . **TCLC 1, 19; SSC 5; WLC**
See also Porter, William Sydney

Henry, Patrick 1736- . . . . **LC 25**
See also CA 145

Henryson, Robert 1430(?)-1506(?). . . . **LC 20**
See also DLB 146

Henry VIII 1491-1547 . . . . **LC 10**

Henschke, Alfred
See Klabund

Hentoff, Nat(han Irving) 1925- . . . . . **CLC 26**
See also AAYA 4; CA 1-4R; CAAS 6;
CANR 5, 25; CLR 1; JRDA; MAICYA;
SATA 42, 69; SATA-Brief 27

Heppenstall, (John) Rayner
1911-1981 . . . . **CLC 10**
See also CA 1-4R; 103; CANR 29

Herbert, Frank (Patrick)
1920-1986 . . . . . . **CLC 12, 23, 35, 44, 85**
See also CA 53-56; 118; CANR 5, 43;
DLB 8; MTCW; SATA 9, 37;
SATA-Obit 47

Herbert, George 1593-1633 . . . . **LC 24; PC 4**
See also CDBLB Before 1660; DLB 126

Herbert, Zbigniew 1924- . . . . **CLC 9, 43**
See also CA 89-92; CANR 36; MTCW

Herbst, Josephine (Frey)
1897-1969 . . . . **CLC 34**
See also CA 5-8R; 25-28R; DLB 9

Hergesheimer, Joseph
1880-1954 . . . . **TCLC 11**
See also CA 109; DLB 102, 9

Herlihy, James Leo 1927-1993 . . . . . . **CLC 6**
See also CA 1-4R; 143; CANR 2

Hermogenes fl. c. 175- . . . . **CMLC 6**

Hernandez, Jose 1834-1886 . . . . . . **NCLC 17**

Herrick, Robert
1591-1674 . . . . **LC 13; DA; PC 9**
See also DLB 126

Herring, Guilles
See Somerville, Edith

Herriot, James 1916- . . . . **CLC 12**
See also Wight, James Alfred
See also AAYA 1; CANR 40

Herrmann, Dorothy 1941- . . . . **CLC 44**
See also CA 107

Herrmann, Taffy
See Herrmann, Dorothy

Hersey, John (Richard)
1914-1993 . . . . **CLC 1, 2, 7, 9, 40, 81**
See also CA 17-20R; 140; CANR 33;
DLB 6; MTCW; SATA 25;
SATA-Obit 76

Herzen, Aleksandr Ivanovich
1812-1870 . . . . **NCLC 10**

Herzl, Theodor 1860-1904 . . . . **TCLC 36**

Herzog, Werner 1942- . . . . **CLC 16**
See also CA 89-92

Hesiod c. 8th cent. B.C.- . . . . **CMLC 5**

Hesse, Hermann
1877-1962 . . . . **CLC 1, 2, 3, 6, 11, 17, 25,**
69; DA; SSC 9; WLC
See also CA 17-18; CAP 2; DLB 66;
MTCW; SATA 50

Hewes, Cady
See De Voto, Bernard (Augustine)

Heyen, William 1940- . . . . **CLC 13, 18**
See also CA 33-36R; CAAS 9; DLB 5

Heyerdahl, Thor 1914- . . . . **CLC 26**
See also CA 5-8R; CANR 5, 22; MTCW;
SATA 2, 52

Heym, Georg (Theodor Franz Arthur)
1887-1912 . . . . **TCLC 9**
See also CA 106

Heym, Stefan 1913- . . . . **CLC 41**
See also CA 9-12R; CANR 4; DLB 69

Heyse, Paul (Johann Ludwig von)
1830-1914 . . . . **TCLC 8**
See also CA 104; DLB 129

Heyward, (Edwin) DuBose
1885-1940 . . . . **TCLC 59**
See also CA 108; DLB 7, 9, 45; SATA 21

Hibbert, Eleanor Alice Burford
1906-1993 . . . . **CLC 7**
See also BEST 90:4; CA 17-20R; 140;
CANR 9, 28; SATA 2; SATA-Obit 74

Higgins, George V(incent)
1939- . . . . **CLC 4, 7, 10, 18**
See also CA 77-80; CAAS 5; CANR 17;
DLB 2; DLBY 81; MTCW

Higginson, Thomas Wentworth
1823-1911 . . . . **TCLC 36**
See also DLB 1, 64

Highet, Helen
See MacInnes, Helen (Clark)

Highsmith, (Mary) Patricia
1921- . . . . **CLC 2, 4, 14, 42**
See also CA 1-4R; CANR 1, 20; MTCW

Highwater, Jamake (Mamake)
1942(?)- . . . . **CLC 12**
See also AAYA 7; CA 65-68; CAAS 7;
CANR 10, 34; CLR 17; DLB 52;
DLBY 85; JRDA; MAICYA; SATA 32,
69; SATA-Brief 30

Higuchi, Ichiyo 1872-1896 . . . . **NCLC 49**

Hijuelos, Oscar 1951- . . . . . . **CLC 65; HLC**
See also BEST 90:1; CA 123; DLB 145; HW

Hikmet, Nazim 1902(?)-1963 . . . . **CLC 40**
See also CA 141; 93-96

Hildesheimer, Wolfgang
1916-1991 . . . . **CLC 49**
See also CA 101; 135; DLB 69, 124

Hill, Geoffrey (William)
1932- . . . . **CLC 5, 8, 18, 45**
See also CA 81-84; CANR 21;
CDBLB 1960 to Present; DLB 40;
MTCW

Hill, George Roy 1921- . . . . **CLC 26**
See also CA 110; 122

Hill, John
See Koontz, Dean R(ay)

Hill, Susan (Elizabeth) 1942- . . . . **CLC 4**
See also CA 33-36R; CANR 29; DLB 14,
139; MTCW

Hillerman, Tony 1925- . . . . **CLC 62**
See also AAYA 6; BEST 89:1; CA 29-32R;
CANR 21, 42; SATA 6

Hillesum, Etty 1914-1943 . . . . **TCLC 49**
See also CA 137

Hilliard, Noel (Harvey) 1929- . . . . . . **CLC 15**
See also CA 9-12R; CANR 7

Hillis, Rick 1956- . . . . **CLC 66**
See also CA 134

Hilton, James 1900-1954 . . . . **TCLC 21**
See also CA 108; DLB 34, 77; SATA 34

Himes, Chester (Bomar)
1909-1984 . . . . **CLC 2, 4, 7, 18, 58; BLC**
See also BW 2; CA 25-28R; 114; CANR 22;
DLB 2, 76, 143; MTCW

Hinde, Thomas . . . . CLC 6, 11
　See also Chitty, Thomas Willes

Hindin, Nathan
　See Bloch, Robert (Albert)

Hine, (William) Daryl　1936- . . . . CLC 15
　See also CA 1-4R; CAAS 15; CANR 1, 20;
　DLB 60

Hinkson, Katharine Tynan
　See Tynan, Katharine

Hinton, S(usan) E(loise)
　1950- . . . . CLC 30; DA
　See also AAYA 2; CA 81-84; CANR 32;
　CLR 3, 23; JRDA; MAICYA; MTCW;
　SATA 19, 58

Hippius, Zinaida . . . . TCLC 9
　See also Gippius, Zinaida (Nikolayevna)

Hiraoka, Kimitake　1925-1970
　See Mishima, Yukio
　See also CA 97-100; 29-32R; MTCW

Hirsch, E(ric) D(onald), Jr.　1928- . . . CLC 79
　See also CA 25-28R; CANR 27; DLB 67;
　MTCW

Hirsch, Edward　1950- . . . . CLC 31, 50
　See also CA 104; CANR 20, 42; DLB 120

Hitchcock, Alfred (Joseph)
　1899-1980 . . . . CLC 16
　See also CA 97-100; SATA 27;
　SATA-Obit 24

Hitler, Adolf　1889-1945 . . . . TCLC 53
　See also CA 117

Hoagland, Edward　1932- . . . . CLC 28
　See also CA 1-4R; CANR 2, 31; DLB 6;
　SATA 51

Hoban, Russell (Conwell)　1925- . . CLC 7, 25
　See also CA 5-8R; CANR 23, 37; CLR 3;
　DLB 52; MAICYA; MTCW; SATA 1,
　40, 78

Hobbs, Perry
　See Blackmur, R(ichard) P(almer)

Hobson, Laura Z(ametkin)
　1900-1986 . . . . CLC 7, 25
　See also CA 17-20R; 118; DLB 28;
　SATA 52

Hochhuth, Rolf　1931- . . . . CLC 4, 11, 18
　See also CA 5-8R; CANR 33; DLB 124;
　MTCW

Hochman, Sandra　1936- . . . . CLC 3, 8
　See also CA 5-8R; DLB 5

Hochwaelder, Fritz　1911-1986 . . . . . . CLC 36
　See also CA 29-32R; 120; CANR 42;
　MTCW

Hochwalder, Fritz
　See Hochwaelder, Fritz

Hocking, Mary (Eunice)　1921- . . . . . CLC 13
　See also CA 101; CANR 18, 40

Hodgins, Jack　1938- . . . . CLC 23
　See also CA 93-96; DLB 60

Hodgson, William Hope
　1877(?)-1918 . . . . TCLC 13
　See also CA 111; DLB 70

Hoffman, Alice　1952- . . . . CLC 51
　See also CA 77-80; CANR 34; MTCW

Hoffman, Daniel (Gerard)
　1923- . . . . CLC 6, 13, 23
　See also CA 1-4R; CANR 4; DLB 5

Hoffman, Stanley　1944- . . . . CLC 5
　See also CA 77-80

Hoffman, William M(oses)　1939- . . . CLC 40
　See also CA 57-60; CANR 11

Hoffmann, E(rnst) T(heodor) A(madeus)
　1776-1822 . . . . NCLC 2; SSC 13
　See also DLB 90; SATA 27

Hofmann, Gert　1931- . . . . CLC 54
　See also CA 128

Hofmannsthal, Hugo von
　1874-1929 . . . . TCLC 11; DC 4
　See also CA 106; DLB 81, 118

Hogan, Linda　1947- . . . . CLC 73
　See also CA 120; CANR 45; NNAL

Hogarth, Charles
　See Creasey, John

Hogg, James　1770-1835 . . . . NCLC 4
　See also DLB 93, 116

Holbach, Paul Henri Thiry Baron
　1723-1789 . . . . LC 14

Holberg, Ludvig　1684-1754 . . . . LC 6

Holden, Ursula　1921- . . . . CLC 18
　See also CA 101; CAAS 8; CANR 22

Holderlin, (Johann Christian) Friedrich
　1770-1843 . . . . NCLC 16; PC 4

Holdstock, Robert
　See Holdstock, Robert P.

Holdstock, Robert P.　1948- . . . . CLC 39
　See also CA 131

Holland, Isabelle　1920- . . . . CLC 21
　See also AAYA 11; CA 21-24R; CANR 10,
　25, 47; JRDA; MAICYA; SATA 8, 70

Holland, Marcus
　See Caldwell, (Janet Miriam) Taylor
　(Holland)

Hollander, John　1929- . . . . . . CLC 2, 5, 8, 14
　See also CA 1-4R; CANR 1; DLB 5;
　SATA 13

Hollander, Paul
　See Silverberg, Robert

Holleran, Andrew　1943(?)- . . . . CLC 38
　See also CA 144

Hollinghurst, Alan　1954- . . . . CLC 55
　See also CA 114

Hollis, Jim
　See Summers, Hollis (Spurgeon, Jr.)

Holmes, John
　See Souster, (Holmes) Raymond

Holmes, John Clellon　1926-1988 . . . . CLC 56
　See also CA 9-12R; 125; CANR 4; DLB 16

Holmes, Oliver Wendell
　1809-1894 . . . . NCLC 14
　See also CDALB 1640-1865; DLB 1;
　SATA 34

Holmes, Raymond
　See Souster, (Holmes) Raymond

Holt, Victoria
　See Hibbert, Eleanor Alice Burford

Holub, Miroslav　1923- . . . . CLC 4
　See also CA 21-24R; CANR 10

Homer　c. 8th cent. B.C.- . . . . . CMLC 1; DA

Honig, Edwin　1919- . . . . CLC 33
　See also CA 5-8R; CAAS 8; CANR 4, 45;
　DLB 5

Hood, Hugh (John Blagdon)
　1928- . . . . CLC 15, 28
　See also CA 49-52; CAAS 17; CANR 1, 33;
　DLB 53

Hood, Thomas　1799-1845 . . . . NCLC 16
　See also DLB 96

Hooker, (Peter) Jeremy　1941- . . . . . . CLC 43
　See also CA 77-80; CANR 22; DLB 40

Hope, A(lec) D(erwent)　1907- . . . . CLC 3, 51
　See also CA 21-24R; CANR 33; MTCW

Hope, Brian
　See Creasey, John

Hope, Christopher (David Tully)
　1944- . . . . CLC 52
　See also CA 106; CANR 47; SATA 62

Hopkins, Gerard Manley
　1844-1889 . . . . NCLC 17; DA; WLC
　See also CDBLB 1890-1914; DLB 35, 57

Hopkins, John (Richard)　1931- . . . . . . CLC 4
　See also CA 85-88

Hopkins, Pauline Elizabeth
　1859-1930 . . . . TCLC 28; BLC
　See also BW 2; CA 141; DLB 50

Hopkinson, Francis　1737-1791 . . . . . . LC 25
　See also DLB 31

Hopley-Woolrich, Cornell George　1903-1968
　See Woolrich, Cornell
　See also CA 13-14; CAP 1

Horatio
　See Proust, (Valentin-Louis-George-Eugene-)
　Marcel

Horgan, Paul　1903- . . . . CLC 9, 53
　See also CA 13-16R; CANR 9, 35;
　DLB 102; DLBY 85; MTCW; SATA 13

Horn, Peter
　See Kuttner, Henry

Hornem, Horace Esq.
　See Byron, George Gordon (Noel)

Hornung, E(rnest) W(illiam)
　1866-1921 . . . . TCLC 59
　See also CA 108; DLB 70

Horovitz, Israel (Arthur)　1939- . . . . . CLC 56
　See also CA 33-36R; CANR 46; DLB 7

Horvath, Odon von
　See Horvath, Oedoen von
　See also DLB 85, 124

Horvath, Oedoen von　1901-1938 . . . TCLC 45
　See also Horvath, Odon von
　See also CA 118

Horwitz, Julius　1920-1986 . . . . CLC 14
　See also CA 9-12R; 119; CANR 12

Hospital, Janette Turner　1942- . . . . . CLC 42
　See also CA 108

Hostos, E. M. de
　See Hostos (y Bonilla), Eugenio Maria de

Hostos, Eugenio M. de
　See Hostos (y Bonilla), Eugenio Maria de

Hostos, Eugenio Maria
　See Hostos (y Bonilla), Eugenio Maria de

Hostos (y Bonilla), Eugenio Maria de
1839-1903 .... **TCLC 24**
See also CA 123; 131; HW

Houdini
See Lovecraft, H(oward) P(hillips)

Hougan, Carolyn 1943- .... **CLC 34**
See also CA 139

Household, Geoffrey (Edward West)
1900-1988 .... **CLC 11**
See also CA 77-80; 126; DLB 87; SATA 14;
SATA-Obit 59

Housman, A(lfred) E(dward)
1859-1936 ...... **TCLC 1, 10; DA; PC 2**
See also CA 104; 125; DLB 19; MTCW

Housman, Laurence 1865-1959 ..... **TCLC 7**
See also CA 106; DLB 10; SATA 25

Howard, Elizabeth Jane 1923- ... **CLC 7, 29**
See also CA 5-8R; CANR 8

Howard, Maureen 1930- ..... **CLC 5, 14, 46**
See also CA 53-56; CANR 31; DLBY 83;
MTCW

Howard, Richard 1929- ...... **CLC 7, 10, 47**
See also AITN 1; CA 85-88; CANR 25;
DLB 5

Howard, Robert Ervin 1906-1936 ... **TCLC 8**
See also CA 105

Howard, Warren F.
See Pohl, Frederik

Howe, Fanny 1940- .... **CLC 47**
See also CA 117; SATA-Brief 52

Howe, Irving 1920-1993 .... **CLC 85**
See also CA 9-12R; 141; CANR 21;
DLB 67; MTCW

Howe, Julia Ward 1819-1910 ..... **TCLC 21**
See also CA 117; DLB 1

Howe, Susan 1937- .... **CLC 72**
See also DLB 120

Howe, Tina 1937- .... **CLC 48**
See also CA 109

Howell, James 1594(?)-1666 .... **LC 13**

Howells, W. D.
See Howells, William Dean

Howells, William D.
See Howells, William Dean

Howells, William Dean
1837-1920 .... **TCLC 7, 17, 41**
See also CA 104; 134; CDALB 1865-1917;
DLB 12, 64, 74, 79

Howes, Barbara 1914- .... **CLC 15**
See also CA 9-12R; CAAS 3; SATA 5

Hrabal, Bohumil 1914- .... **CLC 13, 67**
See also CA 106; CAAS 12

Hsun, Lu .... **TCLC 3**
See also Shu-Jen, Chou

Hubbard, L(afayette) Ron(ald)
1911-1986 .... **CLC 43**
See also CA 77-80; 118; CANR 22

Huch, Ricarda (Octavia)
1864-1947 .... **TCLC 13**
See also CA 111; DLB 66

Huddle, David 1942- .... **CLC 49**
See also CA 57-60; CAAS 20; DLB 130

Hudson, Jeffrey
See Crichton, (John) Michael

Hudson, W(illiam) H(enry)
1841-1922 .... **TCLC 29**
See also CA 115; DLB 98; SATA 35

Hueffer, Ford Madox
See Ford, Ford Madox

Hughart, Barry 1934- .... **CLC 39**
See also CA 137

Hughes, Colin
See Creasey, John

Hughes, David (John) 1930- .... **CLC 48**
See also CA 116; 129; DLB 14

Hughes, (James) Langston
1902-1967 ..... **CLC 1, 5, 10, 15, 35, 44;**
BLC; DA; DC 3; PC 1; SSC 6; WLC
See also AAYA 12; BW 1; CA 1-4R;
25-28R; CANR 1, 34; CDALB 1929-1941;
CLR 17; DLB 4, 7, 48, 51, 86; JRDA;
MAICYA; MTCW; SATA 4, 33

Hughes, Richard (Arthur Warren)
1900-1976 .... **CLC 1, 11**
See also CA 5-8R; 65-68; CANR 4;
DLB 15; MTCW; SATA 8;
SATA-Obit 25

Hughes, Ted
1930- .... **CLC 2, 4, 9, 14, 37; PC 7**
See also CA 1-4R; CANR 1, 33; CLR 3;
DLB 40; MAICYA; MTCW; SATA 49;
SATA-Brief 27

Hugo, Richard F(ranklin)
1923-1982 .... **CLC 6, 18, 32**
See also CA 49-52; 108; CANR 3; DLB 5

Hugo, Victor (Marie)
1802-1885 .. **NCLC 3, 10, 21; DA; WLC**
See also DLB 119; SATA 47

Huidobro, Vicente
See Huidobro Fernandez, Vicente Garcia

Huidobro Fernandez, Vicente Garcia
1893-1948 .... **TCLC 31**
See also CA 131; HW

Hulme, Keri 1947- .... **CLC 39**
See also CA 125

Hulme, T(homas) E(rnest)
1883-1917 .... **TCLC 21**
See also CA 117; DLB 19

Hume, David 1711-1776 .... **LC 7**
See also DLB 104

Humphrey, William 1924- .... **CLC 45**
See also CA 77-80; DLB 6

Humphreys, Emyr Owen 1919- ..... **CLC 47**
See also CA 5-8R; CANR 3, 24; DLB 15

Humphreys, Josephine 1945- .... **CLC 34, 57**
See also CA 121; 127

Hungerford, Pixie
See Brinsmead, H(esba) F(ay)

Hunt, E(verette) Howard, (Jr.)
1918- .... **CLC 3**
See also AITN 1; CA 45-48; CANR 2, 47

Hunt, Kyle
See Creasey, John

Hunt, (James Henry) Leigh
1784-1859 .... **NCLC 1**

Hunt, Marsha 1946- .... **CLC 70**
See also BW 2; CA 143

Hunt, Violet 1866-1942 .... **TCLC 53**

Hunter, E. Waldo
See Sturgeon, Theodore (Hamilton)

Hunter, Evan 1926- .... **CLC 11, 31**
See also CA 5-8R; CANR 5, 38; DLBY 82;
MTCW; SATA 25

Hunter, Kristin (Eggleston) 1931- ... **CLC 35**
See also AITN 1; BW 1; CA 13-16R;
CANR 13; CLR 3; DLB 33; MAICYA;
SAAS 10; SATA 12

Hunter, Mollie 1922- .... **CLC 21**
See also McIlwraith, Maureen Mollie
Hunter
See also AAYA 13; CANR 37; CLR 25;
JRDA; MAICYA; SAAS 7; SATA 54

Hunter, Robert (?)-1734............. **LC 7**

Hurston, Zora Neale
1903-1960 .... **CLC 7, 30, 61; BLC; DA;**
SSC 4
See also BW 1; CA 85-88; DLB 51, 86;
MTCW

Huston, John (Marcellus)
1906-1987 .... **CLC 20**
See also CA 73-76; 123; CANR 34; DLB 26

Hustvedt, Siri 1955-.............. **CLC 76**
See also CA 137

Hutten, Ulrich von 1488-1523....... **LC 16**

Huxley, Aldous (Leonard)
1894-1963 ..... **CLC 1, 3, 4, 5, 8, 11, 18,**
35, 79; DA; WLC
See also AAYA 11; CA 85-88; CANR 44;
CDBLB 1914-1945; DLB 36, 100;
MTCW; SATA 63

Huysmans, Charles Marie Georges
1848-1907
See Huysmans, Joris-Karl
See also CA 104

Huysmans, Joris-Karl.............. TCLC 7
See also Huysmans, Charles Marie Georges
See also DLB 123

Hwang, David Henry
1957-................. **CLC 55; DC 4**
See also CA 127; 132

Hyde, Anthony 1946-............. **CLC 42**
See also CA 136

Hyde, Margaret O(ldroyd) 1917- ... **CLC 21**
See also CA 1-4R; CANR 1, 36; CLR 23;
JRDA; MAICYA; SAAS 8; SATA 1, 42,
76

Hynes, James 1956(?)-............. **CLC 65**

Ian, Janis 1951- .... **CLC 21**
See also CA 105

Ibanez, Vicente Blasco
See Blasco Ibanez, Vicente

Ibarguengoitia, Jorge 1928-1983 .... **CLC 37**
See also CA 124; 113; HW

Ibsen, Henrik (Johan)
1828-1906 .... **TCLC 2, 8, 16, 37, 52;**
DA; DC 2; WLC
See also CA 104; 141

Ibuse Masuji 1898-1993.......... **CLC 22**
See also CA 127; 141

Ichikawa, Kon 1915-.............. **CLC 20**
See also CA 121

Lee, (Nelle) Harper
1926- . . . . **CLC 12, 60; DA; WLC**
See also AAYA 13; CA 13-16R;
CDALB 1941-1968; DLB 6; MTCW;
SATA 11

Lee, Helen Elaine 1959(?)- . . . . **CLC 86**

Lee, Julian
See Latham, Jean Lee

Lee, Larry
See Lee, Lawrence

Lee, Lawrence 1941-1990. . . . . **CLC 34**
See also CA 131; CANR 43

Lee, Manfred B(ennington)
1905-1971 . . . . **CLC 11**
See also Queen, Ellery
See also CA 1-4R; 29-32R; CANR 2;
DLB 137

Lee, Stan 1922- . . . . **CLC 17**
See also AAYA 5; CA 108; 111

Lee, Tanith 1947- . . . . **CLC 46**
See also CA 37-40R; SATA 8

Lee, Vernon . . . . **TCLC 5**
See also Paget, Violet
See also DLB 57

Lee, William
See Burroughs, William S(eward)

Lee, Willy
See Burroughs, William S(eward)

Lee-Hamilton, Eugene (Jacob)
1845-1907 . . . . **TCLC 22**
See also CA 117

Leet, Judith 1935- . . . . **CLC 11**

Le Fanu, Joseph Sheridan
1814-1873 . . . . **NCLC 9; SSC 14**
See also DLB 21, 70

Leffland, Ella 1931- . . . . **CLC 19**
See also CA 29-32R; CANR 35; DLBY 84;
SATA 65

Leger, Alexis
See Leger, (Marie-Rene Auguste) Alexis
Saint-Leger

Leger, (Marie-Rene Auguste) Alexis
Saint-Leger 1887-1975. . . . . **CLC 11**
See also Perse, St.-John
See also CA 13-16R; 61-64; CANR 43;
MTCW

Leger, Saintleger
See Leger, (Marie-Rene Auguste) Alexis
Saint-Leger

Le Guin, Ursula K(roeber)
1929- . . . . **CLC 8, 13, 22, 45, 71; SSC 12**
See also AAYA 9; AITN 1; CA 21-24R;
CANR 9, 32; CDALB 1968-1988; CLR 3,
28; DLB 8, 52; JRDA; MAICYA;
MTCW; SATA 4, 52

Lehmann, Rosamond (Nina)
1901-1990 . . . . **CLC 5**
See also CA 77-80; 131; CANR 8; DLB 15

Leiber, Fritz (Reuter, Jr.)
1910-1992 . . . . **CLC 25**
See also CA 45-48; 139; CANR 2, 40;
DLB 8; MTCW; SATA 45;
SATA-Obit 73

Leimbach, Martha 1963-
See Leimbach, Marti
See also CA 130

Leimbach, Marti . . . . **CLC 65**
See also Leimbach, Martha

Leino, Eino . . . . **TCLC 24**
See also Loennbohm, Armas Eino Leopold

Leiris, Michel (Julien) 1901-1990. . . **CLC 61**
See also CA 119; 128; 132

Leithauser, Brad 1953- . . . . **CLC 27**
See also CA 107; CANR 27; DLB 120

Lelchuk, Alan 1938- . . . . **CLC 5**
See also CA 45-48; CAAS 20; CANR 1

Lem, Stanislaw 1921- . . . . **CLC 8, 15, 40**
See also CA 105; CAAS 1; CANR 32;
MTCW

Lemann, Nancy 1956- . . . . **CLC 39**
See also CA 118; 136

Lemonnier, (Antoine Louis) Camille
1844-1913 . . . . **TCLC 22**
See also CA 121

Lenau, Nikolaus 1802-1850 . . . . . . **NCLC 16**

L'Engle, Madeleine (Camp Franklin)
1918- . . . . **CLC 12**
See also AAYA 1; AITN 2; CA 1-4R;
CANR 3, 21, 39; CLR 1, 14; DLB 52;
JRDA; MAICYA; MTCW; SAAS 15;
SATA 1, 27, 75

Lengyel, Jozsef 1896-1975. . . . . **CLC 7**
See also CA 85-88; 57-60

Lennon, John (Ono)
1940-1980 . . . . **CLC 12, 35**
See also CA 102

Lennox, Charlotte Ramsay
1729(?)-1804 . . . . **NCLC 23**
See also DLB 39

Lentricchia, Frank (Jr.) 1940- . . . . . . **CLC 34**
See also CA 25-28R; CANR 19

Lenz, Siegfried 1926- . . . . **CLC 27**
See also CA 89-92; DLB 75

Leonard, Elmore (John, Jr.)
1925- . . . . **CLC 28, 34, 71**
See also AITN 1; BEST 89:1, 90:4;
CA 81-84; CANR 12, 28; MTCW

Leonard, Hugh . . . . **CLC 19**
See also Byrne, John Keyes
See also DLB 13

Leopardi, (Conte) Giacomo
1798-1837 . . . . **NCLC 22**

Le Reveler
See Artaud, Antonin

Lerman, Eleanor 1952- . . . . **CLC 9**
See also CA 85-88

Lerman, Rhoda 1936- . . . . **CLC 56**
See also CA 49-52

Lermontov, Mikhail Yuryevich
1814-1841 . . . . **NCLC 47**

Leroux, Gaston 1868-1927. . . . . . . **TCLC 25**
See also CA 108; 136; SATA 65

Lesage, Alain-Rene 1668-1747. . . . . . **LC 28**

Leskov, Nikolai (Semyonovich)
1831-1895 . . . . **NCLC 25**

Lessing, Doris (May)
1919- . . . . . **CLC 1, 2, 3, 6, 10, 15, 22, 40;**
DA; SSC 6
See also CA 9-12R; CAAS 14; CANR 33;
CDBLB 1960 to Present; DLB 15, 139;
DLBY 85; MTCW

Lessing, Gotthold Ephraim
1729-1781 . . . . **LC 8**
See also DLB 97

Lester, Richard 1932- . . . . **CLC 20**

Lever, Charles (James)
1806-1872 . . . . **NCLC 23**
See also DLB 21

Leverson, Ada 1865(?)-1936(?) . . . . **TCLC 18**
See also Elaine
See also CA 117

Levertov, Denise
1923- . . . . . . **CLC 1, 2, 3, 5, 8, 15, 28, 66;**
PC 11
See also CA 1-4R; CAAS 19; CANR 3, 29;
DLB 5; MTCW

Levi, Jonathan . . . . **CLC 76**

Levi, Peter (Chad Tigar) 1931- . . . . . **CLC 41**
See also CA 5-8R; CANR 34; DLB 40

Levi, Primo
1919-1987 . . . . **CLC 37, 50; SSC 12**
See also CA 13-16R; 122; CANR 12, 33;
MTCW

Levin, Ira 1929- . . . . **CLC 3, 6**
See also CA 21-24R; CANR 17, 44;
MTCW; SATA 66

Levin, Meyer 1905-1981 . . . . **CLC 7**
See also AITN 1; CA 9-12R; 104;
CANR 15; DLB 9, 28; DLBY 81;
SATA 21; SATA-Obit 27

Levine, Norman 1924- . . . . **CLC 54**
See also CA 73-76; CANR 14; DLB 88

Levine, Philip 1928- . . . **CLC 2, 4, 5, 9, 14, 33**
See also CA 9-12R; CANR 9, 37; DLB 5

Levinson, Deirdre 1931- . . . . **CLC 49**
See also CA 73-76

Levi-Strauss, Claude 1908- . . . . **CLC 38**
See also CA 1-4R; CANR 6, 32; MTCW

Levitin, Sonia (Wolff) 1934- . . . . **CLC 17**
See also AAYA 13; CA 29-32R; CANR 14,
32; JRDA; MAICYA; SAAS 2; SATA 4,
68

Levon, O. U.
See Kesey, Ken (Elton)

Lewes, George Henry
1817-1878 . . . . **NCLC 25**
See also DLB 55, 144

Lewis, Alun 1915-1944. . . . . **TCLC 3**
See also CA 104; DLB 20

Lewis, C. Day
See Day Lewis, C(ecil)

Lewis, C(live) S(taples)
1898-1963 . . . . . **CLC 1, 3, 6, 14, 27; DA;**
WLC
See also AAYA 3; CA 81-84; CANR 33;
CDBLB 1945-1960; CLR 3, 27; DLB 15,
100; JRDA; MAICYA; MTCW;
SATA 13

Lord Byron
See Byron, George Gordon (Noel)

Lorde, Audre (Geraldine)
1934-1992 . . . . **CLC 18, 71; BLC; PC 12**
See also BW 1; CA 25-28R; 142; CANR 16, 26, 46; DLB 41; MTCW

Lord Jeffrey
See Jeffrey, Francis

Lorenzo, Heberto Padilla
See Padilla (Lorenzo), Heberto

Loris
See Hofmannsthal, Hugo von

Loti, Pierre . . . . **TCLC 11**
See also Viaud, (Louis Marie) Julien
See also DLB 123

Louie, David Wong 1954- . . . . **CLC 70**
See also CA 139

Louis, Father M.
See Merton, Thomas

Lovecraft, H(oward) P(hillips)
1890-1937 . . . . **TCLC 4, 22; SSC 3**
See also AAYA 14; CA 104; 133; MTCW

Lovelace, Earl 1935- . . . . **CLC 51**
See also BW 2; CA 77-80; CANR 41; DLB 125; MTCW

Lovelace, Richard 1618-1657 . . . . **LC 24**
See also DLB 131

Lowell, Amy 1874-1925 . . . . **TCLC 1, 8**
See also CA 104; DLB 54, 140

Lowell, James Russell 1819-1891 . . **NCLC 2**
See also CDALB 1640-1865; DLB 1, 11, 64, 79

Lowell, Robert (Traill Spence, Jr.)
1917-1977 . . . **CLC 1, 2, 3, 4, 5, 8, 9, 11, 15, 37; DA; PC 3; WLC**
See also CA 9-12R; 73-76; CABS 2; CANR 26; DLB 5; MTCW

Lowndes, Marie Adelaide (Belloc)
1868-1947 . . . . **TCLC 12**
See also CA 107; DLB 70

Lowry, (Clarence) Malcolm
1909-1957 . . . . **TCLC 6, 40**
See also CA 105; 131; CDBLB 1945-1960; DLB 15; MTCW

Lowry, Mina Gertrude 1882-1966
See Loy, Mina
See also CA 113

Loxsmith, John
See Brunner, John (Kilian Houston)

Loy, Mina . . . . **CLC 28**
See also Lowry, Mina Gertrude
See also DLB 4, 54

Loyson-Bridet
See Schwob, (Mayer Andre) Marcel

Lucas, Craig 1951- . . . . **CLC 64**
See also CA 137

Lucas, George 1944- . . . . **CLC 16**
See also AAYA 1; CA 77-80; CANR 30; SATA 56

Lucas, Hans
See Godard, Jean-Luc

Lucas, Victoria
See Plath, Sylvia

Ludlam, Charles 1943-1987 . . . . . **CLC 46, 50**
See also CA 85-88; 122

Ludlum, Robert 1927- . . . . **CLC 22, 43**
See also AAYA 10; BEST 89:1, 90:3; CA 33-36R; CANR 25, 41; DLBY 82; MTCW

Ludwig, Ken . . . . **CLC 60**

Ludwig, Otto 1813-1865 . . . . **NCLC 4**
See also DLB 129

Lugones, Leopoldo 1874-1938 . . . . . **TCLC 15**
See also CA 116; 131; HW

Lu Hsun 1881-1936 . . . . **TCLC 3**

Lukacs, George . . . . **CLC 24**
See also Lukacs, Gyorgy (Szegeny von)

Lukacs, Gyorgy (Szegeny von) 1885-1971
See Lukacs, George
See also CA 101; 29-32R

Luke, Peter (Ambrose Cyprian)
1919- . . . . **CLC 38**
See also CA 81-84; DLB 13

Lunar, Dennis
See Mungo, Raymond

Lurie, Alison 1926- . . . . **CLC 4, 5, 18, 39**
See also CA 1-4R; CANR 2, 17; DLB 2; MTCW; SATA 46

Lustig, Arnost 1926- . . . . **CLC 56**
See also AAYA 3; CA 69-72; CANR 47; SATA 56

Luther, Martin 1483-1546 . . . . **LC 9**

Luzi, Mario 1914- . . . . **CLC 13**
See also CA 61-64; CANR 9; DLB 128

Lynch, B. Suarez
See Bioy Casares, Adolfo; Borges, Jorge Luis

Lynch, David (K.) 1946- . . . . **CLC 66**
See also CA 124; 129

Lynch, James
See Andreyev, Leonid (Nikolaevich)

Lynch Davis, B.
See Bioy Casares, Adolfo; Borges, Jorge Luis

Lyndsay, Sir David 1490-1555 . . . . . . **LC 20**

Lynn, Kenneth S(chuyler) 1923- . . . . **CLC 50**
See also CA 1-4R; CANR 3, 27

Lynx
See West, Rebecca

Lyons, Marcus
See Blish, James (Benjamin)

Lyre, Pinchbeck
See Sassoon, Siegfried (Lorraine)

Lytle, Andrew (Nelson) 1902- . . . . . . **CLC 22**
See also CA 9-12R; DLB 6

Lyttelton, George 1709-1773 . . . . **LC 10**

Maas, Peter 1929- . . . . **CLC 29**
See also CA 93-96

Macaulay, Rose 1881-1958 . . . . . **TCLC 7, 44**
See also CA 104; DLB 36

Macaulay, Thomas Babington
1800-1859 . . . . **NCLC 42**
See also CDBLB 1832-1890; DLB 32, 55

MacBeth, George (Mann)
1932-1992 . . . . **CLC 2, 5, 9**
See also CA 25-28R; 136; DLB 40; MTCW; SATA 4; SATA-Obit 70

MacCaig, Norman (Alexander)
1910- . . . . **CLC 36**
See also CA 9-12R; CANR 3, 34; DLB 27

MacCarthy, (Sir Charles Otto) Desmond
1877-1952 . . . . **TCLC 36**

MacDiarmid, Hugh
. . . . **CLC 2, 4, 11, 19, 63; PC 9**
See also Grieve, C(hristopher) M(urray)
See also CDBLB 1945-1960; DLB 20

MacDonald, Anson
See Heinlein, Robert A(nson)

Macdonald, Cynthia 1928- . . . . . . **CLC 13, 19**
See also CA 49-52; CANR 4, 44; DLB 105

MacDonald, George 1824-1905 . . . . . **TCLC 9**
See also CA 106; 137; DLB 18; MAICYA; SATA 33

Macdonald, John
See Millar, Kenneth

MacDonald, John D(ann)
1916-1986 . . . . **CLC 3, 27, 44**
See also CA 1-4R; 121; CANR 1, 19; DLB 8; DLBY 86; MTCW

Macdonald, John Ross
See Millar, Kenneth

Macdonald, Ross . . . . . **CLC 1, 2, 3, 14, 34, 41**
See also Millar, Kenneth
See also DLBD 6

MacDougal, John
See Blish, James (Benjamin)

MacEwen, Gwendolyn (Margaret)
1941-1987 . . . . **CLC 13, 55**
See also CA 9-12R; 124; CANR 7, 22; DLB 53; SATA 50; SATA-Obit 55

Macha, Karel Hynek 1810-1846 . . **NCLC 46**

Machado (y Ruiz), Antonio
1875-1939 . . . . **TCLC 3**
See also CA 104; DLB 108

Machado de Assis, Joaquim Maria
1839-1908 . . . . **TCLC 10; BLC**
See also CA 107

Machen, Arthur . . . . **TCLC 4**
See also Jones, Arthur Llewellyn
See also DLB 36

Machiavelli, Niccolo 1469-1527 . . **LC 8; DA**

MacInnes, Colin 1914-1976 . . . . . . **CLC 4, 23**
See also CA 69-72; 65-68; CANR 21; DLB 14; MTCW

MacInnes, Helen (Clark)
1907-1985 . . . . **CLC 27, 39**
See also CA 1-4R; 117; CANR 1, 28; DLB 87; MTCW; SATA 22; SATA-Obit 44

Mackay, Mary 1855-1924
See Corelli, Marie
See also CA 118

Mackenzie, Compton (Edward Montague)
1883-1972 . . . . **CLC 18**
See also CA 21-22; 37-40R; CAP 2; DLB 34, 100

Mackenzie, Henry 1745-1831 . . . . **NCLC 41**
See also DLB 39

Mackintosh, Elizabeth   1896(?)-1952
See Tey, Josephine
See also CA 110

MacLaren, James
See Grieve, C(hristopher) M(urray)

Mac Laverty, Bernard   1942-.......   CLC 31
See also CA 116; 118; CANR 43

MacLean, Alistair (Stuart)
1922-1987 ....   CLC 3, 13, 50, 63
See also CA 57-60; 121; CANR 28; MTCW;
SATA 23; SATA-Obit 50

Maclean, Norman (Fitzroy)
1902-1990 ....   CLC 78; SSC 13
See also CA 102; 132

MacLeish, Archibald
1892-1982 ....   CLC 3, 8, 14, 68
See also CA 9-12R; 106; CANR 33; DLB 4,
7, 45; DLBY 82; MTCW

MacLennan, (John) Hugh
1907-1990 ....   CLC 2, 14
See also CA 5-8R; 142; CANR 33; DLB 68;
MTCW

MacLeod, Alistair   1936- ....   CLC 56
See also CA 123; DLB 60

MacNeice, (Frederick) Louis
1907-1963 ....   CLC 1, 4, 10, 53
See also CA 85-88; DLB 10, 20; MTCW

MacNeill, Dand
See Fraser, George MacDonald

Macpherson, (Jean) Jay   1931-......   CLC 14
See also CA 5-8R; DLB 53

MacShane, Frank   1927-..........   CLC 39
See also CA 9-12R; CANR 3, 33; DLB 111

Macumber, Mari
See Sandoz, Mari(e Susette)

Madach, Imre   1823-1864........   NCLC 19

Madden, (Jerry) David   1933- ....   CLC 5, 15
See also CA 1-4R; CAAS 3; CANR 4, 45;
DLB 6; MTCW

Maddern, Al(an)
See Ellison, Harlan (Jay)

Madhubuti, Haki R.
1942- ....   CLC 6, 73; BLC; PC 5
See also Lee, Don L.
See also BW 2; CA 73-76; CANR 24;
DLB 5, 41; DLBD 8

Maepenn, Hugh
See Kuttner, Henry

Maepenn, K. H.
See Kuttner, Henry

Maeterlinck, Maurice   1862-1949 ...   TCLC 3
See also CA 104; 136; SATA 66

Maginn, William   1794-1842.......   NCLC 8
See also DLB 110

Mahapatra, Jayanta   1928-.........   CLC 33
See also CA 73-76; CAAS 9; CANR 15, 33

Mahfouz, Naguib (Abdel Aziz Al-Sabilgi)
1911(?)-
See Mahfuz, Najib
See also BEST 89:2; CA 128; MTCW

Mahfuz, Najib................   CLC 52, 55
See also Mahfouz, Naguib (Abdel Aziz
Al-Sabilgi)
See also DLBY 88

Mahon, Derek   1941-.............   CLC 27
See also CA 113; 128; DLB 40

Mailer, Norman
1923- ......   CLC 1, 2, 3, 4, 5, 8, 11, 14,
28, 39, 74; DA
See also AITN 2; CA 9-12R; CABS 1;
CANR 28; CDALB 1968-1988; DLB 2,
16, 28; DLBD 3; DLBY 80, 83; MTCW

Maillet, Antonine   1929-..........   CLC 54
See also CA 115; 120; CANR 46; DLB 60

Mais, Roger   1905-1955 ....   TCLC 8
See also BW 1; CA 105; 124; DLB 125;
MTCW

Maistre, Joseph de   1753-1821....   NCLC 37

Maitland, Sara (Louise)   1950-......   CLC 49
See also CA 69-72; CANR 13

Major, Clarence
1936- ....   CLC 3, 19, 48; BLC
See also BW 2; CA 21-24R; CAAS 6;
CANR 13, 25; DLB 33

Major, Kevin (Gerald)   1949-.......   CLC 26
See also CA 97-100; CANR 21, 38;
CLR 11; DLB 60; JRDA; MAICYA;
SATA 32

Maki, James
See Ozu, Yasujiro

Malabaila, Damiano
See Levi, Primo

Malamud, Bernard
1914-1986 ......   CLC 1, 2, 3, 5, 8, 9, 11,
18, 27, 44, 78, 85; DA; SSC 15; WLC
See also CA 5-8R; 118; CABS 1; CANR 28;
CDALB 1941-1968; DLB 2, 28;
DLBY 80, 86; MTCW

Malaparte, Curzio   1898-1957 .....   TCLC 52

Malcolm, Dan
See Silverberg, Robert

Malcolm X.................   CLC 82; BLC
See also Little, Malcolm

Malherbe, Francois de   1555-1628.....   LC 5

Mallarme, Stephane
1842-1898 ....   NCLC 4, 41; PC 4

Mallet-Joris, Francoise   1930-......   CLC 11
See also CA 65-68; CANR 17; DLB 83

Malley, Ern
See McAuley, James Phillip

Mallowan, Agatha Christie
See Christie, Agatha (Mary Clarissa)

Maloff, Saul   1922-................   CLC 5
See also CA 33-36R

Malone, Louis
See MacNeice, (Frederick) Louis

Malone, Michael (Christopher)
1942- ....   CLC 43
See also CA 77-80; CANR 14, 32

Malory, (Sir) Thomas
1410(?)-1471(?) ....   LC 11; DA
See also CDBLB Before 1660; DLB 146;
SATA 59; SATA-Brief 33

Malouf, (George Joseph) David
1934- ....   CLC 28, 86
See also CA 124

Malraux, (Georges-)Andre
1901-1976 ......   CLC 1, 4, 9, 13, 15, 57
See also CA 21-22; 69-72; CANR 34;
CAP 2; DLB 72; MTCW

Malzberg, Barry N(athaniel)   1939-...   CLC 7
See also CA 61-64; CAAS 4; CANR 16;
DLB 8

Mamet, David (Alan)
1947- ....   CLC 9, 15, 34, 46; DC 4
See also AAYA 3; CA 81-84; CABS 3;
CANR 15, 41; DLB 7; MTCW

Mamoulian, Rouben (Zachary)
1897-1987 ....   CLC 16
See also CA 25-28R; 124

Mandelstam, Osip (Emilievich)
1891(?)-1938(?) ....   TCLC 2, 6
See also CA 104

Mander, (Mary) Jane   1877-1949...   TCLC 31

**Mandiargues, Andre Pieyre de.......   CLC 41
See also Pieyre de Mandiargues, Andre
See also DLB 83

Mandrake, Ethel Belle
See Thurman, Wallace (Henry)

Mangan, James Clarence
1803-1849 ....   NCLC 27

Maniere, J.-E.
See Giraudoux, (Hippolyte) Jean

Manley, (Mary) Delariviere
1672(?)-1724 ....   LC 1
See also DLB 39, 80

Mann, Abel
See Creasey, John

Mann, (Luiz) Heinrich   1871-1950...   TCLC 9
See also CA 106; DLB 66

Mann, (Paul) Thomas
1875-1955 ....   TCLC 2, 8, 14, 21, 35, 44;
DA; SSC 5; WLC
See also CA 104; 128; DLB 66; MTCW

Manning, David
See Faust, Frederick (Schiller)

Manning, Frederic   1887(?)-1935...   TCLC 25
See also CA 124

Manning, Olivia   1915-1980......   CLC 5, 19
See also CA 5-8R; 101; CANR 29; MTCW

Mano, D. Keith   1942- ....   CLC 2, 10
See also CA 25-28R; CAAS 6; CANR 26;
DLB 6

Mansfield, Katherine
....   TCLC 2, 8, 39; SSC 9; WLC
See also Beauchamp, Kathleen Mansfield

Manso, Peter   1940- ....   CLC 39
See also CA 29-32R; CANR 44

Mantecon, Juan Jimenez
See Jimenez (Mantecon), Juan Ramon

Manton, Peter
See Creasey, John

Man Without a Spleen, A
See Chekhov, Anton (Pavlovich)

Manzoni, Alessandro   1785-1873 ..   NCLC 29

Mapu, Abraham (ben Jekutiel)
1808-1867 ....   NCLC 18

Mara, Sally
See Queneau, Raymond

Marat, Jean Paul   1743-1793........   LC 10

Maupassant, (Henri Rene Albert) Guy de
1850-1893 .... **NCLC 1, 42; DA; SSC 1;**
WLC
See also DLB 123

Maurhut, Richard
See Traven, B.

Mauriac, Claude 1914-............. **CLC 9**
See also CA 89-92; DLB 83

Mauriac, Francois (Charles)
1885-1970 .... **CLC 4, 9, 56**
See also CA 25-28; CAP 2; DLB 65;
MTCW

Mavor, Osborne Henry 1888-1951
See Bridie, James
See also CA 104

Maxwell, William (Keepers, Jr.)
1908- .... **CLC 19**
See also CA 93-96; DLBY 80

May, Elaine 1932- .... **CLC 16**
See also CA 124; 142; DLB 44

Mayakovski, Vladimir (Vladimirovich)
1893-1930 .... **TCLC 4, 18**
See also CA 104

Mayhew, Henry 1812-1887 ...... **NCLC 31**
See also DLB 18, 55

Maynard, Joyce 1953- .... **CLC 23**
See also CA 111; 129

Mayne, William (James Carter)
1928- .... **CLC 12**
See also CA 9-12R; CANR 37; CLR 25;
JRDA; MAICYA; SAAS 11; SATA 6, 68

Mayo, Jim
See L'Amour, Louis (Dearborn)

Maysles, Albert 1926- .... **CLC 16**
See also CA 29-32R

Maysles, David 1932-............. **CLC 16**

Mazer, Norma Fox 1931- .... **CLC 26**
See also AAYA 5; CA 69-72; CANR 12,
32; CLR 23; JRDA; MAICYA; SAAS 1;
SATA 24, 67

Mazzini, Guiseppe 1805-1872 .... **NCLC 34**

McAuley, James Phillip
1917-1976 .... **CLC 45**
See also CA 97-100

McBain, Ed
See Hunter, Evan

McBrien, William Augustine
1930- .... **CLC 44**
See also CA 107

McCaffrey, Anne (Inez) 1926-...... **CLC 17**
See also AAYA 6; AITN 2; BEST 89:2;
CA 25-28R; CANR 15, 35; DLB 8;
JRDA; MAICYA; MTCW; SAAS 11;
SATA 8, 70

McCall, Nathan 1955(?)- .... **CLC 86**
See also CA 146

McCann, Arthur
See Campbell, John W(ood, Jr.)

McCann, Edson
See Pohl, Frederik

McCarthy, Charles, Jr. 1933-
See McCarthy, Cormac
See also CANR 42

McCarthy, Cormac 1933-..... **CLC 4, 57, 59**
See also McCarthy, Charles, Jr.
See also DLB 6, 143

McCarthy, Mary (Therese)
1912-1989 ... **CLC 1, 3, 5, 14, 24, 39, 59**
See also CA 5-8R; 129; CANR 16; DLB 2;
DLBY 81; MTCW

McCartney, (James) Paul
1942- .... **CLC 12, 35**

McCauley, Stephen (D.) 1955- ..... **CLC 50**
See also CA 141

McClure, Michael (Thomas)
1932- .... **CLC 6, 10**
See also CA 21-24R; CANR 17, 46;
DLB 16

McCorkle, Jill (Collins) 1958- ...... **CLC 51**
See also CA 121; DLBY 87

McCourt, James 1941-............ **CLC 5**
See also CA 57-60

McCoy, Horace (Stanley)
1897-1955 .... **TCLC 28**
See also CA 108; DLB 9

McCrae, John 1872-1918........ **TCLC 12**
See also CA 109; DLB 92

McCreigh, James
See Pohl, Frederik

McCullers, (Lula) Carson (Smith)
1917-1967 .... **CLC 1, 4, 10, 12, 48; DA;**
SSC 9; WLC
See also CA 5-8R; 25-28R; CABS 1, 3;
CANR 18; CDALB 1941-1968; DLB 2, 7;
MTCW; SATA 27

McCulloch, John Tyler
See Burroughs, Edgar Rice

McCullough, Colleen 1938(?)-...... **CLC 27**
See also CA 81-84; CANR 17, 46; MTCW

McElroy, Joseph 1930- .... **CLC 5, 47**
See also CA 17-20R

McEwan, Ian (Russell) 1948- ... **CLC 13, 66**
See also BEST 90:4; CA 61-64; CANR 14,
41; DLB 14; MTCW

McFadden, David 1940-........... **CLC 48**
See also CA 104; DLB 60

McFarland, Dennis 1950- .... **CLC 65**

McGahern, John
1934- .... **CLC 5, 9, 48; SSC 17**
See also CA 17-20R; CANR 29; DLB 14;
MTCW

McGinley, Patrick (Anthony)
1937- .... **CLC 41**
See also CA 120; 127

McGinley, Phyllis 1905-1978 ...... **CLC 14**
See also CA 9-12R; 77-80; CANR 19;
DLB 11, 48; SATA 2, 44; SATA-Obit 24

McGinniss, Joe 1942-............. **CLC 32**
See also AITN 2; BEST 89:2; CA 25-28R;
CANR 26

McGivern, Maureen Daly
See Daly, Maureen

McGrath, Patrick 1950-........... **CLC 55**
See also CA 136

McGrath, Thomas (Matthew)
1916-1990 .... **CLC 28, 59**
See also CA 9-12R; 132; CANR 6, 33;
MTCW; SATA 41; SATA-Obit 66

McGuane, Thomas (Francis III)
1939- ....**CLC 3, 7, 18, 45**
See also AITN 2; CA 49-52; CANR 5, 24;
DLB 2; DLBY 80; MTCW

McGuckian, Medbh 1950-........ **CLC 48**
See also CA 143; DLB 40

McHale, Tom 1942(?)-1982....... **CLC 3, 5**
See also AITN 1; CA 77-80; 106

McIlvanney, William 1936-........ **CLC 42**
See also CA 25-28R; DLB 14

McIlwraith, Maureen Mollie Hunter
See Hunter, Mollie
See also SATA 2

McInerney, Jay 1955- .... **CLC 34**
See also CA 116; 123; CANR 45

McIntyre, Vonda N(eel) 1948- ..... **CLC 18**
See also CA 81-84; CANR 17, 34; MTCW

McKay, Claude ..... **TCLC 7, 41; BLC; PC 2**
See also McKay, Festus Claudius
See also DLB 4, 45, 51, 117

McKay, Festus Claudius 1889-1948
See McKay, Claude
See also BW 1; CA 104; 124; DA; MTCW;
WLC

McKuen, Rod 1933-............. **CLC 1, 3**
See also AITN 1; CA 41-44R; CANR 40

McLoughlin, R. B.
See Mencken, H(enry) L(ouis)

McLuhan, (Herbert) Marshall
1911-1980 .... **CLC 37, 83**
See also CA 9-12R; 102; CANR 12, 34;
DLB 88; MTCW

McMillan, Terry (L.) 1951-..... **CLC 50, 61**
See also BW 2; CA 140

McMurtry, Larry (Jeff)
1936- .... **CLC 2, 3, 7, 11, 27, 44**
See also AITN 2; BEST 89:2; CA 5-8R;
CANR 19, 43; CDALB 1968-1988;
DLB 2, 143; DLBY 80, 87; MTCW

McNally, T. M. 1961-............ **CLC 82**

McNally, Terrence 1939-...... **CLC 4, 7, 41**
See also CA 45-48; CANR 2; DLB 7

McNamer, Deirdre 1950-......... **CLC 70**

McNeile, Herman Cyril 1888-1937
See Sapper
See also DLB 77

McPhee, John (Angus) 1931- ...... **CLC 36**
See also BEST 90:1; CA 65-68; CANR 20,
46; MTCW

McPherson, James Alan
1943- .... **CLC 19, 77**
See also BW 1; CA 25-28R; CAAS 17;
CANR 24; DLB 38; MTCW

McPherson, William (Alexander)
1933- .... **CLC 34**
See also CA 69-72; CANR 28

Mead, Margaret 1901-1978........ **CLC 37**
See also AITN 1; CA 1-4R; 81-84;
CANR 4; MTCW; SATA-Obit 20

Meaker, Marijane (Agnes) 1927-
See Kerr, M. E.
See also CA 107; CANR 37; JRDA;
MAICYA; MTCW; SATA 20, 61

Moritz, Karl Philipp 1756-1793 ...... **LC 2**
See also DLB 94

Morland, Peter Henry
See Faust, Frederick (Schiller)

Morren, Theophil
See Hofmannsthal, Hugo von

Morris, Bill 1952-............... **CLC 76**

Morris, Julian
See West, Morris L(anglo)

Morris, Steveland Judkins 1950(?)-
See Wonder, Stevie
See also CA 111

Morris, William 1834-1896 .... **NCLC 4**
See also CDBLB 1832-1890; DLB 18, 35, 57

Morris, Wright 1910-... **CLC 1, 3, 7, 18, 37**
See also CA 9-12R; CANR 21; DLB 2;
DLBY 81; MTCW

Morrison, Chloe Anthony Wofford
See Morrison, Toni

Morrison, James Douglas 1943-1971
See Morrison, Jim
See also CA 73-76; CANR 40

Morrison, Jim .... **CLC 17**
See also Morrison, James Douglas

Morrison, Toni
1931- .... **CLC 4, 10, 22, 55, 81, 87;
BLC; DA**
See also AAYA 1; BW 2; CA 29-32R;
CANR 27, 42; CDALB 1968-1988;
DLB 6, 33, 143; DLBY 81; MTCW;
SATA 57

Morrison, Van 1945- .... **CLC 21**
See also CA 116

Mortimer, John (Clifford)
1923- .... **CLC 28, 43**
See also CA 13-16R; CANR 21;
CDBLB 1960 to Present; DLB 13;
MTCW

Mortimer, Penelope (Ruth) 1918-.... **CLC 5**
See also CA 57-60; CANR 45

Morton, Anthony
See Creasey, John

Mosher, Howard Frank 1943-...... **CLC 62**
See also CA 139

Mosley, Nicholas 1923 .... **CLC 43, 70**
See also CA 69-72; CANR 41; DLB 14

Moss, Howard
1922-1987 .... **CLC 7, 14, 45, 50**
See also CA 1-4R; 123; CANR 1, 44;
DLB 5

Mossgiel, Rab
See Burns, Robert

Motion, Andrew 1952-........... **CLC 47**
See also DLB 40

Motley, Willard (Francis)
1909-1965 .... **CLC 18**
See also BW 1; CA 117; 106; DLB 76, 143

Motoori, Norinaga 1730-1801 .... **NCLC 45**

Mott, Michael (Charles Alston)
1930- .... **CLC 15, 34**
See also CA 5-8R; CAAS 7; CANR 7, 29

Mowat, Farley (McGill) 1921- ..... **CLC 26**
See also AAYA 1; CA 1-4R; CANR 4, 24,
42; CLR 20; DLB 68; JRDA; MAICYA;
MTCW; SATA 3, 55

Moyers, Bill 1934- .... **CLC 74**
See also AITN 2; CA 61-64; CANR 31

Mphahlele, Es'kia
See Mphahlele, Ezekiel
See also DLB 125

Mphahlele, Ezekiel 1919-..... **CLC 25; BLC**
See also Mphahlele, Es'kia
See also BW 2; CA 81-84; CANR 26

Mqhayi, S(amuel) E(dward) K(rune Loliwe)
1875-1945 .... **TCLC 25; BLC**

Mr. Martin
See Burroughs, William S(eward)

Mrozek, Slawomir 1930-........ **CLC 3, 13**
See also CA 13-16R; CAAS 10; CANR 29;
MTCW

Mrs. Belloc-Lowndes
See Lowndes, Marie Adelaide (Belloc)

Mtwa, Percy (?)-.................. **CLC 47**

Mueller, Lisel 1924-.......... **CLC 13, 51**
See also CA 93-96; DLB 105

Muir, Edwin 1887-1959 .... **TCLC 2**
See also CA 104; DLB 20, 100

Muir, John 1838-1914 .... **TCLC 28**

Mujica Lainez, Manuel
1910-1984 .... **CLC 31**
See also Lainez, Manuel Mujica
See also CA 81-84; 112; CANR 32; HW

Mukherjee, Bharati 1940- .... **CLC 53**
See also BEST 89:2; CA 107; CANR 45;
DLB 60; MTCW

Muldoon, Paul 1951- .... **CLC 32, 72**
See also CA 113; 129; DLB 40

Mulisch, Harry 1927-............ **CLC 42**
See also CA 9-12R; CANR 6, 26

Mull, Martin 1943-.............. **CLC 17**
See also CA 105

Mulock, Dinah Maria
See Craik, Dinah Maria (Mulock)

Munford, Robert 1737(?)-1783 .... **LC 5**
See also DLB 31

Mungo, Raymond 1946-........... **CLC 72**
See also CA 49-52; CANR 2

Munro, Alice
1931- .... **CLC 6, 10, 19, 50; SSC 3**
See also AITN 2; CA 33-36R; CANR 33;
DLB 53; MTCW; SATA 29

Munro, H(ector) H(ugh) 1870-1916
See Saki
See also CA 104; 130; CDBLB 1890-1914;
DA; DLB 34; MTCW; WLC

Murasaki, Lady .... **CMLC 1**

Murdoch, (Jean) Iris
1919- ...... **CLC 1, 2, 3, 4, 6, 8, 11, 15,
22, 31, 51**
See also CA 13-16R; CANR 8, 43;
CDBLB 1960 to Present; DLB 14;
MTCW

Murnau, Friedrich Wilhelm
See Plumpe, Friedrich Wilhelm

Murphy, Richard 1927-........... **CLC 41**
See also CA 29-32R; DLB 40

Murphy, Sylvia 1937-............. **CLC 34**
See also CA 121

Murphy, Thomas (Bernard) 1935-... **CLC 51**
See also CA 101

Murray, Albert L. 1916- .... **CLC 73**
See also BW 2; CA 49-52; CANR 26;
DLB 38

Murray, Les(lie) A(llan) 1938- ..... **CLC 40**
See also CA 21-24R; CANR 11, 27

Murry, J. Middleton
See Murry, John Middleton

Murry, John Middleton
1889-1957 .... **TCLC 16**
See also CA 118

Musgrave, Susan 1951- .... **CLC 13, 54**
See also CA 69-72; CANR 45

Musil, Robert (Edler von)
1880-1942 .... **TCLC 12; SSC 18**
See also CA 109; DLB 81, 124

Musset, (Louis Charles) Alfred de
1810-1857 .... **NCLC 7**

My Brother's Brother
See Chekhov, Anton (Pavlovich)

Myers, L. H. 1881-1944......... **TCLC 59**
See also DLB 15

Myers, Walter Dean 1937- ... **CLC 35; BLC**
See also AAYA 4; BW 2; CA 33-36R;
CANR 20, 42; CLR 4, 16, 35; DLB 33;
JRDA; MAICYA; SAAS 2; SATA 41, 71;
SATA-Brief 27

Myers, Walter M.
See Myers, Walter Dean

Myles, Symon
See Follett, Ken(neth Martin)

Nabokov, Vladimir (Vladimirovich)
1899-1977 ..... **CLC 1, 2, 3, 6, 8, 11, 15,
23, 44, 46, 64; DA; SSC 11; WLC**
See also CA 5-8R; 69-72; CANR 20;
CDALB 1941-1968; DLB 2; DLBD 3;
DLBY 80, 91; MTCW

Nagai Kafu..................... **TCLC 51**
See also Nagai Sokichi

Nagai Sokichi 1879-1959
See Nagai Kafu
See also CA 117

Nagy, Laszlo 1925-1978........... **CLC 7**
See also CA 129; 112

Naipaul, Shiva(dhar Srinivasa)
1945-1985 .... **CLC 32, 39**
See also CA 110; 112; 116; CANR 33;
DLBY 85; MTCW

Naipaul, V(idiadhar) S(urajprasad)
1932- .... **CLC 4, 7, 9, 13, 18, 37**
See also CA 1-4R; CANR 1, 33;
CDBLB 1960 to Present; DLB 125;
DLBY 85; MTCW

Nakos, Lilika 1899(?)-............ **CLC 29**

Narayan, R(asipuram) K(rishnaswami)
1906- .... **CLC 7, 28, 47**
See also CA 81-84; CANR 33; MTCW;
SATA 62

Nova, Craig 1945-.............. CLC **7, 31**
See also CA 45-48; CANR 2

Novak, Joseph
See Kosinski, Jerzy (Nikodem)

Novalis 1772-1801 .... NCLC **13**
See also DLB 90

Nowlan, Alden (Albert) 1933-1983 .. CLC **15**
See also CA 9-12R; CANR 5; DLB 53

Noyes, Alfred 1880-1958 .... TCLC **7**
See also CA 104; DLB 20

Nunn, Kem 19(?)-............... CLC **34**

Nye, Robert 1939- .... CLC **13, 42**
See also CA 33-36R; CANR 29; DLB 14;
MTCW; SATA 6

Nyro, Laura 1947- .... CLC **17**

Oates, Joyce Carol
1938-...... CLC **1, 2, 3, 6, 9, 11, 15, 19,
33, 52; DA; SSC 6; WLC**
See also AITN 1; BEST 89:2; CA 5-8R;
CANR 25, 45; CDALB 1968-1988;
DLB 2, 5, 130, DLDY 81; MTCW

O'Brien, Darcy 1939-............ CLC **11**
See also CA 21-24R; CANR 8

O'Brien, E. G.
See Clarke, Arthur C(harles)

O'Brien, Edna
1936- ... CLC **3, 5, 8, 13, 36, 65; SSC 10**
See also CA 1-4R; CANR 6, 41;
CDBLB 1960 to Present; DLB 14;
MTCW

O'Brien, Fitz-James 1828-1862... NCLC **21**
See also DLB 74

O'Brien, Flann....... CLC **1, 4, 5, 7, 10, 47**
See also O Nuallain, Brian

O'Brien, Richard 1942- .... CLC **17**
See also CA 124

O'Brien, Tim 1946-......... CLC **7, 19, 40**
See also CA 85-88; CANR 40; DLBD 9;
DLBY 80

Obstfelder, Sigbjoern 1866-1900... TCLC **23**
See also CA 123

O'Casey, Sean
1880-1964 .... CLC **1, 5, 9, 11, 15**
See also CA 89-92; CDBLB 1914-1945;
DLB 10; MTCW

O'Cathasaigh, Sean
See O'Casey, Sean

Ochs, Phil 1940-1976............. CLC **17**
See also CA 65-68

O'Connor, Edwin (Greene)
1918-1968 .... CLC **14**
See also CA 93-96; 25-28R

O'Connor, (Mary) Flannery
1925-1964 .... CLC **1, 2, 3, 6, 10, 13, 15,
21, 66; DA; SSC 1; WLC**
See also AAYA 7; CA 1-4R; CANR 3, 41;
CDALB 1941-1968; DLB 2; DLBD 12;
DLBY 80; MTCW

O'Connor, Frank.......... CLC **23; SSC 5**
See also O'Donovan, Michael John

O'Dell, Scott 1898-1989.......... CLC **30**
See also AAYA 3; CA 61-64; 129;
CANR 12, 30; CLR 1, 16; DLB 52;
JRDA; MAICYA; SATA 12, 60

Odets, Clifford 1906-1963 .... CLC **2, 28**
See also CA 85-88; DLB 7, 26; MTCW

O'Doherty, Brian 1934-.......... CLC **76**
See also CA 105

O'Donnell, K. M.
See Malzberg, Barry N(athaniel)

O'Donnell, Lawrence
See Kuttner, Henry

O'Donovan, Michael John
1903-1966 .... CLC **14**
See also O'Connor, Frank
See also CA 93-96

Oe, Kenzaburo 1935-....... CLC **10, 36, 86**
See also CA 97-100; CANR 36; MTCW

O'Faolain, Julia 1932-...... CLC **6, 19, 47**
See also CA 81-84; CAAS 2; CANR 12;
DLB 14; MTCW

O'Faolain, Sean
1900-1991 .... CLC **1, 7, 14, 32, 70;
SSC 13**
See also CA 61-64; 134; CANR 12;
DLB 15; MTCW

O'Flaherty, Liam
1896-1984 .... CLC **5, 34; SSC 6**
See also CA 101; 113; CANR 35; DLB 36;
DLBY 84; MTCW

Ogilvy, Gavin
See Barrie, J(ames) M(atthew)

O'Grady, Standish James
1846-1928 .... TCLC **5**
See also CA 104

O'Grady, Timothy 1951- .... CLC **59**
See also CA 138

O'Hara, Frank
1926-1966 .... CLC **2, 5, 13, 78**
See also CA 9-12R; 25-28R; CANR 33;
DLB 5, 16; MTCW

O'Hara, John (Henry)
1905-1970 .... CLC **1, 2, 3, 6, 11, 42;
SSC 15**
See also CA 5-8R; 25-28R; CANR 31;
CDALB 1929-1941; DLB 9, 86; DLBD 2;
MTCW

O Hehir, Diana 1922- .... CLC **41**
See also CA 93-96

Okigbo, Christopher (Ifenayichukwu)
1932-1967 ..... CLC **25, 84; BLC; PC 7**
See also BW 1; CA 77-80; DLB 125;
MTCW

Okri, Ben 1959- .... CLC **87**
See also BW 2; CA 130; 138

Olds, Sharon 1942-........ CLC **32, 39, 85**
See also CA 101; CANR 18, 41; DLB 120

Oldstyle, Jonathan
See Irving, Washington

Olesha, Yuri (Karlovich)
1899-1960 .... CLC **8**
See also CA 85-88

Oliphant, Laurence
1829(?)-1888 .... NCLC **47**
See also DLB 18

Oliphant, Margaret (Oliphant Wilson)
1828-1897 .... NCLC **11**
See also DLB 18

Oliver, Mary 1935-........... CLC **19, 34**
See also CA 21-24R; CANR 9, 43; DLB 5

Olivier, Laurence (Kerr)
1907-1989 .... CLC **20**
See also CA 111; 129

Olsen, Tillie
1913- .... CLC **4, 13; DA; SSC 11**
See also CA 1-4R; CANR 1, 43; DLB 28;
DLBY 80; MTCW

Olson, Charles (John)
1910-1970 ..... CLC **1, 2, 5, 6, 9, 11, 29**
See also CA 13-16; 25-28R; CABS 2;
CANR 35; CAP 1; DLB 5, 16; MTCW

Olson, Toby 1937- .... CLC **28**
See also CA 65-68; CANR 9, 31

Olyesha, Yuri
See Olesha, Yuri (Karlovich)

Ondaatje, (Philip) Michael
1943- .... CLC **14, 29, 51, 76**
See also CA 77-80; CANR 42; DLB 60

Oneal, Elizabeth 1934-
See Oneal, Zibby
See also CA 106; CANR 28; MAICYA;
SATA 30

Oneal, Zibby .... CLC **30**
See also Oneal, Elizabeth
See also AAYA 5; CLR 13; JRDA

O'Neill, Eugene (Gladstone)
1888-1953 ...... TCLC **1, 6, 27, 49; DA;
WLC**
See also AITN 1; CA 110; 132;
CDALB 1929-1941; DLB 7; MTCW

Onetti, Juan Carlos 1909-1994 ... CLC **7, 10**
See also CA 85-88; 145; CANR 32;
DLB 113; HW; MTCW

O Nuallain, Brian 1911-1966
See O'Brien, Flann
See also CA 21-22; 25-28R; CAP 2

Oppen, George 1908-1984 .... CLC **7, 13, 34**
See also CA 13-16R; 113; CANR 8; DLB 5

Oppenheim, E(dward) Phillips
1866-1946 .... TCLC **45**
See also CA 111; DLB 70

Orlovitz, Gil 1918-1973 .... CLC **22**
See also CA 77-80; 45-48; DLB 2, 5

Orris
See Ingelow, Jean

Ortega y Gasset, Jose
1883-1955 .... TCLC **9; HLC**
See also CA 106; 130; HW; MTCW

Ortiz, Simon J(oseph) 1941- .... CLC **45**
See also CA 134; DLB 120; NNAL

Orton, Joe .... CLC **4, 13, 43; DC 3**
See also Orton, John Kingsley
See also CDBLB 1960 to Present; DLB 13

Orton, John Kingsley 1933-1967
See Orton, Joe
See also CA 85-88; CANR 35; MTCW

Orwell, George
.... TCLC **2, 6, 15, 31, 51; WLC**
See also Blair, Eric (Arthur)
See also CDBLB 1945-1960; DLB 15, 98

Osborne, David
See Silverberg, Robert

Osborne, George
See Silverberg, Robert

Osborne, John (James)
1929- .... CLC **1, 2, 5, 11, 45; DA; WLC**
See also CA 13-16R; CANR 21;
CDBLB 1945-1960; DLB 13; MTCW

Osborne, Lawrence 1958- .... CLC **50**

Oshima, Nagisa 1932- .... CLC **20**
See also CA 116; 121

Oskison, John Milton
1874-1947 .... TCLC **35**
See also CA 144; NNAL

Ossoli, Sarah Margaret (Fuller marchesa d')
1810-1850
See Fuller, Margaret
See also SATA 25

Ostrovsky, Alexander
1823-1886 .... NCLC **30**

Otero, Blas de 1916-1979......... CLC **11**
See also CA 89-92; DLB 134

Otto, Whitney 1955-.............. CLC **70**
See also CA 140

Ouida .... TCLC **43**
See also De La Ramee, (Marie) Louise
See also DLB 18

Ousmane, Sembene 1923- .... CLC **66; BLC**
See also BW 1; CA 117; 125; MTCW

Ovid 43B.C.-18(?)......... CMLC **7; PC 2**

Owen, Hugh
See Faust, Frederick (Schiller)

Owen, Wilfred (Edward Salter)
1893-1918 ...... TCLC **5, 27; DA; WLC**
See also CA 104; 141; CDBLB 1914-1945;
DLB 20

Owens, Rochelle 1936-............. CLC **8**
See also CA 17-20R; CAAS 2; CANR 39

Oz, Amos 1939- ... CLC **5, 8, 11, 27, 33, 54**
See also CA 53-56; CANR 27, 47; MTCW

Ozick, Cynthia
1928- .... CLC **3, 7, 28, 62; SSC 15**
See also BEST 90:1; CA 17-20R; CANR 23;
DLB 28; DLBY 82; MTCW

Ozu, Yasujiro 1903-1963 .... CLC **16**
See also CA 112

Pacheco, C.
See Pessoa, Fernando (Antonio Nogueira)

Pa Chin .... CLC **18**
See also Li Fei-kan

Pack, Robert 1929-.............. CLC **13**
See also CA 1-4R; CANR 3, 44; DLB 5

Padgett, Lewis
See Kuttner, Henry

Padilla (Lorenzo), Heberto 1932-... CLC **38**
See also AITN 1; CA 123; 131; HW

Page, Jimmy 1944-.............. CLC **12**

Page, Louise 1955-.............. CLC **40**
See also CA 140

Page, P(atricia) K(athleen)
1916- .... CLC **7, 18; PC 12**
See also CA 53-56; CANR 4, 22; DLB 68;
MTCW

Paget, Violet 1856-1935
See Lee, Vernon
See also CA 104

Paget-Lowe, Henry
See Lovecraft, H(oward) P(hillips)

Paglia, Camille (Anna) 1947-....... CLC **68**
See also CA 140

Paige, Richard
See Koontz, Dean R(ay)

Pakenham, Antonia
See Fraser, (Lady) Antonia (Pakenham)

Palamas, Kostes 1859-1943 .... TCLC **5**
See also CA 105

Palazzeschi, Aldo 1885-1974 ...... CLC **11**
See also CA 89-92; 53-56; DLB 114

Paley, Grace 1922-.... CLC **4, 6, 37; SSC 8**
See also CA 25-28R; CANR 13, 46;
DLB 28; MTCW

Palin, Michael (Edward) 1943-..... CLC **21**
See also Monty Python
See also CA 107; CANR 35; SATA 67

Palliser, Charles 1947-............ CLC **65**
See also CA 136

Palma, Ricardo 1833-1919....... TCLC **29**

Pancake, Breece Dexter 1952-1979
See Pancake, Breece D'J
See also CA 123; 109

Pancake, Breece D'J.............. CLC **29**
See also Pancake, Breece Dexter
See also DLB 130

Panko, Rudy
See Gogol, Nikolai (Vasilyevich)

Papadiamantis, Alexandros
1851-1911 .... TCLC **29**

Papadiamantopoulos, Johannes 1856-1910
See Moreas, Jean
See also CA 117

Papini, Giovanni 1881-1956...... TCLC **22**
See also CA 121

Paracelsus 1493-1541.............. LC **14**

Parasol, Peter
See Stevens, Wallace

Parfenie, Maria
See Codrescu, Andrei

Parini, Jay (Lee) 1948- .... CLC **54**
See also CA 97-100; CAAS 16; CANR 32

Park, Jordan
See Kornbluth, C(yril) M.; Pohl, Frederik

Parker, Bert
See Ellison, Harlan (Jay)

Parker, Dorothy (Rothschild)
1893-1967 .... CLC **15, 68; SSC 2**
See also CA 19-20; 25-28R; CAP 2;
DLB 11, 45, 86; MTCW

Parker, Robert B(rown) 1932-...... CLC **27**
See also BEST 89:4; CA 49-52; CANR 1,
26; MTCW

Parkin, Frank 1940-.............. CLC **43**

Parkman, Francis, Jr.
1823-1893 .... NCLC **12**
See also DLB 1, 30

Parks, Gordon (Alexander Buchanan)
1912- .... CLC **1, 16; BLC**
See also AITN 2; BW 2; CA 41-44R;
CANR 26; DLB 33; SATA 8

Parnell, Thomas 1679-1718 .... LC **3**
See also DLB 94

Parra, Nicanor 1914- .... CLC **2; HLC**
See also CA 85-88; CANR 32; HW; MTCW

Parrish, Mary Frances
See Fisher, M(ary) F(rances) K(ennedy)

Parson
See Coleridge, Samuel Taylor

Parson Lot
See Kingsley, Charles

Partridge, Anthony
See Oppenheim, E(dward) Phillips

Pascoli, Giovanni 1855-1912 ...... TCLC **45**

Pasolini, Pier Paolo
1922-1975 .... CLC **20, 37**
See also CA 93-96; 61-64; DLB 128;
MTCW

Pasquini
See Silone, Ignazio

Pastan, Linda (Olenik) 1932- ...... CLC **27**
See also CA 61-64; CANR 18, 40; DLB 5

Pasternak, Boris (Leonidovich)
1890-1960 ...... CLC **7, 10, 18, 63; DA;
PC 6; WLC**
See also CA 127; 116; MTCW

Patchen, Kenneth 1911-1972 ... CLC **1, 2, 18**
See also CA 1-4R; 33-36R; CANR 3, 35;
DLB 16, 48; MTCW

Pater, Walter (Horatio)
1839-1894 .... NCLC **7**
See also CDBLB 1832-1890; DLB 57

Paterson, A(ndrew) B(arton)
1864-1941 .... TCLC **32**

Paterson, Katherine (Womeldorf)
1932- .... CLC **12, 30**
See also AAYA 1; CA 21-24R; CANR 28;
CLR 7; DLB 52; JRDA; MAICYA;
MTCW; SATA 13, 53

Patmore, Coventry Kersey Dighton
1823-1896 .... NCLC **9**
See also DLB 35, 98

Paton, Alan (Stewart)
1903-1988 ...... CLC **4, 10, 25, 55; DA;
WLC**
See also CA 13-16; 125; CANR 22; CAP 1;
MTCW; SATA 11; SATA-Obit 56

Paton Walsh, Gillian 1937-
See Walsh, Jill Paton
See also CANR 38; JRDA; MAICYA;
SAAS 3; SATA 4, 72

Paulding, James Kirke 1778-1860.. NCLC **2**
See also DLB 3, 59, 74

Paulin, Thomas Neilson 1949-
See Paulin, Tom
See also CA 123; 128

Paulin, Tom..................... CLC **37**
See also Paulin, Thomas Neilson
See also DLB 40

Paustovsky, Konstantin (Georgievich)
1892-1968 .... CLC **40**
See also CA 93-96; 25-28R

Pavese, Cesare 1908-1950 .... TCLC **3**
See also CA 104; DLB 128

Pavic, Milorad 1929-............. CLC **60**
See also CA 136

Payne, Alan
 See Jakes, John (William)

Paz, Gil
 See Lugones, Leopoldo

Paz, Octavio
 1914- .... **CLC 3, 4, 6, 10, 19, 51, 65;**
 DA; HLC; PC 1; WLC
 See also CA 73-76; CANR 32; DLBY 90;
 HW; MTCW

Peacock, Molly 1947-............ **CLC 60**
 See also CA 103; DLB 120

Peacock, Thomas Love
 1785-1866 .... **NCLC 22**
 See also DLB 96, 116

Peake, Mervyn 1911-1968....... **CLC 7, 54**
 See also CA 5-8R; 25-28R; CANR 3;
 DLB 15; MTCW; SATA 23

Pearce, Philippa .... **CLC 21**
 See also Christie, (Ann) Philippa
 See also CLR 9; MAICYA; SATA 1, 67

Pearl, Eric
 See Elman, Richard

Pearson, T(homas) R(eid) 1956- .... **CLC 39**
 See also CA 120; 130

Peck, Dale 1968(?)- .... **CLC 81**

Peck, John 1941- .... **CLC 3**
 See also CA 49-52; CANR 3

Peck, Richard (Wayne) 1934-...... **CLC 21**
 See also AAYA 1; CA 85-88; CANR 19,
 38; CLR 15; JRDA; MAICYA; SAAS 2;
 SATA 18, 55

Peck, Robert Newton 1928-.... **CLC 17; DA**
 See also AAYA 3; CA 81-84; CANR 31;
 JRDA; MAICYA; SAAS 1; SATA 21, 62

Peckinpah, (David) Sam(uel)
 1925-1984 .... **CLC 20**
 See also CA 109; 114

Pedersen, Knut 1859-1952
 See Hamsun, Knut
 See also CA 104; 119; MTCW

Peeslake, Gaffer
 See Durrell, Lawrence (George)

Peguy, Charles Pierre
 1873-1914 .... **TCLC 10**
 See also CA 107

Pena, Ramon del Valle y
 See Valle-Inclan, Ramon (Maria) del

Pendennis, Arthur Esquir
 See Thackeray, William Makepeace

Penn, William 1644-1718........... **LC 25**
 See also DLB 24

Pepys, Samuel
 1633-1703 .... **LC 11; DA; WLC**
 See also CDBLB 1660-1789; DLB 101

Percy, Walker
 1916-1990 .... **CLC 2, 3, 6, 8, 14, 18, 47,**
 65
 See also CA 1-4R; 131; CANR 1, 23;
 DLB 2; DLBY 80, 90; MTCW

Perec, Georges 1936-1982 .... **CLC 56**
 See also CA 141; DLB 83

Pereda (y Sanchez de Porrua), Jose Maria de
 1833-1906 .... **TCLC 16**
 See also CA 117

Pereda y Porrua, Jose Maria de
 See Pereda (y Sanchez de Porrua), Jose
 Maria de

Peregoy, George Weems
 See Mencken, H(enry) L(ouis)

Perelman, S(idney) J(oseph)
 1904-1979 ... **CLC 3, 5, 9, 15, 23, 44, 49**
 See also AITN 1, 2; CA 73-76; 89-92;
 CANR 18; DLB 11, 44; MTCW

Peret, Benjamin 1899-1959 .... **TCLC 20**
 See also CA 117

Peretz, Isaac Loeb 1851(?)-1915... **TCLC 16**
 See also CA 109

Peretz, Yitzkhok Leibush
 See Peretz, Isaac Loeb

Perez Galdos, Benito 1843-1920... **TCLC 27**
 See also CA 125; HW

Perrault, Charles 1628-1703 .... **LC 2**
 See also MAICYA; SATA 25

Perry, Brighton
 See Sherwood, Robert E(mmet)

Perse, St.-John .... **CLC 4, 11, 46**
 See also Leger, (Marie-Rene Auguste) Alexis
 Saint-Leger

Peseenz, Tulio F.
 See Lopez y Fuentes, Gregorio

Pesetsky, Bette 1932-............ **CLC 28**
 See also CA 133; DLB 130

Peshkov, Alexei Maximovich 1868-1936
 See Gorky, Maxim
 See also CA 105; 141; DA

Pessoa, Fernando (Antonio Nogueira)
 1888-1935 .... **TCLC 27; HLC**
 See also CA 125

Peterkin, Julia Mood 1880-1961.... **CLC 31**
 See also CA 102; DLB 9

Peters, Joan K. 1945-............ **CLC 39**

Peters, Robert L(ouis) 1924-........ **CLC 7**
 See also CA 13-16R; CAAS 8; DLB 105

Petofi, Sandor 1823-1849....... **NCLC 21**

Petrakis, Harry Mark 1923-........ **CLC 3**
 See also CA 9-12R; CANR 4, 30

Petrarch 1304-1374................ **PC 8**

Petrov, Evgeny .... **TCLC 21**
 See also Kataev, Evgeny Petrovich

Petry, Ann (Lane) 1908 ...... **CLC 1, 7, 18**
 See also BW 1; CA 5-8R; CAAS 6;
 CANR 4, 46; CLR 12; DLB 76; JRDA;
 MAICYA; MTCW; SATA 5

Petursson, Halligrimur 1614-1674 .... **LC 8**

Philipson, Morris H. 1926-........ **CLC 53**
 See also CA 1-4R; CANR 4

Phillips, David Graham
 1867-1911 .... **TCLC 44**
 See also CA 108; DLB 9, 12

Phillips, Jack
 See Sandburg, Carl (August)

Phillips, Jayne Anne
 1952-............ **CLC 15, 33; SSC 16**
 See also CA 101; CANR 24; DLBY 80;
 MTCW

Phillips, Richard
 See Dick, Philip K(indred)

Phillips, Robert (Schaeffer) 1938-... **CLC 28**
 See also CA 17-20R; CAAS 13; CANR 8;
 DLB 105

Phillips, Ward
 See Lovecraft, H(oward) P(hillips)

Piccolo, Lucio 1901-1969......... **CLC 13**
 See also CA 97-100; DLB 114

Pickthall, Marjorie L(owry) C(hristie)
 1883-1922 .... **TCLC 21**
 See also CA 107; DLB 92

Pico della Mirandola, Giovanni
 1463-1494 .... **LC 15**

Piercy, Marge
 1936- .... **CLC 3, 6, 14, 18, 27, 62**
 See also CA 21-24R; CAAS 1; CANR 13,
 43; DLB 120; MTCW

Piers, Robert
 See Anthony, Piers

Pieyre de Mandiargues, Andre 1909-1991
 See Mandiargues, Andre Pieyre de
 See also CA 103; 136; CANR 22

Pilnyak, Boris .... **TCLC 23**
 See also Vogau, Boris Andreyevich

Pincherle, Alberto 1907-1990 ... **CLC 11, 18**
 See also Moravia, Alberto
 See also CA 25-28R; 132; CANR 33;
 MTCW

Pinckney, Darryl 1953-........... **CLC 76**
 See also BW 2; CA 143

Pindar 518B.C.-446B.C......... **CMLC 12**

Pineda, Cecile 1942-............. **CLC 39**
 See also CA 118

Pinero, Arthur Wing 1855-1934 ... **TCLC 32**
 See also CA 110; DLB 10

Pinero, Miguel (Antonio Gomez)
 1946-1988 .... **CLC 4, 55**
 See also CA 61-64; 125; CANR 29; HW

Pinget, Robert 1919- .... **CLC 7, 13, 37**
 See also CA 85-88; DLB 83

Pink Floyd
 See Barrett, (Roger) Syd; Gilmour, David;
 Mason, Nick; Waters, Roger; Wright,
 Rick

Pinkney, Edward 1802-1828 ..... **NCLC 31**

Pinkwater, Daniel Manus 1941-.... **CLC 35**
 See also Pinkwater, Manus
 See also AAYA 1; CA 29-32R; CANR 12,
 38; CLR 4; JRDA; MAICYA; SAAS 3;
 SATA 46, 76

Pinkwater, Manus
 See Pinkwater, Daniel Manus
 See also SATA 8

Pinsky, Robert 1940-........ **CLC 9, 19, 38**
 See also CA 29-32R; CAAS 4; DLBY 82

Pinta, Harold
 See Pinter, Harold

Pinter, Harold
 1930- ..... **CLC 1, 3, 6, 9, 11, 15, 27, 58,**
 73; DA; WLC
 See also CA 5-8R; CANR 33; CDBLB 1960
 to Present; DLB 13; MTCW

Pirandello, Luigi
 1867-1936 ..... **TCLC 4, 29; DA; DC 5;**
 WLC
 See also CA 104

Pirsig, Robert M(aynard)
1928- . . . . CLC **4, 6, 73**
See also CA 53-56; CANR 42; MTCW;
SATA 39

Pisarev, Dmitry Ivanovich
1840-1868 . . . . NCLC **25**

Pix, Mary (Griffith) 1666-1709 . . . . . . LC **8**
See also DLB 80

Pixerecourt, Guilbert de
1773-1844 . . . . NCLC **39**

Plaidy, Jean
See Hibbert, Eleanor Alice Burford

Planche, James Robinson
1796-1880 . . . . NCLC **42**

Plant, Robert 1948- . . . . CLC **12**

Plante, David (Robert)
1940- . . . . CLC **7, 23, 38**
See also CA 37-40R; CANR 12, 36;
DLBY 83; MTCW

Plath, Sylvia
1932-1963 . . . . . CLC **1, 2, 3, 5, 9, 11, 14,
17, 50, 51, 62; DA; PC 1; WLC**
See also AAYA 13; CA 19-20; CANR 34;
CAP 2; CDALB 1941-1968; DLB 5, 6;
MTCW

Plato 428(?)B.C.-348(?)B.C.. . . . CMLC **8; DA**

Platonov, Andrei . . . . TCLC **14**
See also Klimentov, Andrei Platonovich

Platt, Kin 1911- . . . . CLC **26**
See also AAYA 11; CA 17-20R; CANR 11;
JRDA; SAAS 17; SATA 21

Plick et Plock
See Simenon, Georges (Jacques Christian)

Plimpton, George (Ames) 1927- . . . . . CLC **36**
See also AITN 1; CA 21-24R; CANR 32;
MTCW; SATA 10

Plomer, William Charles Franklin
1903-1973 . . . . CLC **4, 8**
See also CA 21-22; CANR 34; CAP 2;
DLB 20; MTCW; SATA 24

Plowman, Piers
See Kavanagh, Patrick (Joseph)

Plum, J.
See Wodehouse, P(elham) G(renville)

Plumly, Stanley (Ross) 1939- . . . . . . CLC **33**
See also CA 108; 110; DLB 5

Plumpe, Friedrich Wilhelm
1888-1931 . . . . TCLC **53**
See also CA 112

Poe, Edgar Allan
1809-1849 . . . . . NCLC **1, 16; DA; PC 1;
SSC 1; WLC**
See also AAYA 14; CDALB 1640-1865;
DLB 3, 59, 73, 74; SATA 23

Poet of Titchfield Street, The
See Pound, Ezra (Weston Loomis)

Pohl, Frederik 1919- . . . . CLC **18**
See also CA 61-64; CAAS 1; CANR 11, 37;
DLB 8; MTCW; SATA 24

Poirier, Louis 1910-
See Gracq, Julien
See also CA 122; 126

Poitier, Sidney 1927- . . . . CLC **26**
See also BW 1; CA 117

Polanski, Roman 1933- . . . . CLC **16**
See also CA 77-80

Poliakoff, Stephen 1952- . . . . CLC **38**
See also CA 106; DLB 13

Police, The
See Copeland, Stewart (Armstrong);
Summers, Andrew James; Sumner,
Gordon Matthew

Pollitt, Katha 1949- . . . . CLC **28**
See also CA 120; 122; MTCW

Pollock, (Mary) Sharon 1936- . . . . . . CLC **50**
See also CA 141; DLB 60

Polo, Marco 1254-1324 . . . . CMLC **15:**

Pomerance, Bernard 1940- . . . . CLC **13**
See also CA 101

Ponge, Francis (Jean Gaston Alfred)
1899-1988 . . . . CLC **6, 18**
See also CA 85-88; 126; CANR 40

Pontoppidan, Henrik 1857-1943 . . . TCLC **29**

Poole, Josephine . . . . CLC **17**
See also Helyar, Jane Penelope Josephine
See also SAAS 2; SATA 5

Popa, Vasko 1922- . . . . CLC **19**
See also CA 112

Pope, Alexander
1688-1744 . . . . LC **3; DA; WLC**
See also CDBLB 1660-1789; DLB 95, 101

Porter, Connie (Rose) 1959(?)- . . . . . CLC **70**
See also BW 2; CA 142; SATA 81

Porter, Gene(va Grace) Stratton
1863(?)-1924 . . . . TCLC **21**
See also CA 112

Porter, Katherine Anne
1890-1980 . . . . . . CLC **1, 3, 7, 10, 13, 15,
27; DA; SSC 4**
See also AITN 2; CA 1-4R; 101; CANR 1;
DLB 4, 9, 102; DLBD 12; DLBY 80;
MTCW; SATA 39; SATA-Obit 23

Porter, Peter (Neville Frederick)
1929- . . . . CLC **5, 13, 33**
See also CA 85-88; DLB 40

Porter, William Sydney 1862-1910
See Henry, O.
See also CA 104; 131; CDALB 1865-1917;
DA; DLB 12, 78, 79; MTCW; YABC 2

Portillo (y Pacheco), Jose Lopez
See Lopez Portillo (y Pacheco), Jose

Post, Melville Davisson
1869-1930 . . . . TCLC **39**
See also CA 110

Potok, Chaim 1929- . . . . CLC **2, 7, 14, 26**
See also AITN 1, 2; CA 17-20R; CANR 19,
35; DLB 28; MTCW; SATA 33

Potter, Beatrice
See Webb, (Martha) Beatrice (Potter)
See also MAICYA

Potter, Dennis (Christopher George)
1935-1994 . . . . CLC **58, 86**
See also CA 107; 145; CANR 33; MTCW

Pound, Ezra (Weston Loomis)
1885-1972 . . . . . . CLC **1, 2, 3, 4, 5, 7, 10,
13, 18, 34, 48, 50; DA; PC 4; WLC**
See also CA 5-8R; 37-40R; CANR 40;
CDALB 1917-1929; DLB 4, 45, 63;
MTCW

Povod, Reinaldo 1959-1994 . . . . CLC **44**
See also CA 136; 146

Powell, Anthony (Dymoke)
1905- . . . . CLC **1, 3, 7, 9, 10, 31**
See also CA 1-4R; CANR 1, 32;
CDBLB 1945-1960; DLB 15; MTCW

Powell, Dawn 1897-1965 . . . . CLC **66**
See also CA 5-8R

Powell, Padgett 1952- . . . . CLC **34**
See also CA 126

Powers, J(ames) F(arl)
1917- . . . . CLC **1, 4, 8, 57; SSC 4**
See also CA 1-4R; CANR 2; DLB 130;
MTCW

Powers, John J(ames) 1945-
See Powers, John R.
See also CA 69-72

Powers, John R. . . . . CLC **66**
See also Powers, John J(ames)

Pownall, David 1938- . . . . CLC **10**
See also CA 89-92; CAAS 18; DLB 14

Powys, John Cowper
1872-1963 . . . . CLC **7, 9, 15, 46**
See also CA 85-88; DLB 15; MTCW

Powys, T(heodore) F(rancis)
1875-1953 . . . . TCLC **9**
See also CA 106; DLB 36

Prager, Emily 1952- . . . . CLC **56**

Pratt, E(dwin) J(ohn)
1883(?)-1964 . . . . CLC **19**
See also CA 141; 93-96; DLB 92

Premchand . . . . TCLC **21**
See also Srivastava, Dhanpat Rai

Preussler, Otfried 1923- . . . . CLC **17**
See also CA 77-80; SATA 24

Prevert, Jacques (Henri Marie)
1900-1977 . . . . CLC **15**
See also CA 77-80; 69-72; CANR 29;
MTCW; SATA-Obit 30

Prevost, Abbe (Antoine Francois)
1697-1763 . . . . LC **1**

Price, (Edward) Reynolds
1933- . . . . CLC **3, 6, 13, 43, 50, 63**
See also CA 1-4R; CANR 1, 37; DLB 2

Price, Richard 1949- . . . . CLC **6, 12**
See also CA 49-52; CANR 3; DLBY 81

Prichard, Katharine Susannah
1883-1969 . . . . CLC **46**
See also CA 11-12; CANR 33; CAP 1;
MTCW; SATA 66

Priestley, J(ohn) B(oynton)
1894-1984 . . . . CLC **2, 5, 9, 34**
See also CA 9-12R; 113; CANR 33;
CDBLB 1914-1945; DLB 10, 34, 77, 100,
139; DLBY 84; MTCW

Prince 1958(?)- . . . . CLC **35**

Prince, F(rank) T(empleton) 1912- . . CLC **22**
See also CA 101; CANR 43; DLB 20

Prince Kropotkin
See Kropotkin, Peter (Aleksieevich)

Prior, Matthew 1664-1721 . . . . LC **4**
See also DLB 95

Pritchard, William H(arrison)
1932- . . . . CLC 34
See also CA 65-68; CANR 23; DLB 111

Pritchett, V(ictor) S(awdon)
1900- . . . . . . CLC 5, 13, 15, 41; SSC 14
See also CA 61-64; CANR 31; DLB 15,
139; MTCW

Private 19022
See Manning, Frederic

Probst, Mark   1925- . . . . CLC 59
See also CA 130

Prokosch, Frederic   1908-1989. . . . CLC 4, 48
See also CA 73-76; 128; DLB 48

Prophet, The
See Dreiser, Theodore (Herman Albert)

Prose, Francine   1947-. . . . . CLC 45
See also CA 109; 112; CANR 46

Proudhon
See Cunha, Euclides (Rodrigues Pimenta) da

Proulx, E. Annie   1935 . . . . CLC 81

Proust, (Valentin-Louis-George-Eugene-)
Marcel
1871-1922 . . . TCLC 7, 13, 33; DA; WLC
See also CA 104; 120; DLB 65; MTCW

Prowler, Harley
See Masters, Edgar Lee

Prus, Boleslaw   1845-1912 . . . . TCLC 48

Pryor, Richard (Franklin Lenox Thomas)
1940- . . . . CLC 26
See also CA 122

Przybyszewski, Stanislaw
1868-1927 . . . . TCLC 36
See also DLB 66

Pteleon
See Grieve, C(hristopher) M(urray)

Puckett, Lute
See Masters, Edgar Lee

Puig, Manuel
1932-1990 . . . CLC 3, 5, 10, 28, 65; HLC
See also CA 45-48; CANR 2, 32; DLB 113;
HW; MTCW

Purdy, Al(fred Wellington)
1918- . . . . CLC 3, 6, 14, 50
See also CA 81-84; CAAS 17; CANR 42;
DLB 88

Purdy, James (Amos)
1923- . . . . CLC 2, 4, 10, 28, 52
See also CA 33-36R; CAAS 1; CANR 19;
DLB 2; MTCW

Pure, Simon
See Swinnerton, Frank Arthur

Pushkin, Alexander (Sergeyevich)
1799-1837 . . . . NCLC 3, 27; DA; PC 10;
WLC
See also SATA 61

P'u Sung-ling   1640-1715 . . . . LC 3

Putnam, Arthur Lee
See Alger, Horatio, Jr.

Puzo, Mario   1920- . . . . CLC 1, 2, 6, 36
See also CA 65-68; CANR 4, 42; DLB 6;
MTCW

Pym, Barbara (Mary Crampton)
1913-1980 . . . . CLC 13, 19, 37
See also CA 13-14; 97-100; CANR 13, 34;
CAP 1; DLB 14; DLBY 87; MTCW

Pynchon, Thomas (Ruggles, Jr.)
1937- . . . . . CLC 2, 3, 6, 9, 11, 18, 33, 62,
72; DA; SSC 14; WLC
See also BEST 90:2; CA 17-20R; CANR 22,
46; DLB 2; MTCW

Qian Zhongshu
See Ch'ien Chung-shu

Qroll
See Dagerman, Stig (Halvard)

Quarrington, Paul (Lewis)   1953-. . . . CLC 65
See also CA 129

Quasimodo, Salvatore   1901-1968 . . . CLC 10
See also CA 13-16; 25-28R; CAP 1;
DLB 114; MTCW

Queen, Ellery. . . . . CLC 3, 11
See also Dannay, Frederic; Davidson,
Avram; Lee, Manfred B(ennington);
Sturgeon, Theodore (Hamilton); Vance,
John Holbrook

Queen, Ellery, Jr.
See Dannay, Frederic; Lee, Manfred
B(ennington)

Queneau, Raymond
1903-1976 . . . . CLC 2, 5, 10, 42
See also CA 77-80; 69-72; CANR 32;
DLB 72; MTCW

Quevedo, Francisco de   1580-1645. . . . LC 23

Quiller-Couch, Arthur Thomas
1863-1944 . . . . TCLC 53
See also CA 118; DLB 135

Quin, Ann (Marie)   1936-1973 . . . . . . CLC 6
See also CA 9-12R; 45-48; DLB 14

Quinn, Martin
See Smith, Martin Cruz

Quinn, Simon
See Smith, Martin Cruz

Quiroga, Horacio (Sylvestre)
1878-1937 . . . . TCLC 20; HLC
See also CA 117; 131; HW; MTCW

Quoirez, Francoise   1935-. . . . . CLC 9
See also Sagan, Francoise
See also CA 49-52; CANR 6, 39; MTCW

Raabe, Wilhelm   1831-1910 . . . . TCLC 45
See also DLB 129

Rabe, David (William)   1940-. . . CLC 4, 8, 33
See also CA 85-88; CABS 3; DLB 7

Rabelais, Francois
1483-1553 . . . . LC 5; DA; WLC

Rabinovitch, Sholem   1859-1916
See Aleichem, Sholom
See also CA 104

Racine, Jean   1639-1699 . . . . LC 28

Radcliffe, Ann (Ward)   1764-1823 . . NCLC 6
See also DLB 39

Radiguet, Raymond   1903-1923 . . . . TCLC 29
See also DLB 65

Radnoti, Miklos   1909-1944 . . . . . . TCLC 16
See also CA 118

Rado, James   1939- . . . . CLC 17
See also CA 105

Radvanyi, Netty   1900-1983
See Seghers, Anna
See also CA 85-88; 110

Rae, Ben
See Griffiths, Trevor

Raeburn, John (Hay)   1941-. . . . . CLC 34
See also CA 57-60

Ragni, Gerome   1942-1991 . . . . CLC 17
See also CA 105; 134

Rahv, Philip   1908-1973 . . . . CLC 24
See also Greenberg, Ivan
See also DLB 137

Raine, Craig   1944-. . . . . CLC 32
See also CA 108; CANR 29; DLB 40

Raine, Kathleen (Jessie)   1908- . . . CLC 7, 45
See also CA 85-88; CANR 46; DLB 20;
MTCW

Rainis, Janis   1865-1929. . . . . TCLC 29

Rakosi, Carl. . . . . CLC 47
See also Rawley, Callman
See also CAAS 5

Raleigh, Richard
See Lovecraft, H(oward) P(hillips)

Rallentando, H. P.
See Sayers, Dorothy L(eigh)

Ramal, Walter
See de la Mare, Walter (John)

Ramon, Juan
See Jimenez (Mantecon), Juan Ramon

Ramos, Graciliano   1892-1953 . . . . . TCLC 32

Rampersad, Arnold   1941-. . . . . CLC 44
See also BW 2; CA 127; 133; DLB 111

Rampling, Anne
See Rice, Anne

Ramuz, Charles-Ferdinand
1878-1947 . . . . TCLC 33

Rand, Ayn
1905-1982 . . . . . . CLC 3, 30, 44, 79; DA;
WLC
See also AAYA 10; CA 13-16R; 105;
CANR 27; MTCW

Randall, Dudley (Felker)
1914- . . . . CLC 1; BLC
See also BW 1; CA 25-28R; CANR 23;
DLB 41

Randall, Robert
See Silverberg, Robert

Ranger, Ken
See Creasey, John

Ransom, John Crowe
1888-1974 . . . . CLC 2, 4, 5, 11, 24
See also CA 5-8R; 49-52; CANR 6, 34;
DLB 45, 63; MTCW

Rao, Raja   1909- . . . . CLC 25, 56
See also CA 73-76; MTCW

Raphael, Frederic (Michael)
1931- . . . . CLC 2, 14
See also CA 1-4R; CANR 1; DLB 14

Ratcliffe, James P.
See Mencken, H(enry) L(ouis)

Rathbone, Julian   1935- . . . . CLC 41
See also CA 101; CANR 34

Rattigan, Terence (Mervyn)
1911-1977 . . . . CLC 7
See also CA 85-88; 73-76;
CDBLB 1945-1960; DLB 13; MTCW

Ratushinskaya, Irina 1954- . . . . CLC 54
See also CA 129

Raven, Simon (Arthur Noel)
1927- . . . . CLC 14
See also CA 81-84

Rawley, Callman 1903-
See Rakosi, Carl
See also CA 21-24R; CANR 12, 32

Rawlings, Marjorie Kinnan
1896-1953 . . . . TCLC 4
See also CA 104; 137; DLB 9, 22, 102;
JRDA; MAICYA; YABC 1

Ray, Satyajit 1921-1992 . . . . CLC 16, 76
See also CA 114; 137

Read, Herbert Edward 1893-1968 . . . . CLC 4
See also CA 85-88; 25-28R; DLB 20

Read, Piers Paul 1941- . . . . . . CLC 4, 10, 25
See also CA 21-24R; CANR 38; DLB 14;
SATA 21

Reade, Charles 1814-1884 . . . . NCLC 2
See also DLB 21

Reade, Hamish
See Gray, Simon (James Holliday)

Reading, Peter 1946- . . . . CLC 47
See also CA 103; CANR 46; DLB 40

Reaney, James 1926- . . . . CLC 13
See also CA 41-44R; CAAS 15; CANR 42;
DLB 68; SATA 43

Rebreanu, Liviu 1885-1944 . . . . . . TCLC 28

Rechy, John (Francisco)
1934- . . . . CLC 1, 7, 14, 18; HLC
See also CA 5-8R; CAAS 4; CANR 6, 32;
DLB 122; DLBY 82; HW

Redcam, Tom 1870-1933 . . . . TCLC 25

Reddin, Keith . . . . CLC 67

Redgrove, Peter (William)
1932- . . . . CLC 6, 41
See also CA 1-4R; CANR 3, 39; DLB 40

Redmon, Anne . . . . CLC 22
See also Nightingale, Anne Redmon
See also DLBY 86

Reed, Eliot
See Ambler, Eric

Reed, Ishmael
1938- . . . CLC 2, 3, 5, 6, 13, 32, 60; BLC
See also BW 2; CA 21-24R; CANR 25;
DLB 2, 5, 33; DLBD 8; MTCW

Reed, John (Silas) 1887-1920 . . . . . . TCLC 9
See also CA 106

Reed, Lou . . . . CLC 21
See also Firbank, Louis

Reeve, Clara 1729-1807 . . . . NCLC 19
See also DLB 39

Reich, Wilhelm 1897-1957 . . . . TCLC 57

Reid, Christopher (John) 1949- . . . . . CLC 33
See also CA 140; DLB 40

Reid, Desmond
See Moorcock, Michael (John)

Reid Banks, Lynne 1929-
See Banks, Lynne Reid
See also CA 1-4R; CANR 6, 22, 38;
CLR 24; JRDA; MAICYA; SATA 22, 75

Reilly, William K.
See Creasey, John

Reiner, Max
See Caldwell, (Janet Miriam) Taylor
(Holland)

Reis, Ricardo
See Pessoa, Fernando (Antonio Nogueira)

Remarque, Erich Maria
1898-1970 . . . . CLC 21; DA
See also CA 77-80; 29-32R; DLB 56;
MTCW

Remizov, A.
See Remizov, Aleksei (Mikhailovich)

Remizov, A. M.
See Remizov, Aleksei (Mikhailovich)

Remizov, Aleksei (Mikhailovich)
1877-1957 . . . . TCLC 27
See also CA 125; 133

Renan, Joseph Ernest
1823-1892 . . . . NCLC 26

Renard, Jules 1864-1910 . . . . TCLC 17
See also CA 117

Renault, Mary . . . . CLC 3, 11, 17
See also Challans, Mary
See also DLBY 83

Rendell, Ruth (Barbara) 1930- . . CLC 28, 48
See also Vine, Barbara
See also CA 109; CANR 32; DLB 87;
MTCW

Renoir, Jean 1894-1979 . . . . CLC 20
See also CA 129; 85-88

Resnais, Alain 1922- . . . . CLC 16

Reverdy, Pierre 1889-1960 . . . . CLC 53
See also CA 97-100; 89-92

Rexroth, Kenneth
1905-1982 . . . . . . CLC 1, 2, 6, 11, 22, 49
See also CA 5-8R; 107; CANR 14, 34;
CDALB 1941-1968; DLB 16, 48;
DLBY 82; MTCW

Reyes, Alfonso 1889-1959 . . . . TCLC 33
See also CA 131; HW

Reyes y Basoalto, Ricardo Eliecer Neftali
See Neruda, Pablo

Reymont, Wladyslaw (Stanislaw)
1868(?)-1925 . . . . TCLC 5
See also CA 104

Reynolds, Jonathan 1942- . . . . CLC 6, 38
See also CA 65-68; CANR 28

Reynolds, Joshua 1723-1792 . . . . LC 15
See also DLB 104

Reynolds, Michael Shane 1937- . . . . CLC 44
See also CA 65-68; CANR 9

Reznikoff, Charles 1894-1976 . . . . CLC 9
See also CA 33-36; 61-64; CAP 2; DLB 28,
45

Rezzori (d'Arezzo), Gregor von
1914- . . . . CLC 25
See also CA 122; 136

Rhine, Richard
See Silverstein, Alvin

Rhodes, Eugene Manlove
1869-1934 . . . . TCLC 53

R'hoone
See Balzac, Honore de

Rhys, Jean
1890(?)-1979 . . . . CLC 2, 4, 6, 14, 19, 51
See also CA 25-28R; 85-88; CANR 35;
CDBLB 1945-1960; DLB 36, 117; MTCW

Ribeiro, Darcy 1922- . . . . CLC 34
See also CA 33-36R

Ribeiro, Joao Ubaldo (Osorio Pimentel)
1941- . . . . CLC 10, 67
See also CA 81-84

Ribman, Ronald (Burt) 1932- . . . . CLC 7
See also CA 21-24R; CANR 46

Ricci, Nino 1959- . . . . CLC 70
See also CA 137

Rice, Anne 1941- . . . . CLC 41
See also AAYA 9; BEST 89:2; CA 65-68;
CANR 12, 36

Rice, Elmer (Leopold)
1892-1967 . . . . CLC 7, 49
See also CA 21-22; 25-28R; CAP 2; DLB 4,
7; MTCW

Rice, Tim(othy Miles Bindon)
1944- . . . . CLC 21
See also CA 103; CANR 46

Rich, Adrienne (Cecile)
1929- . . . . CLC 3, 6, 7, 11, 18, 36, 73, 76;
PC 5
See also CA 9-12R; CANR 20; DLB 5, 67;
MTCW

Rich, Barbara
See Graves, Robert (von Ranke)

Rich, Robert
See Trumbo, Dalton

Richards, David Adams 1950- . . . . . . CLC 59
See also CA 93-96; DLB 53

Richards, I(vor) A(rmstrong)
1893-1979 . . . . CLC 14, 24
See also CA 41-44R; 89-92; CANR 34;
DLB 27

Richardson, Anne
See Roiphe, Anne (Richardson)

Richardson, Dorothy Miller
1873-1957 . . . . TCLC 3
See also CA 104; DLB 36

Richardson, Ethel Florence (Lindesay)
1870-1946
See Richardson, Henry Handel
See also CA 105

Richardson, Henry Handel . . . . TCLC 4
See also Richardson, Ethel Florence
(Lindesay)

Richardson, Samuel
1689-1761 . . . . LC 1; DA; WLC
See also CDBLB 1660-1789; DLB 39

Richler, Mordecai
1931- . . . . CLC 3, 5, 9, 13, 18, 46, 70
See also AITN 1; CA 65-68; CANR 31;
CLR 17; DLB 53; MAICYA; MTCW;
SATA 44; SATA-Brief 27

Rosenblatt, Joseph 1933-
See Rosenblatt, Joe
See also CA 89-92

Rosenfeld, Samuel 1896-1963
See Tzara, Tristan
See also CA 89-92

Rosenthal, M(acha) L(ouis) 1917-... CLC 28
See also CA 1-4R; CAAS 6; CANR 4;
DLB 5; SATA 59

Ross, Barnaby
See Dannay, Frederic

Ross, Bernard L.
See Follett, Ken(neth Martin)

Ross, J. H.
See Lawrence, T(homas) E(dward)

Ross, Martin
See Martin, Violet Florence
See also DLB 135

Ross, (James) Sinclair 1908-....... CLC 13
See also CA 73-76; DLB 88

Rossetti, Christina (Georgina)
1830-1894 ... NCLC 2; DA; PC 7; WLC
See also DLB 35; MAICYA; SATA 20

Rossetti, Dante Gabriel
1828-1882 .... NCLC 4; DA; WLC
See also CDBLB 1832-1890; DLB 35

Rossner, Judith (Perelman)
1935- .... CLC 6, 9, 29
See also AITN 2; BEST 90:3; CA 17-20R;
CANR 18; DLB 6; MTCW

Rostand, Edmond (Eugene Alexis)
1868-1918 .... TCLC 6, 37; DA
See also CA 104; 126; MTCW

Roth, Henry 1906-........... CLC 2, 6, 11
See also CA 11-12; CANR 38; CAP 1;
DLB 28; MTCW

Roth, Joseph 1894-1939......... TCLC 33
See also DLB 85

Roth, Philip (Milton)
1933- ...... CLC 1, 2, 3, 4, 6, 9, 15, 22,
31, 47, 66, 86; DA; WLC
See also BEST 90:3; CA 1-4R; CANR 1, 22,
36; CDALB 1968-1988; DLB 2, 28;
DLBY 82; MTCW

Rothenberg, Jerome 1931-....... CLC 6, 57
See also CA 45-48; CANR 1; DLB 5

Roumain, Jacques (Jean Baptiste)
1907-1944 .... TCLC 19; BLC
See also BW 1; CA 117; 125

Rourke, Constance (Mayfield)
1885-1941 .... TCLC 12
See also CA 107; YABC 1

Rousseau, Jean-Baptiste 1671-1741 ... LC 9

Rousseau, Jean-Jacques
1712-1778 .... LC 14; DA; WLC

Roussel, Raymond 1877-1933 ..... TCLC 20
See also CA 117

Rovit, Earl (Herbert) 1927-......... CLC 7
See also CA 5-8R; CANR 12

Rowe, Nicholas 1674-1718.......... LC 8
See also DLB 84

Rowley, Ames Dorrance
See Lovecraft, H(oward) P(hillips)

Rowson, Susanna Haswell
1762(?)-1824 .... NCLC 5
See also DLB 37

Roy, Gabrielle 1909-1983....... CLC 10, 14
See also CA 53-56; 110; CANR 5; DLB 68;
MTCW

Rozewicz, Tadeusz 1921-........ CLC 9, 23
See also CA 108; CANR 36; MTCW

Ruark, Gibbons 1941- .... CLC 3
See also CA 33-36R; CANR 14, 31;
DLB 120

Rubens, Bernice (Ruth) 1923-... CLC 19, 31
See also CA 25-28R; CANR 33; DLB 14;
MTCW

Rudkin, (James) David 1936- ...... CLC 14
See also CA 89-92; DLB 13

Rudnik, Raphael 1933-............. CLC 7
See also CA 29-32R

Ruffian, M.
See Hasek, Jaroslav (Matej Frantisek)

Ruiz, Jose Martinez .... CLC 11
See also Martinez Ruiz, Jose

Rukeyser, Muriel
1913-1980 .... CLC 6, 10, 15, 27; PC 12
See also CA 5-8R; 93-96; CANR 26;
DLB 48; MTCW; SATA-Obit 22

Rule, Jane (Vance) 1931-.......... CLC 27
See also CA 25-28R; CAAS 18; CANR 12;
DLB 60

Rulfo, Juan 1918-1986.... CLC 8, 80; HLC
See also CA 85-88; 118; CANR 26;
DLB 113; HW; MTCW

Runeberg, Johan 1804-1877...... NCLC 41

Runyon, (Alfred) Damon
1884(?)-1946 .... TCLC 10
See also CA 107; DLB 11, 86

Rush, Norman 1933-.............. CLC 44
See also CA 121; 126

Rushdie, (Ahmed) Salman
1947- .... CLC 23, 31, 55
See also BEST 89:3; CA 108; 111;
CANR 33; MTCW

Rushforth, Peter (Scott) 1945- ..... CLC 19
See also CA 101

Ruskin, John 1819-1900.......... TCLC 20
See also CA 114; 129; CDBLB 1832-1890;
DLB 55; SATA 24

Russ, Joanna 1937-.............. CLC 15
See also CA 25-28R; CANR 11, 31; DLB 8;
MTCW

Russell, (Henry) Ken(neth Alfred)
1927- .... CLC 16
See also CA 105

Russell, Willy 1947-.............. CLC 60

Rutherford, Mark .... TCLC 25
See also White, William Hale
See also DLB 18

Ryan, Cornelius (John) 1920-1974 ... CLC 7
See also CA 69-72; 53-56; CANR 38

Ryan, Michael 1946- .... CLC 65
See also CA 49-52; DLBY 82

Rybakov, Anatoli (Naumovich)
1911- .... CLC 23, 53
See also CA 126; 135; SATA 79

Ryder, Jonathan
See Ludlum, Robert

Ryga, George 1932-1987 .... CLC 14
See also CA 101; 124; CANR 43; DLB 60

S. S.
See Sassoon, Siegfried (Lorraine)

Saba, Umberto 1883-1957 .... TCLC 33
See also CA 144; DLB 114

Sabatini, Rafael 1875-1950 .... TCLC 47

Sabato, Ernesto (R.)
1911- .... CLC 10, 23; HLC
See also CA 97-100; CANR 32; DLB 145;
HW; MTCW

Sacastru, Martin
See Bioy Casares, Adolfo

Sacher-Masoch, Leopold von
1836(?)-1895 .... NCLC 31

Sachs, Marilyn (Stickle) 1927- ..... CLC 35
See also AAYA 2; CA 17-20R; CANR 13,
47; CLR 2; JRDA; MAICYA; SAAS 2;
SATA 3, 68

Sachs, Nelly 1891-1970 .... CLC 14
See also CA 17-18; 25-28R; CAP 2

Sackler, Howard (Oliver)
1929-1982 .... CLC 14
See also CA 61-64; 108; CANR 30; DLB 7

Sacks, Oliver (Wolf) 1933- .... CLC 67
See also CA 53-56; CANR 28; MTCW

Sade, Donatien Alphonse Francois Comte
1740-1814 .... NCLC 47

Sadoff, Ira 1945-................. CLC 9
See also CA 53-56; CANR 5, 21; DLB 120

Saetone
See Camus, Albert

Safire, William 1929-............. CLC 10
See also CA 17-20R; CANR 31

Sagan, Carl (Edward) 1934-........ CLC 30
See also AAYA 2; CA 25-28R; CANR 11,
36; MTCW; SATA 58

Sagan, Francoise .... CLC 3, 6, 9, 17, 36
See also Quoirez, Francoise
See also DLB 83

Sahgal, Nayantara (Pandit) 1927-... CLC 41
See also CA 9-12R; CANR 11

Saint, H(arry) F. 1941- .... CLC 50
See also CA 127

St. Aubin de Teran, Lisa 1953-
See Teran, Lisa St. Aubin de
See also CA 118; 126

Sainte-Beuve, Charles Augustin
1804-1869 .... NCLC 5

Saint-Exupery, Antoine (Jean Baptiste Marie
Roger) de
1900-1944 .... TCLC 2, 56; WLC
See also CA 108; 132; CLR 10; DLB 72;
MAICYA; MTCW; SATA 20

St. John, David
See Hunt, E(verette) Howard, (Jr.)

Saint-John Perse
See Leger, (Marie-Rene Auguste) Alexis
Saint-Leger

Saintsbury, George (Edward Bateman)
1845-1933 .... TCLC 31
See also DLB 57

Shacochis, Robert G. 1951-
See Shacochis, Bob
See also CA 119; 124

Shaffer, Anthony (Joshua) 1926-.... **CLC 19**
See also CA 110; 116; DLB 13

Shaffer, Peter (Levin)
1926- .... **CLC 5, 14, 18, 37, 60**
See also CA 25-28R; CANR 25, 47;
CDBLB 1960 to Present; DLB 13;
MTCW

Shakey, Bernard
See Young, Neil

Shalamov, Varlam (Tikhonovich)
1907(?)-1982 .... **CLC 18**
See also CA 129; 105

Shamlu, Ahmad 1925- .... **CLC 10**

Shammas, Anton 1951-............ **CLC 55**

Shange, Ntozake
1948- .... **CLC 8, 25, 38, 74; BLC; DC 3**
See also AAYA 9; BW 2; CA 85-88;
CABS 3; CANR 27; DLB 38; MTCW

Shanley, John Patrick 1950-....... **CLC 75**
See also CA 128; 133

Shapcott, Thomas William 1935- ... **CLC 38**
See also CA 69-72

Shapiro, Jane.................... **CLC 76**

Shapiro, Karl (Jay) 1913- .. **CLC 4, 8, 15, 53**
See also CA 1-4R; CAAS 6; CANR 1, 36;
DLB 48; MTCW

Sharp, William 1855-1905 .... **TCLC 39**

Sharpe, Thomas Ridley 1928-
See Sharpe, Tom
See also CA 114; 122

Sharpe, Tom.................... **CLC 36**
See also Sharpe, Thomas Ridley
See also DLB 14

Shaw, Bernard.................. **TCLC 45**
See also Shaw, George Bernard
See also BW 1

Shaw, G. Bernard
See Shaw, George Bernard

Shaw, George Bernard
1856-1950 .... **TCLC 3, 9, 21; DA; WLC**
See also Shaw, Bernard
See also CA 104; 128; CDBLB 1914-1945;
DLB 10, 57; MTCW

Shaw, Henry Wheeler
1818-1885 .... **NCLC 15**
See also DLB 11

Shaw, Irwin 1913-1984...... **CLC 7, 23, 34**
See also AITN 1; CA 13-16R; 112;
CANR 21; CDALB 1941-1968; DLB 6,
102; DLBY 84; MTCW

Shaw, Robert 1927-1978 .... **CLC 5**
See also AITN 1; CA 1-4R; 81-84;
CANR 4; DLB 13, 14

Shaw, T. E.
See Lawrence, T(homas) E(dward)

Shawn, Wallace 1943- .... **CLC 41**
See also CA 112

Shea, Lisa 1953-................ **CLC 86**

Sheed, Wilfrid (John Joseph)
1930- .... **CLC 2, 4, 10, 53**
See also CA 65-68; CANR 30; DLB 6;
MTCW

Sheldon, Alice Hastings Bradley
1915(?)-1987
See Tiptree, James, Jr.
See also CA 108; 122; CANR 34; MTCW

Sheldon, John
See Bloch, Robert (Albert)

Shelley, Mary Wollstonecraft (Godwin)
1797-1851 .... **NCLC 14; DA; WLC**
See also CDBLB 1789-1832; DLB 110, 116;
SATA 29

Shelley, Percy Bysshe
1792-1822 .... **NCLC 18; DA; WLC**
See also CDBLB 1789-1832; DLB 96, 110

Shepard, Jim 1956-................ **CLC 36**
See also CA 137

Shepard, Lucius 1947- .... **CLC 34**
See also CA 128; 141

Shepard, Sam
1943- .... **CLC 4, 6, 17, 34, 41, 44; DC 5**
See also AAYA 1; CA 69-72; CABS 3;
CANR 22; DLB 7; MTCW

Shepherd, Michael
See Ludlum, Robert

Sherburne, Zoa (Morin) 1912-...... **CLC 30**
See also AAYA 13; CA 1-4R; CANR 3, 37;
MAICYA; SAAS 18; SATA 3

Sheridan, Frances 1724-1766........ **LC 7**
See also DLB 39, 84

Sheridan, Richard Brinsley
1751-1816 ... **NCLC 5; DA; DC 1; WLC**
See also CDBLB 1660-1789; DLB 89

Sherman, Jonathan Marc.......... **CLC 55**

Sherman, Martin 1941(?)-......... **CLC 19**
See also CA 116; 123

Sherwin, Judith Johnson 1936-... **CLC 7, 15**
See also CA 25-28R; CANR 34

Sherwood, Frances 1940-.......... **CLC 81**

Sherwood, Robert E(mmet)
1896-1955 .... **TCLC 3**
See also CA 104; DLB 7, 26

Shestov, Lev 1866-1938 .... **TCLC 56**

Shiel, M(atthew) P(hipps)
1865-1947 .... **TCLC 8**
See also CA 106

Shiga, Naoya 1883-1971.......... **CLC 33**
See also CA 101; 33-36R

Shih, Su 1036-1101............ **CMLC 15:**

Shilts, Randy 1951-1994 .... **CLC 85**
See also CA 115; 127; 144; CANR 45

Shimazaki Haruki 1872-1943
See Shimazaki Toson
See also CA 105; 134

Shimazaki Toson.................. **TCLC 5**
See also Shimazaki Haruki

Sholokhov, Mikhail (Aleksandrovich)
1905-1984 .... **CLC 7, 15**
See also CA 101; 112; MTCW;
SATA-Obit 36

Shone, Patric
See Hanley, James

Shreve, Susan Richards 1939-...... **CLC 23**
See also CA 49-52; CAAS 5; CANR 5, 38;
MAICYA; SATA 46; SATA-Brief 41

Shue, Larry 1946-1985............ **CLC 52**
See also CA 145; 117

Shu-Jen, Chou 1881-1936
See Hsun, Lu
See also CA 104

Shulman, Alix Kates 1932- ...... **CLC 2, 10**
See also CA 29-32R; CANR 43; SATA 7

Shuster, Joe 1914- .... **CLC 21**

Shute, Nevil.................... **CLC 30**
See also Norway, Nevil Shute

Shuttle, Penelope (Diane) 1947-..... **CLC 7**
See also CA 93-96; CANR 39; DLB 14, 40

Sidney, Mary 1561-1621 .... **LC 19**

Sidney, Sir Philip 1554-1586.... **LC 19; DA**
See also CDBLB Before 1660

Siegel, Jerome 1914- .... **CLC 21**
See also CA 116

Siegel, Jerry
See Siegel, Jerome

Sienkiewicz, Henryk (Adam Alexander Pius)
1846-1916 .... **TCLC 3**
See also CA 104; 134

Sierra, Gregorio Martinez
See Martinez Sierra, Gregorio

Sierra, Maria (de la O'LeJarraga) Martinez
See Martinez Sierra, Maria (de la
O'LeJarraga)

Sigal, Clancy 1926-................ **CLC 7**
See also CA 1-4R

Sigourney, Lydia Howard (Huntley)
1791-1865 .... **NCLC 21**
See also DLB 1, 42, 73

Siguenza y Gongora, Carlos de
1645-1700 .... **LC 8**

Sigurjonsson, Johann 1880-1919... **TCLC 27**

Sikelianos, Angelos 1884-1951 .... **TCLC 39**

Silkin, Jon 1930- .... **CLC 2, 6, 43**
See also CA 5-8R; CAAS 5; DLB 27

Silko, Leslie (Marmon)
1948- .... **CLC 23, 74; DA**
See also AAYA 14; CA 115; 122;
CANR 45; DLB 143; NNAL

Sillanpaa, Frans Eemil 1888-1964... **CLC 19**
See also CA 129; 93-96; MTCW

Sillitoe, Alan
1928- .... **CLC 1, 3, 6, 10, 19, 57**
See also AITN 1; CA 9-12R; CAAS 2;
CANR 8, 26; CDBLB 1960 to Present;
DLB 14, 139; MTCW; SATA 61

Silone, Ignazio 1900-1978 .... **CLC 4**
See also CA 25-28; 81-84; CANR 34;
CAP 2; MTCW

Silver, Joan Micklin 1935- .... **CLC 20**
See also CA 114; 121

Silver, Nicholas
See Faust, Frederick (Schiller)

Silverberg, Robert 1935- .... **CLC 7**
See also CA 1-4R; CAAS 3; CANR 1, 20,
36; DLB 8; MAICYA; MTCW; SATA 13

Silverstein, Alvin 1933- . . . . CLC 17
See also CA 49-52; CANR 2; CLR 25;
JRDA; MAICYA; SATA 8, 69

Silverstein, Virginia B(arbara Opshelor)
1937- . . . . CLC 17
See also CA 49-52; CANR 2; CLR 25;
JRDA; MAICYA; SATA 8, 69

Sim, Georges
See Simenon, Georges (Jacques Christian)

Simak, Clifford D(onald)
1904-1988 . . . . CLC 1, 55
See also CA 1-4R; 125; CANR 1, 35;
DLB 8; MTCW; SATA-Obit 56

Simenon, Georges (Jacques Christian)
1903-1989 . . . . . . CLC 1, 2, 3, 8, 18, 47
See also CA 85-88; 129; CANR 35;
DLB 72; DLBY 89; MTCW

Simic, Charles 1938- . . . CLC 6, 9, 22, 49, 68
See also CA 29-32R; CAAS 4; CANR 12,
33; DLB 105

Simmons, Charles (Paul) 1924- . . . . . CLC 57
See also CA 89-92

Simmons, Dan 1948- . . . . CLC 44
See also CA 138

Simmons, James (Stewart Alexander)
1933- . . . . CLC 43
See also CA 105; DLB 40

Simms, William Gilmore
1806-1870 . . . . NCLC 3
See also DLB 3, 30, 59, 73

Simon, Carly 1945- . . . . CLC 26
See also CA 105

Simon, Claude 1913- . . . . . . CLC 4, 9, 15, 39
See also CA 89-92; CANR 33; DLB 83;
MTCW

Simon, (Marvin) Neil
1927- . . . . CLC 6, 11, 31, 39, 70
See also AITN 1; CA 21-24R; CANR 26;
DLB 7; MTCW

Simon, Paul 1942(?)- . . . . CLC 17
See also CA 116

Simonon, Paul 1956(?)- . . . . CLC 30

Simpson, Harriette
See Arnow, Harriette (Louisa) Simpson

Simpson, Louis (Aston Marantz)
1923- . . . . CLC 4, 7, 9, 32
See also CA 1-4R; CAAS 4; CANR 1;
DLB 5; MTCW

Simpson, Mona (Elizabeth) 1957- . . . CLC 44
See also CA 122; 135

Simpson, N(orman) F(rederick)
1919- . . . . CLC 29
See also CA 13-16R; DLB 13

Sinclair, Andrew (Annandale)
1935- . . . . CLC 2, 14
See also CA 9-12R; CAAS 5; CANR 14, 38;
DLB 14; MTCW

Sinclair, Emil
See Hesse, Hermann

Sinclair, Iain 1943- . . . . CLC 76
See also CA 132

Sinclair, Iain MacGregor
See Sinclair, Iain

Sinclair, Mary Amelia St. Clair 1865(?)-1946
See Sinclair, May
See also CA 104

Sinclair, May . . . . TCLC 3, 11
See also Sinclair, Mary Amelia St. Clair
See also DLB 36, 135

Sinclair, Upton (Beall)
1878-1968 . . . . . . CLC 1, 11, 15, 63; DA;
WLC
See also CA 5-8R; 25-28R; CANR 7;
CDALB 1929-1941; DLB 9; MTCW;
SATA 9

Singer, Isaac
See Singer, Isaac Bashevis

Singer, Isaac Bashevis
1904-1991 . . . . CLC 1, 3, 6, 9, 11, 15, 23,
38, 69; DA; SSC 3; WLC
See also AITN 1, 2; CA 1-4R; 134;
CANR 1, 39; CDALB 1941-1968; CLR 1;
DLB 6, 28, 52; DLBY 91; JRDA;
MAICYA; MTCW; SATA 3, 27;
SATA-Obit 68

Singer, Israel Joshua 1893-1944 . . . TCLC 33

Singh, Khushwant 1915- . . . . CLC 11
See also CA 9-12R; CAAS 9; CANR 6

Sinjohn, John
See Galsworthy, John

Sinyavsky, Andrei (Donatevich)
1925- . . . . CLC 8
See also CA 85-88

Sirin, V.
See Nabokov, Vladimir (Vladimirovich)

Sissman, L(ouis) E(dward)
1928-1976 . . . . CLC 9, 18
See also CA 21-24R; 65-68; CANR 13;
DLB 5

Sisson, C(harles) H(ubert) 1914- . . . . . CLC 8
See also CA 1-4R; CAAS 3; CANR 3;
DLB 27

Sitwell, Dame Edith
1887-1964 . . . . CLC 2, 9, 67; PC 3
See also CA 9-12R; CANR 35;
CDBLB 1945-1960; DLB 20; MTCW

Sjoewall, Maj 1935- . . . . CLC 7
See also CA 65-68

Sjowall, Maj
See Sjoewall, Maj

Skelton, Robin 1925- . . . . CLC 13
See also AITN 2; CA 5-8R; CAAS 5;
CANR 28; DLB 27, 53

Skolimowski, Jerzy 1938- . . . . CLC 20
See also CA 128

Skram, Amalie (Bertha)
1847-1905 . . . . TCLC 25

Skvorecky, Josef (Vaclav)
1924- . . . . CLC 15, 39, 69
See also CA 61-64; CAAS 1; CANR 10, 34;
MTCW

Slade, Bernard . . . . CLC 11, 46
See also Newbound, Bernard Slade
See also CAAS 9; DLB 53

Slaughter, Carolyn 1946- . . . . CLC 56
See also CA 85-88

Slaughter, Frank G(ill) 1908- . . . . . . CLC 29
See also AITN 2; CA 5-8R; CANR 5

Slavitt, David R(ytman) 1935- . . . . CLC 5, 14
See also CA 21-24R; CAAS 3; CANR 41;
DLB 5, 6

Slesinger, Tess 1905-1945 . . . . TCLC 10
See also CA 107; DLB 102

Slessor, Kenneth 1901-1971 . . . . CLC 14
See also CA 102; 89-92

Slowacki, Juliusz 1809-1849 . . . . . NCLC 15

Smart, Christopher 1722-1771 . . . . LC 3
See also DLB 109

Smart, Elizabeth 1913-1986 . . . . CLC 54
See also CA 81-84; 118; DLB 88

Smiley, Jane (Graves) 1949- . . . . CLC 53, 76
See also CA 104; CANR 30

Smith, A(rthur) J(ames) M(arshall)
1902-1980 . . . . CLC 15
See also CA 1-4R; 102; CANR 4; DLB 88

Smith, Anna Deavere 1950- . . . . CLC 86
See also CA 133

Smith, Betty (Wehner) 1896-1972 . . . CLC 19
See also CA 5-8R; 33-36R; DLBY 82;
SATA 6

Smith, Charlotte (Turner)
1749-1806 . . . . NCLC 23
See also DLB 39, 109

Smith, Clark Ashton 1893-1961 . . . . CLC 43
See also CA 143

Smith, Dave . . . . CLC 22, 42
See also Smith, David (Jeddie)
See also CAAS 7; DLB 5

Smith, David (Jeddie) 1942-
See Smith, Dave
See also CA 49-52; CANR 1

Smith, Florence Margaret 1902-1971
See Smith, Stevie
See also CA 17-18; 29-32R; CANR 35;
CAP 2; MTCW

Smith, Iain Crichton 1928- . . . . CLC 64
See also CA 21-24R; DLB 40, 139

Smith, John 1580(?)-1631 . . . . LC 9

Smith, Johnston
See Crane, Stephen (Townley)

Smith, Lee 1944- . . . . CLC 25, 73
See also CA 114; 119; CANR 46; DLB 143;
DLBY 83

Smith, Martin
See Smith, Martin Cruz

Smith, Martin Cruz 1942- . . . . CLC 25
See also BEST 89:4; CA 85-88; CANR 6,
23, 43; NNAL

Smith, Mary-Ann Tirone 1944- . . . . . CLC 39
See also CA 118; 136

Smith, Patti 1946- . . . . CLC 12
See also CA 93-96

Smith, Pauline (Urmson)
1882-1959 . . . . TCLC 25

Smith, Rosamond
See Oates, Joyce Carol

Smith, Sheila Kaye
See Kaye-Smith, Sheila

Smith, Stevie . . . . CLC 3, 8, 25, 44; PC 12
See also Smith, Florence Margaret
See also DLB 20

Thoreau, Henry David
1817-1862 ..... NCLC 7, 21; DA; WLC
See also CDALB 1640-1865; DLB 1

Thornton, Hall
See Silverberg, Robert

Thurber, James (Grover)
1894-1961 ... CLC 5, 11, 25; DA; SSC 1
See also CA 73-76; CANR 17, 39;
CDALB 1929-1941; DLB 4, 11, 22, 102;
MAICYA; MTCW; SATA 13

Thurman, Wallace (Henry)
1902-1934 .... TCLC 6; BLC
See also BW 1; CA 104; 124; DLB 51

Ticheburn, Cheviot
See Ainsworth, William Harrison

Tieck, (Johann) Ludwig
1773-1853 .... NCLC 5, 46
See also DLB 90

Tiger, Derry
See Ellison, Harlan (Jay)

Tilghman, Christopher 1948(?)- ..... CLC 65

Tillinghast, Richard (Williford)
1940- .... CLC 29
See also CA 29-32R; CANR 26

Timrod, Henry 1828-1867 .... NCLC 25
See also DLB 3

Tindall, Gillian 1938- .... CLC 7
See also CA 21-24R; CANR 11

Tiptree, James, Jr. .... CLC 48, 50
See also Sheldon, Alice Hastings Bradley
See also DLB 8

Titmarsh, Michael Angelo
See Thackeray, William Makepeace

**Tocqueville, Alexis (Charles Henri Maurice
Clerel Comte)** 1805-1859..... NCLC 7

Tolkien, J(ohn) R(onald) R(euel)
1892-1973 ...... CLC 1, 2, 3, 8, 12, 38;
DA; WLC
See also AAYA 10; AITN 1; CA 17-18;
45-48; CANR 36; CAP 2;
CDBLB 1914-1945; DLB 15; JRDA;
MAICYA; MTCW; SATA 2, 32;
SATA-Obit 24

Toller, Ernst 1893-1939 .... TCLC 10
See also CA 107; DLB 124

Tolson, M. B.
See Tolson, Melvin B(eaunorus)

Tolson, Melvin B(eaunorus)
1898(?)-1966 .... CLC 36; BLC
See also BW 1; CA 124; 89-92; DLB 48, 76

Tolstoi, Aleksei Nikolaevich
See Tolstoy, Alexey Nikolaevich

Tolstoy, Alexey Nikolaevich
1882-1945 .... TCLC 18
See also CA 107

Tolstoy, Count Leo
See Tolstoy, Leo (Nikolaevich)

Tolstoy, Leo (Nikolaevich)
1828-1910 ..... TCLC 4, 11, 17, 28, 44;
DA; SSC 9; WLC
See also CA 104; 123; SATA 26

Tomasi di Lampedusa, Giuseppe 1896-1957
See Lampedusa, Giuseppe (Tomasi) di
See also CA 111

Tomlin, Lily.................... CLC 17
See also Tomlin, Mary Jean

Tomlin, Mary Jean 1939(?)-
See Tomlin, Lily
See also CA 117

Tomlinson, (Alfred) Charles
1927- .... CLC 2, 4, 6, 13, 45
See also CA 5-8R; CANR 33; DLB 40

Tonson, Jacob
See Bennett, (Enoch) Arnold

Toole, John Kennedy
1937-1969 .... CLC 19, 64
See also CA 104; DLBY 81

Toomer, Jean
1894-1967 ...... CLC 1, 4, 13, 22; BLC;
PC 7; SSC 1
See also BW 1; CA 85-88;
CDALB 1917-1929; DLB 45, 51; MTCW

Torley, Luke
See Blish, James (Benjamin)

Tornimparte, Alessandra
See Ginzburg, Natalia

Torre, Raoul della
See Mencken, H(enry) L(ouis)

Torrey, E(dwin) Fuller 1937- .... CLC 34
See also CA 119

Torsvan, Ben Traven
See Traven, B.

Torsvan, Benno Traven
See Traven, B.

Torsvan, Berick Traven
See Traven, B.

Torsvan, Berwick Traven
See Traven, B.

Torsvan, Bruno Traven
See Traven, B.

Torsvan, Traven
See Traven, B.

Tournier, Michel (Edouard)
1924- .... CLC 6, 23, 36
See also CA 49-52; CANR 3, 36; DLB 83;
MTCW; SATA 23

Tournimparte, Alessandra
See Ginzburg, Natalia

Towers, Ivar
See Kornbluth, C(yril) M.

Towne, Robert (Burton) 1936(?)- .... CLC 87
See also CA 108; DLB 44

Townsend, Sue 1946- .... CLC 61
See also CA 119; 127; MTCW; SATA 55;
SATA-Brief 48

Townshend, Peter (Dennis Blandford)
1945- .... CLC 17, 42
See also CA 107

Tozzi, Federigo 1883-1920 .... TCLC 31

Traill, Catharine Parr
1802-1899 .... NCLC 31
See also DLB 99

Trakl, Georg 1887-1914 .... TCLC 5
See also CA 104

Transtroemer, Tomas (Goesta)
1931- .... CLC 52, 65
See also CA 117; 129; CAAS 17

Transtromer, Tomas Gosta
See Transtroemer, Tomas (Goesta)

Traven, B. (?)-1969 .... CLC 8, 11
See also CA 19-20; 25-28R; CAP 2; DLB 9,
56; MTCW

Treitel, Jonathan 1959- .... CLC 70

Tremain, Rose 1943- .... CLC 42
See also CA 97-100; CANR 44; DLB 14

Tremblay, Michel 1942- .... CLC 29
See also CA 116; 128; DLB 60; MTCW

Trevanian .... CLC 29
See also Whitaker, Rod(ney)

Trevor, Glen
See Hilton, James

Trevor, William
1928- .... CLC 7, 9, 14, 25, 71
See also Cox, William Trevor
See also DLB 14, 139

Trifonov, Yuri (Valentinovich)
1925-1981 .... CLC 45
See also CA 126; 103; MTCW

Trilling, Lionel 1905-1975 .... CLC 9, 11, 24
See also CA 9-12R; 61-64; CANR 10;
DLB 28, 63; MTCW

Trimball, W. H.
See Mencken, H(enry) L(ouis)

Tristan
See Gomez de la Serna, Ramon

Tristram
See Housman, A(lfred) E(dward)

Trogdon, William (Lewis) 1939-
See Heat-Moon, William Least
See also CA 115; 119; CANR 47

Trollope, Anthony
1815-1882 ...... NCLC 6, 33; DA; WLC
See also CDBLB 1832-1890; DLB 21, 57;
SATA 22

Trollope, Frances 1779-1863 ..... NCLC 30
See also DLB 21

Trotsky, Leon 1879-1940 .... TCLC 22
See also CA 118

Trotter (Cockburn), Catharine
1679-1749 .... LC 8
See also DLB 84

Trout, Kilgore
See Farmer, Philip Jose

Trow, George W. S. 1943- .... CLC 52
See also CA 126

Troyat, Henri 1911- .... CLC 23
See also CA 45-48; CANR 2, 33; MTCW

Trudeau, G(arretson) B(eekman) 1948-
See Trudeau, Garry B.
See also CA 81-84; CANR 31; SATA 35

Trudeau, Garry B. .... CLC 12
See also Trudeau, G(arretson) B(eekman)
See also AAYA 10; AITN 2

Truffaut, Francois 1932-1984 .... CLC 20
See also CA 81-84; 113; CANR 34

Trumbo, Dalton 1905-1976 .... CLC 19
See also CA 21-24R; 69-72; CANR 10;
DLB 26

Trumbull, John 1750-1831 .... NCLC 30
See also DLB 31

Trundlett, Helen B.
    See Eliot, T(homas) S(tearns)

Tryon, Thomas   1926-1991 . . . . . . CLC 3, 11
    See also AITN 1; CA 29-32R; 135;
    CANR 32; MTCW

Tryon, Tom
    See Tryon, Thomas

Ts'ao Hsueh-ch'in   1715(?)-1763. . . . . . LC 1

Tsushima, Shuji   1909-1948
    See Dazai, Osamu
    See also CA 107

Tsvetaeva (Efron), Marina (Ivanovna)
    1892-1941 . . . . TCLC 7, 35
    See also CA 104; 128; MTCW

Tuck, Lily   1938-. . . . . CLC 70
    See also CA 139

Tu Fu   712-770. . . . . PC 9

Tunis, John R(oberts)   1889-1975 . . . CLC 12
    See also CA 61-64; DLB 22; JRDA;
    MAICYA; SATA 37; SATA-Brief 30

Tuohy, Frank. . . . . CLC 37
    See also Tuohy, John Francis
    See also DLB 14, 139

Tuohy, John Francis   1925-
    See Tuohy, Frank
    See also CA 5-8R; CANR 3, 47

Turco, Lewis (Putnam)   1934- . . . CLC 11, 63
    See also CA 13-16R; CANR 24; DLBY 84

Turgenev, Ivan
    1818-1883 . . . . . . NCLC 21; DA; SSC 7;
                                                        WLC

Turgot, Anne-Robert-Jacques
    1727-1781 . . . . LC 26

Turner, Frederick   1943-. . . . . CLC 48
    See also CA 73-76; CAAS 10; CANR 12,
    30; DLB 40

Tutu, Desmond M(pilo)
    1931- . . . . CLC 80; BLC
    See also BW 1; CA 125

Tutuola, Amos   1920- . . . CLC 5, 14, 29; BLC
    See also BW 2; CA 9-12R; CANR 27;
    DLB 125; MTCW

Twain, Mark
    . . . . . TCLC 6, 12, 19, 36, 48, 59; SSC 6;
                                                        WLC
    See also Clemens, Samuel Langhorne
    See also DLB 11, 12, 23, 64, 74

Tyler, Anne
    1941- . . . . CLC 7, 11, 18, 28, 44, 59
    See also BEST 89:1; CA 9-12R; CANR 11,
    33; DLB 6, 143; DLBY 82; MTCW;
    SATA 7

Tyler, Royall   1757-1826. . . . . NCLC 3
    See also DLB 37

Tynan, Katharine   1861-1931 . . . . . . TCLC 3
    See also CA 104

Tyutchev, Fyodor   1803-1873 . . . . . NCLC 34

Tzara, Tristan . . . . CLC 47
    See also Rosenfeld, Samuel

Uhry, Alfred   1936-. . . . . CLC 55
    See also CA 127; 133

Ulf, Haerved
    See Strindberg, (Johan) August

Ulf, Harved
    See Strindberg, (Johan) August

Ulibarri, Sabine R(eyes)   1919- . . . . . CLC 83
    See also CA 131; DLB 82; HW

Unamuno (y Jugo), Miguel de
    1864-1936 . . . . TCLC 2, 9; HLC; SSC 11
    See also CA 104; 131; DLB 108; HW;
    MTCW

Undercliffe, Errol
    See Campbell, (John) Ramsey

Underwood, Miles
    See Glassco, John

Undset, Sigrid
    1882-1949 . . . . TCLC 3; DA; WLC
    See also CA 104; 129; MTCW

Ungaretti, Giuseppe
    1888-1970 . . . . CLC 7, 11, 15
    See also CA 19-20; 25-28R; CAP 2;
    DLB 114

Unger, Douglas   1952-. . . . . CLC 34
    See also CA 130

Unsworth, Barry (Forster)   1930-. . . . CLC 76
    See also CA 25-28R; CANR 30

Updike, John (Hoyer)
    1932- . . . . . . CLC 1, 2, 3, 5, 7, 9, 13, 15,
                   23, 34, 43, 70; DA; SSC 13; WLC
    See also CA 1-4R; CABS 1; CANR 4, 33;
    CDALB 1968-1988; DLB 2, 5, 143;
    DLBD 3; DLBY 80, 82; MTCW

Upshaw, Margaret Mitchell
    See Mitchell, Margaret (Munnerlyn)

Upton, Mark
    See Sanders, Lawrence

Urdang, Constance (Henriette)
    1922- . . . . CLC 47
    See also CA 21-24R; CANR 9, 24

Uriel, Henry
    See Faust, Frederick (Schiller)

Uris, Leon (Marcus)   1924-. . . . . . . CLC 7, 32
    See also AITN 1, 2; BEST 89:2; CA 1-4R;
    CANR 1, 40; MTCW; SATA 49

Urmuz
    See Codrescu, Andrei

Ustinov, Peter (Alexander)   1921- . . . . CLC 1
    See also AITN 1; CA 13-16R; CANR 25;
    DLB 13

Vaculik, Ludvik   1926- . . . . CLC 7
    See also CA 53-56

Valdez, Luis (Miguel)
    1940- . . . . CLC 84; HLC
    See also CA 101; CANR 32; DLB 122; HW

Valenzuela, Luisa   1938-. . . CLC 31; SSC 14
    See also CA 101; CANR 32; DLB 113; HW

Valera y Alcala-Galiano, Juan
    1824-1905 . . . . TCLC 10
    See also CA 106

Valery, (Ambroise) Paul (Toussaint Jules)
    1871-1945 . . . . TCLC 4, 15; PC 9
    See also CA 104; 122; MTCW

Valle-Inclan, Ramon (Maria) del
    1866-1936 . . . . TCLC 5; HLC
    See also CA 106; DLB 134

Vallejo, Antonio Buero
    See Buero Vallejo, Antonio

Vallejo, Cesar (Abraham)
    1892-1938 . . . . TCLC 3, 56; HLC
    See also CA 105; HW

Valle Y Pena, Ramon del
    See Valle-Inclan, Ramon (Maria) del

Van Ash, Cay   1918-. . . . . CLC 34

Vanbrugh, Sir John   1664-1726 . . . . . . LC 21
    See also DLB 80

Van Campen, Karl
    See Campbell, John W(ood, Jr.)

Vance, Gerald
    See Silverberg, Robert

Vance, Jack. CLC 35
    See also Vance, John Holbrook
    See also DLB 8

Vance, John Holbrook   1916-
    See Queen, Ellery; Vance, Jack
    See also CA 29-32R; CANR 17; MTCW

Van Den Bogarde, Derek Jules Gaspard Ulric
    Niven   1921-
    See Bogarde, Dirk
    See also CA 77-80

Vandenburgh, Jane . . . . CLC 59

Vanderhaeghe, Guy   1951- . . . . CLC 41
    See also CA 113

van der Post, Laurens (Jan)   1906- . . . CLC 5
    See also CA 5-8R; CANR 35

van de Wetering, Janwillem   1931- . . CLC 47
    See also CA 49-52; CANR 4

Van Dine, S. S. . . . . TCLC 23
    See also Wright, Willard Huntington

Van Doren, Carl (Clinton)
    1885-1950 . . . . TCLC 18
    See also CA 111

Van Doren, Mark   1894-1972. . . . . CLC 6, 10
    See also CA 1-4R; 37-40R; CANR 3;
    DLB 45; MTCW

Van Druten, John (William)
    1901-1957 . . . . TCLC 2
    See also CA 104; DLB 10

Van Duyn, Mona (Jane)
    1921-. . . . . CLC 3, 7, 63
    See also CA 9-12R; CANR 7, 38; DLB 5

Van Dyne, Edith
    See Baum, L(yman) Frank

van Itallie, Jean-Claude   1936-. . . . . . . CLC 3
    See also CA 45-48; CAAS 2; CANR 1;
    DLB 7

van Ostaijen, Paul   1896-1928 . . . . . TCLC 33

Van Peebles, Melvin   1932- . . . . . . CLC 2, 20
    See also BW 2; CA 85-88; CANR 27

Vansittart, Peter   1920-. . . . . CLC 42
    See also CA 1-4R; CANR 3

Van Vechten, Carl   1880-1964 . . . . . . CLC 33
    See also CA 89-92; DLB 4, 9, 51

Van Vogt, A(lfred) E(lton)   1912-. . . . . CLC 1
    See also CA 21-24R; CANR 28; DLB 8;
    SATA 14

Varda, Agnes   1928- . . . . CLC 16
    See also CA 116; 122

Vargas Llosa, (Jorge) Mario (Pedro)
1936- .... CLC 3, 6, 9, 10, 15, 31, 42, 85;
DA; HLC
See also CA 73-76; CANR 18, 32, 42;
DLB 145; HW; MTCW

Vasiliu, Gheorghe 1881-1957
See Bacovia, George
See also CA 123

Vassa, Gustavus
See Equiano, Olaudah

Vassilikos, Vassilis 1933-......... CLC 4, 8
See also CA 81-84

Vaughan, Henry 1621-1695 .... LC 27
See also DLB 131

Vaughn, Stephanie................. CLC 62

Vazov, Ivan (Minchov)
1850-1921 .... TCLC 25
See also CA 121; DLB 147

Veblen, Thorstein (Bunde)
1857-1929 .... TCLC 31
See also CA 115

Vega, Lope de 1562-1635........... LC 23

Venison, Alfred
See Pound, Ezra (Weston Loomis)

Verdi, Marie de
See Mencken, H(enry) L(ouis)

Verdu, Matilde
See Cela, Camilo Jose

Verga, Giovanni (Carmelo)
1840-1922 .... TCLC 3
See also CA 104; 123

Vergil
70B.C.-19B.C..... CMLC 9; DA; PC 12

Verhaeren, Emile (Adolphe Gustave)
1855-1916 .... TCLC 12
See also CA 109

Verlaine, Paul (Marie)
1844-1896 .... NCLC 2; PC 2

Verne, Jules (Gabriel)
1828-1905 .... TCLC 6, 52
See also CA 110; 131; DLB 123; JRDA;
MAICYA; SATA 21

Very, Jones 1813-1880........... NCLC 9
See also DLB 1

Vesaas, Tarjei 1897-1970......... CLC 48
See also CA 29-32R

Vialls, Gaston
See Simenon, Georges (Jacques Christian)

Vian, Boris 1920-1959 .... TCLC 9
See also CA 106; DLB 72

Viaud, (Louis Marie) Julien 1850-1923
See Loti, Pierre
See also CA 107

Vicar, Henry
See Felsen, Henry Gregor

Vicker, Angus
See Felsen, Henry Gregor

Vidal, Gore
1925- ..... CLC 2, 4, 6, 8, 10, 22, 33, 72
See also AITN 1; BEST 90:2; CA 5-8R;
CANR 13, 45; DLB 6; MTCW

Viereck, Peter (Robert Edwin)
1916- .... CLC 4
See also CA 1-4R; CANR 1, 47; DLB 5

Vigny, Alfred (Victor) de
1797-1863 .... NCLC 7
See also DLB 119

Vilakazi, Benedict Wallet
1906-1947 .... TCLC 37

Villiers de l'Isle Adam, Jean Marie Mathias Philippe Auguste Comte
1838-1889 .... NCLC 3; SSC 14
See also DLB 123

Vinci, Leonardo da 1452-1519...... LC 12

Vine, Barbara .... CLC 50
See also Rendell, Ruth (Barbara)
See also BEST 90:4

Vinge, Joan D(ennison) 1948-...... CLC 30
See also CA 93-96; SATA 36

Violis, G.
See Simenon, Georges (Jacques Christian)

Visconti, Luchino 1906-1976....... CLC 16
See also CA 81-84; 65-68; CANR 39

Vittorini, Elio 1908-1966...... CLC 6, 9, 14
See also CA 133, 25-28R

Vizinczey, Stephen 1933-.......... CLC 40
See also CA 128

Vliet, R(ussell) G(ordon)
1929-1984 .... CLC 22
See also CA 37-40R; 112; CANR 18

Vogau, Boris Andreyevich 1894-1937(?)
See Pilnyak, Boris
See also CA 123

Vogel, Paula A(nne) 1951-........ CLC 76
See also CA 108

Voight, Ellen Bryant 1943- .... CLC 54
See also CA 69-72; CANR 11, 29; DLB 120

Voigt, Cynthia 1942- .... CLC 30
See also AAYA 3; CA 106; CANR 18, 37,
40; CLR 13; JRDA; MAICYA;
SATA 48, 79; SATA-Brief 33

Voinovich, Vladimir (Nikolaevich)
1932- .... CLC 10, 49
See also CA 81-84; CAAS 12; CANR 33;
MTCW

Voloshinov, V. N.
See Bakhtin, Mikhail Mikhailovich

Voltaire
1694-1778 ... LC 14; DA; SSC 12; WLC

von Aue, Hartmann 1170-1210 .. CMLC 15:

von Daeniken, Erich 1935- .... CLC 30
See also AITN 1; CA 37-40R; CANR 17,
44

von Daniken, Erich
See von Daeniken, Erich

von Heidenstam, (Carl Gustaf) Verner
See Heidenstam, (Carl Gustaf) Verner von

von Heyse, Paul (Johann Ludwig)
See Heyse, Paul (Johann Ludwig von)

von Hofmannsthal, Hugo
See Hofmannsthal, Hugo von

von Horvath, Odon
See Horvath, Oedoen von

von Horvath, Oedoen
See Horvath, Oedoen von

von Liliencron, (Friedrich Adolf Axel) Detlev
See Liliencron, (Friedrich Adolf Axel)
Detlev von

Vonnegut, Kurt, Jr.
1922- ...... CLC 1, 2, 3, 4, 5, 8, 12, 22,
40, 60; DA; SSC 8; WLC
See also AAYA 6; AITN 1; BEST 90:4;
CA 1-4R; CANR 1, 25;
CDALB 1968-1988; DLB 2, 8; DLBD 3;
DLBY 80; MTCW

Von Rachen, Kurt
See Hubbard, L(afayette) Ron(ald)

von Rezzori (d'Arezzo), Gregor
See Rezzori (d'Arezzo), Gregor von

von Sternberg, Josef
See Sternberg, Josef von

Vorster, Gordon 1924-............ CLC 34
See also CA 133

Vosce, Trudie
See Ozick, Cynthia

Voznesensky, Andrei (Andreievich)
1933-................. CLC 1, 15, 57
See also CA 89-92; CANR 37; MTCW

Waddington, Miriam 1917 .... CLC 28
See also CA 21-24R; CANR 12, 30;
DLB 68

Wagman, Fredrica 1937- .... CLC 7
See also CA 97-100

Wagner, Richard 1813-1883....... NCLC 9
See also DLB 129

Wagner-Martin, Linda 1936-....... CLC 50

Wagoner, David (Russell)
1926-.................... CLC 3, 5, 15
See also CA 1-4R; CAAS 3; CANR 2;
DLB 5; SATA 14

Wah, Fred(erick James) 1939-...... CLC 44
See also CA 107; 141; DLB 60

Wahloo, Per 1926-1975 .... CLC 7
See also CA 61-64

Wahloo, Peter
See Wahloo, Per

Wain, John (Barrington)
1925-1994 .... CLC 2, 11, 15, 46
See also CA 5-8R; 145; CAAS 4; CANR 23;
CDBLB 1960 to Present; DLB 15, 27,
139; MTCW

Wajda, Andrzej 1926-............. CLC 16
See also CA 102

Wakefield, Dan 1932-.............. CLC 7
See also CA 21-24R; CAAS 7

Wakoski, Diane
1937- .... CLC 2, 4, 7, 9, 11, 40
See also CA 13-16R; CAAS 1; CANR 9;
DLB 5

Wakoski-Sherbell, Diane
See Wakoski, Diane

Walcott, Derek (Alton)
1930- .... CLC 2, 4, 9, 14, 25, 42, 67, 76;
BLC
See also BW 2; CA 89-92; CANR 26, 47;
DLB 117; DLBY 81; MTCW

Waldman, Anne 1945- .... CLC 7
See also CA 37-40R; CAAS 17; CANR 34;
DLB 16

Waldo, E. Hunter
See Sturgeon, Theodore (Hamilton)

Waldo, Edward Hamilton
See Sturgeon, Theodore (Hamilton)

Walker, Alice (Malsenior)
1944- .... CLC 5, 6, 9, 19, 27, 46, 58;
BLC; DA; SSC 5
See also AAYA 3; BEST 89:4; BW 2;
CA 37-40R; CANR 9, 27;
CDALB 1968-1988; DLB 6, 33, 143;
MTCW; SATA 31

Walker, David Harry 1911-1992.... CLC 14
See also CA 1-4R; 137; CANR 1; SATA 8;
SATA-Obit 71

Walker, Edward Joseph 1934-
See Walker, Ted
See also CA 21-24R; CANR 12, 28

Walker, George F. 1947- .... CLC 44, 61
See also CA 103; CANR 21, 43; DLB 60

Walker, Joseph A. 1935- .... CLC 19
See also BW 1; CA 89-92; CANR 26;
DLB 38

Walker, Margaret (Abigail)
1915- .... CLC 1, 6; BLC
See also BW 2; CA 73-76; CANR 26;
DLB 76; MTCW

Walker, Ted .... CLC 13
See also Walker, Edward Joseph
See also DLB 40

Wallace, David Foster 1962- .... CLC 50
See also CA 132

Wallace, Dexter
See Masters, Edgar Lee

Wallace, (Richard Horatio) Edgar
1875-1932 .... TCLC 57
See also CA 115; DLB 70

Wallace, Irving 1916-1990....... CLC 7, 13
See also AITN 1; CA 1-4R; 132; CAAS 1;
CANR 1, 27; MTCW

Wallant, Edward Lewis
1926-1962 .... CLC 5, 10
See also CA 1-4R; CANR 22; DLB 2, 28,
143; MTCW

Walpole, Horace 1717-1797.......... LC 2
See also DLB 39, 104

Walpole, Hugh (Seymour)
1884-1941 .... TCLC 5
See also CA 104; DLB 34

Walser, Martin 1927-.............. CLC 27
See also CA 57-60; CANR 8, 46; DLB 75,
124

Walser, Robert 1878-1956....... TCLC 18
See also CA 118; DLB 66

Walsh, Jill Paton. .... CLC 35
See also Paton Walsh, Gillian
See also AAYA 11; CLR 2; SAAS 3

Walter, Villiam Christian
See Andersen, Hans Christian

Wambaugh, Joseph (Aloysius, Jr.)
1937- .... CLC 3, 18
See also AITN 1; BEST 89:3; CA 33-36R;
CANR 42; DLB 6; DLBY 83; MTCW

Ward, Arthur Henry Sarsfield 1883-1959
See Rohmer, Sax
See also CA 108

Ward, Douglas Turner 1930-....... CLC 19
See also BW 1; CA 81-84; CANR 27;
DLB 7, 38

Ward, Mary Augusta
See Ward, Mrs. Humphry

Ward, Mrs. Humphry
1851-1920 .... TCLC 55
See also DLB 18

Ward, Peter
See Faust, Frederick (Schiller)

Warhol, Andy 1928(?)-1987........ CLC 20
See also AAYA 12; BEST 89:4; CA 89-92;
121; CANR 34

Warner, Francis (Robert le Plastrier)
1937- .... CLC 14
See also CA 53-56; CANR 11

Warner, Marina 1946-............ CLC 59
See also CA 65-68; CANR 21

Warner, Rex (Ernest) 1905-1986.... CLC 45
See also CA 89-92; 119; DLB 15

Warner, Susan (Bogert)
1819-1885 .... NCLC 31
See also DLB 3, 42

Warner, Sylvia (Constance) Ashton
See Ashton-Warner, Sylvia (Constance)

Warner, Sylvia Townsend
1893-1978 .... CLC 7, 19
See also CA 61-64; 77-80; CANR 16;
DLB 34, 139; MTCW

Warren, Mercy Otis 1728-1814... NCLC 13
See also DLB 31

Warren, Robert Penn
1905-1989 .... CLC 1, 4, 6, 8, 10, 13, 18,
39, 53, 59; DA; SSC 4; WLC
See also AITN 1; CA 13-16R; 129;
CANR 10, 47; CDALB 1968-1988;
DLB 2, 48; DLBY 80, 89; MTCW;
SATA 46; SATA-Obit 63

Warshofsky, Isaac
See Singer, Isaac Bashevis

Warton, Thomas 1728-1790........ LC 15
See also DLB 104, 109

Waruk, Kona
See Harris, (Theodore) Wilson

Warung, Price 1855-1911........ TCLC 45

Warwick, Jarvis
See Garner, Hugh

Washington, Alex
See Harris, Mark

Washington, Booker T(aliaferro)
1856-1915 .... TCLC 10; BLC
See also BW 1; CA 114; 125; SATA 28

Washington, George 1732-1799...... LC 25
See also DLB 31

Wassermann, (Karl) Jakob
1873-1934 .... TCLC 6
See also CA 104; DLB 66

Wasserstein, Wendy
1950- .... CLC 32, 59; DC 4
See also CA 121; 129; CABS 3

Waterhouse, Keith (Spencer)
1929- .... CLC 47
See also CA 5-8R; CANR 38; DLB 13, 15;
MTCW

Waters, Roger 1944-.............. CLC 35

Watkins, Frances Ellen
See Harper, Frances Ellen Watkins

Watkins, Gerrold
See Malzberg, Barry N(athaniel)

Watkins, Paul 1964-.............. CLC 55
See also CA 132

Watkins, Vernon Phillips
1906-1967 .... CLC 43
See also CA 9-10; 25-28R; CAP 1; DLB 20

Watson, Irving S.
See Mencken, H(enry) L(ouis)

Watson, John H.
See Farmer, Philip Jose

Watson, Richard F.
See Silverberg, Robert

Waugh, Auberon (Alexander) 1939- .. CLC 7
See also CA 45-48; CANR 6, 22; DLB 14

Waugh, Evelyn (Arthur St. John)
1903-1966 ...... CLC 1, 3, 8, 13, 19, 27,
44; DA; WLC
See also CA 85-88; 25-28R; CANR 22;
CDBLB 1914-1945; DLB 15; MTCW

Waugh, Harriet 1944- .... CLC 6
See also CA 85-88; CANR 22

Ways, C. R.
See Blount, Roy (Alton), Jr.

Waystaff, Simon
See Swift, Jonathan

Webb, (Martha) Beatrice (Potter)
1858-1943 .... TCLC 22
See also Potter, Beatrice
See also CA 117

Webb, Charles (Richard) 1939-...... CLC 7
See also CA 25-28R

Webb, James H(enry), Jr. 1946-.... CLC 22
See also CA 81-84

Webb, Mary (Gladys Meredith)
1881-1927 .... TCLC 24
See also CA 123; DLB 34

Webb, Mrs. Sidney
See Webb, (Martha) Beatrice (Potter)

Webb, Phyllis 1927-.............. CLC 18
See also CA 104; CANR 23; DLB 53

Webb, Sidney (James)
1859-1947 .... TCLC 22
See also CA 117

Webber, Andrew Lloyd............ CLC 21
See also Lloyd Webber, Andrew

Weber, Lenora Mattingly
1895-1971 .... CLC 12
See also CA 19-20; 29-32R; CAP 1;
SATA 2; SATA-Obit 26

Webster, John 1579(?)-1634(?) .... DC 2
See also CDBLB Before 1660; DA; DLB 58;
WLC

Webster, Noah 1758-1843 .... NCLC 30

Wedekind, (Benjamin) Frank(lin)
1864-1918 .... TCLC 7
See also CA 104; DLB 118

Weidman, Jerome 1913-........... CLC 7
See also AITN 2; CA 1-4R; CANR 1;
DLB 28

Weil, Simone (Adolphine)
1909-1943 .... TCLC 23
See also CA 117

Whittemore, (Edward) Reed (Jr.)
1919- . . . . CLC 4
See also CA 9-12R; CAAS 8; CANR 4;
DLB 5

Whittier, John Greenleaf
1807-1892 . . . . NCLC 8
See also CDALB 1640-1865; DLB 1

Whittlebot, Hernia
See Coward, Noel (Peirce)

Wicker, Thomas Grey   1926-
See Wicker, Tom
See also CA 65-68; CANR 21, 46

Wicker, Tom . . . . CLC 7
See also Wicker, Thomas Grey

Wideman, John Edgar
1941- . . . . CLC 5, 34, 36, 67; BLC
See also BW 2; CA 85-88; CANR 14, 42;
DLB 33, 143

Wiebe, Rudy (Henry)   1934-. . . CLC 6, 11, 14
See also CA 37-40R; CANR 42; DLB 60

Wieland, Christoph Martin
1733-1813 . . . . NCLC 17
See also DLB 97

Wiene, Robert   1881-1938. . . . . TCLC 56

Wieners, John   1934-. . . . . CLC 7
See also CA 13-16R; DLB 16

Wiesel, Elie(zer)
1928- . . . . CLC 3, 5, 11, 37; DA
See also AAYA 7; AITN 1; CA 5-8R;
CAAS 4; CANR 8, 40; DLB 83;
DLBY 87; MTCW; SATA 56

Wiggins, Marianne   1947-. . . . . CLC 57
See also BEST 89:3; CA 130

Wight, James Alfred   1916-
See Herriot, James
See also CA 77-80; SATA 55;
SATA-Brief 44

Wilbur, Richard (Purdy)
1921- . . . . CLC 3, 6, 9, 14, 53; DA
See also CA 1-4R; CABS 2; CANR 2, 29;
DLB 5; MTCW; SATA 9

Wild, Peter   1940-. . . . . CLC 14
See also CA 37-40R; DLB 5

Wilde, Oscar (Fingal O'Flahertie Wills)
1854(?)-1900 . . . . TCLC 1, 8, 23, 41; DA;
SSC 11; WLC
See also CA 104; 119; CDBLB 1890-1914;
DLB 10, 19, 34, 57, 141; SATA 24

Wilder, Billy . . . . CLC 20
See also Wilder, Samuel
See also DLB 26

Wilder, Samuel   1906-
See Wilder, Billy
See also CA 89-92

Wilder, Thornton (Niven)
1897-1975 . . . . . . CLC 1, 5, 6, 10, 15, 35,
82; DA; DC 1; WLC
See also AITN 2; CA 13-16R; 61-64;
CANR 40; DLB 4, 7, 9; MTCW

Wilding, Michael   1942-. . . . . CLC 73
See also CA 104; CANR 24

Wiley, Richard   1944-. . . . . CLC 44
See also CA 121; 129

Wilhelm, Kate . . . . CLC 7
See also Wilhelm, Katie Gertrude
See also CAAS 5; DLB 8

Wilhelm, Katie Gertrude   1928-
See Wilhelm, Kate
See also CA 37-40R; CANR 17, 36; MTCW

Wilkins, Mary
See Freeman, Mary Eleanor Wilkins

Willard, Nancy   1936-. . . . . CLC 7, 37
See also CA 89-92; CANR 10, 39; CLR 5;
DLB 5, 52; MAICYA; MTCW;
SATA 37, 71; SATA-Brief 30

Williams, C(harles) K(enneth)
1936- . . . . CLC 33, 56
See also CA 37-40R; DLB 5

Williams, Charles
See Collier, James L(incoln)

Williams, Charles (Walter Stansby)
1886-1945. . . . . TCLC 1, 11
See also CA 104; DLB 100

Williams, (George) Emlyn
1905-1987 . . . . CLC 15
See also CA 104; 123; CANR 36; DLB 10,
77; MTCW

Williams, Hugo   1942-. . . . . CLC 42
See also CA 17-20R; CANR 45; DLB 40

Williams, J. Walker
See Wodehouse, P(elham) G(renville)

Williams, John A(lfred)
1925-. . . . . CLC 5, 13; BLC
See also BW 2; CA 53-56; CAAS 3;
CANR 6, 26; DLB 2, 33

Williams, Jonathan (Chamberlain)
1929- . . . . CLC 13
See also CA 9-12R; CAAS 12; CANR 8;
DLB 5

Williams, Joy   1944-. . . . . CLC 31
See also CA 41-44R; CANR 22

Williams, Norman   1952- . . . . CLC 39
See also CA 118

Williams, Tennessee
1911-1983 . . . . . CLC 1, 2, 5, 7, 8, 11, 15,
19, 30, 39, 45, 71; DA; DC 4; WLC
See also AITN 1, 2; CA 5-8R; 108;
CABS 3; CANR 31; CDALB 1941-1968;
DLB 7; DLBD 4; DLBY 83; MTCW

Williams, Thomas (Alonzo)
1926-1990 . . . . CLC 14
See also CA 1-4R; 132; CANR 2

Williams, William C.
See Williams, William Carlos

Williams, William Carlos
1883-1963 . . . . CLC 1, 2, 5, 9, 13, 22, 42,
67; DA; PC 7
See also CA 89-92; CANR 34;
CDALB 1917-1929; DLB 4, 16, 54, 86;
MTCW

Williamson, David (Keith)   1942-. . . . CLC 56
See also CA 103; CANR 41

Williamson, Ellen Douglas   1905-1984
See Douglas, Ellen
See also CA 17-20R; 114; CANR 39

Williamson, Jack. . . . . CLC 29
See also Williamson, John Stewart
See also CAAS 8; DLB 8

Williamson, John Stewart   1908-
See Williamson, Jack
See also CA 17-20R; CANR 23

Willie, Frederick
See Lovecraft, H(oward) P(hillips)

Willingham, Calder (Baynard, Jr.)
1922-. . . . . CLC 5, 51
See also CA 5-8R; CANR 3; DLB 2, 44;
MTCW

Willis, Charles
See Clarke, Arthur C(harles)

Willy
See Colette, (Sidonie-Gabrielle)

Willy, Colette
See Colette, (Sidonie-Gabrielle)

Wilson, A(ndrew) N(orman)   1950- . . CLC 33
See also CA 112; 122; DLB 14

Wilson, Angus (Frank Johnstone)
1913-1991 . . . . CLC 2, 3, 5, 25, 34
See also CA 5-8R; 134; CANR 21; DLB 15,
139; MTCW

Wilson, August
1945-. . CLC 39, 50, 63; BLC; DA; DC 2
See also BW 2; CA 115; 122; CANR 42;
MTCW

Wilson, Brian   1942-. . . . . CLC 12

Wilson, Colin   1931-. . . . . CLC 3, 14
See also CA 1-4R; CAAS 5; CANR 1, 22,
33; DLB 14; MTCW

Wilson, Dirk
See Pohl, Frederik

Wilson, Edmund
1895-1972 . . . . CLC 1, 2, 3, 8, 24
See also CA 1-4R; 37-40R; CANR 1, 46;
DLB 63; MTCW

Wilson, Ethel Davis (Bryant)
1888(?)-1980 . . . . CLC 13
See also CA 102; DLB 68; MTCW

Wilson, John   1785-1854. . . . . NCLC 5

Wilson, John (Anthony) Burgess   1917-1993
See Burgess, Anthony
See also CA 1-4R; 143; CANR 2, 46;
MTCW

Wilson, Lanford   1937-. . . . . . . CLC 7, 14, 36
See also CA 17-20R; CABS 3; CANR 45;
DLB 7

Wilson, Robert M.   1944-. . . . . CLC 7, 9
See also CA 49-52; CANR 2, 41; MTCW

Wilson, Robert McLiam   1964-. . . . . CLC 59
See also CA 132

Wilson, Sloan   1920-. . . . . CLC 32
See also CA 1-4R; CANR 1, 44

Wilson, Snoo   1948-. . . . . CLC 33
See also CA 69-72

Wilson, William S(mith)   1932- . . . . . CLC 49
See also CA 81-84

Winchilsea, Anne (Kingsmill) Finch Counte
1661-1720 . . . . LC 3

Windham, Basil
See Wodehouse, P(elham) G(renville)

Wingrove, David (John)   1954-. . . . . . CLC 68
See also CA 133

Author Index

Literary Criticism Series
Cumulative Topic Index

This index lists all topic entries in the Gale Literary Criticism Series *Classical and Medieval Literature Criticism, Contemporary Literary Criticism, Literature Criticism from 1400 to 1800, Nineteenth-Century Literature Criticism,* and *Twentieth-Century Literary Criticism.*

Topic Index

Topic Index

NCLC Cumulative Nationality Index

AMERICAN

Alcott, Amos Bronson 1
Alcott, Louisa May 6
Alger, Horatio Jr. 8
Allston, Washington 2
Audubon, John James 47
Barlow, Joel 23
Beecher, Catharine Esther 30
Bellamy, Edward 4
Bird, Robert Montgomery 1
Brackenridge, Hugh Henry 7
Brentano, Clemens (Maria) 1
Brown, Charles Brockden 22
Brown, William Wells 2
Bryant, William Cullen 6, 46
Burney, Fanny 12
Calhoun, John Caldwell 15
Channing, William Ellery 17
Child, Lydia Maria 6
Chivers, Thomas Holley 49
Cooke, John Esten 5
Cooper, James Fenimore 1, 27
Crockett, David 8
Dickinson, Emily (Elizabeth) 21
Douglass, Frederick 7
Dunlap, William 2
Dwight, Timothy 13
Emerson, Ralph Waldo 1, 38
Field, Eugene 3
Foster, Stephen Collins 26
Frederic, Harold 10
Freneau, Philip Morin 1
Fuller, Margaret 5
Halleck, Fitz-Greene 47
Hamilton, Alexander 49
Hammon, Jupiter 5
Harris, George Washington 23
Hawthorne, Nathaniel 2, 10, 17, 23, 39
Holmes, Oliver Wendell 14

Irving, Washington 2, 19
Jefferson, Thomas 11
Kennedy, John Pendleton 2
Lanier, Sidney 6
Lazarus, Emma 8
Lincoln, Abraham 18
Longfellow, Henry Wadsworth 2, 45
Lowell, James Russell 2
Melville, Herman 3, 12, 29, 45, 49
Parkman, Francis Jr. 12
Paulding, James Kirke 2
Pinkney, Edward 31
Poe, Edgar Allan 1, 16
Rowson, Susanna Haswell 5
Sedgwick, Catharine Maria 19
Shaw, Henry Wheeler 15
Sheridan, Richard Brinsley 5
Sigourney, Lydia Howard (Huntley) 21
Simms, William Gilmore 3
Southworth, Emma Dorothy Eliza Nevitte 26
Stowe, Harriet (Elizabeth) Beecher 3
Thoreau, Henry David 7, 21
Timrod, Henry 25
Trumbull, John 30
Tyler, Royall 3
Very, Jones 9
Warner, Susan (Bogert) 31
Warren, Mercy Otis 13
Webster, Noah 30
Whitman, Sarah Helen (Power) 19
Whitman, Walt(er) 4, 31
Whittier, John Greenleaf 8

ARGENTINIAN

Echeverria, (Jose) Esteban (Antonino) 18
Hernandez, Jose 17

AUSTRALIAN

Adams, Francis 33
Clarke, Marcus (Andrew Hislop) 19
Gordon, Adam Lindsay 21
Kendall, Henry 12

AUSTRIAN

Grillparzer, Franz 1
Lenau, Nikolaus 16
Nestroy, Johann 42
Sacher-Masoch, Leopold von 31
Stifter, Adalbert 41

CANADIAN

Crawford, Isabella Valancy 12
Haliburton, Thomas Chandler 15
Lampman, Archibald 25
Moodie, Susanna (Strickland) 14
Traill, Catharine Parr 31

CZECH

Macha, Karel Hynek 46

DANISH

Andersen, Hans Christian 7
Grundtvig, Nicolai Frederik Severin 1
Jacobsen, Jens Peter 34
Kierkegaard, Soren 34

ENGLISH

Ainsworth, William Harrison 13
Arnold, Matthew 6, 29
Arnold, Thomas 18
Austen, Jane 1, 13, 19, 33
Bagehot, Walter 10
Beardsley, Aubrey 6
Beckford, William 16
Beddoes, Thomas Lovell 3
Bentham, Jeremy 38

Nationality Index

NCLC-49 Title Index

Title Index

ISBN 0-8103-8940-1

90000